Acknowledged by *The Times* of London as "the greatest historian of the comics and graphic novel form in this country", Paul Gravett is a writer, lecturer and broadcaster about international comics and director of the Comica festival at London's Institute of Contemporary Arts. Other books by Paul Gravett, co-authored with Peter Stanbury, include *Manga: Sixty Years of Japanese Comics* (2004), *Graphic Novels: Stories to Change Your Life* (2005), and *Great British Comics* (2006).

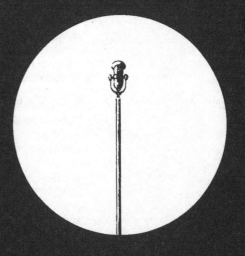

ALSO AVAILABLE

The Mammoth Book of 20th Century Science Fiction
The Mammoth Book of Best British Mysteries
The Mammoth Book of Best Horror Comics
The Mammoth Book of the Best of Best New SF
The Mammoth Book of Best New Erotica 7
The Mammoth Book of Best New Manga 2
The Mammoth Book of Best New SF 20
The Mammoth Book of Best War Comics
The Mammoth Book of Bikers
The Mammoth Book of Boys' Own Stuff
The Mammoth Book of Brain Workouts
The Mammoth Book of Celebrity Murders
The Mammoth Book of Comic Fantasy
The Mammoth Book of Comic Quotes
The Mammoth Book of Cover-Ups
The Mammoth Book of CSI
The Mammoth Book of the Deep
The Mammoth Book of Dirty, Sick, X-Rated & Politically Incorrect Jokes
The Mammoth Book of Dickensian Whodunnits
The Mammoth Book of Egyptian Whodunnits
The Mammoth Book of Erotic Online Diaries
The Mammoth Book of Erotic Women
The Mammoth Book of Extreme Fantasy
The Mammoth Book of Funniest Cartoons of All Time
The Mammoth Book of Hard Men
The Mammoth Book of Historical Whodunnits
The Mammoth Book of Illustrated True Crime
The Mammoth Book of Inside the Elite Forces
The Mammoth Book of International Erotica
The Mammoth Book of Jack the Ripper
The Mammoth Book of Jacobean Whodunnits
The Mammoth Book of Killers at Large
The Mammoth Book of King Arthur
The Mammoth Book of Lesbian Erotica
The Mammoth Book of Maneaters
The Mammoth Book of Modern Ghost Stories
The Mammoth Book of Monsters
The Mammoth Book of Mountain Disasters
The Mammoth Book of New Gay Erotica
The Mammoth Book of New Terror
The Mammoth Book of On the Road
The Mammoth Book of Pirates
The Mammoth Book of Poker
The Mammoth Book of Prophecies
The Mammoth Book of Roaring Twenties Whodunnits
The Mammoth Book of Sex, Drugs and Rock 'N' Roll
The Mammoth Book of Short Spy Novels
The Mammoth Book of Sorcerers' Tales
The Mammoth Book of True Crime
The Mammoth Book of True War Stories
The Mammoth Book of Unsolved Crimes
The Mammoth Book of Vintage Whodunnits
The Mammoth Book of Women Who Kill

The Mammoth Book of

Best

Crime
Comics

Edited by Paul Gravett

RUNNING PRESS
PHILADELPHIA · LONDON

ROBINSON

This book is dedicated to the unknown writers and artists
of these comics, who despite much research have evaded recognition,
may they be remembered, and rediscovered, very soon.

Constable & Robinson Ltd
3 The Lanchesters
162 Fulham Palace Road
London W6 9ER
www.constablerobinson.com

First published in the UK by Robinson,
an imprint of Constable & Robinson, 2008

Selection and introductory material © Paul Gravett 2008.
www.paulgravett.com

Copyright in stories as listed on pages 6–7.

The right of Paul Gravett to be identified as the
author of this work has been asserted by him in accordance
with the Copyright, Designs & Patents Act 1988.

Cover and book design by Peter Stanbury.
Cover illustration by Jordi Bernet.

A copy of the British Library Cataloguing in Publication
Data is available from the British Library

UK ISBN 978-1-84529-710-7

1 3 5 7 9 10 8 6 4 2

First published in the United States in 2008 by Running Press Book Publishers

9 8 7 6 5 4 3 2 1
Digit on the right indicates the number of this printing

US Library of Congress number: 2008926155
US ISBN 978-0-7624-3394-0

Running Press Book Publishers
2300 Chestnut Street
Philadelphia, PA 19103-4371

Visit us on the web!
www.runningpress.com

Printed and bound in the EU

CONTENTS

Acknowledgments

Copyright © 2008 in restored artwork: Peter Stanbury except for *Murder, Morphine and Me*, restored by Michael T. Gilbert and Roger Stewart, and *Lily-white Joe*, restored by Lou Copeland and Greg Sadowski.

Cover: *Torpedo 1936*, copyright © 2008 Jordi Bernet / Enrique Sánchez Abulí. Copyright © Ediciones Glénat España S.L.

Old Gangsters Never Die, copyright © 1983 Alan Moore & Lloyd Thatcher. Originally published on the fold-out sleeve to the single by *The Sinister Ducks*. Reprinted by permission of the authors.

Torpedo 1936: The Switch, copyright © 2008 Jordi Bernet / Enrique Sánchez Abulí. Copyright © Ediciones Glénat España S.L. Published in English by Catalan Communications, 1984 and translated by David H. Rosenthal and Karol Blazer.

The Money-Making Machine Swindlers, copyright © 2008 Joseph H. Simon & Jack Kirby. All Rights Reserved. Originally published in *Justice Traps the Guilty* Number 6, September 1948.

87th Precinct: Blind Man's Bluff, copyright © 1962 Dell Publishing Co.. Originally published in *Four Color* Number 1309, April–June 1962. Reprinted in Britain in *87th Precinct* Number 1, 1962. Adapted from the *87th Precinct* series by Ed McBain. Reprinted by arrangement with Gelfman Schneider Literary Agents, Inc.

The Murderer of Hung, copyright © 1982 Dominique Grange and Jacques Tardi. Originally published in *L'Echo des Savanes* Number 84 bis, Special New York, in 1982. Translated by Mathew Screech and lettered by Woodrow Phoenix in *Escape* Magazine Number 8, 1986. Reprinted by permission of the authors.

Murder, Morphine and Me, copyright © 1948 Magazine Village. Originally published in *True Crime* Number 3, July–August 1948. Art reconstruction by Michael T. Gilbert (www.michaelgilbert.com) and Roger Stewart.

El Borbah: Love in Vein, copyright © 1987 Charles Burns. Reprinted by permission of the author.

The Spirit: The Portier Fortune, copyright © Will Eisner Studios, Inc. Originally published on 1 December 1946. Reproduced by arrangement with Denis Kitchen from the reprint published by Kitchen Sink Press in *The Spirit* Magazine Number 33 in 1982.

Secret Agent X-9, originally published by King Features Syndicate, 1934. Reproduced by arrangement with Denis Kitchen from the reprint compilation published by Kitchen Sink Press in 1990.

Commissario Spada: Strada [Street], copyright © 1979 Gianluigi Gonano & Gianni De Luca. Originally published in *Il Giornalino* Number 36.

Every Shade of Noir

IF your only real exposure so far to crime comics has been the *Sin City* graphic novels by Frank Miller or maybe their faithful big-screen adaptations, you'd better fasten your seat belt, you're in for a foot-to-the-floor ride through this compendium of the cream of crime comics. Along the way, you'll see how several of Miller's acknowledged masters and peers enthral with their pacing, atmosphere and verbal and visual panache. You'll also see how Miller's battered, bandaged Marvin belongs in a long line-up of lean, mean machismo going back to the 1930s and before, when gangsters fought the cops for control of America's cities.

It was a war back then, fought on the streets and in the strips. Newspaper comics may have started out as "The Funnies" offering mainly light relief from the grim front pages, but all that changed on 13 August 1931. After ten years of rejections, cartoonist Chester Gould received the telegram he'd been waiting for: publisher Captain Joseph Patterson of the *Chicago Tribune* syndicate wanted to see him about his latest ideas for a strip, *Plainclothes Tracy*: "I decided that if that police couldn't catch the gangsters, I'd create a fellow who could." Gould kept that telegram framed on the wall as his most cherished possession, after Patterson signed up Gould's concept, shrewdly shortening the name to the punchier *Dick Tracy*, who rapidly became a circulation-boosting phenomenon.

Rival press baron William Randolph Hearst at King Features struck back in 1933 in his typical fashion, paying whatever it cost to buy the very best. For $500 a week, Hearst secured the hugely popular author Dashiell Hammett, who was in need of ready cash to finance his spendthrift lifestyle. Once more, Hammett, an ex-field operative for San Francisco's Pinkerton Detective Agency, remixed his genuine experiences to devise a fresh hero for the newspaper strips. In trench-coat and snap-brim hat, the keen-witted, determined mystery man *Secret Agent X-9* was assigned to Alex Raymond. This rising young illustrator was set to launch *Flash Gordon* and *Jungle Jim* in the colour Sunday pages on 7 January 1934. The very next day, what was to be Hammett's last novel, *The Thin Man*, hit the bookstores.

Building on all this publicity, X-9 burst into the daily papers on 22 January. That day, Hammett wrote to his wife, "I'm writing a story for a cartoon strip for Hearst's syndicate which will bring me a regular and, I hope, growing income perhaps forever." It was not to last, however; once he fell behind with scripts, King Features meddled with them and Hollywood beckoned. Even so, in its prime, and in the climactic twenty weeks of his first long serial resurrected here, *X-9* ranks, according to his biographer William F. Nolan, as "...Hammett at his pulpy best. The author's never-equalled mastery of understatement and his dead-pan but deliberate use of self-parody are in abundance here and seem to indicate that Hammett was having a ball." It marked Hammett's last words printed in his lifetime; from now on, his writing would be for the movies.

It wasn't long before *X-9*, *Tracy* and other detective strips were repackaged in comic books, the emerging 10-cent novelties that turned into a multi-million dollar industry with the success of *Superman*, *Batman* and the rest. Before them, however, their New York publishers had set up a company called Detective Comics, Inc. in 1936 to publish one of the first single-theme anthologies, *Detective Comics*. This was not only the birthplace of The Dark Knight and his home to this day, but also the source of DC Comics' initials. During the Second World War, while superheroes, essentially costumed crimefighters, dominated comic books, the crime genre developed elsewhere in America, for example in Will Eisner's newspaper supplement *The Spirit*, a veritable weekly primer on how to expand the audience and expressive power of the medium.

Publisher Leverett Gleason also recognized that the readership was changing and ageing, so in 1942 he took a gamble on a novel approach from cartoonist-editors Charles Biro and Bob Wood. They took the sort of real-life, supposedly "true" prose accounts of murderers and criminals which had sold pulp magazines in the 1920s and were a staple of the tabloid press and on the big screen, and reinterpreted them as comics, where every lurid detail could be visualized and fixed on the page. The first, and for several years, the only "All True" crime comic book in America, *Crime Does Not Pay* slowly but steadily sold more each year. As demobbed troops increased the adult audience, by 1948 it topped one million copies per month. Multiply that by the "pass-along" rate and Gleason could justify the cover line, "More Than 6,000,000 readers monthly!" No wonder that year triggered a sudden two-year surge in crime comic books. Gleason's competitors would range from the delectable sleaze of Fox's *Crimes By Women* or Magazine Village's *True Crime* to the classier acts of EC or Simon and Kirby, all represented here.

Although the genre never reached such a peak, overtaken from 1950 by booms in romance and horror, it was these unrestrained crime comics that first stirred up a moral panic about their power to corrupt young minds and turn them into juvenile delinquents. Vilified in the media, the target of local bans and boycotts, subjected to televised Congressional hearings, comic books became a burning issue of the day, literally as parents, teachers and pressurized kids threw piles of them onto public bonfires. To avert legislation, most of the big players in the industry ganged up in 1954 to appoint an independent Comics Code Authority to apply the strictest self-imposed code of content on any medium. Twelve clauses cleaned up crime comics overnight by outlawing, among other things, "excessive violence", "kidnapping", "unique details and methods of a crime" and "disrespect for authority" and insisting that "in every instance good shall triumph over evil". It was no better in the newspapers at this time, when complaints about a bondage scene in Mickey Spillane's *Mike Hammer* strip forced its cancellation.

Constraints like these meant that crime definitely did not pay for America's comic book publishers and the genre all but vanished by 1959 as superheroes took over once more. Readers looked for their crime thrills in books, films and television cop shows, which from the early 1960s were spun off into comic books. In that era before videos, DVDs and countless channels running repeats, comics like these allowed viewers to enjoy new episodes of their favourite shows anytime, anywhere. The majority were put out by wholesome company Dell and were pretty tame, but at least one of their uncredited writers was a total maverick, as proven by his *87th Precinct* story based on the TV series and Ed McBain's novels.

Apart from brave one-off experiments like Gil Kane's *Savage*, Jack Kirby's *In the Days of the Mob* or Jim Steranko's *Chandler*, darker, more mature crime comics struggled in America, but they would flourish elsewhere. From *fumetti neri* or pocket-sized black comics in Italy to the French revolution in quality *bande dessinée* magazines and albums, it was European-based creators starting in the 1970s, like Jacques Tardi, Abuli & Bernet, Gonano & De Luca, and Muñoz & Sampayo, who were largely free from censorship to explore the many shades of noir in truly sophisticated narratives for adults.

Meanwhile, back in Code-approved America, nobody was publishing crime when a fledgling Frank Miller broke into comics. The only game in town was superheroes. So in 1979 when he landed the pencilling and then writing jobs on a languishing Marvel B-feature *Daredevil*, Miller stripped it back to its essence of a lone blind man fighting for justice as a lawyer and costumed vigilante. It was as close as he could get to the crime comic he had always dreamt of producing.

There were always limits when working under the Comics Code, still restricting news-stand comics. But the Code became irrelevant when another market emerged in specialist comic shops, allowing publishers big and small to sell directly to fans. Out of this explosion, Max Allan Collins & Terry Beatty paved the way in 1981 with avenging widow *Ms. Tree*, as brutal as *Hammer* but a good deal smarter. Ten years later, Miller took the plunge and created his own universe to play in, Sin City. Thanks to the graphic novel positioning comics into bookstores, libraries and the bestseller lists, the diversity and quality of today's crime comics are unprecedented. Once more, acclaimed novelists such as Greg Rucka, Jerome Charyn and Ian Rankin are taking up the challenges of scripting comics. At last crime really can pay, and not just the publishers but the writers and artists as well.

It's a different world from those heydays of classic newspaper strips and comics. Their often stratospheric print runs might lead you to assume that there's a plentiful supply still in existence. The fact is, millions of pages of fading newsprint have been disposed of, thrown onto those anti-comics campaigners' pyres, recycled in war-time paper drives, sent far afield as ships' ballast, dumped even from overloaded libraries in the rush to microfilm or digitize. To the point where today surviving original copies are few, fragile and highly prized and priced. Rarer still are the unique original artworks. So I want to thank Martin Barker, Max Allan Collins, George Hagenauer, Denis Kitchen, Frank Motler, Ian Rakoff, Roger Sabin, Greg Sadowski and all the other connoisseurs who helped me to rescue and research these treasures for this compilation and most of all Peter Stanbury for dedicating such care and skill to their restoration and presentation. And, of course, my gratitude goes to the writers and artists for their brilliant work. Comics are both a vital part of our cultural heritage and the sharpest cutting edge of twenty-first century literature. This is one story that is definitely "to be continued".

Paul Gravett

"...or turn their faces up,
like so, receiving Death
as if it were a Mother's kiss..."

Pull up a front-row seat and join tonight's
spectral audience. The curtains part and
your host steps out into the spotlight for this
evening's elegy to gangland lives and deaths.
If his snarling repartee has an air of cabaret
about it, it's because his words started life
as the lyrics for a song by Alan Moore, with
music by David J of British gothic rock band
Bauhaus and performed by them both in the
group *The Sinister Ducks*. Moore and Lloyd
Thatcher adapted it into a comic for the
single's fold-out record sleeve, although it was
not printed at a proper size or quality until
this version, revised by the artist. With a nod
to V *for Vendetta* from the same period, this
mood piece taps into Moore's ongoing passion
for the theatrical, from his participation in
Northampton's Seventies Arts Lab to his
one-off magic-inspired performances.

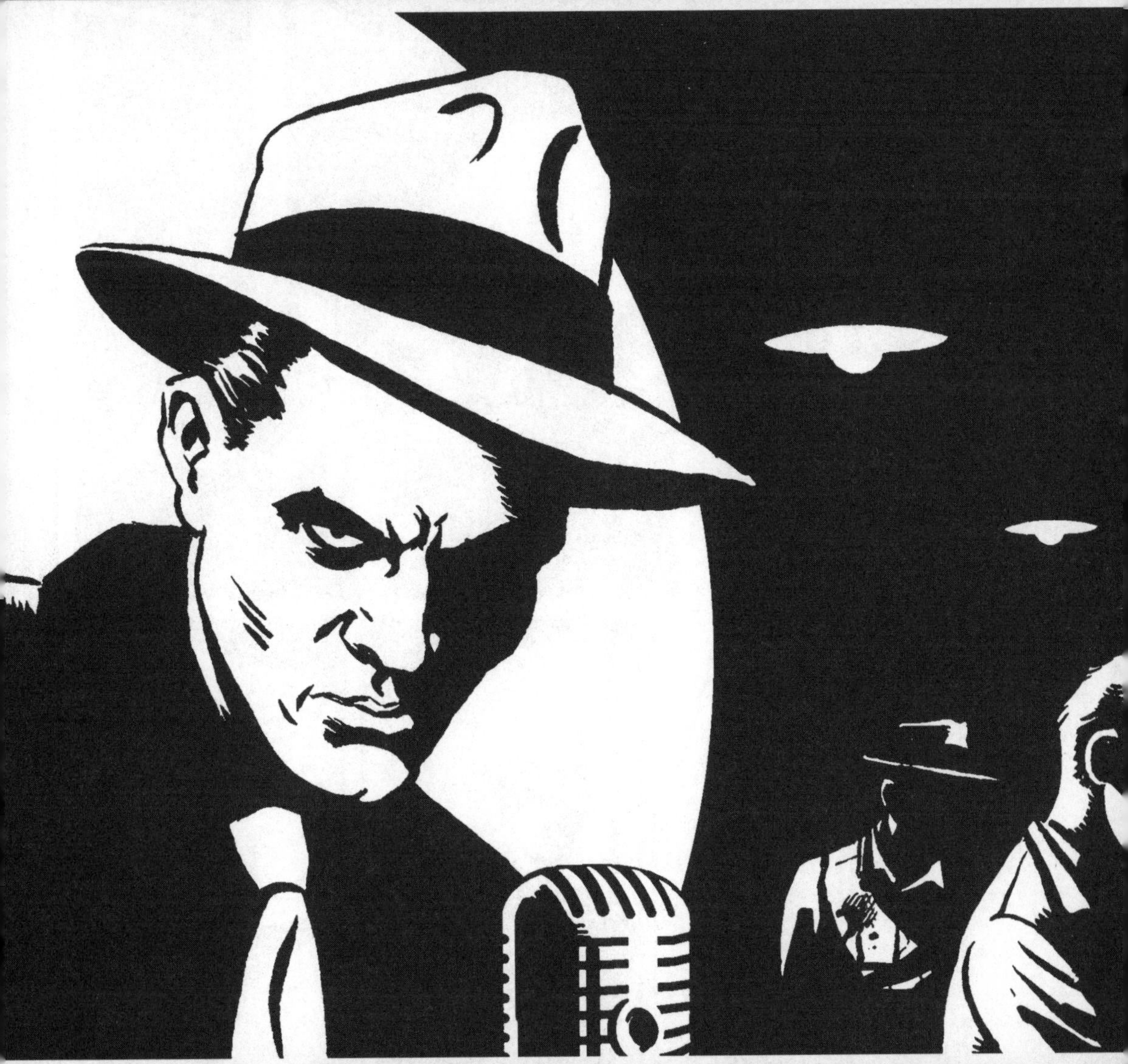

Old Gangsters Never Die

Alan Moore (script) and Lloyd Thatcher (art) 1983

Old Gangsters never die

By Alan Moore & Lloyd Thatcher

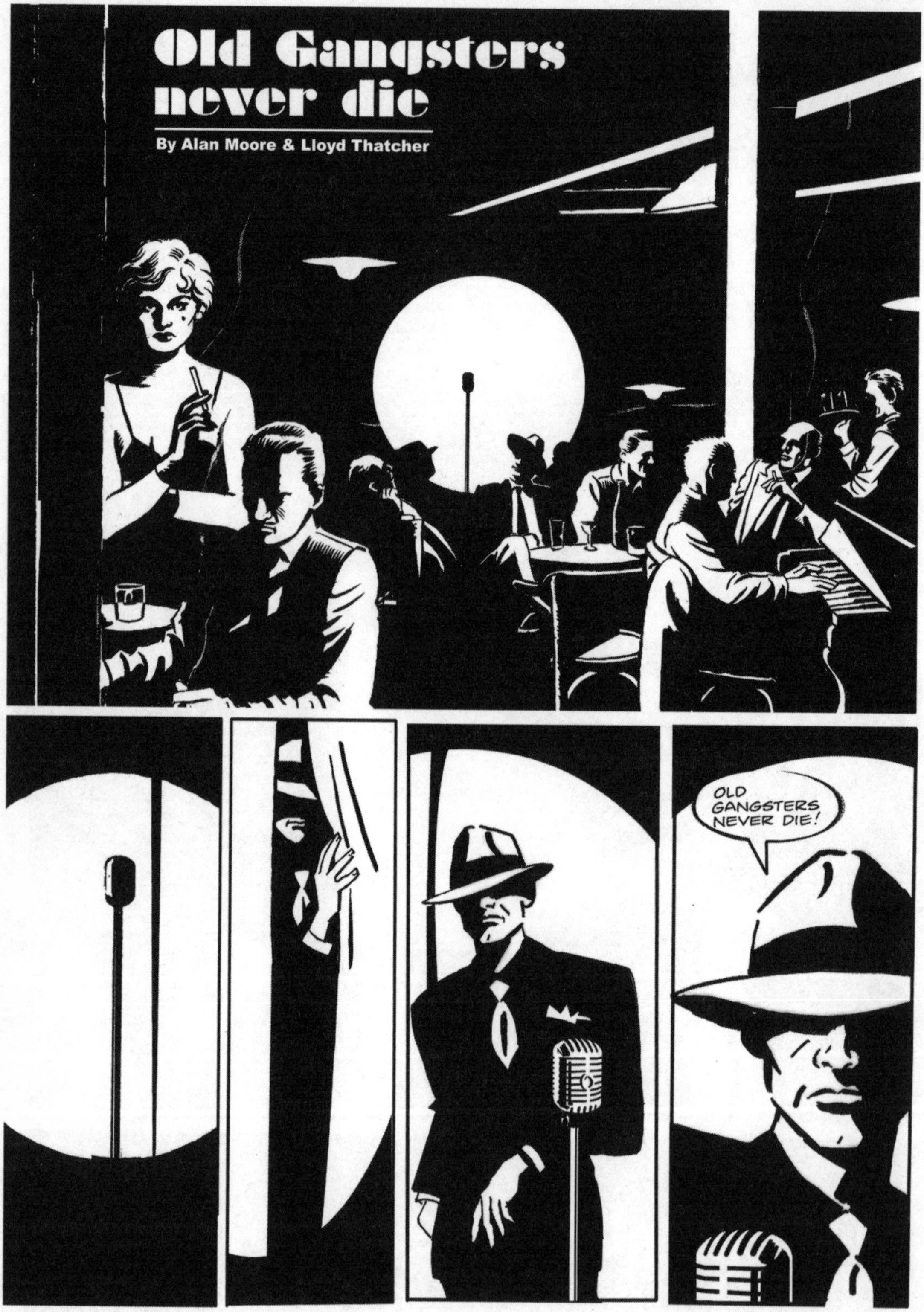
OLD GANGSTERS NEVER DIE!

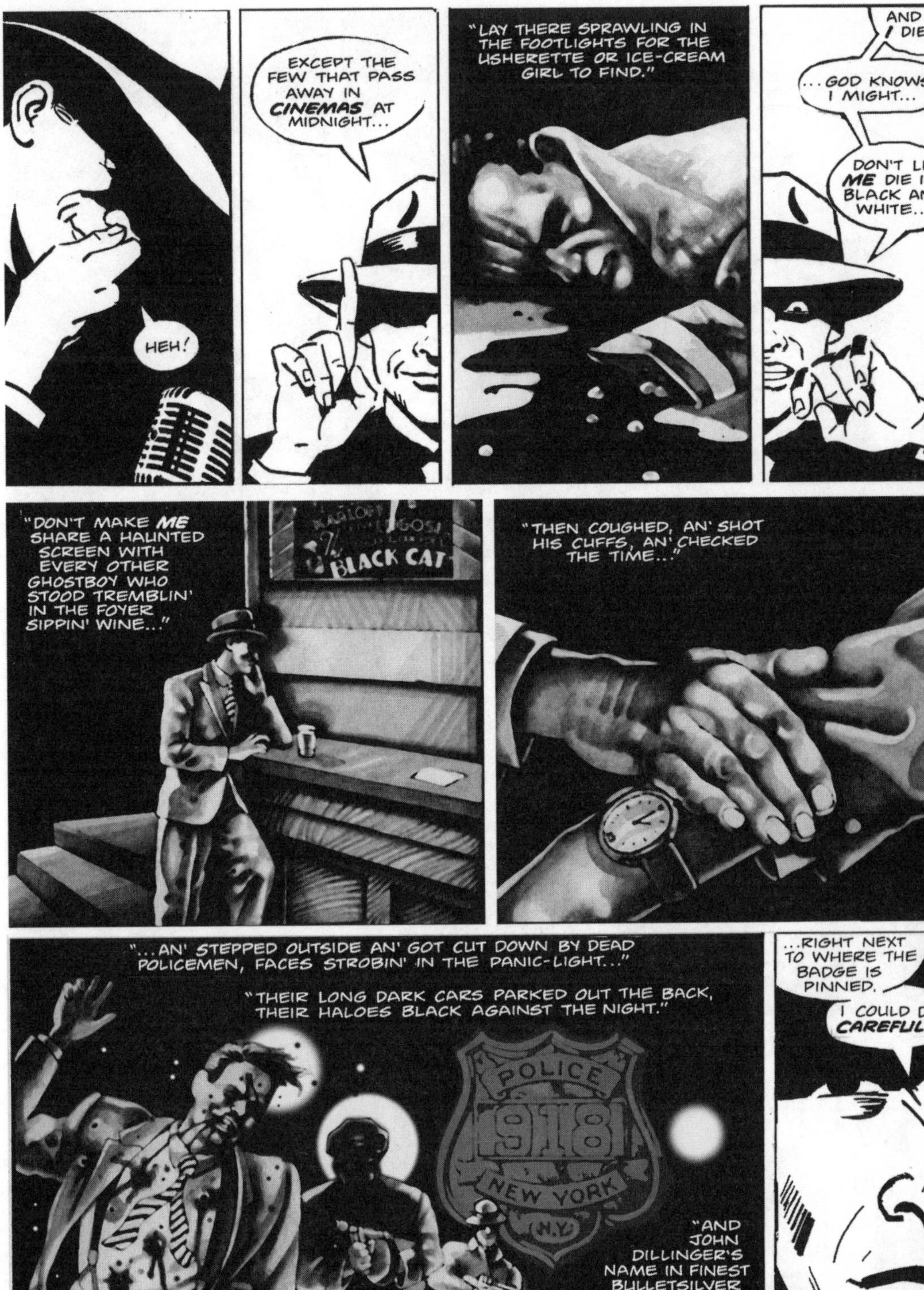
HEH!
EXCEPT THE FEW THAT PASS AWAY IN CINEMAS AT MIDNIGHT...
"LAY THERE SPRAWLING IN THE FOOTLIGHTS FOR THE USHERETTE OR ICE-CREAM GIRL TO FIND."
AND IF I DIE...
...GOD KNOWS, I MIGHT...
DON'T LET ME DIE IN BLACK AND WHITE...
"DON'T MAKE ME SHARE A HAUNTED SCREEN WITH EVERY OTHER GHOSTBOY WHO STOOD TREMBLIN' IN THE FOYER SIPPIN' WINE..."
BLACK CAT
"THEN COUGHED, AN' SHOT HIS CUFFS, AN' CHECKED THE TIME..."
"...AN' STEPPED OUTSIDE AN' GOT CUT DOWN BY DEAD POLICEMEN, FACES STROBIN' IN THE PANIC-LIGHT..."
"THEIR LONG DARK CARS PARKED OUT THE BACK, THEIR HALOES BLACK AGAINST THE NIGHT."
POLICE
918
NEW YORK
N.Y.
"AND JOHN DILLINGER'S NAME IN FINEST BULLETSILVER ETCHED UPON THEIR HEARTS A COLD TATTOO UPON THEIR SKIN..."
...RIGHT NEXT TO WHERE THE BADGE IS PINNED.
I COULD DIE CAREFULLY.
AT DUSK.

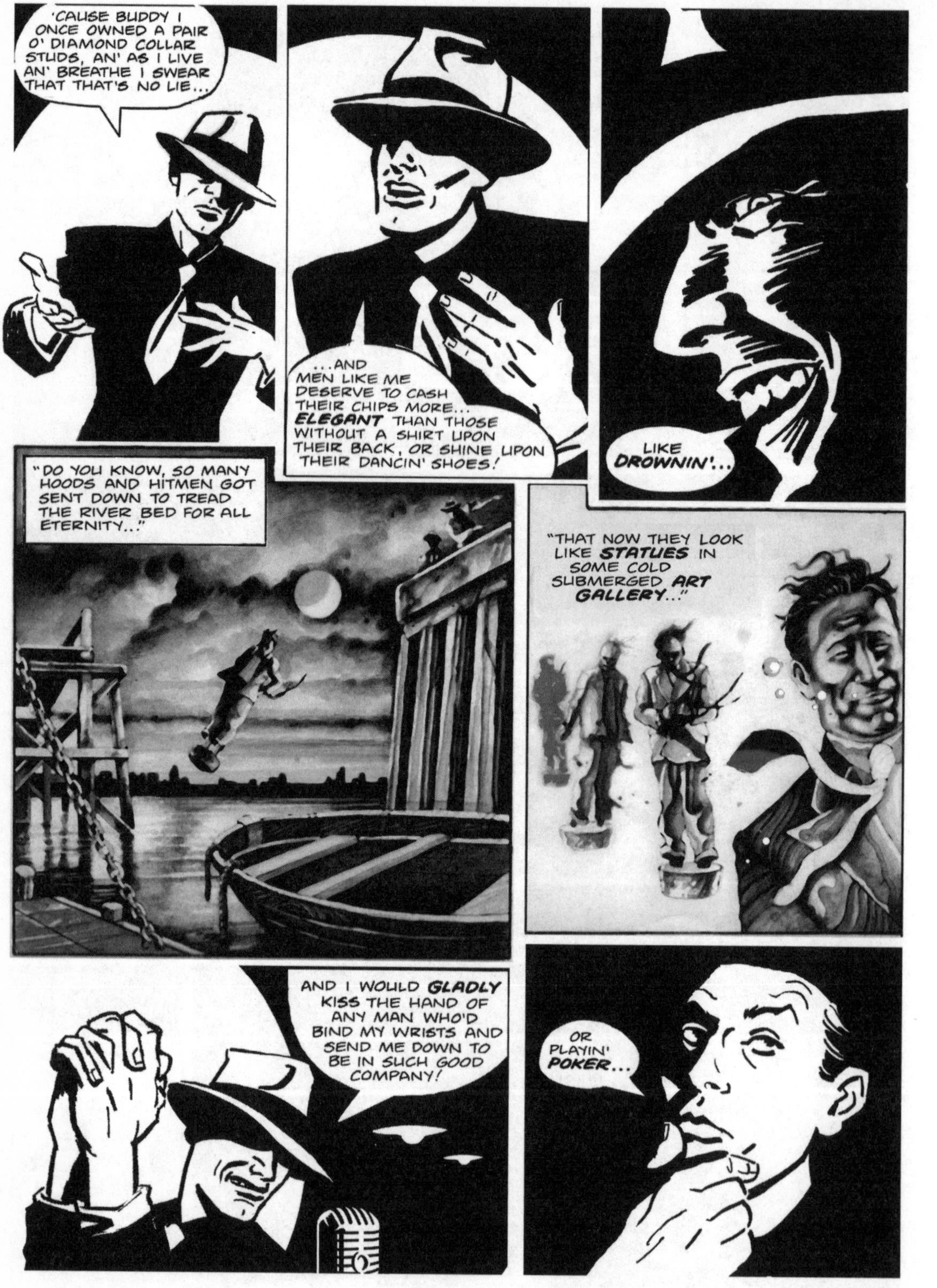
'CAUSE BUDDY I ONCE OWNED A PAIR O' DIAMOND COLLAR STUDS, AN' AS I LIVE AN' BREATHE I SWEAR THAT THAT'S NO LIE...
...AND MEN LIKE ME DESERVE TO CASH THEIR CHIPS MORE... ELEGANT THAN THOSE WITHOUT A SHIRT UPON THEIR BACK, OR SHINE UPON THEIR DANCIN' SHOES!
LIKE DROWNIN'...
"DO YOU KNOW, SO MANY HOODS AND HITMEN GOT SENT DOWN TO TREAD THE RIVER BED FOR ALL ETERNITY..."
"THAT NOW THEY LOOK LIKE STATUES IN SOME COLD SUBMERGED ART GALLERY..."
AND I WOULD GLADLY KISS THE HAND OF ANY MAN WHO'D BIND MY WRISTS AND SEND ME DOWN TO BE IN SUCH GOOD COMPANY!
OR PLAYIN' POKER...

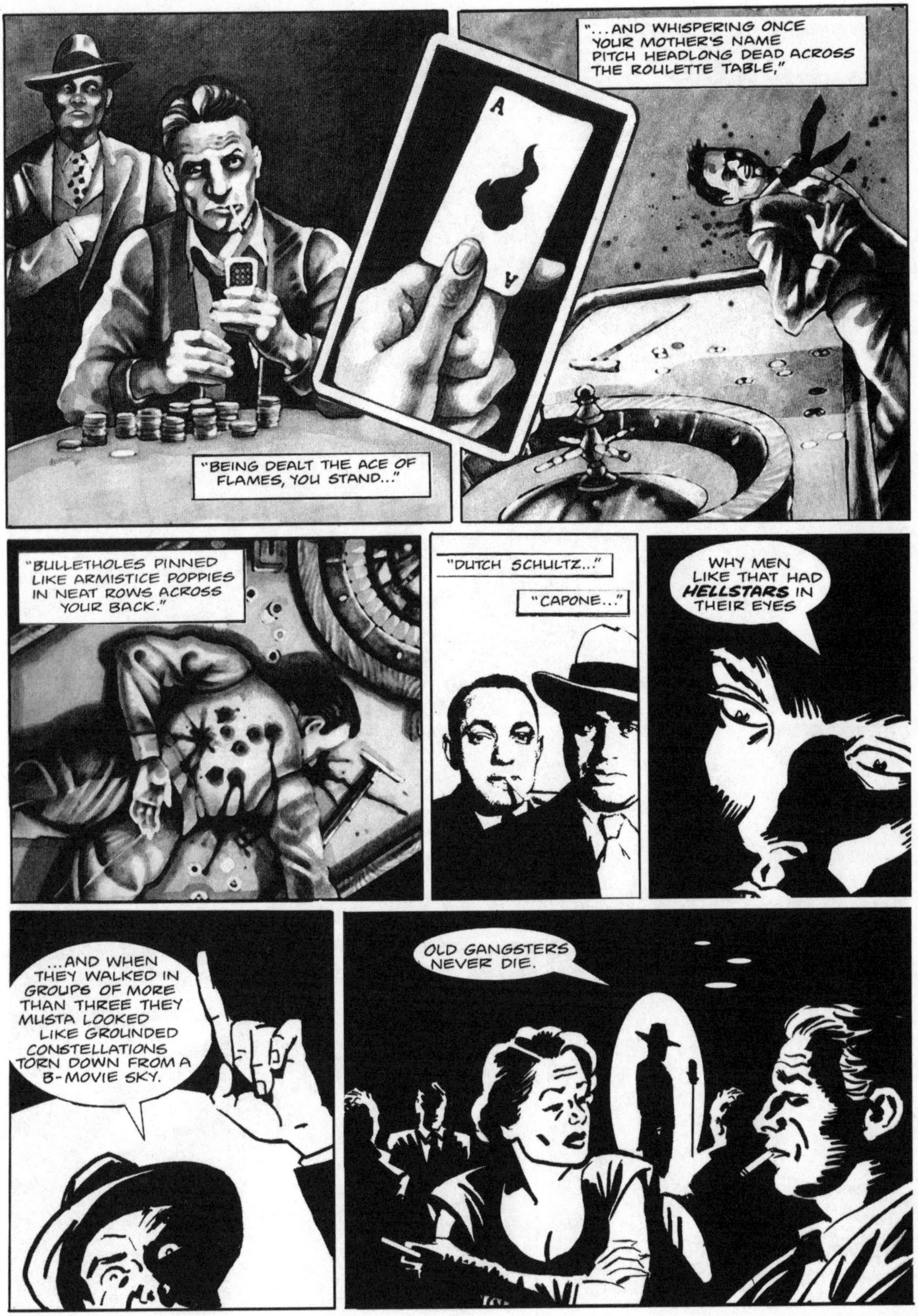

"BEING DEALT THE ACE OF FLAMES, YOU STAND..."
A
A
"...AND WHISPERING ONCE YOUR MOTHER'S NAME PITCH HEADLONG DEAD ACROSS THE ROULETTE TABLE,"
"BULLETHOLES PINNED LIKE ARMISTICE POPPIES IN NEAT ROWS ACROSS YOUR BACK."
"DUTCH SCHULTZ..."
"CAPONE..."
WHY MEN LIKE THAT HAD **HELLSTARS** IN THEIR EYES
...AND WHEN THEY WALKED IN GROUPS OF MORE THAN THREE THEY MUSTA LOOKED LIKE GROUNDED CONSTELLATIONS TORN DOWN FROM A B-MOVIE SKY.
OLD GANGSTERS NEVER DIE.

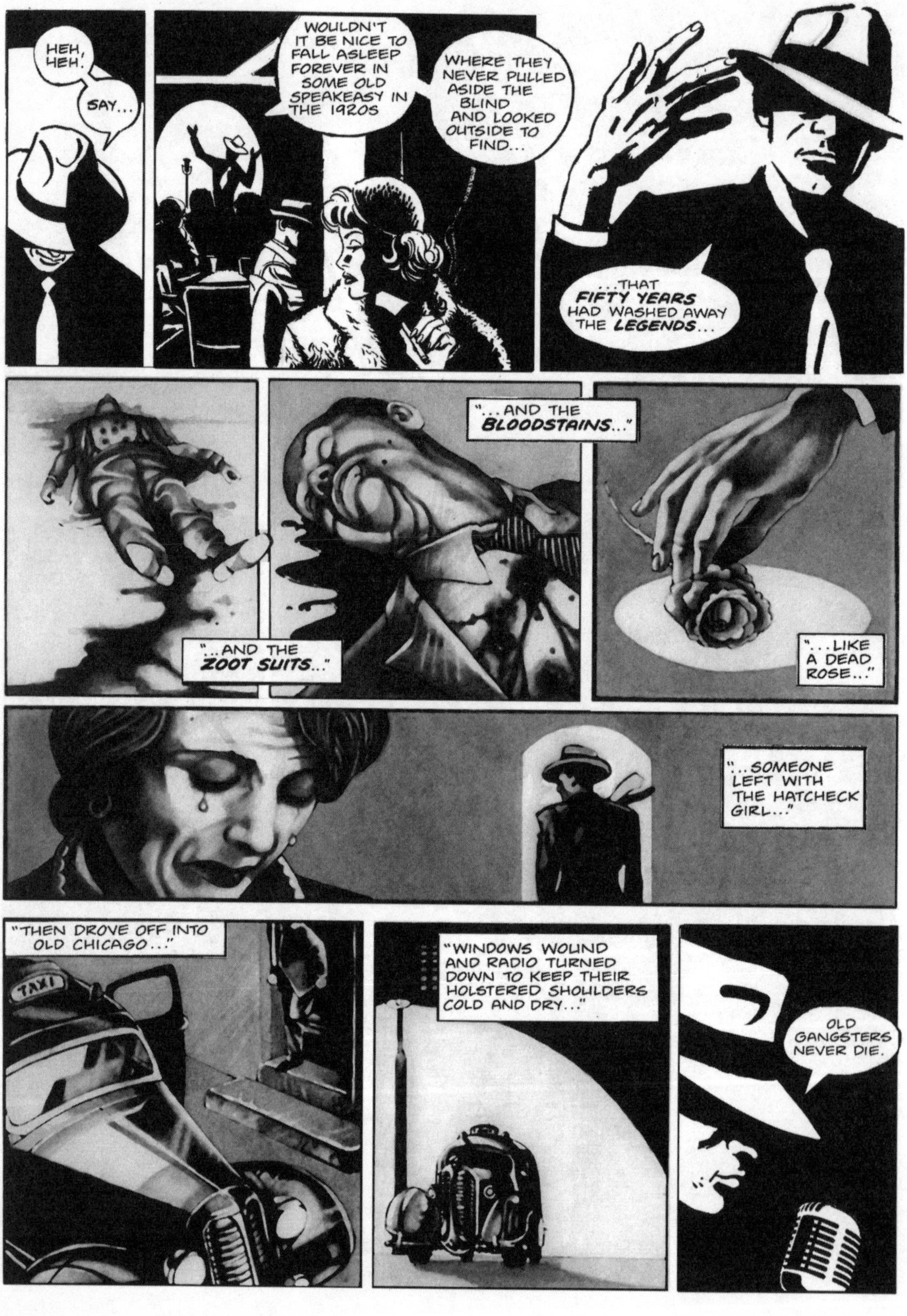
HEH, HEH.
SAY...
WOULDN'T IT BE NICE TO FALL ASLEEP FOREVER IN SOME OLD SPEAKEASY IN THE 1920S
WHERE THEY NEVER PULLED ASIDE THE BLIND AND LOOKED OUTSIDE TO FIND...
...THAT **FIFTY YEARS** HAD WASHED AWAY THE **LEGENDS**...
"...AND THE **ZOOT SUITS**..."
"...AND THE **BLOODSTAINS**..."
"...LIKE A DEAD ROSE..."
"...SOMEONE LEFT WITH THE HATCHECK GIRL..."
"THEN DROVE OFF INTO OLD CHICAGO..."
TAXI
"WINDOWS WOUND AND RADIO TURNED DOWN TO KEEP THEIR HOLSTERED SHOULDERS COLD AND DRY..."
OLD GANGSTERS NEVER DIE.

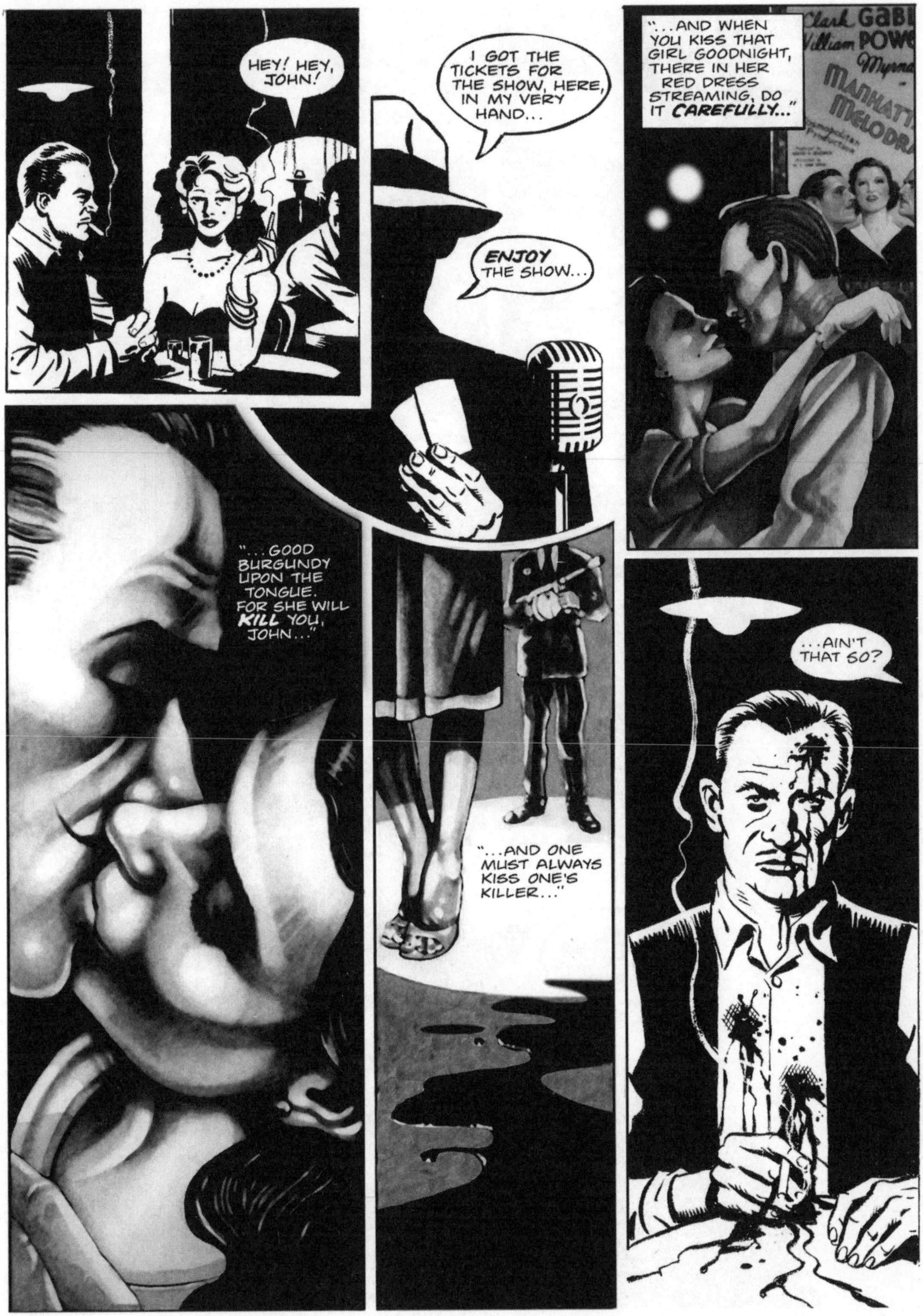
HEY! HEY, JOHN!
I GOT THE TICKETS FOR THE SHOW, HERE, IN MY VERY HAND...
ENJOY THE SHOW...
"...AND WHEN YOU KISS THAT GIRL GOODNIGHT, THERE IN HER RED DRESS STREAMING, DO IT CAREFULLY..."
Clark Gable
William Powell
Myrna
MANHATTAN MELODRAMA
"...GOOD BURGUNDY UPON THE TONGUE. FOR SHE WILL KILL YOU, JOHN..."
"...AND ONE MUST ALWAYS KISS ONE'S KILLER..."
...AIN'T THAT SO?

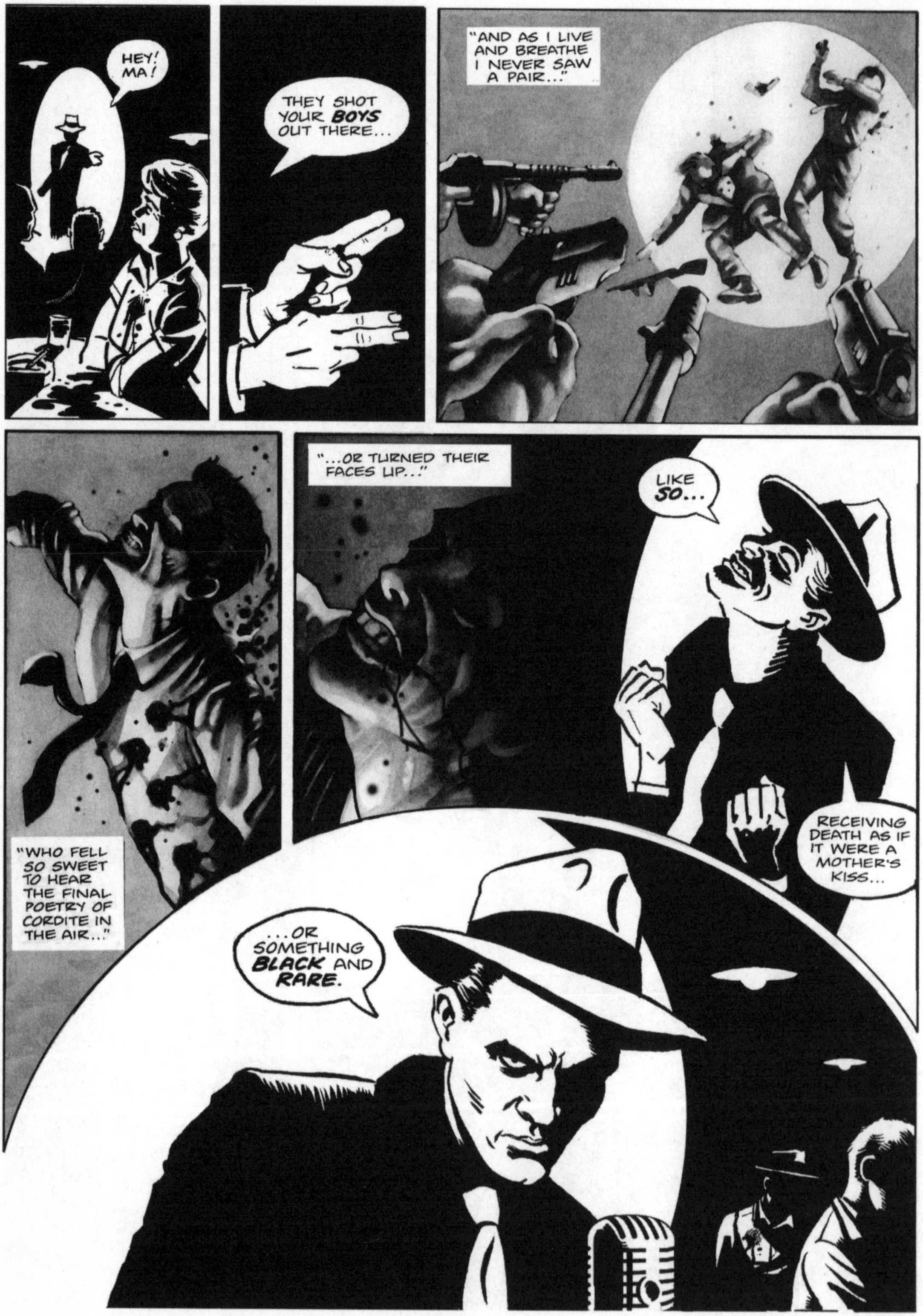
HEY! MA!
THEY SHOT YOUR **BOYS** OUT THERE...
"AND AS I LIVE AND BREATHE I NEVER SAW A PAIR..."
"WHO FELL SO SWEET TO HEAR THE FINAL POETRY OF CORDITE IN THE AIR..."
"...OR TURNED THEIR FACES UP..."
LIKE **SO**...
RECEIVING DEATH AS IF IT WERE A MOTHER'S KISS...
...OR SOMETHING **BLACK** AND **RARE**.

HEY, FELLAS. IS IT COLD THERE IN THAT MOVIE-HOUSE TONIGHT?

C'MONNNN...

LET'S PASS OUT THAT JACK DANIELS...

...AND WE'LL TALK ABOUT OLD MURDERS...

...DOUBLE-CROSSES...

...AND DEAD BLONDES...

...AND SAY "HERE'S LOOKIN' ATCHA!"

"HERE'S BLOOD IN YA EYE!"

OLD GHOSTS SIT IN THE BACKROOM.

OLD BODIES DON'T TELL STORIES.

OLD DREAMS WEAR DUSTY CLOTHING.

OLD GANGSTERS...

...NEVER DIE.

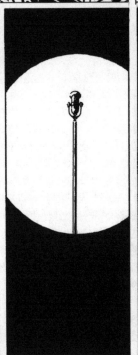

CLICK!

21

"You don't look right.
You look at me
with distorted eyes."

It's "an eye for an eye" in this tale of devious,
determined revenge, grounded in the gritty
accuracy of New York during the Great
Depression. There's a sadistic streak to Sicilian-
born Luca Torelli and one police inspector finds
out the hard way that it pays not to mess with
this torpedo or hitman-for-hire. It was in 1981
that acclaimed Spanish writer Sanchez Abuli
wrote *Torpedo 1936* for American artist Alex
Toth, but Toth grew unhappy with Abuli's
dark, ironic view of humanity and decided
to leave after two episodes. The Spanish
illustrator Jordi Bernet more than filled his
shoes, developing the series with Abuli over
15 volumes into one of Europe's modern
classics. They were awarded in 1986 with
the Best Foreign Album Award at France's
Angoulême International Comics Festival.

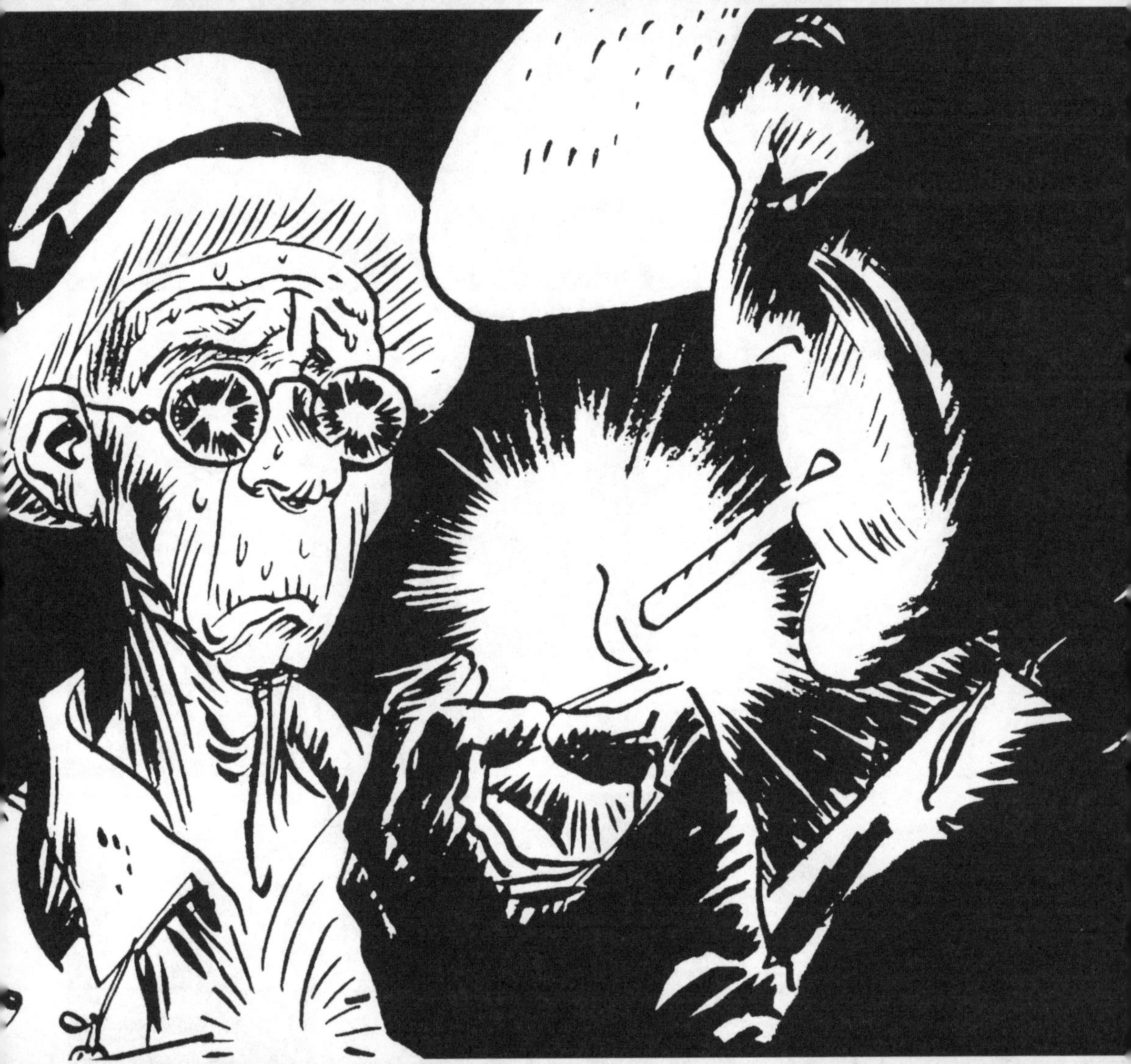

Torpedo 1936: The Switch

Sanchez Abuli (script) and Jordi Bernet (art) 1982

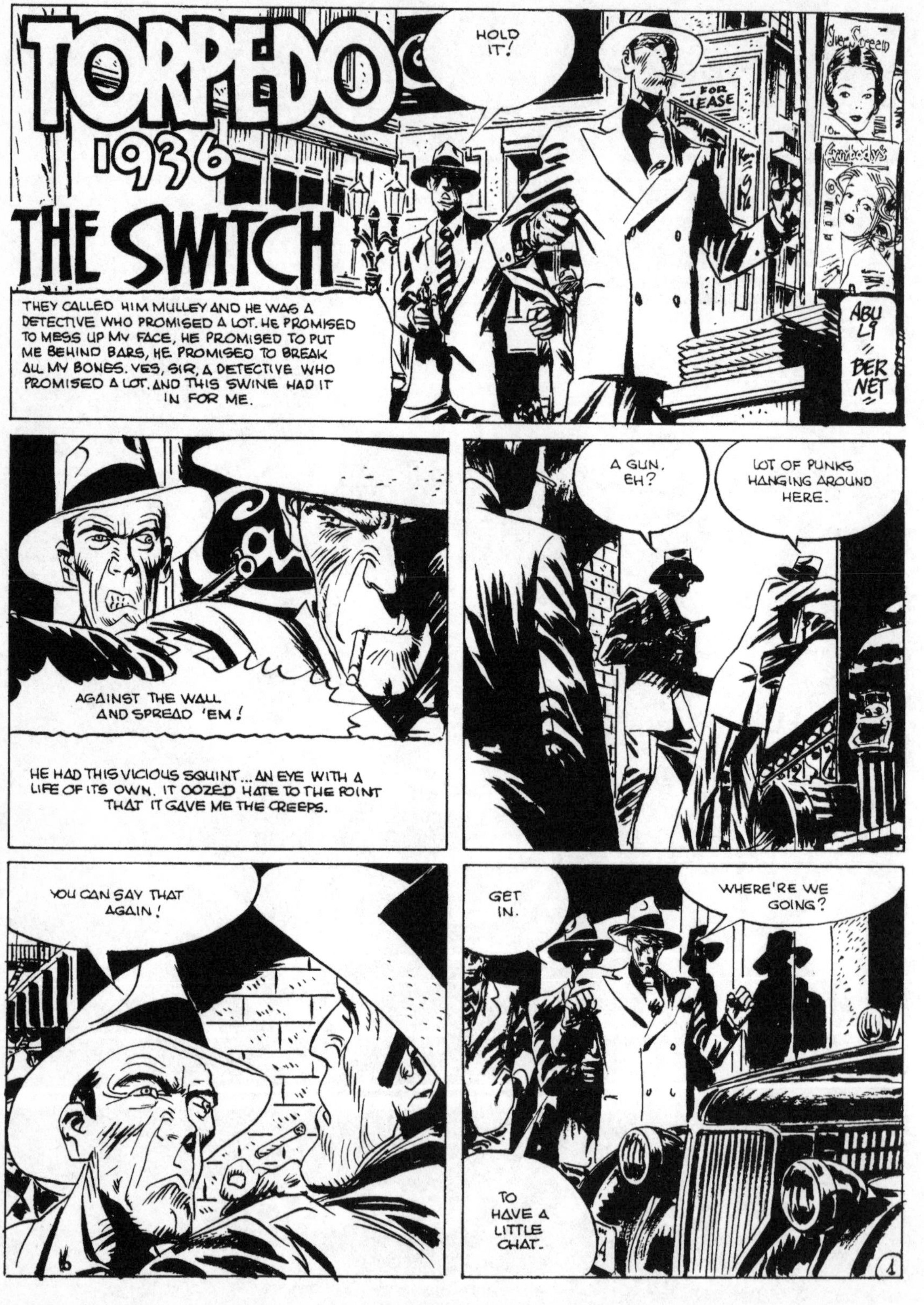
TORPEDO
1936
THE SWITCH
HOLD IT!
FOR LEASE
THEY CALLED HIM MULLEY AND HE WAS A DETECTIVE WHO PROMISED A LOT. HE PROMISED TO MESS UP MY FACE, HE PROMISED TO PUT ME BEHIND BARS, HE PROMISED TO BREAK ALL MY BONES. YES, SIR, A DETECTIVE WHO PROMISED A LOT. AND THIS SWINE HAD IT IN FOR ME.
ABULI BERNET
AGAINST THE WALL AND SPREAD 'EM!
HE HAD THIS VICIOUS SQUINT... AN EYE WITH A LIFE OF ITS OWN. IT OOZED HATE TO THE POINT THAT IT GAVE ME THE CREEPS.
A GUN, EH?
LOT OF PUNKS HANGING AROUND HERE.
YOU CAN SAY THAT AGAIN!
GET IN.
WHERE'RE WE GOING?
TO HAVE A LITTLE CHAT.

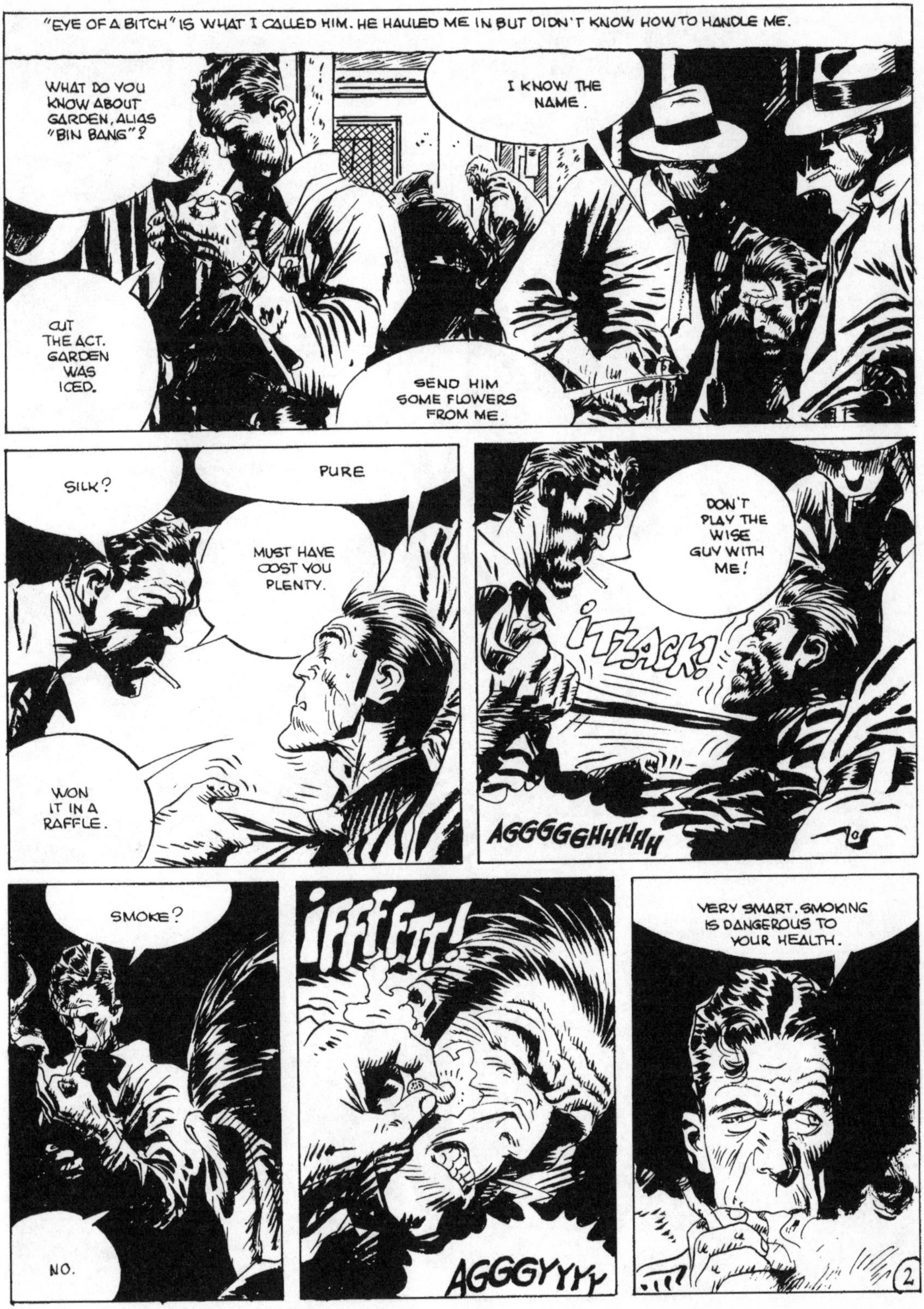
"EYE OF A BITCH" IS WHAT I CALLED HIM. HE HAULED ME IN BUT DIDN'T KNOW HOW TO HANDLE ME.
WHAT DO YOU KNOW ABOUT GARDEN, ALIAS "BIN BANG"?
I KNOW THE NAME.
CUT THE ACT. GARDEN WAS ICED.
SEND HIM SOME FLOWERS FROM ME.
SILK?
PURE
MUST HAVE COST YOU PLENTY.
WON IT IN A RAFFLE.
DON'T PLAY THE WISE GUY WITH ME!
ITZACK!
AGGGGGHHHHH
SMOKE?
NO.
IFFFFTT!
AGGGYYYY
VERY SMART. SMOKING IS DANGEROUS TO YOUR HEALTH.
2

WELL, I DON'T HAVE ANYTHING ON YOU NOW, NOT YET. BUT THE DAY I CATCH YOU REDHANDED, I PROMISE...

AFTER A LOT OF PROMISES, "EYE OF A BITCH" LET ME GO. WITH MY TEMPERAMENT, I CAN'T STAND ALL THIS MESSING AROUND. FROM NOW ON IT WAS WAR. AND EITHER I WOULD WIN OR HE WOULD LOSE. I PROMISE.

ZOWEE! WHOSE BEEN DOING YOUR MAKEUP, BOSS?

BEAUTY PARLOR

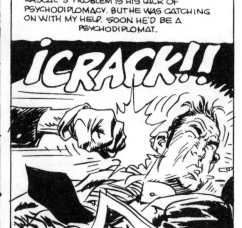

RASCAL'S PROBLEM IS HIS LACK OF PSYCHODIPLOMACY. BUT HE WAS CATCHING ON WITH MY HELP. SOON HE'D BE A PSYCHODIPLOMAT.

¡CRACK!!

MY REVENGE WAS REACHING FEVER PITCH. "EYE OF A BITCH" EVEN APPEARED IN MY NIGHTMARES. EVEN AT A DISTANCE, HIS SICKENING EYE WOULD DRIP POISON.

I WON'T PLUG HIM... THE WHOLE N.Y.P.D. WOULD HIT ME LIKE A TON OF BRICKS. IT HAS TO LOOK LIKE AN ACCIDENT.

WELL, MAYBE ONE OF THESE DAYS HIS GUN WILL GO OFF AND KILL HIM.

¡BAM!

THAT'S IT!! OF COURSE! HIS GUN WILL GO OFF!

3

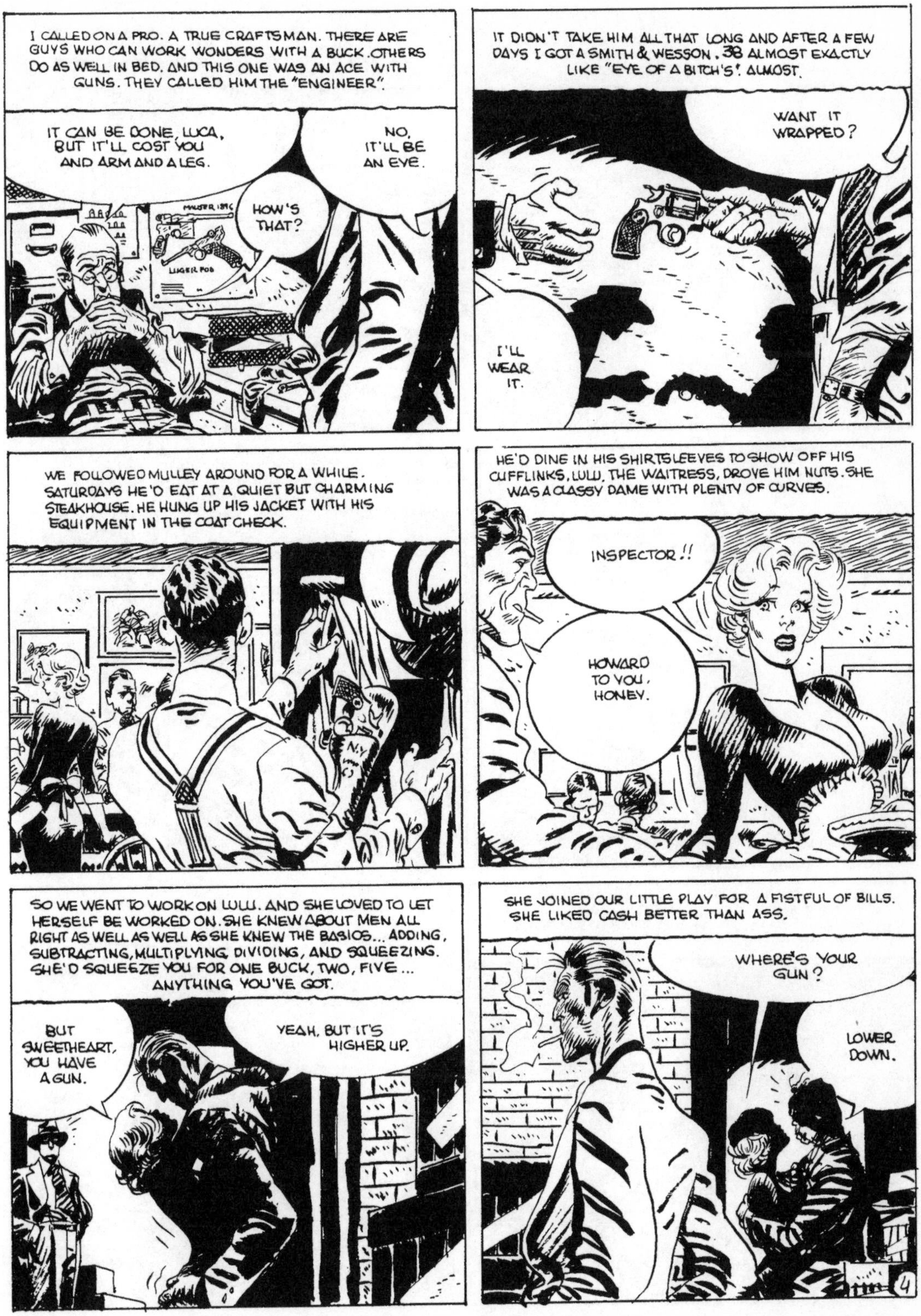
I CALLED ON A PRO. A TRUE CRAFTSMAN. THERE ARE GUYS WHO CAN WORK WONDERS WITH A BUCK. OTHERS DO AS WELL IN BED. AND THIS ONE WAS AN ACE WITH GUNS. THEY CALLED HIM THE "ENGINEER".
IT CAN BE DONE, LUCA, BUT IT'LL COST YOU AND ARM AND A LEG.
HOW'S THAT?
NO, IT'LL BE AN EYE.
IT DIDN'T TAKE HIM ALL THAT LONG AND AFTER A FEW DAYS I GOT A SMITH & WESSON .38 ALMOST EXACTLY LIKE "EYE OF A BITCH'S". ALMOST.
WANT IT WRAPPED?
I'LL WEAR IT.
WE FOLLOWED MULLEY AROUND FOR A WHILE. SATURDAYS HE'D EAT AT A QUIET BUT CHARMING STEAKHOUSE. HE HUNG UP HIS JACKET WITH HIS EQUIPMENT IN THE COAT CHECK.
HE'D DINE IN HIS SHIRTSLEEVES TO SHOW OFF HIS CUFFLINKS. LULU, THE WAITRESS, DROVE HIM NUTS. SHE WAS A CLASSY DAME WITH PLENTY OF CURVES.
INSPECTOR!!
HOWARD TO YOU, HONEY.
SO WE WENT TO WORK ON LULU. AND SHE LOVED TO LET HERSELF BE WORKED ON. SHE KNEW ABOUT MEN ALL RIGHT AS WELL AS WELL AS SHE KNEW THE BASICS... ADDING, SUBTRACTING, MULTIPLYING, DIVIDING, AND SQUEEZING. SHE'D SQUEEZE YOU FOR ONE BUCK, TWO, FIVE... ANYTHING YOU'VE GOT.
BUT SWEETHEART, YOU HAVE A GUN.
YEAH, BUT IT'S HIGHER UP.
SHE JOINED OUR LITTLE PLAY FOR A FISTFUL OF BILLS. SHE LIKED CASH BETTER THAN ASS.
WHERE'S YOUR GUN?
LOWER DOWN.

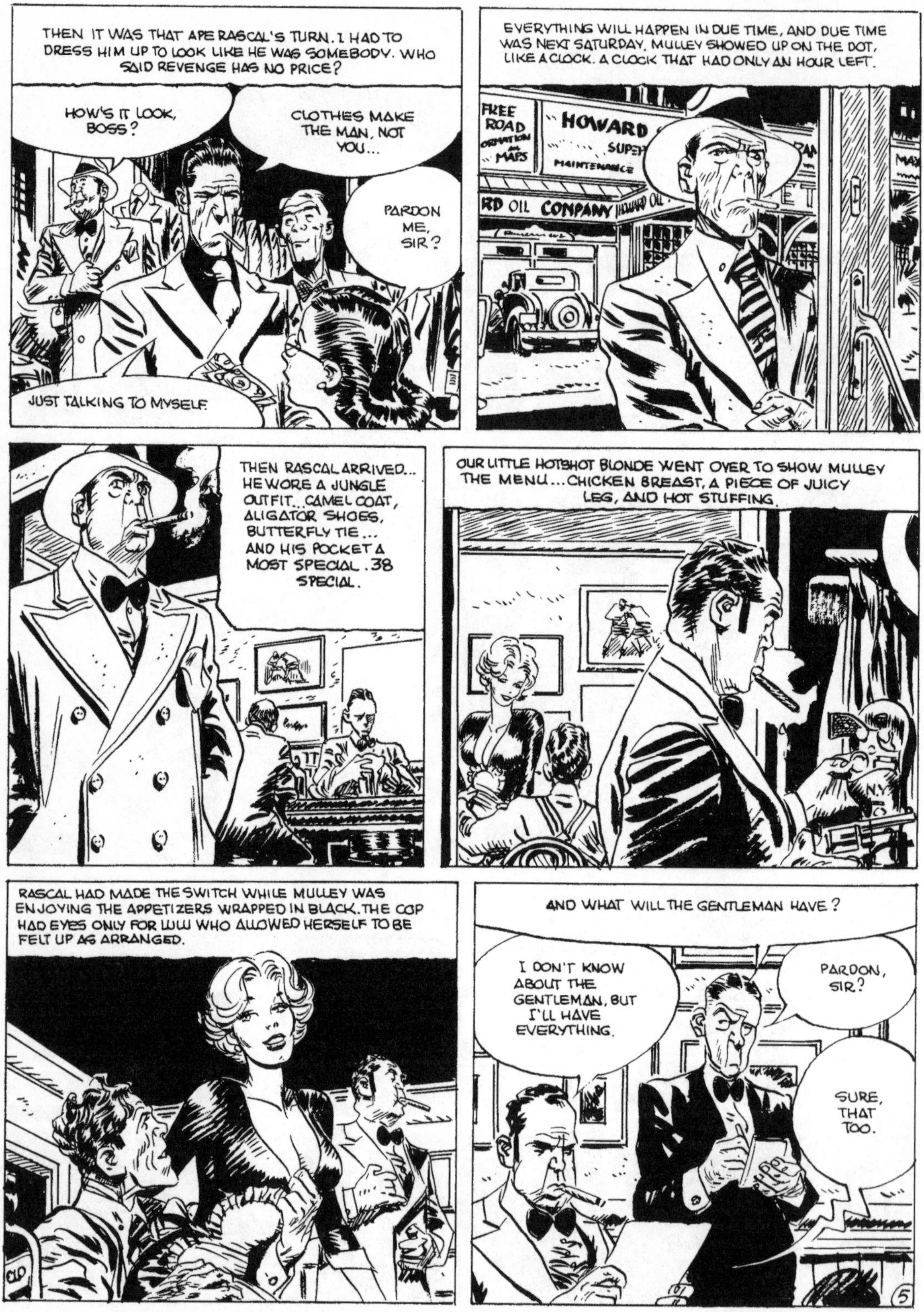
THEN IT WAS THAT APE RASCAL'S TURN. I HAD TO DRESS HIM UP TO LOOK LIKE HE WAS SOMEBODY. WHO SAID REVENGE HAS NO PRICE?
HOW'S IT LOOK, BOSS?
CLOTHES MAKE THE MAN, NOT YOU...
PARDON ME, SIR?
JUST TALKING TO MYSELF.
EVERYTHING WILL HAPPEN IN DUE TIME, AND DUE TIME WAS NEXT SATURDAY. MULLEY SHOWED UP ON THE DOT, LIKE A CLOCK. A CLOCK THAT HAD ONLY AN HOUR LEFT.
FREE ROAD
HOWARD
MAPS
MAINTENANCE
OIL COMPANY
THEN RASCAL ARRIVED... HE WORE A JUNGLE OUTFIT... CAMEL COAT, ALIGATOR SHOES, BUTTERFLY TIE... AND HIS POCKET A MOST SPECIAL .38 SPECIAL.
OUR LITTLE HOTSHOT BLONDE WENT OVER TO SHOW MULLEY THE MENU... CHICKEN BREAST, A PIECE OF JUICY LEG, AND HOT STUFFING.
RASCAL HAD MADE THE SWITCH WHILE MULLEY WAS ENJOYING THE APPETIZERS WRAPPED IN BLACK. THE COP HAD EYES ONLY FOR LULU WHO ALLOWED HERSELF TO BE FELT UP AS ARRANGED.
AND WHAT WILL THE GENTLEMAN HAVE?
I DON'T KNOW ABOUT THE GENTLEMAN, BUT I'LL HAVE EVERYTHING.
PARDON, SIR?
SURE, THAT TOO.
5

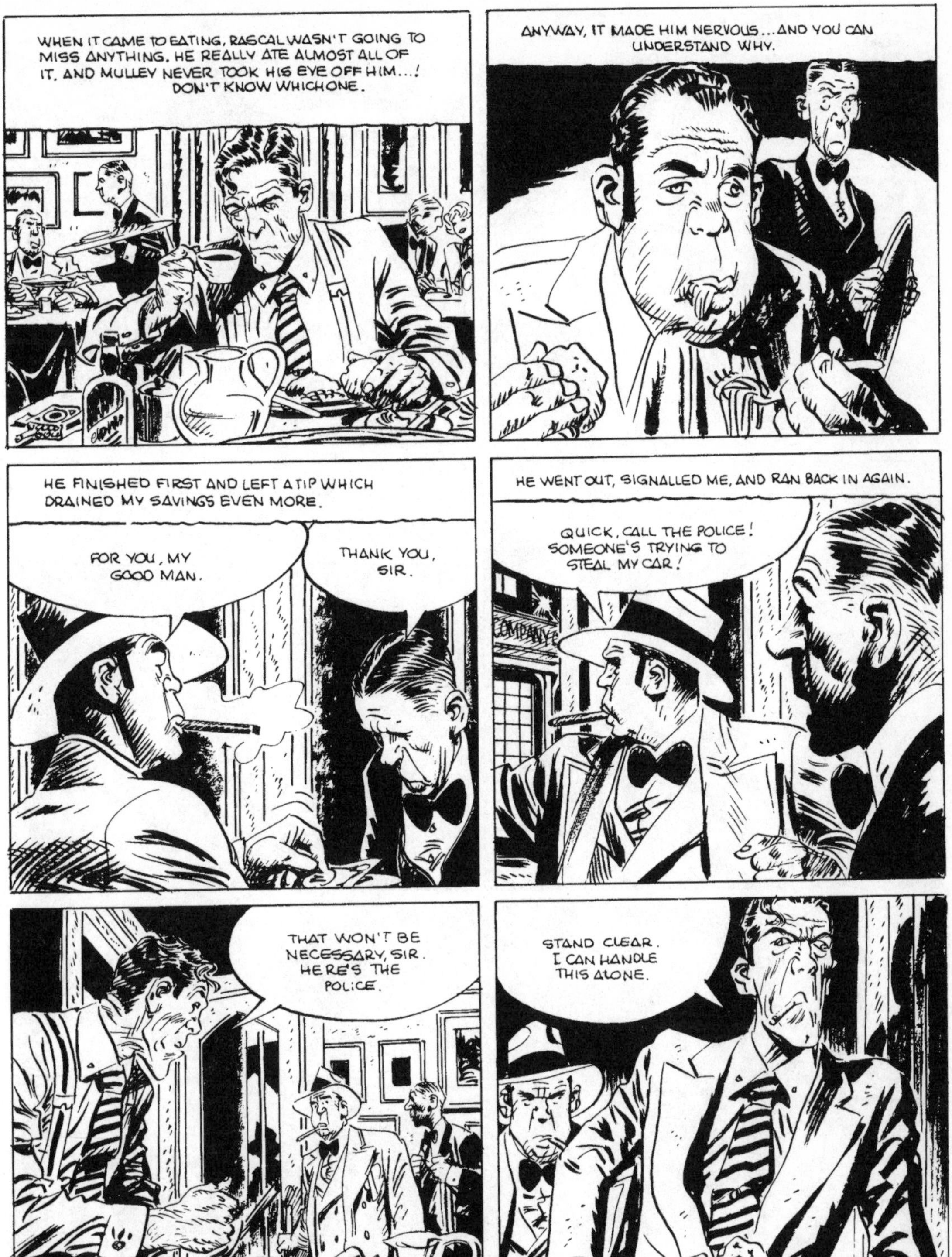
WHEN IT CAME TO EATING, RASCAL WASN'T GOING TO MISS ANYTHING. HE REALLY ATE ALMOST ALL OF IT, AND MULLEY NEVER TOOK HIS EYE OFF HIM...! DON'T KNOW WHICH ONE.
ANYWAY, IT MADE HIM NERVOUS... AND YOU CAN UNDERSTAND WHY.
HE FINISHED FIRST AND LEFT A TIP WHICH DRAINED MY SAVINGS EVEN MORE.
FOR YOU, MY GOOD MAN.
THANK YOU, SIR.
HE WENT OUT, SIGNALLED ME, AND RAN BACK IN AGAIN.
QUICK, CALL THE POLICE! SOMEONE'S TRYING TO STEAL MY CAR!
THAT WON'T BE NECESSARY, SIR. HERE'S THE POLICE.
STAND CLEAR. I CAN HANDLE THIS ALONE.
6

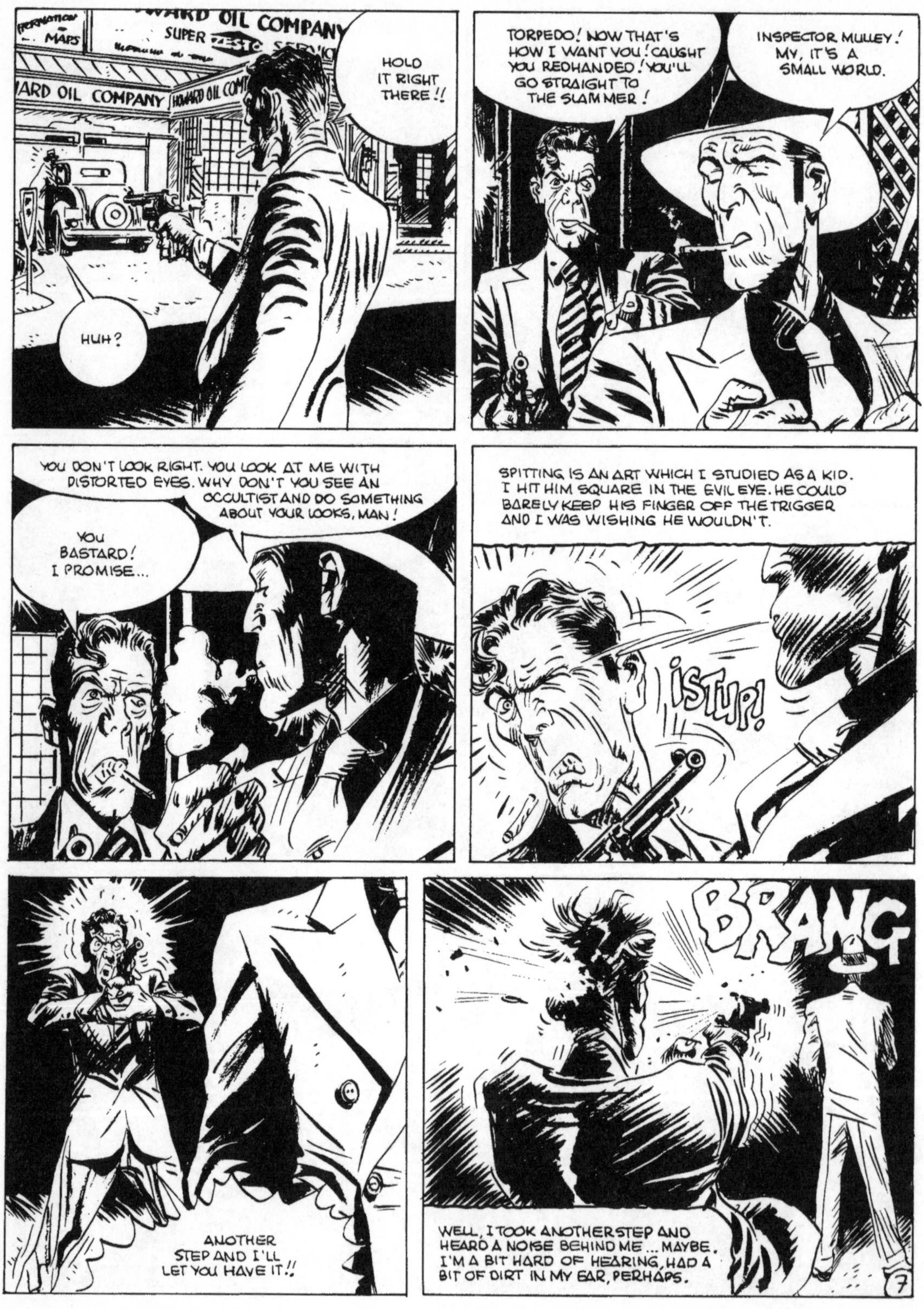
HOWARD OIL COMPANY
SUPER ZESTO SERVICE
MAPS
HOWARD OIL COMPANY
HOWARD OIL COMPANY
HOLD IT RIGHT THERE!!
HUH?
TORPEDO! NOW THAT'S HOW I WANT YOU! CAUGHT YOU REDHANDED! YOU'LL GO STRAIGHT TO THE SLAMMER!
INSPECTOR MULLEY! MY, IT'S A SMALL WORLD.
YOU DON'T LOOK RIGHT. YOU LOOK AT ME WITH DISTORTED EYES. WHY DON'T YOU SEE AN OCCULTIST AND DO SOMETHING ABOUT YOUR LOOKS, MAN!
YOU BASTARD! I PROMISE...
SPITTING IS AN ART WHICH I STUDIED AS A KID. I HIT HIM SQUARE IN THE EVIL EYE. HE COULD BARELY KEEP HIS FINGER OFF THE TRIGGER AND I WAS WISHING HE WOULDN'T.
ISTUP!
ANOTHER STEP AND I'LL LET YOU HAVE IT!!
BRANG
WELL, I TOOK ANOTHER STEP AND HEARD A NOISE BEHIND ME ... MAYBE. I'M A BIT HARD OF HEARING, HAD A BIT OF DIRT IN MY EAR, PERHAPS.
7

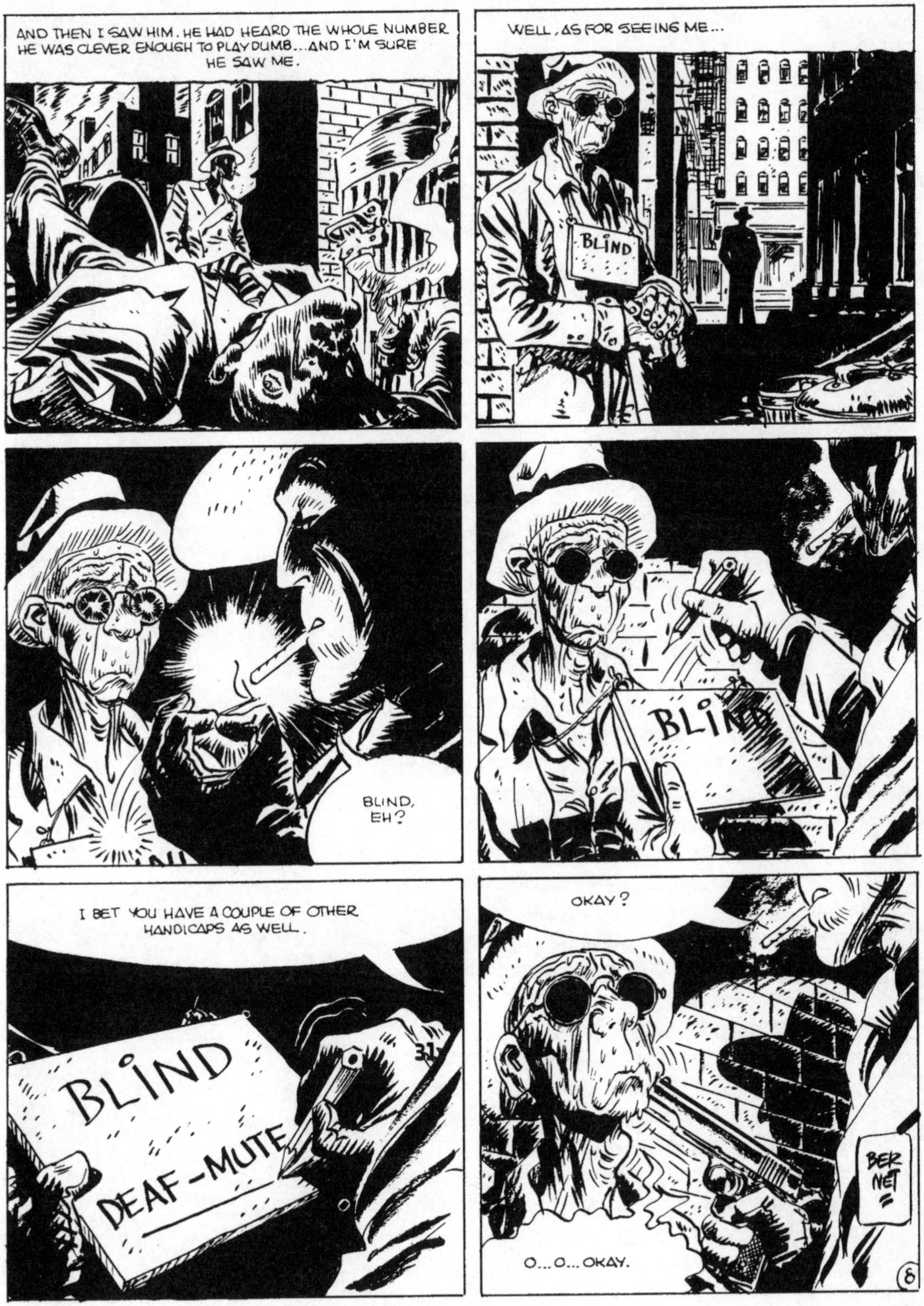
AND THEN I SAW HIM. HE HAD HEARD THE WHOLE NUMBER
HE WAS CLEVER ENOUGH TO PLAY DUMB... AND I'M SURE HE SAW ME.
WELL, AS FOR SEEING ME...
BLIND
BLIND, EH?
BLIND
I BET YOU HAVE A COUPLE OF OTHER HANDICAPS AS WELL.
BLIND
DEAF-MUTE
OKAY?
O... O... OKAY.
BERNET
8

"A man could make
a fortune in a few days!
I'll pay anything for it – anything!"

In the first-person style of *True Confessions*
magazine, Stella Brady tells her story from
behind bars of how she becomes an accomplice
in a scheme to fleece suckers gullible enough
to believe in a machine that could crank out
freshly minted cash.
Joe Simon and Jack Kirby are one of the
greatest partnerships in comic books, kick-
starting whole genres in America like kid
gangs or romance. When these Jewish New
Yorkers started getting anti-Semitic death
threats for creating their Hitler-punching
super-patriot *Captain America* in 1941, Mayor
LaGuardia himself arranged round-the-clock
protection for their studio. Raised in the
Bowery, Kirby could not help coming across
crime on New York's streets, escaping thanks
to his innate artistic talent. His forte for
science fiction and mechanical design, seen so
well in the *Fantastic Four* and other Marvel
co-creations with Stan Lee, makes his phony
contraption here almost believable.

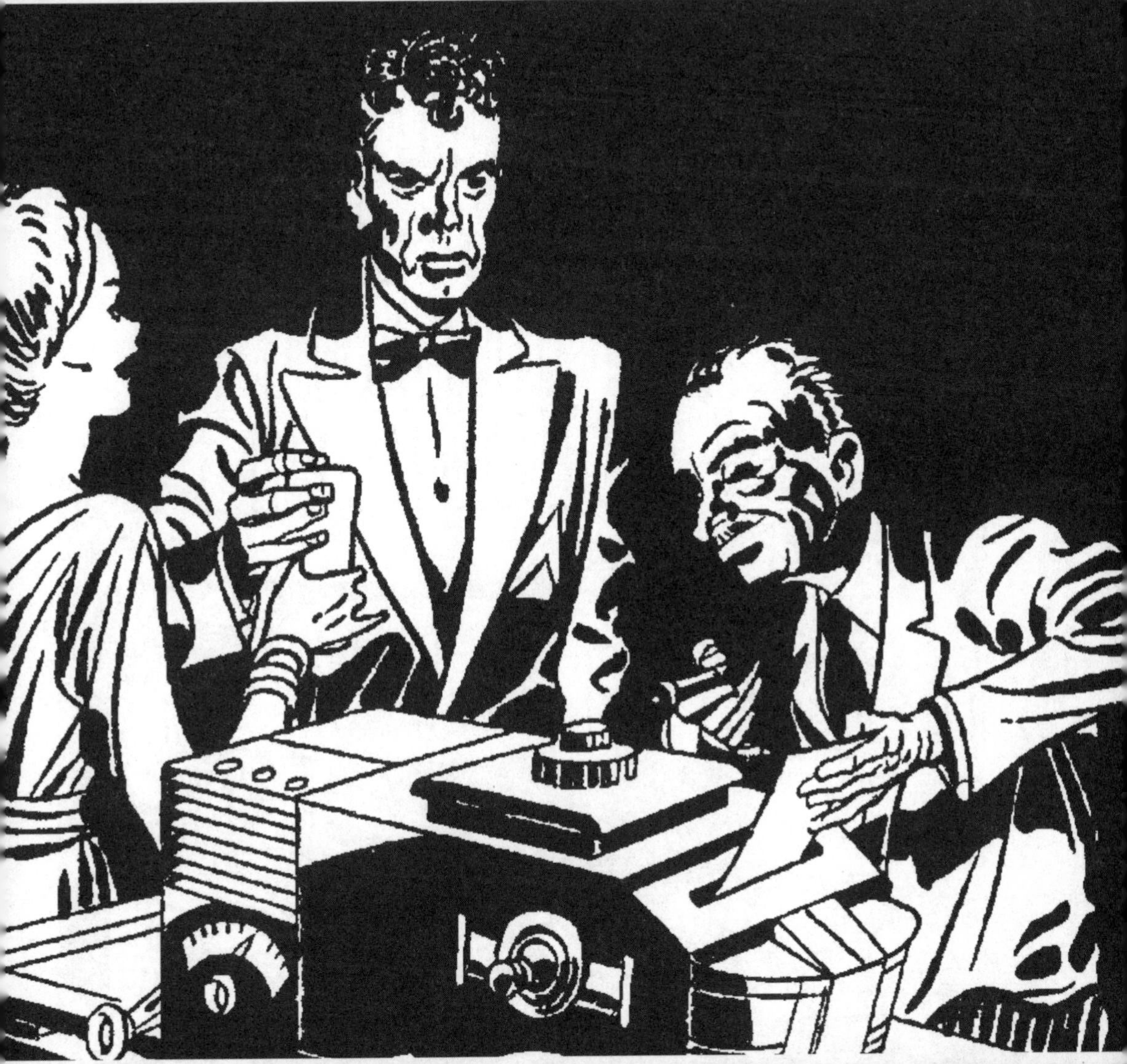

The Money-Making Machine Swindlers

Joe Simon & Jack Kirby (script and art) 1948

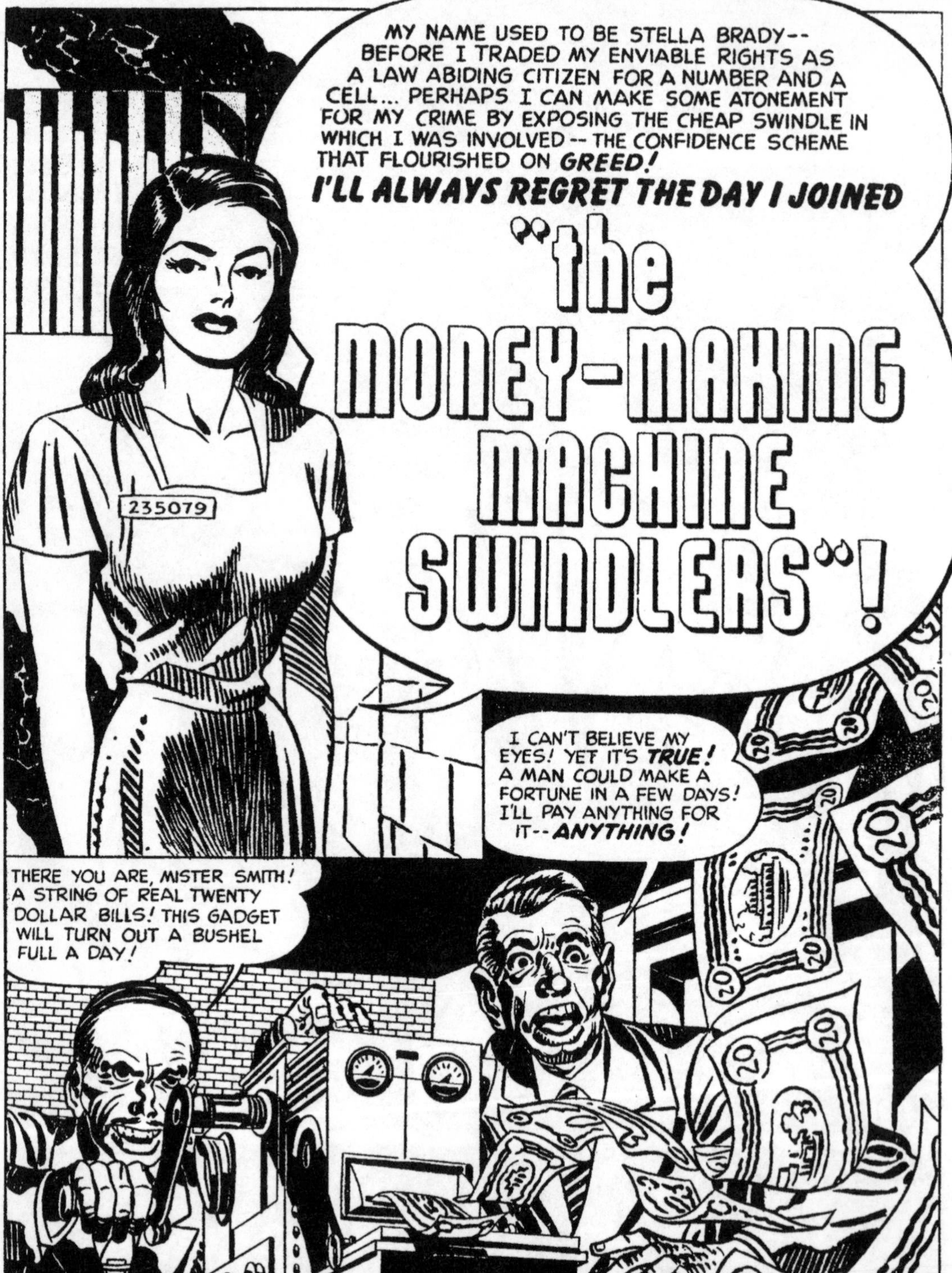

MY NAME USED TO BE STELLA BRADY-- BEFORE I TRADED MY ENVIABLE RIGHTS AS A LAW ABIDING CITIZEN FOR A NUMBER AND A CELL... PERHAPS I CAN MAKE SOME ATONEMENT FOR MY CRIME BY EXPOSING THE CHEAP SWINDLE IN WHICH I WAS INVOLVED -- THE CONFIDENCE SCHEME THAT FLOURISHED ON ***GREED!***
I'LL ALWAYS REGRET THE DAY I JOINED
"the MONEY-MAKING MACHINE SWINDLERS"!
235079
THERE YOU ARE, MISTER SMITH! A STRING OF REAL TWENTY DOLLAR BILLS! THIS GADGET WILL TURN OUT A BUSHEL FULL A DAY!
I CAN'T BELIEVE MY EYES! YET IT'S ***TRUE!*** A MAN COULD MAKE A FORTUNE IN A FEW DAYS! I'LL PAY ANYTHING FOR IT--***ANYTHING!***

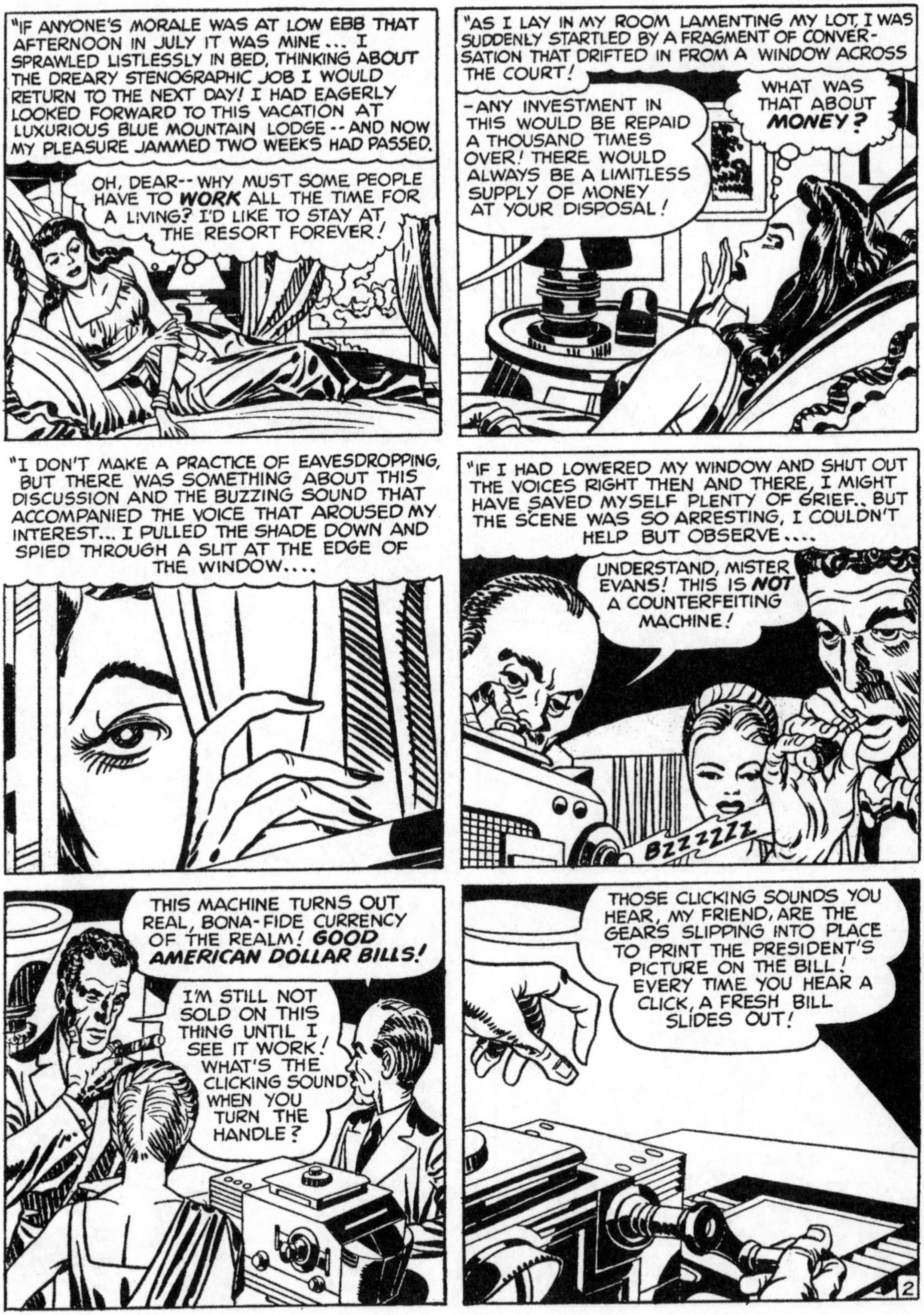
"IF ANYONE'S MORALE WAS AT LOW EBB THAT AFTERNOON IN JULY IT WAS MINE ... I SPRAWLED LISTLESSLY IN BED, THINKING ABOUT THE DREARY STENOGRAPHIC JOB I WOULD RETURN TO THE NEXT DAY! I HAD EAGERLY LOOKED FORWARD TO THIS VACATION AT LUXURIOUS BLUE MOUNTAIN LODGE -- AND NOW MY PLEASURE JAMMED TWO WEEKS HAD PASSED.
OH, DEAR-- WHY MUST SOME PEOPLE HAVE TO **WORK** ALL THE TIME FOR A LIVING? I'D LIKE TO STAY AT THE RESORT FOREVER!
"AS I LAY IN MY ROOM LAMENTING MY LOT, I WAS SUDDENLY STARTLED BY A FRAGMENT OF CONVERSATION THAT DRIFTED IN FROM A WINDOW ACROSS THE COURT!
-ANY INVESTMENT IN THIS WOULD BE REPAID A THOUSAND TIMES OVER! THERE WOULD ALWAYS BE A LIMITLESS SUPPLY OF MONEY AT YOUR DISPOSAL!
WHAT WAS THAT ABOUT **MONEY?**
"I DON'T MAKE A PRACTICE OF EAVESDROPPING, BUT THERE WAS SOMETHING ABOUT THIS DISCUSSION AND THE BUZZING SOUND THAT ACCOMPANIED THE VOICE THAT AROUSED MY INTEREST... I PULLED THE SHADE DOWN AND SPIED THROUGH A SLIT AT THE EDGE OF THE WINDOW....
"IF I HAD LOWERED MY WINDOW AND SHUT OUT THE VOICES RIGHT THEN AND THERE, I MIGHT HAVE SAVED MYSELF PLENTY OF GRIEF.. BUT THE SCENE WAS SO ARRESTING, I COULDN'T HELP BUT OBSERVE....
UNDERSTAND, MISTER EVANS! THIS IS **NOT** A COUNTERFEITING MACHINE!
BZZZZZZ
THIS MACHINE TURNS OUT REAL, BONA-FIDE CURRENCY OF THE REALM! **GOOD AMERICAN DOLLAR BILLS!**
I'M STILL NOT SOLD ON THIS THING UNTIL I SEE IT WORK! WHAT'S THE CLICKING SOUND WHEN YOU TURN THE HANDLE?
THOSE CLICKING SOUNDS YOU HEAR, MY FRIEND, ARE THE GEARS SLIPPING INTO PLACE TO PRINT THE PRESIDENT'S PICTURE ON THE BILL! EVERY TIME YOU HEAR A CLICK, A FRESH BILL SLIDES OUT!
2

THESE FOUR SMALL ELETRIC BULBS REPRODUCE THE REST OF THE CHARACTERISTICS ON THE PAPER BY A PHOTOGRAPHIC PROCESS...

ALL RIGHT--OKAY--THAT'S ENOUGH OF A SALES TALK! I WANT TO SEE THE GADGET TURN OUT *GREENBACKS!*

WON'T YOU HAVE A COKE, MISTER EVANS?

THANKS!

IT'S ABSURDLY SIMPLE! I TAKE THIS SPECIAL BOND PAPER WHICH HAS BEEN CUT TO PROPER SIZE--PLACE IT IN THE RECEIVING SLOT--AND

"FROM MY WINDOW, ACROSS THE COURT, I GAZED INCREDULOUSLY AS THE LITTLE MAN TURNED THE CRANK HANDLE IN TUNE WITH A SUCCESSION OF MECHANICAL SOUNDS--AND THAT FANTASTIC MACHINE DISGORGED TWO NEW DOLLAR BILLS.

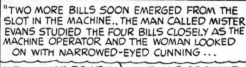

THERE YOU ARE, MISTER EVANS TRY AND FIND FAULT WITH THOSE TWO LEAVES OF LETTUCE!

TURN OUT A COUPLE MORE, MONTGOMERY. --THESE ARE VERY INTERESTING!

I'LL HAVE TO REPLENISH THE INK HOPPERS FIRST...--GOT TO HAVE JUST THE RIGHT MIXTURE TO GET A LEGITIMATE TINT ON THE BILL!

LIGHT, MISTER EVANS?

"TWO MORE BILLS SOON EMERGED FROM THE SLOT IN THE MACHINE.. THE MAN CALLED MISTER EVANS STUDIED THE FOUR BILLS CLOSELY AS THE MACHINE OPERATOR AND THE WOMAN LOOKED ON WITH NARROWED-EYED CUNNING...

WELL, WHAT DO YOU THINK, MISTER EVANS?

WHAT KIND OF CHUMP DO YOU TAKE ME FOR, MONTY?

THE SERIAL NUMBERS ON THESE BILLS ARE AS FAR APART AS THE FOUR POINTS OF THE COMPASS! IF THIS MACHINE *REALLY* PRINTED MONEY, THE SERIAL NUMBERS WOULD BE IN CONSECUTIVE ORDER!--

3

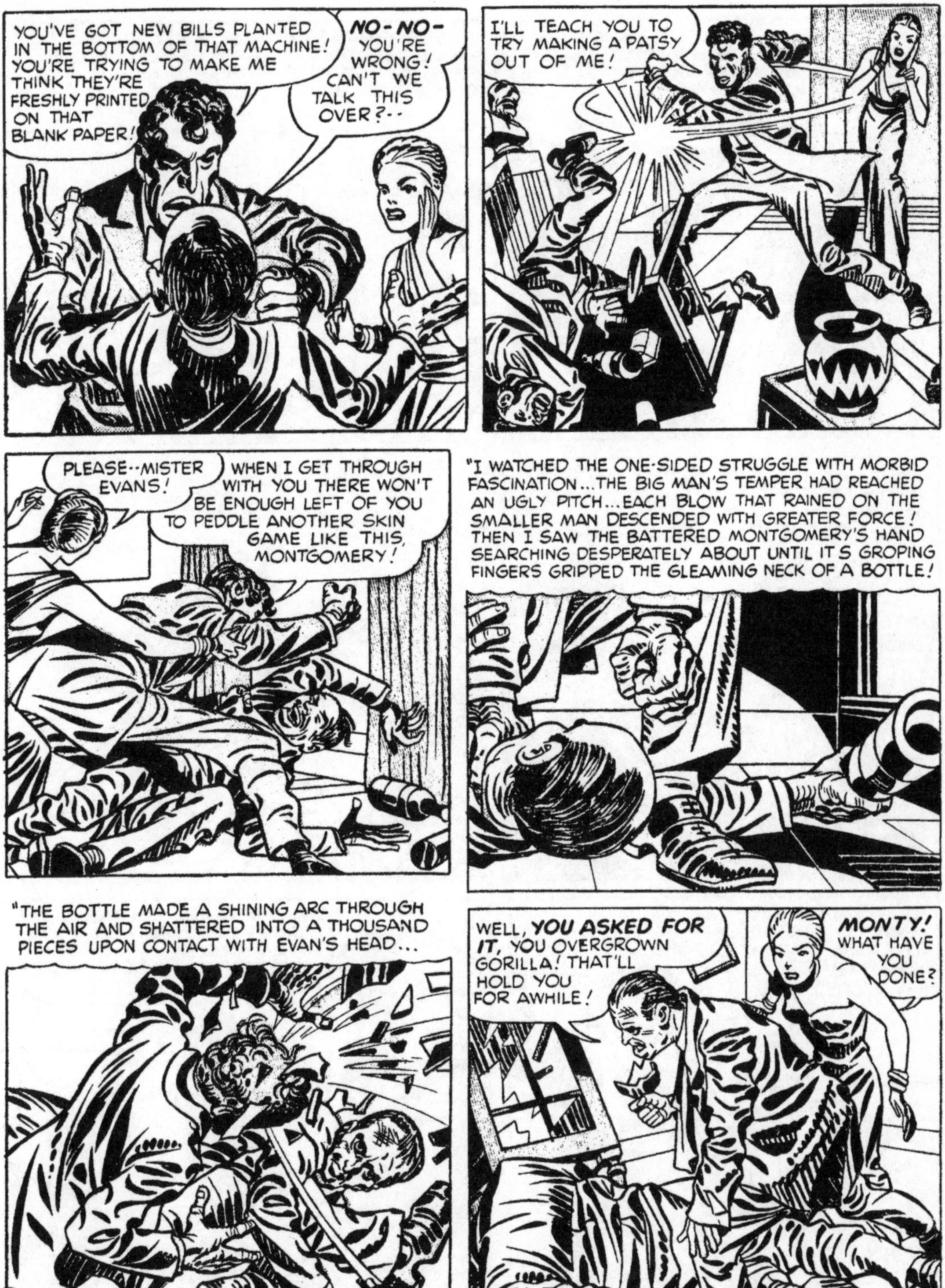
YOU'VE GOT NEW BILLS PLANTED IN THE BOTTOM OF THAT MACHINE! YOU'RE TRYING TO MAKE ME THINK THEY'RE FRESHLY PRINTED ON THAT BLANK PAPER!
NO-NO- YOU'RE WRONG! CAN'T WE TALK THIS OVER?--
I'LL TEACH YOU TO TRY MAKING A PATSY OUT OF ME!
PLEASE--MISTER EVANS!
WHEN I GET THROUGH WITH YOU THERE WON'T BE ENOUGH LEFT OF YOU TO PEDDLE ANOTHER SKIN GAME LIKE THIS, MONTGOMERY!
"I WATCHED THE ONE-SIDED STRUGGLE WITH MORBID FASCINATION...THE BIG MAN'S TEMPER HAD REACHED AN UGLY PITCH...EACH BLOW THAT RAINED ON THE SMALLER MAN DESCENDED WITH GREATER FORCE! THEN I SAW THE BATTERED MONTGOMERY'S HAND SEARCHING DESPERATELY ABOUT UNTIL IT'S GROPING FINGERS GRIPPED THE GLEAMING NECK OF A BOTTLE!
"THE BOTTLE MADE A SHINING ARC THROUGH THE AIR AND SHATTERED INTO A THOUSAND PIECES UPON CONTACT WITH EVAN'S HEAD...
WELL, **YOU ASKED FOR IT,** YOU OVERGROWN GORILLA! THAT'LL HOLD YOU FOR AWHILE!
MONTY! WHAT HAVE YOU DONE?
4

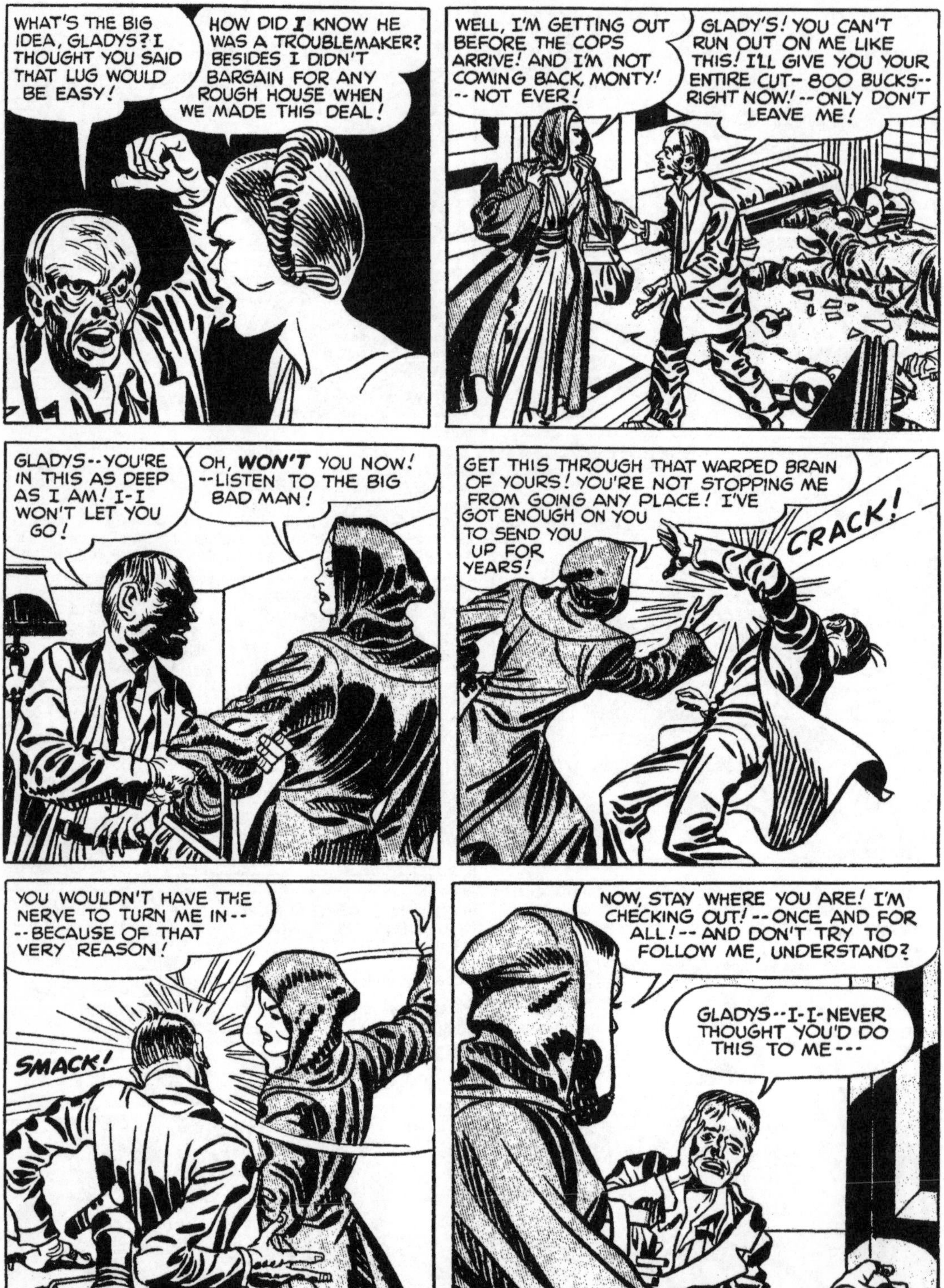
WHAT'S THE BIG IDEA, GLADYS? I THOUGHT YOU SAID THAT LUG WOULD BE EASY!
HOW DID I KNOW HE WAS A TROUBLEMAKER? BESIDES I DIDN'T BARGAIN FOR ANY ROUGH HOUSE WHEN WE MADE THIS DEAL!
WELL, I'M GETTING OUT BEFORE THE COPS ARRIVE! AND I'M NOT COMING BACK, MONTY! --NOT EVER!
GLADY'S! YOU CAN'T RUN OUT ON ME LIKE THIS! I'LL GIVE YOU YOUR ENTIRE CUT- 800 BUCKS-- RIGHT NOW! --ONLY DON'T LEAVE ME!
GLADYS--YOU'RE IN THIS AS DEEP AS I AM! I-I WON'T LET YOU GO!
OH, WON'T YOU NOW! --LISTEN TO THE BIG BAD MAN!
GET THIS THROUGH THAT WARPED BRAIN OF YOURS! YOU'RE NOT STOPPING ME FROM GOING ANY PLACE! I'VE GOT ENOUGH ON YOU TO SEND YOU UP FOR YEARS!
CRACK!
YOU WOULDN'T HAVE THE NERVE TO TURN ME IN-- --BECAUSE OF THAT VERY REASON!
SMACK!
NOW, STAY WHERE YOU ARE! I'M CHECKING OUT! --ONCE AND FOR ALL!-- AND DON'T TRY TO FOLLOW ME, UNDERSTAND?
GLADYS--I-I-NEVER THOUGHT YOU'D DO THIS TO ME---
5

"AT THIS POINT I FOUND MYSELF TORN BETWEEN TWO EMOTIONS... A DEEP SENSE OF REPROACH FOR WHAT I WAS THINKING AND THE DESIRE TO PUT MY THOUGHTS INTO ACTION...

MONTGOMERY'S WORK IS OBVIOUSLY A RACKET--YET IT MAY BE MY CHANCE TO MAKE REAL MONEY! I'M GOING TO LOOK INTO THIS!

"I DIDN'T HAVE TO KNOCK ON MONTGOMERY'S DOOR BECAUSE IT WAS STILL OPEN FROM GLADY'S STORMY EXIT! THE LITTLE MAN SAT DEJECTEDLY IN A CORNER ---SLOWLY TURNING HIS BRUISED, GNOMISH HEAD IN MY DIRECTION AS I CROSSED THE THRESHOLD!

GO AWAY, SISTER, I'VE GOT TROUBLES OF MY OWN...

"THE SHARP EDGE TO MONTGOMERY'S TONE SOFTENED ABRUPTLY WHEN HE LOOKED UP AT ME... BUT I THINK MY FRIENDLINESS MEANT MORE TO HIM AT THAT MOMENT THAN FEMININE ALLURE...

I'M YOUR NEIGHBOR ACROSS THE COURT.. MY WINDOW IS DIRECTLY OPPOSITE YOURS... I- I ACCIDENTALLY WITNESSED THE SCENE THAT JUST TOOK PLACE HERE--

WELL--? WELL--! WON'T YOU SIT DOWN?

IT WAS ALL SO TERRIBLE! I JUST HAD TO COME IN AND FIND OUT IF THERE WASN'T ANYTHING I COULD DO TO HELP YOU?

HMMM-I SEE! I WISH GLADYS HAD YOUR ATTITUDE... THINGS WOULD BE RUNNING SMOOTHLY.. HOWEVER, I DON'T SEE WHY THEY STILL CAN'T!

WE MIGHT AS WELL INTRODUCE OURSELVES.. I'M STELLA BRADY ABOUT TO GO BACK TO A BORING JOB IN THE CITY--AND VERY MUCH INTERESTED IN A NEW VOCATION WITH THESE SURROUNDINGS!

I GET YOU, HONEY! YOU'VE GOT A DEAL! TOGETHER WE CAN WORK THE SUMMER RESORTS AND CLEAN UP A FORTUNE! I'M WILLIE MONTGOMERY--- MONTY-- TO YOU!

I OVERHEARD YOUR UNRULY CLIENT DEBUNKING YOUR MONEY-MAKING MACHINE! I DON'T IMAGINE HE WAS WRONG... IT IS A FAKE, ISN'T IT?

6

39

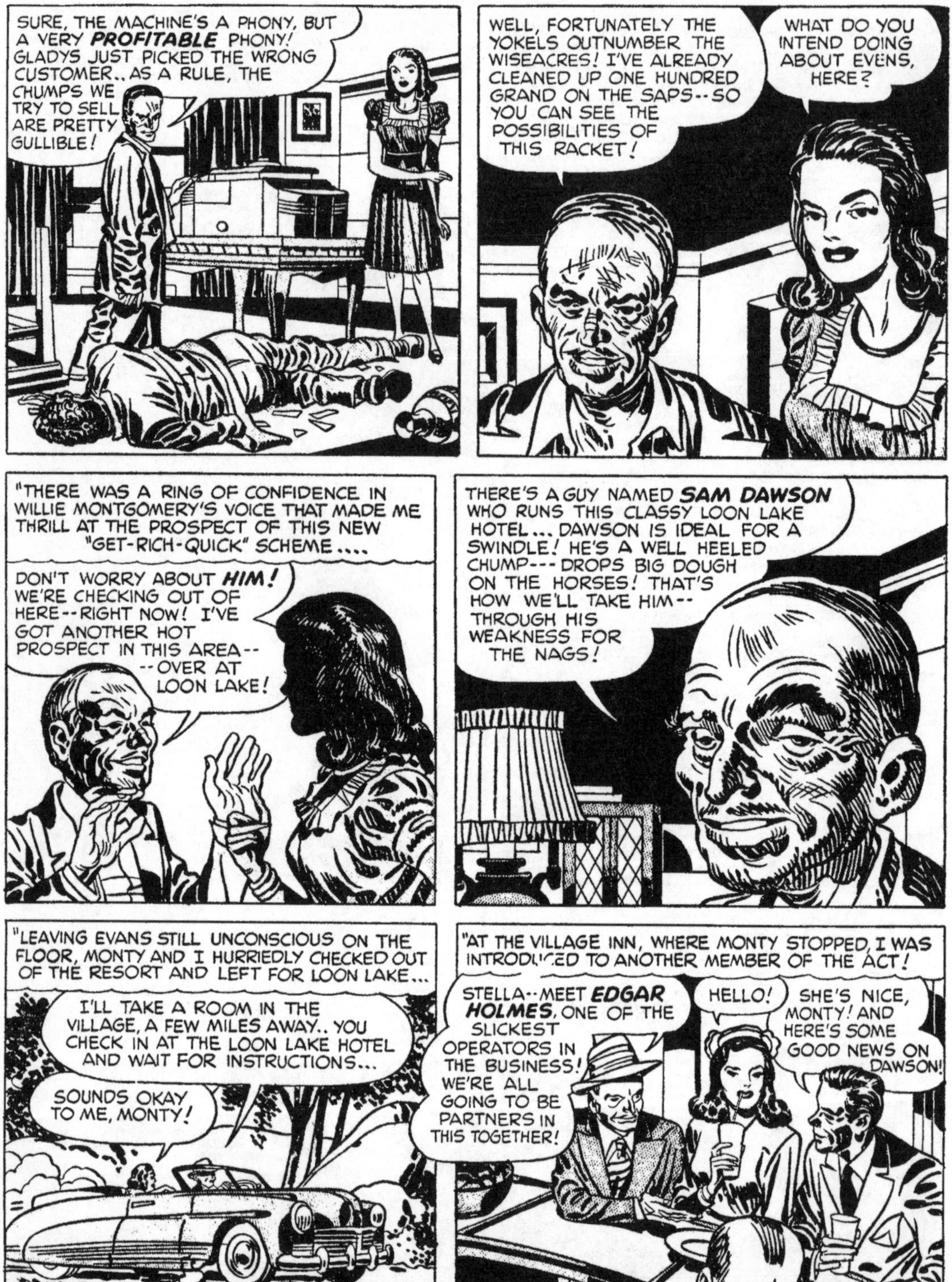
SURE, THE MACHINE'S A PHONY, BUT A VERY PROFITABLE PHONY! GLADYS JUST PICKED THE WRONG CUSTOMER.. AS A RULE, THE CHUMPS WE TRY TO SELL ARE PRETTY GULLIBLE!
WELL, FORTUNATELY THE YOKELS OUTNUMBER THE WISEACRES! I'VE ALREADY CLEANED UP ONE HUNDRED GRAND ON THE SAPS--SO YOU CAN SEE THE POSSIBILITIES OF THIS RACKET!
WHAT DO YOU INTEND DOING ABOUT EVENS, HERE?
"THERE WAS A RING OF CONFIDENCE IN WILLIE MONTGOMERY'S VOICE THAT MADE ME THRILL AT THE PROSPECT OF THIS NEW "GET-RICH-QUICK" SCHEME....
DON'T WORRY ABOUT HIM! WE'RE CHECKING OUT OF HERE--RIGHT NOW! I'VE GOT ANOTHER HOT PROSPECT IN THIS AREA-- --OVER AT LOON LAKE!
THERE'S A GUY NAMED SAM DAWSON WHO RUNS THIS CLASSY LOON LAKE HOTEL... DAWSON IS IDEAL FOR A SWINDLE! HE'S A WELL HEELED CHUMP---DROPS BIG DOUGH ON THE HORSES! THAT'S HOW WE'LL TAKE HIM--THROUGH HIS WEAKNESS FOR THE NAGS!
"LEAVING EVANS STILL UNCONSCIOUS ON THE FLOOR, MONTY AND I HURRIEDLY CHECKED OUT OF THE RESORT AND LEFT FOR LOON LAKE...
I'LL TAKE A ROOM IN THE VILLAGE, A FEW MILES AWAY.. YOU CHECK IN AT THE LOON LAKE HOTEL AND WAIT FOR INSTRUCTIONS...
SOUNDS OKAY TO ME, MONTY!
"AT THE VILLAGE INN, WHERE MONTY STOPPED, I WAS INTRODUCED TO ANOTHER MEMBER OF THE ACT!
STELLA--MEET EDGAR HOLMES, ONE OF THE SLICKEST OPERATORS IN THE BUSINESS! WE'RE ALL GOING TO BE PARTNERS IN THIS TOGETHER!
HELLO!
SHE'S NICE, MONTY! AND HERE'S SOME GOOD NEWS ON DAWSON!
7

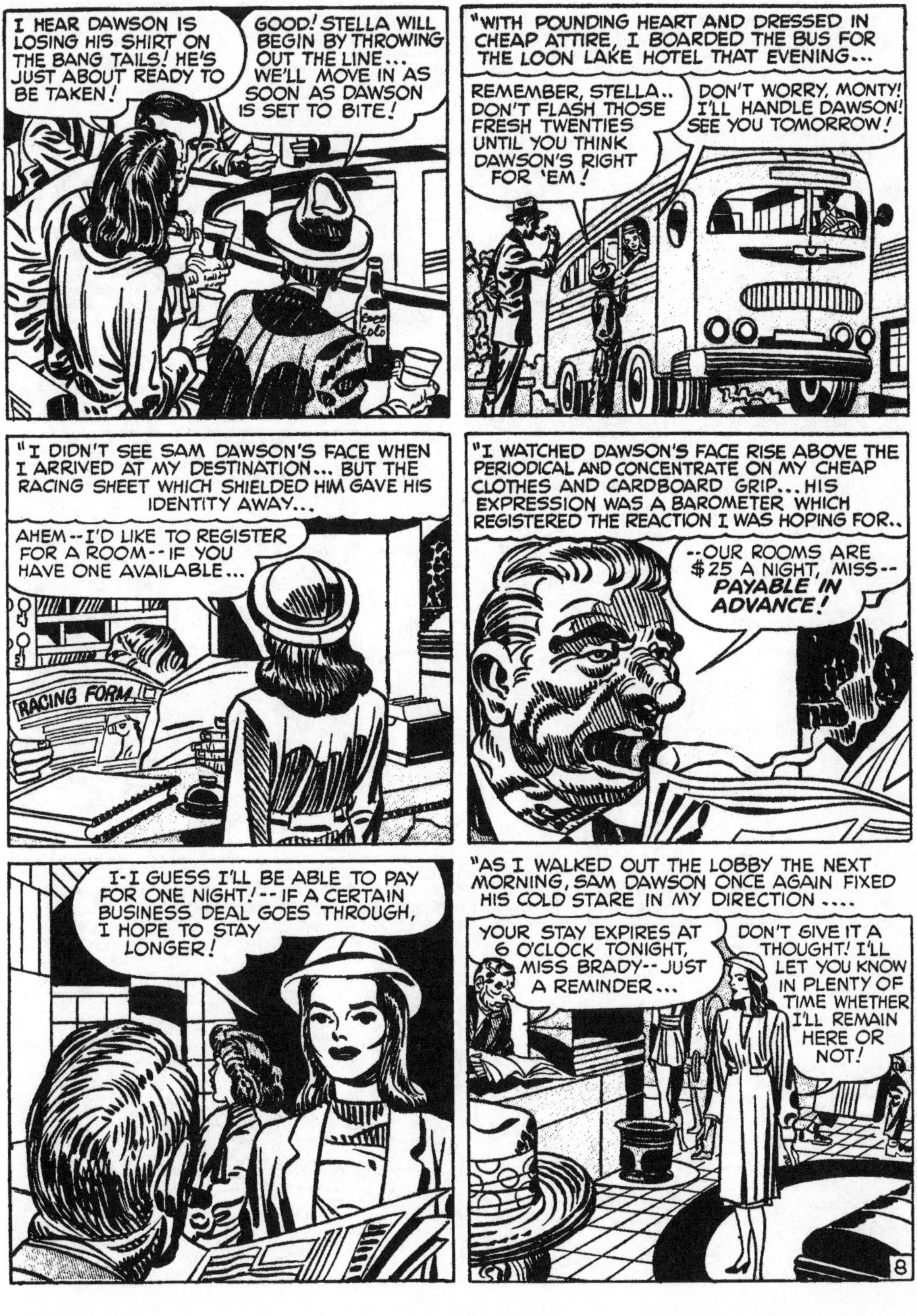

I HEAR DAWSON IS LOSING HIS SHIRT ON THE BANG TAILS! HE'S JUST ABOUT READY TO BE TAKEN!
GOOD! STELLA WILL BEGIN BY THROWING OUT THE LINE... WE'LL MOVE IN AS SOON AS DAWSON IS SET TO BITE!
"WITH POUNDING HEART AND DRESSED IN CHEAP ATTIRE, I BOARDED THE BUS FOR THE LOON LAKE HOTEL THAT EVENING...
REMEMBER, STELLA.. DON'T FLASH THOSE FRESH TWENTIES UNTIL YOU THINK DAWSON'S RIGHT FOR 'EM!
DON'T WORRY, MONTY! I'LL HANDLE DAWSON! SEE YOU TOMORROW!
"I DIDN'T SEE SAM DAWSON'S FACE WHEN I ARRIVED AT MY DESTINATION... BUT THE RACING SHEET WHICH SHIELDED HIM GAVE HIS IDENTITY AWAY...
AHEM--I'D LIKE TO REGISTER FOR A ROOM--IF YOU HAVE ONE AVAILABLE...
RACING FORM
"I WATCHED DAWSON'S FACE RISE ABOVE THE PERIODICAL AND CONCENTRATE ON MY CHEAP CLOTHES AND CARDBOARD GRIP... HIS EXPRESSION WAS A BAROMETER WHICH REGISTERED THE REACTION I WAS HOPING FOR..
--OUR ROOMS ARE $25 A NIGHT, MISS-- ***PAYABLE IN ADVANCE!***
I-I GUESS I'LL BE ABLE TO PAY FOR ONE NIGHT!--IF A CERTAIN BUSINESS DEAL GOES THROUGH, I HOPE TO STAY LONGER!
"AS I WALKED OUT THE LOBBY THE NEXT MORNING, SAM DAWSON ONCE AGAIN FIXED HIS COLD STARE IN MY DIRECTION ....
YOUR STAY EXPIRES AT 6 O'CLOCK TONIGHT, MISS BRADY--JUST A REMINDER...
DON'T GIVE IT A THOUGHT! I'LL LET YOU KNOW IN PLENTY OF TIME WHETHER I'LL REMAIN HERE OR NOT!
8

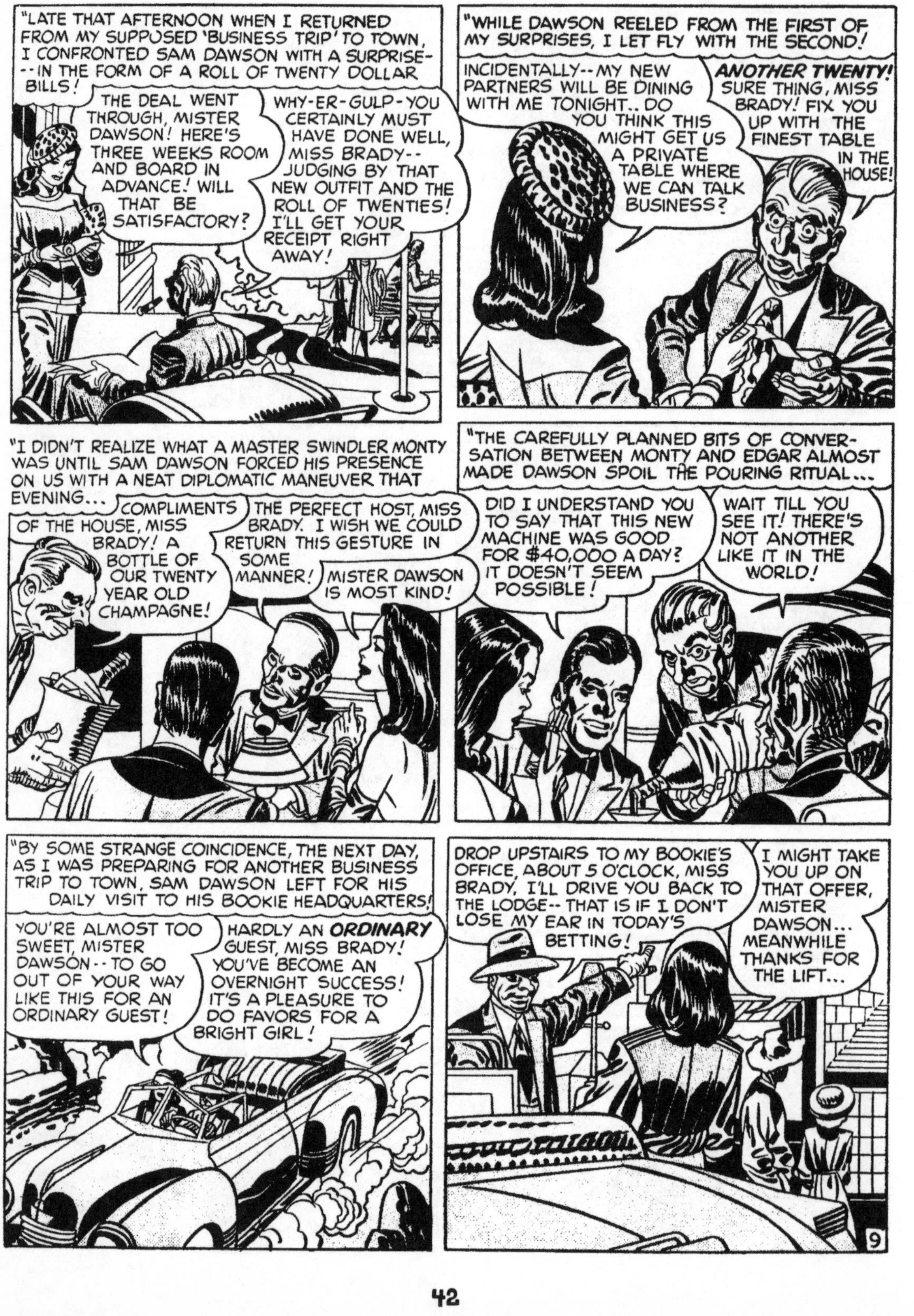
"LATE THAT AFTERNOON WHEN I RETURNED FROM MY SUPPOSED 'BUSINESS TRIP' TO TOWN, I CONFRONTED SAM DAWSON WITH A SURPRISE--IN THE FORM OF A ROLL OF TWENTY DOLLAR BILLS!
THE DEAL WENT THROUGH, MISTER DAWSON! HERE'S THREE WEEKS ROOM AND BOARD IN ADVANCE! WILL THAT BE SATISFACTORY?
WHY-ER-GULP-YOU CERTAINLY MUST HAVE DONE WELL, MISS BRADY--JUDGING BY THAT NEW OUTFIT AND THE ROLL OF TWENTIES! I'LL GET YOUR RECEIPT RIGHT AWAY!
"WHILE DAWSON REELED FROM THE FIRST OF MY SURPRISES, I LET FLY WITH THE SECOND!
INCIDENTALLY--MY NEW PARTNERS WILL BE DINING WITH ME TONIGHT.. DO YOU THINK THIS MIGHT GET US A PRIVATE TABLE WHERE WE CAN TALK BUSINESS?
ANOTHER TWENTY! SURE THING, MISS BRADY! FIX YOU UP WITH THE FINEST TABLE IN THE HOUSE!
"I DIDN'T REALIZE WHAT A MASTER SWINDLER MONTY WAS UNTIL SAM DAWSON FORCED HIS PRESENCE ON US WITH A NEAT DIPLOMATIC MANEUVER THAT EVENING...
COMPLIMENTS OF THE HOUSE, MISS BRADY! A BOTTLE OF OUR TWENTY YEAR OLD CHAMPAGNE!
THE PERFECT HOST, MISS BRADY. I WISH WE COULD RETURN THIS GESTURE IN SOME MANNER!
MISTER DAWSON IS MOST KIND!
"THE CAREFULLY PLANNED BITS OF CONVERSATION BETWEEN MONTY AND EDGAR ALMOST MADE DAWSON SPOIL THE POURING RITUAL...
DID I UNDERSTAND YOU TO SAY THAT THIS NEW MACHINE WAS GOOD FOR $40,000 A DAY? IT DOESN'T SEEM POSSIBLE!
WAIT TILL YOU SEE IT! THERE'S NOT ANOTHER LIKE IT IN THE WORLD!
"BY SOME STRANGE COINCIDENCE, THE NEXT DAY, AS I WAS PREPARING FOR ANOTHER BUSINESS TRIP TO TOWN, SAM DAWSON LEFT FOR HIS DAILY VISIT TO HIS BOOKIE HEADQUARTERS!
YOU'RE ALMOST TOO SWEET, MISTER DAWSON--TO GO OUT OF YOUR WAY LIKE THIS FOR AN ORDINARY GUEST!
HARDLY AN ORDINARY GUEST, MISS BRADY! YOU'VE BECOME AN OVERNIGHT SUCCESS! IT'S A PLEASURE TO DO FAVORS FOR A BRIGHT GIRL!
DROP UPSTAIRS TO MY BOOKIE'S OFFICE, ABOUT 5 O'CLOCK, MISS BRADY, I'LL DRIVE YOU BACK TO THE LODGE--THAT IS IF I DON'T LOSE MY EAR IN TODAY'S BETTING!
I MIGHT TAKE YOU UP ON THAT OFFER, MISTER DAWSON... MEANWHILE THANKS FOR THE LIFT...
9

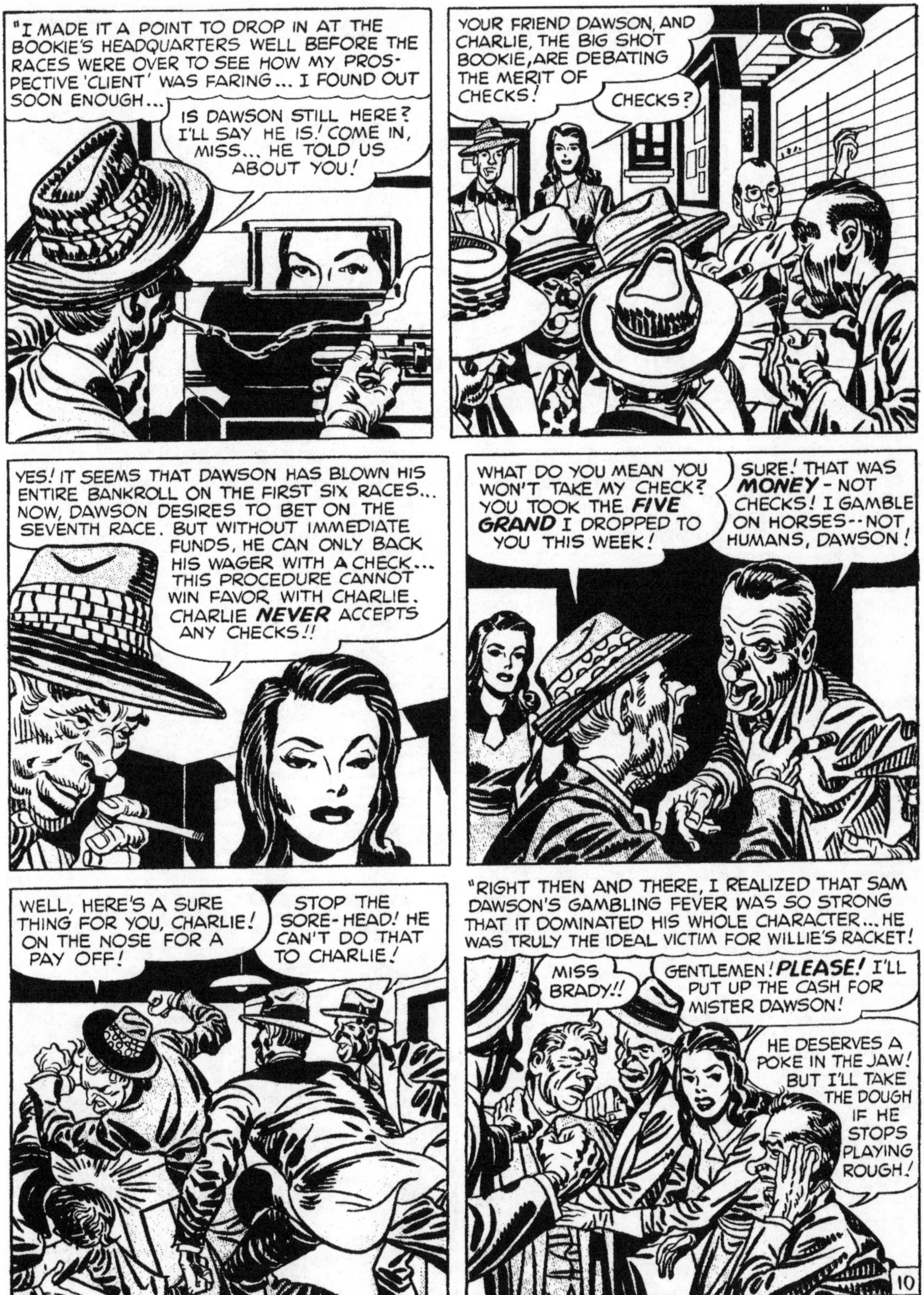
"I MADE IT A POINT TO DROP IN AT THE BOOKIE'S HEADQUARTERS WELL BEFORE THE RACES WERE OVER TO SEE HOW MY PROSPECTIVE 'CLIENT' WAS FARING... I FOUND OUT SOON ENOUGH...
IS DAWSON STILL HERE?
I'LL SAY HE IS! COME IN, MISS... HE TOLD US ABOUT YOU!
YOUR FRIEND DAWSON, AND CHARLIE, THE BIG SHOT BOOKIE, ARE DEBATING THE MERIT OF CHECKS!
CHECKS?
YES! IT SEEMS THAT DAWSON HAS BLOWN HIS ENTIRE BANKROLL ON THE FIRST SIX RACES... NOW, DAWSON DESIRES TO BET ON THE SEVENTH RACE. BUT WITHOUT IMMEDIATE FUNDS, HE CAN ONLY BACK HIS WAGER WITH A CHECK... THIS PROCEDURE CANNOT WIN FAVOR WITH CHARLIE. CHARLIE **NEVER** ACCEPTS ANY CHECKS!!
WHAT DO YOU MEAN YOU WON'T TAKE MY CHECK? YOU TOOK THE **FIVE GRAND** I DROPPED TO YOU THIS WEEK!
SURE! THAT WAS **MONEY** - NOT CHECKS! I GAMBLE ON HORSES--NOT HUMANS, DAWSON!
WELL, HERE'S A SURE THING FOR YOU, CHARLIE! ON THE NOSE FOR A PAY OFF!
STOP THE SORE-HEAD! HE CAN'T DO THAT TO CHARLIE!
"RIGHT THEN AND THERE, I REALIZED THAT SAM DAWSON'S GAMBLING FEVER WAS SO STRONG THAT IT DOMINATED HIS WHOLE CHARACTER... HE WAS TRULY THE IDEAL VICTIM FOR WILLIE'S RACKET!
MISS BRADY!!
GENTLEMEN! **PLEASE!** I'LL PUT UP THE CASH FOR MISTER DAWSON!
HE DESERVES A POKE IN THE JAW! BUT I'LL TAKE THE DOUGH IF HE STOPS PLAYING ROUGH!
10

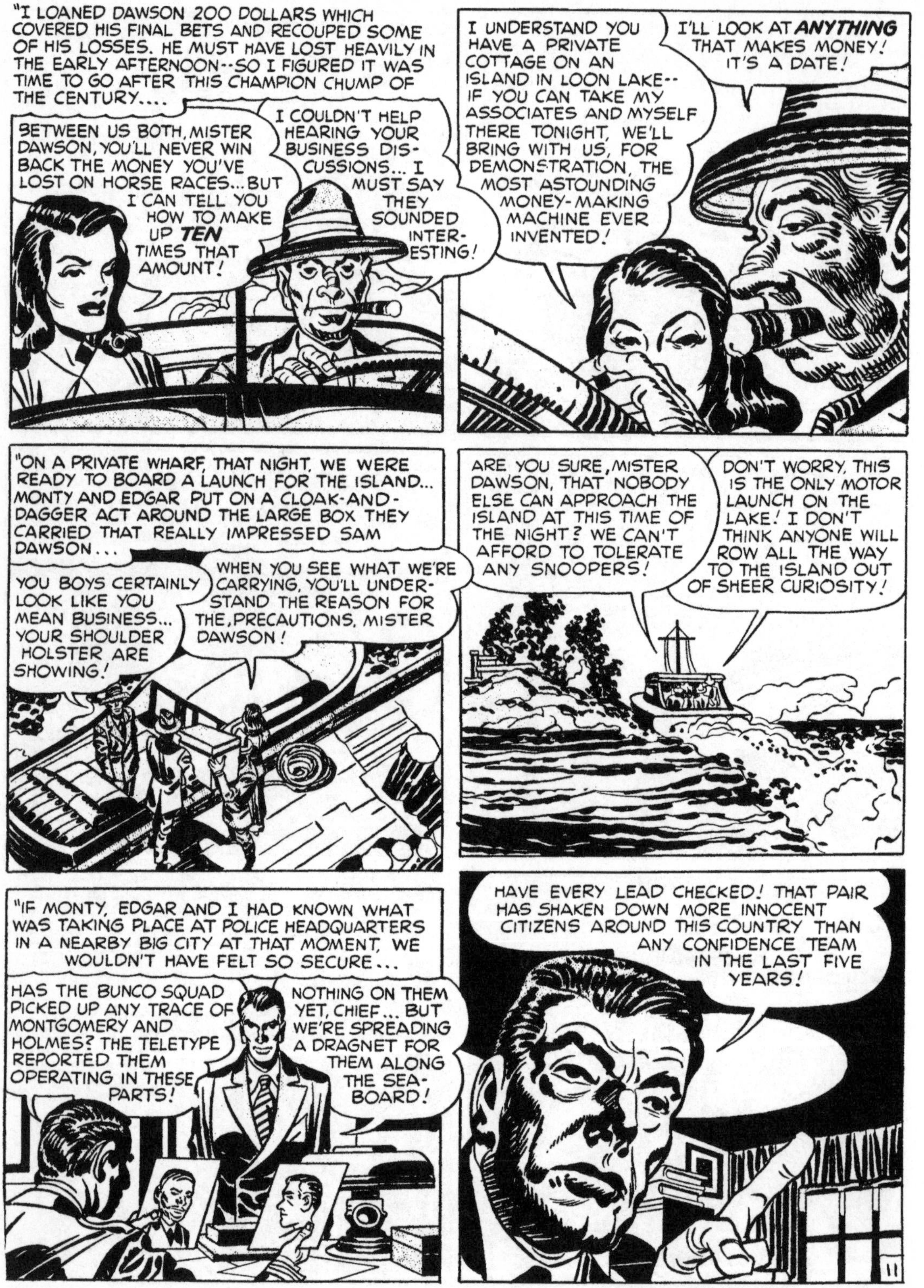
"I LOANED DAWSON 200 DOLLARS WHICH COVERED HIS FINAL BETS AND RECOUPED SOME OF HIS LOSSES. HE MUST HAVE LOST HEAVILY IN THE EARLY AFTERNOON--SO I FIGURED IT WAS TIME TO GO AFTER THIS CHAMPION CHUMP OF THE CENTURY....
BETWEEN US BOTH, MISTER DAWSON, YOU'LL NEVER WIN BACK THE MONEY YOU'VE LOST ON HORSE RACES...BUT I CAN TELL YOU HOW TO MAKE UP **TEN** TIMES THAT AMOUNT!
I COULDN'T HELP HEARING YOUR BUSINESS DISCUSSIONS... I MUST SAY THEY SOUNDED INTERESTING!
I UNDERSTAND YOU HAVE A PRIVATE COTTAGE ON AN ISLAND IN LOON LAKE-- IF YOU CAN TAKE MY ASSOCIATES AND MYSELF THERE TONIGHT, WE'LL BRING WITH US, FOR DEMONSTRATION, THE MOST ASTOUNDING MONEY-MAKING MACHINE EVER INVENTED!
I'LL LOOK AT **ANYTHING** THAT MAKES MONEY! IT'S A DATE!
"ON A PRIVATE WHARF, THAT NIGHT, WE WERE READY TO BOARD A LAUNCH FOR THE ISLAND... MONTY AND EDGAR PUT ON A CLOAK-AND-DAGGER ACT AROUND THE LARGE BOX THEY CARRIED THAT REALLY IMPRESSED SAM DAWSON...
YOU BOYS CERTAINLY LOOK LIKE YOU MEAN BUSINESS... YOUR SHOULDER HOLSTER ARE SHOWING!
WHEN YOU SEE WHAT WE'RE CARRYING, YOU'LL UNDERSTAND THE REASON FOR THE,PRECAUTIONS, MISTER DAWSON!
ARE YOU SURE, MISTER DAWSON, THAT NOBODY ELSE CAN APPROACH THE ISLAND AT THIS TIME OF THE NIGHT? WE CAN'T AFFORD TO TOLERATE ANY SNOOPERS!
DON'T WORRY, THIS IS THE ONLY MOTOR LAUNCH ON THE LAKE! I DON'T THINK ANYONE WILL ROW ALL THE WAY TO THE ISLAND OUT OF SHEER CURIOSITY!
"IF MONTY, EDGAR AND I HAD KNOWN WHAT WAS TAKING PLACE AT POLICE HEADQUARTERS IN A NEARBY BIG CITY AT THAT MOMENT, WE WOULDN'T HAVE FELT SO SECURE...
HAS THE BUNCO SQUAD PICKED UP ANY TRACE OF MONTGOMERY AND HOLMES? THE TELETYPE REPORTED THEM OPERATING IN THESE PARTS!
NOTHING ON THEM YET, CHIEF... BUT WE'RE SPREADING A DRAGNET FOR THEM ALONG THE SEABOARD!
HAVE EVERY LEAD CHECKED! THAT PAIR HAS SHAKEN DOWN MORE INNOCENT CITIZENS AROUND THIS COUNTRY THAN ANY CONFIDENCE TEAM IN THE LAST FIVE YEARS!
11

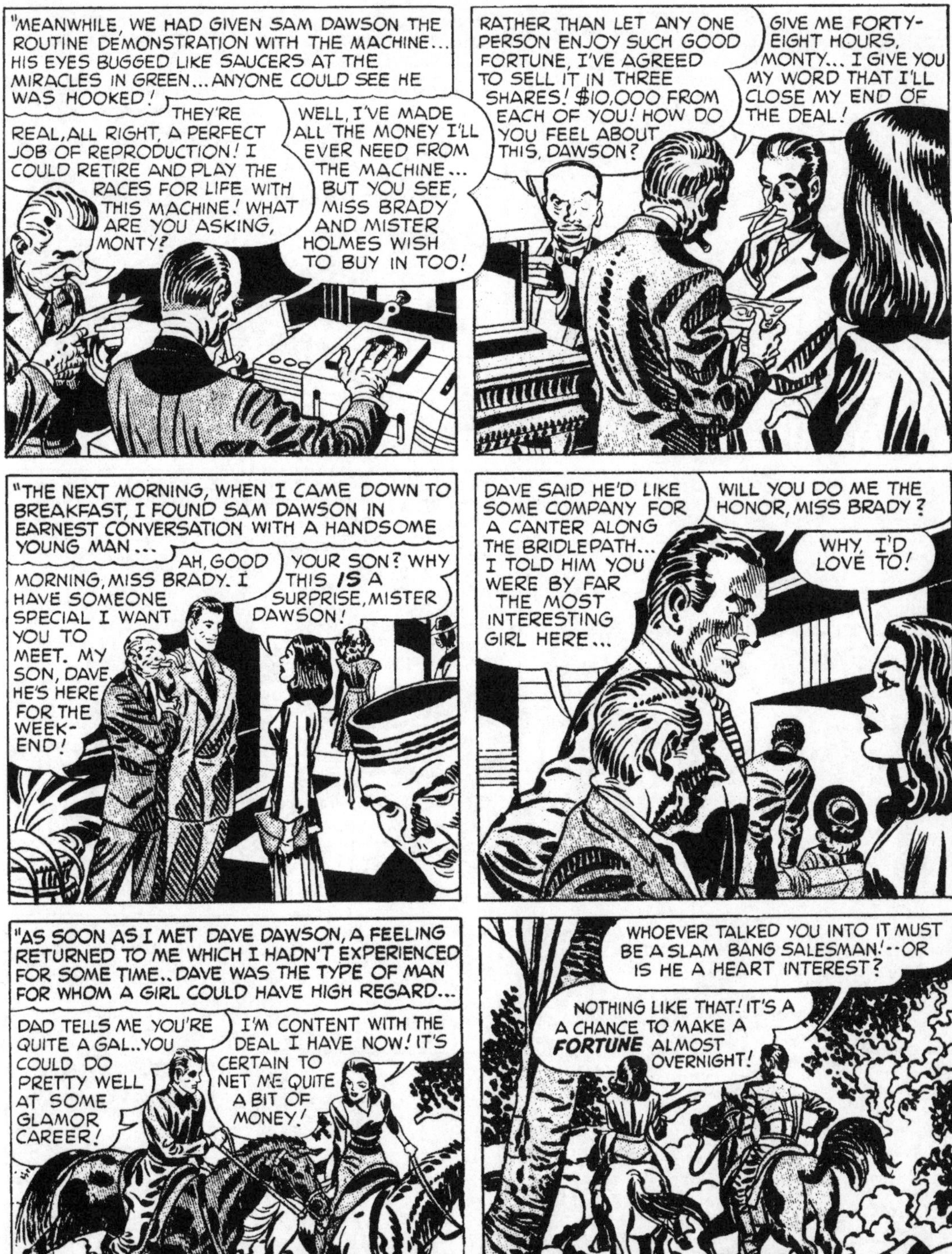
"MEANWHILE, WE HAD GIVEN SAM DAWSON THE ROUTINE DEMONSTRATION WITH THE MACHINE... HIS EYES BUGGED LIKE SAUCERS AT THE MIRACLES IN GREEN... ANYONE COULD SEE HE WAS HOOKED!
THEY'RE REAL, ALL RIGHT, A PERFECT JOB OF REPRODUCTION! I COULD RETIRE AND PLAY THE RACES FOR LIFE WITH THIS MACHINE! WHAT ARE YOU ASKING, MONTY?
WELL, I'VE MADE ALL THE MONEY I'LL EVER NEED FROM THE MACHINE... BUT YOU SEE, MISS BRADY AND MISTER HOLMES WISH TO BUY IN TOO!
RATHER THAN LET ANY ONE PERSON ENJOY SUCH GOOD FORTUNE, I'VE AGREED TO SELL IT IN THREE SHARES! $10,000 FROM EACH OF YOU! HOW DO YOU FEEL ABOUT THIS, DAWSON?
GIVE ME FORTY-EIGHT HOURS, MONTY... I GIVE YOU MY WORD THAT I'LL CLOSE MY END OF THE DEAL!
"THE NEXT MORNING, WHEN I CAME DOWN TO BREAKFAST, I FOUND SAM DAWSON IN EARNEST CONVERSATION WITH A HANDSOME YOUNG MAN...
AH, GOOD MORNING, MISS BRADY. I HAVE SOMEONE SPECIAL I WANT YOU TO MEET. MY SON, DAVE. HE'S HERE FOR THE WEEK-END!
YOUR SON? WHY THIS IS A SURPRISE, MISTER DAWSON!
DAVE SAID HE'D LIKE SOME COMPANY FOR A CANTER ALONG THE BRIDLEPATH... I TOLD HIM YOU WERE BY FAR THE MOST INTERESTING GIRL HERE...
WILL YOU DO ME THE HONOR, MISS BRADY?
WHY, I'D LOVE TO!
"AS SOON AS I MET DAVE DAWSON, A FEELING RETURNED TO ME WHICH I HADN'T EXPERIENCED FOR SOME TIME.. DAVE WAS THE TYPE OF MAN FOR WHOM A GIRL COULD HAVE HIGH REGARD...
DAD TELLS ME YOU'RE QUITE A GAL..YOU COULD DO PRETTY WELL AT SOME GLAMOR CAREER!
I'M CONTENT WITH THE DEAL I HAVE NOW! IT'S CERTAIN TO NET ME QUITE A BIT OF MONEY!
WHOEVER TALKED YOU INTO IT MUST BE A SLAM BANG SALESMAN!--OR IS HE A HEART INTEREST?
NOTHING LIKE THAT! IT'S A A CHANCE TO MAKE A FORTUNE ALMOST OVERNIGHT!
12

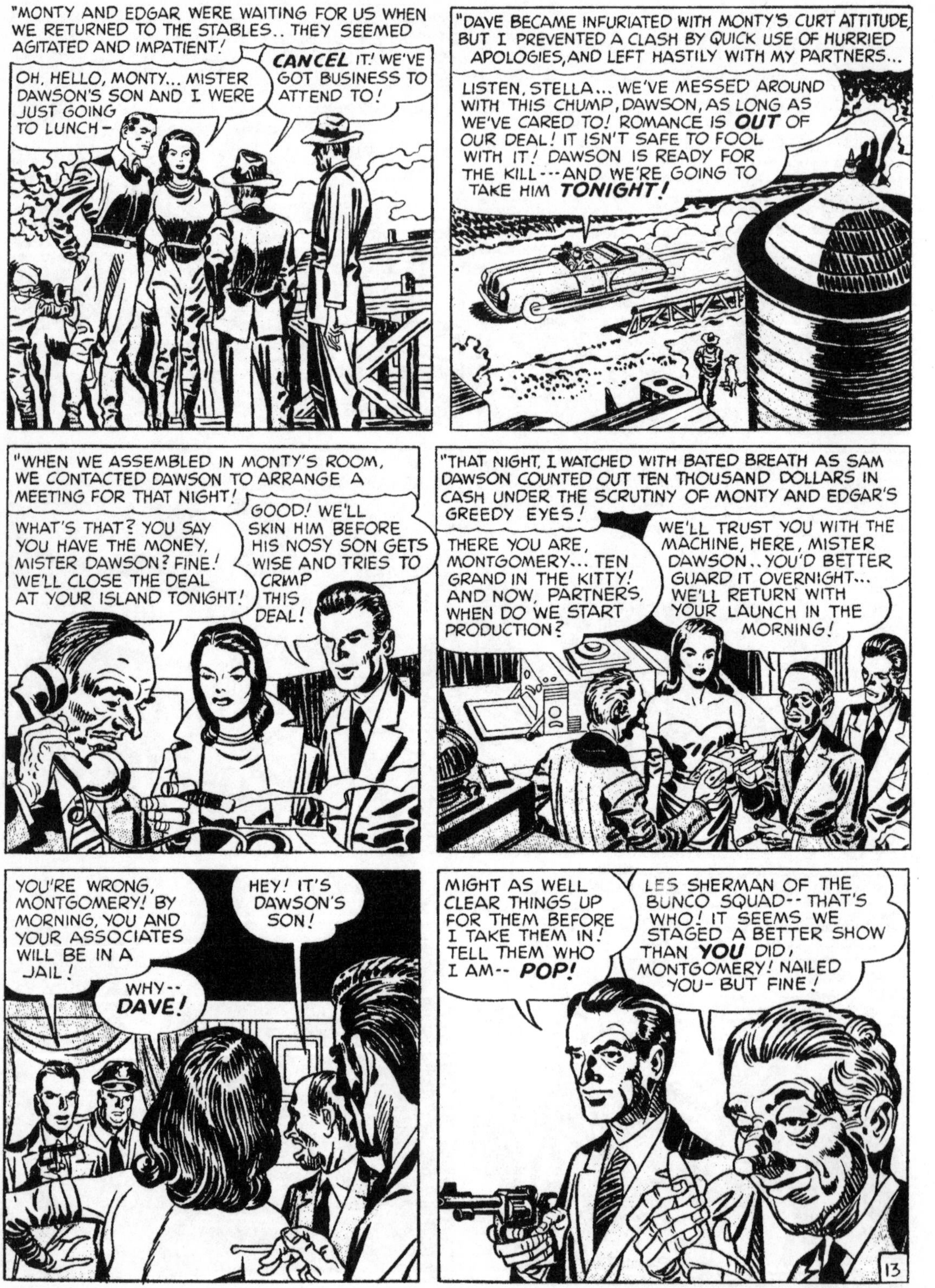
"MONTY AND EDGAR WERE WAITING FOR US WHEN WE RETURNED TO THE STABLES.. THEY SEEMED AGITATED AND IMPATIENT!
OH, HELLO, MONTY... MISTER DAWSON'S SON AND I WERE JUST GOING TO LUNCH-
CANCEL IT! WE'VE GOT BUSINESS TO ATTEND TO!
"DAVE BECAME INFURIATED WITH MONTY'S CURT ATTITUDE, BUT I PREVENTED A CLASH BY QUICK USE OF HURRIED APOLOGIES, AND LEFT HASTILY WITH MY PARTNERS...
LISTEN, STELLA... WE'VE MESSED AROUND WITH THIS CHUMP, DAWSON, AS LONG AS WE'VE CARED TO! ROMANCE IS OUT OF OUR DEAL! IT ISN'T SAFE TO FOOL WITH IT! DAWSON IS READY FOR THE KILL---AND WE'RE GOING TO TAKE HIM TONIGHT!
"WHEN WE ASSEMBLED IN MONTY'S ROOM, WE CONTACTED DAWSON TO ARRANGE A MEETING FOR THAT NIGHT!
WHAT'S THAT? YOU SAY YOU HAVE THE MONEY, MISTER DAWSON? FINE! WE'LL CLOSE THE DEAL AT YOUR ISLAND TONIGHT!
GOOD! WE'LL SKIN HIM BEFORE HIS NOSY SON GETS WISE AND TRIES TO CRIMP THIS DEAL!
"THAT NIGHT, I WATCHED WITH BATED BREATH AS SAM DAWSON COUNTED OUT TEN THOUSAND DOLLARS IN CASH UNDER THE SCRUTINY OF MONTY AND EDGAR'S GREEDY EYES!
THERE YOU ARE, MONTGOMERY... TEN GRAND IN THE KITTY! AND NOW, PARTNERS, WHEN DO WE START PRODUCTION?
WE'LL TRUST YOU WITH THE MACHINE, HERE, MISTER DAWSON.. YOU'D BETTER GUARD IT OVERNIGHT... WE'LL RETURN WITH YOUR LAUNCH IN THE MORNING!
YOU'RE WRONG, MONTGOMERY! BY MORNING, YOU AND YOUR ASSOCIATES WILL BE IN A JAIL!
HEY! IT'S DAWSON'S SON!
WHY-- DAVE!
MIGHT AS WELL CLEAR THINGS UP FOR THEM BEFORE I TAKE THEM IN! TELL THEM WHO I AM-- POP!
LES SHERMAN OF THE BUNCO SQUAD-- THAT'S WHO! IT SEEMS WE STAGED A BETTER SHOW THAN YOU DID, MONTGOMERY! NAILED YOU- BUT FINE!
13

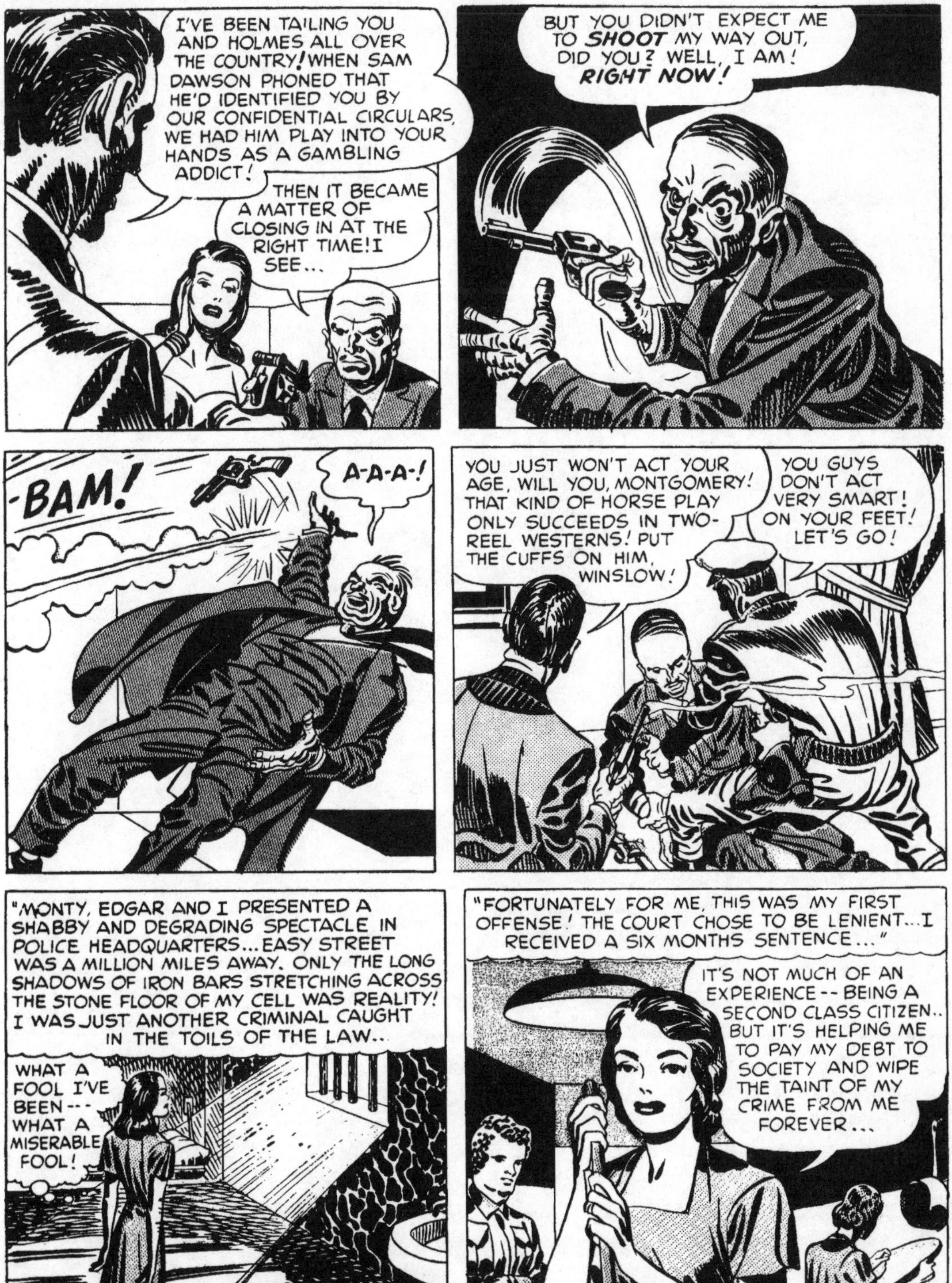
I'VE BEEN TAILING YOU AND HOLMES ALL OVER THE COUNTRY! WHEN SAM DAWSON PHONED THAT HE'D IDENTIFIED YOU BY OUR CONFIDENTIAL CIRCULARS, WE HAD HIM PLAY INTO YOUR HANDS AS A GAMBLING ADDICT!
THEN IT BECAME A MATTER OF CLOSING IN AT THE RIGHT TIME! I SEE...
BUT YOU DIDN'T EXPECT ME TO SHOOT MY WAY OUT, DID YOU? WELL, I AM! RIGHT NOW!
-BAM!
A-A-A-!
YOU JUST WON'T ACT YOUR AGE, WILL YOU, MONTGOMERY! THAT KIND OF HORSE PLAY ONLY SUCCEEDS IN TWO-REEL WESTERNS! PUT THE CUFFS ON HIM, WINSLOW!
YOU GUYS DON'T ACT VERY SMART! ON YOUR FEET! LET'S GO!
"MONTY, EDGAR AND I PRESENTED A SHABBY AND DEGRADING SPECTACLE IN POLICE HEADQUARTERS... EASY STREET WAS A MILLION MILES AWAY. ONLY THE LONG SHADOWS OF IRON BARS STRETCHING ACROSS THE STONE FLOOR OF MY CELL WAS REALITY! I WAS JUST ANOTHER CRIMINAL CAUGHT IN THE TOILS OF THE LAW..
WHAT A FOOL I'VE BEEN--- WHAT A MISERABLE FOOL!
"FORTUNATELY FOR ME, THIS WAS MY FIRST OFFENSE! THE COURT CHOSE TO BE LENIENT... I RECEIVED A SIX MONTHS SENTENCE..."
IT'S NOT MUCH OF AN EXPERIENCE -- BEING A SECOND CLASS CITIZEN.. BUT IT'S HELPING ME TO PAY MY DEBT TO SOCIETY AND WIPE THE TAINT OF MY CRIME FROM ME FOREVER...

"It was as if the body
of the person appeared
on the canvas itself.
And all I had to do
was lay on the paint!"

Ed McBain, alias Evan Hunter, born Salvatore
Lombino, introduced 87th Precinct in his
1956 novel *Cop Hater*. Set in the thinly
disguised Manhattan of "Isola", it was adapted
in 1961 for television, and to cash in, a
series of tie-in comic books was started with
original stories involving McBain's characters.
Only two appeared and the first highlights
McBain's supporting player, Detective Steve
Carella's deaf-mute wife Carella, in the
strange case of a blinded beatnik painter
driven to extreme perfectionism. Illustrated
by the EC Comics genius Bernie Krigstein,
it was described by him as "...the most
fantastically absurd story that has ever been
typed or presented to an artist...". A painter
himself at the time, Krigstein quit the series
after rejecting the unknown writer's second
script and pursued his art career, sadly never
to draw comics again. Despite his misgivings,
his swansong has a bizarre fascination to it.

87th Precinct: Blind Man's Bluff

Bernie Krigstein (art), writer unknown   1962

87TH PRECINCT BLIND MAN'S BLUFF...

AT PRECINCT 87, THE DESK PHONE OF DETECTIVE STEVE CARELLA RANG. A NEIGHBOR OF ARCHITECT DOLAN SAYLES WAS CALLING TO SAY THAT TWO HOUNDS WERE HOWLING...WHICH WAS VERY UNUSUAL. DETECTIVES CARELLA AND HAVILLAND SMELLED TROUBLE...AND THEY WERE RIGHT. THE ARCHITECT WAS DEAD!

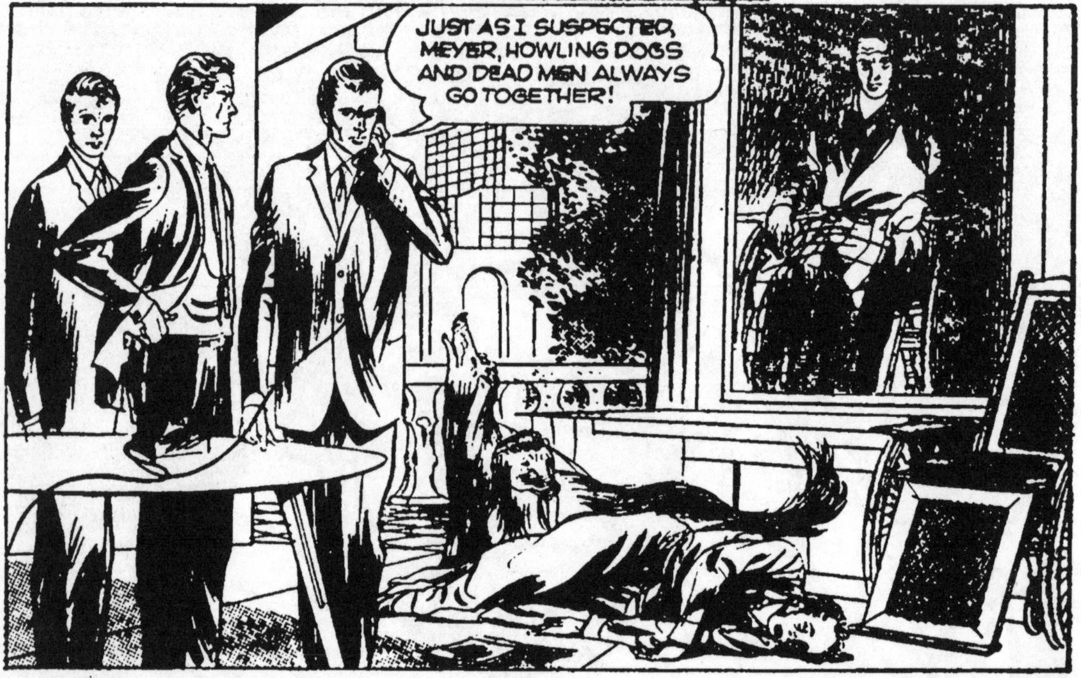
JUST AS I SUSPECTED, MEYER, HOWLING DOGS AND DEAD MEN ALWAYS GO TOGETHER!

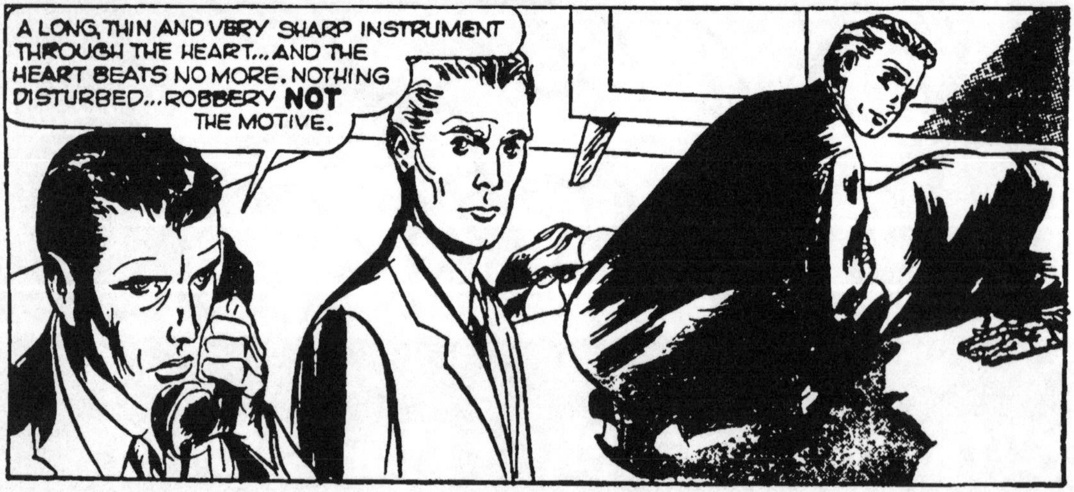
A LONG, THIN AND VERY SHARP INSTRUMENT THROUGH THE HEART... AND THE HEART BEATS NO MORE. NOTHING DISTURBED... ROBBERY **NOT** THE MOTIVE.

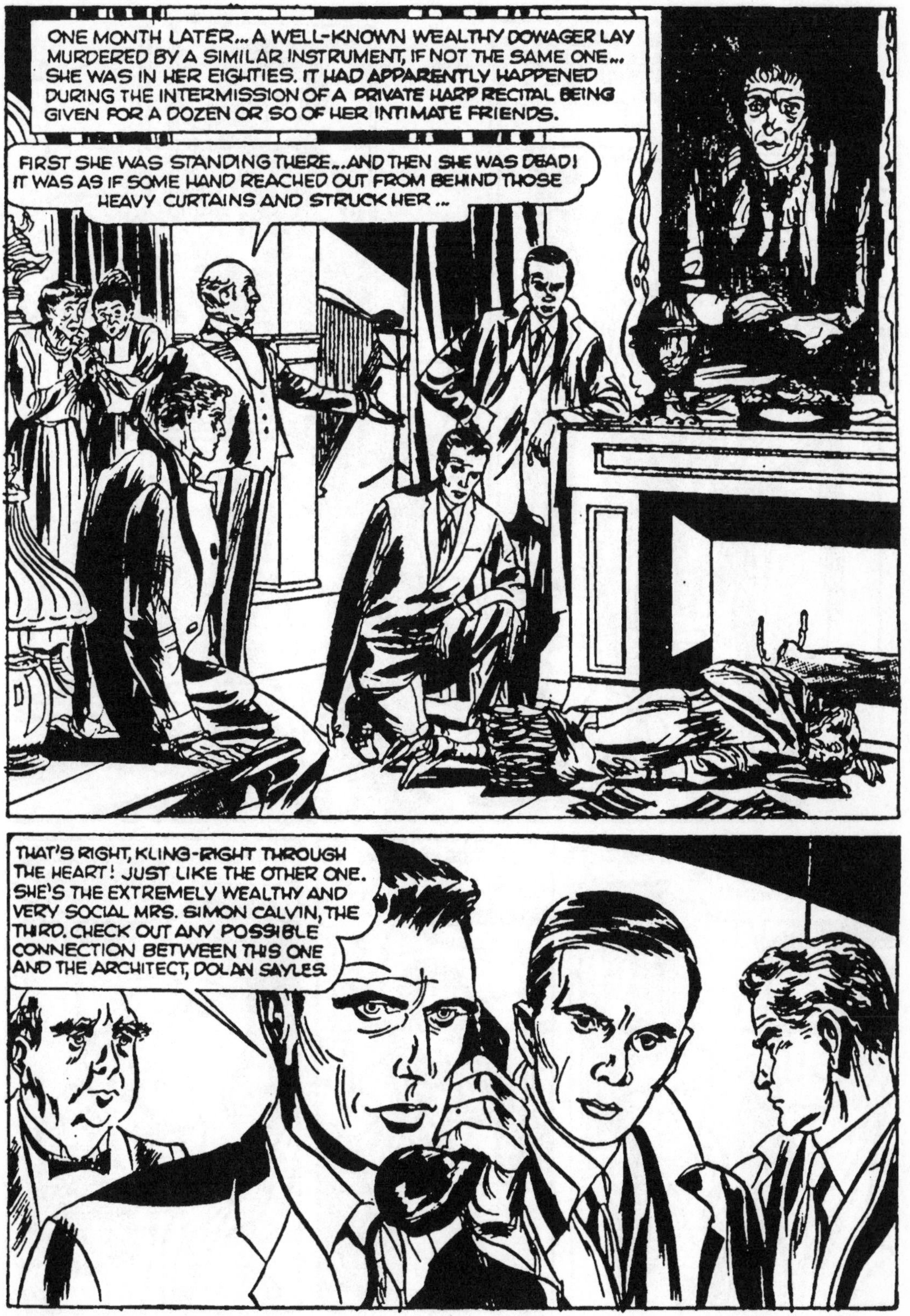

ONE MONTH LATER... A WELL-KNOWN WEALTHY DOWAGER LAY MURDERED BY A SIMILAR INSTRUMENT, IF NOT THE SAME ONE... SHE WAS IN HER EIGHTIES. IT HAD APPARENTLY HAPPENED DURING THE INTERMISSION OF A PRIVATE HARP RECITAL BEING GIVEN FOR A DOZEN OR SO OF HER INTIMATE FRIENDS.
FIRST SHE WAS STANDING THERE...AND THEN SHE WAS DEAD! IT WAS AS IF SOME HAND REACHED OUT FROM BEHIND THOSE HEAVY CURTAINS AND STRUCK HER...
THAT'S RIGHT, KLING-RIGHT THROUGH THE HEART! JUST LIKE THE OTHER ONE. SHE'S THE EXTREMELY WEALTHY AND VERY SOCIAL MRS. SIMON CALVIN, THE THIRD. CHECK OUT ANY POSSIBLE CONNECTION BETWEEN THIS ONE AND THE ARCHITECT, DOLAN SAYLES.

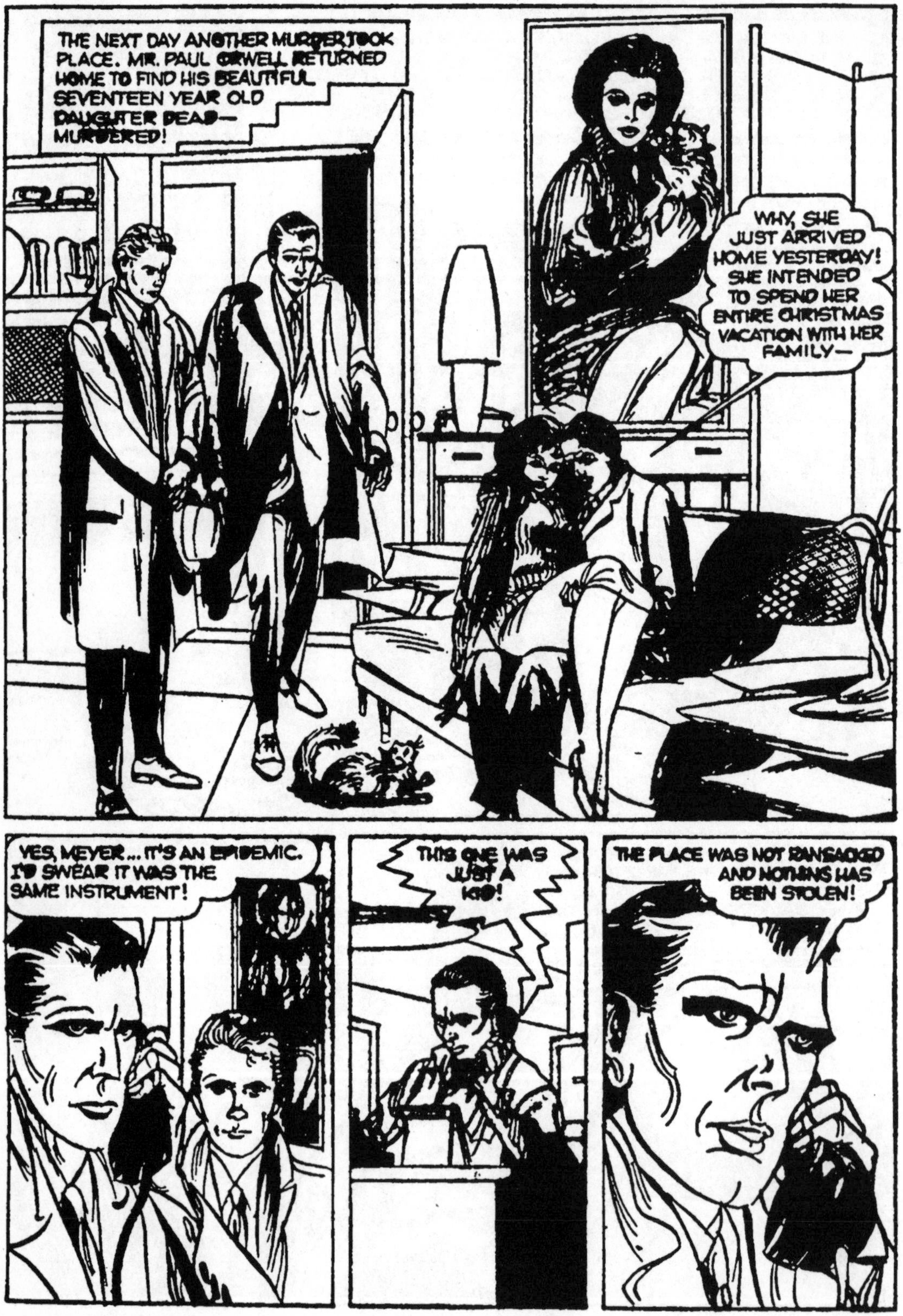
THE NEXT DAY ANOTHER MURDER TOOK PLACE. MR. PAUL ORWELL RETURNED HOME TO FIND HIS BEAUTIFUL SEVENTEEN YEAR OLD DAUGHTER DEAD— MURDERED!
WHY, SHE JUST ARRIVED HOME YESTERDAY! SHE INTENDED TO SPEND HER ENTIRE CHRISTMAS VACATION WITH HER FAMILY—
YES, MEYER... IT'S AN EPIDEMIC. I'D SWEAR IT WAS THE SAME INSTRUMENT!
THIS ONE WAS JUST A KID!
THE PLACE WAS NOT RANSACKED AND NOTHING HAS BEEN STOLEN!

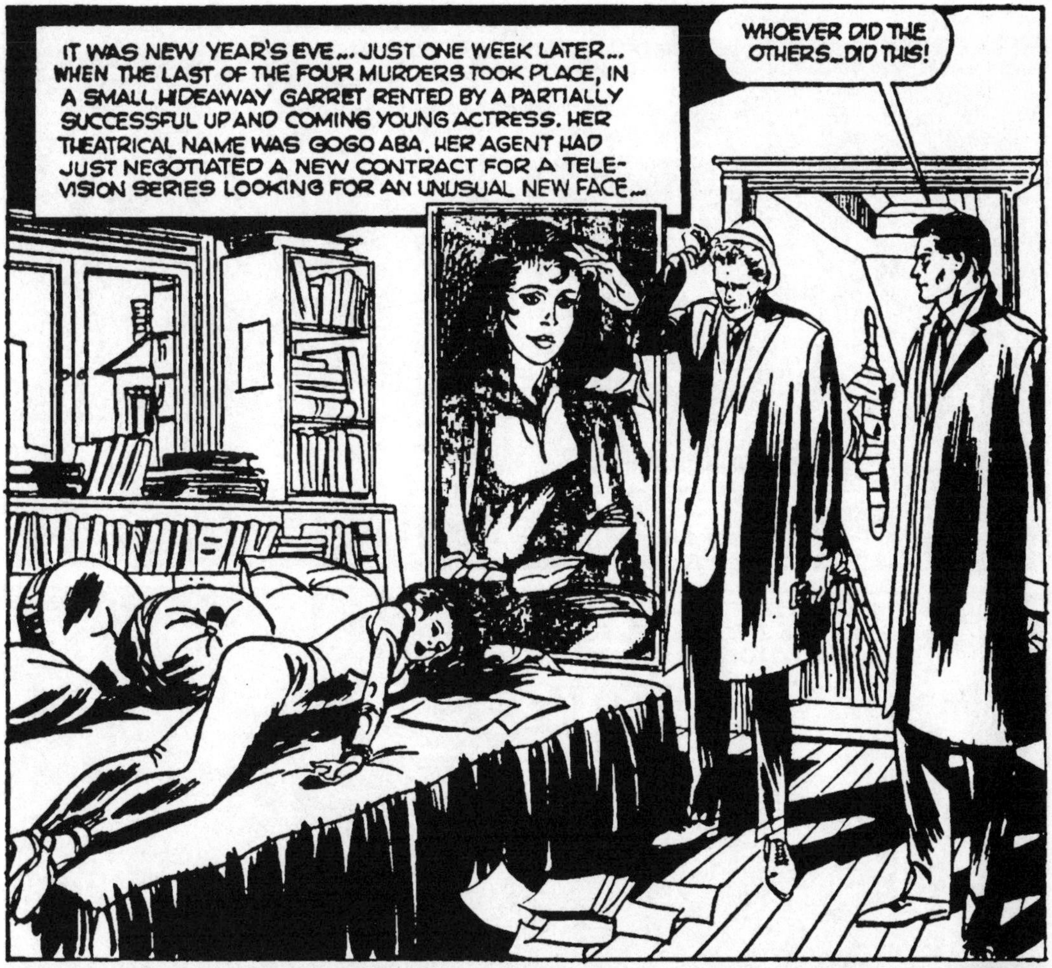
IT WAS NEW YEAR'S EVE... JUST ONE WEEK LATER... WHEN THE LAST OF THE FOUR MURDERS TOOK PLACE, IN A SMALL HIDEAWAY GARRET RENTED BY A PARTIALLY SUCCESSFUL UP AND COMING YOUNG ACTRESS. HER THEATRICAL NAME WAS GOGO ABA. HER AGENT HAD JUST NEGOTIATED A NEW CONTRACT FOR A TELE-VISION SERIES LOOKING FOR AN UNUSUAL NEW FACE...
WHOEVER DID THE OTHERS...DID THIS!

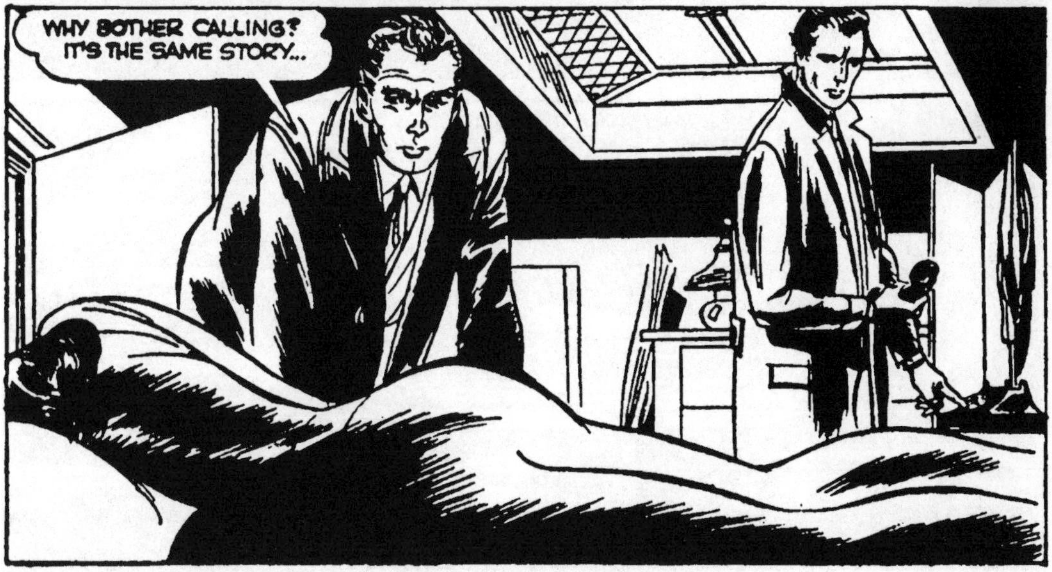
WHY BOTHER CALLING? IT'S THE SAME STORY...

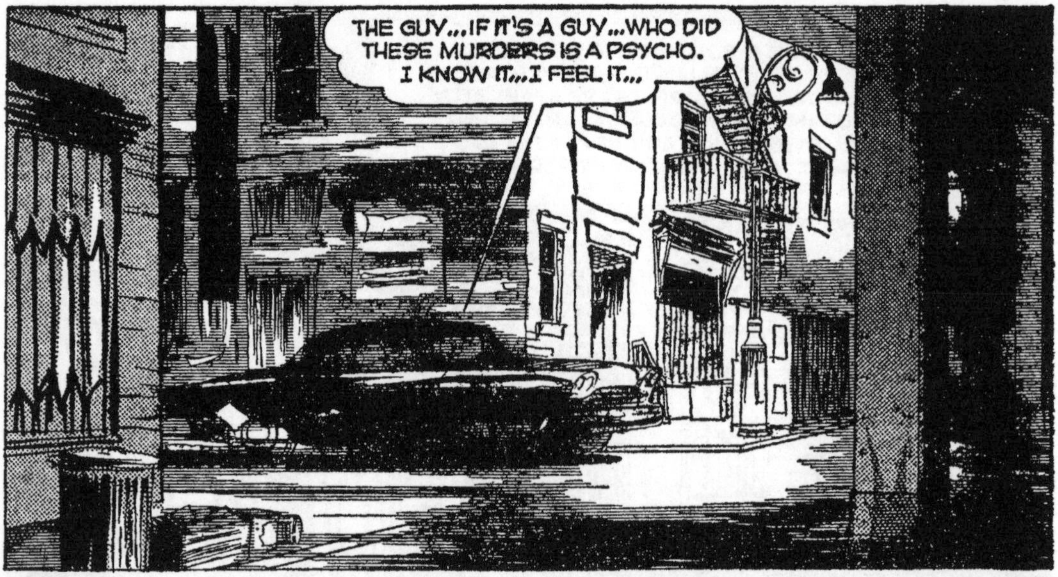
THE GUY...IF IT'S A GUY...WHO DID THESE MURDERS IS A PSYCHO. I KNOW IT...I FEEL IT...
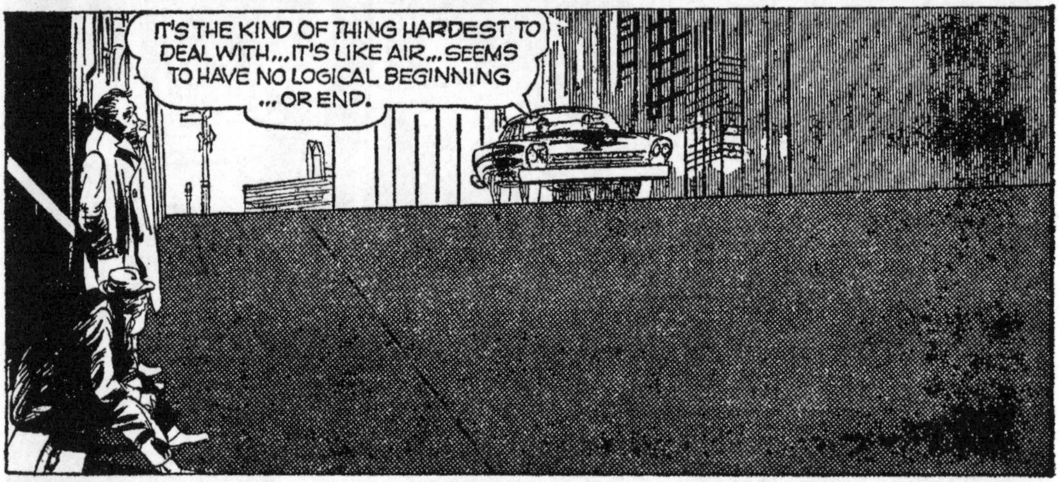
IT'S THE KIND OF THING HARDEST TO DEAL WITH...IT'S LIKE AIR...SEEMS TO HAVE NO LOGICAL BEGINNING ...OR END.
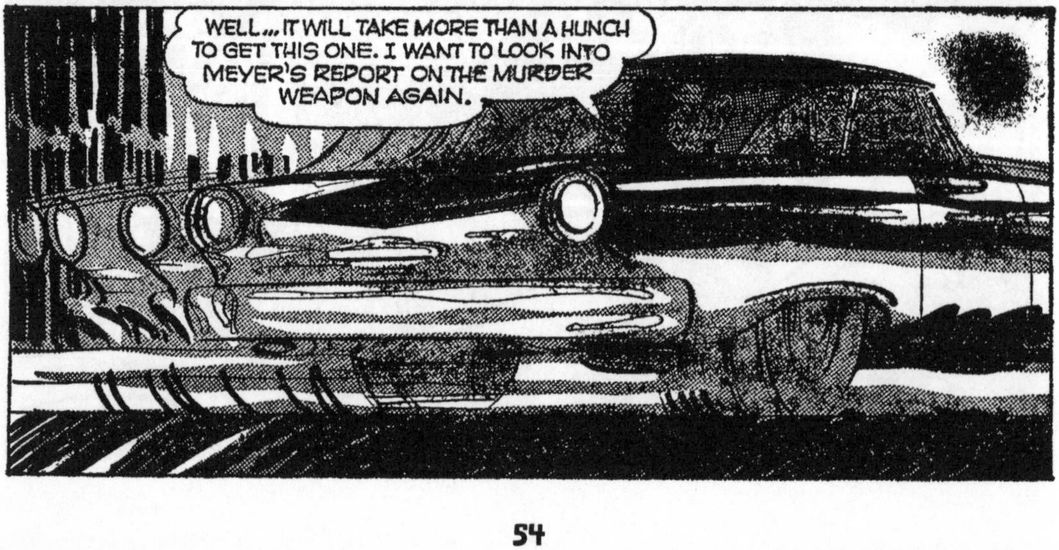
WELL... IT WILL TAKE MORE THAN A HUNCH TO GET THIS ONE. I WANT TO LOOK INTO MEYER'S REPORT ON THE MURDER WEAPON AGAIN.

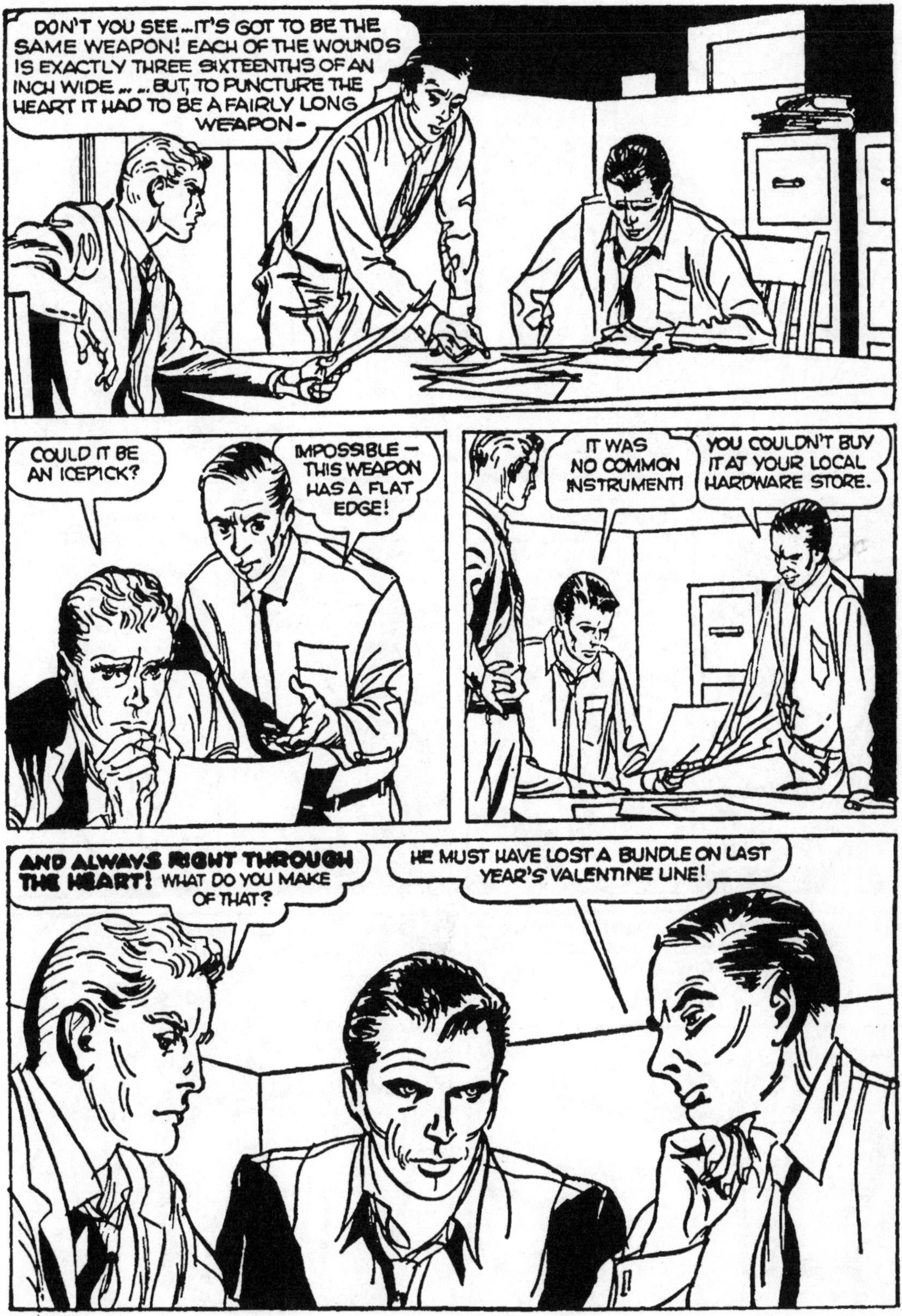
DON'T YOU SEE...IT'S GOT TO BE THE SAME WEAPON! EACH OF THE WOUNDS IS EXACTLY THREE SIXTEENTHS OF AN INCH WIDE ... ...BUT, TO PUNCTURE THE HEART IT HAD TO BE A FAIRLY LONG WEAPON-
COULD IT BE AN ICEPICK?
IMPOSSIBLE — THIS WEAPON HAS A FLAT EDGE!
IT WAS NO COMMON INSTRUMENT!
YOU COULDN'T BUY IT AT YOUR LOCAL HARDWARE STORE.
AND ALWAYS RIGHT THROUGH THE HEART! WHAT DO YOU MAKE OF THAT?
HE MUST HAVE LOST A BUNDLE ON LAST YEAR'S VALENTINE LINE!

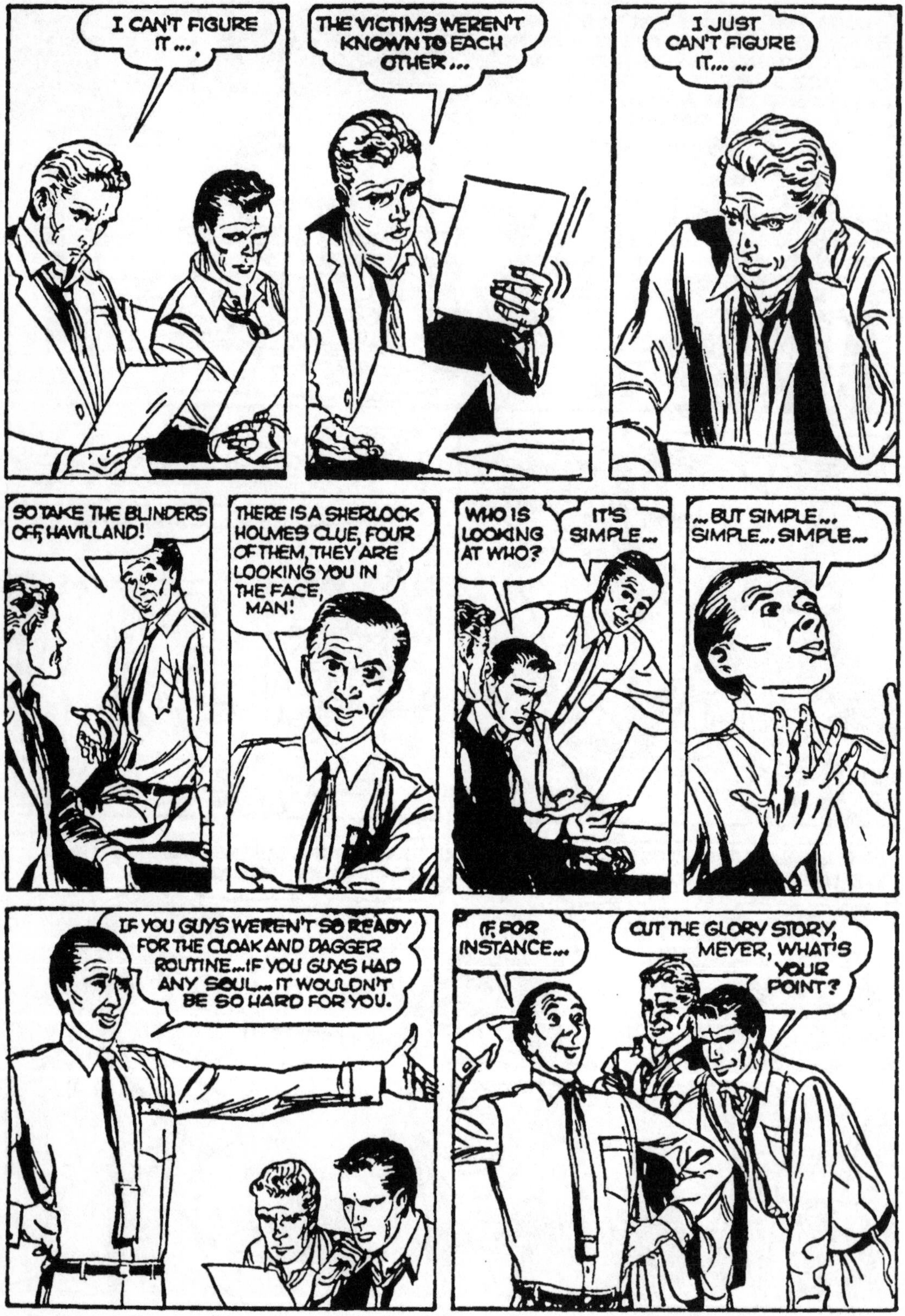
I CAN'T FIGURE IT ... .
THE VICTIMS WEREN'T KNOWN TO EACH OTHER ...
I JUST CAN'T FIGURE IT... ...
SO TAKE THE BLINDERS OFF, HAVILLAND!
THERE IS A SHERLOCK HOLMES CLUE, FOUR OF THEM, THEY ARE LOOKING YOU IN THE FACE, MAN!
WHO IS LOOKING AT WHO?
IT'S SIMPLE...
...BUT SIMPLE... SIMPLE... SIMPLE...
IF YOU GUYS WEREN'T SO READY FOR THE CLOAK AND DAGGER ROUTINE...IF YOU GUYS HAD ANY SOUL... IT WOULDN'T BE SO HARD FOR YOU.
IF, FOR INSTANCE...
CUT THE GLORY STORY, MEYER, WHAT'S YOUR POINT?

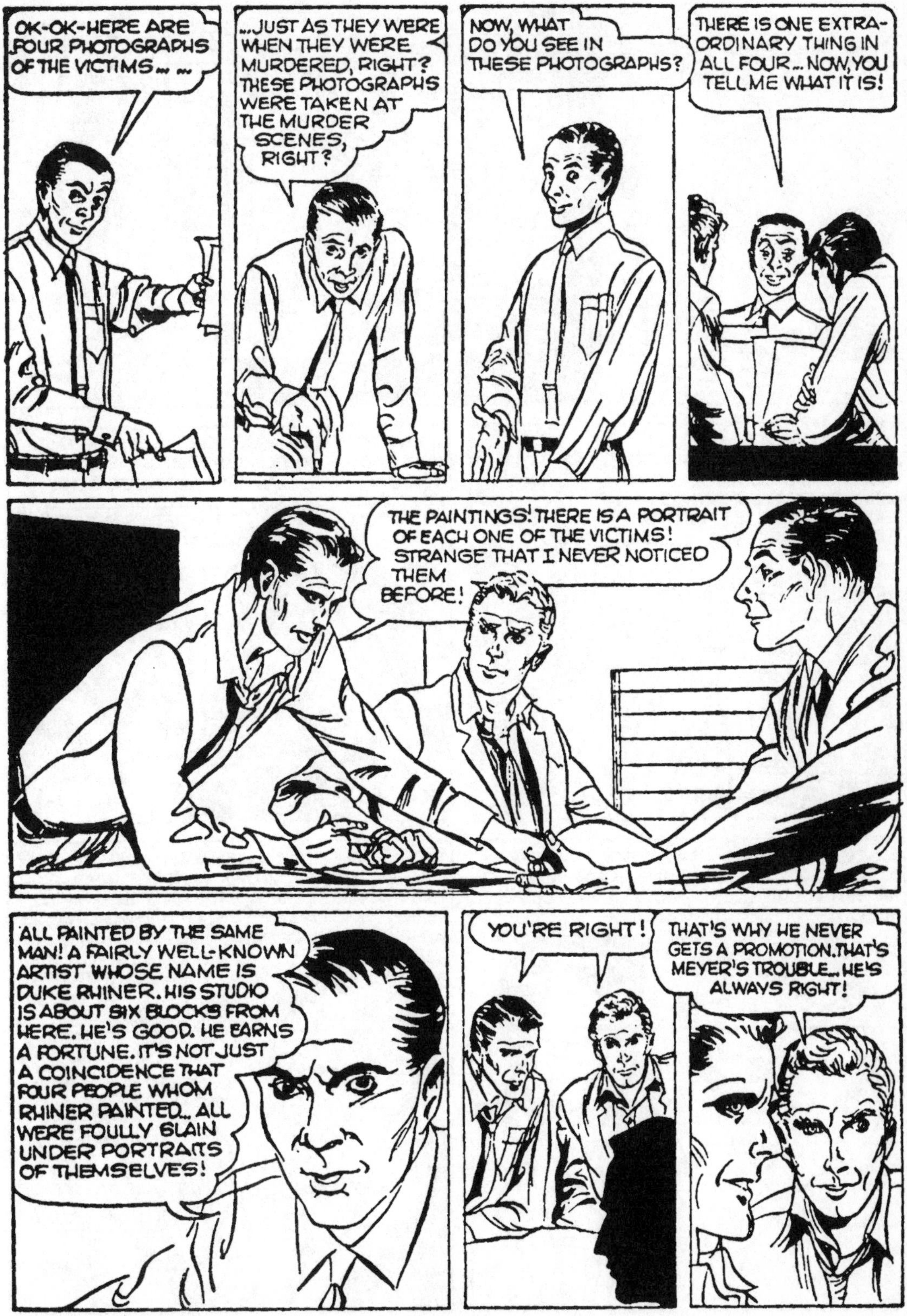
OK-OK-HERE ARE FOUR PHOTOGRAPHS OF THE VICTIMS... ...
...JUST AS THEY WERE WHEN THEY WERE MURDERED, RIGHT? THESE PHOTOGRAPHS WERE TAKEN AT THE MURDER SCENES, RIGHT?
NOW, WHAT DO YOU SEE IN THESE PHOTOGRAPHS?
THERE IS ONE EXTRA-ORDINARY THING IN ALL FOUR... NOW, YOU TELL ME WHAT IT IS!
THE PAINTINGS! THERE IS A PORTRAIT OF EACH ONE OF THE VICTIMS! STRANGE THAT I NEVER NOTICED THEM BEFORE!
ALL PAINTED BY THE SAME MAN! A FAIRLY WELL-KNOWN ARTIST WHOSE NAME IS DUKE RHINER. HIS STUDIO IS ABOUT SIX BLOCKS FROM HERE. HE'S GOOD. HE EARNS A FORTUNE. IT'S NOT JUST A COINCIDENCE THAT FOUR PEOPLE WHOM RHINER PAINTED... ALL WERE FOULLY SLAIN UNDER PORTRAITS OF THEMSELVES!
YOU'RE RIGHT!
THAT'S WHY HE NEVER GETS A PROMOTION. THAT'S MEYER'S TROUBLE... HE'S ALWAYS RIGHT!

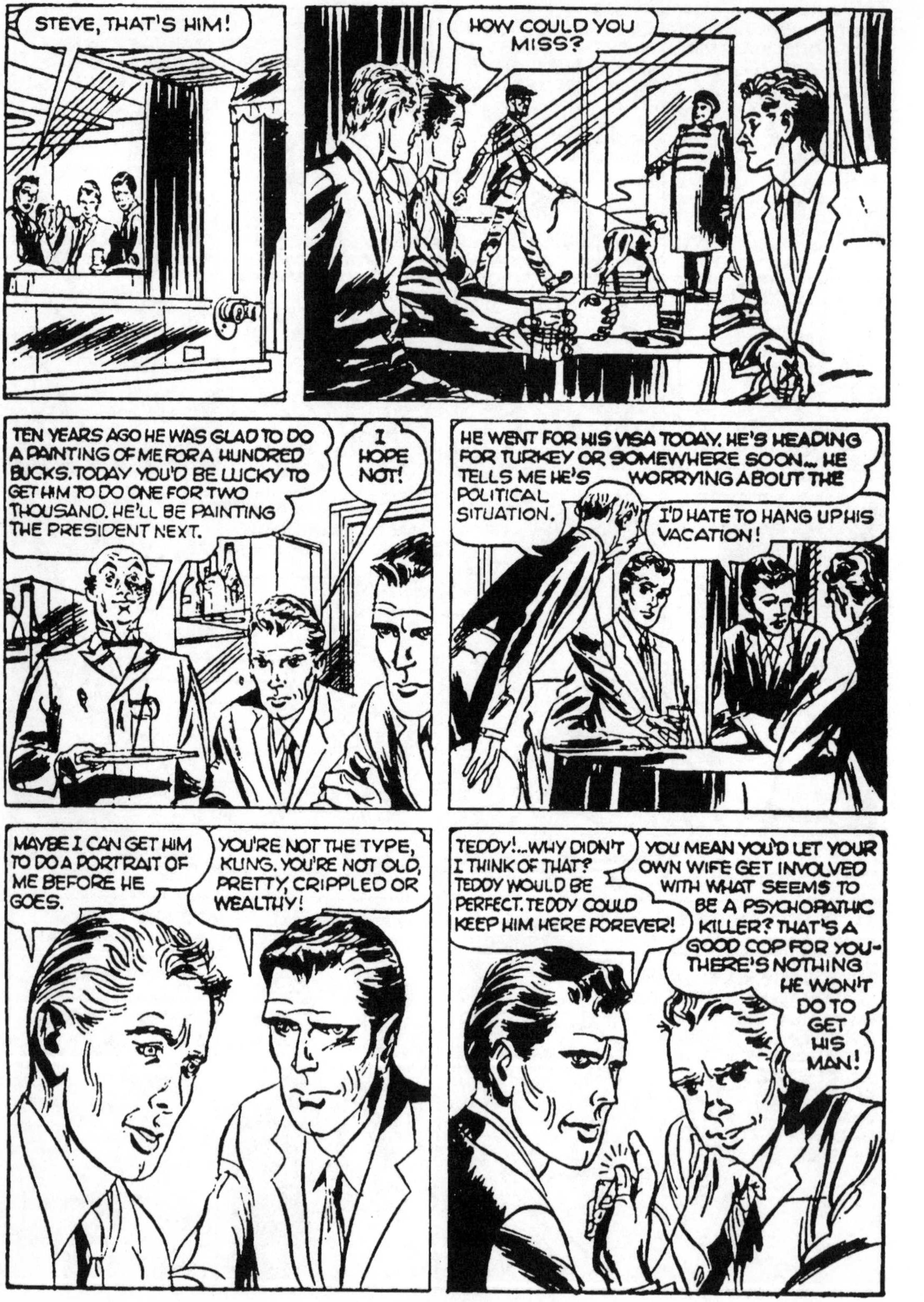
STEVE, THAT'S HIM!
HOW COULD YOU MISS?
TEN YEARS AGO HE WAS GLAD TO DO A PAINTING OF ME FOR A HUNDRED BUCKS. TODAY YOU'D BE LUCKY TO GET HIM TO DO ONE FOR TWO THOUSAND. HE'LL BE PAINTING THE PRESIDENT NEXT.
I HOPE NOT!
HE WENT FOR HIS VISA TODAY. HE'S HEADING FOR TURKEY OR SOMEWHERE SOON... HE TELLS ME HE'S WORRYING ABOUT THE POLITICAL SITUATION.
I'D HATE TO HANG UP HIS VACATION!
MAYBE I CAN GET HIM TO DO A PORTRAIT OF ME BEFORE HE GOES.
YOU'RE NOT THE TYPE, KLING. YOU'RE NOT OLD, PRETTY, CRIPPLED OR WEALTHY!
TEDDY!...WHY DIDN'T I THINK OF THAT? TEDDY WOULD BE PERFECT. TEDDY COULD KEEP HIM HERE FOREVER!
YOU MEAN YOU'D LET YOUR OWN WIFE GET INVOLVED WITH WHAT SEEMS TO BE A PSYCHOPATHIC KILLER? THAT'S A GOOD COP FOR YOU- THERE'S NOTHING HE WON'T DO TO GET HIS MAN!

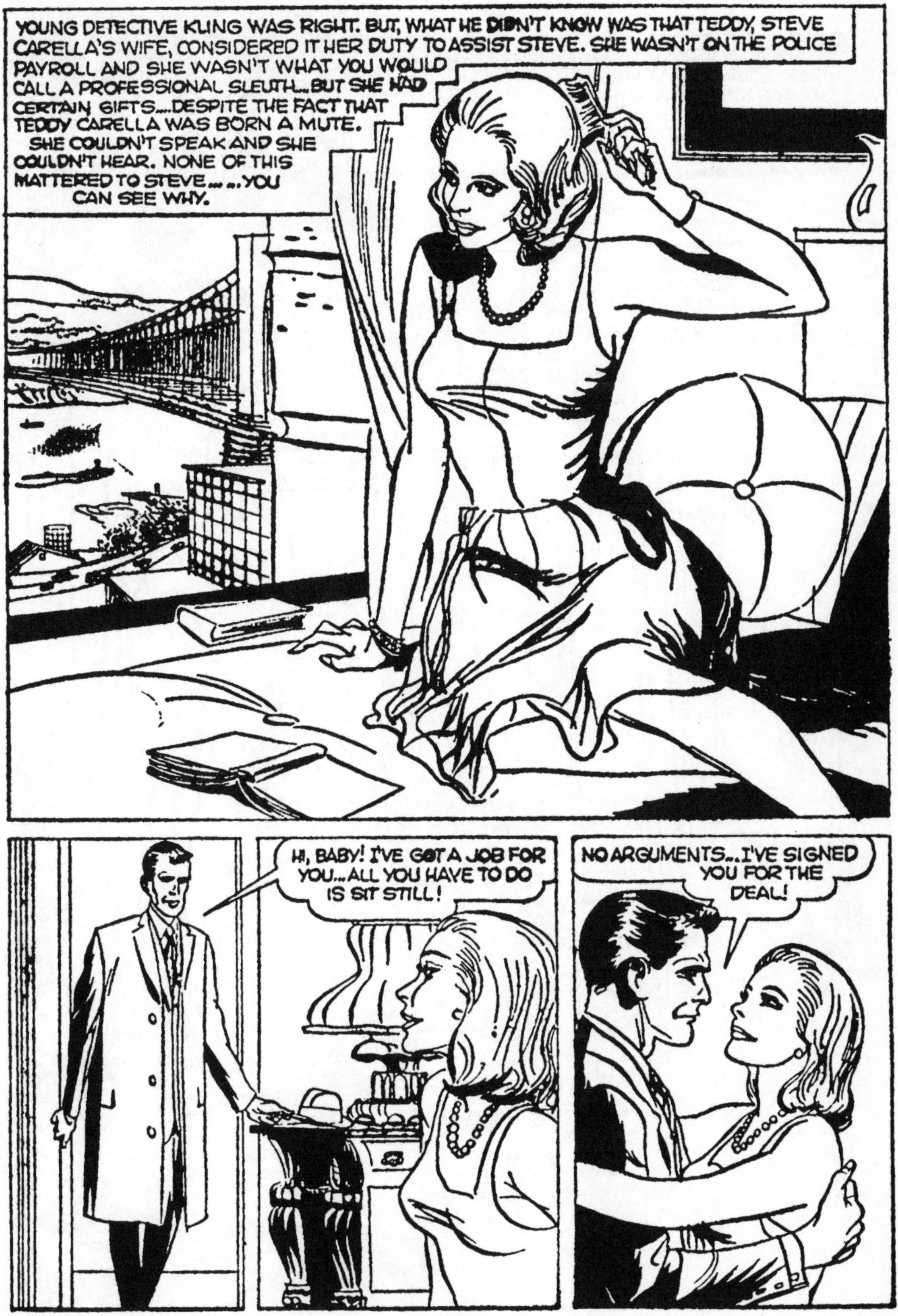
YOUNG DETECTIVE KLING WAS RIGHT. BUT, WHAT HE DIDN'T KNOW WAS THAT TEDDY, STEVE CARELLA'S WIFE, CONSIDERED IT HER DUTY TO ASSIST STEVE. SHE WASN'T ON THE POLICE PAYROLL AND SHE WASN'T WHAT YOU WOULD CALL A PROFESSIONAL SLEUTH...BUT SHE HAD CERTAIN GIFTS....DESPITE THE FACT THAT TEDDY CARELLA WAS BORN A MUTE. SHE COULDN'T SPEAK AND SHE COULDN'T HEAR. NONE OF THIS MATTERED TO STEVE......YOU CAN SEE WHY.
HI, BABY! I'VE GOT A JOB FOR YOU...ALL YOU HAVE TO DO IS SIT STILL!
NO ARGUMENTS...I'VE SIGNED YOU FOR THE DEAL!

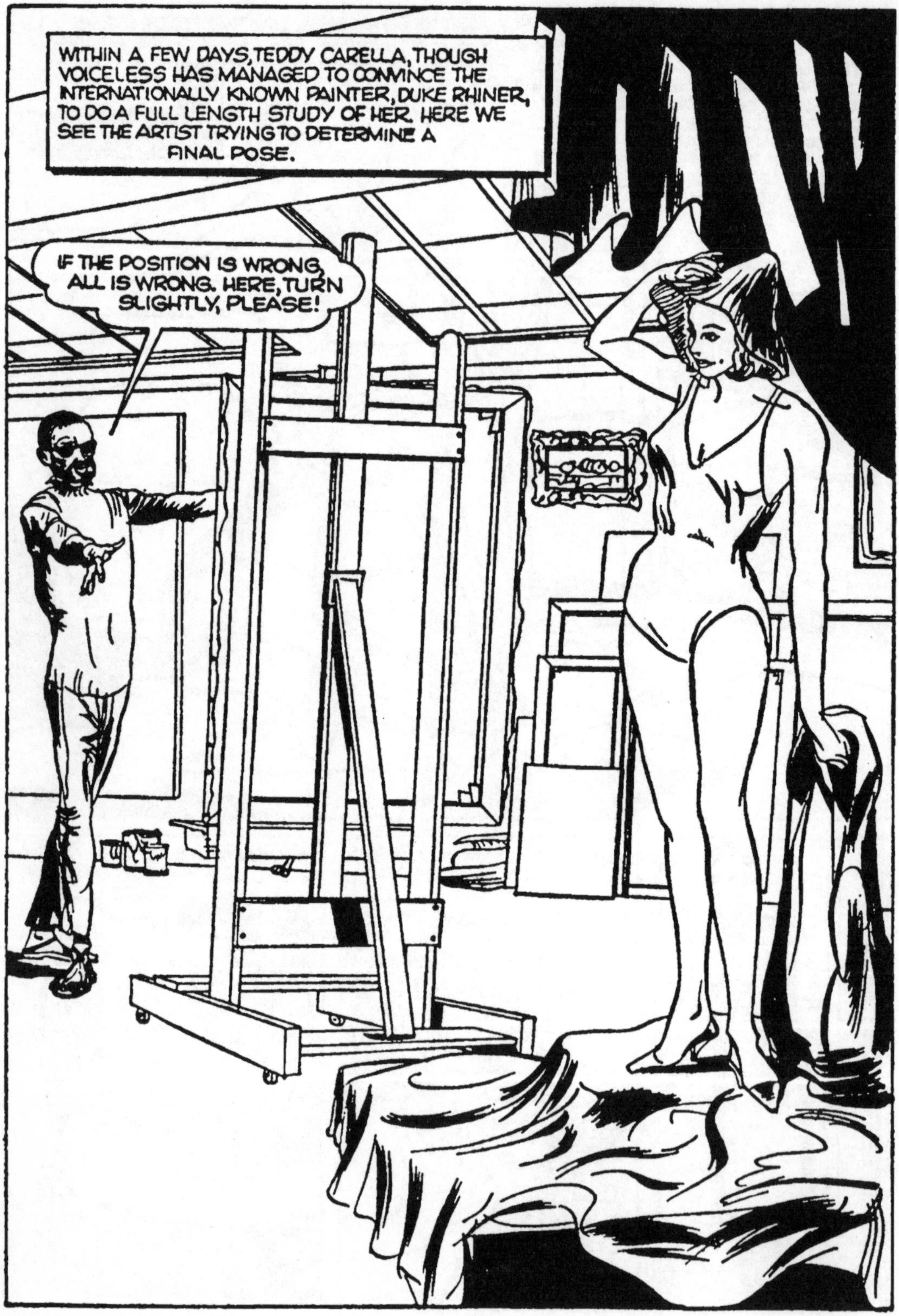
WITHIN A FEW DAYS, TEDDY CARELLA, THOUGH VOICELESS HAS MANAGED TO CONVINCE THE INTERNATIONALLY KNOWN PAINTER, DUKE RHINER, TO DO A FULL LENGTH STUDY OF HER. HERE WE SEE THE ARTIST TRYING TO DETERMINE A FINAL POSE.
IF THE POSITION IS WRONG, ALL IS WRONG. HERE, TURN SLIGHTLY, PLEASE!

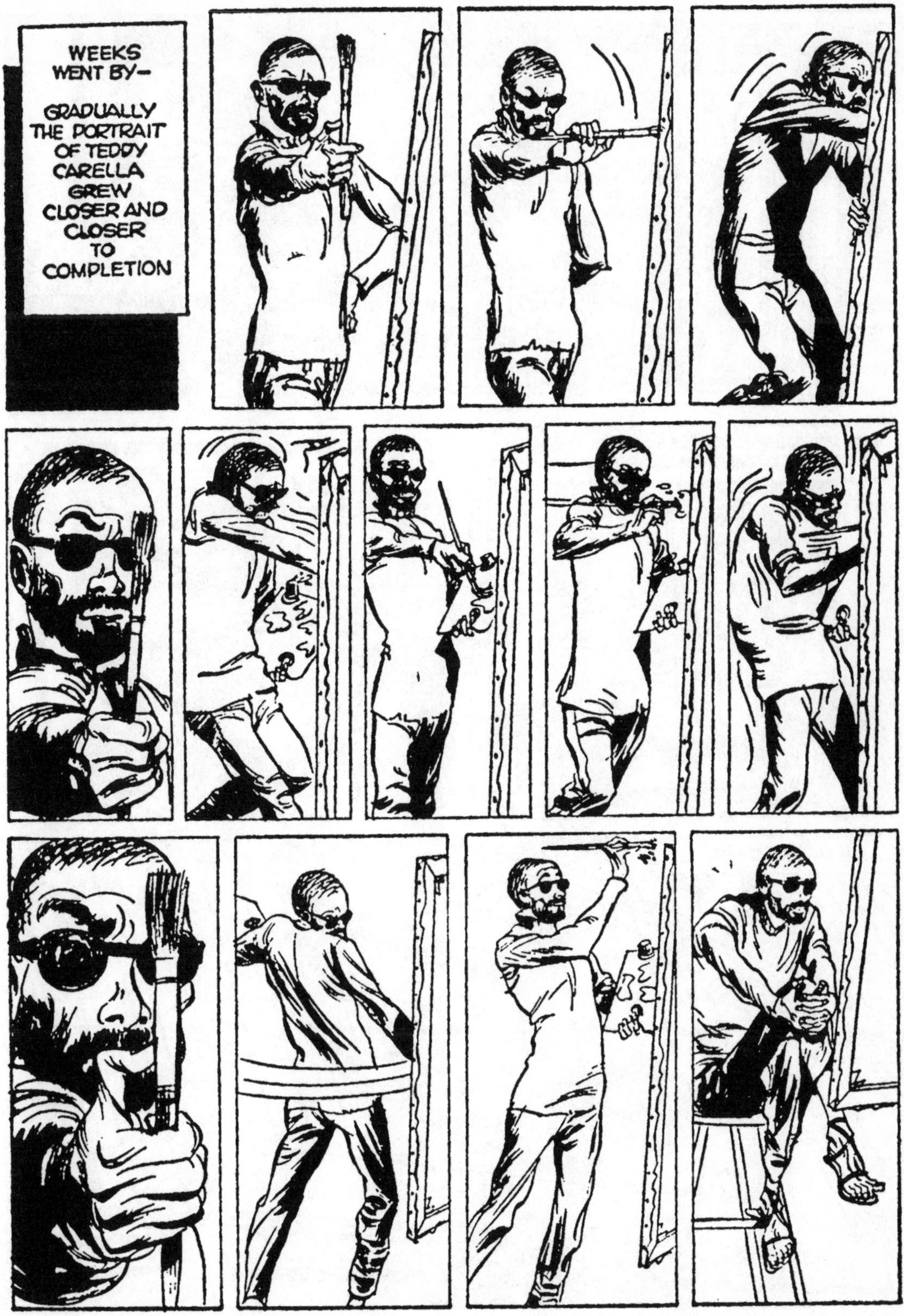
WEEKS WENT BY— GRADUALLY THE PORTRAIT OF TEDDY CARELLA GREW CLOSER AND CLOSER TO COMPLETION

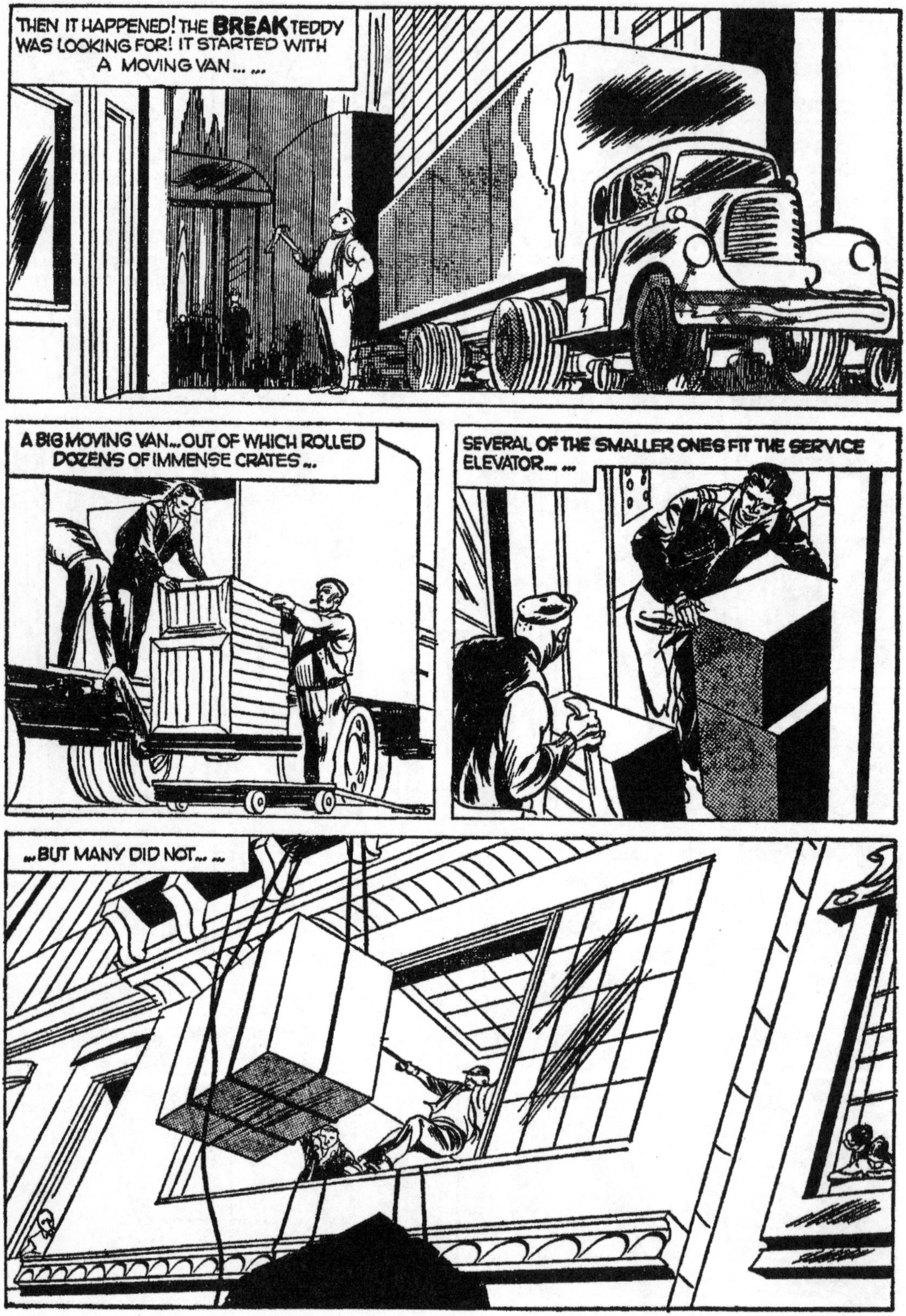
THEN IT HAPPENED! THE BREAK TEDDY WAS LOOKING FOR! IT STARTED WITH A MOVING VAN... ...
A BIG MOVING VAN...OUT OF WHICH ROLLED DOZENS OF IMMENSE CRATES...
SEVERAL OF THE SMALLER ONES FIT THE SERVICE ELEVATOR... ...
...BUT MANY DID NOT... ...

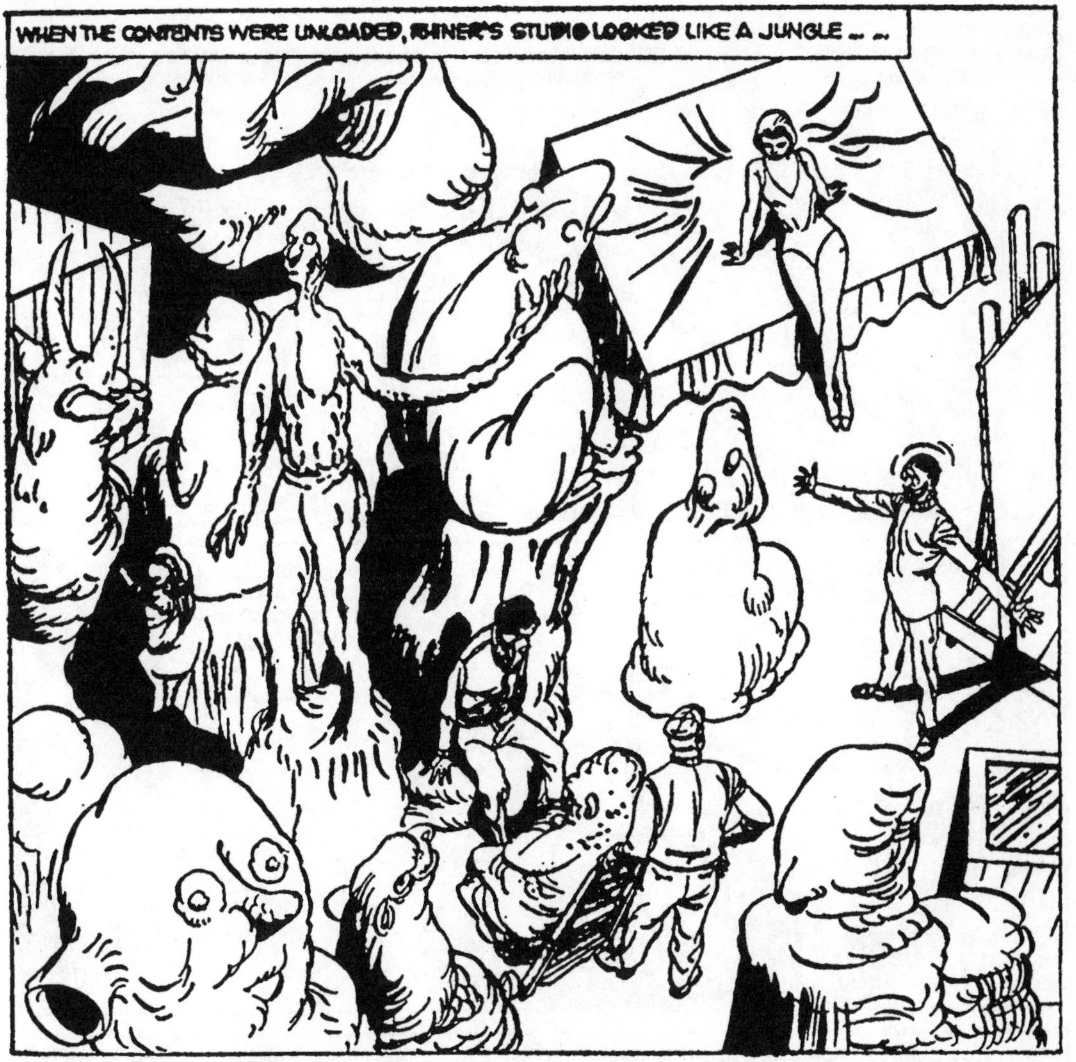
WHEN THE CONTENTS WERE UNLOADED, RHINER'S STUDIO LOOKED LIKE A JUNGLE ... ...

AN EXHIBIT OF RHINER'S EARLY SCULPTURE...IN WHICH HE EXCELLED BEFORE HE TOOK PORTRAITURE ... JUST RETURNED FROM A WORLD TOUR... RATHER UNEXPECTEDLY... RHINER WAS IN A FIT. HE SEEMED ABNORMALLY DISTURBED BY THE CLUTTER!

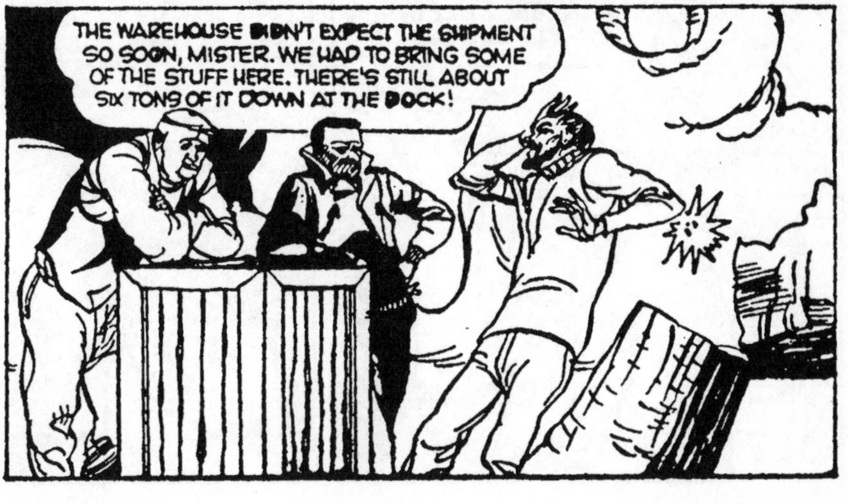
THE WAREHOUSE DIDN'T EXPECT THE SHIPMENT SO SOON, MISTER. WE HAD TO BRING SOME OF THE STUFF HERE. THERE'S STILL ABOUT SIX TONS OF IT DOWN AT THE DOCK!

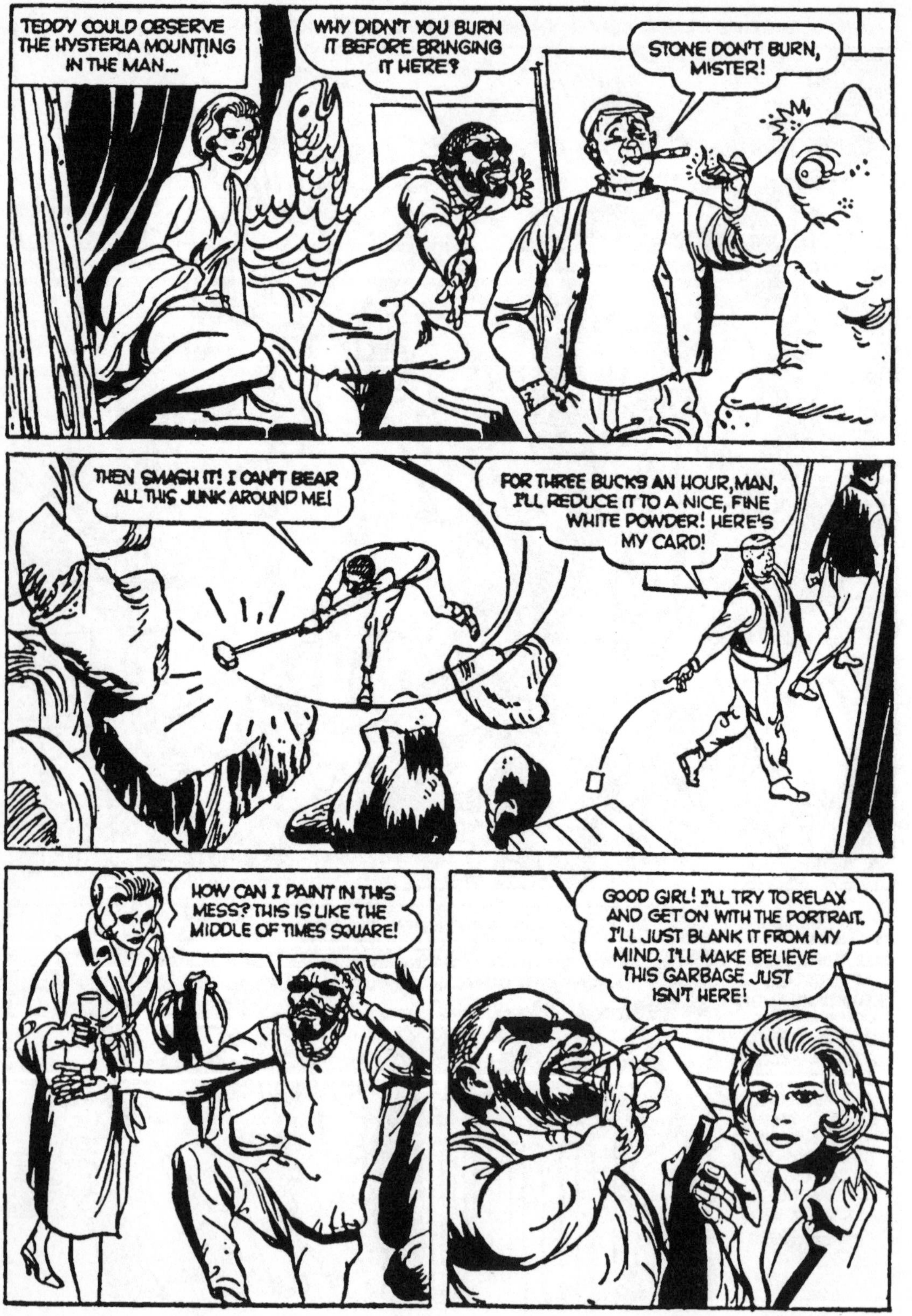
TEDDY COULD OBSERVE THE HYSTERIA MOUNTING IN THE MAN...
WHY DIDN'T YOU BURN IT BEFORE BRINGING IT HERE?
STONE DON'T BURN, MISTER!
THEN SMASH IT! I CAN'T BEAR ALL THIS JUNK AROUND ME!
FOR THREE BUCKS AN HOUR, MAN, I'LL REDUCE IT TO A NICE, FINE WHITE POWDER! HERE'S MY CARD!
HOW CAN I PAINT IN THIS MESS? THIS IS LIKE THE MIDDLE OF TIMES SQUARE!
GOOD GIRL! I'LL TRY TO RELAX AND GET ON WITH THE PORTRAIT. I'LL JUST BLANK IT FROM MY MIND. I'LL MAKE BELIEVE THIS GARBAGE JUST ISN'T HERE!

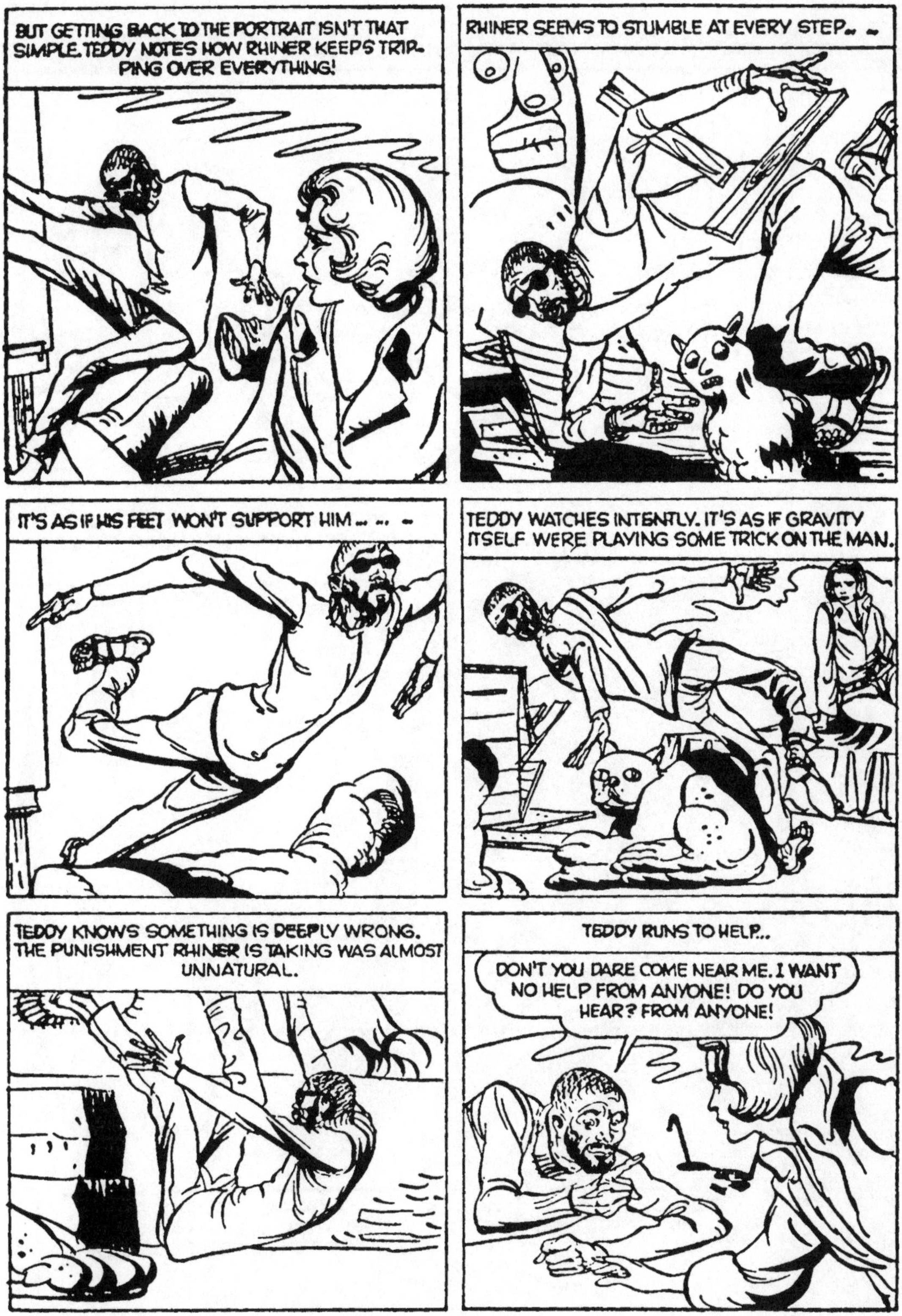

BUT GETTING BACK TO THE PORTRAIT ISN'T THAT SIMPLE. TEDDY NOTES HOW RHINER KEEPS TRIP-PING OVER EVERYTHING!
RHINER SEEMS TO STUMBLE AT EVERY STEP... ..
IT'S AS IF HIS FEET WON'T SUPPORT HIM... ... ..
TEDDY WATCHES INTENTLY. IT'S AS IF GRAVITY ITSELF WERE PLAYING SOME TRICK ON THE MAN.
TEDDY KNOWS SOMETHING IS DEEPLY WRONG. THE PUNISHMENT RHINER IS TAKING WAS ALMOST UNNATURAL.
TEDDY RUNS TO HELP...
DON'T YOU DARE COME NEAR ME. I WANT NO HELP FROM ANYONE! DO YOU HEAR? FROM ANYONE!

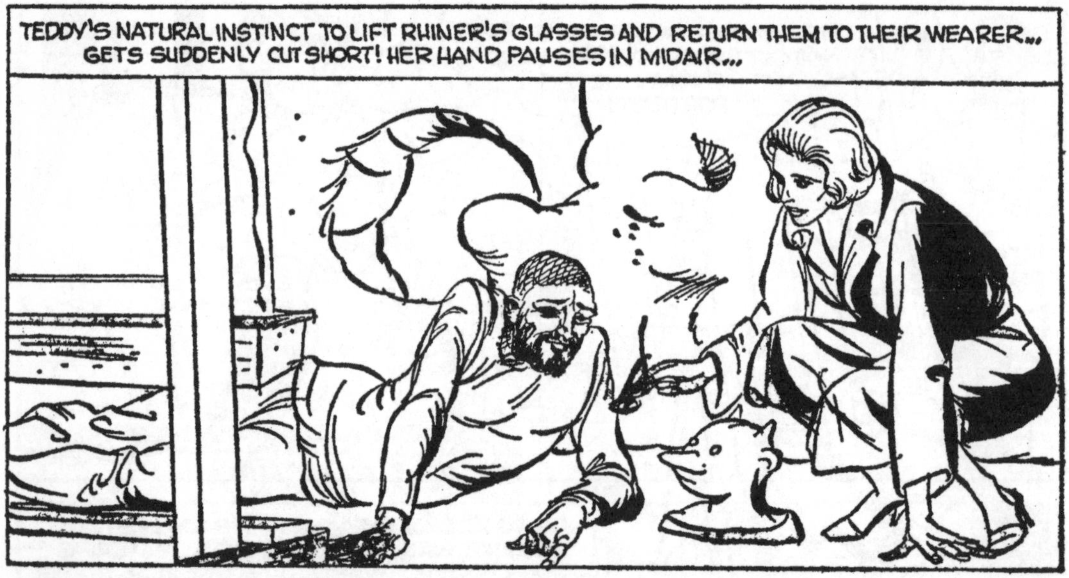
TEDDY'S NATURAL INSTINCT TO LIFT RHINER'S GLASSES AND RETURN THEM TO THEIR WEARER... GETS SUDDENLY CUT SHORT! HER HAND PAUSES IN MIDAIR...

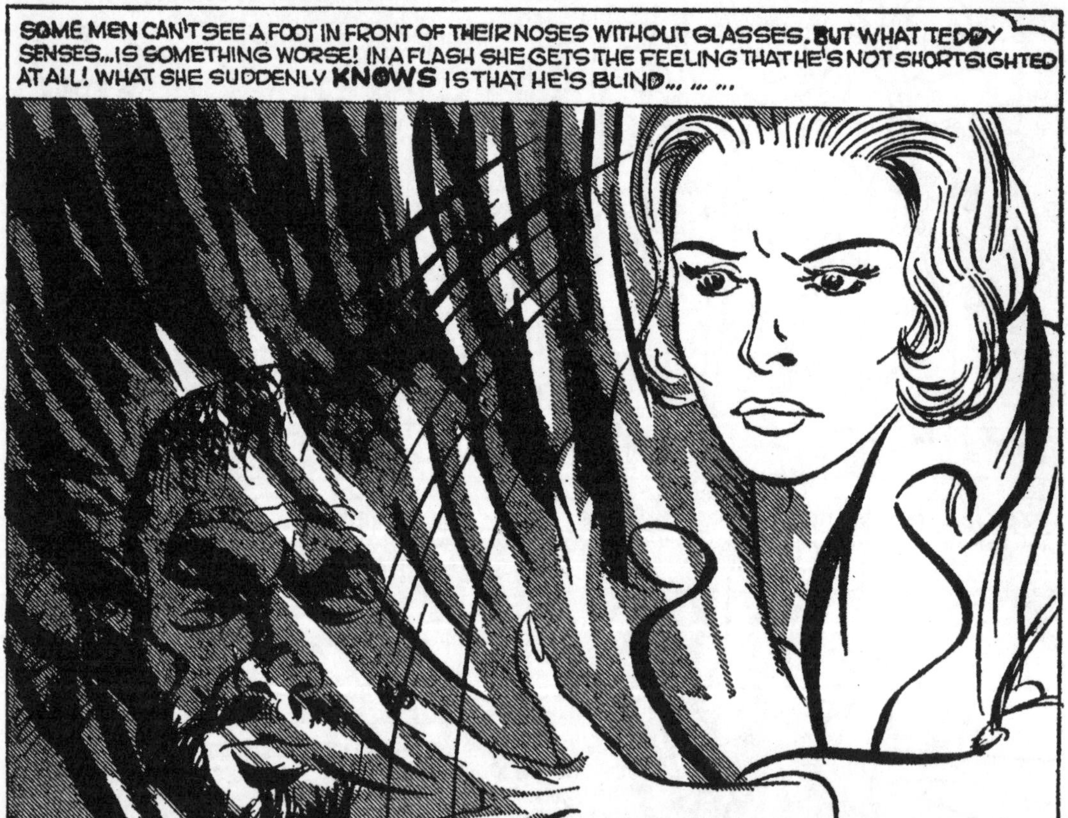
SOME MEN CAN'T SEE A FOOT IN FRONT OF THEIR NOSES WITHOUT GLASSES. BUT WHAT TEDDY SENSES...IS SOMETHING WORSE! IN A FLASH SHE GETS THE FEELING THAT HE'S NOT SHORTSIGHTED AT ALL! WHAT SHE SUDDENLY **KNOWS** IS THAT HE'S BLIND... ... ...
FLUTTERING HER HAND FOR A RESPONSE FROM RHINER... PROVES IT...HE SEES NOTHING AT ALL!

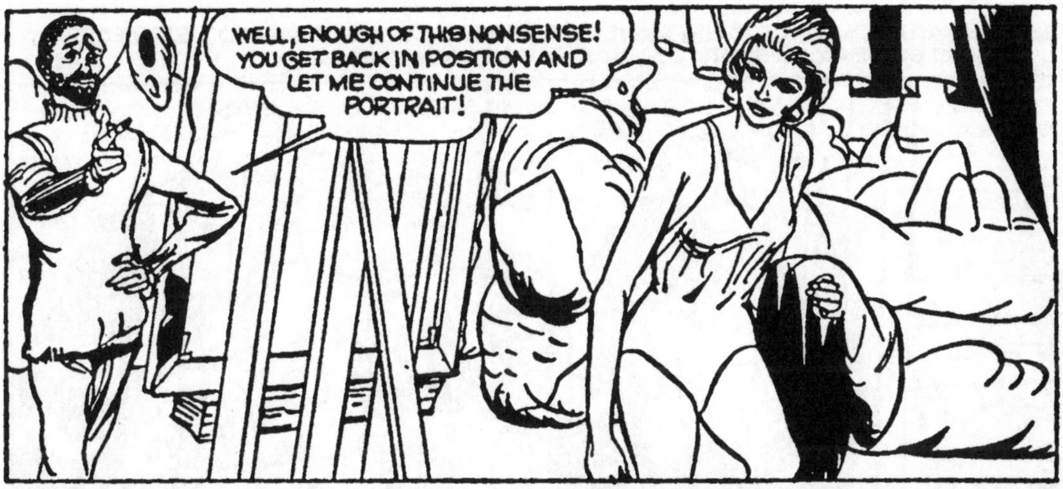
WELL, ENOUGH OF THIS NONSENSE! YOU GET BACK IN POSITION AND LET ME CONTINUE THE PORTRAIT!

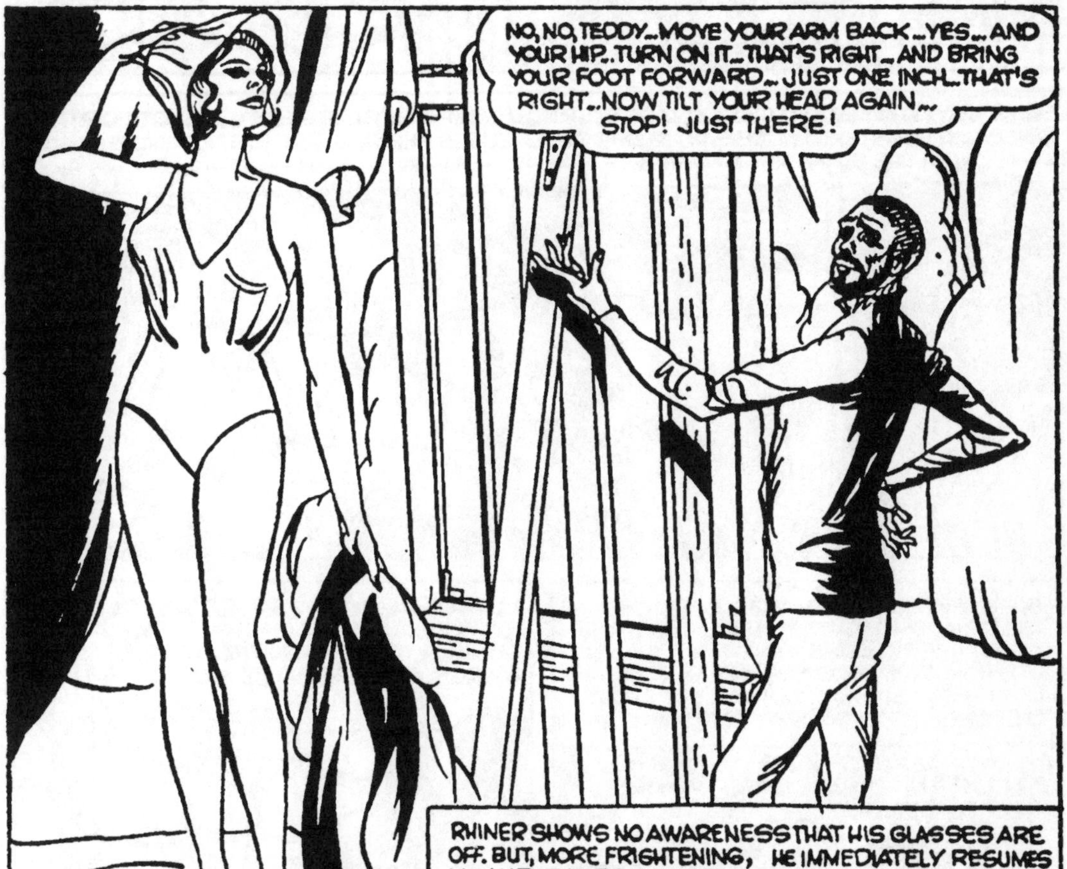
NO, NO, TEDDY...MOVE YOUR ARM BACK...YES... AND YOUR HIP...TURN ON IT...THAT'S RIGHT... AND BRING YOUR FOOT FORWARD... JUST ONE INCH...THAT'S RIGHT...NOW TILT YOUR HEAD AGAIN... STOP! JUST THERE!
RHINER SHOWS NO AWARENESS THAT HIS GLASSES ARE OFF. BUT, MORE FRIGHTENING, HE IMMEDIATELY RESUMES HIS NATURAL BEHAVIOR... AND ACTS AS IF ALL WERE PERFECTLY OKAY...AND THAT NOTHING, IS WRONG. TEDDY IS AMAZED AND TERRIFIED! ONLY A MADMAN COULD BE SO PERFECT AN ACTOR! ONLY A MAN, MAD, COULD BE STONE BLIND AND PAINT REALISTIC PORTRAITS OF PEOPLE HE DOESN'T EVEN SEE!

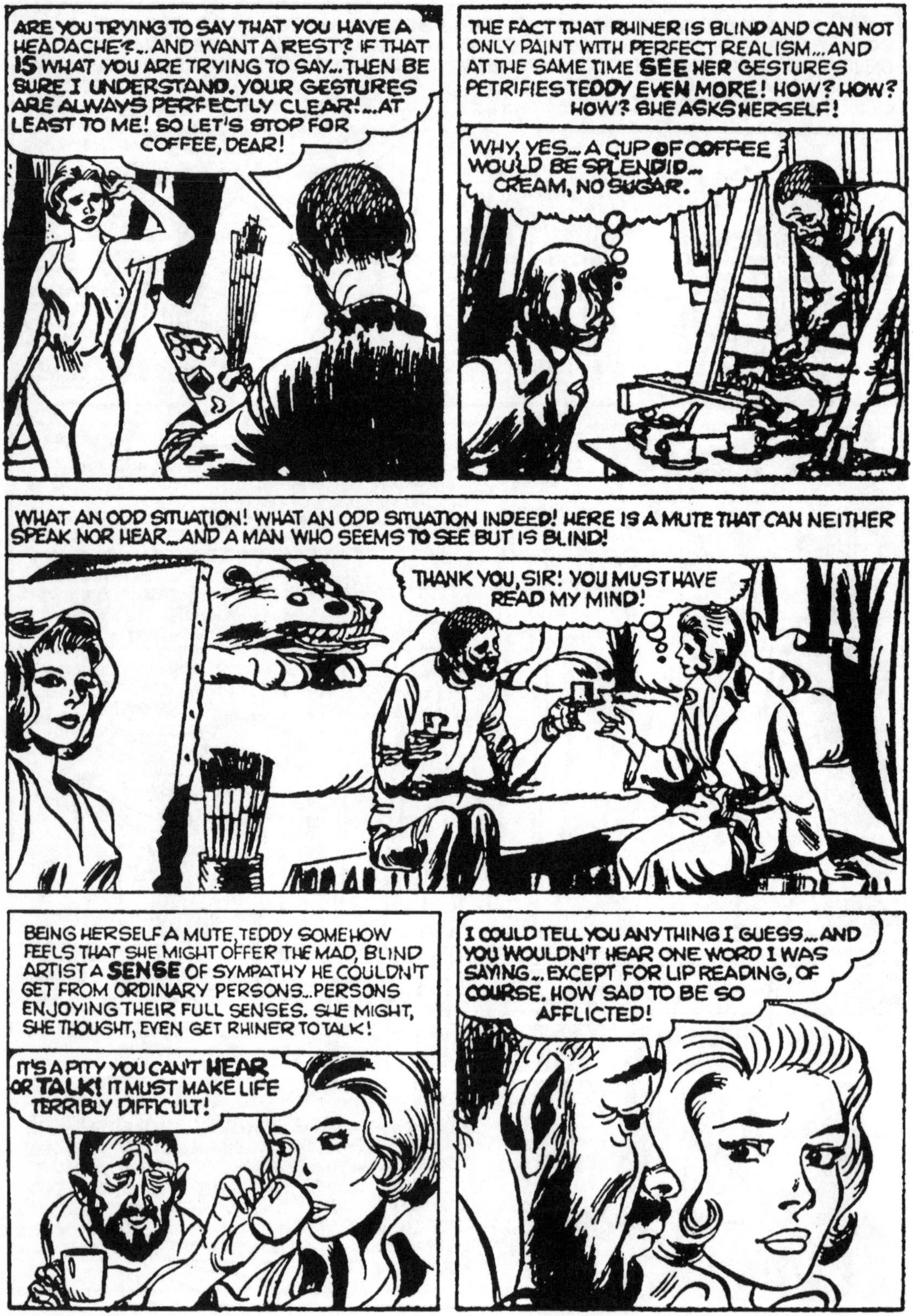
ARE YOU TRYING TO SAY THAT YOU HAVE A HEADACHE?...AND WANT A REST? IF THAT IS WHAT YOU ARE TRYING TO SAY...THEN BE SURE I UNDERSTAND. YOUR GESTURES ARE ALWAYS PERFECTLY CLEAR!...AT LEAST TO ME! SO LET'S STOP FOR COFFEE, DEAR!
THE FACT THAT RHINER IS BLIND AND CAN NOT ONLY PAINT WITH PERFECT REALISM...AND AT THE SAME TIME SEE HER GESTURES PETRIFIES TEDDY EVEN MORE! HOW? HOW? HOW? SHE ASKS HERSELF!
WHY, YES... A CUP OF COFFEE WOULD BE SPLENDID... CREAM, NO SUGAR.
WHAT AN ODD SITUATION! WHAT AN ODD SITUATION INDEED! HERE IS A MUTE THAT CAN NEITHER SPEAK NOR HEAR...AND A MAN WHO SEEMS TO SEE BUT IS BLIND!
THANK YOU, SIR! YOU MUST HAVE READ MY MIND!
BEING HERSELF A MUTE, TEDDY SOMEHOW FEELS THAT SHE MIGHT OFFER THE MAD, BLIND ARTIST A SENSE OF SYMPATHY HE COULDN'T GET FROM ORDINARY PERSONS...PERSONS ENJOYING THEIR FULL SENSES. SHE MIGHT, SHE THOUGHT, EVEN GET RHINER TO TALK!
IT'S A PITY YOU CAN'T HEAR OR TALK! IT MUST MAKE LIFE TERRIBLY DIFFICULT!
I COULD TELL YOU ANYTHING I GUESS...AND YOU WOULDN'T HEAR ONE WORD I WAS SAYING... EXCEPT FOR LIP READING, OF COURSE. HOW SAD TO BE SO AFFLICTED!

DON'T CRY, MY DEAR! SOME PEOPLE GET THE BREAKS AND SOME DON'T! I CAN UNDERSTAND BELIEVE ME! WHAT IT MEANS TO BE DEPRIVED OF ONE'S NORMAL ABILITY TO SEE...OR HEAR, EVEN TALK! IT'S A TERRIBLE CURSE!

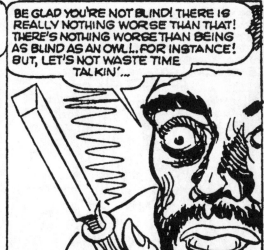

BE GLAD YOU'RE NOT BLIND! THERE IS REALLY NOTHING WORSE THAN THAT! THERE'S NOTHING WORSE THAN BEING AS BLIND AS AN OWL!..FOR INSTANCE! BUT, LET'S NOT WASTE TIME TALKIN'...

WE MAY ALL BE DEAD TOMORROW! AND EVERY MINUTE COUNTS! SO, RESUME YOUR POSE, TEDDY!

AS RHINER APPLIES THE FINISHING TOUCHES TO THE SUPER REALISTIC PORTRAIT OF TEDDY HE WAXES PHILOSOPHICAL... TEDDY'S PLIGHT HAS TOUCHED HIM, APPARENTLY! IT'S SO LIKE HIS OWN!

DEATH IS OUR ONLY CONSOLATION! IT MAKES UP FOR ALL THE PAIN!

WITH ALL MY MONEY, MY SUCCESS, MY FAME... IT'S NOTHING...ADDS UP TO NOTHING! IT ALL WINDS UP IN A PITCH BLACK PLACE... AN EMPTY, BLIND PIT!

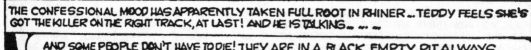

THE CONFESSIONAL MOOD HAS APPARENTLY TAKEN FULL ROOT IN RHINER... TEDDY FEELS SHE'S GOT THE KILLER ON THE RIGHT TRACK, AT LAST! AND HE IS TALKING... ~ ~

AND SOME PEOPLE DON'T HAVE TO DIE! THEY ARE IN A BLACK, EMPTY PIT ALWAYS... WITH NOTHING BUT CONTINUAL DARKNESS EVERY HOUR OF THE LIVING DAY... AND NIGHT!

LIKE **ME**! LIKE **ME**! I'M ONE OF THOSE PEOPLE. DAY AND NIGHT—NIGHT AND DAY I AM IN THE ABYSS. IN THE EMPTY PIT! I SEE NOTHING! I AM BLIND! **BLIND**! **BLIND**!

BLIND! BLIND! BLIND!

YOU'RE HORRIFIED AREN'T YOU? YOU WONDER HOW THE GREAT DUKE RHINER CAN BE **BLIND** AND YET SUCCEED IN PAINTING A PORTRAIT OF YOU WITH A REALISM NOT EVEN A CAMERA COULD CAPTURE! MYSTERIOUS, ISN'T IT?

WELL, I'LL LET YOU IN ON THE MYSTERY... TEDDY GIRL! I'LL TELL YOU HOW THE BLIND CAN SEE BETTER THAN THE SEEING! JUST LOOK... THE PORTRAIT LOOKS MORE LIKE YOU THAN YOU LOOK LIKE YOURSELF!

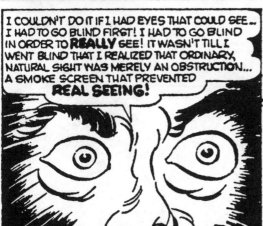

I COULDN'T DO IT IF I HAD EYES THAT COULD SEE... I HAD TO GO BLIND FIRST! I HAD TO GO BLIND IN ORDER TO **REALLY** SEE! IT WASN'T TILL I WENT BLIND THAT I REALIZED THAT ORDINARY, NATURAL SIGHT WAS MERELY AN OBSTRUCTION... A SMOKE SCREEN THAT PREVENTED **REAL SEEING!**

MY BLINDNESS STRUCK ME SUDDENLY, WITHOUT WARNING! I WAS INVITED TO A FRIEND'S ESTATE FOR PHEASANT HUNTING SOMETIME LAST YEAR!

BANG!
BANG!— o POW!

A MEAN, OVERSIZED HAWK KEPT CONTINUALLY GETTING IN THE WAY OF THINGS! HE SEEMED TO BE COMPETING WITH US... ...

THERE SEEMED TO BE A DEMON IN THAT BIRD... HE HAUNTED US...

POW!

I WAS DETERMINED TO GET HIM...
KER-POW!
I HUNTED THAT BEAST OF A BIRD FOR THREE DAYS...WITH NO LUCK!
BANG!
BAM
POW
BANG!
POW
BAM!
BLA
BANG!
ON THE FOURTH DAY, JUST AS THE SUN CAME UP...I GOT MY CHANCE! HE SWOOPED ABOUT TEN FEET OVER MY HEAD... WHILE SCULPTING ON A PIECE I HAD BEEN COMMISSIONED TO DO FOR THIS SAME FRIEND... ... ...
THEN HE SWOOPED AGAIN...THIS TIME ALMOST IN MY FACE...
HE CAME CLOSER...CLOSER... SWIFTLY... HE SEEMED TO STARE STRAIGHT INTO MY EYES!
I FELT A SEARING PAIN IN MY BRAIN...I MUST HAVE FAINTED FROM THE SHOCK...

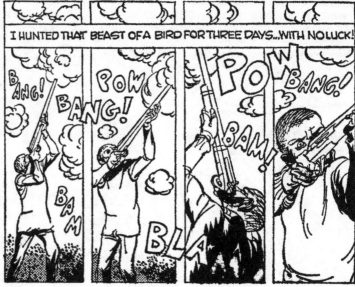

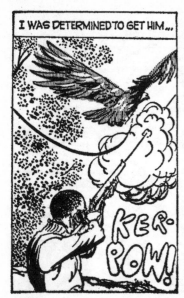

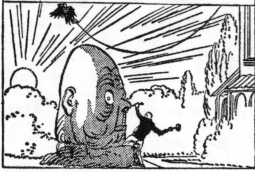

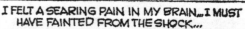

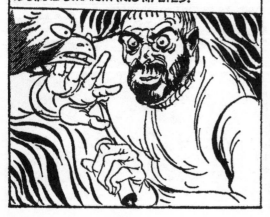

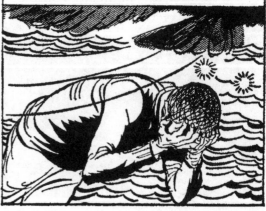

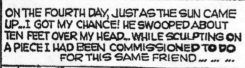

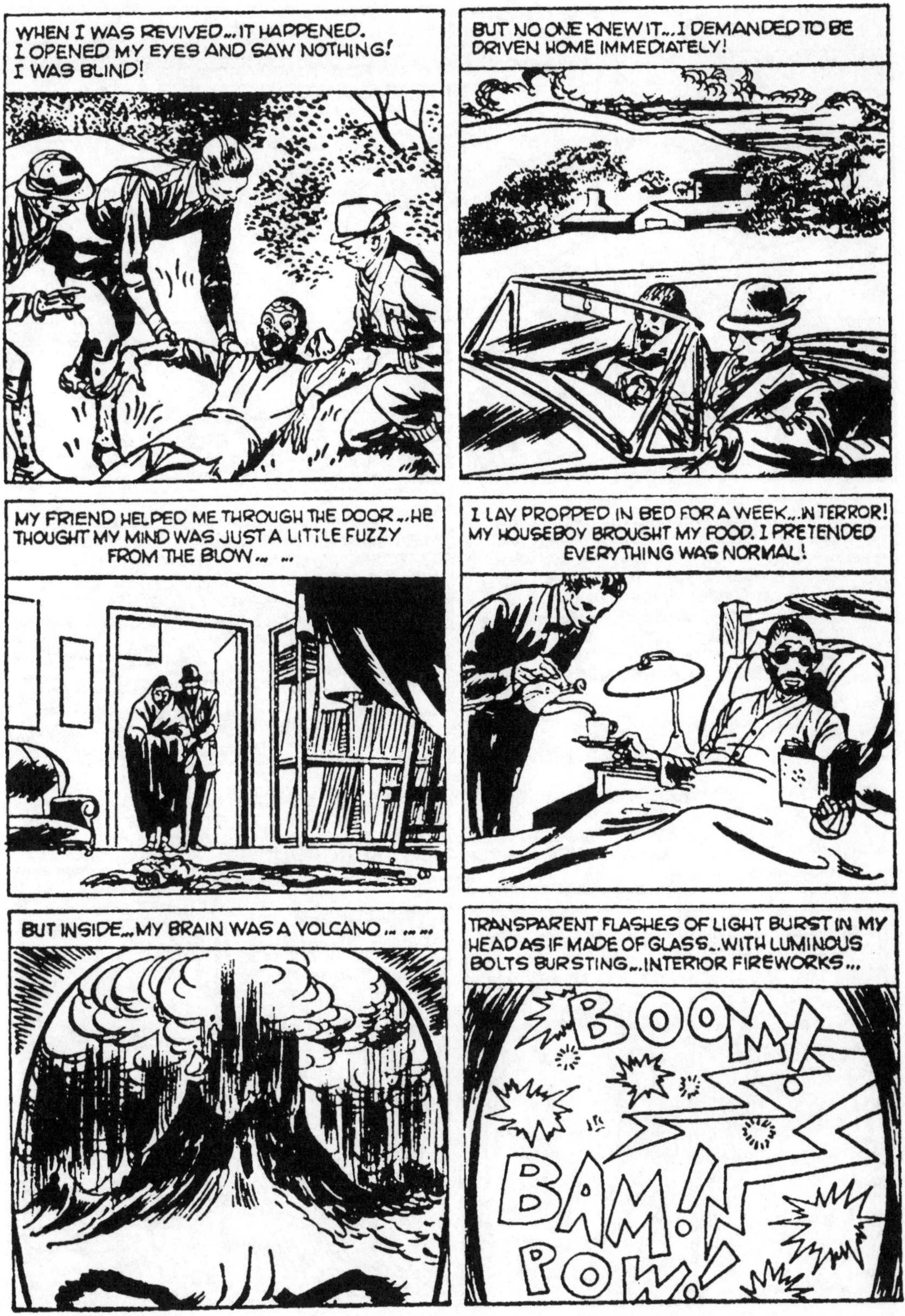
WHEN I WAS REVIVED... IT HAPPENED. I OPENED MY EYES AND SAW NOTHING! I WAS BLIND!
BUT NO ONE KNEW IT... I DEMANDED TO BE DRIVEN HOME IMMEDIATELY!
MY FRIEND HELPED ME THROUGH THE DOOR... HE THOUGHT MY MIND WAS JUST A LITTLE FUZZY FROM THE BLOW... ...
I LAY PROPPED IN BED FOR A WEEK... IN TERROR! MY HOUSEBOY BROUGHT MY FOOD. I PRETENDED EVERYTHING WAS NORMAL!
BUT INSIDE... MY BRAIN WAS A VOLCANO... ... ...
TRANSPARENT FLASHES OF LIGHT BURST IN MY HEAD AS IF MADE OF GLASS... WITH LUMINOUS BOLTS BURSTING... INTERIOR FIREWORKS...
BOOM!
BAM!
POW!

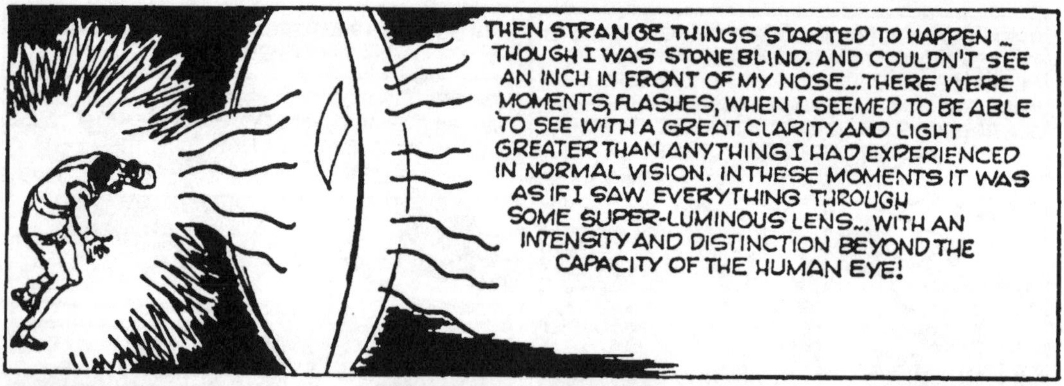
THEN STRANGE THINGS STARTED TO HAPPEN... THOUGH I WAS STONE BLIND. AND COULDN'T SEE AN INCH IN FRONT OF MY NOSE... THERE WERE MOMENTS, FLASHES, WHEN I SEEMED TO BE ABLE TO SEE WITH A GREAT CLARITY AND LIGHT GREATER THAN ANYTHING I HAD EXPERIENCED IN NORMAL VISION. IN THESE MOMENTS IT WAS AS IF I SAW EVERYTHING THROUGH SOME SUPER-LUMINOUS LENS... WITH AN INTENSITY AND DISTINCTION BEYOND THE CAPACITY OF THE HUMAN EYE!

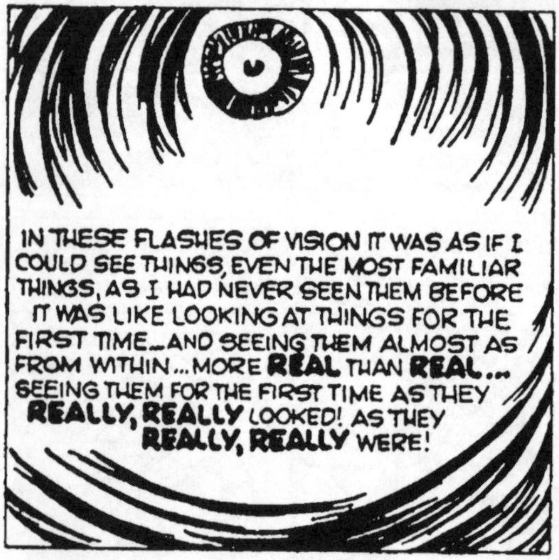
IN THESE FLASHES OF VISION IT WAS AS IF I COULD SEE THINGS, EVEN THE MOST FAMILIAR THINGS, AS I HAD NEVER SEEN THEM BEFORE IT WAS LIKE LOOKING AT THINGS FOR THE FIRST TIME... AND SEEING THEM ALMOST AS FROM WITHIN... MORE **REAL** THAN **REAL...** SEEING THEM FOR THE FIRST TIME AS THEY **REALLY, REALLY** LOOKED! AS THEY **REALLY, REALLY** WERE!

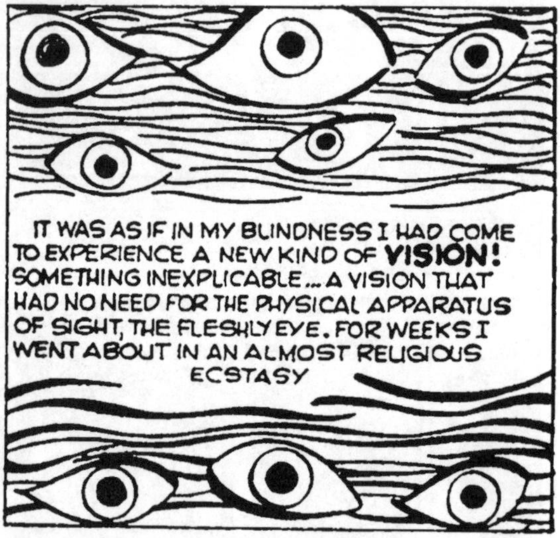
IT WAS AS IF IN MY BLINDNESS I HAD COME TO EXPERIENCE A NEW KIND OF **VISION!** SOMETHING INEXPLICABLE... A VISION THAT HAD NO NEED FOR THE PHYSICAL APPARATUS OF SIGHT, THE FLESHLY EYE. FOR WEEKS I WENT ABOUT IN AN ALMOST RELIGIOUS ECSTASY

AT THE TIME THERE WERE FOUR UNFINISHED PORTRAITS I WAS DOING. ONE OF AN ARCHITECT, A CRIPPLED ARCHITECT. ONE OF A YOUNG GIRL... ONE OF AN OLD DOWAGER... AND ONE OF SOME TRAGEDY-FATED YOUNG ACTRESS. I HAD TAKEN SIZABLE MONETARY ADVANCES ON ALL OF THEM AND THEY SIMPLY HAD TO BE COMPLETED!

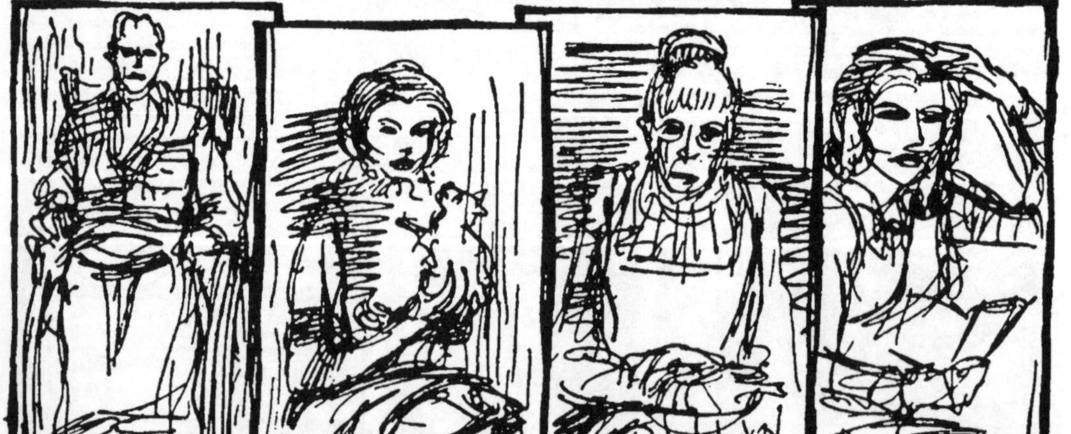

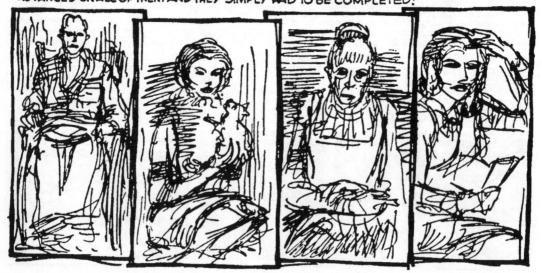

THEN AND THERE I DECIDED TO PUT MY NEW VISION TO THE TEST. EITHER I HAD TO RESIGN MYSELF TO BLINDNESS AND THE LOSS OF MY CAREER... OR I WOULD ATTEMPT TO PAINT THROUGH THESE FLASHES OF SUPER-SIGHT THAT WOULD COME TO ME OUT OF THE DARKNESS...

MY SUCCESS WAS GREATER THAN I BELIEVED POSSIBLE...

RHINER, THIS PORTRAIT IS UNBELIEVABLE. IT LOOKS MORE LIKE ME THAN I DO. YOUR GENIUS SEEMS TO HAVE TAKEN A NEW TURN. THE REALISM IS FRIGHTENING... IT'S UNCANNY!

AND HE NEVER REALIZED I WAS BLIND... STONE BLIND!

THE OLD LADY WAS EQUALLY ELATED.

RHINER, YOU ARE NOT AN ARTIST, YOU ARE A MAGICIAN... AN ADEPT... A MASTER! IT'S IMPOSSIBLE TO BELIEVE... I COULDN'T BELIEVE IT MYSELF!

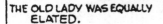

AND I DON'T KNOW HOW I DID IT...

IT WAS AS IF I COULD SEE THESE PEOPLE IN ONE FLASH... ...SO PERFECTLY CLEAR... AS IF IT WERE THEIR SOULS I SAW!

AND MY HAND MOVED AUTOMATICALLY AS IF CONTROLLED BY THE SAME FORCES THAT GENERATED THIS NEW INNER VISION!

IT WAS IF THE BODY OF THE PERSON APPEARED ON THE CANVAS ITSELF!

AND ALL I HAD TO DO WAS LAY ON THE PAINT! LIKE SOME SORT OF SKIN... THE PICTURE SIMPLY MADE ITSELF!

ALL I HAD TO DO WAS TRACE OVER WHAT WAS ALREADY THERE!

I DIDN'T HAVE TO THINK! I DIDN'T HAVE TO SEE! THE PICTURE AND MY BRUSH WERE SIMPLY DRAWN TOGETHER AS IF BY SOME MAGNET! ALL I HAD TO DO WAS NOT RESIST!

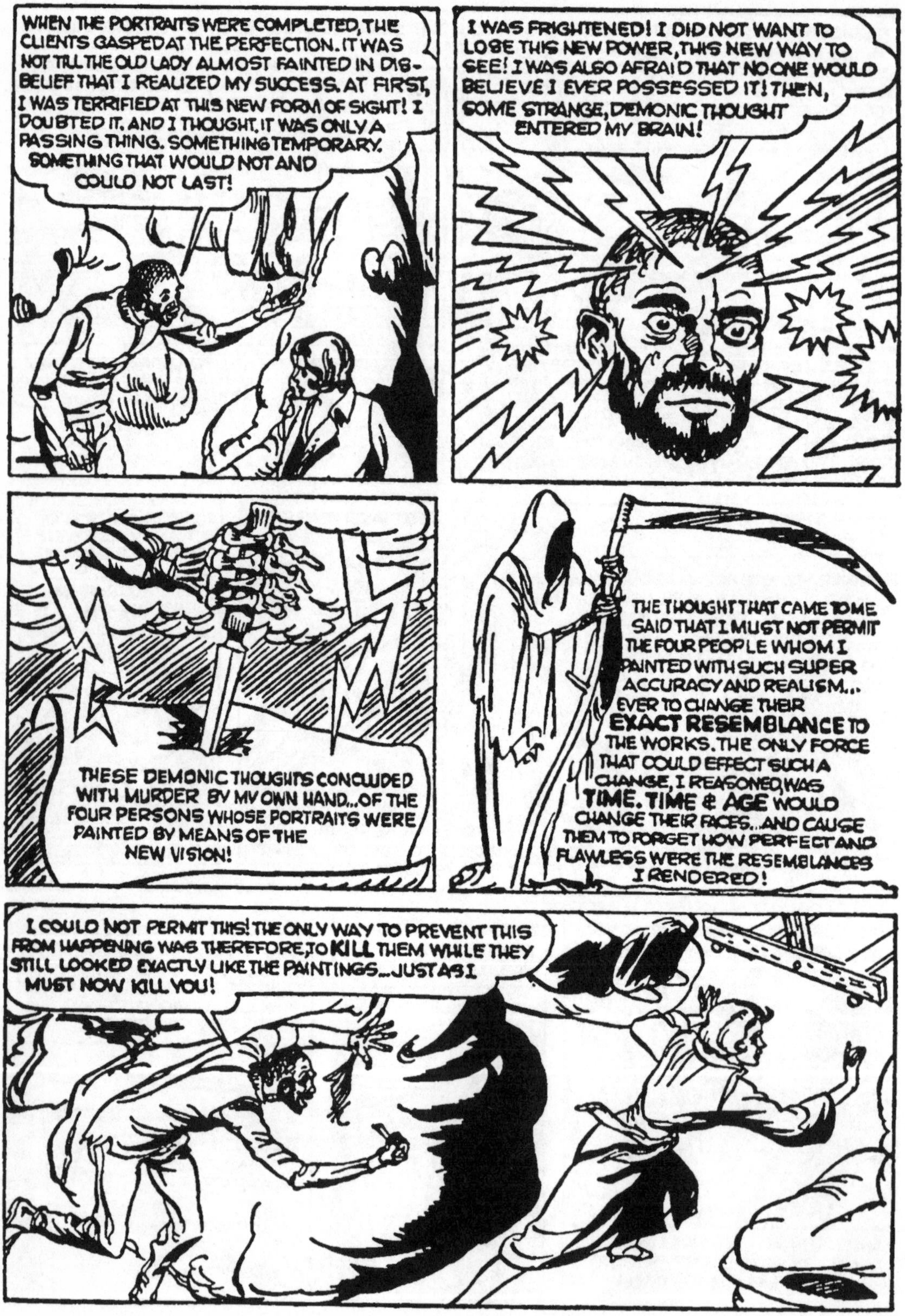
WHEN THE PORTRAITS WERE COMPLETED, THE CLIENTS GASPED AT THE PERFECTION. IT WAS NOT TILL THE OLD LADY ALMOST FAINTED IN DIS-BELIEF THAT I REALIZED MY SUCCESS. AT FIRST, I WAS TERRIFIED AT THIS NEW FORM OF SIGHT! I DOUBTED IT, AND I THOUGHT, IT WAS ONLY A PASSING THING. SOMETHING TEMPORARY. SOMETHING THAT WOULD NOT AND COULD NOT LAST!
I WAS FRIGHTENED! I DID NOT WANT TO LOSE THIS NEW POWER, THIS NEW WAY TO SEE! I WAS ALSO AFRAID THAT NO ONE WOULD BELIEVE I EVER POSSESSED IT! THEN, SOME STRANGE, DEMONIC THOUGHT ENTERED MY BRAIN!
THESE DEMONIC THOUGHTS CONCLUDED WITH MURDER BY MY OWN HAND... OF THE FOUR PERSONS WHOSE PORTRAITS WERE PAINTED BY MEANS OF THE NEW VISION!
THE THOUGHT THAT CAME TO ME SAID THAT I MUST NOT PERMIT THE FOUR PEOPLE WHOM I PAINTED WITH SUCH SUPER ACCURACY AND REALISM... EVER TO CHANGE THEIR EXACT RESEMBLANCE TO THE WORKS. THE ONLY FORCE THAT COULD EFFECT SUCH A CHANGE, I REASONED, WAS TIME. TIME & AGE WOULD CHANGE THEIR FACES... AND CAUSE THEM TO FORGET HOW PERFECT AND FLAWLESS WERE THE RESEMBLANCES I RENDERED!
I COULD NOT PERMIT THIS! THE ONLY WAY TO PREVENT THIS FROM HAPPENING WAS THEREFORE, TO KILL THEM WHILE THEY STILL LOOKED EXACTLY LIKE THE PAINTINGS... JUST AS I MUST NOW KILL YOU!

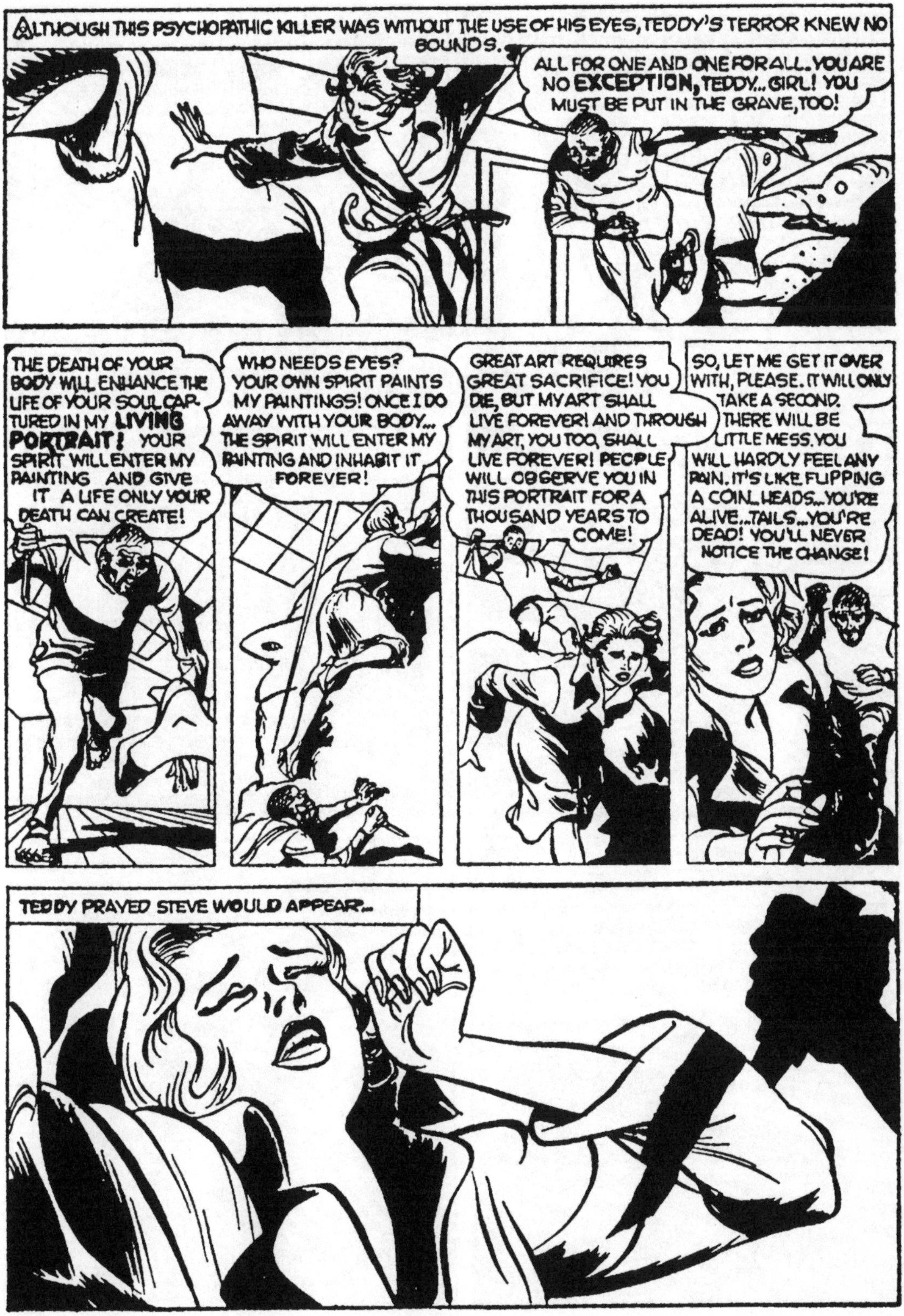
ALTHOUGH THIS PSYCHOPATHIC KILLER WAS WITHOUT THE USE OF HIS EYES, TEDDY'S TERROR KNEW NO BOUNDS...
ALL FOR ONE AND ONE FOR ALL.. YOU ARE NO EXCEPTION, TEDDY... GIRL! YOU MUST BE PUT IN THE GRAVE, TOO!
THE DEATH OF YOUR BODY WILL ENHANCE THE LIFE OF YOUR SOUL CAPTURED IN MY LIVING PORTRAIT! YOUR SPIRIT WILL ENTER MY PAINTING AND GIVE IT A LIFE ONLY YOUR DEATH CAN CREATE!
WHO NEEDS EYES? YOUR OWN SPIRIT PAINTS MY PAINTINGS! ONCE I DO AWAY WITH YOUR BODY... THE SPIRIT WILL ENTER MY PAINTING AND INHABIT IT FOREVER!
GREAT ART REQUIRES GREAT SACRIFICE! YOU DIE, BUT MY ART SHALL LIVE FOREVER! AND THROUGH MY ART, YOU TOO, SHALL LIVE FOREVER! PEOPLE WILL OBSERVE YOU IN THIS PORTRAIT FOR A THOUSAND YEARS TO COME!
SO, LET ME GET IT OVER WITH, PLEASE. IT WILL ONLY TAKE A SECOND. THERE WILL BE LITTLE MESS. YOU WILL HARDLY FEEL ANY PAIN. IT'S LIKE FLIPPING A COIN. HEADS... YOU'RE ALIVE... TAILS... YOU'RE DEAD! YOU'LL NEVER NOTICE THE CHANGE!
TEDDY PRAYED STEVE WOULD APPEAR...

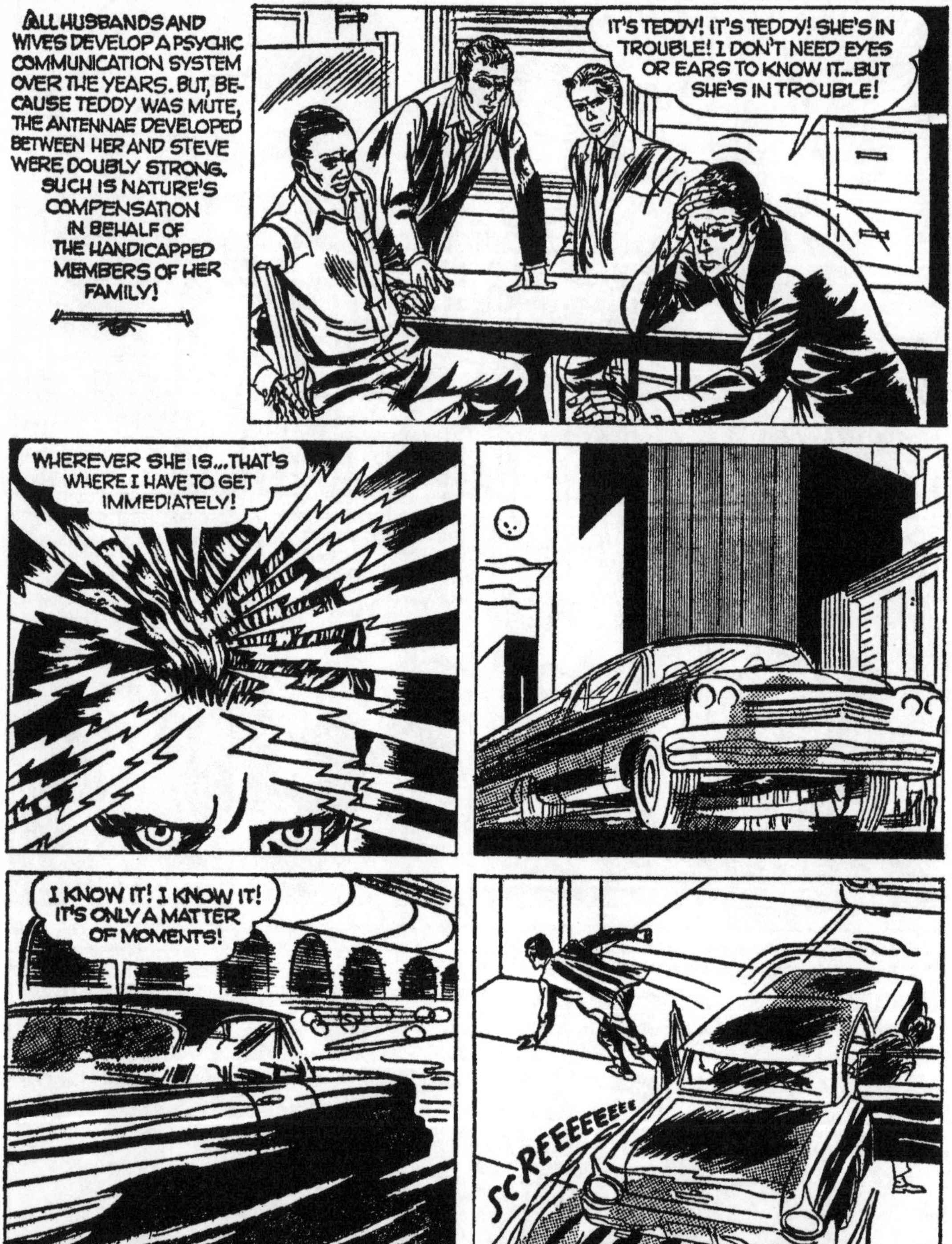
ALL HUSBANDS AND WIVES DEVELOP A PSYCHIC COMMUNICATION SYSTEM OVER THE YEARS. BUT, BECAUSE TEDDY WAS MUTE, THE ANTENNAE DEVELOPED BETWEEN HER AND STEVE WERE DOUBLY STRONG. SUCH IS NATURE'S COMPENSATION IN BEHALF OF THE HANDICAPPED MEMBERS OF HER FAMILY!
IT'S TEDDY! IT'S TEDDY! SHE'S IN TROUBLE! I DON'T NEED EYES OR EARS TO KNOW IT...BUT SHE'S IN TROUBLE!
WHEREVER SHE IS...THAT'S WHERE I HAVE TO GET IMMEDIATELY!
I KNOW IT! I KNOW IT! IT'S ONLY A MATTER OF MOMENTS!
SCREEEEEEEE

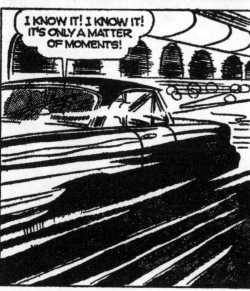

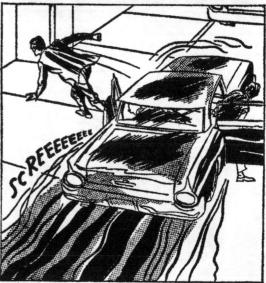

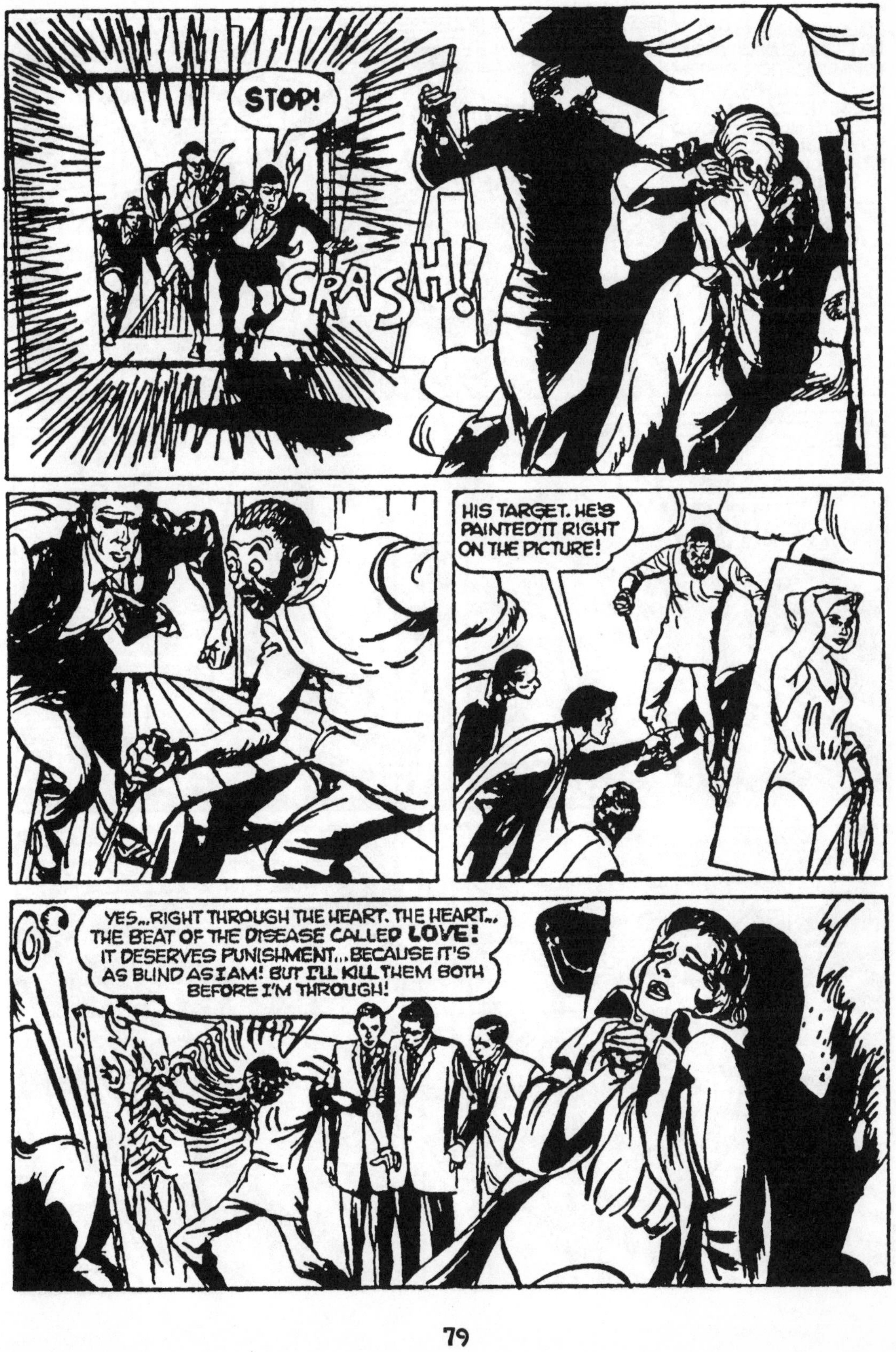
STOP!
CRASH!
HIS TARGET. HE'S PAINTED IT RIGHT ON THE PICTURE!
YES... RIGHT THROUGH THE HEART. THE HEART... THE BEAT OF THE DISEASE CALLED **LOVE!** IT DESERVES PUNISHMENT... BECAUSE IT'S AS BLIND AS I AM! BUT I'LL KILL THEM BOTH BEFORE I'M THROUGH!

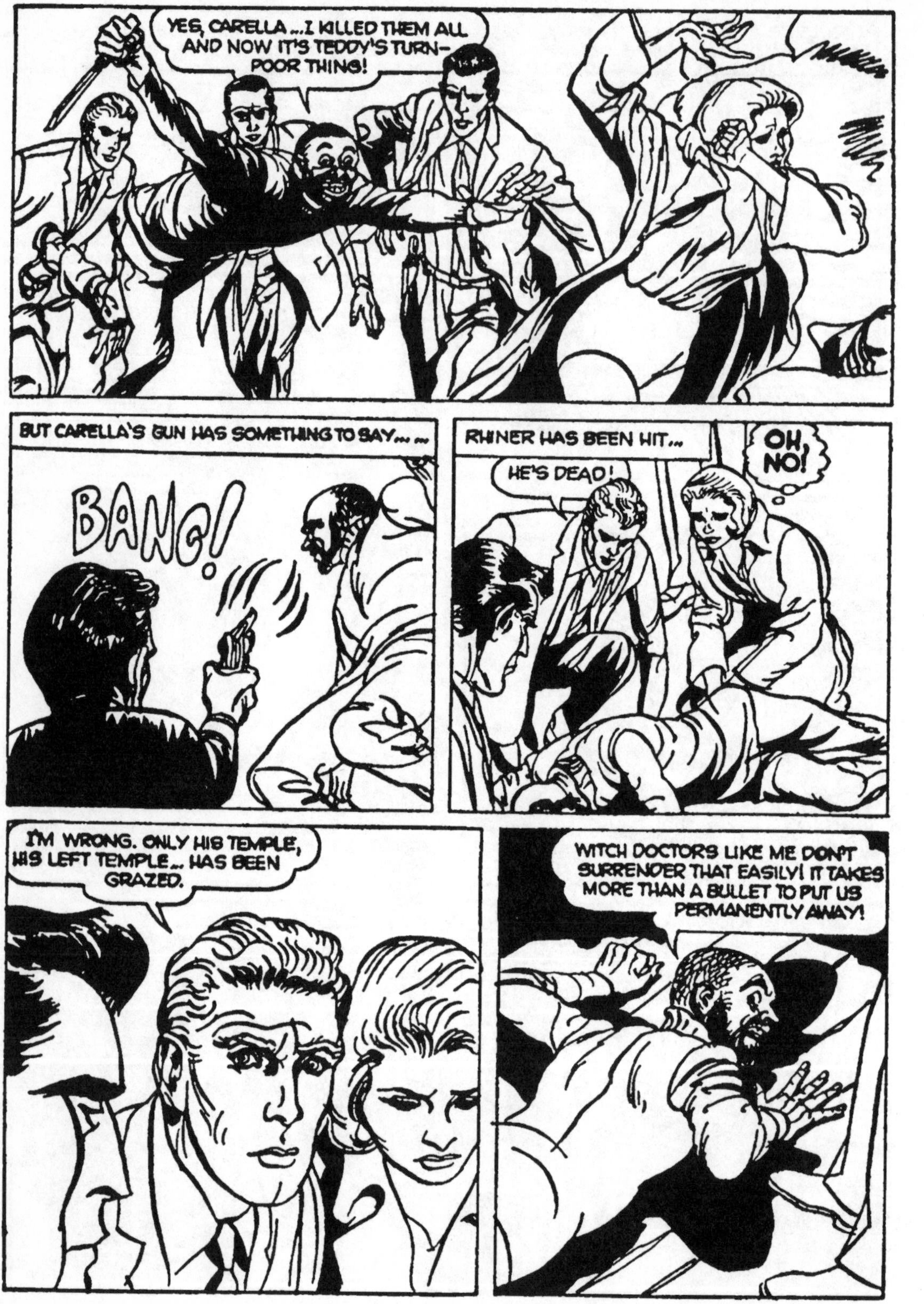
YES, CARELLA ...I KILLED THEM ALL AND NOW IT'S TEDDY'S TURN- POOR THING!
BUT CARELLA'S GUN HAS SOMETHING TO SAY... ...
BANG!
RHINER HAS BEEN HIT...
HE'S DEAD!
OH, NO!
I'M WRONG. ONLY HIS TEMPLE, HIS LEFT TEMPLE... HAS BEEN GRAZED.
WITCH DOCTORS LIKE ME DON'T SURRENDER THAT EASILY! IT TAKES MORE THAN A BULLET TO PUT US PERMANENTLY AWAY!

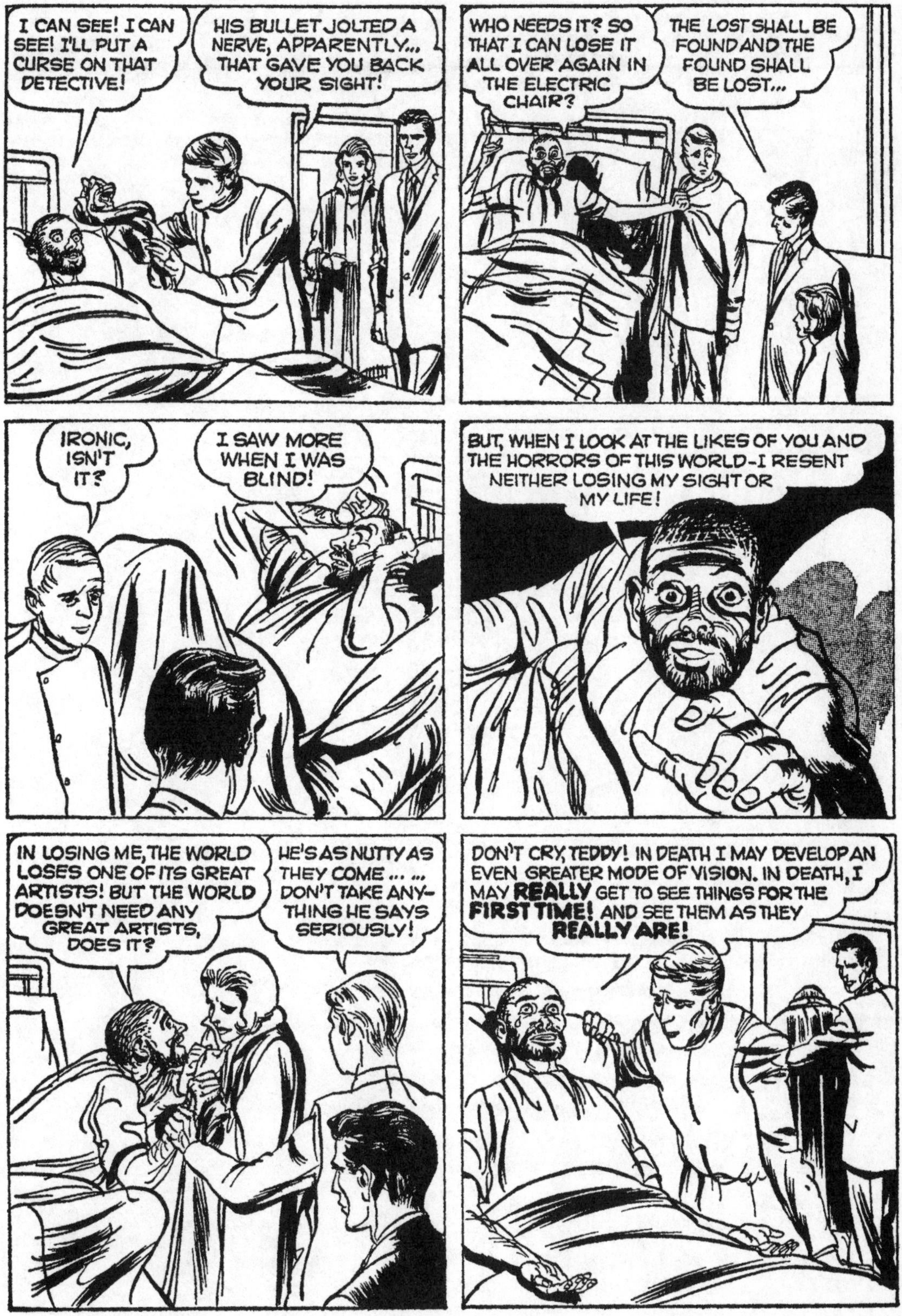

I CAN SEE! I CAN SEE! I'LL PUT A CURSE ON THAT DETECTIVE!
HIS BULLET JOLTED A NERVE, APPARENTLY... THAT GAVE YOU BACK YOUR SIGHT!
WHO NEEDS IT? SO THAT I CAN LOSE IT ALL OVER AGAIN IN THE ELECTRIC CHAIR?
THE LOST SHALL BE FOUND AND THE FOUND SHALL BE LOST...
IRONIC, ISN'T IT?
I SAW MORE WHEN I WAS BLIND!
BUT, WHEN I LOOK AT THE LIKES OF YOU AND THE HORRORS OF THIS WORLD-I RESENT NEITHER LOSING MY SIGHT OR MY LIFE!
IN LOSING ME, THE WORLD LOSES ONE OF ITS GREAT ARTISTS! BUT THE WORLD DOESN'T NEED ANY GREAT ARTISTS, DOES IT?
HE'S AS NUTTY AS THEY COME ... ... DON'T TAKE ANY-THING HE SAYS SERIOUSLY!
DON'T CRY, TEDDY! IN DEATH I MAY DEVELOP AN EVEN GREATER MODE OF VISION. IN DEATH, I MAY REALLY GET TO SEE THINGS FOR THE FIRST TIME! AND SEE THEM AS THEY REALLY ARE!

"Since we've been after that brute, his trail leads down and down. I never knew there were so many hotels and slums full of sleaze..."

Haunted since childhood by his grandfather's recollections of the First World War, Jacques Tardi regularly returns to the horrors of war in his understated yet powerful graphic novels. Here he is joined by his wife Dominique Grange who writes this tale of the Vietnam conflict and its terrible legacy. They portray the Big Apple with a seedy atmosphere and a toned photo-reference realism, reminiscent of Martin Scorsese's *Taxi Driver* (1976). Preferring pathos to hysteria, they question the true value of vengeance. Tardi is a great French master of *bande dessinée*, hailed for his Belle Epoque female investigator of the occult, Adèle Blanc-Sec, and his adaptations of Léo Malet's novels, and his own original stories, about the Parisian detective Nestor Burma.

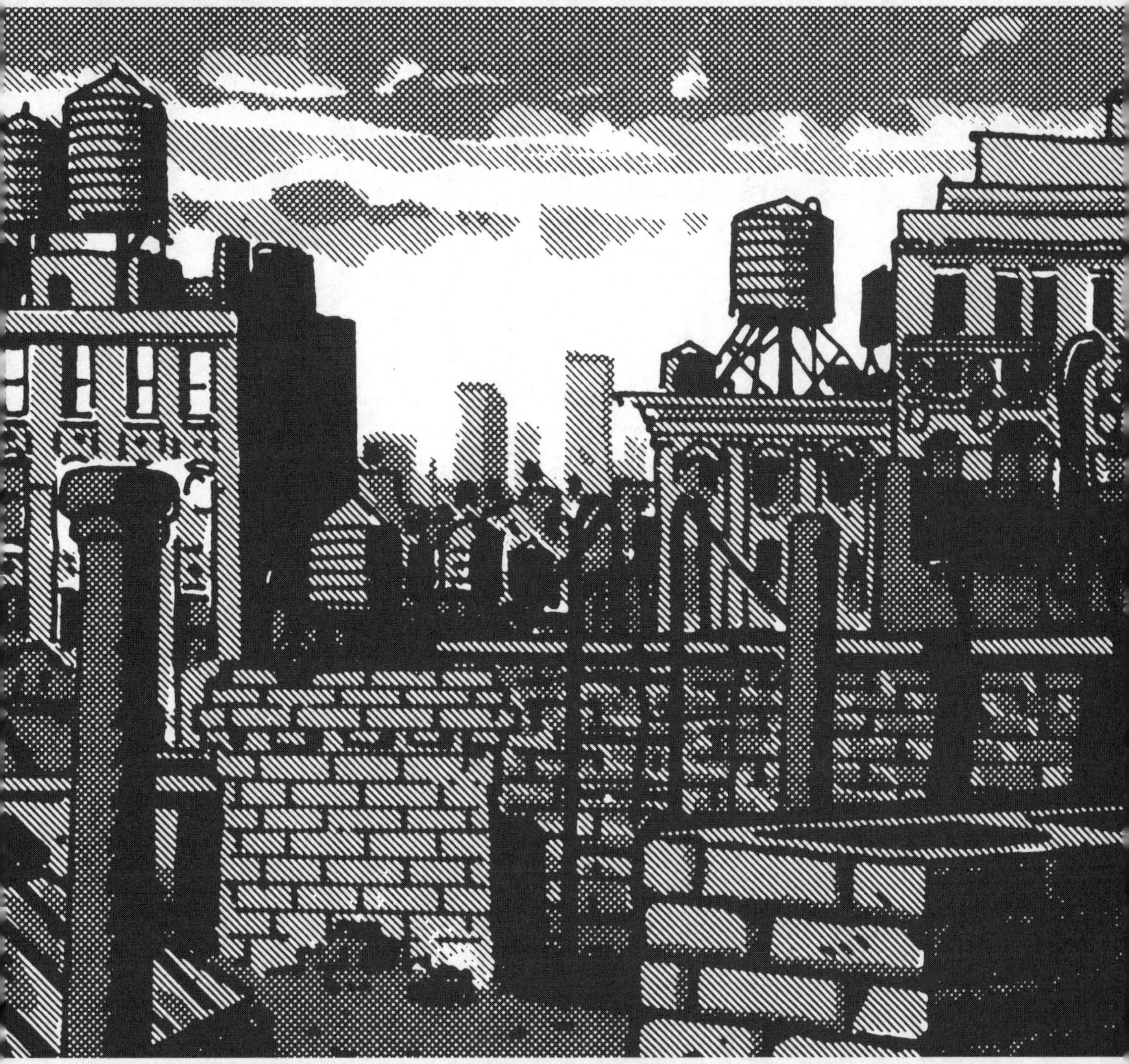

The Murderer of Hung

Dominique Grange (script) and Jacques Tardi (art) 1982

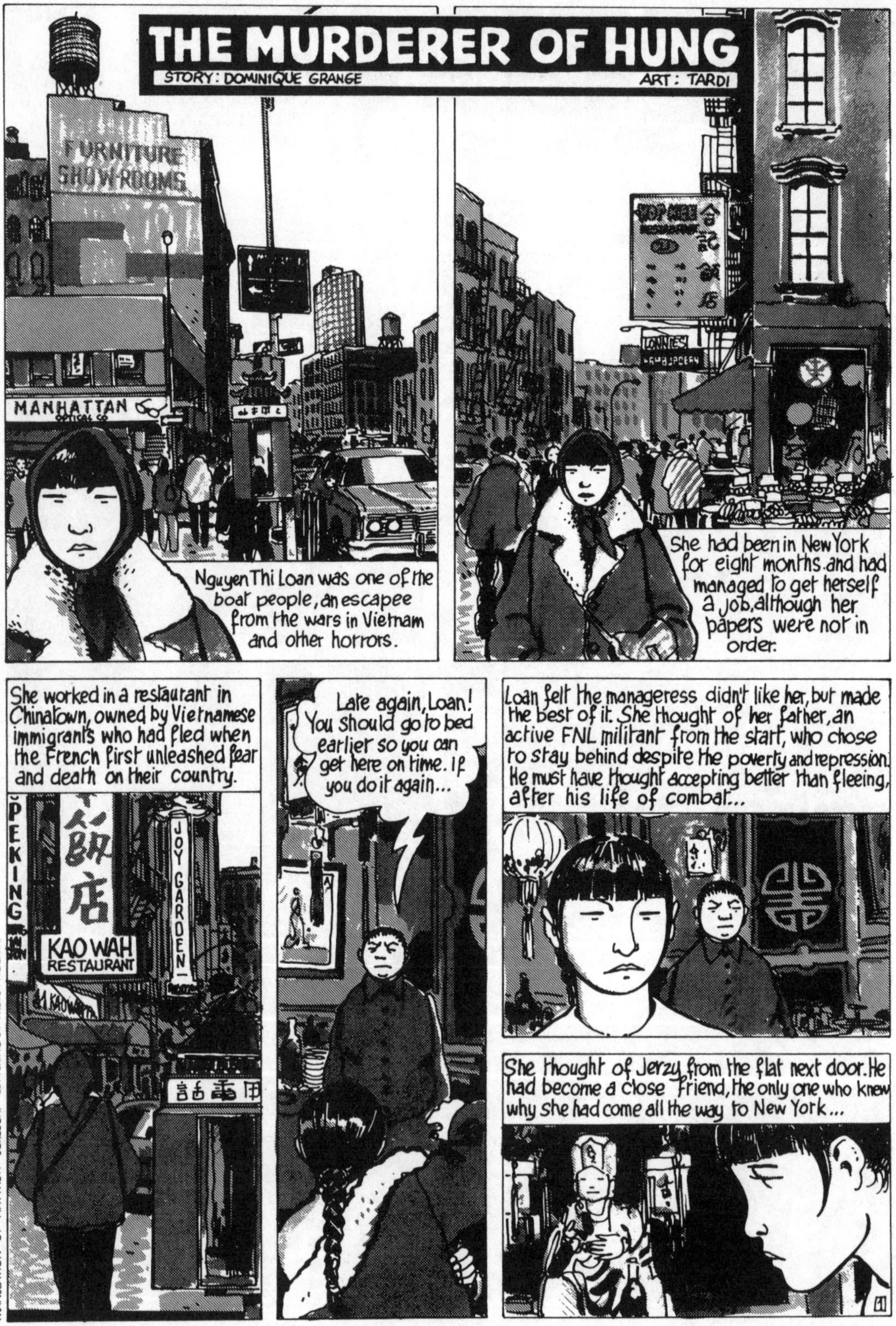
THE MURDERER OF HUNG
STORY: DOMINIQUE GRANGE
ART: TARDI
FURNITURE SHOWROOMS
MANHATTAN OPTICAL CO
Nguyen Thi Loan was one of the boat people, an escapee from the wars in Vietnam and other horrors.
LONNIE'S
She had been in New York for eight months and had managed to get herself a job, although her papers were not in order.
She worked in a restaurant in Chinatown, owned by Vietnamese immigrants who had fled when the French first unleashed fear and death on their country.
PEKING
KAO WAH RESTAURANT
JOY GARDEN
Late again, Loan! You should go to bed earlier so you can get here on time. If you do it again...
Loan felt the manageress didn't like her, but made the best of it. She thought of her father, an active FNL militant from the start, who chose to stay behind despite the poverty and repression. He must have thought accepting better than fleeing, after his life of combat...
She thought of Jerzy from the flat next door. He had become a close friend, the only one who knew why she had come all the way to New York...

TRANSLATION BY MATTHEW SCREECH. LETTERING BY TREVS PHOENIX.

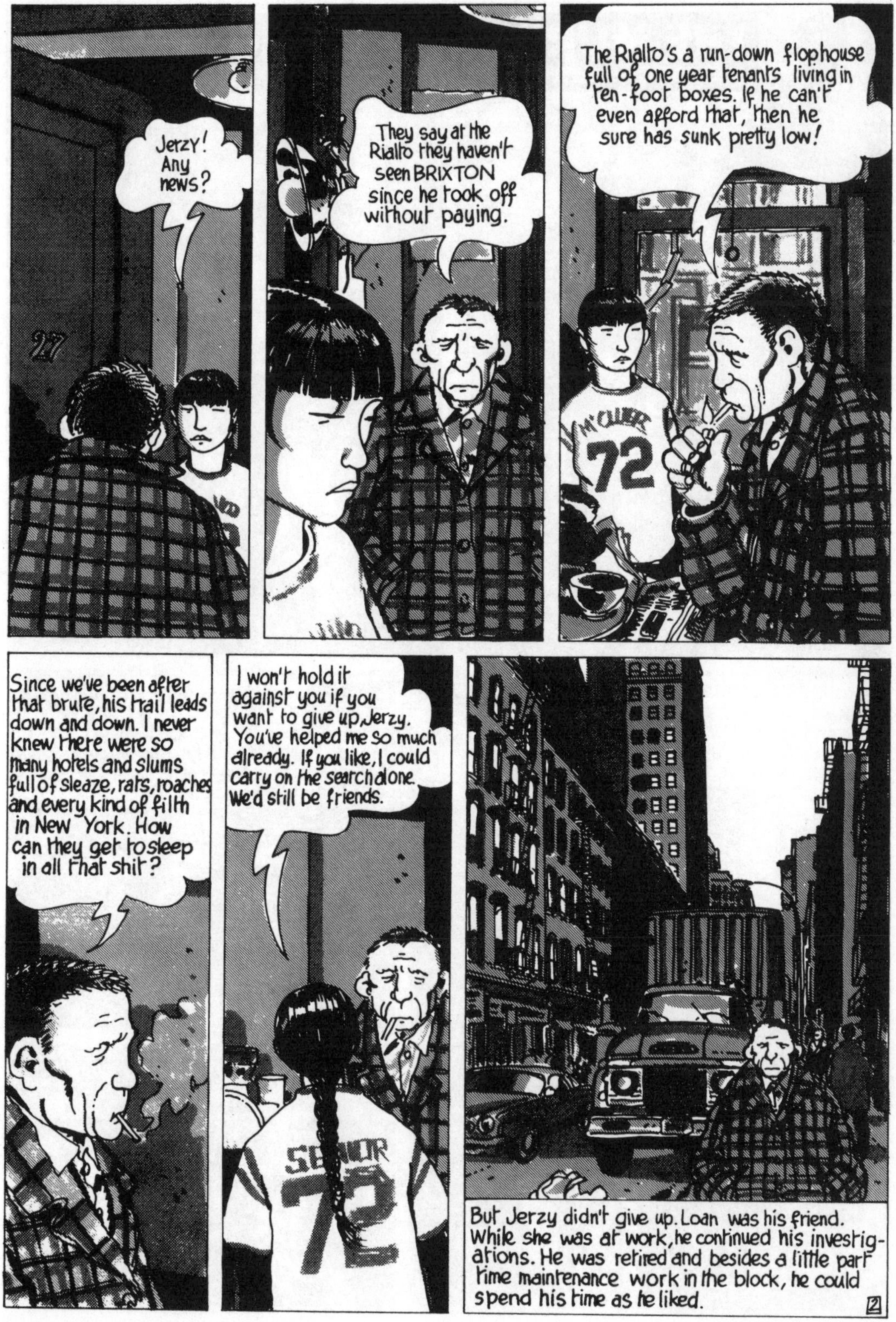
Jerzy! Any news?
They say at the Rialto they haven't seen BRIXTON since he took off without paying.
The Rialto's a run-down flophouse full of one year tenants living in ten-foot boxes. If he can't even afford that, then he sure has sunk pretty low!
Since we've been after that brute, his trail leads down and down. I never knew there were so many hotels and slums full of sleaze, rats, roaches and every kind of filth in New York. How can they get to sleep in all that shit?
I won't hold it against you if you want to give up, Jerzy. You've helped me so much already. If you like, I could carry on the search alone. We'd still be friends.
But Jerzy didn't give up. Loan was his friend. While she was at work, he continued his investigations. He was retired and besides a little part time maintenance work in the block, he could spend his time as he liked.
2

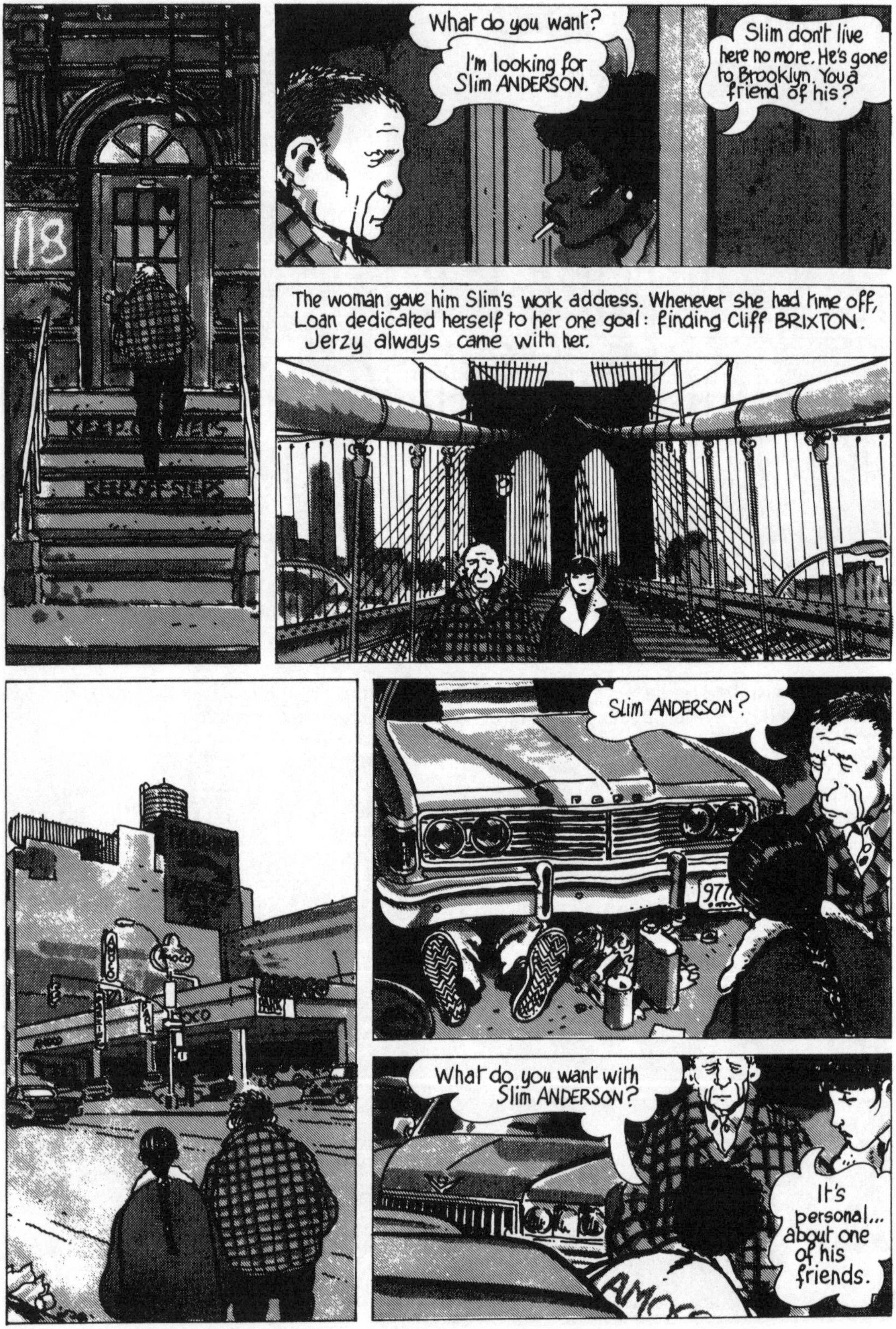

118
What do you want?
I'm looking for Slim ANDERSON.
Slim don't live here no more. He's gone to Brooklyn. You a friend of his?
The woman gave him Slim's work address. Whenever she had time off, Loan dedicated herself to her one goal: finding Cliff BRIXTON. Jerzy always came with her.
Slim ANDERSON?
What do you want with Slim ANDERSON?
It's personal... about one of his friends.

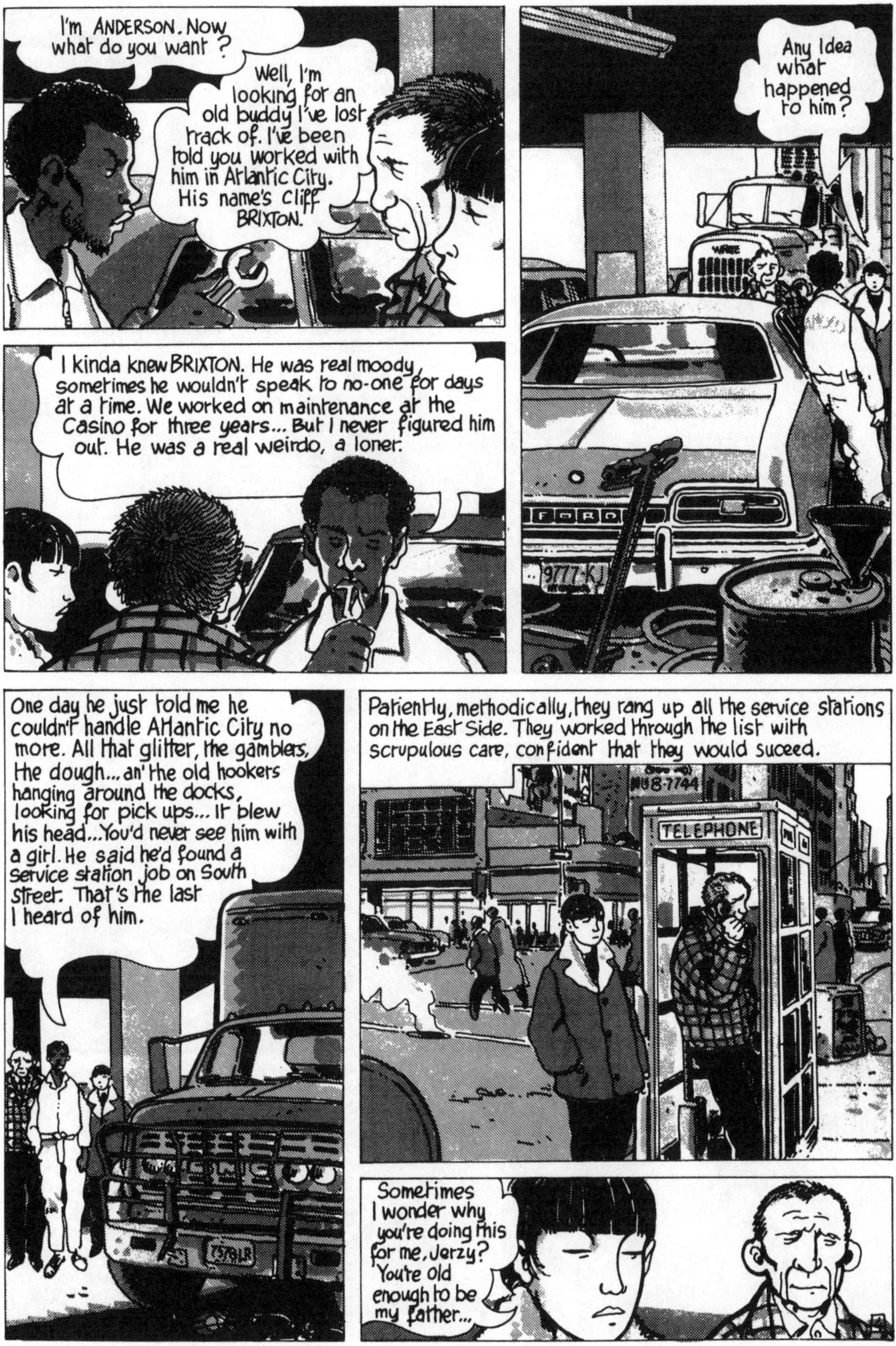
I'm ANDERSON. Now what do you want?
Well, I'm looking for an old buddy I've lost track of. I've been told you worked with him in Atlantic City. His name's Cliff BRIXTON.
I kinda knew BRIXTON. He was real moody, sometimes he wouldn't speak to no-one for days at a time. We worked on maintenance at the Casino for three years... But I never figured him out. He was a real weirdo, a loner.
Any Idea what happened to him?
FORD
One day he just told me he couldn't handle Atlantic City no more. All that glitter, the gamblers, the dough... an' the old hookers hanging around the docks, looking for pick ups... It blew his head... You'd never see him with a girl. He said he'd found a service station job on South street. That's the last I heard of him.
Patiently, methodically, they rang up all the service stations on the East Side. They worked through the list with scrupulous care, confident that they would suceed.
TELEPHONE
Sometimes I wonder why you're doing this for me, Jerzy? You're old enough to be my father...

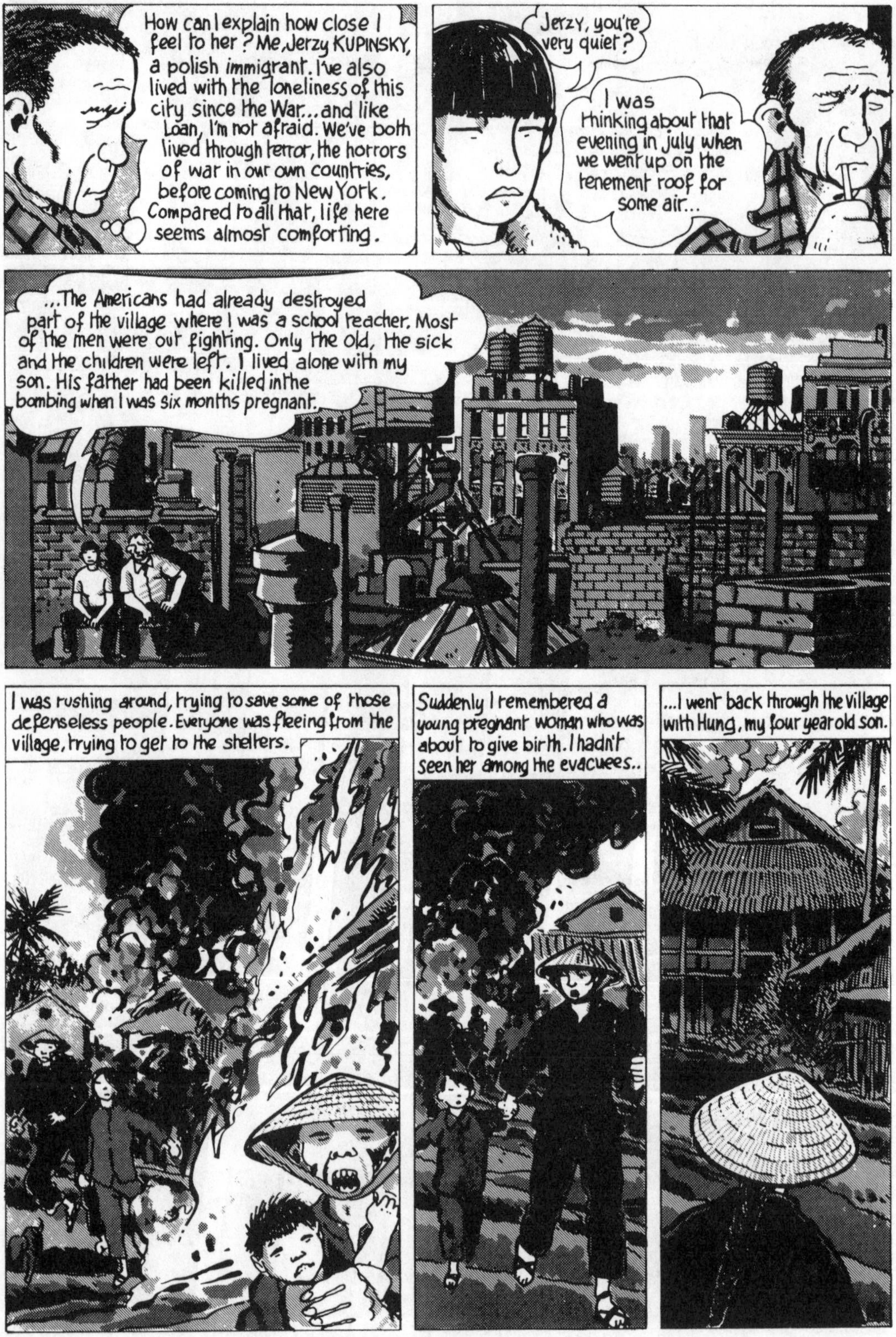
How can I explain how close I feel to her? Me, Jerzy KUPINSKY, a polish immigrant. I've also lived with the loneliness of this city since the War... and like Loan, I'm not afraid. We've both lived through terror, the horrors of war in our own countries, before coming to New York. Compared to all that, life here seems almost comforting.
Jerzy, you're very quiet?
I was thinking about that evening in july when we went up on the tenement roof for some air...
...The Americans had already destroyed part of the village where I was a school teacher. Most of the men were out fighting. Only the old, the sick and the children were left. I lived alone with my son. His father had been killed in the bombing when I was six months pregnant.
I was rushing around, trying to save some of those defenseless people. Everyone was fleeing from the village, trying to get to the shelters.
Suddenly I remembered a young pregnant woman who was about to give birth. I hadn't seen her among the evacuees..
...I went back through the village with Hung, my four year old son.

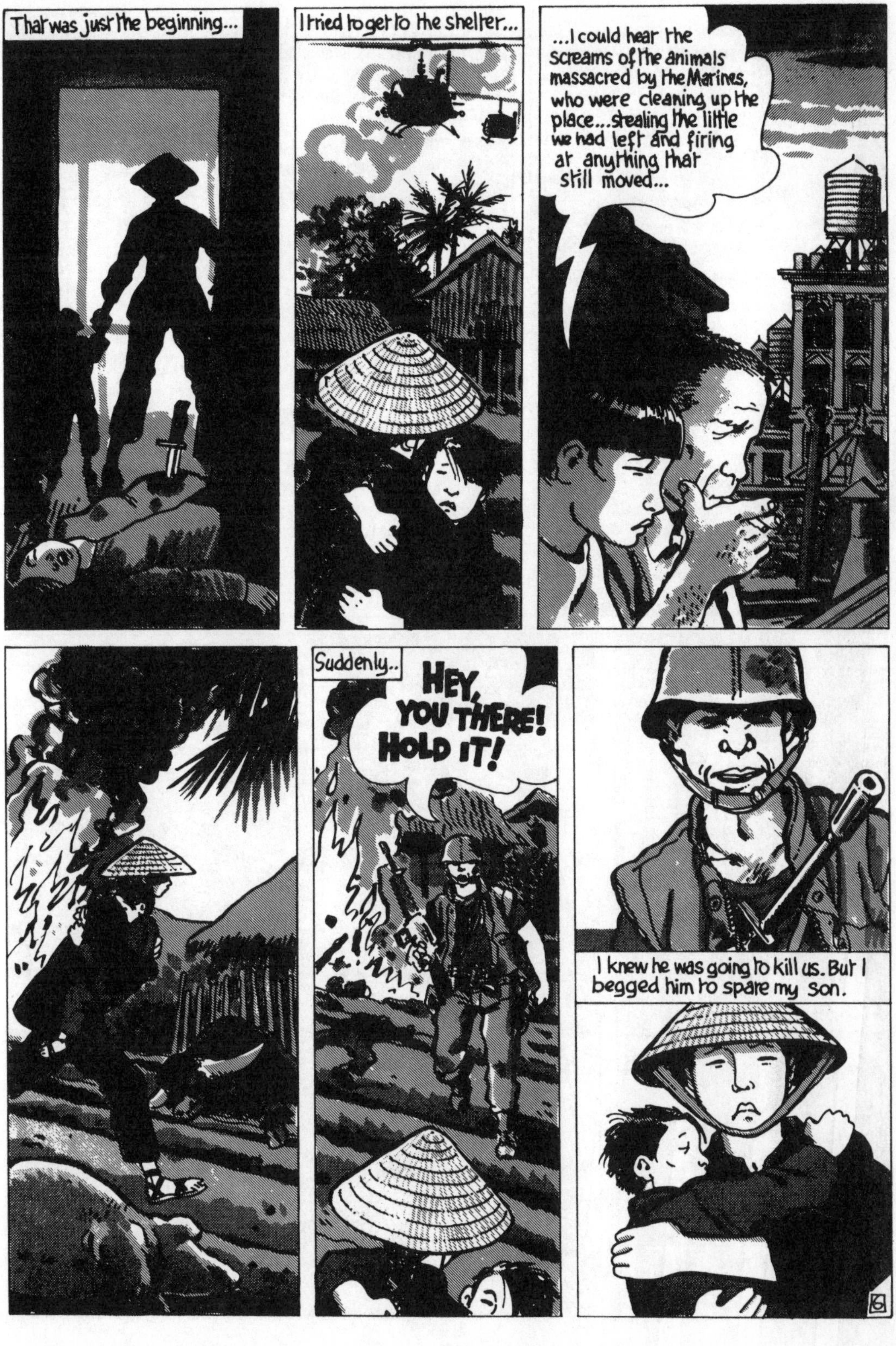

That was just the beginning...
I tried to get to the shelter...
...I could hear the screams of the animals massacred by the Marines, who were cleaning up the place...stealing the little we had left and firing at anything that still moved...
Suddenly..
HEY, YOU THERE! HOLD IT!
I knew he was going to kill us. But I begged him to spare my son.

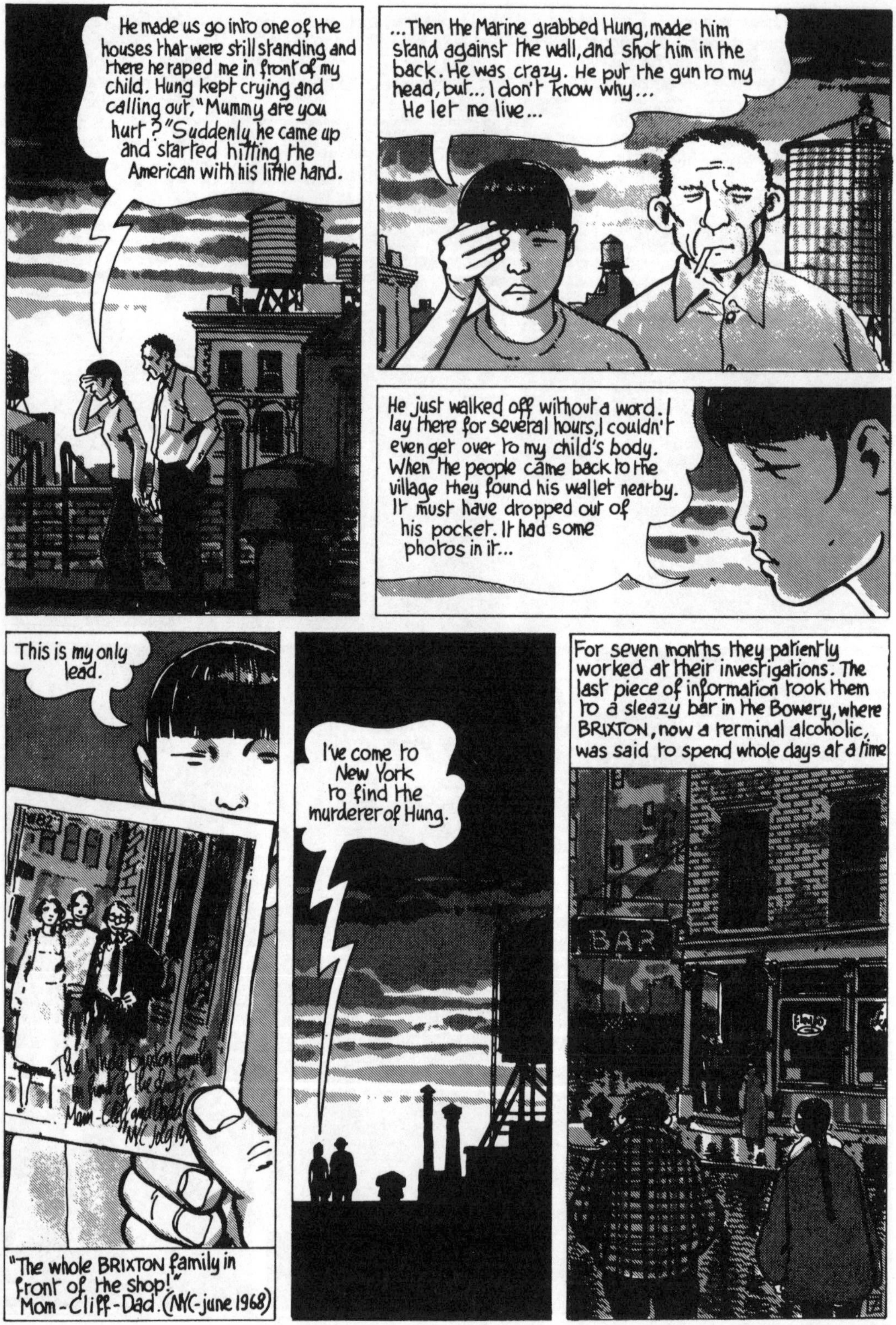
He made us go into one of the houses that were still standing and there he raped me in front of my child. Hung kept crying and calling out, "Mummy are you hurt?" Suddenly he came up and started hitting the American with his little hand.
...Then the Marine grabbed Hung, made him stand against the wall, and shot him in the back. He was crazy. He put the gun to my head, but... I don't know why... He let me live...
He just walked off without a word. I lay there for several hours, I couldn't even get over to my child's body. When the people came back to the village they found his wallet nearby. It must have dropped out of his pocket. It had some photos in it...
This is my only lead.
"The whole BRIXTON family in front of the shop!" Mom - Cliff - Dad. (NYC - june 1968)
I've come to New York to find the murderer of Hung.
For seven months they patiently worked at their investigations. The last piece of information took them to a sleazy bar in the Bowery, where BRIXTON, now a terminal alcoholic, was said to spend whole days at a time
BAR

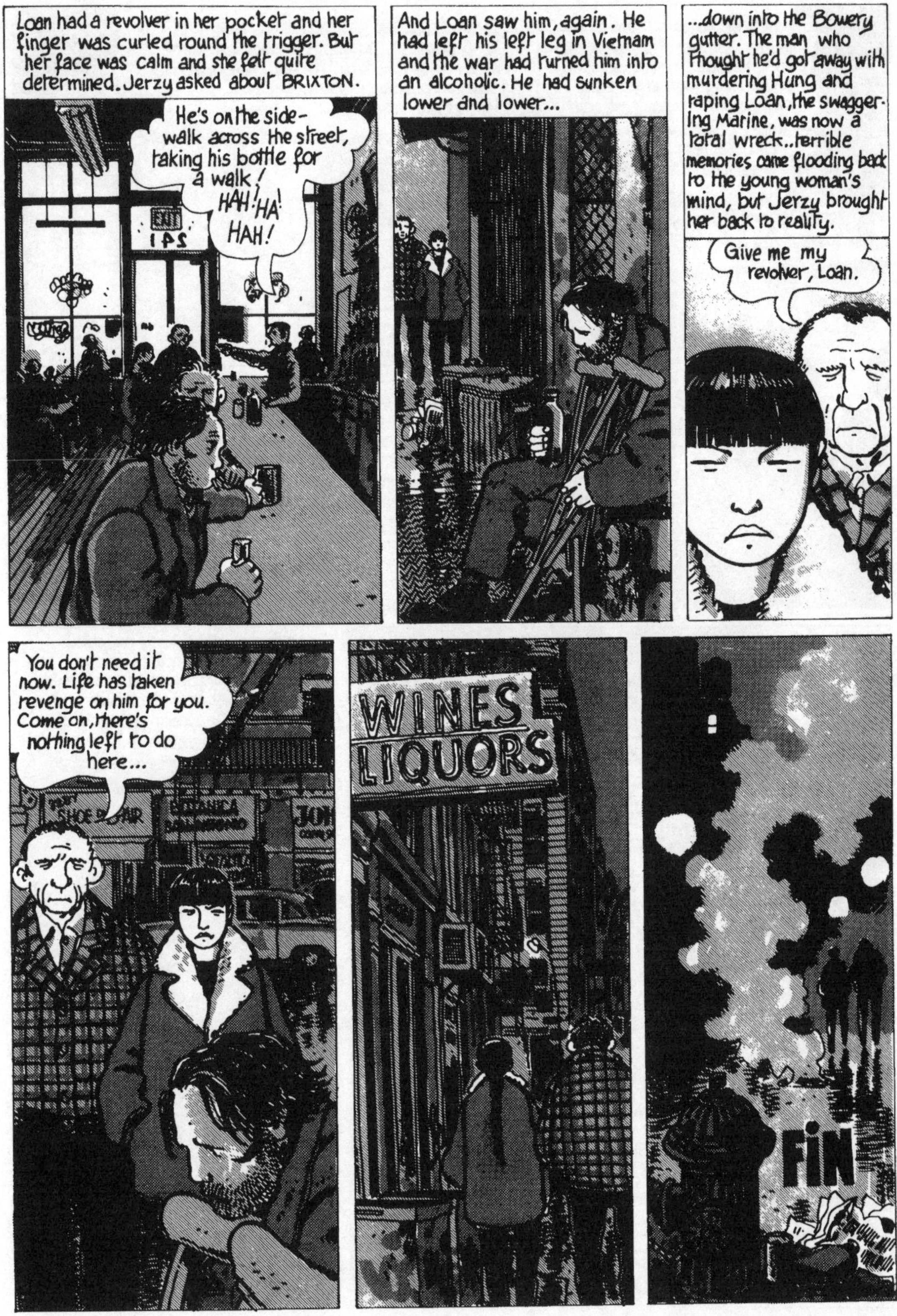
Loan had a revolver in her pocket and her finger was curled round the trigger. But her face was calm and she felt quite determined. Jerzy asked about BRIXTON.
He's on the side-walk across the street, taking his bottle for a walk!
HAH! HA! HAH!
EXIT
And Loan saw him, again. He had left his left leg in Vietnam and the war had turned him into an alcoholic. He had sunken lower and lower...
...down into the Bowery gutter. The man who thought he'd got away with murdering Hung and raping Loan, the swaggering Marine, was now a total wreck.. terrible memories came flooding back to the young woman's mind, but Jerzy brought her back to reality.
Give me my revolver, Loan.
You don't need it now. Life has taken revenge on him for you. Come on, there's nothing left to do here...
WINES
LIQUORS
FIN

"Oh, Geeze...
ain't there anyone
in the world
ya can trust??"

For sheer heart-thumping, lip-quivering
histrionics, where panels literally quake
with shock and dialogue and balloons vibrate
with emotion, nothing comes close to Jack
Cole's fever-pitch gem of a confessional.
Tormented by her dope-induced nightmares,
Mary Kennedy breaks down and confesses
her sordid history. The alarming panel on the
second page of a needle about to be injected
into poor Mary's eye gained notoriety when
psychiatrist Dr Fredric Wertham highlighted
it out of context in his panic-raising diatribe,
Seduction of the Innocent, as "a sample of the
injury-to-the-eye motif". While this comes
as the climax of a nightmare, it seems it did
really happen during an evening ordeal which
Mary cannot forget. The creator of the zany,
pliable Plastic Man, Jack Cole was at the
height of his career in 1958 as a cartoonist for
Playboy and his own syndicated newspaper
strip, when he took his own life.

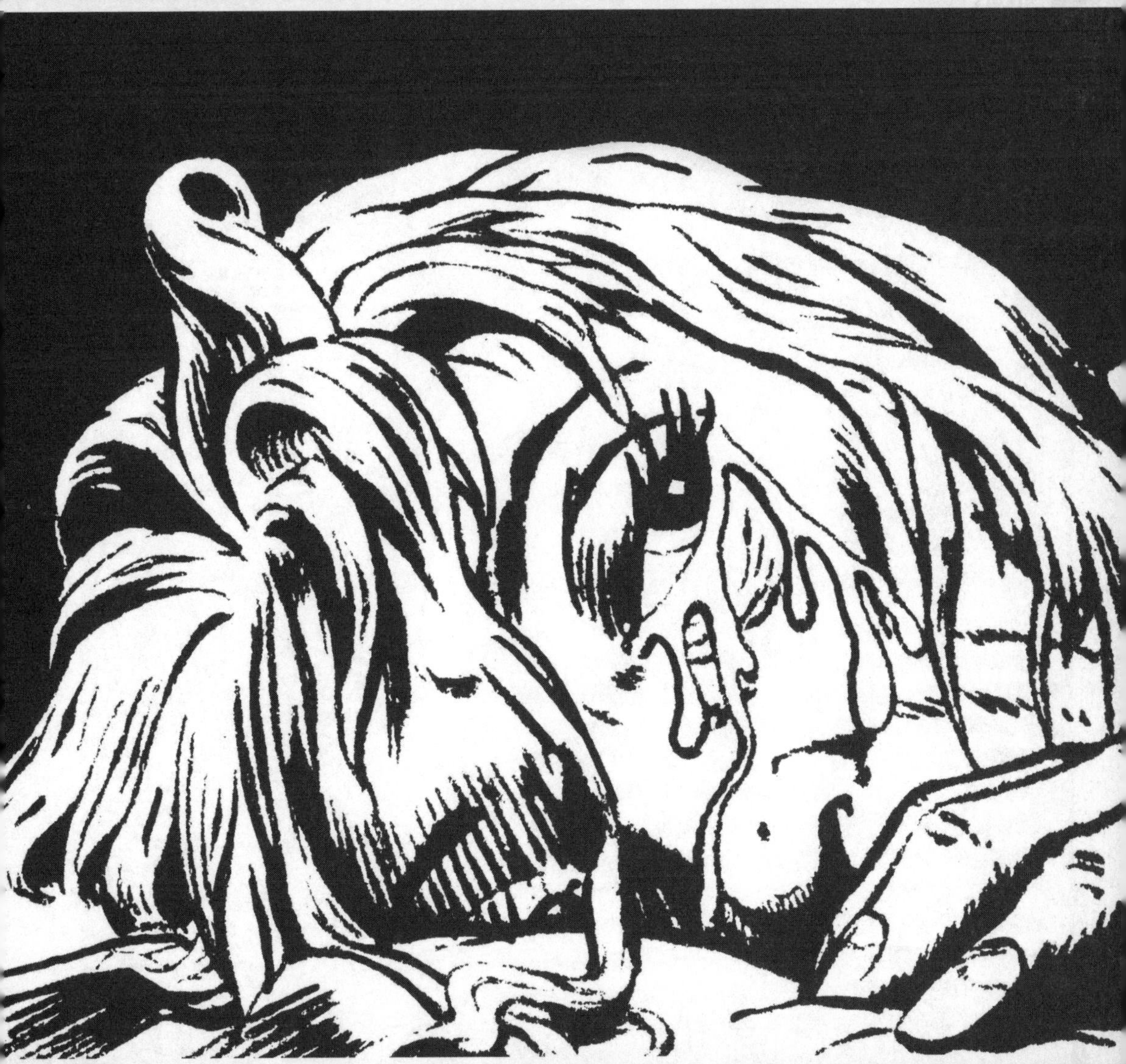

Murder, Morphine and Me!

Jack Cole (script and art) 1948

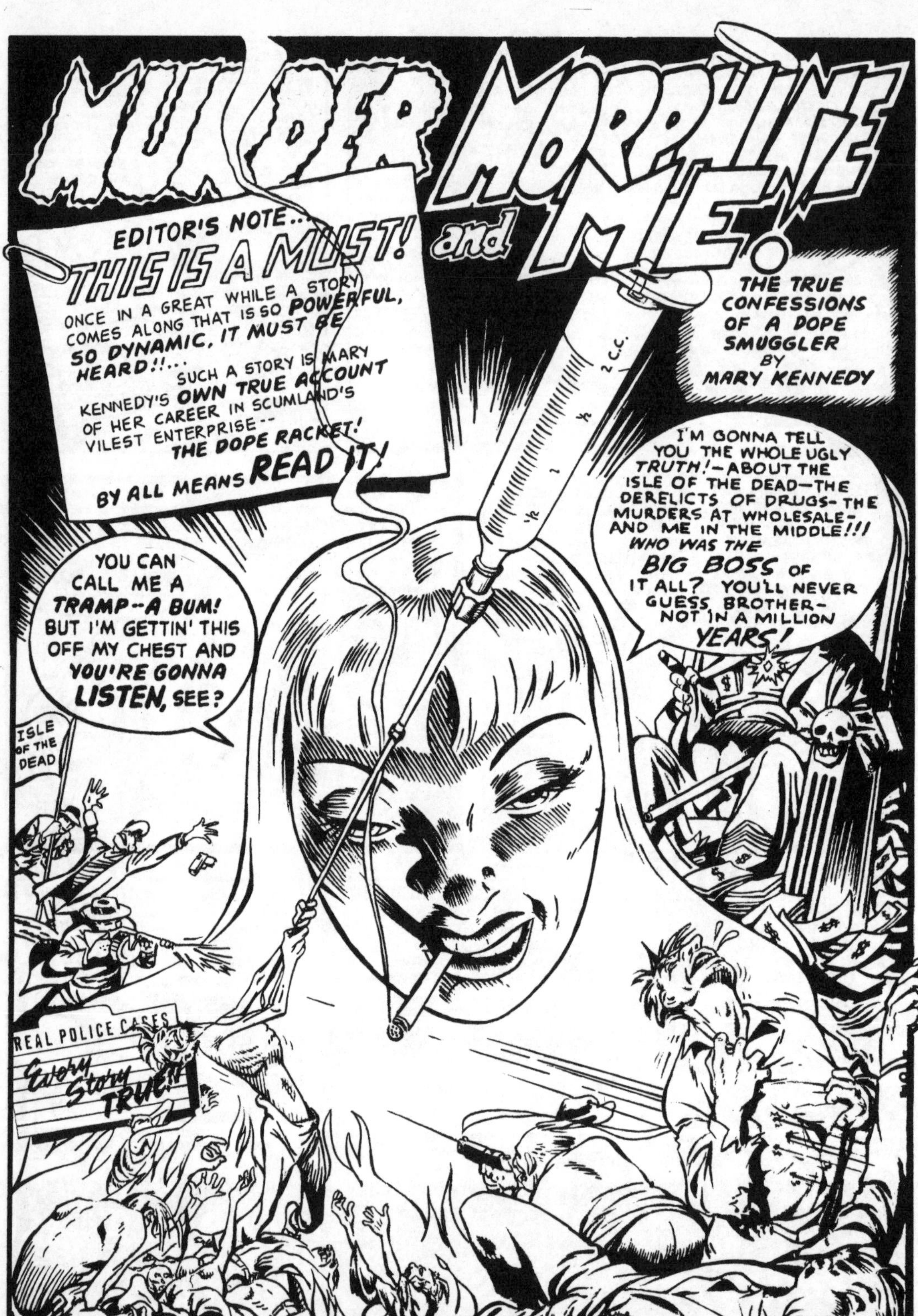

MURDER MORPHINE and ME!
EDITOR'S NOTE... THIS IS A MUST! ONCE IN A GREAT WHILE A STORY COMES ALONG THAT IS SO POWERFUL, SO DYNAMIC, IT MUST BE HEARD!!... SUCH A STORY IS MARY KENNEDY'S OWN TRUE ACCOUNT OF HER CAREER IN SCUMLAND'S VILEST ENTERPRISE -- THE DOPE RACKET! BY ALL MEANS READ IT!
THE TRUE CONFESSIONS OF A DOPE SMUGGLER BY MARY KENNEDY
2 C.C.
YOU CAN CALL ME A TRAMP--A BUM! BUT I'M GETTIN' THIS OFF MY CHEST AND YOU'RE GONNA LISTEN, SEE?
I'M GONNA TELL YOU THE WHOLE UGLY TRUTH!—ABOUT THE ISLE OF THE DEAD—THE DERELICTS OF DRUGS—THE MURDERS AT WHOLESALE—AND ME IN THE MIDDLE!!! WHO WAS THE BIG BOSS OF IT ALL? YOU'LL NEVER GUESS BROTHER—NOT IN A MILLION YEARS!
ISLE OF THE DEAD
REAL POLICE CASES
Every Story TRUE!!

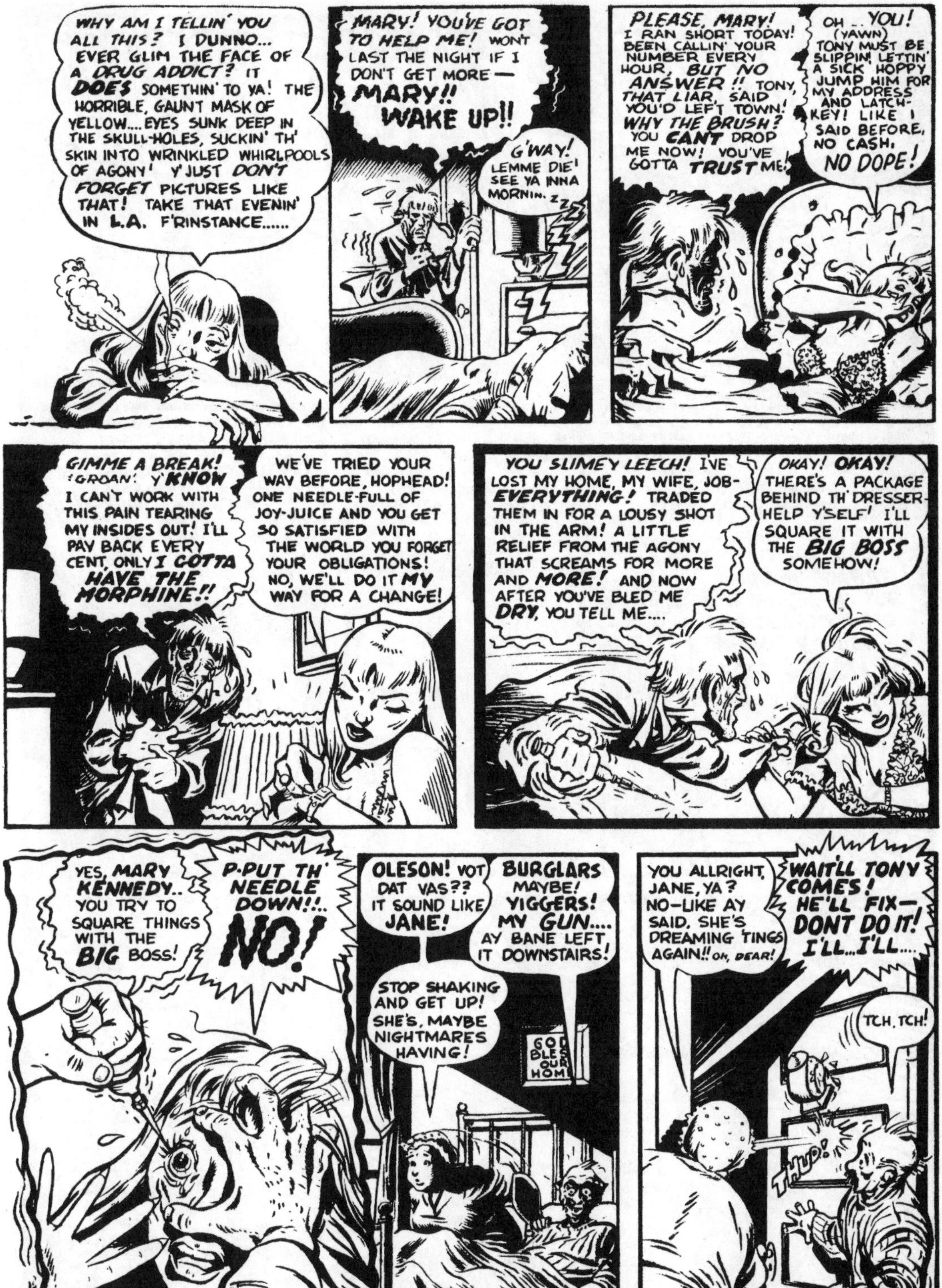
WHY AM I TELLIN' YOU ALL THIS? I DUNNO... EVER GLIM THE FACE OF A DRUG ADDICT? IT DOES SOMETHIN' TO YA! THE HORRIBLE, GAUNT MASK OF YELLOW.... EYES SUNK DEEP IN THE SKULL-HOLES, SUCKIN' TH' SKIN INTO WRINKLED WHIRLPOOLS OF AGONY! Y'JUST DON'T FORGET PICTURES LIKE THAT! TAKE THAT EVENIN' IN L.A. F'RINSTANCE......
MARY! YOU'VE GOT TO HELP ME! WON'T LAST THE NIGHT IF I DON'T GET MORE— MARY!! WAKE UP!!
G'WAY! LEMME DIE! SEE YA INNA MORNIN. Z Z
PLEASE, MARY! I RAN SHORT TODAY! BEEN CALLIN' YOUR NUMBER EVERY HOUR, BUT NO ANSWER!! TONY, THAT LIAR, SAID YOU'D LEFT TOWN! WHY THE BRUSH? YOU CAN'T DROP ME NOW! YOU'VE GOTTA TRUST ME!
OH... YOU! (YAWN) TONY MUST BE SLIPPIN' LETTIN' A SICK HOPPY JUMP HIM FOR MY ADDRESS AND LATCH-KEY! LIKE I SAID BEFORE, NO CASH, NO DOPE!
GIMME A BREAK! 'GROAN' Y'KNOW I CAN'T WORK WITH THIS PAIN TEARING MY INSIDES OUT! I'LL PAY BACK EVERY CENT, ONLY I GOTTA HAVE THE MORPHINE!!
WE'VE TRIED YOUR WAY BEFORE, HOPHEAD! ONE NEEDLE-FULL OF JOY-JUICE AND YOU GET SO SATISFIED WITH THE WORLD YOU FORGET YOUR OBLIGATIONS! NO, WE'LL DO IT MY WAY FOR A CHANGE!
YOU SLIMEY LEECH! I'VE LOST MY HOME, MY WIFE, JOB-EVERYTHING! TRADED THEM IN FOR A LOUSY SHOT IN THE ARM! A LITTLE RELIEF FROM THE AGONY THAT SCREAMS FOR MORE AND MORE! AND NOW AFTER YOU'VE BLED ME DRY, YOU TELL ME....
OKAY! OKAY! THERE'S A PACKAGE BEHIND TH' DRESSER-HELP Y'SELF! I'LL SQUARE IT WITH THE BIG BOSS SOMEHOW!
YES, MARY KENNEDY.. YOU TRY TO SQUARE THINGS WITH THE BIG BOSS!
P-PUT TH' NEEDLE DOWN!!.. NO!
OLESON! VOT DAT VAS?? IT SOUND LIKE JANE!
BURGLARS MAYBE! YIGGERS! MY GUN.... AY BANE LEFT IT DOWNSTAIRS!
STOP SHAKING AND GET UP! SHE'S, MAYBE NIGHTMARES HAVING!
GOD BLESS OUR HOME
YOU ALLRIGHT, JANE, YA? NO-LIKE AY SAID, SHE'S DREAMING TINGS AGAIN!! OH, DEAR!
WAIT'LL TONY COMES! HE'LL FIX— DONT DO IT! I'LL...I'LL....
TCH, TCH!
THUD!
2

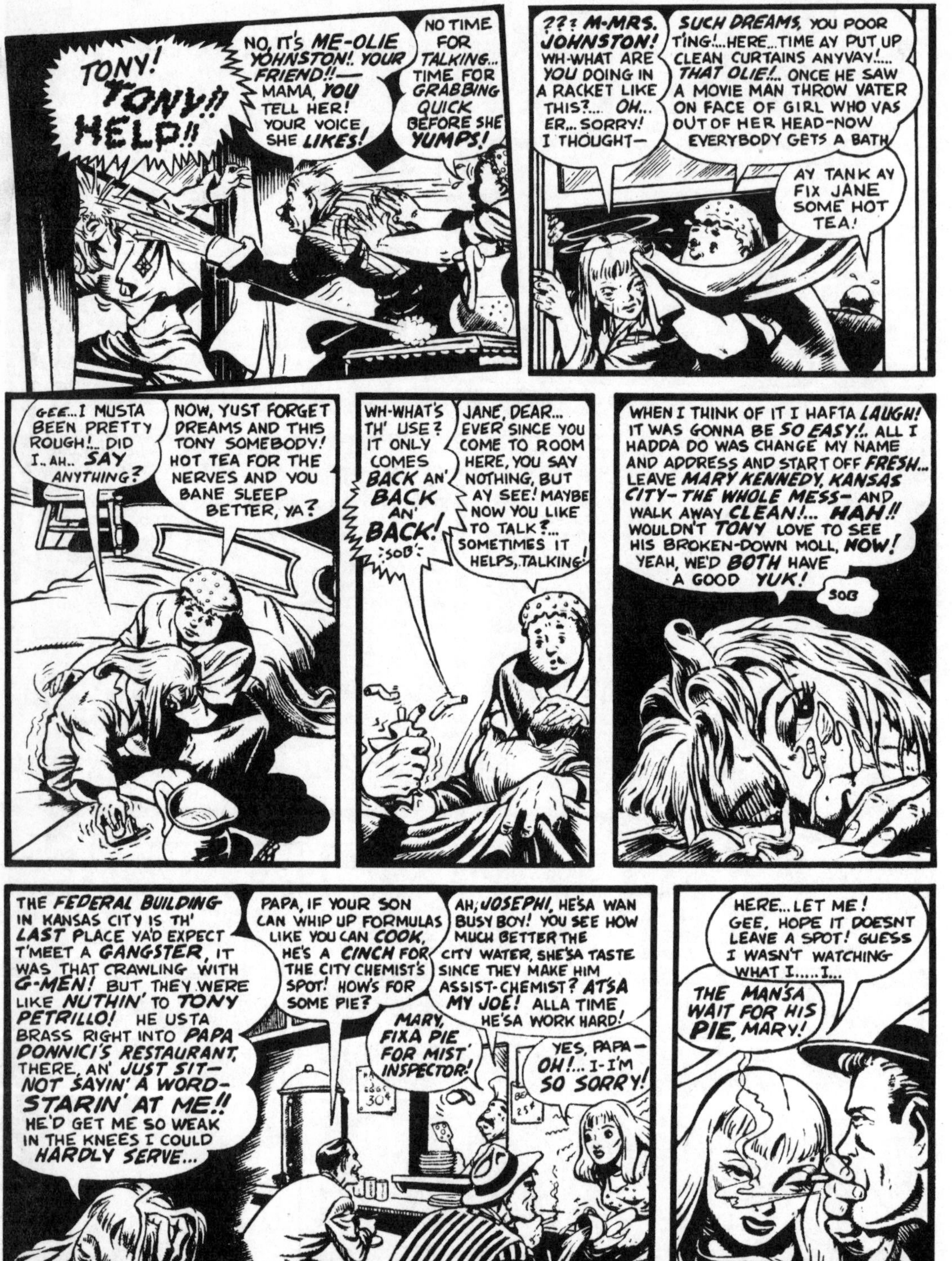
TONY! TONY!! HELP!!
NO, IT'S ME-OLIE YOHNSTON!. YOUR FRIEND!!— MAMA, YOU TELL HER! YOUR VOICE SHE LIKES!
NO TIME FOR TALKING... TIME FOR GRABBING QUICK BEFORE SHE YUMPS!
??? M-MRS. JOHNSTON! WH-WHAT ARE YOU DOING IN A RACKET LIKE THIS?.... OH... ER... SORRY! I THOUGHT—
SUCH DREAMS, YOU POOR TING!...HERE...TIME AY PUT UP CLEAN CURTAINS ANYVAY!.... THAT OLIE!... ONCE HE SAW A MOVIE MAN THROW VATER ON FACE OF GIRL WHO VAS OUT OF HER HEAD-NOW EVERYBODY GETS A BATH
AY TANK AY FIX JANE SOME HOT TEA!
GEE...I MUSTA BEEN PRETTY ROUGH!... DID I.. AH.. SAY ANYTHING?
NOW, YUST FORGET DREAMS AND THIS TONY SOMEBODY! HOT TEA FOR THE NERVES AND YOU BANE SLEEP BETTER, YA?
WH-WHAT'S TH' USE? IT ONLY COMES BACK AN' BACK AN' BACK!
SOB
JANE, DEAR... EVER SINCE YOU COME TO ROOM HERE, YOU SAY NOTHING, BUT AY SEE! MAYBE NOW YOU LIKE TO TALK?... SOMETIMES IT HELPS, TALKING!
WHEN I THINK OF IT I HAFTA LAUGH! IT WAS GONNA BE SO EASY!.. ALL I HADDA DO WAS CHANGE MY NAME AND ADDRESS AND START OFF FRESH... LEAVE MARY KENNEDY, KANSAS CITY- THE WHOLE MESS- AND WALK AWAY CLEAN!... HAH!! WOULDN'T TONY LOVE TO SEE HIS BROKEN-DOWN MOLL, NOW! YEAH, WE'D BOTH HAVE A GOOD YUK!
SOB
THE FEDERAL BUILDING IN KANSAS CITY IS TH' LAST PLACE YA'D EXPECT T'MEET A GANGSTER, IT WAS THAT CRAWLING WITH G-MEN! BUT THEY WERE LIKE NUTHIN' TO TONY PETRILLO! HE USTA BRASS RIGHT INTO PAPA DONNICI'S RESTAURANT, THERE, AN' JUST SIT- NOT SAYIN' A WORD- STARIN' AT ME!! HE'D GET ME SO WEAK IN THE KNEES I COULD HARDLY SERVE...
PAPA, IF YOUR SON CAN WHIP UP FORMULAS LIKE YOU CAN COOK, HE'S A CINCH FOR THE CITY CHEMIST'S SPOT! HOW'S FOR SOME PIE?
AH, JOSEPHI, HE'SA WAN BUSY BOY! YOU SEE HOW MUCH BETTER THE CITY WATER, SHE'SA TASTE SINCE THEY MAKE HIM ASSIST-CHEMIST? ATSA MY JOE! ALLA TIME, HE'SA WORK HARD!
MARY, FIXA PIE FOR MIST' INSPECTOR!
YES, PAPA- OH!... I-I'M SO SORRY!
EGGS 30¢
25¢
HERE...LET ME! GEE, HOPE IT DOESNT LEAVE A SPOT! GUESS I WASN'T WATCHING WHAT I..... I...
THE MAN'SA WAIT FOR HIS PIE, MARY!
3

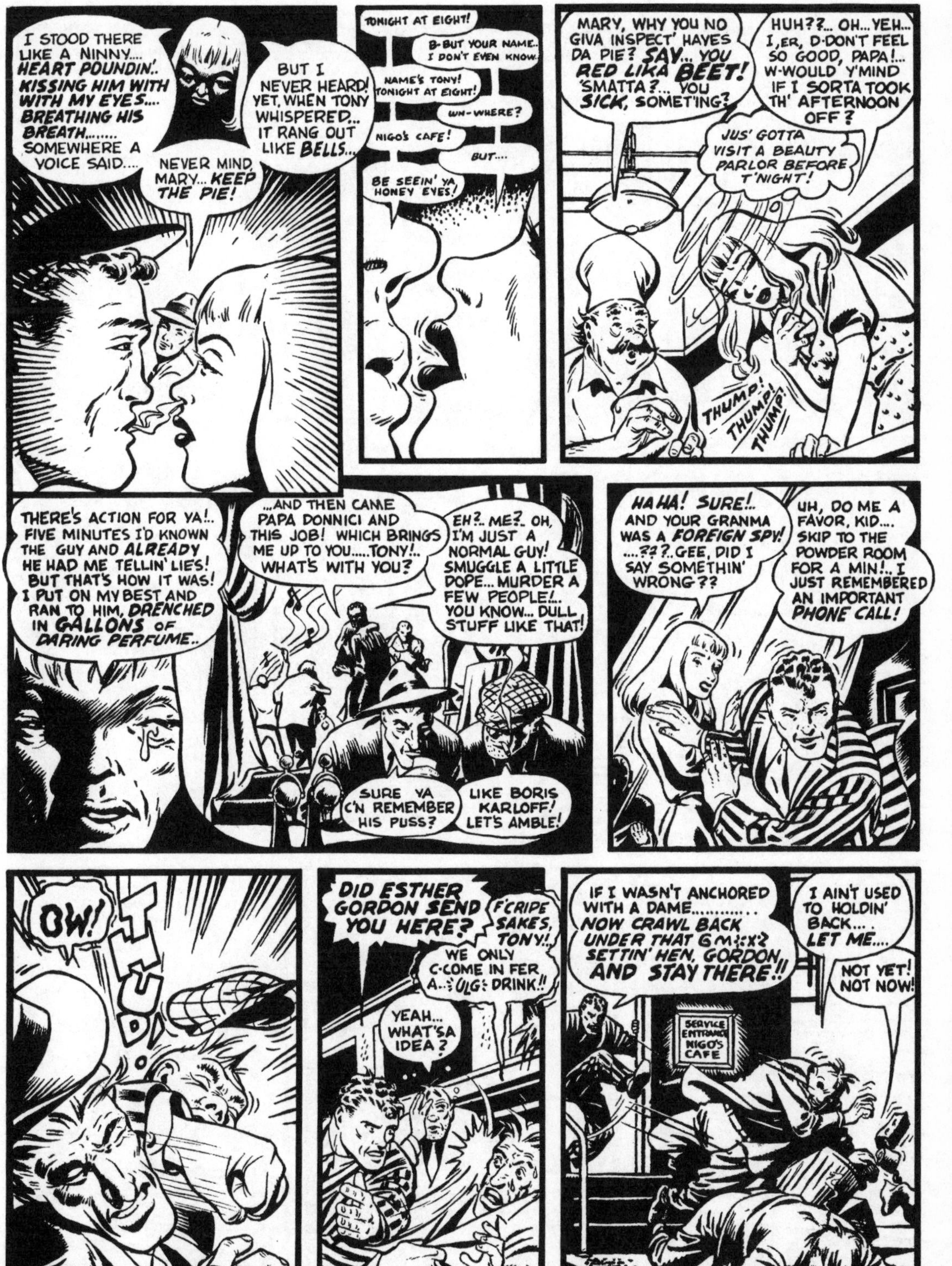
I STOOD THERE LIKE A NINNY.... HEART POUNDIN'.. KISSING HIM WITH WITH MY EYES.... BREATHING HIS BREATH........ SOMEWHERE A VOICE SAID....
NEVER MIND, MARY... KEEP THE PIE!
BUT I NEVER HEARD! YET, WHEN TONY WHISPERED... IT RANG OUT LIKE BELLS...
TONIGHT AT EIGHT!
B-BUT YOUR NAME.. I DON'T EVEN KNOW.
NAME'S TONY! TONIGHT AT EIGHT!
WH-WHERE?
NIGO'S CAFE!
BUT....
BE SEEIN' YA, HONEY EYES!
MARY, WHY YOU NO GIVA INSPECT' HAYES DA PIE? SAY... YOU RED LIKA BEET! 'SMATTA?... YOU SICK, SOMET'ING?
HUH??... OH... YEH... I, ER, D-DON'T FEEL SO GOOD, PAPA!... W-WOULD' Y'MIND IF I SORTA TOOK TH' AFTERNOON OFF?
JUS' GOTTA VISIT A BEAUTY PARLOR BEFORE T'NIGHT!
THUMP! THUMP! THUMP!
THERE'S ACTION FOR YA!.. FIVE MINUTES I'D KNOWN THE GUY AND ALREADY HE HAD ME TELLIN' LIES! BUT THAT'S HOW IT WAS! I PUT ON MY BEST AND RAN TO HIM, DRENCHED IN GALLONS OF DARING PERFUME..
...AND THEN CAME PAPA DONNICI AND THIS JOB! WHICH BRINGS ME UP TO YOU.....TONY!.. WHAT'S WITH YOU?
EH?.. ME?.. OH, I'M JUST A NORMAL GUY! SMUGGLE A LITTLE DOPE... MURDER A FEW PEOPLE!.. YOU KNOW... DULL STUFF LIKE THAT!
SURE YA C'N REMEMBER HIS PUSS?
LIKE BORIS KARLOFF! LET'S AMBLE!
HA HA! SURE!... AND YOUR GRANMA WAS A FOREIGN SPY! ....???.. GEE, DID I SAY SOMETHIN' WRONG??
UH, DO ME A FAVOR, KID.... SKIP TO THE POWDER ROOM FOR A MIN!.. I JUST REMEMBERED AN IMPORTANT PHONE CALL!
OW!
THUD
DID ESTHER GORDON SEND YOU HERE?
F'CRIPE SAKES, TONY!.. WE ONLY C-COME IN FER A..ULG! DRINK!!
YEAH... WHAT'SA IDEA?
IF I WASN'T ANCHORED WITH A DAME........... NOW CRAWL BACK UNDER THAT G M:X? SETTIN' HEN, GORDON, AND STAY THERE!!
SERVICE ENTRANCE NIGO'S CAFE
I AIN'T USED TO HOLDIN' BACK.... LET ME....
NOT YET! NOT NOW!

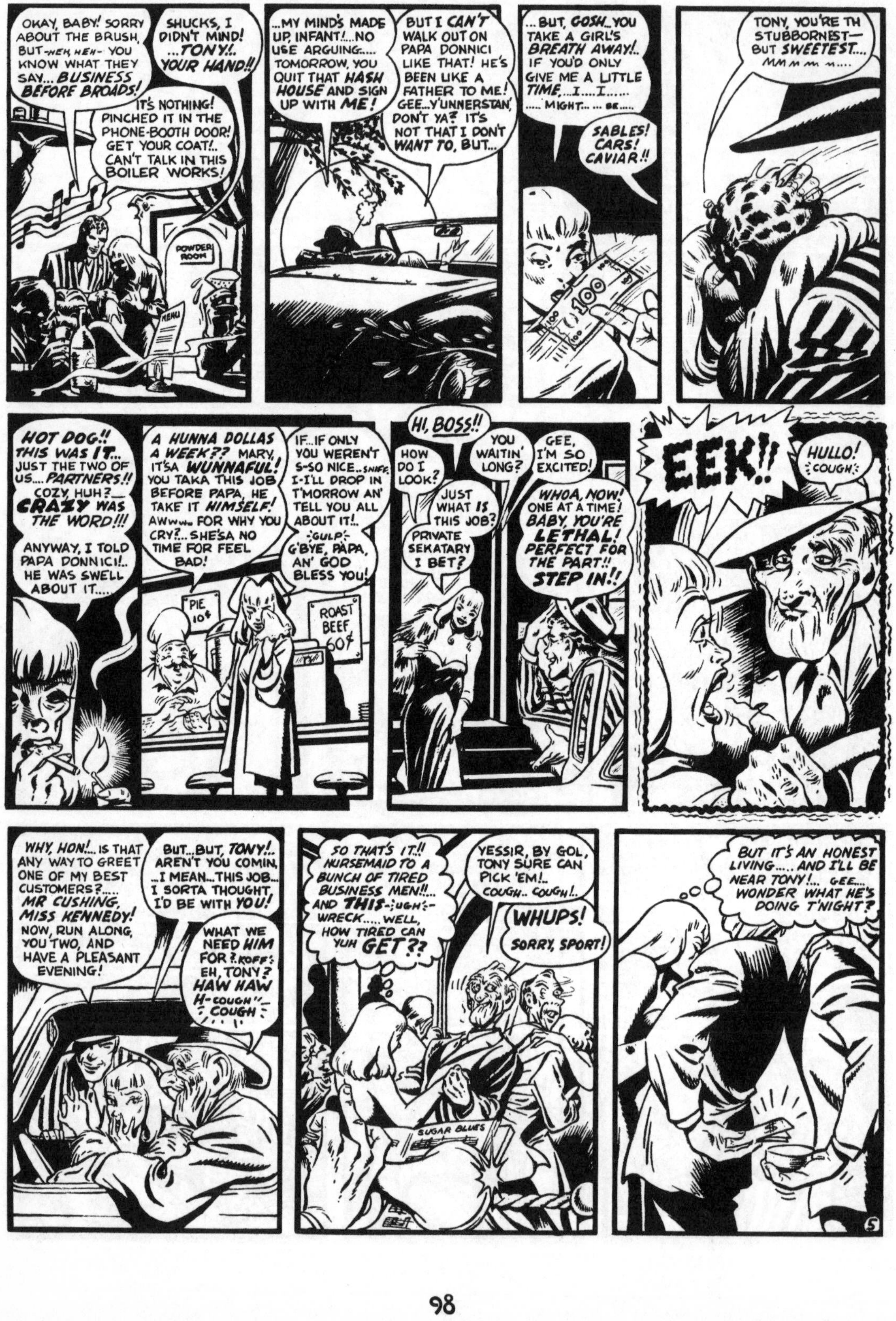
OKAY, BABY! SORRY ABOUT THE BRUSH, BUT -HEH, HEH- YOU KNOW WHAT THEY SAY... BUSINESS BEFORE BROADS!
SHUCKS, I DIDN'T MIND! ...TONY!.. YOUR HAND!!
IT'S NOTHING! PINCHED IT IN THE PHONE-BOOTH DOOR! GET YOUR COAT!.. CAN'T TALK IN THIS BOILER WORKS!
POWDER ROOM
MENU
...MY MIND'S MADE UP, INFANT!...NO USE ARGUING..... TOMORROW, YOU QUIT THAT HASH HOUSE AND SIGN UP WITH ME!
BUT I CAN'T WALK OUT ON PAPA DONNICI LIKE THAT! HE'S BEEN LIKE A FATHER TO ME! GEE...Y'UNNERSTAN', DON'T YA? IT'S NOT THAT I DON'T WANT TO, BUT...
...BUT, GOSH...YOU TAKE A GIRL'S BREATH AWAY!.. IF YOU'D ONLY GIVE ME A LITTLE TIME,...I....I..... ..... MIGHT... ... BE.....
SABLES! CARS! CAVIAR!!
100
TONY, YOU'RE TH STUBBORNEST— BUT SWEETEST.... MMMMM.....
HOT DOG!! THIS WAS IT... JUST THE TWO OF US....PARTNERS!! COZY, HUH?__ CRAZY WAS THE WORD!!!
ANYWAY, I TOLD PAPA DONNICI!.. HE WAS SWELL ABOUT IT.....
A HUNNA DOLLAS A WEEK?? MARY, IT'SA WUNNAFUL! YOU TAKA THIS JOB BEFORE PAPA, HE TAKE IT HIMSELF! AWW... FOR WHY YOU CRY?... SHE'SA NO TIME FOR FEEL BAD!
IF...IF ONLY YOU WEREN'T S-SO NICE... SNIFF. I-I'LL DROP IN T'MORROW AN' TELL YOU ALL ABOUT IT!.. -GULP- G'BYE, PAPA, AN' GOD BLESS YOU!
PIE 10¢
ROAST BEEF 60¢
HI, BOSS!!
HOW DO I LOOK?
YOU WAITIN' LONG?
GEE, I'M SO EXCITED!
JUST WHAT IS THIS JOB?
PRIVATE SEKATARY I BET?
WHOA, NOW! ONE AT A TIME! BABY, YOU'RE LETHAL! PERFECT FOR THE PART!! STEP IN!!
EEK!!
HULLO! -COUGH-
WHY, HON!... IS THAT ANY WAY TO GREET ONE OF MY BEST CUSTOMERS?..... MR CUSHING, MISS KENNEDY! NOW, RUN ALONG, YOU TWO, AND HAVE A PLEASANT EVENING!
BUT...BUT, TONY!.. AREN'T YOU COMIN, ...I MEAN...THIS JOB... I SORTA THOUGHT, I'D BE WITH YOU!
WHAT WE NEED HIM FOR?.KOFF.. EH, TONY? HAW HAW H-COUGH- COUGH
SO THAT'S IT!! NURSEMAID TO A BUNCH OF TIRED BUSINESS MEN!!... AND THIS -UGH- WRECK..... WELL, HOW TIRED CAN YUH GET??
YESSIR, BY GOL, TONY SURE CAN PICK 'EM!.. COUGH.. COUGH!..
WHUPS! SORRY, SPORT!
SUGAR BLUES
BUT IT'S AN HONEST LIVING..... AND I'LL BE NEAR TONY!... GEE... WONDER WHAT HE'S DOING T'NIGHT?
5

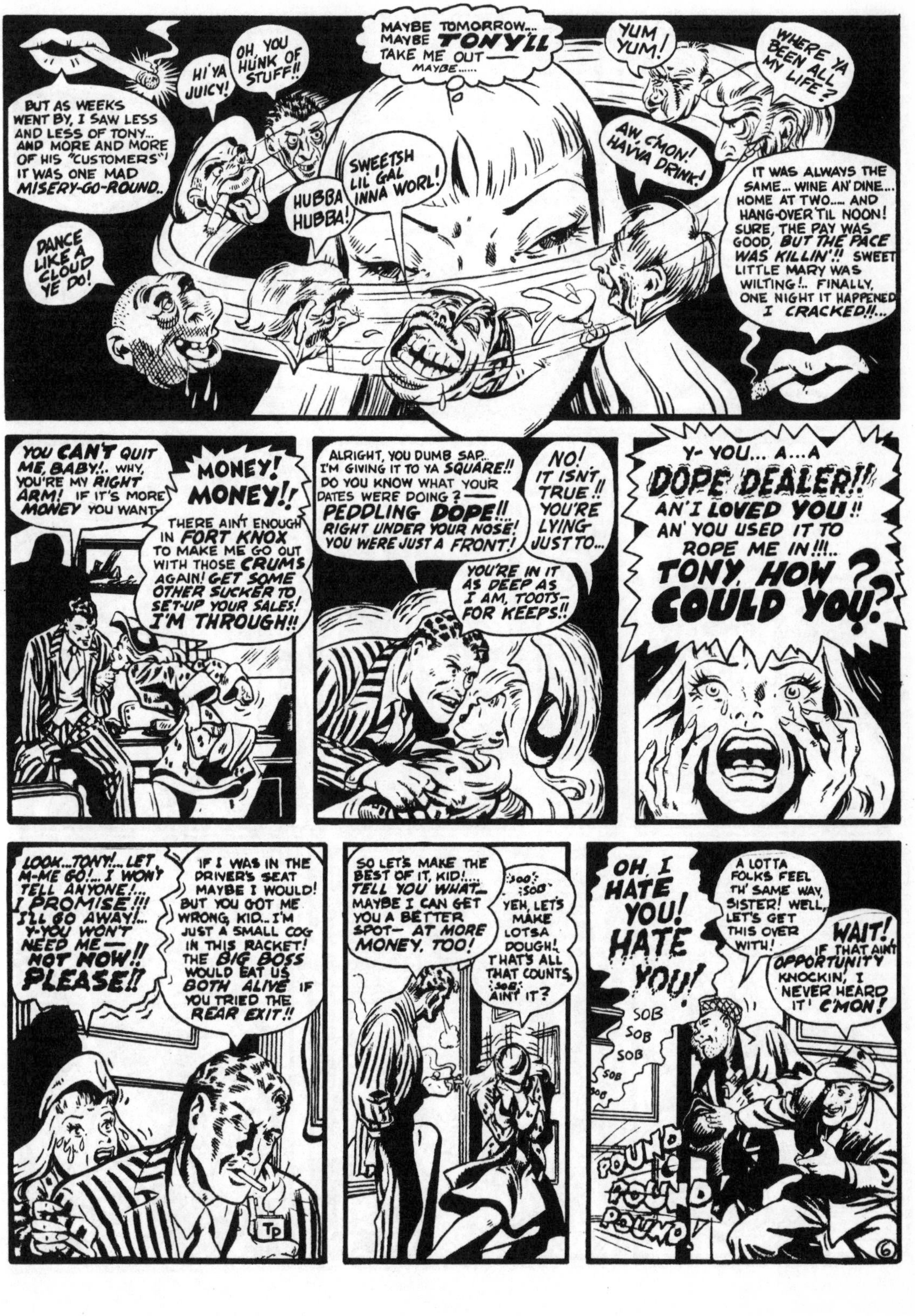
BUT AS WEEKS WENT BY, I SAW LESS AND LESS OF TONY... AND MORE AND MORE OF HIS "CUSTOMERS"! IT WAS ONE MAD MISERY-GO-ROUND..
HI'YA JUICY!
OH, YOU HUNK OF STUFF!!
MAYBE TOMORROW... MAYBE TONY'LL TAKE ME OUT— MAYBE......
YUM YUM!
WHERE YA BEEN ALL MY LIFE?
AW, C'MON! HAVVA DRINK!
SWEETSH LIL GAL INNA WORL!
HUBBA HUBBA!
DANCE LIKE A CLOUD YE DO!
IT WAS ALWAYS THE SAME... WINE AN' DINE... HOME AT TWO.... AND HANG-OVER 'TIL NOON! SURE, THE PAY WAS GOOD, BUT THE PACE WAS KILLIN'!! SWEET LITTLE MARY WAS WILTING!.. FINALLY, ONE NIGHT IT HAPPENED I CRACKED!!...
YOU CAN'T QUIT ME, BABY!.. WHY, YOU'RE MY RIGHT ARM! IF IT'S MORE MONEY YOU WANT-
MONEY! MONEY!!
THERE AIN'T ENOUGH IN FORT KNOX TO MAKE ME GO OUT WITH THOSE CRUMS AGAIN! GET SOME OTHER SUCKER TO SET-UP YOUR SALES! I'M THROUGH!!
ALRIGHT, YOU DUMB SAP.. I'M GIVING IT TO YA SQUARE!! DO YOU KNOW WHAT YOUR DATES WERE DOING?— PEDDLING DOPE!!... RIGHT UNDER YOUR NOSE! YOU WERE JUST A FRONT!
NO! IT ISN'T TRUE!! YOU'RE LYING JUST TO...
YOU'RE IN IT AS DEEP AS I AM, TOOTS- FOR KEEPS!!
Y- YOU... A...A DOPE DEALER!! AN' I LOVED YOU!! AN' YOU USED IT TO ROPE ME IN!!!.. TONY, HOW COULD YOU??
LOOK...TONY!... LET M-ME GO!...I WON'T TELL ANYONE!... I PROMISE!!! I'LL GO AWAY!... Y-YOU WON'T NEED ME— NOT NOW!! PLEASE!!
IF I WAS IN THE DRIVER'S SEAT MAYBE I WOULD! BUT YOU GOT ME WRONG, KID.. I'M JUST A SMALL COG IN THIS RACKET! THE BIG BOSS WOULD EAT US BOTH ALIVE IF YOU TRIED THE REAR EXIT!!
TD
SO LET'S MAKE THE BEST OF IT, KID!... TELL YOU WHAT... MAYBE I CAN GET YOU A BETTER SPOT— AT MORE MONEY, TOO!
SOB SOB YEH, LET'S MAKE LOTSA DOUGH! THAT'S ALL THAT COUNTS, SOB AIN'T IT?
OH, I HATE YOU! HATE YOU!
SOB SOB SOB SOB SOB
A LOTTA FOLKS FEEL TH' SAME WAY, SISTER! WELL, LET'S GET THIS OVER WITH!
WAIT! IF THAT AIN'T OPPORTUNITY KNOCKIN', I NEVER HEARD IT! C'MON!
POUND POUND POUND!
6

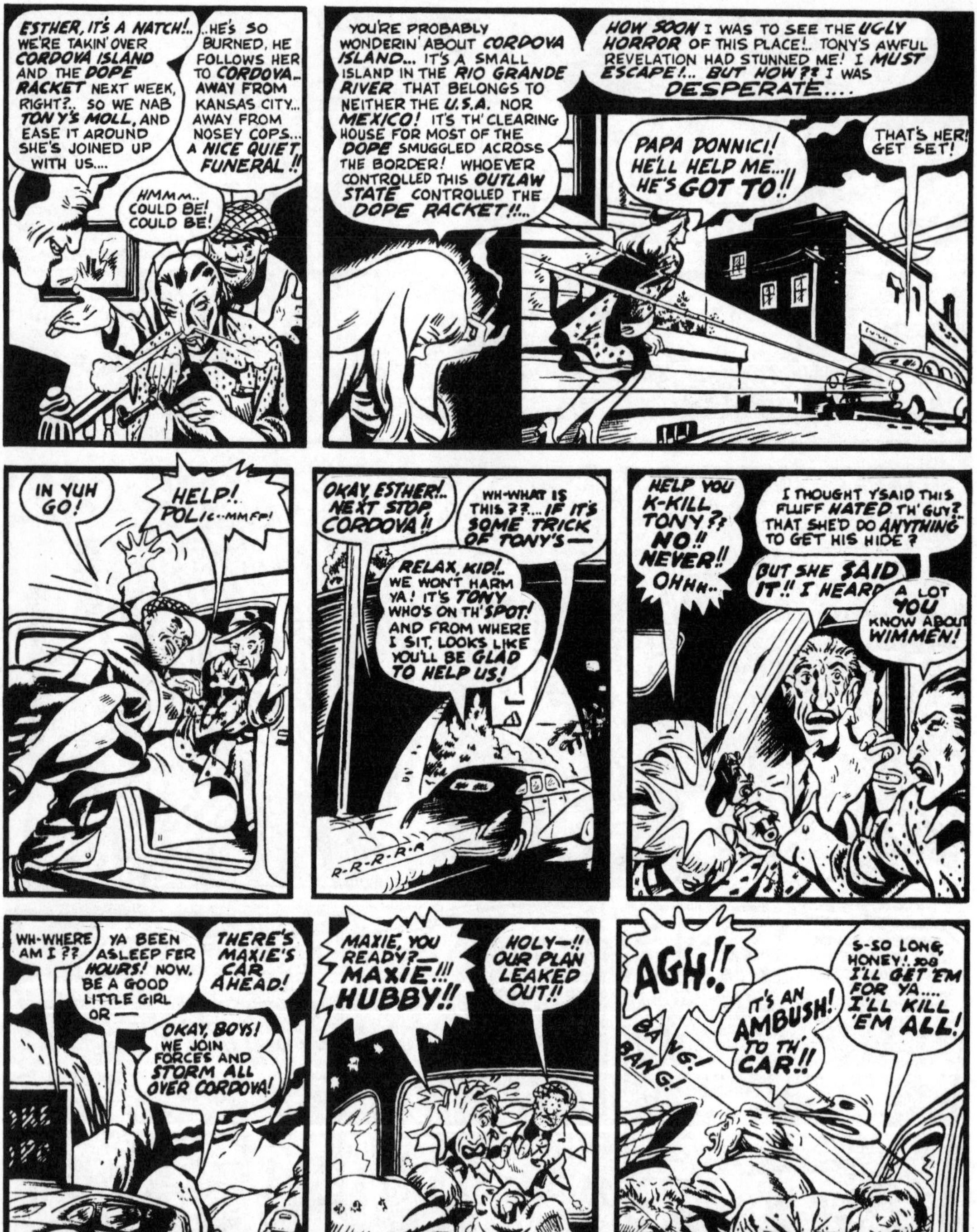
ESTHER, IT'S A NATCH!.. WE'RE TAKIN' OVER CORDOVA ISLAND AND THE DOPE RACKET NEXT WEEK, RIGHT?.. SO WE NAB TONY'S MOLL, AND EASE IT AROUND SHE'S JOINED UP WITH US....
..HE'S SO BURNED, HE FOLLOWS HER TO CORDOVA.. AWAY FROM KANSAS CITY... AWAY FROM NOSEY COPS... A NICE QUIET FUNERAL!!
HMMM.. COULD BE! COULD BE!
YOU'RE PROBABLY WONDERIN' ABOUT CORDOVA ISLAND... IT'S A SMALL ISLAND IN THE RIO GRANDE RIVER THAT BELONGS TO NEITHER THE U.S.A. NOR MEXICO! IT'S TH' CLEARING HOUSE FOR MOST OF THE DOPE SMUGGLED ACROSS THE BORDER! WHOEVER CONTROLLED THIS OUTLAW STATE CONTROLLED THE DOPE RACKET!!...
HOW SOON I WAS TO SEE THE UGLY HORROR OF THIS PLACE!.. TONY'S AWFUL REVELATION HAD STUNNED ME! I MUST ESCAPE!... BUT HOW?? I WAS DESPERATE....
PAPA DONNICI! HE'LL HELP ME... HE'S GOT TO!!
THAT'S HER! GET SET!
IN YUH GO!
HELP!.. POLIC--MMFF!
OKAY, ESTHER!.. NEXT STOP CORDOVA!!
WH-WHAT IS THIS??... IF IT'S SOME TRICK OF TONY'S—
RELAX, KID!.. WE WON'T HARM YA! IT'S TONY WHO'S ON TH' SPOT! AND FROM WHERE I SIT, LOOKS LIKE YOU'LL BE GLAD TO HELP US!
R-R-R-R-R
HELP YOU K-KILL TONY?? NO!! NEVER!! OHHH..
I THOUGHT Y'SAID THIS FLUFF HATED TH' GUY?.. THAT SHE'D DO ANYTHING TO GET HIS HIDE?
BUT SHE SAID IT!! I HEARD
A LOT YOU KNOW ABOUT WIMMEN!
WH-WHERE AM I??
YA BEEN ASLEEP FER HOURS! NOW. BE A GOOD LITTLE GIRL OR—
THERE'S MAXIE'S CAR AHEAD!
OKAY, BOYS! WE JOIN FORCES AND STORM ALL OVER CORDOVA!
EL PASO TEXAS 5 MI
MAXIE, YOU READY?— MAXIE!!! HUBBY!!
HOLY—!! OUR PLAN LEAKED OUT!!
AGH!!
BANG! BANG!
IT'S AN AMBUSH! TO TH' CAR!!
S-SO LONG, HONEY! SOB I'LL GET 'EM FOR YA.... I'LL KILL 'EM ALL!
7

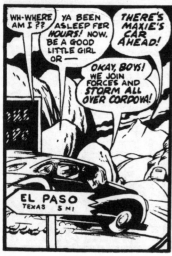

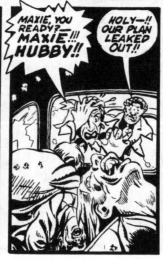

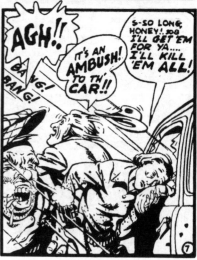

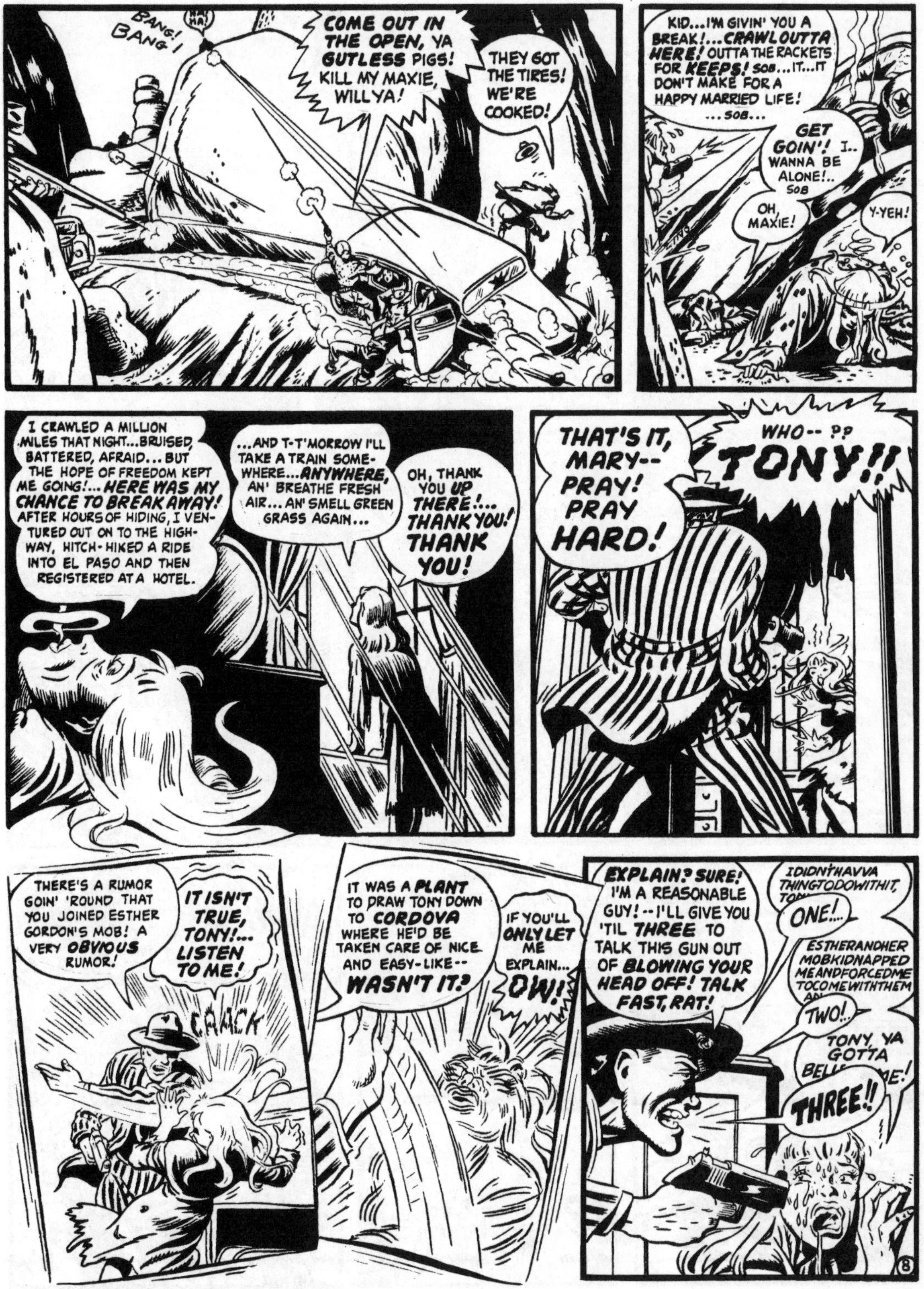
BANG! BANG!
HA! HA!
COME OUT IN THE OPEN, YA GUTLESS PIGS! KILL MY MAXIE, WILLYA!
THEY GOT THE TIRES! WE'RE COOKED!
KID...I'M GIVIN' YOU A BREAK!...CRAWL OUTTA HERE! OUTTA THE RACKETS FOR KEEPS! SOB...IT...IT DON'T MAKE FOR A HAPPY MARRIED LIFE! ...SOB...
GET GOIN'! I.. WANNA BE ALONE!.. SOB
OH, MAXIE!
Y-YEH!
I CRAWLED A MILLION MILES THAT NIGHT...BRUISED, BATTERED, AFRAID...BUT THE HOPE OF FREEDOM KEPT ME GOING!...HERE WAS MY CHANCE TO BREAK AWAY! AFTER HOURS OF HIDING, I VENTURED OUT ON TO THE HIGHWAY, HITCH-HIKED A RIDE INTO EL PASO AND THEN REGISTERED AT A HOTEL.
...AND T-T'MORROW I'LL TAKE A TRAIN SOMEWHERE...ANYWHERE, AN' BREATHE FRESH AIR...AN' SMELL GREEN GRASS AGAIN...
OH, THANK YOU UP THERE!... THANK YOU! THANK YOU!
THAT'S IT, MARY-- PRAY! PRAY HARD!
WHO-- ?? TONY!!
THERE'S A RUMOR GOIN' 'ROUND THAT YOU JOINED ESTHER GORDON'S MOB! A VERY OBVIOUS RUMOR!
IT ISN'T TRUE, TONY!... LISTEN TO ME!
CRACK
IT WAS A PLANT TO DRAW TONY DOWN TO CORDOVA WHERE HE'D BE TAKEN CARE OF NICE AND EASY-LIKE-- WASN'T IT?
IF YOU'LL ONLY LET ME EXPLAIN... OW!
EXPLAIN? SURE! I'M A REASONABLE GUY! --I'LL GIVE YOU 'TIL THREE TO TALK THIS GUN OUT OF BLOWING YOUR HEAD OFF! TALK FAST, RAT!
IDIDN'THAVVA THINGTODOWITHIT,
ONE!...
ESTHERANDHER MOBKIDNAPPED MEANDFORCEDME TOCOMEWITHTHEM
TWO!..
TONY, YA GOTTA
THREE!!
8

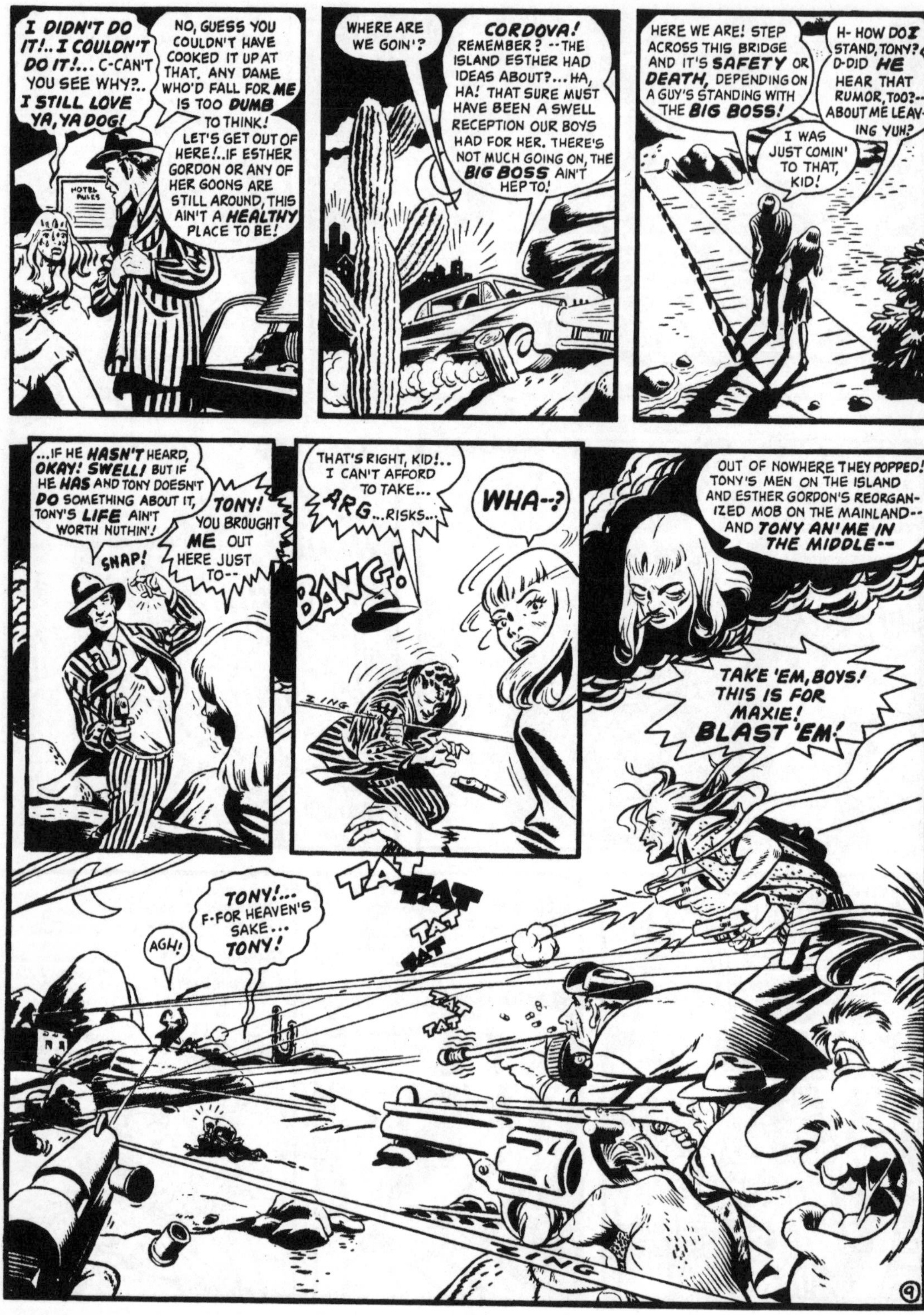
I DIDN'T DO IT!.. I COULDN'T DO IT!... C-CAN'T YOU SEE WHY?.. I STILL LOVE YA, YA DOG!
NO, GUESS YOU COULDN'T HAVE COOKED IT UP AT THAT. ANY DAME WHO'D FALL FOR ME IS TOO DUMB TO THINK!
LET'S GET OUT OF HERE!..IF ESTHER GORDON OR ANY OF HER GOONS ARE STILL AROUND, THIS AIN'T A HEALTHY PLACE TO BE!
HOTEL RULES
WHERE ARE WE GOIN'?
CORDOVA! REMEMBER? --THE ISLAND ESTHER HAD IDEAS ABOUT?... HA, HA! THAT SURE MUST HAVE BEEN A SWELL RECEPTION OUR BOYS HAD FOR HER. THERE'S NOT MUCH GOING ON, THE BIG BOSS AIN'T HEP TO!
HERE WE ARE! STEP ACROSS THIS BRIDGE AND IT'S SAFETY OR DEATH, DEPENDING ON A GUY'S STANDING WITH THE BIG BOSS!
H- HOW DO I STAND, TONY? D-DID HE HEAR THAT RUMOR, TOO?-- ABOUT ME LEAVING YUH?
I WAS JUST COMIN' TO THAT, KID!
...IF HE HASN'T HEARD, OKAY! SWELL! BUT IF HE HAS AND TONY DOESN'T DO SOMETHING ABOUT IT, TONY'S LIFE AIN'T WORTH NUTHIN'!
SNAP!
TONY! YOU BROUGHT ME OUT HERE JUST TO--
THAT'S RIGHT, KID!.. I CAN'T AFFORD TO TAKE... ARG...RISKS...
BANG!
WHA--?
ZING
OUT OF NOWHERE THEY POPPED! TONY'S MEN ON THE ISLAND AND ESTHER GORDON'S REORGANIZED MOB ON THE MAINLAND-- AND TONY AN' ME IN THE MIDDLE--
TAKE 'EM, BOYS! THIS IS FOR MAXIE! BLAST 'EM!
TAT TAT TAT TAT
TONY!... F-FOR HEAVEN'S SAKE... TONY!
AGH!
TAT TAT
ZING
9

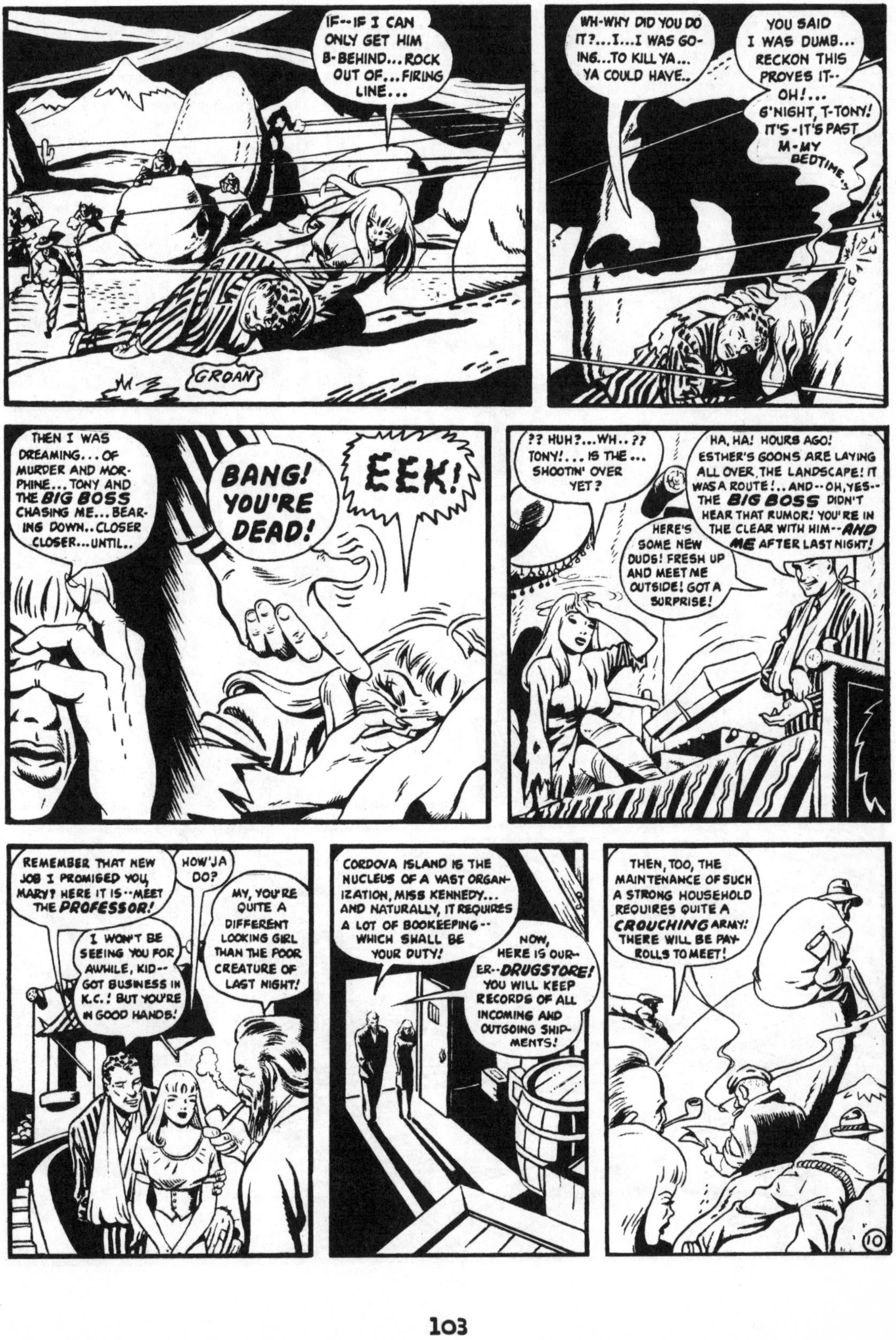
IF--IF I CAN ONLY GET HIM B-BEHIND...ROCK OUT OF...FIRING LINE...
GROAN
WH-WHY DID YOU DO IT?...I...I WAS GOING...TO KILL YA...YA COULD HAVE..
YOU SAID I WAS DUMB... RECKON THIS PROVES IT--OH!... G'NIGHT, T-TONY! IT'S-IT'S PAST M-MY BEDTIME...
THEN I WAS DREAMING... OF MURDER AND MORPHINE... TONY AND THE BIG BOSS CHASING ME... BEARING DOWN.. CLOSER CLOSER... UNTIL..
BANG! YOU'RE DEAD!
EEK!
?? HUH?...WH..?? TONY!... IS THE... SHOOTIN' OVER YET?
HA, HA! HOURS AGO! ESTHER'S GOONS ARE LAYING ALL OVER THE LANDSCAPE! IT WAS A ROUTE!...AND--OH, YES--THE BIG BOSS DIDN'T HEAR THAT RUMOR! YOU'RE IN THE CLEAR WITH HIM--AND ME AFTER LAST NIGHT!
HERE'S SOME NEW DUDS! FRESH UP AND MEET ME OUTSIDE! GOT A SURPRISE!
REMEMBER THAT NEW JOB I PROMISED YOU, MARY? HERE IT IS--MEET THE PROFESSOR!
HOW'JA DO?
MY, YOU'RE QUITE A DIFFERENT LOOKING GIRL THAN THE POOR CREATURE OF LAST NIGHT!
I WON'T BE SEEING YOU FOR AWHILE, KID--GOT BUSINESS IN K.C.! BUT YOU'RE IN GOOD HANDS!
CORDOVA ISLAND IS THE NUCLEUS OF A VAST ORGANIZATION, MISS KENNEDY... AND NATURALLY, IT REQUIRES A LOT OF BOOKEEPING--WHICH SHALL BE YOUR DUTY!
NOW, HERE IS OUR-ER--DRUGSTORE! YOU WILL KEEP RECORDS OF ALL INCOMING AND OUTGOING SHIPMENTS!
THEN, TOO, THE MAINTENANCE OF SUCH A STRONG HOUSEHOLD REQUIRES QUITE A CROUCHING ARMY! THERE WILL BE PAYROLLS TO MEET!
10

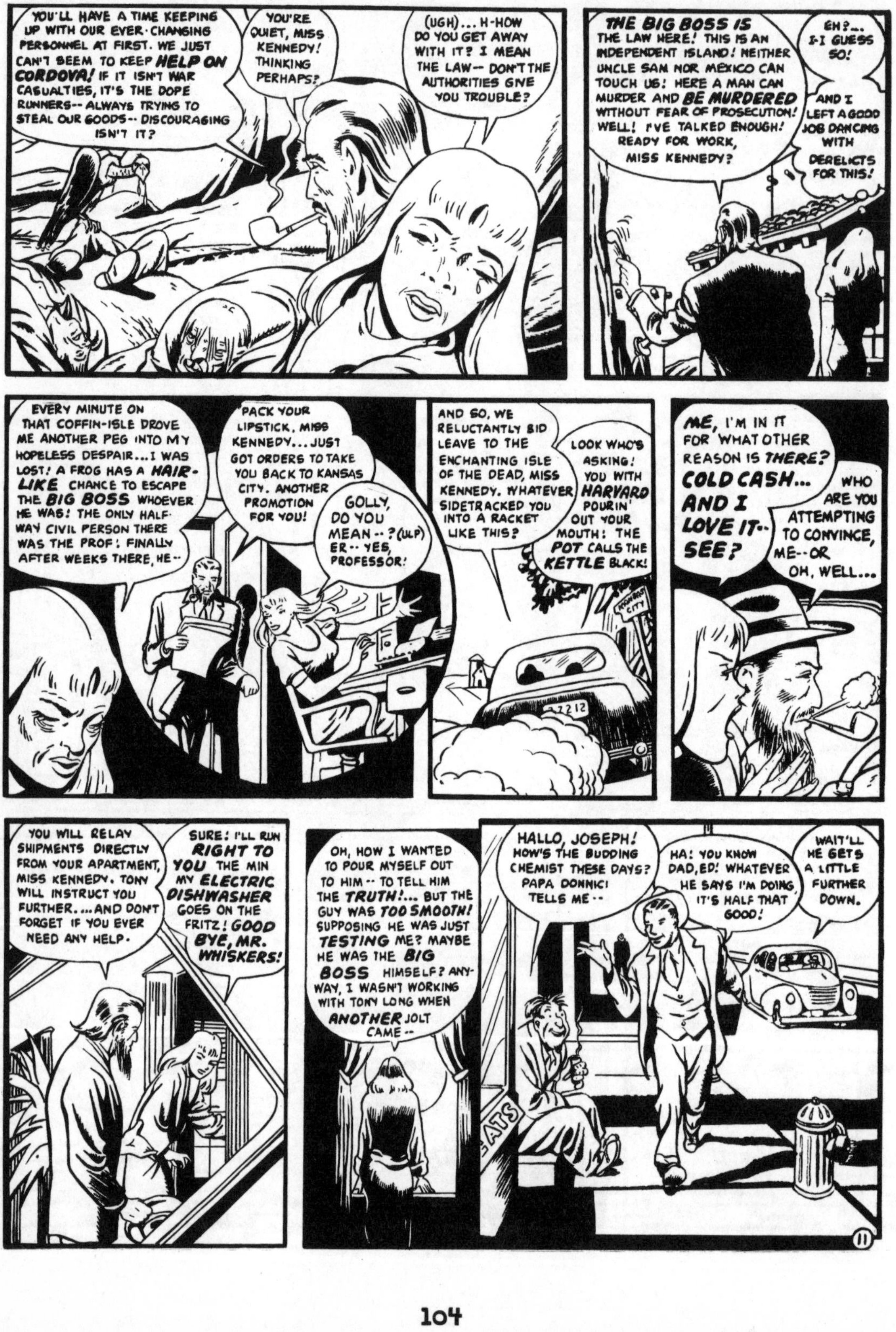
YOU'LL HAVE A TIME KEEPING UP WITH OUR EVER-CHANGING PERSONNEL AT FIRST. WE JUST CAN'T SEEM TO KEEP HELP ON CORDOVA! IF IT ISN'T WAR CASUALTIES, IT'S THE DOPE RUNNERS-- ALWAYS TRYING TO STEAL OUR GOODS-- DISCOURAGING ISN'T IT?
YOU'RE QUIET, MISS KENNEDY! THINKING PERHAPS?
(UGH)... H-HOW DO YOU GET AWAY WITH IT? I MEAN THE LAW-- DON'T THE AUTHORITIES GIVE YOU TROUBLE?
THE BIG BOSS IS THE LAW HERE! THIS IS AN INDEPENDENT ISLAND! NEITHER UNCLE SAM NOR MEXICO CAN TOUCH US! HERE A MAN CAN MURDER AND BE MURDERED WITHOUT FEAR OF PROSECUTION! WELL! I'VE TALKED ENOUGH! READY FOR WORK, MISS KENNEDY?
EH?... I-I GUESS SO!
AND I LEFT A GOOD JOB DANCING WITH DERELICTS FOR THIS!
EVERY MINUTE ON THAT COFFIN-ISLE DROVE ME ANOTHER PEG INTO MY HOPELESS DESPAIR... I WAS LOST! A FROG HAS A HAIR-LIKE CHANCE TO ESCAPE THE BIG BOSS WHOEVER HE WAS! THE ONLY HALF-WAY CIVIL PERSON THERE WAS THE PROF! FINALLY AFTER WEEKS THERE, HE--
PACK YOUR LIPSTICK, MISS KENNEDY... JUST GOT ORDERS TO TAKE YOU BACK TO KANSAS CITY. ANOTHER PROMOTION FOR YOU!
GOLLY, DO YOU MEAN--? (ULP) ER-- YES, PROFESSOR!
AND SO, WE RELUCTANTLY BID LEAVE TO THE ENCHANTING ISLE OF THE DEAD, MISS KENNEDY. WHATEVER SIDETRACKED YOU INTO A RACKET LIKE THIS?
LOOK WHO'S ASKING! YOU WITH HARVARD POURIN' OUT YOUR MOUTH! THE POT CALLS THE KETTLE BLACK!
ME, I'M IN IT FOR WHAT OTHER REASON IS THERE? COLD CASH... AND I LOVE IT-- SEE?
WHO ARE YOU ATTEMPTING TO CONVINCE, ME--OR OH, WELL...
YOU WILL RELAY SHIPMENTS DIRECTLY FROM YOUR APARTMENT, MISS KENNEDY. TONY WILL INSTRUCT YOU FURTHER.... AND DON'T FORGET IF YOU EVER NEED ANY HELP.
SURE! I'LL RUN RIGHT TO YOU THE MIN MY ELECTRIC DISHWASHER GOES ON THE FRITZ! GOOD BYE, MR. WHISKERS!
OH, HOW I WANTED TO POUR MYSELF OUT TO HIM -- TO TELL HIM THE TRUTH!... BUT THE GUY WAS TOO SMOOTH! SUPPOSING HE WAS JUST TESTING ME? MAYBE HE WAS THE BIG BOSS HIMSELF? ANYWAY, I WASN'T WORKING WITH TONY LONG WHEN ANOTHER JOLT CAME--
HALLO, JOSEPH! HOW'S THE BUDDING CHEMIST THESE DAYS? PAPA DONNICI TELLS ME--
HA! YOU KNOW DAD, ED! WHATEVER HE SAYS I'M DOING, IT'S HALF THAT GOOD!
WAIT'LL HE GETS A LITTLE FURTHER DOWN.
EATS
11

MIO DIO! IT'S PAPA DONNICI'S BOY!

GLG!

GOOD HEAVENS! IT CAN'T BE!

DAILY EXPRESS
CITY CHEMIST
JOSEPH DONNICI KILLED BY GANGSTERS!
BELIEVED VICTIM OF MISTAKEN IDENTITY

PAPA! IT'S ME-- MARY!... I JUST HEARD THE HORRIBLE NEWS... WHY, YOU POOR DEAR! YOU SHOULDN'T HAVE TO DO THAT NOW! GIVE ME YOUR APRON!

IT'SA HOKAY, MARY... SOB... I DO SOMETING OR I GO CRAZY! SOB... SOB... SOB... WHO JOEY HARM? GERMS MAYBE... NOBODY ELSE... SOB... SOB...

DA PAPER SHE'SA SAY MY JOEY SHOT BY MISTAKE!...SOB...SOB... PLEESA EXCUSE... SO SORRY! IT'SA ALL RIGHT-- I GOT LOTSA JOEYS! HE'SA GROW ON TREES! SOB...

PAPA, I--

ALLA TIME HE'SA ASK 'BOUT YOU, MARY! "HOW'S MARY'S NEW LOTSA MONEY JOB," HE SAY!... LONGA TIME YOU NO COME SEE US...SNIFF ...I TELL HIM YOU ONE BUSY GIRL AND HAPPY, YES?

EVERYTHING'S FINE, PAPA! JUST D-DANDY! IF THERE'S ANYTHING I CAN DO FOR YOU...

I- I COULDN'T TELL PAPA THE TRUTH! WHAT IF IT WAS TONY'S MOB --MY MOB--WHO KILLED JOE? OH, GLORY, IF IT WAS... IF SOMETHING DOESN'T BREAK SOON, ILL DIE!

SOMEBODY IMPORTANT MUST HAVE HEARD MY PRAYERS THAT NIGHT, FOR SOON AFTER THE AUTHORITIES BEGAN RAIDING TH' DOPE RING'S BRANCH OFFICES ALL OVER THE NATION!

FIRST THEY STRUCK IN CHICAGO...

...THEN NEW YORK...

..AND LOS ANGELES...

...IT HAPPENED SO QUICKLY-- SO SILENTLY THAT ALMOST BEFORE ANYONE KNEW IT.

12

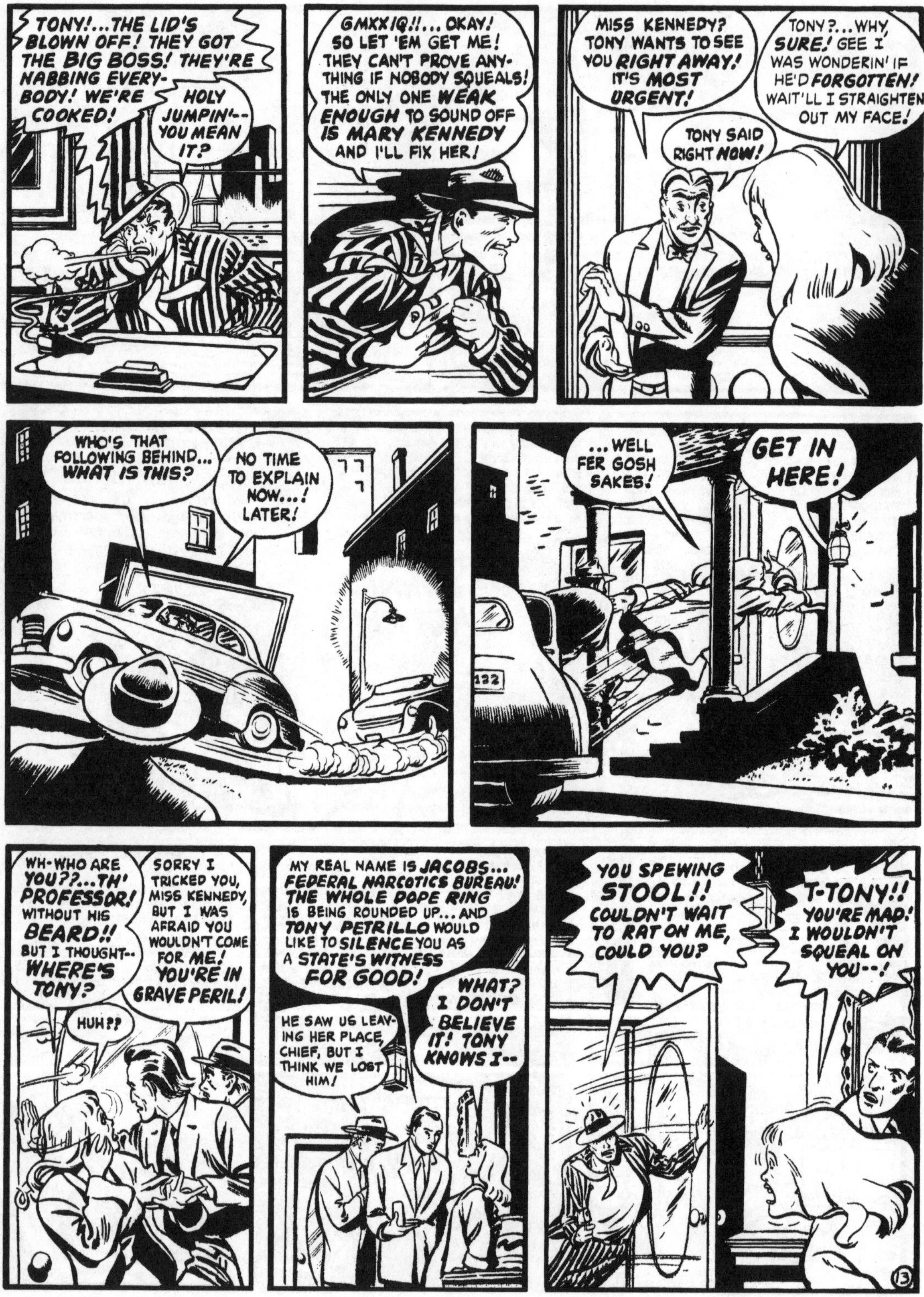
TONY!...THE LID'S BLOWN OFF! THEY GOT THE BIG BOSS! THEY'RE NABBING EVERY-BODY! WE'RE COOKED!
HOLY JUMPIN'-- YOU MEAN IT?
GMXXIQ!!... OKAY! SO LET 'EM GET ME! THEY CAN'T PROVE ANY-THING IF NOBODY SQUEALS! THE ONLY ONE WEAK ENOUGH TO SOUND OFF IS MARY KENNEDY AND I'LL FIX HER!
MISS KENNEDY? TONY WANTS TO SEE YOU RIGHT AWAY! IT'S MOST URGENT!
TONY?...WHY, SURE! GEE I WAS WONDERIN' IF HE'D FORGOTTEN! WAIT'LL I STRAIGHTEN OUT MY FACE!
TONY SAID RIGHT NOW!
WHO'S THAT FOLLOWING BEHIND... WHAT IS THIS?
NO TIME TO EXPLAIN NOW...! LATER!
...WELL FER GOSH SAKES!
GET IN HERE!
WH-WHO ARE YOU??...TH' PROFESSOR! WITHOUT HIS BEARD!! BUT I THOUGHT-- WHERE'S TONY?
SORRY I TRICKED YOU, MISS KENNEDY, BUT I WAS AFRAID YOU WOULDN'T COME FOR ME! YOU'RE IN GRAVE PERIL!
HUH??
MY REAL NAME IS JACOBS... FEDERAL NARCOTICS BUREAU! THE WHOLE DOPE RING IS BEING ROUNDED UP... AND TONY PETRILLO WOULD LIKE TO SILENCE YOU AS A STATE'S WITNESS FOR GOOD!
HE SAW US LEAV-ING HER PLACE, CHIEF, BUT I THINK WE LOST HIM!
WHAT? I DON'T BELIEVE IT! TONY KNOWS I--
YOU SPEWING STOOL!! COULDN'T WAIT TO RAT ON ME, COULD YOU?
T-TONY!! YOU'RE MAD! I WOULDN'T SQUEAL ON YOU--!
13

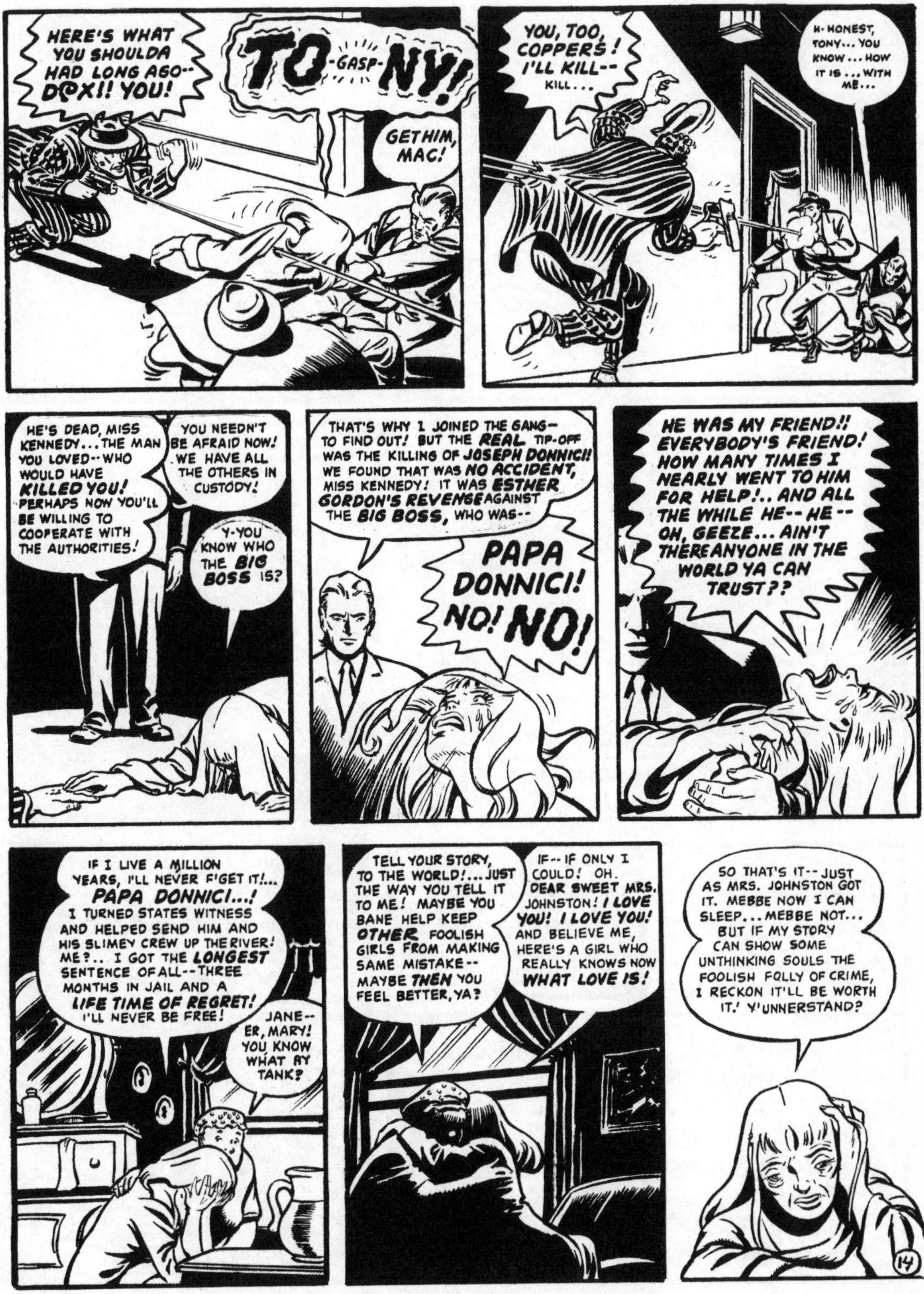
HERE'S WHAT YOU SHOULDA HAD LONG AGO-- D@X!! YOU!
TO-GASP-NY!
GET HIM, MAC!
YOU, TOO, COPPERS! I'LL KILL-- KILL...
H-HONEST, TONY... YOU KNOW... HOW IT IS... WITH ME...
HE'S DEAD, MISS KENNEDY... THE MAN YOU LOVED--WHO WOULD HAVE KILLED YOU! PERHAPS NOW YOU'LL BE WILLING TO COOPERATE WITH THE AUTHORITIES!
YOU NEEDN'T BE AFRAID NOW! WE HAVE ALL THE OTHERS IN CUSTODY!
Y-YOU KNOW WHO THE BIG BOSS IS?
THAT'S WHY I JOINED THE GANG-- TO FIND OUT! BUT THE REAL TIP-OFF WAS THE KILLING OF JOSEPH DONNICI! WE FOUND THAT WAS NO ACCIDENT, MISS KENNEDY! IT WAS ESTHER GORDON'S REVENGE AGAINST THE BIG BOSS, WHO WAS--
PAPA DONNICI! NO! NO!
HE WAS MY FRIEND!! EVERYBODY'S FRIEND! HOW MANY TIMES I NEARLY WENT TO HIM FOR HELP!.. AND ALL THE WHILE HE-- HE-- OH, GEEZE... AIN'T THERE ANYONE IN THE WORLD YA CAN TRUST??
IF I LIVE A MILLION YEARS, I'LL NEVER F'GET IT!... PAPA DONNICI...! I TURNED STATES WITNESS AND HELPED SEND HIM AND HIS SLIMEY CREW UP THE RIVER! ME?... I GOT THE LONGEST SENTENCE OF ALL--THREE MONTHS IN JAIL AND A LIFE TIME OF REGRET! I'LL NEVER BE FREE!
JANE-- ER, MARY! YOU KNOW WHAT RY TANK?
TELL YOUR STORY, TO THE WORLD!... JUST THE WAY YOU TELL IT TO ME! MAYBE YOU BANE HELP KEEP OTHER FOOLISH GIRLS FROM MAKING SAME MISTAKE-- MAYBE THEN YOU FEEL BETTER, YA?
IF-- IF ONLY I COULD! OH. DEAR SWEET MRS. JOHNSTON! I LOVE YOU! I LOVE YOU! AND BELIEVE ME, HERE'S A GIRL WHO REALLY KNOWS NOW WHAT LOVE IS!
SO THAT'S IT-- JUST AS MRS. JOHNSTON GOT IT. MEBBE NOW I CAN SLEEP... MEBBE NOT... BUT IF MY STORY CAN SHOW SOME UNTHINKING SOULS THE FOOLISH FOLLY OF CRIME, I RECKON IT'LL BE WORTH IT.' Y'UNNERSTAND?
14

"Jee-zus...
Jesus creeping Christ on a cross!"

**Real-life masked wrestlers like El Santo are
part of a tradition of heavyweight
champions of the people in modern Mexico.
Not El Borbah. He is 400 pounds of money-
grubbing private eye with a short fuse and
big stomach, hooked on cigarettes, junk food
and porn. Weird science, sharp satire and
bad hairdos combine in this mystery about a
misbehaving brat, a sperm bank and a sinister
cult turning children against their parents.
The creator of *Big Baby*, *Dog Boy* and the
teen plague chiller *Black Hole*, Charles Burns
brings an inhumanly perfect polish to his
world of creeps, geeks and freaks.**

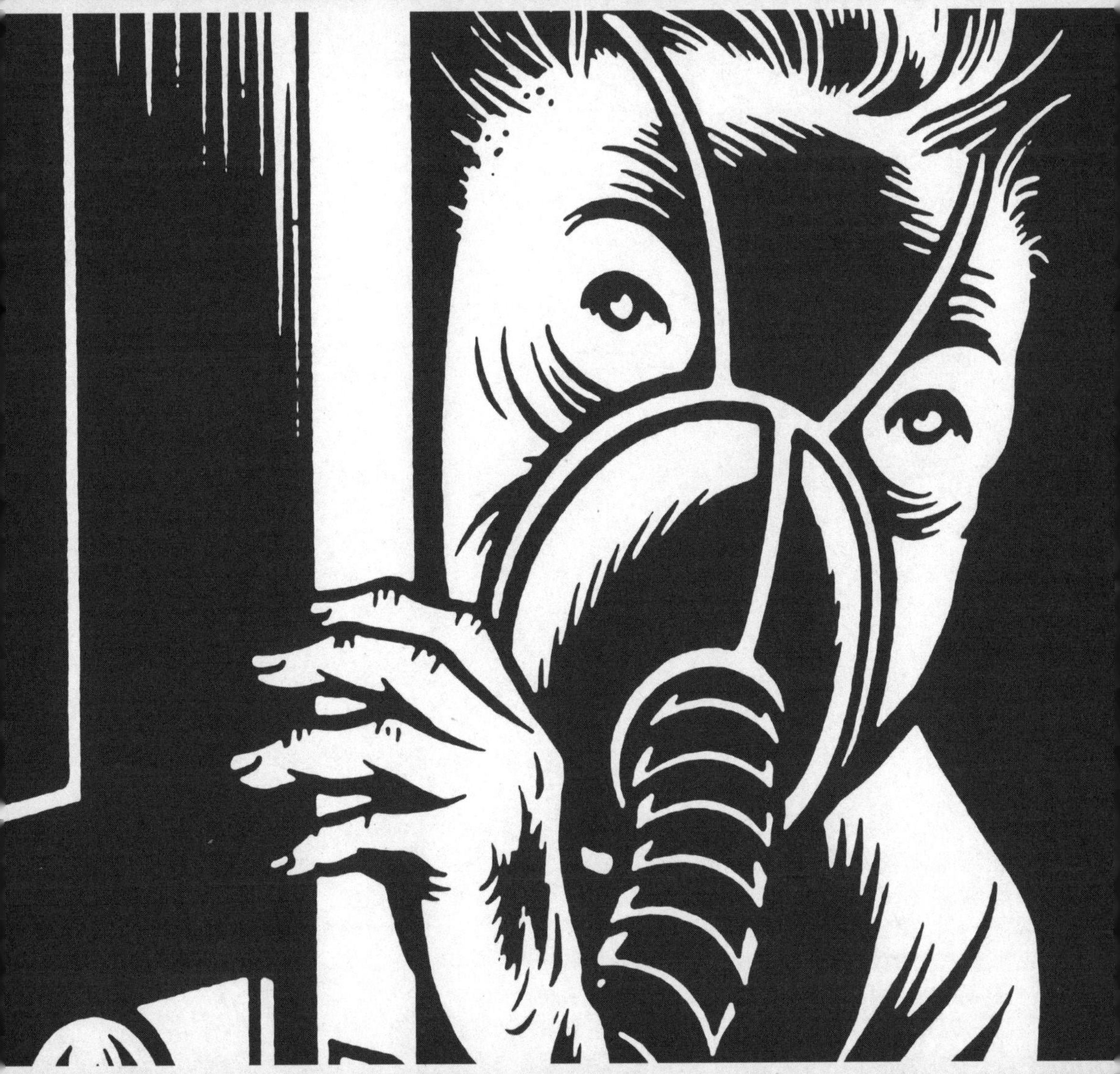

El Borbah: Love in Vein

Charles Burns (script & art)   1987

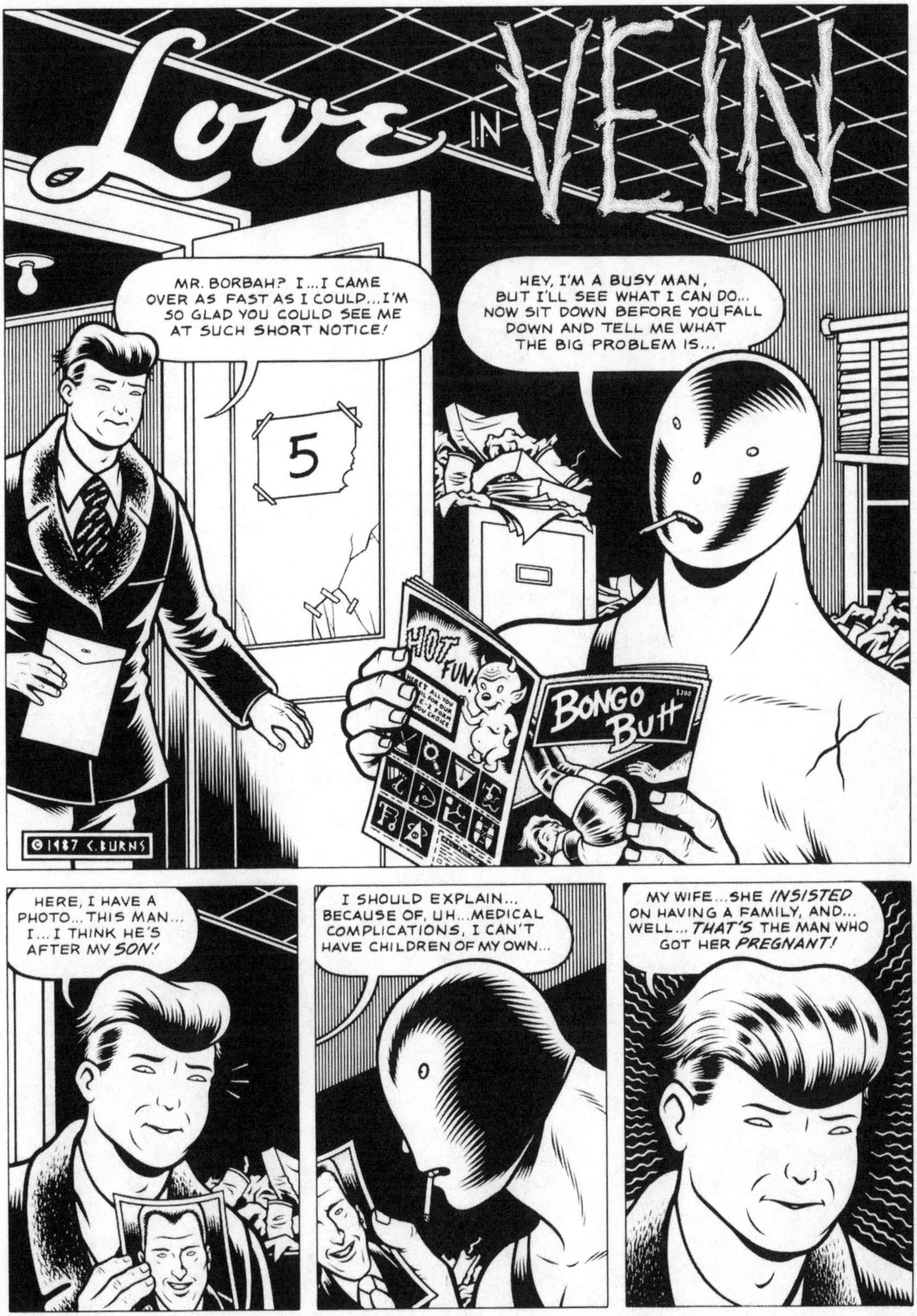
Love IN VEIN
MR. BORBAH? I...I CAME OVER AS FAST AS I COULD...I'M SO GLAD YOU COULD SEE ME AT SUCH SHORT NOTICE!
HEY, I'M A BUSY MAN, BUT I'LL SEE WHAT I CAN DO... NOW SIT DOWN BEFORE YOU FALL DOWN AND TELL ME WHAT THE BIG PROBLEM IS...
5
HOT FUN!
BONGO BUtt
©1987 C.BURNS
HERE, I HAVE A PHOTO...THIS MAN... I...I THINK HE'S AFTER MY *SON!*
I SHOULD EXPLAIN... BECAUSE OF, UH...MEDICAL COMPLICATIONS, I CAN'T HAVE CHILDREN OF MY OWN...
MY WIFE...SHE *INSISTED* ON HAVING A FAMILY, AND... WELL...*THAT'S* THE MAN WHO GOT HER *PREGNANT!*

LEMME GET THIS STRAIGHT...YOUR EQUIPMENT ISN'T IN WORKIN' ORDER, SO YOU LET *THIS* GUY KNOCK UP YOUR WIFE?

NO, NO...HE WAS THE DONOR WE PICKED OUT AT *SPERM 'N' STUFF*...

UM...SPERM 'N' STUFF...RIGHT.

THEY'RE A COMMERCIAL SPERM BANK WITH OUTLETS ALL OVER THE COUNTRY...AFTER MY WIFE AND I TRIED EVERYTHING ELSE WE WENT TO THEM.

THEY SEEMED VERY PROFESSIONAL AND ASSURED US EVERYTHING WOULD BE HELD IN STRICT CONFIDENCE...

THE PROCEDURE IS QUITE SIMPLE...YOU CAN GET STARTED BY SELECTING YOUR DONOR...

EACH OF THE DONORS HAD A FILE WITH A PHOTO AND A COMPLETE MEDICAL HISTORY...

HOW ABOUT THIS ONE ARNOLD? SIX TWO, ONE EIGHTY, NO SEX DISEASES OR GENETIC DAMAGE, AND...AND I *LIKE* HIS SMILE...

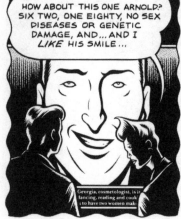

Georgia, cosmetologist, is i[...] [...]ancing, reading and cook [...] to have two women mak[...]

THE PREGNANCY WENT SMOOTHLY, AND LIANNA GAVE BIRTH TO A BEAUTIFUL EIGHT-POUND BOY...

HE...HE HAS *YOUR* EYES, DARLING...

OUR SON JOSHUA HAS ALWAYS BEEN A FINE, WELL-BEHAVED YOUNGSTER... UNTIL A FEW WEEKS AGO...

BE A GOOD BOY AND GO WASH UP FOR DINNER...

I DON'T *HAVE* TO! *YOU'RE* NOT MY FATHER! ONLY MY *REAL* FATHER CAN TELL ME WHAT TO DO!

MY WIFE TOLD ME SHE HAD SAID ABSOLUTELY *NOTHING* TO JOSHUA ABOUT THE ARTIFICIAL INSEMINATION.

THEN HOW COULD HE KNOW? UNLESS THAT...THAT *DONOR* HAS SOMEHOW TRACKED US DOWN, AND...AND HE'S BEEN TALKING TO JOSH!

IT'S THE ONLY LOGICAL EXPLANATION! HE'S AFTER MY SON AND *YOU'VE* GOT TO STOP HIM! I'LL DO *ANYTHING* TO PROTECT MY FAMILY!

ANYTHING? DOES THAT INCLUDE FORKIN' OVER SOME BIG BUCKS?

MISS BONGO BUTT

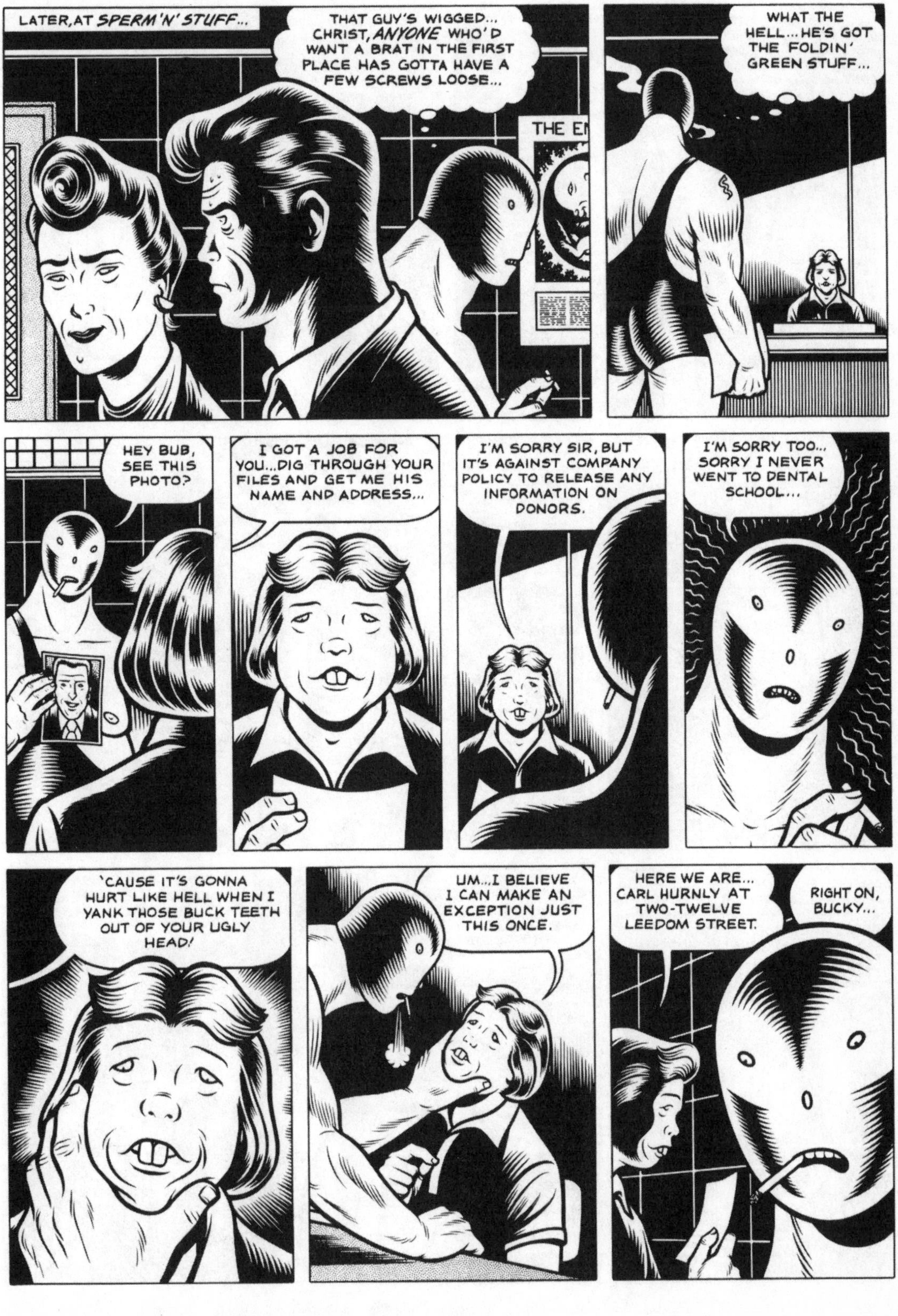

LATER, AT SPERM 'N' STUFF...
THAT GUY'S WIGGED... CHRIST, ANYONE WHO'D WANT A BRAT IN THE FIRST PLACE HAS GOTTA HAVE A FEW SCREWS LOOSE...
THE EN
WHAT THE HELL... HE'S GOT THE FOLDIN' GREEN STUFF...
HEY BUB, SEE THIS PHOTO?
I GOT A JOB FOR YOU...DIG THROUGH YOUR FILES AND GET ME HIS NAME AND ADDRESS...
I'M SORRY SIR, BUT IT'S AGAINST COMPANY POLICY TO RELEASE ANY INFORMATION ON DONORS.
I'M SORRY TOO... SORRY I NEVER WENT TO DENTAL SCHOOL...
'CAUSE IT'S GONNA HURT LIKE HELL WHEN I YANK THOSE BUCK TEETH OUT OF YOUR UGLY HEAD!
UM...I BELIEVE I CAN MAKE AN EXCEPTION JUST THIS ONCE.
HERE WE ARE... CARL HURNLY AT TWO-TWELVE LEEDOM STREET.
RIGHT ON, BUCKY...

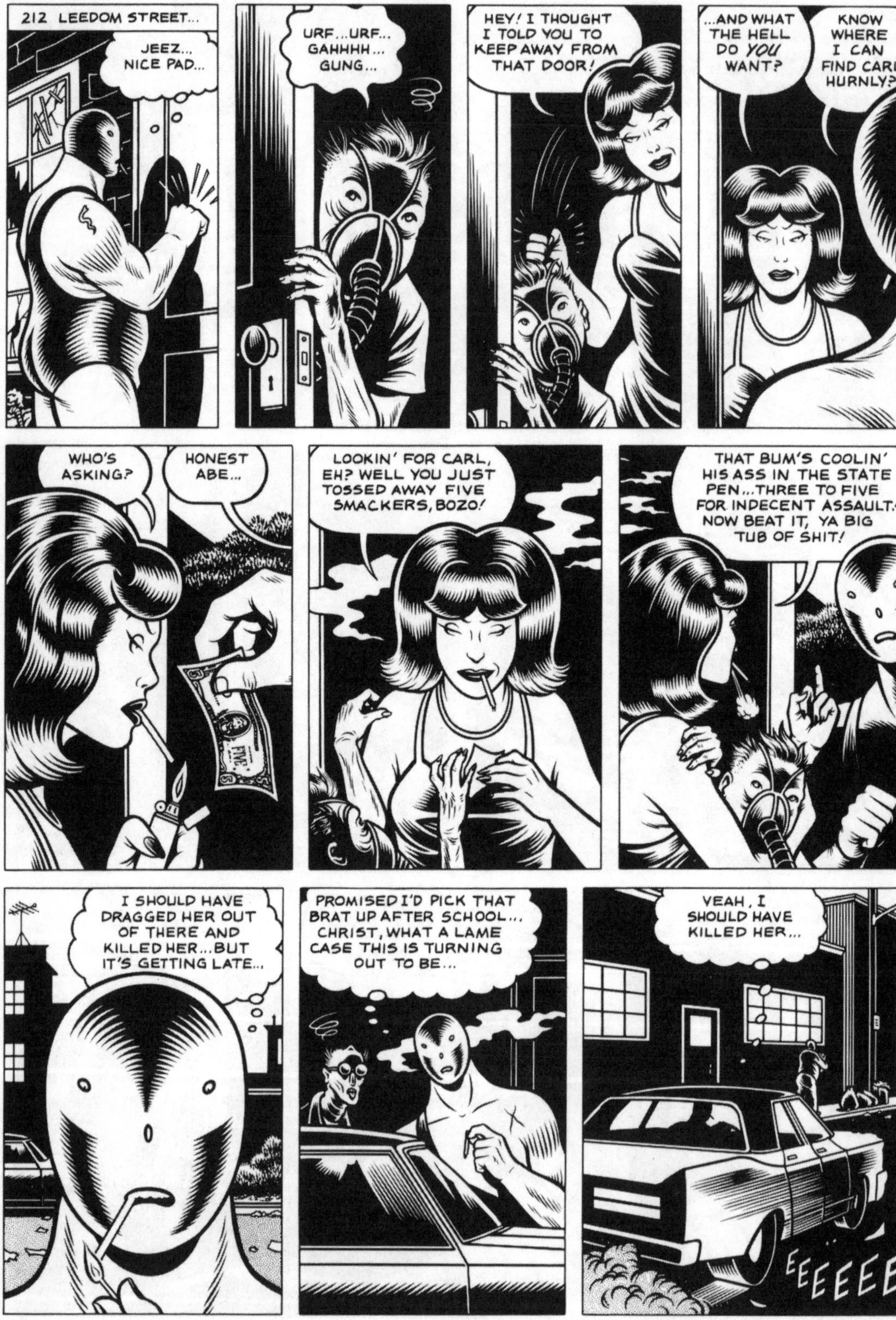

212 LEEDOM STREET...
JEEZ... NICE PAD...
URF...URF... GAHHHH... GUNG...
HEY! I THOUGHT I TOLD YOU TO KEEP AWAY FROM THAT DOOR!
...AND WHAT THE HELL DO YOU WANT?
KNOW WHERE I CAN FIND CARL HURNLY?
WHO'S ASKING?
HONEST ABE...
LOOKIN' FOR CARL, EH? WELL YOU JUST TOSSED AWAY FIVE SMACKERS, BOZO!
THAT BUM'S COOLIN' HIS ASS IN THE STATE PEN...THREE TO FIVE FOR INDECENT ASSAULT! NOW BEAT IT, YA BIG TUB OF SHIT!
I SHOULD HAVE DRAGGED HER OUT OF THERE AND KILLED HER...BUT IT'S GETTING LATE...
PROMISED I'D PICK THAT BRAT UP AFTER SCHOOL... CHRIST, WHAT A LAME CASE THIS IS TURNING OUT TO BE...
VEAH, I SHOULD HAVE KILLED HER...
EEEEEE

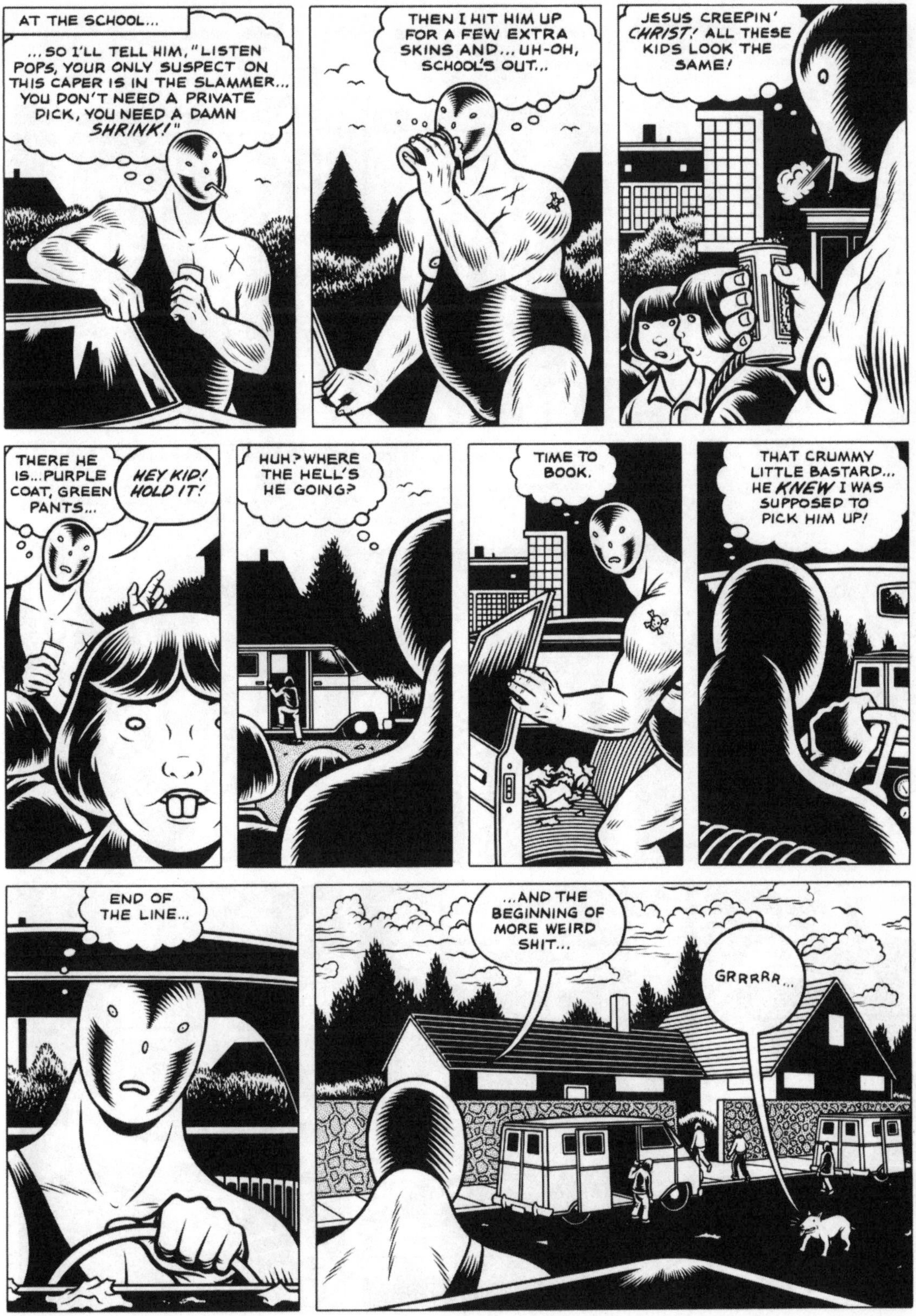
AT THE SCHOOL...
...SO I'LL TELL HIM, "LISTEN POPS, YOUR ONLY SUSPECT ON THIS CAPER IS IN THE SLAMMER... YOU DON'T NEED A PRIVATE DICK, YOU NEED A DAMN SHRINK!"
THEN I HIT HIM UP FOR A FEW EXTRA SKINS AND... UH-OH, SCHOOL'S OUT...
JESUS CREEPIN' CHRIST! ALL THESE KIDS LOOK THE SAME!
THERE HE IS...PURPLE COAT, GREEN PANTS...
HEY KID! HOLD IT!
HUH? WHERE THE HELL'S HE GOING?
TIME TO BOOK.
THAT CRUMMY LITTLE BASTARD... HE KNEW I WAS SUPPOSED TO PICK HIM UP!
END OF THE LINE...
...AND THE BEGINNING OF MORE WEIRD SHIT...
GRRRRR...

AT THE HOUSE...

COOL IT BOSKO... I KNOW A GOOD RECIPE FOR HIND LEG OF DOG...

WILL SOMEONE TURN OUT THE LIGHTS?

LOOK, MY CHILDREN...GAZE UPON THE OCEAN...THE SUN IS SETTING AND A GREAT DARKNESS IS FALLING ON THE EARTH...

THIS DARKNESS IS SLOWLY ENVELOPING OUR ONCE GREAT NATION...WE ARE DYING, DECAYING... FROM LUST, GREED, AND WICKEDNESS!

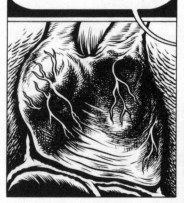

NOW GAZE AT MY HEART...A GIFT FROM *GOD!* A HUGE, PERFECTLY CONSTRUCTED MUSCLE THAT PUMPS BLOOD AND... AND *TRUTH!*

YOU, MY CHILDREN! *YOU* ARE MY BLOOD! VESSELS OF PERFECTION MADE IN *MY* IMAGE...CARRYING *MY* BLOOD!

THE DARKNESS IS FALLING, BUT WITH PURE YOUNG BLOOD PUMPING THROUGH YOUR VEINS AND MY STRONG HEART TO GUIDE YOU... WE WILL *SURVIVE!*

ENOUGH OF THIS SHIT...

WAM! WAM!

COME HERE JIVE-ASS...

OH, NO, I SHOULD HAVE GUESSED... BUCKY.

116

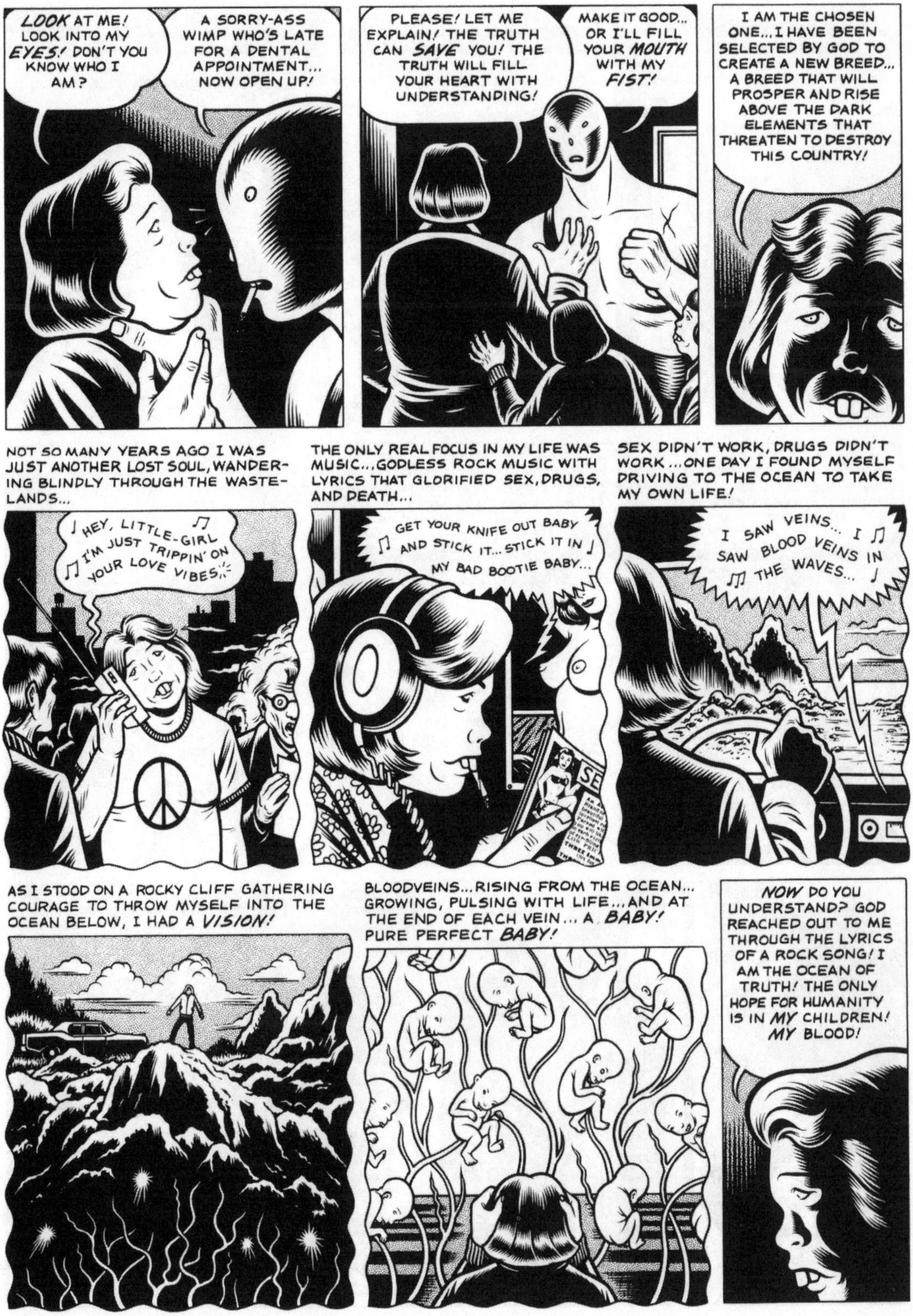
LOOK AT ME! LOOK INTO MY EYES! DON'T YOU KNOW WHO I AM?
A SORRY-ASS WIMP WHO'S LATE FOR A DENTAL APPOINTMENT... NOW OPEN UP!
PLEASE! LET ME EXPLAIN! THE TRUTH CAN SAVE YOU! THE TRUTH WILL FILL YOUR HEART WITH UNDERSTANDING!
MAKE IT GOOD... OR I'LL FILL YOUR MOUTH WITH MY FIST!
I AM THE CHOSEN ONE... I HAVE BEEN SELECTED BY GOD TO CREATE A NEW BREED... A BREED THAT WILL PROSPER AND RISE ABOVE THE DARK ELEMENTS THAT THREATEN TO DESTROY THIS COUNTRY!
NOT SO MANY YEARS AGO I WAS JUST ANOTHER LOST SOUL, WANDERING BLINDLY THROUGH THE WASTELANDS...
HEY, LITTLE-GIRL I'M JUST TRIPPIN' ON YOUR LOVE VIBES
THE ONLY REAL FOCUS IN MY LIFE WAS MUSIC... GODLESS ROCK MUSIC WITH LYRICS THAT GLORIFIED SEX, DRUGS, AND DEATH...
GET YOUR KNIFE OUT BABY AND STICK IT... STICK IT IN MY BAD BOOTIE BABY...
SEX DIDN'T WORK, DRUGS DIDN'T WORK ... ONE DAY I FOUND MYSELF DRIVING TO THE OCEAN TO TAKE MY OWN LIFE!
I SAW VEINS... I SAW BLOOD VEINS IN THE WAVES...
AS I STOOD ON A ROCKY CLIFF GATHERING COURAGE TO THROW MYSELF INTO THE OCEAN BELOW, I HAD A VISION!
BLOODVEINS... RISING FROM THE OCEAN... GROWING, PULSING WITH LIFE... AND AT THE END OF EACH VEIN... A BABY! PURE PERFECT BABY!
NOW DO YOU UNDERSTAND? GOD REACHED OUT TO ME THROUGH THE LYRICS OF A ROCK SONG! I AM THE OCEAN OF TRUTH! THE ONLY HOPE FOR HUMANITY IS IN MY CHILDREN! MY BLOOD!

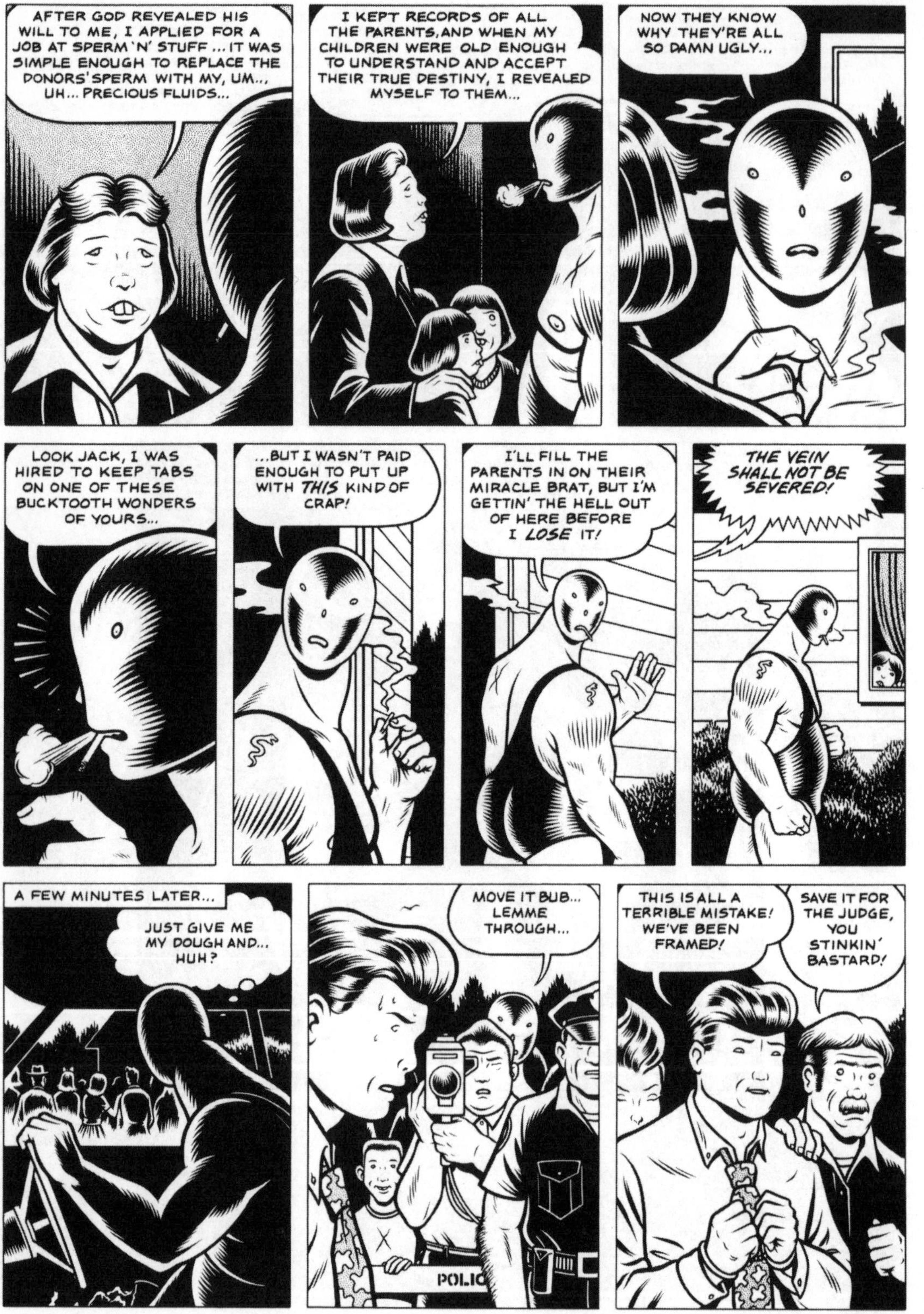
AFTER GOD REVEALED HIS WILL TO ME, I APPLIED FOR A JOB AT SPERM 'N' STUFF ... IT WAS SIMPLE ENOUGH TO REPLACE THE DONORS' SPERM WITH MY, UM... UH... PRECIOUS FLUIDS...
I KEPT RECORDS OF ALL THE PARENTS, AND WHEN MY CHILDREN WERE OLD ENOUGH TO UNDERSTAND AND ACCEPT THEIR TRUE DESTINY, I REVEALED MYSELF TO THEM...
NOW THEY KNOW WHY THEY'RE ALL SO DAMN UGLY...
LOOK JACK, I WAS HIRED TO KEEP TABS ON ONE OF THESE BUCKTOOTH WONDERS OF YOURS...
...BUT I WASN'T PAID ENOUGH TO PUT UP WITH *THIS* KIND OF CRAP!
I'LL FILL THE PARENTS IN ON THEIR MIRACLE BRAT, BUT I'M GETTIN' THE HELL OUT OF HERE BEFORE I *LOSE* IT!
THE VEIN SHALL NOT BE SEVERED!
A FEW MINUTES LATER...
JUST GIVE ME MY DOUGH AND... HUH?
MOVE IT BUB... LEMME THROUGH...
POLIC
THIS IS ALL A TERRIBLE MISTAKE! WE'VE BEEN FRAMED!
SAVE IT FOR THE JUDGE, YOU STINKIN' BASTARD!

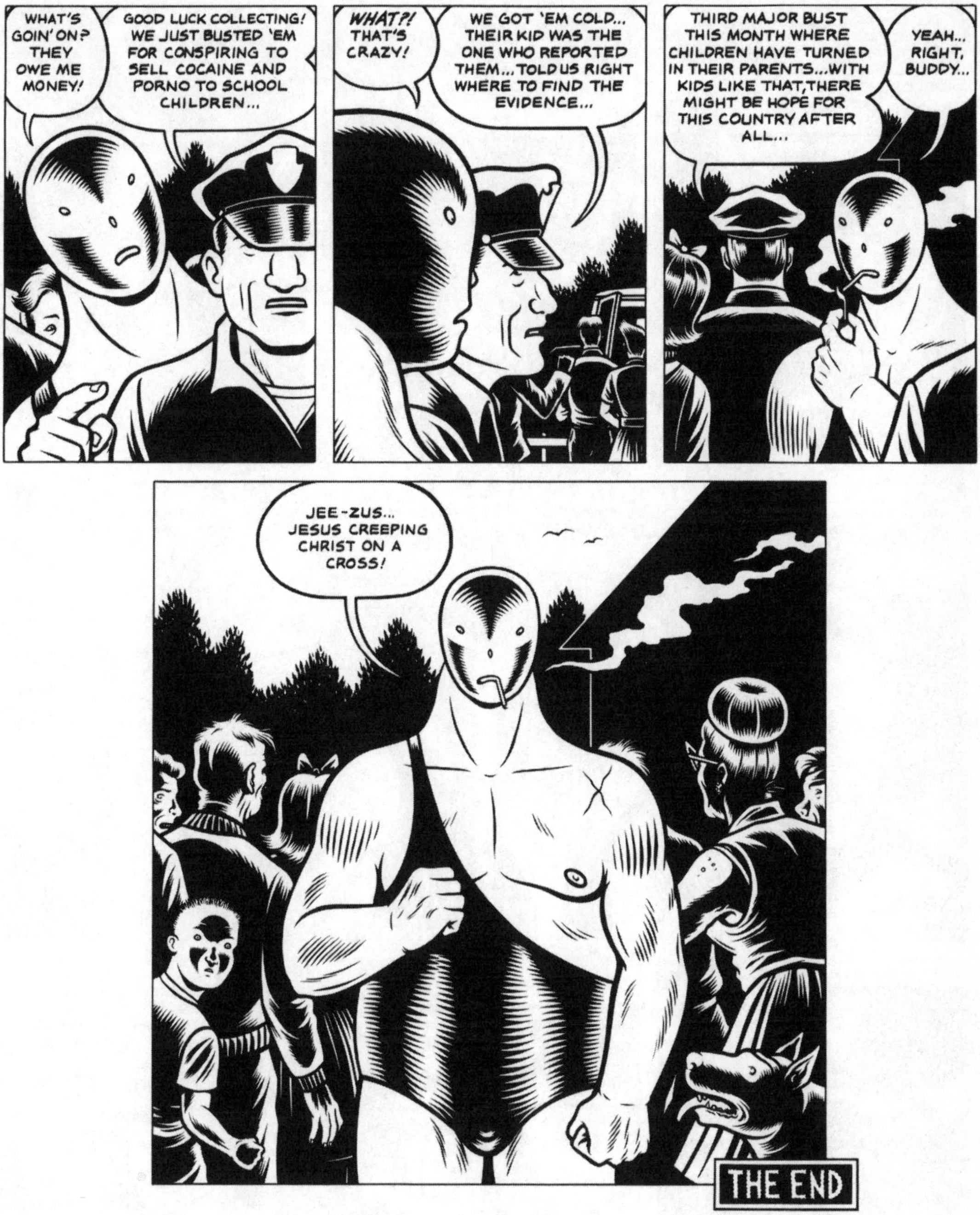
WHAT'S GOIN' ON? THEY OWE ME MONEY!
GOOD LUCK COLLECTING! WE JUST BUSTED 'EM FOR CONSPIRING TO SELL COCAINE AND PORNO TO SCHOOL CHILDREN...
WHAT?! THAT'S CRAZY!
WE GOT 'EM COLD... THEIR KID WAS THE ONE WHO REPORTED THEM... TOLD US RIGHT WHERE TO FIND THE EVIDENCE...
THIRD MAJOR BUST THIS MONTH WHERE CHILDREN HAVE TURNED IN THEIR PARENTS... WITH KIDS LIKE THAT, THERE MIGHT BE HOPE FOR THIS COUNTRY AFTER ALL...
YEAH... RIGHT, BUDDY...
JEE-ZUS... JESUS CREEPING CHRIST ON A CROSS!
THE END

"Please don't think me immodest,
but Waldo was so grateful for my...
ah...intellectual companionship,
he left me the key
to the family strong box!"

Police detective Denny Colt has returned
from the dead as mystery man The Spirit,
his costume merely a modest eyemask, his
purpose to help beleaguered Commissioner
Dolan foil the deadliest criminals. The Spirit's
great nemesis is The Octopus, identified only
by his tell-tale gloves. As for his many femmes
fatales, none compares to gorgeous gold-
digger P'Gell for film-star glamour and nerve.
Brilliant at pacing, composition and arch
humour, Will Eisner rewrote the rulebook of
comics, expanding the medium's capacities
week after week from 1940 to 1952 in his
compact fables given away free with Sunday
newspapers. The Spirit and his cast are
coming to the big screen directed by graphic
novelist Frank Miller.

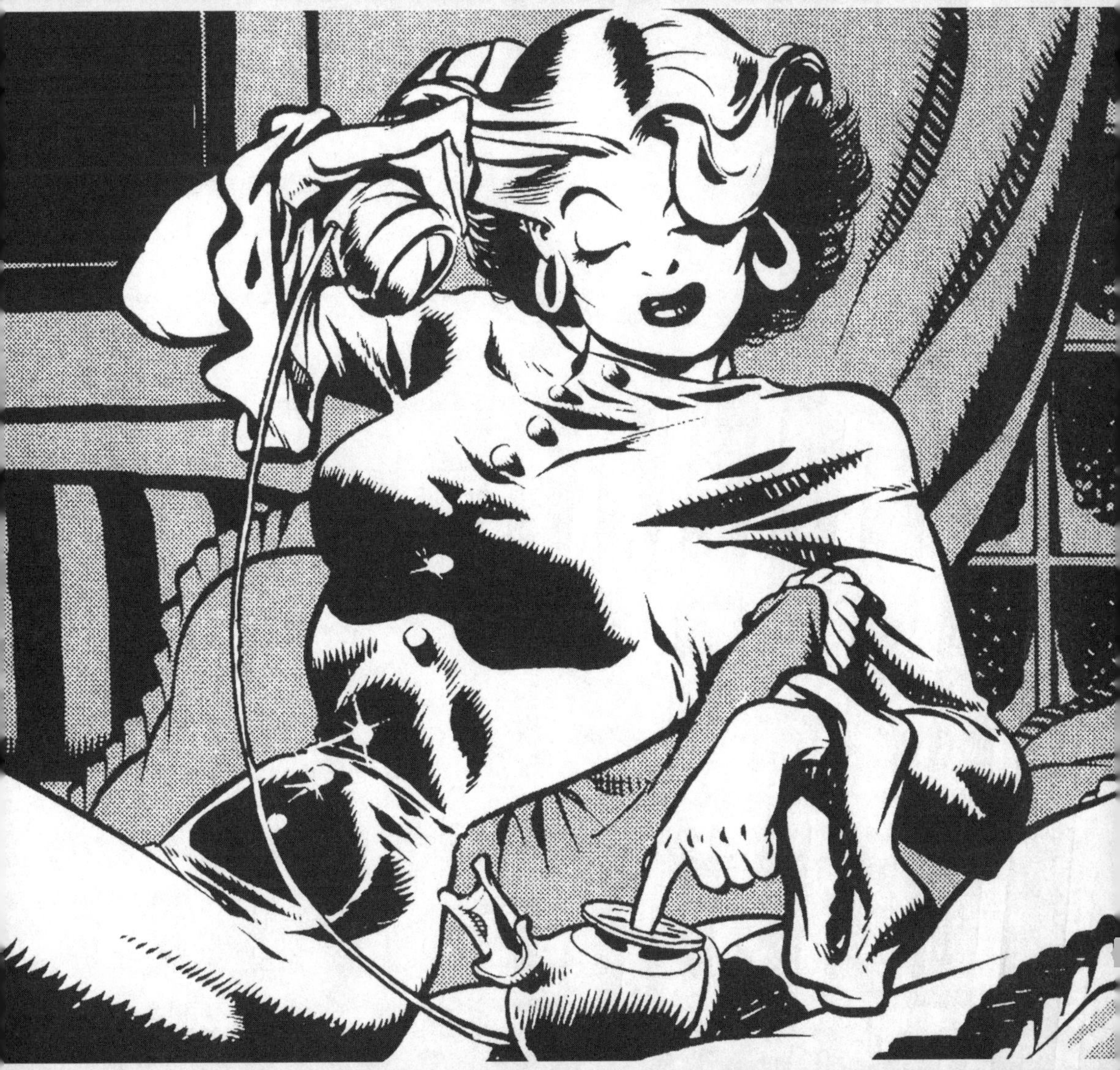

The Spirit: The Portier Fortune

Will Eisner (script & art) 1946

The PORTIER FORTUNE

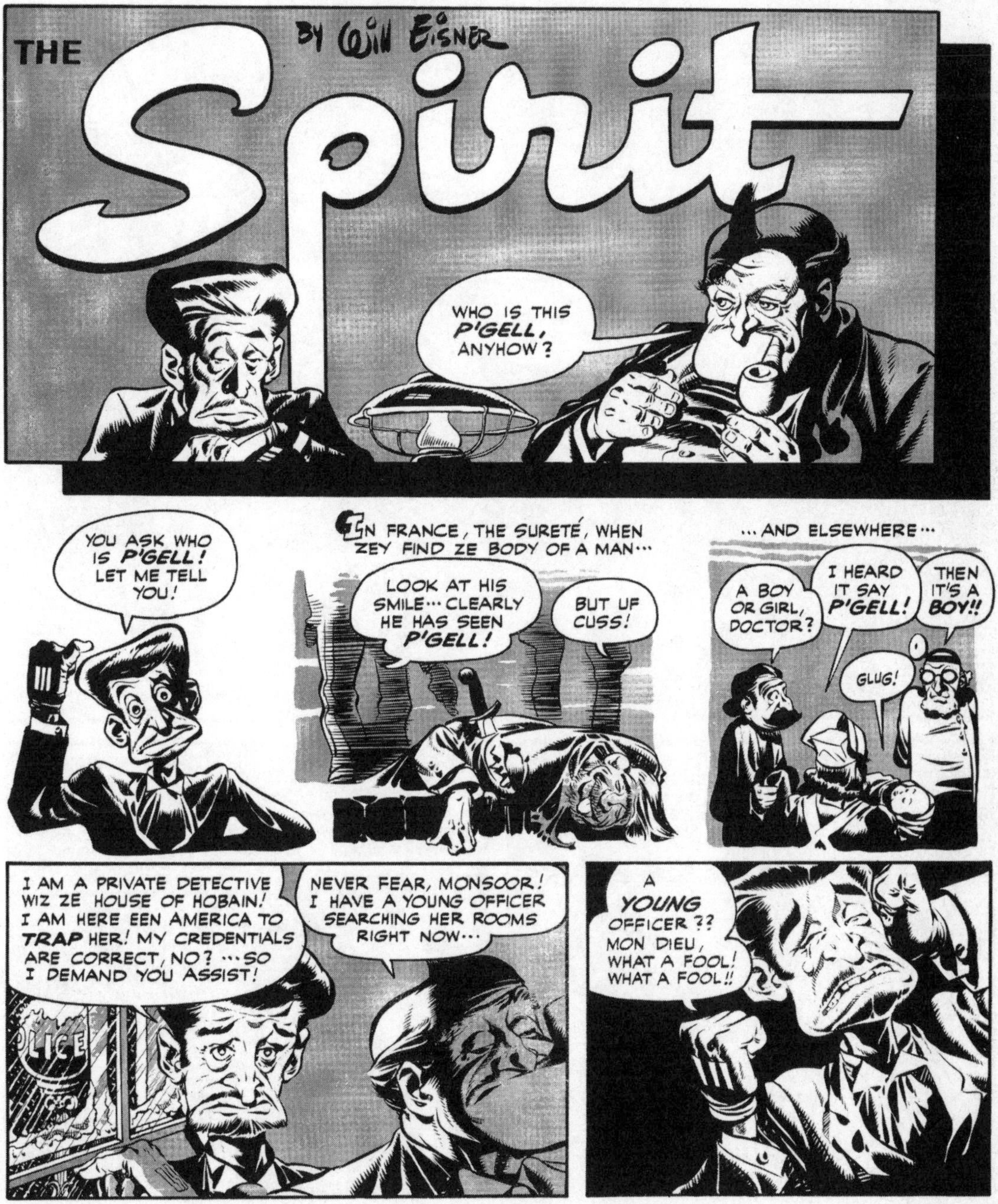

BY WILL EISNER
THE Spirit
WHO IS THIS **P'GELL,** ANYHOW?
YOU ASK WHO IS **P'GELL!** LET ME TELL YOU!
IN FRANCE, THE SURETÉ, WHEN ZEY FIND ZE BODY OF A MAN...
LOOK AT HIS SMILE... CLEARLY HE HAS SEEN **P'GELL!**
BUT UF CUSS!
...AND ELSEWHERE...
A BOY OR GIRL, DOCTOR?
I HEARD IT SAY **P'GELL!**
THEN IT'S A **BOY!!**
GLUG!
I AM A PRIVATE DETECTIVE WIZ ZE HOUSE OF HOBAIN! I AM HERE EEN AMERICA TO **TRAP** HER! MY CREDENTIALS ARE CORRECT, NO? ...SO I DEMAND YOU ASSIST!
NEVER FEAR, MONSOOR! I HAVE A YOUNG OFFICER SEARCHING HER ROOMS RIGHT NOW...
A **YOUNG** OFFICER?? MON DIEU, WHAT A FOOL! WHAT A FOOL!!

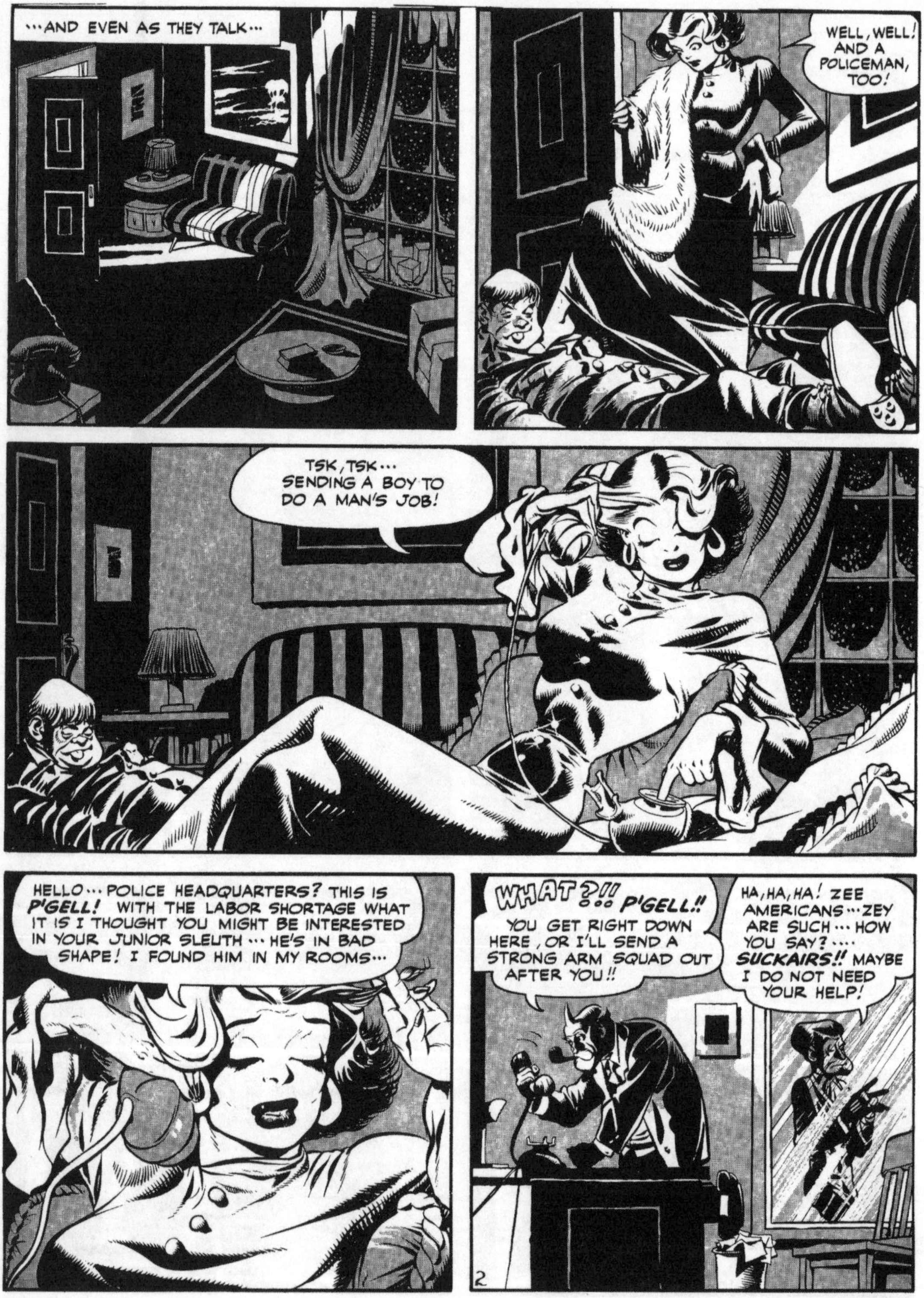

...AND EVEN AS THEY TALK...
WELL, WELL! AND A POLICEMAN, TOO!
TSK, TSK... SENDING A BOY TO DO A MAN'S JOB!
HELLO... POLICE HEADQUARTERS? THIS IS **P'GELL!** WITH THE LABOR SHORTAGE WHAT IT IS I THOUGHT YOU MIGHT BE INTERESTED IN YOUR JUNIOR SLEUTH... HE'S IN BAD SHAPE! I FOUND HIM IN MY ROOMS...
WHAT?!! ... P'GELL!! YOU GET RIGHT DOWN HERE, OR I'LL SEND A STRONG ARM SQUAD OUT AFTER YOU!!
HA, HA, HA! ZEE AMERICANS... ZEY ARE SUCH... HOW YOU SAY?.... **SUCKAIRS!!** MAYBE I DO NOT NEED YOUR HELP!

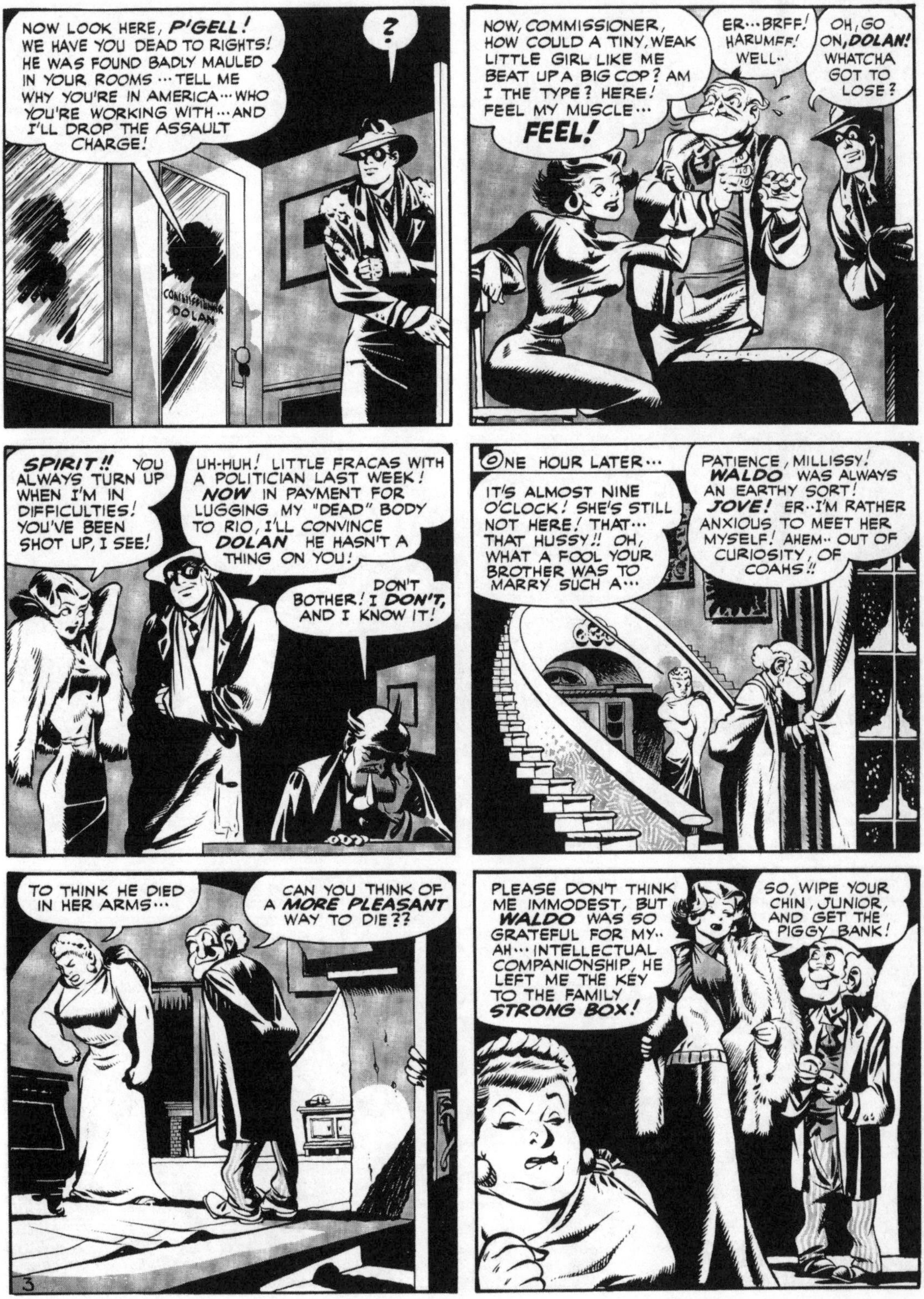
NOW LOOK HERE, P'GELL! WE HAVE YOU DEAD TO RIGHTS! HE WAS FOUND BADLY MAULED IN YOUR ROOMS ··· TELL ME WHY YOU'RE IN AMERICA ··· WHO YOU'RE WORKING WITH ··· AND I'LL DROP THE ASSAULT CHARGE!
?
COMMISSIONER DOLAN
NOW, COMMISSIONER, HOW COULD A TINY, WEAK LITTLE GIRL LIKE ME BEAT UP A BIG COP? AM I THE TYPE? HERE! FEEL MY MUSCLE ··· FEEL!
ER··· BRFF! HARUMFF! WELL··
OH, GO ON, DOLAN! WHATCHA GOT TO LOSE?
SPIRIT!! YOU ALWAYS TURN UP WHEN I'M IN DIFFICULTIES! YOU'VE BEEN SHOT UP, I SEE!
UH-HUH! LITTLE FRACAS WITH A POLITICIAN LAST WEEK! NOW IN PAYMENT FOR LUGGING MY "DEAD" BODY TO RIO, I'LL CONVINCE DOLAN HE HASN'T A THING ON YOU!
DON'T BOTHER! I DON'T, AND I KNOW IT!
ONE HOUR LATER···
IT'S ALMOST NINE O'CLOCK! SHE'S STILL NOT HERE! THAT··· THAT HUSSY!! OH, WHAT A FOOL YOUR BROTHER WAS TO MARRY SUCH A···
PATIENCE, MILLISSY! WALDO WAS ALWAYS AN EARTHY SORT! JOVE! ER··I'M RATHER ANXIOUS TO MEET HER MYSELF! AHEM·· OUT OF CURIOSITY, OF COAHS!!
TO THINK HE DIED IN HER ARMS···
CAN YOU THINK OF A MORE PLEASANT WAY TO DIE??
3
PLEASE DON'T THINK ME IMMODEST, BUT WALDO WAS SO GRATEFUL FOR MY·· AH··· INTELLECTUAL COMPANIONSHIP, HE LEFT ME THE KEY TO THE FAMILY STRONG BOX!
SO, WIPE YOUR CHIN, JUNIOR, AND GET THE PIGGY BANK!

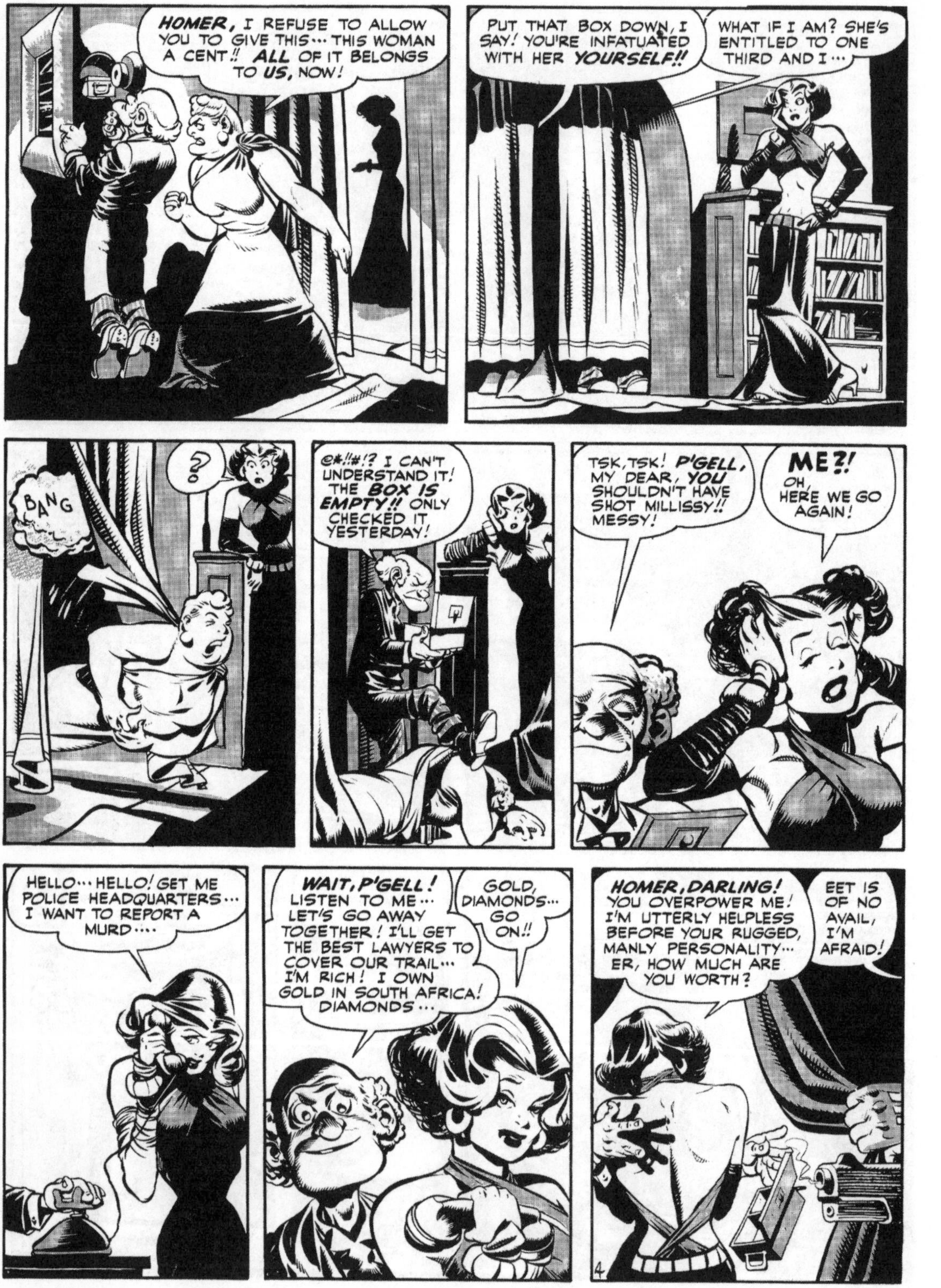
HOMER, I REFUSE TO ALLOW YOU TO GIVE THIS··· THIS WOMAN A CENT!! ALL OF IT BELONGS TO US, NOW!
PUT THAT BOX DOWN, I SAY! YOU'RE INFATUATED WITH HER YOURSELF!!
WHAT IF I AM? SHE'S ENTITLED TO ONE THIRD AND I···
BANG
?
@*!!#!? I CAN'T UNDERSTAND IT! THE BOX IS EMPTY!! ONLY CHECKED IT YESTERDAY!
TSK, TSK! P'GELL, MY DEAR, YOU SHOULDN'T HAVE SHOT MILLISSY!! MESSY!
ME?! OH, HERE WE GO AGAIN!
HELLO··· HELLO! GET ME POLICE HEADQUARTERS··· I WANT TO REPORT A MURD····
WAIT, P'GELL! LISTEN TO ME··· LET'S GO AWAY TOGETHER! I'LL GET THE BEST LAWYERS TO COVER OUR TRAIL··· I'M RICH! I OWN GOLD IN SOUTH AFRICA! DIAMONDS···
GOLD, DIAMONDS··· GO ON!!
HOMER, DARLING! YOU OVERPOWER ME! I'M UTTERLY HELPLESS BEFORE YOUR RUGGED, MANLY PERSONALITY··· ER, HOW MUCH ARE YOU WORTH?
EET IS OF NO AVAIL, I'M AFRAID!
4

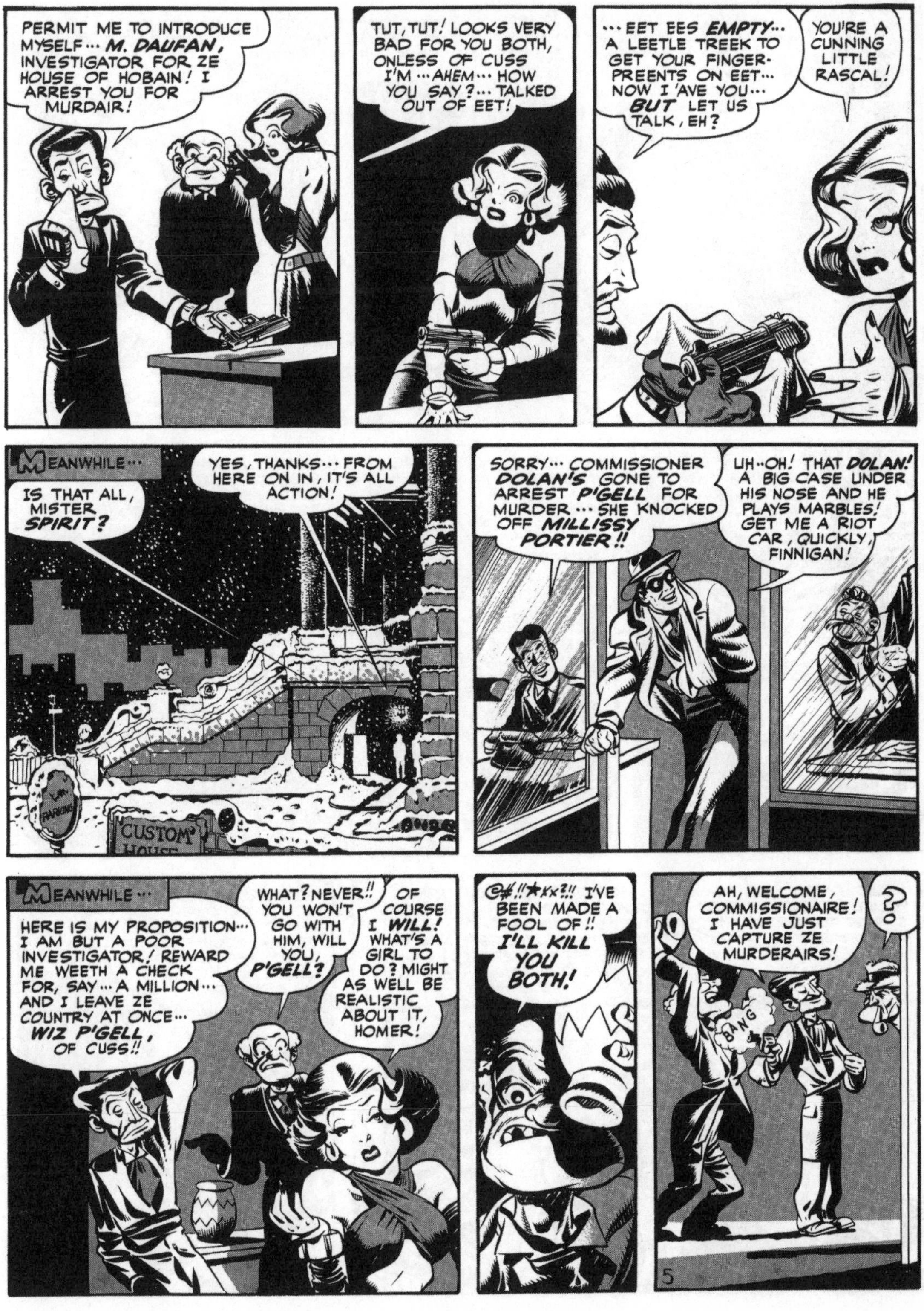
PERMIT ME TO INTRODUCE MYSELF... M. DAUFAN, INVESTIGATOR FOR ZE HOUSE OF HOBAIN! I ARREST YOU FOR MURDAIR!
TUT, TUT! LOOKS VERY BAD FOR YOU BOTH, ONLESS OF CUSS I'M ... AHEM ... HOW YOU SAY? ... TALKED OUT OF EET!
... EET EES EMPTY ... A LEETLE TREEK TO GET YOUR FINGER-PREENTS ON EET ... NOW I 'AVE YOU ... BUT LET US TALK, EH?
YOU'RE A CUNNING LITTLE RASCAL!
MEANWHILE...
IS THAT ALL, MISTER SPIRIT?
YES, THANKS ... FROM HERE ON IN, IT'S ALL ACTION!
SORRY ... COMMISSIONER DOLAN'S GONE TO ARREST P'GELL FOR MURDER ... SHE KNOCKED OFF MILLISSY PORTIER!!
UH-OH! THAT DOLAN! A BIG CASE UNDER HIS NOSE AND HE PLAYS MARBLES! GET ME A RIOT CAR, QUICKLY, FINNIGAN!
MEANWHILE...
HERE IS MY PROPOSITION ... I AM BUT A POOR INVESTIGATOR! REWARD ME WEETH A CHECK FOR, SAY ... A MILLION ... AND I LEAVE ZE COUNTRY AT ONCE ... WIZ P'GELL, OF CUSS!!
WHAT? NEVER!! YOU WON'T GO WITH HIM, WILL YOU, P'GELL?
OF COURSE I WILL! WHAT'S A GIRL TO DO? MIGHT AS WELL BE REALISTIC ABOUT IT, HOMER!
@#!!★xx?!! I'VE BEEN MADE A FOOL OF!! I'LL KILL YOU BOTH!
AH, WELCOME, COMMISSIONAIRE! I HAVE JUST CAPTURE ZE MURDERAIRS!
?
BANG

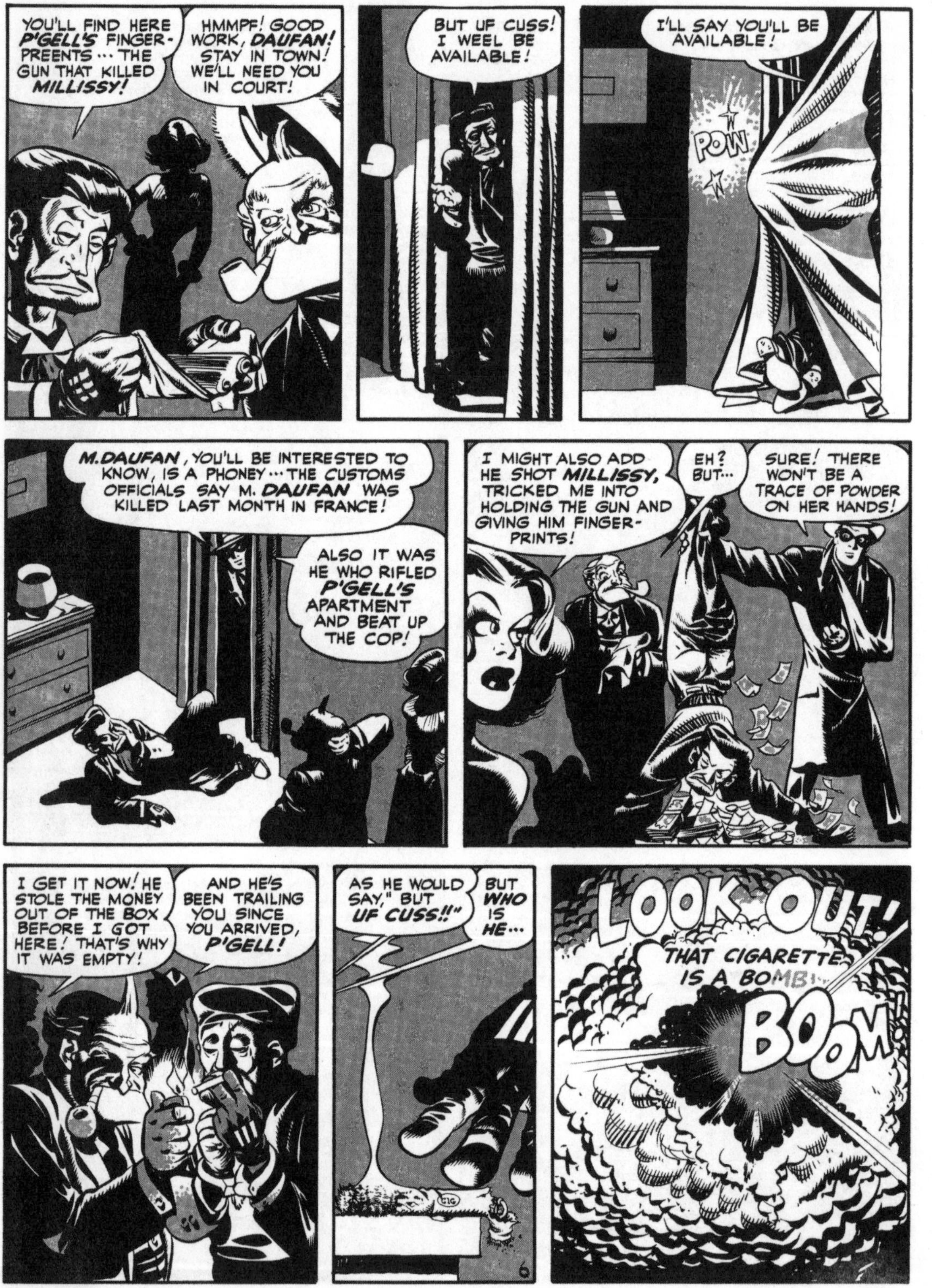
YOU'LL FIND HERE P'GELL'S FINGER-PREENTS ... THE GUN THAT KILLED MILLISSY!
HMMPF! GOOD WORK, DAUFAN! STAY IN TOWN! WE'LL NEED YOU IN COURT!
BUT UF CUSS! I WEEL BE AVAILABLE!
I'LL SAY YOU'LL BE AVAILABLE!
POW
M. DAUFAN, YOU'LL BE INTERESTED TO KNOW, IS A PHONEY ... THE CUSTOMS OFFICIALS SAY M. DAUFAN WAS KILLED LAST MONTH IN FRANCE!
ALSO IT WAS HE WHO RIFLED P'GELL'S APARTMENT AND BEAT UP THE COP!
I MIGHT ALSO ADD HE SHOT MILLISSY, TRICKED ME INTO HOLDING THE GUN AND GIVING HIM FINGER-PRINTS!
EH? BUT...
SURE! THERE WON'T BE A TRACE OF POWDER ON HER HANDS!
I GET IT NOW! HE STOLE THE MONEY OUT OF THE BOX BEFORE I GOT HERE! THAT'S WHY IT WAS EMPTY!
AND HE'S BEEN TRAILING YOU SINCE YOU ARRIVED, P'GELL!
AS HE WOULD SAY," BUT UF CUSS!!"
BUT WHO IS HE...
LOOK-OUT!
THAT CIGARETTE IS A BOMB
BOOM!

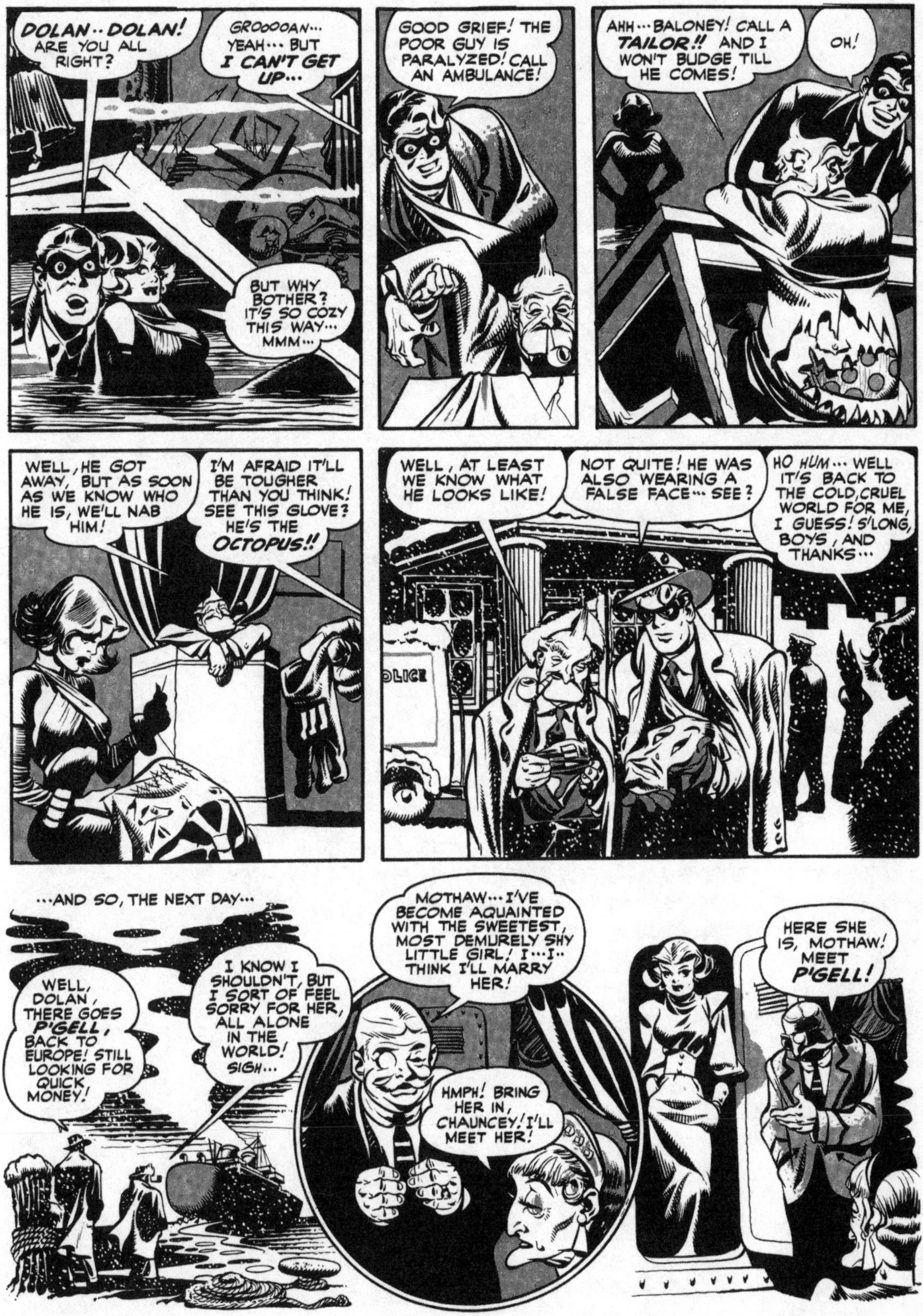
DOLAN.. DOLAN! ARE YOU ALL RIGHT?
GROOOOAN... YEAH... BUT I CAN'T GET UP...
BUT WHY BOTHER? IT'S SO COZY THIS WAY... MMM...
GOOD GRIEF! THE POOR GUY IS PARALYZED! CALL AN AMBULANCE!
AHH... BALONEY! CALL A TAILOR!! AND I WON'T BUDGE TILL HE COMES!
OH!
WELL, HE GOT AWAY, BUT AS SOON AS WE KNOW WHO HE IS, WE'LL NAB HIM!
I'M AFRAID IT'LL BE TOUGHER THAN YOU THINK! SEE THIS GLOVE? HE'S THE OCTOPUS!!
WELL, AT LEAST WE KNOW WHAT HE LOOKS LIKE!
NOT QUITE! HE WAS ALSO WEARING A FALSE FACE... SEE?
HO HUM... WELL IT'S BACK TO THE COLD, CRUEL WORLD FOR ME, I GUESS! S'LONG, BOYS, AND THANKS...
...AND SO, THE NEXT DAY...
WELL, DOLAN, THERE GOES P'GELL, BACK TO EUROPE! STILL LOOKING FOR QUICK MONEY!
I KNOW I SHOULDN'T, BUT I SORT OF FEEL SORRY FOR HER, ALL ALONE IN THE WORLD! SIGH...
MOTHAW... I'VE BECOME AQUAINTED WITH THE SWEETEST, MOST DEMURELY SHY LITTLE GIRL! I...I... THINK I'LL MARRY HER!
HMPH! BRING HER IN, CHAUNCEY! I'LL MEET HER!
HERE SHE IS, MOTHAW! MEET P'GELL!

"But there was somebody
I don't want to hurt!
Who was it?
I... I can't remember!"

As gripping as any 1930s movie serial but
delivered six days a week, Mondays to
Saturdays, Dashiell Hammett's newspaper
strip begins by introducing his hero and
racing through several plotlines over the first
eighty episodes which eventually converge.
It is from this point we join the story, when
Hammett concentrates on the convoluted
hunt by X-9, alias Dexter, for the mysterious
criminal mastermind The Top and for the
true inheritor of the recently deceased
Tarlton Powers' fortune. Hammett cuts loose
with richer characterization and dialogue,
admirably assisted by talented newcomer Alex
Raymond's lush faces and figures, many based
on models, to create a sense of realism and
glamour. Together they bring their cast to life,
including rugged, relentless detective Dexter,
colourful coward Sydney Carp, and the
alluring but ambiguous widow Grace Powers.
The story picks up as she conspires with
wily Alfred Hall, her lover...

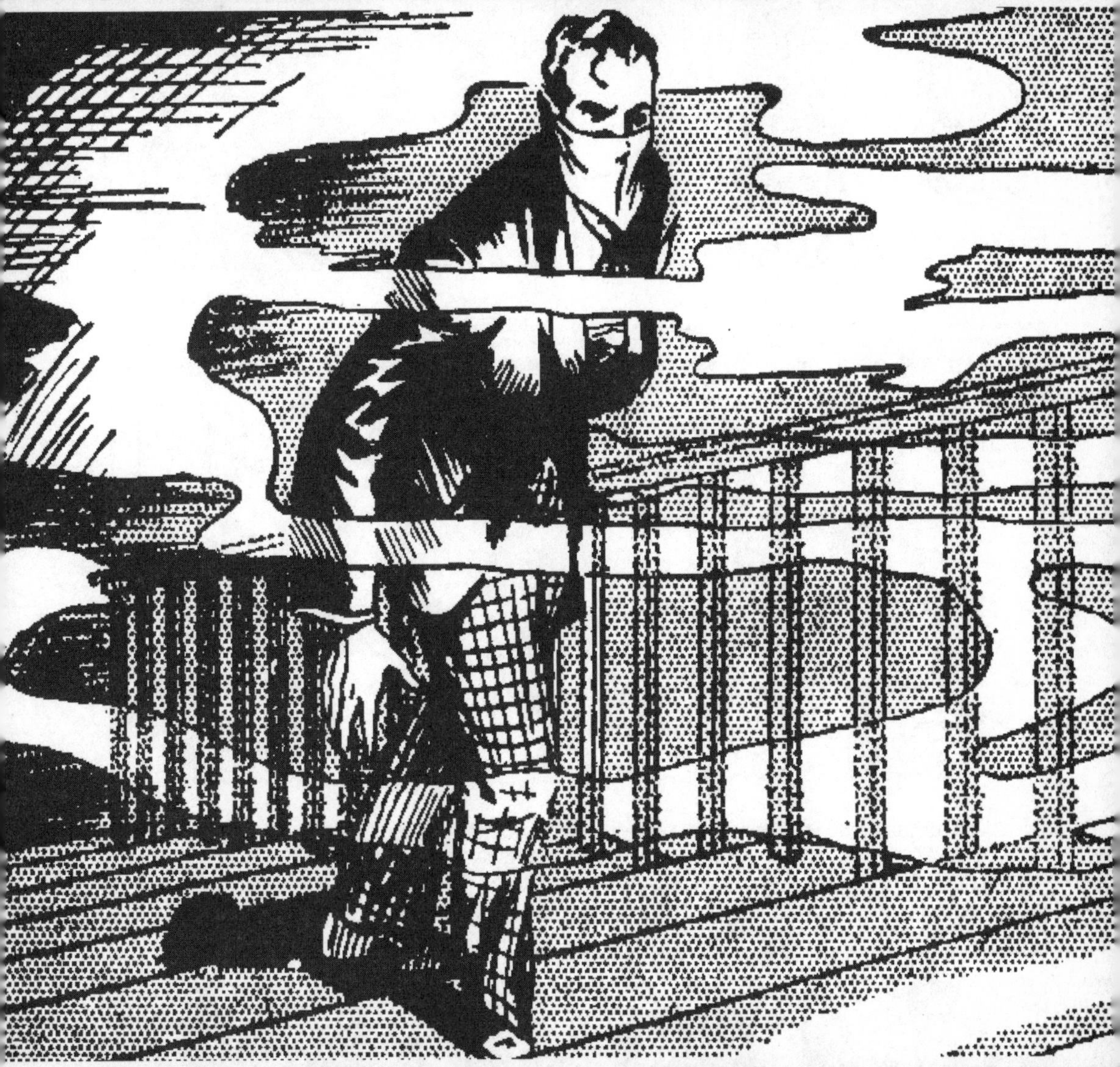

Secret Agent X-9

Dashiell Hammett (script) and Alex Raymond (art) 1934

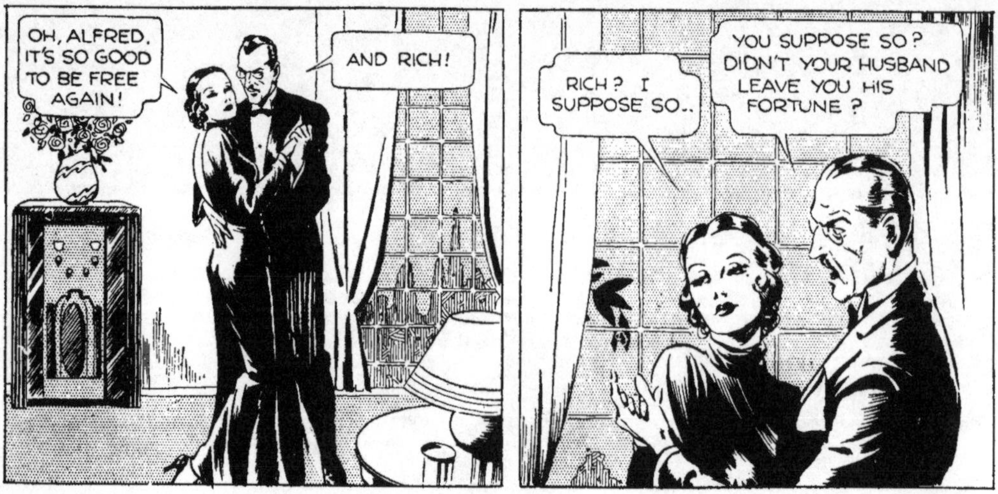
OH, ALFRED. IT'S SO GOOD TO BE FREE AGAIN!
AND RICH!
RICH? I SUPPOSE SO..
YOU SUPPOSE SO? DIDN'T YOUR HUSBAND LEAVE YOU HIS FORTUNE?

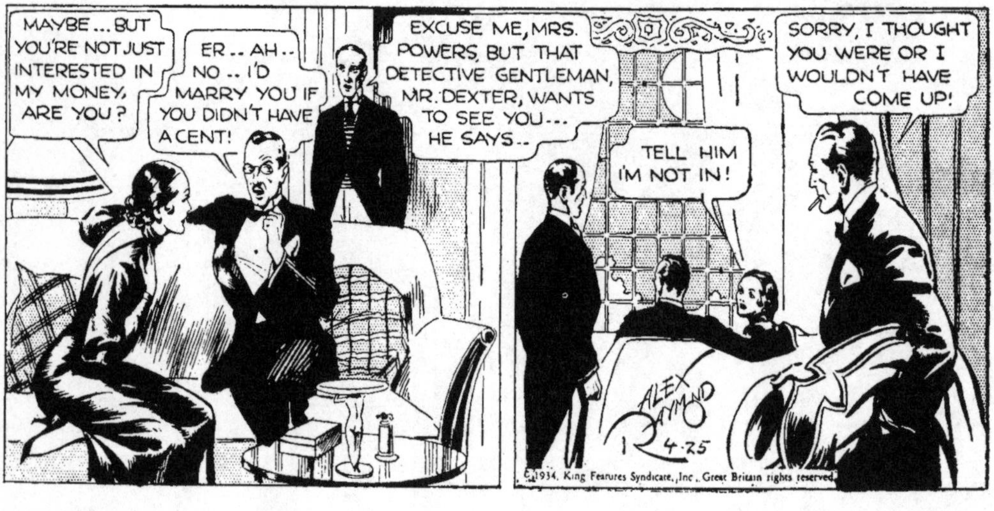
MAYBE ... BUT YOU'RE NOT JUST INTERESTED IN MY MONEY, ARE YOU?
ER .. AH .. NO .. I'D MARRY YOU IF YOU DIDN'T HAVE A CENT!
EXCUSE ME, MRS. POWERS, BUT THAT DETECTIVE GENTLEMAN, MR. DEXTER, WANTS TO SEE YOU ... HE SAYS ..
TELL HIM I'M NOT IN!
SORRY, I THOUGHT YOU WERE OR I WOULDN'T HAVE COME UP!
ALEX RAYMOND 4-25
©1934, King Features Syndicate, Inc., Great Britain rights reserved.

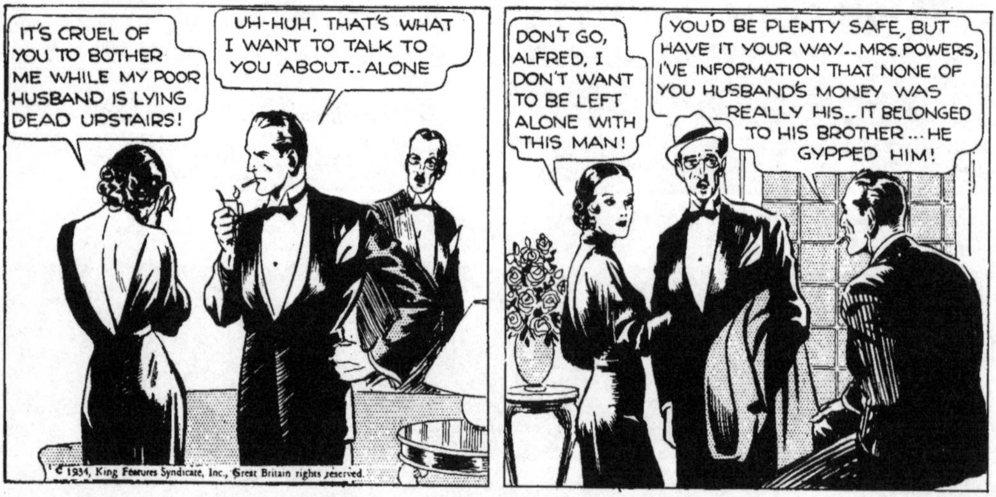
IT'S CRUEL OF YOU TO BOTHER ME WHILE MY POOR HUSBAND IS LYING DEAD UPSTAIRS!
UH-HUH. THAT'S WHAT I WANT TO TALK TO YOU ABOUT.. ALONE
©1934, King Features Syndicate, Inc., Great Britain rights reserved.
DON'T GO, ALFRED, I DON'T WANT TO BE LEFT ALONE WITH THIS MAN!
YOU'D BE PLENTY SAFE, BUT HAVE IT YOUR WAY.. MRS. POWERS, I'VE INFORMATION THAT NONE OF YOU HUSBAND'S MONEY WAS REALLY HIS.. IT BELONGED TO HIS BROTHER ... HE GYPPED HIM!

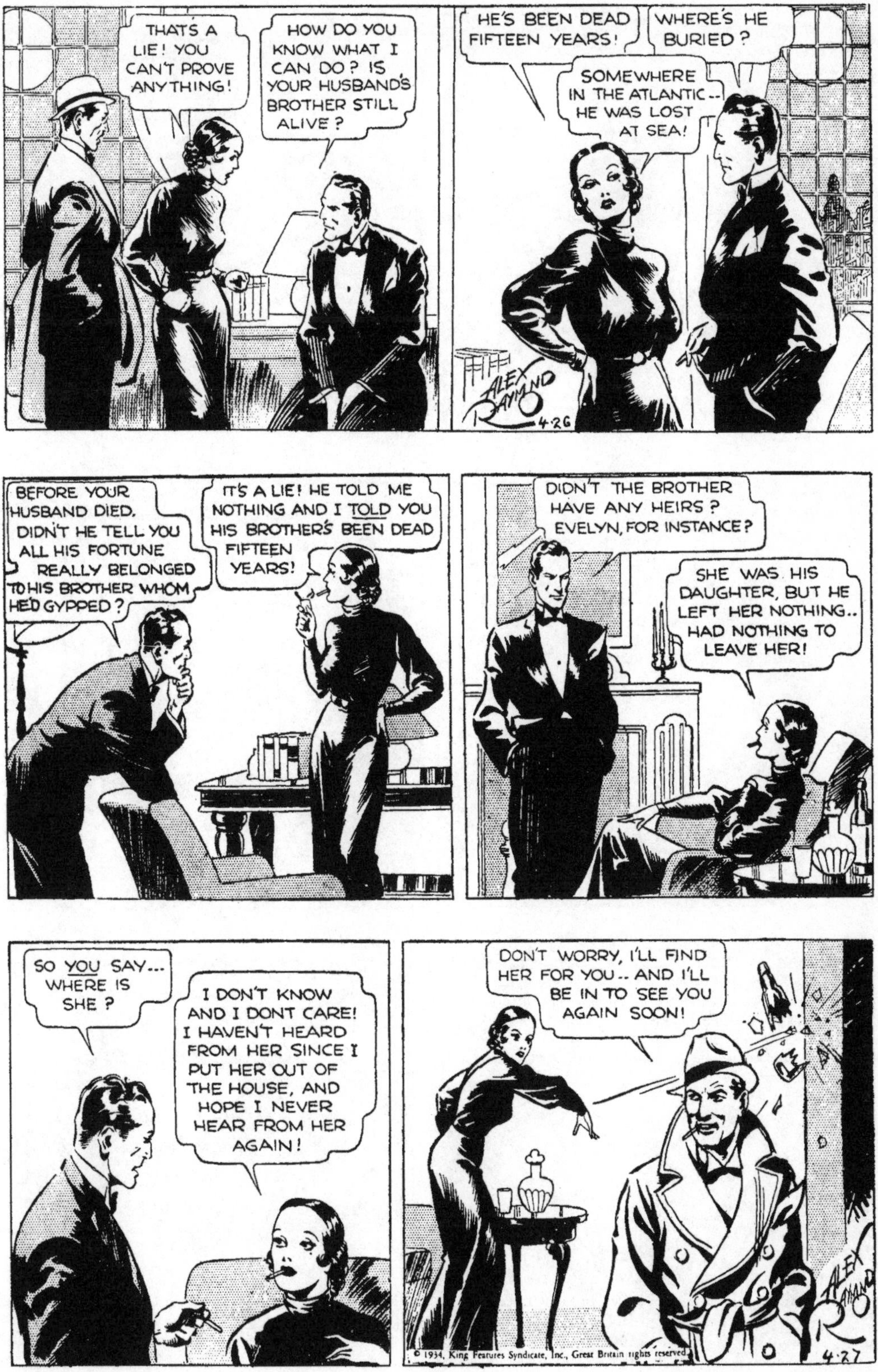
THAT'S A LIE! YOU CAN'T PROVE ANYTHING!
HOW DO YOU KNOW WHAT I CAN DO? IS YOUR HUSBAND'S BROTHER STILL ALIVE?
HE'S BEEN DEAD FIFTEEN YEARS!
WHERE'S HE BURIED?
SOMEWHERE IN THE ATLANTIC -- HE WAS LOST AT SEA!
ALEX RAYMOND 4·26
BEFORE YOUR HUSBAND DIED, DIDN'T HE TELL YOU ALL HIS FORTUNE REALLY BELONGED TO HIS BROTHER WHOM HE'D GYPPED?
IT'S A LIE! HE TOLD ME NOTHING AND I TOLD YOU HIS BROTHER'S BEEN DEAD FIFTEEN YEARS!
DIDN'T THE BROTHER HAVE ANY HEIRS? EVELYN, FOR INSTANCE?
SHE WAS HIS DAUGHTER, BUT HE LEFT HER NOTHING.. HAD NOTHING TO LEAVE HER!
SO YOU SAY... WHERE IS SHE?
I DON'T KNOW AND I DONT CARE! I HAVEN'T HEARD FROM HER SINCE I PUT HER OUT OF THE HOUSE, AND HOPE I NEVER HEAR FROM HER AGAIN!
DON'T WORRY, I'LL FIND HER FOR YOU.. AND I'LL BE IN TO SEE YOU AGAIN SOON!
ALEX RAYMOND 4·27
© 1934, King Features Syndicate, Inc., Great Britain rights reserved.

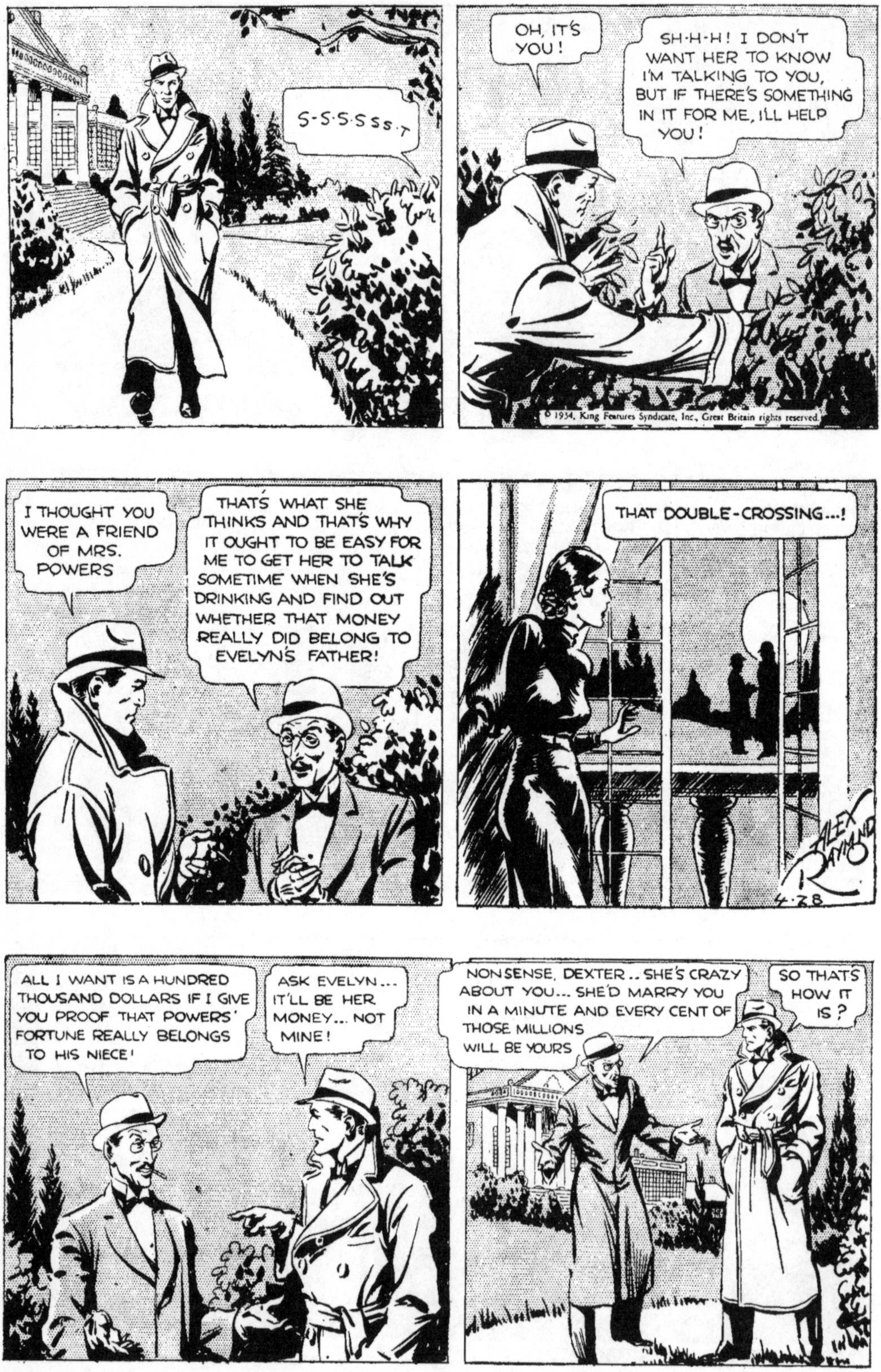

S-S-S-S-S-S-S-T
OH, IT'S YOU!
SH-H-H! I DON'T WANT HER TO KNOW I'M TALKING TO YOU, BUT IF THERE'S SOMETHING IN IT FOR ME, I'LL HELP YOU!
© 1934, King Features Syndicate, Inc., Great Britain rights reserved.
I THOUGHT YOU WERE A FRIEND OF MRS. POWERS
THAT'S WHAT SHE THINKS AND THAT'S WHY IT OUGHT TO BE EASY FOR ME TO GET HER TO TALK SOMETIME WHEN SHE'S DRINKING AND FIND OUT WHETHER THAT MONEY REALLY DID BELONG TO EVELYN'S FATHER!
THAT DOUBLE-CROSSING...!
ALEX RAYMOND
4-28
ALL I WANT IS A HUNDRED THOUSAND DOLLARS IF I GIVE YOU PROOF THAT POWERS' FORTUNE REALLY BELONGS TO HIS NIECE!
ASK EVELYN... IT'LL BE HER MONEY... NOT MINE!
NONSENSE, DEXTER.. SHE'S CRAZY ABOUT YOU... SHE'D MARRY YOU IN A MINUTE AND EVERY CENT OF THOSE MILLIONS WILL BE YOURS
SO THAT'S HOW IT IS?

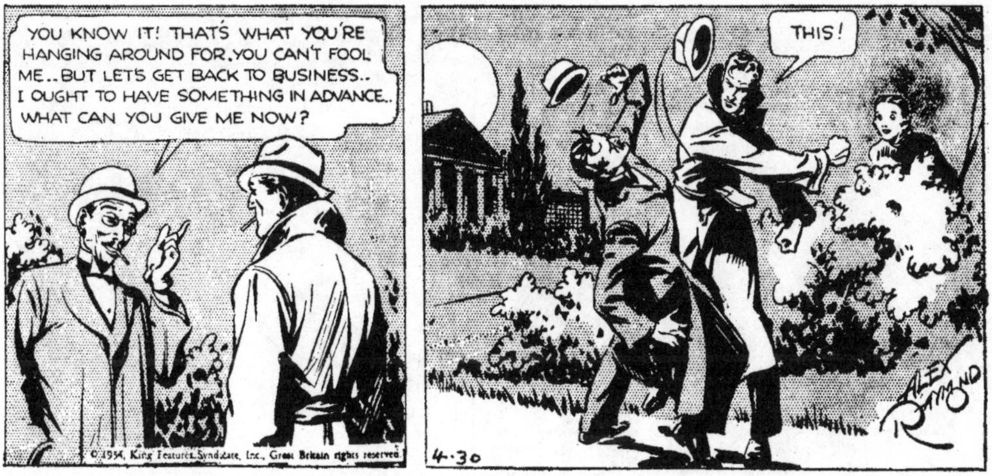
YOU KNOW IT! THAT'S WHAT YOU'RE HANGING AROUND FOR. YOU CAN'T FOOL ME.. BUT LET'S GET BACK TO BUSINESS.. I OUGHT TO HAVE SOMETHING IN ADVANCE.. WHAT CAN YOU GIVE ME NOW?
© 1934, King Features Syndicate, Inc., Great Britain rights reserved
THIS!
ALEX RAYMOND
4·30

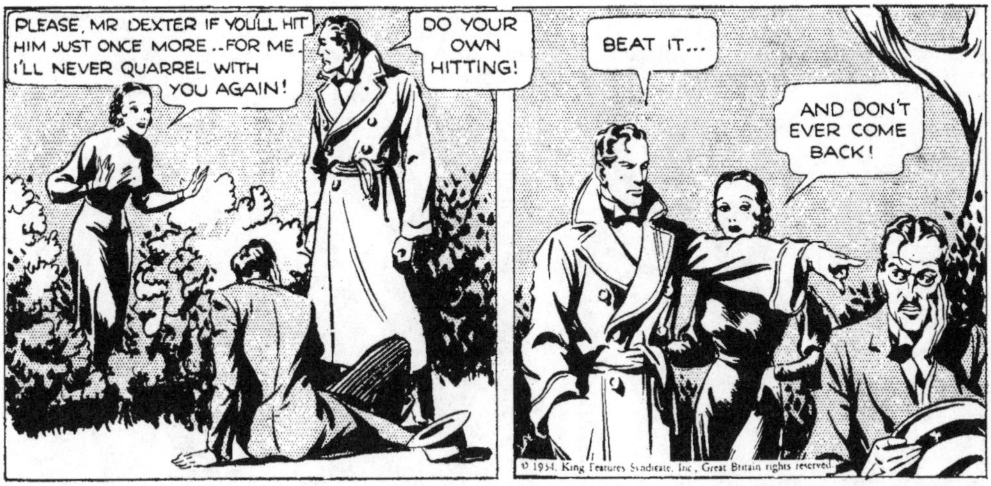
PLEASE, MR DEXTER IF YOU'LL HIT HIM JUST ONCE MORE .. FOR ME. I'LL NEVER QUARREL WITH YOU AGAIN!
DO YOUR OWN HITTING!
BEAT IT...
AND DON'T EVER COME BACK!
© 1934, King Features Syndicate, Inc., Great Britain rights reserved

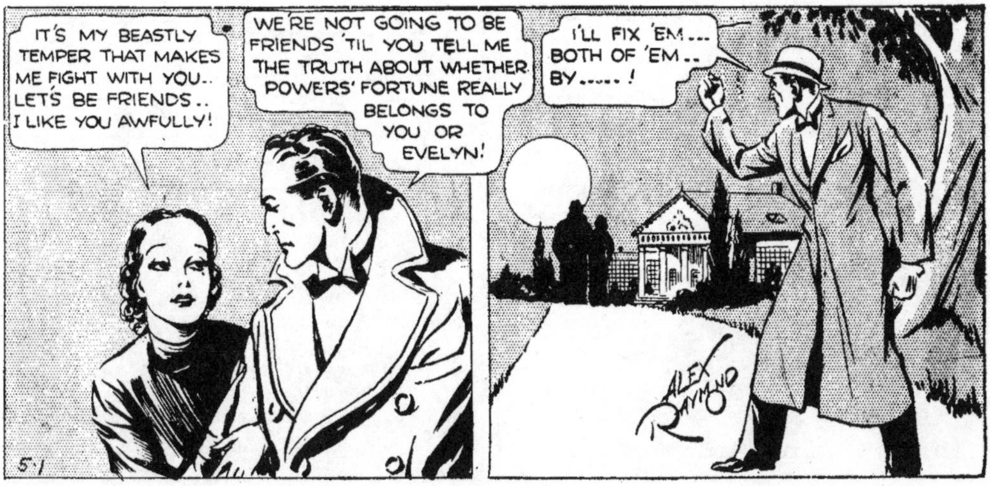
IT'S MY BEASTLY TEMPER THAT MAKES ME FIGHT WITH YOU.. LET'S BE FRIENDS.. I LIKE YOU AWFULLY!
WE'RE NOT GOING TO BE FRIENDS 'TIL YOU TELL ME THE TRUTH ABOUT WHETHER POWERS' FORTUNE REALLY BELONGS TO YOU OR EVELYN!
5·1
I'LL FIX 'EM... BOTH OF 'EM.. BY.....!
ALEX RAYMOND

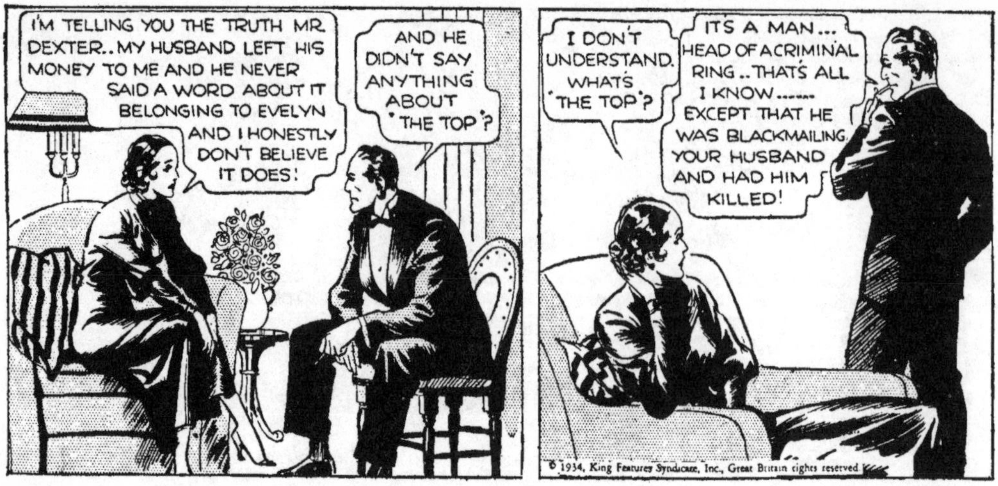
I'M TELLING YOU THE TRUTH MR. DEXTER.. MY HUSBAND LEFT HIS MONEY TO ME AND HE NEVER SAID A WORD ABOUT IT BELONGING TO EVELYN AND I HONESTLY DON'T BELIEVE IT DOES!
AND HE DIDN'T SAY ANYTHING ABOUT "THE TOP"?
I DON'T UNDERSTAND. WHAT'S "THE TOP"?
IT'S A MAN... HEAD OF A CRIMINAL RING.. THAT'S ALL I KNOW...... EXCEPT THAT HE WAS BLACKMAILING YOUR HUSBAND AND HAD HIM KILLED!
© 1934, King Features Syndicate, Inc., Great Britain rights reserved

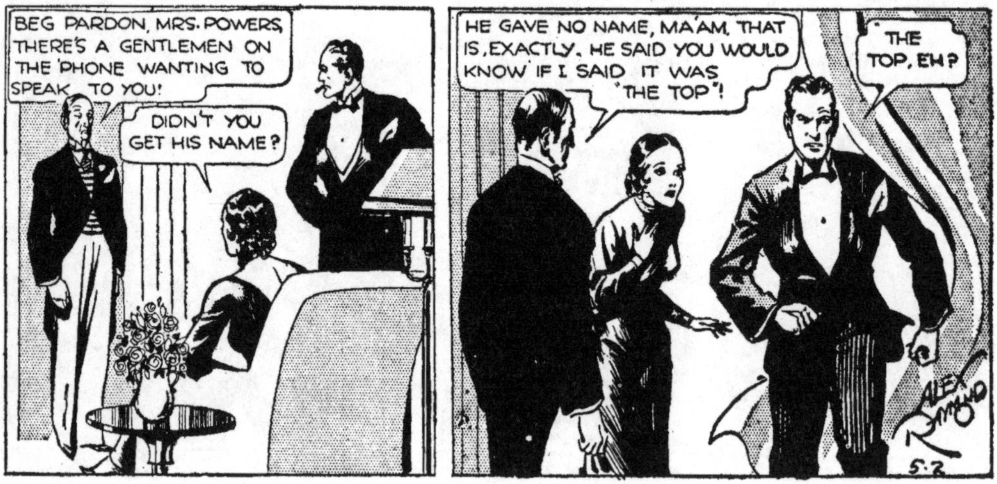
BEG PARDON, MRS. POWERS, THERE'S A GENTLEMEN ON THE PHONE WANTING TO SPEAK TO YOU!
DIDN'T YOU GET HIS NAME?
HE GAVE NO NAME, MA'AM, THAT IS, EXACTLY. HE SAID YOU WOULD KNOW IF I SAID IT WAS "THE TOP"!
"THE TOP, EH?
ALEX RAYMOND
5-2

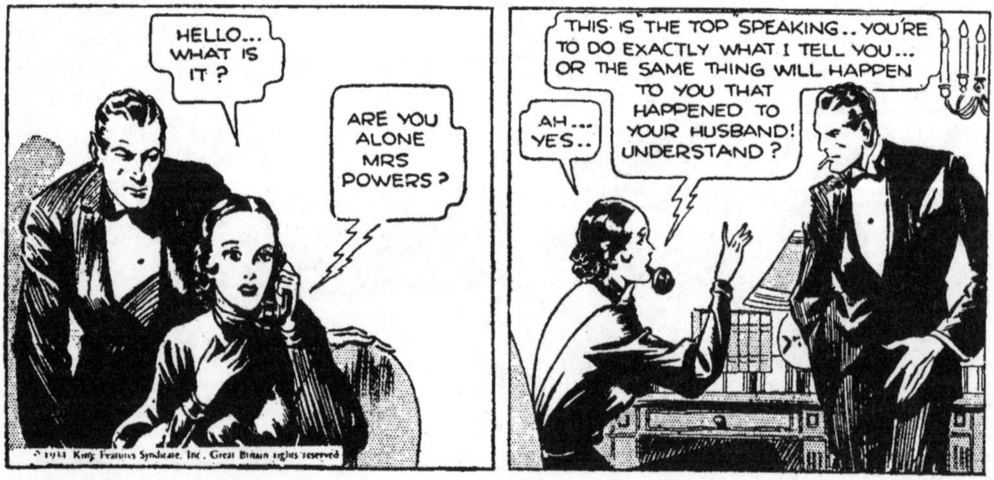
HELLO... WHAT IS IT?
ARE YOU ALONE MRS POWERS?
© 1934 King Features Syndicate, Inc., Great Britain rights reserved
THIS IS "THE TOP" SPEAKING.. YOU'RE TO DO EXACTLY WHAT I TELL YOU... OR THE SAME THING WILL HAPPEN TO YOU THAT HAPPENED TO YOUR HUSBAND! UNDERSTAND?
AH... YES..

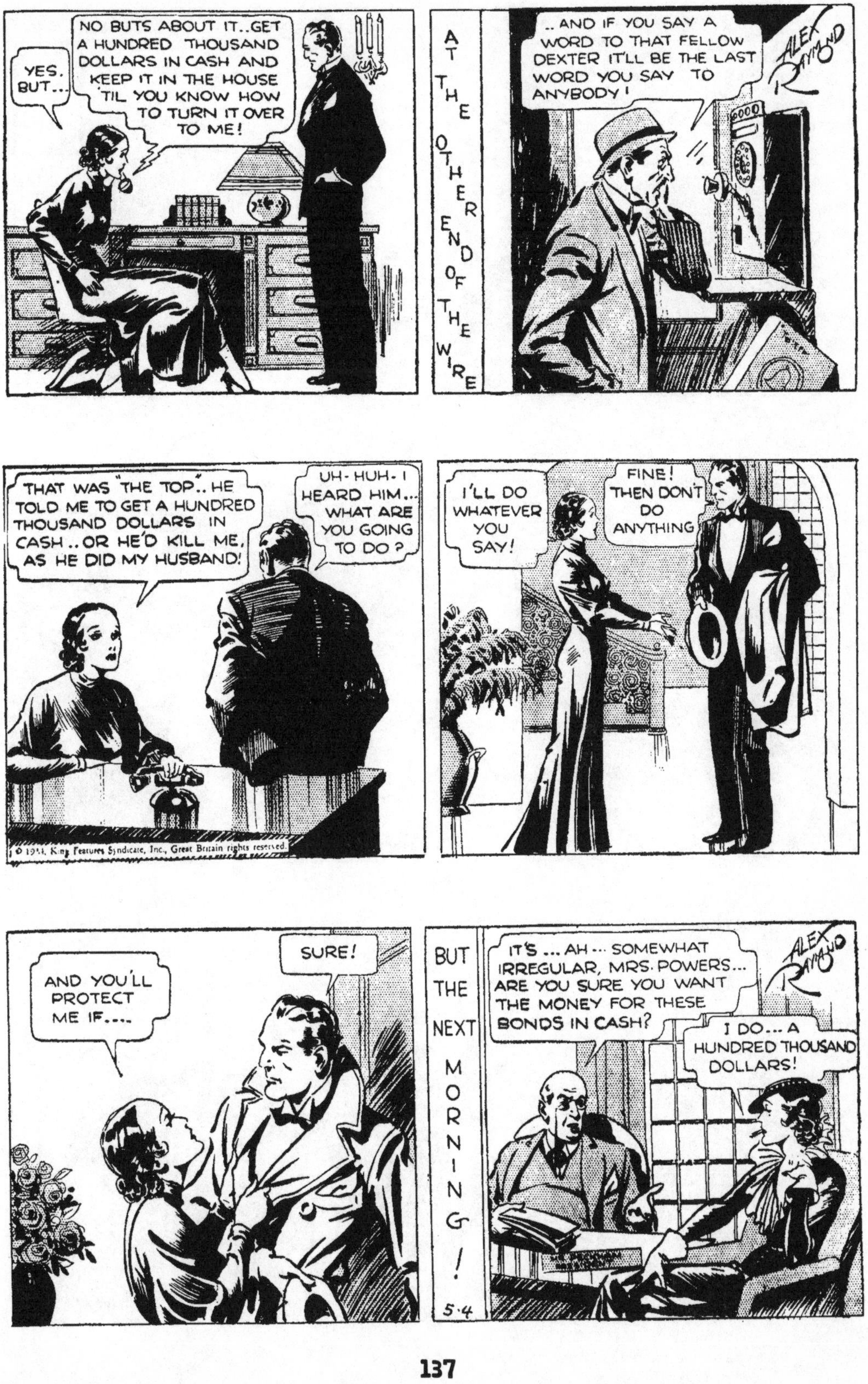
YES. BUT...
NO BUTS ABOUT IT..GET A HUNDRED THOUSAND DOLLARS IN CASH AND KEEP IT IN THE HOUSE 'TIL YOU KNOW HOW TO TURN IT OVER TO ME!
AT THE OTHER END OF THE WIRE
..AND IF YOU SAY A WORD TO THAT FELLOW DEXTER IT'LL BE THE LAST WORD YOU SAY TO ANYBODY!
ALEX RAYMOND
THAT WAS "THE TOP".. HE TOLD ME TO GET A HUNDRED THOUSAND DOLLARS IN CASH..OR HE'D KILL ME, AS HE DID MY HUSBAND!
UH-HUH-I HEARD HIM... WHAT ARE YOU GOING TO DO?
© 1934, King Features Syndicate, Inc., Great Britain rights reserved.
I'LL DO WHATEVER YOU SAY!
FINE! THEN DON'T DO ANYTHING
AND YOU'LL PROTECT ME IF....
SURE!
BUT THE NEXT MORNING!
IT'S ... AH --- SOMEWHAT IRREGULAR, MRS. POWERS... ARE YOU SURE YOU WANT THE MONEY FOR THESE BONDS IN CASH?
ALEX RAYMOND
I DO... A HUNDRED THOUSAND DOLLARS!
5·4

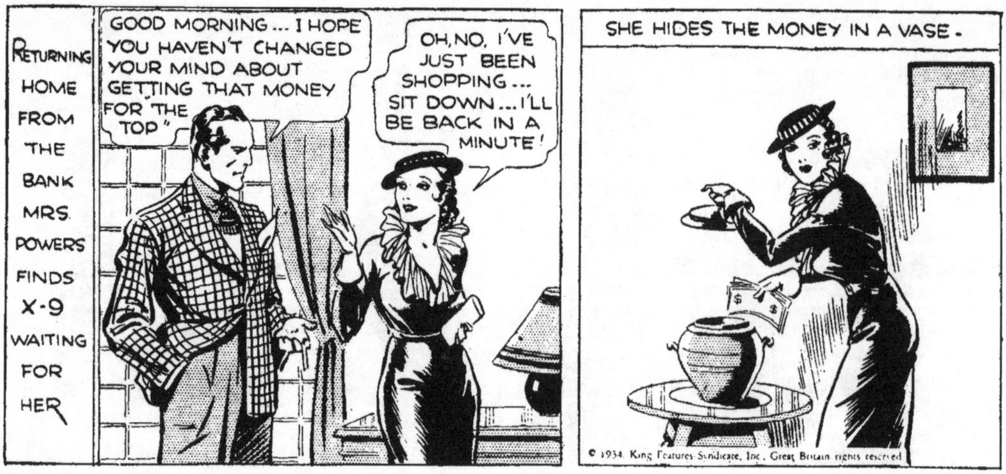
RETURNING HOME FROM THE BANK MRS. POWERS FINDS X-9 WAITING FOR HER
GOOD MORNING... I HOPE YOU HAVEN'T CHANGED YOUR MIND ABOUT GETTING THAT MONEY FOR "THE TOP"
OH, NO, I'VE JUST BEEN SHOPPING... SIT DOWN... I'LL BE BACK IN A MINUTE!
SHE HIDES THE MONEY IN A VASE.
© 1934, King Features Syndicate, Inc., Great Britain rights reserved

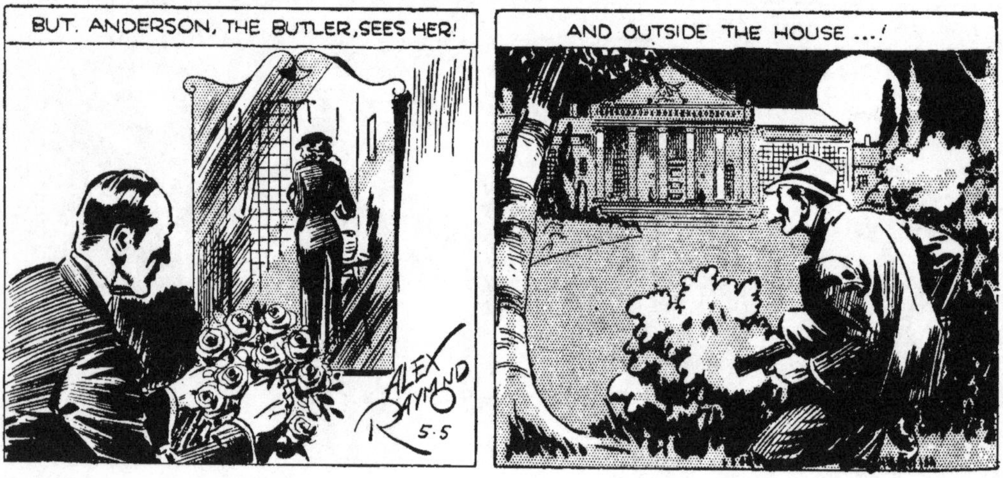
BUT. ANDERSON, THE BUTLER, SEES HER!
ALEX RAYMOND 5-5
AND OUTSIDE THE HOUSE ...!

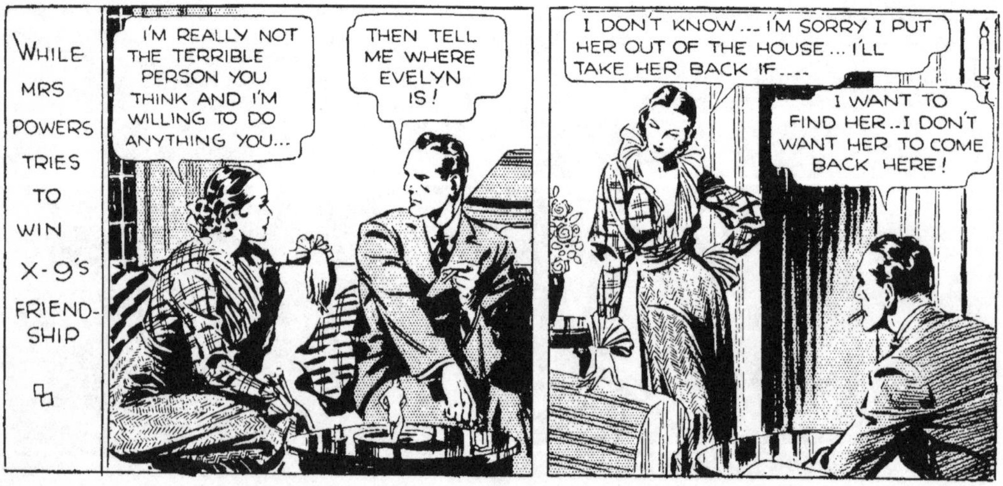
WHILE MRS POWERS TRIES TO WIN X-9'S FRIENDSHIP
I'M REALLY NOT THE TERRIBLE PERSON YOU THINK AND I'M WILLING TO DO ANYTHING YOU...
THEN TELL ME WHERE EVELYN IS!
I DON'T KNOW... I'M SORRY I PUT HER OUT OF THE HOUSE... I'LL TAKE HER BACK IF....
I WANT TO FIND HER.. I DON'T WANT HER TO COME BACK HERE!

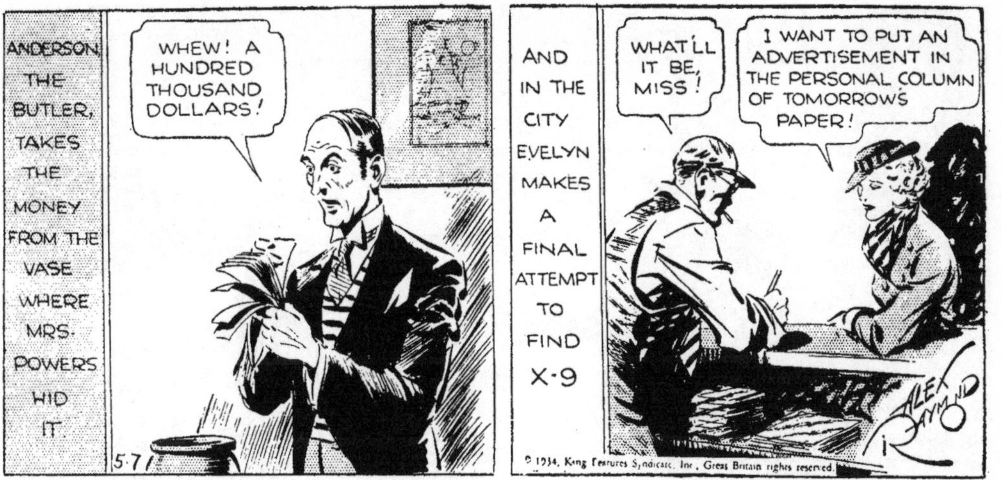

ANDERSON, THE BUTLER, TAKES THE MONEY FROM THE VASE WHERE MRS. POWERS HID IT
WHEW! A HUNDRED THOUSAND DOLLARS!
5·7
AND IN THE CITY EVELYN MAKES A FINAL ATTEMPT TO FIND X-9
WHAT'LL IT BE, MISS!
I WANT TO PUT AN ADVERTISEMENT IN THE PERSONAL COLUMN OF TOMORROW'S PAPER!
ALEX RAYMOND
© 1934, King Features Syndicate, Inc., Great Britain rights reserved.

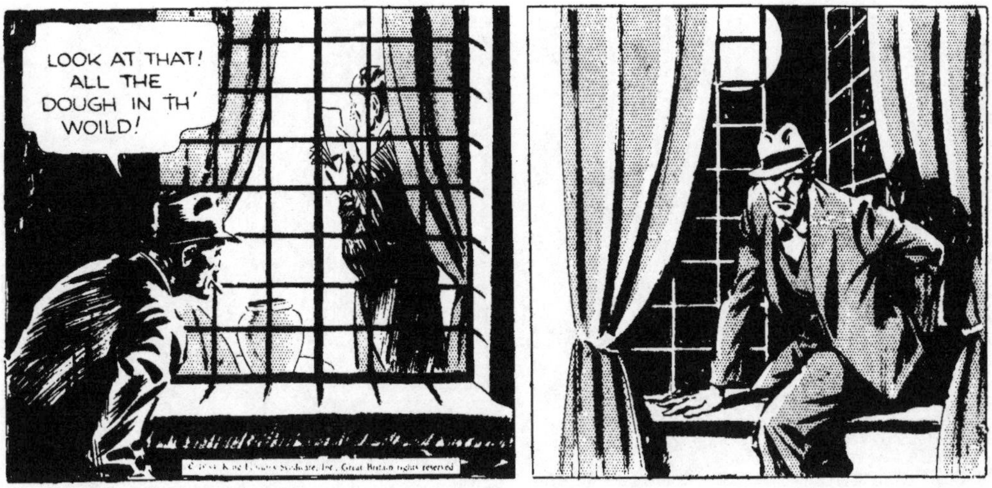

LOOK AT THAT! ALL THE DOUGH IN TH' WOILD!

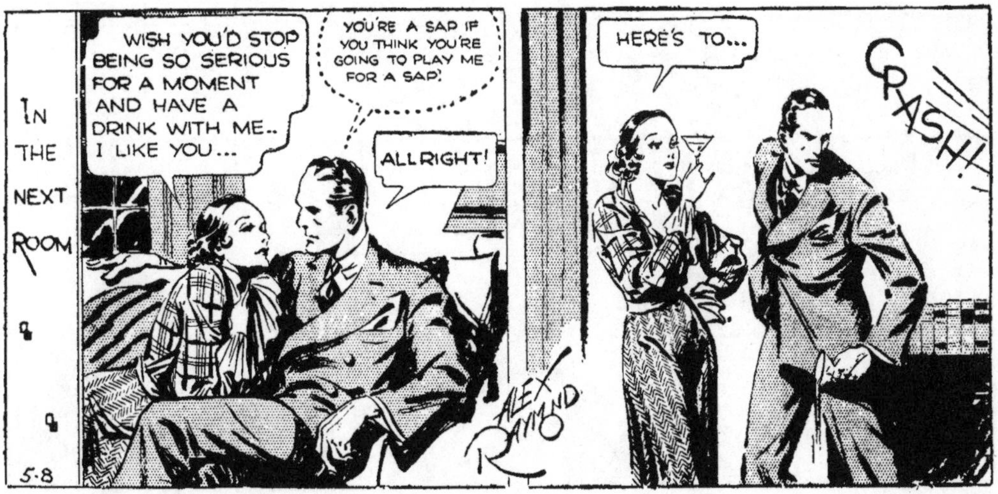

IN THE NEXT ROOM
WISH YOU'D STOP BEING SO SERIOUS FOR A MOMENT AND HAVE A DRINK WITH ME.. I LIKE YOU...
YOU'RE A SAP IF YOU THINK YOU'RE GOING TO PLAY ME FOR A SAP!
ALLRIGHT!
5·8
ALEX RAYMOND
HERE'S TO...
CRASH!!

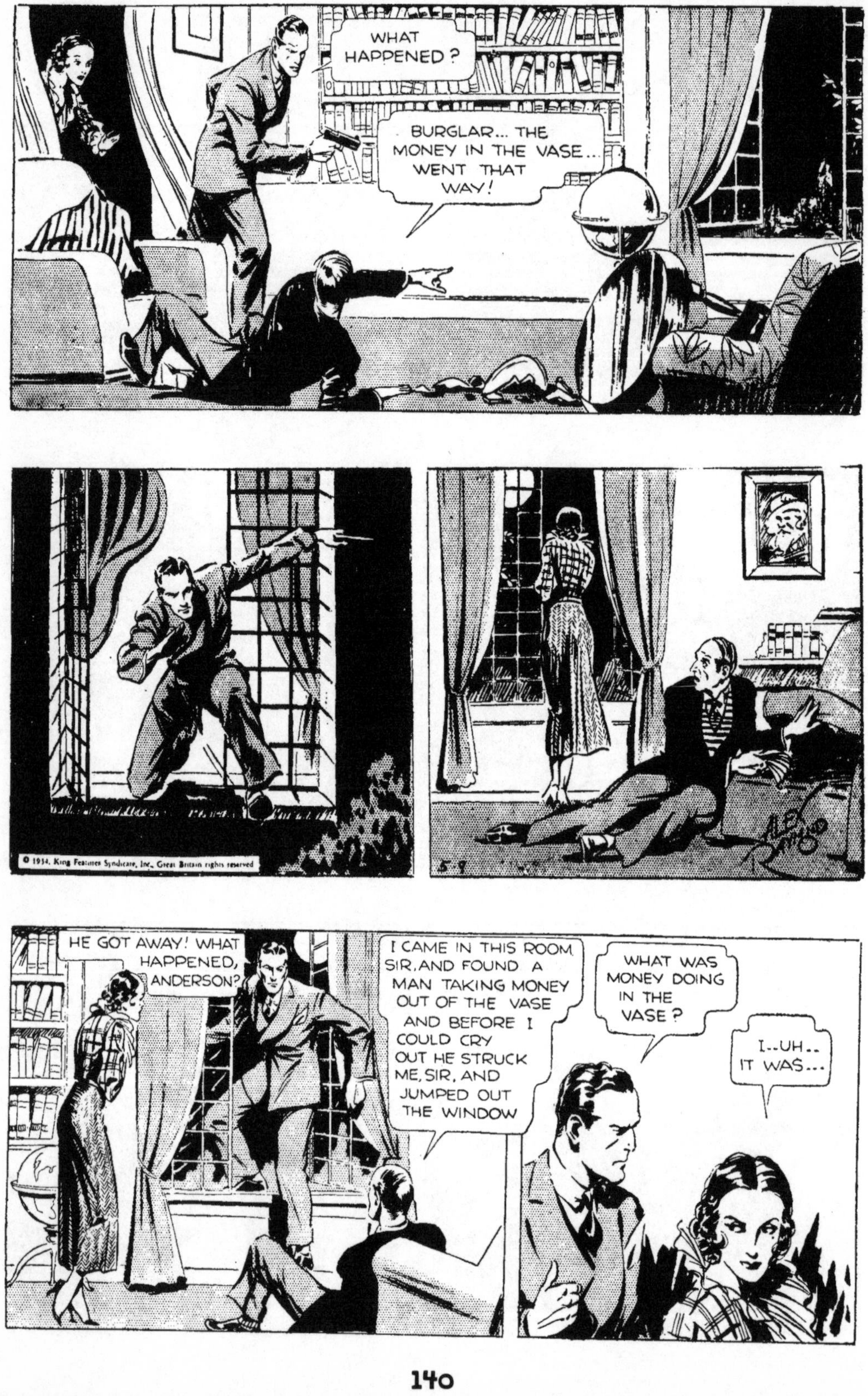
WHAT HAPPENED ?
BURGLAR... THE MONEY IN THE VASE... WENT THAT WAY!
© 1934, King Features Syndicate, Inc., Great Britain rights reserved
5-9
HE GOT AWAY! WHAT HAPPENED, ANDERSON?
I CAME IN THIS ROOM SIR, AND FOUND A MAN TAKING MONEY OUT OF THE VASE AND BEFORE I COULD CRY OUT HE STRUCK ME, SIR, AND JUMPED OUT THE WINDOW
WHAT WAS MONEY DOING IN THE VASE ?
I..UH.. IT WAS...

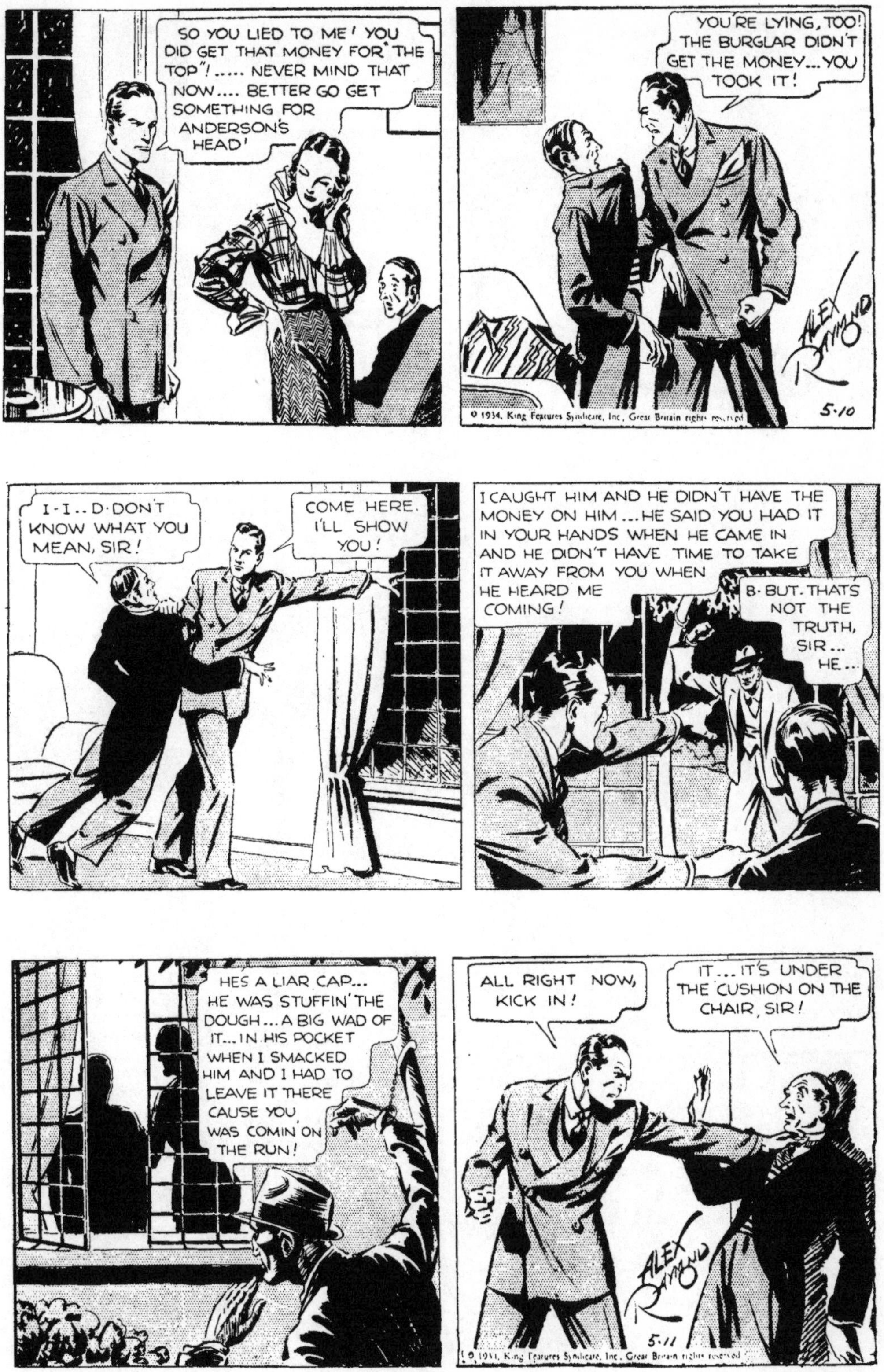
SO YOU LIED TO ME! YOU DID GET THAT MONEY FOR "THE TOP"!..... NEVER MIND THAT NOW.... BETTER GO GET SOMETHING FOR ANDERSON'S HEAD!
YOU'RE LYING, TOO! THE BURGLAR DIDN'T GET THE MONEY... YOU TOOK IT!
ALEX RAYMOND
© 1934, King Features Syndicate, Inc., Great Britain rights reserved
5-10
I-I.. D-DON'T KNOW WHAT YOU MEAN, SIR!
COME HERE. I'LL SHOW YOU!
I CAUGHT HIM AND HE DIDN'T HAVE THE MONEY ON HIM... HE SAID YOU HAD IT IN YOUR HANDS WHEN HE CAME IN AND HE DIDN'T HAVE TIME TO TAKE IT AWAY FROM YOU WHEN HE HEARD ME COMING!
B-BUT-THAT'S NOT THE TRUTH, SIR... HE...
HES A LIAR CAP... HE WAS STUFFIN' THE DOUGH... A BIG WAD OF IT... IN HIS POCKET WHEN I SMACKED HIM AND I HAD TO LEAVE IT THERE CAUSE YOU WAS COMIN' ON THE RUN!
ALL RIGHT NOW, KICK IN!
IT... IT'S UNDER THE CUSHION ON THE CHAIR, SIR!
ALEX RAYMOND
5-11
© 1934, King Features Syndicate, Inc., Great Britain rights reserved

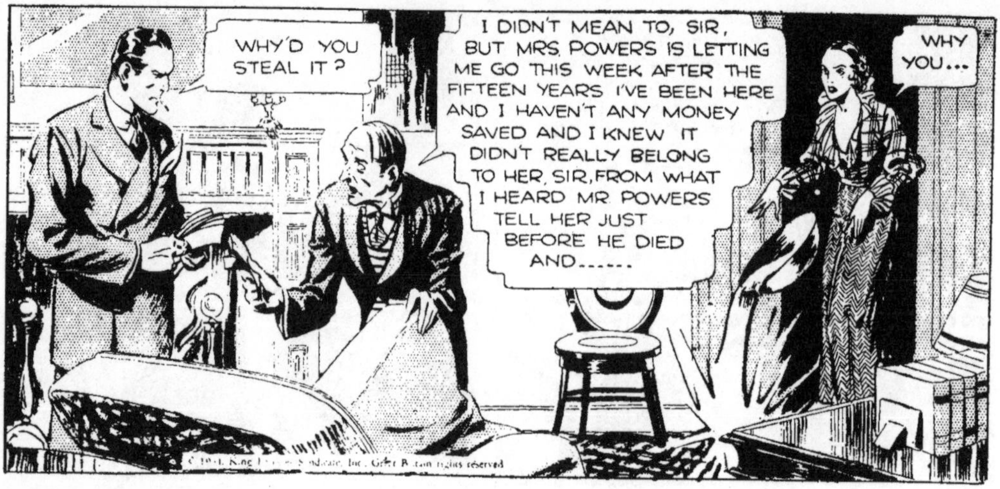
WHY'D YOU STEAL IT ?
I DIDN'T MEAN TO, SIR, BUT MRS. POWERS IS LETTING ME GO THIS WEEK AFTER THE FIFTEEN YEARS I'VE BEEN HERE AND I HAVEN'T ANY MONEY SAVED AND I KNEW IT DIDN'T REALLY BELONG TO HER, SIR, FROM WHAT I HEARD MR. POWERS TELL HER JUST BEFORE HE DIED AND......
WHY YOU...

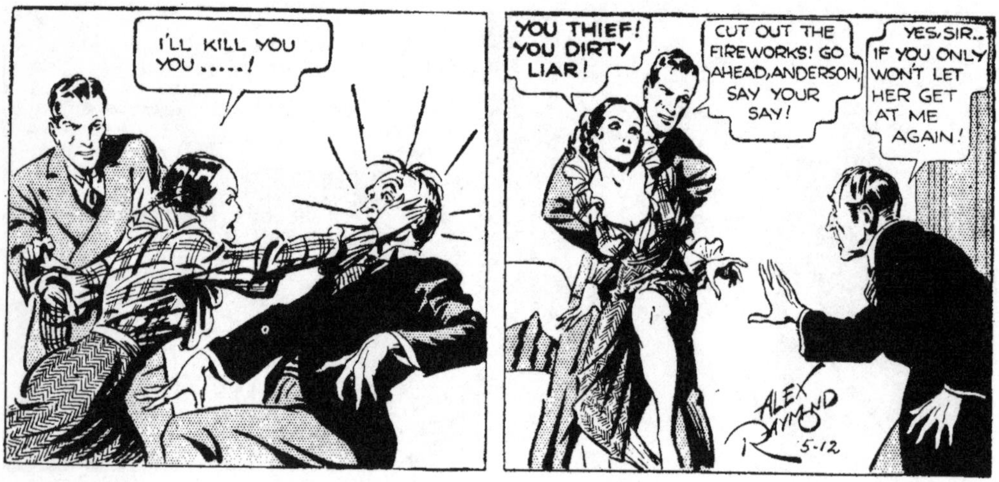
I'LL KILL YOU YOU.....!
YOU THIEF! YOU DIRTY LIAR!
CUT OUT THE FIREWORKS! GO AHEAD, ANDERSON, SAY YOUR SAY!
YES, SIR.. IF YOU ONLY WON'T LET HER GET AT ME AGAIN!
ALEX RAYMOND
5-12

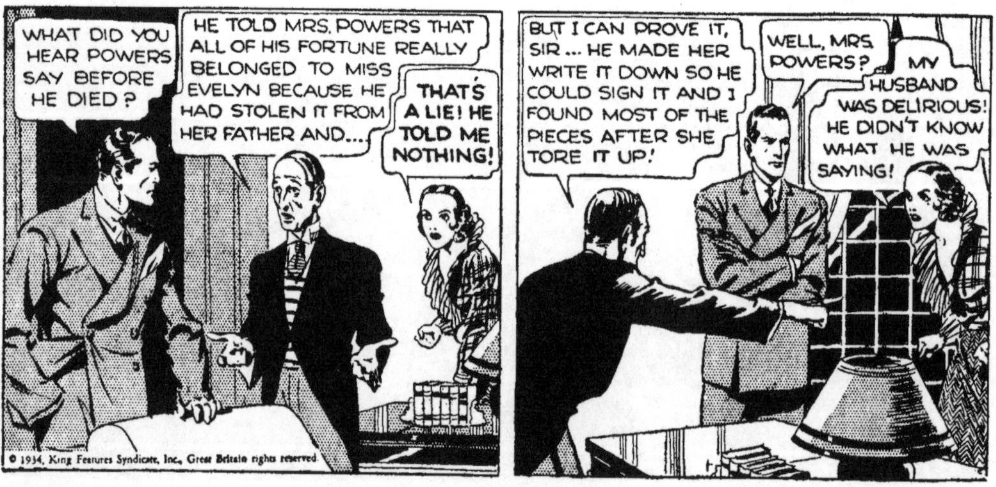
WHAT DID YOU HEAR POWERS SAY BEFORE HE DIED ?
HE TOLD MRS. POWERS THAT ALL OF HIS FORTUNE REALLY BELONGED TO MISS EVELYN BECAUSE HE HAD STOLEN IT FROM HER FATHER AND...
THAT'S A LIE! HE TOLD ME NOTHING!
BUT I CAN PROVE IT, SIR ... HE MADE HER WRITE IT DOWN SO HE COULD SIGN IT AND I FOUND MOST OF THE PIECES AFTER SHE TORE IT UP!
WELL, MRS. POWERS ?
MY HUSBAND WAS DELIRIOUS! HE DIDN'T KNOW WHAT HE WAS SAYING!
© 1934, King Features Syndicate, Inc., Great Britain rights reserved.

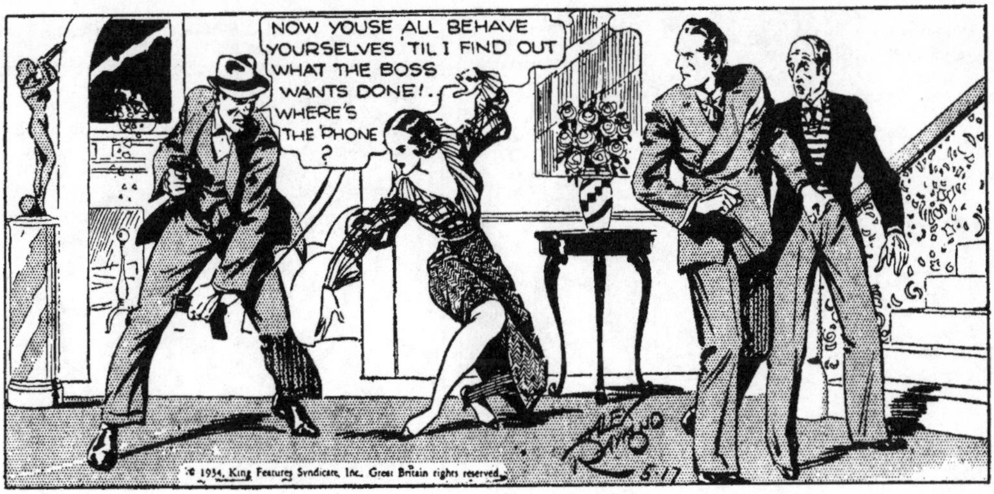
NOW YOUSE ALL BEHAVE YOURSELVES 'TIL I FIND OUT WHAT THE BOSS WANTS DONE!.. WHERE'S THE PHONE ?
© 1934, King Features Syndicate, Inc., Great Britain rights reserved.

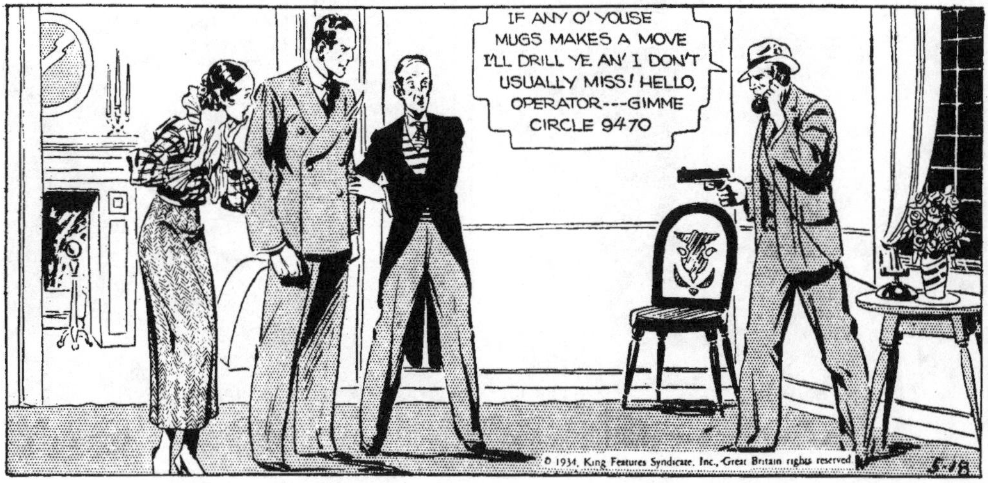
IF ANY O' YOUSE MUGS MAKES A MOVE I'LL DRILL YE AN' I DON'T USUALLY MISS! HELLO, OPERATOR---GIMME CIRCLE 9470
© 1934, King Features Syndicate, Inc., Great Britain rights reserved

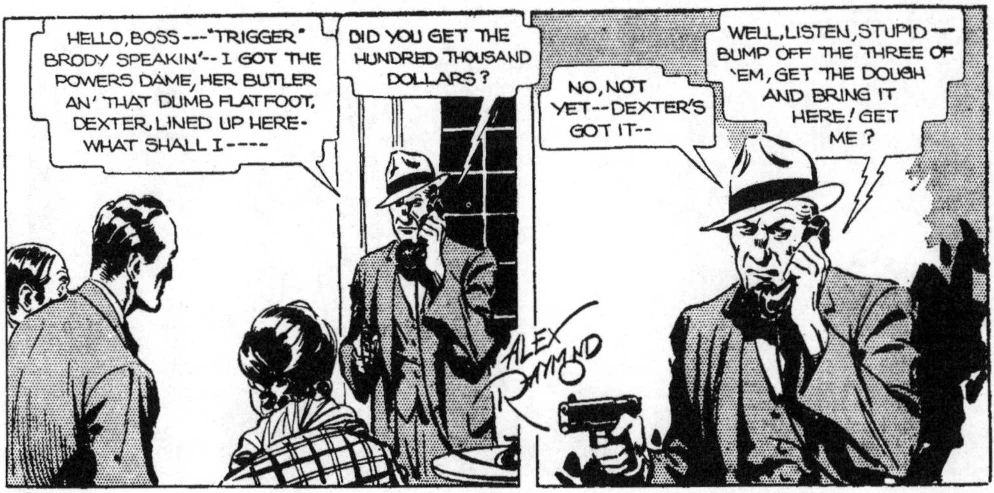
HELLO, BOSS---"TRIGGER" BRODY SPEAKIN'-- I GOT THE POWERS DAME, HER BUTLER AN' THAT DUMB FLATFOOT, DEXTER, LINED UP HERE- WHAT SHALL I ----
DID YOU GET THE HUNDRED THOUSAND DOLLARS ?
NO, NOT YET--DEXTER'S GOT IT--
WELL, LISTEN, STUPID -- BUMP OFF THE THREE OF 'EM, GET THE DOUGH AND BRING IT HERE! GET ME ?
ALEX RAYMOND

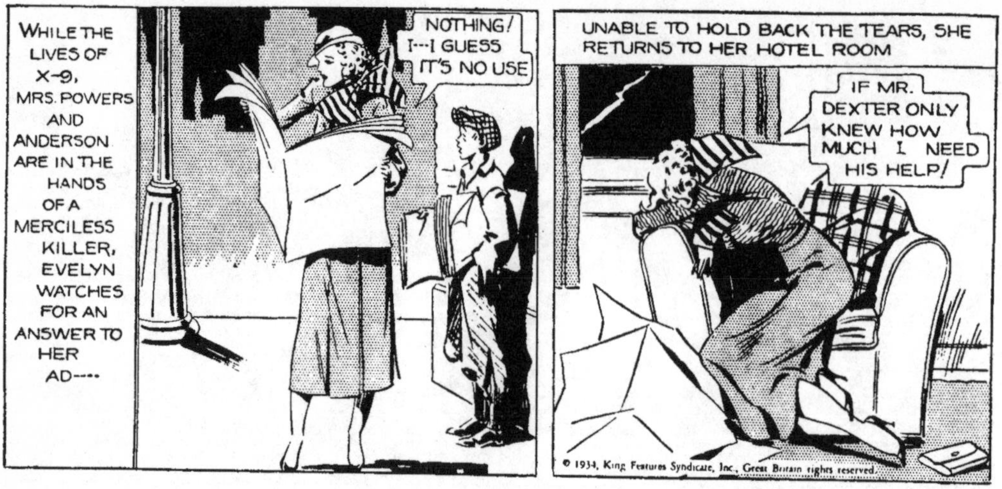
WHILE THE LIVES OF X-9, MRS. POWERS AND ANDERSON ARE IN THE HANDS OF A MERCILESS KILLER, EVELYN WATCHES FOR AN ANSWER TO HER AD----
NOTHING! I---I GUESS IT'S NO USE
UNABLE TO HOLD BACK THE TEARS, SHE RETURNS TO HER HOTEL ROOM
IF MR. DEXTER ONLY KNEW HOW MUCH I NEED HIS HELP!
© 1934, King Features Syndicate, Inc., Great Britain rights reserved.

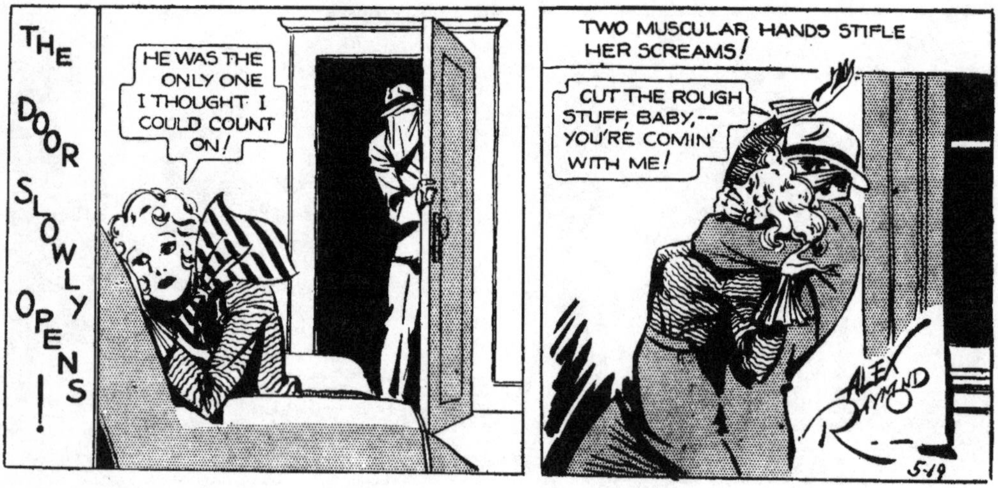
THE DOOR SLOWLY OPENS!
HE WAS THE ONLY ONE I THOUGHT I COULD COUNT ON!
TWO MUSCULAR HANDS STIFLE HER SCREAMS!
CUT THE ROUGH STUFF, BABY,-- YOU'RE COMIN' WITH ME!
ALEX RAYMOND
5-19

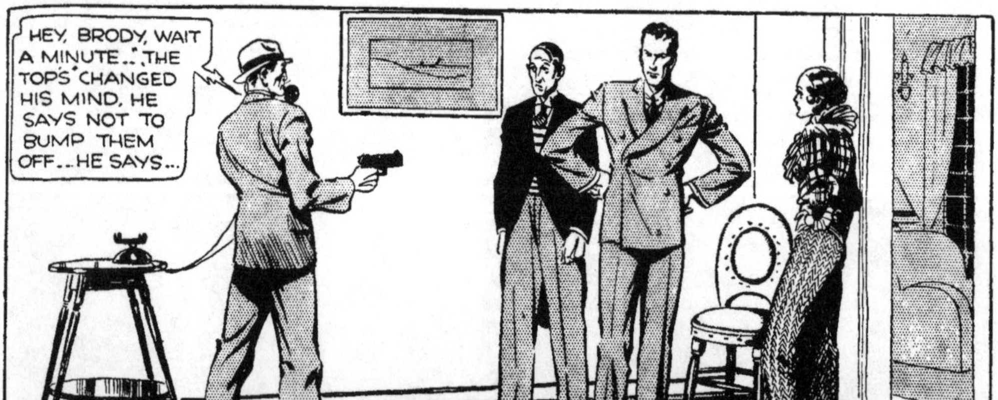
HEY, BRODY, WAIT A MINUTE..."THE TOP'S" CHANGED HIS MIND, HE SAYS NOT TO BUMP THEM OFF...HE SAYS...

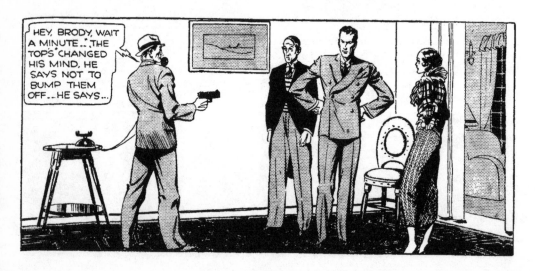

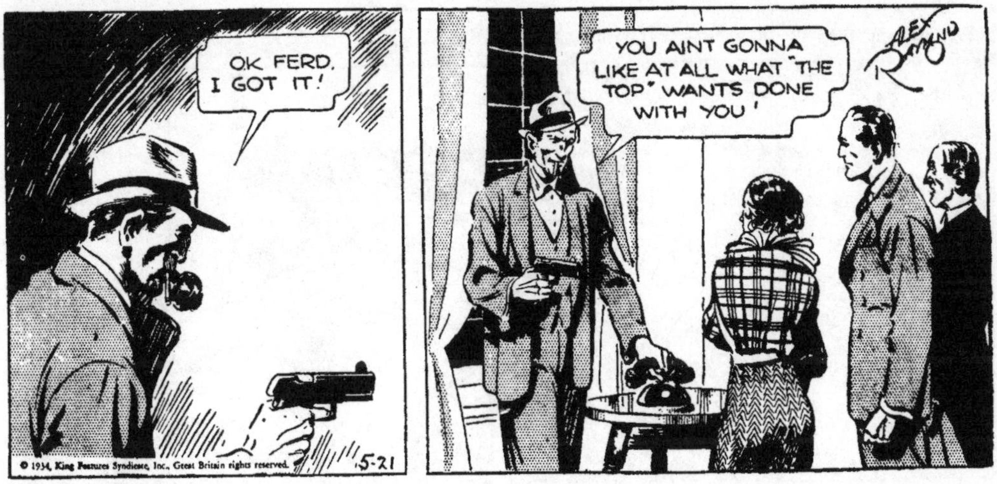
OK FERD, I GOT IT!
© 1934, King Features Syndicate, Inc., Great Britain rights reserved.
5-21
YOU AINT GONNA LIKE AT ALL WHAT "THE TOP" WANTS DONE WITH YOU!
ALEX RAYMOND

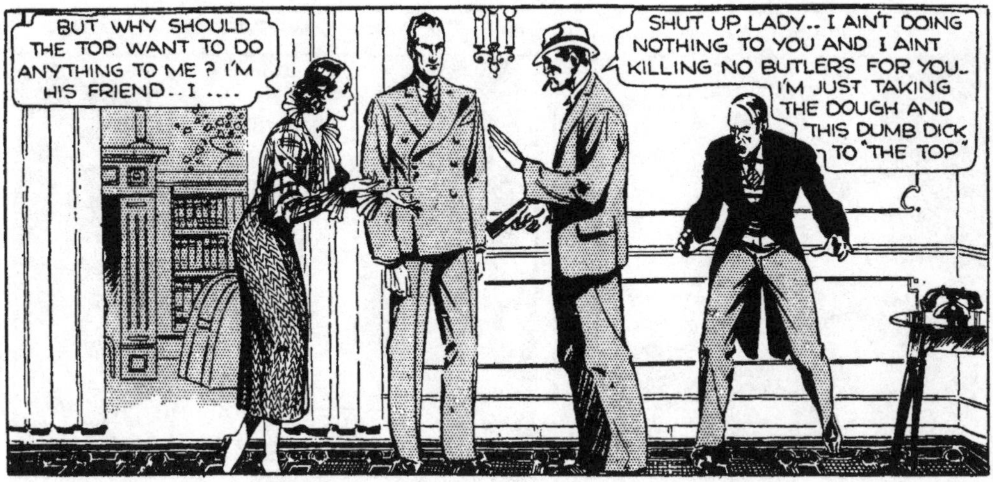
BUT WHY SHOULD THE TOP WANT TO DO ANYTHING TO ME? I'M HIS FRIEND.. I ....
SHUT UP, LADY.. I AIN'T DOING NOTHING TO YOU AND I AINT KILLING NO BUTLERS FOR YOU.. I'M JUST TAKING THE DOUGH AND THIS DUMB DICK TO "THE TOP"

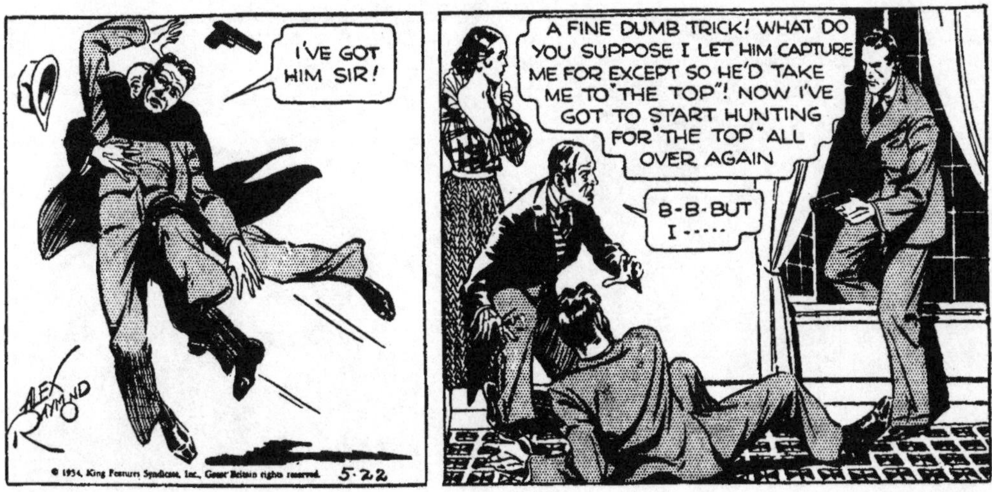
I'VE GOT HIM SIR!
ALEX RAYMOND
© 1934, King Features Syndicate, Inc., Great Britain rights reserved.
5-22
A FINE DUMB TRICK! WHAT DO YOU SUPPOSE I LET HIM CAPTURE ME FOR EXCEPT SO HE'D TAKE ME TO "THE TOP"! NOW I'VE GOT TO START HUNTING FOR "THE TOP" ALL OVER AGAIN
B-B-BUT I -----

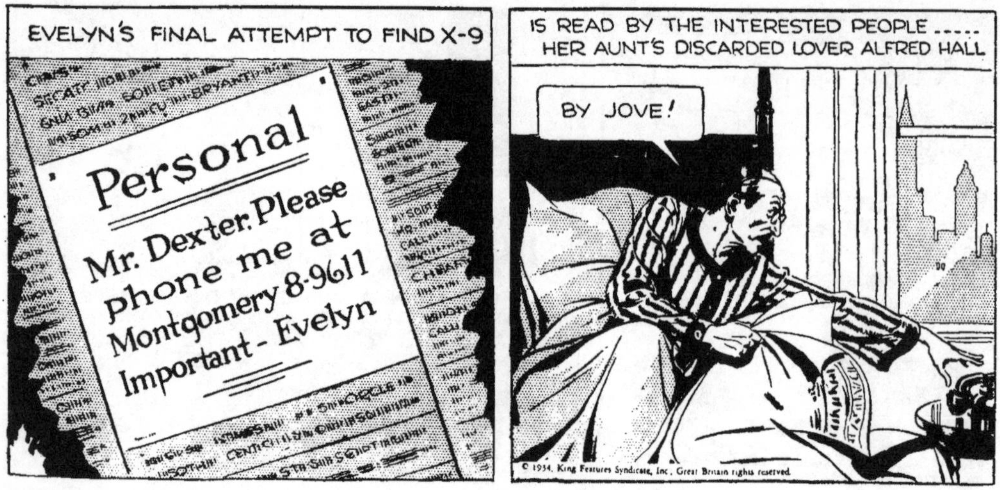
EVELYN'S FINAL ATTEMPT TO FIND X-9
Personal
Mr. Dexter, Please phone me at Montgomery 8-9611 Important - Evelyn
IS READ BY THE INTERESTED PEOPLE ----- HER AUNT'S DISCARDED LOVER ALFRED HALL
BY JOVE!
© 1934, King Features Syndicate, Inc., Great Britain rights reserved.

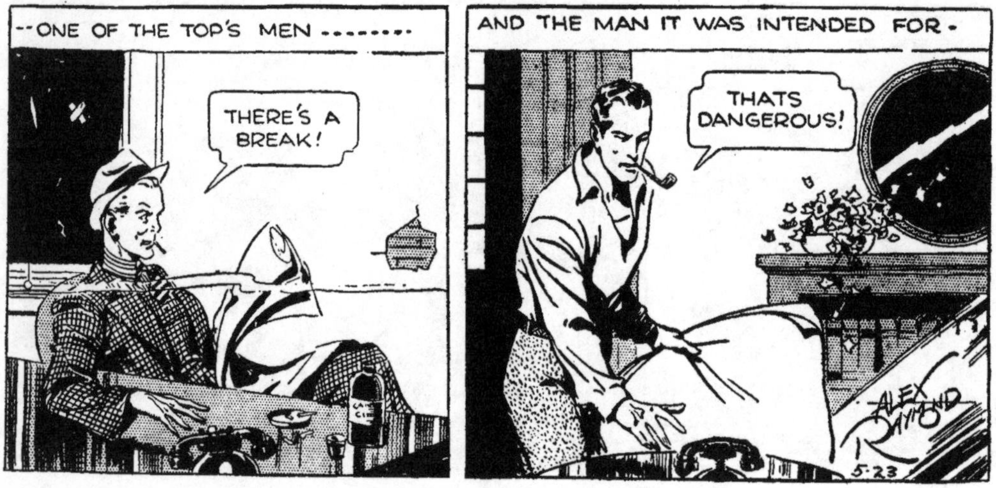
--ONE OF THE TOP'S MEN --------
THERE'S A BREAK!
AND THE MAN IT WAS INTENDED FOR -
THATS DANGEROUS!
ALEX RAYMOND
5-23

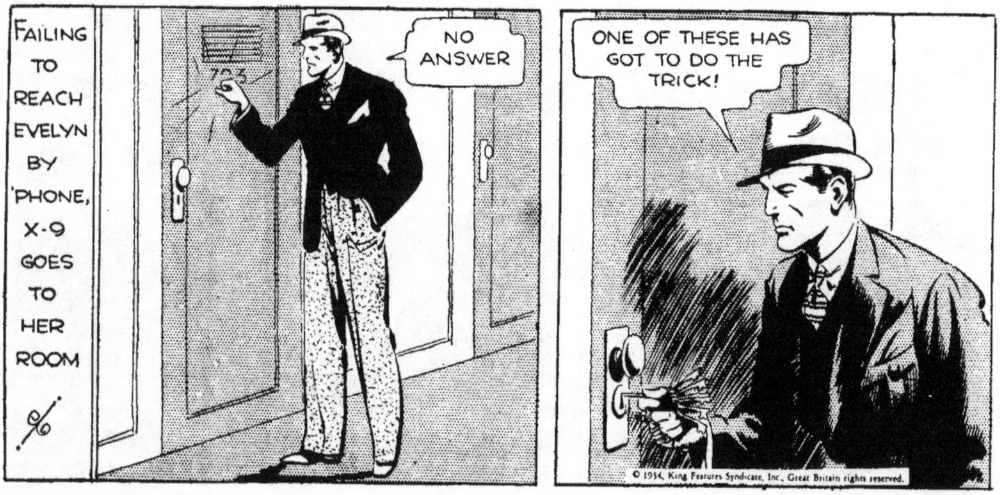
FAILING TO REACH EVELYN BY 'PHONE, X-9 GOES TO HER ROOM
NO ANSWER
ONE OF THESE HAS GOT TO DO THE TRICK!
© 1934, King Features Syndicate, Inc., Great Britain rights reserved.

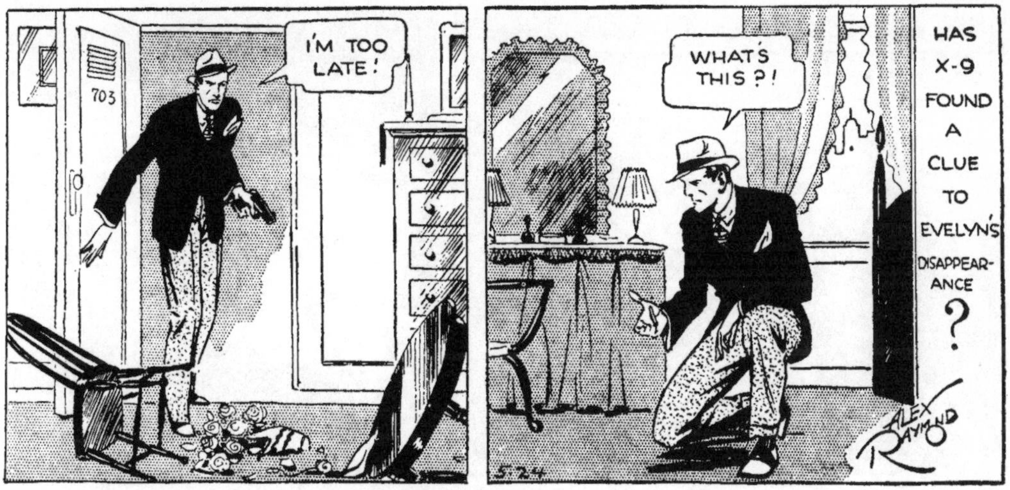
I'M TOO LATE!
WHAT'S THIS ?!
HAS X-9 FOUND A CLUE TO EVELYN'S DISAPPEAR-ANCE ?
ALEX RAYMOND
5-24

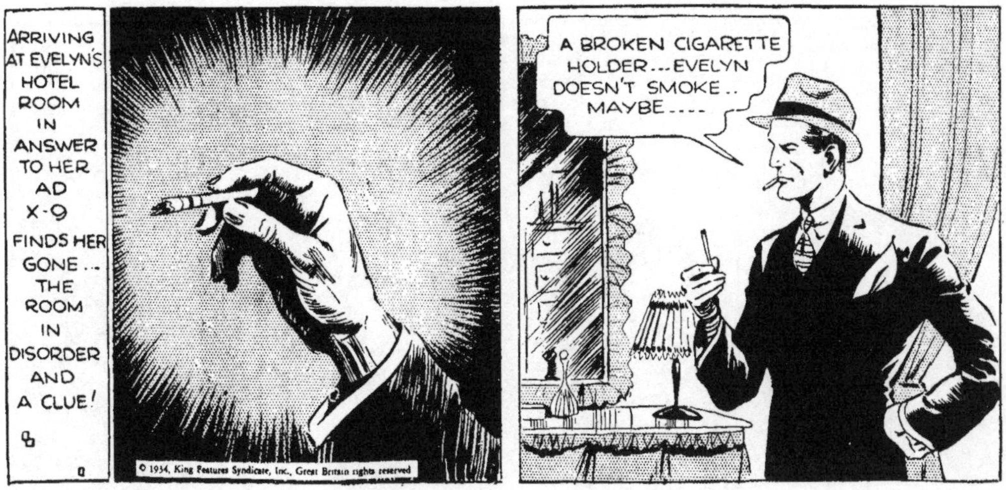
ARRIVING AT EVELYN'S HOTEL ROOM IN ANSWER TO HER AD X-9 FINDS HER GONE... THE ROOM IN DISORDER AND A CLUE!
© 1934, King Features Syndicate, Inc., Great Britain rights reserved
A BROKEN CIGARETTE HOLDER... EVELYN DOESN'T SMOKE.. MAYBE....

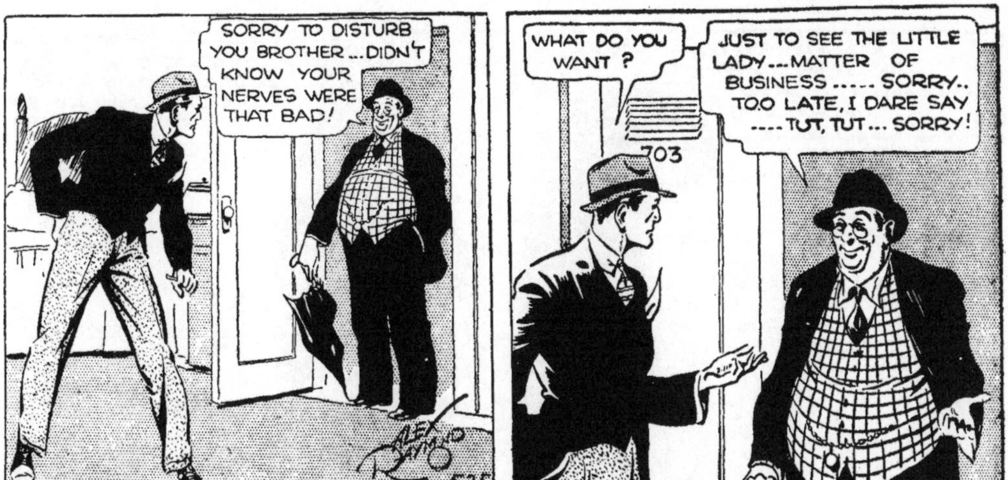
SORRY TO DISTURB YOU BROTHER... DIDN'T KNOW YOUR NERVES WERE THAT BAD!
ALEX RAYMOND
5-25
WHAT DO YOU WANT ?
JUST TO SEE THE LITTLE LADY... MATTER OF BUSINESS...... SORRY.. TO.O LATE, I DARE SAY ---- TUT, TUT... SORRY!
703

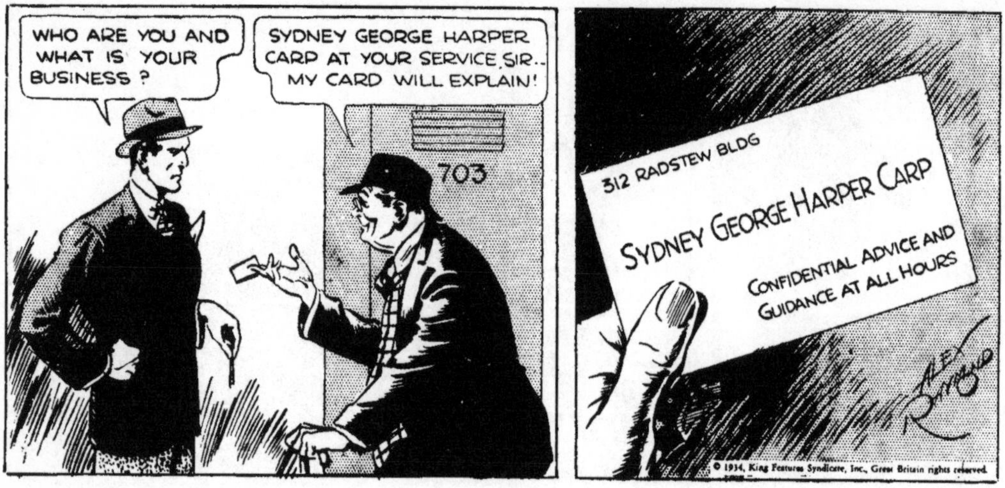
WHO ARE YOU AND WHAT IS YOUR BUSINESS ?
SYDNEY GEORGE HARPER CARP AT YOUR SERVICE, SIR.. MY CARD WILL EXPLAIN!
703
312 RADSTEW BLDG
SYDNEY GEORGE HARPER CARP
CONFIDENTIAL ADVICE AND GUIDANCE AT ALL HOURS
© 1934, King Features Syndicate, Inc., Great Britain rights reserved.

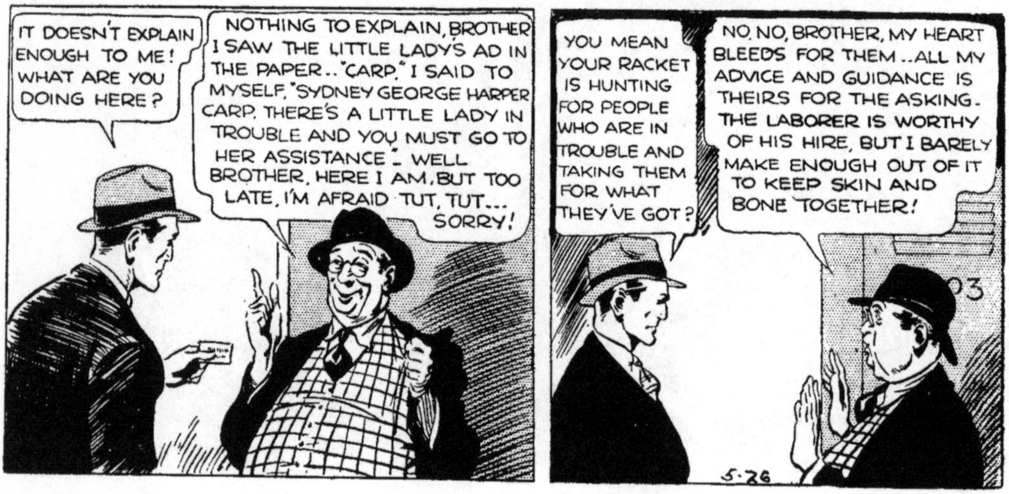
IT DOESN'T EXPLAIN ENOUGH TO ME! WHAT ARE YOU DOING HERE ?
NOTHING TO EXPLAIN, BROTHER I SAW THE LITTLE LADY'S AD IN THE PAPER.. "CARP," I SAID TO MYSELF, "SYDNEY GEORGE HARPER CARP, THERE'S A LITTLE LADY IN TROUBLE AND YOU MUST GO TO HER ASSISTANCE".. WELL BROTHER, HERE I AM, BUT TOO LATE, I'M AFRAID. TUT, TUT... SORRY!
YOU MEAN YOUR RACKET IS HUNTING FOR PEOPLE WHO ARE IN TROUBLE AND TAKING THEM FOR WHAT THEY'VE GOT ?
NO, NO, BROTHER, MY HEART BLEEDS FOR THEM .. ALL MY ADVICE AND GUIDANCE IS THEIRS FOR THE ASKING. THE LABORER IS WORTHY OF HIS HIRE, BUT I BARELY MAKE ENOUGH OUT OF IT TO KEEP SKIN AND BONE TOGETHER!
5-26

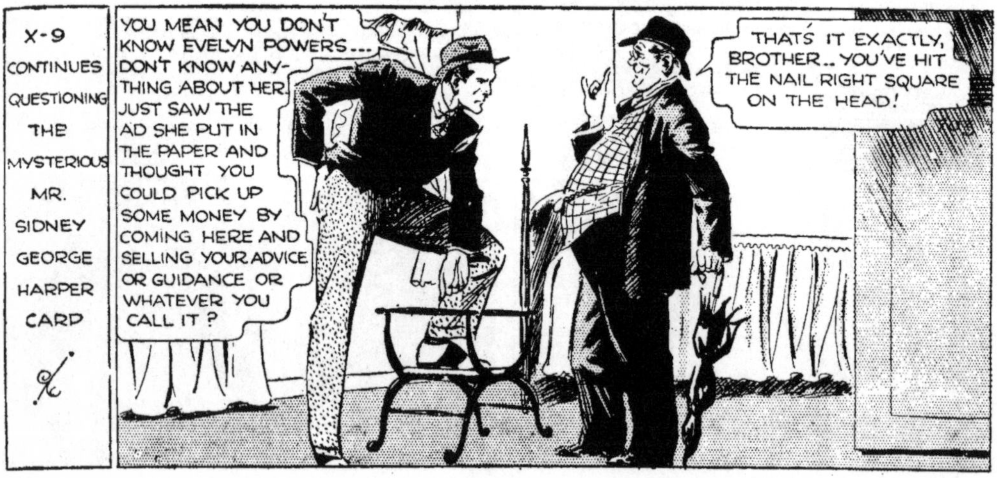
X-9 CONTINUES QUESTIONING THE MYSTERIOUS MR. SIDNEY GEORGE HARPER CARD
YOU MEAN YOU DON'T KNOW EVELYN POWERS... DON'T KNOW ANYTHING ABOUT HER. JUST SAW THE AD SHE PUT IN THE PAPER AND THOUGHT YOU COULD PICK UP SOME MONEY BY COMING HERE AND SELLING YOUR ADVICE OR GUIDANCE OR WHATEVER YOU CALL IT ?
THAT'S IT EXACTLY, BROTHER .. YOU'VE HIT THE NAIL RIGHT SQUARE ON THE HEAD!

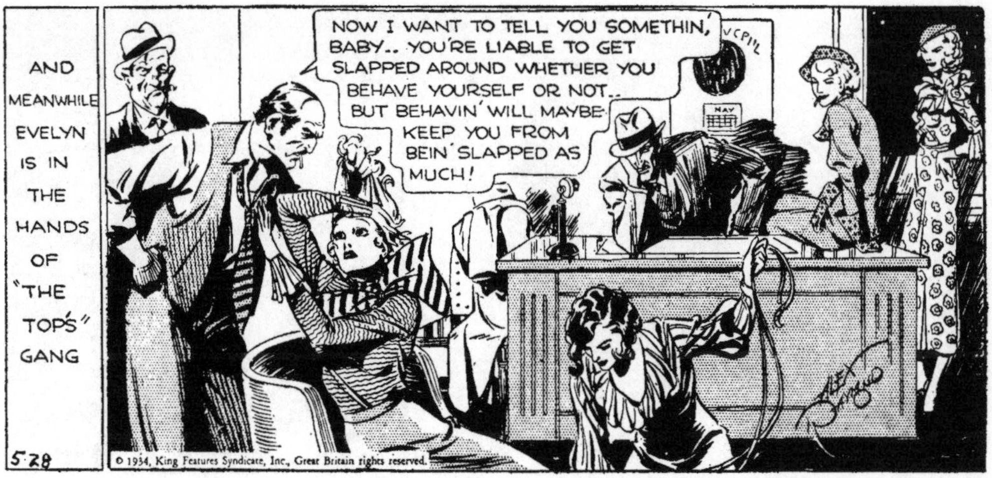
AND MEANWHILE EVELYN IS IN THE HANDS OF "THE TOPS'" GANG
5-28
NOW I WANT TO TELL YOU SOMETHIN', BABY.. YOU'RE LIABLE TO GET SLAPPED AROUND WHETHER YOU BEHAVE YOURSELF OR NOT.. BUT BEHAVIN' WILL MAYBE KEEP YOU FROM BEIN' SLAPPED AS MUCH!
MAY
© 1934, King Features Syndicate, Inc., Great Britain rights reserved.

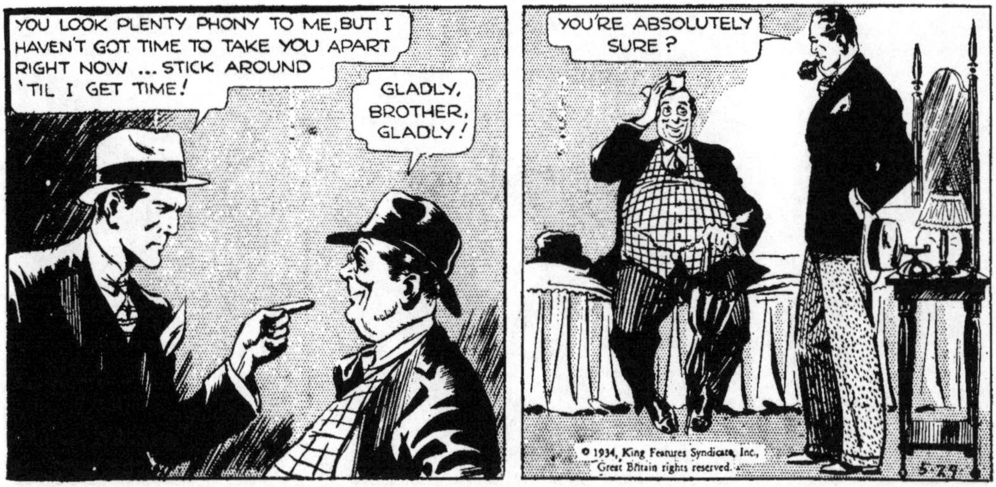
YOU LOOK PLENTY PHONY TO ME, BUT I HAVEN'T GOT TIME TO TAKE YOU APART RIGHT NOW ... STICK AROUND 'TIL I GET TIME!
GLADLY, BROTHER, GLADLY!
YOU'RE ABSOLUTELY SURE?
© 1934, King Features Syndicate, Inc., Great Britain rights reserved.
5-29

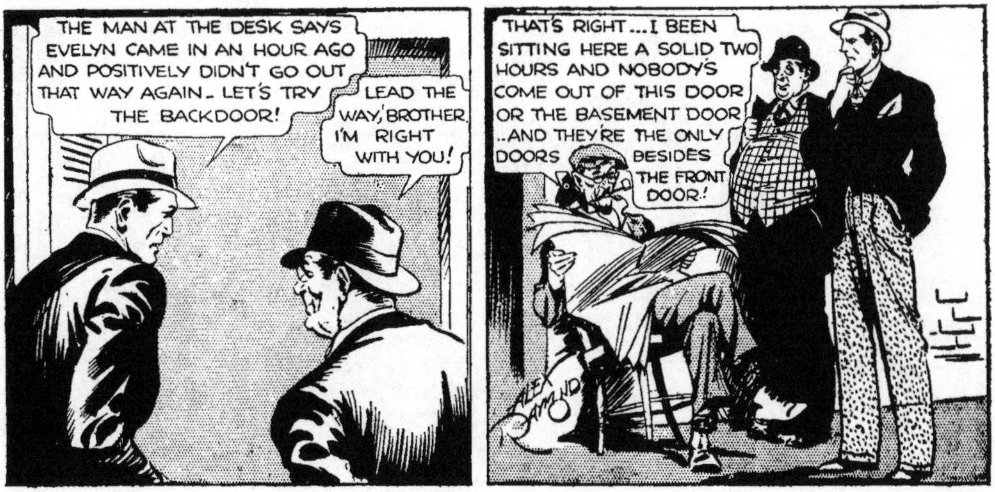
THE MAN AT THE DESK SAYS EVELYN CAME IN AN HOUR AGO AND POSITIVELY DIDN'T GO OUT THAT WAY AGAIN.. LET'S TRY THE BACKDOOR!
LEAD THE WAY, BROTHER, I'M RIGHT WITH YOU!
THAT'S RIGHT... I BEEN SITTING HERE A SOLID TWO HOURS AND NOBODY'S COME OUT OF THIS DOOR OR THE BASEMENT DOOR ..AND THEY'RE THE ONLY DOORS BESIDES THE FRONT DOOR!

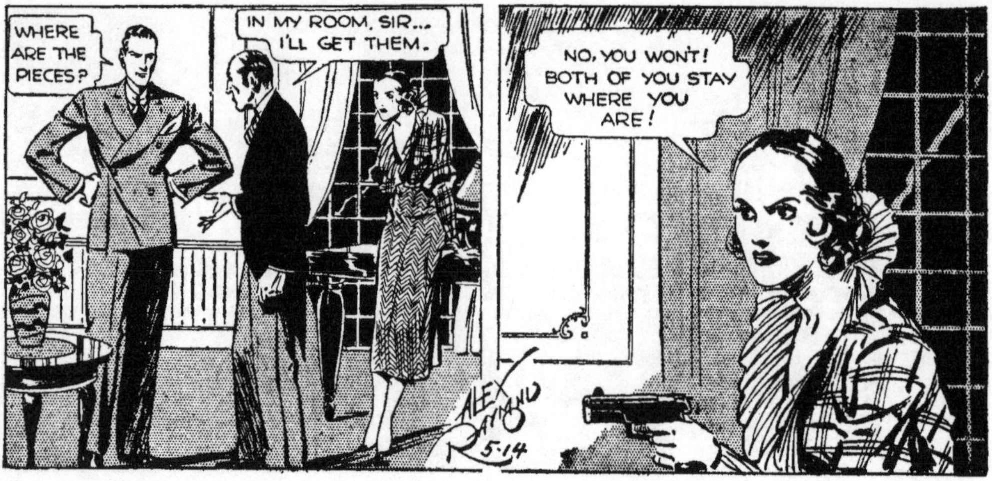
WHERE ARE THE PIECES?
IN MY ROOM, SIR... I'LL GET THEM.
NO, YOU WON'T! BOTH OF YOU STAY WHERE YOU ARE!
ALEX RAYMOND 5-14

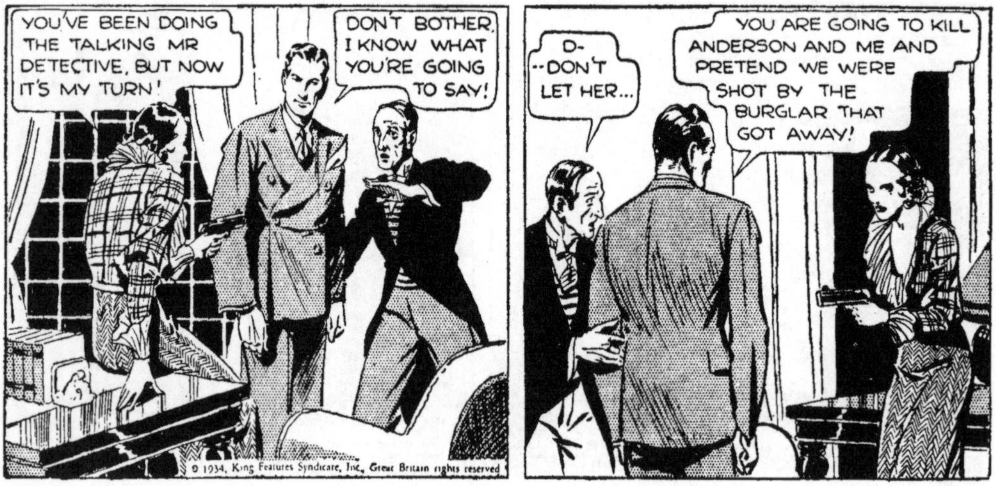
YOU'VE BEEN DOING THE TALKING MR DETECTIVE, BUT NOW IT'S MY TURN!
DON'T BOTHER, I KNOW WHAT YOU'RE GOING TO SAY!
© 1934, King Features Syndicate, Inc., Great Britain rights reserved
D- --DON'T LET HER...
YOU ARE GOING TO KILL ANDERSON AND ME AND PRETEND WE WERE SHOT BY THE BURGLAR THAT GOT AWAY!

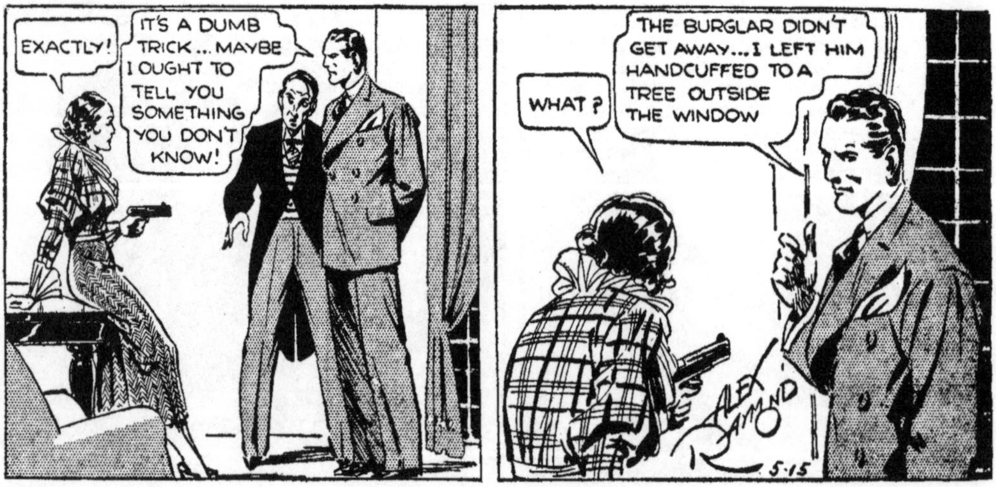
EXACTLY!
IT'S A DUMB TRICK... MAYBE I OUGHT TO TELL YOU SOMETHING YOU DON'T KNOW!
WHAT?
THE BURGLAR DIDN'T GET AWAY... I LEFT HIM HANDCUFFED TO A TREE OUTSIDE THE WINDOW
ALEX RAYMOND 5-15

MRS POWERS FORCES X-9 TO RELEASE HIS PRISONER %

AND MAKES THE PRISONER AN OFFER %

YOU CAN HAVE THE MONEY YOU TRIED TO STEAL IF YOU'LL KILL THESE TWO MEN!

FOR ALL THAT DOUGH? SURE, LADY!

NO, NO.. I BEG YOU.. PLEASE

ALEX RAYMOND 5-16

© 1934, King Features Syndicate Inc. Great Britain rights reserved

WHAT DO I KILL 'EM WITH?

HE'S PROBABLY GOT A GUN... GET IT!

WE BETTER KILL 'EM INDOORS... IT'LL LOOK BETTER —

YES!

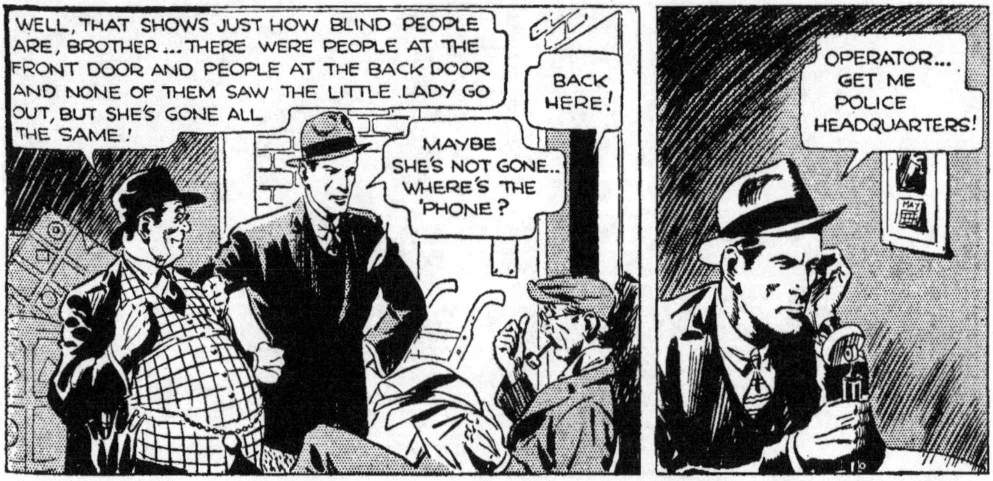
WELL, THAT SHOWS JUST HOW BLIND PEOPLE ARE, BROTHER ... THERE WERE PEOPLE AT THE FRONT DOOR AND PEOPLE AT THE BACK DOOR AND NONE OF THEM SAW THE LITTLE LADY GO OUT, BUT SHE'S GONE ALL THE SAME!
BACK HERE!
MAYBE SHE'S NOT GONE.. WHERE'S THE 'PHONE?
OPERATOR... GET ME POLICE HEADQUARTERS!

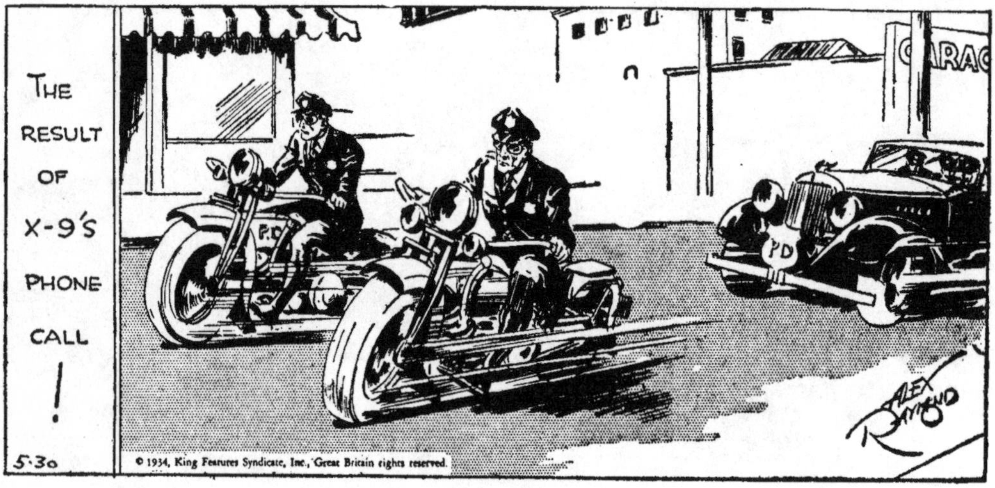
THE RESULT OF X-9'S PHONE CALL !
GARAG
P.D.
PD
ALEX RAYMOND
5·30
© 1934, King Features Syndicate, Inc., Great Britain rights reserved.

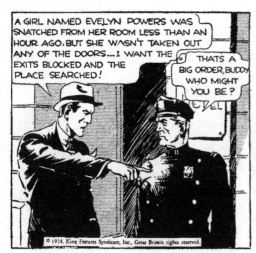

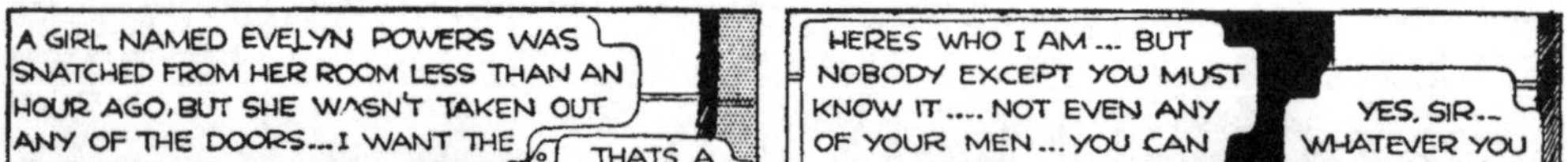
A GIRL NAMED EVELYN POWERS WAS SNATCHED FROM HER ROOM LESS THAN AN HOUR AGO, BUT SHE WASN'T TAKEN OUT ANY OF THE DOORS...I WANT THE EXITS BLOCKED AND THE PLACE SEARCHED!
THATS A BIG ORDER, BUDDY WHO MIGHT YOU BE?
© 1934, King Features Syndicate, Inc., Great Britain rights reserved.
HERES WHO I AM ... BUT NOBODY EXCEPT YOU MUST KNOW IT .... NOT EVEN ANY OF YOUR MEN ... YOU CAN CALL ME DEXTER!
YES, SIR.. WHATEVER YOU SAY, SIR!
HOTEL

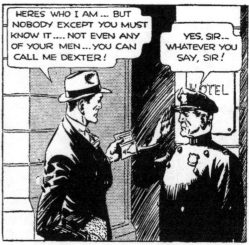

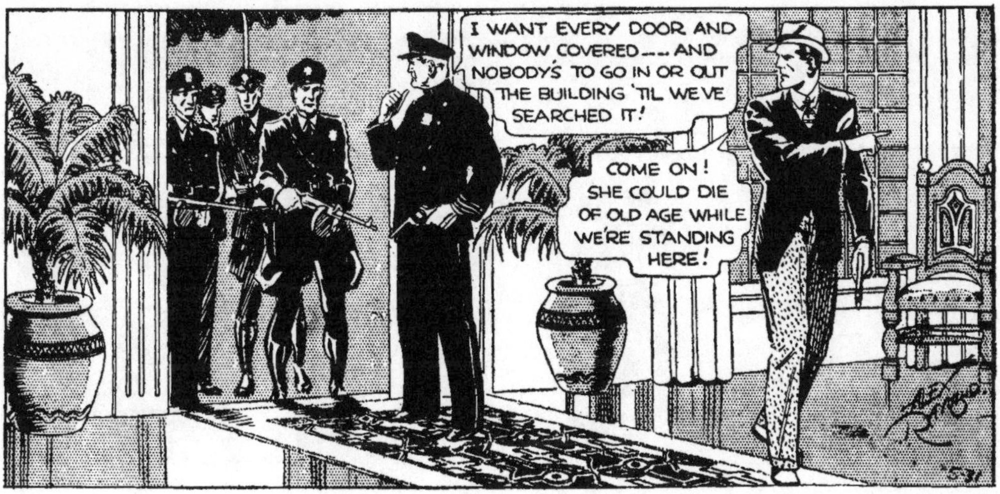
I WANT EVERY DOOR AND WINDOW COVERED--- AND NOBODY'S TO GO IN OR OUT THE BUILDING 'TIL WE'VE SEARCHED IT!
COME ON! SHE COULD DIE OF OLD AGE WHILE WE'RE STANDING HERE!
5-31
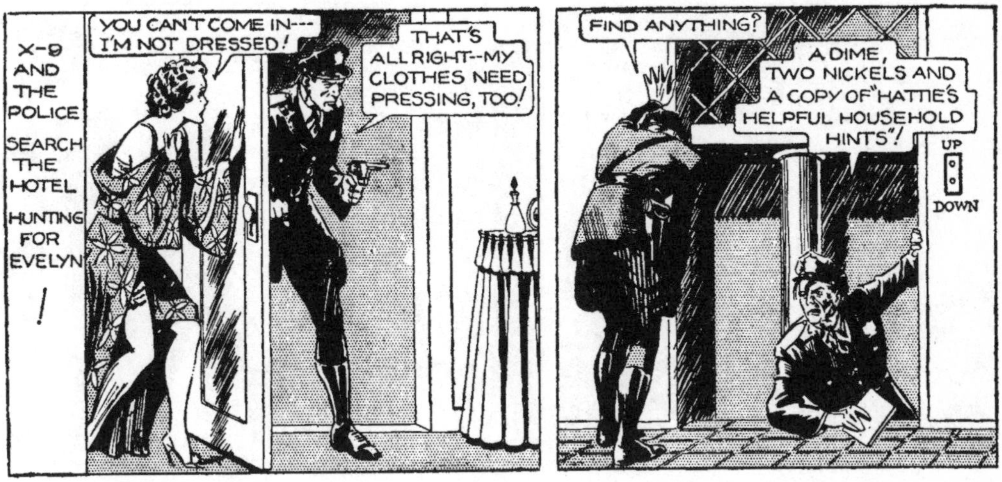
X-9 AND THE POLICE SEARCH THE HOTEL HUNTING FOR EVELYN !
YOU CAN'T COME IN--- I'M NOT DRESSED!
THAT'S ALL RIGHT--MY CLOTHES NEED PRESSING, TOO!
FIND ANYTHING?
A DIME, TWO NICKELS AND A COPY OF "HATTIE'S HELPFUL HOUSEHOLD HINTS"!
UP
DOWN
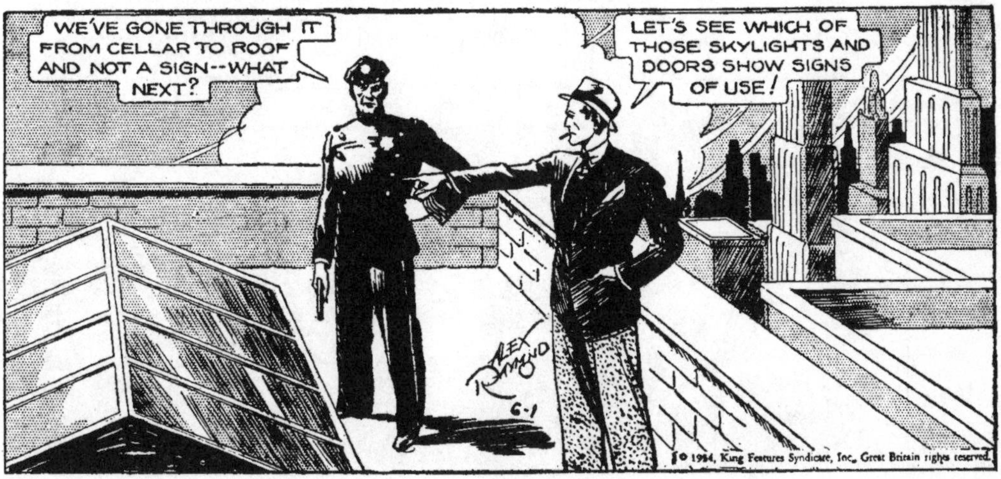
WE'VE GONE THROUGH IT FROM CELLAR TO ROOF AND NOT A SIGN--WHAT NEXT?
LET'S SEE WHICH OF THOSE SKYLIGHTS AND DOORS SHOW SIGNS OF USE!
6-1
© 1934, King Features Syndicate, Inc., Great Britain rights reserved.

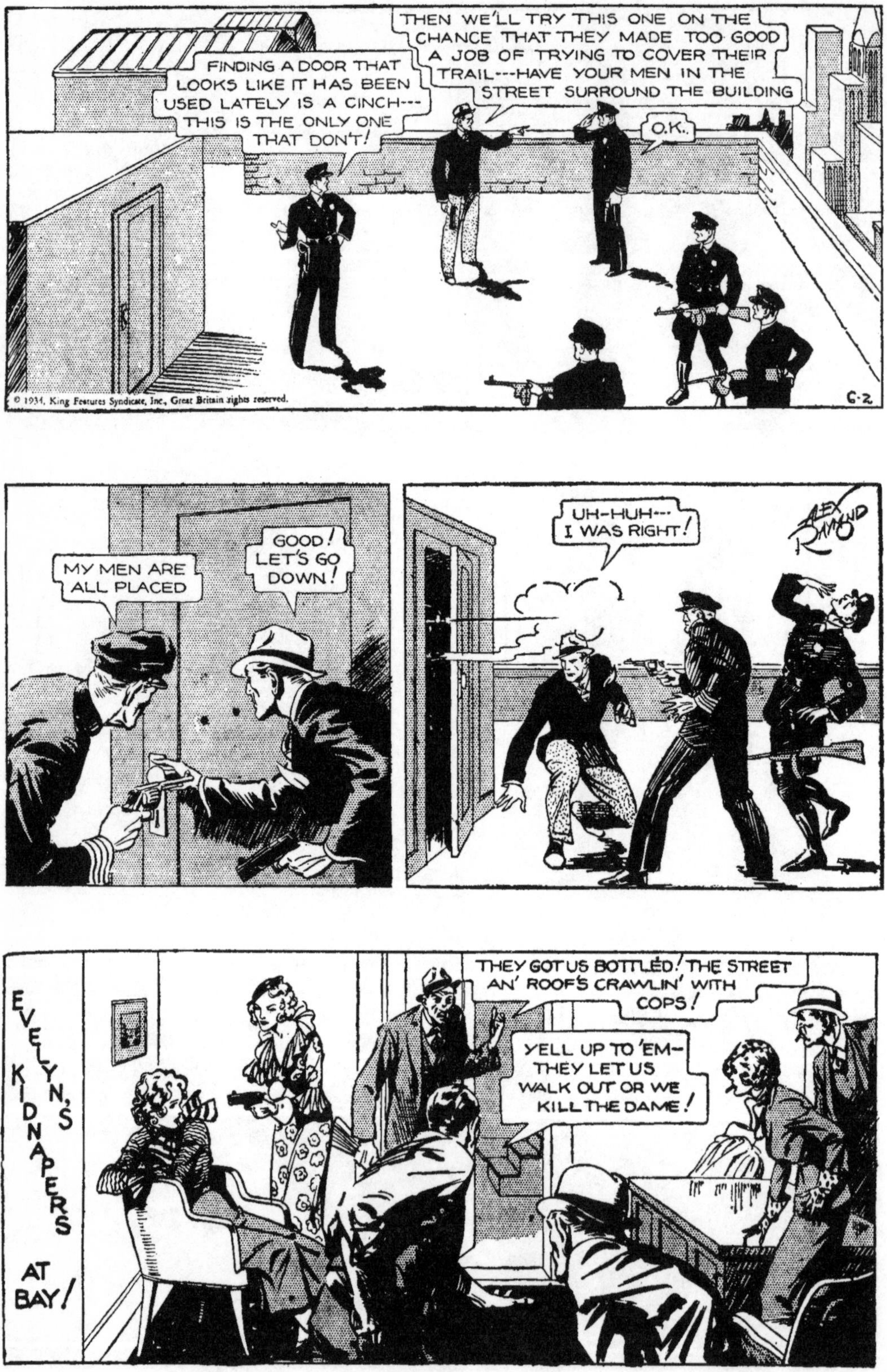
FINDING A DOOR THAT LOOKS LIKE IT HAS BEEN USED LATELY IS A CINCH--- THIS IS THE ONLY ONE THAT DON'T!
THEN WE'LL TRY THIS ONE ON THE CHANCE THAT THEY MADE TOO GOOD A JOB OF TRYING TO COVER THEIR TRAIL---HAVE YOUR MEN IN THE STREET SURROUND THE BUILDING
O.K.
© 1934, King Features Syndicate, Inc., Great Britain rights reserved.
6-2
MY MEN ARE ALL PLACED
GOOD! LET'S GO DOWN!
UH-HUH--- I WAS RIGHT!
ALEX RAYMOND
EVELYN'S KIDNAPERS AT BAY!
THEY GOT US BOTTLED! THE STREET AN' ROOF'S CRAWLIN' WITH COPS!
YELL UP TO 'EM- THEY LET US WALK OUT OR WE KILL THE DAME!

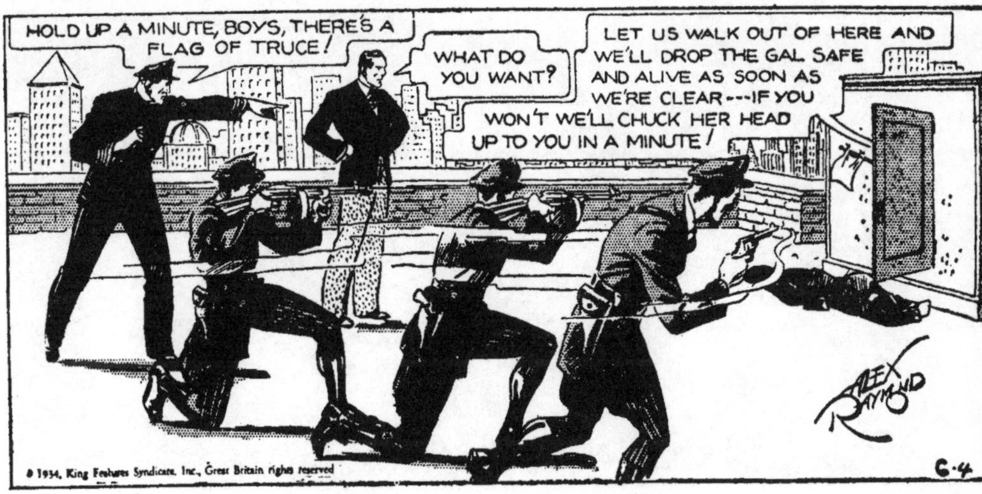
HOLD UP A MINUTE, BOYS, THERE'S A FLAG OF TRUCE!
WHAT DO YOU WANT?
LET US WALK OUT OF HERE AND WE'LL DROP THE GAL SAFE AND ALIVE AS SOON AS WE'RE CLEAR---IF YOU WON'T WE'LL CHUCK HER HEAD UP TO YOU IN A MINUTE!
ALEX RAYMOND
© 1934, King Features Syndicate, Inc., Great Britain rights reserved
6-4

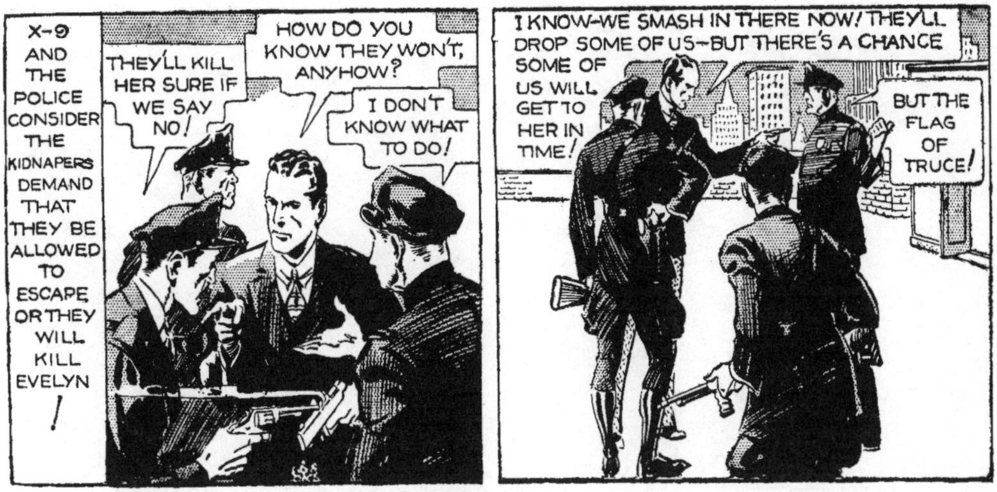
X-9 AND THE POLICE CONSIDER THE KIDNAPERS DEMAND THAT THEY BE ALLOWED TO ESCAPE OR THEY WILL KILL EVELYN!
THEY'LL KILL HER SURE IF WE SAY NO!
HOW DO YOU KNOW THEY WON'T, ANYHOW?
I DON'T KNOW WHAT TO DO!
I KNOW-WE SMASH IN THERE NOW! THEY'LL DROP SOME OF US-BUT THERE'S A CHANCE SOME OF US WILL GET TO HER IN TIME!
BUT THE FLAG OF TRUCE!

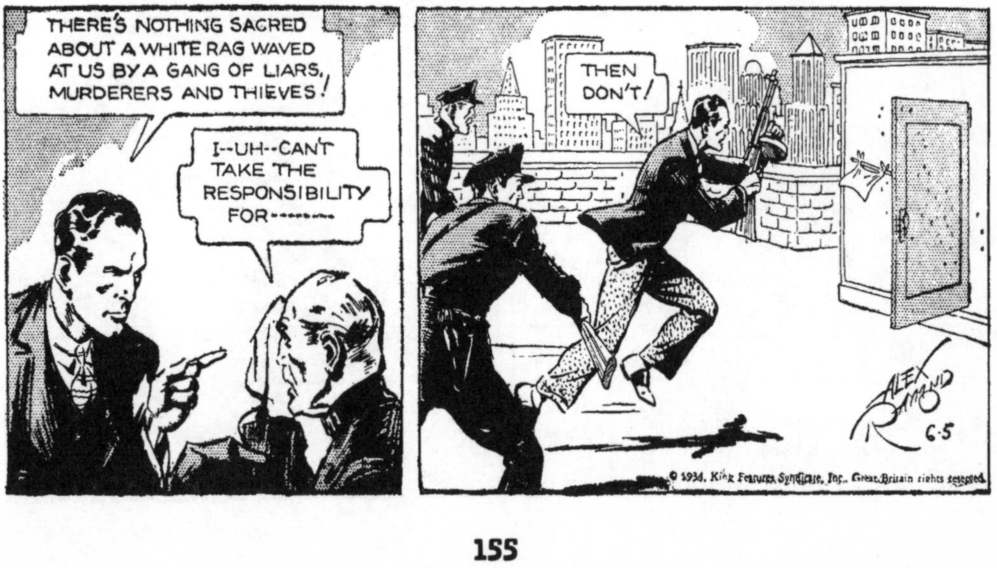
THERE'S NOTHING SACRED ABOUT A WHITE RAG WAVED AT US BY A GANG OF LIARS, MURDERERS AND THIEVES!
I--UH--CAN'T TAKE THE RESPONSIBILITY FOR--------
THEN DON'T!
ALEX RAYMOND
6-5
© 1934, King Features Syndicate, Inc., Great Britain rights reserved.

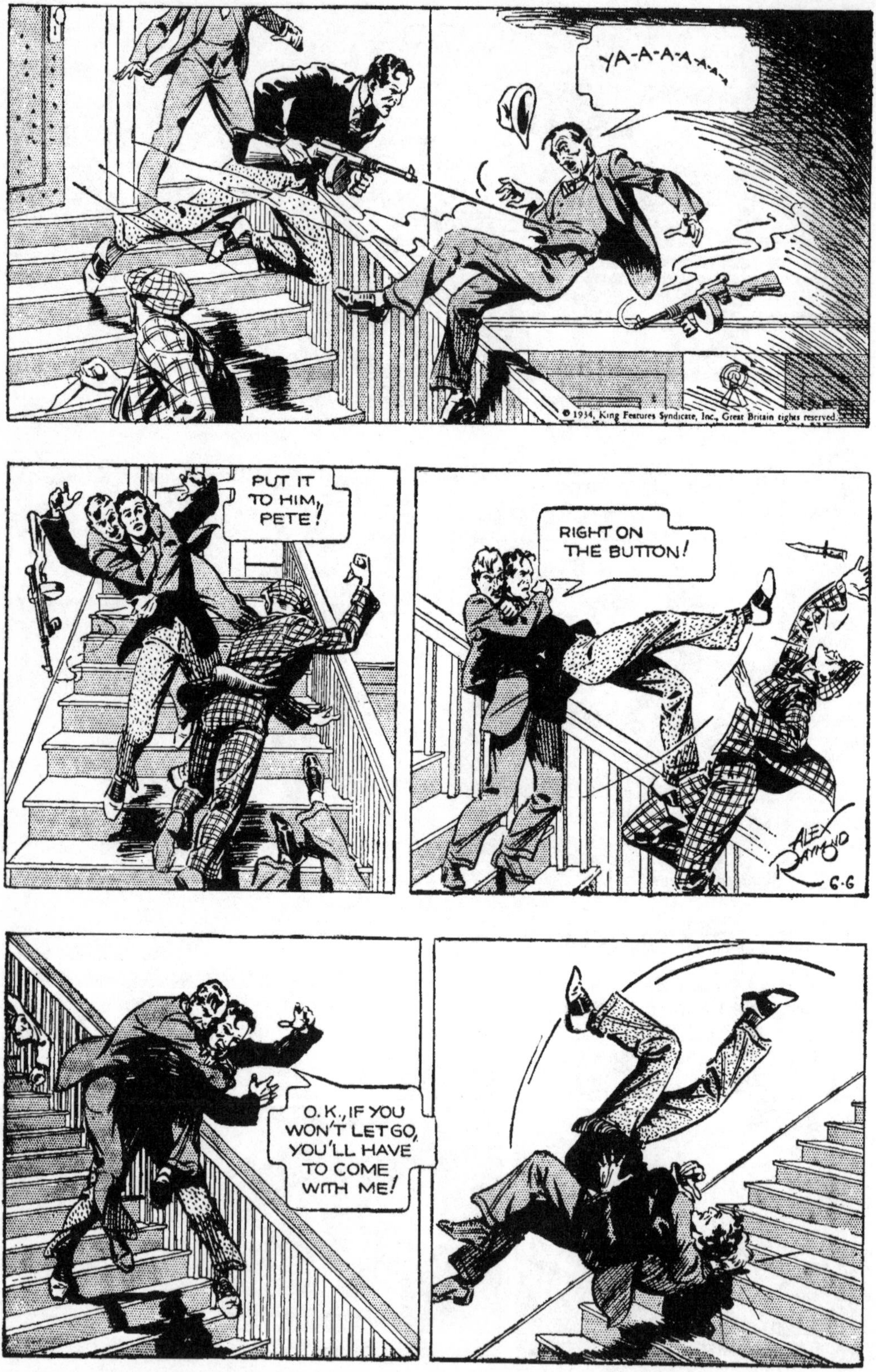
YA-A-A-A-A-A-A
© 1934, King Features Syndicate, Inc., Great Britain rights reserved.
PUT IT TO HIM, PETE!
RIGHT ON THE BUTTON!
ALEX RAYMOND
6-6
O.K., IF YOU WON'T LET GO, YOU'LL HAVE TO COME WITH ME!

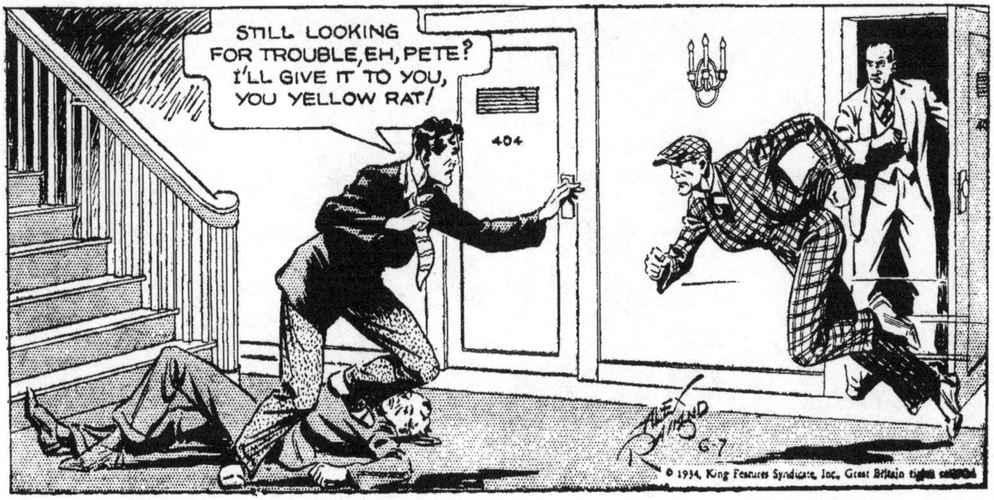
STILL LOOKING FOR TROUBLE, EH, PETE? I'LL GIVE IT TO YOU, YOU YELLOW RAT!
© 1934, King Features Syndicate, Inc., Great Britain

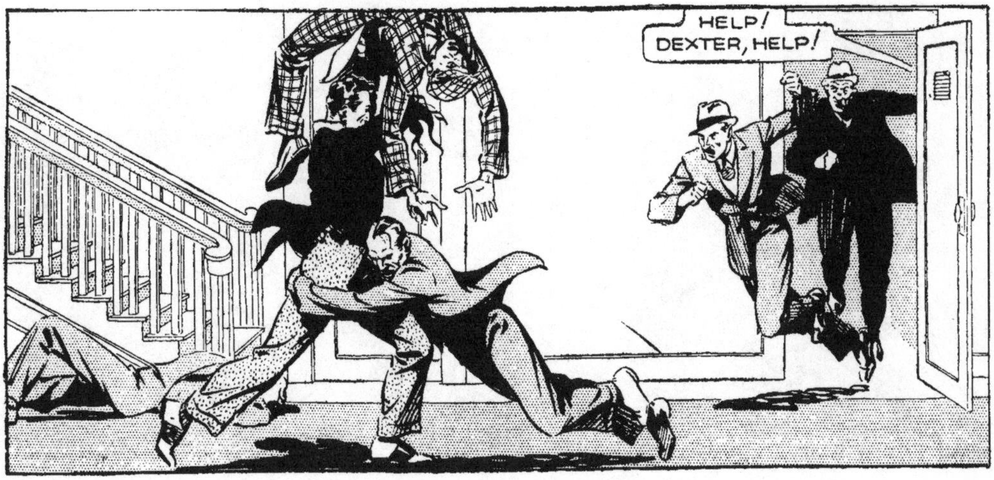
HELP! DEXTER, HELP!

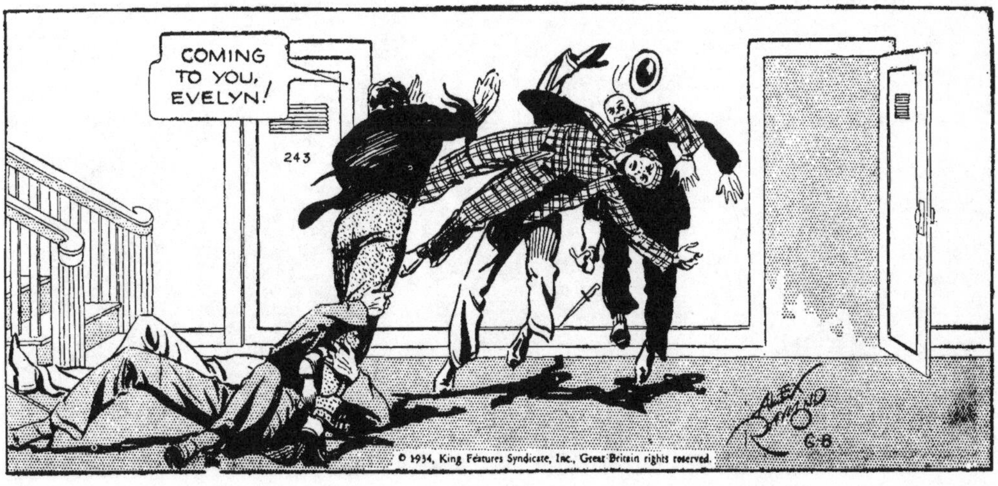
COMING TO YOU, EVELYN!
© 1934, King Features Syndicate, Inc., Great Britain rights reserved.

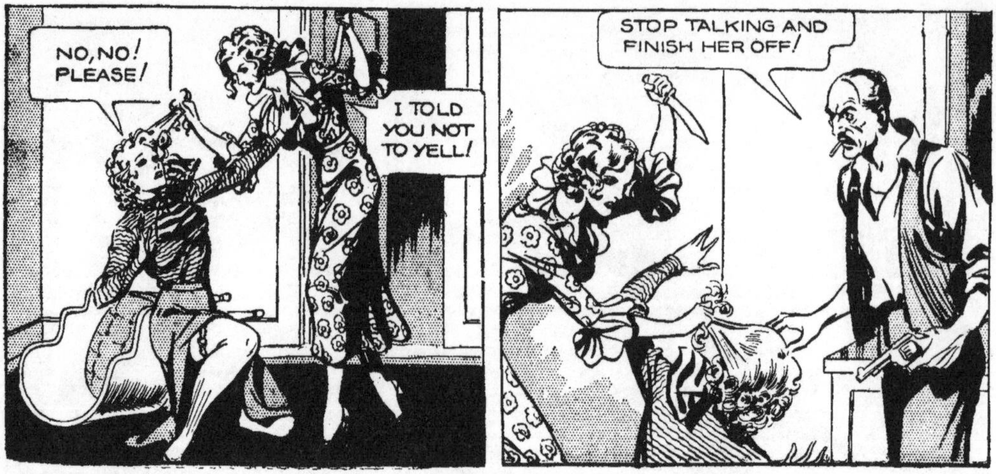
NO, NO! PLEASE!
I TOLD YOU NOT TO YELL!
STOP TALKING AND FINISH HER OFF!

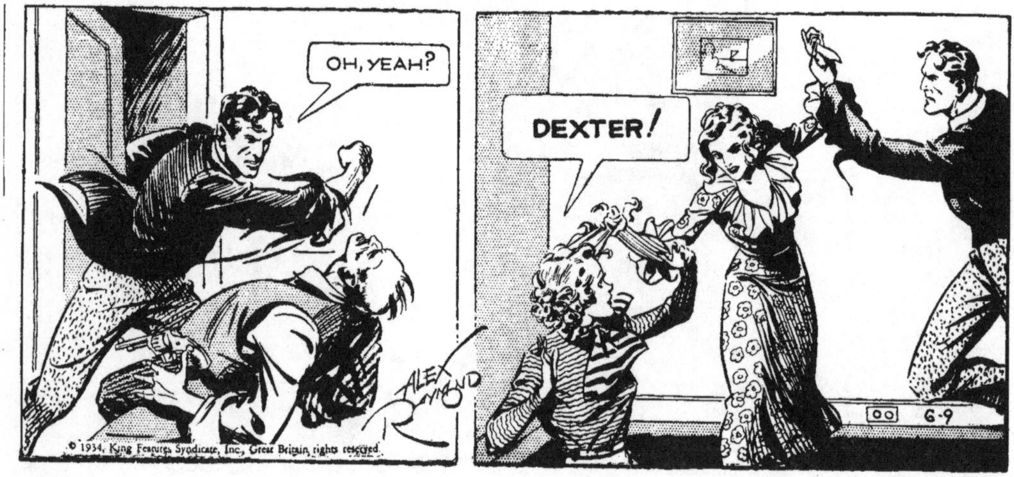
OH, YEAH?
ALEX RAYMOND
© 1934, King Features Syndicate, Inc., Great Britain rights reserved.
DEXTER!
00 6-9

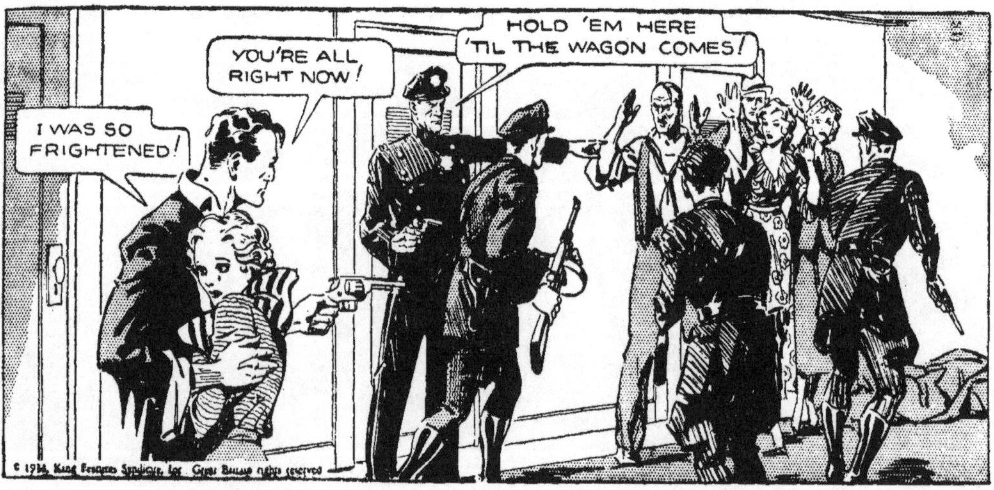
I WAS SO FRIGHTENED!
YOU'RE ALL RIGHT NOW!
HOLD 'EM HERE 'TIL THE WAGON COMES!
© 1934, King Features Syndicate, Inc. Great Britain rights reserved

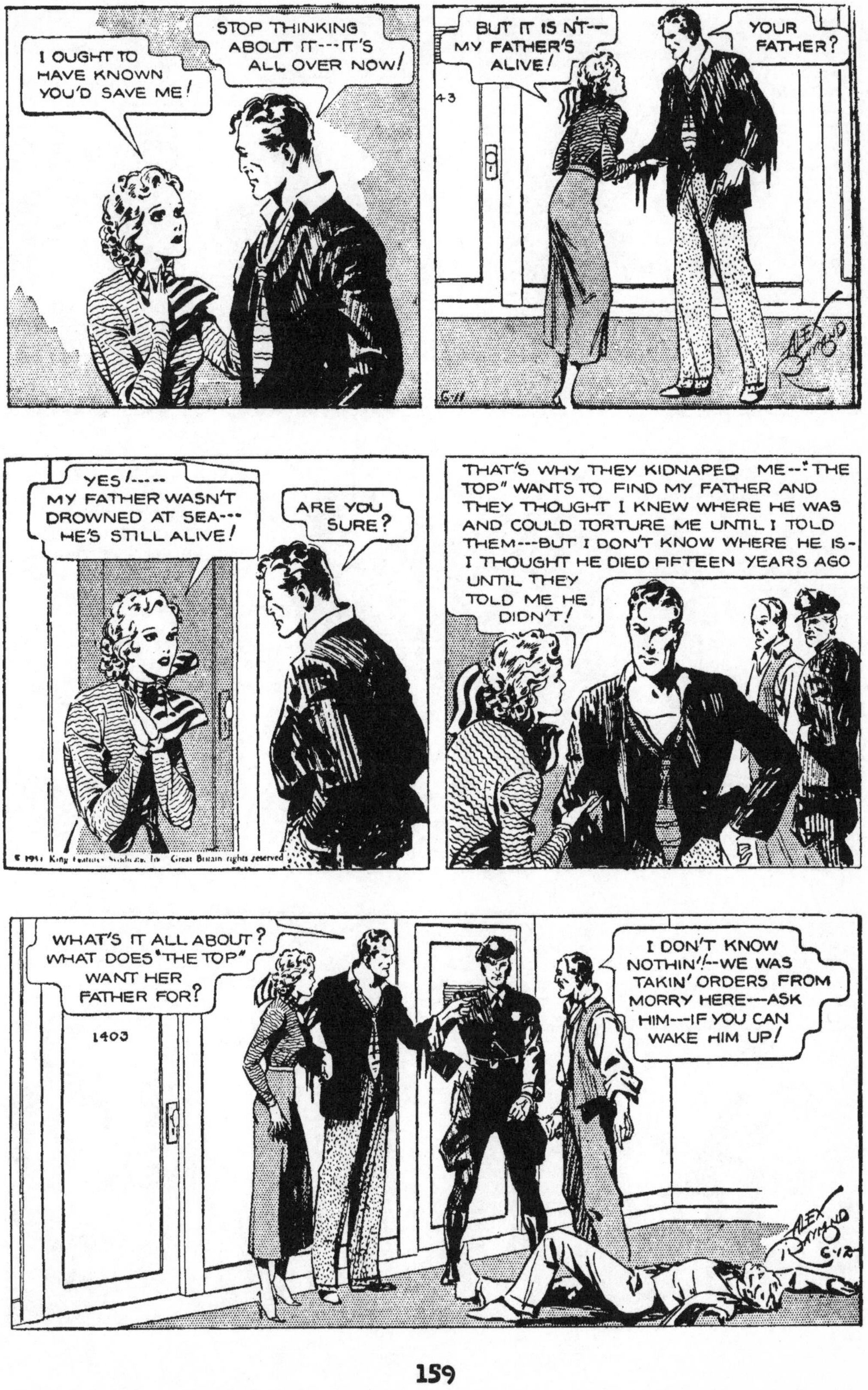
I OUGHT TO HAVE KNOWN YOU'D SAVE ME!
STOP THINKING ABOUT IT---IT'S ALL OVER NOW!
BUT IT IS N'T--- MY FATHER'S ALIVE!
YOUR FATHER?
6-11
YES!----- MY FATHER WASN'T DROWNED AT SEA--- HE'S STILL ALIVE!
ARE YOU SURE?
King Features Syndicate, Inc. Great Britain rights reserved
THAT'S WHY THEY KIDNAPED ME--"THE TOP" WANTS TO FIND MY FATHER AND THEY THOUGHT I KNEW WHERE HE WAS AND COULD TORTURE ME UNTIL I TOLD THEM---BUT I DON'T KNOW WHERE HE IS- I THOUGHT HE DIED FIFTEEN YEARS AGO UNTIL THEY TOLD ME HE DIDN'T!
WHAT'S IT ALL ABOUT? WHAT DOES "THE TOP" WANT HER FATHER FOR?
1403
I DON'T KNOW NOTHIN'!--WE WAS TAKIN' ORDERS FROM MORRY HERE---ASK HIM---IF YOU CAN WAKE HIM UP!
ALEX RAYMOND
6-12

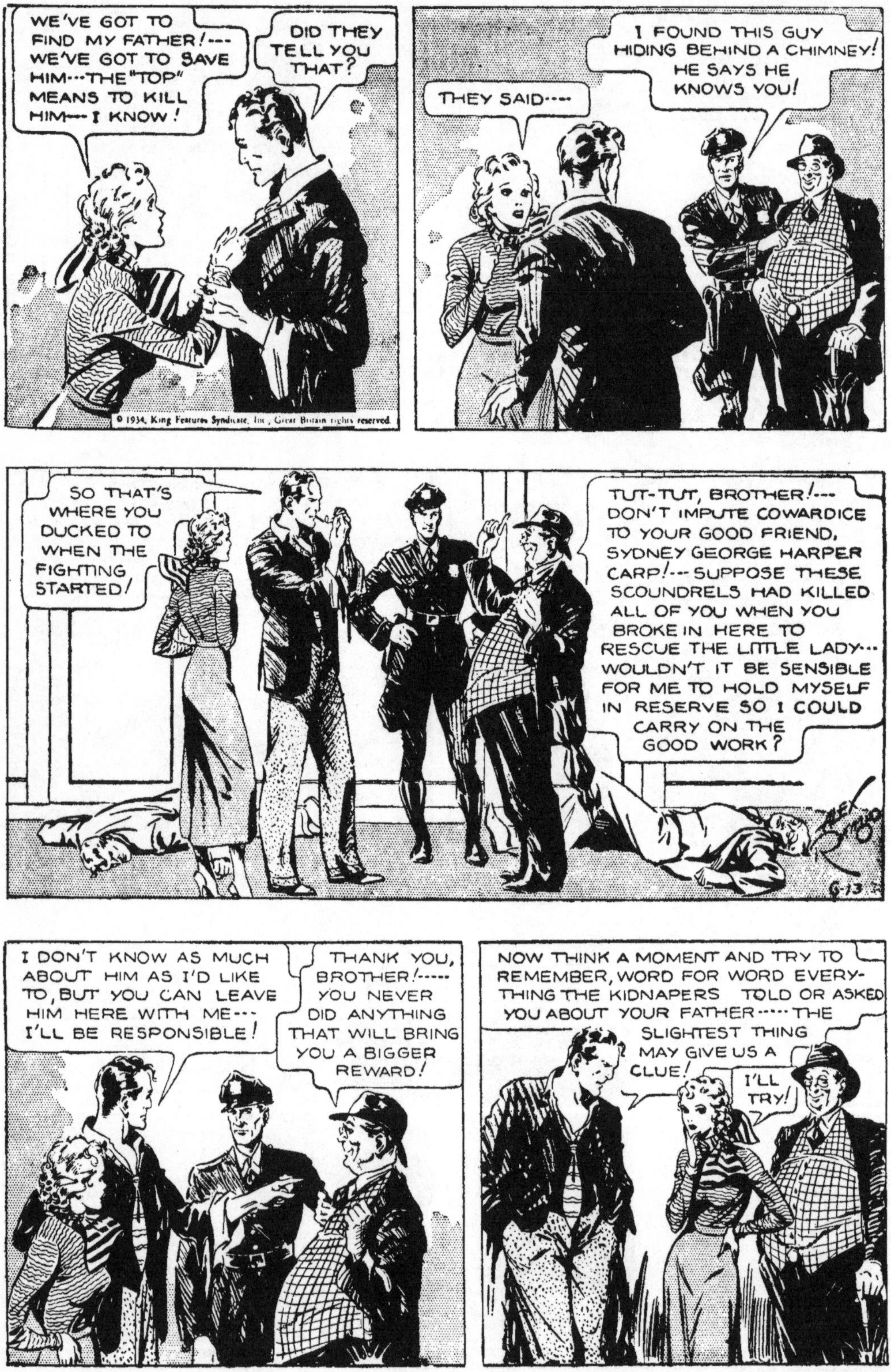
WE'VE GOT TO FIND MY FATHER!--- WE'VE GOT TO SAVE HIM---THE "TOP" MEANS TO KILL HIM--- I KNOW!
DID THEY TELL YOU THAT?
© 1934, King Features Syndicate, Inc., Great Britain rights reserved.
THEY SAID----
I FOUND THIS GUY HIDING BEHIND A CHIMNEY! HE SAYS HE KNOWS YOU!
SO THAT'S WHERE YOU DUCKED TO WHEN THE FIGHTING STARTED!
TUT-TUT, BROTHER!--- DON'T IMPUTE COWARDICE TO YOUR GOOD FRIEND, SYDNEY GEORGE HARPER CARP!--- SUPPOSE THESE SCOUNDRELS HAD KILLED ALL OF YOU WHEN YOU BROKE IN HERE TO RESCUE THE LITTLE LADY... WOULDN'T IT BE SENSIBLE FOR ME TO HOLD MYSELF IN RESERVE SO I COULD CARRY ON THE GOOD WORK?
I DON'T KNOW AS MUCH ABOUT HIM AS I'D LIKE TO, BUT YOU CAN LEAVE HIM HERE WITH ME--- I'LL BE RESPONSIBLE!
THANK YOU, BROTHER!----- YOU NEVER DID ANYTHING THAT WILL BRING YOU A BIGGER REWARD!
NOW THINK A MOMENT AND TRY TO REMEMBER, WORD FOR WORD EVERYTHING THE KIDNAPERS TOLD OR ASKED YOU ABOUT YOUR FATHER----- THE SLIGHTEST THING MAY GIVE US A CLUE!
I'LL TRY!

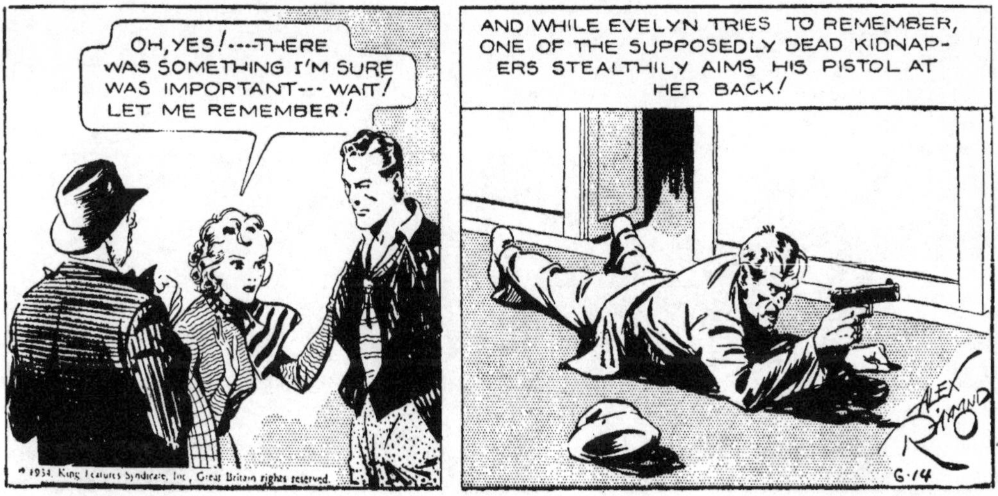
OH, YES!----THERE WAS SOMETHING I'M SURE WAS IMPORTANT--- WAIT! LET ME REMEMBER!
© 1934, King Features Syndicate, Inc., Great Britain rights reserved.
AND WHILE EVELYN TRIES TO REMEMBER, ONE OF THE SUPPOSEDLY DEAD KIDNAPERS STEALTHILY AIMS HIS PISTOL AT HER BACK!
ALEX RAYMOND
6-14

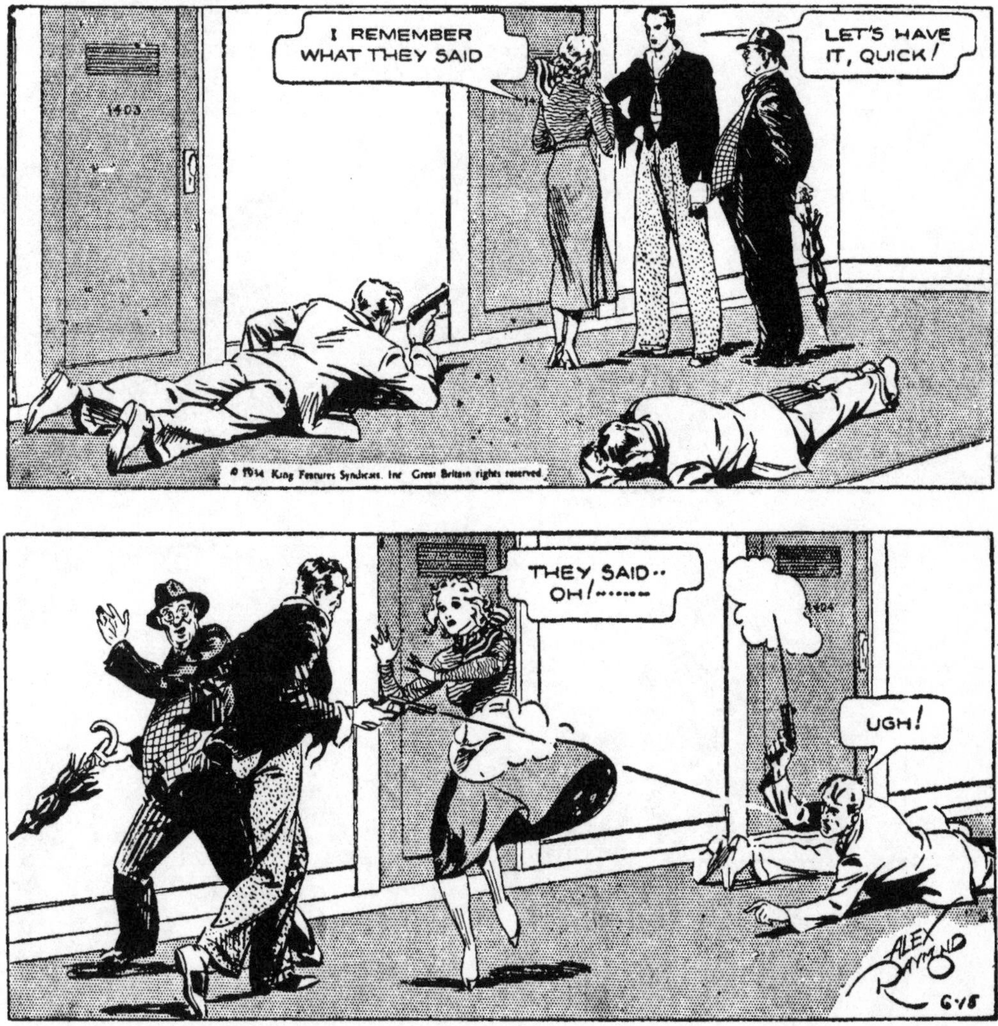
1403
I REMEMBER WHAT THEY SAID
LET'S HAVE IT, QUICK!
© 1934 King Features Syndicate, Inc. Great Britain rights reserved.
THEY SAID.. OH!.......
1404
UGH!
ALEX RAYMOND
6-15

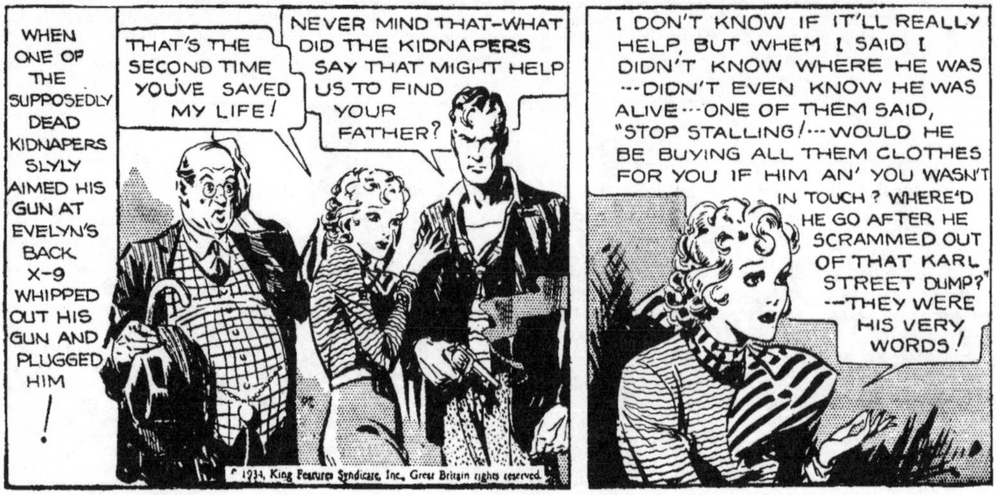
WHEN ONE OF THE SUPPOSEDLY DEAD KIDNAPERS SLYLY AIMED HIS GUN AT EVELYN'S BACK X-9 WHIPPED OUT HIS GUN AND PLUGGED HIM!
THAT'S THE SECOND TIME YOU'VE SAVED MY LIFE!
NEVER MIND THAT—WHAT DID THE KIDNAPERS SAY THAT MIGHT HELP US TO FIND YOUR FATHER?
© 1934, King Features Syndicate, Inc., Great Britain rights reserved.
I DON'T KNOW IF IT'LL REALLY HELP, BUT WHEM I SAID I DIDN'T KNOW WHERE HE WAS ---DIDN'T EVEN KNOW HE WAS ALIVE---ONE OF THEM SAID, "STOP STALLING!---WOULD HE BE BUYING ALL THEM CLOTHES FOR YOU IF HIM AN' YOU WASN'T IN TOUCH? WHERE'D HE GO AFTER HE SCRAMMED OUT OF THAT KARL STREET DUMP?" --THEY WERE HIS VERY WORDS!

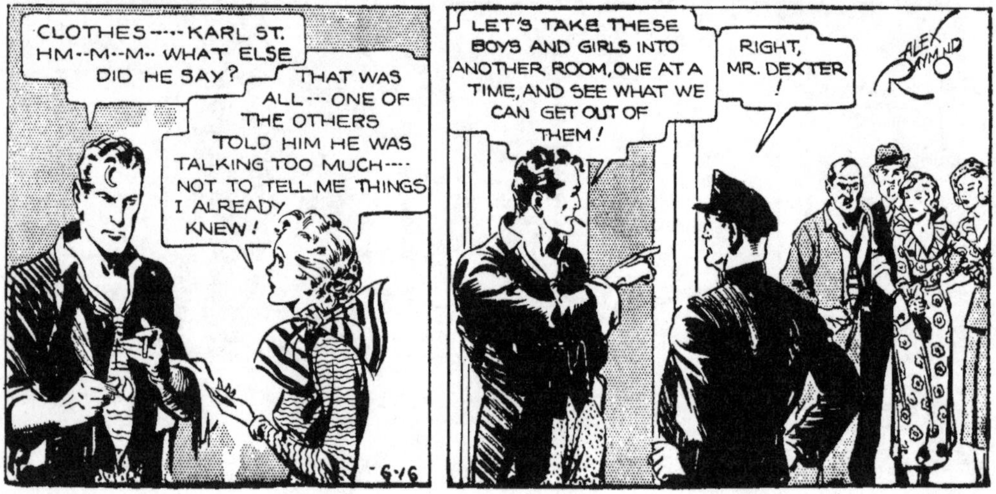
CLOTHES----KARL ST. HM--M--M-- WHAT ELSE DID HE SAY?
THAT WAS ALL---ONE OF THE OTHERS TOLD HIM HE WAS TALKING TOO MUCH---- NOT TO TELL ME THINGS I ALREADY KNEW!
6-16
LET'S TAKE THESE BOYS AND GIRLS INTO ANOTHER ROOM, ONE AT A TIME, AND SEE WHAT WE CAN GET OUT OF THEM!
RIGHT, MR. DEXTER!
ALEX RAYMOND

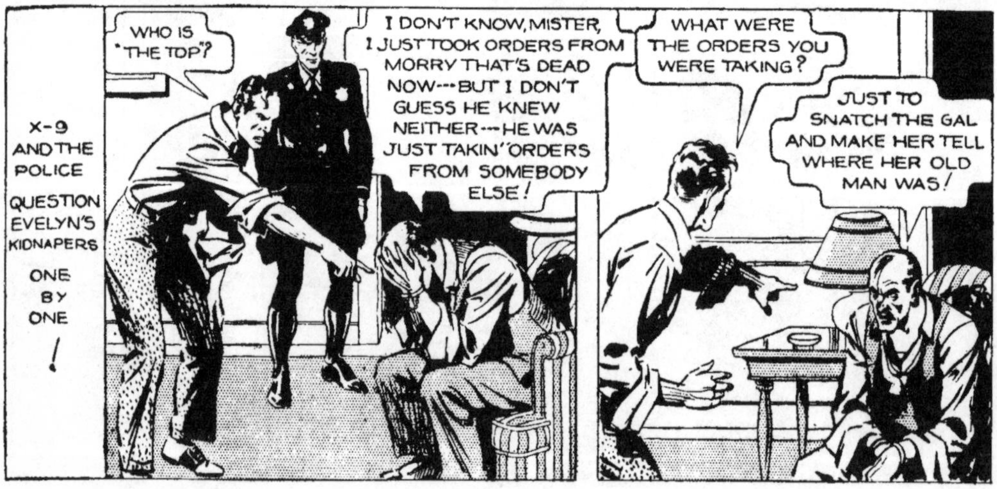
X-9 AND THE POLICE QUESTION EVELYN'S KIDNAPERS ONE BY ONE!
WHO IS "THE TOP"?
I DON'T KNOW, MISTER, I JUST TOOK ORDERS FROM MORRY THAT'S DEAD NOW---BUT I DON'T GUESS HE KNEW NEITHER---HE WAS JUST TAKIN' ORDERS FROM SOMEBODY ELSE!
WHAT WERE THE ORDERS YOU WERE TAKING?
JUST TO SNATCH THE GAL AND MAKE HER TELL WHERE HER OLD MAN WAS!

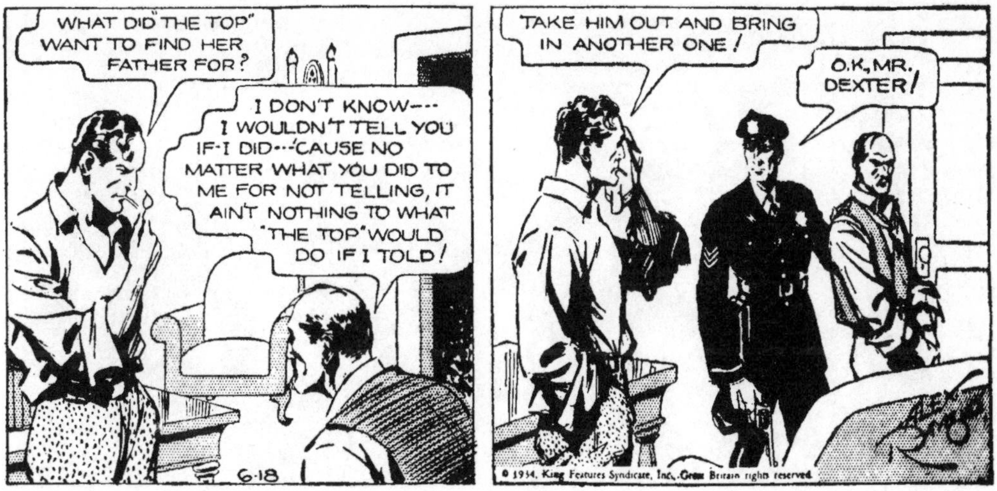
WHAT DID "THE TOP" WANT TO FIND HER FATHER FOR?
I DON'T KNOW--- I WOULDN'T TELL YOU IF I DID---'CAUSE NO MATTER WHAT YOU DID TO ME FOR NOT TELLING, IT AIN'T NOTHING TO WHAT "THE TOP" WOULD DO IF I TOLD!
6-18
TAKE HIM OUT AND BRING IN ANOTHER ONE!
O.K., MR. DEXTER!
© 1934, King Features Syndicate, Inc., Great Britain rights reserved.

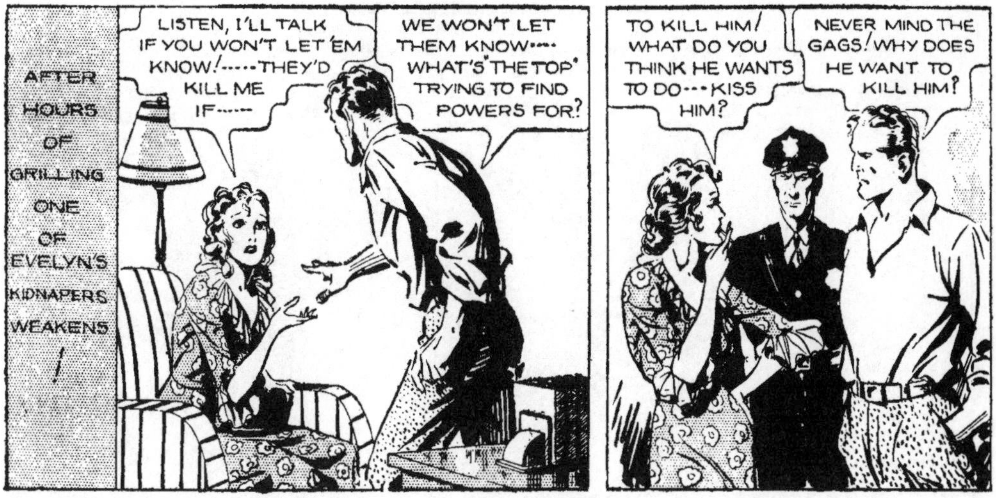
AFTER HOURS OF GRILLING ONE OF EVELYN'S KIDNAPERS WEAKENS!
LISTEN, I'LL TALK IF YOU WON'T LET 'EM KNOW!-----THEY'D KILL ME IF-----
WE WON'T LET THEM KNOW----- WHAT'S "THE TOP" TRYING TO FIND POWERS FOR?
TO KILL HIM! WHAT DO YOU THINK HE WANTS TO DO---KISS HIM?
NEVER MIND THE GAGS! WHY DOES HE WANT TO KILL HIM?

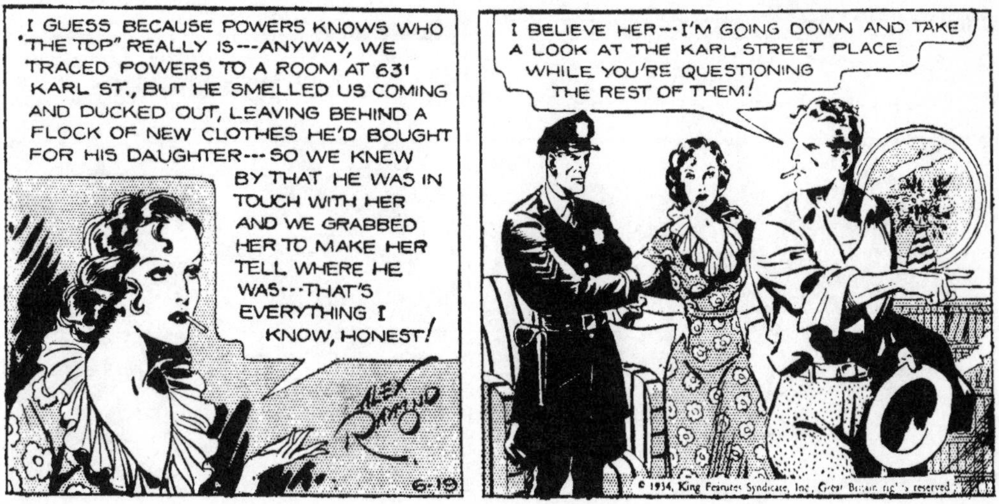
I GUESS BECAUSE POWERS KNOWS WHO "THE TOP" REALLY IS---ANYWAY, WE TRACED POWERS TO A ROOM AT 631 KARL ST., BUT HE SMELLED US COMING AND DUCKED OUT, LEAVING BEHIND A FLOCK OF NEW CLOTHES HE'D BOUGHT FOR HIS DAUGHTER---SO WE KNEW BY THAT HE WAS IN TOUCH WITH HER AND WE GRABBED HER TO MAKE HER TELL WHERE HE WAS---THAT'S EVERYTHING I KNOW, HONEST!
6-19
I BELIEVE HER---I'M GOING DOWN AND TAKE A LOOK AT THE KARL STREET PLACE WHILE YOU'RE QUESTIONING THE REST OF THEM!
© 1934, King Features Syndicate, Inc., Great Britain rights reserved.

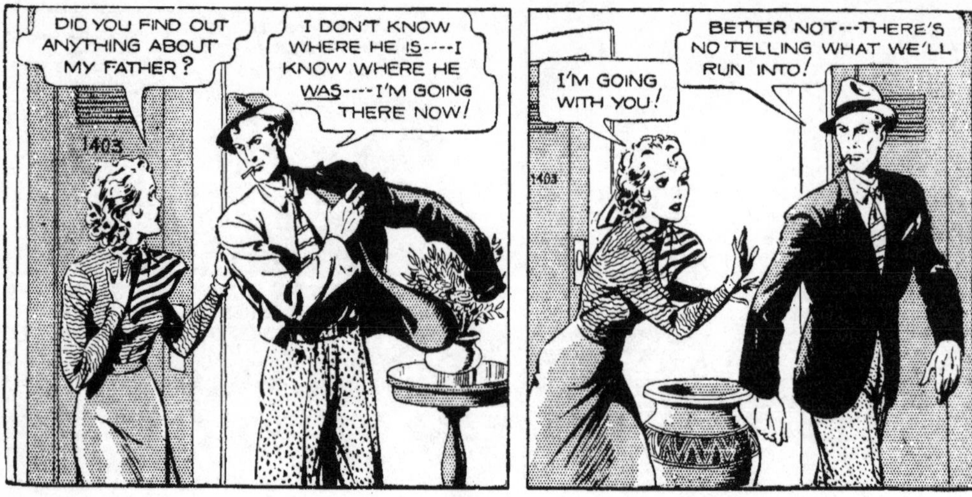
DID YOU FIND OUT ANYTHING ABOUT MY FATHER?
I DON'T KNOW WHERE HE IS----I KNOW WHERE HE WAS----I'M GOING THERE NOW!
1403
I'M GOING WITH YOU!
BETTER NOT---THERE'S NO TELLING WHAT WE'LL RUN INTO!

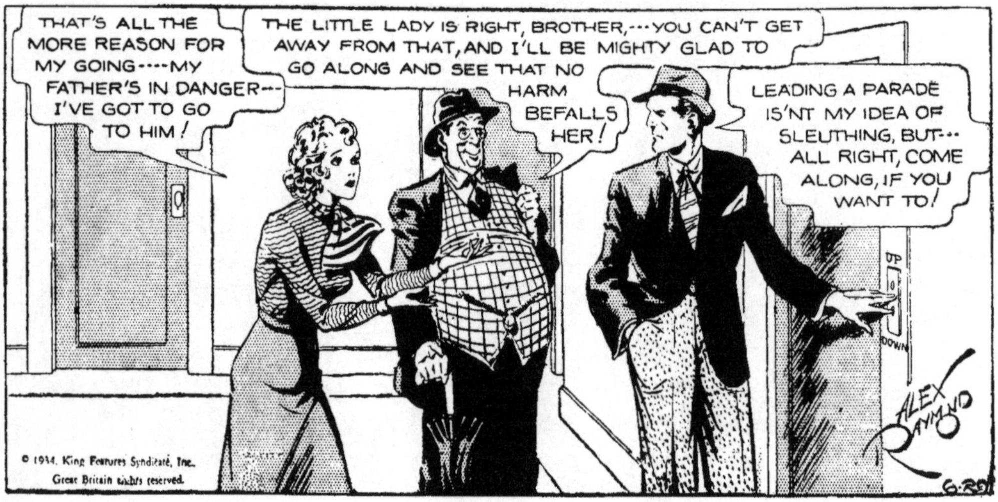
THAT'S ALL THE MORE REASON FOR MY GOING----MY FATHER'S IN DANGER--- I'VE GOT TO GO TO HIM!
THE LITTLE LADY IS RIGHT, BROTHER,---YOU CAN'T GET AWAY FROM THAT, AND I'LL BE MIGHTY GLAD TO GO ALONG AND SEE THAT NO HARM BEFALLS HER!
LEADING A PARADE IS'NT MY IDEA OF SLEUTHING, BUT--- ALL RIGHT, COME ALONG, IF YOU WANT TO!
UP
DOWN
ALEX RAYMOND
© 1934, King Features Syndicate, Inc. Great Britain rights reserved.

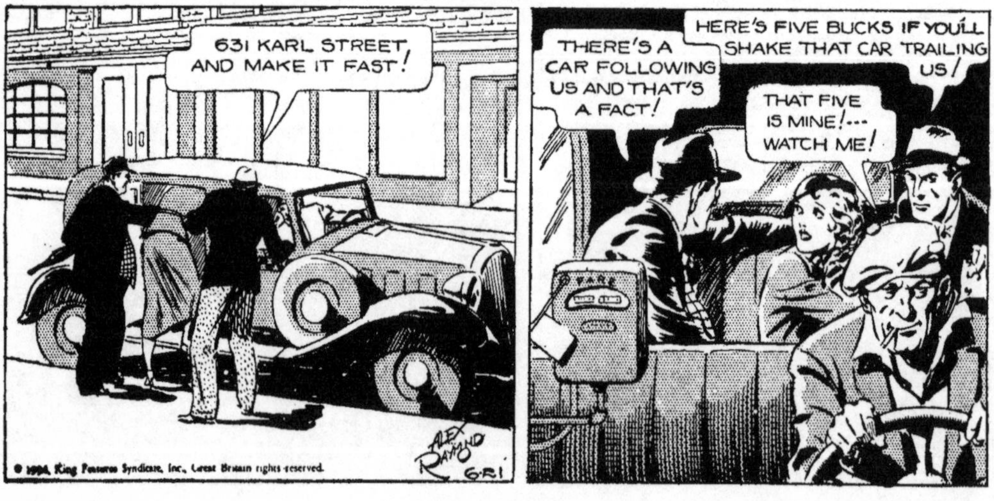
631 KARL STREET, AND MAKE IT FAST!
ALEX RAYMOND
© 1934, King Features Syndicate, Inc., Great Britain rights reserved.
THERE'S A CAR FOLLOWING US AND THAT'S A FACT!
HERE'S FIVE BUCKS IF YOU'LL SHAKE THAT CAR TRAILING US!
THAT FIVE IS MINE!--- WATCH ME!
FARE

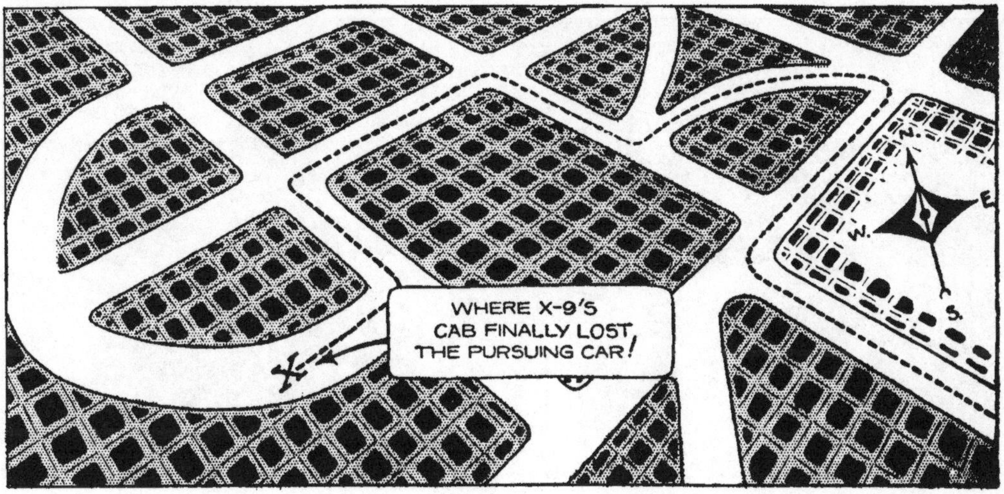
WHERE X-9'S CAB FINALLY LOST THE PURSUING CAR!
X
N.
E.
W.
S.

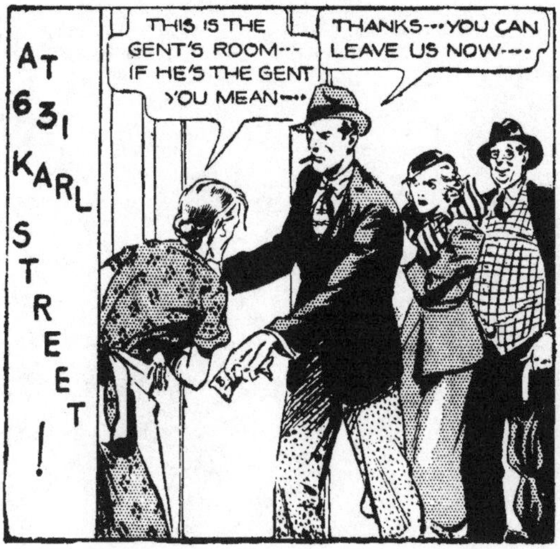
AT 631 KARL STREET!
THIS IS THE GENT'S ROOM--- IF HE'S THE GENT YOU MEAN---
THANKS--- YOU CAN LEAVE US NOW----

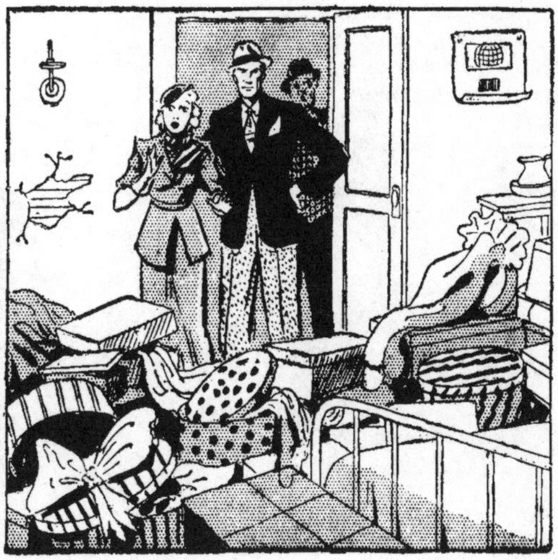

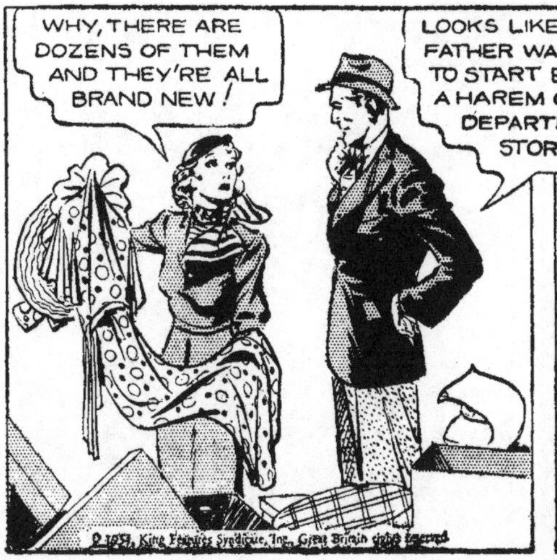
WHY, THERE ARE DOZENS OF THEM AND THEY'RE ALL BRAND NEW!
LOOKS LIKE YOUR FATHER WAS GOING TO START EITHER A HAREM OR A DEPARTMENT STORE!
King Features Syndicate, Inc., Great Britain rights reserved

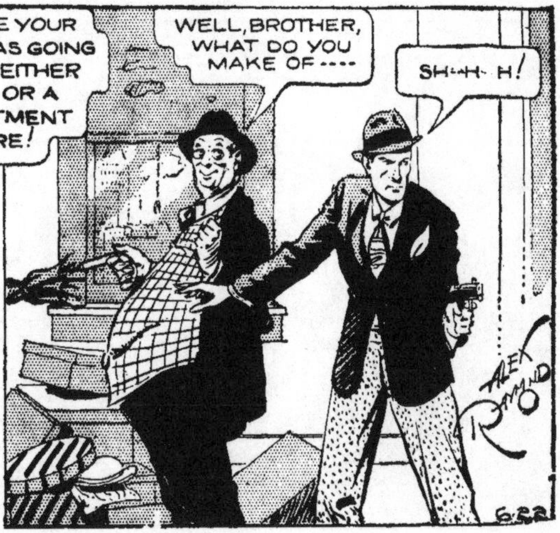
WELL, BROTHER, WHAT DO YOU MAKE OF ----
SH--H- H!
ALEX RAYMOND
6-22

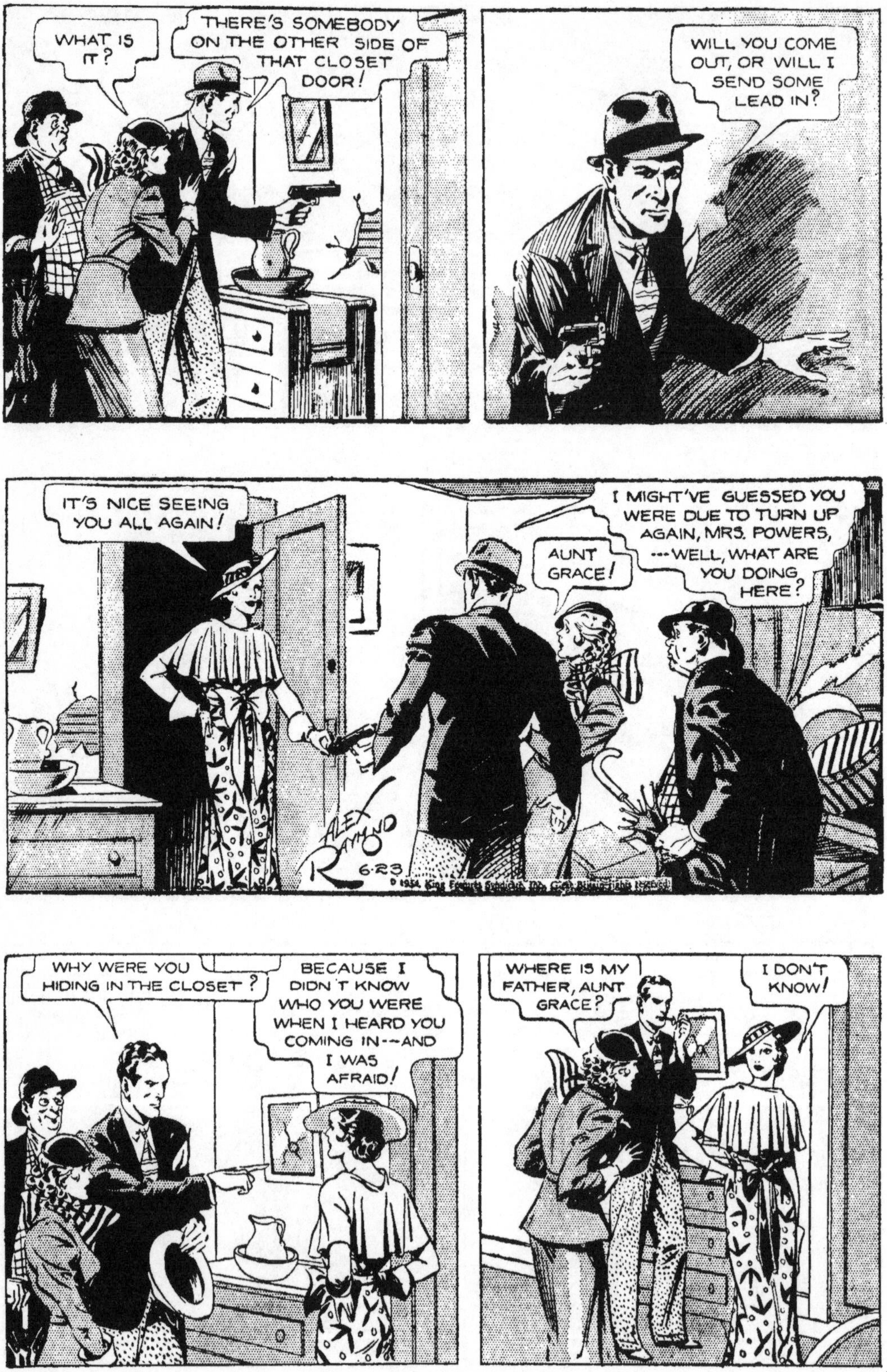
WHAT IS IT?
THERE'S SOMEBODY ON THE OTHER SIDE OF THAT CLOSET DOOR!
WILL YOU COME OUT, OR WILL I SEND SOME LEAD IN?
IT'S NICE SEEING YOU ALL AGAIN!
I MIGHT'VE GUESSED YOU WERE DUE TO TURN UP AGAIN, MRS. POWERS, ---WELL, WHAT ARE YOU DOING HERE?
AUNT GRACE!
ALEX RAYMOND
6-23
WHY WERE YOU HIDING IN THE CLOSET?
BECAUSE I DIDN'T KNOW WHO YOU WERE WHEN I HEARD YOU COMING IN--AND I WAS AFRAID!
WHERE IS MY FATHER, AUNT GRACE?
I DON'T KNOW!

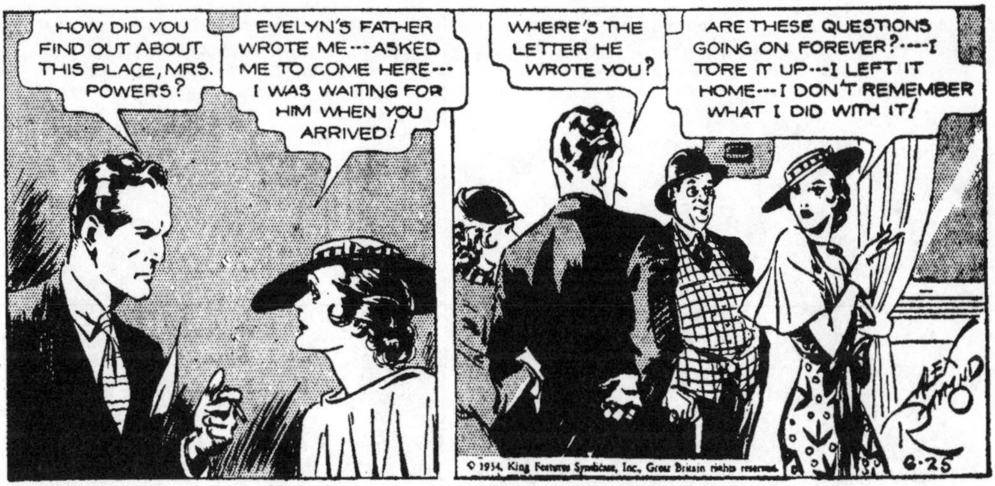
HOW DID YOU FIND OUT ABOUT THIS PLACE, MRS. POWERS?
EVELYN'S FATHER WROTE ME---ASKED ME TO COME HERE--- I WAS WAITING FOR HIM WHEN YOU ARRIVED!
WHERE'S THE LETTER HE WROTE YOU?
ARE THESE QUESTIONS GOING ON FOREVER?----I TORE IT UP---I LEFT IT HOME---I DON'T REMEMBER WHAT I DID WITH IT!
© 1934, King Features Syndicate, Inc., Great Britain rights reserved.
6-25

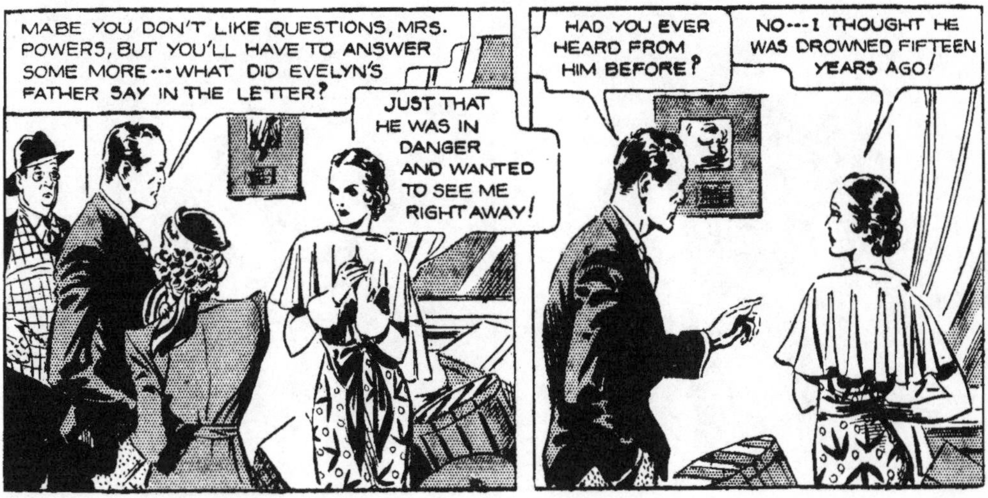
MABE YOU DON'T LIKE QUESTIONS, MRS. POWERS, BUT YOU'LL HAVE TO ANSWER SOME MORE---WHAT DID EVELYN'S FATHER SAY IN THE LETTER?
JUST THAT HE WAS IN DANGER AND WANTED TO SEE ME RIGHT AWAY!
HAD YOU EVER HEARD FROM HIM BEFORE?
NO---I THOUGHT HE WAS DROWNED FIFTEEN YEARS AGO!

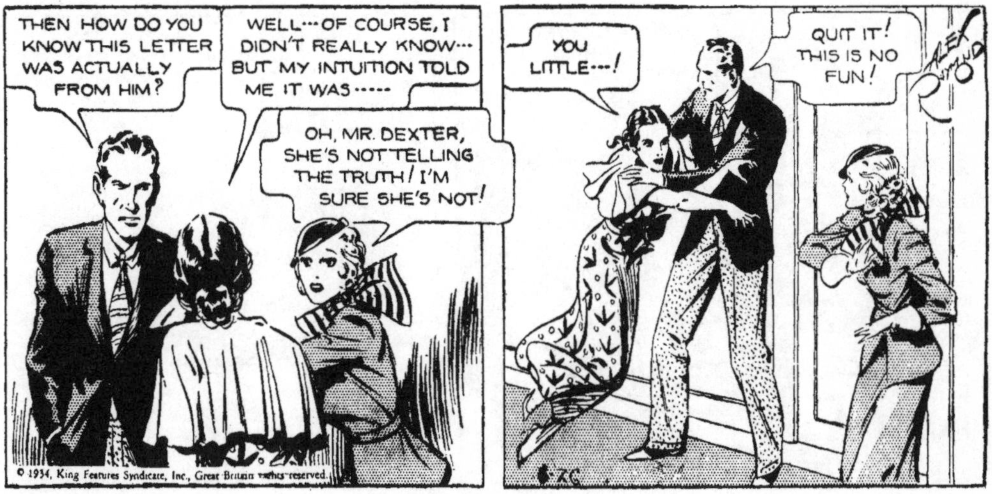
THEN HOW DO YOU KNOW THIS LETTER WAS ACTUALLY FROM HIM?
WELL---OF COURSE, I DIDN'T REALLY KNOW--- BUT MY INTUITION TOLD ME IT WAS-----
OH, MR. DEXTER, SHE'S NOT TELLING THE TRUTH! I'M SURE SHE'S NOT!
© 1934, King Features Syndicate, Inc., Great Britain rights reserved.
YOU LITTLE---!
QUIT IT! THIS IS NO FUN!

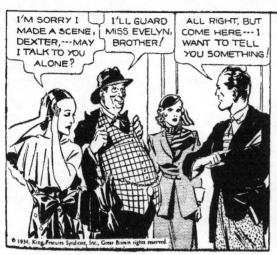

I'M SORRY I MADE A SCENE, DEXTER,---MAY I TALK TO YOU ALONE?
I'LL GUARD MISS EVELYN, BROTHER!
ALL RIGHT, BUT COME HERE---I WANT TO TELL YOU SOMETHING!
© 1934, King Features Syndicate, Inc., Great Britain rights reserved.
NOW LISTEN, MY FAT FRIEND---IF YOU LET ANYTHING HAPPEN TO EVELYN I'LL WHITTLE YOU DOWN TO KINDLING SIZE! TAKE HER INTO THE NEXT ROOM AND KEEP HER THERE UNTIL I FIND OUT WHAT HER AUNT IS UP TO!
BROTHER, YOU CAN TRUST SYDNEY GEORGE HARPER CARP TO THE LAST DROP!
WHAT DID DEXTER WHISPER TO YOU?
HE WANTS US TO SNEAK OUT OF HERE AND WAIT FOR HIM IN A PLACE ON THE OTHER SIDE OF TOWN!
BUT I-----!
SH--H--H! 'TIL WE GET OUTSIDE!---MR. DEXTER IS A MAN WHO KNOWS WHAT HE'S DOING AND WE WON'T GO WRONG OBEYING HIS ORDERS!
6-27
WHILE CARP, CONTRARY TO X-9'S ORDERS, TRICKS EVELYN INTO GOING OFF WITH HIM!
BUT WHERE ARE WE GOING?
WHERE DEXTER TOLD ME TO TAKE YOU----DON'T YOU WORRY, LITTLE LADY---JUST LEAVE IT TO US!
BUT I'VE GOT TO FIND MY FATHER---HE'S IN DANGER AND----
----AND YOU CAN LEAVE THAT TO US, TOO, DEXTER AND CARP'S A TEAM THAT NEVER FAILS-----NEVER!

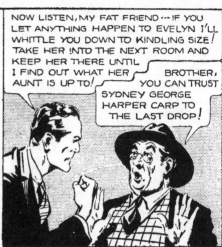

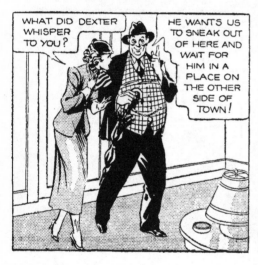

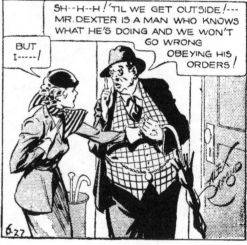

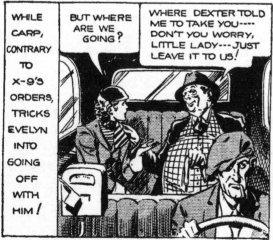

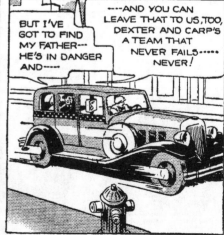

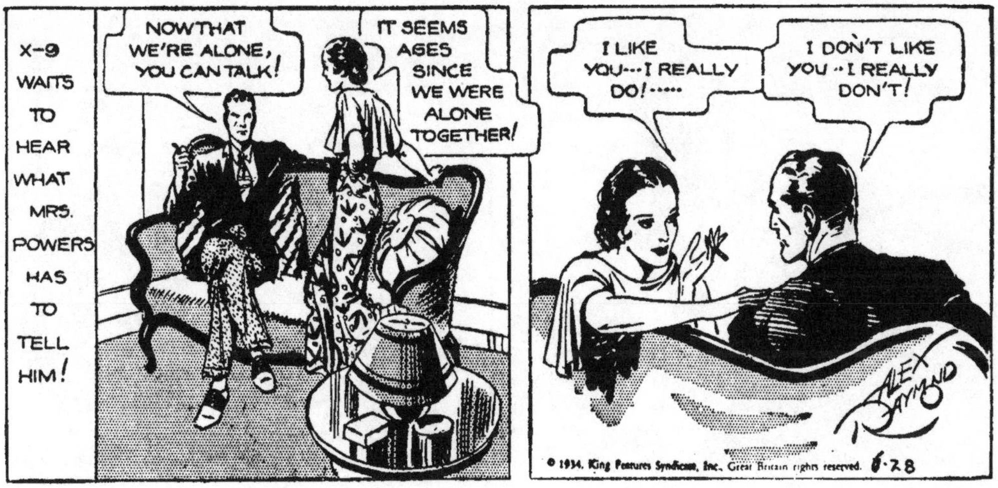
X-9 WAITS TO HEAR WHAT MRS. POWERS HAS TO TELL HIM!
NOW THAT WE'RE ALONE, YOU CAN TALK!
IT SEEMS AGES SINCE WE WERE ALONE TOGETHER!
I LIKE YOU---I REALLY DO!-----
I DON'T LIKE YOU --I REALLY DON'T!
ALEX RAYMOND
© 1934, King Features Syndicate, Inc., Great Britain rights reserved. 6·28

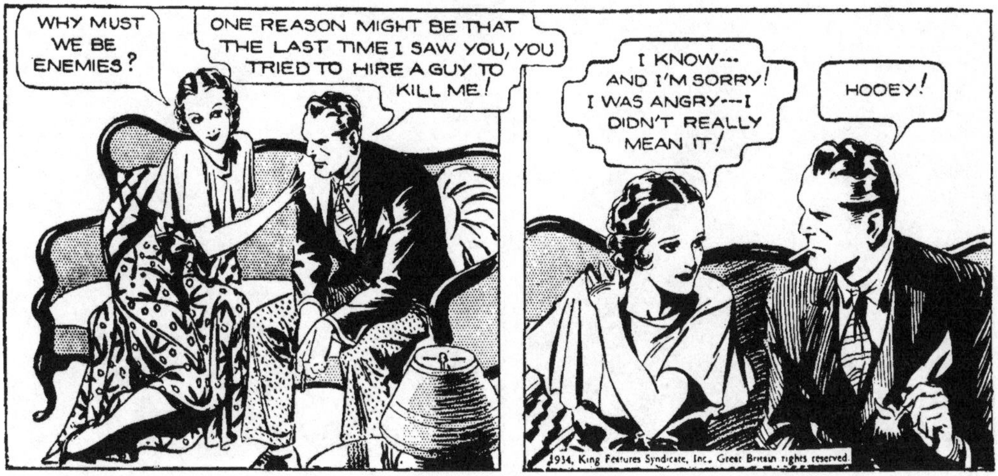
WHY MUST WE BE ENEMIES?
ONE REASON MIGHT BE THAT THE LAST TIME I SAW YOU, YOU TRIED TO HIRE A GUY TO KILL ME!
I KNOW--- AND I'M SORRY! I WAS ANGRY---I DIDN'T REALLY MEAN IT!
HOOEY!
1934, King Features Syndicate, Inc., Great Britain rights reserved.

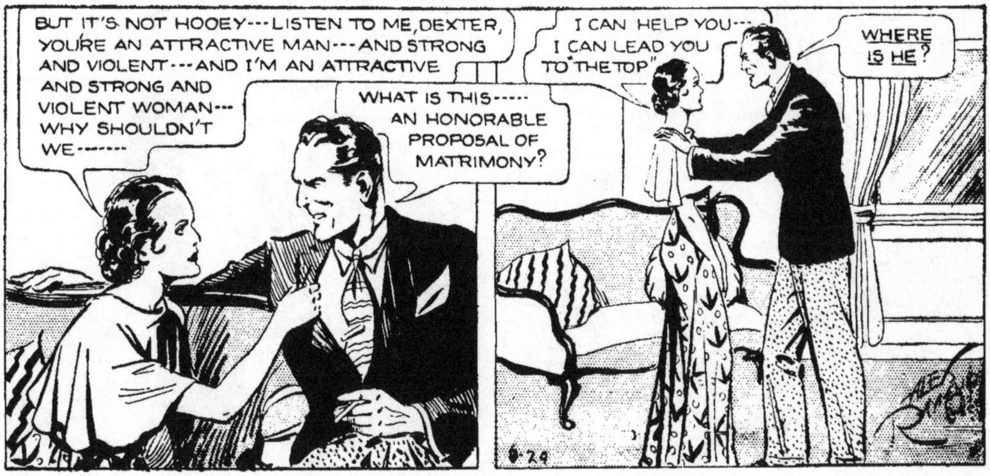
BUT IT'S NOT HOOEY---LISTEN TO ME, DEXTER, YOU'RE AN ATTRACTIVE MAN---AND STRONG AND VIOLENT---AND I'M AN ATTRACTIVE AND STRONG AND VIOLENT WOMAN--- WHY SHOULDN'T WE-------
WHAT IS THIS----- AN HONORABLE PROPOSAL OF MATRIMONY?
I CAN HELP YOU--- I CAN LEAD YOU TO "THE TOP"
WHERE IS HE?
6·29

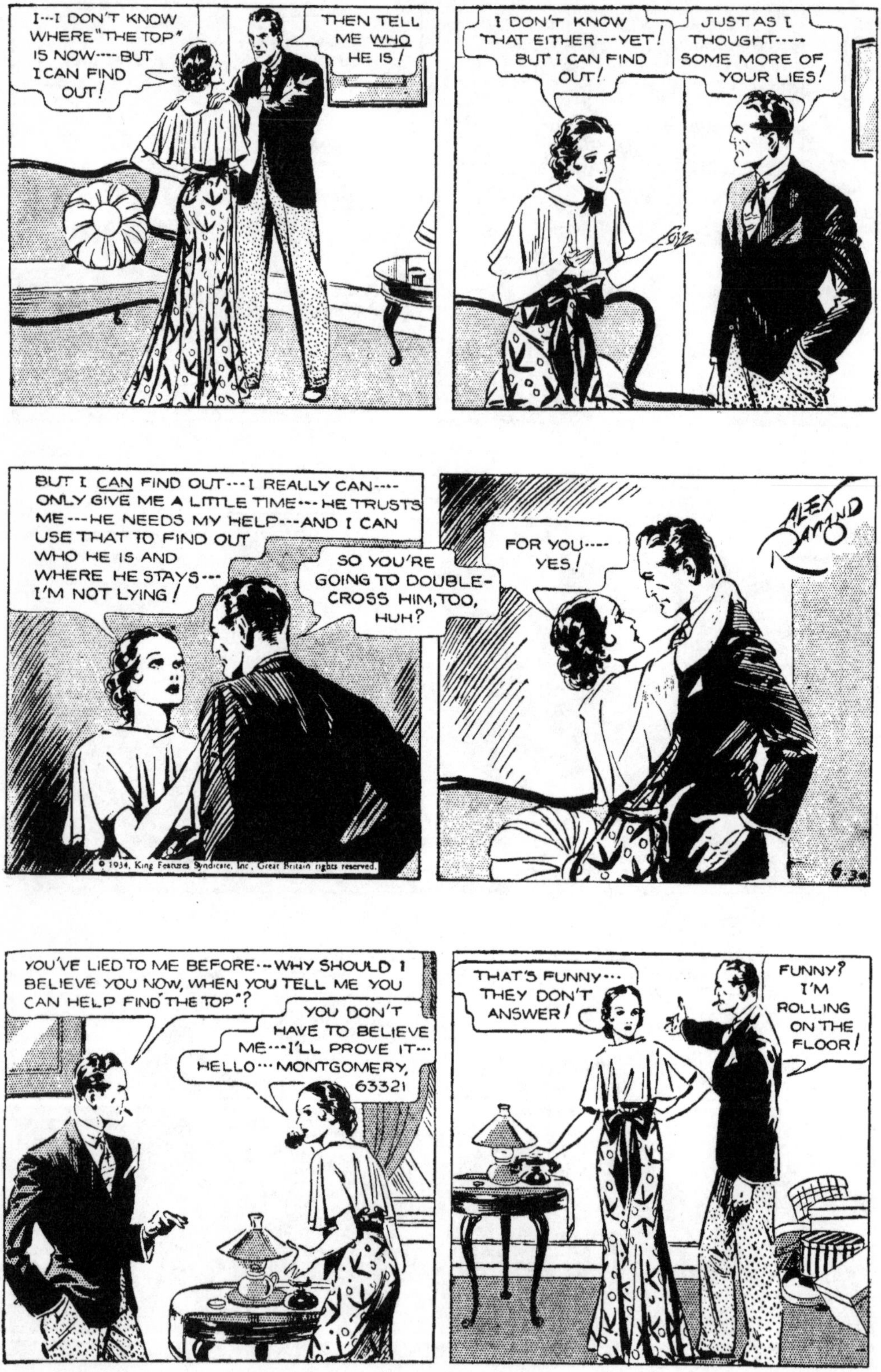

I---I DON'T KNOW WHERE "THE TOP" IS NOW---- BUT I CAN FIND OUT!
THEN TELL ME WHO HE IS!
I DON'T KNOW THAT EITHER---YET! BUT I CAN FIND OUT!
JUST AS I THOUGHT---- SOME MORE OF YOUR LIES!
BUT I CAN FIND OUT---I REALLY CAN---- ONLY GIVE ME A LITTLE TIME--- HE TRUSTS ME---HE NEEDS MY HELP---AND I CAN USE THAT TO FIND OUT WHO HE IS AND WHERE HE STAYS--- I'M NOT LYING!
SO YOU'RE GOING TO DOUBLE-CROSS HIM, TOO, HUH?
© 1934, King Features Syndicate, Inc., Great Britain rights reserved.
ALEX RAYMOND
FOR YOU---- YES!
6-30
YOU'VE LIED TO ME BEFORE--WHY SHOULD I BELIEVE YOU NOW, WHEN YOU TELL ME YOU CAN HELP FIND "THE TOP"?
YOU DON'T HAVE TO BELIEVE ME---I'LL PROVE IT--- HELLO---MONTGOMERY, 63321
THAT'S FUNNY--- THEY DON'T ANSWER!
FUNNY? I'M ROLLING ON THE FLOOR!

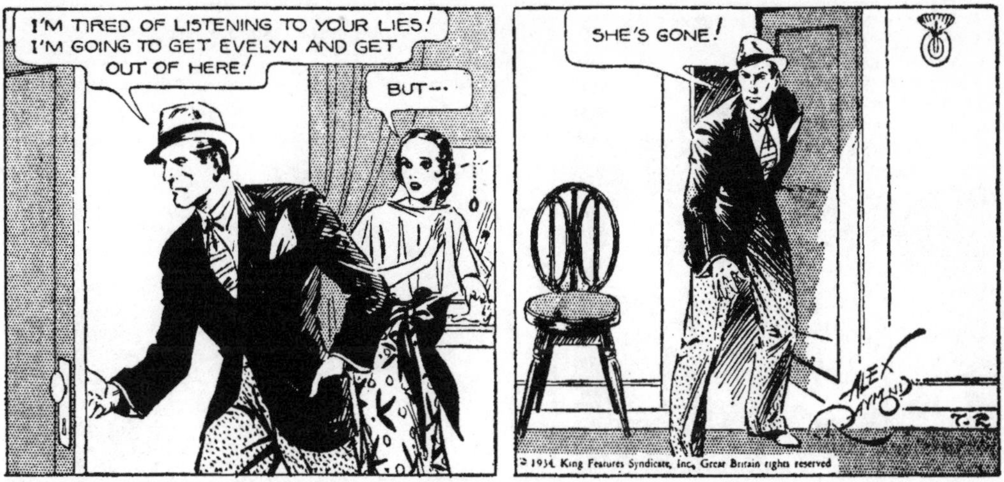
I'M TIRED OF LISTENING TO YOUR LIES! I'M GOING TO GET EVELYN AND GET OUT OF HERE!
BUT---
SHE'S GONE!
ALEX RAYMOND
T. R
© 1934, King Features Syndicate, Inc., Great Britain rights reserved

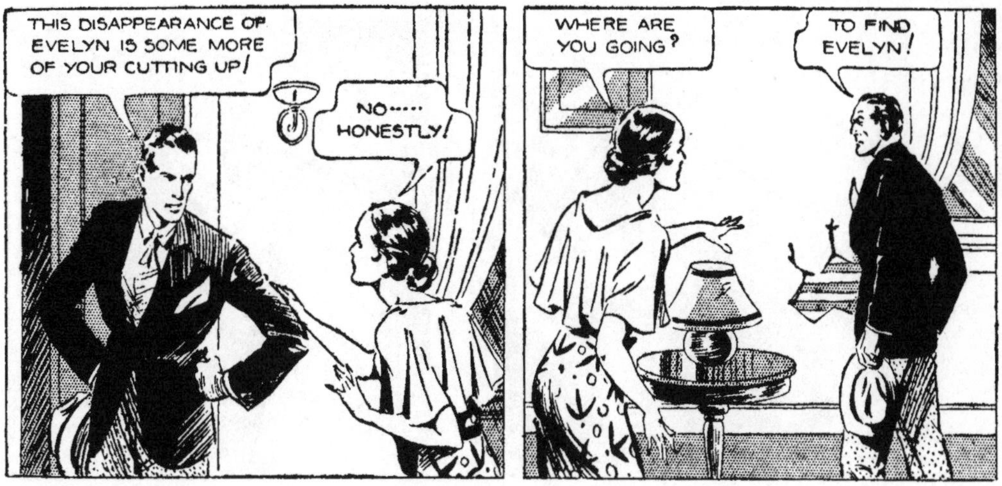
THIS DISAPPEARANCE OF EVELYN IS SOME MORE OF YOUR CUTTING UP!
NO----- HONESTLY!
WHERE ARE YOU GOING?
TO FIND EVELYN!

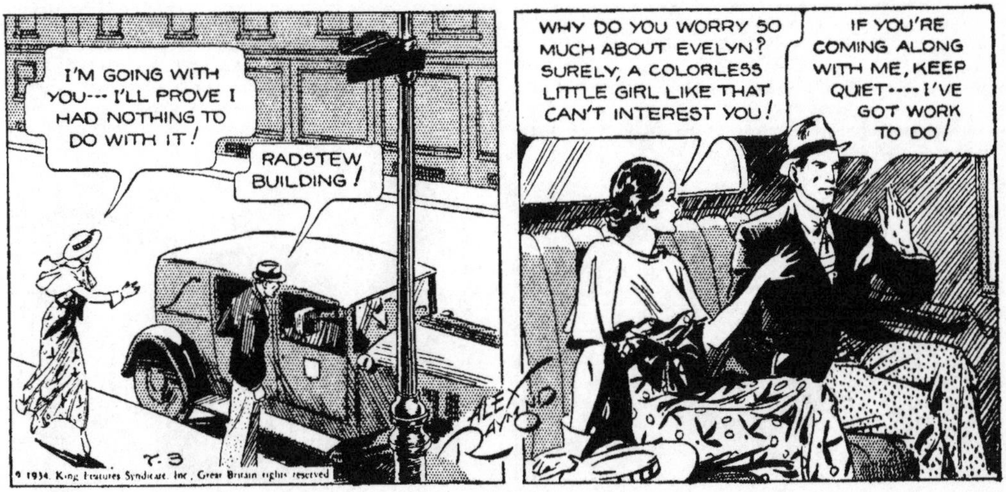
I'M GOING WITH YOU--- I'LL PROVE I HAD NOTHING TO DO WITH IT!
RADSTEW BUILDING!
T. 3
© 1934, King Features Syndicate, Inc., Great Britain rights reserved
ALEX RAYMOND
WHY DO YOU WORRY SO MUCH ABOUT EVELYN? SURELY, A COLORLESS LITTLE GIRL LIKE THAT CAN'T INTEREST YOU!
IF YOU'RE COMING ALONG WITH ME, KEEP QUIET----I'VE GOT WORK TO DO!

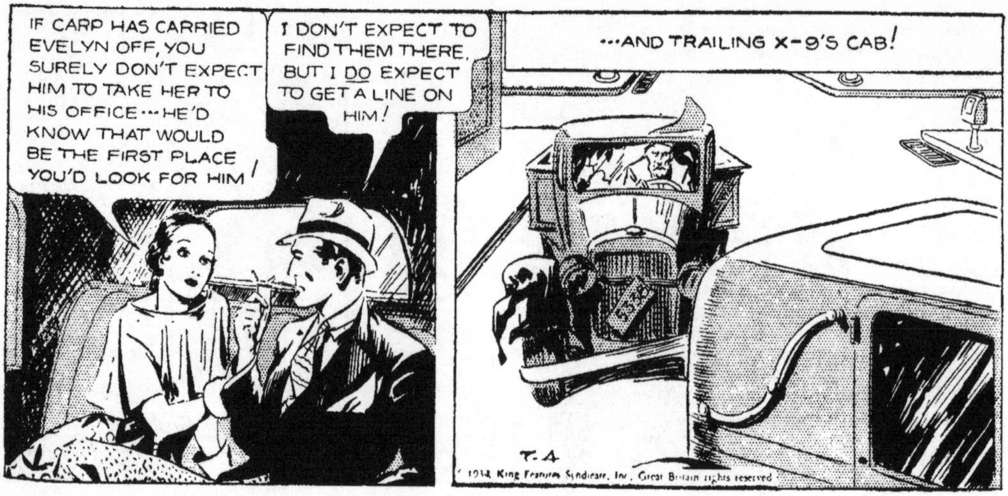
IF CARP HAS CARRIED EVELYN OFF, YOU SURELY DON'T EXPECT HIM TO TAKE HER TO HIS OFFICE --- HE'D KNOW THAT WOULD BE THE FIRST PLACE YOU'D LOOK FOR HIM!
I DON'T EXPECT TO FIND THEM THERE, BUT I DO EXPECT TO GET A LINE ON HIM!
--- AND TRAILING X-9'S CAB!
T-4
© 1934 King Features Syndicate, Inc., Great Britain rights reserved

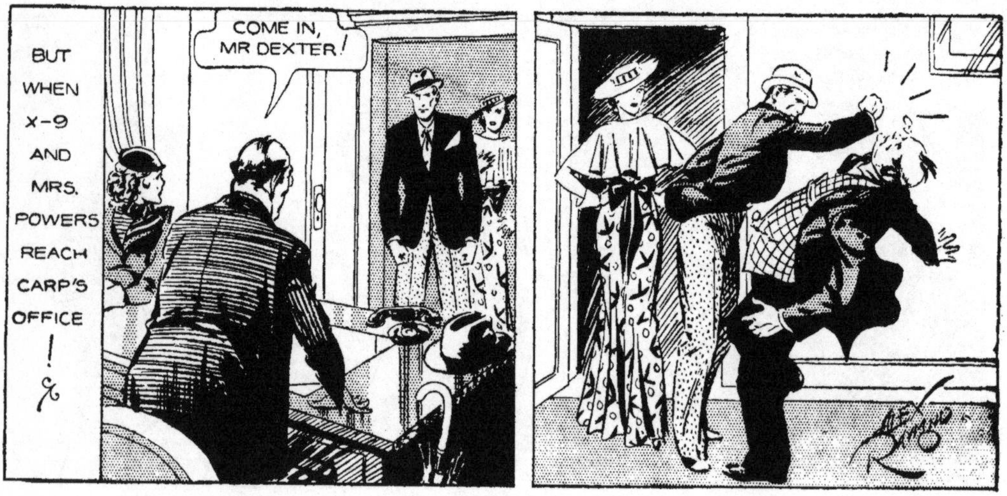
BUT WHEN X-9 AND MRS. POWERS REACH CARP'S OFFICE!
COME IN, MR DEXTER!
ALEX RAYMOND

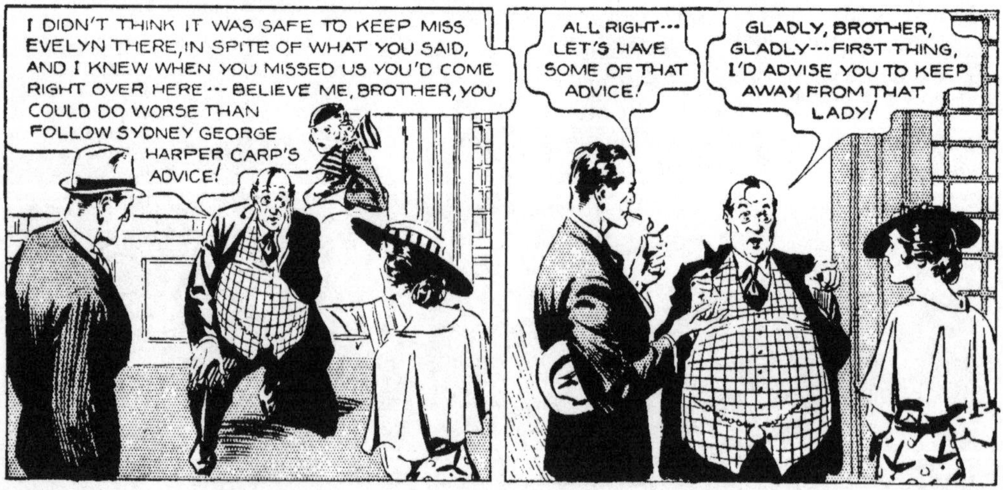
I DIDN'T THINK IT WAS SAFE TO KEEP MISS EVELYN THERE, IN SPITE OF WHAT YOU SAID, AND I KNEW WHEN YOU MISSED US YOU'D COME RIGHT OVER HERE --- BELIEVE ME, BROTHER, YOU COULD DO WORSE THAN FOLLOW SYDNEY GEORGE HARPER CARP'S ADVICE!
ALL RIGHT --- LET'S HAVE SOME OF THAT ADVICE!
GLADLY, BROTHER, GLADLY --- FIRST THING, I'D ADVISE YOU TO KEEP AWAY FROM THAT LADY!

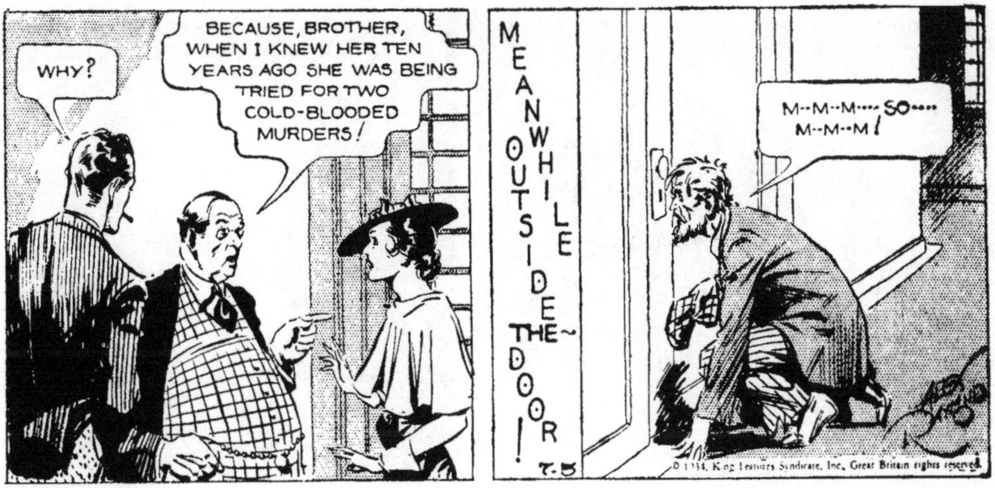
WHY?
BECAUSE, BROTHER, WHEN I KNEW HER TEN YEARS AGO SHE WAS BEING TRIED FOR TWO COLD-BLOODED MURDERS!
MEANWHILE OUTSIDE THE~ DOOR!
M--M--M---- SO---- M--M--M!
7-5
© 1934, King Features Syndicate, Inc., Great Britain rights reserved

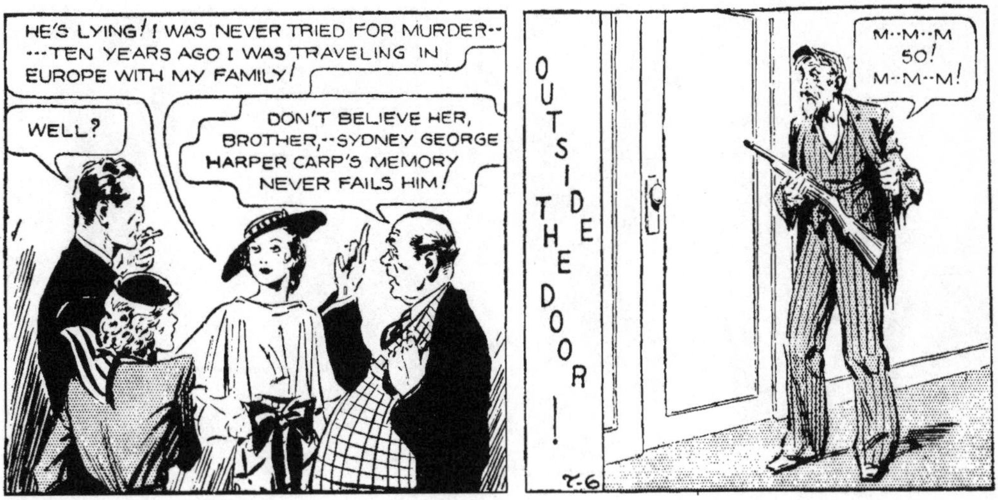
HE'S LYING! I WAS NEVER TRIED FOR MURDER-- ---TEN YEARS AGO I WAS TRAVELING IN EUROPE WITH MY FAMILY!
WELL?
DON'T BELIEVE HER, BROTHER,--SYDNEY GEORGE HARPER CARP'S MEMORY NEVER FAILS HIM!
OUTSIDE THE DOOR!
M--M--M SO! M--M--M!
7-6

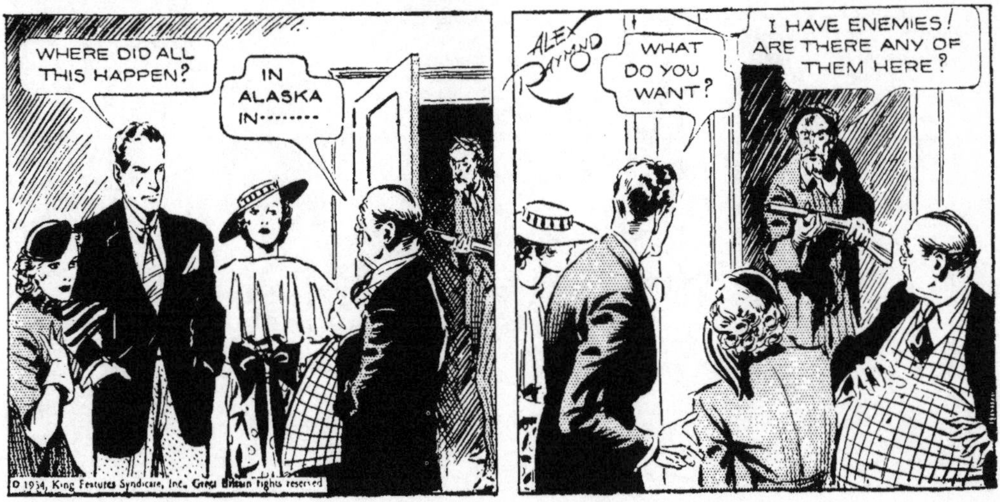
WHERE DID ALL THIS HAPPEN?
IN ALASKA IN--------
© 1934, King Features Syndicate, Inc., Great Britain rights reserved
ALEX RAYMOND
WHAT DO YOU WANT?
I HAVE ENEMIES! ARE THERE ANY OF THEM HERE?

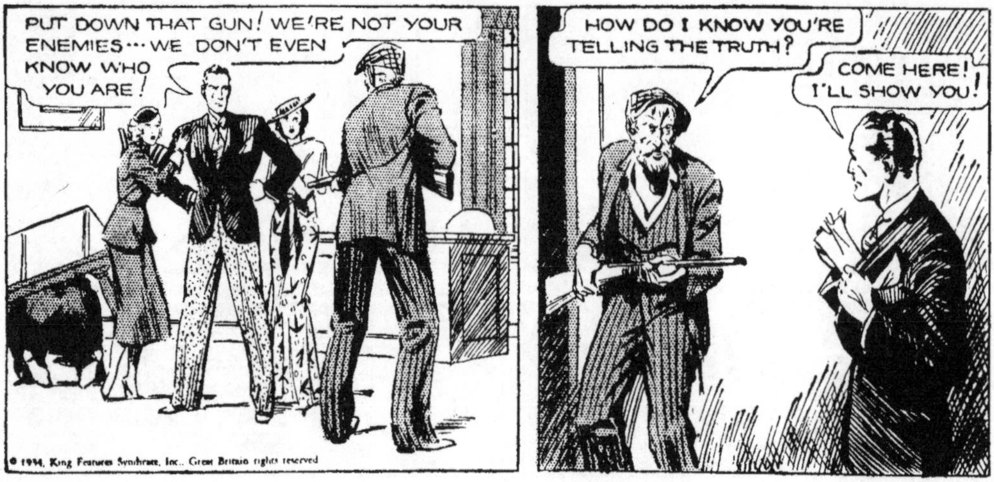
PUT DOWN THAT GUN! WE'RE NOT YOUR ENEMIES--- WE DON'T EVEN KNOW WHO YOU ARE!
HOW DO I KNOW YOU'RE TELLING THE TRUTH?
COME HERE! I'LL SHOW YOU!

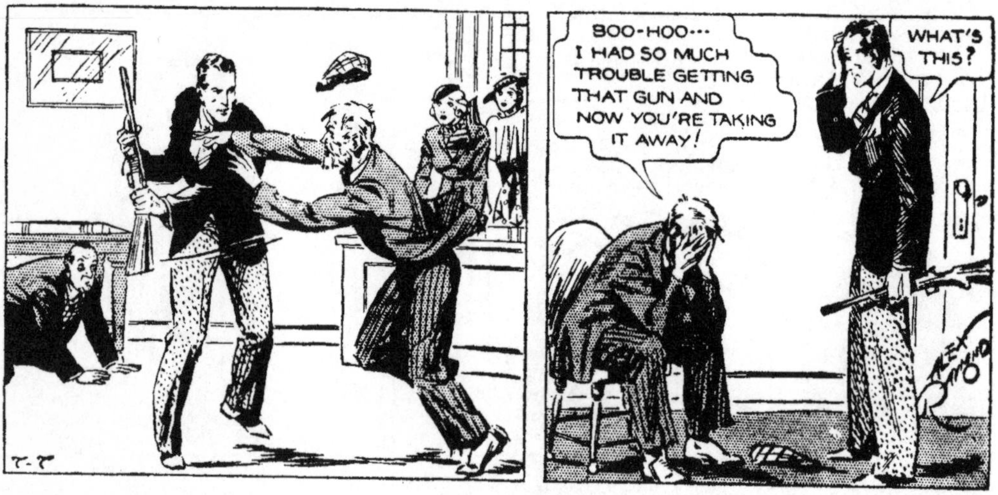
BOO-HOO--- I HAD SO MUCH TROUBLE GETTING THAT GUN AND NOW YOU'RE TAKING IT AWAY!
WHAT'S THIS?

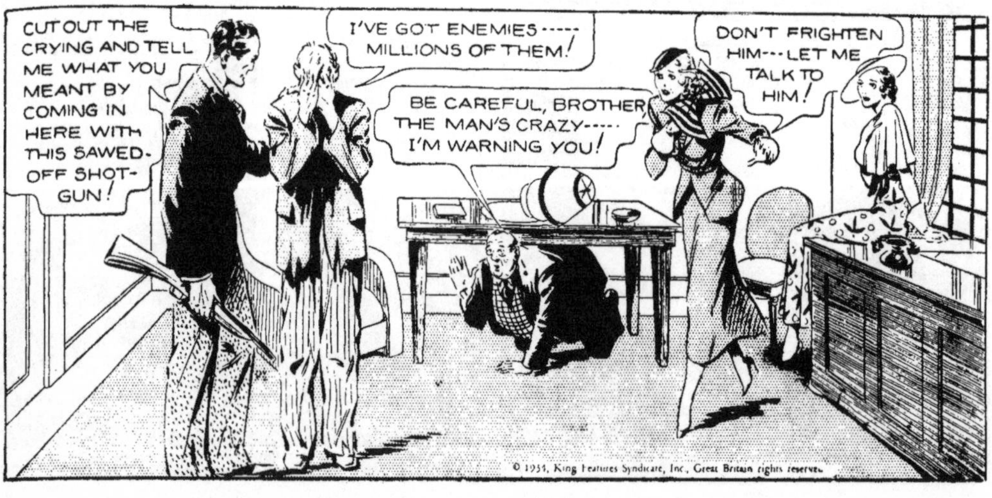
CUT OUT THE CRYING AND TELL ME WHAT YOU MEANT BY COMING IN HERE WITH THIS SAWED-OFF SHOT-GUN!
I'VE GOT ENEMIES ----- MILLIONS OF THEM!
BE CAREFUL, BROTHER THE MAN'S CRAZY----- I'M WARNING YOU!
DON'T FRIGHTEN HIM---LET ME TALK TO HIM!

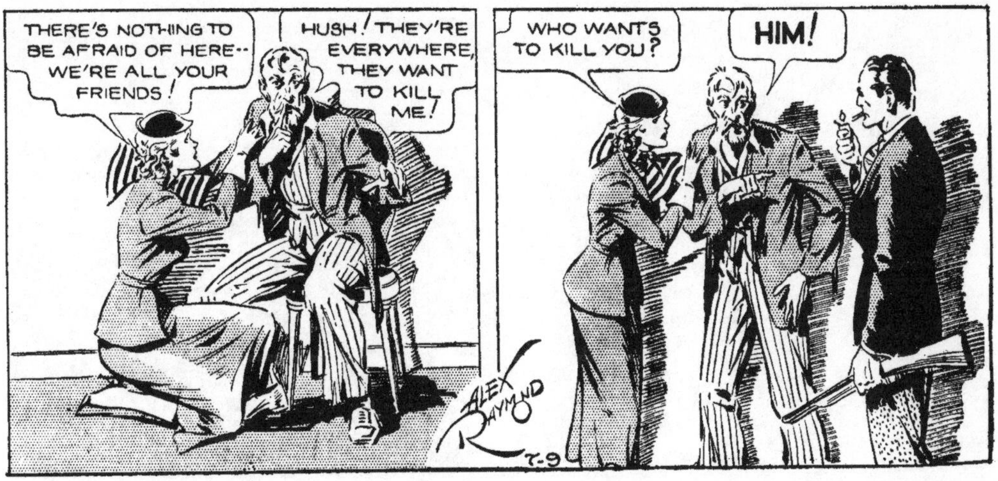
THERE'S NOTHING TO BE AFRAID OF HERE-- WE'RE ALL YOUR FRIENDS!
HUSH! THEY'RE EVERYWHERE, THEY WANT TO KILL ME!
WHO WANTS TO KILL YOU?
HIM!

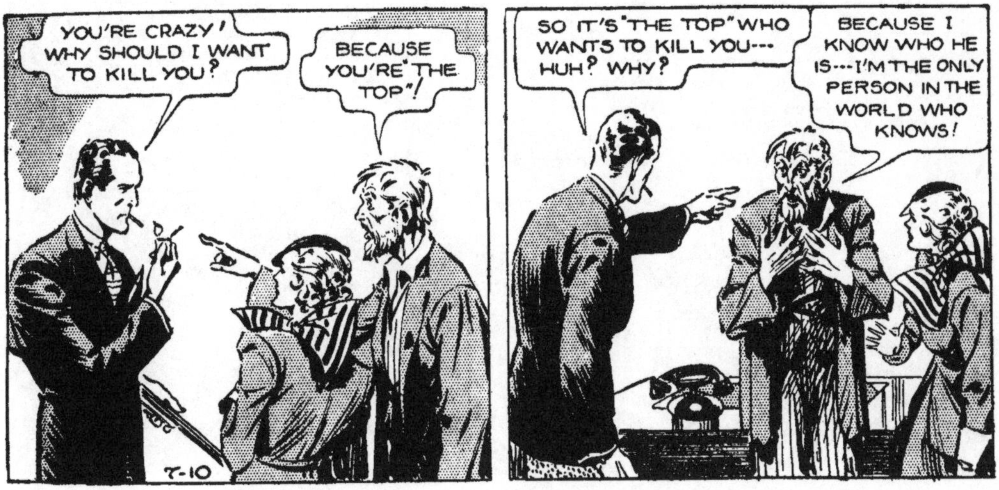
YOU'RE CRAZY! WHY SHOULD I WANT TO KILL YOU?
BECAUSE YOU'RE "THE TOP"!
SO IT'S "THE TOP" WHO WANTS TO KILL YOU--- HUH? WHY?
BECAUSE I KNOW WHO HE IS---I'M THE ONLY PERSON IN THE WORLD WHO KNOWS!

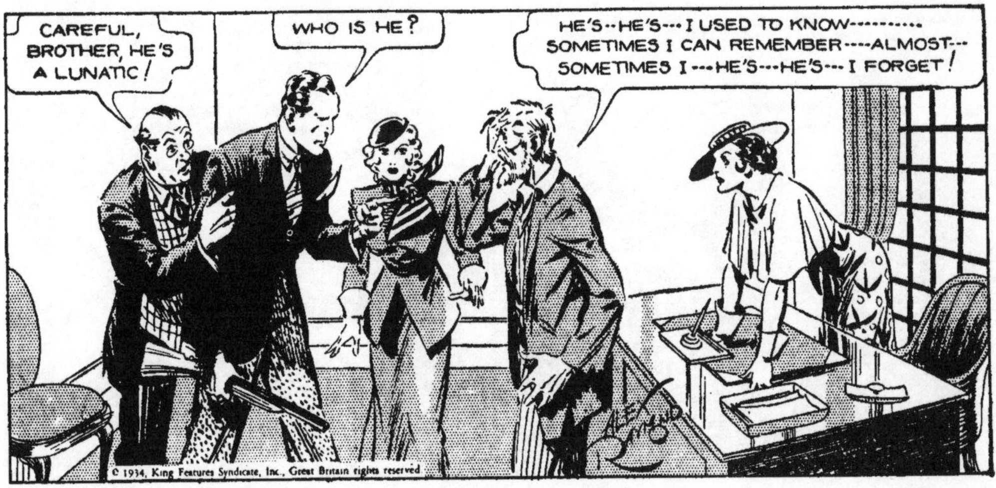
CAREFUL, BROTHER, HE'S A LUNATIC!
WHO IS HE?
HE'S--HE'S--- I USED TO KNOW---------- SOMETIMES I CAN REMEMBER----ALMOST--- SOMETIMES I ---HE'S---HE'S--- I FORGET!
© 1934, King Features Syndicate, Inc., Great Britain rights reserved

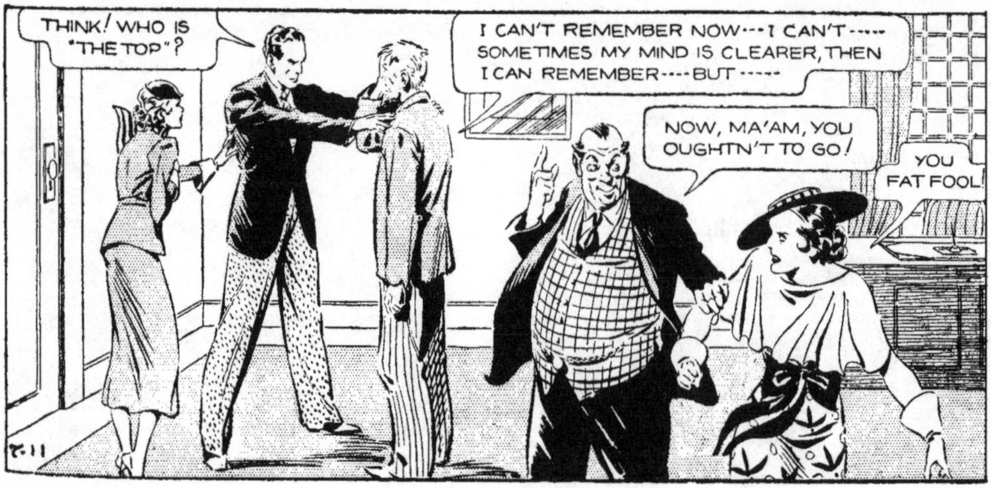
THINK! WHO IS "THE TOP"?
I CAN'T REMEMBER NOW---I CAN'T----- SOMETIMES MY MIND IS CLEARER, THEN I CAN REMEMBER----BUT-----
NOW, MA'AM, YOU OUGHTN'T TO GO!
YOU FAT FOOL!
7-11

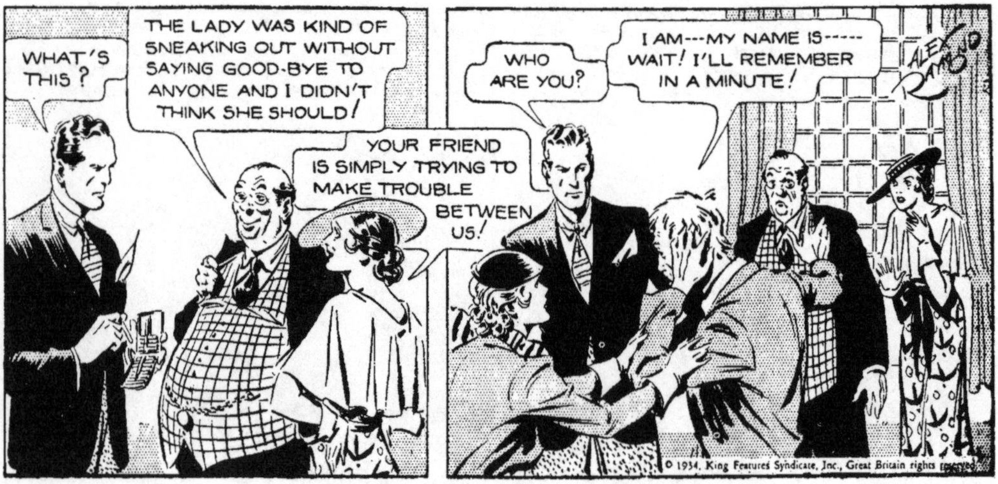
WHAT'S THIS?
THE LADY WAS KIND OF SNEAKING OUT WITHOUT SAYING GOOD-BYE TO ANYONE AND I DIDN'T THINK SHE SHOULD!
YOUR FRIEND IS SIMPLY TRYING TO MAKE TROUBLE BETWEEN US!
WHO ARE YOU?
I AM---MY NAME IS----- WAIT! I'LL REMEMBER IN A MINUTE!
ALEX RAYMOND
© 1934, King Features Syndicate, Inc., Great Britain rights reserved.

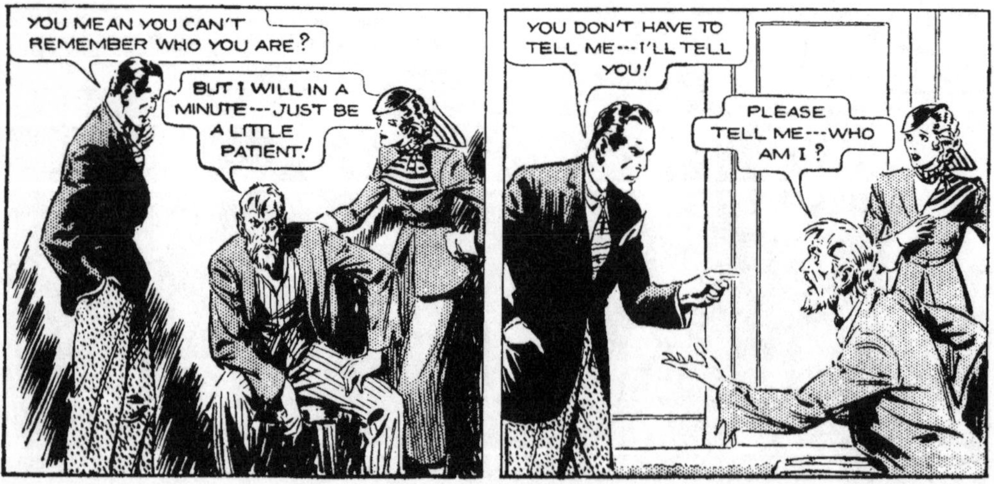
YOU MEAN YOU CAN'T REMEMBER WHO YOU ARE?
BUT I WILL IN A MINUTE---JUST BE A LITTLE PATIENT!
YOU DON'T HAVE TO TELL ME---I'LL TELL YOU!
PLEASE TELL ME---WHO AM I?

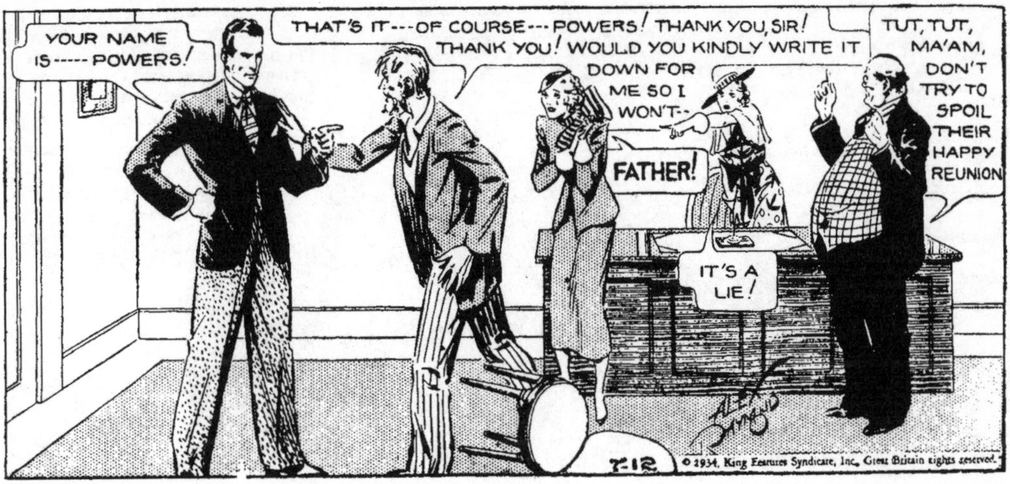
YOUR NAME IS----- POWERS!
THAT'S IT---OF COURSE---POWERS! THANK YOU, SIR! THANK YOU! WOULD YOU KINDLY WRITE IT DOWN FOR ME SO I WON'T-
FATHER!
IT'S A LIE!
TUT, TUT, MA'AM, DON'T TRY TO SPOIL THEIR HAPPY REUNION
ALEX RAYMOND
7-12
© 1934, King Features Syndicate, Inc., Great Britain rights reserved.

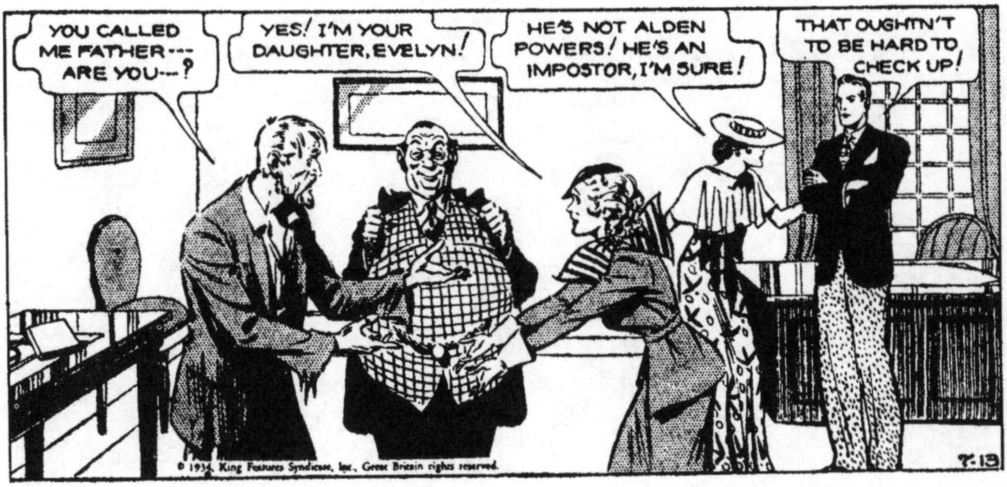
YOU CALLED ME FATHER--- ARE YOU---?
YES! I'M YOUR DAUGHTER, EVELYN!
HE'S NOT ALDEN POWERS! HE'S AN IMPOSTOR, I'M SURE!
THAT OUGHTN'T TO BE HARD TO CHECK UP!
© 1934, King Features Syndicate, Inc., Great Britain rights reserved.
7-13

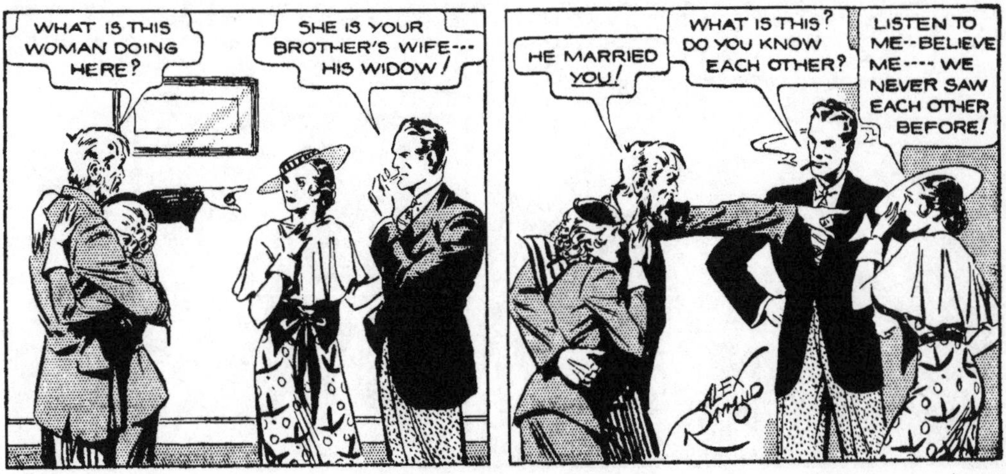
WHAT IS THIS WOMAN DOING HERE?
SHE IS YOUR BROTHER'S WIFE--- HIS WIDOW!
HE MARRIED YOU!
WHAT IS THIS? DO YOU KNOW EACH OTHER?
LISTEN TO ME--BELIEVE ME---- WE NEVER SAW EACH OTHER BEFORE!
ALEX RAYMOND

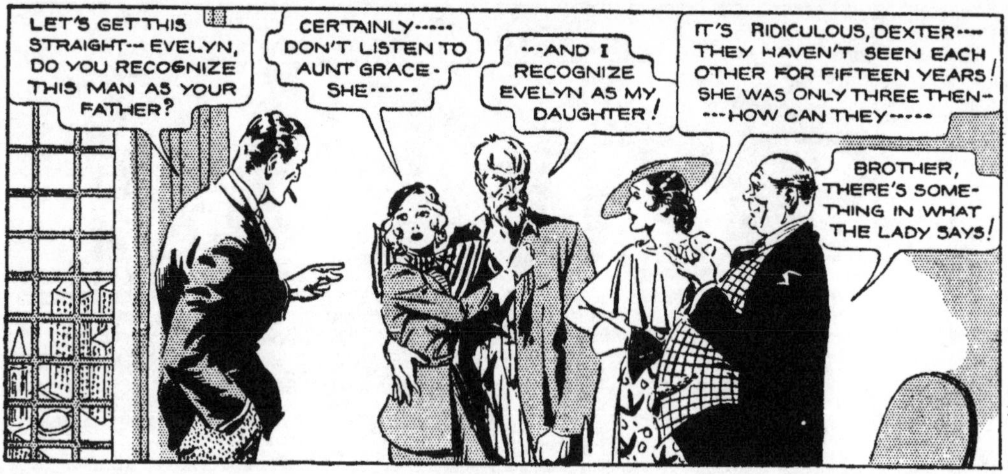
LET'S GET THIS STRAIGHT-- EVELYN, DO YOU RECOGNIZE THIS MAN AS YOUR FATHER?
CERTAINLY----- DON'T LISTEN TO AUNT GRACE- SHE------
---AND I RECOGNIZE EVELYN AS MY DAUGHTER!
IT'S RIDICULOUS, DEXTER---- THEY HAVEN'T SEEN EACH OTHER FOR FIFTEEN YEARS! SHE WAS ONLY THREE THEN-- ---HOW CAN THEY-----
BROTHER, THERE'S SOMETHING IN WHAT THE LADY SAYS!

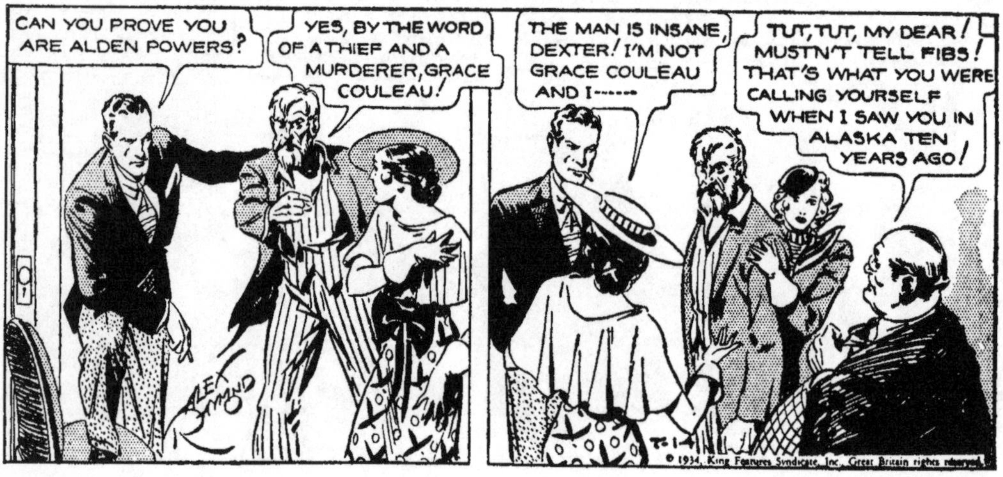
CAN YOU PROVE YOU ARE ALDEN POWERS?
YES, BY THE WORD OF A THIEF AND A MURDERER, GRACE COULEAU!
ALEX RAYMOND
THE MAN IS INSANE, DEXTER! I'M NOT GRACE COULEAU AND I------
TUT, TUT, MY DEAR! MUSTN'T TELL FIBS! THAT'S WHAT YOU WERE CALLING YOURSELF WHEN I SAW YOU IN ALASKA TEN YEARS AGO!
7-14
© 1934, King Features Syndicate, Inc., Great Britain rights reserved.

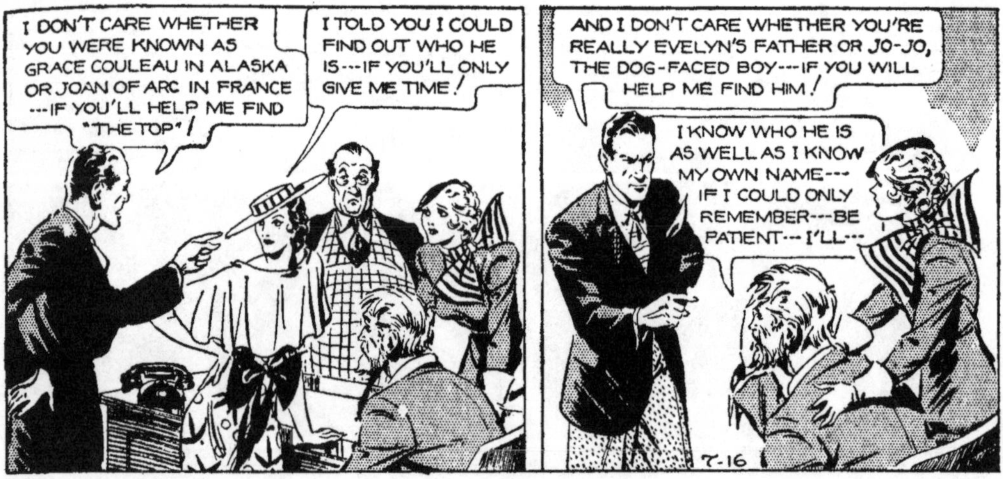
I DON'T CARE WHETHER YOU WERE KNOWN AS GRACE COULEAU IN ALASKA OR JOAN OF ARC IN FRANCE ---IF YOU'LL HELP ME FIND "THE TOP"!
I TOLD YOU I COULD FIND OUT WHO HE IS---IF YOU'LL ONLY GIVE ME TIME!
AND I DON'T CARE WHETHER YOU'RE REALLY EVELYN'S FATHER OR JO-JO, THE DOG-FACED BOY---IF YOU WILL HELP ME FIND HIM!
I KNOW WHO HE IS AS WELL AS I KNOW MY OWN NAME--- IF I COULD ONLY REMEMBER---BE PATIENT--- I'LL---
7-16

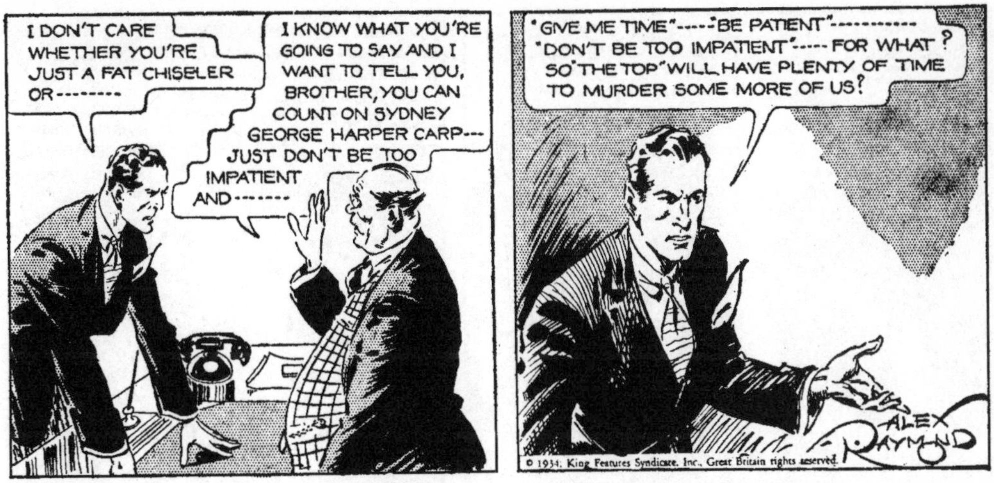
I DON'T CARE WHETHER YOU'RE JUST A FAT CHISELER OR --------
I KNOW WHAT YOU'RE GOING TO SAY AND I WANT TO TELL YOU, BROTHER, YOU CAN COUNT ON SYDNEY GEORGE HARPER CARP--- JUST DON'T BE TOO IMPATIENT AND -------
"GIVE ME TIME"-----"BE PATIENT"----------- "DON'T BE TOO IMPATIENT"----- FOR WHAT ? SO "THE TOP" WILL HAVE PLENTY OF TIME TO MURDER SOME MORE OF US?
ALEX RAYMOND
© 1934, King Features Syndicate, Inc., Great Britain rights reserved.

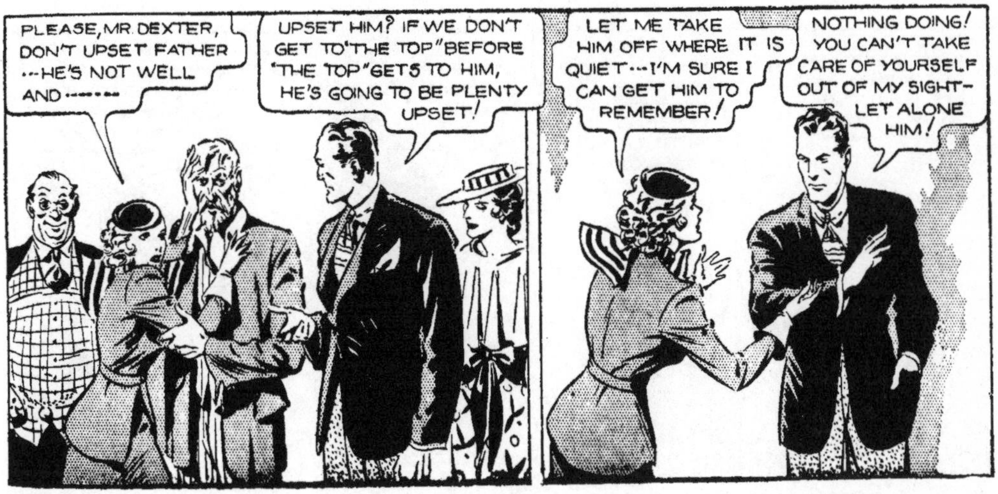
PLEASE, MR. DEXTER, DON'T UPSET FATHER ---HE'S NOT WELL AND -------
UPSET HIM? IF WE DON'T GET TO "THE TOP" BEFORE "THE TOP" GETS TO HIM, HE'S GOING TO BE PLENTY UPSET!
LET ME TAKE HIM OFF WHERE IT IS QUIET---I'M SURE I CAN GET HIM TO REMEMBER!
NOTHING DOING! YOU CAN'T TAKE CARE OF YOURSELF OUT OF MY SIGHT- LET ALONE HIM!

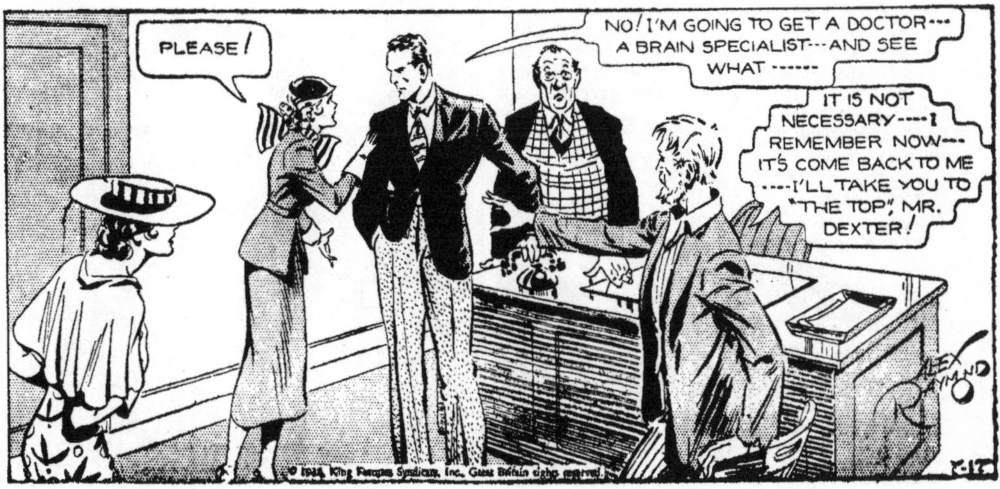
PLEASE!
NO! I'M GOING TO GET A DOCTOR--- A BRAIN SPECIALIST---AND SEE WHAT ------
IT IS NOT NECESSARY----I REMEMBER NOW--- IT'S COME BACK TO ME ----I'LL TAKE YOU TO "THE TOP", MR. DEXTER!
ALEX RAYMOND
© 1934, King Features Syndicate, Inc., Great Britain rights reserved.
7-17

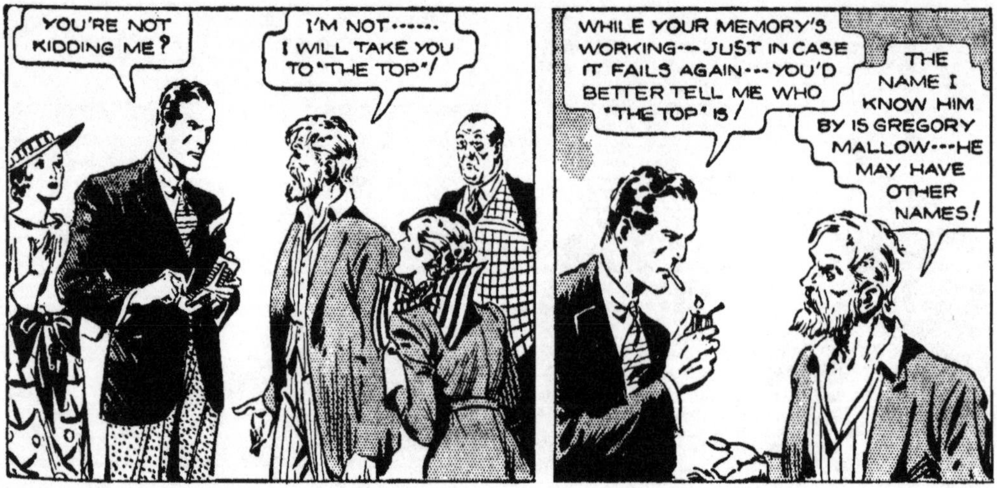
YOU'RE NOT KIDDING ME?
I'M NOT------ I WILL TAKE YOU TO "THE TOP"!
WHILE YOUR MEMORY'S WORKING--- JUST IN CASE IT FAILS AGAIN--- YOU'D BETTER TELL ME WHO "THE TOP" IS!
THE NAME I KNOW HIM BY IS GREGORY MALLOW---HE MAY HAVE OTHER NAMES!

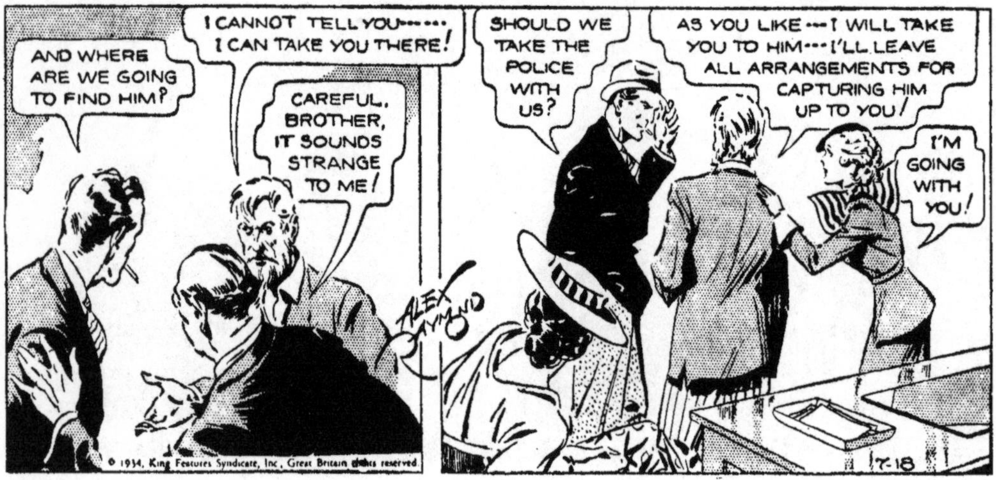
AND WHERE ARE WE GOING TO FIND HIM?
I CANNOT TELL YOU------ I CAN TAKE YOU THERE!
CAREFUL, BROTHER, IT SOUNDS STRANGE TO ME!
© 1934, King Features Syndicate, Inc., Great Britain rights reserved.
ALEX RAYMOND
SHOULD WE TAKE THE POLICE WITH US?
AS YOU LIKE---I WILL TAKE YOU TO HIM---I'LL LEAVE ALL ARRANGEMENTS FOR CAPTURING HIM UP TO YOU!
I'M GOING WITH YOU!
7-18

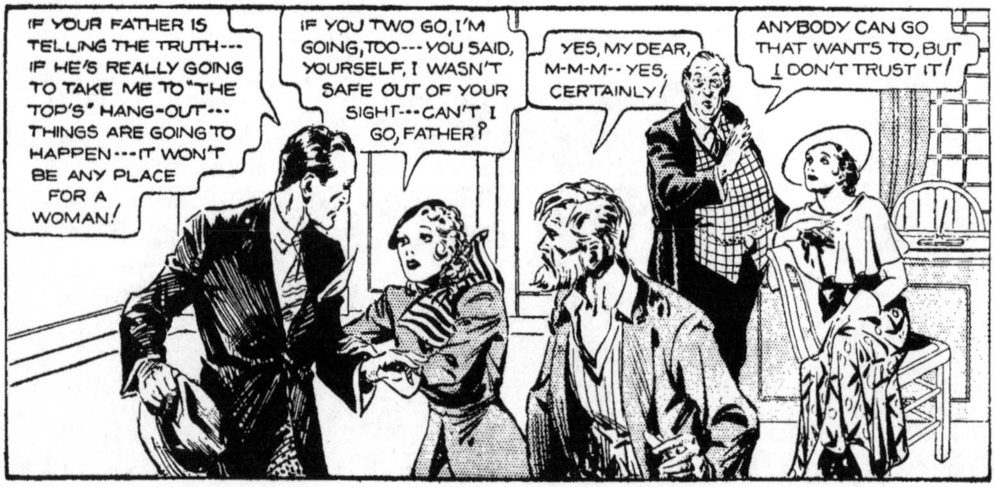
IF YOUR FATHER IS TELLING THE TRUTH--- IF HE'S REALLY GOING TO TAKE ME TO "THE TOP'S" HANG-OUT--- THINGS ARE GOING TO HAPPEN---IT WON'T BE ANY PLACE FOR A WOMAN!
IF YOU TWO GO, I'M GOING, TOO--- YOU SAID, YOURSELF, I WASN'T SAFE OUT OF YOUR SIGHT---CAN'T I GO, FATHER?
YES, MY DEAR, M-M-M-- YES, CERTAINLY!
ANYBODY CAN GO THAT WANTS TO, BUT I DON'T TRUST IT!

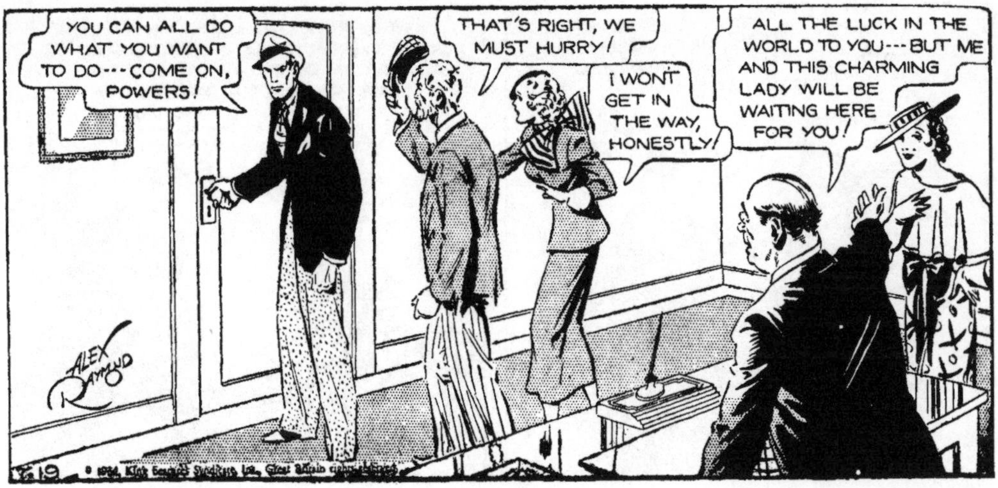

YOU CAN ALL DO WHAT YOU WANT TO DO---COME ON, POWERS!
ALEX RAYMOND
THAT'S RIGHT, WE MUST HURRY!
I WON'T GET IN THE WAY, HONESTLY!
ALL THE LUCK IN THE WORLD TO YOU---BUT ME AND THIS CHARMING LADY WILL BE WAITING HERE FOR YOU!

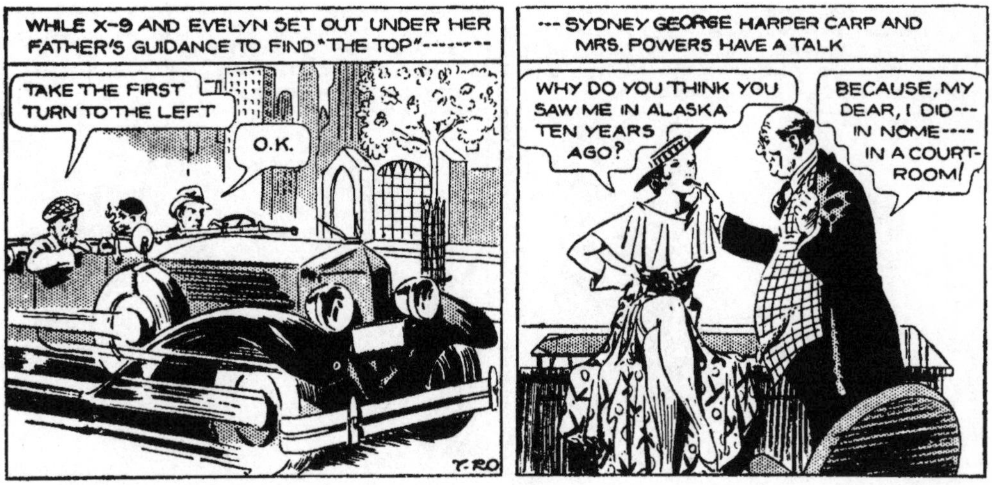

WHILE X-9 AND EVELYN SET OUT UNDER HER FATHER'S GUIDANCE TO FIND "THE TOP"--------
TAKE THE FIRST TURN TO THE LEFT
O.K.
---SYDNEY GEORGE HARPER CARP AND MRS. POWERS HAVE A TALK
WHY DO YOU THINK YOU SAW ME IN ALASKA TEN YEARS AGO?
BECAUSE, MY DEAR, I DID---IN NOME----IN A COURT-ROOM!

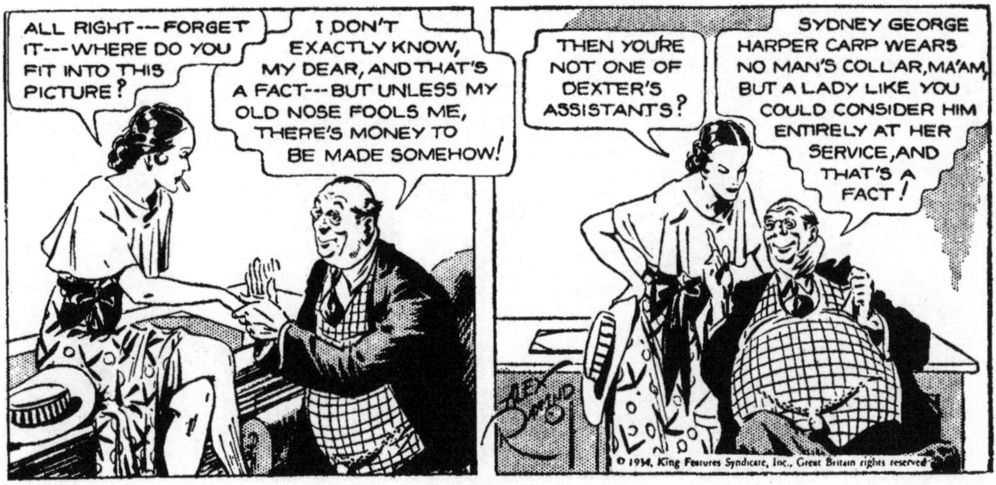

ALL RIGHT---FORGET IT---WHERE DO YOU FIT INTO THIS PICTURE?
I DON'T EXACTLY KNOW, MY DEAR, AND THAT'S A FACT---BUT UNLESS MY OLD NOSE FOOLS ME, THERE'S MONEY TO BE MADE SOMEHOW!
THEN YOU'RE NOT ONE OF DEXTER'S ASSISTANTS?
SYDNEY GEORGE HARPER CARP WEARS NO MAN'S COLLAR, MA'AM, BUT A LADY LIKE YOU COULD CONSIDER HIM ENTIRELY AT HER SERVICE, AND THAT'S A FACT!
ALEX RAYMOND
© 1934, King Features Syndicate, Inc., Great Britain rights reserved

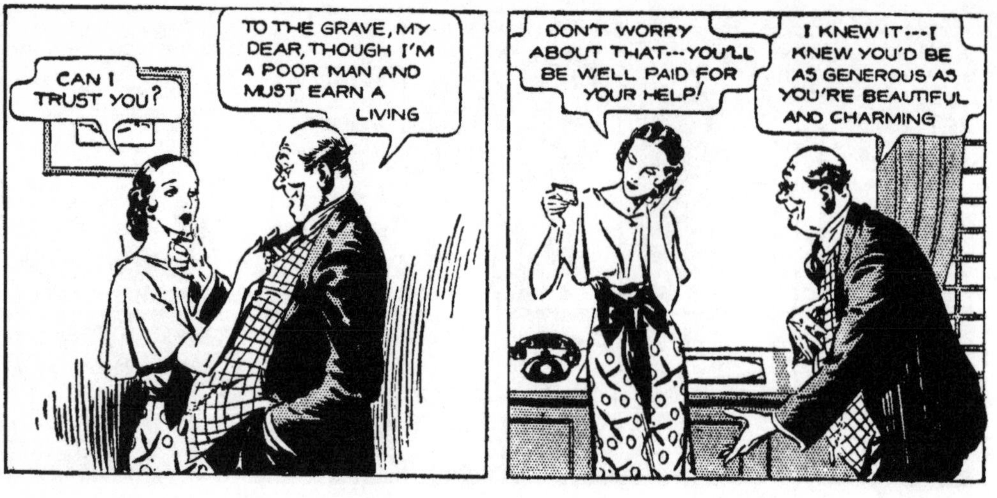
CAN I TRUST YOU?
TO THE GRAVE, MY DEAR, THOUGH I'M A POOR MAN AND MUST EARN A LIVING
DON'T WORRY ABOUT THAT---YOU'LL BE WELL PAID FOR YOUR HELP!
I KNEW IT---I KNEW YOU'D BE AS GENEROUS AS YOU'RE BEAUTIFUL AND CHARMING

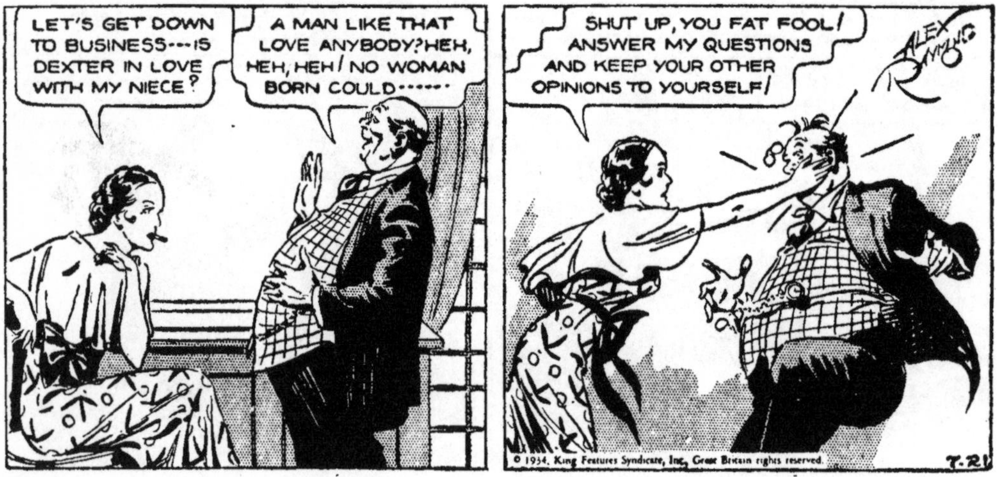
LET'S GET DOWN TO BUSINESS---IS DEXTER IN LOVE WITH MY NIECE?
A MAN LIKE THAT LOVE ANYBODY? HEH, HEH, HEH! NO WOMAN BORN COULD------
SHUT UP, YOU FAT FOOL! ANSWER MY QUESTIONS AND KEEP YOUR OTHER OPINIONS TO YOURSELF!
ALEX RAYMOND
© 1934, King Features Syndicate, Inc. Great Britain rights reserved.
7-21

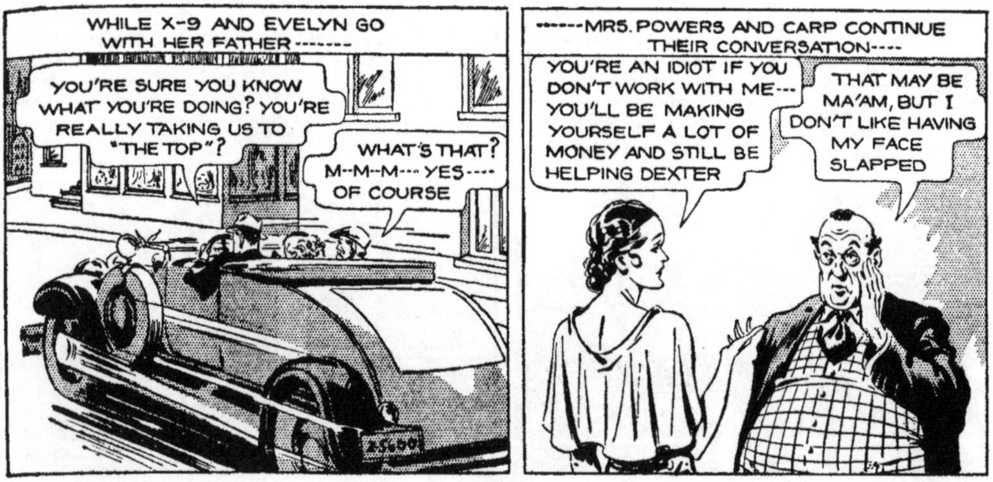
WHILE X-9 AND EVELYN GO WITH HER FATHER-------
YOU'RE SURE YOU KNOW WHAT YOU'RE DOING? YOU'RE REALLY TAKING US TO "THE TOP"?
WHAT'S THAT? M--M--M--- YES---- OF COURSE
------MRS. POWERS AND CARP CONTINUE THEIR CONVERSATION----
YOU'RE AN IDIOT IF YOU DON'T WORK WITH ME--- YOU'LL BE MAKING YOURSELF A LOT OF MONEY AND STILL BE HELPING DEXTER
THAT MAY BE MA'AM, BUT I DON'T LIKE HAVING MY FACE SLAPPED

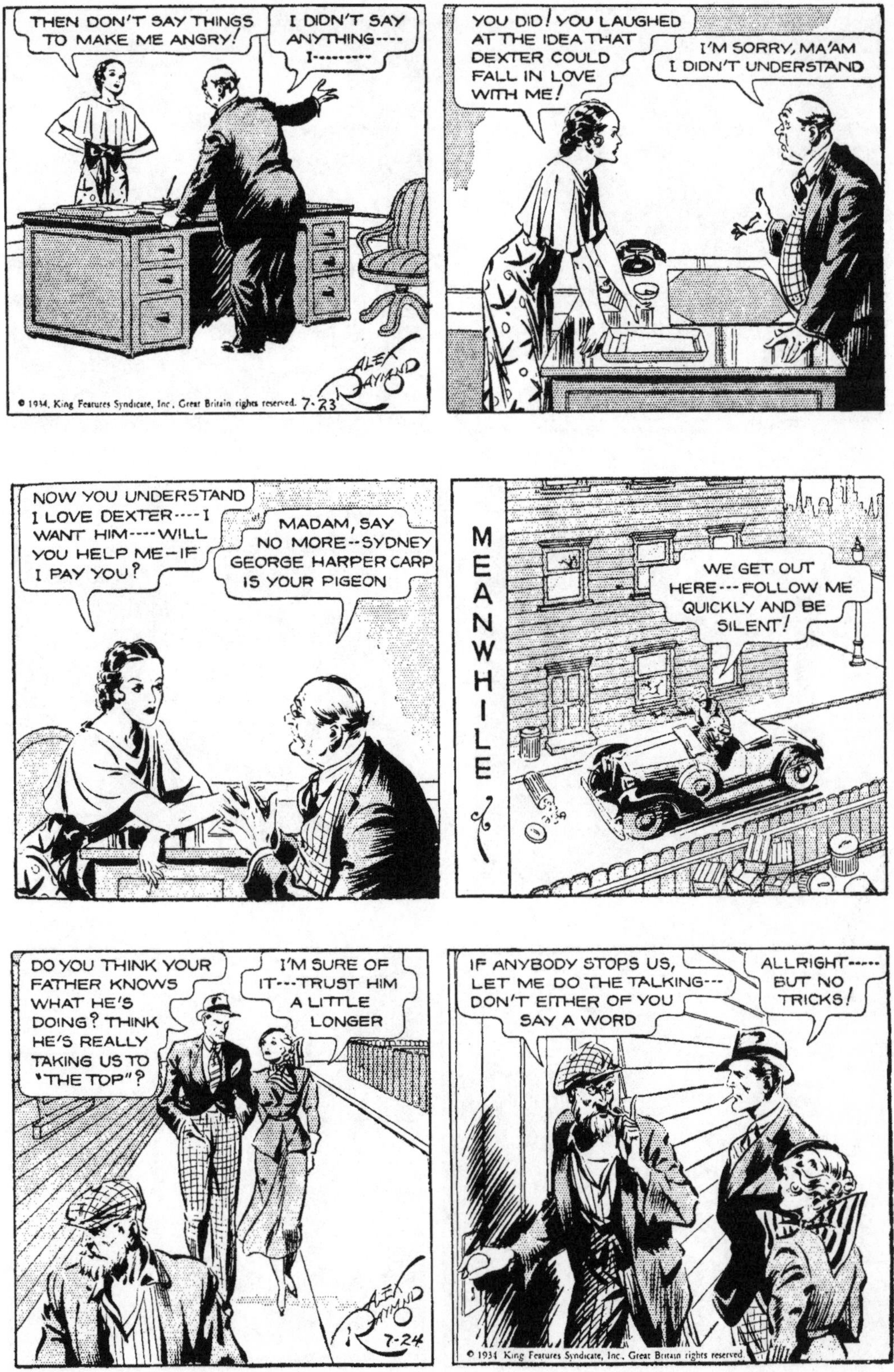
THEN DON'T SAY THINGS TO MAKE ME ANGRY!
I DIDN'T SAY ANYTHING---- I---------
ALEX RAYMOND 7-23
© 1934, King Features Syndicate, Inc., Great Britain rights reserved.
YOU DID! YOU LAUGHED AT THE IDEA THAT DEXTER COULD FALL IN LOVE WITH ME!
I'M SORRY, MA'AM I DIDN'T UNDERSTAND
NOW YOU UNDERSTAND I LOVE DEXTER----I WANT HIM----WILL YOU HELP ME—IF I PAY YOU?
MADAM, SAY NO MORE--SYDNEY GEORGE HARPER CARP IS YOUR PIGEON
MEANWHILE
WE GET OUT HERE---FOLLOW ME QUICKLY AND BE SILENT!
DO YOU THINK YOUR FATHER KNOWS WHAT HE'S DOING? THINK HE'S REALLY TAKING US TO "THE TOP"?
I'M SURE OF IT---TRUST HIM A LITTLE LONGER
ALEX RAYMOND 7-24
IF ANYBODY STOPS US, LET ME DO THE TALKING--- DON'T EITHER OF YOU SAY A WORD
ALLRIGHT----- BUT NO TRICKS!
© 1934 King Features Syndicate, Inc., Great Britain rights reserved.

SH-H-H!
7-25
© 1934, King Features Syndicate, Inc., Great Britain rights reserved.
BE CAREFUL--- THIS LADDER ISN'T VERY STRONG
QUIET NOW, WE'RE ALMOST THERE---
I HOPE SO!
ALEX RAYMOND
NOTHING DOING--- WE STAY TOGETHER!
OH, WHY CAN'T YOU TRUST HIM?
WAIT HERE 'TIL I-----
I TRUST YOU ALLRIGHT, POWERS, BUT I'M NOT LETTING YOU OUT OF MY SIGHT
M-M-M--- SO--- YOU'D BE SAFER WAITING HERE 'TIL I FOUND OUT-- BUT COME ON!
'TIL YOU FOUND OUT WHAT?
SH-H-H!
© 1934, King Features Syndicate, Inc., Great Britain rights reserved.
7-26

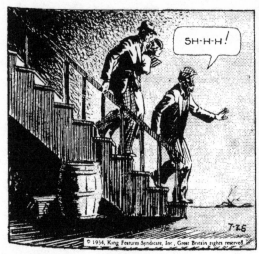

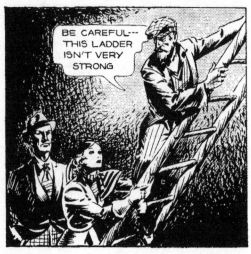

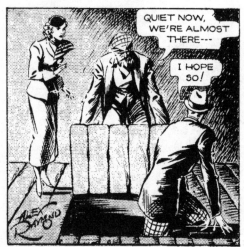

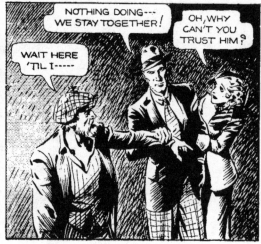

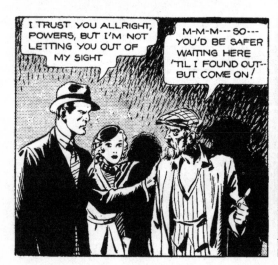

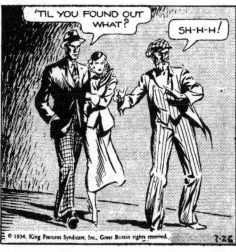

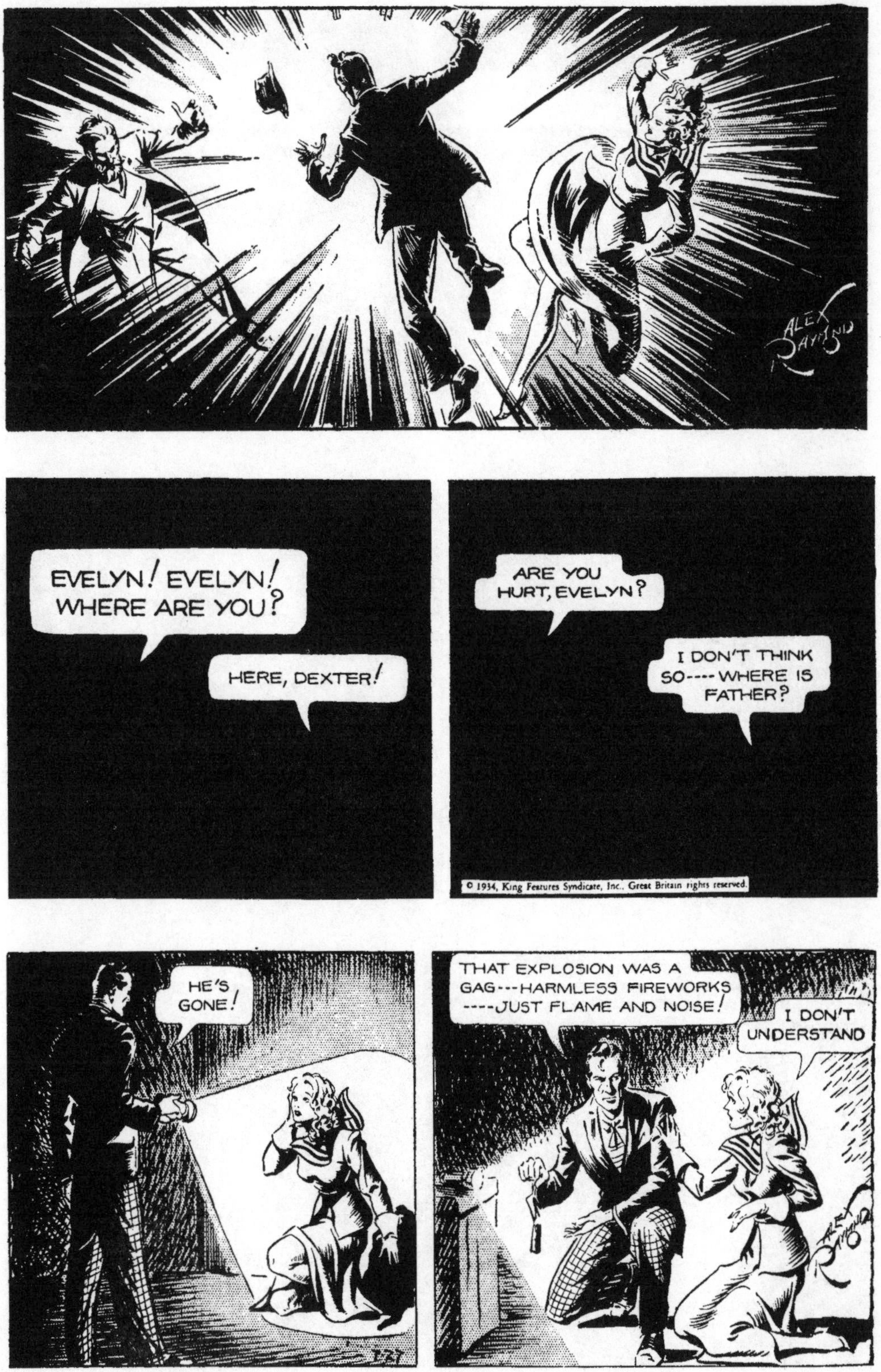
EVELYN! EVELYN! WHERE ARE YOU?
HERE, DEXTER!
ARE YOU HURT, EVELYN?
I DON'T THINK SO---- WHERE IS FATHER?
© 1934, King Features Syndicate, Inc., Great Britain rights reserved.
HE'S GONE!
THAT EXPLOSION WAS A GAG---HARMLESS FIREWORKS ----JUST FLAME AND NOISE!
I DON'T UNDERSTAND

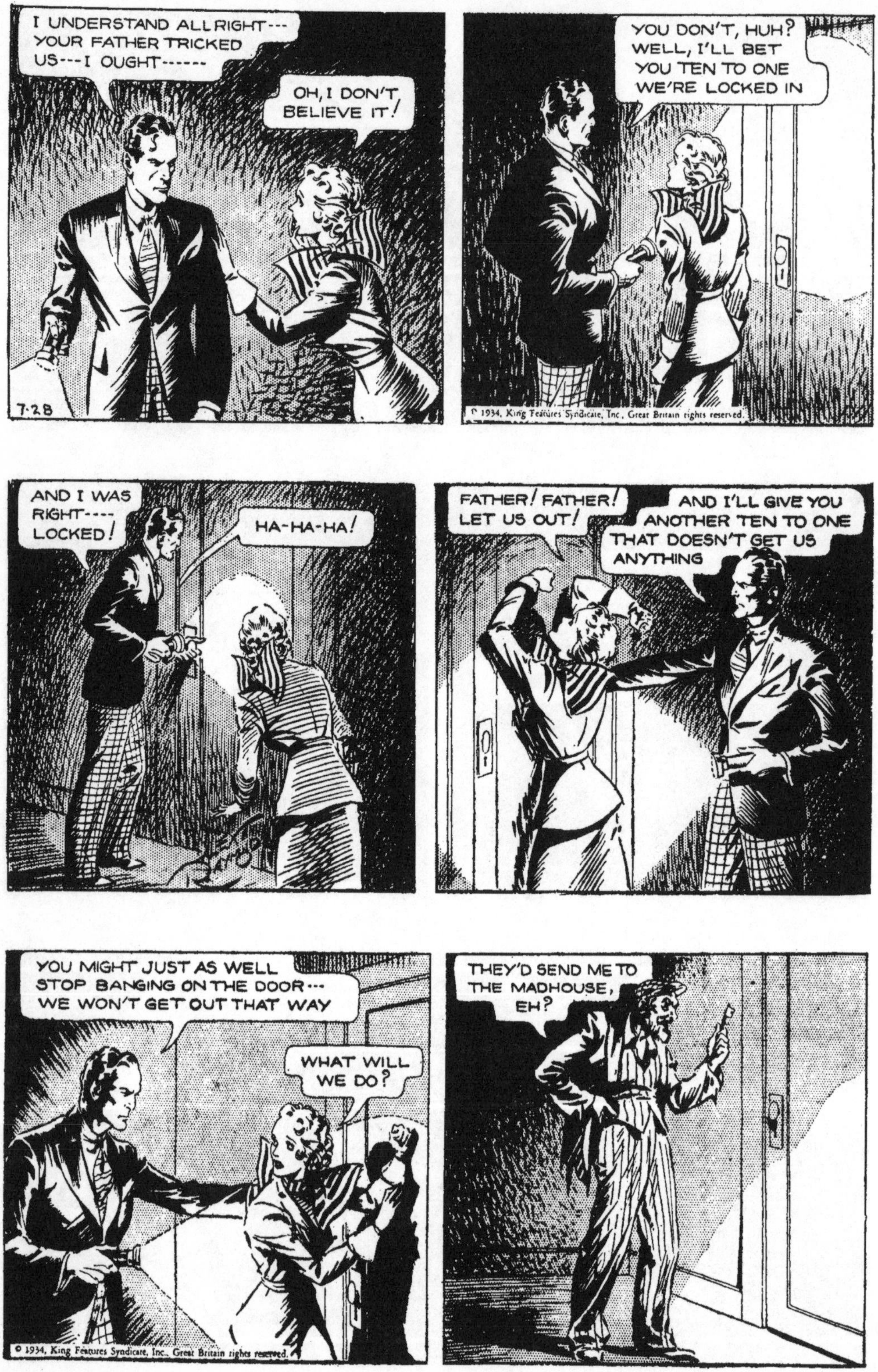

I UNDERSTAND ALL RIGHT--- YOUR FATHER TRICKED US---I OUGHT------
OH, I DON'T BELIEVE IT!
7-28
YOU DON'T, HUH? WELL, I'LL BET YOU TEN TO ONE WE'RE LOCKED IN
© 1934, King Features Syndicate, Inc., Great Britain rights reserved.
AND I WAS RIGHT---- LOCKED!
HA-HA-HA!
FATHER! FATHER! LET US OUT!
AND I'LL GIVE YOU ANOTHER TEN TO ONE THAT DOESN'T GET US ANYTHING
YOU MIGHT JUST AS WELL STOP BANGING ON THE DOOR--- WE WON'T GET OUT THAT WAY
WHAT WILL WE DO?
© 1934, King Features Syndicate, Inc., Great Britain rights reserved.
THEY'D SEND ME TO THE MADHOUSE, EH?

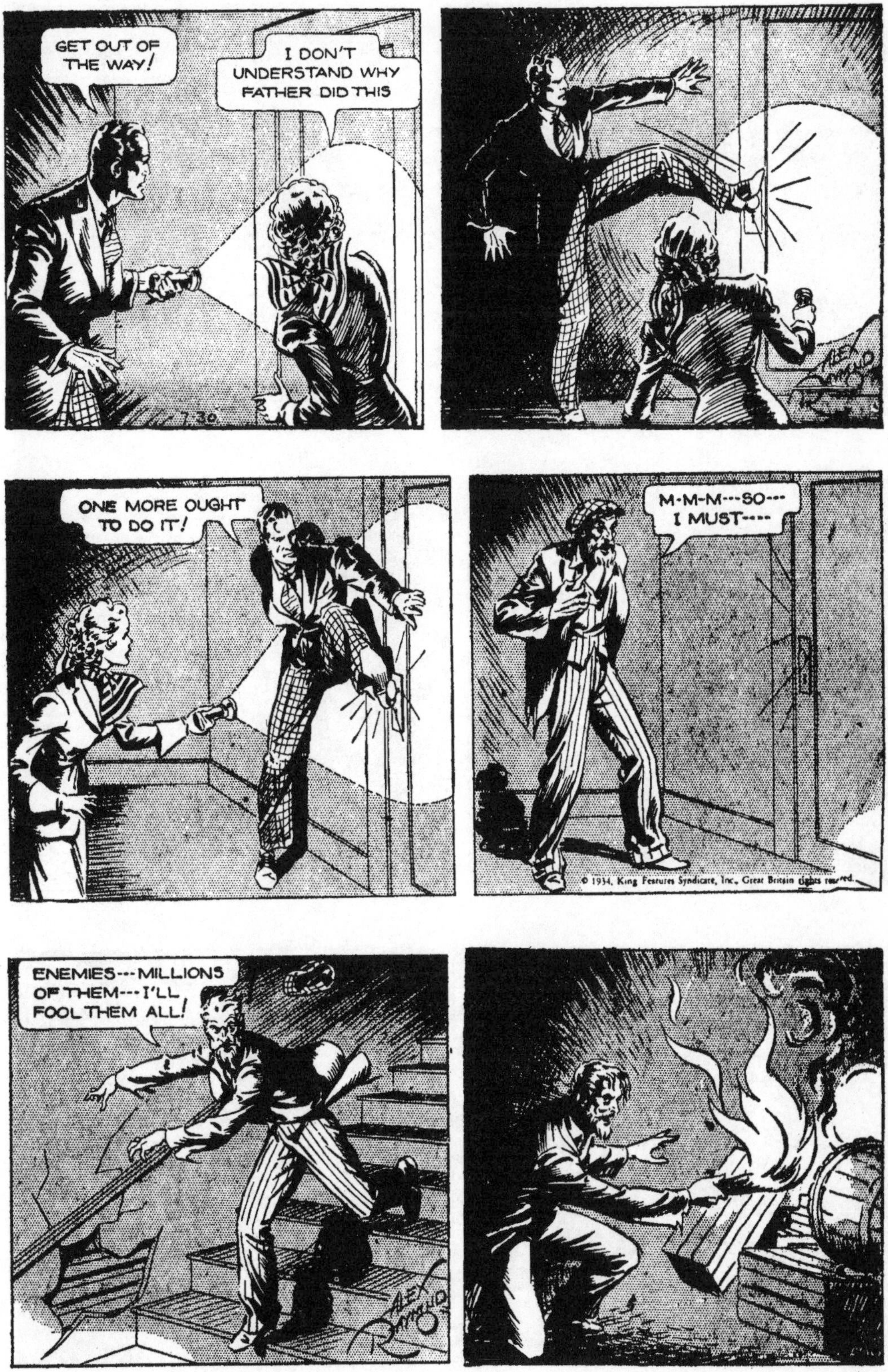
GET OUT OF THE WAY!
I DON'T UNDERSTAND WHY FATHER DID THIS
ONE MORE OUGHT TO DO IT!
M-M-M---SO--- I MUST----
© 1934, King Features Syndicate, Inc., Great Britain rights reserved.
ENEMIES---MILLIONS OF THEM---I'LL FOOL THEM ALL!

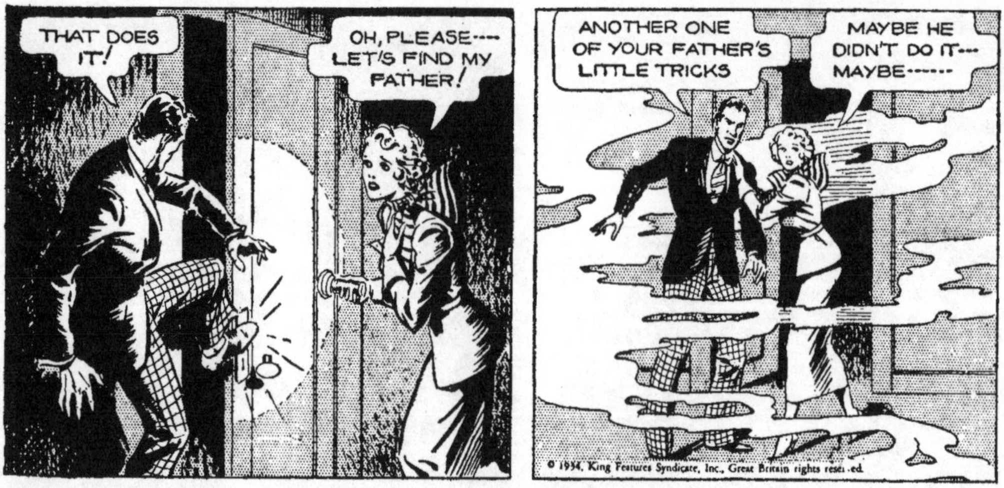
THAT DOES IT!
OH, PLEASE---- LET'S FIND MY FATHER!
ANOTHER ONE OF YOUR FATHER'S LITTLE TRICKS
MAYBE HE DIDN'T DO IT--- MAYBE------
© 1934, King Features Syndicate, Inc., Great Britain rights reserved.

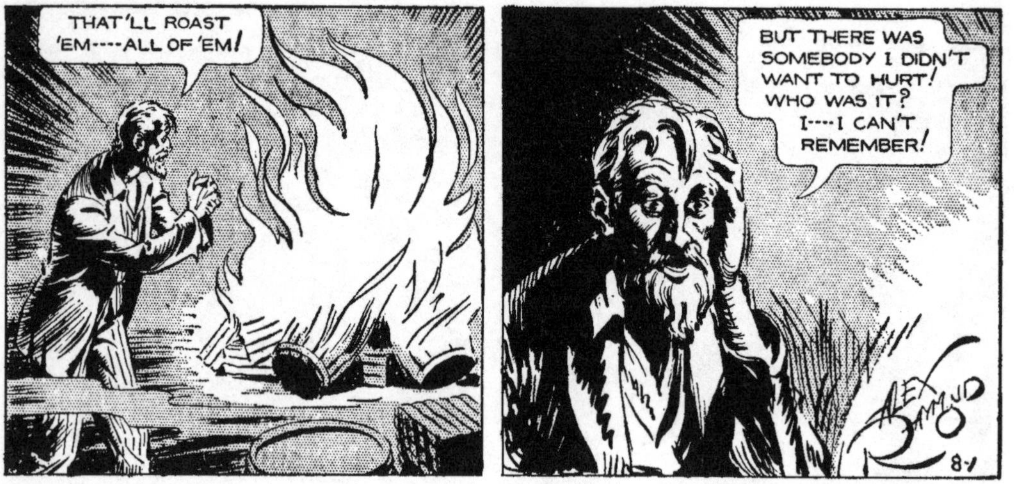
THAT'LL ROAST 'EM----ALL OF 'EM!
BUT THERE WAS SOMEBODY I DIDN'T WANT TO HURT! WHO WAS IT? I---- I CAN'T REMEMBER!
ALEX RAYMOND
8-1

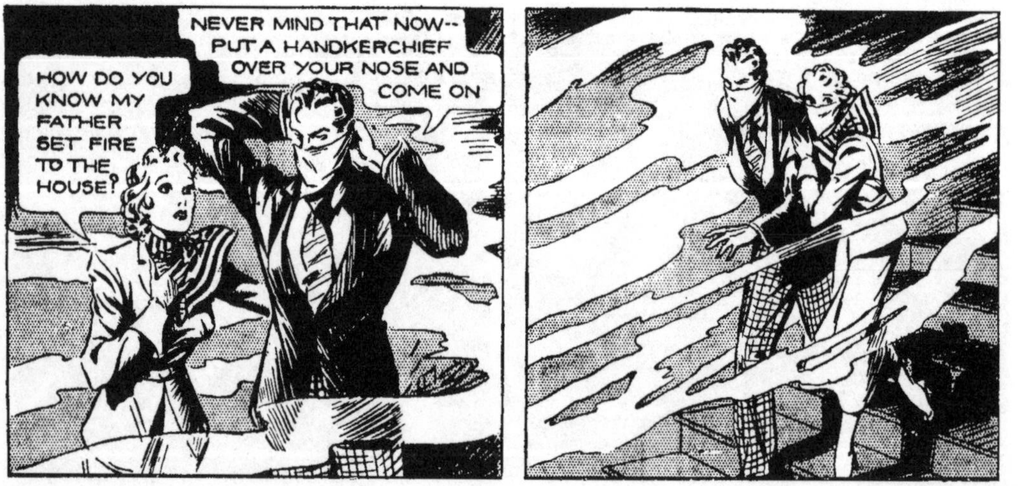
HOW DO YOU KNOW MY FATHER SET FIRE TO THE HOUSE?
NEVER MIND THAT NOW-- PUT A HANDKERCHIEF OVER YOUR NOSE AND COME ON

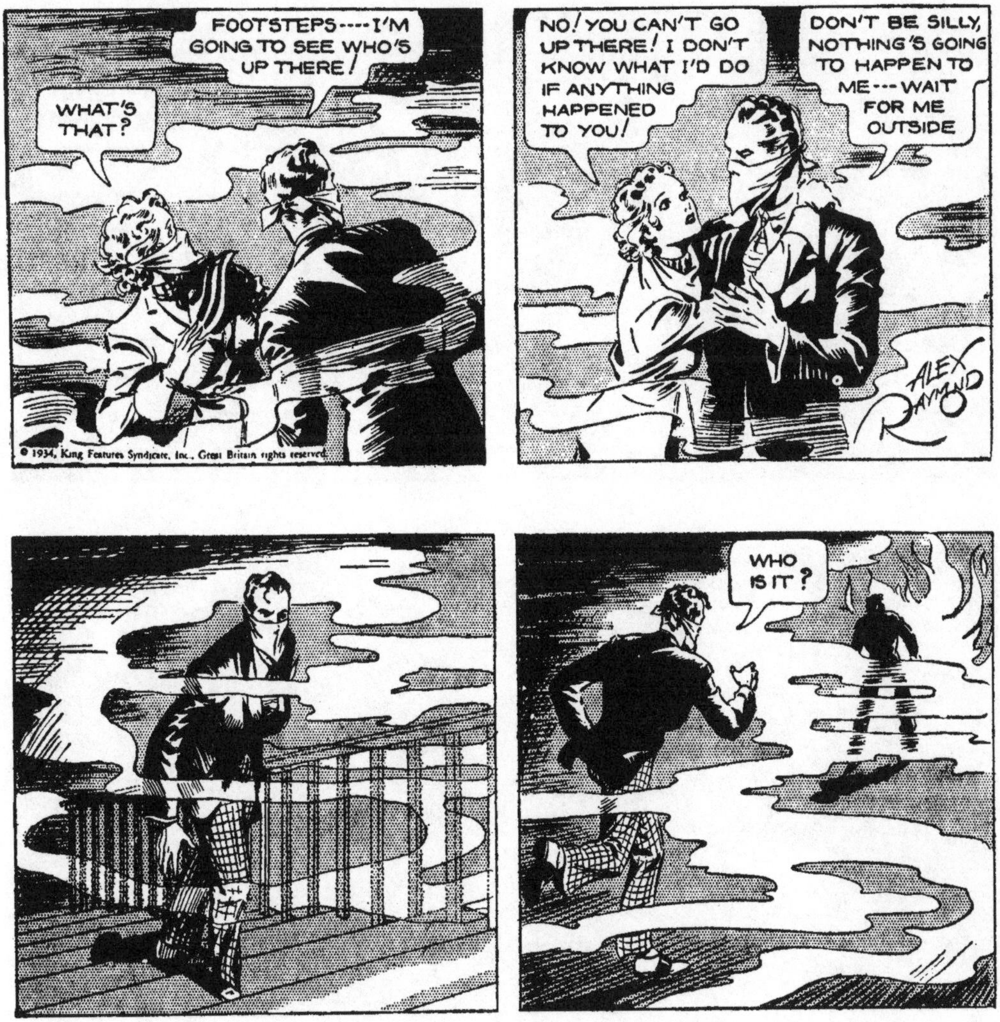
FOOTSTEPS----I'M GOING TO SEE WHO'S UP THERE!
WHAT'S THAT?
© 1934, King Features Syndicate, Inc., Great Britain rights reserved.
NO! YOU CAN'T GO UP THERE! I DON'T KNOW WHAT I'D DO IF ANYTHING HAPPENED TO YOU!
DON'T BE SILLY, NOTHING'S GOING TO HAPPEN TO ME---WAIT FOR ME OUTSIDE
ALEX RAYMOND
WHO IS IT?

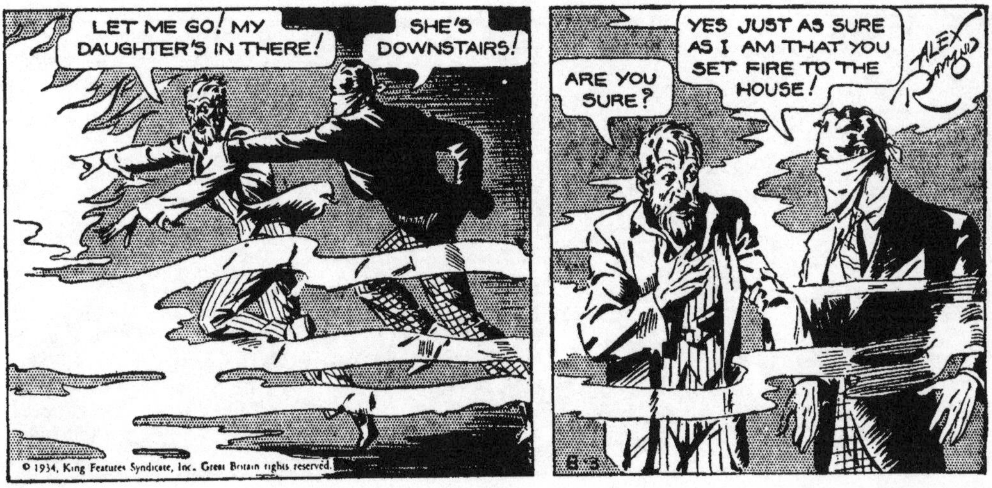
LET ME GO! MY DAUGHTER'S IN THERE!
SHE'S DOWNSTAIRS!
© 1934, King Features Syndicate, Inc. Great Britain rights reserved.
ARE YOU SURE?
YES JUST AS SURE AS I AM THAT YOU SET FIRE TO THE HOUSE!
ALEX RAYMOND

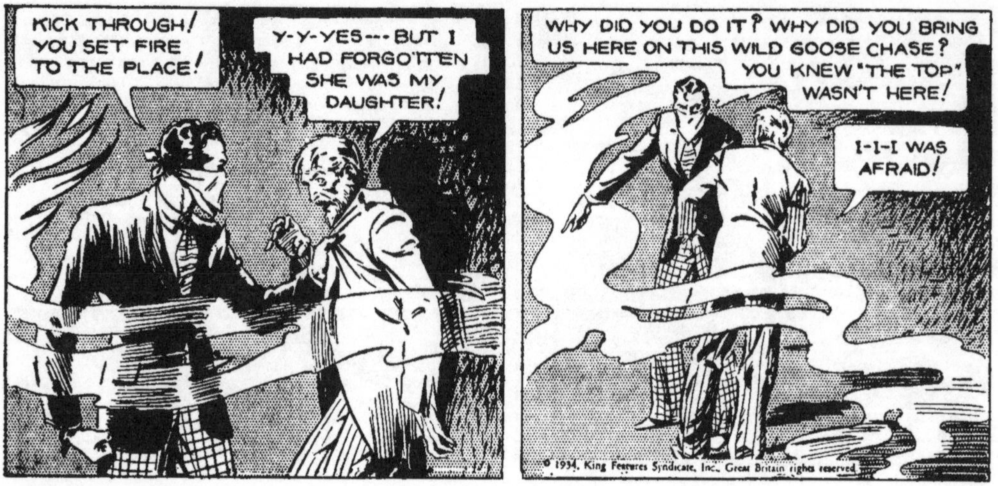
KICK THROUGH! YOU SET FIRE TO THE PLACE!
Y-Y-YES--- BUT I HAD FORGOTTEN SHE WAS MY DAUGHTER!
WHY DID YOU DO IT? WHY DID YOU BRING US HERE ON THIS WILD GOOSE CHASE? YOU KNEW "THE TOP" WASN'T HERE!
I-I-I WAS AFRAID!
© 1934, King Features Syndicate, Inc., Great Britain rights reserved.

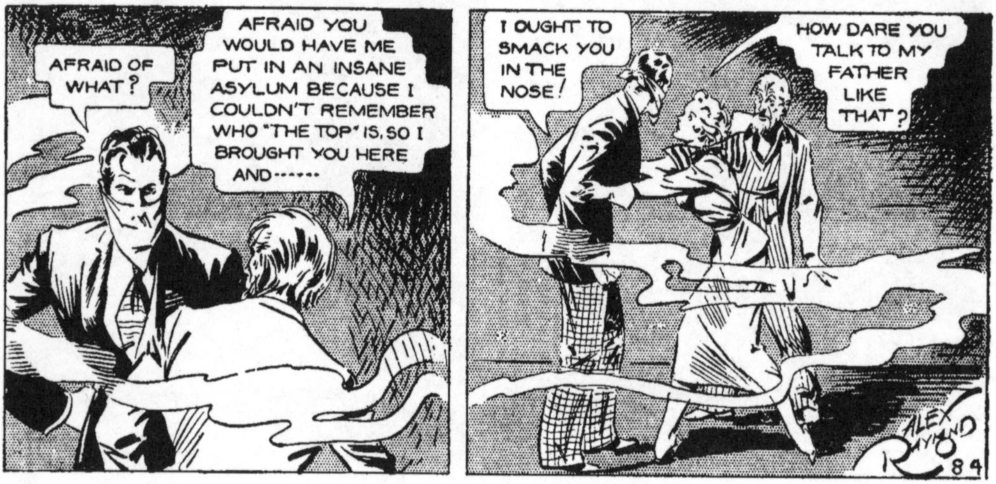
AFRAID OF WHAT?
AFRAID YOU WOULD HAVE ME PUT IN AN INSANE ASYLUM BECAUSE I COULDN'T REMEMBER WHO "THE TOP" IS, SO I BROUGHT YOU HERE AND------
I OUGHT TO SMACK YOU IN THE NOSE!
HOW DARE YOU TALK TO MY FATHER LIKE THAT?
ALEX RAYMOND
8 4

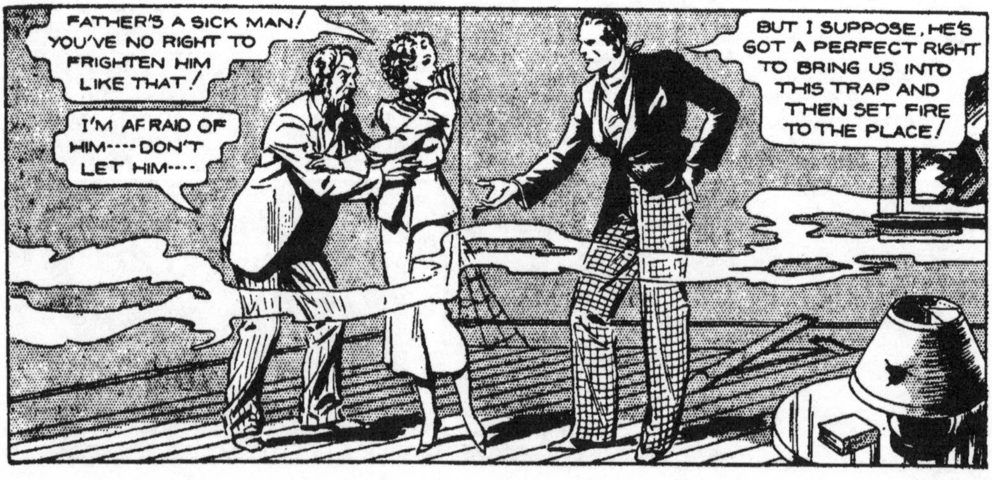
FATHER'S A SICK MAN! YOU'VE NO RIGHT TO FRIGHTEN HIM LIKE THAT!
I'M AFRAID OF HIM---- DON'T LET HIM----
BUT I SUPPOSE, HE'S GOT A PERFECT RIGHT TO BRING US INTO THIS TRAP AND THEN SET FIRE TO THE PLACE!

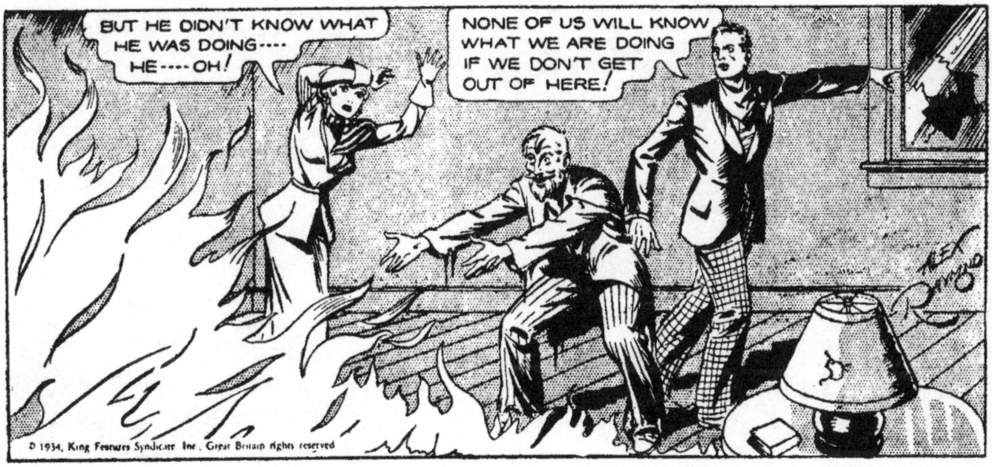
BUT HE DIDN'T KNOW WHAT HE WAS DOING---- HE----OH!
NONE OF US WILL KNOW WHAT WE ARE DOING IF WE DON'T GET OUT OF HERE!
© 1934, King Features Syndicate Inc., Great Britain rights reserved

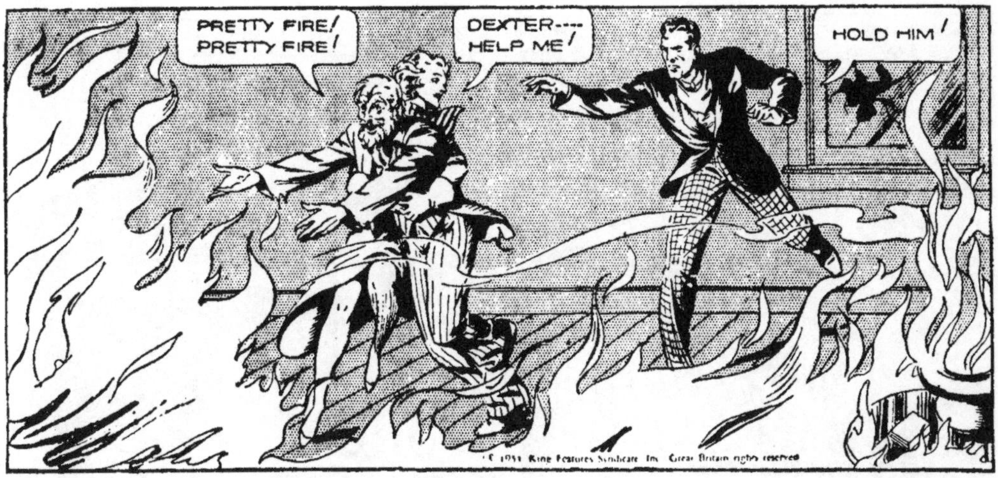
PRETTY FIRE! PRETTY FIRE!
DEXTER---- HELP ME!
HOLD HIM!

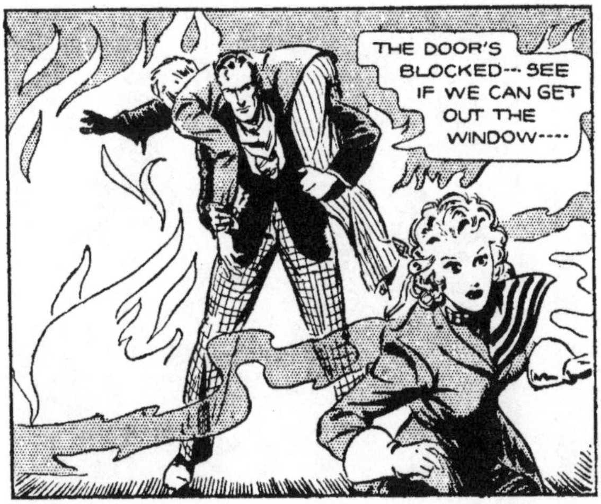
THE DOOR'S BLOCKED--- SEE IF WE CAN GET OUT THE WINDOW----

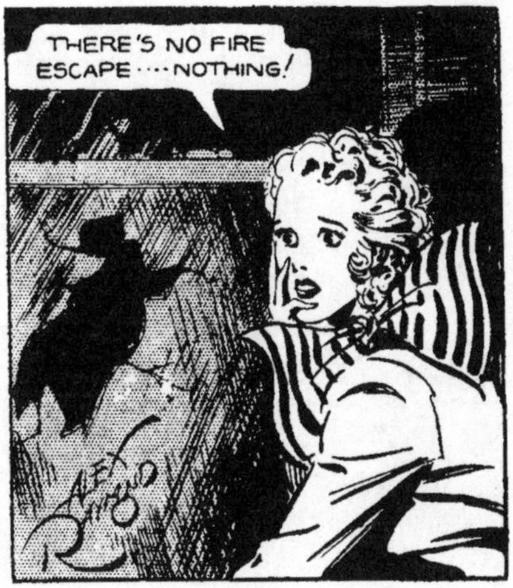
THERE'S NO FIRE ESCAPE ----NOTHING!

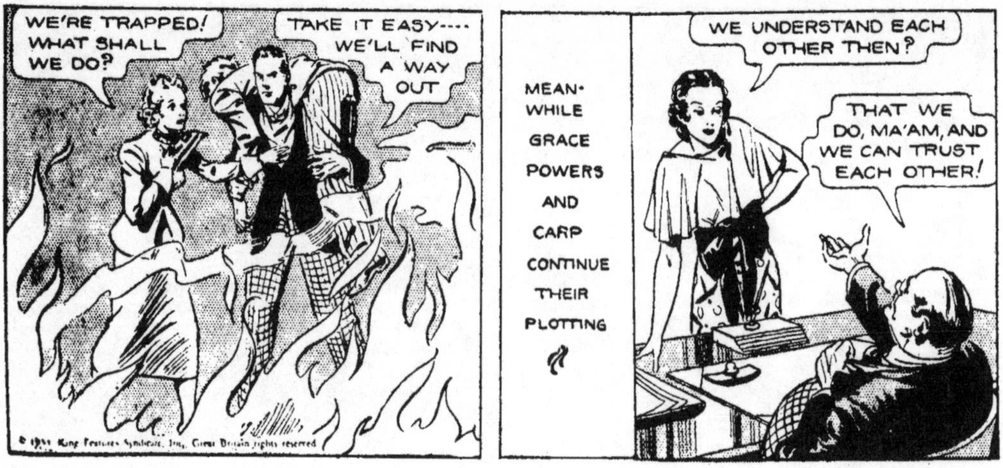
WE'RE TRAPPED! WHAT SHALL WE DO?
TAKE IT EASY---- WE'LL FIND A WAY OUT
© 1934 King Features Syndicate, Inc., Great Britain rights reserved
MEAN-WHILE GRACE POWERS AND CARP CONTINUE THEIR PLOTTING
WE UNDERSTAND EACH OTHER THEN?
THAT WE DO, MA'AM, AND WE CAN TRUST EACH OTHER!

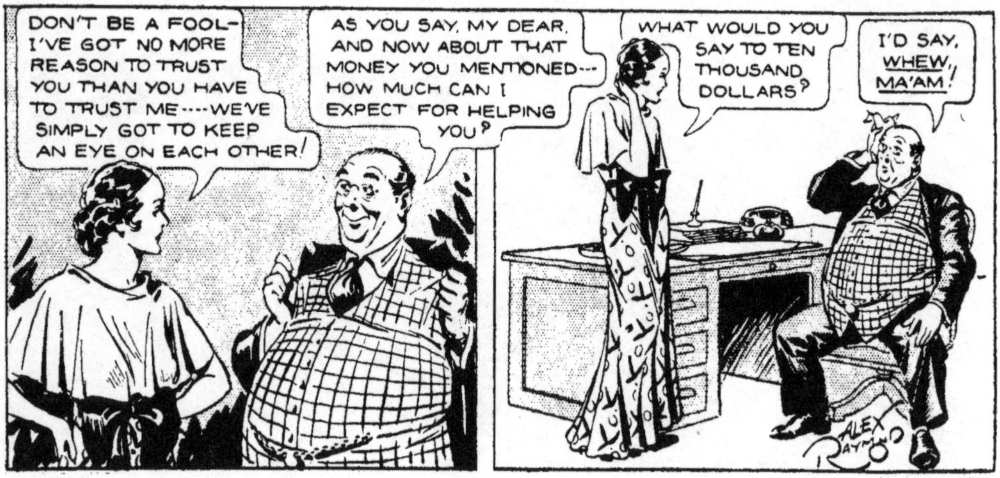
DON'T BE A FOOL- I'VE GOT NO MORE REASON TO TRUST YOU THAN YOU HAVE TO TRUST ME----WE'VE SIMPLY GOT TO KEEP AN EYE ON EACH OTHER!
AS YOU SAY, MY DEAR, AND NOW ABOUT THAT MONEY YOU MENTIONED--- HOW MUCH CAN I EXPECT FOR HELPING YOU?
WHAT WOULD YOU SAY TO TEN THOUSAND DOLLARS?
I'D SAY, WHEW, MA'AM!
ALEX RAYMOND

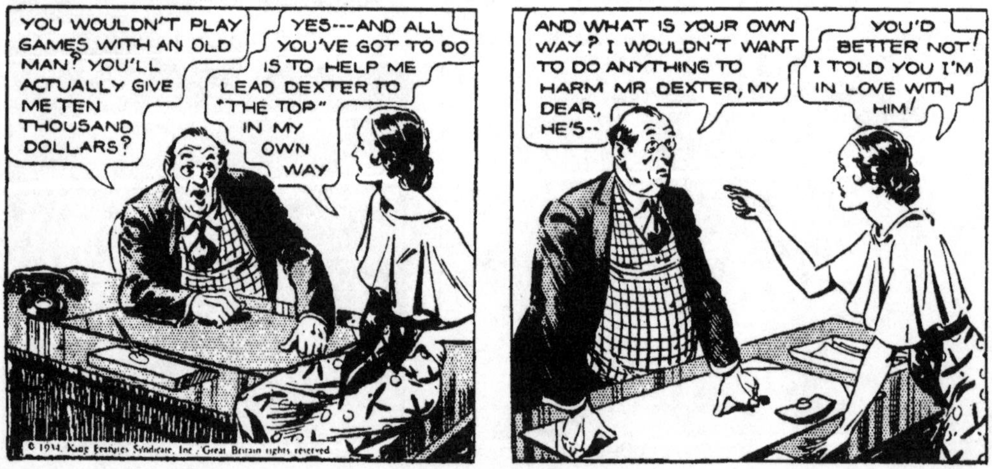
YOU WOULDN'T PLAY GAMES WITH AN OLD MAN? YOU'LL ACTUALLY GIVE ME TEN THOUSAND DOLLARS?
YES---AND ALL YOU'VE GOT TO DO IS TO HELP ME LEAD DEXTER TO "THE TOP" IN MY OWN WAY
© 1934, King Features Syndicate, Inc., Great Britain rights reserved
AND WHAT IS YOUR OWN WAY? I WOULDN'T WANT TO DO ANYTHING TO HARM MR DEXTER, MY DEAR, HE'S--
YOU'D BETTER NOT! I TOLD YOU I'M IN LOVE WITH HIM!

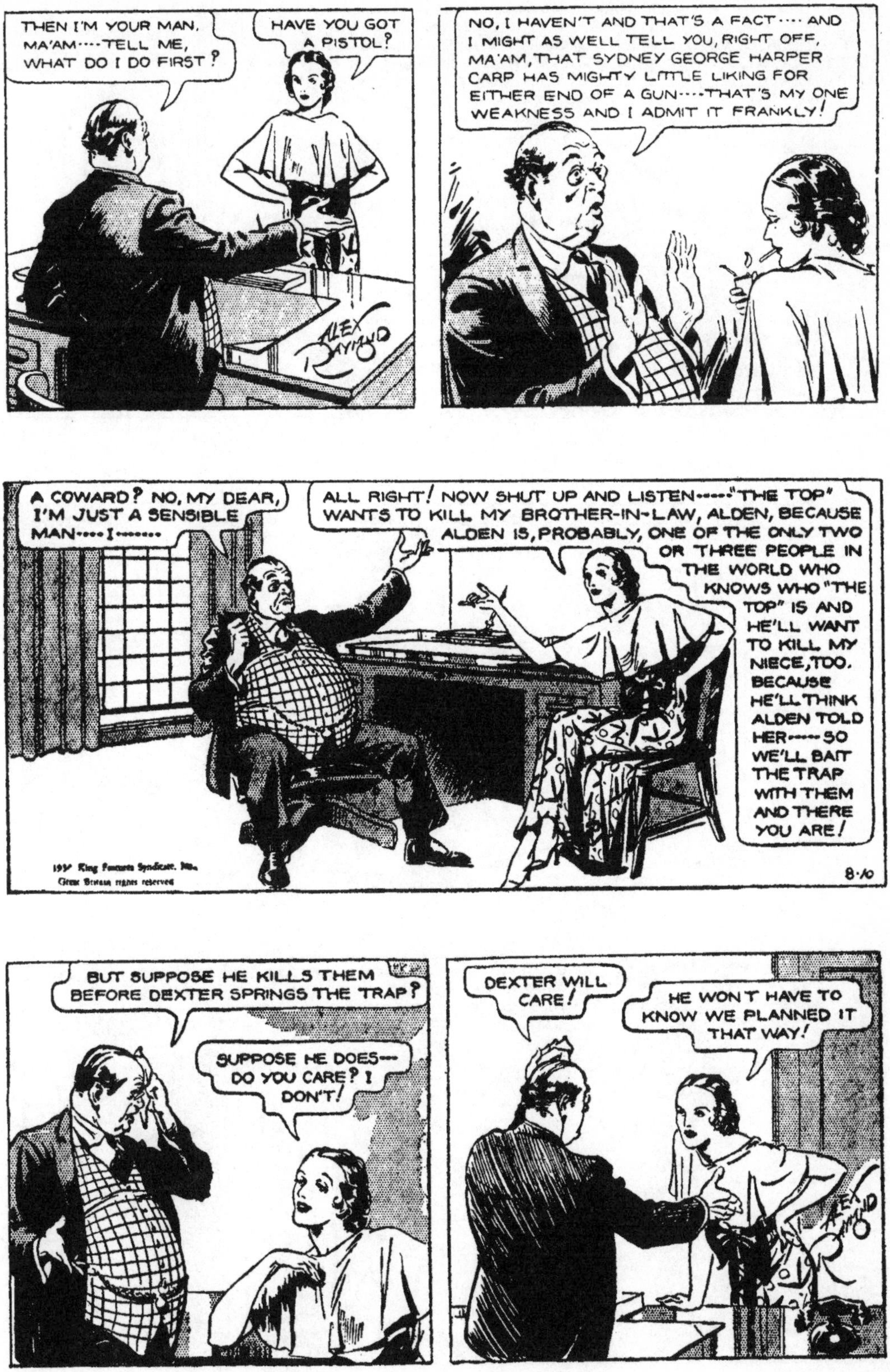
THEN I'M YOUR MAN, MA'AM····TELL ME, WHAT DO I DO FIRST?
HAVE YOU GOT A PISTOL?
ALEX RAYMOND
NO, I HAVEN'T AND THAT'S A FACT···· AND I MIGHT AS WELL TELL YOU, RIGHT OFF, MA'AM, THAT SYDNEY GEORGE HARPER CARP HAS MIGHTY LITTLE LIKING FOR EITHER END OF A GUN····THAT'S MY ONE WEAKNESS AND I ADMIT IT FRANKLY!
A COWARD? NO, MY DEAR, I'M JUST A SENSIBLE MAN····I·······
ALL RIGHT! NOW SHUT UP AND LISTEN·····"THE TOP" WANTS TO KILL MY BROTHER-IN-LAW, ALDEN, BECAUSE ALDEN IS, PROBABLY, ONE OF THE ONLY TWO OR THREE PEOPLE IN THE WORLD WHO KNOWS WHO "THE TOP" IS AND HE'LL WANT TO KILL MY NIECE, TOO. BECAUSE HE'LL THINK ALDEN TOLD HER·····SO WE'LL BAIT THE TRAP WITH THEM AND THERE YOU ARE!
8-10
BUT SUPPOSE HE KILLS THEM BEFORE DEXTER SPRINGS THE TRAP?
SUPPOSE HE DOES--- DO YOU CARE? I DON'T!
DEXTER WILL CARE!
HE WON'T HAVE TO KNOW WE PLANNED IT THAT WAY!
ALEX RAYMOND

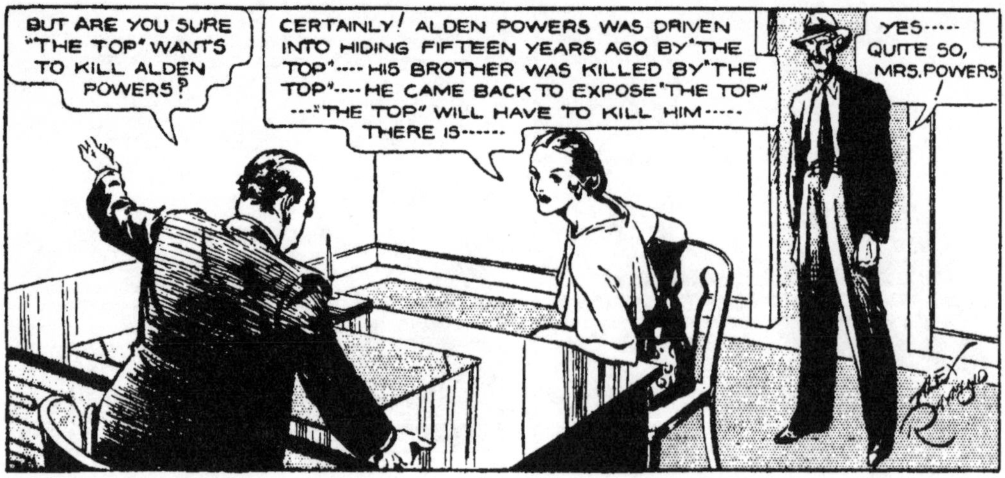
BUT ARE YOU SURE "THE TOP" WANTS TO KILL ALDEN POWERS?
CERTAINLY! ALDEN POWERS WAS DRIVEN INTO HIDING FIFTEEN YEARS AGO BY "THE TOP"---- HIS BROTHER WAS KILLED BY "THE TOP"---- HE CAME BACK TO EXPOSE "THE TOP" ---"THE TOP" WILL HAVE TO KILL HIM----- THERE IS------
YES----- QUITE SO, MRS. POWERS!

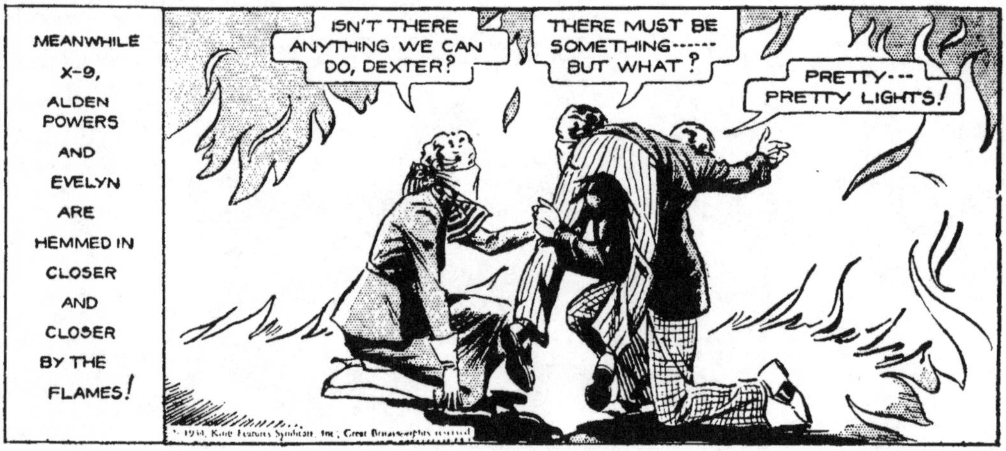
MEANWHILE X-9, ALDEN POWERS AND EVELYN ARE HEMMED IN CLOSER AND CLOSER BY THE FLAMES!
ISN'T THERE ANYTHING WE CAN DO, DEXTER?
THERE MUST BE SOMETHING------ BUT WHAT?
PRETTY--- PRETTY LIGHTS!

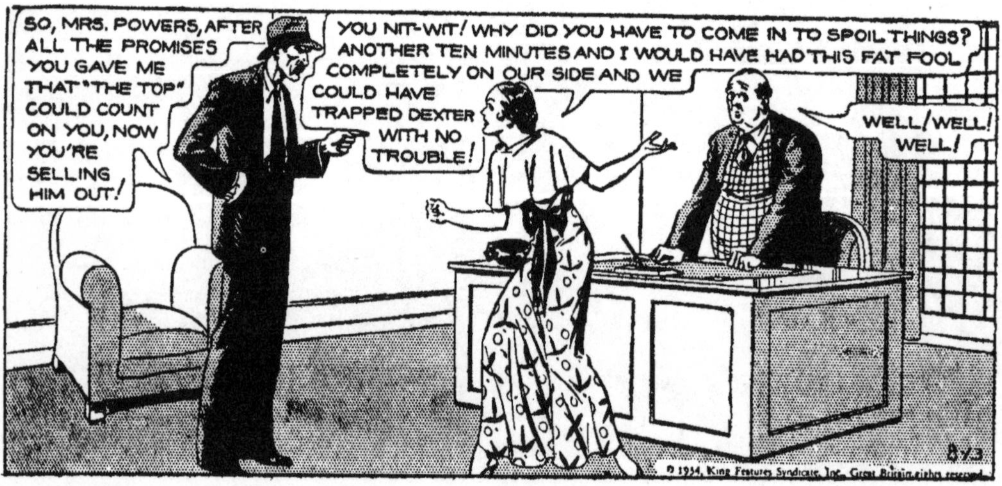
SO, MRS. POWERS, AFTER ALL THE PROMISES YOU GAVE ME THAT "THE TOP" COULD COUNT ON YOU, NOW YOU'RE SELLING HIM OUT!
YOU NIT-WIT! WHY DID YOU HAVE TO COME IN TO SPOIL THINGS? ANOTHER TEN MINUTES AND I WOULD HAVE HAD THIS FAT FOOL COMPLETELY ON OUR SIDE AND WE COULD HAVE TRAPPED DEXTER WITH NO TROUBLE!
WELL! WELL! WELL!

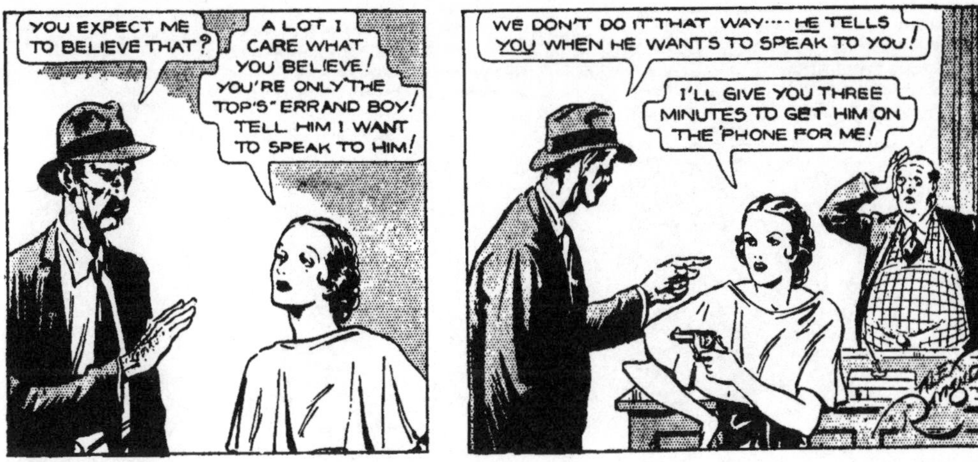
YOU EXPECT ME TO BELIEVE THAT?
A LOT I CARE WHAT YOU BELIEVE! YOU'RE ONLY "THE TOP'S" ERRAND BOY! TELL HIM I WANT TO SPEAK TO HIM!
WE DON'T DO IT THAT WAY.... HE TELLS YOU WHEN HE WANTS TO SPEAK TO YOU!
I'LL GIVE YOU THREE MINUTES TO GET HIM ON THE 'PHONE FOR ME!

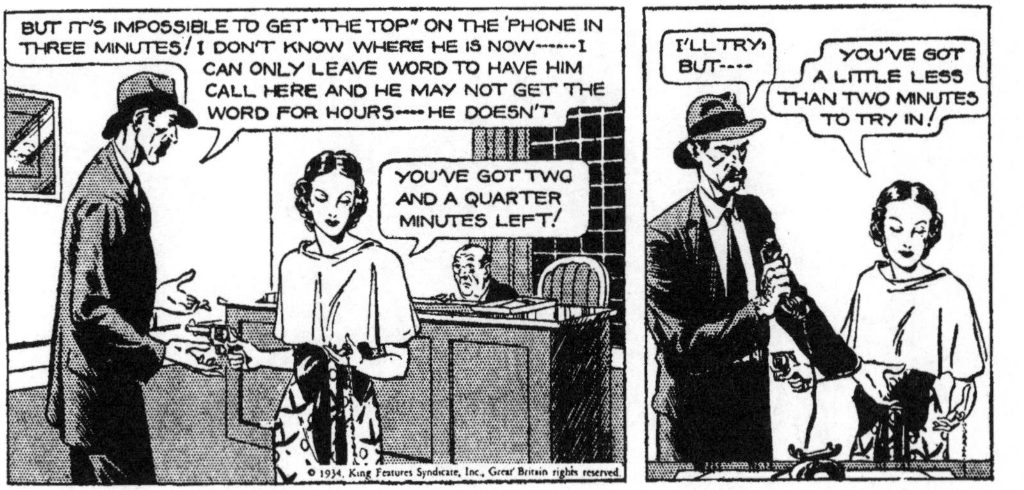
BUT IT'S IMPOSSIBLE TO GET "THE TOP" ON THE 'PHONE IN THREE MINUTES! I DON'T KNOW WHERE HE IS NOW------I CAN ONLY LEAVE WORD TO HAVE HIM CALL HERE AND HE MAY NOT GET THE WORD FOR HOURS---- HE DOESN'T
YOU'VE GOT TWO AND A QUARTER MINUTES LEFT!
© 1934, King Features Syndicate, Inc., Great Britain rights reserved
I'LL TRY! BUT----
YOU'VE GOT A LITTLE LESS THAN TWO MINUTES TO TRY IN!

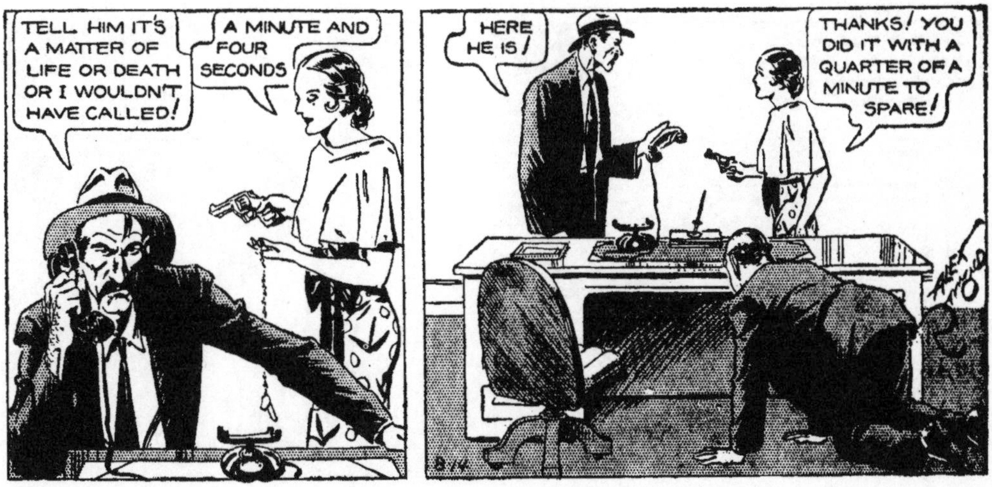
TELL HIM IT'S A MATTER OF LIFE OR DEATH OR I WOULDN'T HAVE CALLED!
A MINUTE AND FOUR SECONDS
HERE HE IS!
THANKS! YOU DID IT WITH A QUARTER OF A MINUTE TO SPARE!

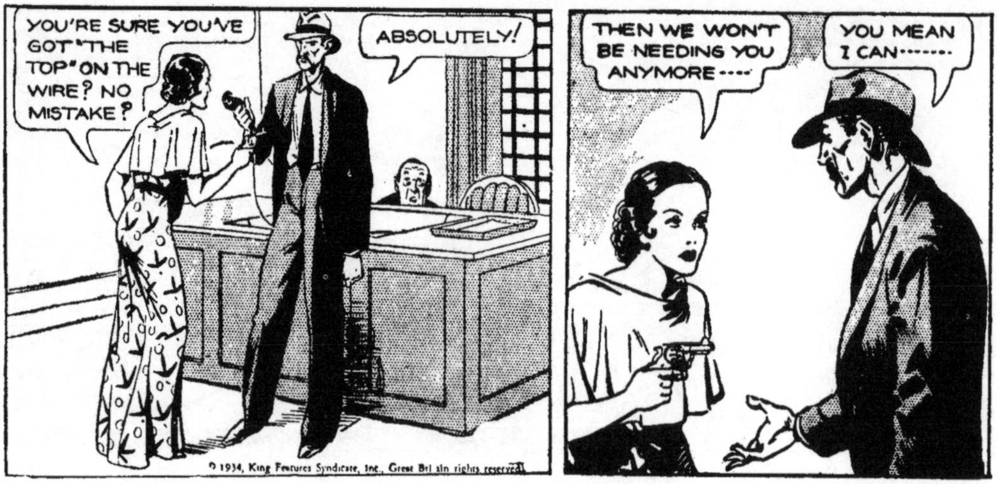
YOU'RE SURE YOU'VE GOT "THE TOP" ON THE WIRE? NO MISTAKE?
ABSOLUTELY!
© 1934, King Features Syndicate, Inc., Great Britain rights reserved
THEN WE WON'T BE NEEDING YOU ANYMORE----
YOU MEAN I CAN-------

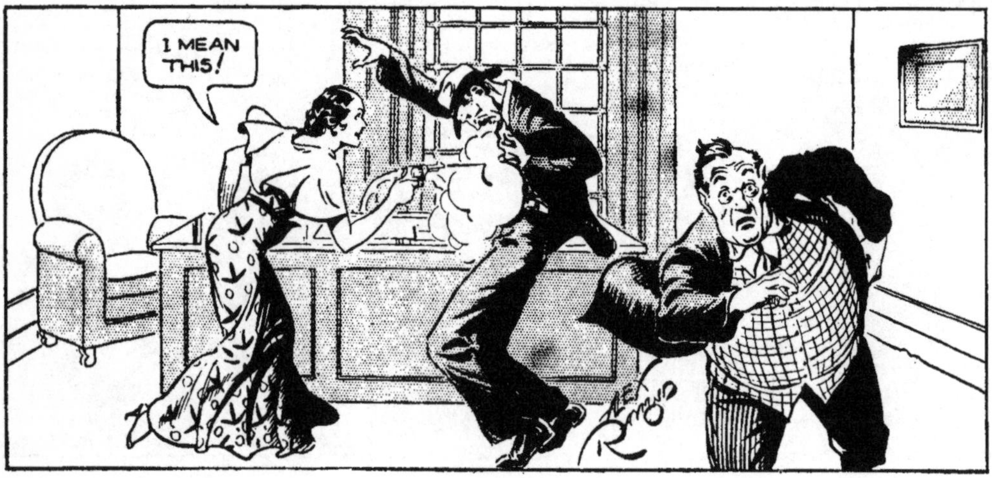
I MEAN THIS!

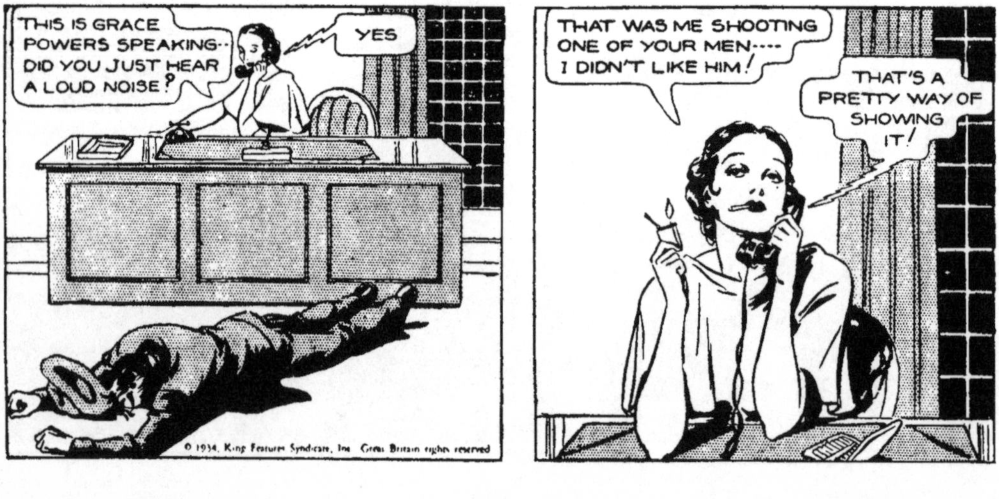
THIS IS GRACE POWERS SPEAKING-- DID YOU JUST HEAR A LOUD NOISE?
YES
© 1934, King Features Syndicate, Inc. Great Britain rights reserved
THAT WAS ME SHOOTING ONE OF YOUR MEN---- I DIDN'T LIKE HIM!
THAT'S A PRETTY WAY OF SHOWING IT!

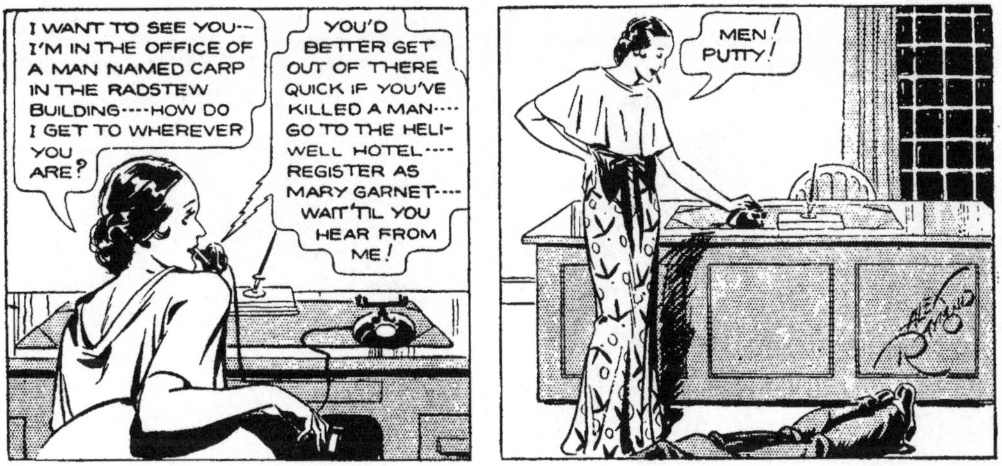
I WANT TO SEE YOU-- I'M IN THE OFFICE OF A MAN NAMED CARP IN THE RADSTEW BUILDING----HOW DO I GET TO WHEREVER YOU ARE?
YOU'D BETTER GET OUT OF THERE QUICK IF YOU'VE KILLED A MAN---- GO TO THE HELI-WELL HOTEL---- REGISTER AS MARY GARNET---- WAIT 'TIL YOU HEAR FROM ME!
MEN! PUTTY!

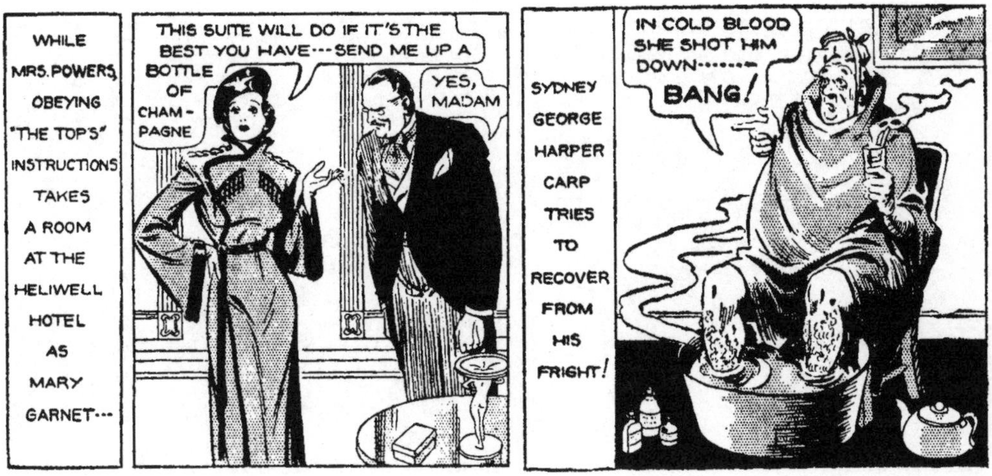
WHILE MRS. POWERS, OBEYING "THE TOP'S" INSTRUCTIONS TAKES A ROOM AT THE HELIWELL HOTEL AS MARY GARNET---
THIS SUITE WILL DO IF IT'S THE BEST YOU HAVE---SEND ME UP A BOTTLE OF CHAMPAGNE
YES, MADAM
SYDNEY GEORGE HARPER CARP TRIES TO RECOVER FROM HIS FRIGHT!
IN COLD BLOOD SHE SHOT HIM DOWN------- BANG!

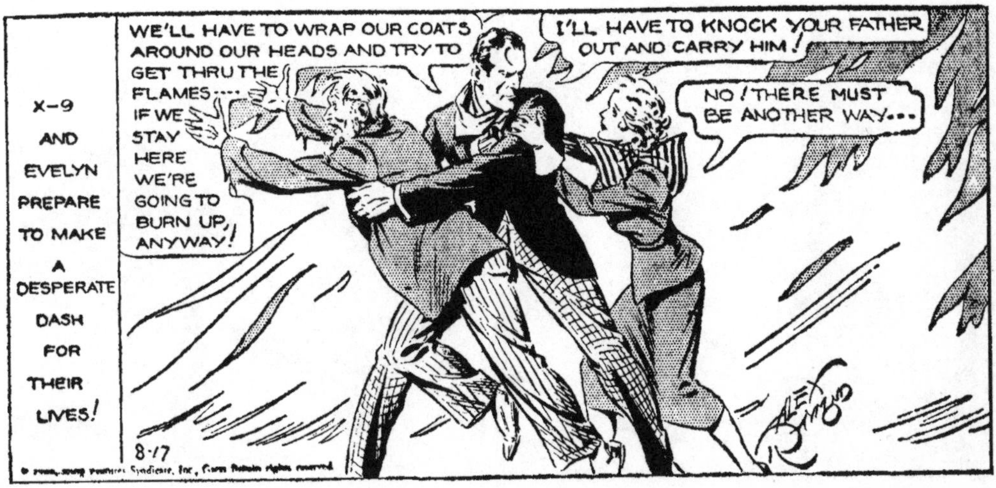
X-9 AND EVELYN PREPARE TO MAKE A DESPERATE DASH FOR THEIR LIVES!
WE'LL HAVE TO WRAP OUR COATS AROUND OUR HEADS AND TRY TO GET THRU THE FLAMES---- IF WE STAY HERE WE'RE GOING TO BURN UP, ANYWAY!
I'LL HAVE TO KNOCK YOUR FATHER OUT AND CARRY HIM!
NO! THERE MUST BE ANOTHER WAY...
8-17

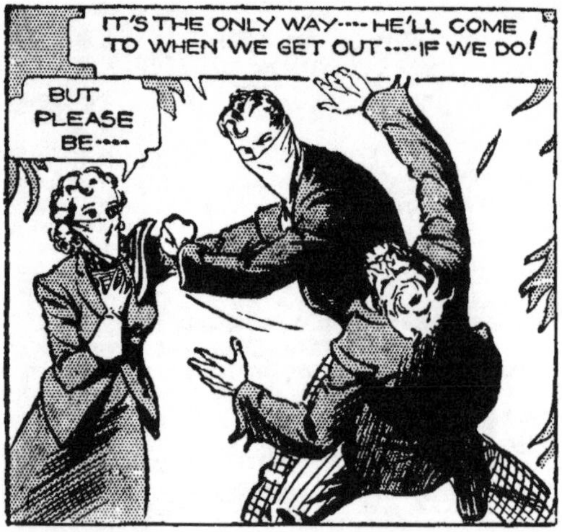
IT'S THE ONLY WAY---- HE'LL COME TO WHEN WE GET OUT----IF WE DO!
BUT PLEASE BE----
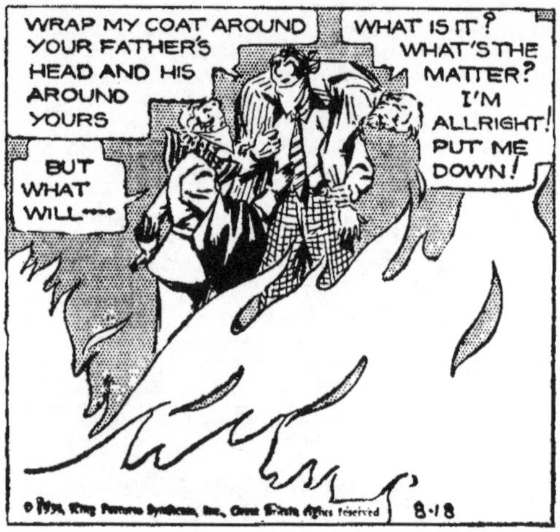
WRAP MY COAT AROUND YOUR FATHER'S HEAD AND HIS AROUND YOURS
WHAT IS IT? WHAT'S THE MATTER? I'M ALLRIGHT! PUT ME DOWN!
BUT WHAT WILL----
8-18
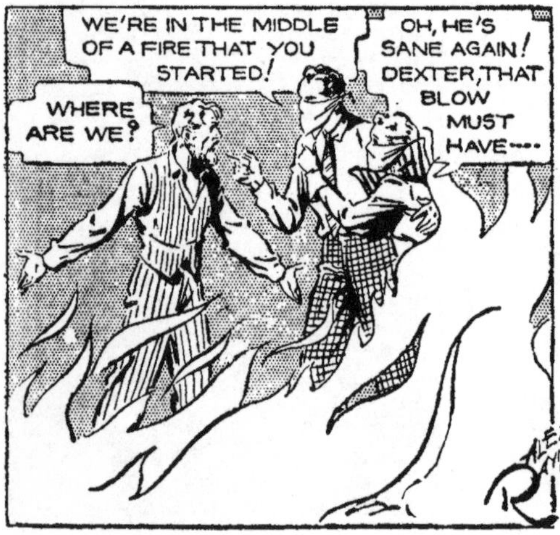
WE'RE IN THE MIDDLE OF A FIRE THAT YOU STARTED!
OH, HE'S SANE AGAIN! DEXTER, THAT BLOW MUST HAVE----
WHERE ARE WE?
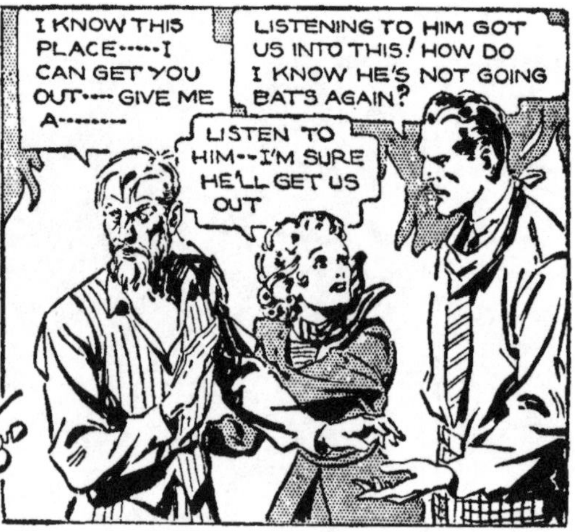
I KNOW THIS PLACE-----I CAN GET YOU OUT---- GIVE ME A--------
LISTENING TO HIM GOT US INTO THIS! HOW DO I KNOW HE'S NOT GOING BATS AGAIN?
LISTEN TO HIM--I'M SURE HE'LL GET US OUT
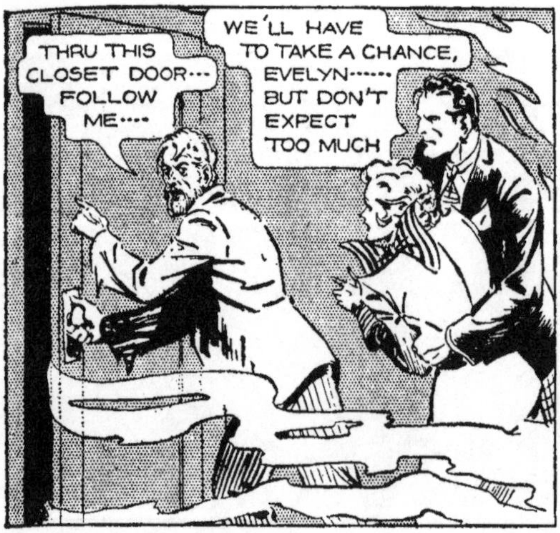
THRU THIS CLOSET DOOR--- FOLLOW ME----
WE'LL HAVE TO TAKE A CHANCE, EVELYN------ BUT DON'T EXPECT TOO MUCH
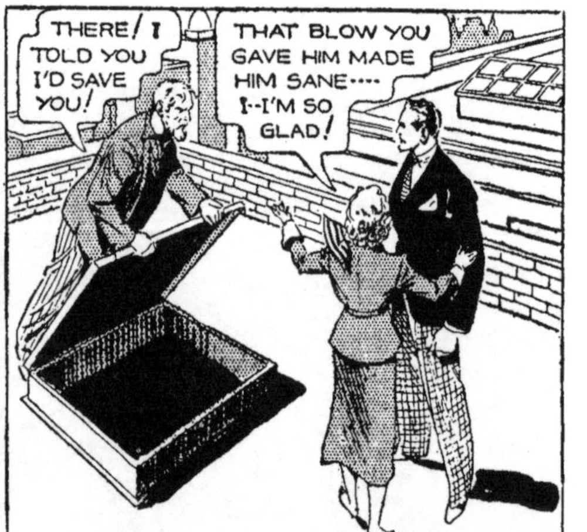
THERE! I TOLD YOU I'D SAVE YOU!
THAT BLOW YOU GAVE HIM MADE HIM SANE---- I--I'M SO GLAD!

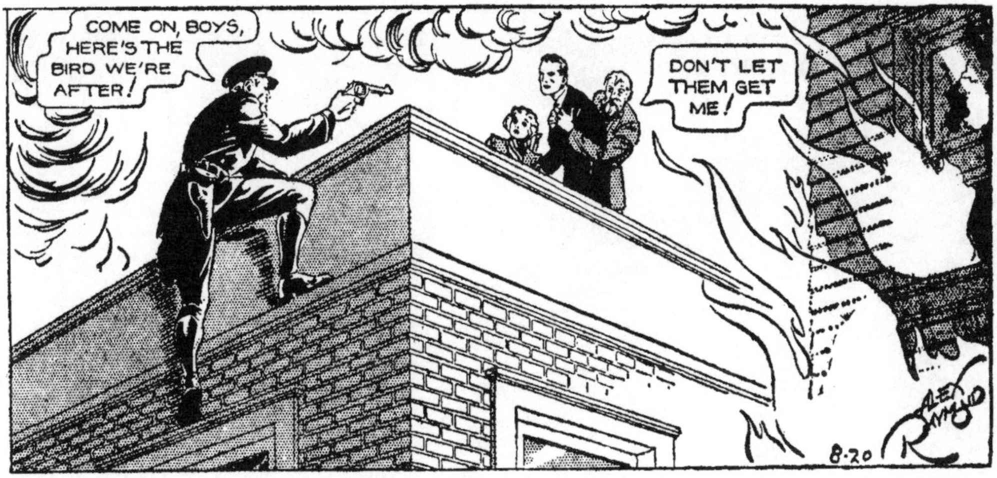
COME ON, BOYS, HERE'S THE BIRD WE'RE AFTER!
DON'T LET THEM GET ME!
ALEX RAYMOND
8-20

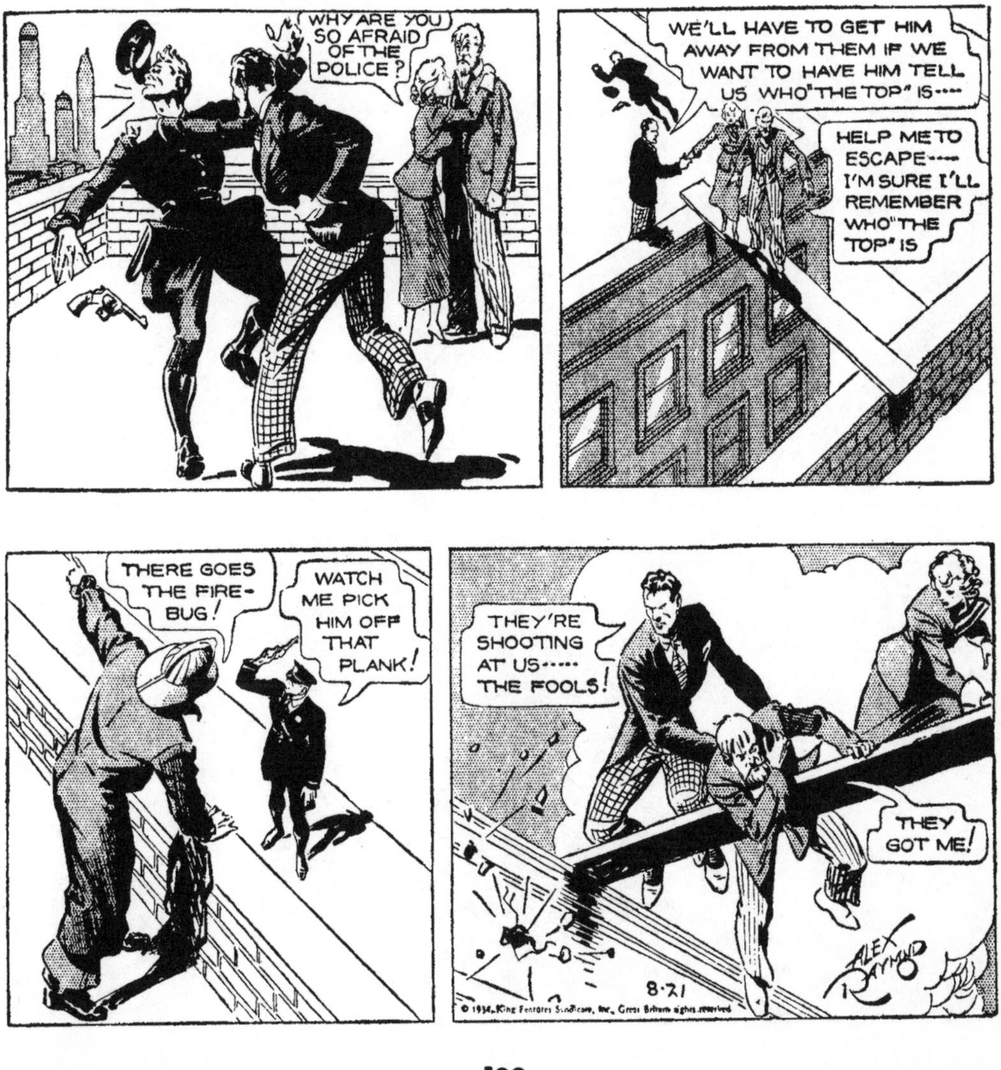
WHY ARE YOU SO AFRAID OF THE POLICE?
WE'LL HAVE TO GET HIM AWAY FROM THEM IF WE WANT TO HAVE HIM TELL US WHO "THE TOP" IS----
HELP ME TO ESCAPE---- I'M SURE I'LL REMEMBER WHO "THE TOP" IS
THERE GOES THE FIRE-BUG!
WATCH ME PICK HIM OFF THAT PLANK!
THEY'RE SHOOTING AT US----- THE FOOLS!
THEY GOT ME!
ALEX RAYMOND
8-21
© 1934, King Features Syndicate, Inc., Great Britain rights reserved

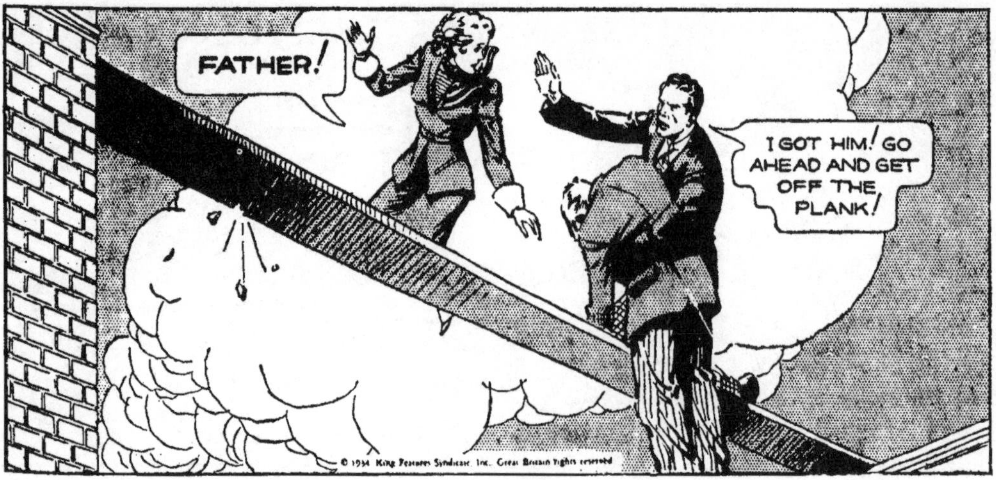
FATHER!
I GOT HIM! GO AHEAD AND GET OFF THE PLANK!
© 1934 King Features Syndicate, Inc., Great Britain rights reserved

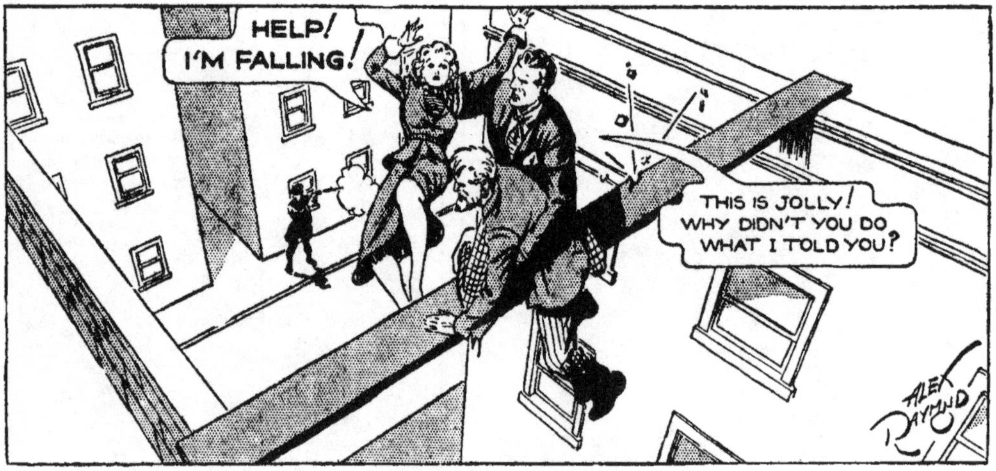
HELP! I'M FALLING!
THIS IS JOLLY! WHY DIDN'T YOU DO WHAT I TOLD YOU?
ALEX RAYMOND

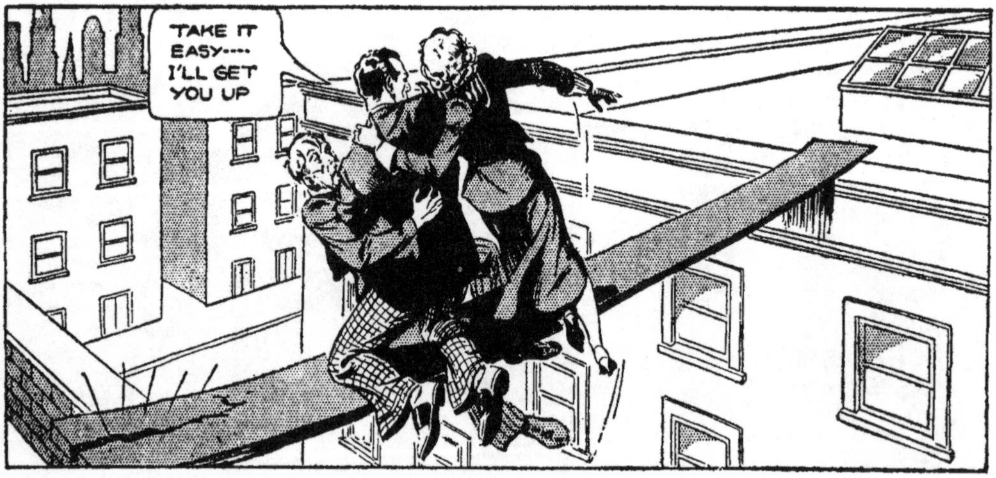
TAKE IT EASY---- I'LL GET YOU UP

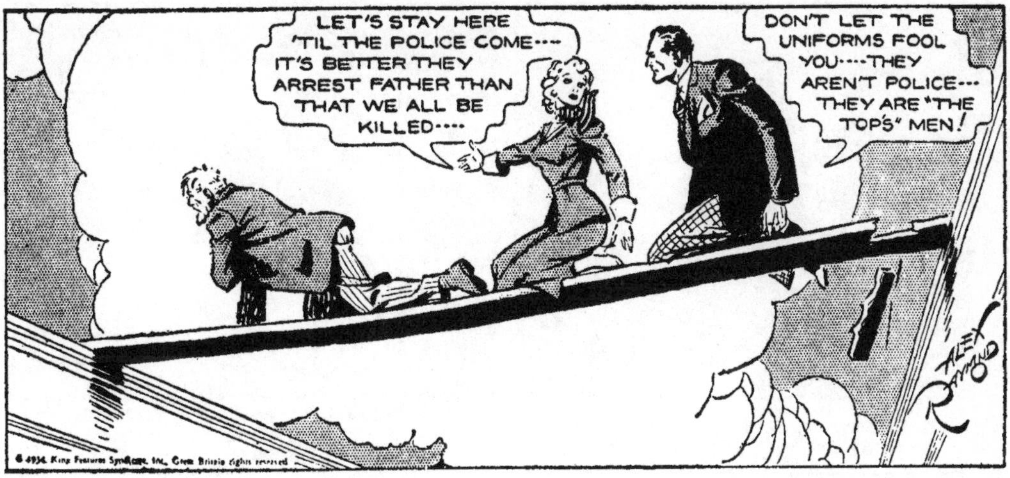
LET'S STAY HERE 'TIL THE POLICE COME---- IT'S BETTER THEY ARREST FATHER THAN THAT WE ALL BE KILLED----
DON'T LET THE UNIFORMS FOOL YOU----THEY AREN'T POLICE--- THEY ARE "THE TOP'S" MEN!
ALEX RAYMOND
© 1934, King Features Syndicate, Inc., Great Britain rights reserved

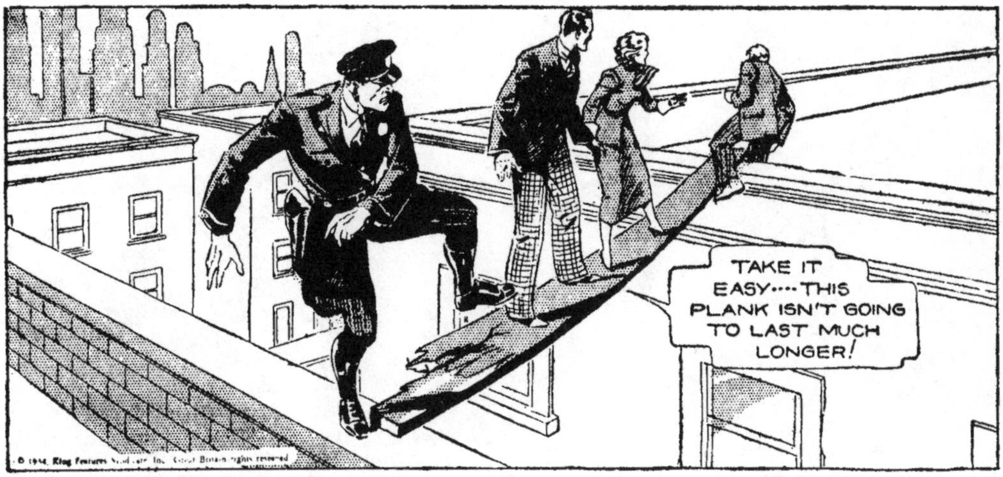
TAKE IT EASY----THIS PLANK ISN'T GOING TO LAST MUCH LONGER!
© 1934, King Features Syndicate, Inc., Great Britain rights reserved

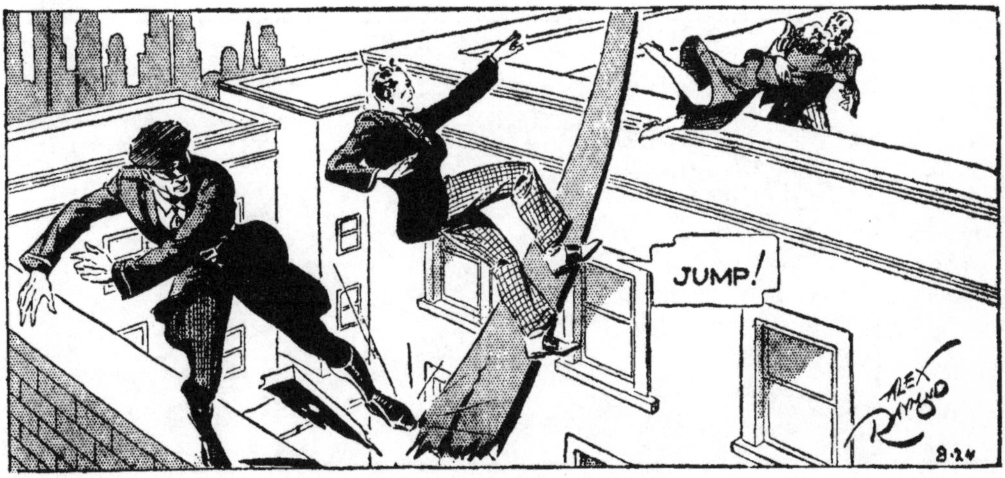
JUMP!
ALEX RAYMOND
8-24

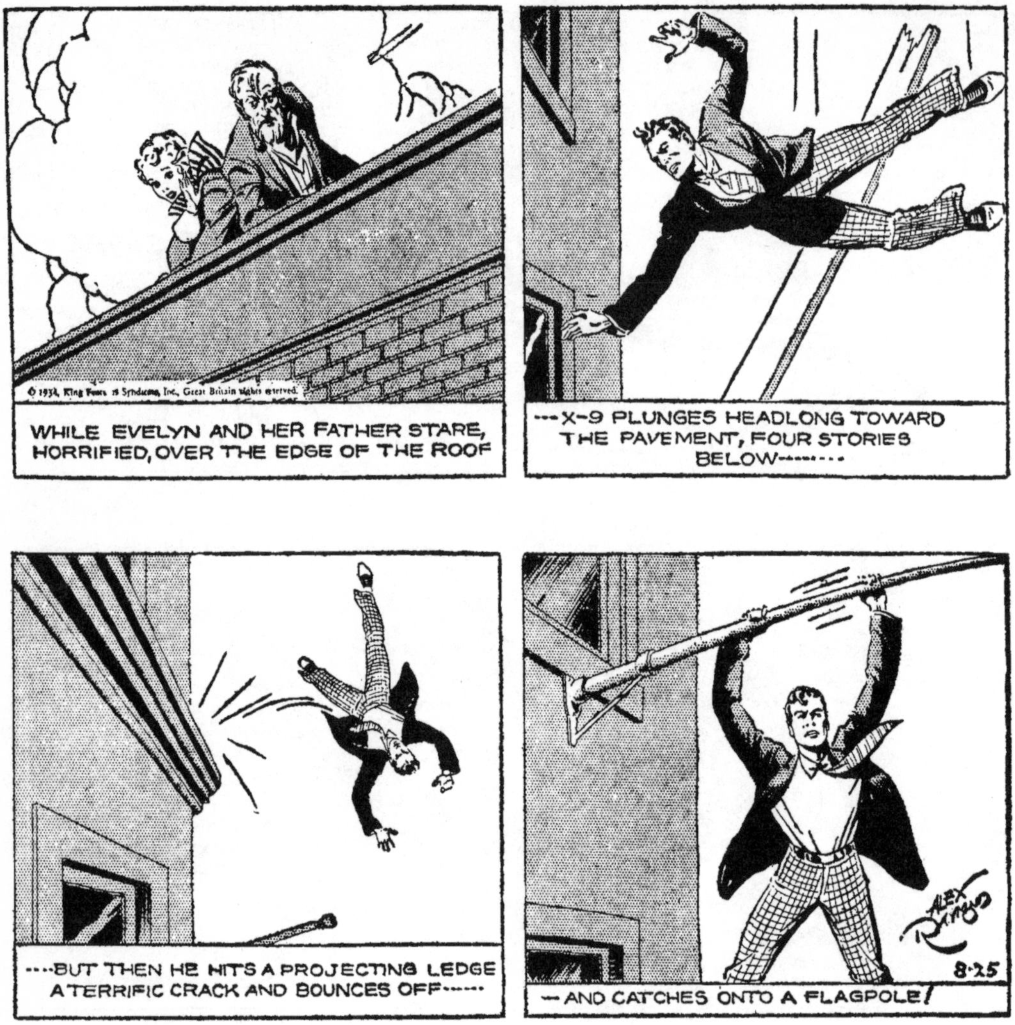
© 1934, King Features Syndicate, Inc., Great Britain rights reserved.
WHILE EVELYN AND HER FATHER STARE, HORRIFIED, OVER THE EDGE OF THE ROOF
---X-9 PLUNGES HEADLONG TOWARD THE PAVEMENT, FOUR STORIES BELOW--------
----BUT THEN HE HITS A PROJECTING LEDGE A TERRIFIC CRACK AND BOUNCES OFF------
ALEX RAYMOND
8-25
--AND CATCHES ONTO A FLAGPOLE!

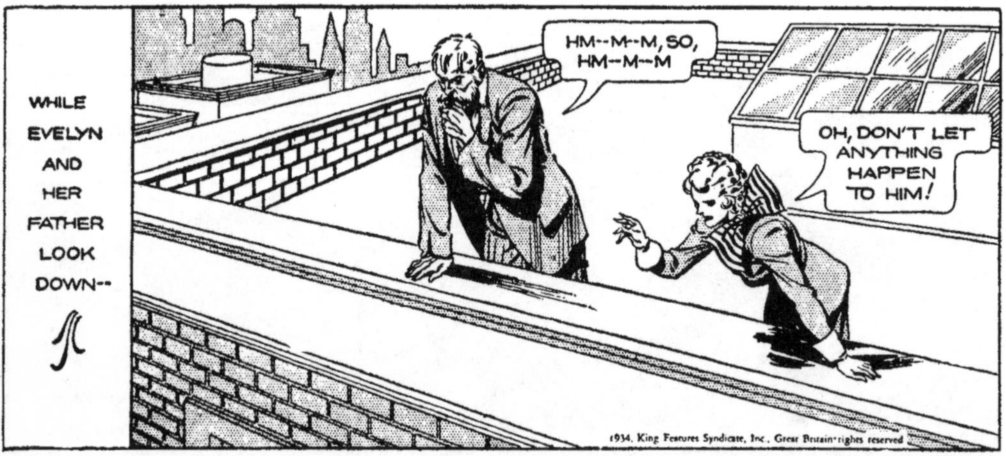
WHILE EVELYN AND HER FATHER LOOK DOWN--
HM--M--M, SO, HM--M--M
OH, DON'T LET ANYTHING HAPPEN TO HIM!
1934, King Features Syndicate, Inc., Great Britain rights reserved

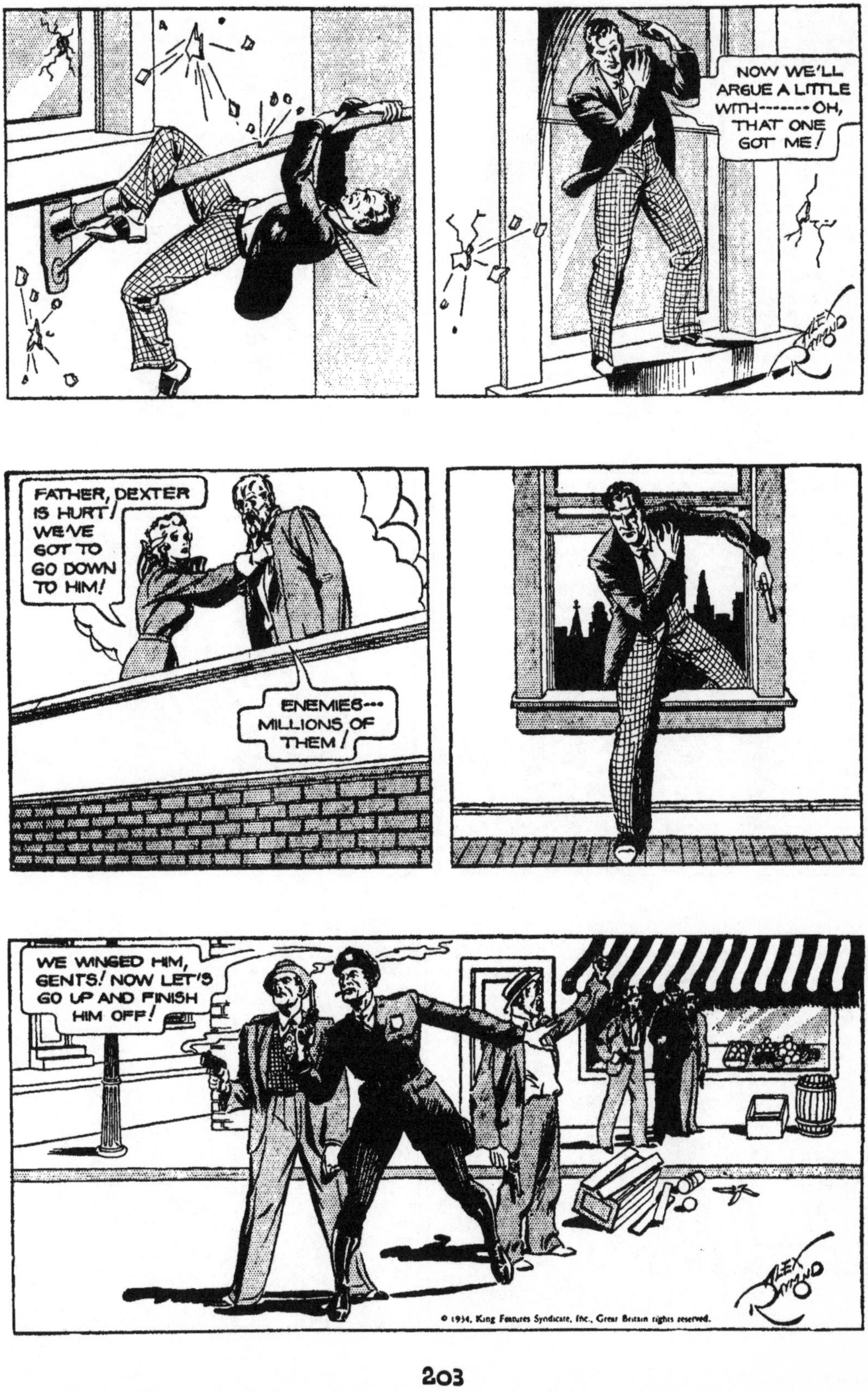
NOW WE'LL ARGUE A LITTLE WITH------- OH, THAT ONE GOT ME!
FATHER, DEXTER IS HURT! WE'VE GOT TO GO DOWN TO HIM!
ENEMIES--- MILLIONS OF THEM!
WE WINGED HIM, GENTS! NOW LET'S GO UP AND FINISH HIM OFF!
© 1934, King Features Syndicate, Inc., Great Britain rights reserved.

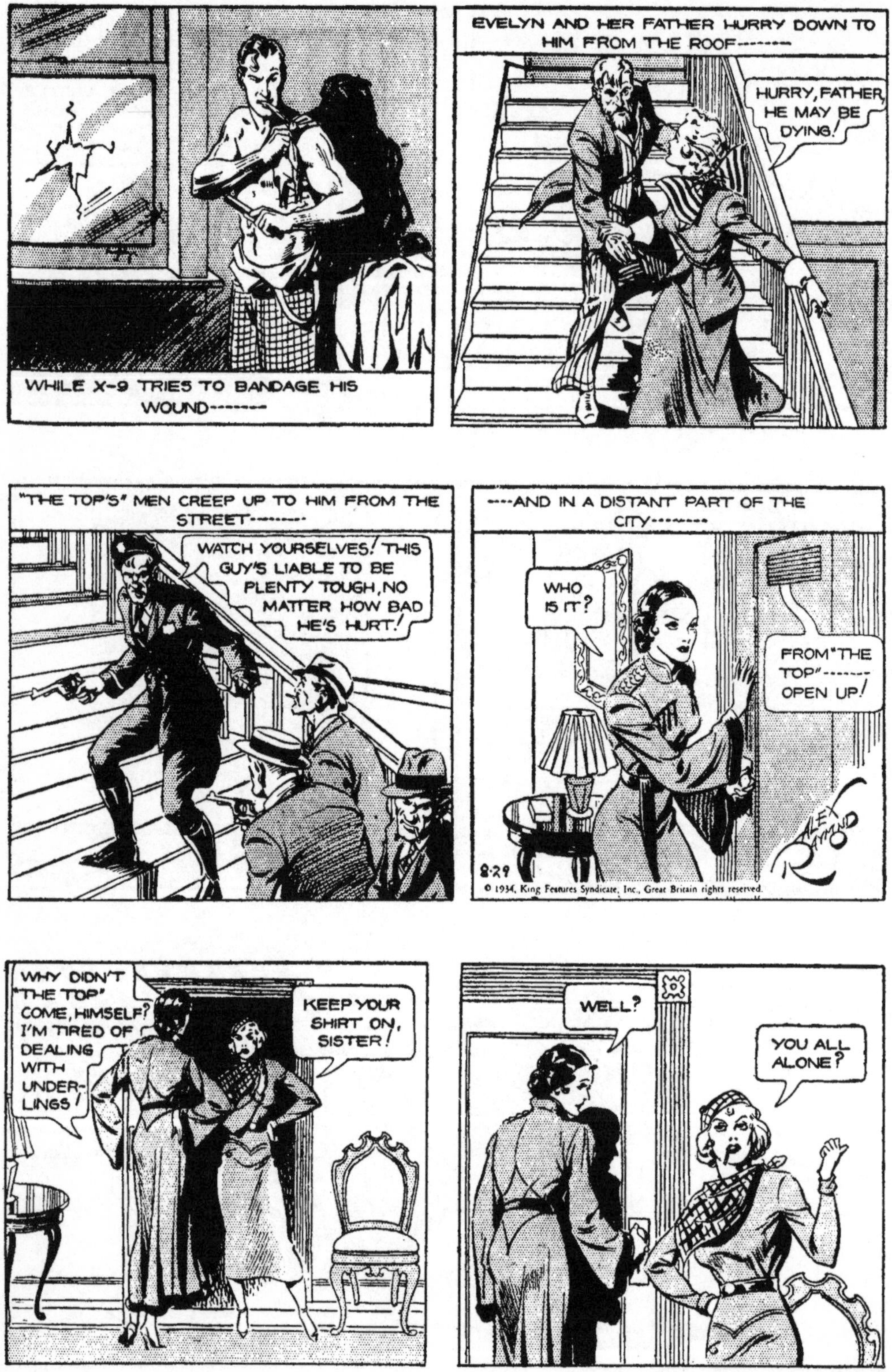
WHILE X-9 TRIES TO BANDAGE HIS WOUND-------
EVELYN AND HER FATHER HURRY DOWN TO HIM FROM THE ROOF-------
HURRY, FATHER, HE MAY BE DYING!
"THE TOP'S" MEN CREEP UP TO HIM FROM THE STREET--------
WATCH YOURSELVES! THIS GUY'S LIABLE TO BE PLENTY TOUGH, NO MATTER HOW BAD HE'S HURT!
----AND IN A DISTANT PART OF THE CITY--------
WHO IS IT?
FROM "THE TOP"------- OPEN UP!
ALEX RAYMOND
8-29
© 1934, King Features Syndicate, Inc., Great Britain rights reserved.
WHY DIDN'T "THE TOP" COME, HIMSELF? I'M TIRED OF DEALING WITH UNDER-LINGS!
KEEP YOUR SHIRT ON, SISTER!
WELL?
YOU ALL ALONE?

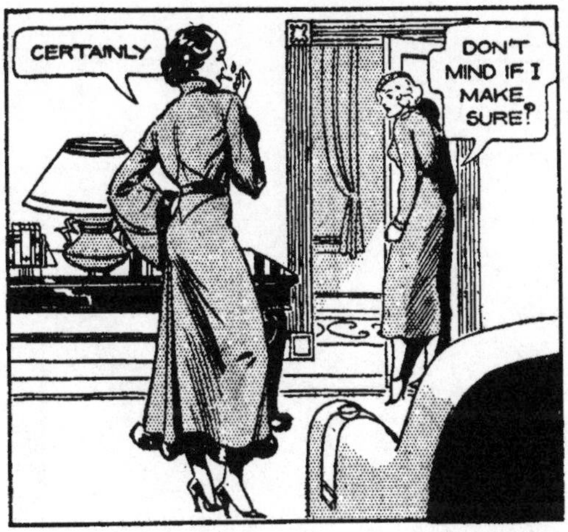
CERTAINLY
DON'T MIND IF I MAKE SURE?

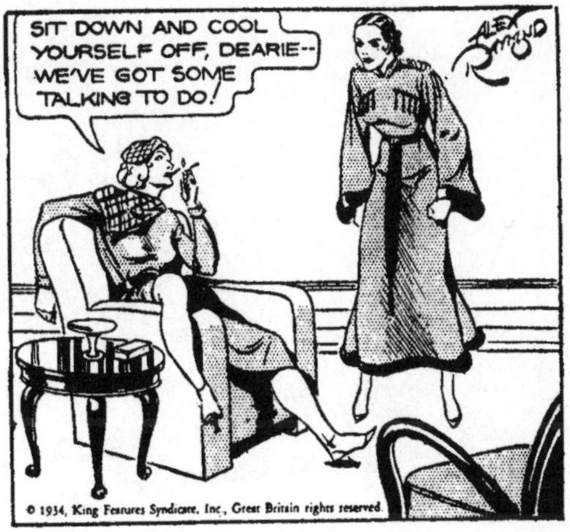
SIT DOWN AND COOL YOURSELF OFF, DEARIE-- WE'VE GOT SOME TALKING TO DO!
ALEX RAYMOND
© 1934, King Features Syndicate, Inc., Great Britain rights reserved.

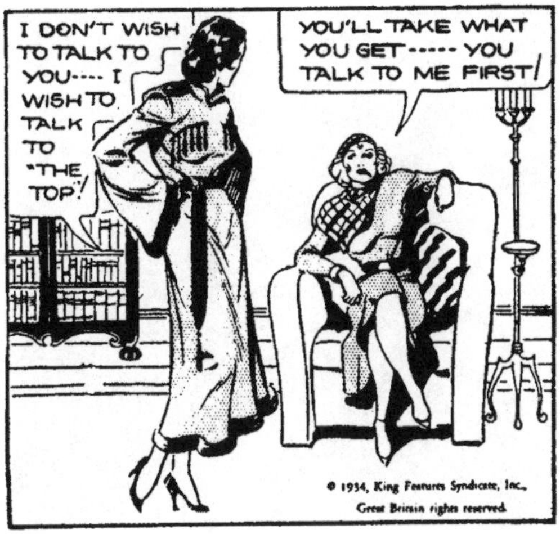
I DON'T WISH TO TALK TO YOU---- I WISH TO TALK TO "THE TOP"!
YOU'LL TAKE WHAT YOU GET ----- YOU TALK TO ME FIRST!
© 1934, King Features Syndicate, Inc., Great Britain rights reserved.

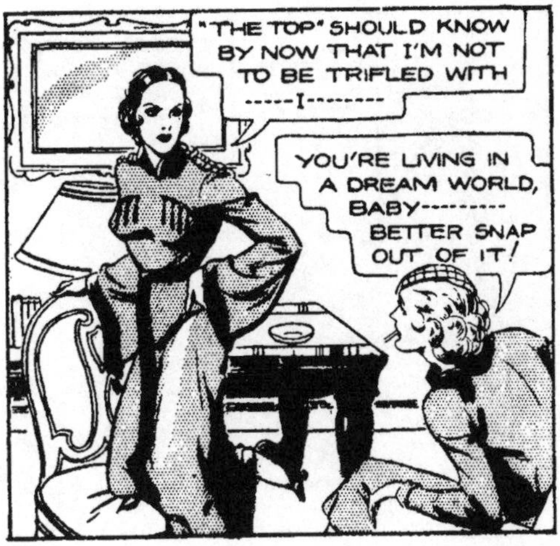
"THE TOP" SHOULD KNOW BY NOW THAT I'M NOT TO BE TRIFLED WITH -----I--------
YOU'RE LIVING IN A DREAM WORLD, BABY--------- BETTER SNAP OUT OF IT!

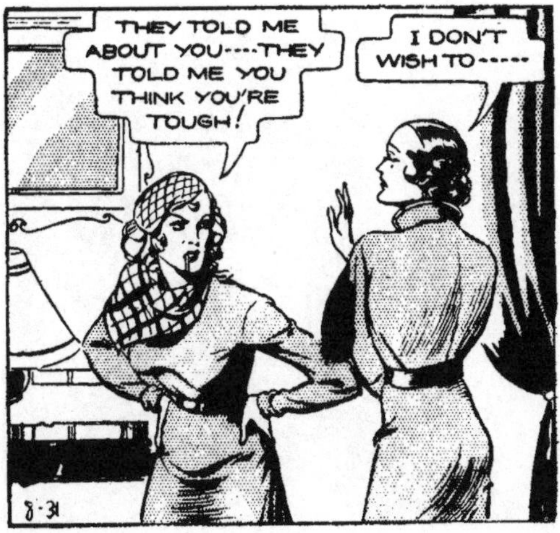
THEY TOLD ME ABOUT YOU----THEY TOLD ME YOU THINK YOU'RE TOUGH!
I DON'T WISH TO-----
8-31

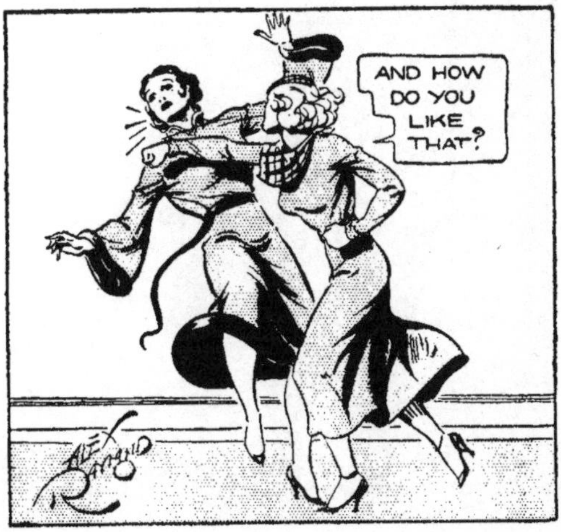
AND HOW DO YOU LIKE THAT?
ALEX RAYMOND

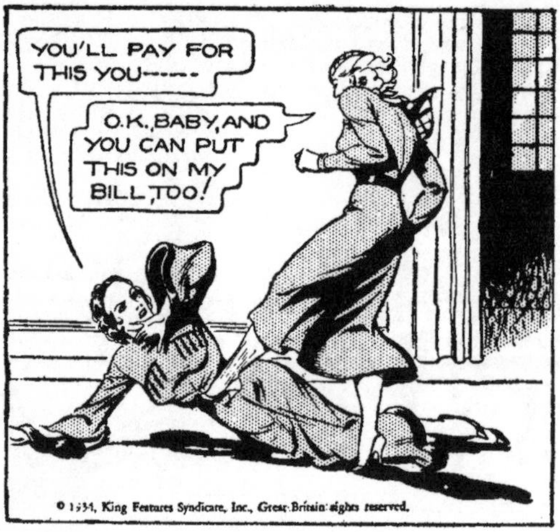
YOU'LL PAY FOR THIS YOU------
O.K., BABY, AND YOU CAN PUT THIS ON MY BILL, TOO!
© 1934, King Features Syndicate, Inc., Great Britain rights reserved.

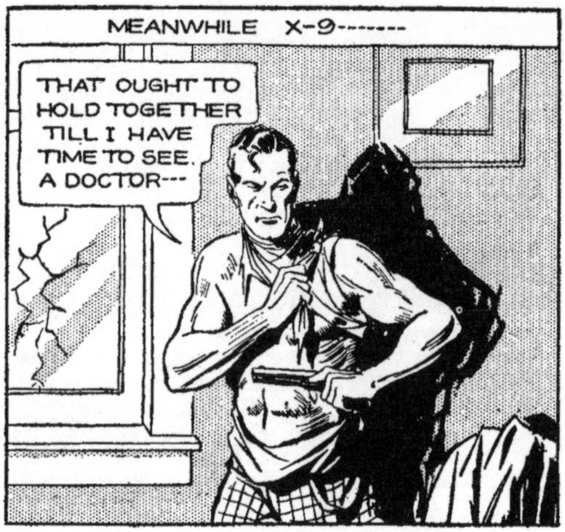
MEANWHILE X-9-------
THAT OUGHT TO HOLD TOGETHER TILL I HAVE TIME TO SEE A DOCTOR---

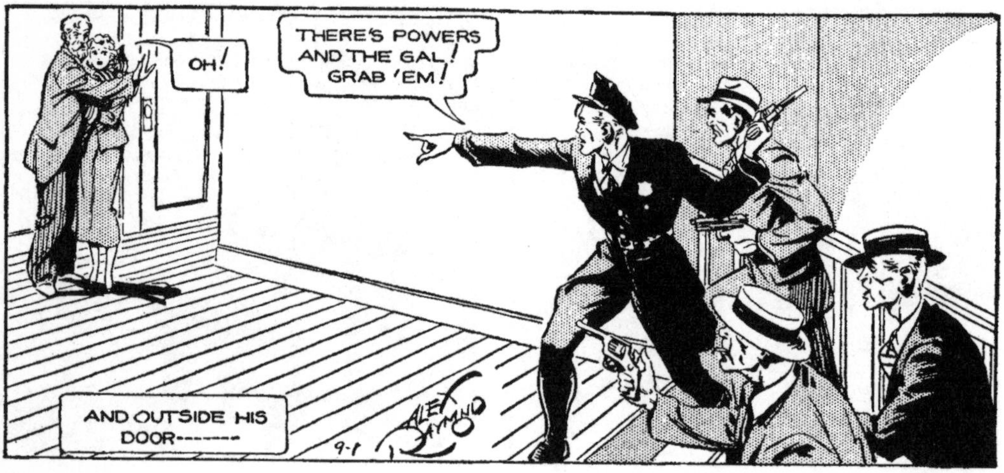
OH!
THERE'S POWERS AND THE GAL! GRAB 'EM!
AND OUTSIDE HIS DOOR-------

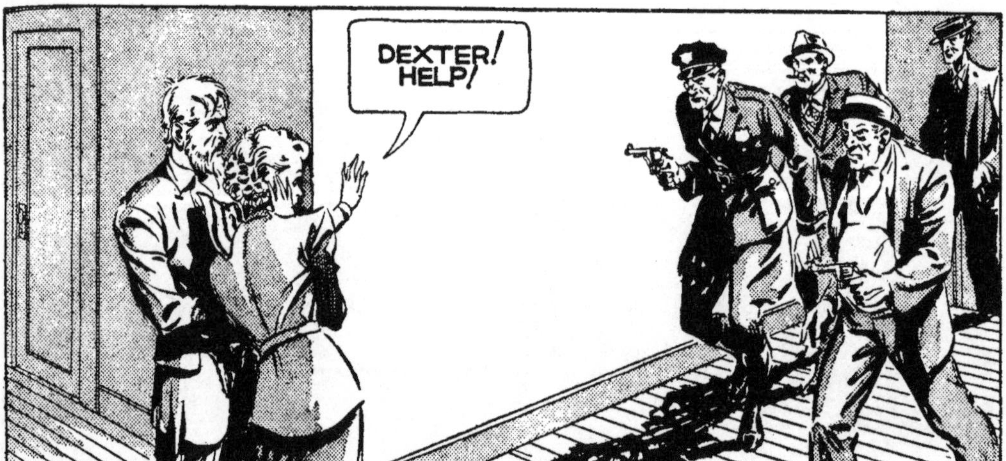
DEXTER! HELP!

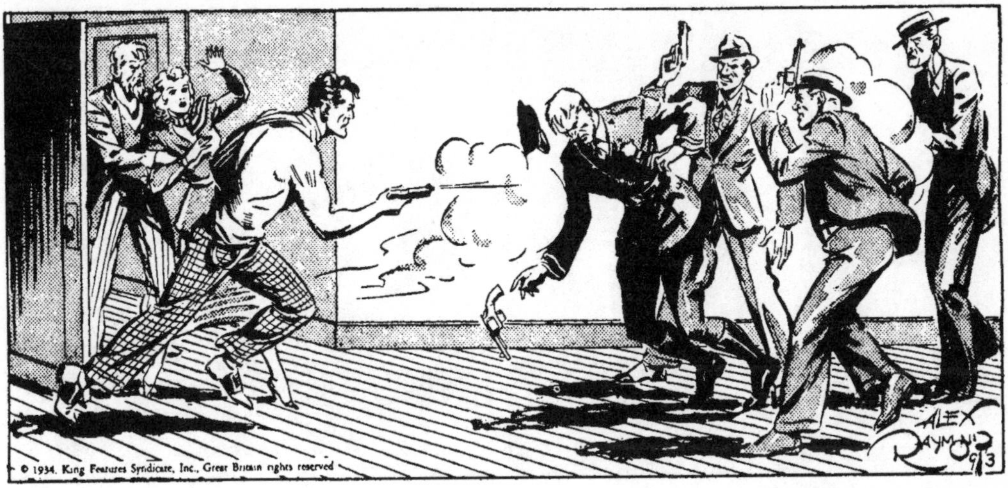
© 1934, King Features Syndicate, Inc., Great Britain rights reserved

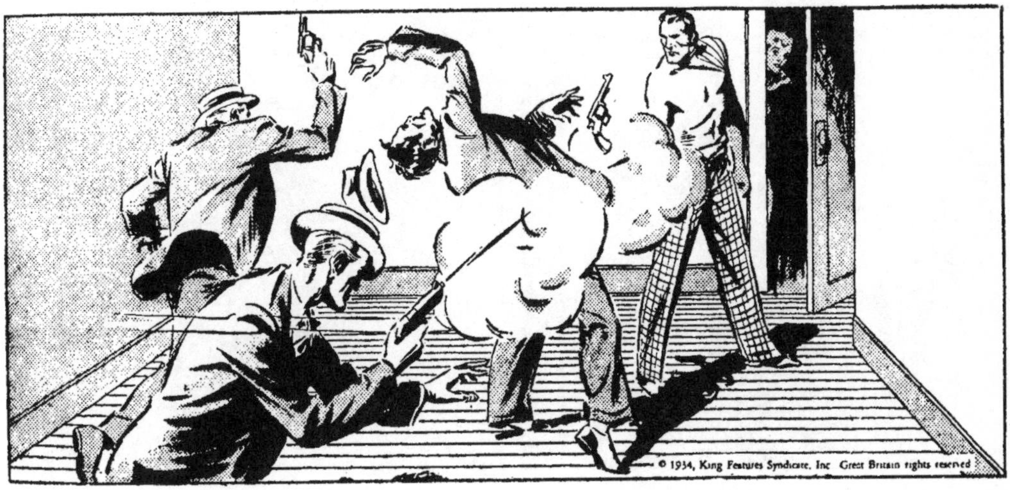
© 1934, King Features Syndicate, Inc Great Britain rights reserved

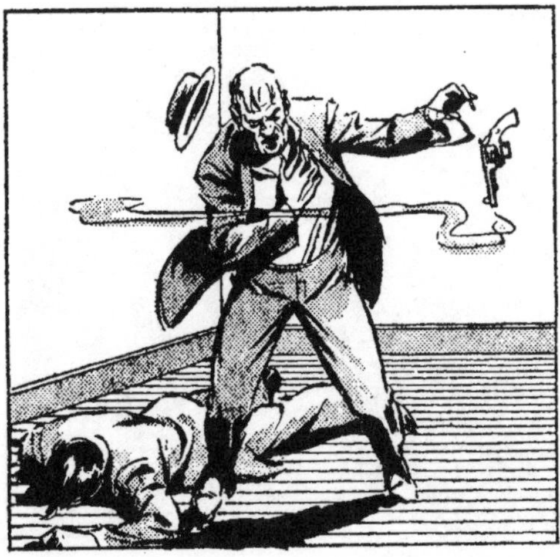

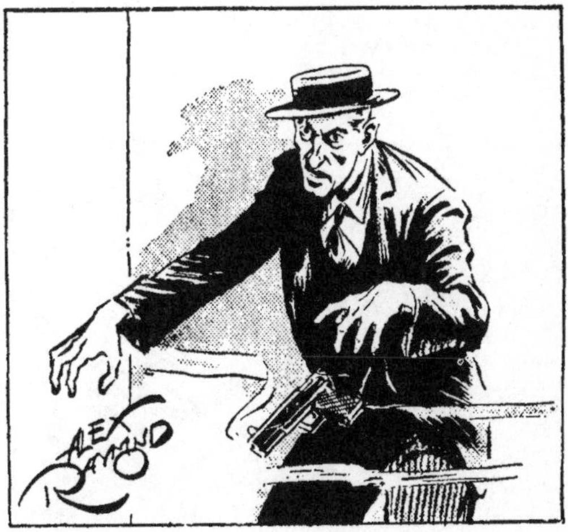

DEXTER! YOU'RE HURT!
THAT'S ALL RIGHT---- THE COAST'S CLEAR NOW--- GET YOUR FATHER AND GET OUT OF HERE---
© 1934, King Features Syndicate, Inc., Great Britain rights reserved.
BUT WE CAN'T GO LIKE THIS---YOU'RE---
DON'T WORRY ABOUT ME---GET GOING
9·5
YOU CAN'T MEAN YOU'RE NOT GOING WITH US!
THAT'S EXACTLY WHAT I MEAN!
ALEX RAYMOND
BUT YOU'RE WOUNDED--- WOUNDED SAVING OUR LIVES AGAIN! WE CAN'T DESERT YOU NOW!
THAT'S THE POINT--- I'M TIRED OF SAVING YOUR LIVES!
© 1934, King Features Syndicate, Inc., Great Britain rights reserved
WHAT?
LISTEN, EVELYN---YOU'RE A NICE GIRL AND I LIKE YOU, BUT I'VE GOT A TOUGH JOB ON MY HANDS TRYING TO FIND "THE TOP"---FOR A WHILE I THOUGHT YOU AND YOUR FATHER COULD HELP ME AND---

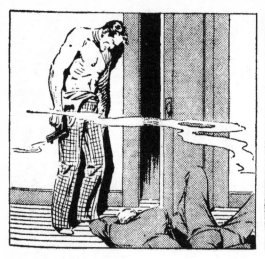

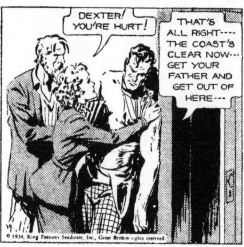

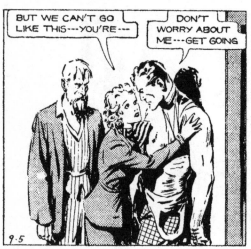

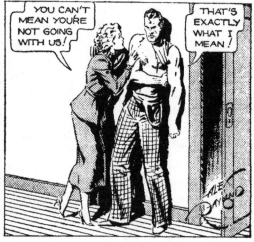

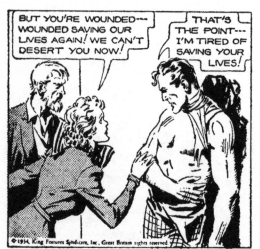

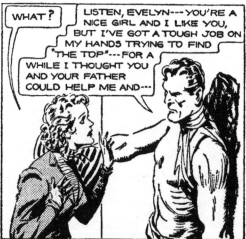

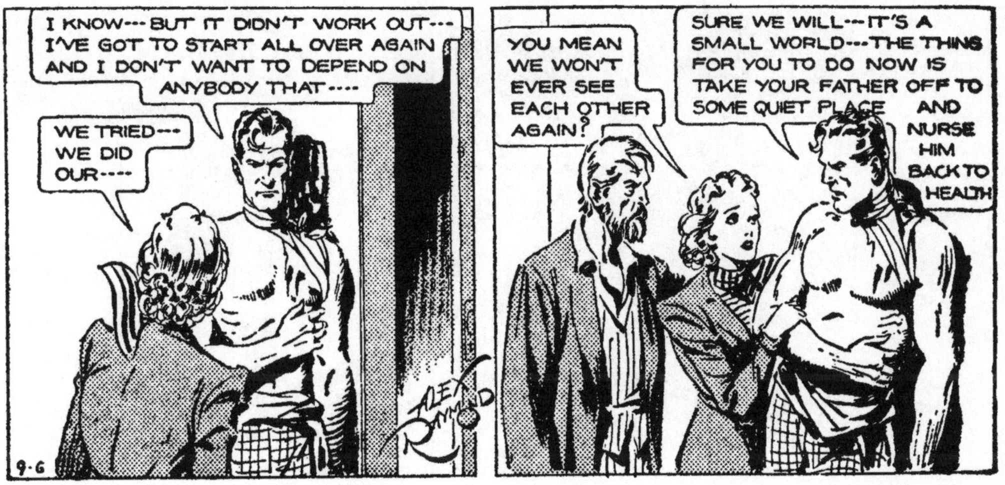
I KNOW--- BUT IT DIDN'T WORK OUT--- I'VE GOT TO START ALL OVER AGAIN AND I DON'T WANT TO DEPEND ON ANYBODY THAT----
WE TRIED--- WE DID OUR----
ALEX RAYMOND
9-6
YOU MEAN WE WON'T EVER SEE EACH OTHER AGAIN?
SURE WE WILL--- IT'S A SMALL WORLD--- THE THING FOR YOU TO DO NOW IS TAKE YOUR FATHER OFF TO SOME QUIET PLACE AND NURSE HIM BACK TO HEALTH

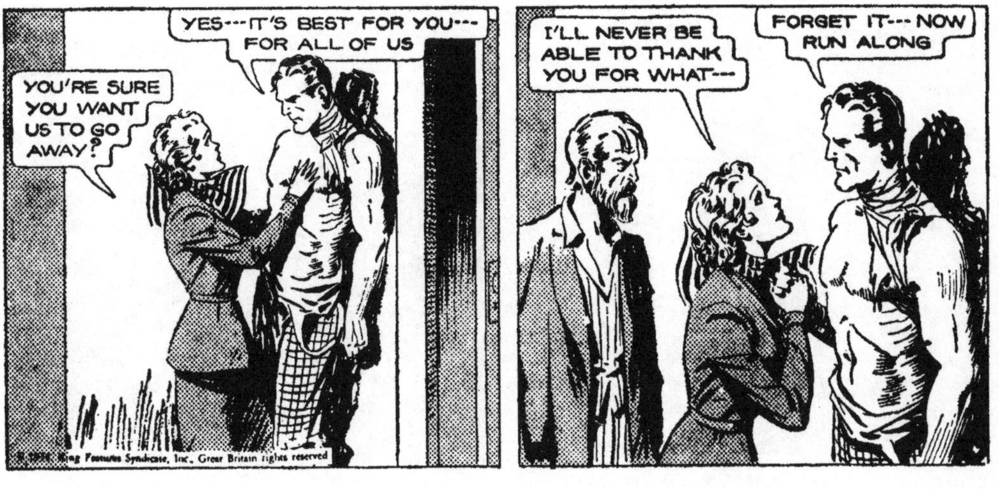
YES--- IT'S BEST FOR YOU--- FOR ALL OF US
YOU'RE SURE YOU WANT US TO GO AWAY?
© 1936, King Features Syndicate, Inc., Great Britain rights reserved
I'LL NEVER BE ABLE TO THANK YOU FOR WHAT---
FORGET IT--- NOW RUN ALONG

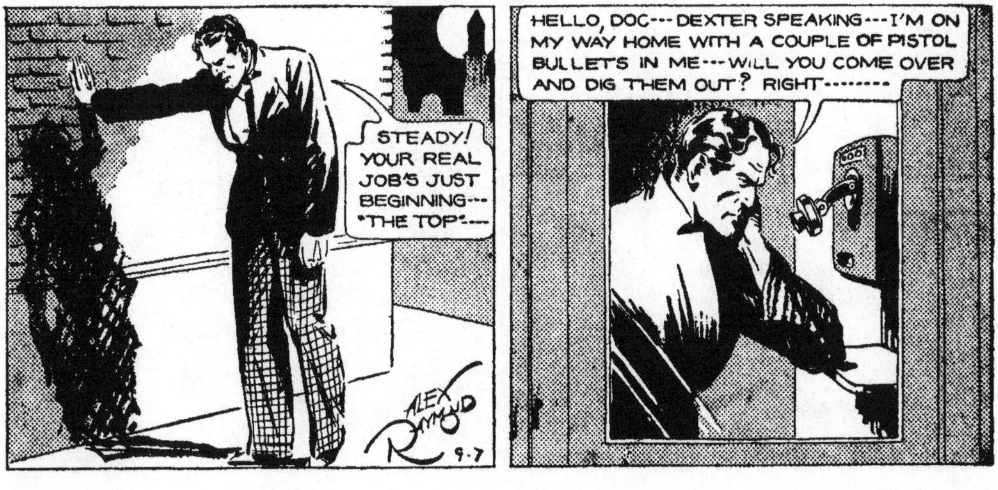
STEADY! YOUR REAL JOB'S JUST BEGINNING--- "THE TOP"---
ALEX RAYMOND
9-7
HELLO, DOC--- DEXTER SPEAKING--- I'M ON MY WAY HOME WITH A COUPLE OF PISTOL BULLETS IN ME--- WILL YOU COME OVER AND DIG THEM OUT? RIGHT--------

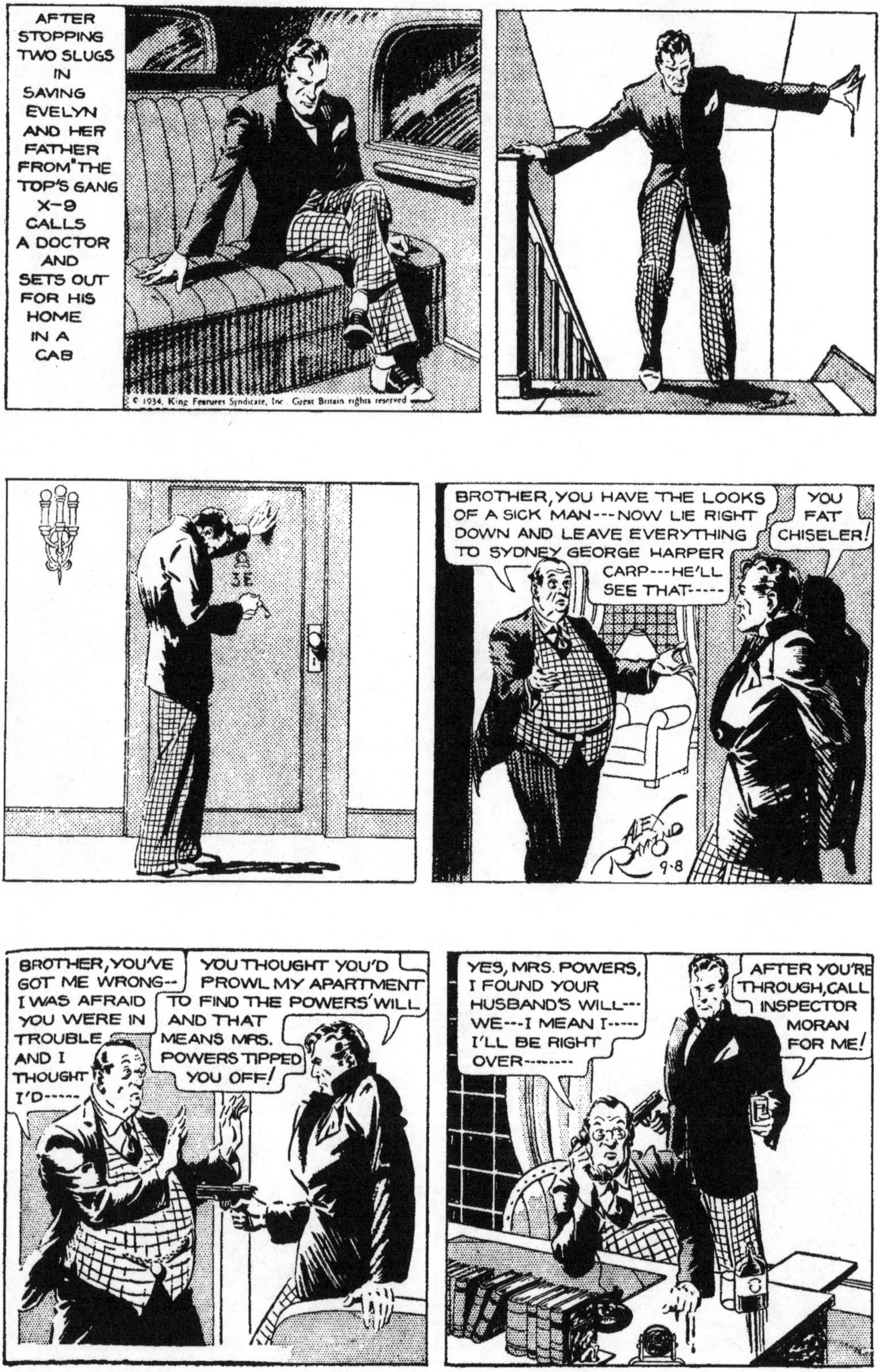
AFTER STOPPING TWO SLUGS IN SAVING EVELYN AND HER FATHER FROM "THE TOP'S GANG X-9 CALLS A DOCTOR AND SETS OUT FOR HIS HOME IN A CAB
© 1934, King Features Syndicate, Inc., Great Britain rights reserved
3E
BROTHER, YOU HAVE THE LOOKS OF A SICK MAN---NOW LIE RIGHT DOWN AND LEAVE EVERYTHING TO SYDNEY GEORGE HARPER CARP---HE'LL SEE THAT-----
YOU FAT CHISELER!
ALEX RAYMOND 9-8
BROTHER, YOU'VE GOT ME WRONG-- I WAS AFRAID YOU WERE IN TROUBLE AND I THOUGHT I'D-----
YOU THOUGHT YOU'D PROWL MY APARTMENT TO FIND THE POWERS' WILL AND THAT MEANS MRS. POWERS TIPPED YOU OFF!
YES, MRS. POWERS, I FOUND YOUR HUSBAND'S WILL--- WE---I MEAN I----- I'LL BE RIGHT OVER--------
AFTER YOU'RE THROUGH, CALL INSPECTOR MORAN FOR ME!

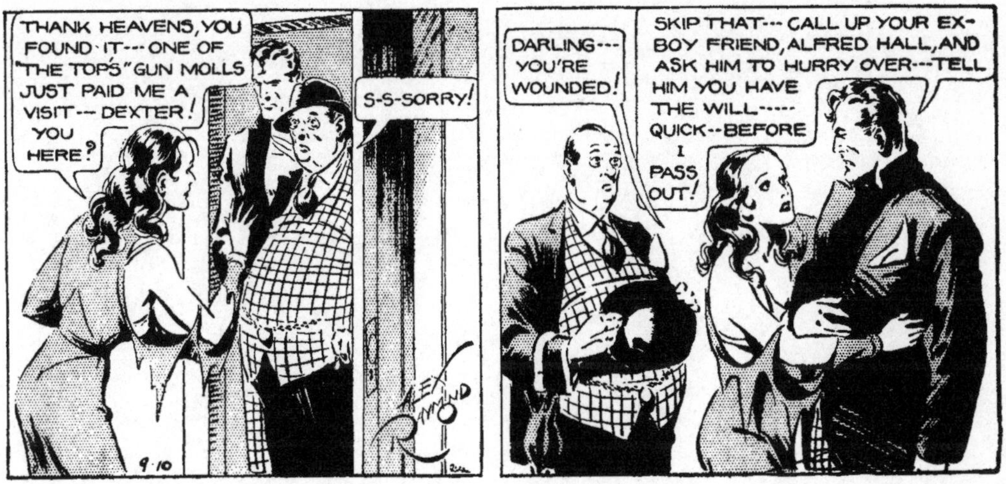
THANK HEAVENS, YOU FOUND IT--- ONE OF "THE TOP'S" GUN MOLLS JUST PAID ME A VISIT--- DEXTER! YOU HERE?
S-S-SORRY!
ALEX RAYMOND
9-10
DARLING--- YOU'RE WOUNDED!
SKIP THAT--- CALL UP YOUR EX-BOY FRIEND, ALFRED HALL, AND ASK HIM TO HURRY OVER---TELL HIM YOU HAVE THE WILL----- QUICK--BEFORE I PASS OUT!

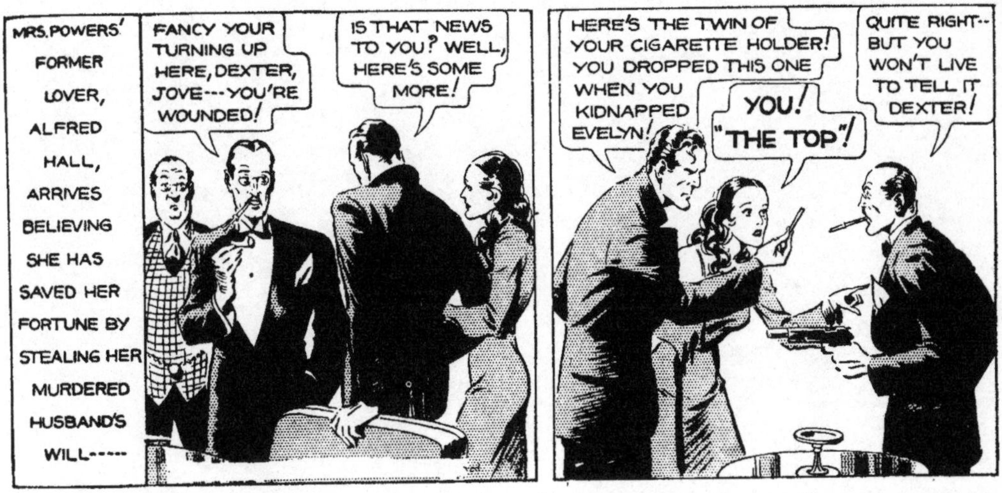
MRS. POWERS' FORMER LOVER, ALFRED HALL, ARRIVES BELIEVING SHE HAS SAVED HER FORTUNE BY STEALING HER MURDERED HUSBAND'S WILL-----
FANCY YOUR TURNING UP HERE, DEXTER, JOVE---YOU'RE WOUNDED!
IS THAT NEWS TO YOU? WELL, HERE'S SOME MORE!
HERE'S THE TWIN OF YOUR CIGARETTE HOLDER! YOU DROPPED THIS ONE WHEN YOU KIDNAPPED EVELYN!
YOU! "THE TOP"!
QUITE RIGHT-- BUT YOU WON'T LIVE TO TELL IT DEXTER!

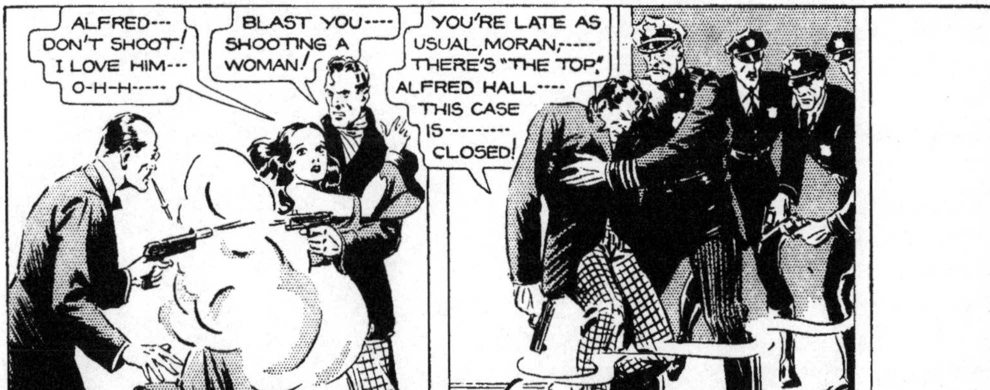
ALFRED--- DON'T SHOOT! I LOVE HIM--- O-H-H-----
BLAST YOU---- SHOOTING A WOMAN!
YOU'RE LATE AS USUAL, MORAN,----- THERE'S "THE TOP," ALFRED HALL---- THIS CASE IS--------- CLOSED!
ALEX RAYMOND
The End

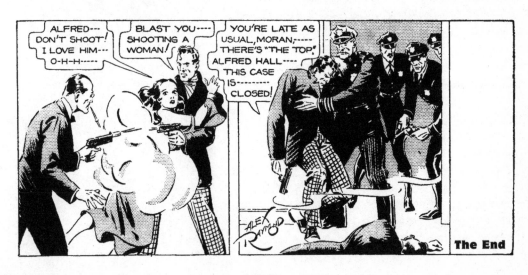

"Look carefully at this street.
Does anything catch your eye?
Nothing? All looks normal?"

Commissario Spada (or "Commissioner
Sword") must have the best detective's nose
since Dick Tracy. His flattened profile was
the result of a serious car crash while chasing
crooks. Spada is an Interpol agent based in
Milan as well as a widower-father of a teenage
son, who would sometimes get involved
in his cases. For a series published in the
Catholic children's weekly *Il Giornalino* (*Little
Newspaper*), it could be surprisingly hard-
hitting, dealing with drugs and terrorism.
This short story may be more low-key, but
it exposes the web of everyday dishonesty
beneath the surface of a big city and the flaws
in the memories and perceptions of witnesses.
It marks the first time any of De Luca's
extraordinarily innovative *fumetti* have been
translated into English.

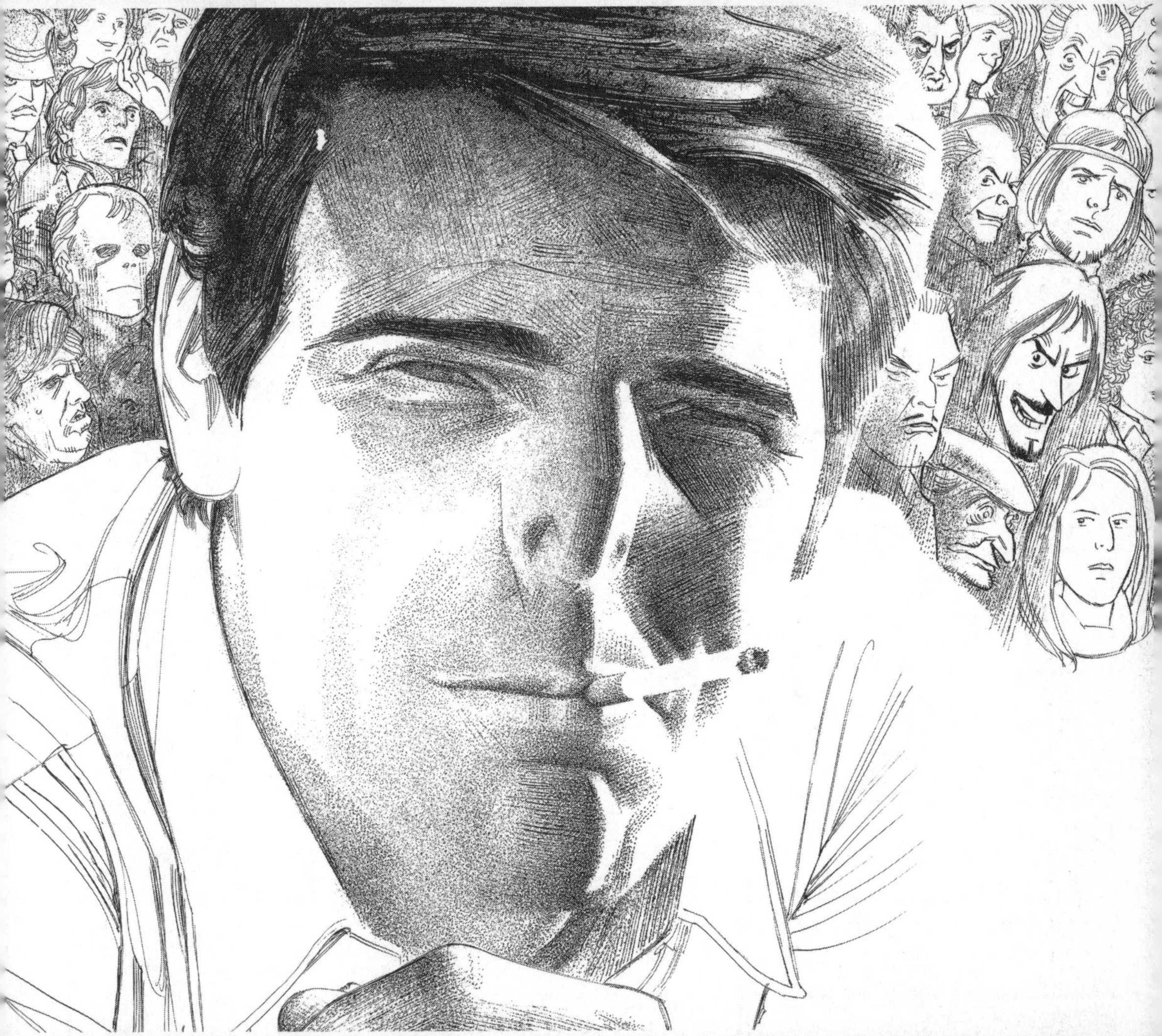

Commissario Spada: Strada [Street]

Gianluigi Gonano (script) and Gianni De Luca (art) 1979

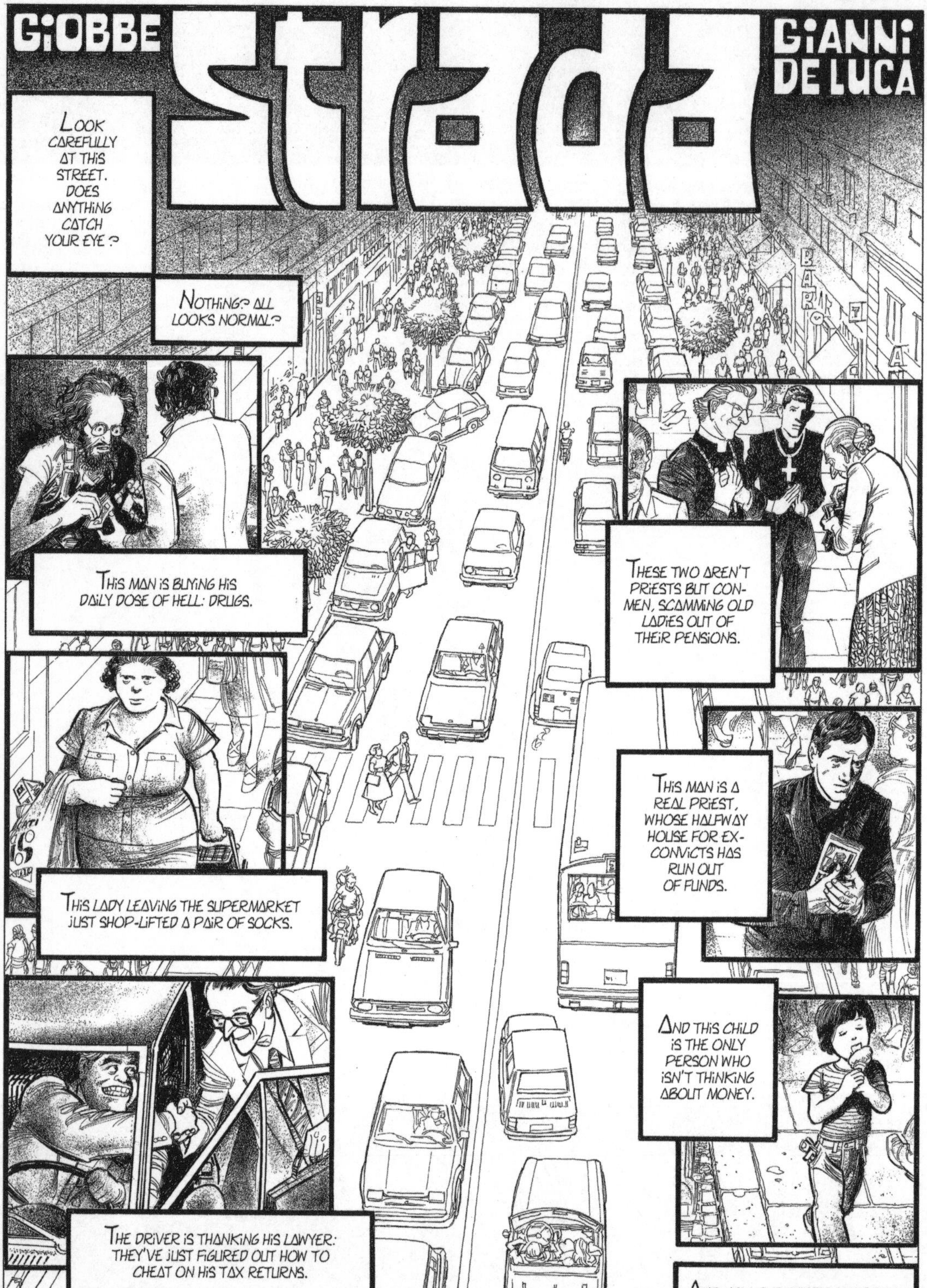
GiOBBE
strada
GiANNi DE LUCA
LOOK CAREFULLY AT THIS STREET. DOES ANYTHING CATCH YOUR EYE?
NOTHING? ALL LOOKS NORMAL?
THIS MAN IS BUYING HIS DAILY DOSE OF HELL: DRUGS.
THESE TWO AREN'T PRIESTS BUT CON-MEN, SCAMMING OLD LADIES OUT OF THEIR PENSIONS.
THIS LADY LEAVING THE SUPERMARKET JUST SHOP-LIFTED A PAIR OF SOCKS.
THIS MAN IS A REAL PRIEST, WHOSE HALFWAY HOUSE FOR EX-CONVICTS HAS RUN OUT OF FUNDS.
THE DRIVER IS THANKING HIS LAWYER: THEY'VE JUST FIGURED OUT HOW TO CHEAT ON HIS TAX RETURNS.
AND THIS CHILD IS THE ONLY PERSON WHO ISN'T THINKING ABOUT MONEY.
AND NOW OUR STORY CAN BEGIN.

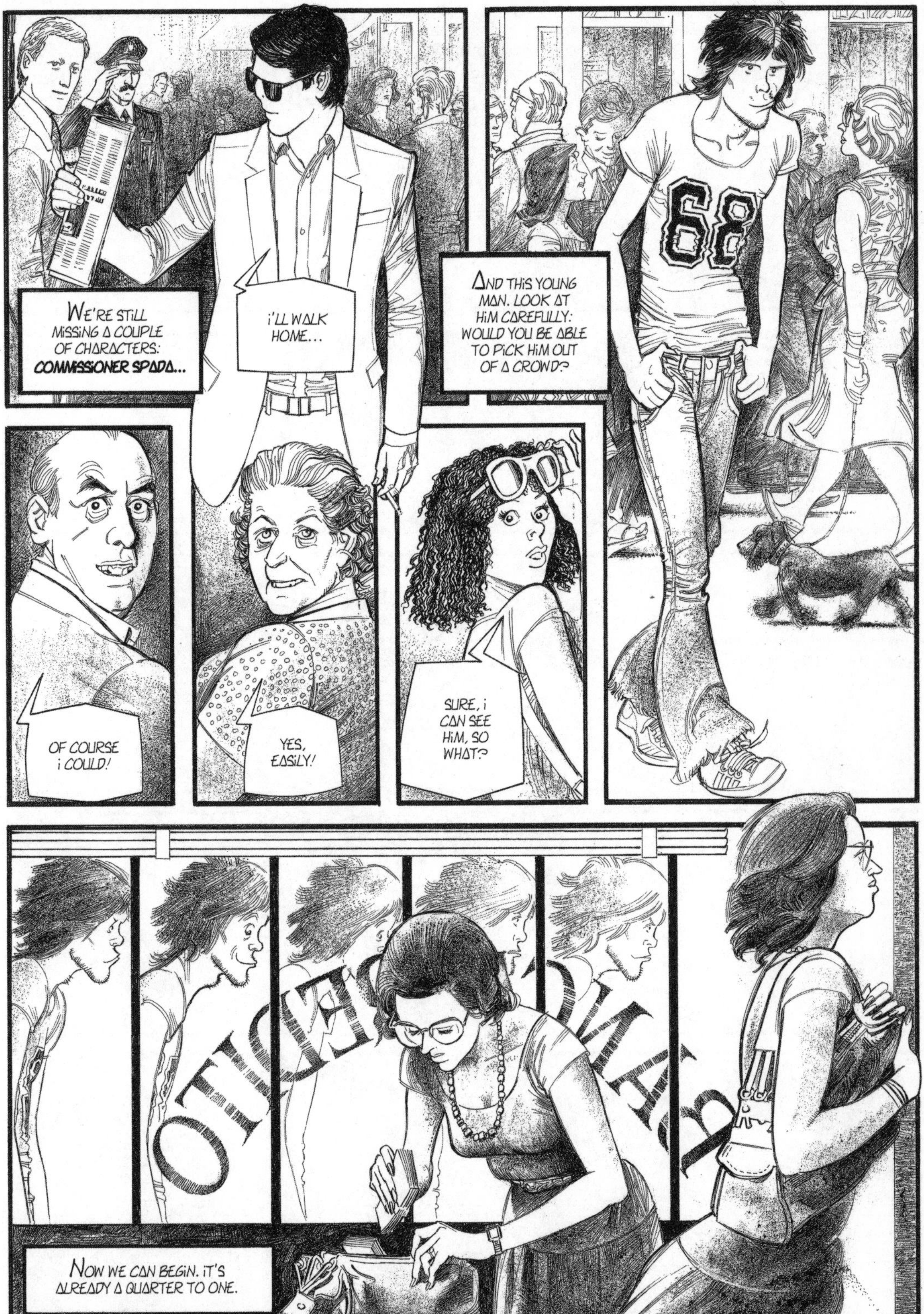
WE'RE STILL MISSING A COUPLE OF CHARACTERS: **COMMISSIONER SPADA...**
I'LL WALK HOME...
AND THIS YOUNG MAN. LOOK AT HIM CAREFULLY: WOULD YOU BE ABLE TO PICK HIM OUT OF A CROWD?
OF COURSE I COULD!
YES, EASILY!
SURE, I CAN SEE HIM, SO WHAT?
NOW WE CAN BEGIN. IT'S ALREADY A QUARTER TO ONE.

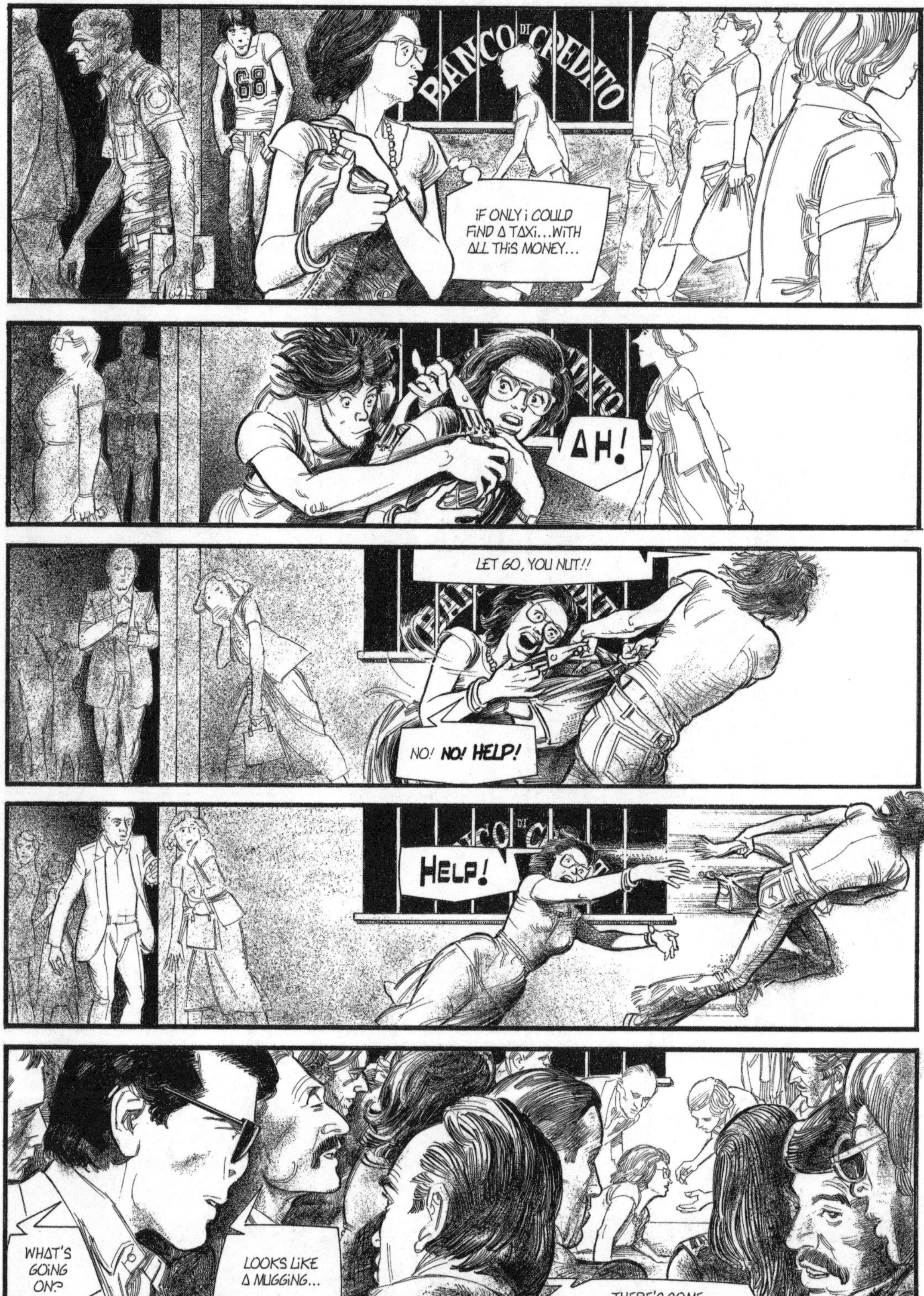
BANCO DI CREDITO
iF ONLY i COULD FiND A TAXi...WiTH ALL THiS MONEY...
AH!
LET GO, YOU NUT!!
NO! NO! HELP!
HELP!
WHAT'S GOiNG ON?
LOOKS LiKE A MUGGiNG...
THERE'S SOME LADY ON THE GROUND...

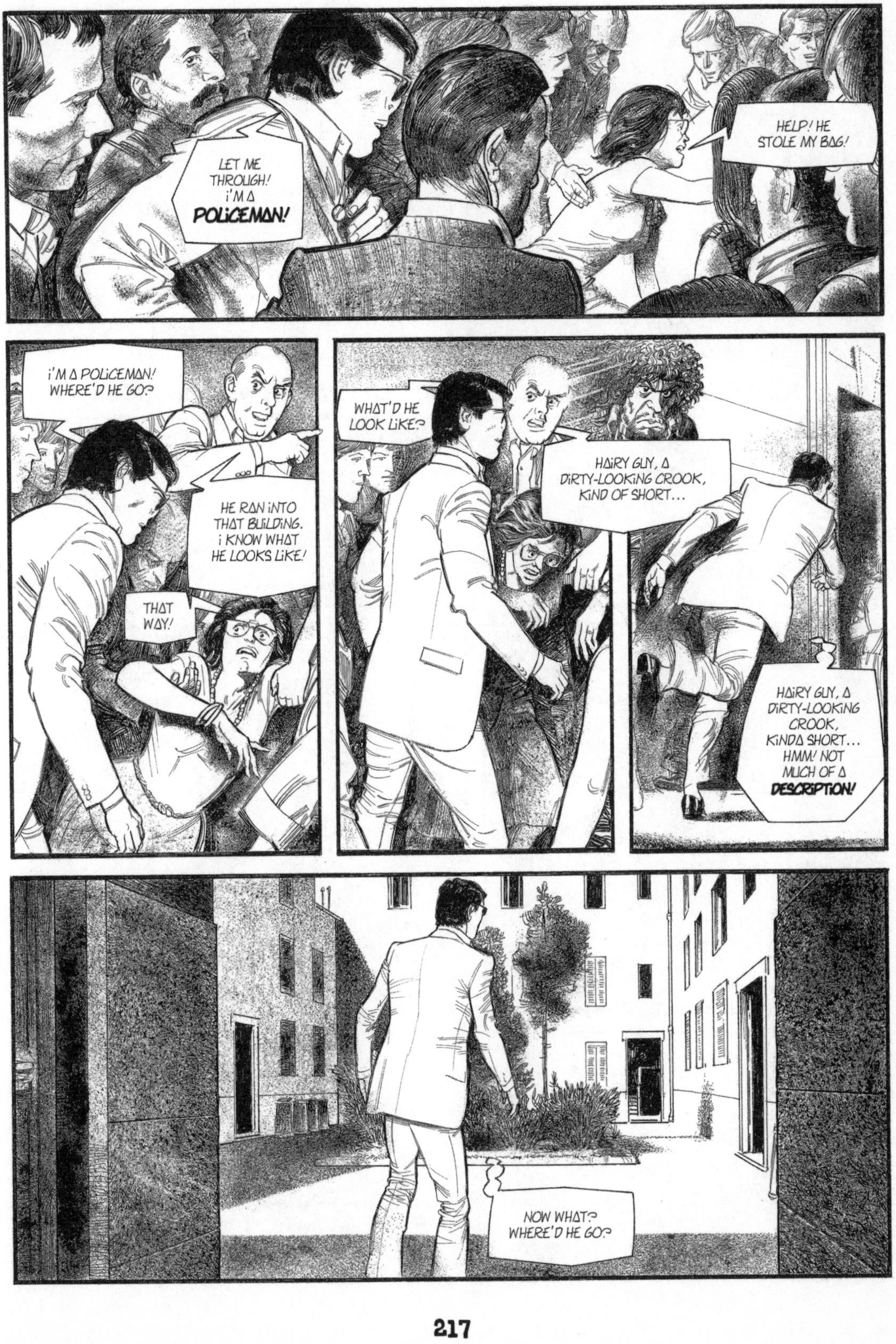
LET ME THROUGH! I'M A **POLICEMAN!**
HELP! HE STOLE MY BAG!
I'M A POLICEMAN! WHERE'D HE GO?
HE RAN INTO THAT BUILDING. I KNOW WHAT HE LOOKS LIKE!
THAT WAY!
WHAT'D HE LOOK LIKE?
HAIRY GUY, A DIRTY-LOOKING CROOK, KIND OF SHORT...
HAIRY GUY, A DIRTY-LOOKING CROOK, KINDA SHORT... HMM! NOT MUCH OF A **DESCRIPTION!**
NOW WHAT? WHERE'D HE GO?

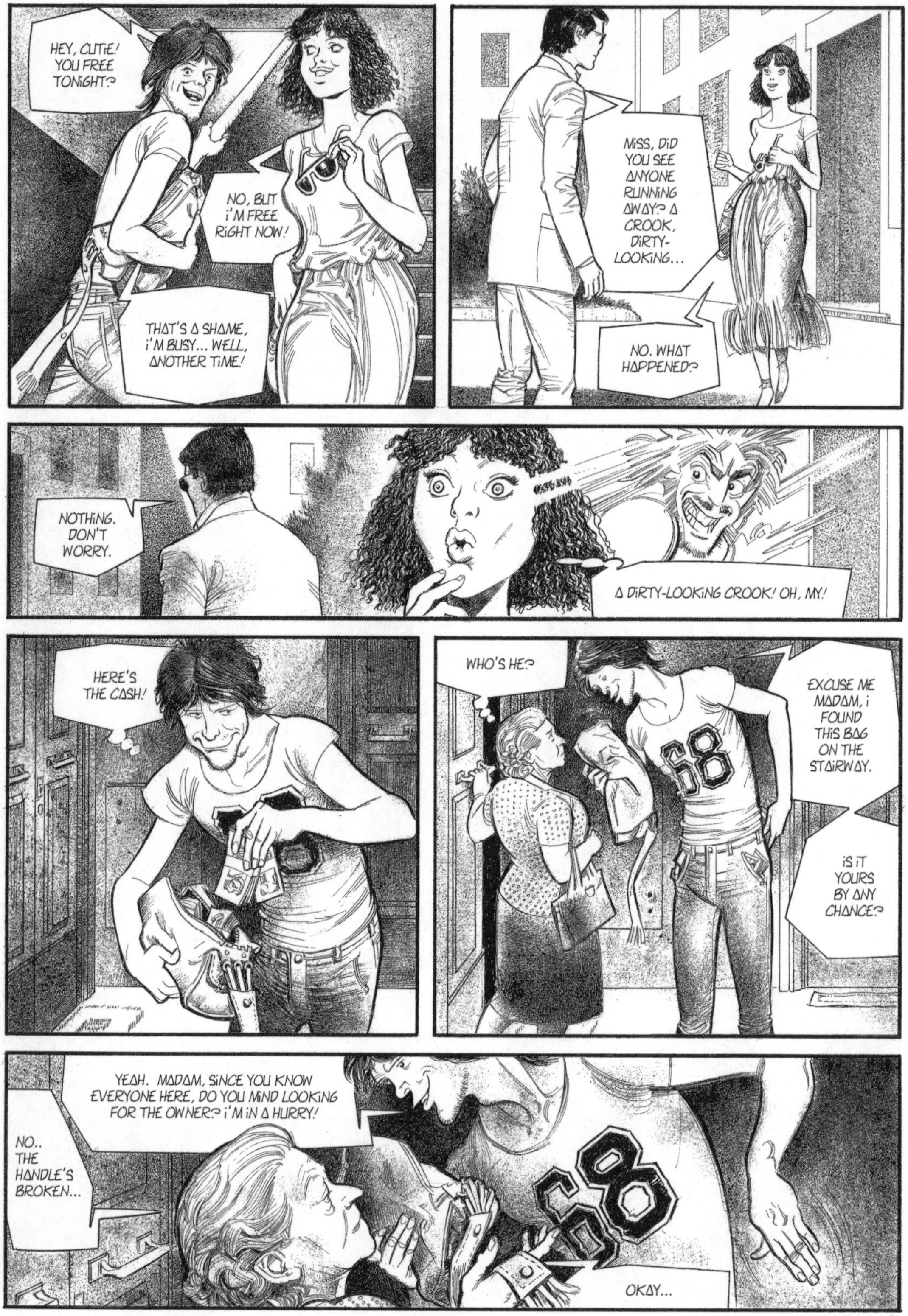
HEY, CUTIE! YOU FREE TONIGHT?
NO, BUT I'M FREE RIGHT NOW!
THAT'S A SHAME, I'M BUSY... WELL, ANOTHER TIME!
MISS, DID YOU SEE ANYONE RUNNING AWAY? A CROOK, DIRTY-LOOKING...
NO. WHAT HAPPENED?
NOTHING. DON'T WORRY.
A DIRTY-LOOKING CROOK! OH, MY!
HERE'S THE CASH!
WHO'S HE?
EXCUSE ME MADAM, I FOUND THIS BAG ON THE STAIRWAY.
IS IT YOURS BY ANY CHANCE?
YEAH. MADAM, SINCE YOU KNOW EVERYONE HERE, DO YOU MIND LOOKING FOR THE OWNER? I'M IN A HURRY!
NO.. THE HANDLE'S BROKEN...
OKAY...

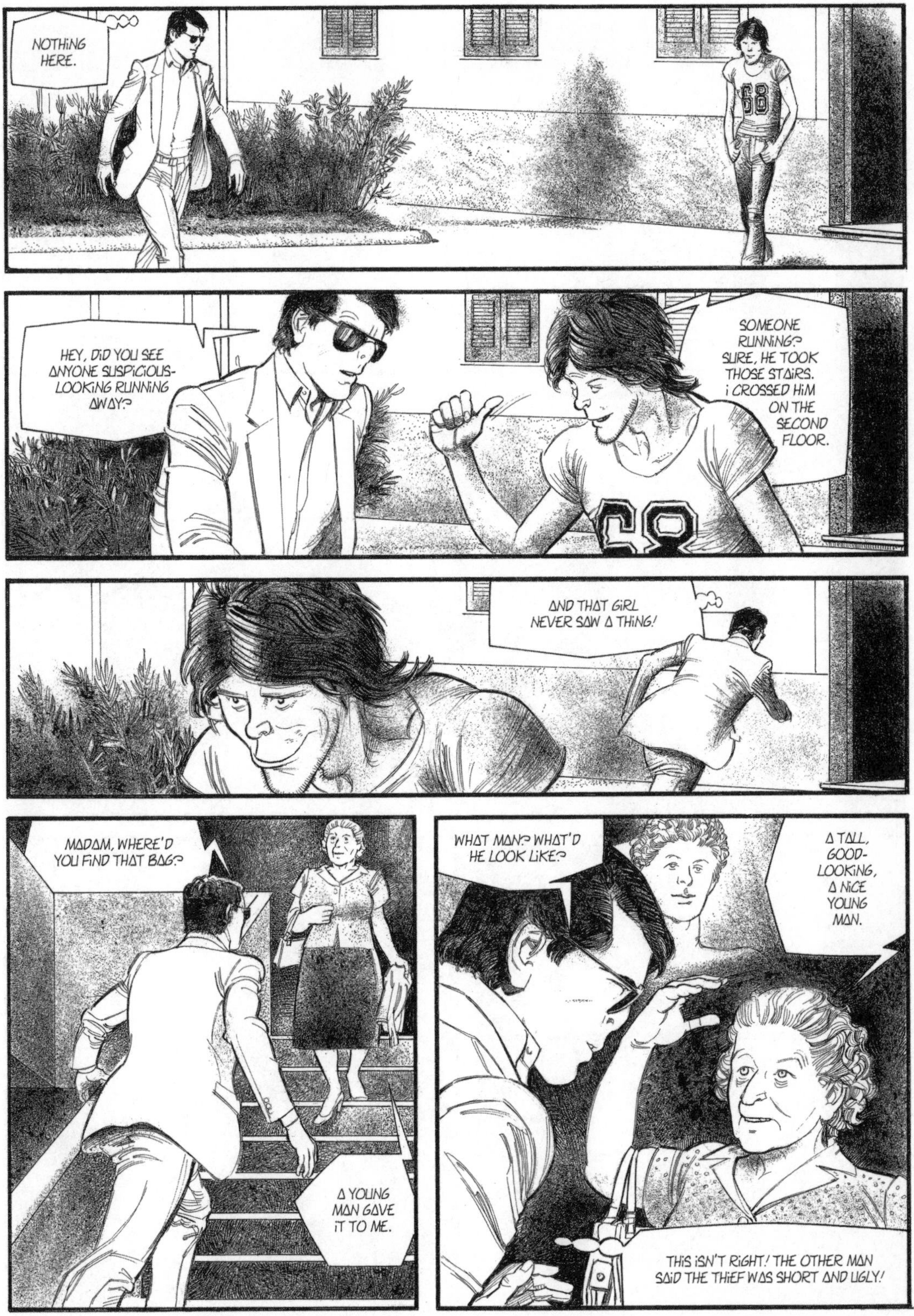
NOTHING HERE.
HEY, DID YOU SEE ANYONE SUSPICIOUS-LOOKING RUNNING AWAY?
SOMEONE RUNNING? SURE, HE TOOK THOSE STAIRS. I CROSSED HIM ON THE SECOND FLOOR.
AND THAT GIRL NEVER SAW A THING!
MADAM, WHERE'D YOU FIND THAT BAG?
A YOUNG MAN GAVE IT TO ME.
WHAT MAN? WHAT'D HE LOOK LIKE?
A TALL, GOOD-LOOKING, A NICE YOUNG MAN.
THIS ISN'T RIGHT! THE OTHER MAN SAID THE THIEF WAS SHORT AND UGLY!

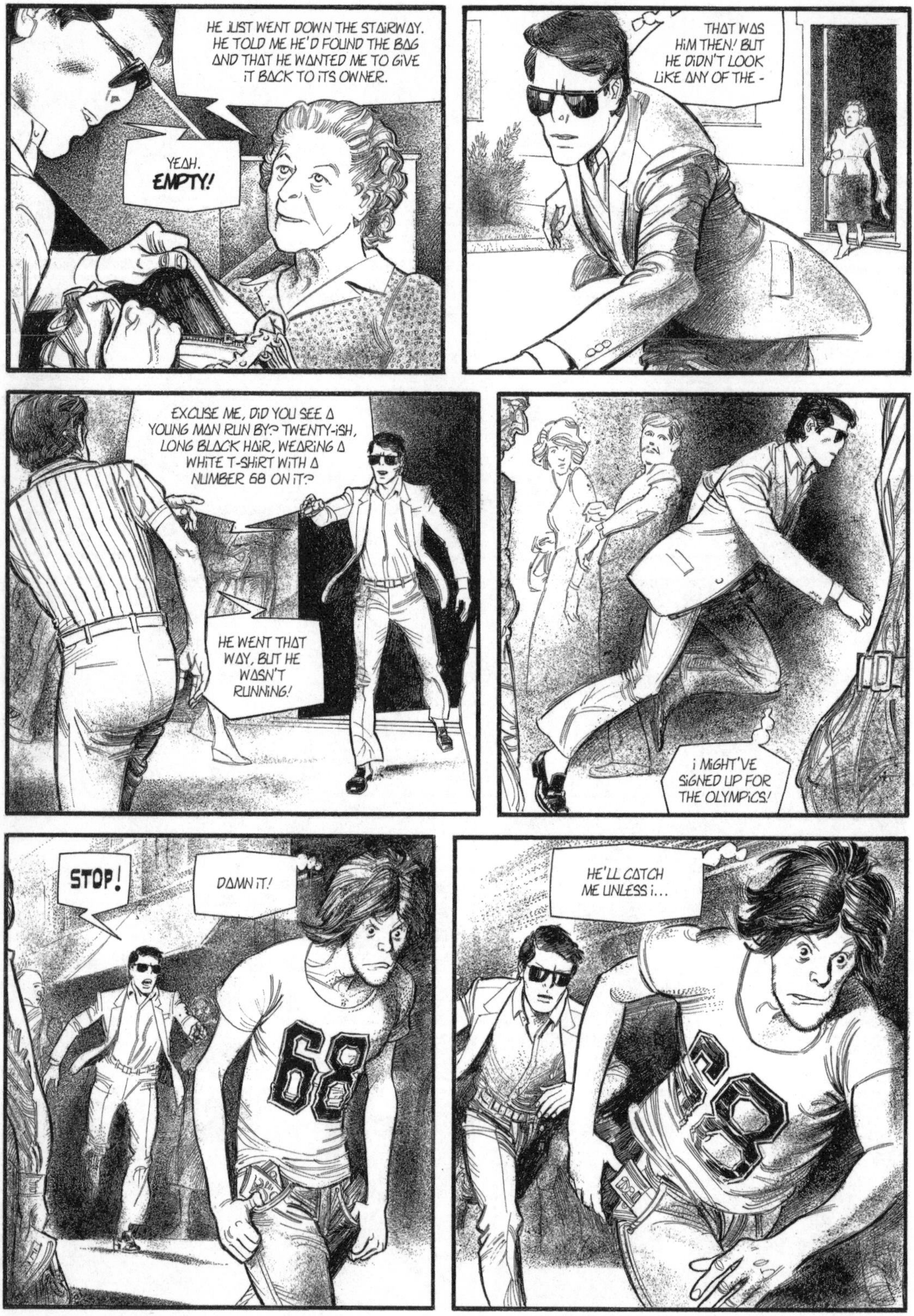
HE JUST WENT DOWN THE STAIRWAY. HE TOLD ME HE'D FOUND THE BAG AND THAT HE WANTED ME TO GIVE IT BACK TO ITS OWNER.
YEAH. EMPTY!
THAT WAS HIM THEN! BUT HE DIDN'T LOOK LIKE ANY OF THE -
EXCUSE ME, DID YOU SEE A YOUNG MAN RUN BY? TWENTY-ISH, LONG BLACK HAIR, WEARING A WHITE T-SHIRT WITH A NUMBER 68 ON IT?
HE WENT THAT WAY, BUT HE WASN'T RUNNING!
I MIGHT'VE SIGNED UP FOR THE OLYMPICS!
STOP!
DAMN IT!
HE'LL CATCH ME UNLESS I...

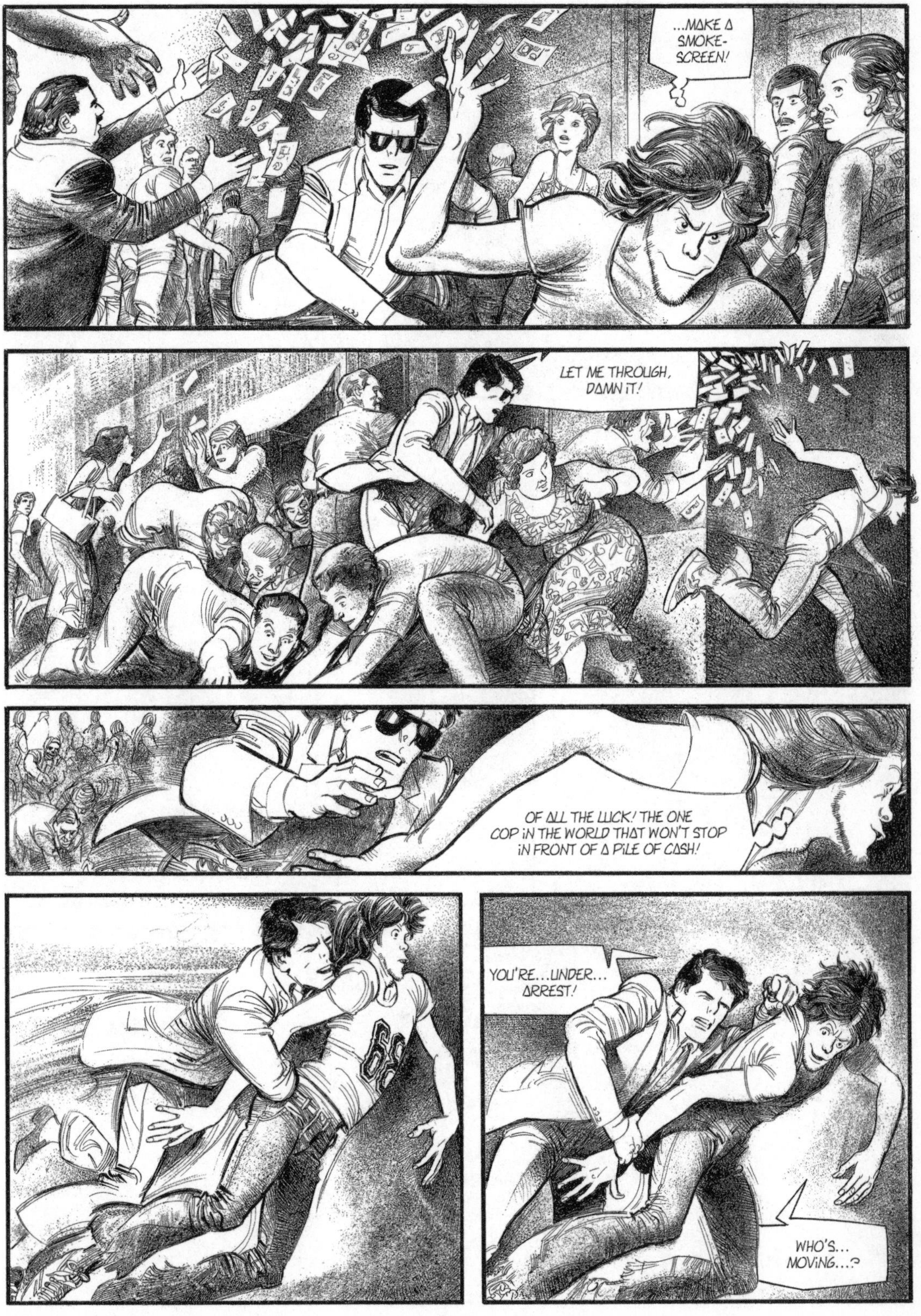
...MAKE A SMOKE-SCREEN!
LET ME THROUGH, DAMN IT!
OF ALL THE LUCK! THE ONE COP IN THE WORLD THAT WON'T STOP IN FRONT OF A PILE OF CASH!
YOU'RE...UNDER... ARREST!
WHO'S... MOVING...?

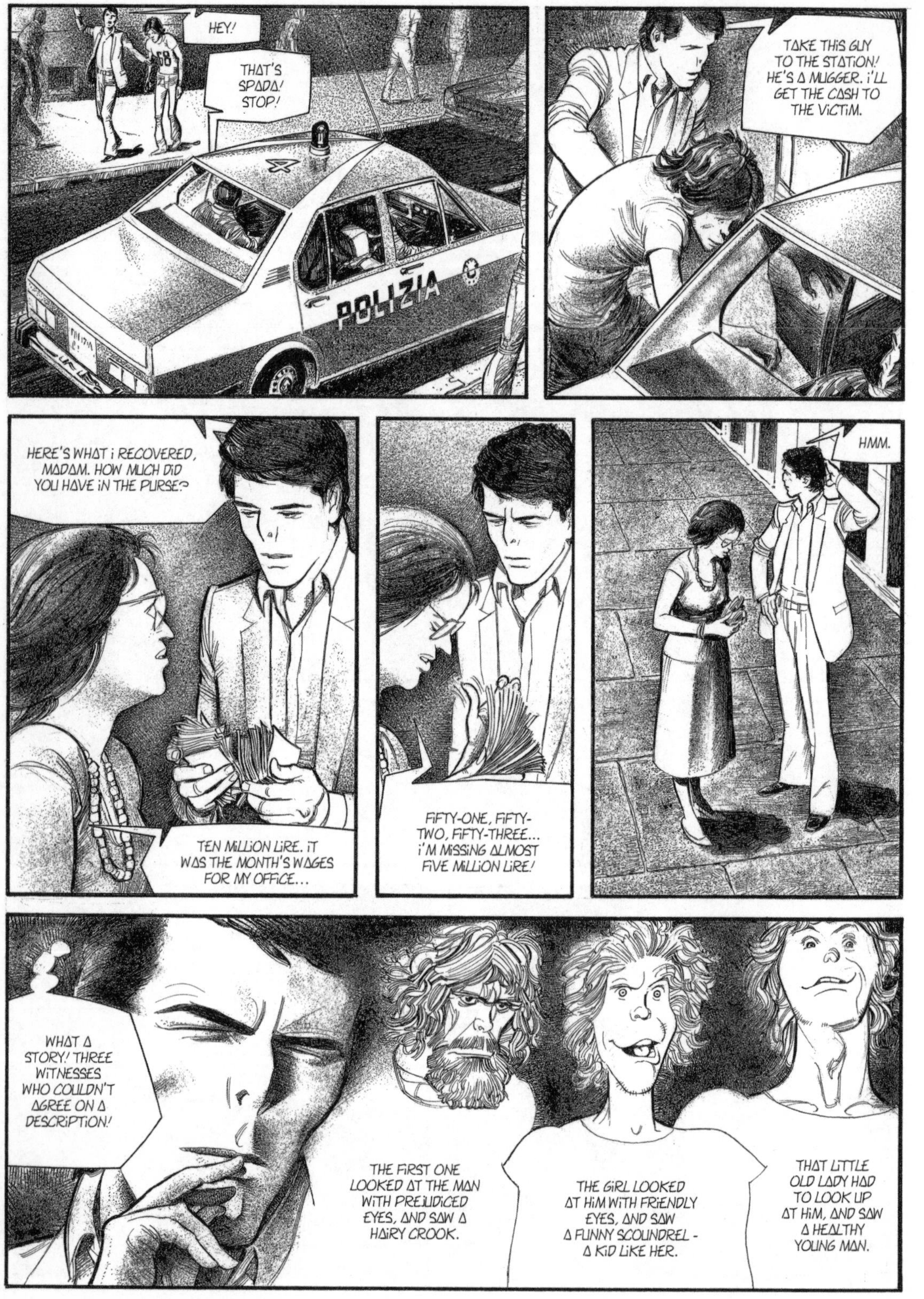
HEY!
THAT'S SPADA! STOP!
POLIZIA
TAKE THIS GUY TO THE STATION! HE'S A MUGGER. I'LL GET THE CASH TO THE VICTIM.
HERE'S WHAT I RECOVERED, MADAM. HOW MUCH DID YOU HAVE IN THE PURSE?
TEN MILLION LIRE. IT WAS THE MONTH'S WAGES FOR MY OFFICE...
FIFTY-ONE, FIFTY-TWO, FIFTY-THREE... I'M MISSING ALMOST FIVE MILLION LIRE!
HMM.
WHAT A STORY! THREE WITNESSES WHO COULDN'T AGREE ON A DESCRIPTION!
THE FIRST ONE LOOKED AT THE MAN WITH PREJUDICED EYES, AND SAW A HAIRY CROOK.
THE GIRL LOOKED AT HIM WITH FRIENDLY EYES, AND SAW A FUNNY SCOUNDREL - A KID LIKE HER.
THAT LITTLE OLD LADY HAD TO LOOK UP AT HIM, AND SAW A HEALTHY YOUNG MAN.

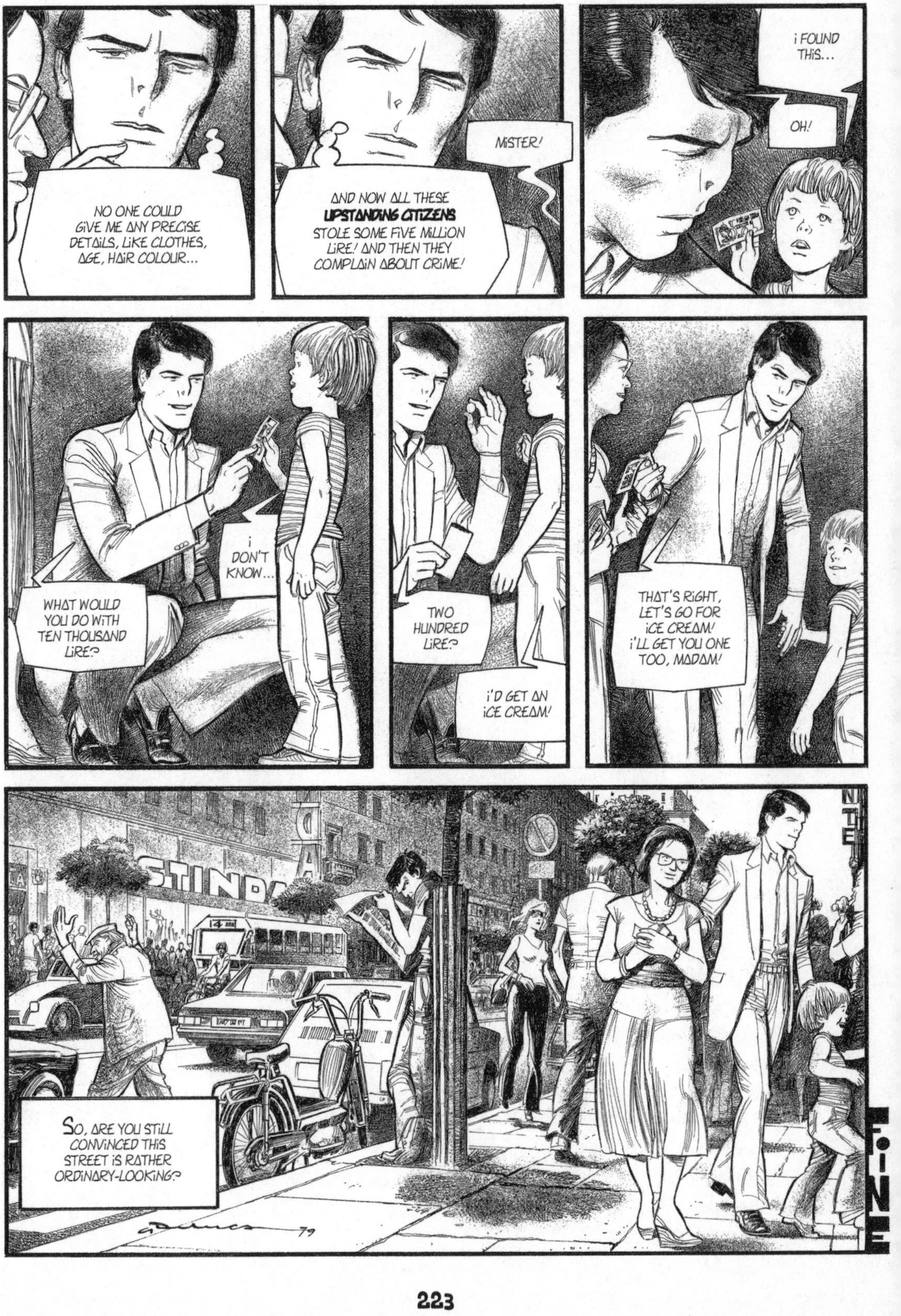
NO ONE COULD GIVE ME ANY PRECISE DETAILS, LIKE CLOTHES, AGE, HAIR COLOUR...
AND NOW ALL THESE **UPSTANDING CITIZENS** STOLE SOME FIVE MILLION LIRE! AND THEN THEY COMPLAIN ABOUT CRIME!
MISTER!
I FOUND THIS...
OH!
WHAT WOULD YOU DO WITH TEN THOUSAND LIRE?
I DON'T KNOW...
TWO HUNDRED LIRE?
I'D GET AN ICE CREAM!
THAT'S RIGHT, LET'S GO FOR ICE CREAM! I'LL GET YOU ONE TOO, MADAM!
SO, ARE YOU STILL CONVINCED THIS STREET IS RATHER ORDINARY-LOOKING?
FINE

"I'm a respectable businessman...
I went into this on business terms.
He can't treat me this way.
I'll show him..."

Respectability means everything to
obsequious restaurateur Joe Rivers,
but can he stay as pure as the driven snow
when he starts silently investing in
a criminal racket? In this morality play,
there is no turning back once you've taken
that first small step and strayed from the
straight and narrow. Renowned for his later
work at EC Comics, here Krigstein is already
refining his distinctive approach and expertly
capturing his characters' facial expressions
and body language.

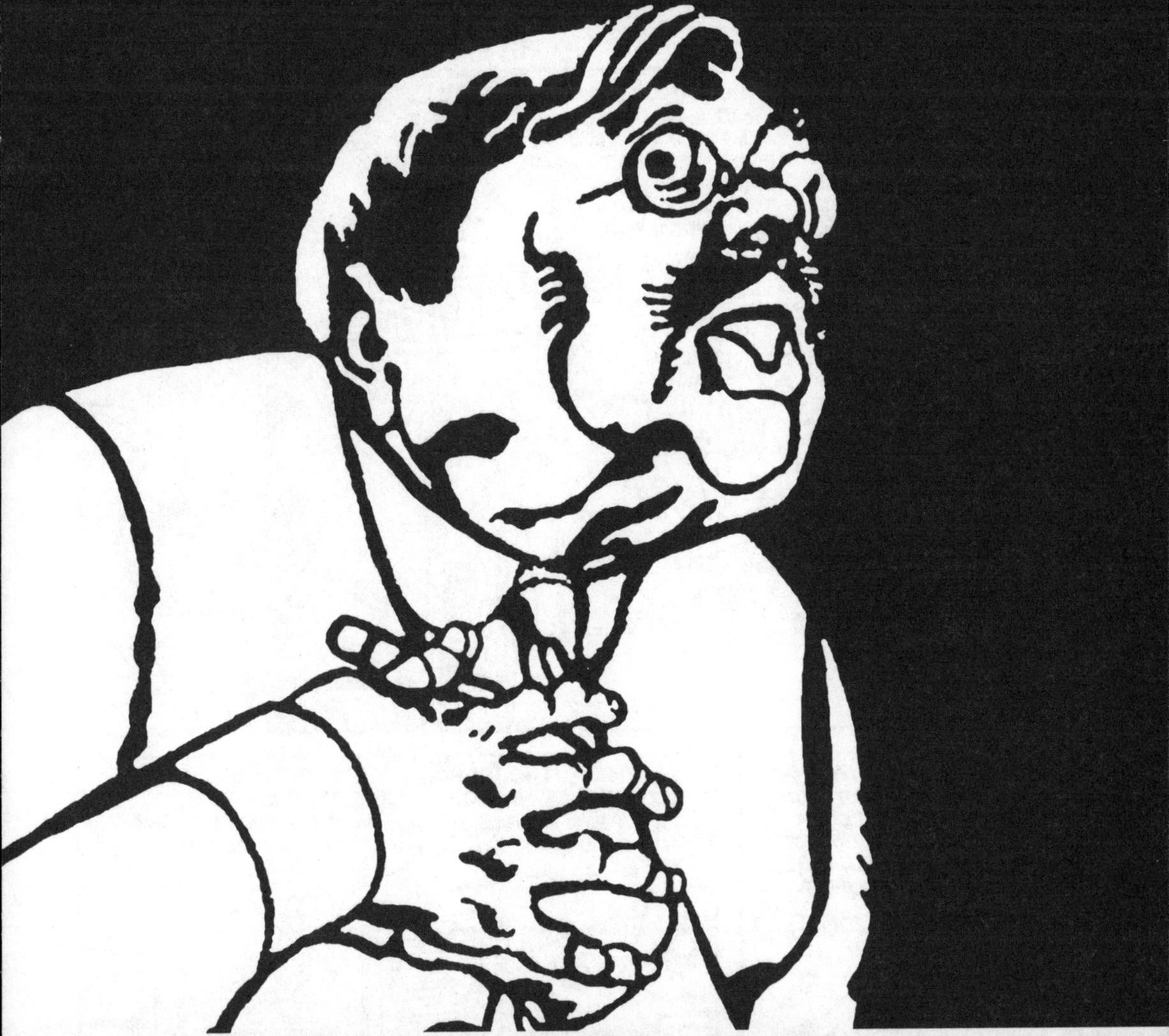

Lily-white Joe

Bernie Krigstein (art), writer unknown 1950

Lily-white Joe

JOE RIVERS WAS A HYPOCRITE– HE OWNED A RESTAURANT AND HE LIKED TO KID HIMSELF THAT HE WAS A NICE RESPECTABLE BUSINESSMAN.... BUT JOE NEVER OVERLOOKED THE CHANCE TO MAKE A SHADY BUCK..., THAT'S WHY WE NOW SEE HIM IN QUIET CONVERSATION WITH A GAMBLER CHARACTER NAMED MARC RINALD...

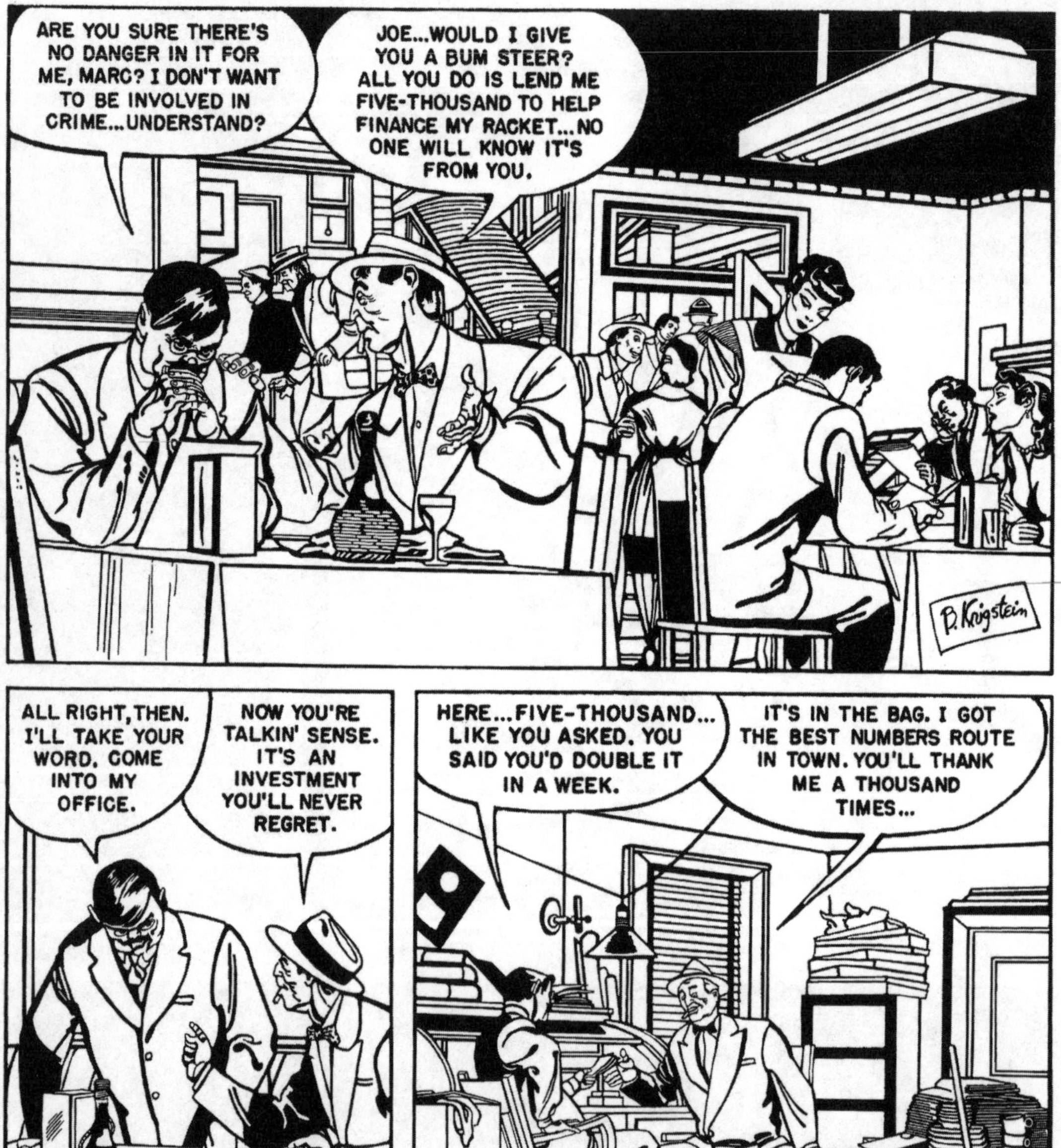
ARE YOU SURE THERE'S NO DANGER IN IT FOR ME, MARC? I DON'T WANT TO BE INVOLVED IN CRIME...UNDERSTAND?
JOE...WOULD I GIVE YOU A BUM STEER? ALL YOU DO IS LEND ME FIVE-THOUSAND TO HELP FINANCE MY RACKET...NO ONE WILL KNOW IT'S FROM YOU.
B. Krigstein
ALL RIGHT, THEN. I'LL TAKE YOUR WORD. COME INTO MY OFFICE.
NOW YOU'RE TALKIN' SENSE. IT'S AN INVESTMENT YOU'LL NEVER REGRET.
HERE...FIVE-THOUSAND... LIKE YOU ASKED. YOU SAID YOU'D DOUBLE IT IN A WEEK.
IT'S IN THE BAG. I GOT THE BEST NUMBERS ROUTE IN TOWN. YOU'LL THANK ME A THOUSAND TIMES...

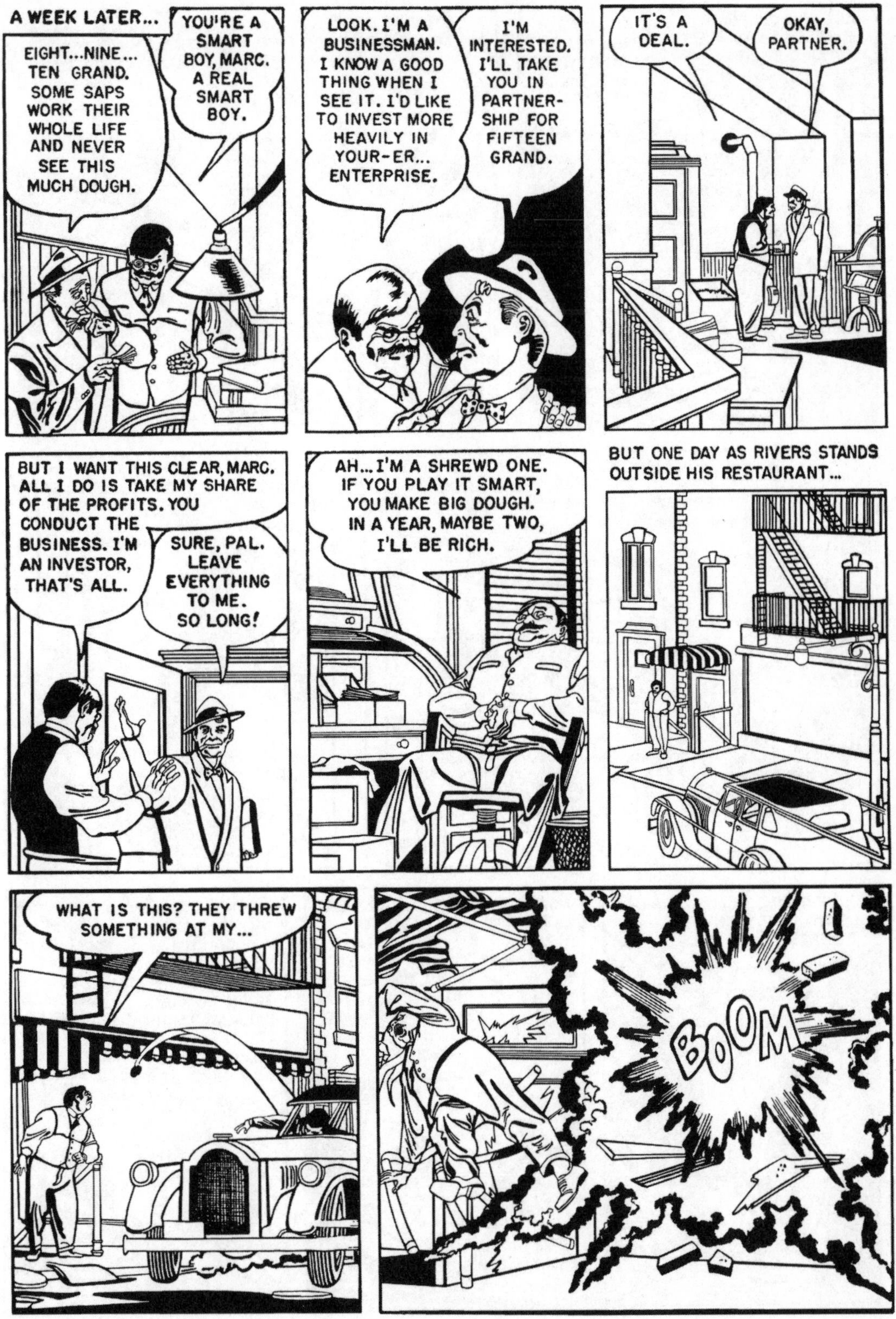
A WEEK LATER...
EIGHT...NINE... TEN GRAND. SOME SAPS WORK THEIR WHOLE LIFE AND NEVER SEE THIS MUCH DOUGH.
YOU'RE A SMART BOY, MARC. A REAL SMART BOY.
LOOK. I'M A BUSINESSMAN. I KNOW A GOOD THING WHEN I SEE IT. I'D LIKE TO INVEST MORE HEAVILY IN YOUR-ER... ENTERPRISE.
I'M INTERESTED. I'LL TAKE YOU IN PARTNERSHIP FOR FIFTEEN GRAND.
IT'S A DEAL.
OKAY, PARTNER.
BUT I WANT THIS CLEAR, MARC. ALL I DO IS TAKE MY SHARE OF THE PROFITS. YOU CONDUCT THE BUSINESS. I'M AN INVESTOR, THAT'S ALL.
SURE, PAL. LEAVE EVERYTHING TO ME. SO LONG!
AH... I'M A SHREWD ONE. IF YOU PLAY IT SMART, YOU MAKE BIG DOUGH. IN A YEAR, MAYBE TWO, I'LL BE RICH.
BUT ONE DAY AS RIVERS STANDS OUTSIDE HIS RESTAURANT...
WHAT IS THIS? THEY THREW SOMETHING AT MY...
BOOM

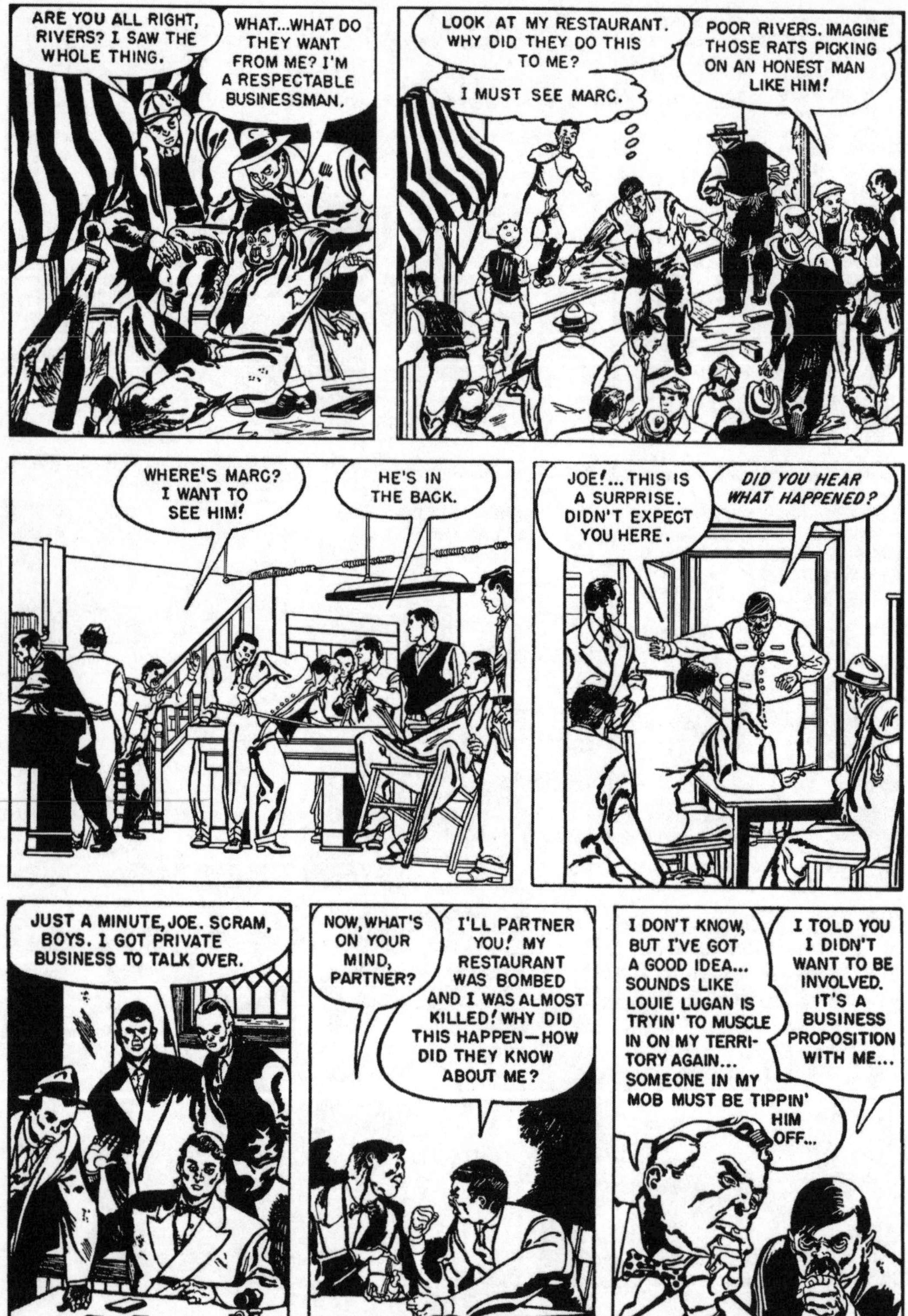
ARE YOU ALL RIGHT, RIVERS? I SAW THE WHOLE THING.
WHAT...WHAT DO THEY WANT FROM ME? I'M A RESPECTABLE BUSINESSMAN.
LOOK AT MY RESTAURANT. WHY DID THEY DO THIS TO ME?
I MUST SEE MARC.
POOR RIVERS. IMAGINE THOSE RATS PICKING ON AN HONEST MAN LIKE HIM!
WHERE'S MARC? I WANT TO SEE HIM!
HE'S IN THE BACK.
JOE!... THIS IS A SURPRISE. DIDN'T EXPECT YOU HERE.
DID YOU HEAR WHAT HAPPENED?
JUST A MINUTE, JOE. SCRAM, BOYS. I GOT PRIVATE BUSINESS TO TALK OVER.
NOW, WHAT'S ON YOUR MIND, PARTNER?
I'LL PARTNER YOU! MY RESTAURANT WAS BOMBED AND I WAS ALMOST KILLED! WHY DID THIS HAPPEN—HOW DID THEY KNOW ABOUT ME?
I DON'T KNOW, BUT I'VE GOT A GOOD IDEA... SOUNDS LIKE LOUIE LUGAN IS TRYIN' TO MUSCLE IN ON MY TERRITORY AGAIN... SOMEONE IN MY MOB MUST BE TIPPIN' HIM OFF...
I TOLD YOU I DIDN'T WANT TO BE INVOLVED. IT'S A BUSINESS PROPOSITION WITH ME...

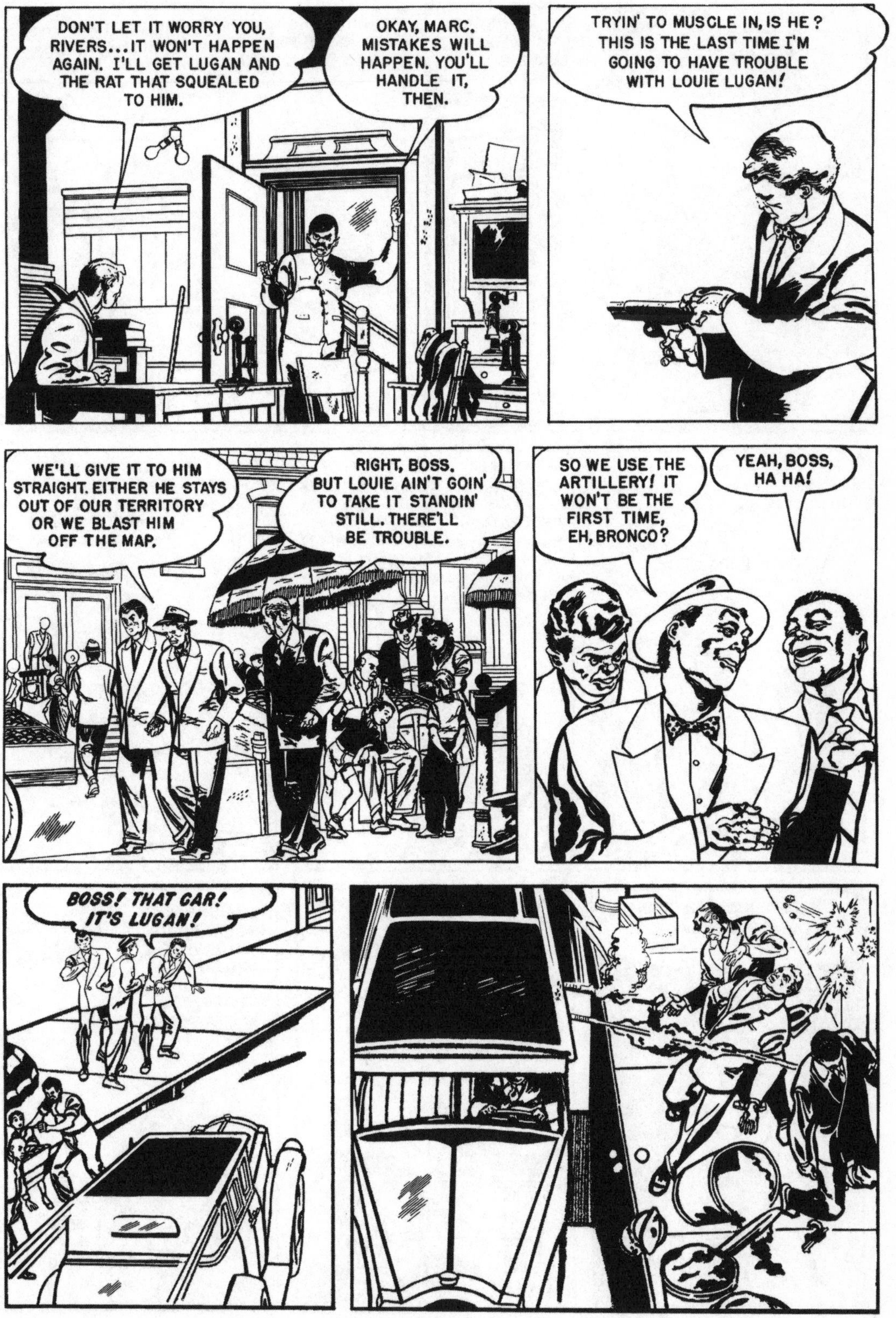
DON'T LET IT WORRY YOU, RIVERS...IT WON'T HAPPEN AGAIN. I'LL GET LUGAN AND THE RAT THAT SQUEALED TO HIM.
OKAY, MARC. MISTAKES WILL HAPPEN. YOU'LL HANDLE IT, THEN.
TRYIN' TO MUSCLE IN, IS HE? THIS IS THE LAST TIME I'M GOING TO HAVE TROUBLE WITH LOUIE LUGAN!
WE'LL GIVE IT TO HIM STRAIGHT. EITHER HE STAYS OUT OF OUR TERRITORY OR WE BLAST HIM OFF THE MAP.
RIGHT, BOSS. BUT LOUIE AIN'T GOIN' TO TAKE IT STANDIN' STILL. THERE'LL BE TROUBLE.
SO WE USE THE ARTILLERY! IT WON'T BE THE FIRST TIME, EH, BRONCO?
YEAH, BOSS, HA HA!
BOSS! THAT CAR! IT'S LUGAN!

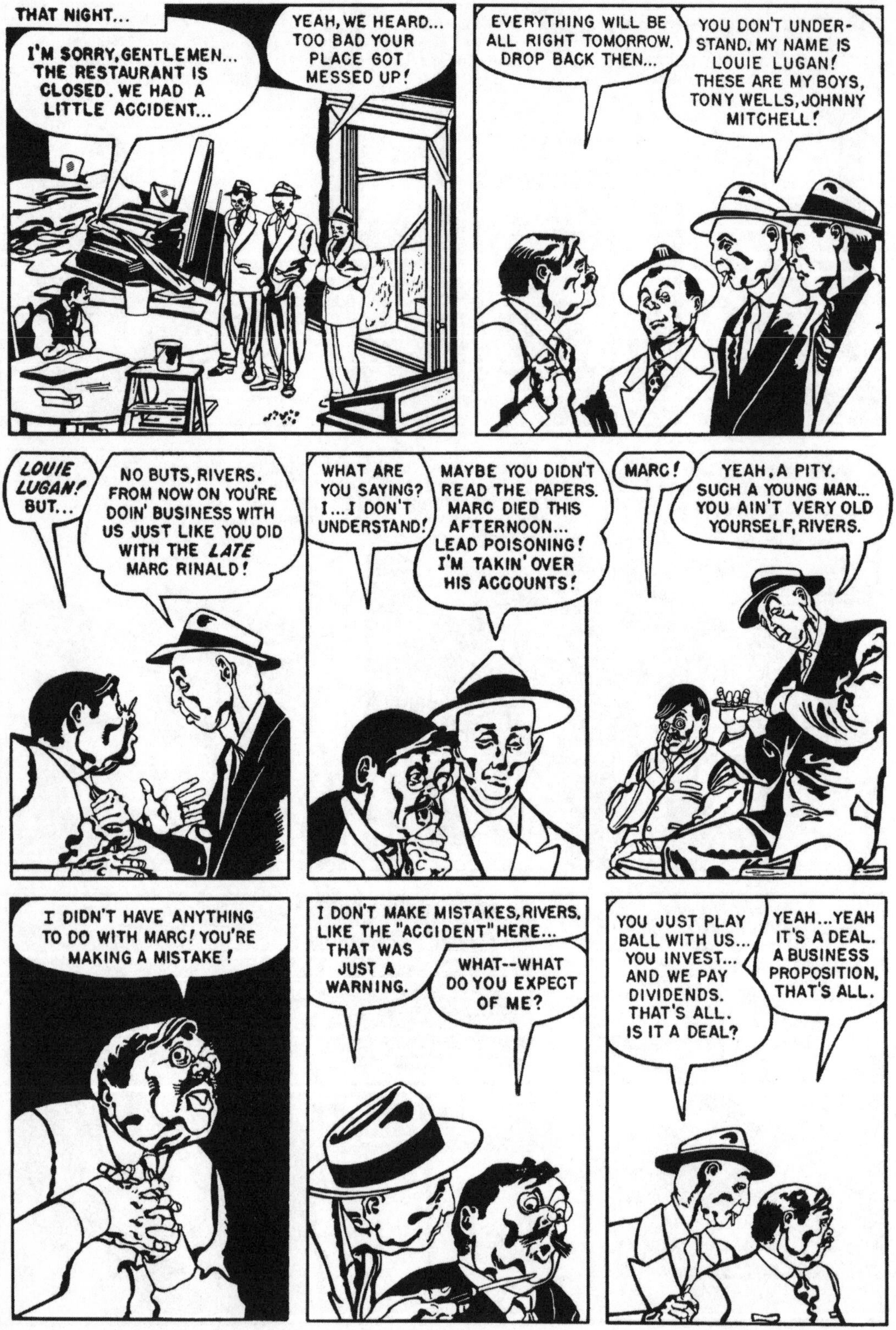
THAT NIGHT...
I'M SORRY, GENTLEMEN... THE RESTAURANT IS CLOSED. WE HAD A LITTLE ACCIDENT...
YEAH, WE HEARD... TOO BAD YOUR PLACE GOT MESSED UP!
EVERYTHING WILL BE ALL RIGHT TOMORROW. DROP BACK THEN...
YOU DON'T UNDER-STAND. MY NAME IS LOUIE LUGAN! THESE ARE MY BOYS, TONY WELLS, JOHNNY MITCHELL!
LOUIE LUGAN! BUT...
NO BUTS, RIVERS. FROM NOW ON YOU'RE DOIN' BUSINESS WITH US JUST LIKE YOU DID WITH THE LATE MARC RINALD!
WHAT ARE YOU SAYING? I...I DON'T UNDERSTAND!
MAYBE YOU DIDN'T READ THE PAPERS. MARC DIED THIS AFTERNOON... LEAD POISONING! I'M TAKIN' OVER HIS ACCOUNTS!
MARC!
YEAH, A PITY. SUCH A YOUNG MAN... YOU AIN'T VERY OLD YOURSELF, RIVERS.
I DIDN'T HAVE ANYTHING TO DO WITH MARC! YOU'RE MAKING A MISTAKE!
I DON'T MAKE MISTAKES, RIVERS. LIKE THE "ACCIDENT" HERE... THAT WAS JUST A WARNING.
WHAT--WHAT DO YOU EXPECT OF ME?
YOU JUST PLAY BALL WITH US... YOU INVEST... AND WE PAY DIVIDENDS. THAT'S ALL. IS IT A DEAL?
YEAH...YEAH IT'S A DEAL. A BUSINESS PROPOSITION, THAT'S ALL.

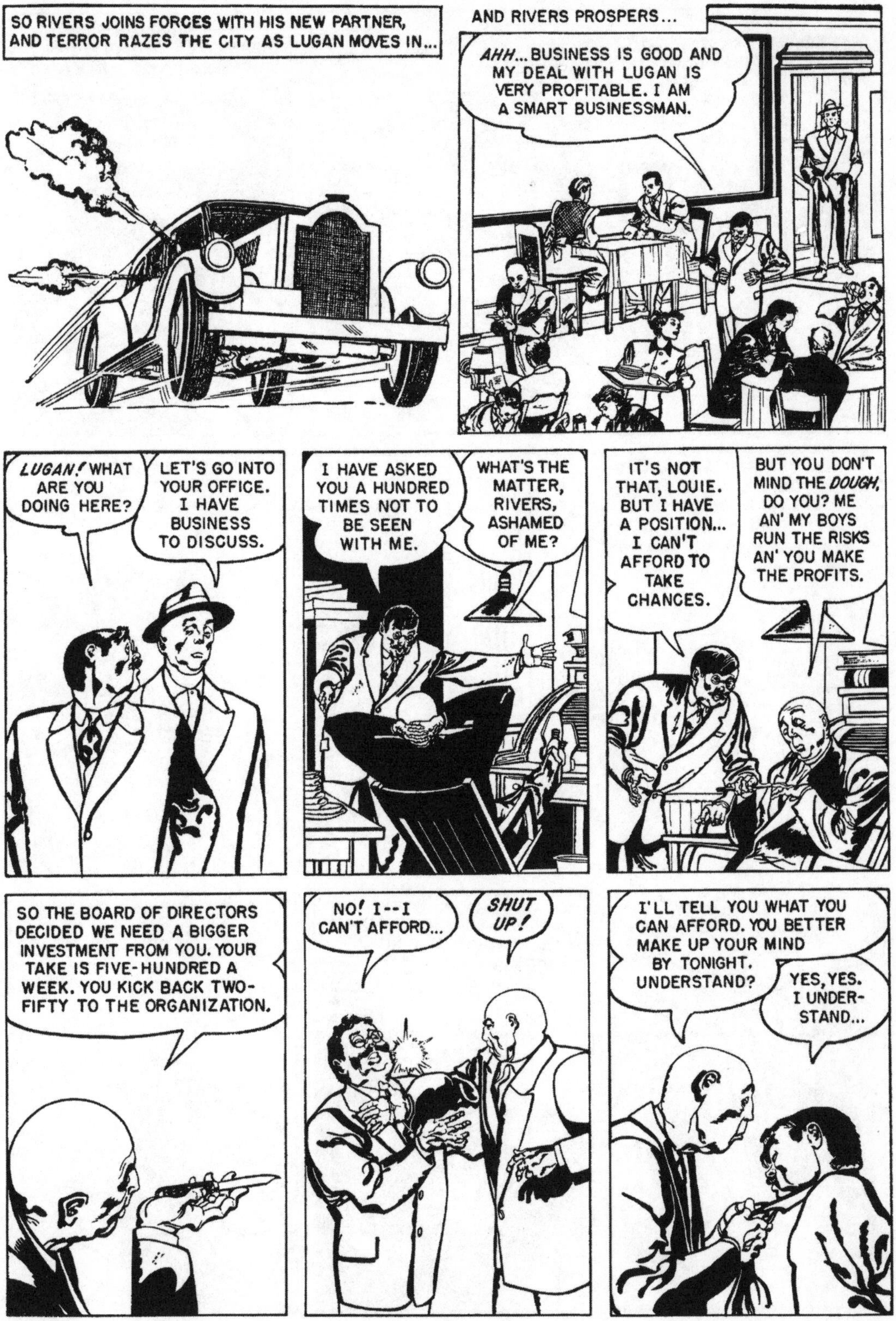
SO RIVERS JOINS FORCES WITH HIS NEW PARTNER, AND TERROR RAZES THE CITY AS LUGAN MOVES IN...
AND RIVERS PROSPERS...
AHH... BUSINESS IS GOOD AND MY DEAL WITH LUGAN IS VERY PROFITABLE. I AM A SMART BUSINESSMAN.
LUGAN! WHAT ARE YOU DOING HERE?
LET'S GO INTO YOUR OFFICE. I HAVE BUSINESS TO DISCUSS.
I HAVE ASKED YOU A HUNDRED TIMES NOT TO BE SEEN WITH ME.
WHAT'S THE MATTER, RIVERS, ASHAMED OF ME?
IT'S NOT THAT, LOUIE. BUT I HAVE A POSITION... I CAN'T AFFORD TO TAKE CHANCES.
BUT YOU DON'T MIND THE DOUGH, DO YOU? ME AN' MY BOYS RUN THE RISKS AN' YOU MAKE THE PROFITS.
SO THE BOARD OF DIRECTORS DECIDED WE NEED A BIGGER INVESTMENT FROM YOU. YOUR TAKE IS FIVE-HUNDRED A WEEK. YOU KICK BACK TWO-FIFTY TO THE ORGANIZATION.
NO! I--I CAN'T AFFORD...
SHUT UP!
I'LL TELL YOU WHAT YOU CAN AFFORD. YOU BETTER MAKE UP YOUR MIND BY TONIGHT. UNDERSTAND?
YES, YES. I UNDER-STAND...

I'M...I'M A RESPECTABLE BUSINESSMAN... I WENT INTO THIS ON BUSINESS TERMS. HE CAN'T TREAT ME THIS WAY. I'LL SHOW HIM...

I'LL TAKE THIS WITH ME ...JUST IN CASE.

THERE'S ENOUGH MONEY HERE. I'LL TAKE OFF. HE'LL NEVER FIND ME...NEVER!

WON'T HE FEEL STUPID WHEN HE SEES THAT I'VE SKIPPED. I OUTSMARTED HIM. YEAH... I OUTSMARTED THEM ALL.

I FIGURED YOU'D TRY A RUN-OUT. VERY CONVENIENT, RIGHT HERE IN THE ALLEY.

YOU'RE WRONG... I... I...

MAKE IT GOOD, PAL. IT'S THE LAST CHANCE YOU'LL HAVE.

YOU CAN'T STOP ME! NOBODY CAN! I WON'T LET YOU!

DON'T BE A FOOL, RIVERS!

RIVERS IS NOT THE FOOL! YOU ARE!

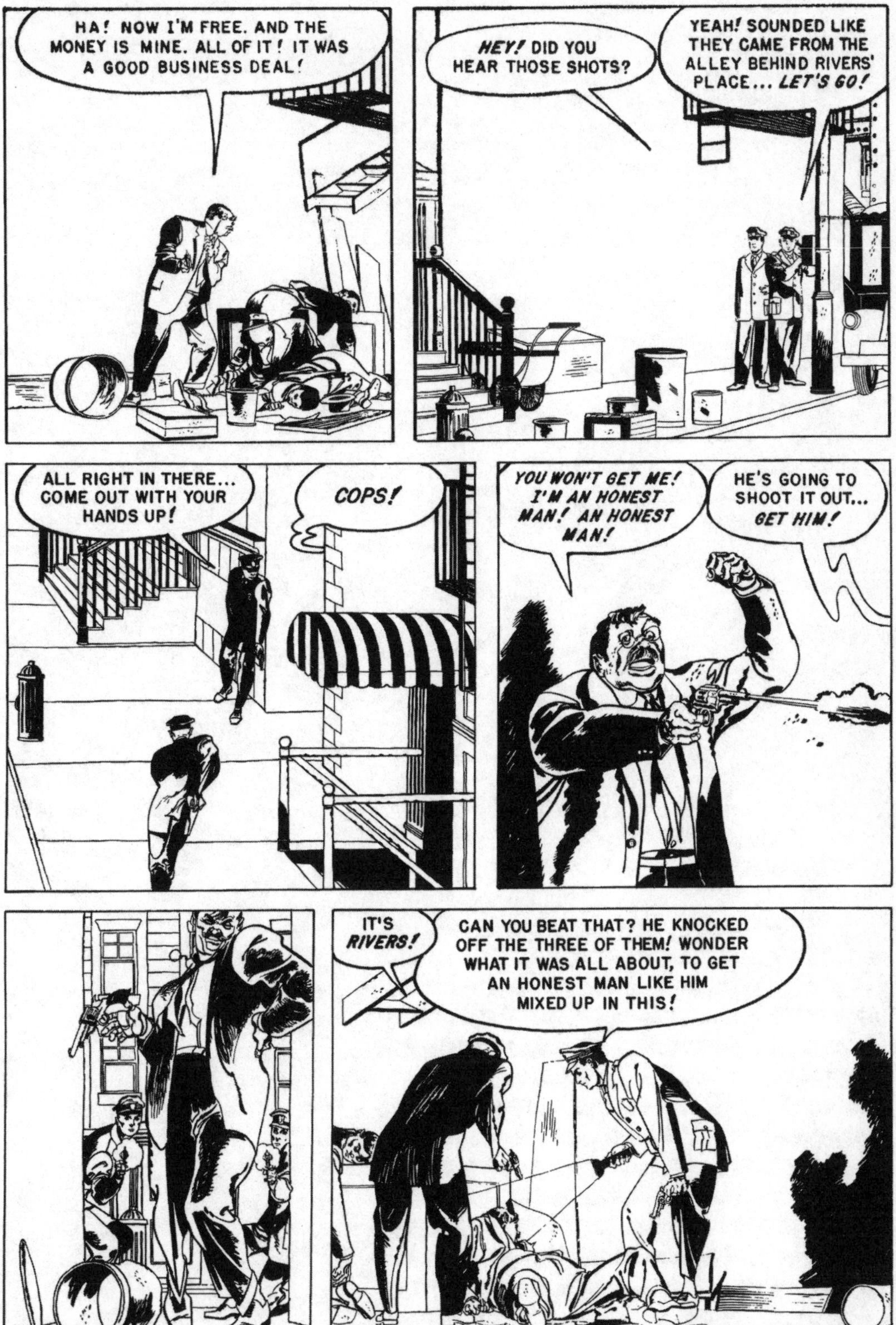
HA! NOW I'M FREE. AND THE MONEY IS MINE. ALL OF IT! IT WAS A GOOD BUSINESS DEAL!
HEY! DID YOU HEAR THOSE SHOTS?
YEAH! SOUNDED LIKE THEY CAME FROM THE ALLEY BEHIND RIVERS' PLACE... LET'S GO!
ALL RIGHT IN THERE... COME OUT WITH YOUR HANDS UP!
COPS!
YOU WON'T GET ME! I'M AN HONEST MAN! AN HONEST MAN!
HE'S GOING TO SHOOT IT OUT... GET HIM!
IT'S RIVERS!
CAN YOU BEAT THAT? HE KNOCKED OFF THE THREE OF THEM! WONDER WHAT IT WAS ALL ABOUT, TO GET AN HONEST MAN LIKE HIM MIXED UP IN THIS!

"Who does she think she is,
dancin' with 'im?
She's like all the rest!
I'll show 'em — both of 'em"

Paranoia was sweeping through early 1950s
America rocked by the rise of the rebellious
teenager, hormones raging out of control.
Parallel to this there was the growing
fascination with psychiatry as a way to
diagnose, if not cure, such delinquents. Could
treatment have helped young Johnny Faber?
Like a junior James Cagney, Doctor Crane's
latest subject seems to have been psychopathic
from day one, a volatile obsessive whose only
way to cope with the world going against
him is to lash out. Alex Toth brings a fresh
modernity to post-war American comic books,
based not on repeating others' clichés but on
acute observation and arresting composition,
cropping, silhouettes and expressive hand
gestures. This is regarded as one of Toth's
finest and was a personal favourite of his.

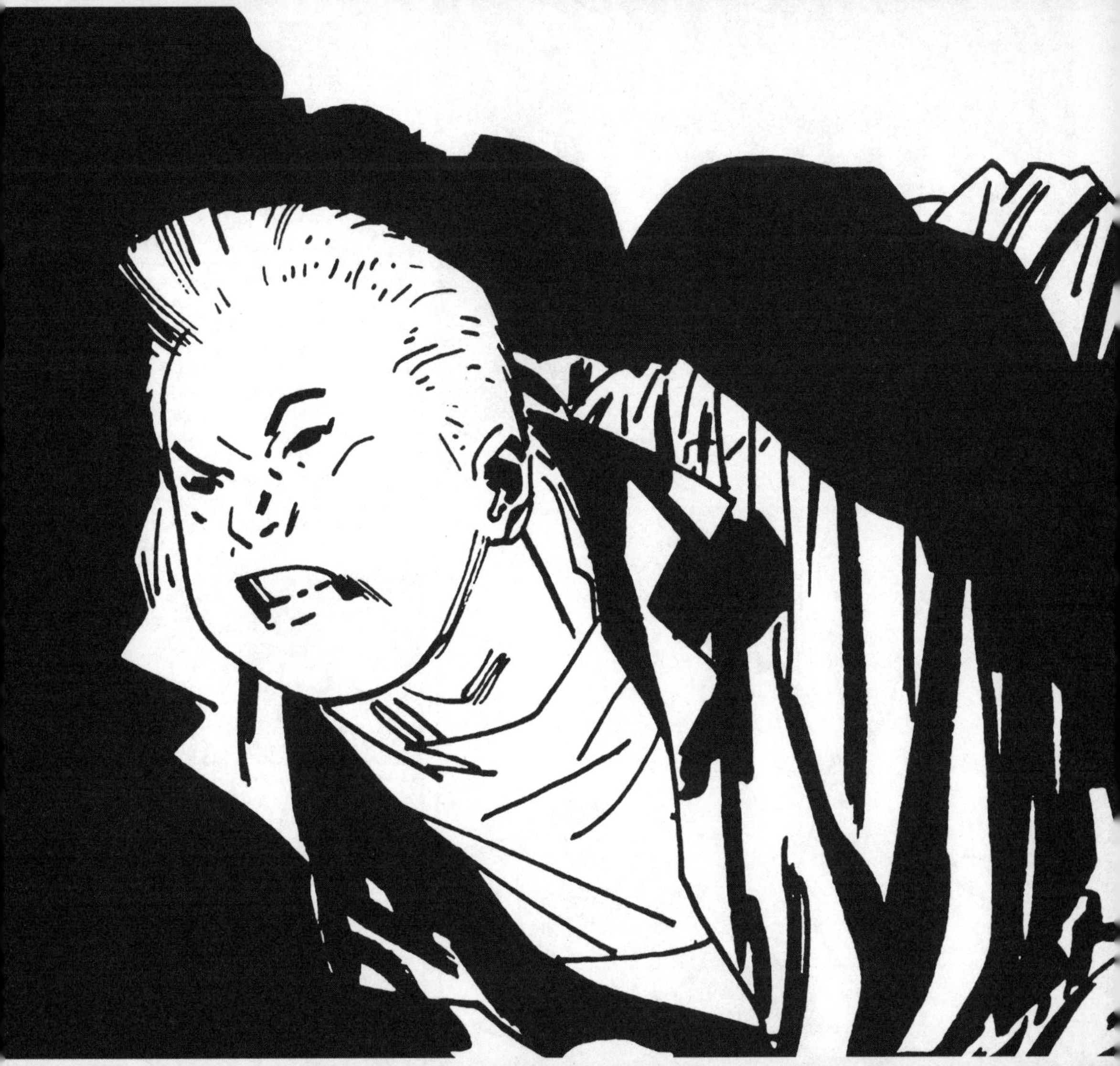

The Crushed Gardenia

Alex Toth (art), writer unknown 1953

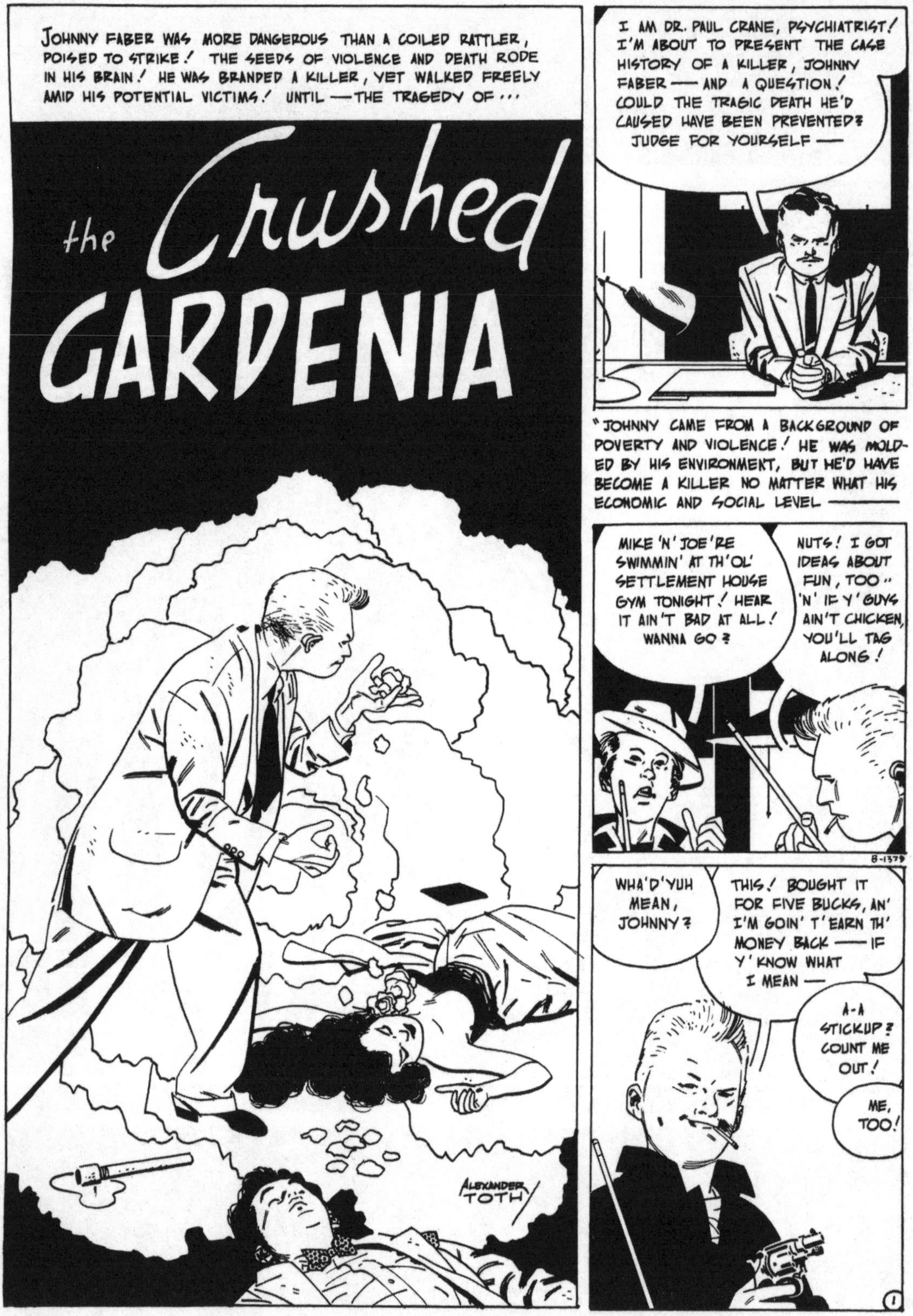
JOHNNY FABER WAS MORE DANGEROUS THAN A COILED RATTLER, POISED TO STRIKE! THE SEEDS OF VIOLENCE AND DEATH RODE IN HIS BRAIN! HE WAS BRANDED A KILLER, YET WALKED FREELY AMID HIS POTENTIAL VICTIMS! UNTIL —THE TRAGEDY OF . . .
the Crushed GARDENIA
ALEXANDER TOTH
I AM DR. PAUL CRANE, PSYCHIATRIST! I'M ABOUT TO PRESENT THE CASE HISTORY OF A KILLER, JOHNNY FABER — AND A QUESTION! COULD THE TRAGIC DEATH HE'D CAUSED HAVE BEEN PREVENTED? JUDGE FOR YOURSELF —
"JOHNNY CAME FROM A BACKGROUND OF POVERTY AND VIOLENCE! HE WAS MOLDED BY HIS ENVIRONMENT, BUT HE'D HAVE BECOME A KILLER NO MATTER WHAT HIS ECONOMIC AND SOCIAL LEVEL —
MIKE 'N' JOE'RE SWIMMIN' AT TH' OL' SETTLEMENT HOUSE GYM TONIGHT! HEAR IT AIN'T BAD AT ALL! WANNA GO?
NUTS! I GOT IDEAS ABOUT FUN, TOO .. 'N' IF Y' GUYS AIN'T CHICKEN, YOU'LL TAG ALONG!
B-1379
WHA'D'YUH MEAN, JOHNNY?
THIS! BOUGHT IT FOR FIVE BUCKS, AN' I'M GOIN' T'EARN TH' MONEY BACK — IF Y' KNOW WHAT I MEAN —
A-A STICKUP? COUNT ME OUT!
ME, TOO!
1

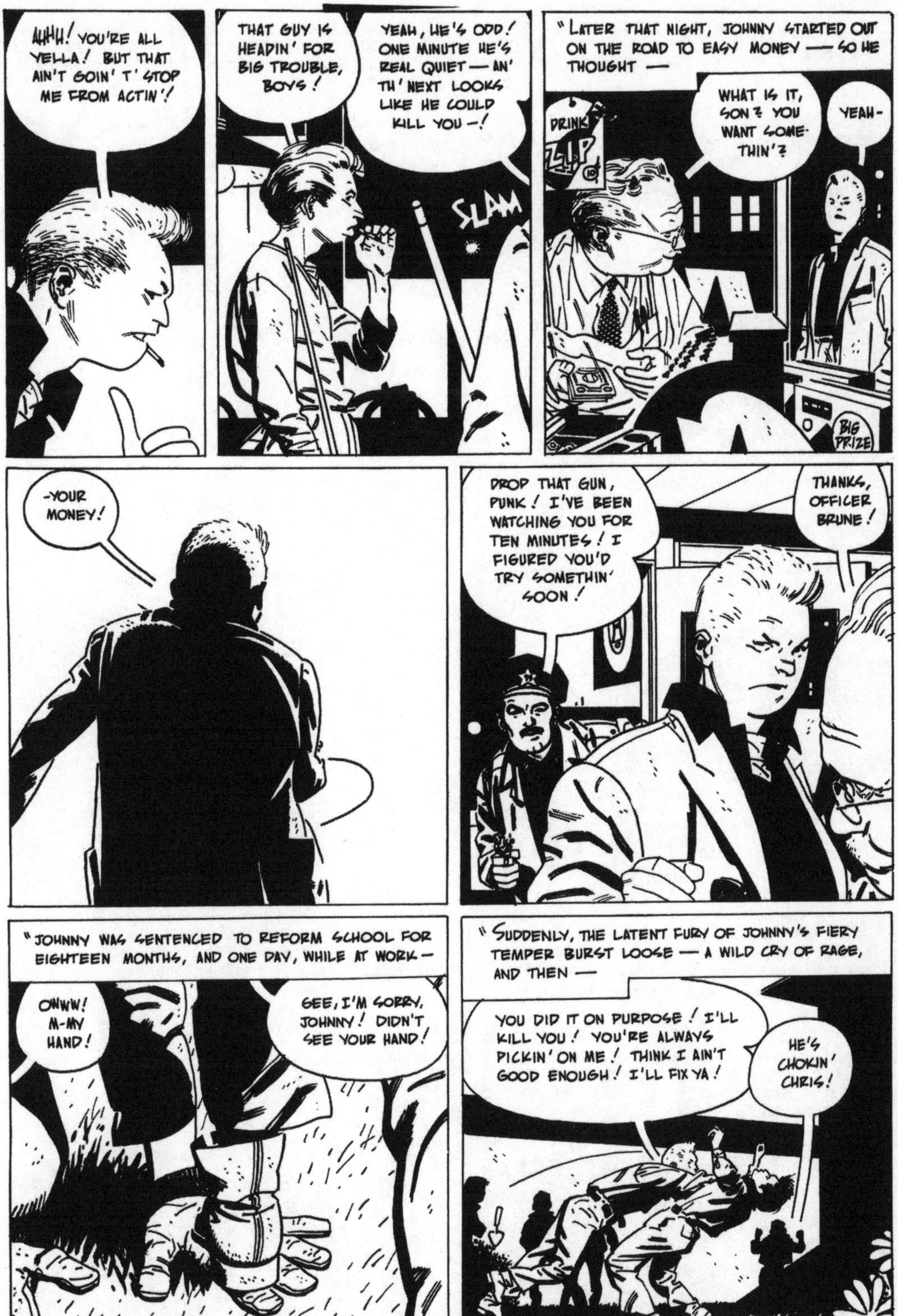
AHHH! YOU'RE ALL YELLA! BUT THAT AIN'T GOIN' T' STOP ME FROM ACTIN'!
THAT GUY IS HEADIN' FOR BIG TROUBLE, BOYS!
YEAH, HE'S ODD! ONE MINUTE HE'S REAL QUIET — AN' TH' NEXT LOOKS LIKE HE COULD KILL YOU —!
SLAM
"LATER THAT NIGHT, JOHNNY STARTED OUT ON THE ROAD TO EASY MONEY — SO HE THOUGHT —
DRINK ZIP
WHAT IS IT, SON? YOU WANT SOMETHIN'?
YEAH-
BIG PRIZE
-YOUR MONEY!
DROP THAT GUN, PUNK! I'VE BEEN WATCHING YOU FOR TEN MINUTES! I FIGURED YOU'D TRY SOMETHIN' SOON!
THANKS, OFFICER BRUNE!
"JOHNNY WAS SENTENCED TO REFORM SCHOOL FOR EIGHTEEN MONTHS, AND ONE DAY, WHILE AT WORK—
OWWW! M-MY HAND!
GEE, I'M SORRY, JOHNNY! DIDN'T SEE YOUR HAND!
"SUDDENLY, THE LATENT FURY OF JOHNNY'S FIERY TEMPER BURST LOOSE — A WILD CRY OF RAGE, AND THEN —
YOU DID IT ON PURPOSE! I'LL KILL YOU! YOU'RE ALWAYS PICKIN' ON ME! THINK I AIN'T GOOD ENOUGH! I'LL FIX YA!
HE'S CHOKIN' CHRIS!
2

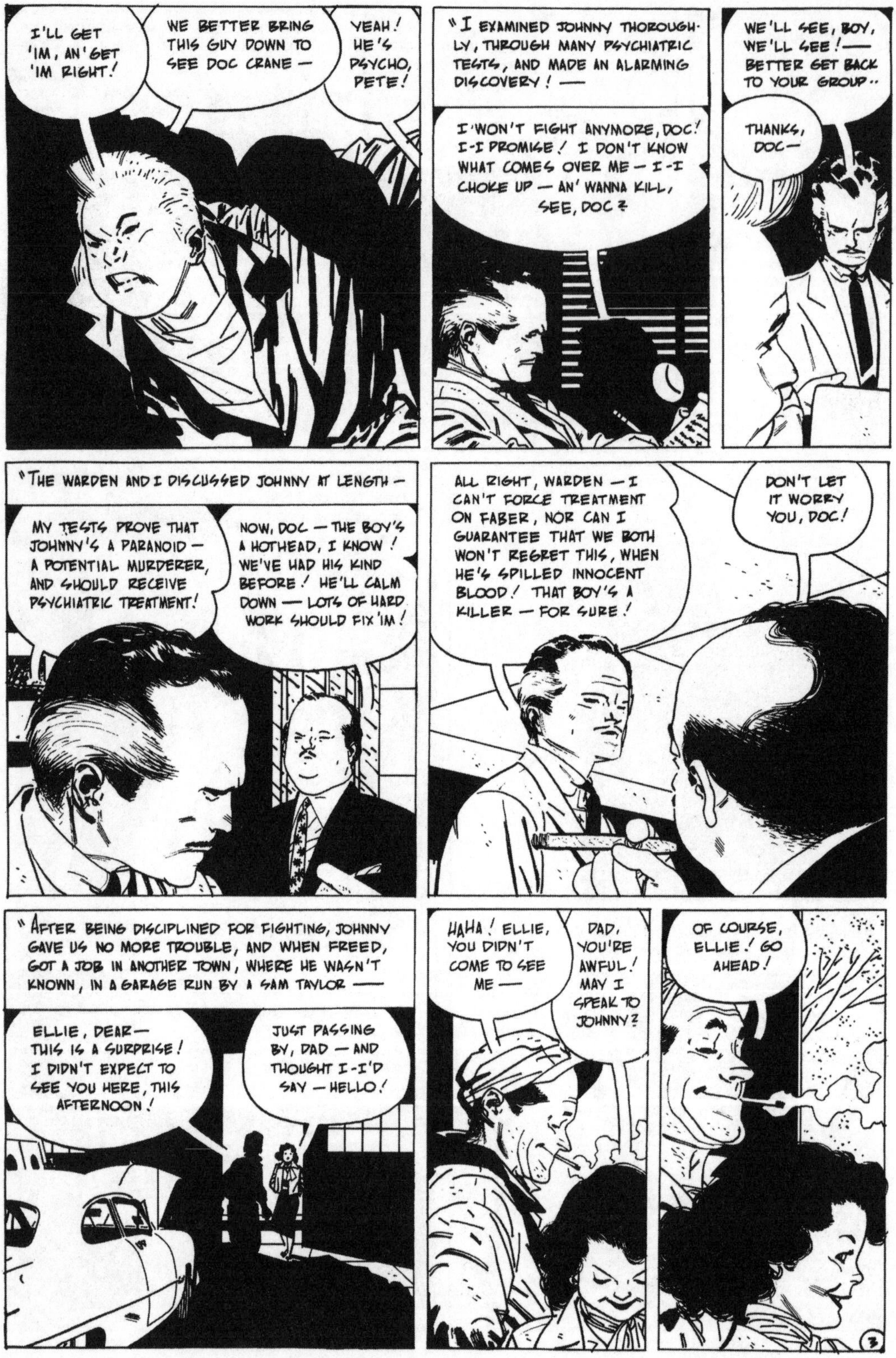
I'LL GET 'IM, AN' GET 'IM RIGHT!
WE BETTER BRING THIS GUY DOWN TO SEE DOC CRANE —
YEAH! HE'S PSYCHO, PETE!
"I EXAMINED JOHNNY THOROUGHLY, THROUGH MANY PSYCHIATRIC TESTS, AND MADE AN ALARMING DISCOVERY! —
I WON'T FIGHT ANYMORE, DOC! I-I PROMISE! I DON'T KNOW WHAT COMES OVER ME — I-I CHOKE UP — AN' WANNA KILL, SEE, DOC?
WE'LL SEE, BOY, WE'LL SEE! — BETTER GET BACK TO YOUR GROUP..
THANKS, DOC—
"THE WARDEN AND I DISCUSSED JOHNNY AT LENGTH —
MY TESTS PROVE THAT JOHNNY'S A PARANOID — A POTENTIAL MURDERER, AND SHOULD RECEIVE PSYCHIATRIC TREATMENT!
NOW, DOC — THE BOY'S A HOTHEAD, I KNOW! WE'VE HAD HIS KIND BEFORE! HE'LL CALM DOWN — LOTS OF HARD WORK SHOULD FIX 'IM!
ALL RIGHT, WARDEN — I CAN'T FORCE TREATMENT ON FABER, NOR CAN I GUARANTEE THAT WE BOTH WON'T REGRET THIS, WHEN HE'S SPILLED INNOCENT BLOOD! THAT BOY'S A KILLER — FOR SURE!
DON'T LET IT WORRY YOU, DOC!
"AFTER BEING DISCIPLINED FOR FIGHTING, JOHNNY GAVE US NO MORE TROUBLE, AND WHEN FREED, GOT A JOB IN ANOTHER TOWN, WHERE HE WASN'T KNOWN, IN A GARAGE RUN BY A SAM TAYLOR —
ELLIE, DEAR— THIS IS A SURPRISE! I DIDN'T EXPECT TO SEE YOU HERE, THIS AFTERNOON!
JUST PASSING BY, DAD — AND THOUGHT I-I'D SAY — HELLO!
HAHA! ELLIE, YOU DIDN'T COME TO SEE ME —
DAD, YOU'RE AWFUL! MAY I SPEAK TO JOHNNY?
OF COURSE, ELLIE! GO AHEAD!
3

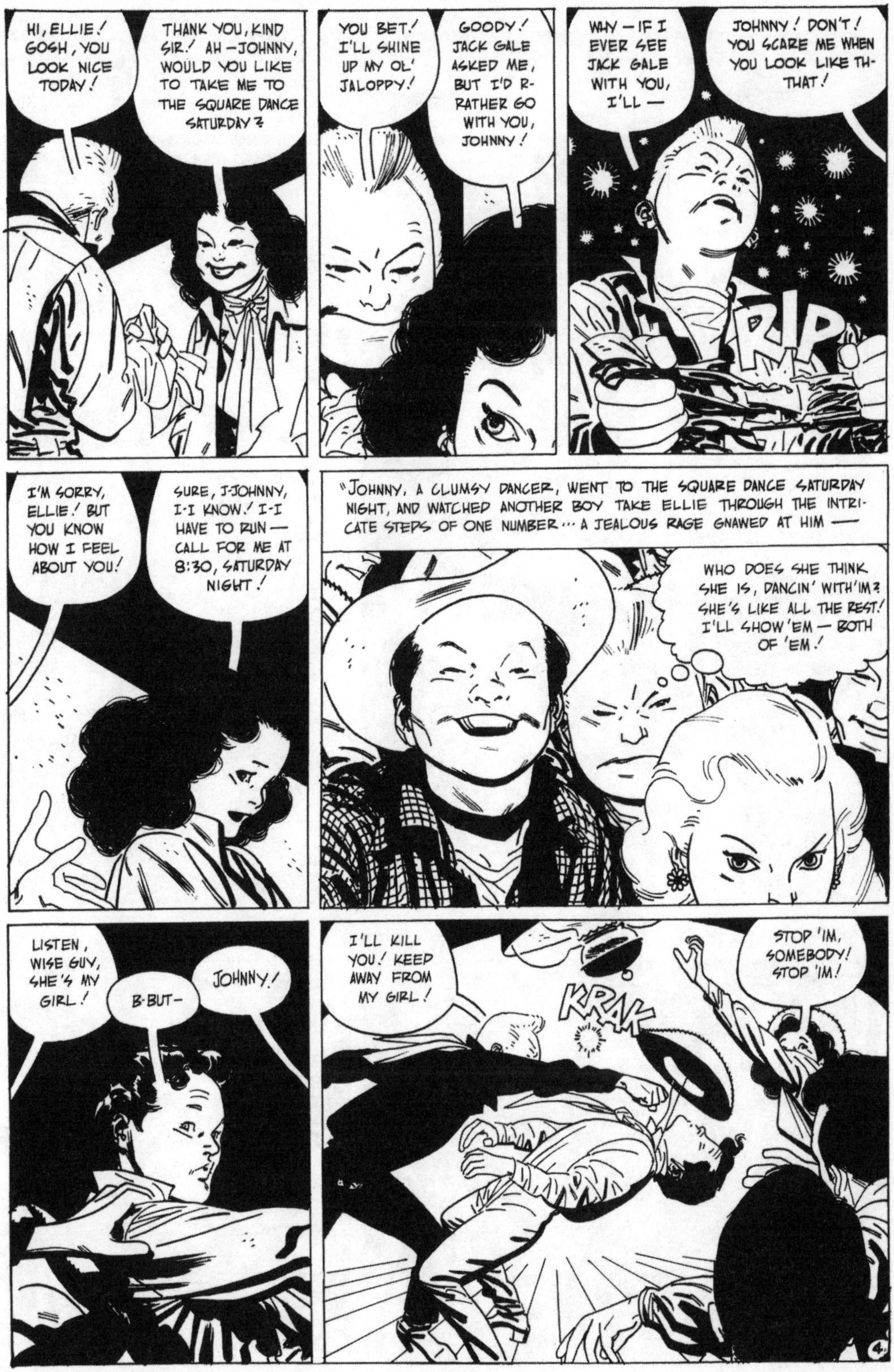
HI, ELLIE! GOSH, YOU LOOK NICE TODAY!
THANK YOU, KIND SIR! AH—JOHNNY, WOULD YOU LIKE TO TAKE ME TO THE SQUARE DANCE SATURDAY?
YOU BET! I'LL SHINE UP MY OL' JALOPPY!
GOODY! JACK GALE ASKED ME, BUT I'D R-RATHER GO WITH YOU, JOHNNY!
WHY—IF I EVER SEE JACK GALE WITH YOU, I'LL—
JOHNNY! DON'T! YOU SCARE ME WHEN YOU LOOK LIKE TH-THAT!
RIP!
I'M SORRY, ELLIE! BUT YOU KNOW HOW I FEEL ABOUT YOU!
SURE, J-JOHNNY, I-I KNOW! I-I HAVE TO RUN—CALL FOR ME AT 8:30, SATURDAY NIGHT!
"JOHNNY, A CLUMSY DANCER, WENT TO THE SQUARE DANCE SATURDAY NIGHT, AND WATCHED ANOTHER BOY TAKE ELLIE THROUGH THE INTRICATE STEPS OF ONE NUMBER... A JEALOUS RAGE GNAWED AT HIM—
WHO DOES SHE THINK SHE IS, DANCIN' WITH'IM? SHE'S LIKE ALL THE REST! I'LL SHOW 'EM—BOTH OF 'EM!
LISTEN, WISE GUY, SHE'S MY GIRL!
B-BUT-
JOHNNY!
I'LL KILL YOU! KEEP AWAY FROM MY GIRL!
KRAK
STOP 'IM, SOMEBODY! STOP 'IM!
4.

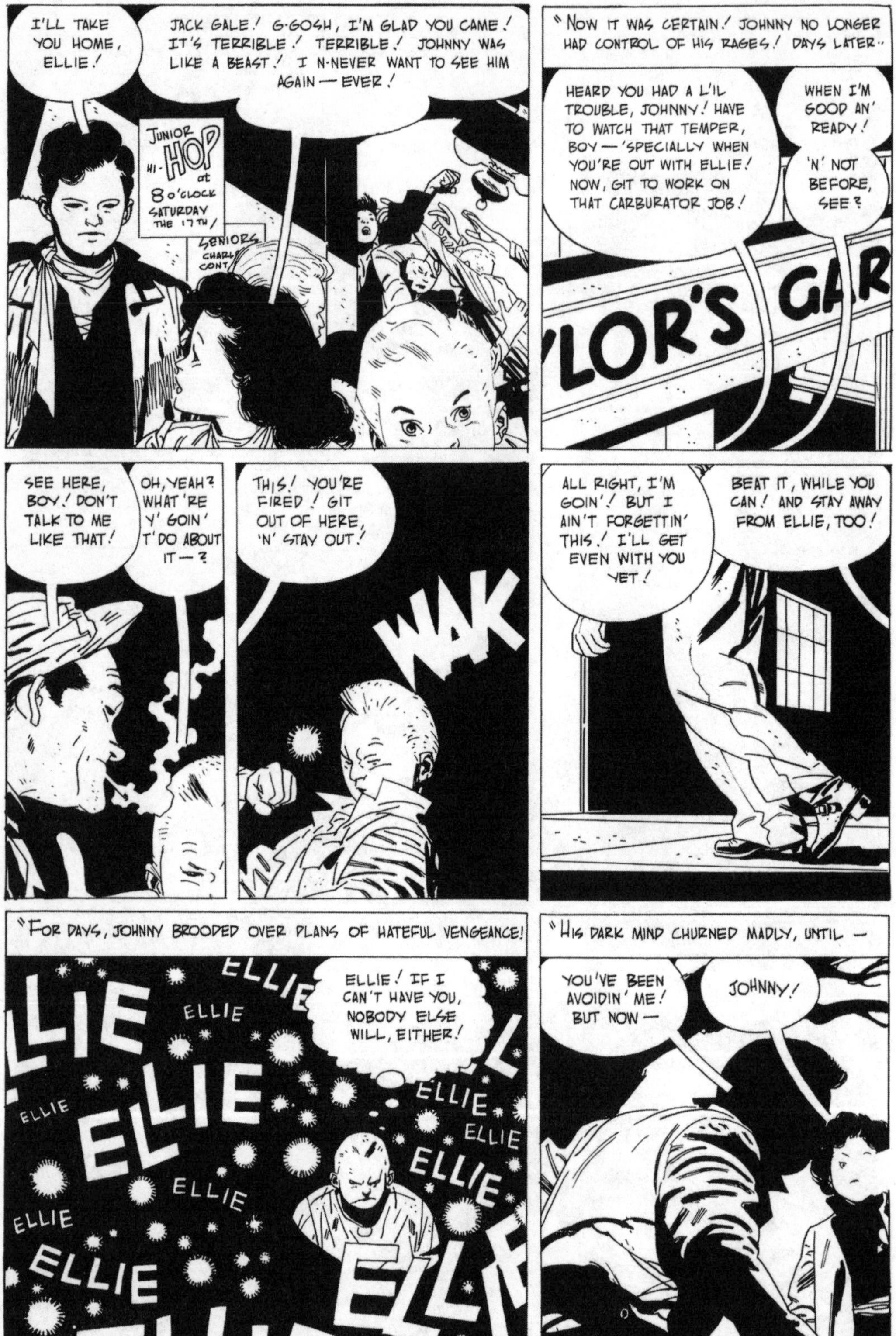
I'LL TAKE YOU HOME, ELLIE!
JACK GALE! G-GOSH, I'M GLAD YOU CAME! IT'S TERRIBLE! TERRIBLE! JOHNNY WAS LIKE A BEAST! I N-NEVER WANT TO SEE HIM AGAIN — EVER!
JUNIOR HI-HOP at 8 O'CLOCK SATURDAY THE 17TH!
SENIORS
"NOW IT WAS CERTAIN! JOHNNY NO LONGER HAD CONTROL OF HIS RAGES! DAYS LATER..
HEARD YOU HAD A L'IL TROUBLE, JOHNNY! HAVE TO WATCH THAT TEMPER, BOY — 'SPECIALLY WHEN YOU'RE OUT WITH ELLIE! NOW, GIT TO WORK ON THAT CARBURATOR JOB!
WHEN I'M GOOD AN' READY!
'N' NOT BEFORE, SEE?
YLOR'S GAR
SEE HERE, BOY! DON'T TALK TO ME LIKE THAT!
OH, YEAH? WHAT'RE Y' GOIN' T'DO ABOUT IT —?
THIS! YOU'RE FIRED! GIT OUT OF HERE, 'N' STAY OUT!
WAK
ALL RIGHT, I'M GOIN'! BUT I AIN'T FORGETTIN' THIS! I'LL GET EVEN WITH YOU YET!
BEAT IT, WHILE YOU CAN! AND STAY AWAY FROM ELLIE, TOO!
"FOR DAYS, JOHNNY BROODED OVER PLANS OF HATEFUL VENGEANCE!
ELLIE! IF I CAN'T HAVE YOU, NOBODY ELSE WILL, EITHER!
ELLIE ELLIE ELLIE ELLIE ELLIE ELLIE ELLIE ELLIE ELLIE ELLIE ELLIE
"HIS DARK MIND CHURNED MADLY, UNTIL —
YOU'VE BEEN AVOIDIN' ME! BUT NOW —
JOHNNY!
5

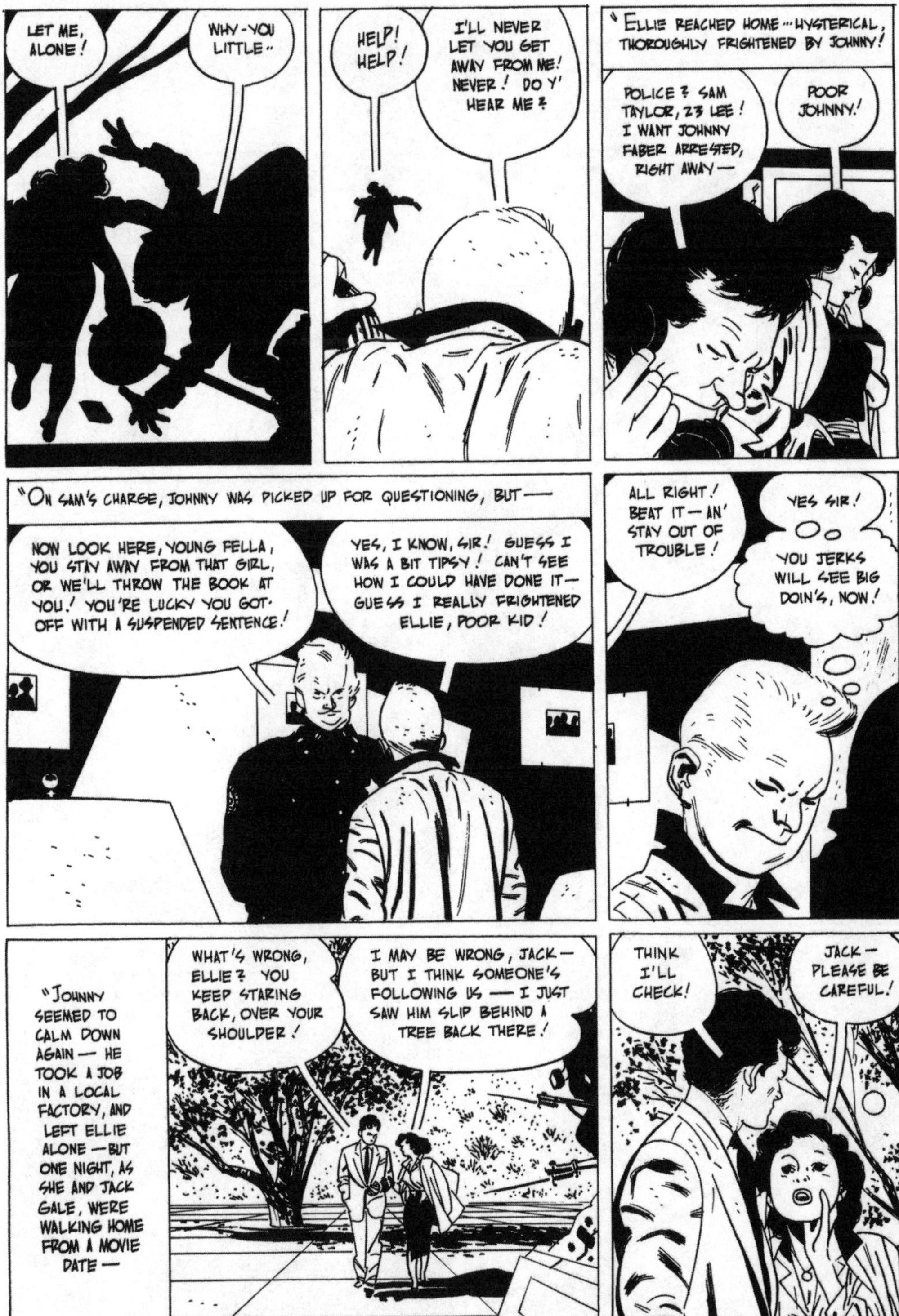
LET ME, ALONE!
WHY-YOU LITTLE..
HELP! HELP!
I'LL NEVER LET YOU GET AWAY FROM ME! NEVER! DO Y' HEAR ME?
"ELLIE REACHED HOME... HYSTERICAL, THOROUGHLY FRIGHTENED BY JOHNNY!
POLICE? SAM TAYLOR, 23 LEE! I WANT JOHNNY FABER ARRESTED, RIGHT AWAY—
POOR JOHNNY!
"ON SAM'S CHARGE, JOHNNY WAS PICKED UP FOR QUESTIONING, BUT—
NOW LOOK HERE, YOUNG FELLA, YOU STAY AWAY FROM THAT GIRL, OR WE'LL THROW THE BOOK AT YOU! YOU'RE LUCKY YOU GOT OFF WITH A SUSPENDED SENTENCE!
YES, I KNOW, SIR! GUESS I WAS A BIT TIPSY! CAN'T SEE HOW I COULD HAVE DONE IT— GUESS I REALLY FRIGHTENED ELLIE, POOR KID!
ALL RIGHT! BEAT IT— AN' STAY OUT OF TROUBLE!
YES SIR!
YOU JERKS WILL SEE BIG DOIN'S, NOW!
"JOHNNY SEEMED TO CALM DOWN AGAIN — HE TOOK A JOB IN A LOCAL FACTORY, AND LEFT ELLIE ALONE — BUT ONE NIGHT, AS SHE AND JACK GALE, WERE WALKING HOME FROM A MOVIE DATE —
WHAT'S WRONG, ELLIE? YOU KEEP STARING BACK, OVER YOUR SHOULDER!
I MAY BE WRONG, JACK— BUT I THINK SOMEONE'S FOLLOWING US — I JUST SAW HIM SLIP BEHIND A TREE BACK THERE!
THINK I'LL CHECK!
JACK— PLEASE BE CAREFUL!
6

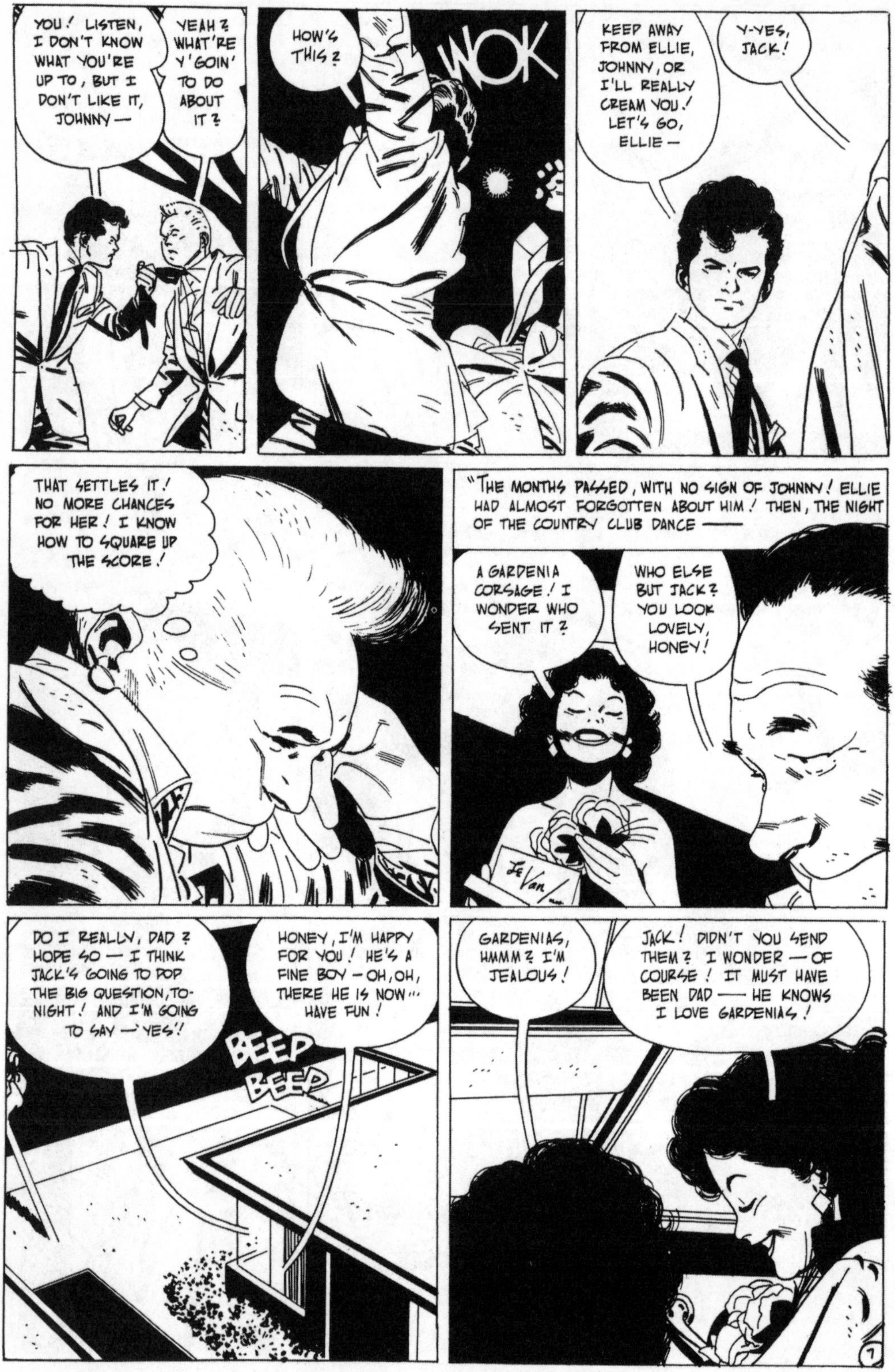
YOU! LISTEN, I DON'T KNOW WHAT YOU'RE UP TO, BUT I DON'T LIKE IT, JOHNNY—
YEAH? WHAT'RE Y'GOIN' TO DO ABOUT IT?
HOW'S THIS?
WOK
KEEP AWAY FROM ELLIE, JOHNNY, OR I'LL REALLY CREAM YOU! LET'S GO, ELLIE—
Y-YES, JACK!
THAT SETTLES IT! NO MORE CHANCES FOR HER! I KNOW HOW TO SQUARE UP THE SCORE!
"THE MONTHS PASSED, WITH NO SIGN OF JOHNNY! ELLIE HAD ALMOST FORGOTTEN ABOUT HIM! THEN, THE NIGHT OF THE COUNTRY CLUB DANCE——
A GARDENIA CORSAGE! I WONDER WHO SENT IT?
WHO ELSE BUT JACK? YOU LOOK LOVELY, HONEY!
DO I REALLY, DAD? HOPE SO — I THINK JACK'S GOING TO POP THE BIG QUESTION, TO-NIGHT! AND I'M GOING TO SAY — YES!
HONEY, I'M HAPPY FOR YOU! HE'S A FINE BOY — OH, OH, THERE HE IS NOW... HAVE FUN!
BEEP BEEP
GARDENIAS, HMMM? I'M JEALOUS!
JACK! DIDN'T YOU SEND THEM? I WONDER — OF COURSE! IT MUST HAVE BEEN DAD —— HE KNOWS I LOVE GARDENIAS!
7

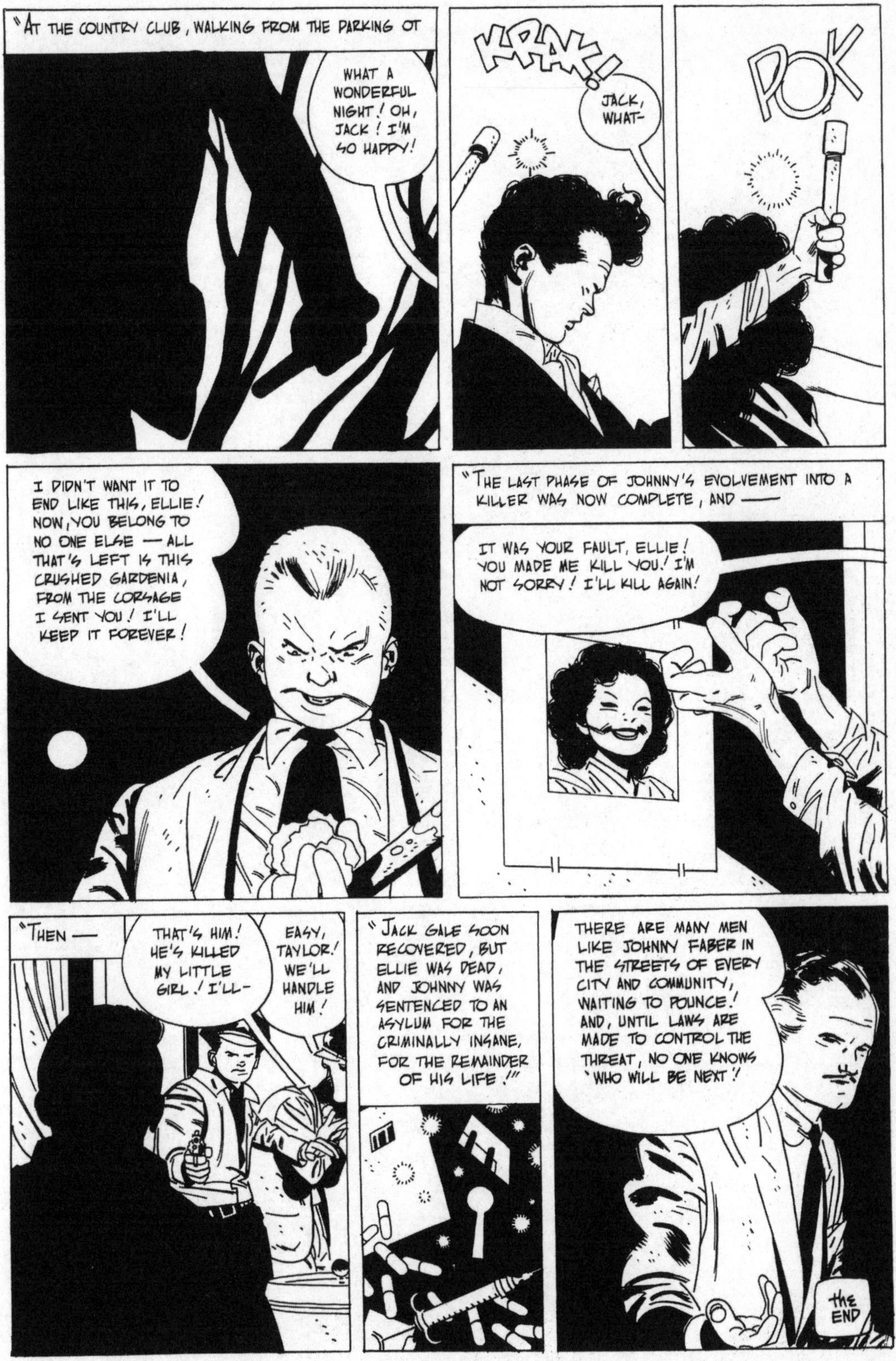
"AT THE COUNTRY CLUB, WALKING FROM THE PARKING OT
WHAT A WONDERFUL NIGHT! OH, JACK! I'M SO HAPPY!
KRAK!
JACK, WHAT-
POK
I DIDN'T WANT IT TO END LIKE THIS, ELLIE! NOW, YOU BELONG TO NO ONE ELSE — ALL THAT'S LEFT IS THIS CRUSHED GARDENIA, FROM THE CORSAGE I SENT YOU! I'LL KEEP IT FOREVER!
"THE LAST PHASE OF JOHNNY'S EVOLVEMENT INTO A KILLER WAS NOW COMPLETE, AND —
IT WAS YOUR FAULT, ELLIE! YOU MADE ME KILL YOU! I'M NOT SORRY! I'LL KILL AGAIN!
"THEN —
THAT'S HIM! HE'S KILLED MY LITTLE GIRL! I'LL-
EASY, TAYLOR! WE'LL HANDLE HIM!
"JACK GALE SOON RECOVERED, BUT ELLIE WAS DEAD, AND JOHNNY WAS SENTENCED TO AN ASYLUM FOR THE CRIMINALLY INSANE, FOR THE REMAINDER OF HIS LIFE!"
THERE ARE MANY MEN LIKE JOHNNY FABER IN THE STREETS OF EVERY CITY AND COMMUNITY, WAITING TO POUNCE! AND, UNTIL LAWS ARE MADE TO CONTROL THE THREAT, NO ONE KNOWS 'WHO WILL BE NEXT'!
THE END

"I just killed two morons and my water broke"

Before Sue Grafton's Kinsey Millhone or Sara Paretsky's V.I. Warshawski, to find a tough female detective you turned to comic books and Michael Tree. Yes, she's a woman, real name Michelle, usually called Ms. Tree, who took over her husband Michael's name and business, Tree Investigations, Inc., when she sought revenge for his murder on their wedding night by the criminal Muerta family. She is also a mother to her stepson, Mike Jr., and to her second child, due in less than a month. Writer Max Allan Collins has explained that Ms. Tree is a female, smarter version of Mike Hammer, although Spillane's hero never had to deal with being nine months pregnant. Collins collaborated with Chester Gould on *Dick Tracy*, taking over as scripter after Gould's death from 1977 to 1993, and wrote the graphic novel *Road to Perdition* filmed by Sam Mendes. After around 75 issues of *Ms. Tree* from 1981 to 1993, Collins resurrected her in 2007 in a new novel, *Dearly Beloved*, and a movie is in development.

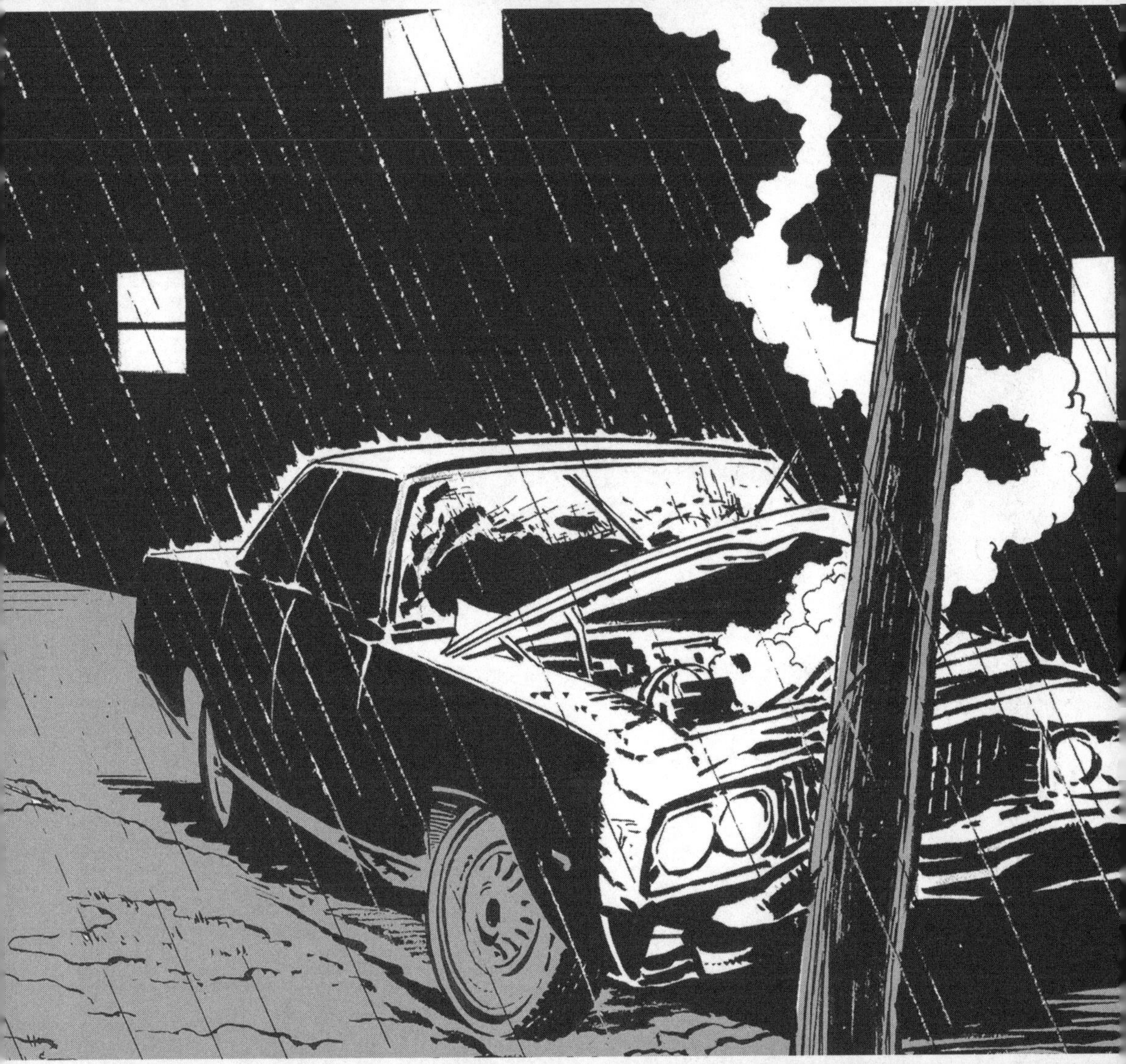

Ms. Tree: Maternity Leave

Max Allan Collins (script) and Terry Beatty (art) 1992

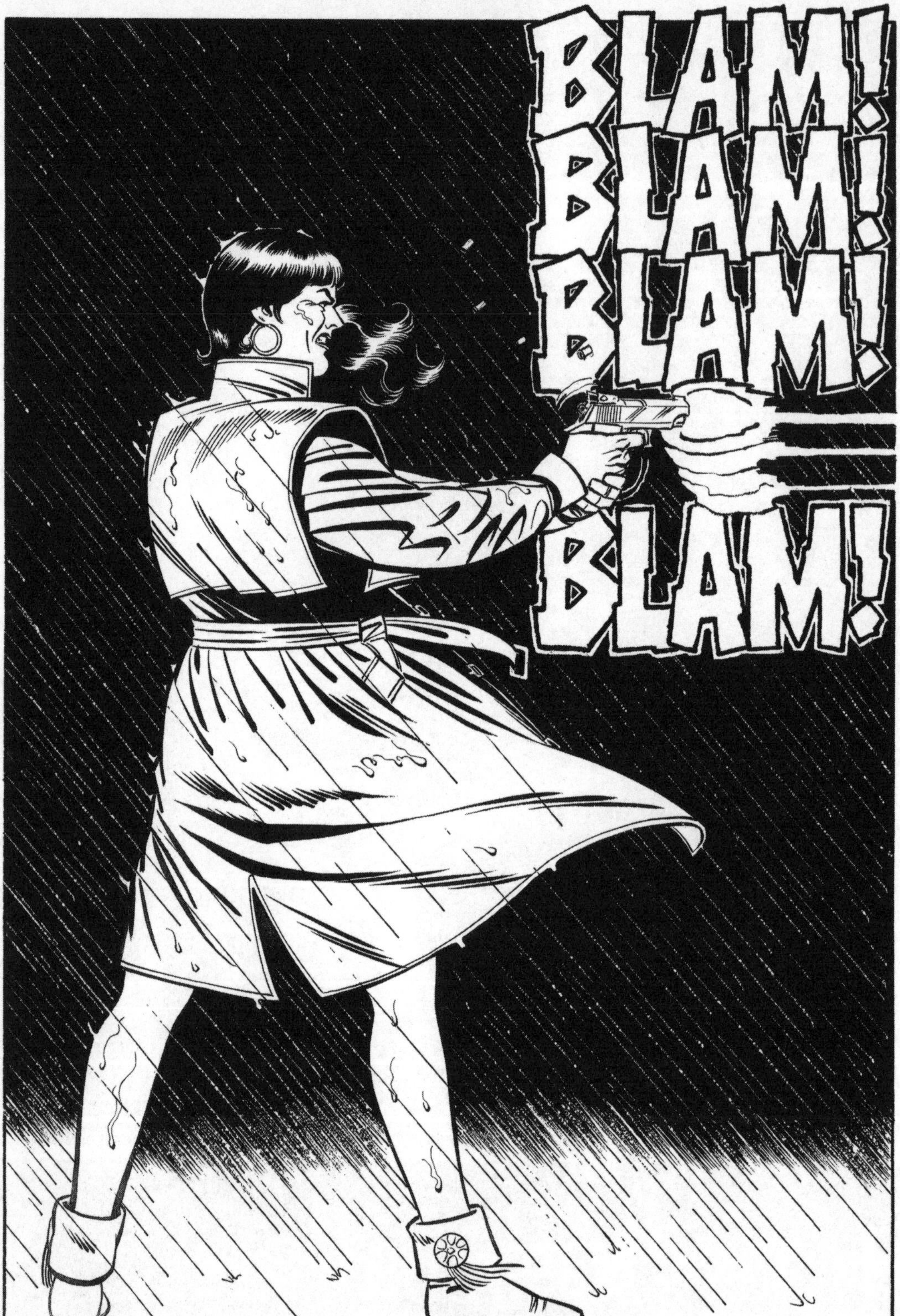
BLAM! BLAM! BLAM!
BLAM!

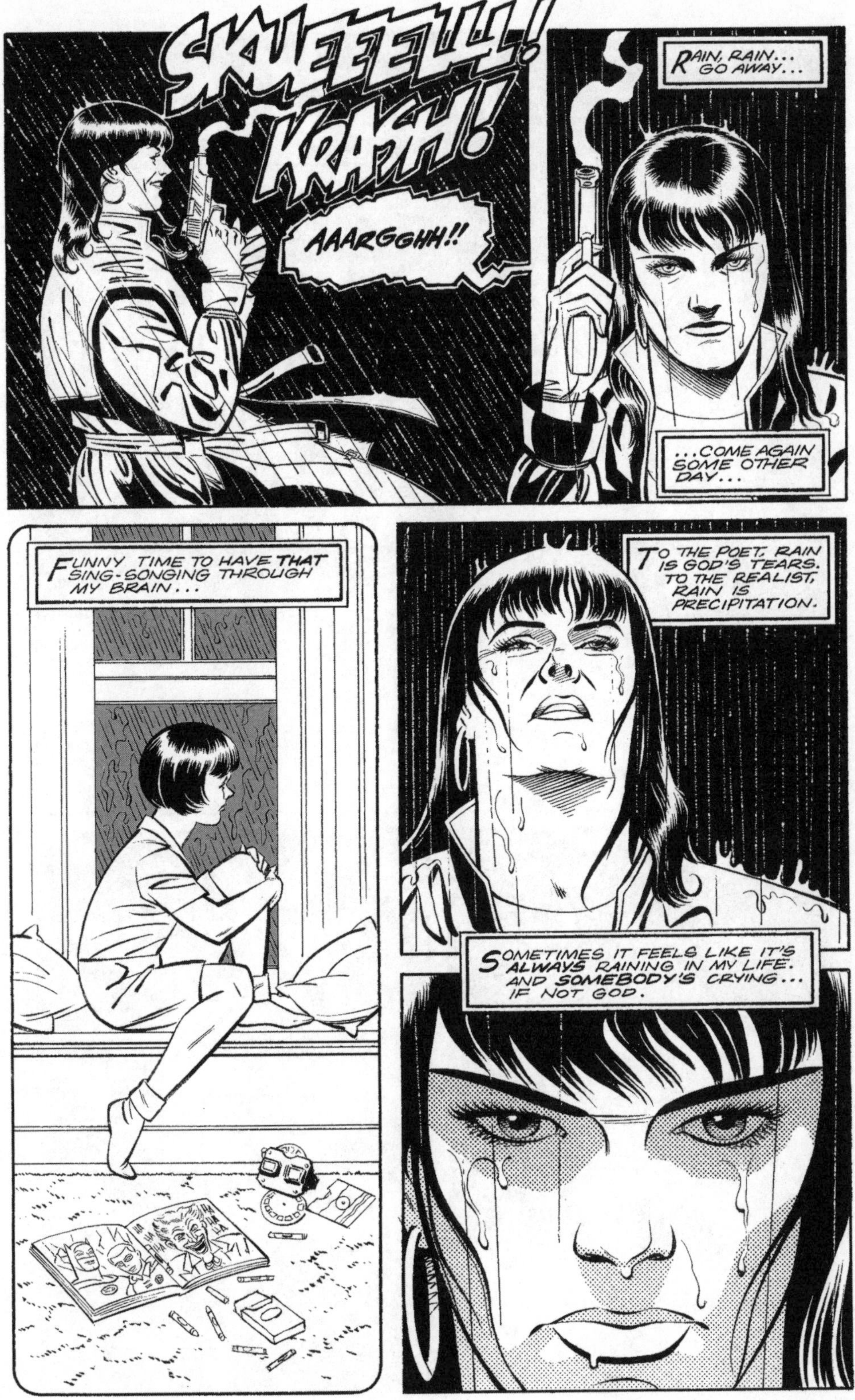
SKWEEELLL!
KRASH!
AAARGGHH!!
RAIN, RAIN... GO AWAY...
...COME AGAIN SOME OTHER DAY...
FUNNY TIME TO HAVE THAT SING-SONGING THROUGH MY BRAIN...
TO THE POET, RAIN IS GOD'S TEARS. TO THE REALIST, RAIN IS PRECIPITATION.
SOMETIMES IT FEELS LIKE IT'S ALWAYS RAINING IN MY LIFE. AND SOMEBODY'S CRYING... IF NOT GOD.

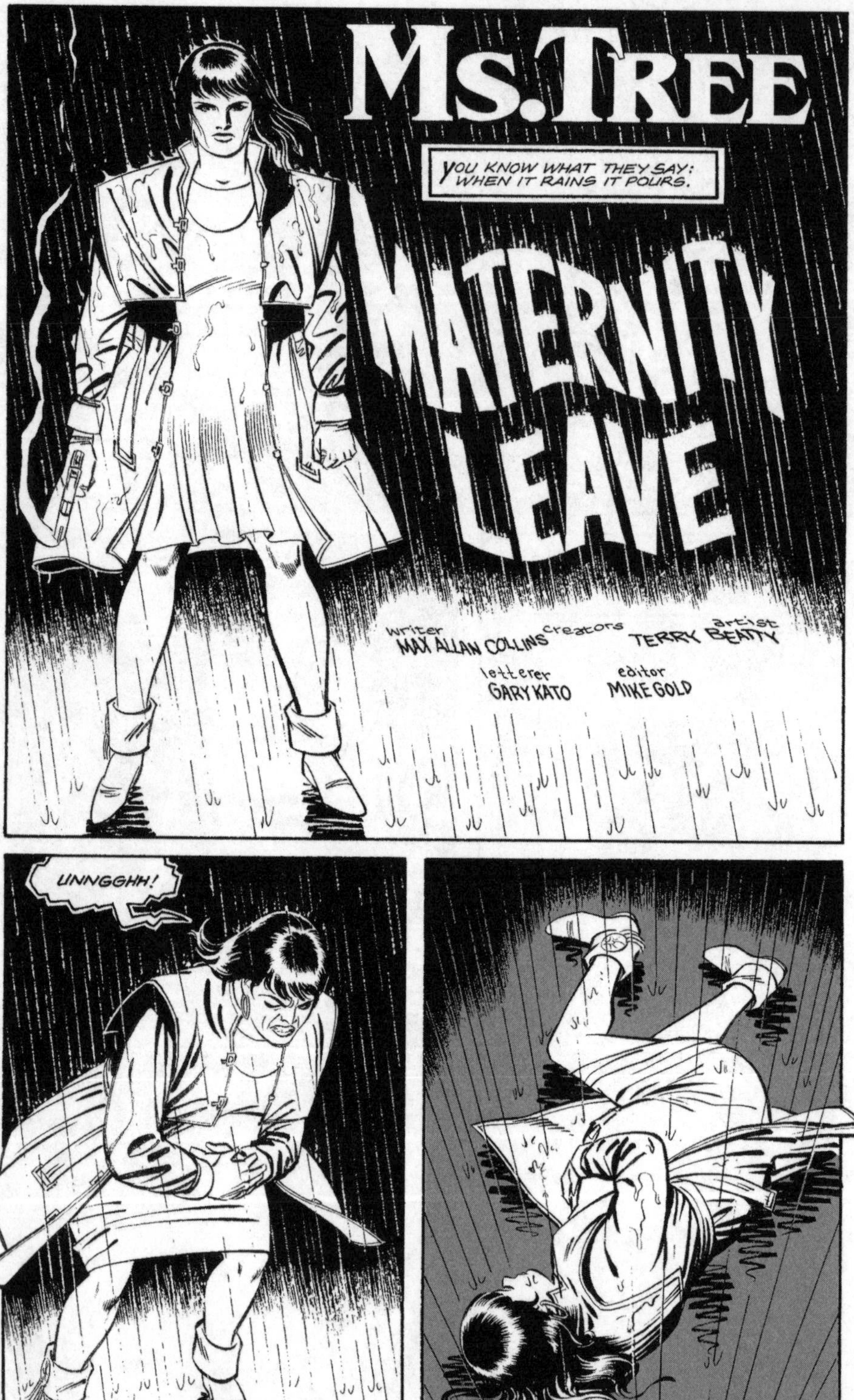
MS. TREE
YOU KNOW WHAT THEY SAY: WHEN IT RAINS IT POURS.
MATERNITY LEAVE
creators
writer MAX ALLAN COLLINS
artist TERRY BEATTY
letterer GARY KATO
editor MIKE GOLD
UNNGGHH!

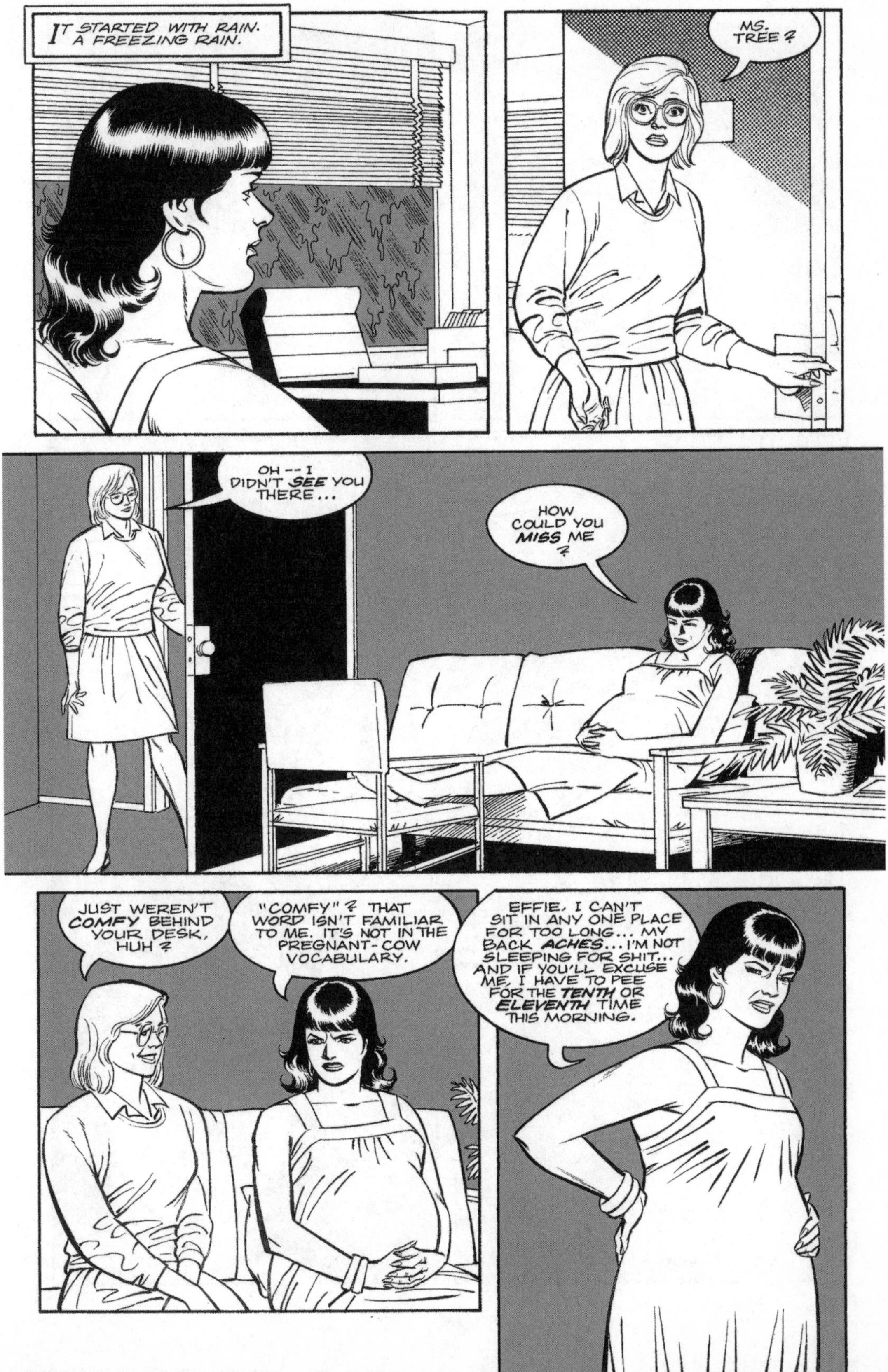
IT STARTED WITH RAIN. A FREEZING RAIN.
MS. TREE?
OH -- I DIDN'T SEE YOU THERE...
HOW COULD YOU MISS ME ?
JUST WEREN'T COMFY BEHIND YOUR DESK, HUH ?
"COMFY"? THAT WORD ISN'T FAMILIAR TO ME. IT'S NOT IN THE PREGNANT-COW VOCABULARY.
EFFIE, I CAN'T SIT IN ANY ONE PLACE FOR TOO LONG... MY BACK ACHES... I'M NOT SLEEPING FOR SHIT... AND IF YOU'LL EXCUSE ME, I HAVE TO PEE FOR THE TENTH OR ELEVENTH TIME THIS MORNING.

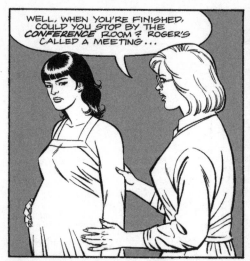

WELL, WHEN YOU'RE FINISHED, COULD YOU STOP BY THE *CONFERENCE* ROOM? ROGER'S CALLED A MEETING...

I CALL THE MEETINGS AROUND HERE!

I JOINED THE TREE INVESTIGATIONS, INC. STAFF AS SOON AS I COULD...

WHO PUT *YOU* IN CHARGE, MR. FREEMONT? WHAT IS THIS, A *GODDAMN MUTINY?*

YES.

YOU'RE *NOT* GETTING ANY WORK DONE. YOUR SOLE FUNCTION HERE, FOR THE LAST COUPLE OF WEEKS, IS TO BE A CRANKY *PAIN* IN THE ASS.

WHAT DO YOU SUGGEST I *DO?* GO HOME AND *NEST?*

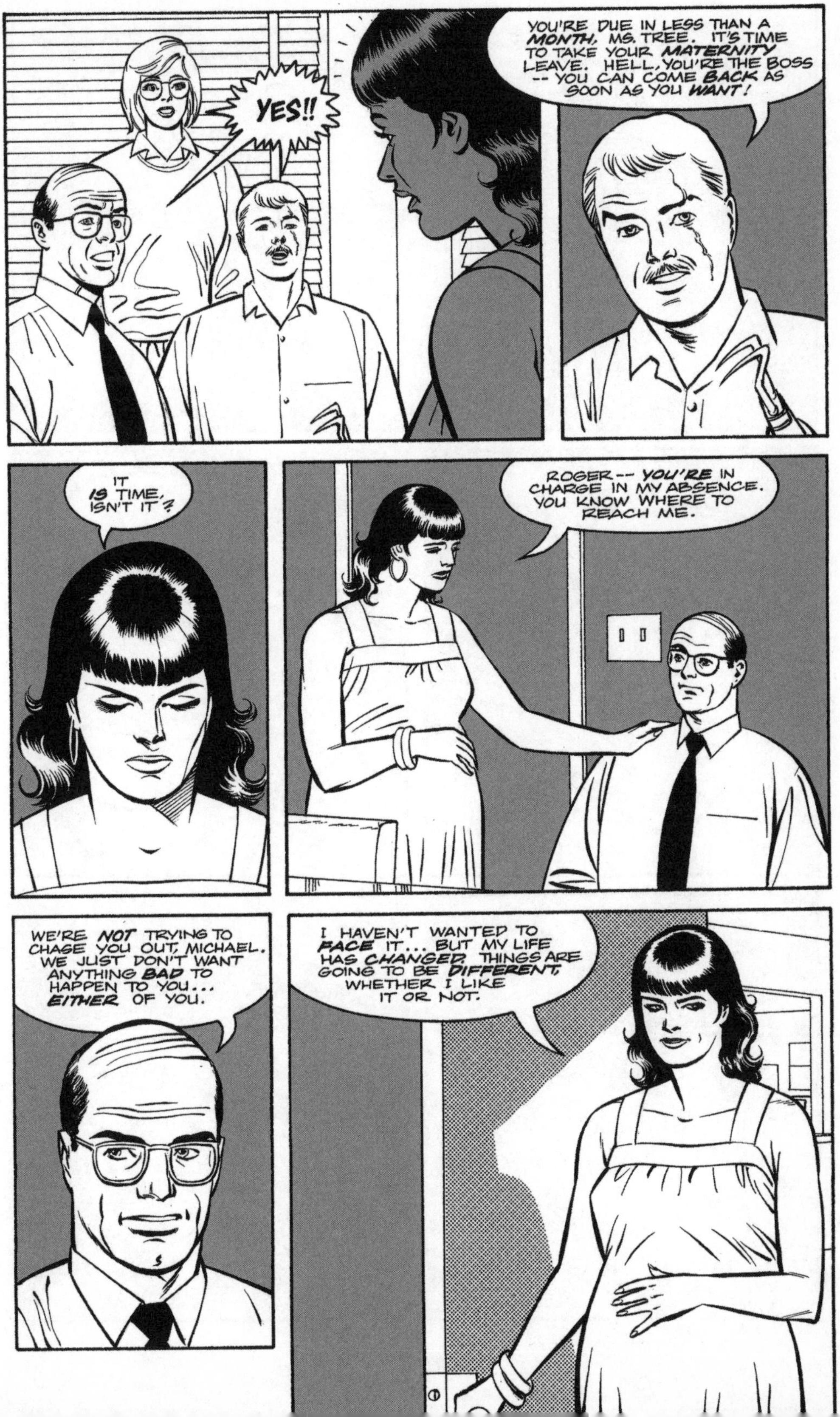
YES!!
YOU'RE DUE IN LESS THAN A MONTH, MS. TREE. IT'S TIME TO TAKE YOUR MATERNITY LEAVE. HELL, YOU'RE THE BOSS -- YOU CAN COME BACK AS SOON AS YOU WANT!
IT IS TIME, ISN'T IT?
ROGER -- YOU'RE IN CHARGE IN MY ABSENCE. YOU KNOW WHERE TO REACH ME.
WE'RE NOT TRYING TO CHASE YOU OUT, MICHAEL. WE JUST DON'T WANT ANYTHING BAD TO HAPPEN TO YOU... EITHER OF YOU.
I HAVEN'T WANTED TO FACE IT... BUT MY LIFE HAS CHANGED. THINGS ARE GOING TO BE DIFFERENT, WHETHER I LIKE IT OR NOT.

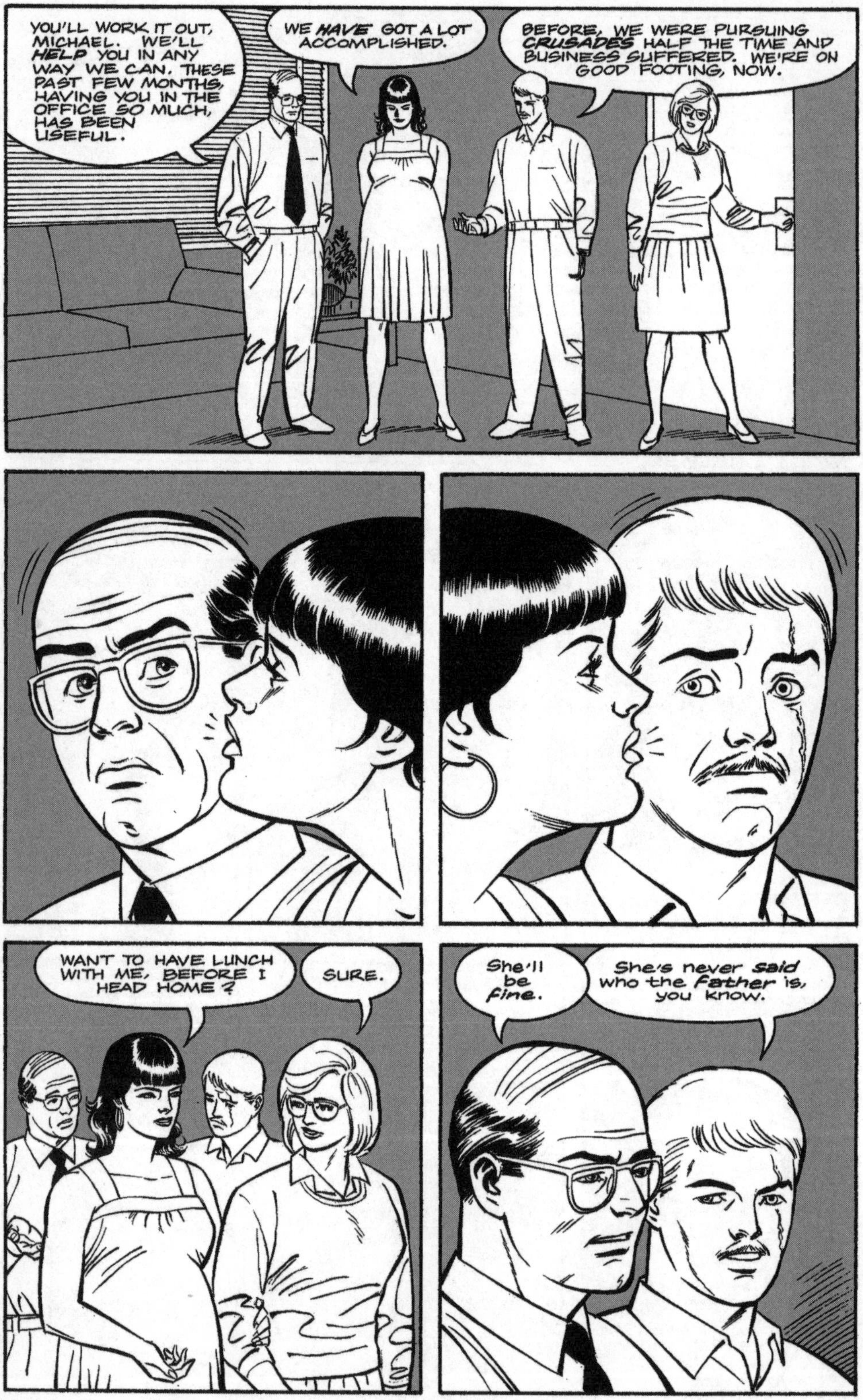
YOU'LL WORK IT OUT, MICHAEL. WE'LL *HELP* YOU IN ANY WAY WE CAN. THESE PAST FEW MONTHS, HAVING YOU IN THE OFFICE SO MUCH, HAS BEEN USEFUL.
WE *HAVE* GOT A LOT ACCOMPLISHED.
BEFORE, WE WERE PURSUING *CRUSADES* HALF THE TIME AND BUSINESS SUFFERED. WE'RE ON GOOD FOOTING, NOW.
WANT TO HAVE LUNCH WITH ME, BEFORE I HEAD HOME?
SURE.
She'll be *fine*.
She's never *said* who the *father* is, you know.

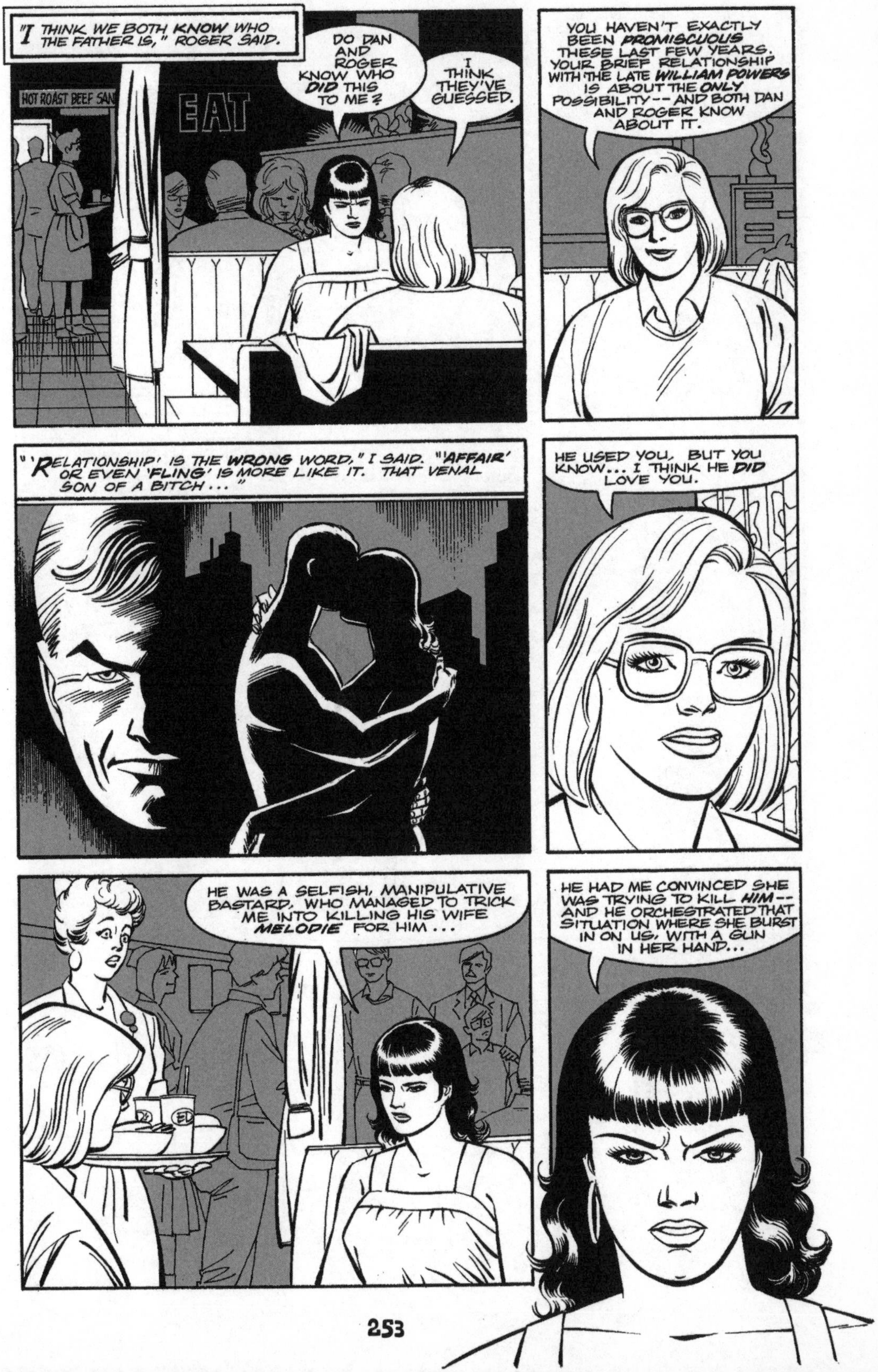
"I THINK WE BOTH KNOW WHO THE FATHER IS," ROGER SAID.
HOT ROAST BEEF SAN
EAT
DO DAN AND ROGER KNOW WHO DID THIS TO ME?
I THINK THEY'VE GUESSED.
YOU HAVEN'T EXACTLY BEEN PROMISCUOUS THESE LAST FEW YEARS. YOUR BRIEF RELATIONSHIP WITH THE LATE WILLIAM POWERS IS ABOUT THE ONLY POSSIBILITY -- AND BOTH DAN AND ROGER KNOW ABOUT IT.
"'RELATIONSHIP' IS THE WRONG WORD," I SAID. "'AFFAIR' OR EVEN 'FLING' IS MORE LIKE IT. THAT VENAL SON OF A BITCH ..."
HE USED YOU, BUT YOU KNOW... I THINK HE DID LOVE YOU.
HE WAS A SELFISH, MANIPULATIVE BASTARD, WHO MANAGED TO TRICK ME INTO KILLING HIS WIFE MELODIE FOR HIM ...
HE HAD ME CONVINCED SHE WAS TRYING TO KILL HIM -- AND HE ORCHESTRATED THAT SITUATION WHERE SHE BURST IN ON US, WITH A GUN IN HER HAND...

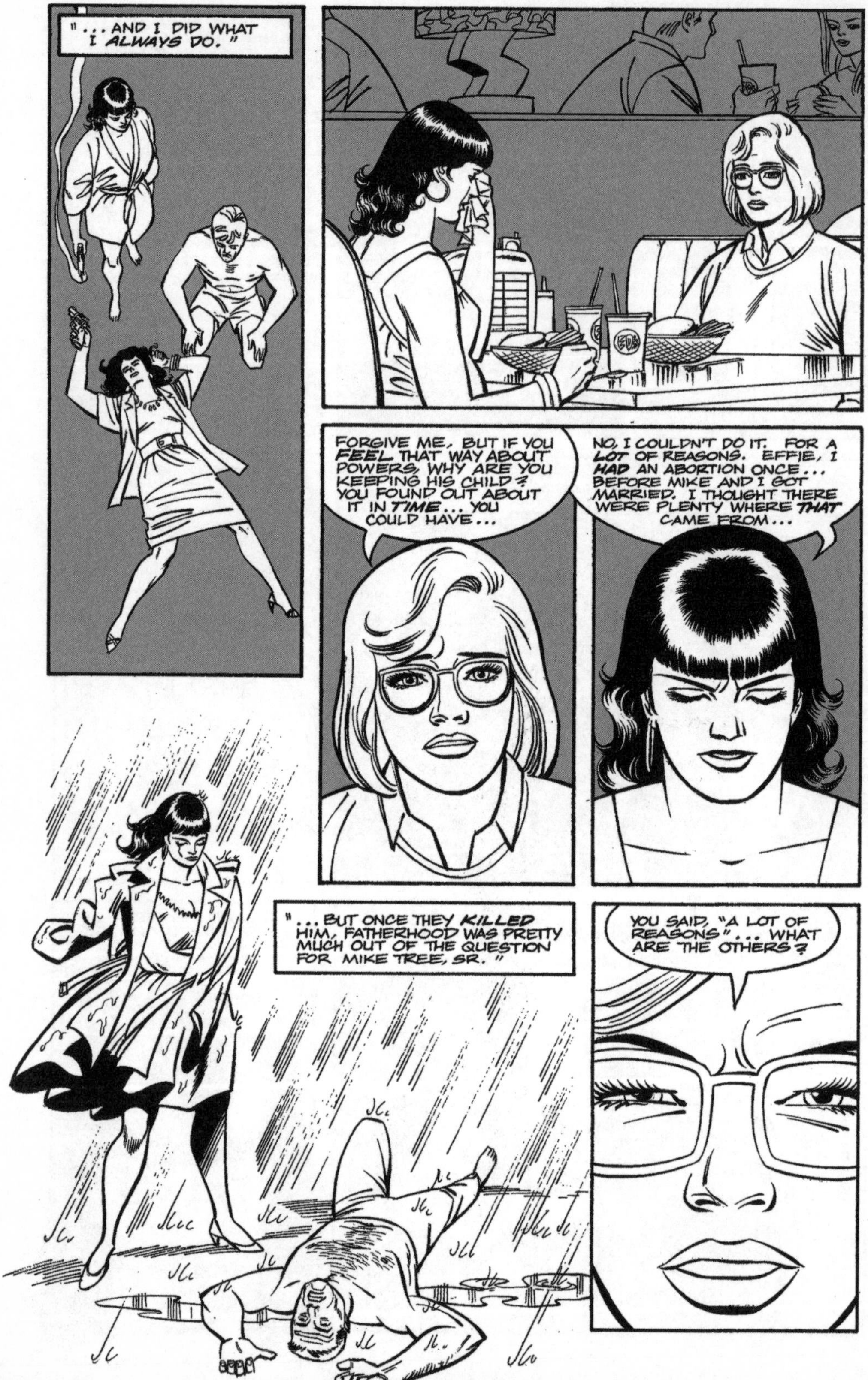
"... AND I DID WHAT I *ALWAYS* DO."
FORGIVE ME, BUT IF YOU *FEEL* THAT WAY ABOUT POWERS, WHY ARE YOU KEEPING HIS CHILD? YOU FOUND OUT ABOUT IT IN *TIME*... YOU COULD HAVE...
NO, I COULDN'T DO IT. FOR A *LOT* OF REASONS. EFFIE, I *HAD* AN ABORTION ONCE... BEFORE MIKE AND I GOT MARRIED. I THOUGHT THERE WERE PLENTY WHERE *THAT* CAME FROM...
"... BUT ONCE THEY *KILLED* HIM, FATHERHOOD WAS PRETTY MUCH OUT OF THE QUESTION FOR MIKE TREE, SR."
YOU SAID, "A LOT OF REASONS"... WHAT ARE THE OTHERS?

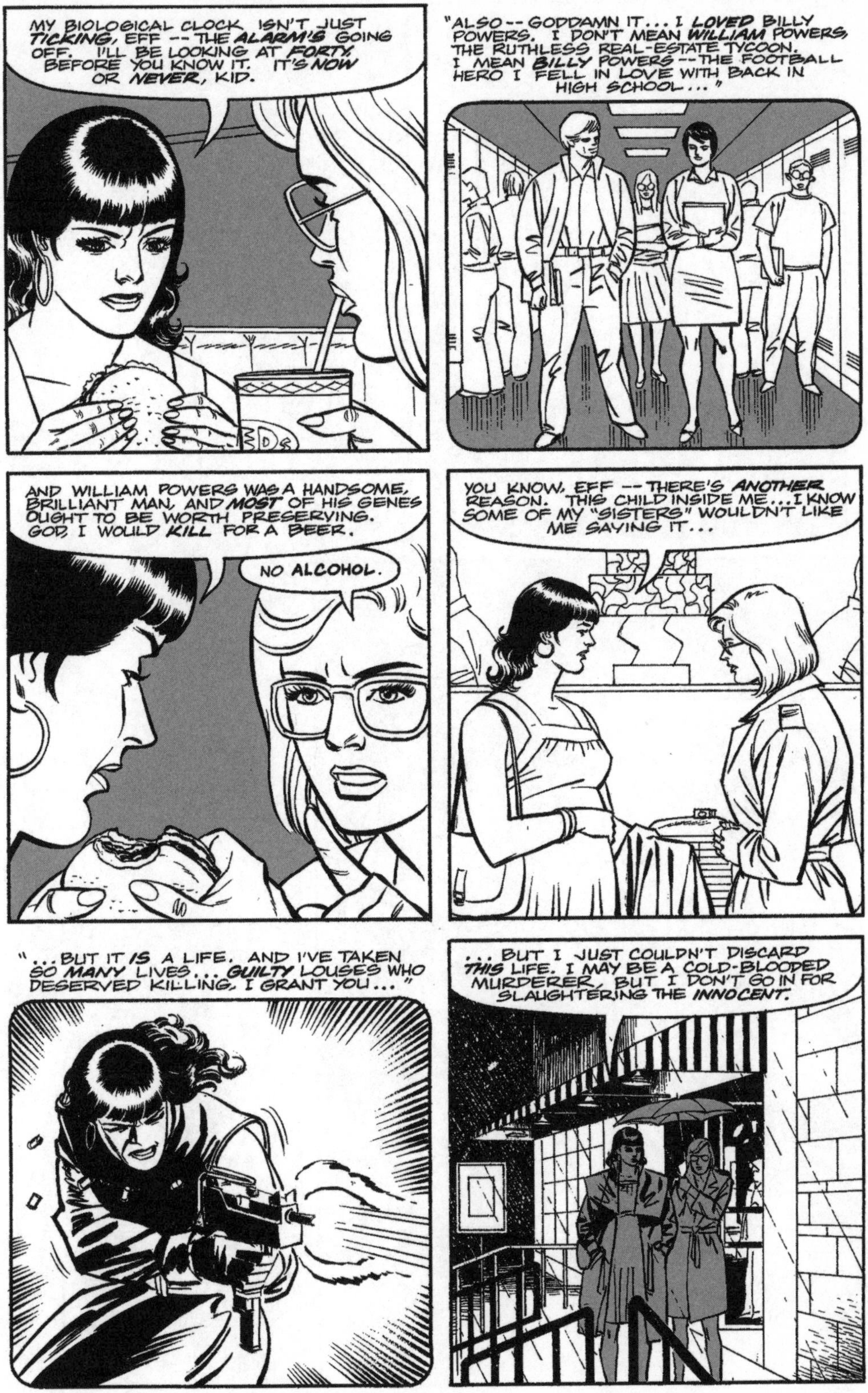
MY BIOLOGICAL CLOCK ISN'T JUST TICKING, EFF -- THE ALARM'S GOING OFF. I'LL BE LOOKING AT FORTY BEFORE YOU KNOW IT. IT'S NOW OR NEVER, KID.
"ALSO -- GODDAMN IT... I LOVED BILLY POWERS. I DON'T MEAN WILLIAM POWERS, THE RUTHLESS REAL-ESTATE TYCOON. I MEAN BILLY POWERS -- THE FOOTBALL HERO I FELL IN LOVE WITH BACK IN HIGH SCHOOL..."
AND WILLIAM POWERS WAS A HANDSOME, BRILLIANT MAN, AND MOST OF HIS GENES OUGHT TO BE WORTH PRESERVING. GOD, I WOULD KILL FOR A BEER.
NO ALCOHOL.
YOU KNOW, EFF -- THERE'S ANOTHER REASON. THIS CHILD INSIDE ME... I KNOW SOME OF MY "SISTERS" WOULDN'T LIKE ME SAYING IT...
"...BUT IT IS A LIFE. AND I'VE TAKEN SO MANY LIVES... GUILTY LOUSES WHO DESERVED KILLING, I GRANT YOU..."
...BUT I JUST COULDN'T DISCARD THIS LIFE. I MAY BE A COLD-BLOODED MURDERER, BUT I DON'T GO IN FOR SLAUGHTERING THE INNOCENT.

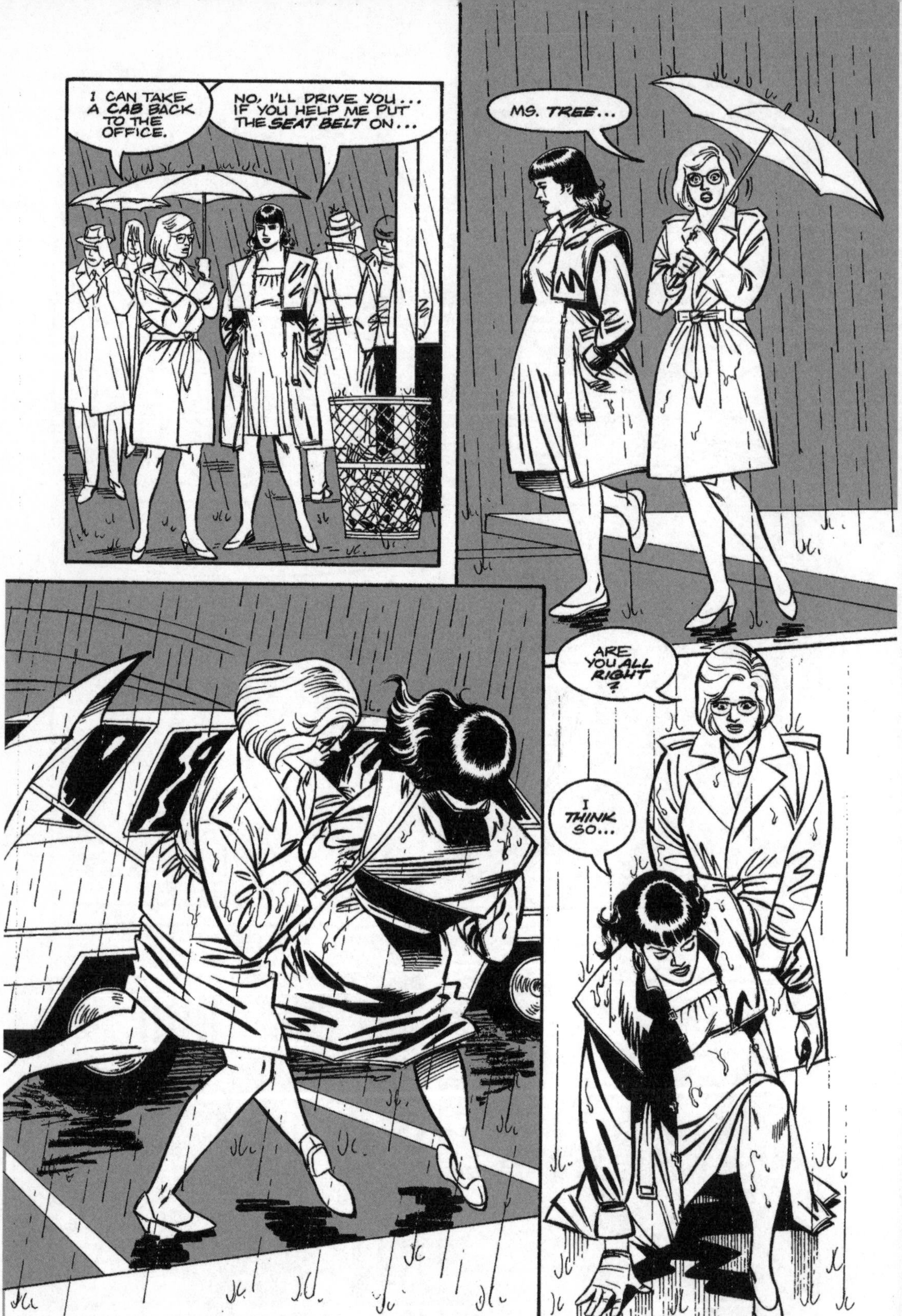

I CAN TAKE A CAB BACK TO THE OFFICE.
NO, I'LL DRIVE YOU... IF YOU HELP ME PUT THE SEAT BELT ON...
MS. TREE...
ARE YOU ALL RIGHT?
I THINK SO...

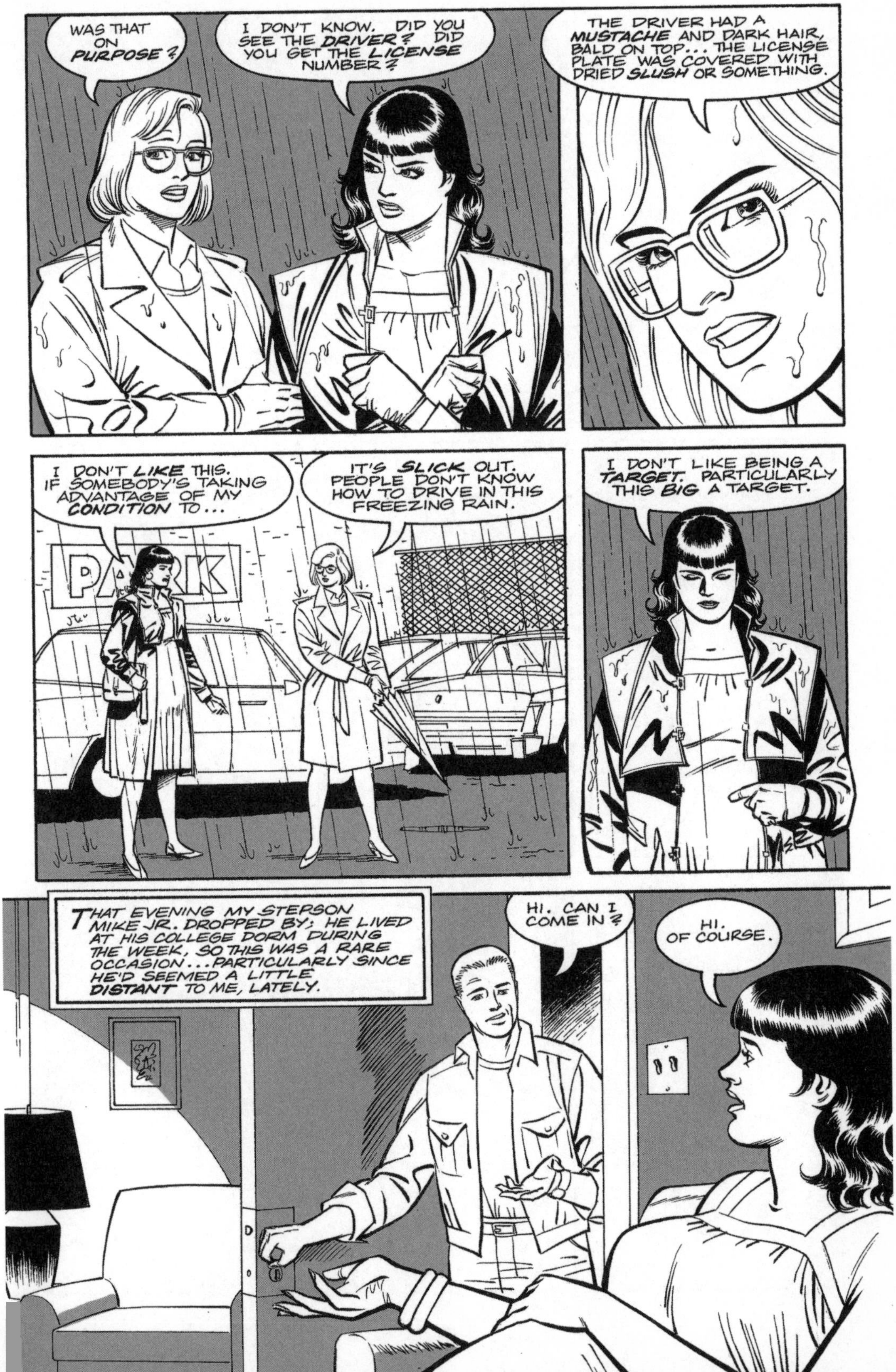
WAS THAT ON PURPOSE?
I DON'T KNOW. DID YOU SEE THE DRIVER? DID YOU GET THE LICENSE NUMBER?
THE DRIVER HAD A MUSTACHE AND DARK HAIR, BALD ON TOP... THE LICENSE PLATE WAS COVERED WITH DRIED SLUSH OR SOMETHING.
I DON'T LIKE THIS. IF SOMEBODY'S TAKING ADVANTAGE OF MY CONDITION TO...
PARK
IT'S SLICK OUT. PEOPLE DON'T KNOW HOW TO DRIVE IN THIS FREEZING RAIN.
I DON'T LIKE BEING A TARGET. PARTICULARLY THIS BIG A TARGET.
THAT EVENING MY STERSON MIKE JR. DROPPED BY; HE LIVED AT HIS COLLEGE DORM DURING THE WEEK, SO THIS WAS A RARE OCCASION... PARTICULARLY SINCE HE'D SEEMED A LITTLE DISTANT TO ME, LATELY.
HI. CAN I COME IN?
HI. OF COURSE.

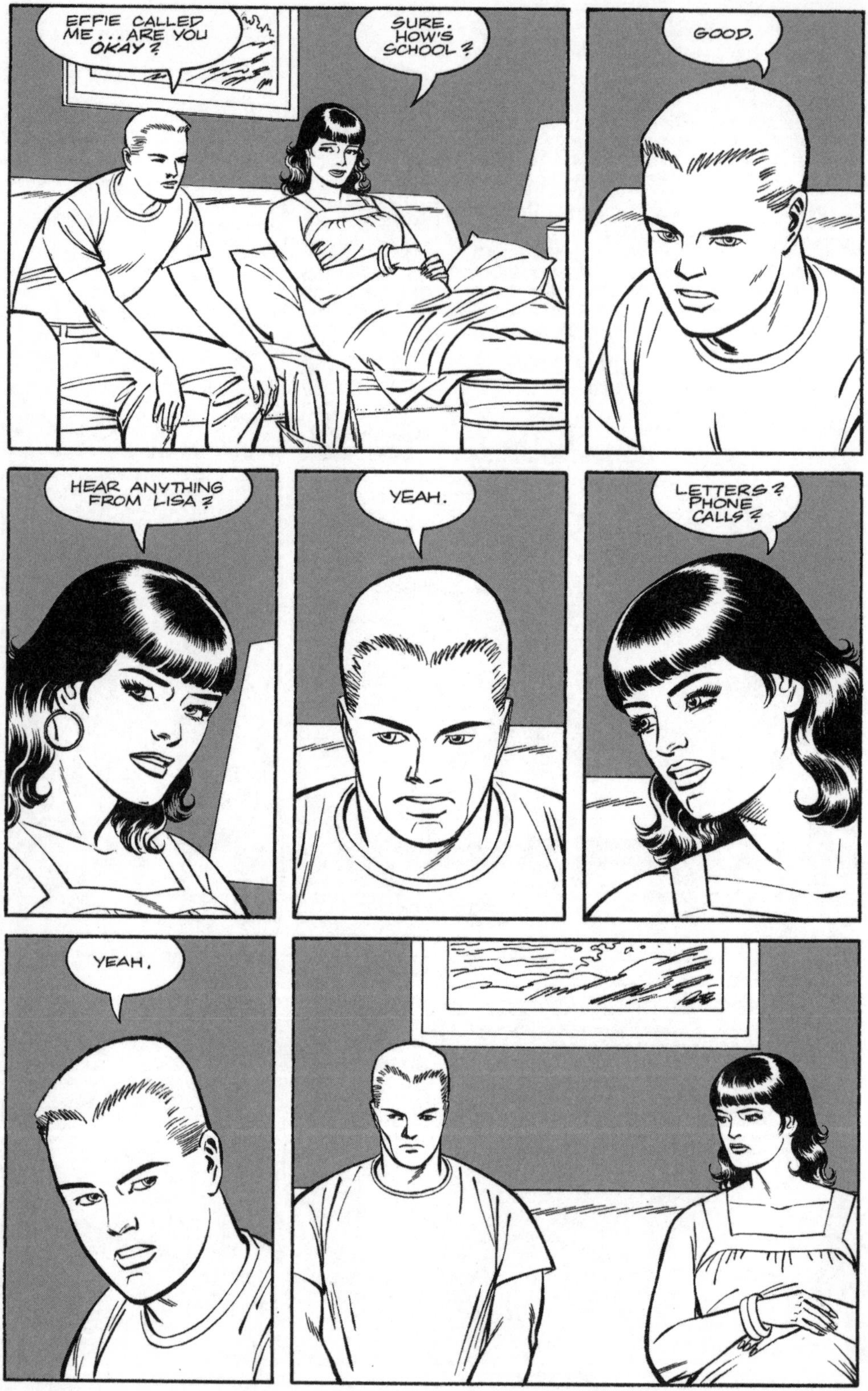
EFFIE CALLED ME... ARE YOU *OKAY*?
SURE. HOW'S SCHOOL?
GOOD.
HEAR ANYTHING FROM LISA?
YEAH.
LETTERS? PHONE CALLS?
YEAH.

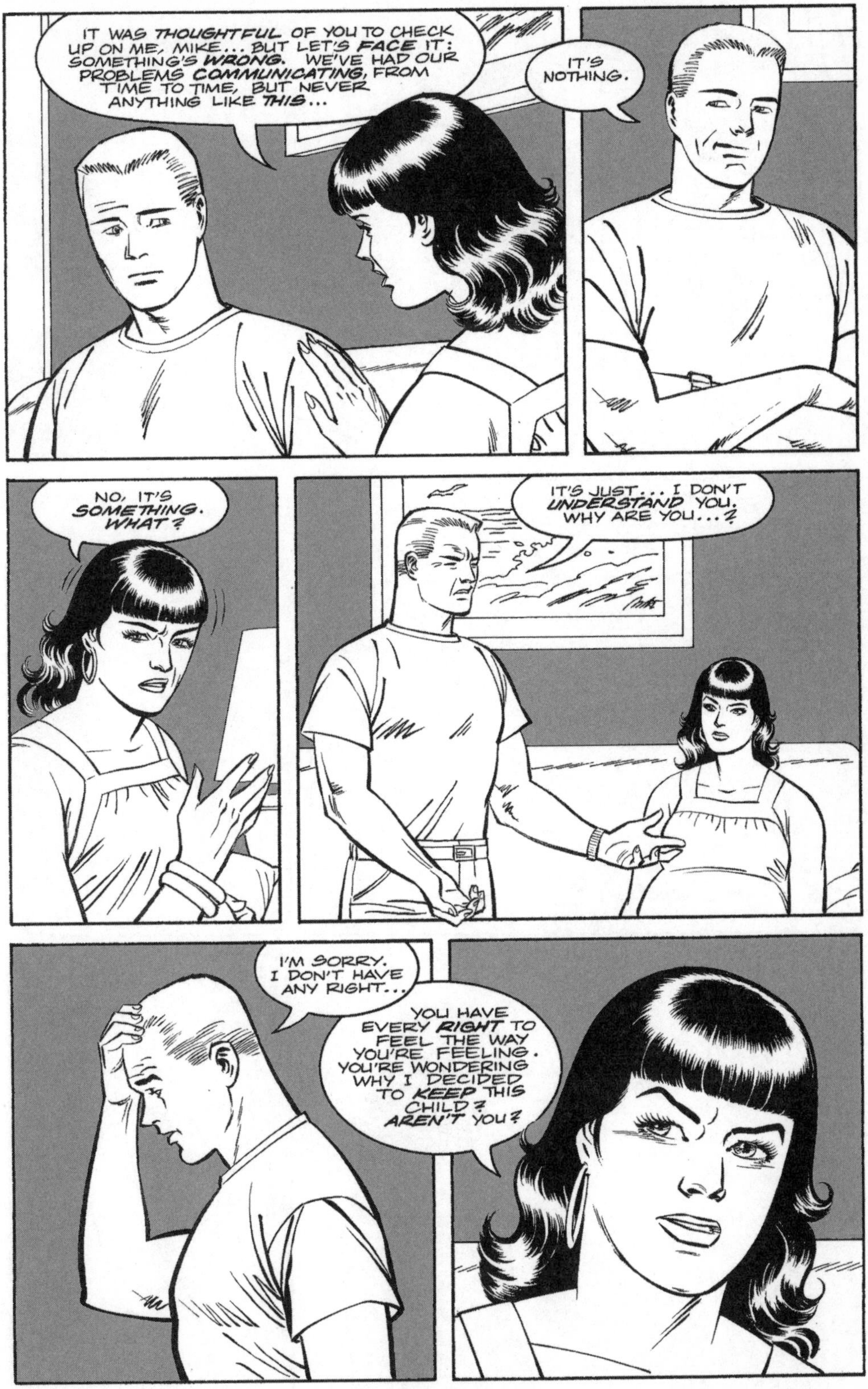
IT WAS THOUGHTFUL OF YOU TO CHECK UP ON ME, MIKE... BUT LET'S FACE IT: SOMETHING'S WRONG. WE'VE HAD OUR PROBLEMS COMMUNICATING, FROM TIME TO TIME, BUT NEVER ANYTHING LIKE THIS...
IT'S NOTHING.
NO, IT'S SOMETHING. WHAT?
IT'S JUST... I DON'T UNDERSTAND YOU. WHY ARE YOU...?
I'M SORRY. I DON'T HAVE ANY RIGHT...
YOU HAVE EVERY RIGHT TO FEEL THE WAY YOU'RE FEELING. YOU'RE WONDERING WHY I DECIDED TO KEEP THIS CHILD? AREN'T YOU?

I DON'T HAVE *ANY* RIGHT! IT'S NOT *MY* BUSINESS...

IT *IS* YOUR BUSINESS. I'M ALL THE FAMILY YOU'VE GOT RIGHT NOW. SAY IT. I CAN TAKE IT.

YOU'RE SUPPOSED TO BE IN *LOVE* WITH MY *DAD!* THAT'S WHAT YOU'VE ALWAYS *SAID...* WHY WOULD YOU HAVE THE CHILD OF THAT TRASHY *IMMORAL* ASSHOLE, *WILLIAM POWERS* ?!?

"IT'S... AN *INSULT* TO DAD'S MEMORY."

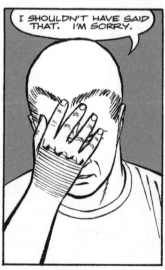

I SHOULDN'T HAVE SAID THAT. I'M SORRY.

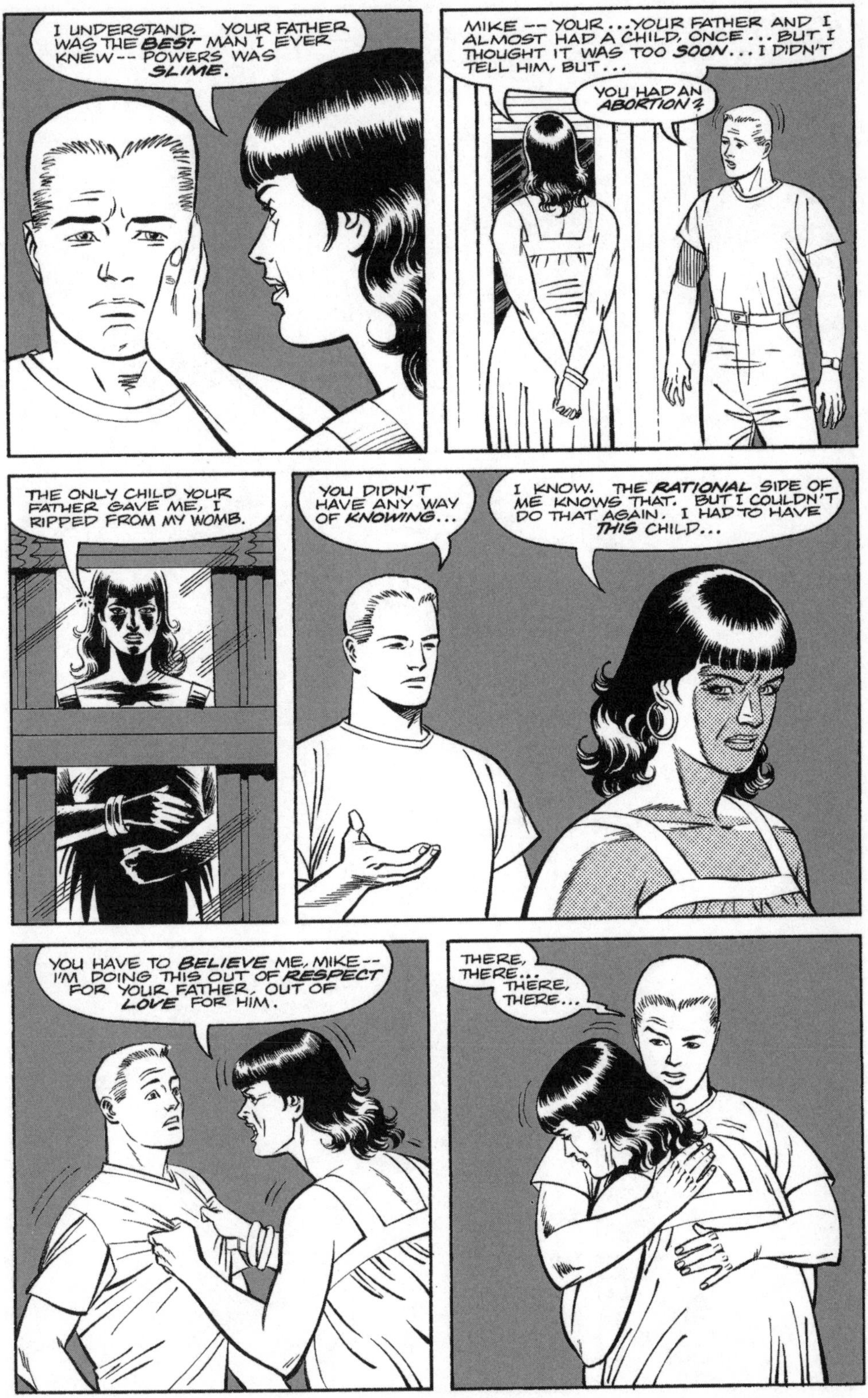
I UNDERSTAND. YOUR FATHER WAS THE BEST MAN I EVER KNEW-- POWERS WAS SLIME.
MIKE -- YOUR... YOUR FATHER AND I ALMOST HAD A CHILD, ONCE... BUT I THOUGHT IT WAS TOO SOON... I DIDN'T TELL HIM, BUT...
YOU HAD AN ABORTION?
THE ONLY CHILD YOUR FATHER GAVE ME, I RIPPED FROM MY WOMB.
YOU DIDN'T HAVE ANY WAY OF KNOWING...
I KNOW. THE RATIONAL SIDE OF ME KNOWS THAT. BUT I COULDN'T DO THAT AGAIN. I HAD TO HAVE THIS CHILD...
YOU HAVE TO BELIEVE ME, MIKE-- I'M DOING THIS OUT OF RESPECT FOR YOUR FATHER, OUT OF LOVE FOR HIM.
THERE, THERE... THERE, THERE...

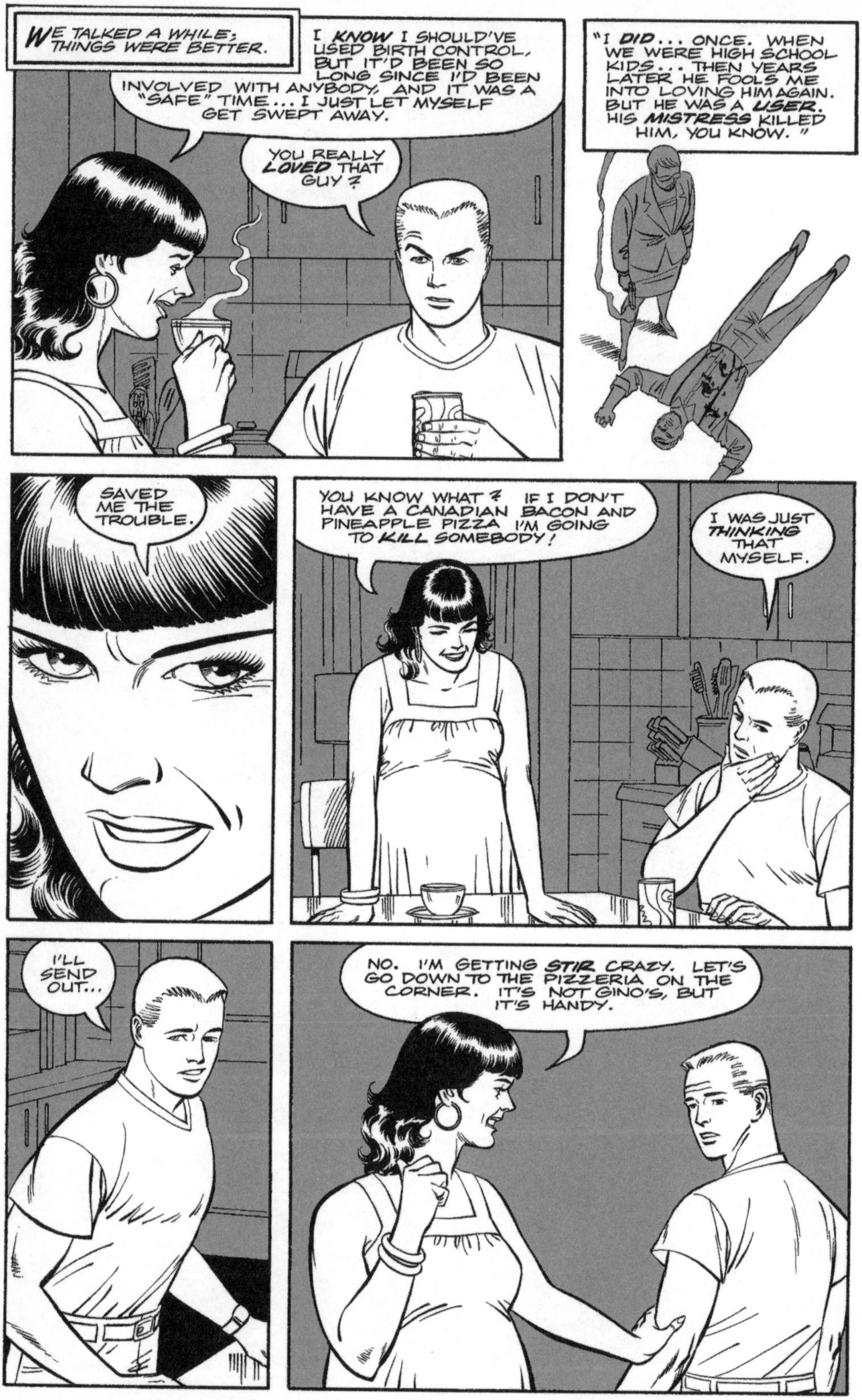
WE TALKED A WHILE; THINGS WERE BETTER.
I KNOW I SHOULD'VE USED BIRTH CONTROL, BUT IT'D BEEN SO LONG SINCE I'D BEEN INVOLVED WITH ANYBODY, AND IT WAS A "SAFE" TIME... I JUST LET MYSELF GET SWEPT AWAY.
YOU REALLY LOVED THAT GUY ?
"I DID... ONCE. WHEN WE WERE HIGH SCHOOL KIDS... THEN YEARS LATER HE FOOLS ME INTO LOVING HIM AGAIN. BUT HE WAS A USER. HIS MISTRESS KILLED HIM, YOU KNOW."
SAVED ME THE TROUBLE.
YOU KNOW WHAT ? IF I DON'T HAVE A CANADIAN BACON AND PINEAPPLE PIZZA I'M GOING TO KILL SOMEBODY!
I WAS JUST THINKING THAT MYSELF.
I'LL SEND OUT...
NO. I'M GETTING STIR CRAZY. LET'S GO DOWN TO THE PIZZERIA ON THE CORNER. IT'S NOT GINO'S, BUT IT'S HANDY.

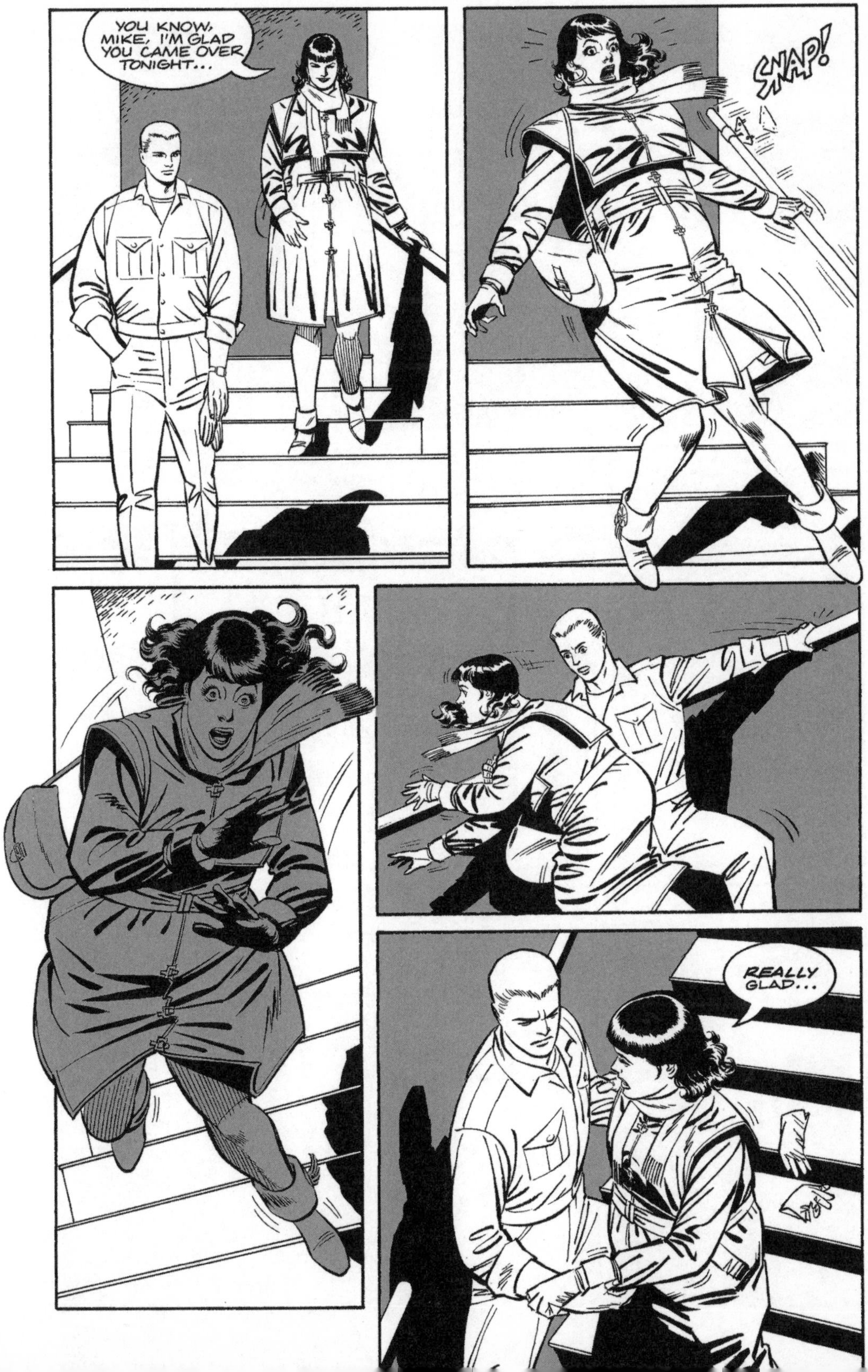
YOU KNOW, MIKE, I'M GLAD YOU CAME OVER TONIGHT...
SNAP!
REALLY GLAD...

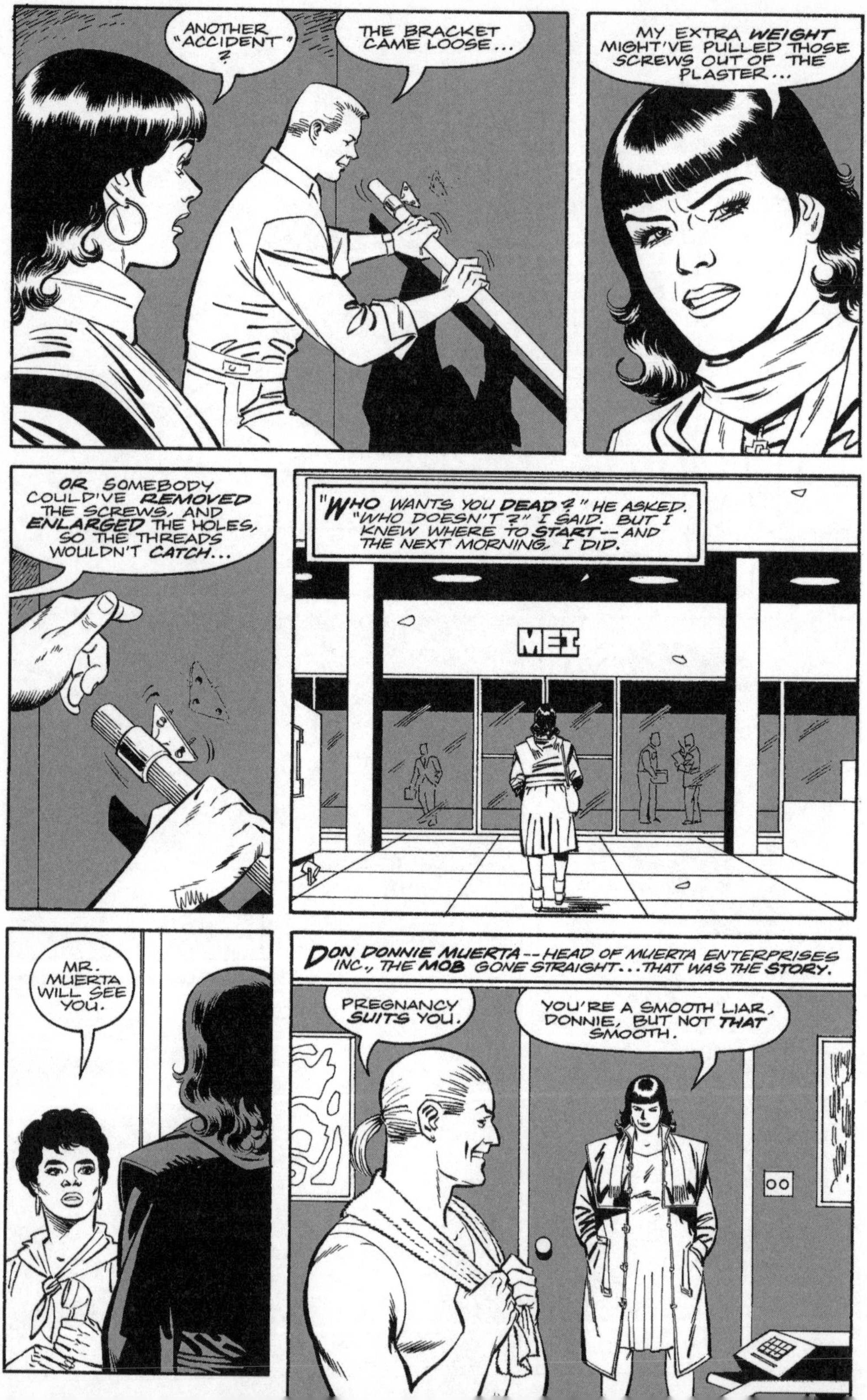
ANOTHER "ACCIDENT"?
THE BRACKET CAME LOOSE...
MY EXTRA WEIGHT MIGHT'VE PULLED THOSE SCREWS OUT OF THE PLASTER...
OR SOMEBODY COULD'VE REMOVED THE SCREWS, AND ENLARGED THE HOLES, SO THE THREADS WOULDN'T CATCH...
"WHO WANTS YOU DEAD?" HE ASKED. "WHO DOESN'T?" I SAID. BUT I KNEW WHERE TO START-- AND THE NEXT MORNING, I DID.
MEI
MR. MUERTA WILL SEE YOU.
DON DONNIE MUERTA--HEAD OF MUERTA ENTERPRISES INC., THE MOB GONE STRAIGHT...THAT WAS THE STORY.
PREGNANCY SUITS YOU.
YOU'RE A SMOOTH LIAR, DONNIE, BUT NOT THAT SMOOTH.

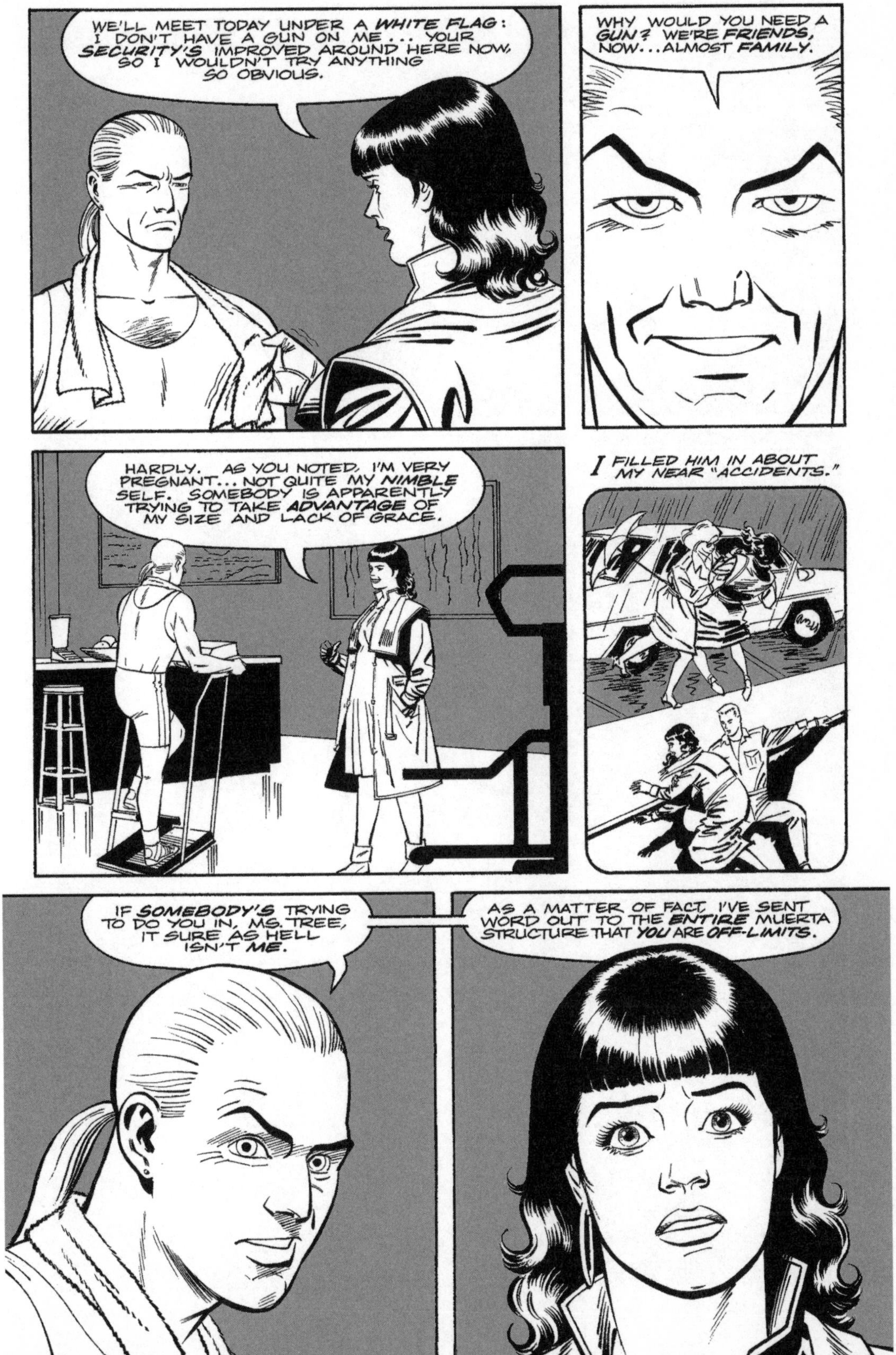
WE'LL MEET TODAY UNDER A WHITE FLAG: I DON'T HAVE A GUN ON ME... YOUR SECURITY'S IMPROVED AROUND HERE NOW, SO I WOULDN'T TRY ANYTHING SO OBVIOUS.
WHY WOULD YOU NEED A GUN? WE'RE FRIENDS, NOW... ALMOST FAMILY.
HARDLY. AS YOU NOTED, I'M VERY PREGNANT... NOT QUITE MY NIMBLE SELF. SOMEBODY IS APPARENTLY TRYING TO TAKE ADVANTAGE OF MY SIZE AND LACK OF GRACE.
I FILLED HIM IN ABOUT MY NEAR "ACCIDENTS."
IF SOMEBODY'S TRYING TO DO YOU IN, MS. TREE, IT SURE AS HELL ISN'T ME.
AS A MATTER OF FACT, I'VE SENT WORD OUT TO THE ENTIRE MUERTA STRUCTURE THAT YOU ARE OFF-LIMITS.

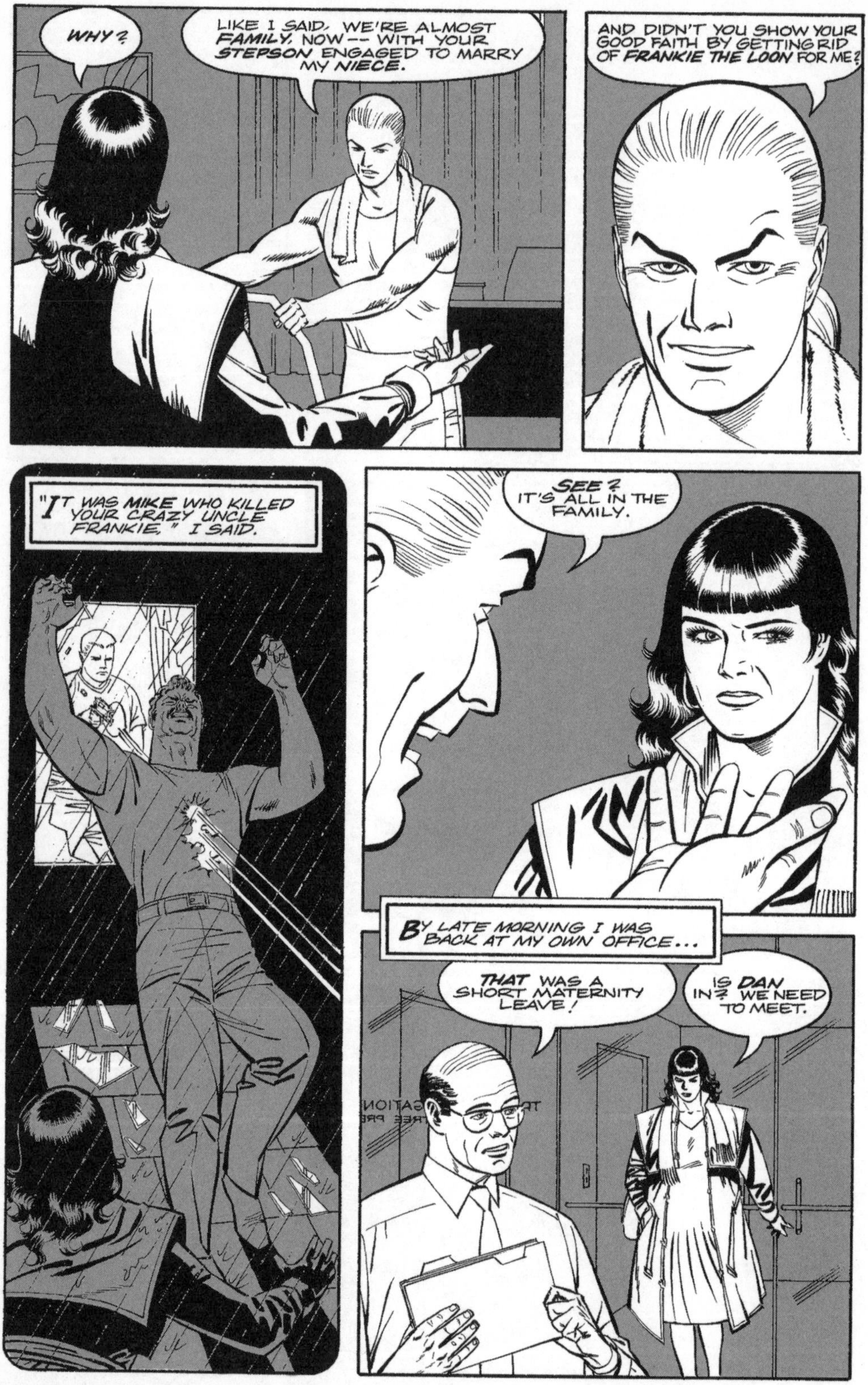
WHY?
LIKE I SAID, WE'RE ALMOST FAMILY, NOW -- WITH YOUR STEPSON ENGAGED TO MARRY MY NIECE.
AND DIDN'T YOU SHOW YOUR GOOD FAITH BY GETTING RID OF FRANKIE THE LOON FOR ME?
"IT WAS MIKE WHO KILLED YOUR CRAZY UNCLE FRANKIE," I SAID.
SEE? IT'S ALL IN THE FAMILY.
BY LATE MORNING I WAS BACK AT MY OWN OFFICE...
THAT WAS A SHORT MATERNITY LEAVE!
IS DAN IN? WE NEED TO MEET.

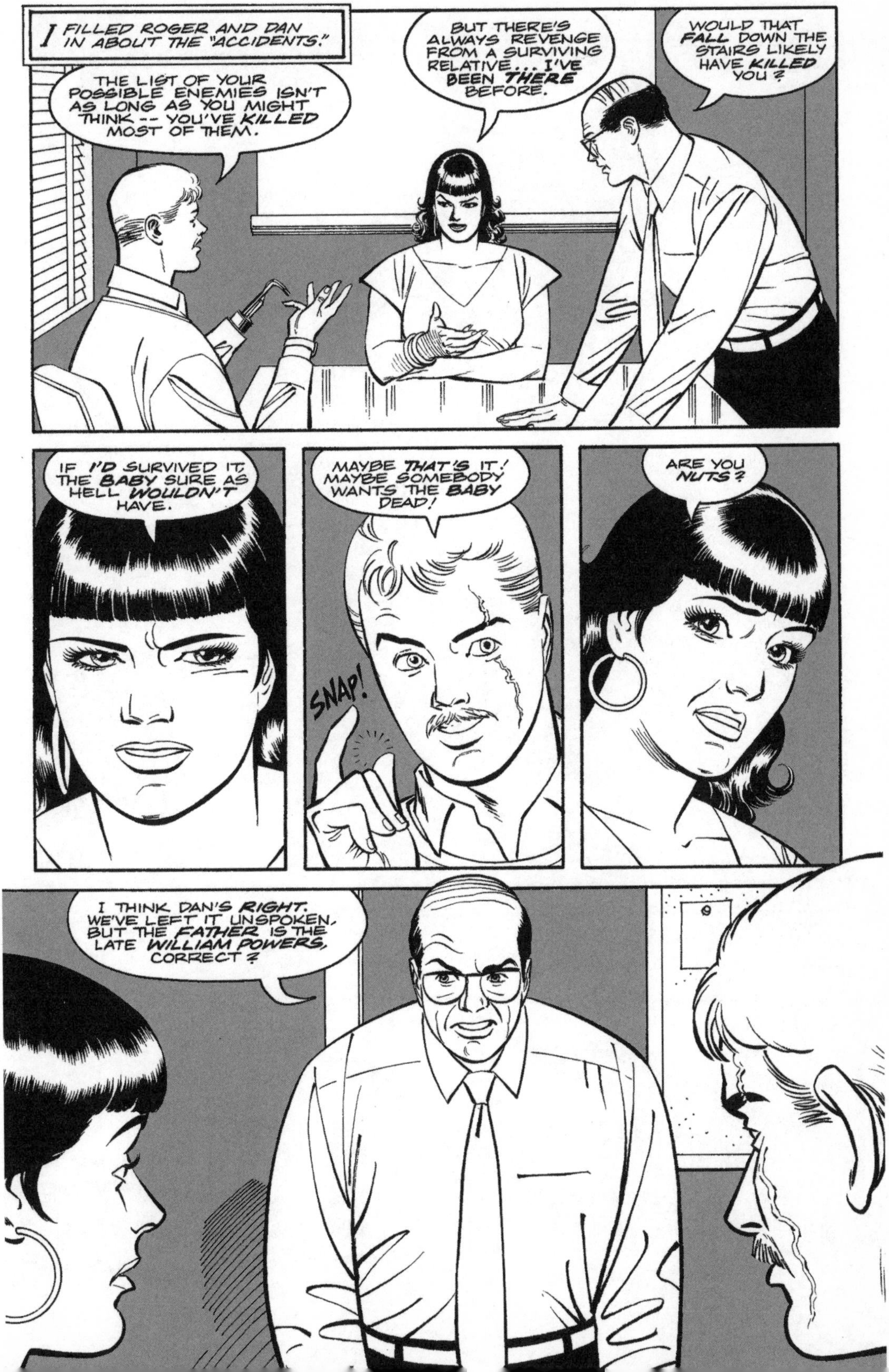
I FILLED ROGER AND DAN IN ABOUT THE "ACCIDENTS."
THE LIST OF YOUR POSSIBLE ENEMIES ISN'T AS LONG AS YOU MIGHT THINK -- YOU'VE KILLED MOST OF THEM.
BUT THERE'S ALWAYS REVENGE FROM A SURVIVING RELATIVE... I'VE BEEN THERE BEFORE.
WOULD THAT FALL DOWN THE STAIRS LIKELY HAVE KILLED YOU?
IF I'D SURVIVED IT, THE BABY SURE AS HELL WOULDN'T HAVE.
MAYBE THAT'S IT! MAYBE SOMEBODY WANTS THE BABY DEAD!
SNAP!
ARE YOU NUTS?
I THINK DAN'S RIGHT. WE'VE LEFT IT UNSPOKEN, BUT THE FATHER IS THE LATE WILLIAM POWERS, CORRECT?

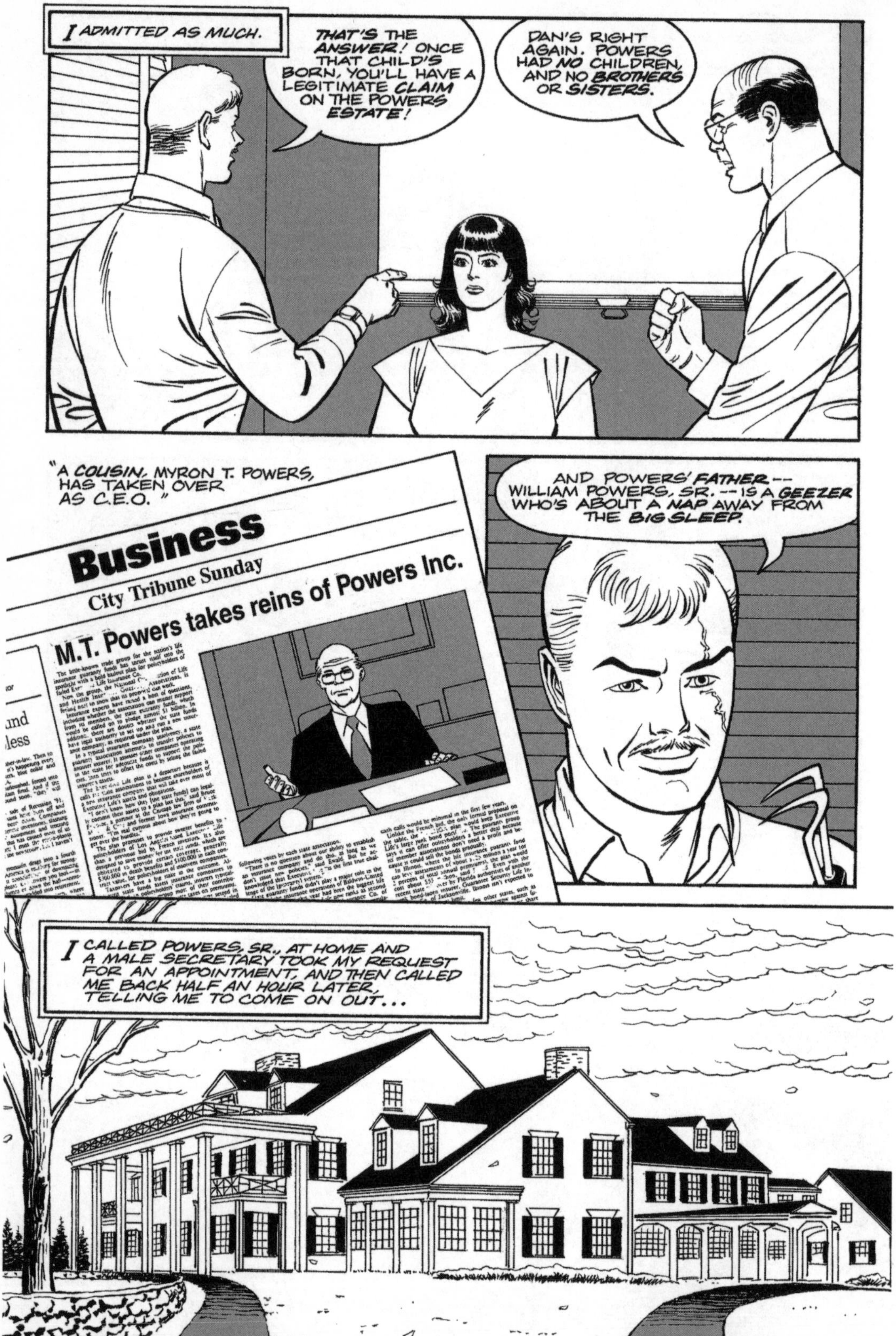
I ADMITTED AS MUCH.
THAT'S THE ANSWER! ONCE THAT CHILD'S BORN, YOU'LL HAVE A LEGITIMATE CLAIM ON THE POWERS ESTATE!
DAN'S RIGHT AGAIN. POWERS HAD NO CHILDREN, AND NO BROTHERS OR SISTERS.
"A COUSIN, MYRON T. POWERS, HAS TAKEN OVER AS C.E.O."
Business
City Tribune Sunday
M.T. Powers takes reins of Powers Inc.
AND POWERS' FATHER -- WILLIAM POWERS, SR. -- IS A GEEZER WHO'S ABOUT A NAP AWAY FROM THE BIG SLEEP.
I CALLED POWERS, SR., AT HOME AND A MALE SECRETARY TOOK MY REQUEST FOR AN APPOINTMENT, AND THEN CALLED ME BACK HALF AN HOUR LATER, TELLING ME TO COME ON OUT...

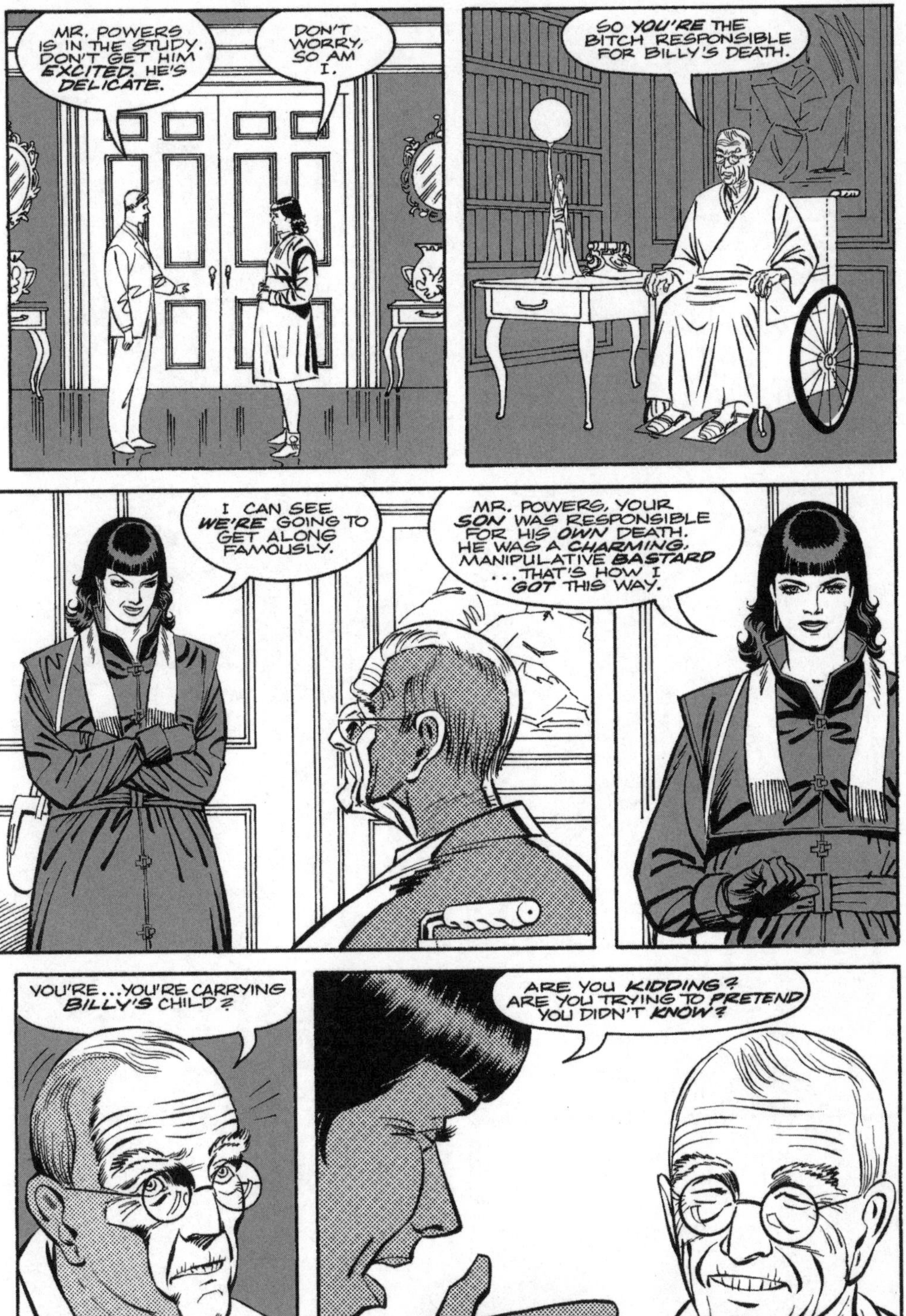
MR. POWERS IS IN THE STUDY. DON'T GET HIM EXCITED. HE'S DELICATE.
DON'T WORRY, SO AM I.
SO YOU'RE THE BITCH RESPONSIBLE FOR BILLY'S DEATH.
I CAN SEE WE'RE GOING TO GET ALONG FAMOUSLY.
MR. POWERS, YOUR SON WAS RESPONSIBLE FOR HIS OWN DEATH. HE WAS A CHARMING, MANIPULATIVE BASTARD ...THAT'S HOW I GOT THIS WAY.
YOU'RE...YOU'RE CARRYING BILLY'S CHILD?
ARE YOU KIDDING? ARE YOU TRYING TO PRETEND YOU DIDN'T KNOW?

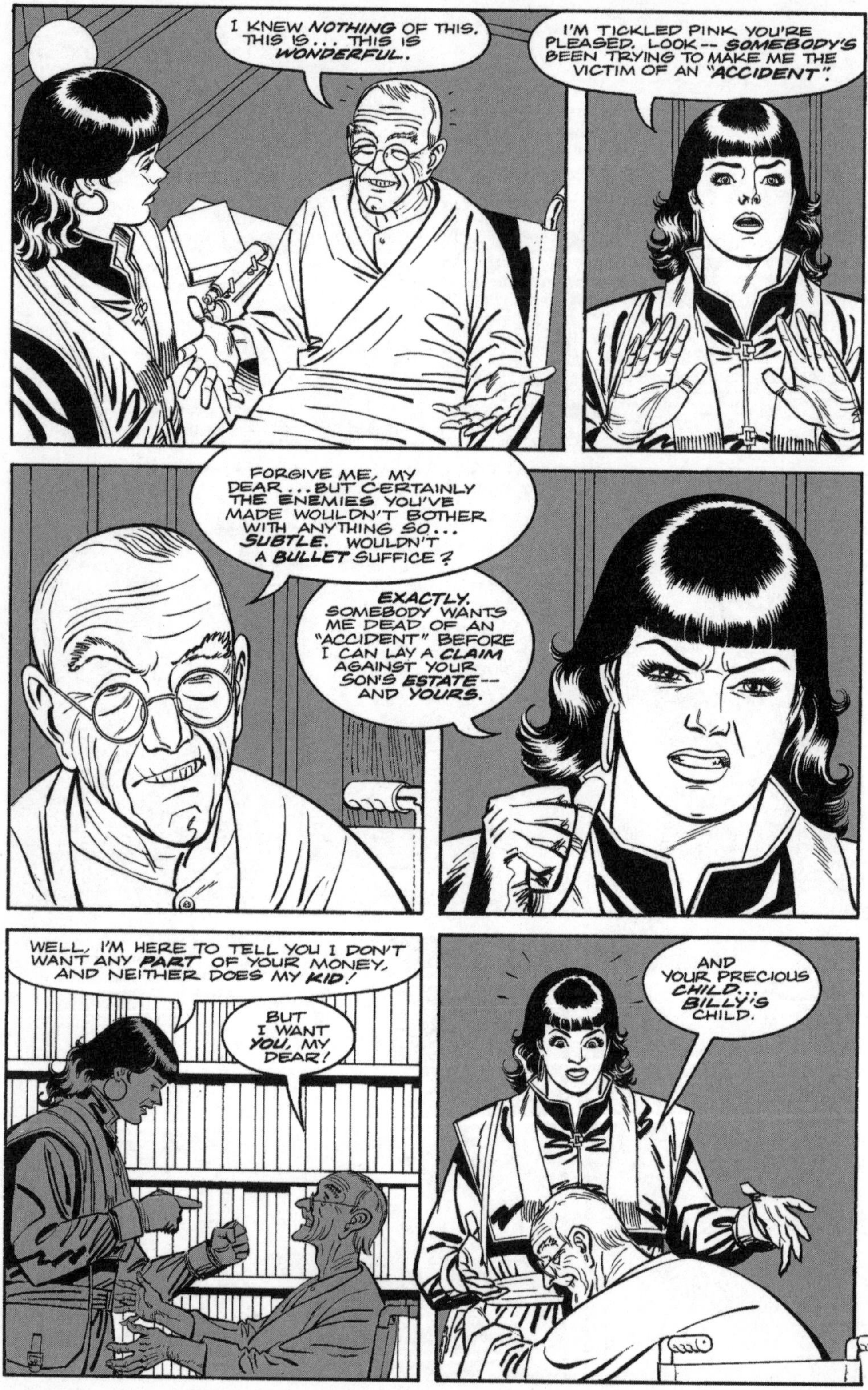
I KNEW NOTHING OF THIS. THIS IS... THIS IS WONDERFUL.
I'M TICKLED PINK YOU'RE PLEASED. LOOK-- SOMEBODY'S BEEN TRYING TO MAKE ME THE VICTIM OF AN "ACCIDENT".
FORGIVE ME, MY DEAR...BUT CERTAINLY THE ENEMIES YOU'VE MADE WOULDN'T BOTHER WITH ANYTHING SO... SUBTLE. WOULDN'T A BULLET SUFFICE?
EXACTLY. SOMEBODY WANTS ME DEAD OF AN "ACCIDENT" BEFORE I CAN LAY A CLAIM AGAINST YOUR SON'S ESTATE-- AND YOURS.
WELL, I'M HERE TO TELL YOU I DON'T WANT ANY PART OF YOUR MONEY, AND NEITHER DOES MY KID!
BUT I WANT YOU, MY DEAR!
AND YOUR PRECIOUS CHILD... BILLY'S CHILD.

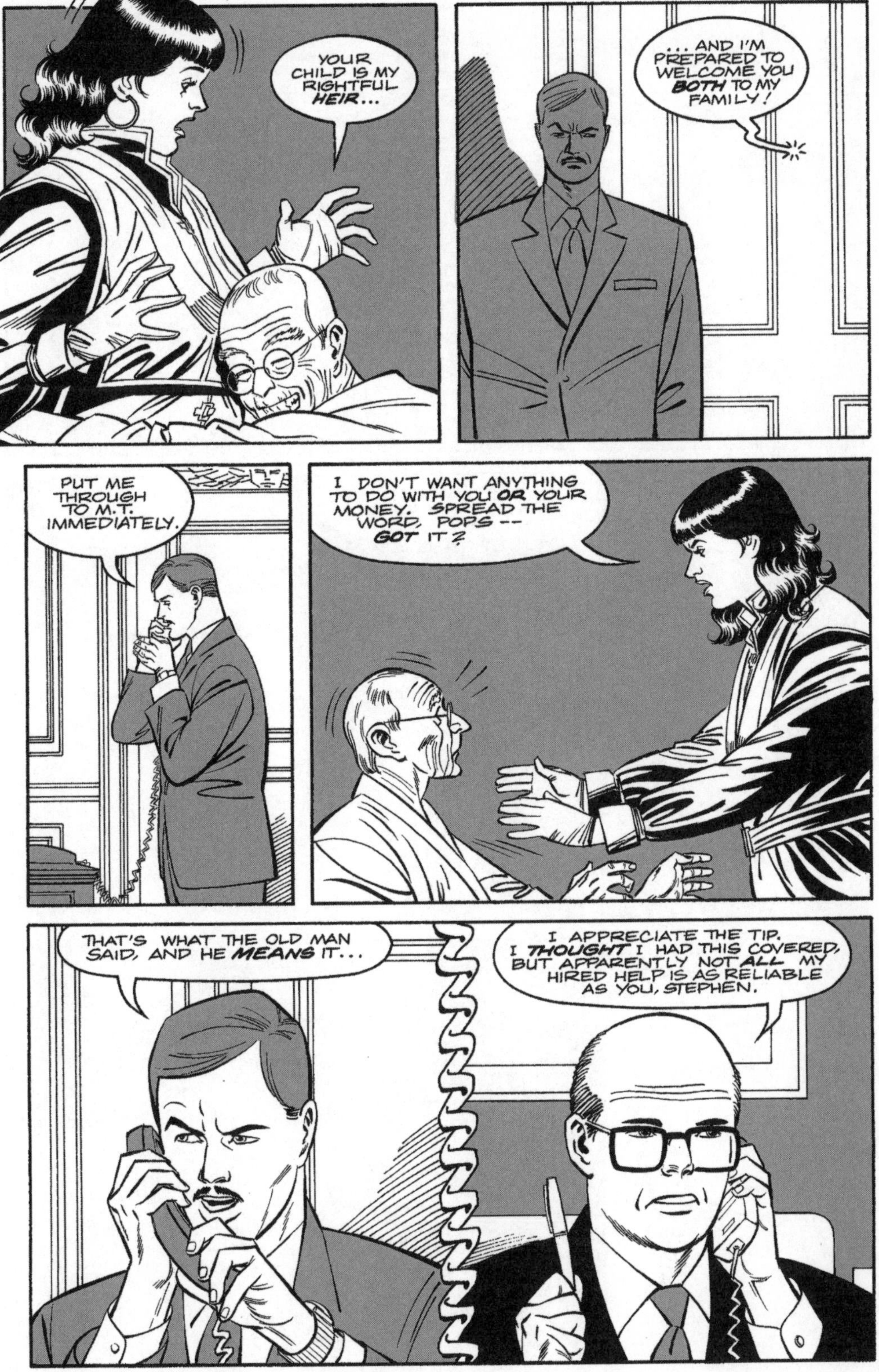
YOUR CHILD IS MY RIGHTFUL *HEIR*...
... AND I'M PREPARED TO WELCOME YOU *BOTH* TO MY FAMILY!
PUT ME THROUGH TO M.T. IMMEDIATELY.
I DON'T WANT ANYTHING TO DO WITH YOU *OR* YOUR MONEY. SPREAD THE WORD, POPS -- *GOT* IT?
THAT'S WHAT THE OLD MAN SAID, AND HE *MEANS* IT...
I APPRECIATE THE TIP. I *THOUGHT* I HAD THIS COVERED, BUT APPARENTLY NOT *ALL* MY HIRED HELP IS AS RELIABLE AS YOU, STEPHEN.

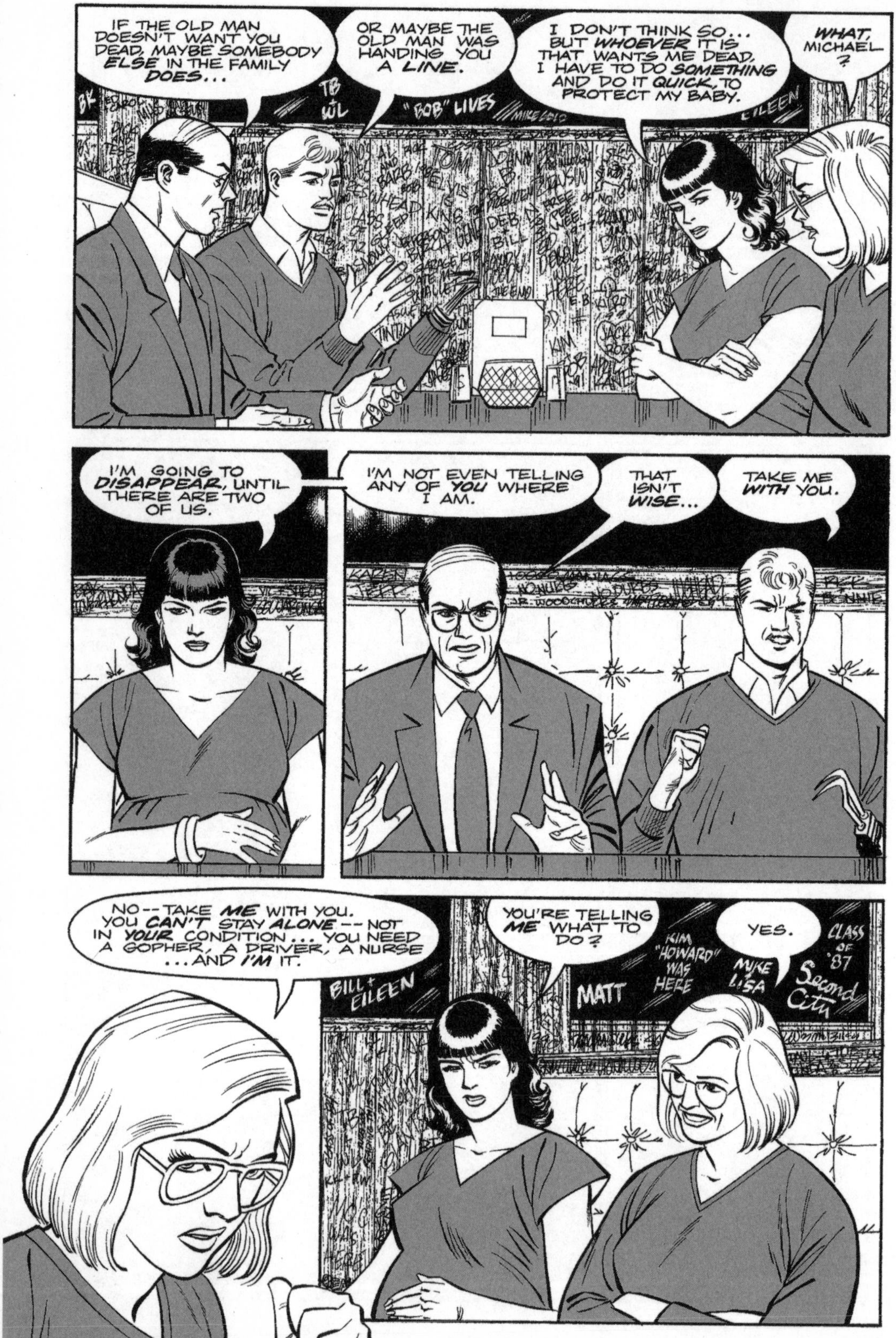
IF THE OLD MAN DOESN'T WANT YOU DEAD, MAYBE SOMEBODY ELSE IN THE FAMILY DOES...
OR MAYBE THE OLD MAN WAS HANDING YOU A LINE.
I DON'T THINK SO... BUT WHOEVER IT IS THAT WANTS ME DEAD, I HAVE TO DO SOMETHING AND DO IT QUICK, TO PROTECT MY BABY.
WHAT, MICHAEL?
"BOB" LIVES
EILEEN
I'M GOING TO DISAPPEAR, UNTIL THERE ARE TWO OF US.
I'M NOT EVEN TELLING ANY OF YOU WHERE I AM.
THAT ISN'T WISE...
TAKE ME WITH YOU.
NO--TAKE ME WITH YOU. YOU CAN'T STAY ALONE--NOT IN YOUR CONDITION... YOU NEED A GOPHER, A DRIVER, A NURSE ...AND I'M IT.
YOU'RE TELLING ME WHAT TO DO?
YES.
BILL + EILEEN
MATT
KIM "HOWARD" WAS HERE
MIKE LISA
CLASS OF '87
Second City

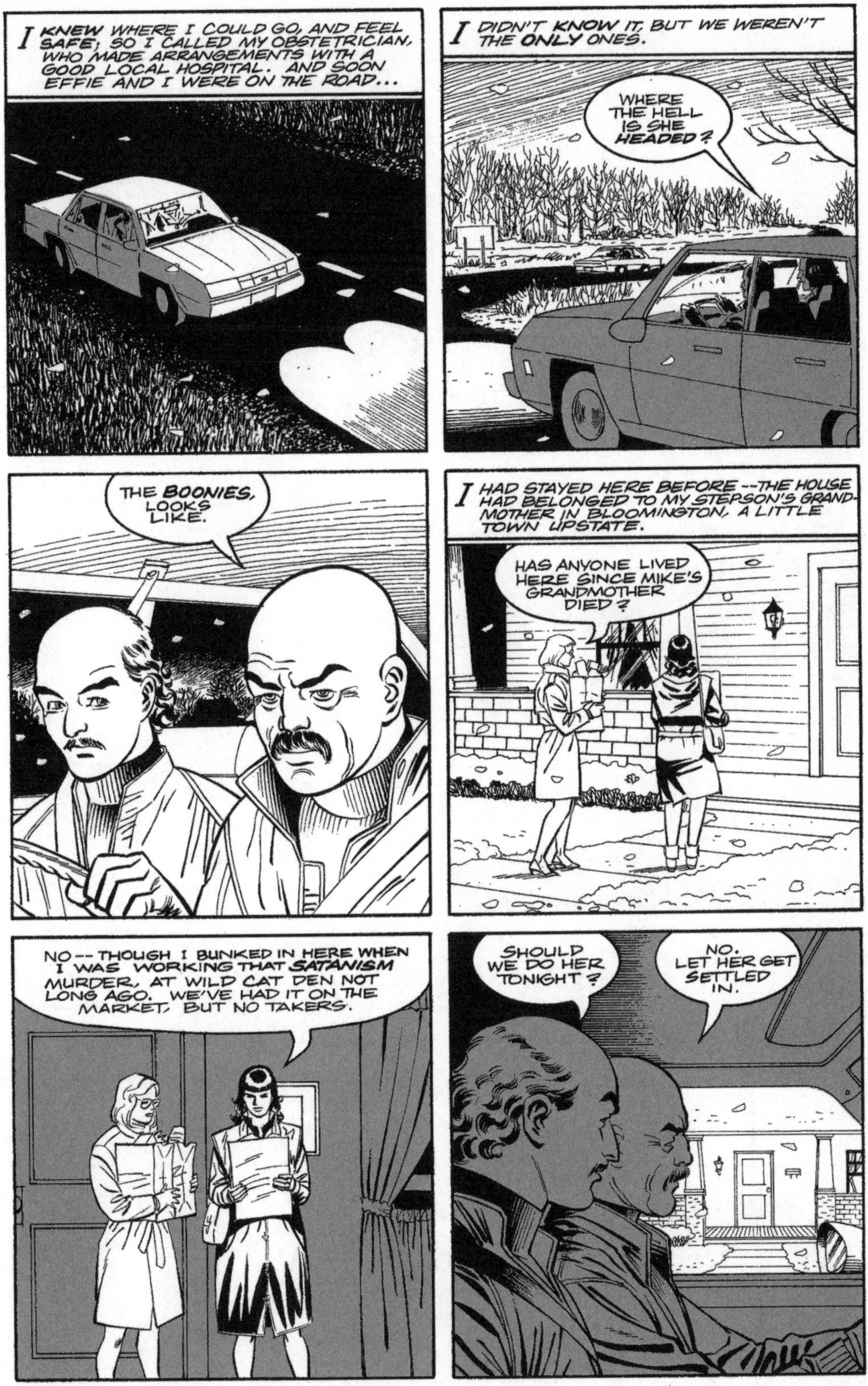
I KNEW WHERE I COULD GO, AND FEEL SAFE; SO I CALLED MY OBSTETRICIAN, WHO MADE ARRANGEMENTS WITH A GOOD LOCAL HOSPITAL. AND SOON EFFIE AND I WERE ON THE ROAD...
I DIDN'T KNOW IT, BUT WE WEREN'T THE ONLY ONES.
WHERE THE HELL IS SHE HEADED?
THE BOONIES, LOOKS LIKE.
I HAD STAYED HERE BEFORE--THE HOUSE HAD BELONGED TO MY STEPSON'S GRANDMOTHER IN BLOOMINGTON, A LITTLE TOWN UPSTATE.
HAS ANYONE LIVED HERE SINCE MIKE'S GRANDMOTHER DIED?
NO--THOUGH I BUNKED IN HERE WHEN I WAS WORKING THAT SATANISM MURDER, AT WILD CAT DEN NOT LONG AGO. WE'VE HAD IT ON THE MARKET, BUT NO TAKERS.
SHOULD WE DO HER TONIGHT?
NO. LET HER GET SETTLED IN.

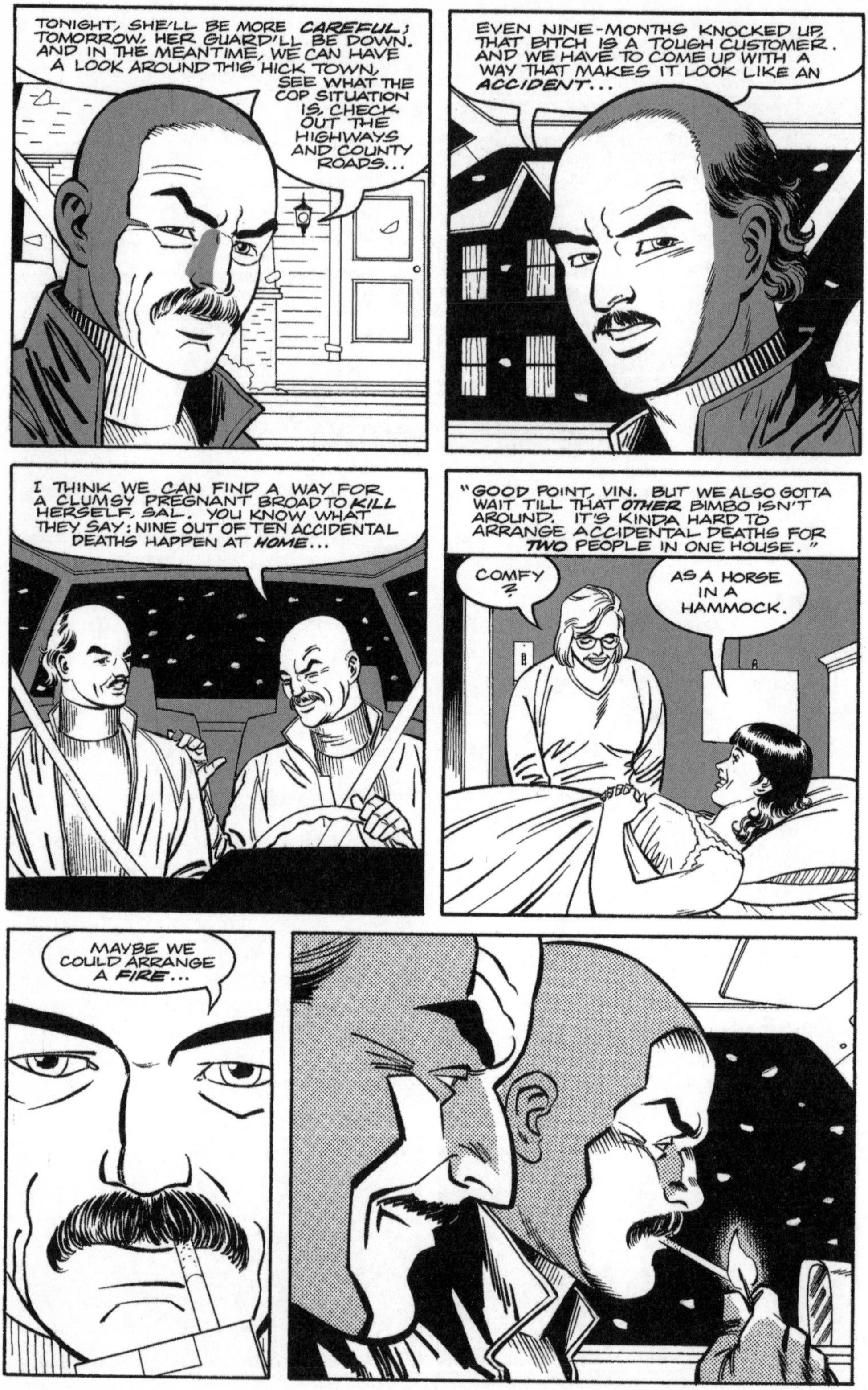
TONIGHT, SHE'LL BE MORE CAREFUL; TOMORROW, HER GUARD'LL BE DOWN. AND IN THE MEANTIME, WE CAN HAVE A LOOK AROUND THIS HICK TOWN, SEE WHAT THE COP SITUATION IS, CHECK OUT THE HIGHWAYS AND COUNTY ROADS...
EVEN NINE-MONTHS KNOCKED UP, THAT BITCH IS A TOUGH CUSTOMER. AND WE HAVE TO COME UP WITH A WAY THAT MAKES IT LOOK LIKE AN ACCIDENT...
I THINK WE CAN FIND A WAY FOR A CLUMSY PREGNANT BROAD TO KILL HERSELF, SAL. YOU KNOW WHAT THEY SAY: NINE OUT OF TEN ACCIDENTAL DEATHS HAPPEN AT HOME...
"GOOD POINT, VIN. BUT WE ALSO GOTTA WAIT TILL THAT OTHER BIMBO ISN'T AROUND. IT'S KINDA HARD TO ARRANGE ACCIDENTAL DEATHS FOR TWO PEOPLE IN ONE HOUSE."
COMFY?
AS A HORSE IN A HAMMOCK.
MAYBE WE COULD ARRANGE A FIRE...

BEAUTIFUL DAY OUT THERE... A LITTLE OVERCAST, THOUGH.

"MICHAEL," EFFIE SAID, "WHY DON'T WE BUNDLE UP AND TAKE A WALK AND GET SOME FRESH AIR?"

I DON'T WANT TO ATTRACT ANY ATTENTION. IS THIS DECAF?

YES.

DAMN.

KNOK! KNOK!

WHAT'S THAT?

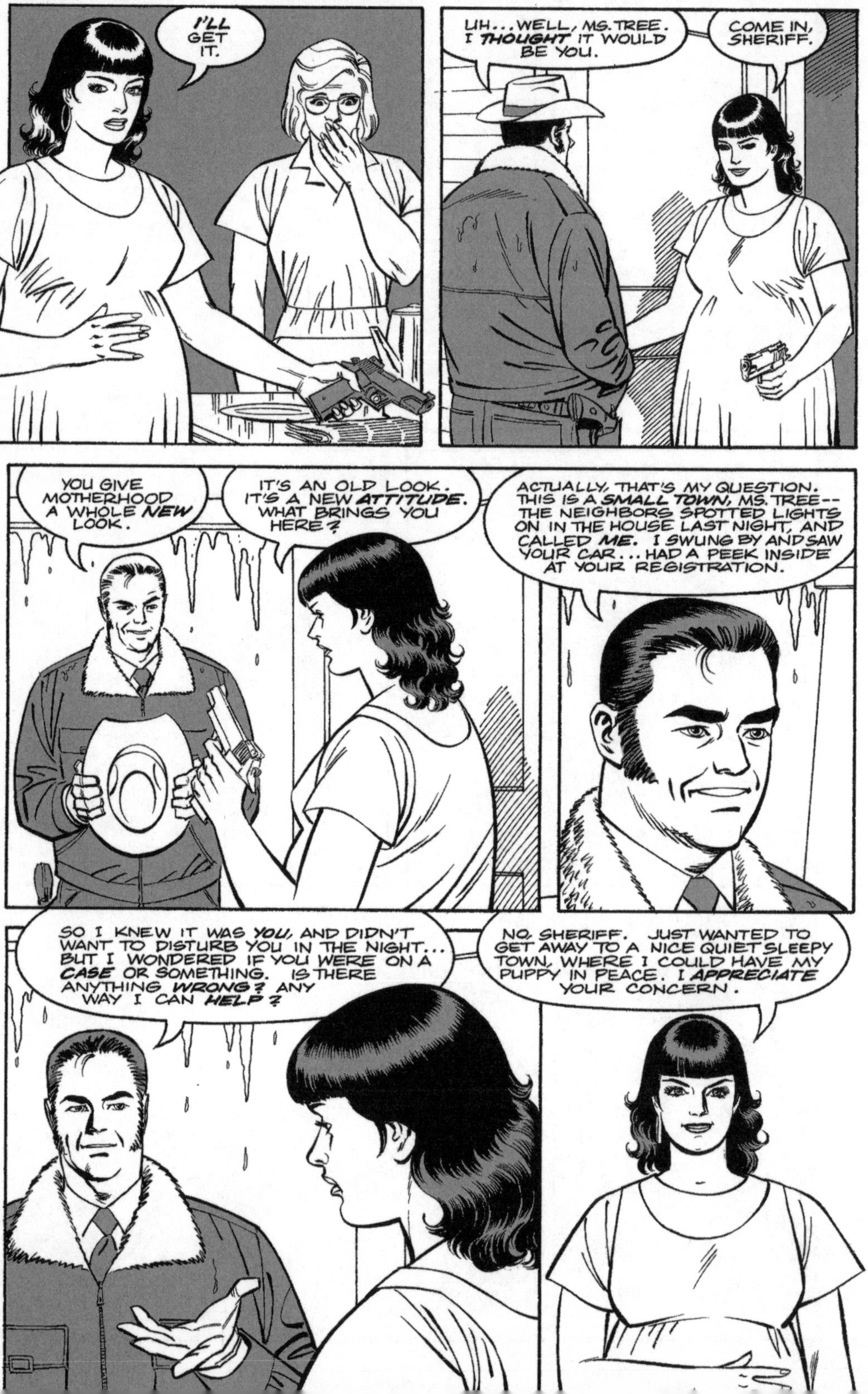
I'LL GET IT.
UH...WELL, MS. TREE. I THOUGHT IT WOULD BE YOU.
COME IN, SHERIFF.
YOU GIVE MOTHERHOOD A WHOLE NEW LOOK.
IT'S AN OLD LOOK. IT'S A NEW ATTITUDE. WHAT BRINGS YOU HERE?
ACTUALLY, THAT'S MY QUESTION. THIS IS A SMALL TOWN, MS. TREE-- THE NEIGHBORS SPOTTED LIGHTS ON IN THE HOUSE LAST NIGHT, AND CALLED ME. I SWUNG BY AND SAW YOUR CAR... HAD A PEEK INSIDE AT YOUR REGISTRATION.
SO I KNEW IT WAS YOU, AND DIDN'T WANT TO DISTURB YOU IN THE NIGHT... BUT I WONDERED IF YOU WERE ON A CASE OR SOMETHING. IS THERE ANYTHING WRONG? ANY WAY I CAN HELP?
NO, SHERIFF. JUST WANTED TO GET AWAY TO A NICE QUIET SLEEPY TOWN, WHERE I COULD HAVE MY PUPPY IN PEACE. I APPRECIATE YOUR CONCERN.

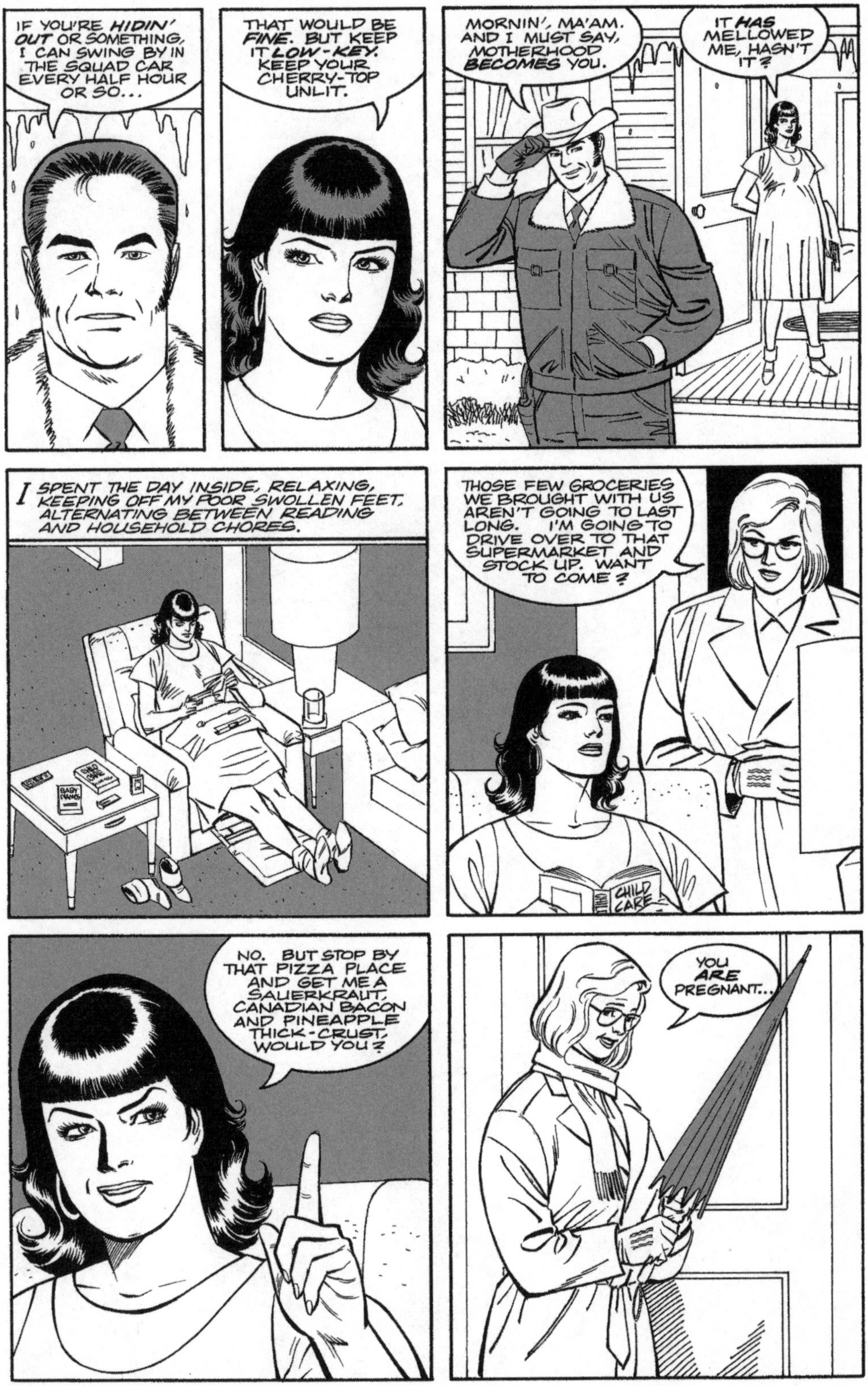
IF YOU'RE HIDIN' OUT OR SOMETHING, I CAN SWING BY IN THE SQUAD CAR EVERY HALF HOUR OR SO...
THAT WOULD BE FINE. BUT KEEP IT LOW-KEY. KEEP YOUR CHERRY-TOP UNLIT.
MORNIN', MA'AM. AND I MUST SAY, MOTHERHOOD BECOMES YOU.
IT HAS MELLOWED ME, HASN'T IT?
I SPENT THE DAY INSIDE, RELAXING, KEEPING OFF MY POOR SWOLLEN FEET, ALTERNATING BETWEEN READING AND HOUSEHOLD CHORES.
BABY NAMES
CHILD CARE
THOSE FEW GROCERIES WE BROUGHT WITH US AREN'T GOING TO LAST LONG. I'M GOING TO DRIVE OVER TO THAT SUPERMARKET AND STOCK UP. WANT TO COME?
CHILD CARE
NO. BUT STOP BY THAT PIZZA PLACE AND GET ME A SAUERKRAUT, CANADIAN BACON AND PINEAPPLE THICK-CRUST, WOULD YOU?
YOU ARE PREGNANT...

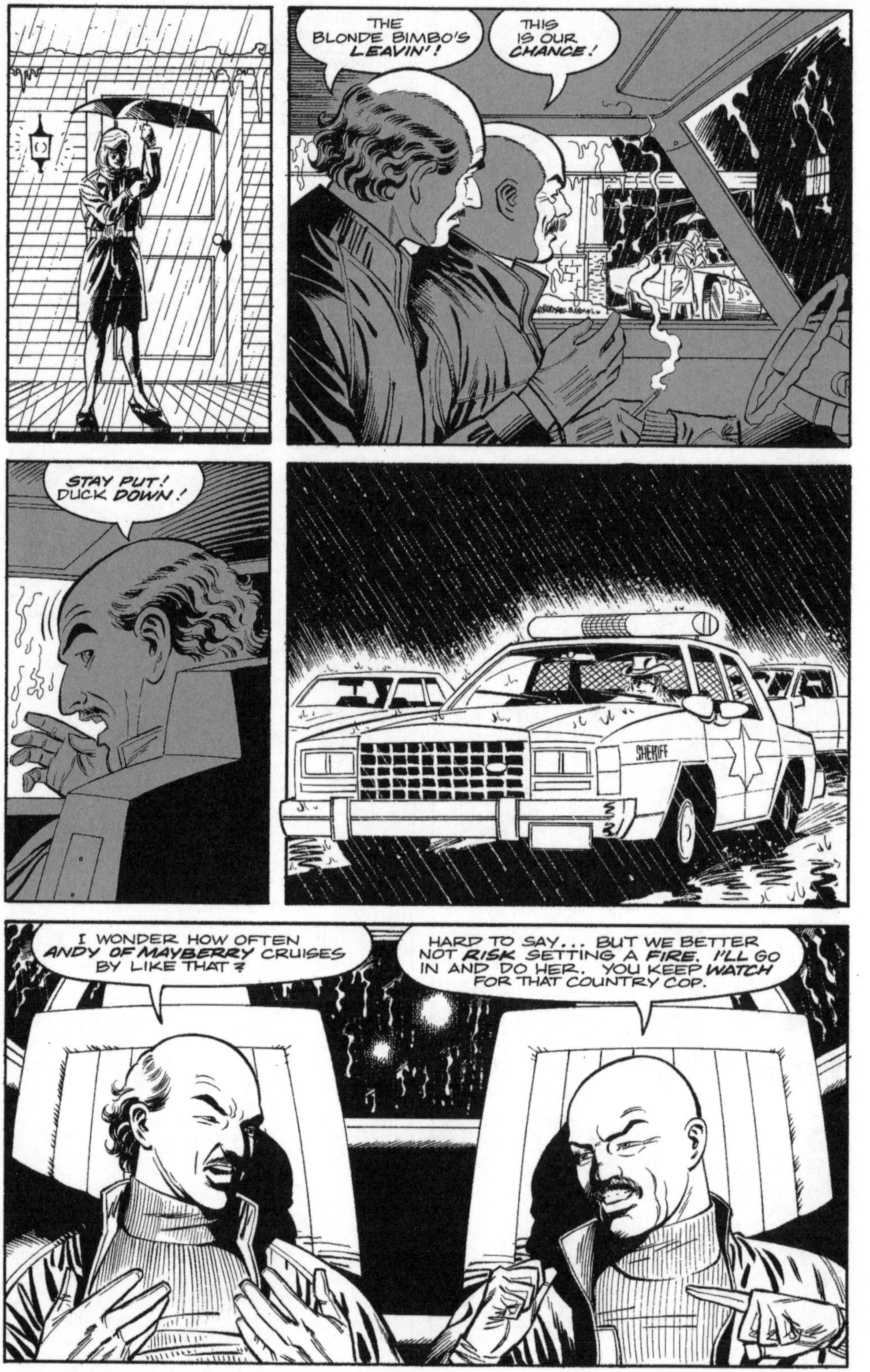
THE BLONDE BIMBO'S LEAVIN'!
THIS IS OUR CHANCE!
STAY PUT! DUCK DOWN!
SHERIFF
I WONDER HOW OFTEN ANDY OF MAYBERRY CRUISES BY LIKE THAT?
HARD TO SAY... BUT WE BETTER NOT RISK SETTING A FIRE. I'LL GO IN AND DO HER. YOU KEEP WATCH FOR THAT COUNTRY COP.

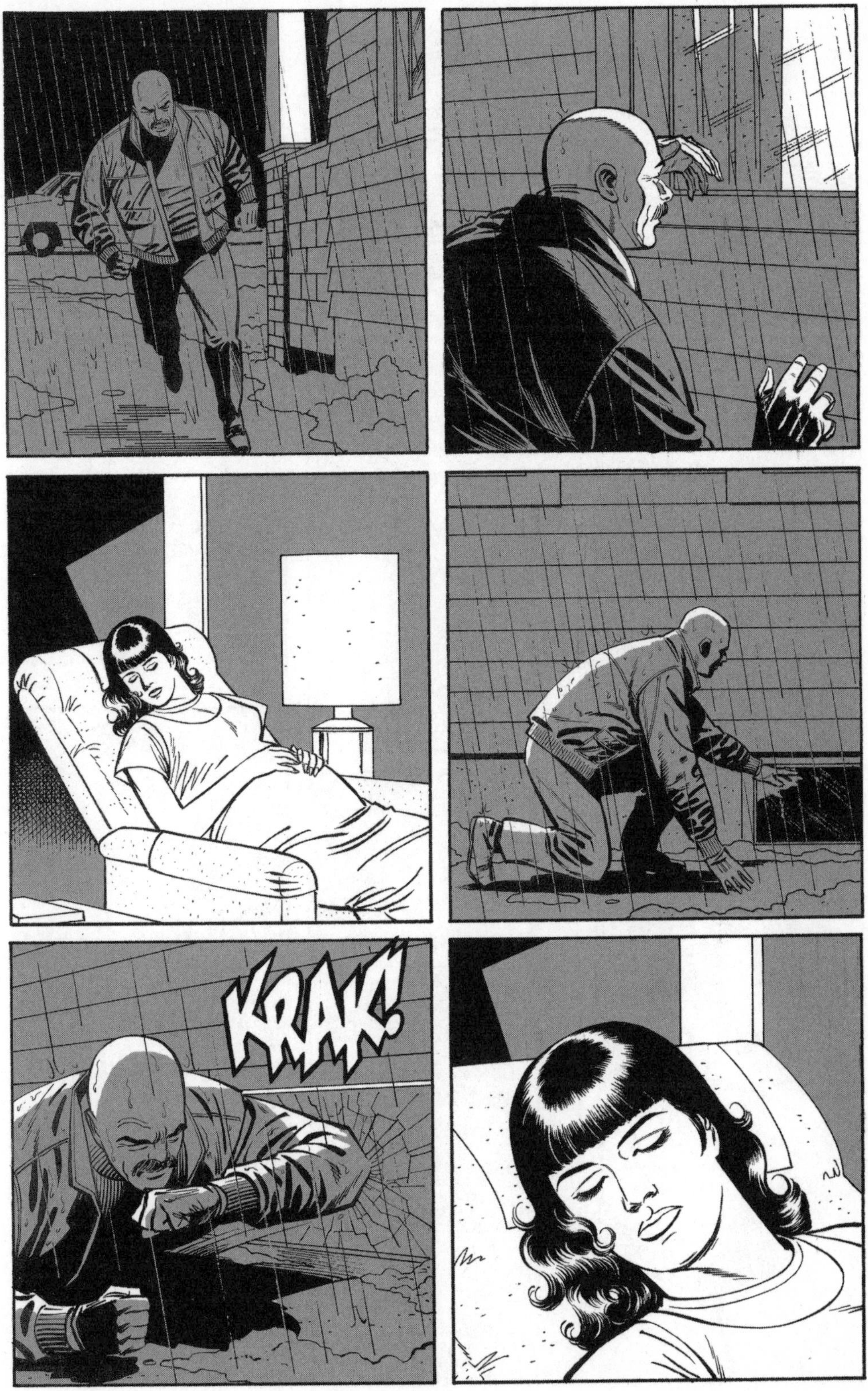
KRAK!

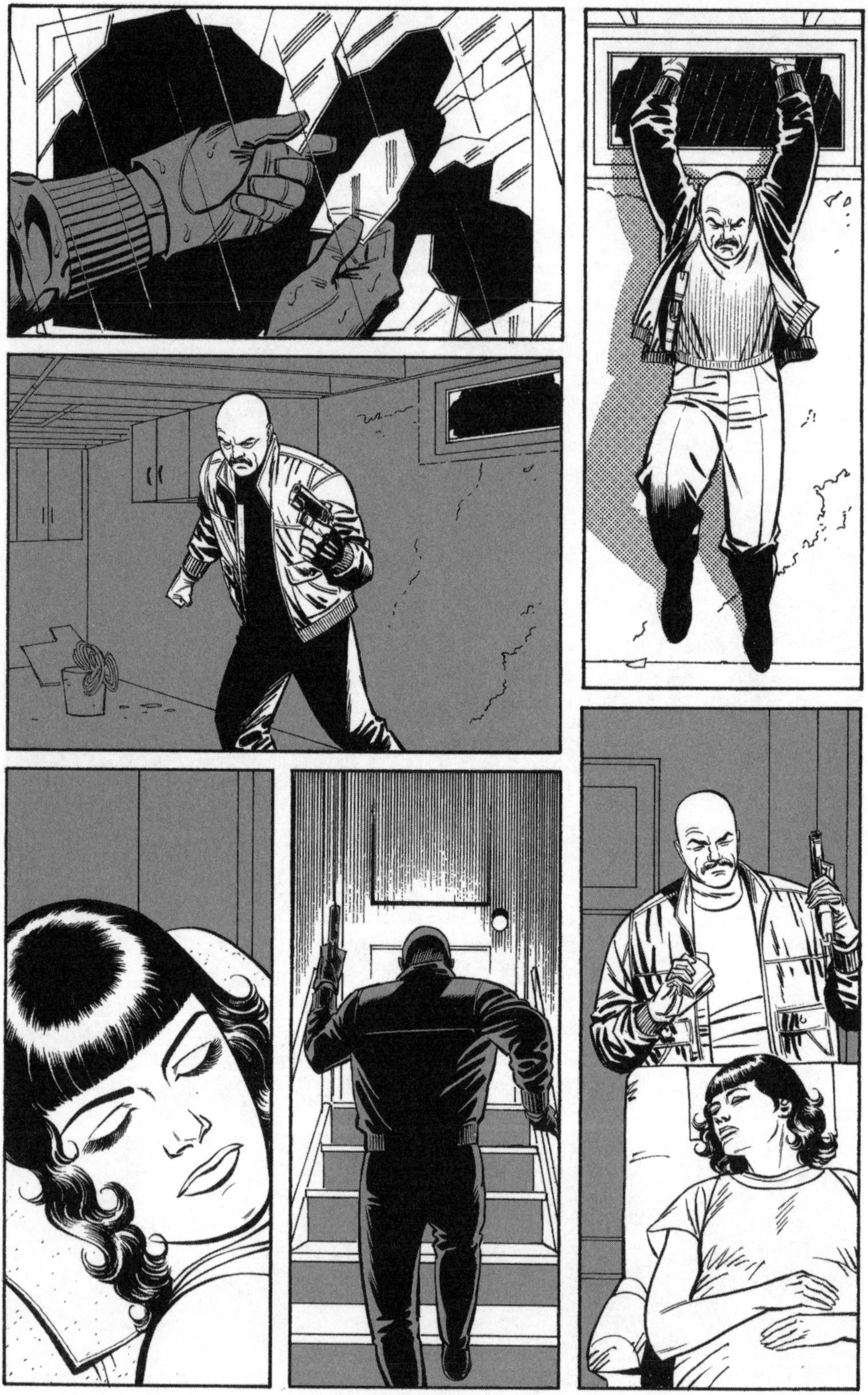

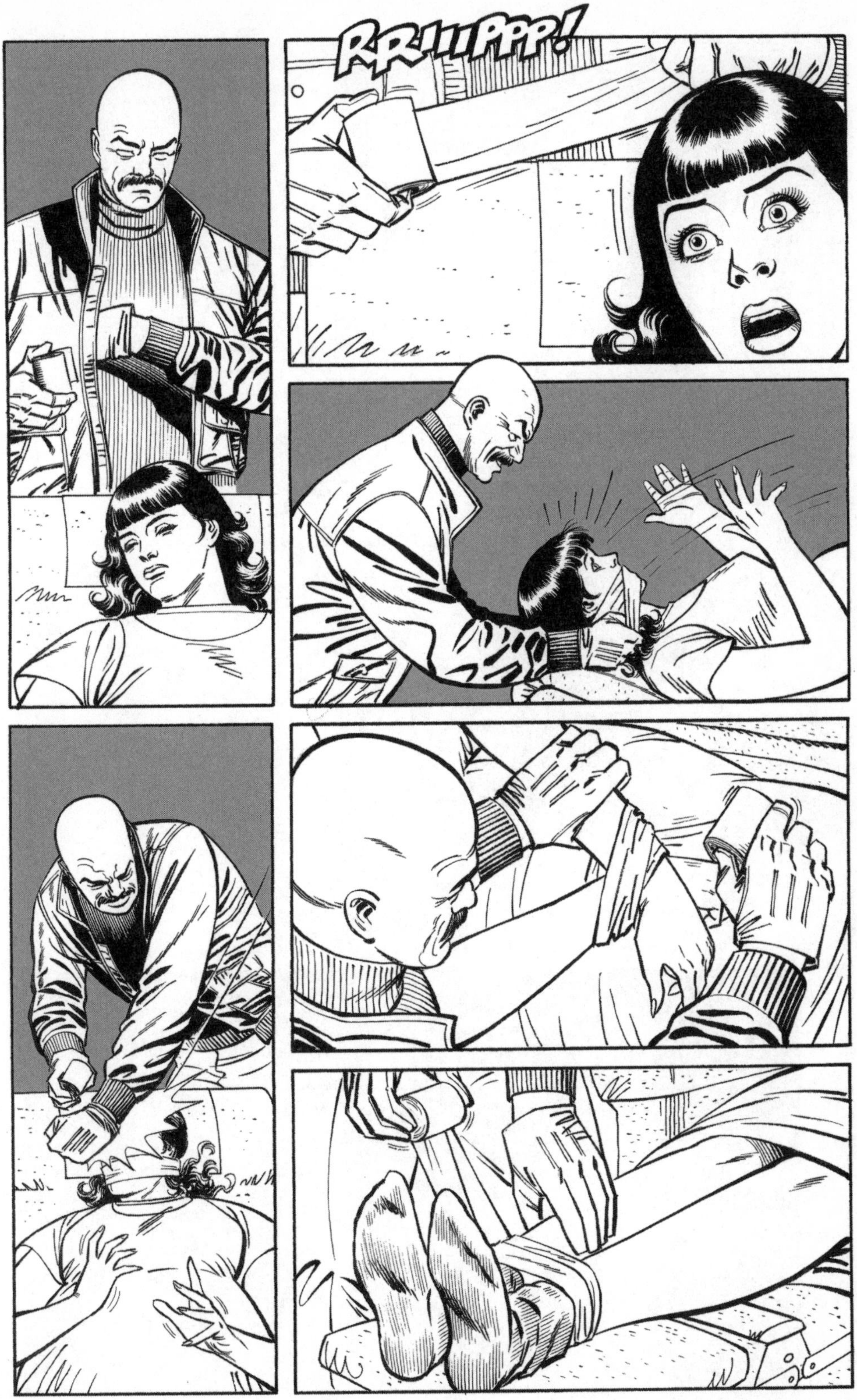
RRIIIPPP!

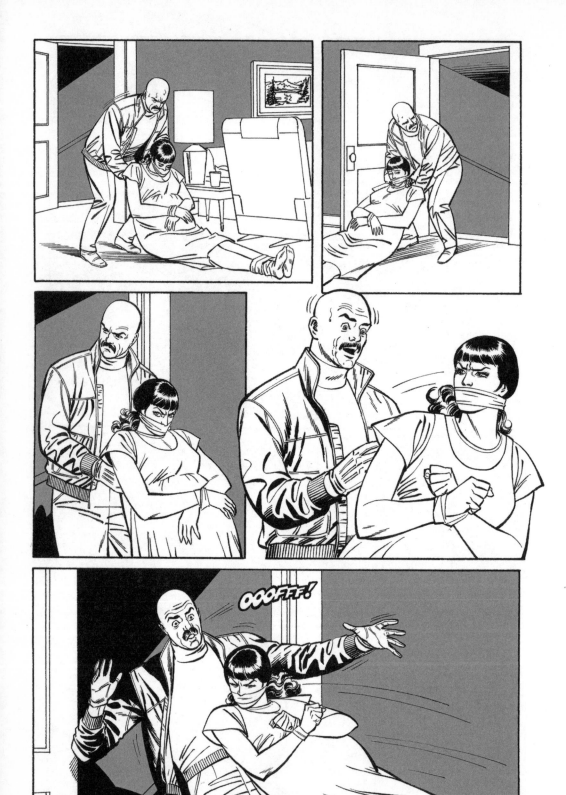

OOOFFF!

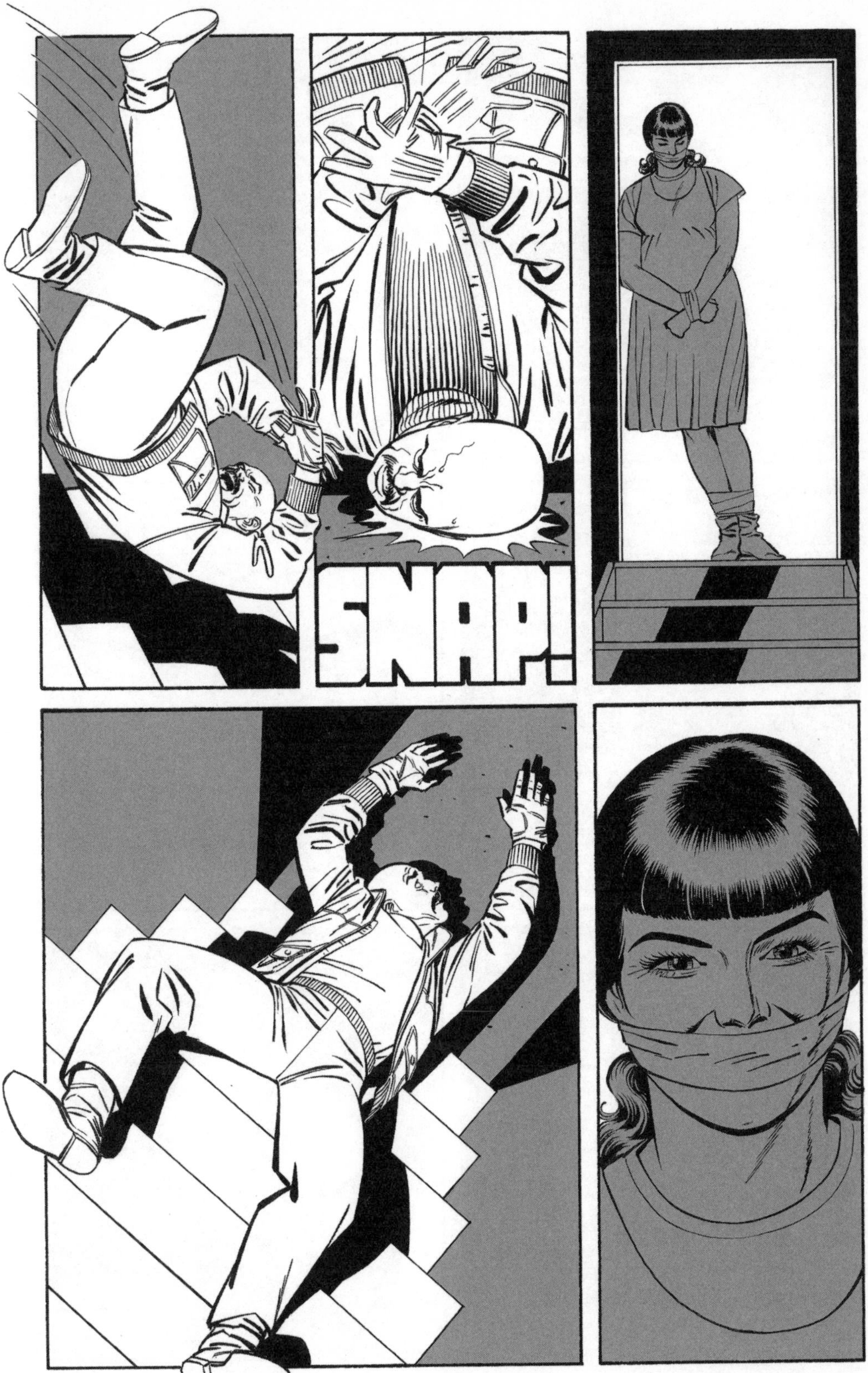
SNAP!

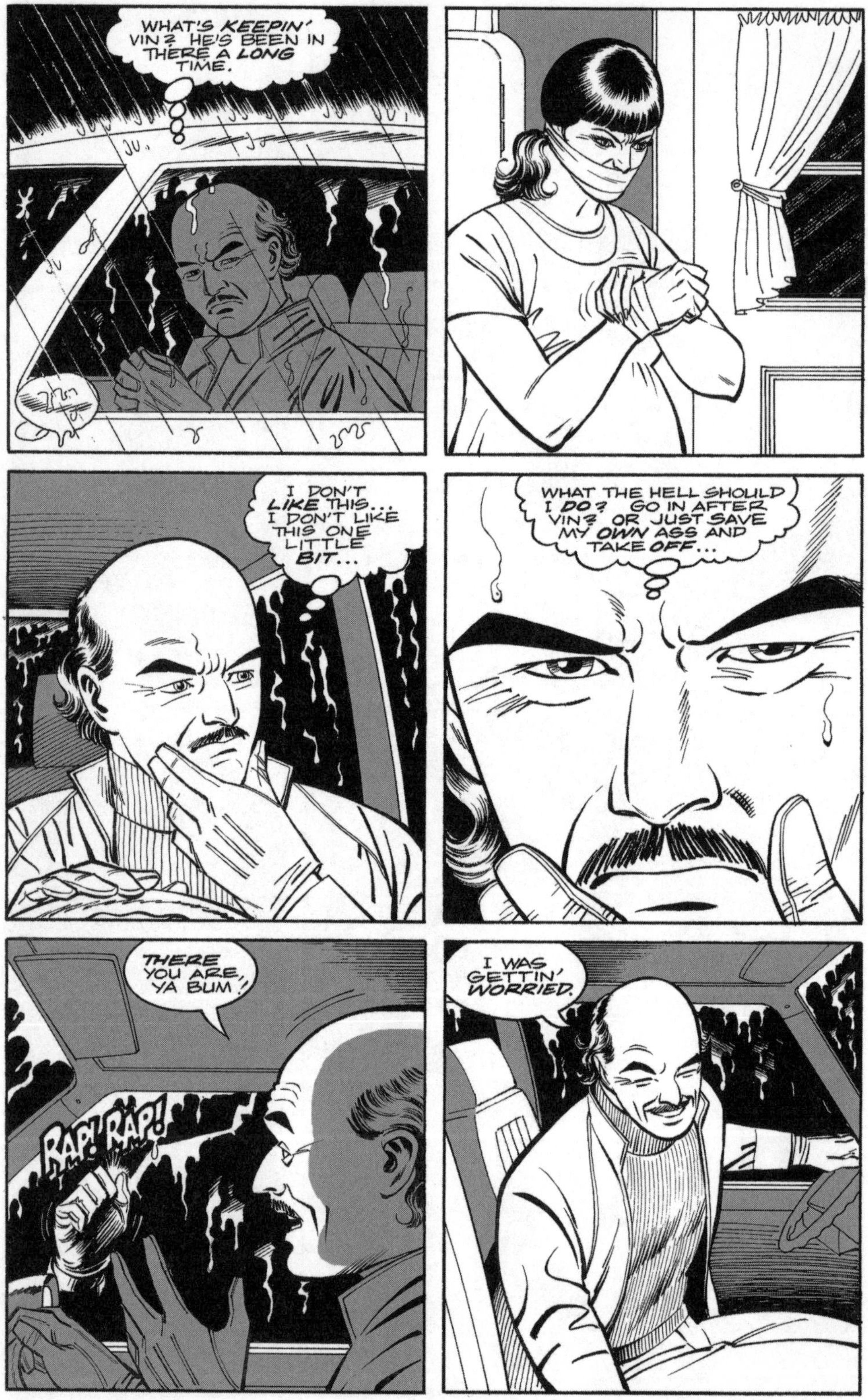
WHAT'S KEEPIN' VIN? HE'S BEEN IN THERE A LONG TIME.
I DON'T LIKE THIS... I DON'T LIKE THIS ONE LITTLE BIT...
WHAT THE HELL SHOULD I DO? GO IN AFTER VIN? OR JUST SAVE MY OWN ASS AND TAKE OFF...
THERE YOU ARE, YA BUM!
RAP! RAP!
I WAS GETTIN' WORRIED.

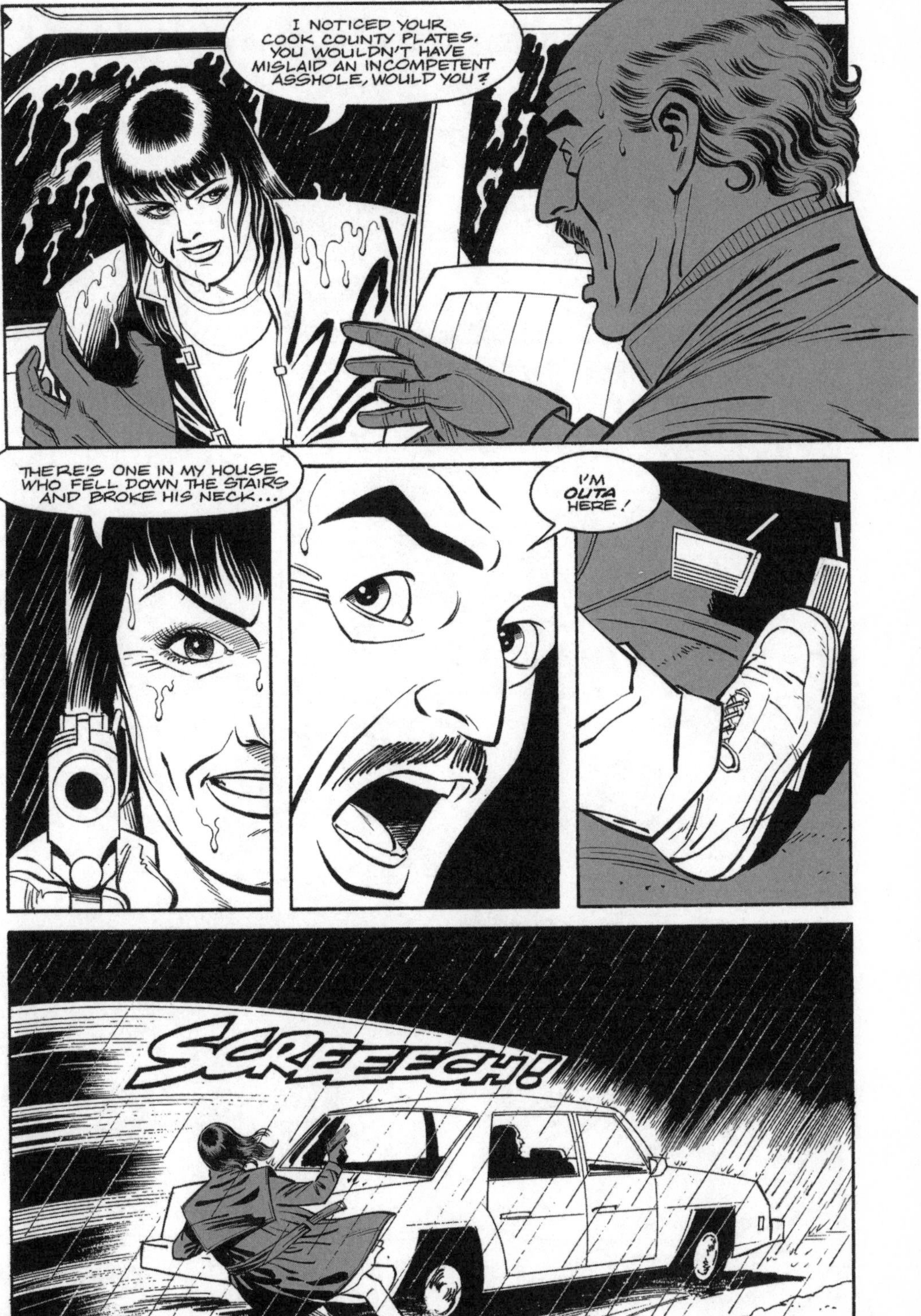
I NOTICED YOUR COOK COUNTY PLATES. YOU WOULDN'T HAVE MISLAID AN INCOMPETENT ASSHOLE, WOULD YOU?
THERE'S ONE IN MY HOUSE WHO FELL DOWN THE STAIRS AND BROKE HIS NECK...
I'M OUTA HERE!
SCREEEECH!

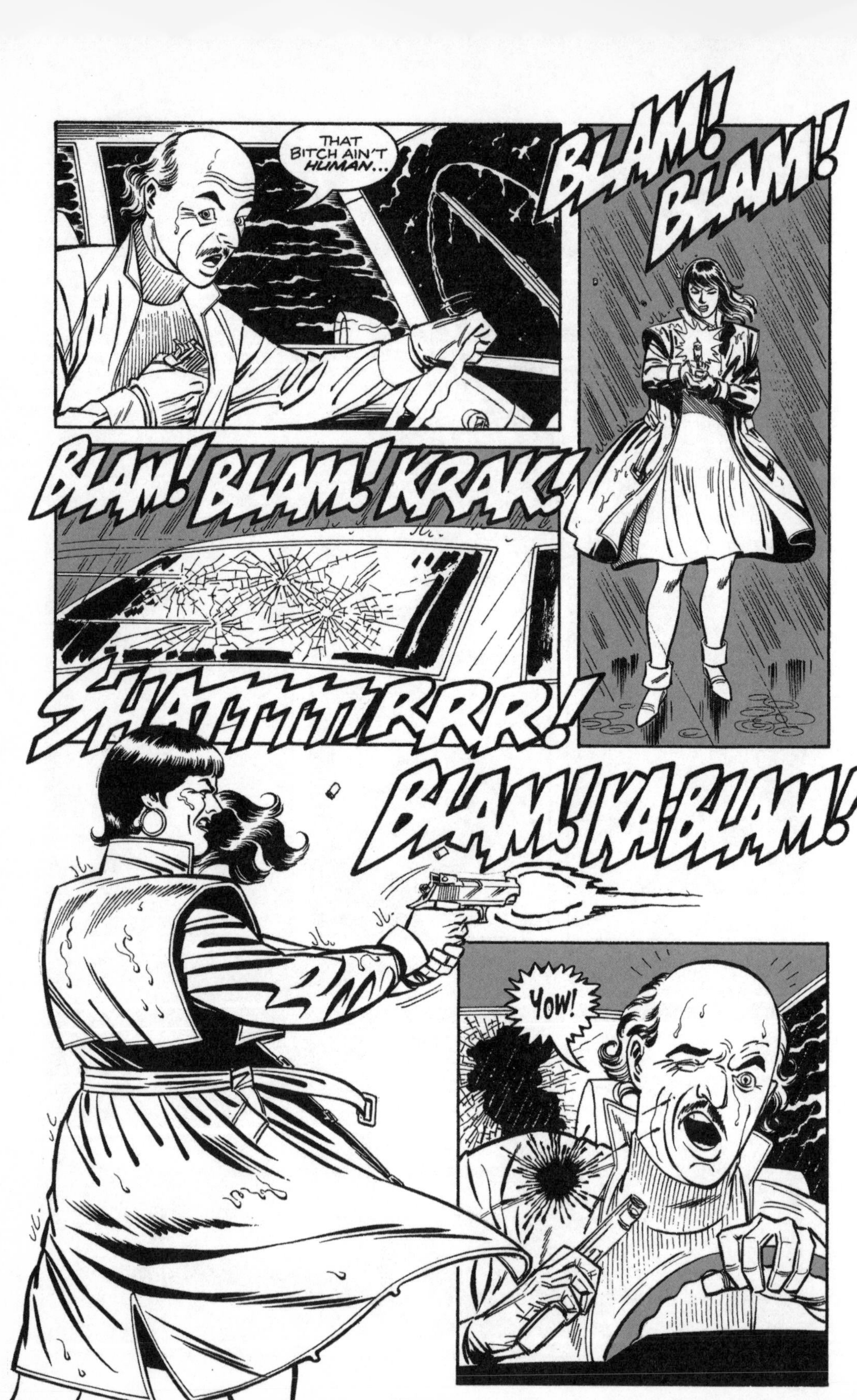
THAT BITCH AIN'T *HUMAN*...
BLAM! BLAM! KRAK!
SHATTTTTRRR!
BLAM! BLAM!
BLAM! KA-BLAM!
YOW!

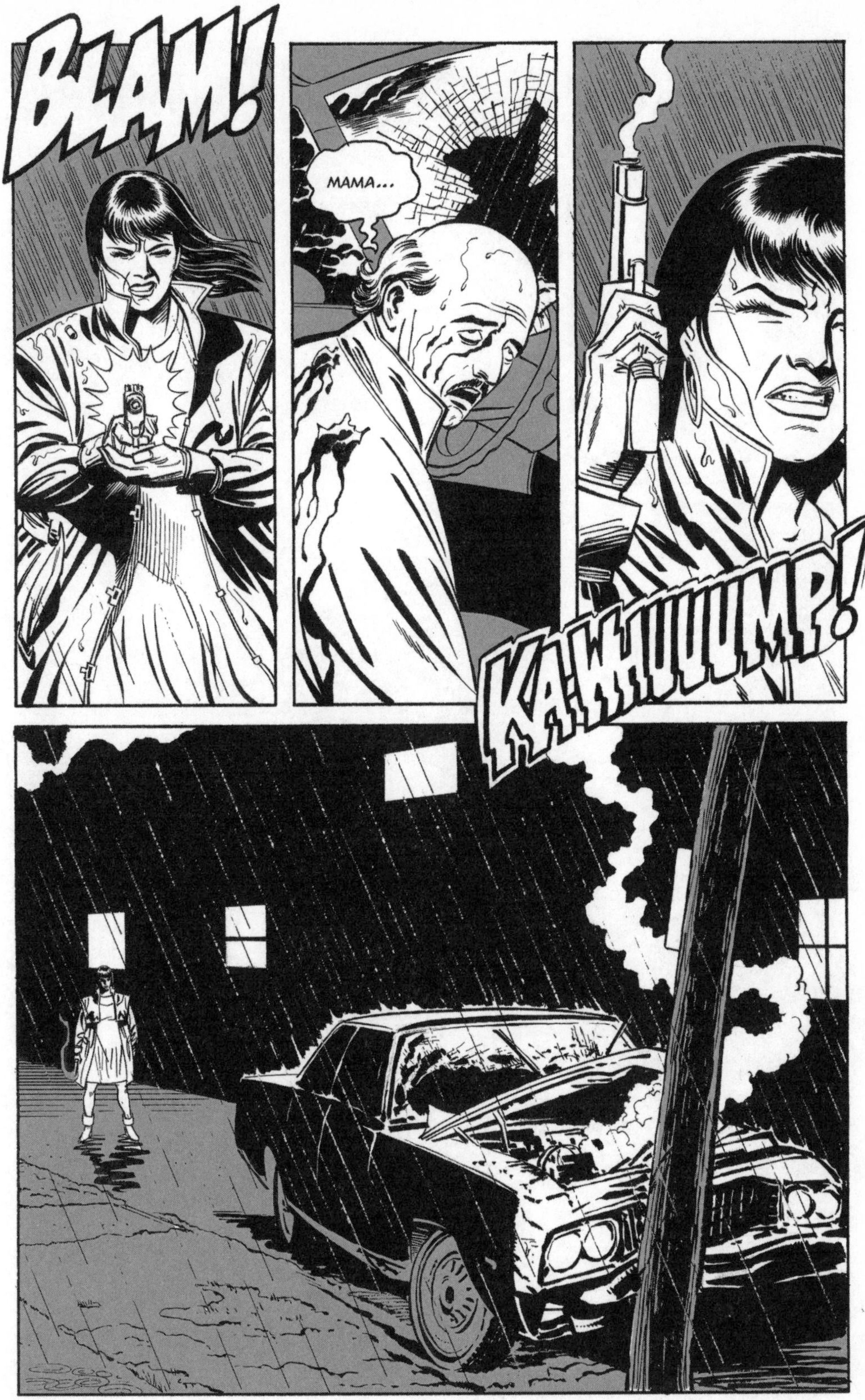
BLAM!
MAMA...
KA-WHUUUMP!

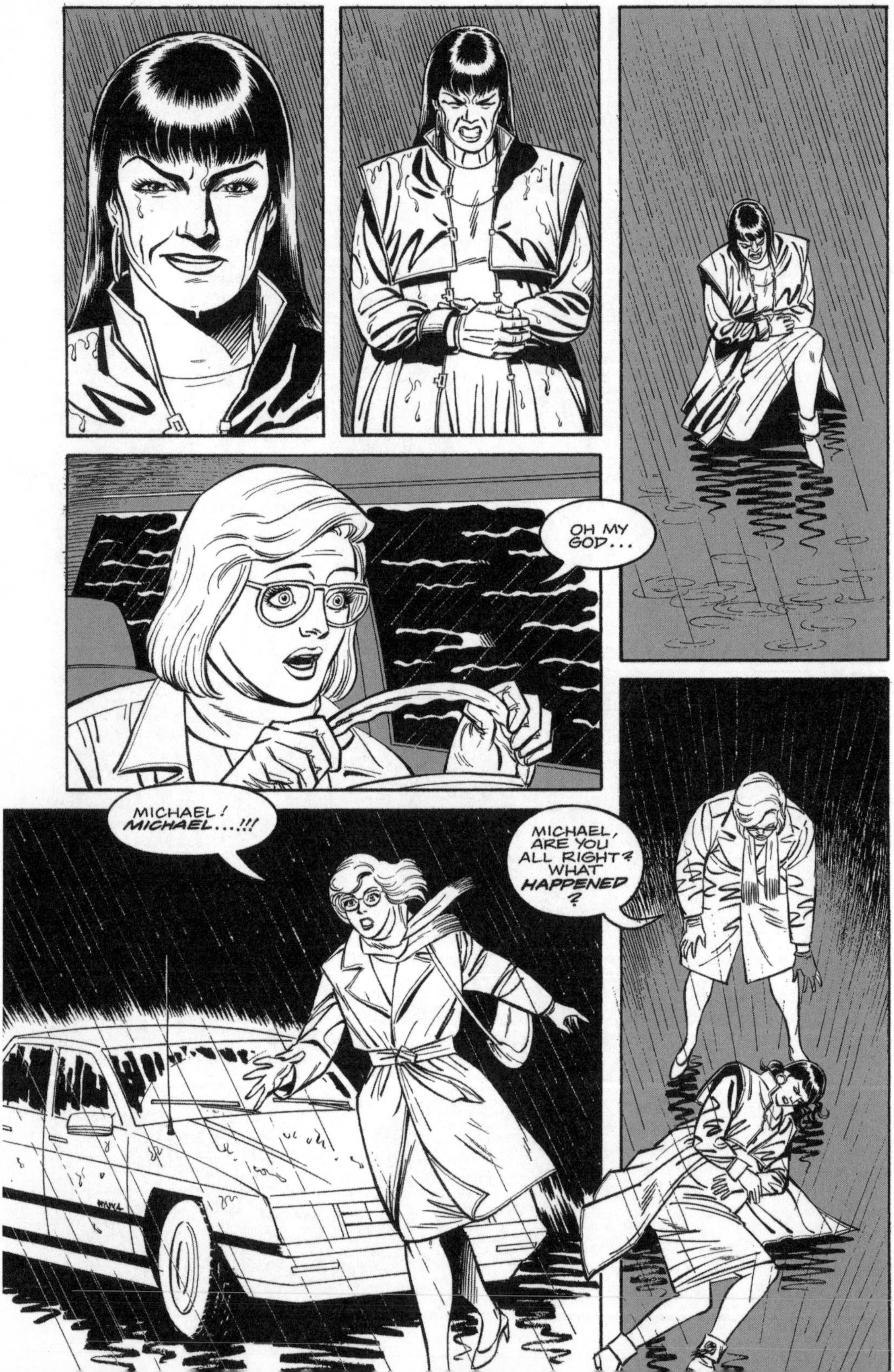

OH MY GOD...
MICHAEL! MICHAEL...!!!
MICHAEL, ARE YOU ALL RIGHT? WHAT HAPPENED?

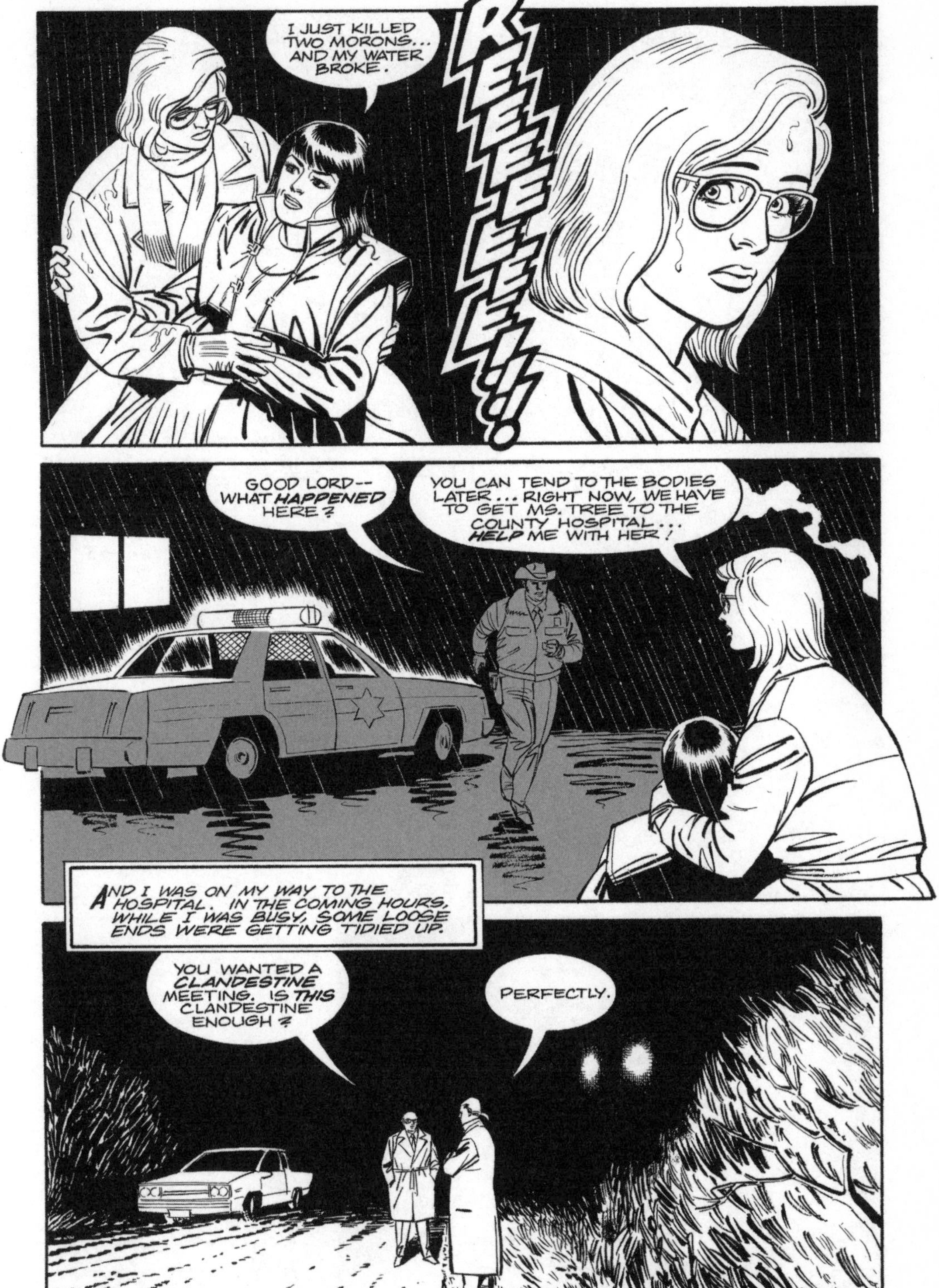
I JUST KILLED TWO MORONS... AND MY WATER BROKE.
REEEEEEEEEE!!!
GOOD LORD-- WHAT HAPPENED HERE?
YOU CAN TEND TO THE BODIES LATER... RIGHT NOW, WE HAVE TO GET MS. TREE TO THE COUNTY HOSPITAL... HELP ME WITH HER!
AND I WAS ON MY WAY TO THE HOSPITAL. IN THE COMING HOURS, WHILE I WAS BUSY, SOME LOOSE ENDS WERE GETTING TIDIED UP.
YOU WANTED A CLANDESTINE MEETING. IS THIS CLANDESTINE ENOUGH?
PERFECTLY.

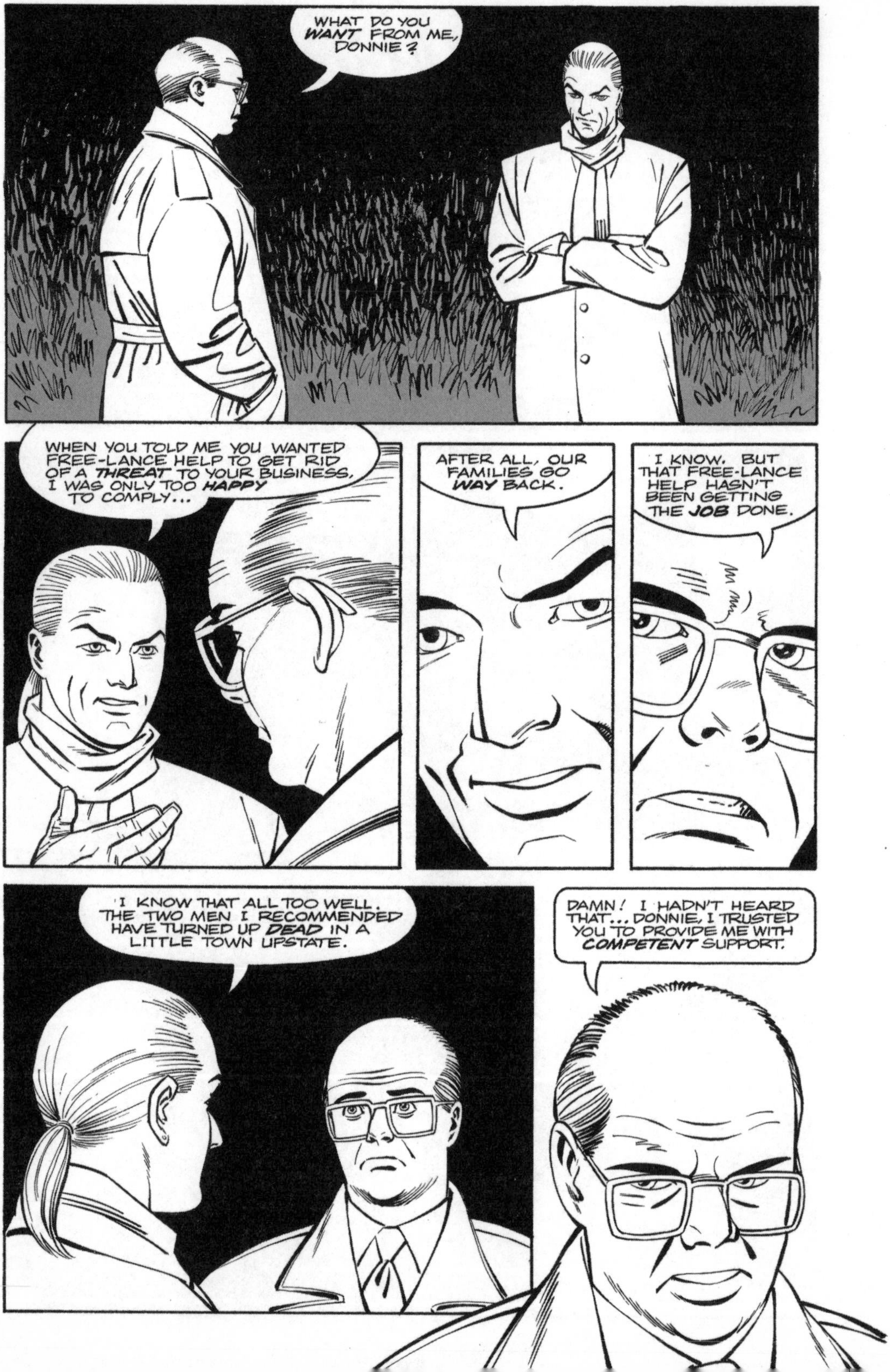
WHAT DO YOU WANT FROM ME, DONNIE?
WHEN YOU TOLD ME YOU WANTED FREE-LANCE HELP TO GET RID OF A THREAT TO YOUR BUSINESS, I WAS ONLY TOO HAPPY TO COMPLY...
AFTER ALL, OUR FAMILIES GO WAY BACK.
I KNOW. BUT THAT FREE-LANCE HELP HASN'T BEEN GETTING THE JOB DONE.
I KNOW THAT ALL TOO WELL. THE TWO MEN I RECOMMENDED HAVE TURNED UP DEAD IN A LITTLE TOWN UPSTATE.
DAMN! I HADN'T HEARD THAT... DONNIE, I TRUSTED YOU TO PROVIDE ME WITH COMPETENT SUPPORT.

SOMEBODY'S GOT TO ANSWER FOR THIS!
SOMEBODY WILL.
YOU DIDN'T TELL ME IT WAS MS. TREE YOU WANTED RID OF.
WHY SHOULD YOU CARE? SHE'S BEEN THE BANE OF YOUR FAMILY'S EXISTENCE FOR ALMOST TEN YEARS!
"NOT ANY MORE, M.T. SHE IS FAMILY, NOW, OR SOON WILL BE... HER STEPSON IS ENGAGED TO MARRY MY NIECE."
KILLING A PREGNANT WOMAN? HAVE YOU NO SHAME, POWERS?

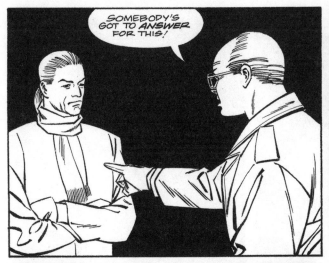

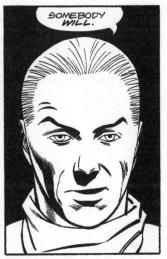

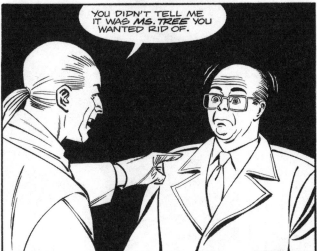

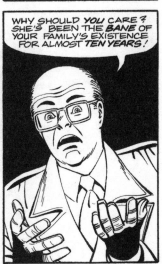

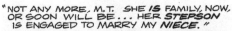

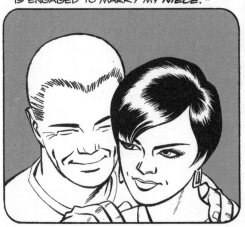

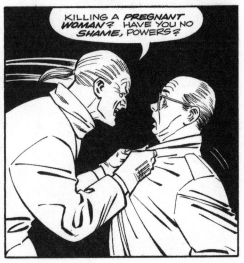

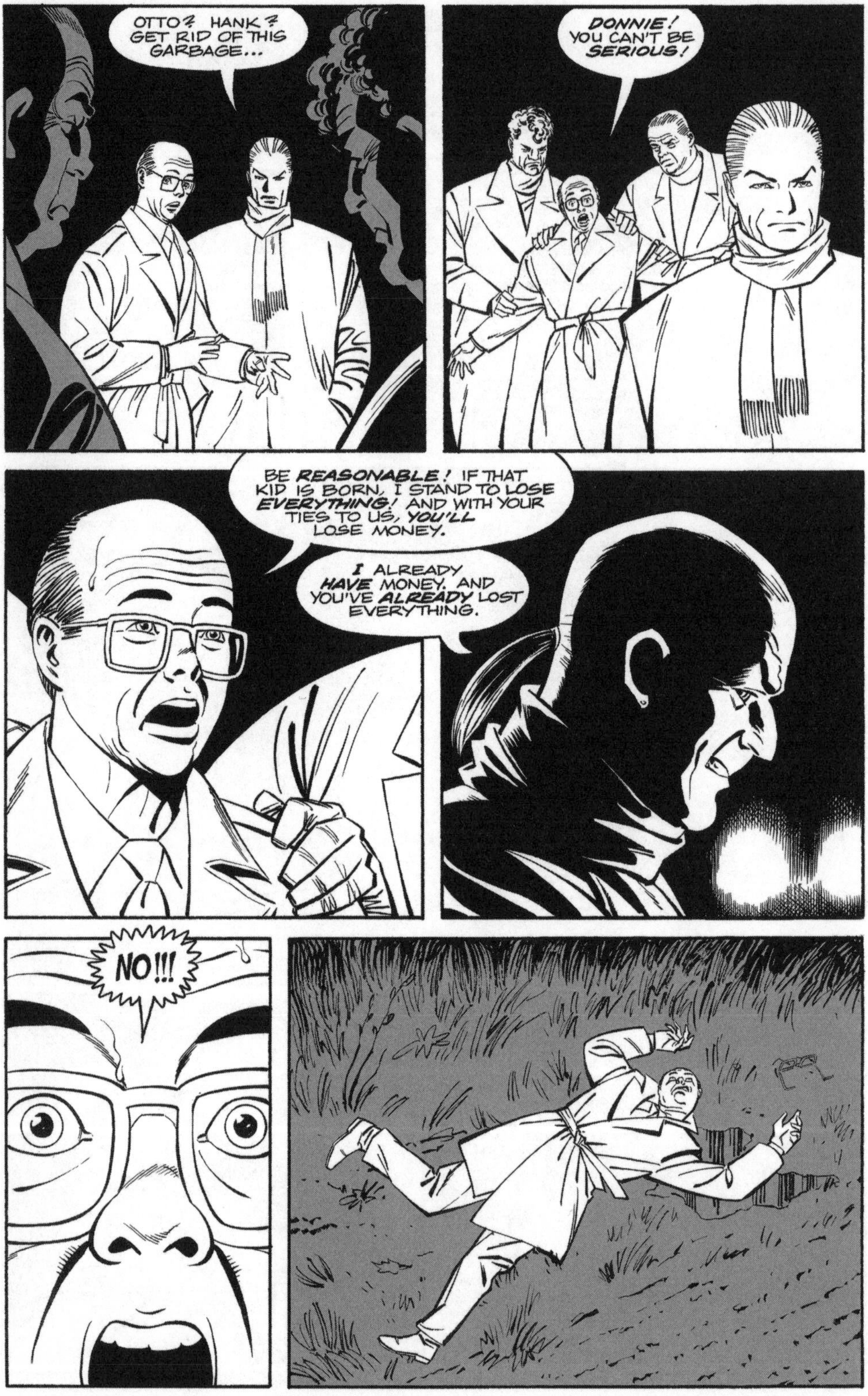
OTTO? HANK? GET RID OF THIS GARBAGE...
DONNIE! YOU CAN'T BE SERIOUS!
BE REASONABLE! IF THAT KID IS BORN, I STAND TO LOSE EVERYTHING! AND WITH YOUR TIES TO US, YOU'LL LOSE MONEY.
I ALREADY HAVE MONEY, AND YOU'VE ALREADY LOST EVERYTHING.
NO!!!

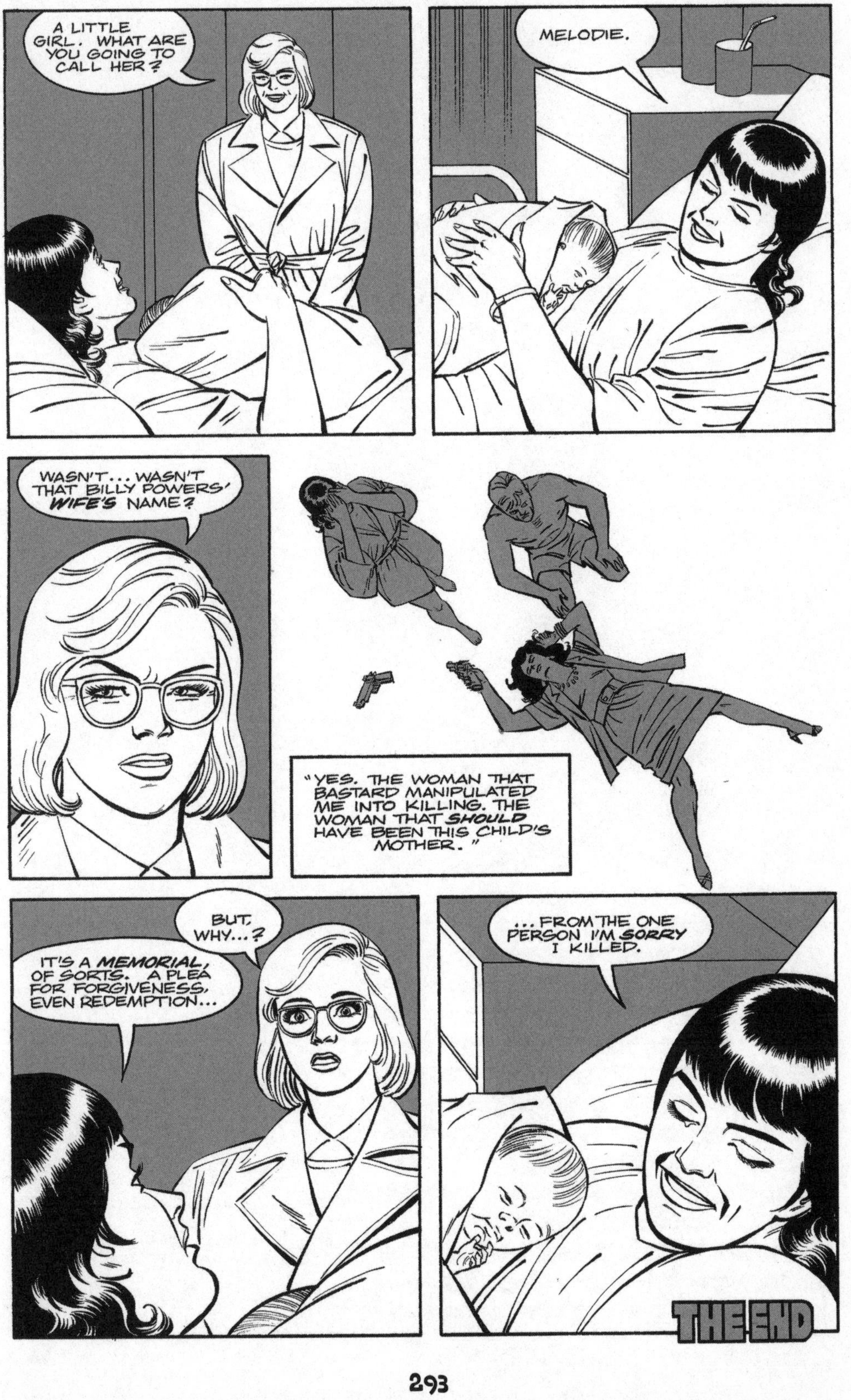
A LITTLE GIRL. WHAT ARE YOU GOING TO CALL HER?
MELODIE.
WASN'T... WASN'T THAT BILLY POWERS' *WIFE'S* NAME?
"YES. THE WOMAN THAT BASTARD MANIPULATED ME INTO KILLING. THE WOMAN THAT *SHOULD* HAVE BEEN THIS CHILD'S MOTHER."
BUT, WHY...?
IT'S A *MEMORIAL*, OF SORTS. A PLEA FOR FORGIVENESS, EVEN REDEMPTION...
...FROM THE ONE PERSON I'M *SORRY* I KILLED.
THE END

"Sure was smart of you Dutch coming in at a place like Blackpool"

Britons in the early 1950s were still recovering from the war and coping with even stricter rationing, yet they flocked to Blackpool, England's most popular holiday destination, for its famous beaches, tower and illuminations. These serve as more than a seaside setting for this art-heist thriller, with echoes of Graham Greene's *Brighton Rock* filmed in 1947.

An artist of precision detail, Denis McLoughlin (1918–2002) was one of Britain's finest painters of pulp magazine and crime novel covers. He and his brother Colin created *Roy Carson* comics for Boardman Books from February 1948 to 1954, as well as crafting the bestselling *Buffalo Bill Wild West Annuals* and space explorer *Swift Morgan*.

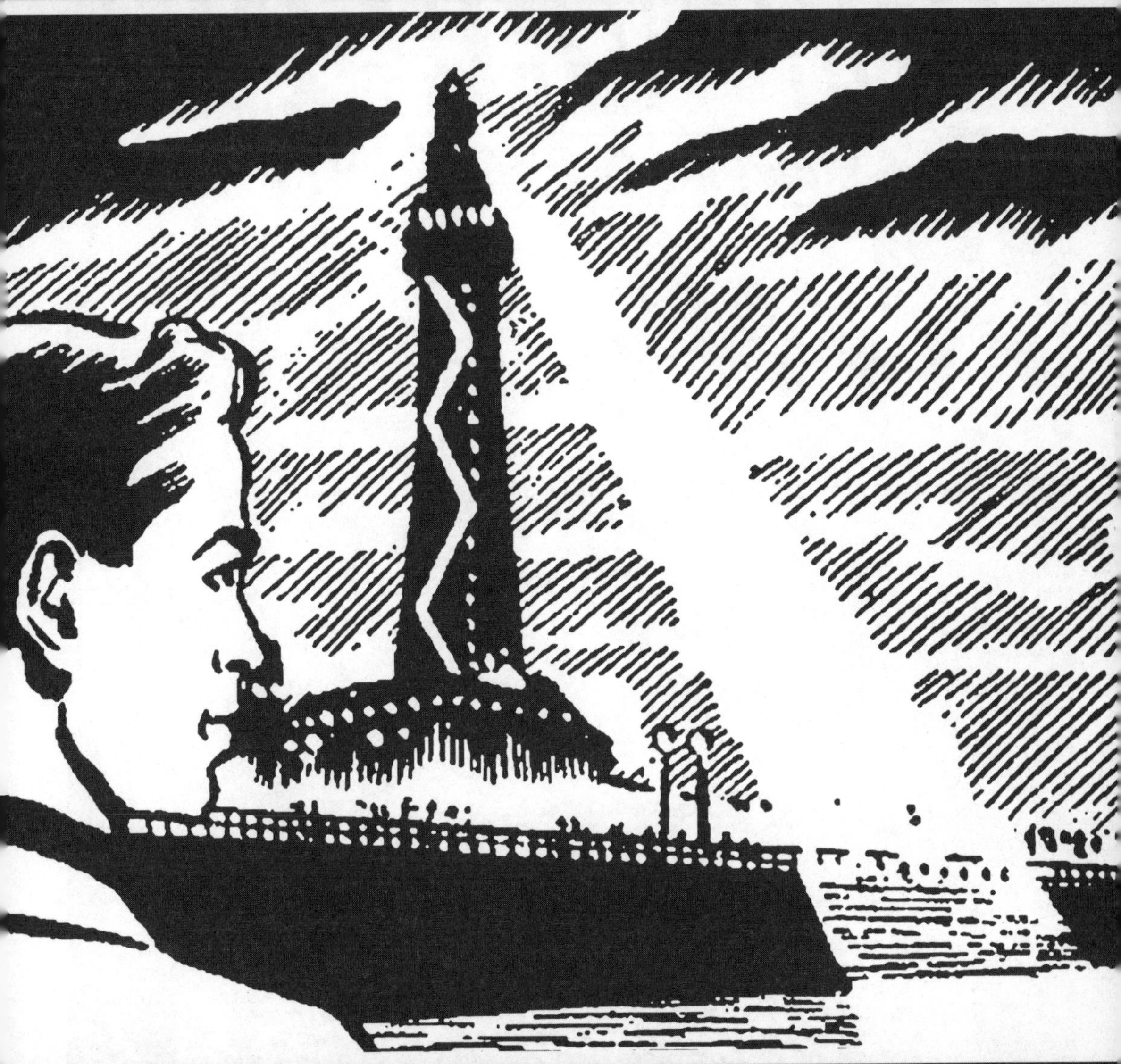

Roy Carson and the Old Master

Colin McLoughlin (script) and Denis McLoughlin (art) 1953

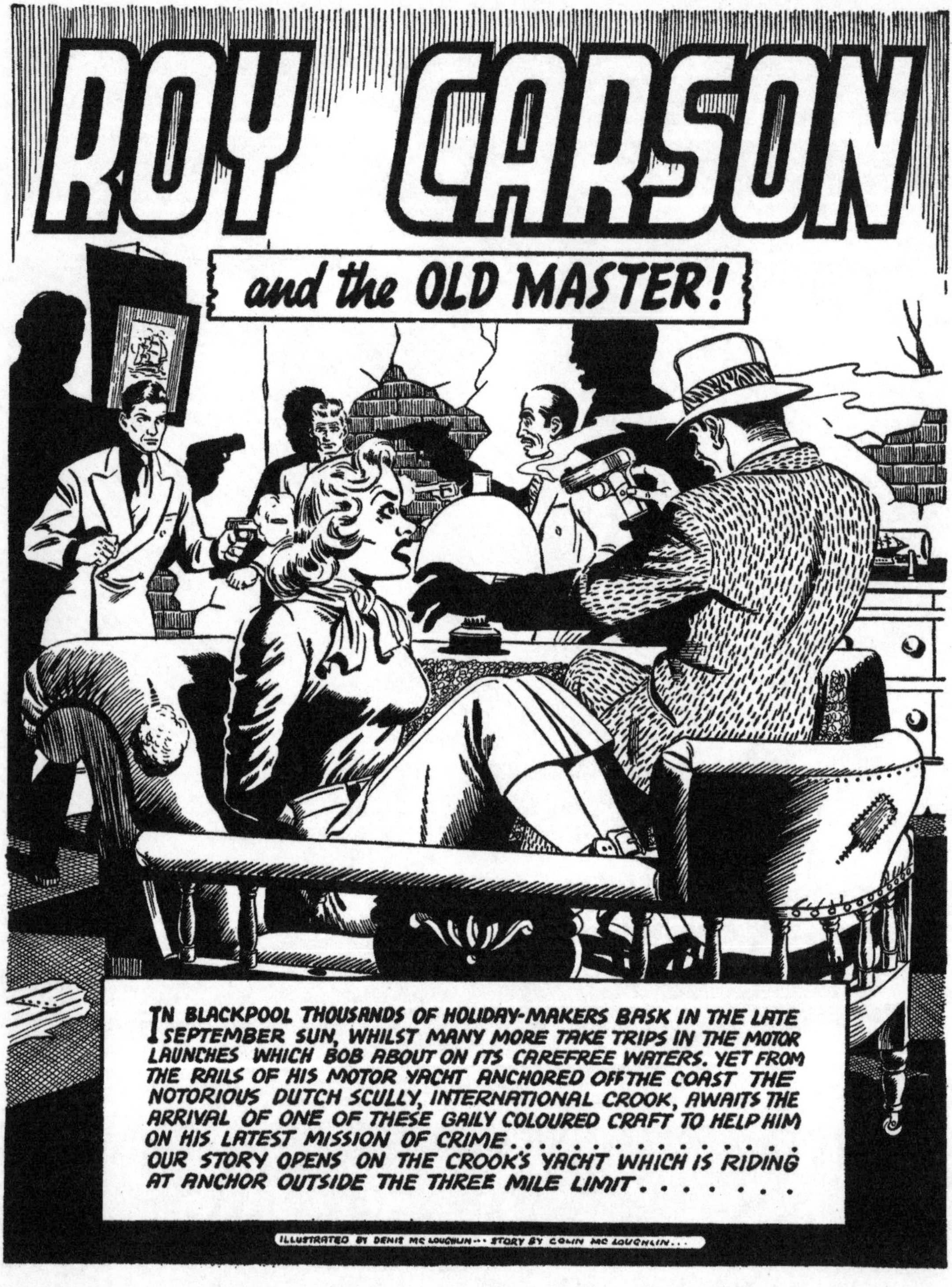

ROY CARSON
and the OLD MASTER!
IN BLACKPOOL THOUSANDS OF HOLIDAY-MAKERS BASK IN THE LATE SEPTEMBER SUN, WHILST MANY MORE TAKE TRIPS IN THE MOTOR LAUNCHES WHICH BOB ABOUT ON ITS CAREFREE WATERS. YET FROM THE RAILS OF HIS MOTOR YACHT ANCHORED OFF THE COAST THE NOTORIOUS DUTCH SCULLY, INTERNATIONAL CROOK, AWAITS THE ARRIVAL OF ONE OF THESE GAILY COLOURED CRAFT TO HELP HIM ON HIS LATEST MISSION OF CRIME..............
OUR STORY OPENS ON THE CROOK'S YACHT WHICH IS RIDING AT ANCHOR OUTSIDE THE THREE MILE LIMIT.......
ILLUSTRATED BY DENIS MC LOUGHLIN... STORY BY COLIN MC LOUGHLIN...

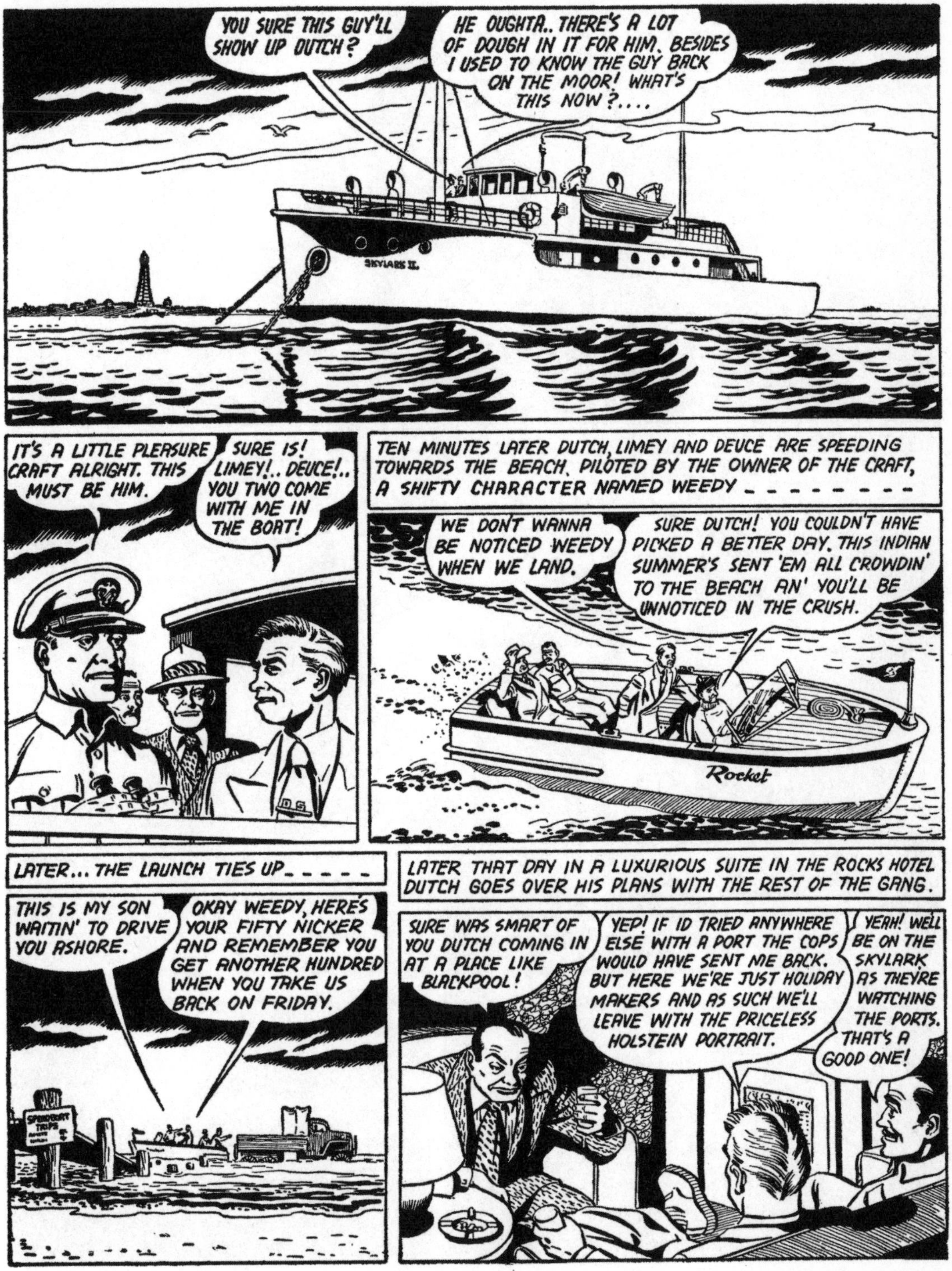
YOU SURE THIS GUY'LL SHOW UP DUTCH?
HE OUGHTA.. THERE'S A LOT OF DOUGH IN IT FOR HIM. BESIDES I USED TO KNOW THE GUY BACK ON THE MOOR! WHAT'S THIS NOW?....
SKYLARK II.
IT'S A LITTLE PLERSURE CRAFT ALRIGHT. THIS MUST BE HIM.
SURE IS! LIMEY!.. DEUCE!.. YOU TWO COME WITH ME IN THE BOAT!
TEN MINUTES LATER DUTCH, LIMEY AND DEUCE ARE SPEEDING TOWARDS THE BEACH, PILOTED BY THE OWNER OF THE CRAFT, A SHIFTY CHARACTER NAMED WEEDY - - - - - - -
WE DON'T WANNA BE NOTICED WEEDY WHEN WE LAND.
SURE DUTCH! YOU COULDN'T HAVE PICKED A BETTER DAY. THIS INDIAN SUMMER'S SENT 'EM ALL CROWDIN' TO THE BEACH AN' YOU'LL BE UNNOTICED IN THE CRUSH.
Rocket
LATER... THE LAUNCH TIES UP- - - - -
THIS IS MY SON WAITIN' TO DRIVE YOU ASHORE.
OKAY WEEDY, HERE'S YOUR FIFTY NICKER AND REMEMBER YOU GET ANOTHER HUNDRED WHEN YOU TAKE US BACK ON FRIDAY.
LATER THAT DAY IN A LUXURIOUS SUITE IN THE ROCKS HOTEL DUTCH GOES OVER HIS PLANS WITH THE REST OF THE GANG.
SURE WAS SMART OF YOU DUTCH COMING IN AT A PLACE LIKE BLACKPOOL!
YEP! IF ID TRIED ANYWHERE ELSE WITH A PORT THE COPS WOULD HAVE SENT ME BACK. BUT HERE WE'RE JUST HOLIDAY MAKERS AND AS SUCH WE'LL LEAVE WITH THE PRICELESS HOLSTEIN PORTRAIT.
YEAH! WE'LL BE ON THE SKYLARK AS THEY'RE WATCHING THE PORTS. THAT'S A GOOD ONE!

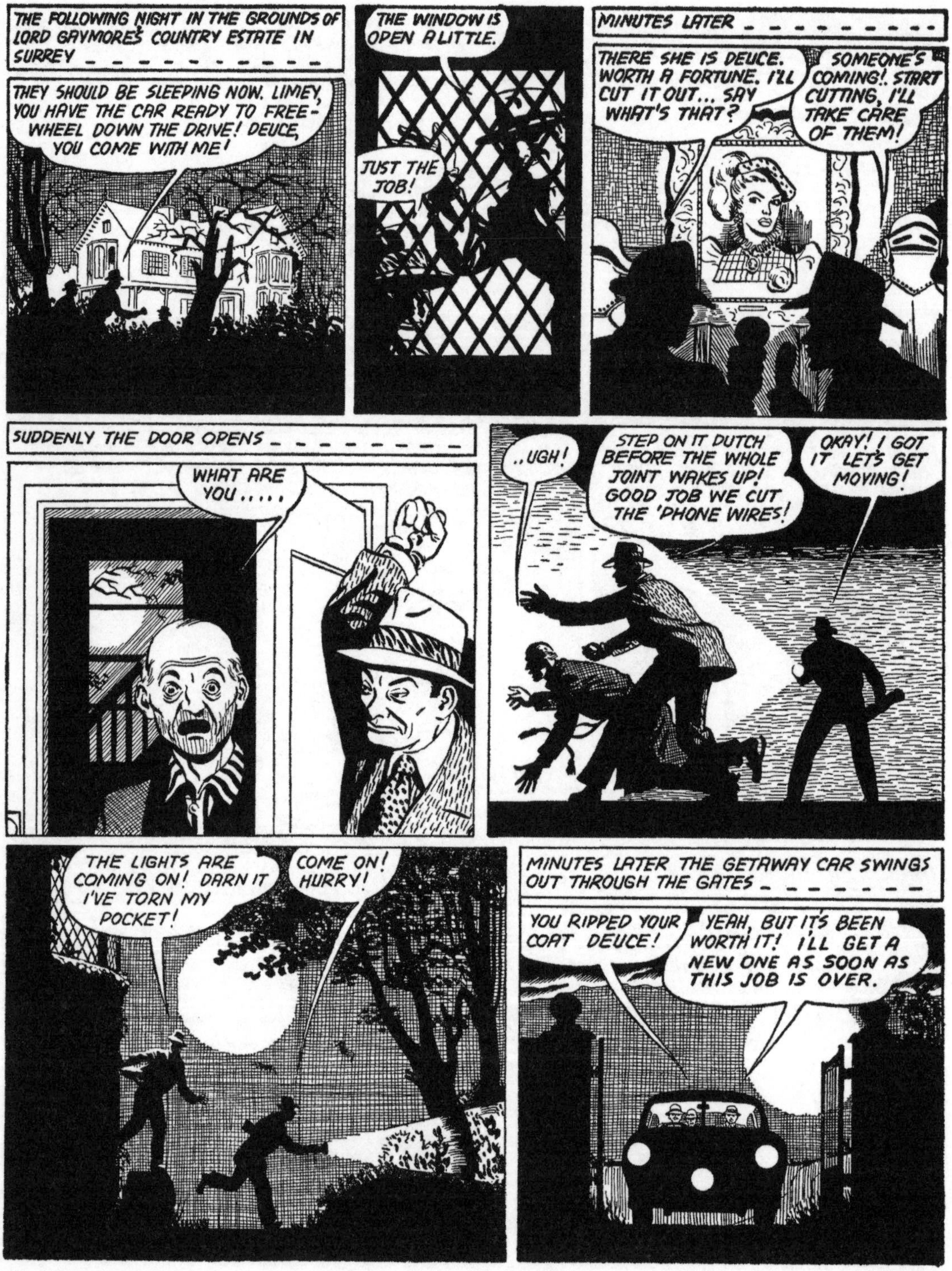
THE FOLLOWING NIGHT IN THE GROUNDS OF LORD GAYMORE'S COUNTRY ESTATE IN SURREY
THEY SHOULD BE SLEEPING NOW. LIMEY, YOU HAVE THE CAR READY TO FREE-WHEEL DOWN THE DRIVE! DEUCE, YOU COME WITH ME!
THE WINDOW IS OPEN A LITTLE.
JUST THE JOB!
MINUTES LATER
THERE SHE IS DEUCE. WORTH A FORTUNE. I'LL CUT IT OUT... SAY WHAT'S THAT?
SOMEONE'S COMING! START CUTTING, I'LL TAKE CARE OF THEM!
SUDDENLY THE DOOR OPENS
WHAT ARE YOU.....
..UGH!
STEP ON IT DUTCH BEFORE THE WHOLE JOINT WAKES UP! GOOD JOB WE CUT THE 'PHONE WIRES!
OKAY! I GOT IT LET'S GET MOVING!
THE LIGHTS ARE COMING ON! DARN IT I'VE TORN MY POCKET!
COME ON! HURRY!
MINUTES LATER THE GETAWAY CAR SWINGS OUT THROUGH THE GATES
YOU RIPPED YOUR COAT DEUCE!
YEAH, BUT IT'S BEEN WORTH IT! I'LL GET A NEW ONE AS SOON AS THIS JOB IS OVER.

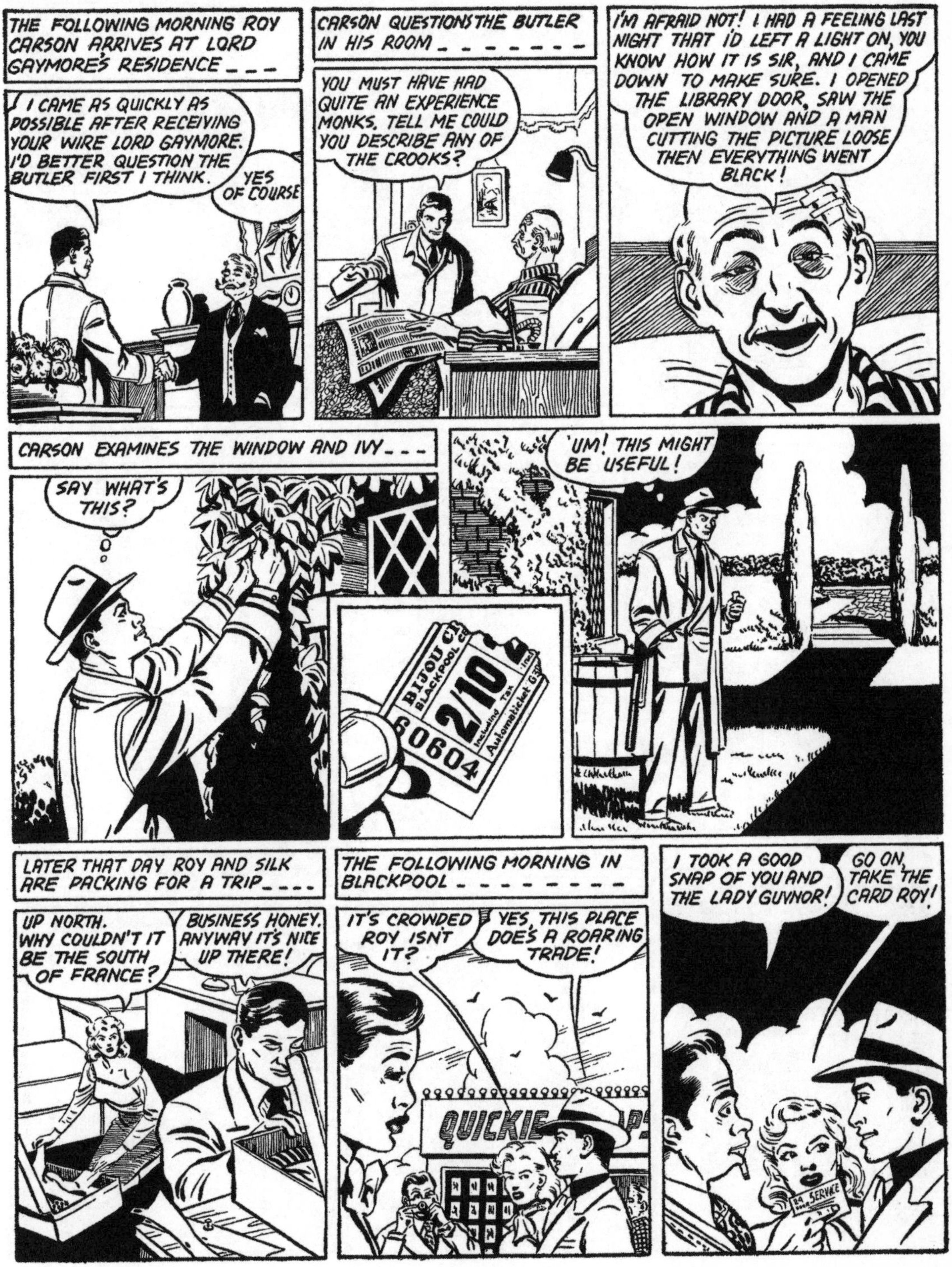
THE FOLLOWING MORNING ROY CARSON ARRIVES AT LORD GAYMORE'S RESIDENCE ---
I CAME AS QUICKLY AS POSSIBLE AFTER RECEIVING YOUR WIRE LORD GAYMORE. I'D BETTER QUESTION THE BUTLER FIRST I THINK.
YES OF COURSE
CARSON QUESTIONS THE BUTLER IN HIS ROOM -------
YOU MUST HAVE HAD QUITE AN EXPERIENCE MONKS. TELL ME COULD YOU DESCRIBE ANY OF THE CROOKS?
I'M AFRAID NOT! I HAD A FEELING LAST NIGHT THAT I'D LEFT A LIGHT ON, YOU KNOW HOW IT IS SIR, AND I CAME DOWN TO MAKE SURE. I OPENED THE LIBRARY DOOR, SAW THE OPEN WINDOW AND A MAN CUTTING THE PICTURE LOOSE THEN EVERYTHING WENT BLACK!
CARSON EXAMINES THE WINDOW AND IVY ---
SAY WHAT'S THIS?
BIJOU CL
BLACKPOOL
2/10
Including Tax
60604
'UM! THIS MIGHT BE USEFUL!
LATER THAT DAY ROY AND SILK ARE PACKING FOR A TRIP ----
UP NORTH. WHY COULDN'T IT BE THE SOUTH OF FRANCE?
BUSINESS HONEY. ANYWAY IT'S NICE UP THERE!
THE FOLLOWING MORNING IN BLACKPOOL -------
IT'S CROWDED ROY ISN'T IT?
YES, THIS PLACE DOES A ROARING TRADE!
QUICKIE
I TOOK A GOOD SNAP OF YOU AND THE LADY GUVNOR!
GO ON, TAKE THE CARD ROY!
24 SERVICE

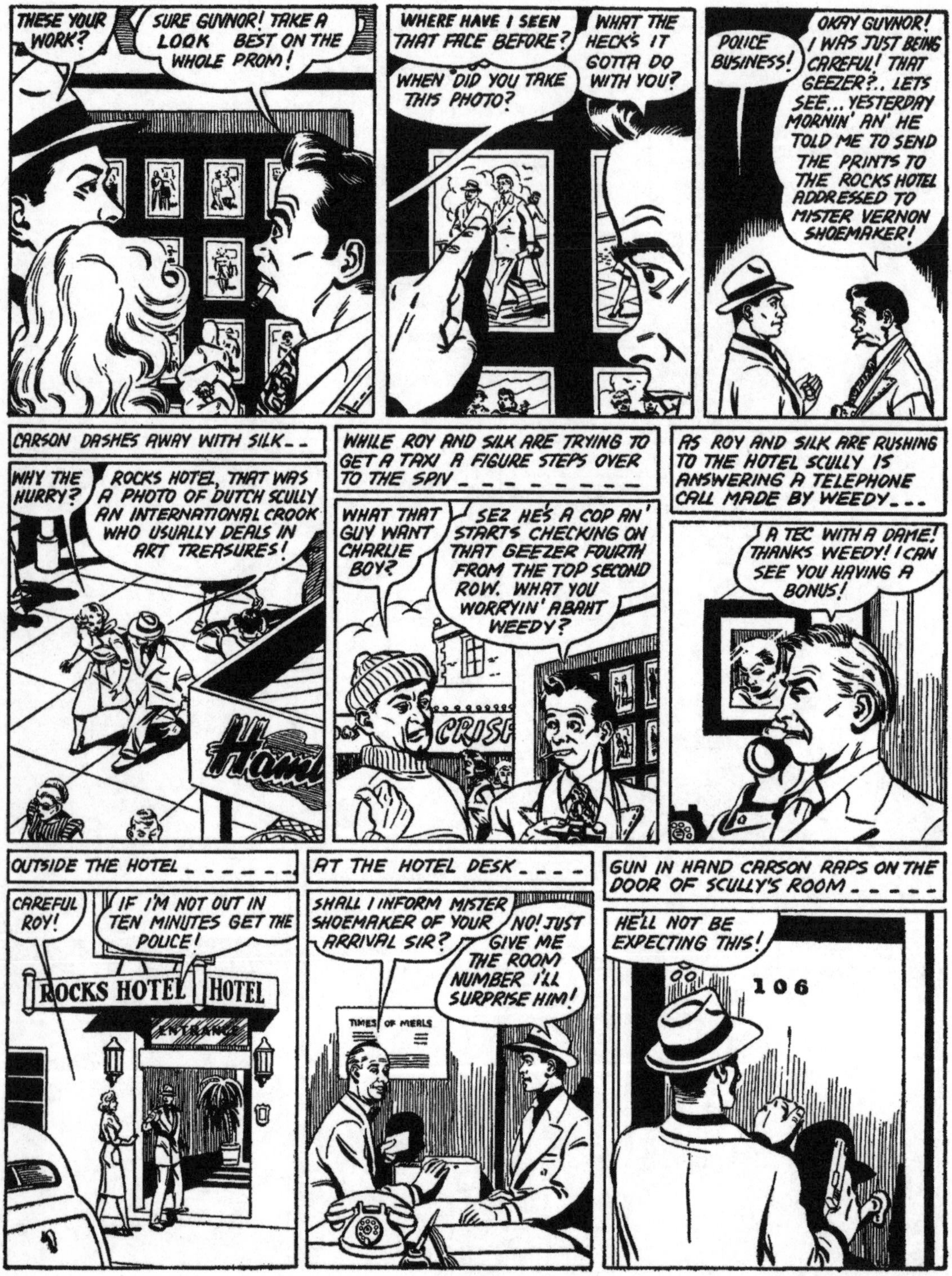
THESE YOUR WORK?
SURE GUVNOR! TAKE A LOOK BEST ON THE WHOLE PROM!
WHERE HAVE I SEEN THAT FACE BEFORE?
WHEN DID YOU TAKE THIS PHOTO?
WHAT THE HECK'S IT GOTTA DO WITH YOU?
POLICE BUSINESS!
OKAY GUVNOR! I WAS JUST BEING CAREFUL! THAT GEEZER?.. LETS SEE... YESTERDAY MORNIN' AN' HE TOLD ME TO SEND THE PRINTS TO THE ROCKS HOTEL ADDRESSED TO MISTER VERNON SHOEMAKER!
CARSON DASHES AWAY WITH SILK--
WHY THE HURRY?
ROCKS HOTEL, THAT WAS A PHOTO OF DUTCH SCULLY AN INTERNATIONAL CROOK WHO USUALLY DEALS IN ART TREASURES!
WHILE ROY AND SILK ARE TRYING TO GET A TAXI A FIGURE STEPS OVER TO THE SPIV --------
WHAT THAT GUY WANT CHARLIE BOY?
SEZ HE'S A COP AN' STARTS CHECKING ON THAT GEEZER FOURTH FROM THE TOP SECOND ROW. WHAT YOU WORRYIN' ABAHT WEEDY?
AS ROY AND SILK ARE RUSHING TO THE HOTEL SCULLY IS ANSWERING A TELEPHONE CALL MADE BY WEEDY---
A TEC WITH A DAME! THANKS WEEDY! I CAN SEE YOU HAVING A BONUS!
OUTSIDE THE HOTEL ------
CAREFUL ROY!
IF I'M NOT OUT IN TEN MINUTES GET THE POLICE!
ROCKS HOTEL
HOTEL
AT THE HOTEL DESK ----
SHALL I INFORM MISTER SHOEMAKER OF YOUR ARRIVAL SIR?
NO! JUST GIVE ME THE ROOM NUMBER I'LL SURPRISE HIM!
TIMES OF MEALS
GUN IN HAND CARSON RAPS ON THE DOOR OF SCULLY'S ROOM ----
HE'LL NOT BE EXPECTING THIS!
106

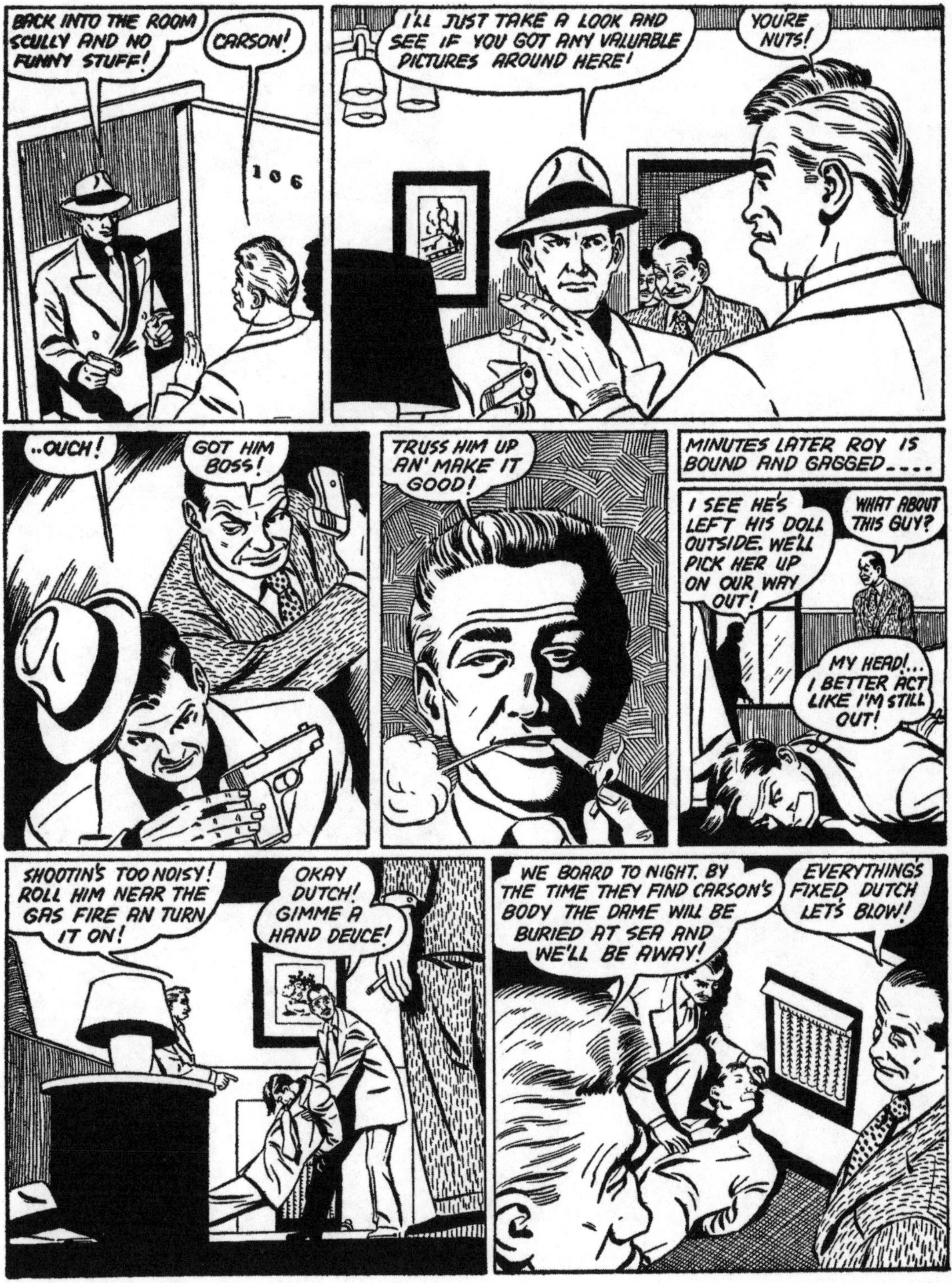
BACK INTO THE ROOM SCULLY AND NO FUNNY STUFF!
CARSON!
106
I'LL JUST TAKE A LOOK AND SEE IF YOU GOT ANY VALUABLE PICTURES AROUND HERE!
YOU'RE NUTS!
..OUCH!
GOT HIM BOSS!
TRUSS HIM UP AN' MAKE IT GOOD!
MINUTES LATER ROY IS BOUND AND GAGGED....
I SEE HE'S LEFT HIS DOLL OUTSIDE. WE'LL PICK HER UP ON OUR WAY OUT!
WHAT ABOUT THIS GUY?
MY HEAD!... I BETTER ACT LIKE I'M STILL OUT!
SHOOTIN'S TOO NOISY! ROLL HIM NEAR THE GAS FIRE AN TURN IT ON!
OKAY DUTCH! GIMME A HAND DEUCE!
WE BOARD TO NIGHT. BY THE TIME THEY FIND CARSON'S BODY THE DAME WILL BE BURIED AT SEA AND WE'LL BE AWAY!
EVERYTHING'S FIXED DUTCH LET'S BLOW!

OUTSIDE THE HOTEL _ _ _ _ _ _ _ _ _

THIS ISN'T A PIPE IN MY POCKET SISTER. GET INTO THE CAR BY THE KERB!

WHAT HAVE YOU DONE WITH ROY?

GET MOVIN'!

...IF ONLY ID PHONED THE POLICE!

THANKS! SO ONLY CARSON AND YOU KNOW I'M IN THIS COUNTRY! JUST AS I THOUGHT. WITH YOU TWO OUT OF THE WAY I'M IN THE CLEAR!

TEN MINUTES LATER THEY ENTER WEEDY'S LITTLE COTTAGE _ _ _ _ _ _ _ _ _

COME IN FELLERS! WHERE'S THE GUY I SAW WITH THIS DAME?

DEAD BY NOW I RECKON!

I DON'T WANT ANTHIN' TO DO WITH MURDER. GET OUT!

YOU YELLOW LIVERED.....!!

LAY OFF MY OLD MAN!

.. AAH!

TIE THE OLD MAN AN' THE DAME UP. I DON'T THINK ANYONE WILL HAVE NOTICED THAT SHOT!

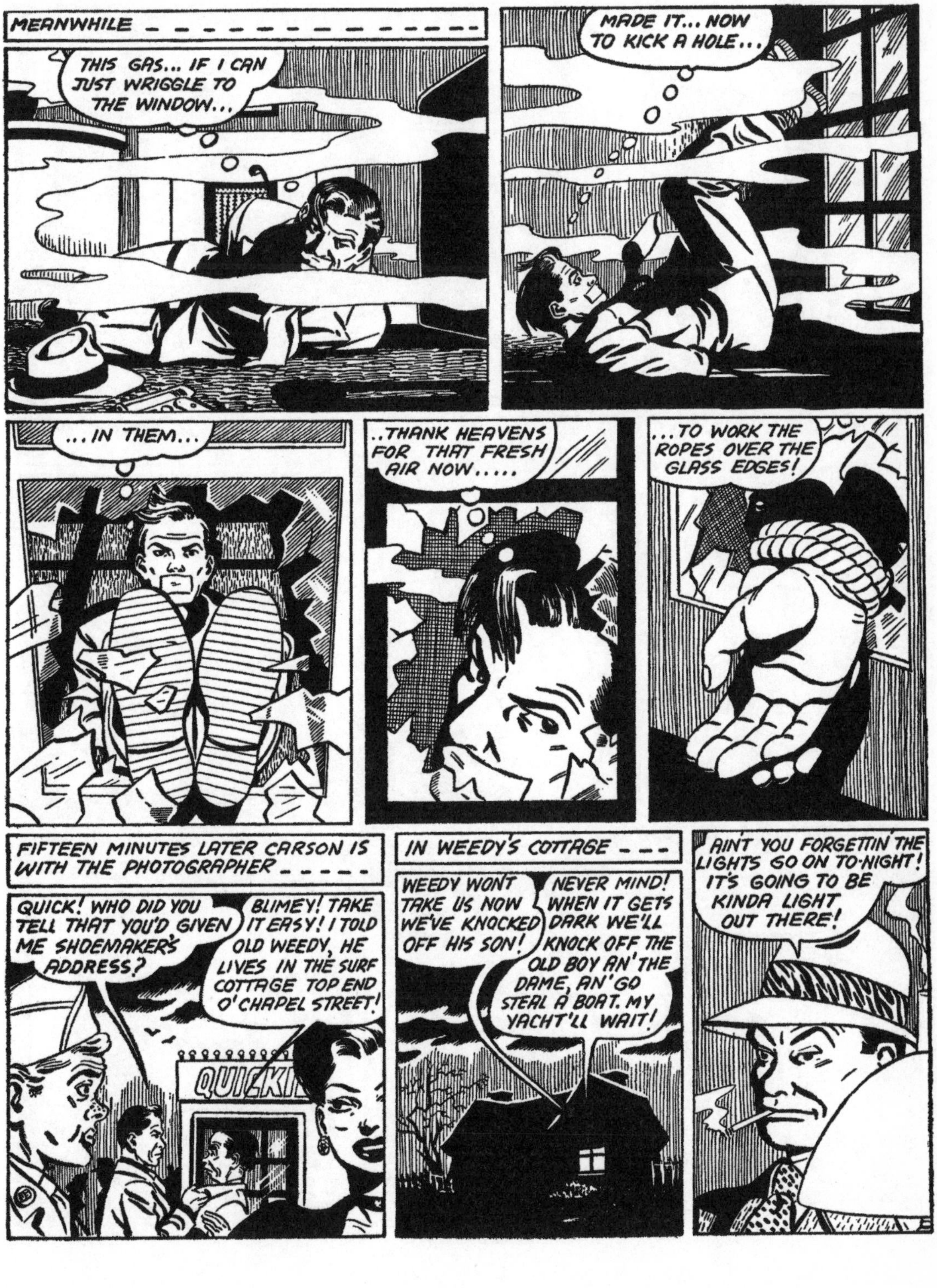
MEANWHILE
THIS GAS... IF I CAN JUST WRIGGLE TO THE WINDOW...
MADE IT... NOW TO KICK A HOLE...
... IN THEM...
..THANK HEAVENS FOR THAT FRESH AIR NOW.....
...TO WORK THE ROPES OVER THE GLASS EDGES!
FIFTEEN MINUTES LATER CARSON IS WITH THE PHOTOGRAPHER
QUICK! WHO DID YOU TELL THAT YOU'D GIVEN ME SHOEMAKER'S ADDRESS?
BLIMEY! TAKE IT EASY! I TOLD OLD WEEDY, HE LIVES IN THE SURF COTTAGE TOP END O' CHAPEL STREET!
IN WEEDY'S COTTAGE
WEEDY WON'T TAKE US NOW WE'VE KNOCKED OFF HIS SON!
NEVER MIND! WHEN IT GETS DARK WE'LL KNOCK OFF THE OLD BOY AN' THE DAME, AN' GO STEAL A BOAT. MY YACHT'LL WAIT!
AIN'T YOU FORGETTIN' THE LIGHTS GO ON TO-NIGHT! IT'S GOING TO BE KINDA LIGHT OUT THERE!

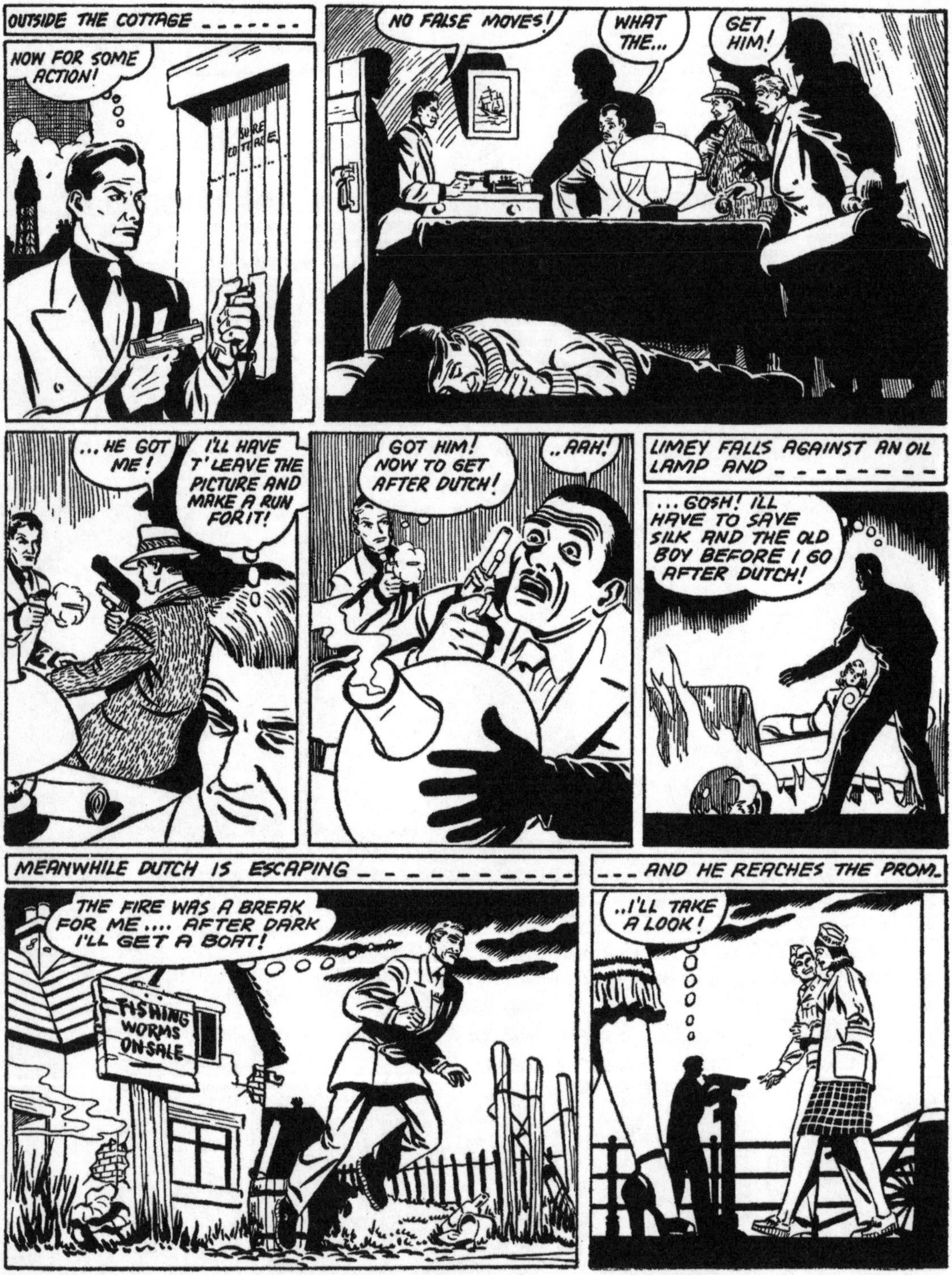
OUTSIDE THE COTTAGE - - - - - - -
NOW FOR SOME ACTION!
SURE COTTAGE
NO FALSE MOVES!
WHAT THE...
GET HIM!
...HE GOT ME!
I'LL HAVE T' LEAVE THE PICTURE AND MAKE A RUN FOR IT!
GOT HIM! NOW TO GET AFTER DUTCH!
..AAH!
LIMEY FALLS AGAINST AN OIL LAMP AND - - - - - - - -
...GOSH! I'LL HAVE TO SAVE SILK AND THE OLD BOY BEFORE I GO AFTER DUTCH!
MEANWHILE DUTCH IS ESCAPING - - - - - - - - - -
THE FIRE WAS A BREAK FOR ME.... AFTER DARK I'LL GET A BOAT!
FISHING WORMS ON SALE
- - - AND HE REACHES THE PROM.
..I'LL TAKE A LOOK!

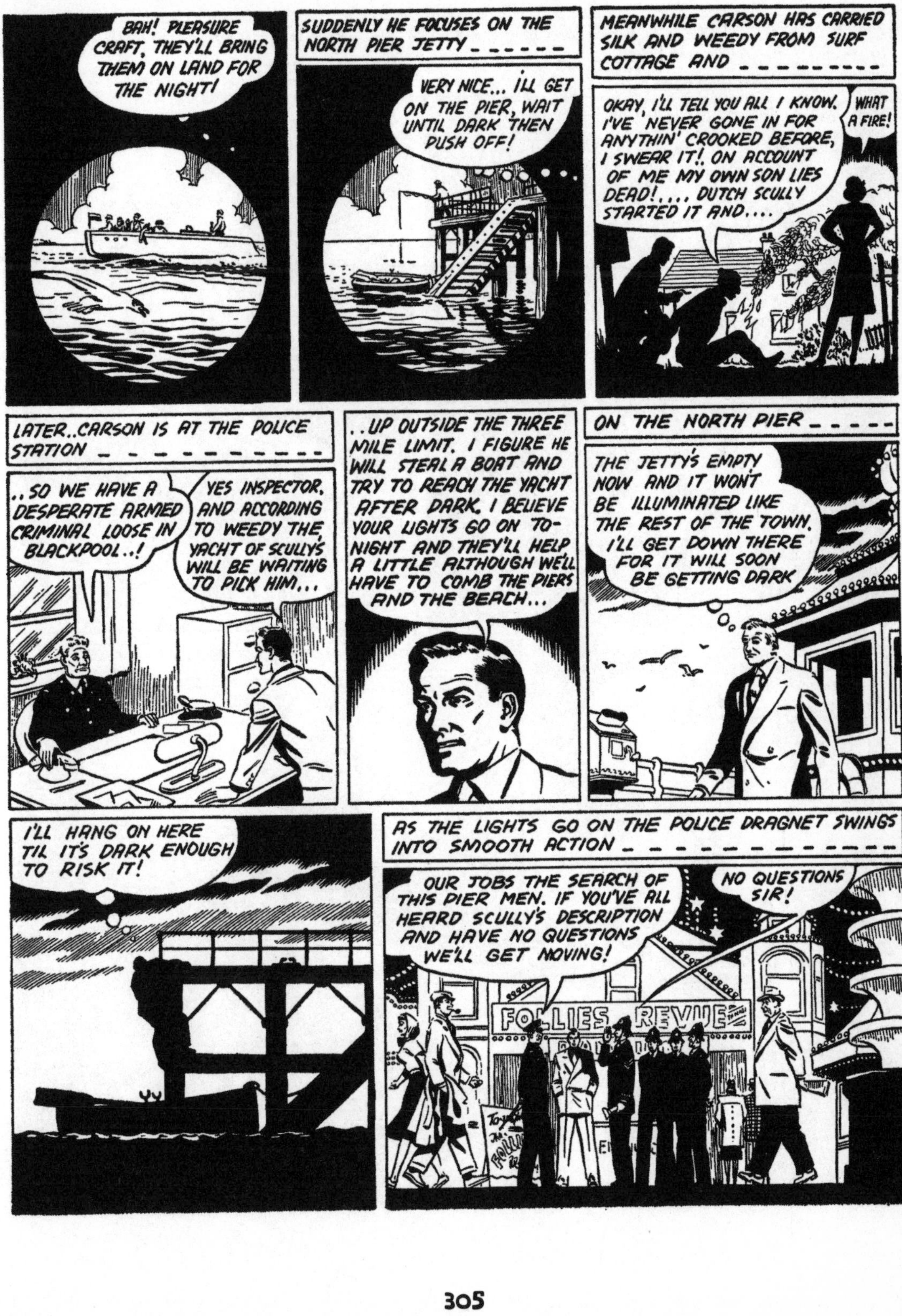
BAH! PLEASURE CRAFT, THEY'LL BRING THEM ON LAND FOR THE NIGHT!
SUDDENLY HE FOCUSES ON THE NORTH PIER JETTY _ _ _ _ _
VERY NICE... I'LL GET ON THE PIER, WAIT UNTIL DARK THEN PUSH OFF!
MEANWHILE CARSON HAS CARRIED SILK AND WEEDY FROM SURF COTTAGE AND _ _ _ _ _ _ _
OKAY, I'LL TELL YOU ALL I KNOW. I'VE NEVER GONE IN FOR ANYTHIN' CROOKED BEFORE, I SWEAR IT!, ON ACCOUNT OF ME MY OWN SON LIES DEAD!..., DUTCH SCULLY STARTED IT AND....
WHAT A FIRE!
LATER..CARSON IS AT THE POLICE STATION _ _ _ _ _ _ _ _ _
..SO WE HAVE A DESPERATE ARMED CRIMINAL LOOSE IN BLACKPOOL..!
YES INSPECTOR, AND ACCORDING TO WEEDY THE, YACHT OF SCULLY'S WILL BE WAITING TO PICK HIM...
..UP OUTSIDE THE THREE MILE LIMIT. I FIGURE HE WILL STEAL A BOAT AND TRY TO REACH THE YACHT AFTER DARK. I BELIEVE YOUR LIGHTS GO ON TO-NIGHT AND THEY'LL HELP A LITTLE ALTHOUGH WE'LL HAVE TO COMB THE PIERS AND THE BEACH...
ON THE NORTH PIER _ _ _ _ _
THE JETTY'S EMPTY NOW AND IT WON'T BE ILLUMINATED LIKE THE REST OF THE TOWN. I'LL GET DOWN THERE FOR IT WILL SOON BE GETTING DARK
I'LL HANG ON HERE TIL IT'S DARK ENOUGH TO RISK IT!
AS THE LIGHTS GO ON THE POLICE DRAGNET SWINGS INTO SMOOTH ACTION _ _ _ _ _ _ _ _ _ _
OUR JOBS THE SEARCH OF THIS PIER MEN. IF YOU'VE ALL HEARD SCULLY'S DESCRIPTION AND HAVE NO QUESTIONS WE'LL GET MOVING!
NO QUESTIONS SIR!
FOLLIES REVUE

THE POLICE CHECK CONTINUES, SOMETIMES CAUSING EMBARRASSMENT AND ANNOYANCE TO INNOCENT HOLIDAY MAKERS _ _ _ _ _ _ _ _ _ _ _ _ _ _ _ _ _ _

WHAT THE...

OKAY SON CARRY ON!

SAY WHAT IS THIS...?

POLICE CHECK! YOU'RE OKAY!

DOESN'T SEEM TO BE ANYONE DOWN HERE!

PIER'S CRAWLIN WITH COPPERS PHEW!

WE NEED MORE LIGHT. GOT IT! THE TOWER SEARCHLIGHT!

CONSTABLE!.. FIND THE INSPECTOR AND ASK HIM TO REQUEST, THE TOWER TO PLAY ITS SEARCHLIGHT ALONG THE BEACH!

RIGHT AWAY MISTER CARSON!

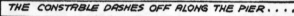

THE CONSTABLE DASHES OFF ALONG THE PIER....

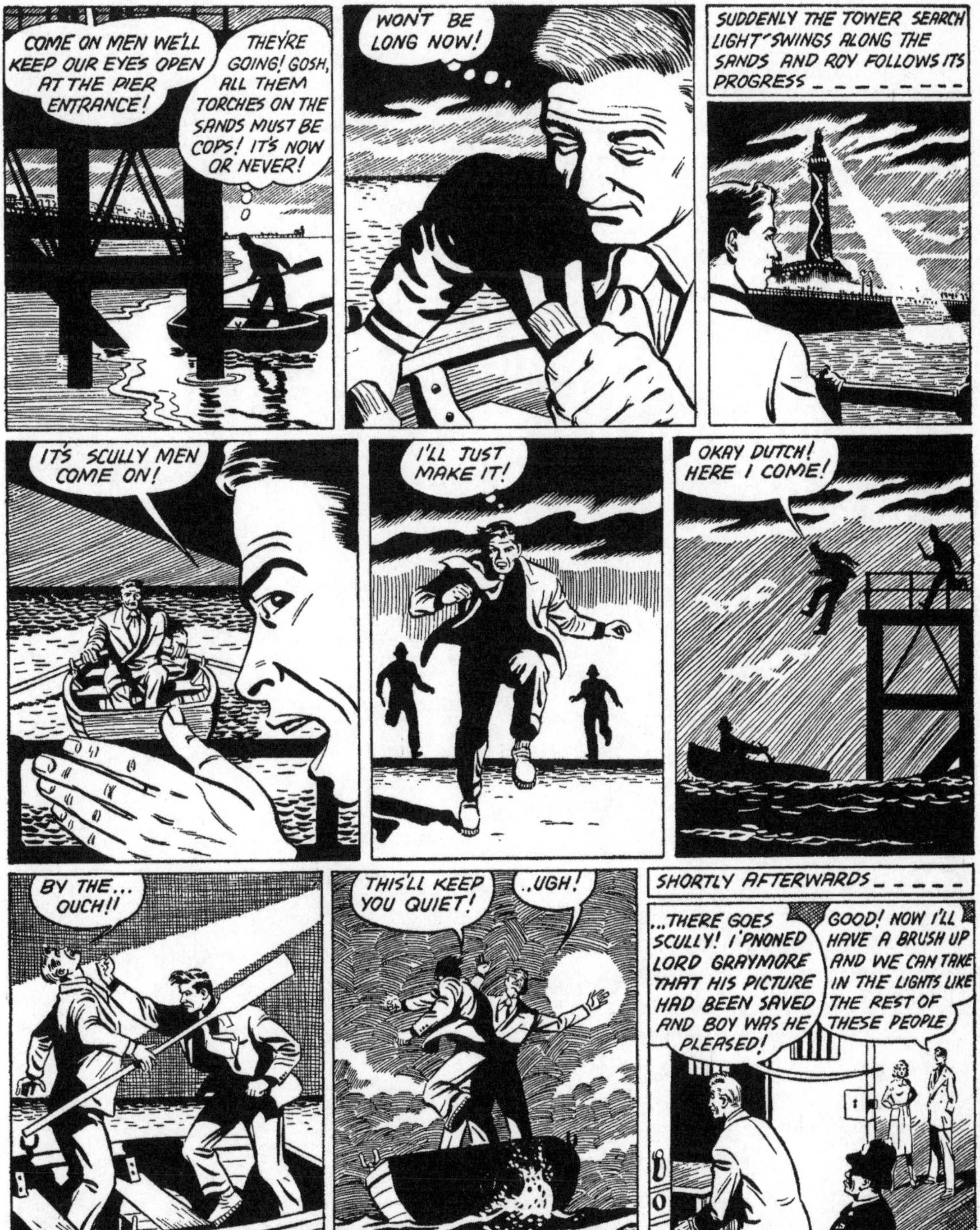
COME ON MEN WE'LL KEEP OUR EYES OPEN AT THE PIER ENTRANCE!
THEY'RE GOING! GOSH, ALL THEM TORCHES ON THE SANDS MUST BE COPS! IT'S NOW OR NEVER!
WON'T BE LONG NOW!
SUDDENLY THE TOWER SEARCH LIGHT SWINGS ALONG THE SANDS AND ROY FOLLOWS ITS PROGRESS ________
IT'S SCULLY MEN COME ON!
I'LL JUST MAKE IT!
OKAY DUTCH! HERE I COME!
BY THE... OUCH!!
THIS'LL KEEP YOU QUIET!
..UGH!
SHORTLY AFTERWARDS ____
...THERE GOES SCULLY! I'PNONED LORD GRAYMORE THAT HIS PICTURE HAD BEEN SAVED AND BOY WAS HE PLEASED!
GOOD! NOW I'LL HAVE A BRUSH UP AND WE CAN TAKE IN THE LIGHTS LIKE THE REST OF THESE PEOPLE

"I know exactly what I'm doing!
I've waited for this moment for so long!
Now what good is your money
going to do you Walter...
Now what good!"

As an accountant for DC Comics, British-born
Victor Fox was so impressed by their comic
book profits that he started his own company
in 1939. The short, loud, self-proclaimed "King
of Comics" pumped out whatever was selling
and hit on a winner in the mix of buxom
broads and bullets in *Crimes By Women*. In this
John Waters-esque melodrama, a listless wife
schemes to rid herself of her dull but wealthy
husband. Crudely compulsive, the uncredited
artwork pours on the tawdry sleaze and
shapely legs. There's even a clever parallel
between two external overhead shots through
windows, the one into Mary's home as she
celebrates her triumph, the other into prison

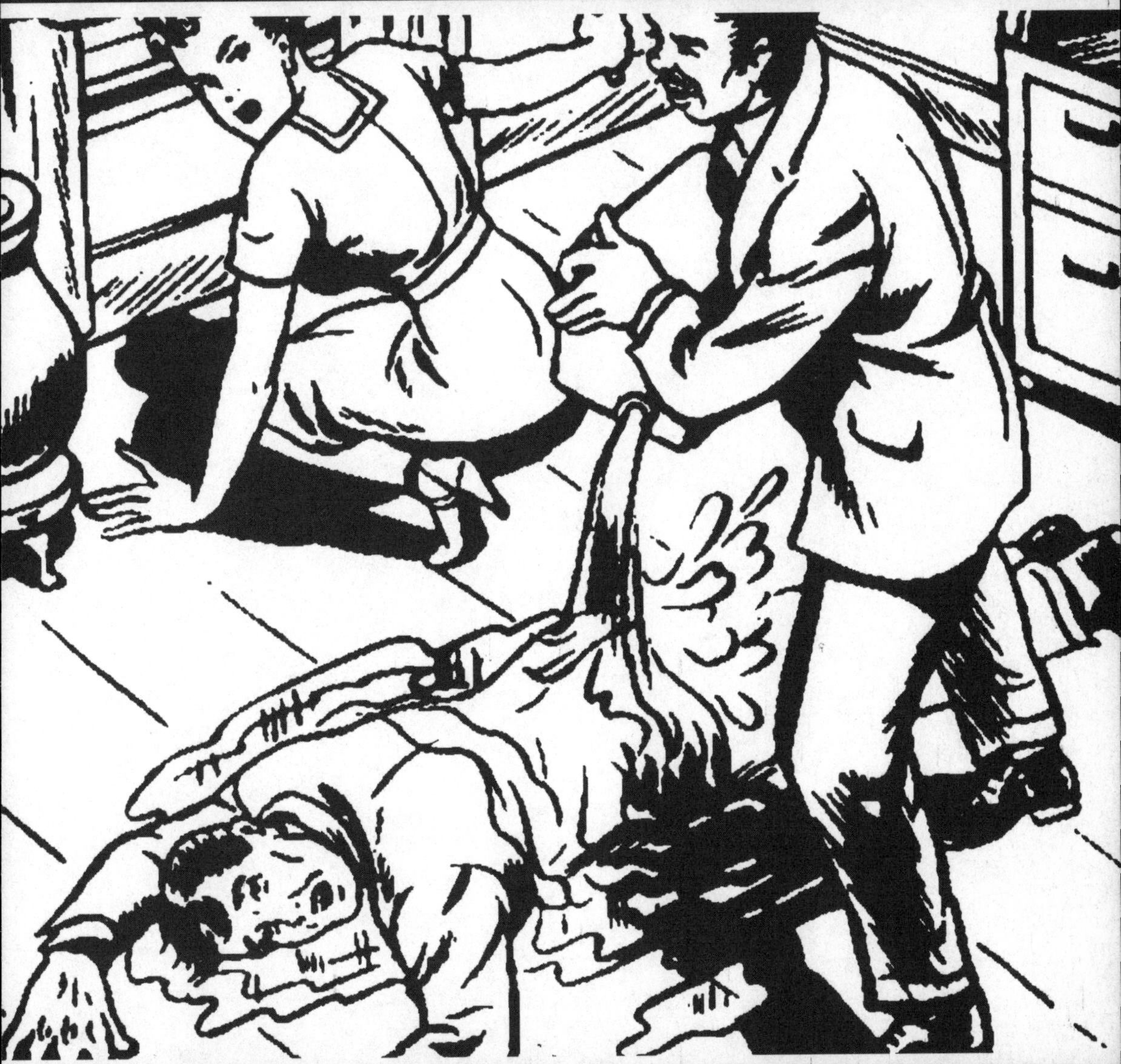

Mary Spratchet

Writer and artist unknown 1949

MARY SPRATCHET

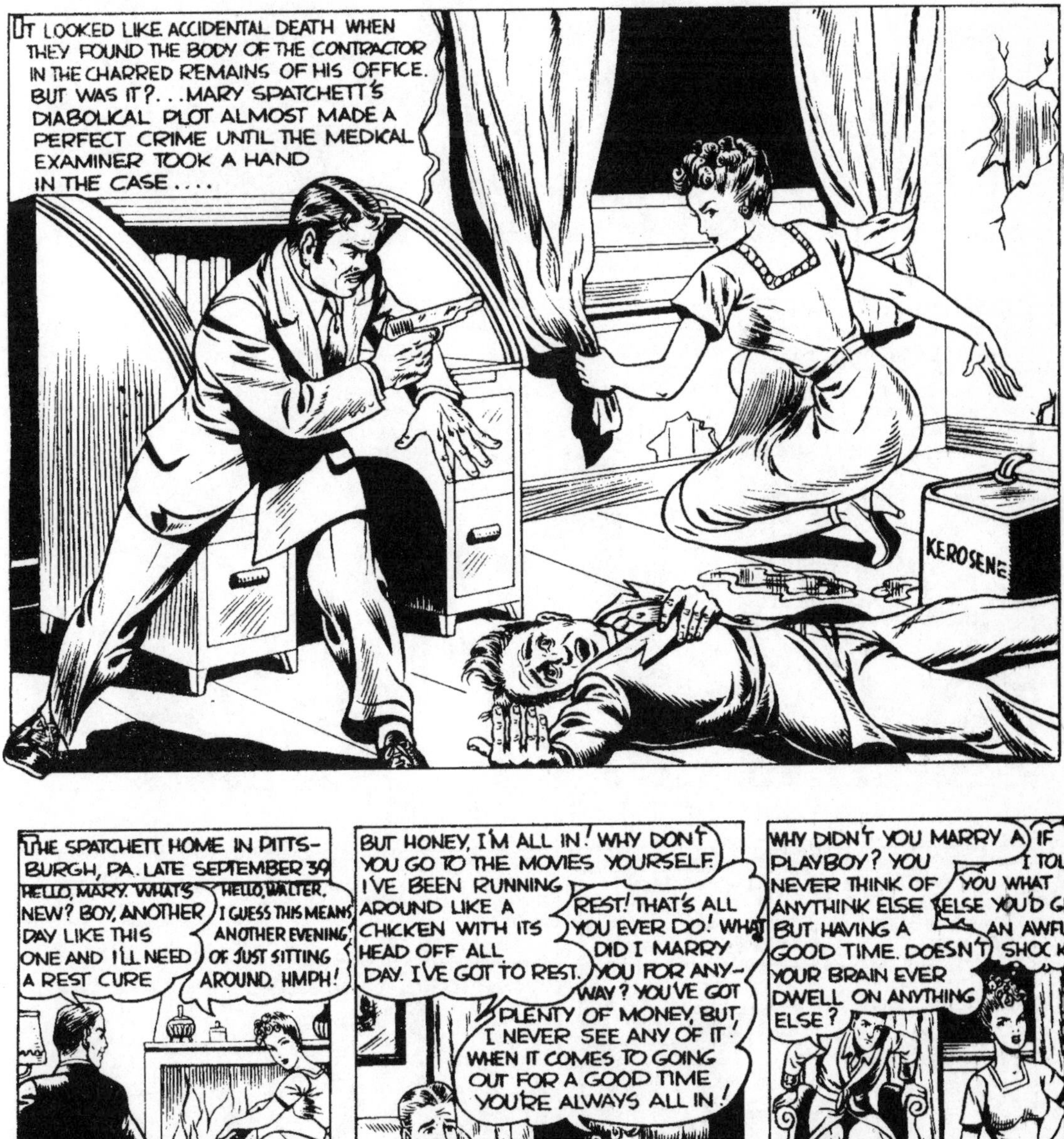
IT LOOKED LIKE ACCIDENTAL DEATH WHEN THEY FOUND THE BODY OF THE CONTRACTOR IN THE CHARRED REMAINS OF HIS OFFICE. BUT WAS IT?... MARY SPATCHETT'S DIABOLICAL PLOT ALMOST MADE A PERFECT CRIME UNTIL THE MEDICAL EXAMINER TOOK A HAND IN THE CASE....
KEROSENE
THE SPATCHETT HOME IN PITTSBURGH, PA. LATE SEPTEMBER 39
HELLO, MARY. WHAT'S NEW? BOY, ANOTHER DAY LIKE THIS ONE AND I'LL NEED A REST CURE
HELLO, WALTER. I GUESS THIS MEANS ANOTHER EVENING OF JUST SITTING AROUND. HMPH!
BUT HONEY, I'M ALL IN! WHY DON'T YOU GO TO THE MOVIES YOURSELF. I'VE BEEN RUNNING AROUND LIKE A CHICKEN WITH ITS HEAD OFF ALL DAY. I'VE GOT TO REST.
REST! THAT'S ALL YOU EVER DO! WHAT DID I MARRY YOU FOR ANYWAY? YOU'VE GOT PLENTY OF MONEY, BUT I NEVER SEE ANY OF IT! WHEN IT COMES TO GOING OUT FOR A GOOD TIME YOU'RE ALWAYS ALL IN!
WHY DIDN'T YOU MARRY A PLAYBOY? YOU NEVER THINK OF ANYTHINK ELSE BUT HAVING A GOOD TIME. DOESN'T YOUR BRAIN EVER DWELL ON ANYTHING ELSE?
IF I TOLD YOU WHAT ELSE YOU'D GET AN AWFUL SHOCK!

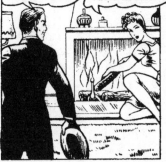

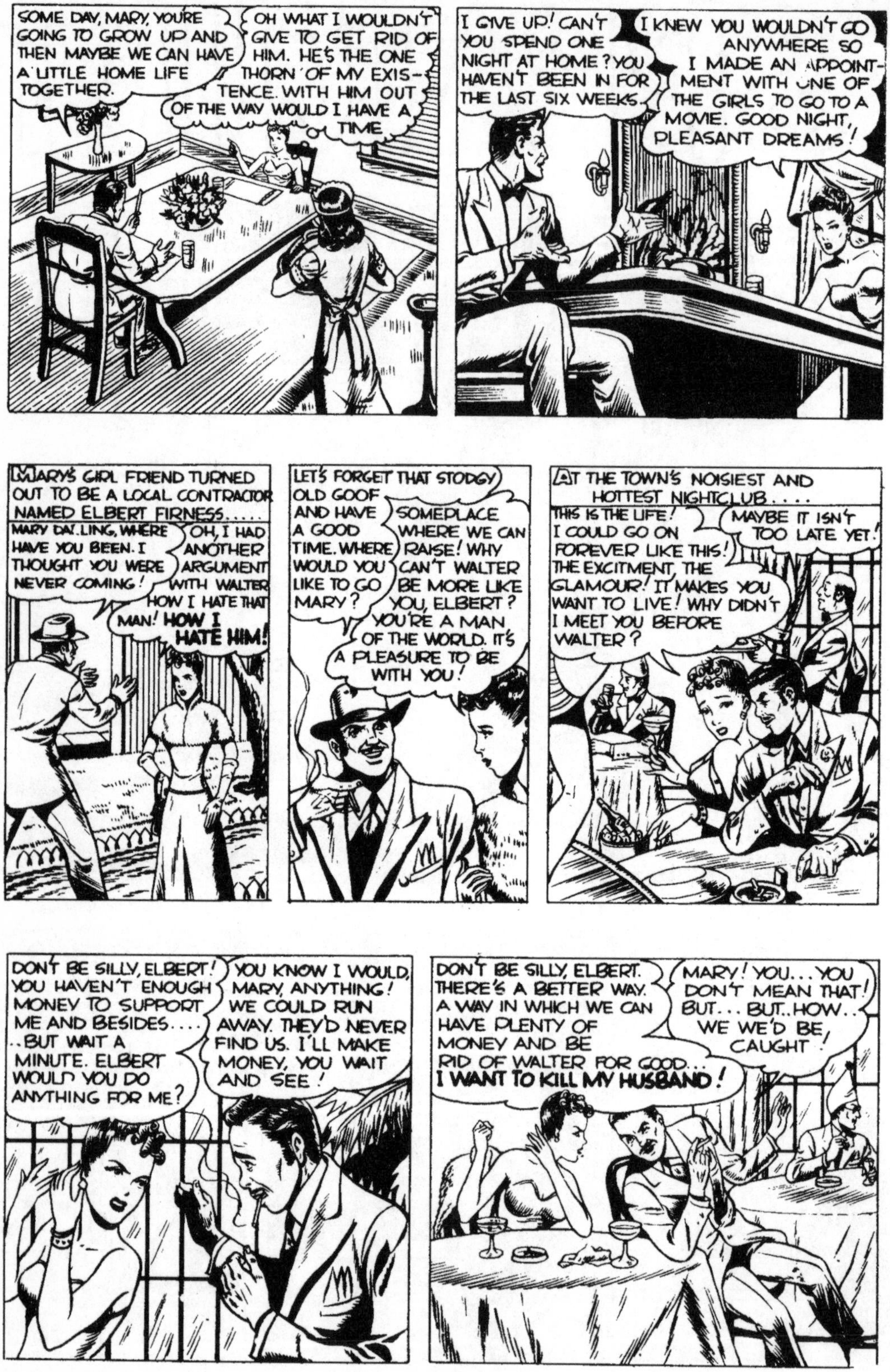
SOME DAY, MARY, YOU'RE GOING TO GROW UP AND THEN MAYBE WE CAN HAVE A LITTLE HOME LIFE TOGETHER.
OH WHAT I WOULDN'T GIVE TO GET RID OF HIM. HE'S THE ONE THORN OF MY EXISTENCE. WITH HIM OUT OF THE WAY WOULD I HAVE A TIME
I GIVE UP! CAN'T YOU SPEND ONE NIGHT AT HOME? YOU HAVEN'T BEEN IN FOR THE LAST SIX WEEKS.
I KNEW YOU WOULDN'T GO ANYWHERE SO I MADE AN APPOINTMENT WITH ONE OF THE GIRLS TO GO TO A MOVIE. GOOD NIGHT, PLEASANT DREAMS!
MARY'S GIRL FRIEND TURNED OUT TO BE A LOCAL CONTRACTOR NAMED ELBERT FIRNESS.....
MARY DARLING, WHERE HAVE YOU BEEN. I THOUGHT YOU WERE NEVER COMING!
OH, I HAD ANOTHER ARGUMENT WITH WALTER HOW I HATE THAT MAN! HOW I HATE HIM!
LET'S FORGET THAT STODGY OLD GOOF AND HAVE A GOOD TIME. WHERE WOULD YOU LIKE TO GO MARY?
SOMEPLACE WHERE WE CAN RAISE! WHY CAN'T WALTER BE MORE LIKE YOU, ELBERT? YOU'RE A MAN OF THE WORLD. IT'S A PLEASURE TO BE WITH YOU!
AT THE TOWN'S NOISIEST AND HOTTEST NIGHTCLUB....
THIS IS THE LIFE! I COULD GO ON FOREVER LIKE THIS! THE EXCITMENT, THE GLAMOUR! IT MAKES YOU WANT TO LIVE! WHY DIDN'T I MEET YOU BEFORE WALTER?
MAYBE IT ISN'T TOO LATE YET!
DON'T BE SILLY, ELBERT! YOU HAVEN'T ENOUGH MONEY TO SUPPORT ME AND BESIDES.... ..BUT WAIT A MINUTE. ELBERT WOULD YOU DO ANYTHING FOR ME?
YOU KNOW I WOULD, MARY, ANYTHING! WE COULD RUN AWAY. THEY'D NEVER FIND US. I'LL MAKE MONEY, YOU WAIT AND SEE!
DON'T BE SILLY, ELBERT. THERE'S A BETTER WAY. A WAY IN WHICH WE CAN HAVE PLENTY OF MONEY AND BE RID OF WALTER FOR GOOD... I WANT TO KILL MY HUSBAND!
MARY! YOU... YOU DON'T MEAN THAT! BUT... BUT..HOW.. WE WE'D BE CAUGHT!

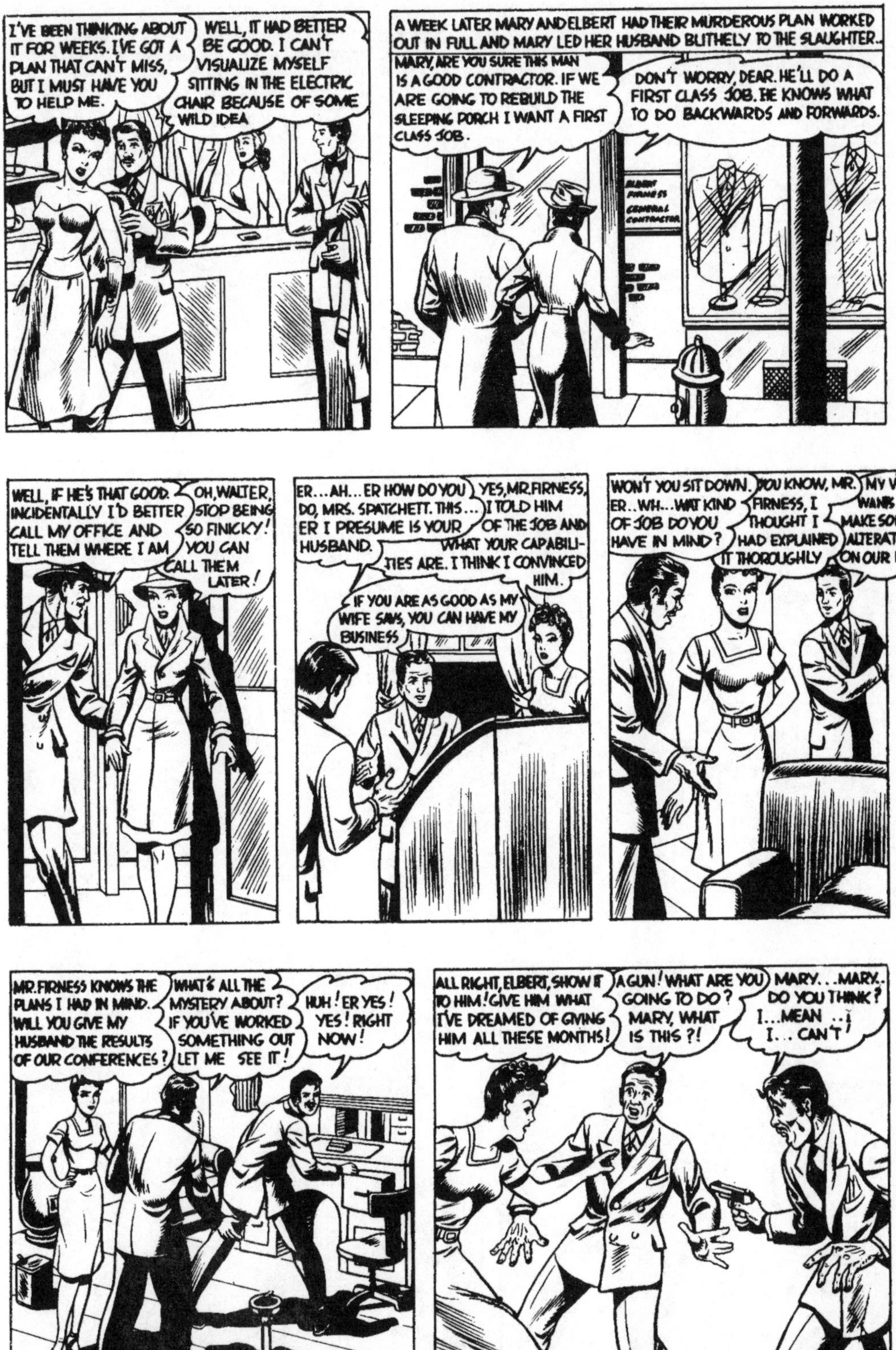
I'VE BEEN THINKING ABOUT IT FOR WEEKS. I'VE GOT A PLAN THAT CAN'T MISS, BUT I MUST HAVE YOU TO HELP ME.
WELL, IT HAD BETTER BE GOOD. I CAN'T VISUALIZE MYSELF SITTING IN THE ELECTRIC CHAIR BECAUSE OF SOME WILD IDEA
A WEEK LATER MARY AND ELBERT HAD THEIR MURDEROUS PLAN WORKED OUT IN FULL AND MARY LED HER HUSBAND BLITHELY TO THE SLAUGHTER..
MARY, ARE YOU SURE THIS MAN IS A GOOD CONTRACTOR. IF WE ARE GOING TO REBUILD THE SLEEPING PORCH I WANT A FIRST CLASS JOB.
DON'T WORRY, DEAR. HE'LL DO A FIRST CLASS JOB. HE KNOWS WHAT TO DO BACKWARDS AND FORWARDS.
WELL, IF HE'S THAT GOOD. INCIDENTALLY I'D BETTER CALL MY OFFICE AND TELL THEM WHERE I AM
OH, WALTER, STOP BEING SO FINICKY! YOU CAN CALL THEM LATER!
ER...AH...ER HOW DO YOU DO, MRS. SPATCHETT. THIS... ER I PRESUME IS YOUR HUSBAND.
YES, MR. FIRNESS, I TOLD HIM OF THE JOB AND WHAT YOUR CAPABILITIES ARE. I THINK I CONVINCED HIM.
IF YOU ARE AS GOOD AS MY WIFE SAYS, YOU CAN HAVE MY BUSINESS
WON'T YOU SIT DOWN. ER..WH...WAT KIND OF JOB DO YOU HAVE IN MIND?
YOU KNOW, MR. FIRNESS, I THOUGHT I HAD EXPLAINED IT THOROUGHLY
MY WIFE WANTS TO MAKE SOME ALTERATIONS ON OUR HOUSE
MR. FIRNESS KNOWS THE PLANS I HAD IN MIND. WILL YOU GIVE MY HUSBAND THE RESULTS OF OUR CONFERENCES?
WHAT'S ALL THE MYSTERY ABOUT? IF YOU'VE WORKED SOMETHING OUT LET ME SEE IT!
HUH! ER YES! YES! RIGHT NOW!
ALL RIGHT, ELBERT, SHOW IT TO HIM! GIVE HIM WHAT I'VE DREAMED OF GIVING HIM ALL THESE MONTHS!
A GUN! WHAT ARE YOU GOING TO DO? MARY, WHAT IS THIS?!
MARY...MARY.. DO YOU THINK? I...MEAN... I... CAN'T
3

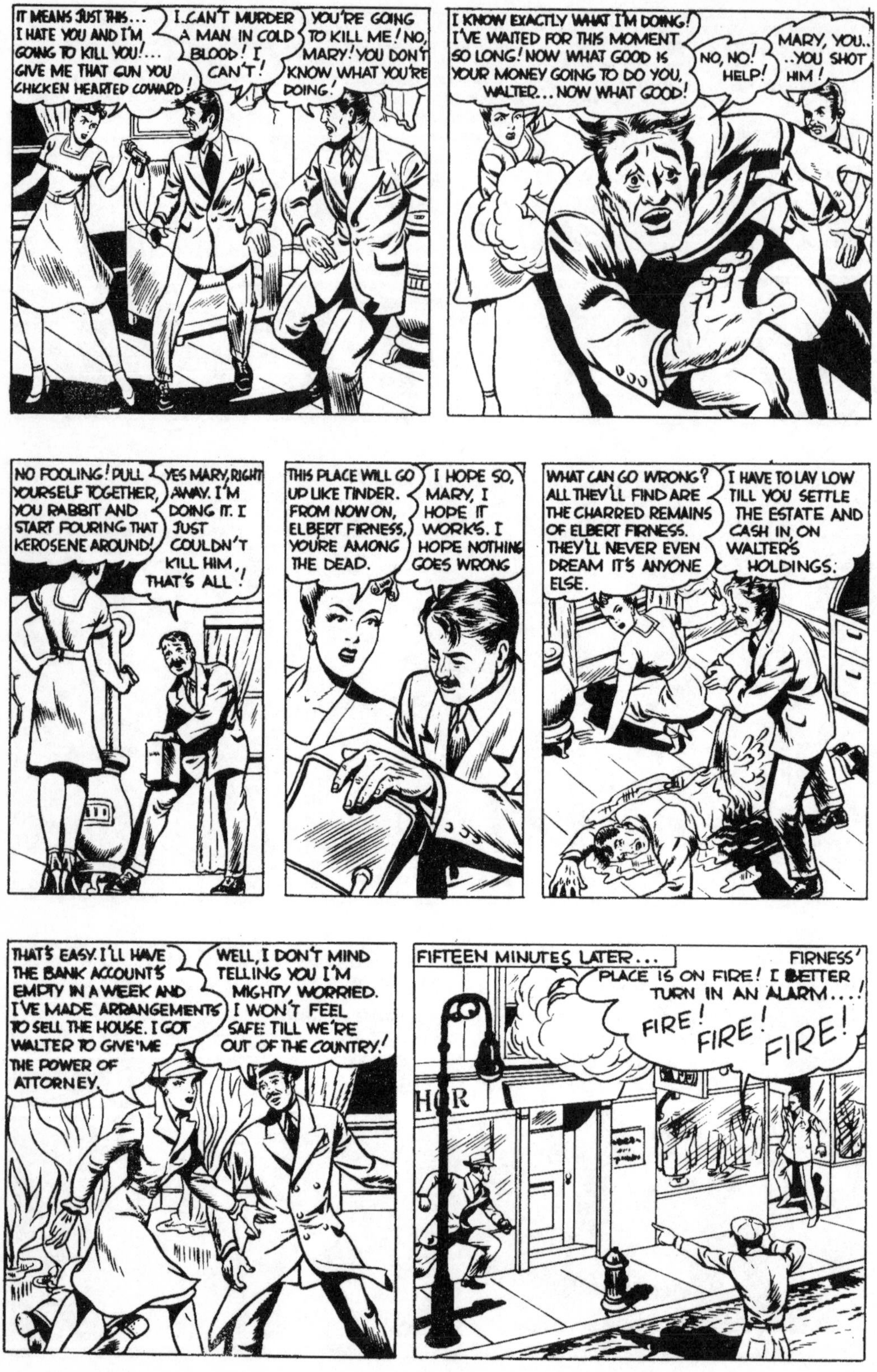
IT MEANS JUST THIS... I HATE YOU AND I'M GOING TO KILL YOU!... GIVE ME THAT GUN YOU CHICKEN HEARTED COWARD!
I..CAN'T MURDER A MAN IN COLD BLOOD! I CAN'T!
YOU'RE GOING TO KILL ME! NO, MARY! YOU DON'T KNOW WHAT YOU'RE DOING!
I KNOW EXACTLY WHAT I'M DOING! I'VE WAITED FOR THIS MOMENT SO LONG! NOW WHAT GOOD IS YOUR MONEY GOING TO DO YOU, WALTER... NOW WHAT GOOD!
NO, NO! HELP!
MARY, YOU.. ..YOU SHOT HIM!
NO FOOLING! PULL YOURSELF TOGETHER, YOU RABBIT AND START POURING THAT KEROSENE AROUND!
YES MARY, RIGHT AWAY. I'M DOING IT. I JUST COULDN'T KILL HIM, THAT'S ALL!
THIS PLACE WILL GO UP LIKE TINDER. FROM NOW ON, ELBERT FIRNESS, YOU'RE AMONG THE DEAD.
I HOPE SO, MARY, I HOPE IT WORKS. I HOPE NOTHING GOES WRONG
WHAT CAN GO WRONG? ALL THEY'LL FIND ARE THE CHARRED REMAINS OF ELBERT FIRNESS. THEY'LL NEVER EVEN DREAM IT'S ANYONE ELSE.
I HAVE TO LAY LOW TILL YOU SETTLE THE ESTATE AND CASH IN ON WALTER'S HOLDINGS.
THAT'S EASY. I'LL HAVE THE BANK ACCOUNT'S EMPTY IN A WEEK AND I'VE MADE ARRANGEMENTS TO SELL THE HOUSE. I GOT WALTER TO GIVE ME THE POWER OF ATTORNEY.
WELL, I DON'T MIND TELLING YOU I'M MIGHTY WORRIED. I WON'T FEEL SAFE TILL WE'RE OUT OF THE COUNTRY!
FIFTEEN MINUTES LATER...
FIRNESS' PLACE IS ON FIRE! I BETTER TURN IN AN ALARM...! FIRE! FIRE! FIRE!
HOR

WHEN THE ENGINES ARRIVE THE OFFICE IS A BLAZING INFERNO. WHEW! LOOK AT THAT! THERE WON'T BE A STICK LEFT. POOR ELBERT!

POOR ELBERT IS RIGHT. THEY THINK HE WAS TRAPPED INSIDE. IF HE WAS HE'S DONE FOR!

I HAVEN'T SEEN A BLAZE LIKE THIS IN TWENTY YEARS. WE NEVER HAD A CHANCE TO CHECK IT.

WONDER IF THE POOR GUY CAUGHT. WELL WE'LL KNOW IN A MINUTE.

UGH! HE WAS CAUGHT ALL RIGHT. YOU'D NEVER EVEN KNOW IT WAS A HUMAN BEING!

YOU SAID IT. LET'S REPORT TO THE CHIEF SO THEY CAN GET THE BOYS TO MOVE HIM! THIS KIND OF THING MAKES ME SORRY I EVER BECAME A FIREMAN

LATER AT THE CITY MORGUE.... THIS WAY PLEASE. THERE ISN'T MUCH TO IDENTIFY!

WE UNDERSTAND

OHH! THIS IS TERRIBLE! POOR ELBERT!

CAN YOU RECOGNIZE ANYTHING THAT WILL GIVE HIS IDENTIFY.

OHH! ITS ELBERT, ALL RIGHT. HE WAS THAT SIZE AND...THAT'S ENOUGH.. I...I'M SURE. IT COULD NOT BE ANYONE ELSE

THAT'S RIGHT. ELBERT ISN'T HOME OR ANYWHERE. IT'S HE WITHOUT A DOUBT!

WHAT A HORRIBLE WAY TO DIE. WHEN CAN WE CLAIM THE BODY FOR BURIAL.

OHH, JOE TAKE ME HOME, TAKE ME OUT OF HERE

NOT TILL AFTER THE MEDICAL EXAMINER FINISHES HIS AUTOPSY

MEANWHILE MARY AND ELBERT ARE CELEBRATING THE SUCCESS OF THEIR FIENDISH CRIME.... THIS IS WONDERFUL. IN A WEEK WE CAN LEAVE. NO ONE WILL SUSPECT ANYTHING. I TOLD WALTER'S OFFICE HE WAS TAKING A WEEK OFF AND WAS GOING OUT OF TOWN.

MARY, THE SERVANTS, WHAT ABOUT THEM?

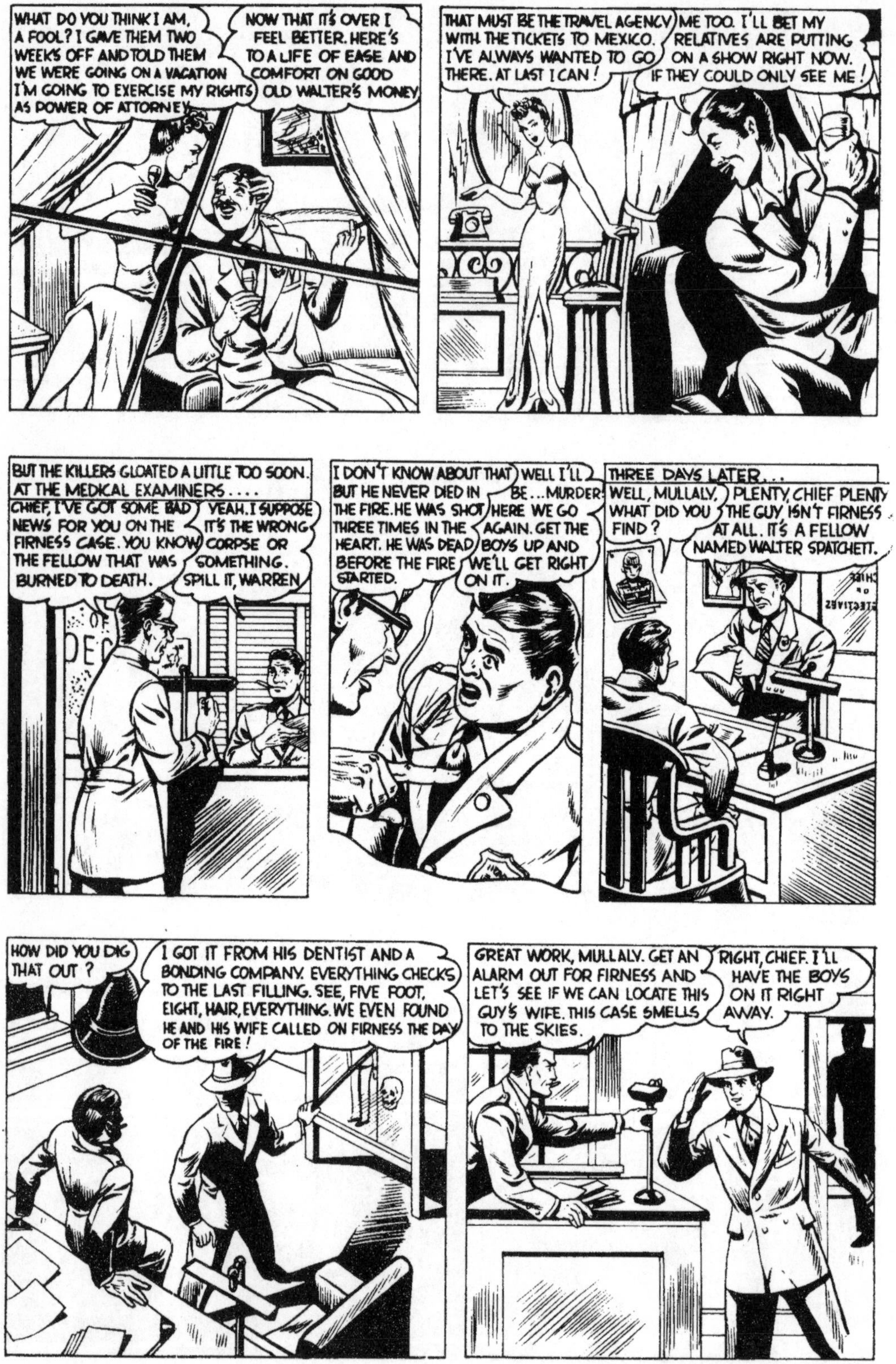
WHAT DO YOU THINK I AM, A FOOL? I GAVE THEM TWO WEEKS OFF AND TOLD THEM WE WERE GOING ON A VACATION I'M GOING TO EXERCISE MY RIGHTS AS POWER OF ATTORNEY.
NOW THAT IT'S OVER I FEEL BETTER. HERE'S TO A LIFE OF EASE AND COMFORT ON GOOD OLD WALTER'S MONEY
THAT MUST BE THE TRAVEL AGENCY WITH THE TICKETS TO MEXICO. I'VE ALWAYS WANTED TO GO THERE. AT LAST I CAN!
ME TOO. I'LL BET MY RELATIVES ARE PUTTING ON A SHOW RIGHT NOW. IF THEY COULD ONLY SEE ME!
BUT THE KILLERS GLOATED A LITTLE TOO SOON. AT THE MEDICAL EXAMINERS....
CHIEF, I'VE GOT SOME BAD NEWS FOR YOU ON THE FIRNESS CASE. YOU KNOW THE FELLOW THAT WAS BURNED TO DEATH.
YEAH. I SUPPOSE IT'S THE WRONG CORPSE OR SOMETHING. SPILL IT, WARREN.
I DON'T KNOW ABOUT THAT BUT HE NEVER DIED IN THE FIRE. HE WAS SHOT THREE TIMES IN THE HEART. HE WAS DEAD BEFORE THE FIRE STARTED.
WELL I'LL BE...MURDER! HERE WE GO AGAIN. GET THE BOYS UP AND WE'LL GET RIGHT ON IT.
THREE DAYS LATER...
WELL, MULLALY, WHAT DID YOU FIND?
PLENTY, CHIEF PLENTY THE GUY ISN'T FIRNESS AT ALL. IT'S A FELLOW NAMED WALTER SPATCHETT.
HOW DID YOU DIG THAT OUT?
I GOT IT FROM HIS DENTIST AND A BONDING COMPANY. EVERYTHING CHECKS TO THE LAST FILLING. SEE, FIVE FOOT, EIGHT, HAIR, EVERYTHING. WE EVEN FOUND HE AND HIS WIFE CALLED ON FIRNESS THE DAY OF THE FIRE!
GREAT WORK, MULLALY. GET AN ALARM OUT FOR FIRNESS AND LET'S SEE IF WE CAN LOCATE THIS GUY'S WIFE. THIS CASE SMELLS TO THE SKIES.
RIGHT, CHIEF. I'LL HAVE THE BOYS ON IT RIGHT AWAY.

BUT UNFORTUNATELY THE NEWSPAPERS GOT THE STORY AND THAT AFTERNOON....
HI, MARY. HOW MUCH LONGER DO WE HAVE TO HANG AROUND HERE ANYWAY. I'M BEGINNING TO GET JITTERY COOPED UP LIKE THIS!
JUST ANOTHER DAY OR TWO HERE, I BROUGHT YOU THE PAPERS.
OKAY, BUT... MARY! LOOK!
ELBERT! WHAT'S WRONG? WHAT'S HAPPENED?
I KNEW THIS WOULD HAPPEN! NOW WE'LL GO TO THE CHAIR IT'S ALL YOUR FAULT!
OH SHUT UP YOU NINNY! THEY HAVEN'T GOT US YET. I'VE GOT PLENTY OF CASH AND THE CAR IS OUTSIDE.
SHORTLY AFTER...
ELBERT! WILL YOU STOP ACTING LIKE A HUNTED CRIMINAL IN A MOVIE. GET IN THAT CAR BEFORE WE'RE ARRESTED!
YES, MARY, OKAY. I'M GETTING IN. JUST LET'S GET OUT OF HERE.
WE'LL HEAD ACROSS COUNTRY AND TRY AND MAKE THE BORDER. IF THINGS GET TO HOT WE'LL HOLE UP IN SOME SMALL RESORT.
ANYTHING, ANYTHING! AS LONG AS WE GO. THEY'RE NOT GOING TO BURN ME. I DIDN'T KILL HIM!
TEN MINUTES LATER....
THIS IS THE PLACE. LOOKS AS THOUGH NO ONE IS HOME.
SURE DOES, MAYBE THEY FLEW THE COOP. THOSE NEWSPAPERS, THE CHIEF COULD WRING THEIR NECKS!... HEY, WHAT'S THIS DAME WANT?
OH, MR. POLICEMAN! MR. POLICEMAN!
IF YOU'RE LOOKING FOR MRS. SPATCHETT SHE AND A MAN DROVE OFF IN HER CAR TEN MINUTES AGO. I NEVER DID TRUST THAT WOMEN!
I KNEW IT! THANKS LADY FOR THE TIP. YOU STAY HERE, AL WHILE I GO BACK AND REPORT
OKAY, THEY MIGHT COME BACK.. MAYBE!

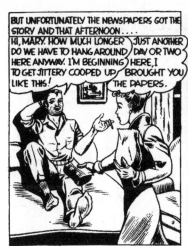

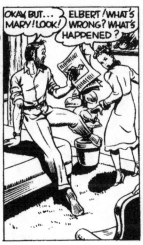

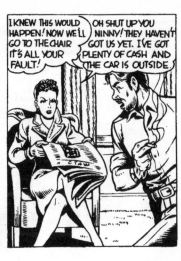

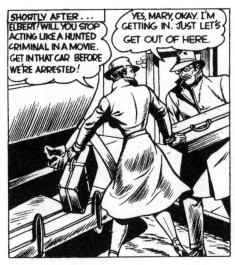

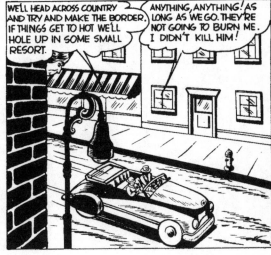

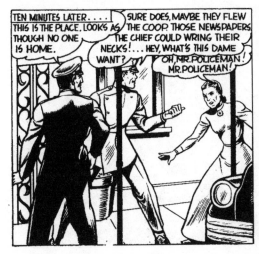

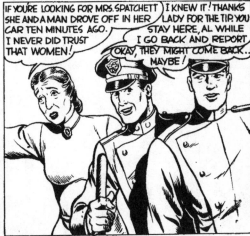

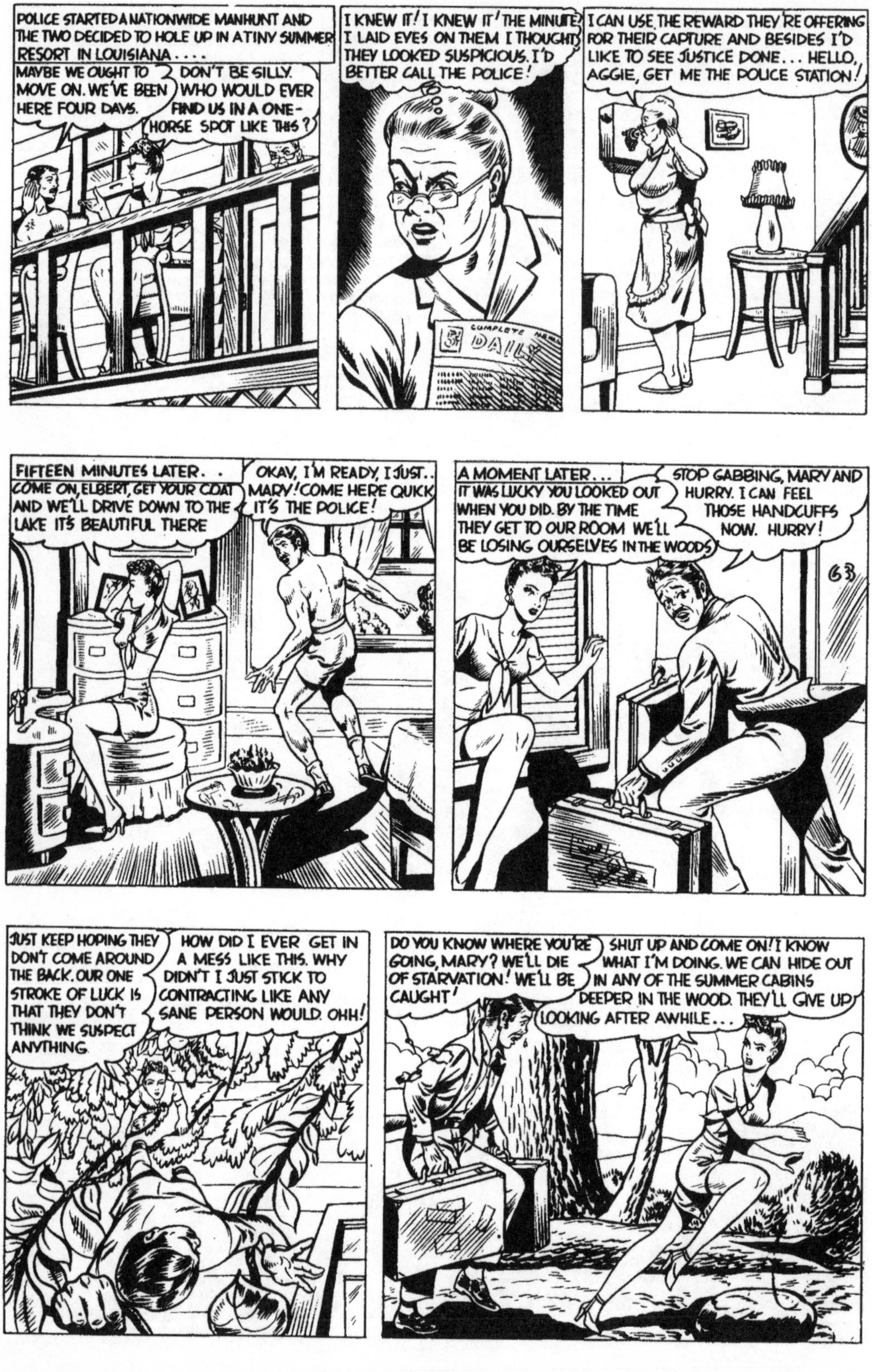
POLICE STARTED A NATIONWIDE MANHUNT AND THE TWO DECIDED TO HOLE UP IN A TINY SUMMER RESORT IN LOUISIANA . . . .
MAYBE WE OUGHT TO MOVE ON. WE'VE BEEN HERE FOUR DAYS.
DON'T BE SILLY. WHO WOULD EVER FIND US IN A ONE-HORSE SPOT LIKE THIS?
I KNEW IT! I KNEW IT! THE MINUTE I LAID EYES ON THEM I THOUGHT THEY LOOKED SUSPICIOUS. I'D BETTER CALL THE POLICE!
COMPLETE NEWS
DAILY
I CAN USE THE REWARD THEY'RE OFFERING FOR THEIR CAPTURE AND BESIDES I'D LIKE TO SEE JUSTICE DONE... HELLO, AGGIE, GET ME THE POLICE STATION!
FIFTEEN MINUTES LATER. .
COME ON, ELBERT, GET YOUR COAT AND WE'LL DRIVE DOWN TO THE LAKE IT'S BEAUTIFUL THERE
OKAY, I'M READY, I JUST.. MARY! COME HERE QUICK IT'S THE POLICE!
A MOMENT LATER...
IT WAS LUCKY YOU LOOKED OUT WHEN YOU DID. BY THE TIME THEY GET TO OUR ROOM WE'LL BE LOSING OURSELVES IN THE WOODS
STOP GABBING, MARY AND HURRY. I CAN FEEL THOSE HANDCUFFS NOW. HURRY!
63
JUST KEEP HOPING THEY DON'T COME AROUND THE BACK. OUR ONE STROKE OF LUCK IS THAT THEY DON'T THINK WE SUSPECT ANYTHING.
HOW DID I EVER GET IN A MESS LIKE THIS. WHY DIDN'T I JUST STICK TO CONTRACTING LIKE ANY SANE PERSON WOULD. OHH!
DO YOU KNOW WHERE YOU'RE GOING, MARY? WE'LL DIE OF STARVATION! WE'LL BE CAUGHT!
SHUT UP AND COME ON! I KNOW WHAT I'M DOING. WE CAN HIDE OUT IN ANY OF THE SUMMER CABINS DEEPER IN THE WOOD. THEY'LL GIVE UP LOOKING AFTER AWHILE...

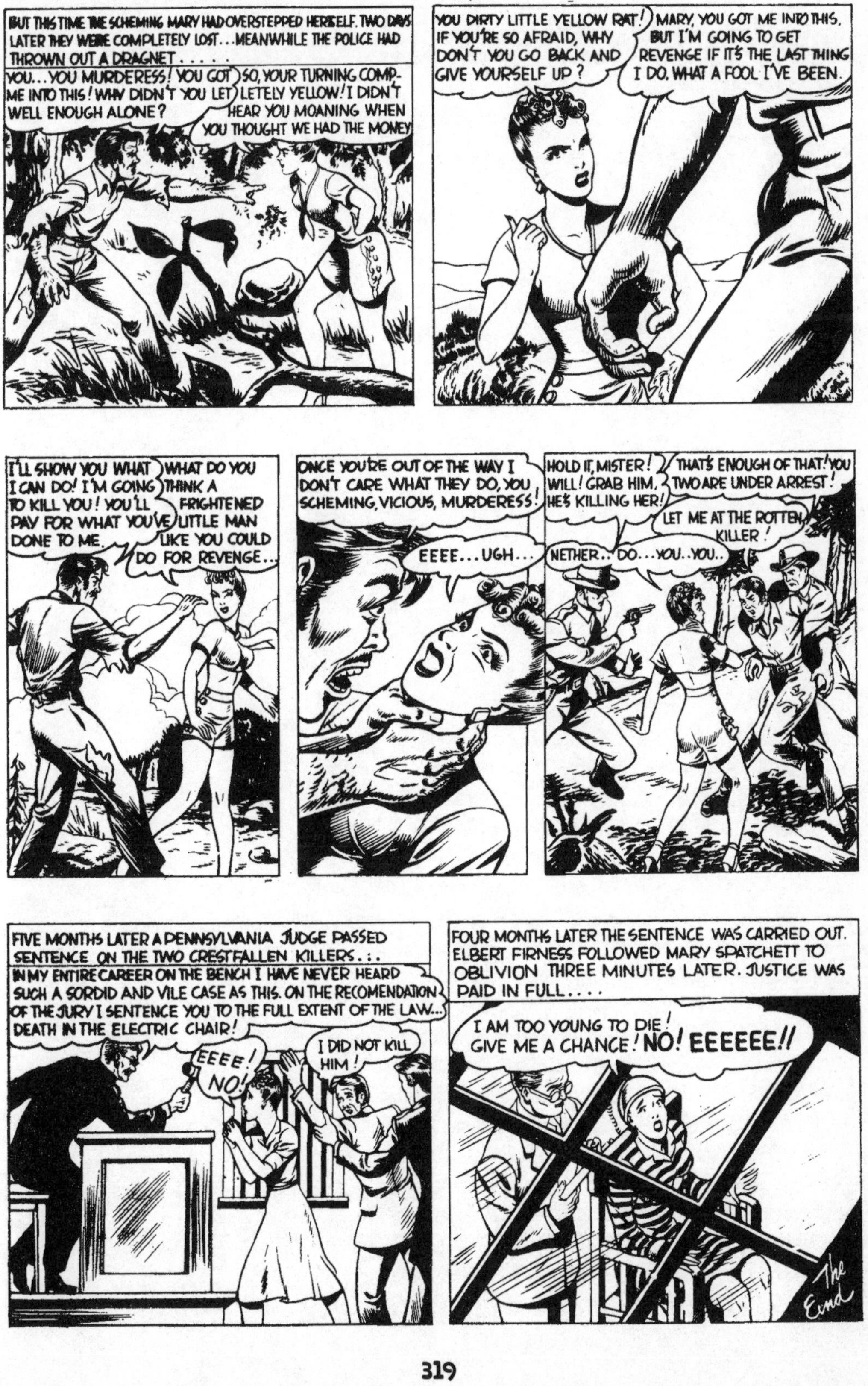

BUT THIS TIME THE SCHEMING MARY HAD OVERSTEPPED HERSELF. TWO DAYS LATER THEY WERE COMPLETELY LOST... MEANWHILE THE POLICE HAD THROWN OUT A DRAGNET . . . . .
YOU... YOU MURDERESS! YOU GOT ME INTO THIS! WHY DIDN'T YOU LET WELL ENOUGH ALONE?
SO, YOUR TURNING COMPLETELY YELLOW! I DIDN'T HEAR YOU MOANING WHEN YOU THOUGHT WE HAD THE MONEY
YOU DIRTY LITTLE YELLOW RAT! IF YOU'RE SO AFRAID, WHY DON'T YOU GO BACK AND GIVE YOURSELF UP?
MARY, YOU GOT ME INTO THIS, BUT I'M GOING TO GET REVENGE IF IT'S THE LAST THING I DO. WHAT A FOOL I'VE BEEN.
I'LL SHOW YOU WHAT I CAN DO! I'M GOING TO KILL YOU! YOU'LL PAY FOR WHAT YOU'VE DONE TO ME.
WHAT DO YOU THINK A FRIGHTENED LITTLE MAN LIKE YOU COULD DO FOR REVENGE...
ONCE YOU'RE OUT OF THE WAY I DON'T CARE WHAT THEY DO, YOU SCHEMING, VICIOUS, MURDERESS!
EEEE...UGH...
HOLD IT, MISTER! WILL! GRAB HIM, HE'S KILLING HER!
THAT'S ENOUGH OF THAT! YOU TWO ARE UNDER ARREST!
LET ME AT THE ROTTEN KILLER!
NETHER.. DO...YOU..YOU..
FIVE MONTHS LATER A PENNSYLVANIA JUDGE PASSED SENTENCE ON THE TWO CRESTFALLEN KILLERS. : .
IN MY ENTIRE CAREER ON THE BENCH I HAVE NEVER HEARD SUCH A SORDID AND VILE CASE AS THIS. ON THE RECOMENDATION OF THE JURY I SENTENCE YOU TO THE FULL EXTENT OF THE LAW... DEATH IN THE ELECTRIC CHAIR!
EEEE! NO!
I DID NOT KILL HIM!
FOUR MONTHS LATER THE SENTENCE WAS CARRIED OUT. ELBERT FIRNESS FOLLOWED MARY SPATCHETT TO OBLIVION THREE MINUTES LATER. JUSTICE WAS PAID IN FULL. . . .
I AM TOO YOUNG TO DIE! GIVE ME A CHANCE! NO! EEEEEE!!
The End

"So... what did you do?"

Principles come cheap if you want to get ahead in the police force. José Muñoz and Carlos Sampayo knew about corruption in the highest places when they quit a deteriorating Argentina in 1972 and became political exiles in Europe. Their second meeting near Barcelona in 1974 instigated a close creative friendship which nurtured their greatest character, Alack Sinner. Considering the vividness of their portrayal of New York, it's a surprise that neither of them had ever visited the Big Apple when they developed the *Sinner* saga. By relying instead on the almost mythical metropolis familiar from the media, they conjured up a startlingly convincing cityscape, and a troubled, sympathetic detective. Tonight he needs to do some serious drinking and get off his chest to someone how he gave up being a cop, so that he could live with himself again.

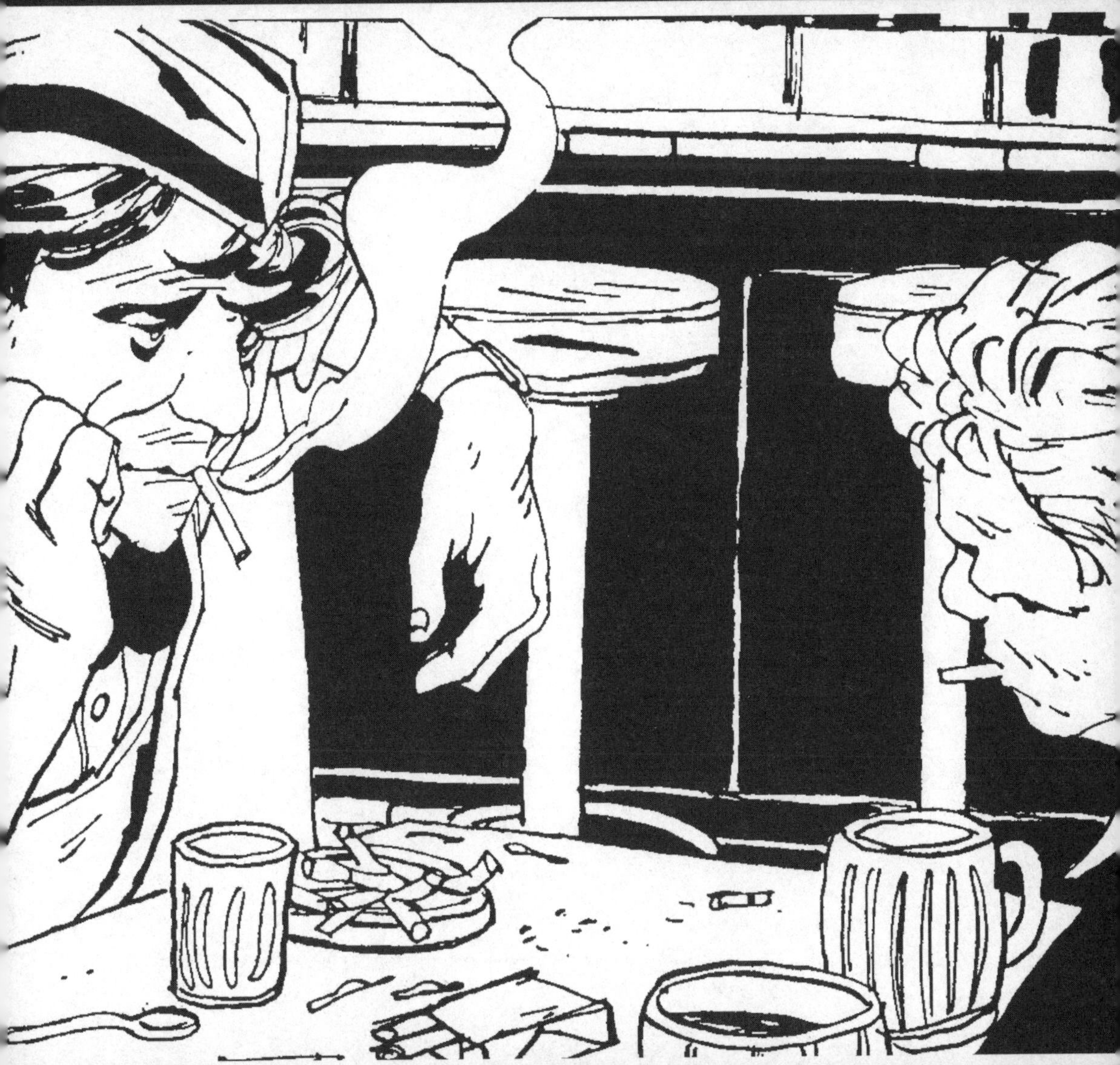

Alack Sinner: Talkin' With Joe

Carlos Sampayo (script) and José Muñoz (art) 1975

SINNER

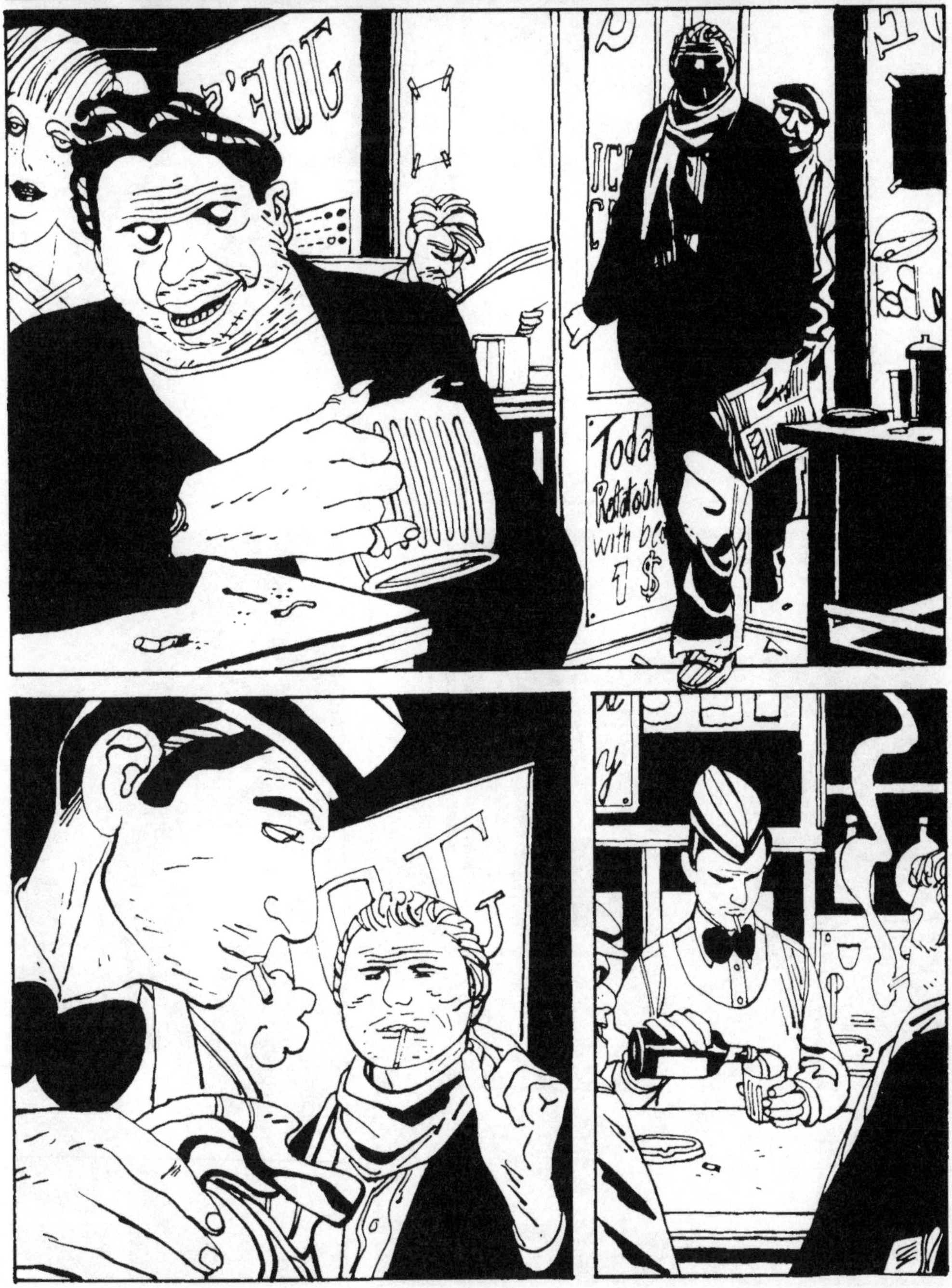

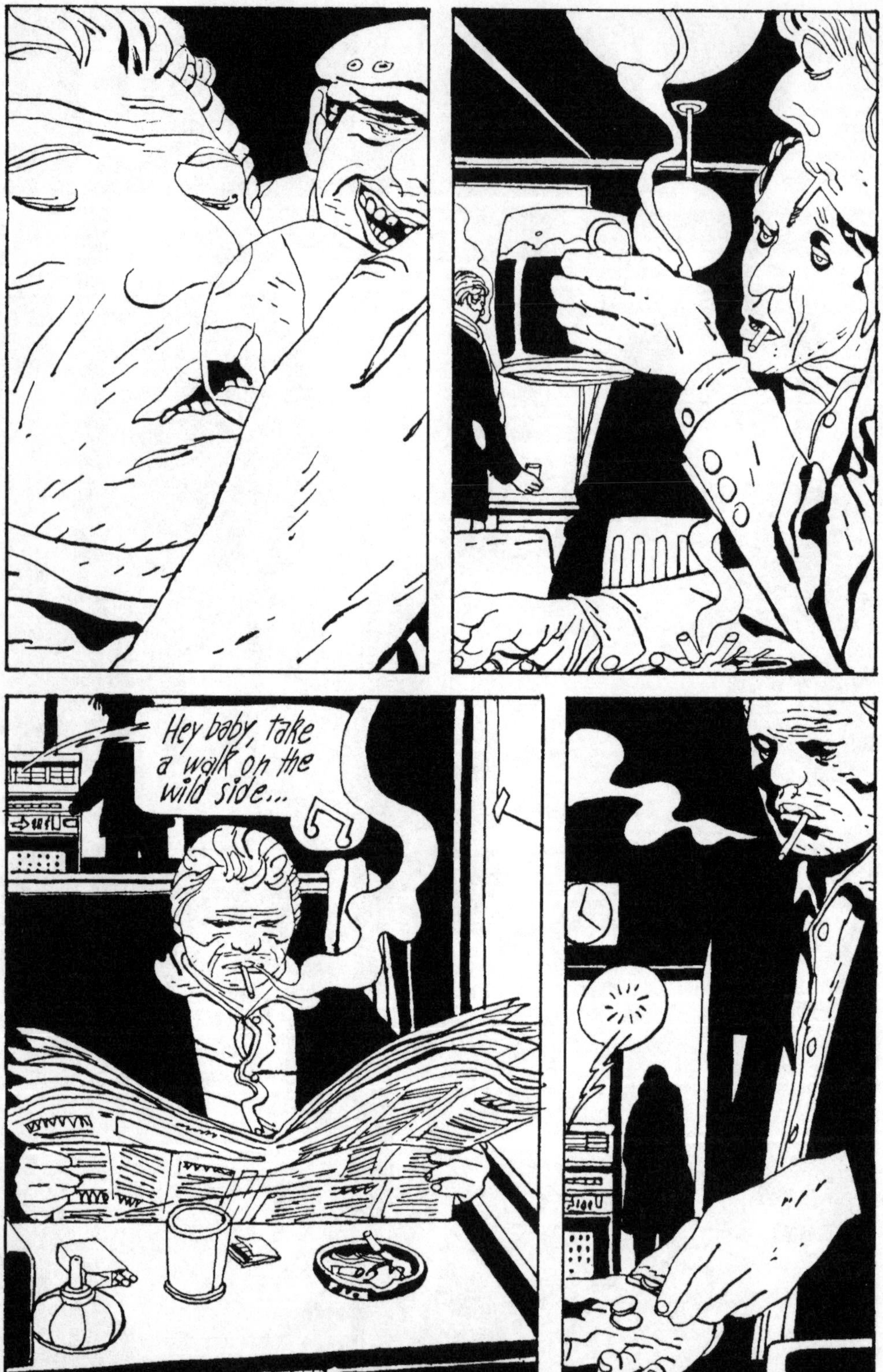
Hey baby, take a walk on the wild side...

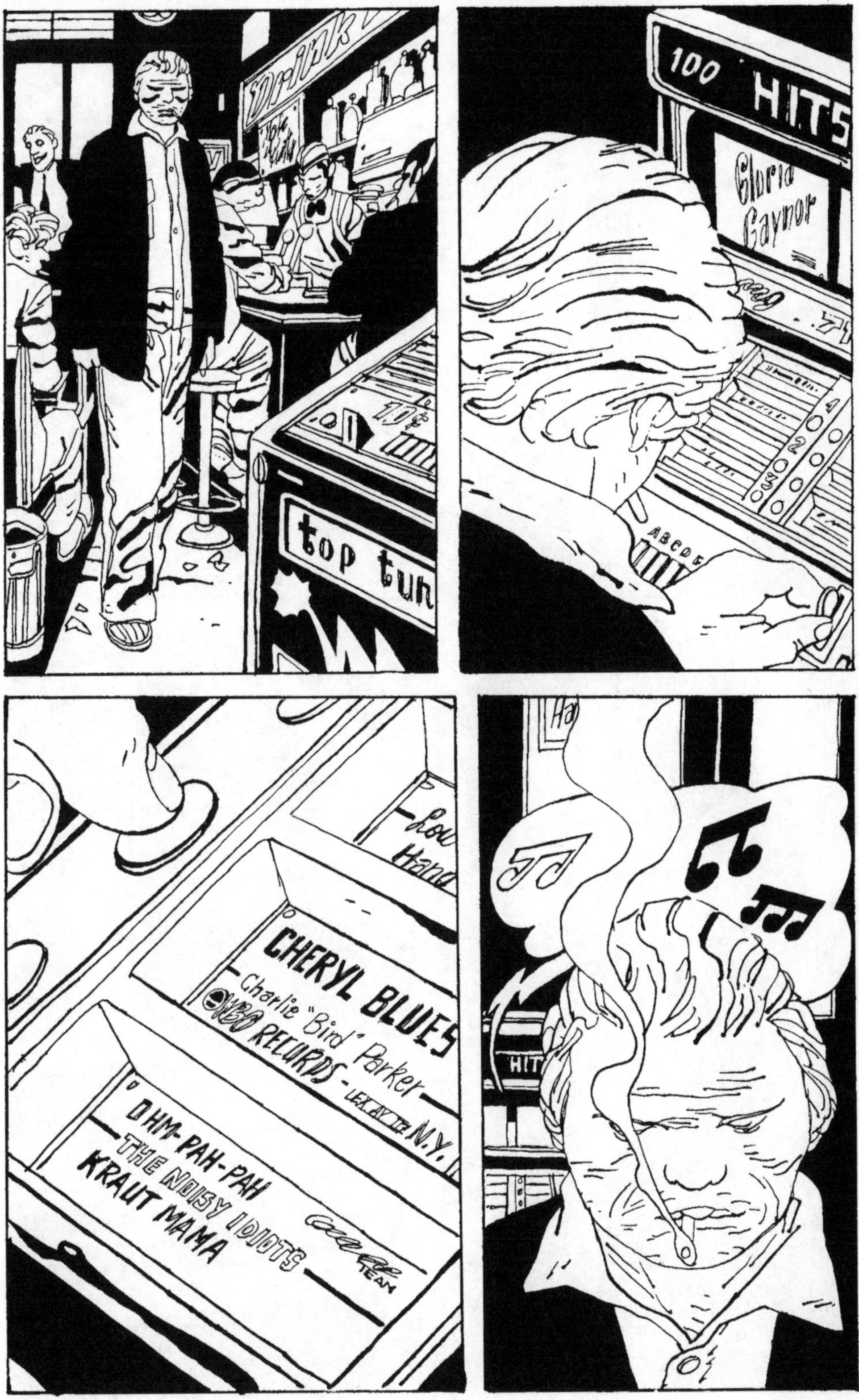
10¢
top tun
100 HITS
Gloria Gaynor
ABCDE
CHERYL BLUES
Charlie "Bird" Parker
RECORDS
N.Y.
OHM-PAH-PAH
THE NOISY IDIOTS
KRAUT MAMA
HITS

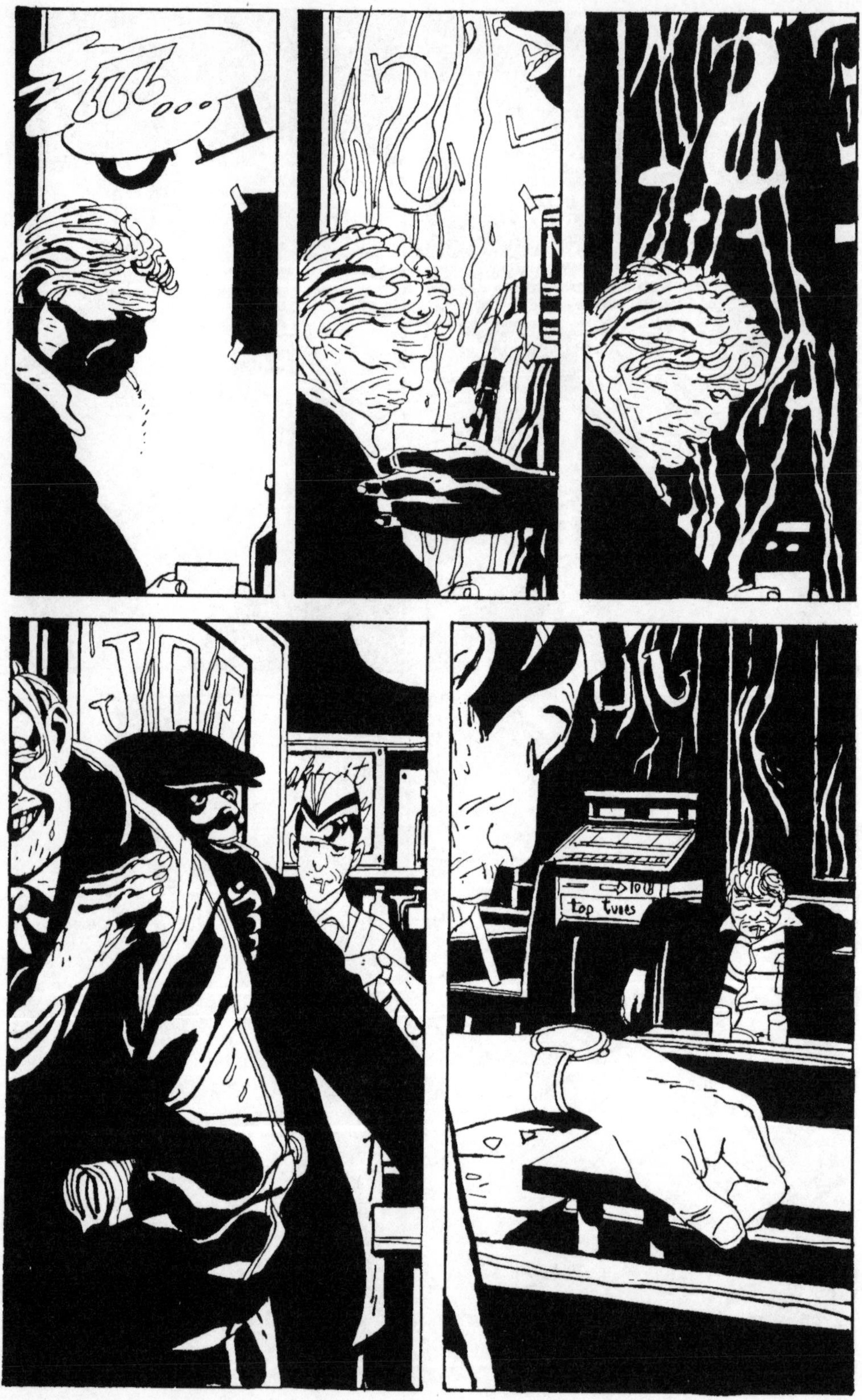
ZZZ...
top tunes

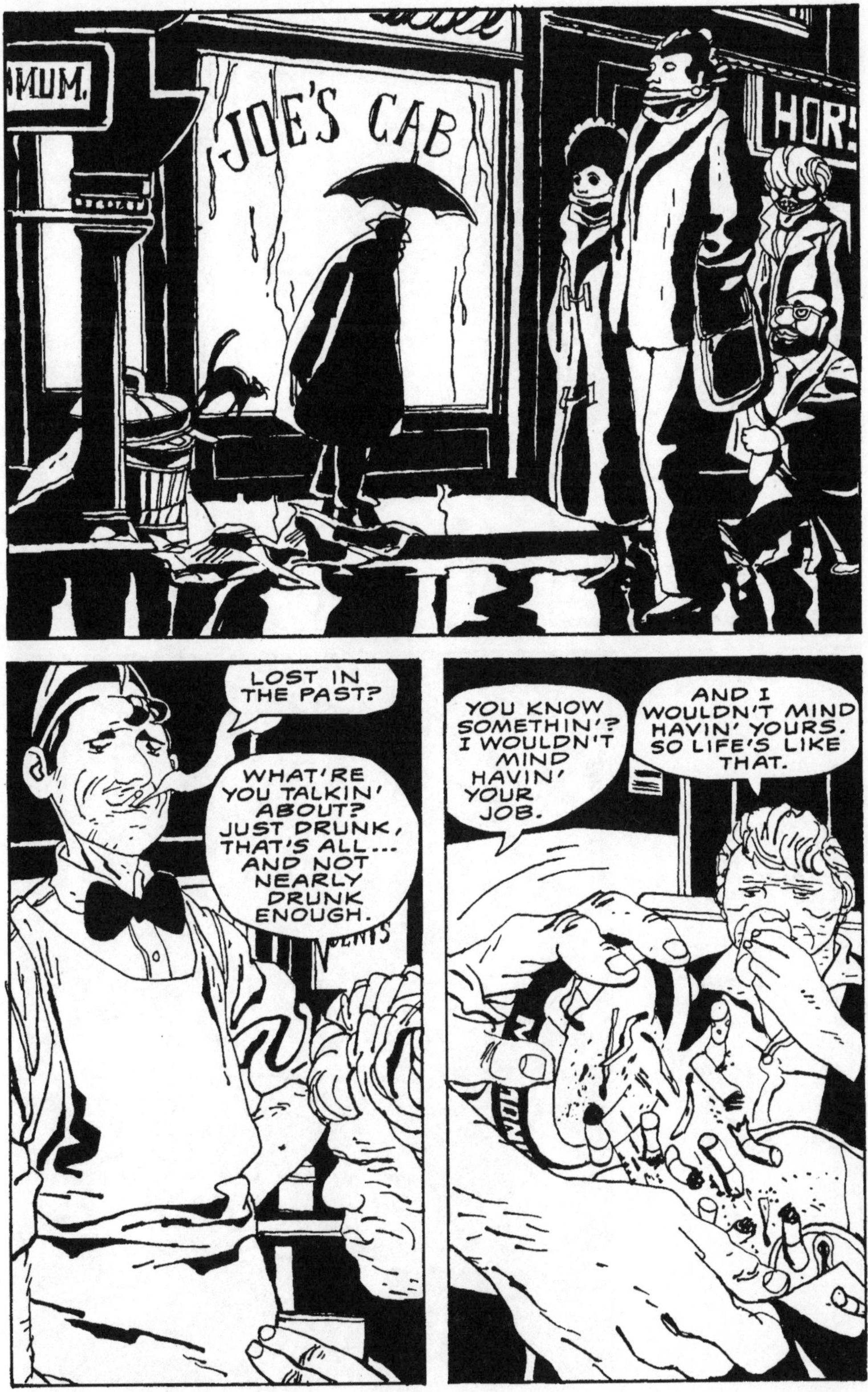
MUM.
JOE'S CAB
LOST IN THE PAST?
WHAT'RE YOU TALKIN' ABOUT? JUST DRUNK, THAT'S ALL... AND NOT NEARLY DRUNK ENOUGH.
YOU KNOW SOMETHIN'? I WOULDN'T MIND HAVIN' YOUR JOB.
AND I WOULDN'T MIND HAVIN' YOURS. SO LIFE'S LIKE THAT.

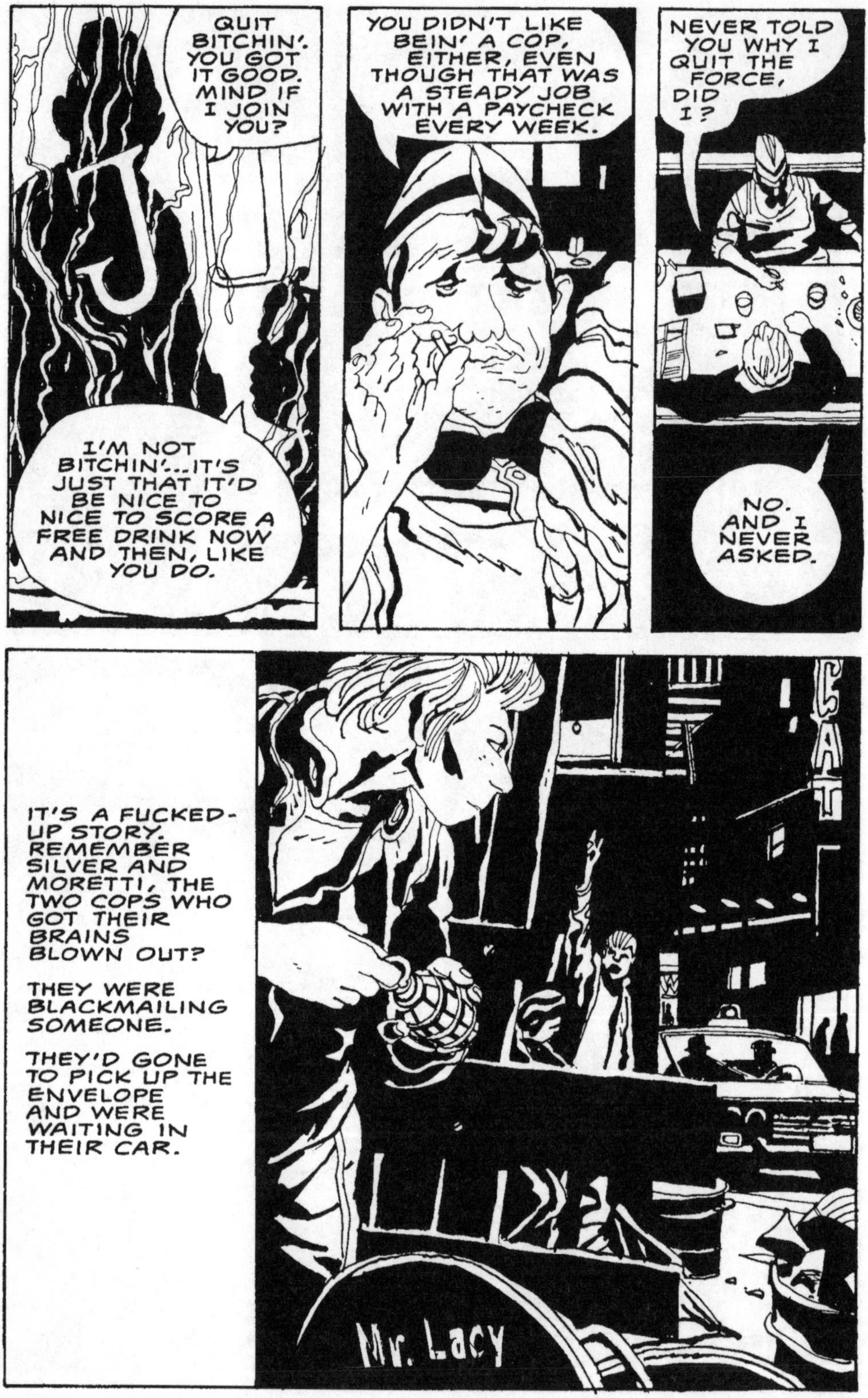
QUIT BITCHIN'. YOU GOT IT GOOD. MIND IF I JOIN YOU?
I'M NOT BITCHIN'...IT'S JUST THAT IT'D BE NICE TO NICE TO SCORE A FREE DRINK NOW AND THEN, LIKE YOU DO.
YOU DIDN'T LIKE BEIN' A COP, EITHER, EVEN THOUGH THAT WAS A STEADY JOB WITH A PAYCHECK EVERY WEEK.
NEVER TOLD YOU WHY I QUIT THE FORCE, DID I?
NO. AND I NEVER ASKED.
IT'S A FUCKED-UP STORY. REMEMBER SILVER AND MORETTI, THE TWO COPS WHO GOT THEIR BRAINS BLOWN OUT?
THEY WERE BLACKMAILING SOMEONE.
THEY'D GONE TO PICK UP THE ENVELOPE AND WERE WAITING IN THEIR CAR.
Mr. Lacy

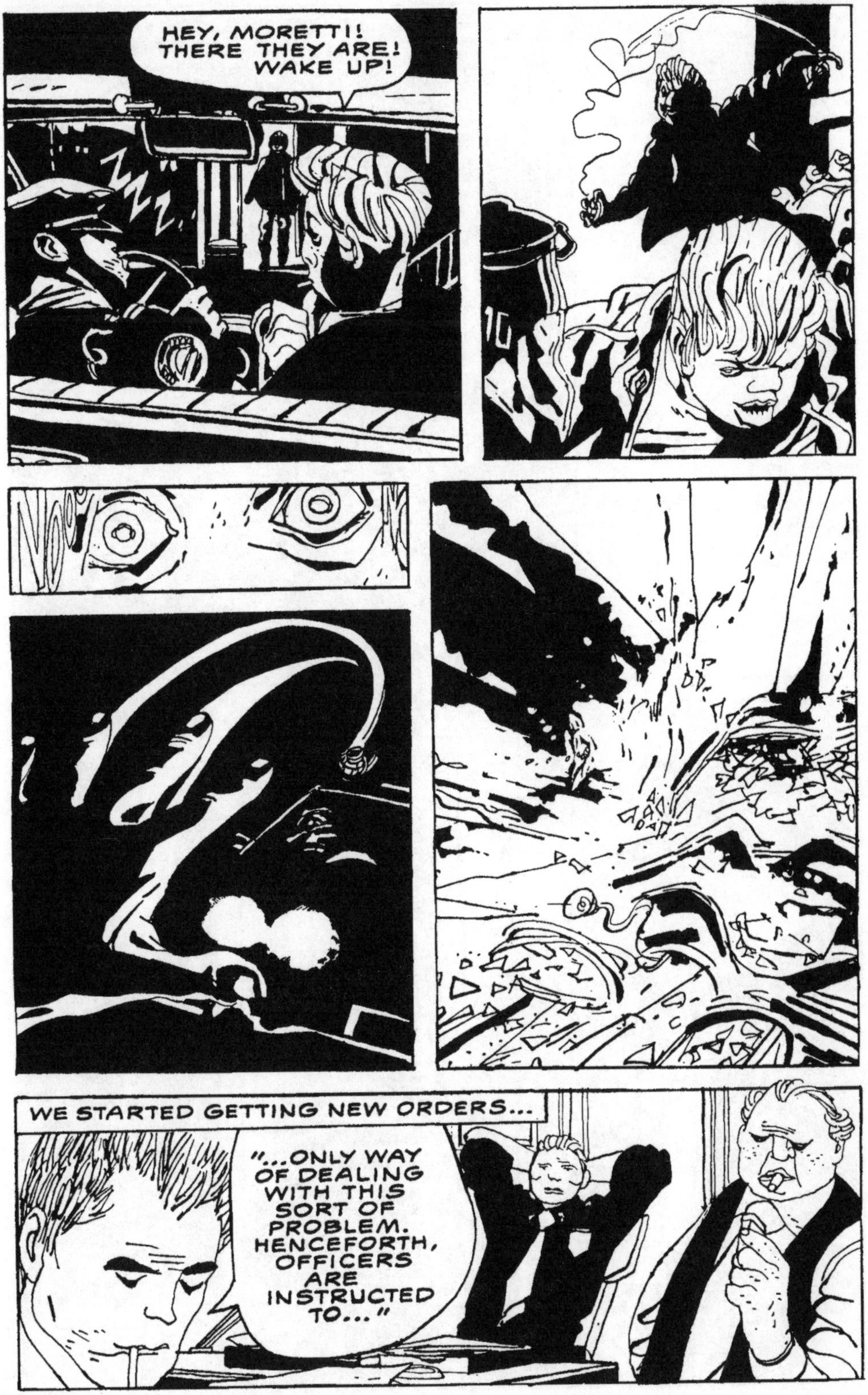
HEY, MORETTI! THERE THEY ARE! WAKE UP!
ZZZ
WE STARTED GETTING NEW ORDERS...
"...ONLY WAY OF DEALING WITH THIS SORT OF PROBLEM. HENCEFORTH, OFFICERS ARE INSTRUCTED TO..."

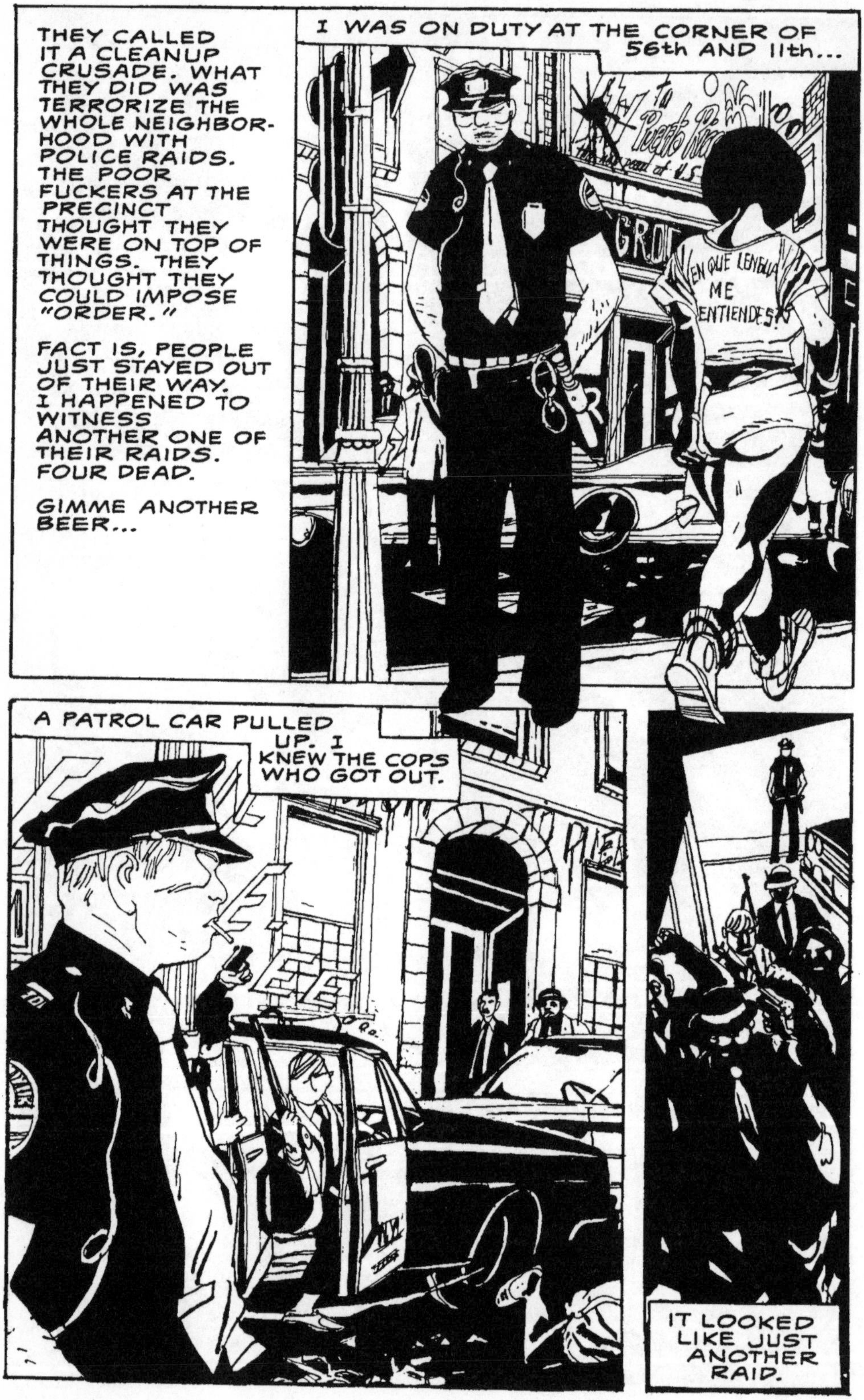
THEY CALLED IT A CLEANUP CRUSADE. WHAT THEY DID WAS TERRORIZE THE WHOLE NEIGHBORHOOD WITH POLICE RAIDS. THE POOR FUCKERS AT THE PRECINCT THOUGHT THEY WERE ON TOP OF THINGS. THEY THOUGHT THEY COULD IMPOSE "ORDER."
FACT IS, PEOPLE JUST STAYED OUT OF THEIR WAY. I HAPPENED TO WITNESS ANOTHER ONE OF THEIR RAIDS. FOUR DEAD.
GIMME ANOTHER BEER...
I WAS ON DUTY AT THE CORNER OF 56th AND 11th...
EN QUE LENGUA ME ENTIENDES?
A PATROL CAR PULLED UP. I KNEW THE COPS WHO GOT OUT.
IT LOOKED LIKE JUST ANOTHER RAID.

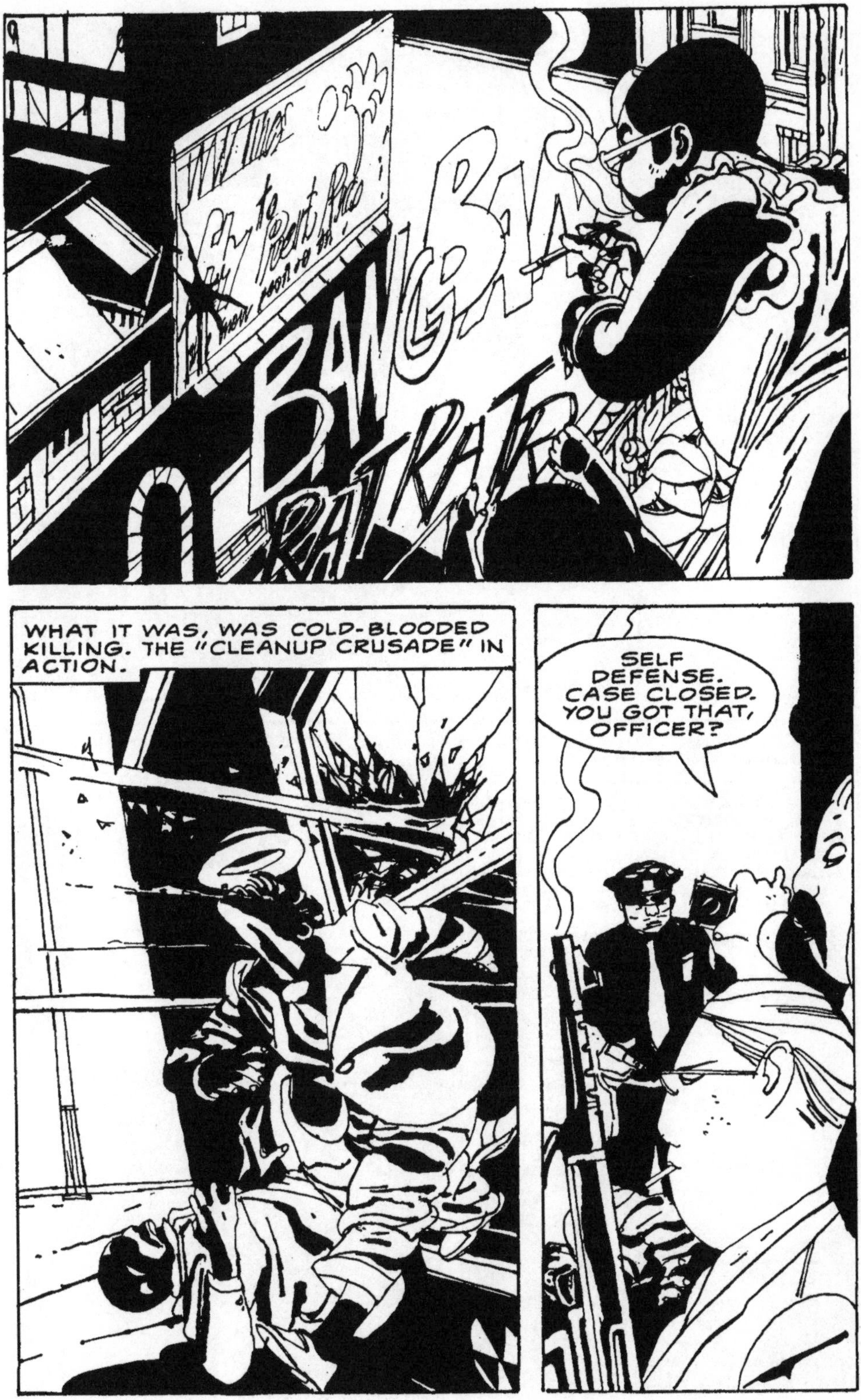
BANG
BAM
RATRAT
WHAT IT WAS, WAS COLD-BLOODED KILLING. THE "CLEANUP CRUSADE" IN ACTION.
SELF DEFENSE. CASE CLOSED. YOU GOT THAT, OFFICER?

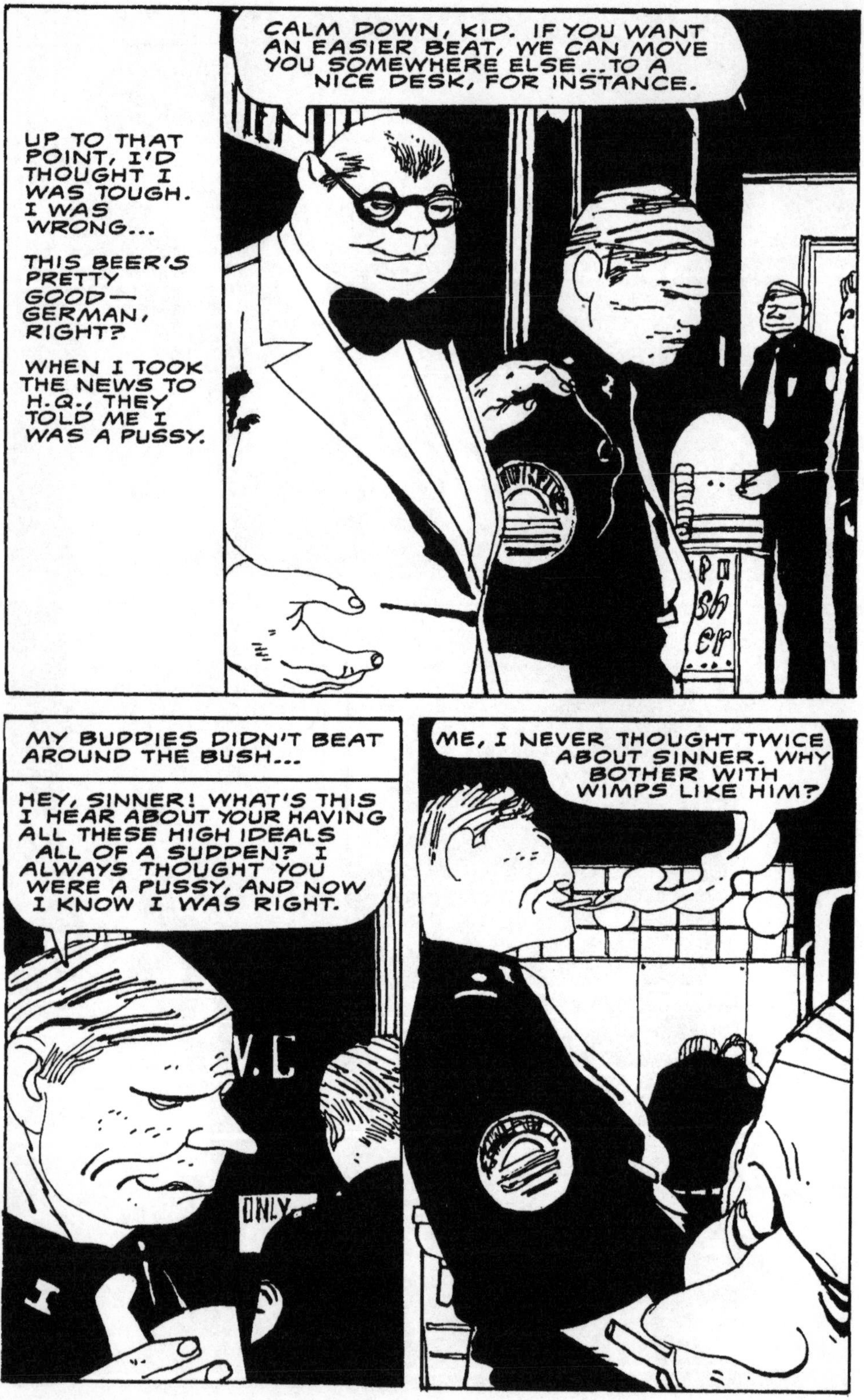
UP TO THAT POINT, I'D THOUGHT I WAS TOUGH. I WAS WRONG...
THIS BEER'S PRETTY GOOD— GERMAN, RIGHT?
WHEN I TOOK THE NEWS TO H.Q., THEY TOLD ME I WAS A PUSSY.
CALM DOWN, KID. IF YOU WANT AN EASIER BEAT, WE CAN MOVE YOU SOMEWHERE ELSE...TO A NICE DESK, FOR INSTANCE.
MY BUDDIES DIDN'T BEAT AROUND THE BUSH...
HEY, SINNER! WHAT'S THIS I HEAR ABOUT YOUR HAVING ALL THESE HIGH IDEALS ALL OF A SUDDEN? I ALWAYS THOUGHT YOU WERE A PUSSY, AND NOW I KNOW I WAS RIGHT.
ONLY
ME, I NEVER THOUGHT TWICE ABOUT SINNER. WHY BOTHER WITH WIMPS LIKE HIM?

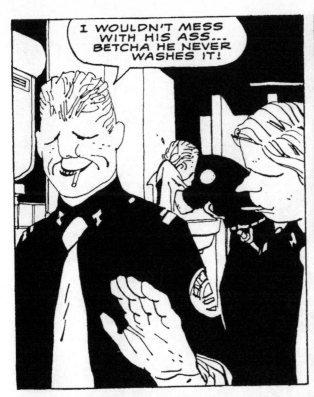

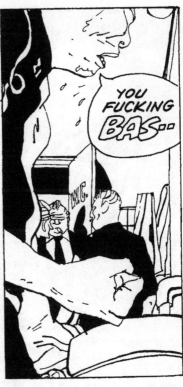

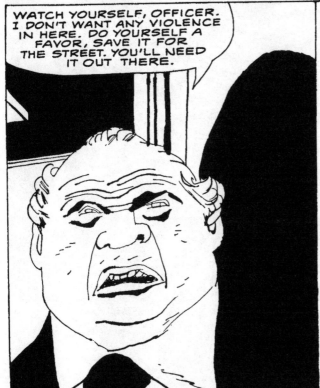

I WOULDN'T MESS WITH HIS ASS... BETCHA HE NEVER WASHES IT!
YOU FUCKING BAS..
WATCH YOURSELF, OFFICER. I DON'T WANT ANY VIOLENCE IN HERE. DO YOURSELF A FAVOR, SAVE IT FOR THE STREET. YOU'LL NEED IT OUT THERE.
THE OTHER COPS... IT WAS A WASTE OF TIME TO GET PISSED WITH THEM.
IF I LOST MY COOL, I WAS JUST GIVIN' 'EM WHAT THEY WANTED.
CHEERS.

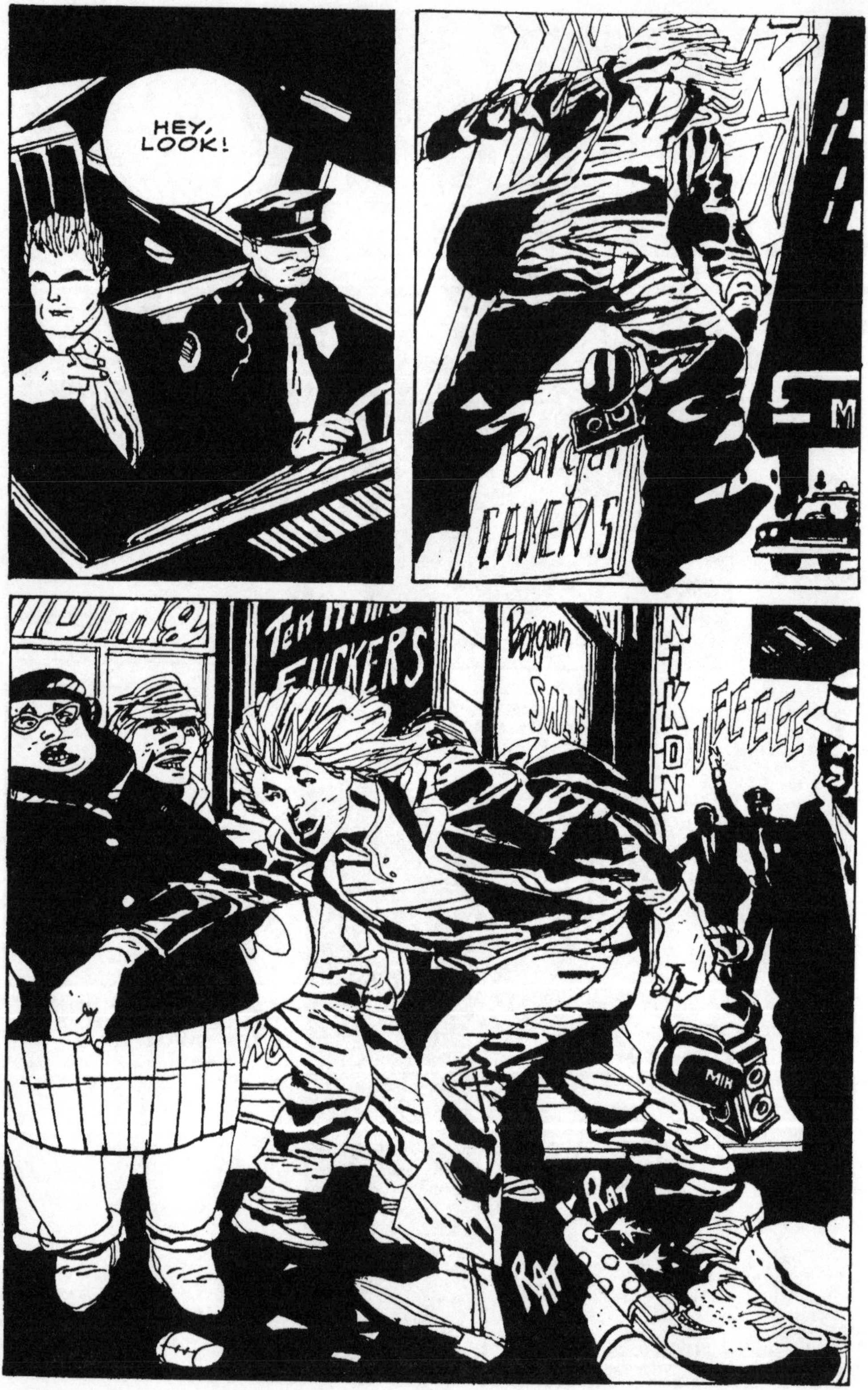
HEY, LOOK!
Bargain
CAMERAS
FUCKERS
Bargain
SALE
NIKON
UEEEEEE
RAT
RAT

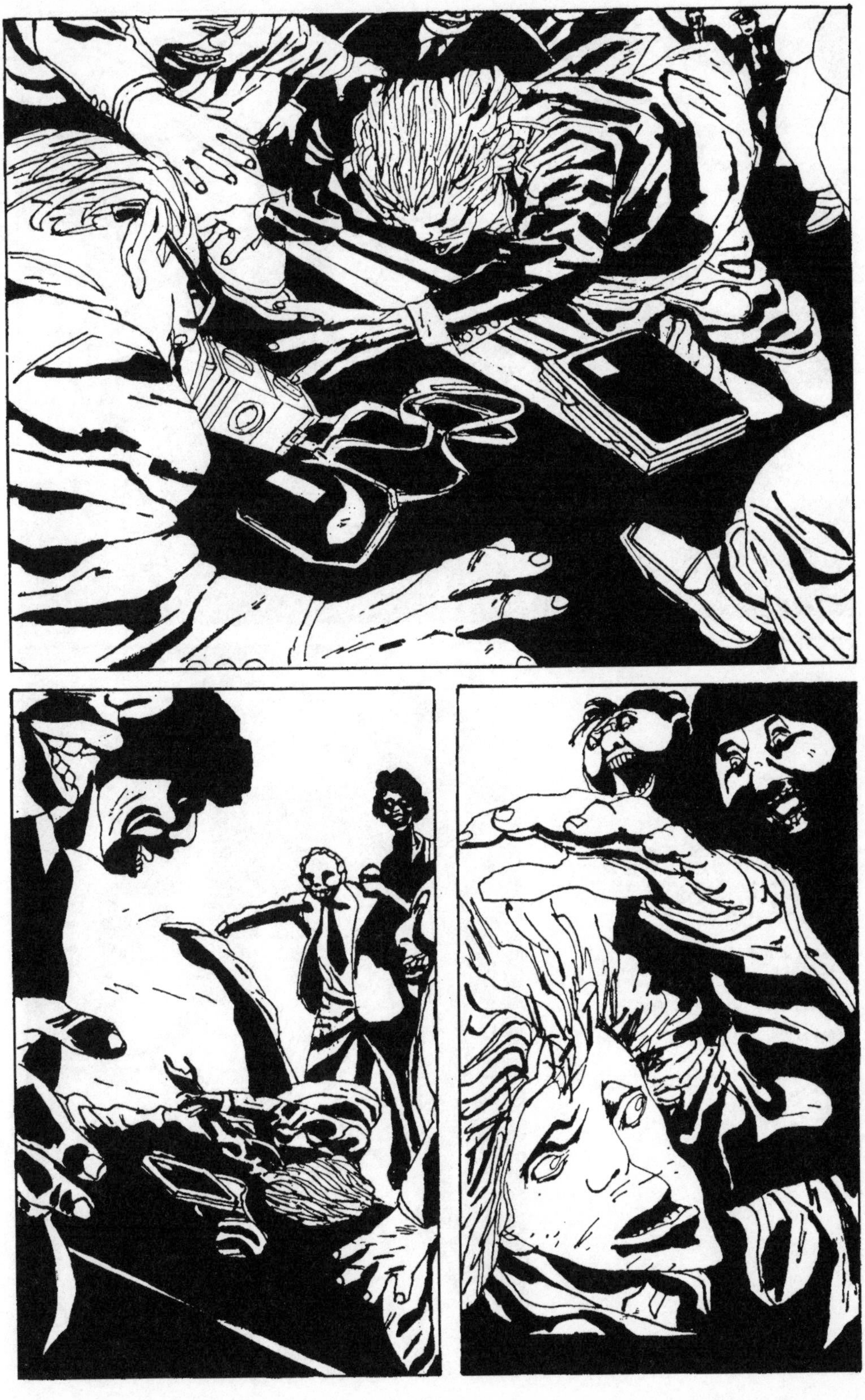

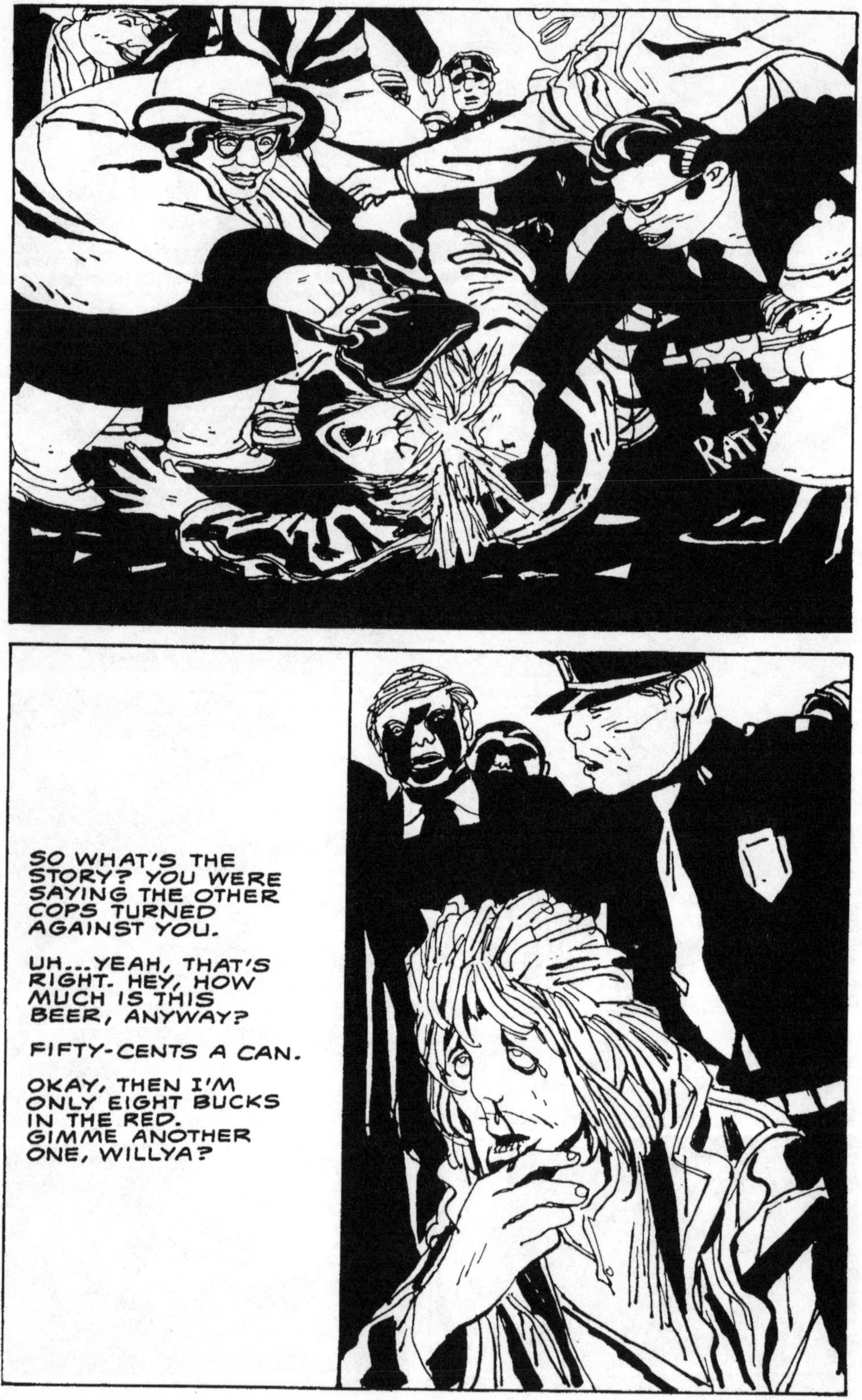
SO WHAT'S THE STORY? YOU WERE SAYING THE OTHER COPS TURNED AGAINST YOU.
UH...YEAH, THAT'S RIGHT. HEY, HOW MUCH IS THIS BEER, ANYWAY?
FIFTY-CENTS A CAN.
OKAY, THEN I'M ONLY EIGHT BUCKS IN THE RED. GIMME ANOTHER ONE, WILLYA?

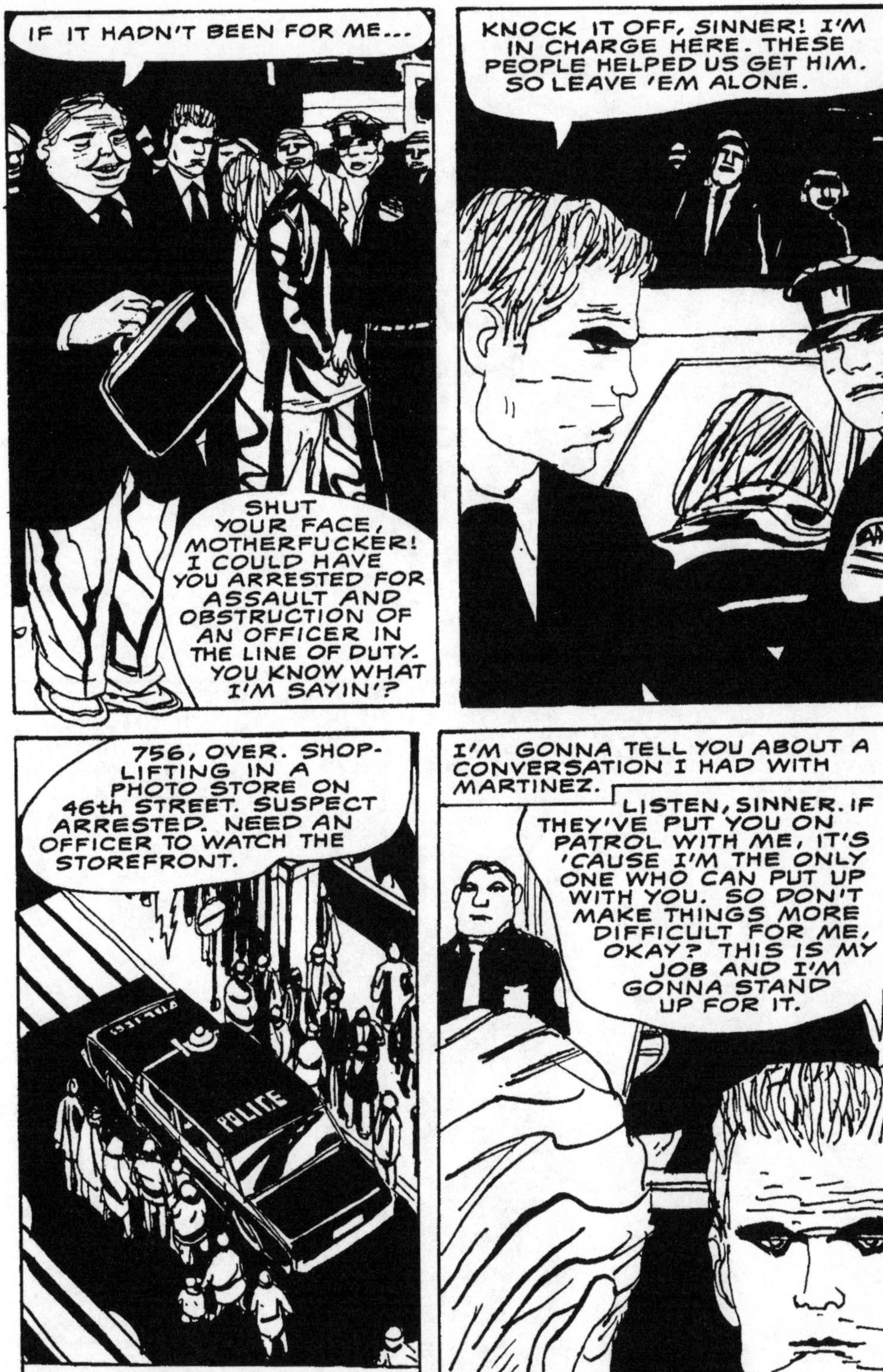
IF IT HADN'T BEEN FOR ME...
SHUT YOUR FACE, MOTHERFUCKER! I COULD HAVE YOU ARRESTED FOR ASSAULT AND OBSTRUCTION OF AN OFFICER IN THE LINE OF DUTY. YOU KNOW WHAT I'M SAYIN'?
KNOCK IT OFF, SINNER! I'M IN CHARGE HERE. THESE PEOPLE HELPED US GET HIM. SO LEAVE 'EM ALONE.
756, OVER. SHOPLIFTING IN A PHOTO STORE ON 46th STREET. SUSPECT ARRESTED. NEED AN OFFICER TO WATCH THE STOREFRONT.
POLICE
THE CITIZENS WERE ALL FOR THE "CLEANUP CRUSADE." AT LEAST *THOSE* WERE.
I'M GONNA TELL YOU ABOUT A CONVERSATION I HAD WITH MARTINEZ.
LISTEN, SINNER. IF THEY'VE PUT YOU ON PATROL WITH ME, IT'S 'CAUSE I'M THE ONLY ONE WHO CAN PUT UP WITH YOU. SO DON'T MAKE THINGS MORE DIFFICULT FOR ME, OKAY? THIS IS MY JOB AND I'M GONNA STAND UP FOR IT.

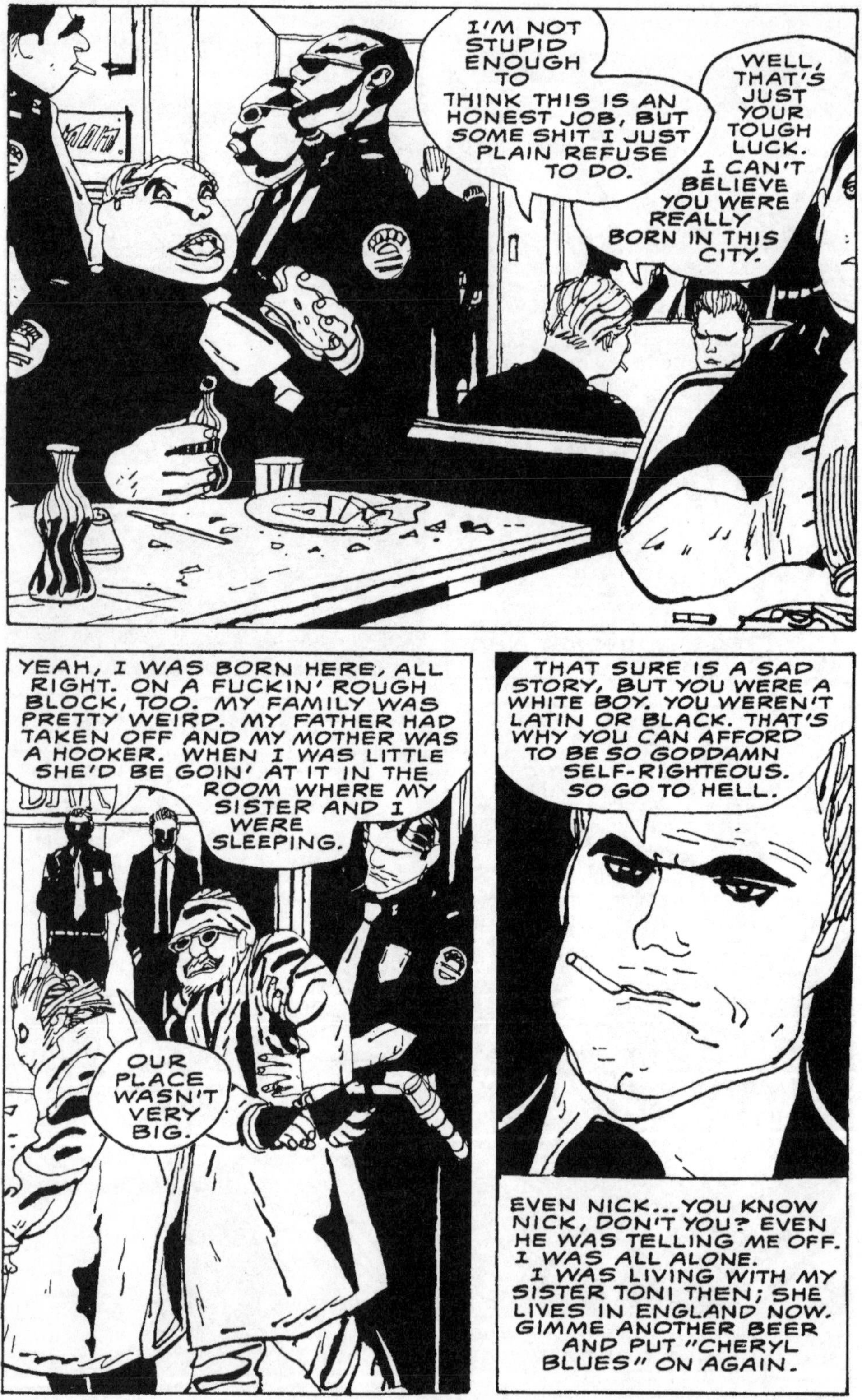
I'M NOT STUPID ENOUGH TO THINK THIS IS AN HONEST JOB, BUT SOME SHIT I JUST PLAIN REFUSE TO DO.
WELL, THAT'S JUST YOUR TOUGH LUCK. I CAN'T BELIEVE YOU WERE REALLY BORN IN THIS CITY.
YEAH, I WAS BORN HERE, ALL RIGHT. ON A FUCKIN' ROUGH BLOCK, TOO. MY FAMILY WAS PRETTY WEIRD. MY FATHER HAD TAKEN OFF AND MY MOTHER WAS A HOOKER. WHEN I WAS LITTLE SHE'D BE GOIN' AT IT IN THE ROOM WHERE MY SISTER AND I WERE SLEEPING.
OUR PLACE WASN'T VERY BIG.
THAT SURE IS A SAD STORY, BUT YOU WERE A WHITE BOY. YOU WEREN'T LATIN OR BLACK. THAT'S WHY YOU CAN AFFORD TO BE SO GODDAMN SELF-RIGHTEOUS. SO GO TO HELL.
EVEN NICK...YOU KNOW NICK, DON'T YOU? EVEN HE WAS TELLING ME OFF. I WAS ALL ALONE. I WAS LIVING WITH MY SISTER TONI THEN; SHE LIVES IN ENGLAND NOW. GIMME ANOTHER BEER AND PUT "CHERYL BLUES" ON AGAIN.

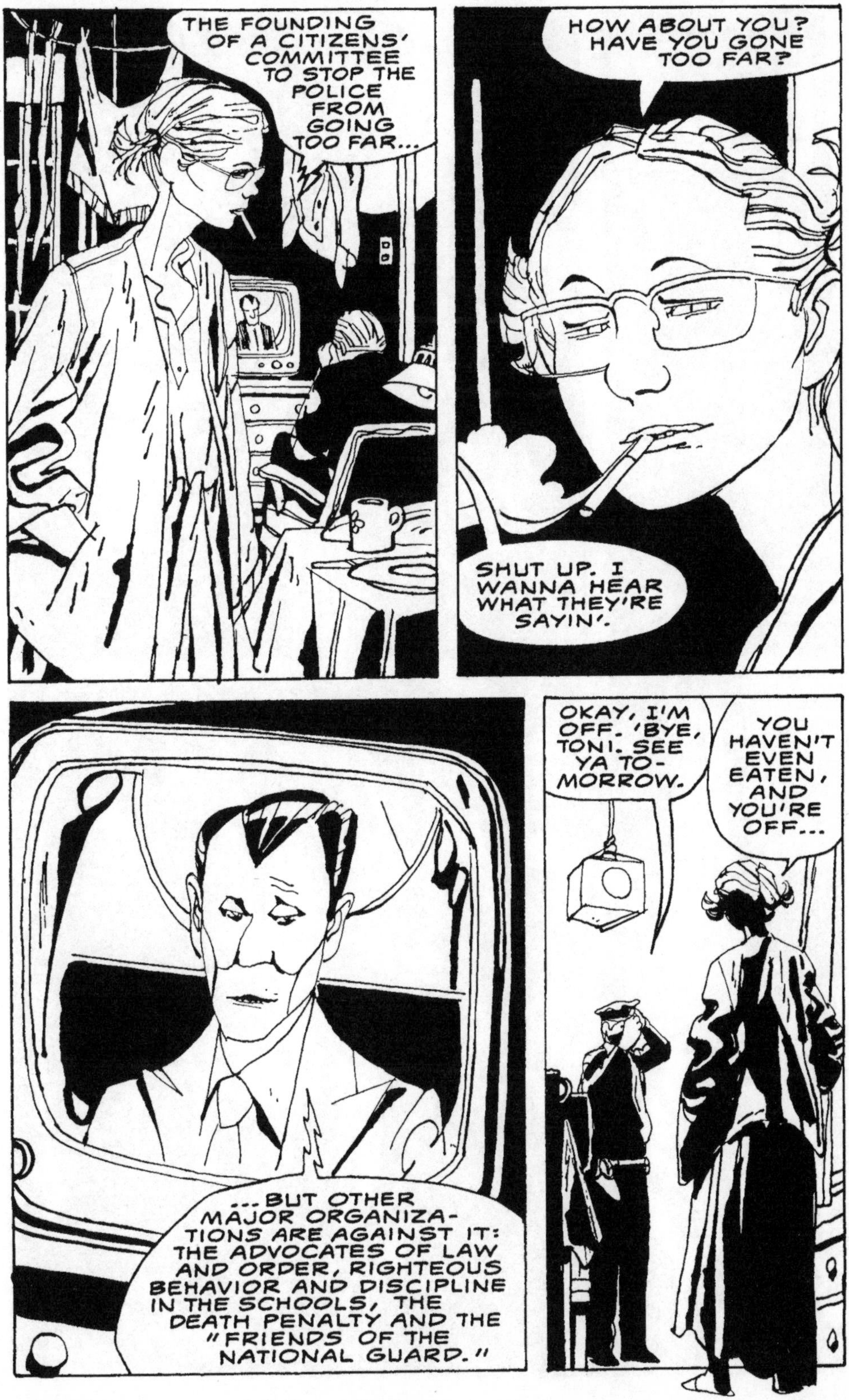
THE FOUNDING OF A CITIZENS' COMMITTEE TO STOP THE POLICE FROM GOING TOO FAR...
HOW ABOUT YOU? HAVE YOU GONE TOO FAR?
SHUT UP. I WANNA HEAR WHAT THEY'RE SAYIN'.
...BUT OTHER MAJOR ORGANIZATIONS ARE AGAINST IT: THE ADVOCATES OF LAW AND ORDER, RIGHTEOUS BEHAVIOR AND DISCIPLINE IN THE SCHOOLS, THE DEATH PENALTY AND THE "FRIENDS OF THE NATIONAL GUARD."
OKAY, I'M OFF. 'BYE, TONI. SEE YA TOMORROW.
YOU HAVEN'T EVEN EATEN, AND YOU'RE OFF...

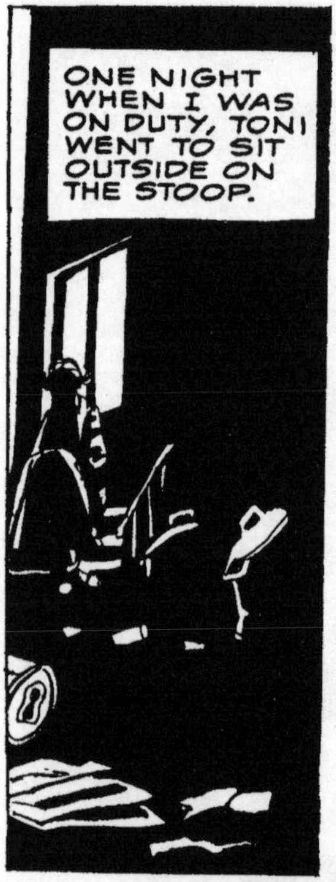
ONE NIGHT WHEN I WAS ON DUTY, TONI WENT TO SIT OUTSIDE ON THE STOOP.

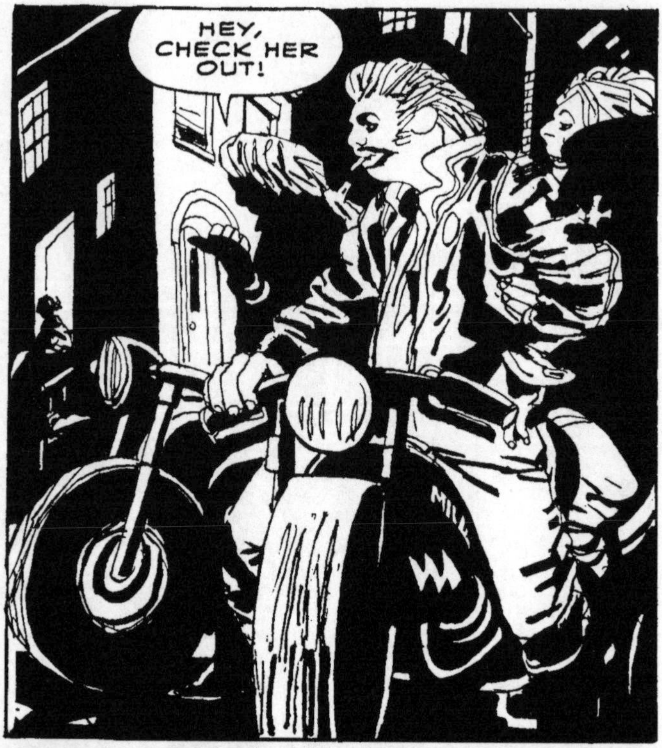
HEY, CHECK HER OUT!

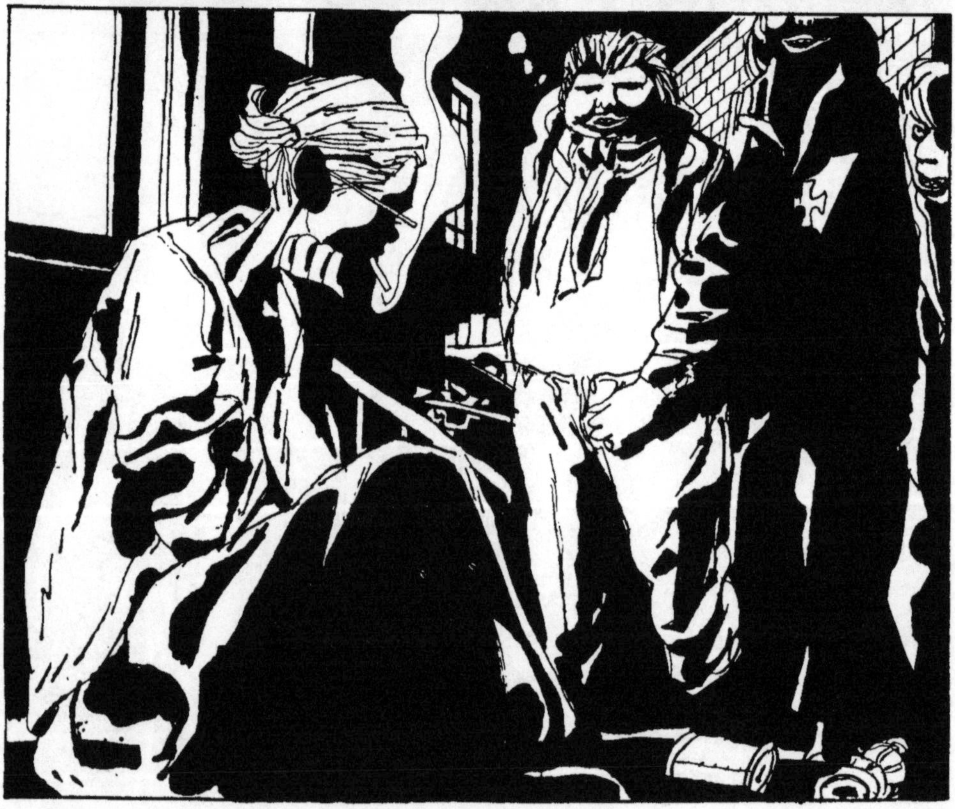

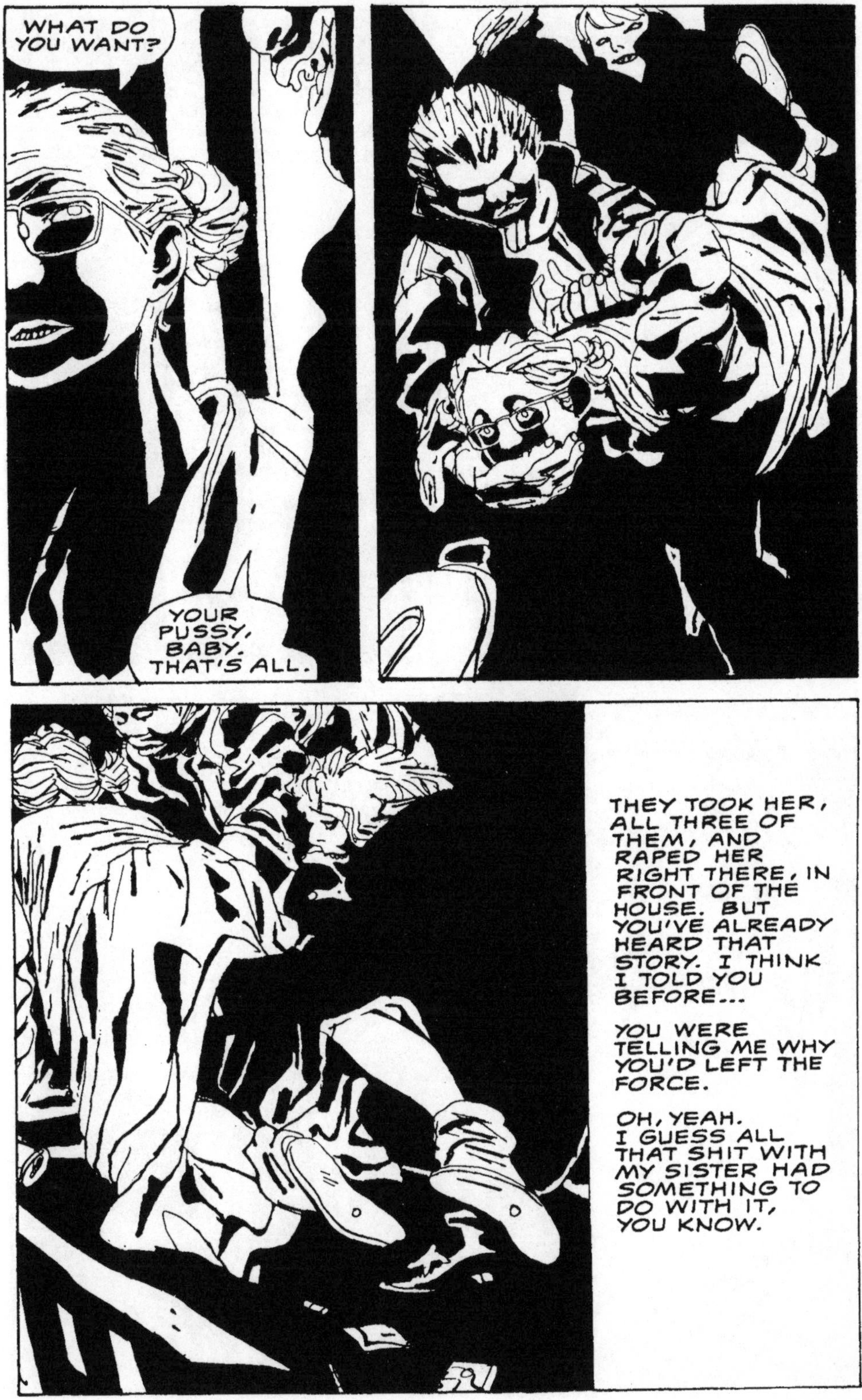
WHAT DO YOU WANT?
YOUR PUSSY, BABY. THAT'S ALL.
THEY TOOK HER, ALL THREE OF THEM, AND RAPED HER RIGHT THERE, IN FRONT OF THE HOUSE. BUT YOU'VE ALREADY HEARD THAT STORY. I THINK I TOLD YOU BEFORE...
YOU WERE TELLING ME WHY YOU'D LEFT THE FORCE.
OH, YEAH. I GUESS ALL THAT SHIT WITH MY SISTER HAD SOMETHING TO DO WITH IT, YOU KNOW.

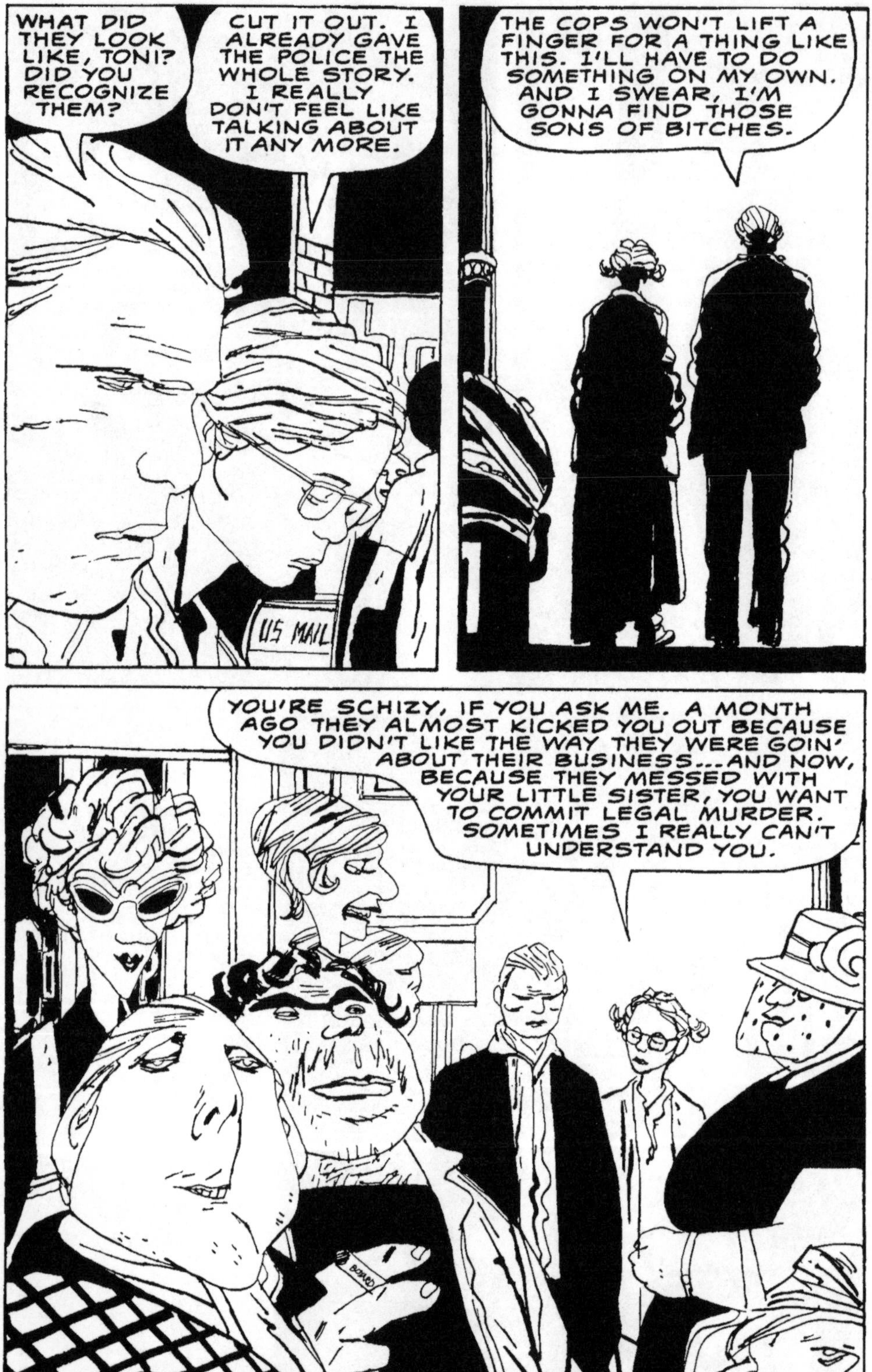
WHAT DID THEY LOOK LIKE, TONI? DID YOU RECOGNIZE THEM?
CUT IT OUT. I ALREADY GAVE THE POLICE THE WHOLE STORY. I REALLY DON'T FEEL LIKE TALKING ABOUT IT ANY MORE.
US MAIL
THE COPS WON'T LIFT A FINGER FOR A THING LIKE THIS. I'LL HAVE TO DO SOMETHING ON MY OWN. AND I SWEAR, I'M GONNA FIND THOSE SONS OF BITCHES.
YOU'RE SCHIZY, IF YOU ASK ME. A MONTH AGO THEY ALMOST KICKED YOU OUT BECAUSE YOU DIDN'T LIKE THE WAY THEY WERE GOIN' ABOUT THEIR BUSINESS... AND NOW, BECAUSE THEY MESSED WITH YOUR LITTLE SISTER, YOU WANT TO COMMIT LEGAL MURDER. SOMETIMES I REALLY CAN'T UNDERSTAND YOU.

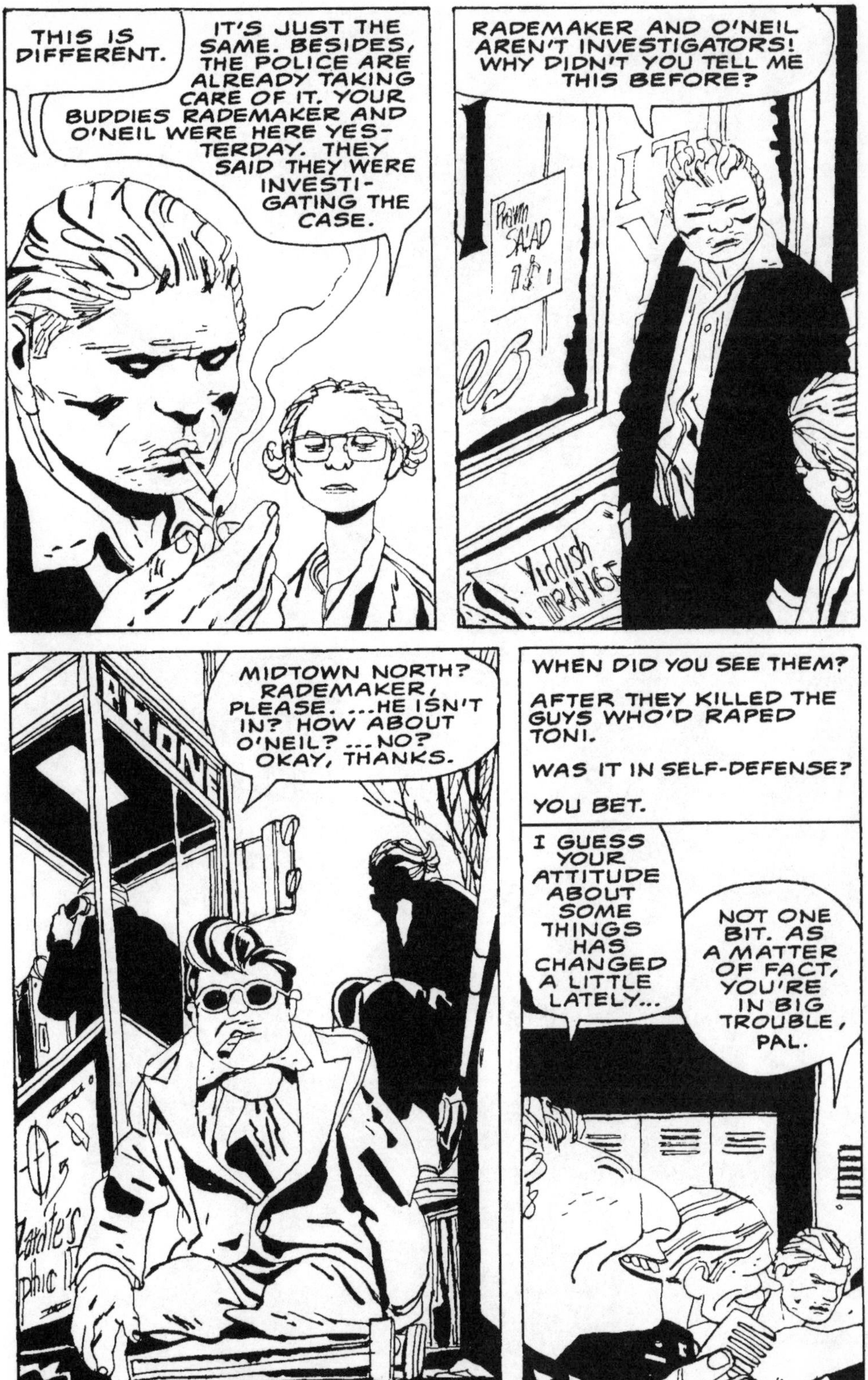
THIS IS DIFFERENT.
IT'S JUST THE SAME. BESIDES, THE POLICE ARE ALREADY TAKING CARE OF IT. YOUR BUDDIES RADEMAKER AND O'NEIL WERE HERE YES-TERDAY. THEY SAID THEY WERE INVESTI-GATING THE CASE.
RADEMAKER AND O'NEIL AREN'T INVESTIGATORS! WHY DIDN'T YOU TELL ME THIS BEFORE?
Prawn SALAD
Yiddish
MIDTOWN NORTH? RADEMAKER, PLEASE. ...HE ISN'T IN? HOW ABOUT O'NEIL? ...NO? OKAY, THANKS.
WHEN DID YOU SEE THEM?
AFTER THEY KILLED THE GUYS WHO'D RAPED TONI.
WAS IT IN SELF-DEFENSE?
YOU BET.
I GUESS YOUR ATTITUDE ABOUT SOME THINGS HAS CHANGED A LITTLE LATELY...
NOT ONE BIT. AS A MATTER OF FACT, YOU'RE IN BIG TROUBLE, PAL.

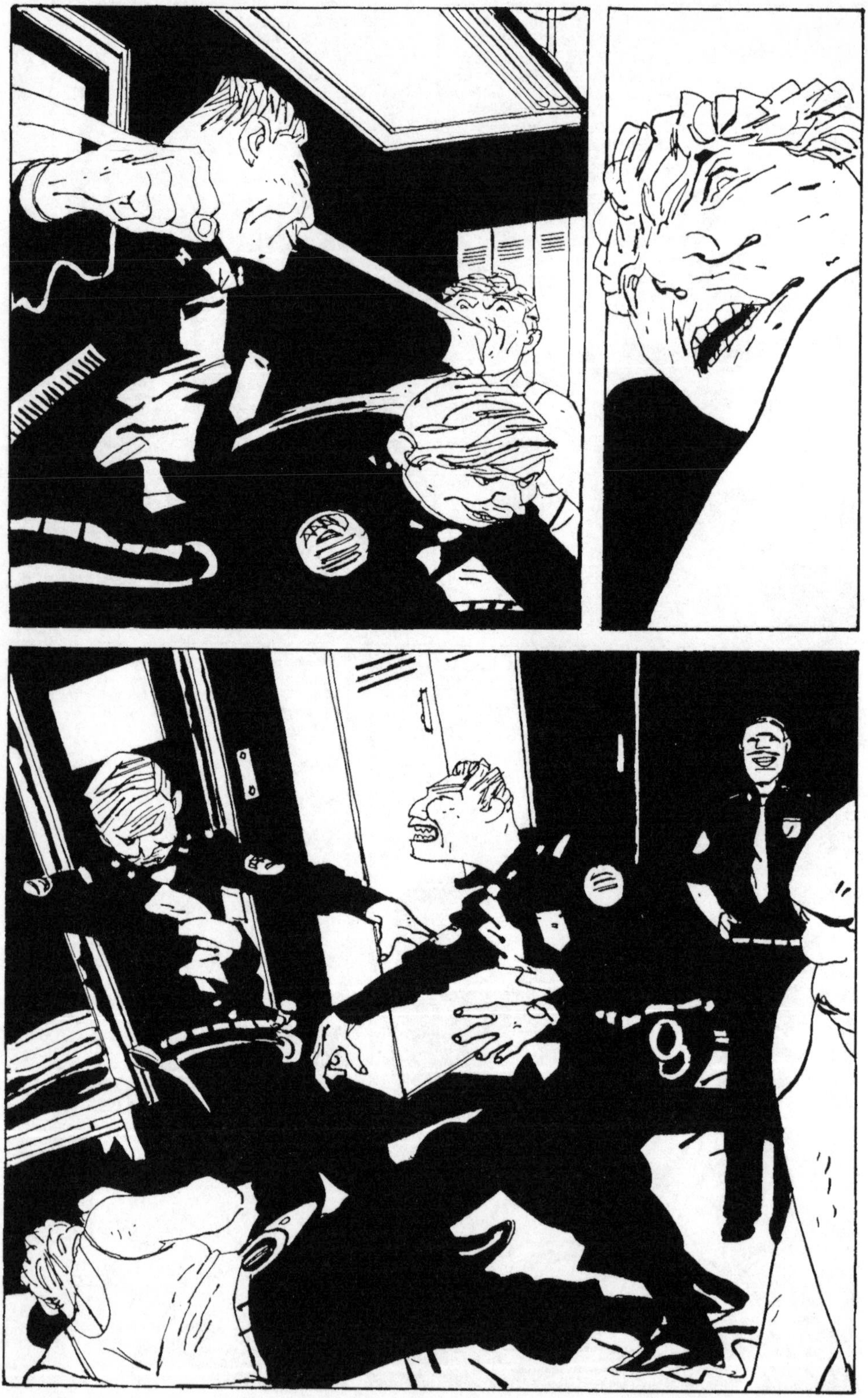

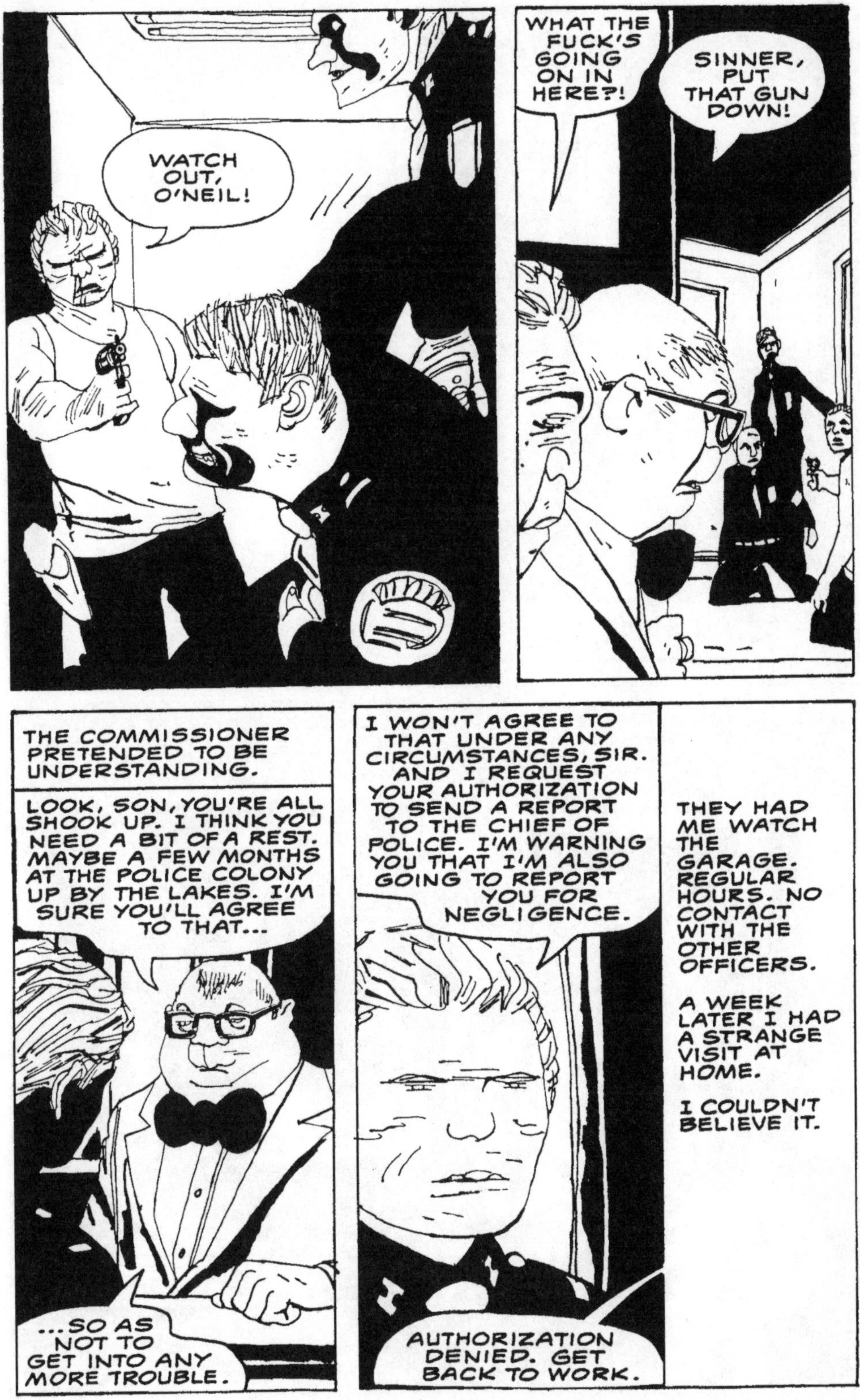
WATCH OUT, O'NEIL!
WHAT THE FUCK'S GOING ON IN HERE?!
SINNER, PUT THAT GUN DOWN!
THE COMMISSIONER PRETENDED TO BE UNDERSTANDING.
LOOK, SON, YOU'RE ALL SHOOK UP. I THINK YOU NEED A BIT OF A REST. MAYBE A FEW MONTHS AT THE POLICE COLONY UP BY THE LAKES. I'M SURE YOU'LL AGREE TO THAT...
...SO AS NOT TO GET INTO ANY MORE TROUBLE.
I WON'T AGREE TO THAT UNDER ANY CIRCUMSTANCES, SIR. AND I REQUEST YOUR AUTHORIZATION TO SEND A REPORT TO THE CHIEF OF POLICE. I'M WARNING YOU THAT I'M ALSO GOING TO REPORT YOU FOR NEGLIGENCE.
AUTHORIZATION DENIED. GET BACK TO WORK.
THEY HAD ME WATCH THE GARAGE. REGULAR HOURS. NO CONTACT WITH THE OTHER OFFICERS.
A WEEK LATER I HAD A STRANGE VISIT AT HOME.
I COULDN'T BELIEVE IT.

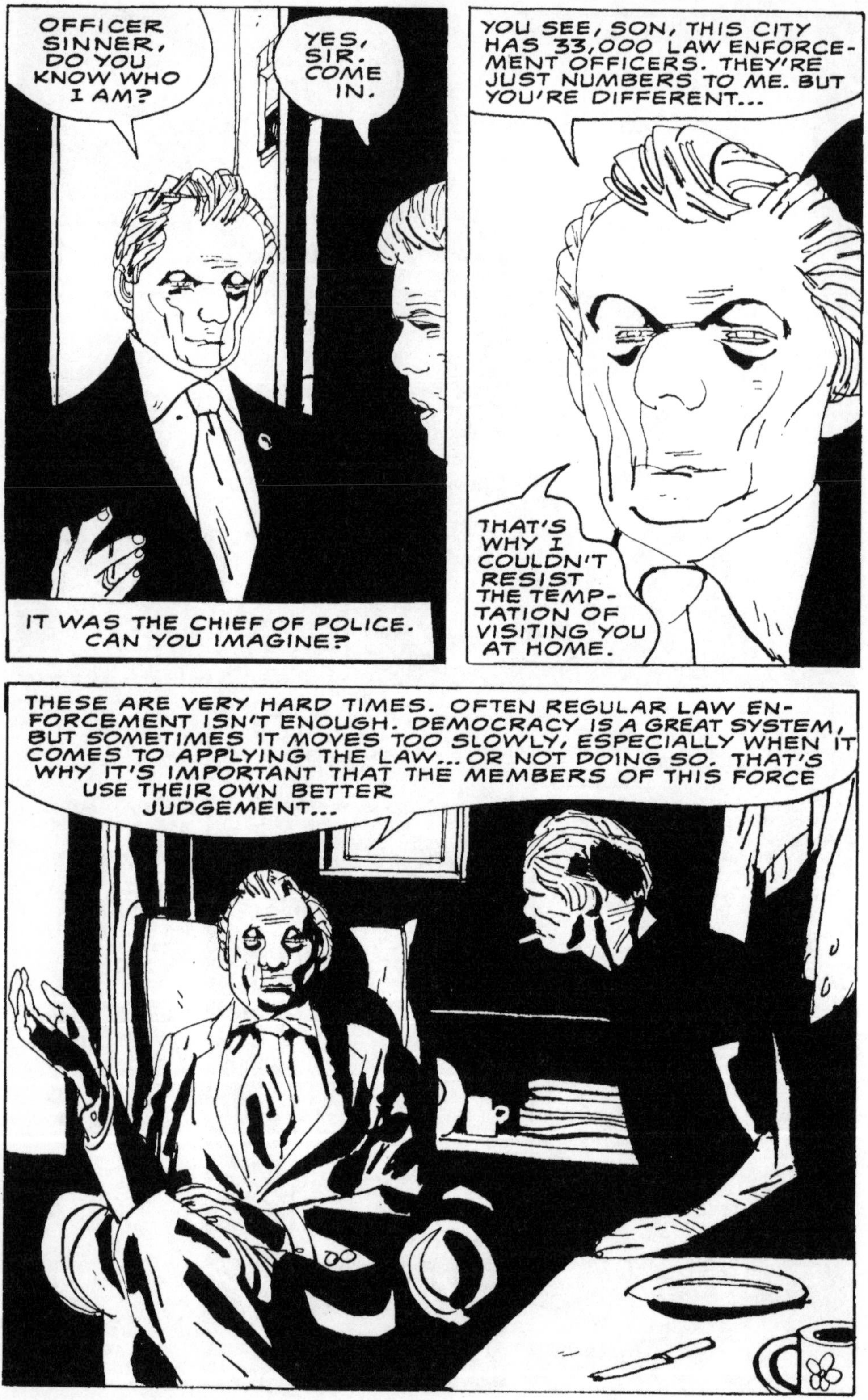
OFFICER SINNER, DO YOU KNOW WHO I AM?
YES, SIR. COME IN.
IT WAS THE CHIEF OF POLICE. CAN YOU IMAGINE?
YOU SEE, SON, THIS CITY HAS 33,000 LAW ENFORCE-MENT OFFICERS. THEY'RE JUST NUMBERS TO ME. BUT YOU'RE DIFFERENT...
THAT'S WHY I COULDN'T RESIST THE TEMP-TATION OF VISITING YOU AT HOME.
THESE ARE VERY HARD TIMES. OFTEN REGULAR LAW EN-FORCEMENT ISN'T ENOUGH. DEMOCRACY IS A GREAT SYSTEM, BUT SOMETIMES IT MOVES TOO SLOWLY, ESPECIALLY WHEN IT COMES TO APPLYING THE LAW... OR NOT DOING SO. THAT'S WHY IT'S IMPORTANT THAT THE MEMBERS OF THIS FORCE USE THEIR OWN BETTER JUDGEMENT...

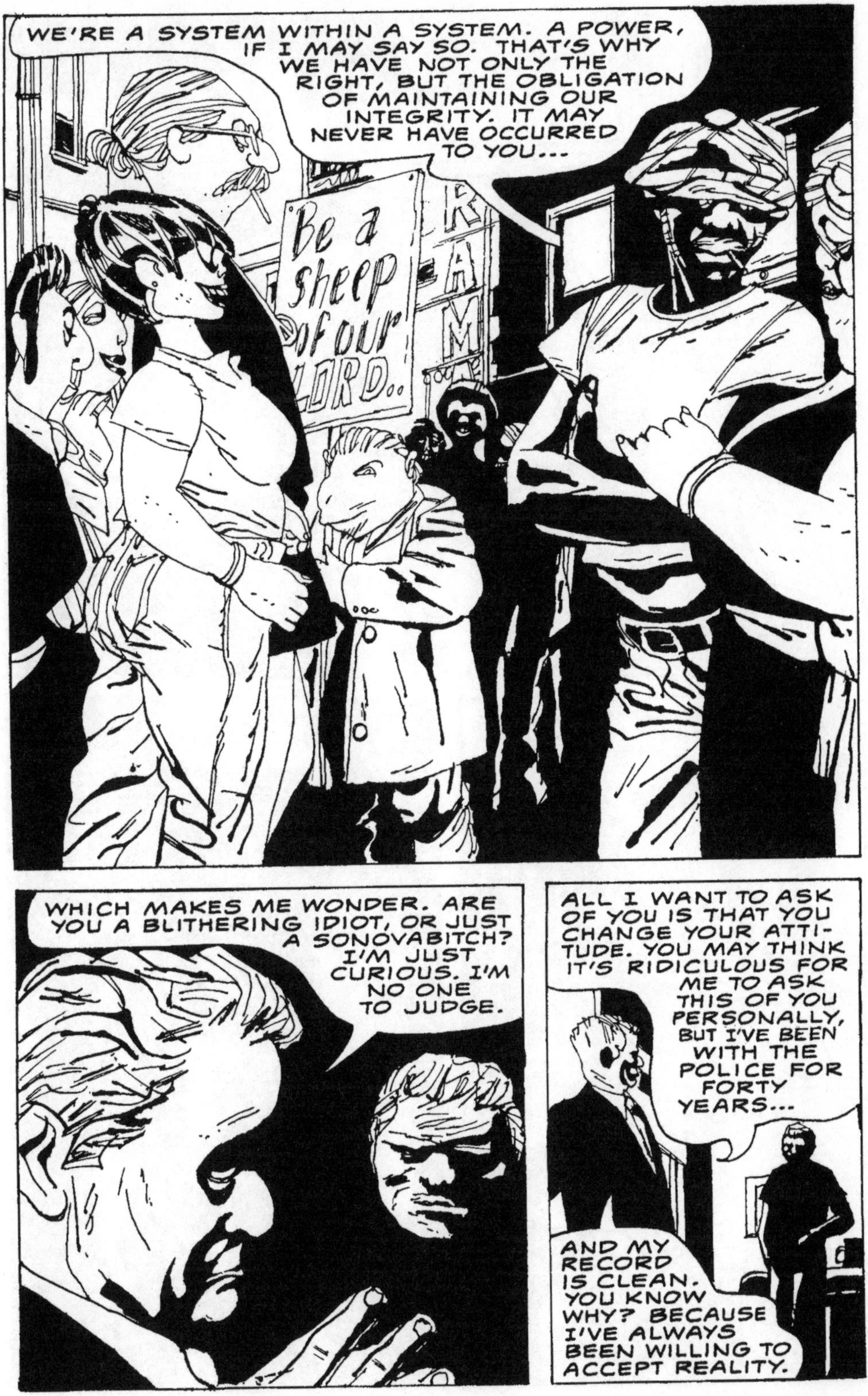
WE'RE A SYSTEM WITHIN A SYSTEM. A POWER, IF I MAY SAY SO. THAT'S WHY WE HAVE NOT ONLY THE RIGHT, BUT THE OBLIGATION OF MAINTAINING OUR INTEGRITY. IT MAY NEVER HAVE OCCURRED TO YOU...
Be a sheep of our LORD..
WHICH MAKES ME WONDER. ARE YOU A BLITHERING IDIOT, OR JUST A SONOVABITCH? I'M JUST CURIOUS. I'M NO ONE TO JUDGE.
ALL I WANT TO ASK OF YOU IS THAT YOU CHANGE YOUR ATTITUDE. YOU MAY THINK IT'S RIDICULOUS FOR ME TO ASK THIS OF YOU PERSONALLY, BUT I'VE BEEN WITH THE POLICE FOR FORTY YEARS...
AND MY RECORD IS CLEAN. YOU KNOW WHY? BECAUSE I'VE ALWAYS BEEN WILLING TO ACCEPT REALITY.

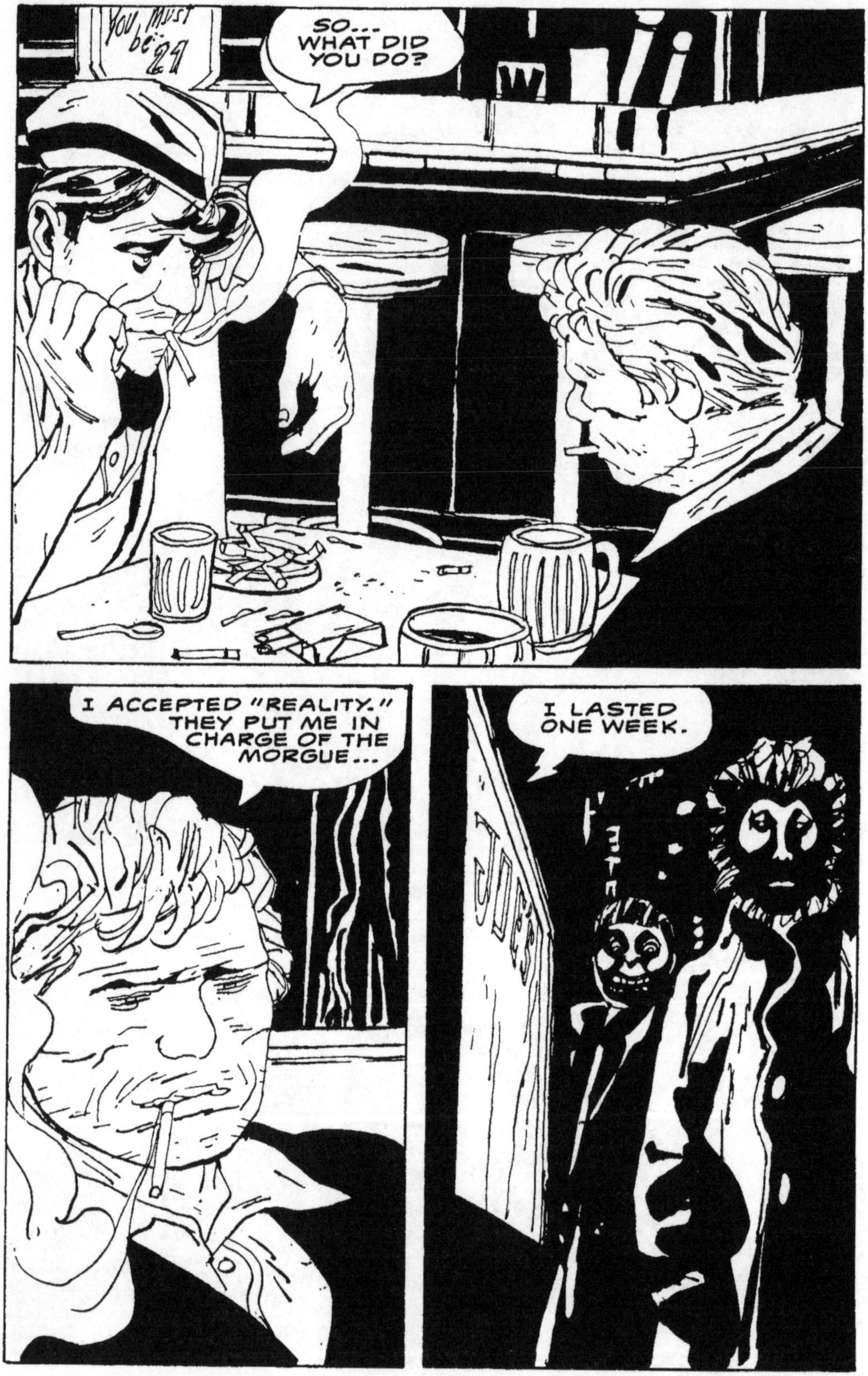
You must be 21
SO... WHAT DID YOU DO?
I ACCEPTED "REALITY." THEY PUT ME IN CHARGE OF THE MORGUE...
I LASTED ONE WEEK.
JOE'S

AND THEN?

I ASKED TO BE DISMISSED FROM THE FORCE, AND LEFT WITHOUT A SINGLE MEDAL, AS ANONYMOUSLY AS I HAD BEEN THERE.

WAS THAT WHEN YOU STARTED DOIN' DETECTIVE WORK?

FOR A MONTH I DIDN'T KNOW *WHAT* TO DO. NICK SUGGESTED THAT I WORK AS A PRIVATE EYE; IT TURNED OUT HE WAS REAL WORRIED ABOUT ME. I HAD NO TROUBLE GETTING A LICENSE... OH, AND GET THIS! DEMETRIUS SIGNED IT—!!

SO HOW DID THAT WORK OUT?

OKAY, I GUESS. I STARTED OFF LOOKING INTO SOME MINOR CASES. TAILING PEOPLE, UNFAITHFUL WIVES WHO OFTEN WALKED FASTER THAN I DID. NO BIG DEAL. BUT ONE THING WAS REALLY WEIRD... FOR MORE THAN A YEAR I COULDN'T LOOK AT MY FACE IN THE MIRROR. I ENDED UP FORGETTING WHAT I LOOKED LIKE.

AND THEN WHAT HAPPENED?

THEN I GOT THE WEBSTER CASE, MY FIRST BIG JOB. IT WAS REAL HEAVY... BUT ENOUGH SOB STORIES. GIMME ANOTHER BEER.

CAN'T. GOTTA CLOSE UP. HEY, DID YOU START LOOKIN' AT YOURSELF IN THE MIRROR AGAIN AFTER THAT?

YEAH. LATER ON I DID.

"They're right!
You can't be too careful!
The smallest thing
might give you away!"

Some of the cleverest work in Lev Gleason's
pair of bestsellers, *Crime Does Not Pay* and
Crime and Punishment, were the shorter
supporting features. Like this neat twist-
ending vignette about a smart-aleck street
robber desperate not to leave the tiniest
incriminating clue at the scene of the crime.
Artist Bill Everett demonstrates his superb
realization of characterful faces. He conceived
Marvel's monarch of the seas, the Sub-Mariner,
and was a direct descendent of British
visionary William Blake.

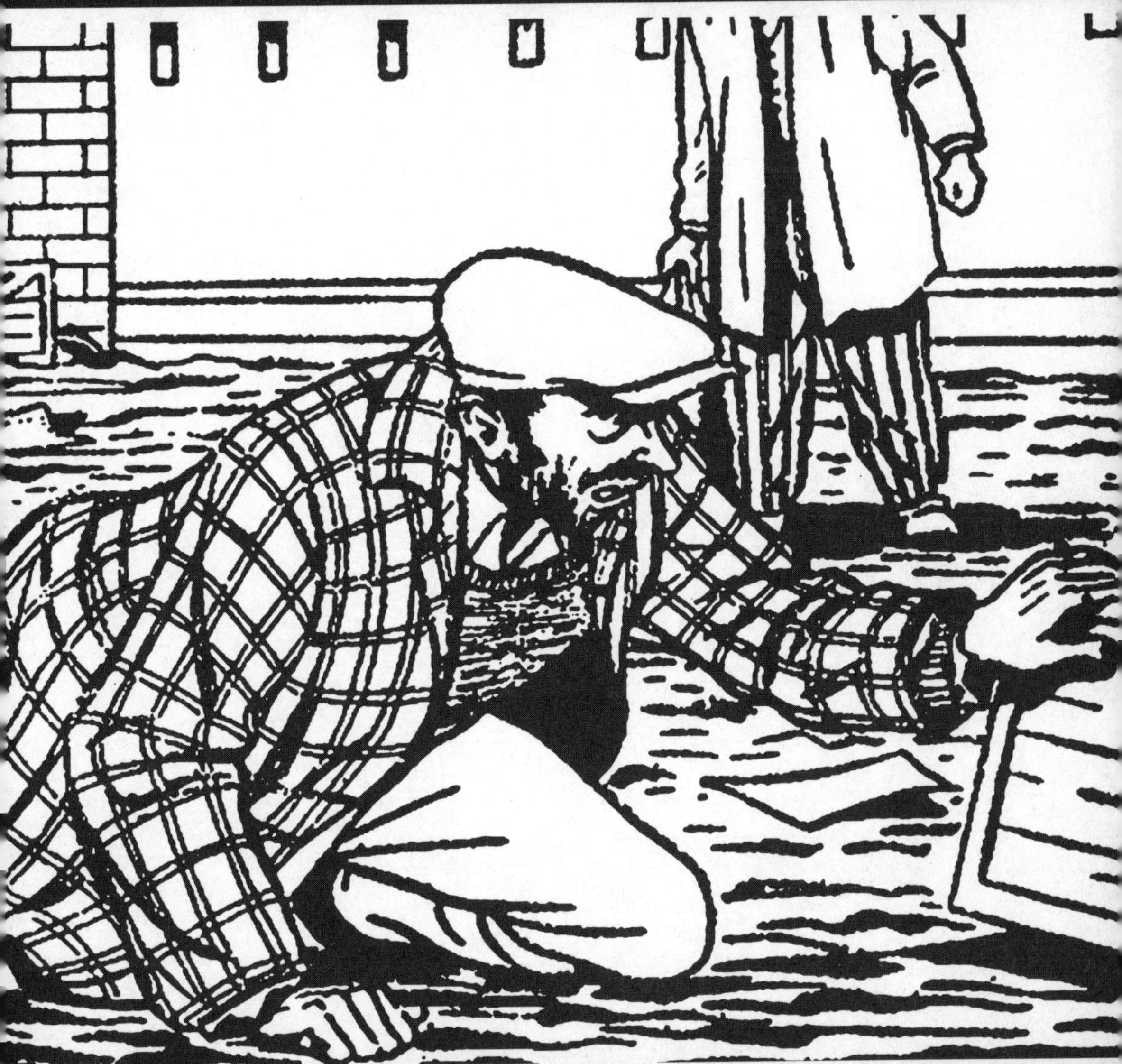

The Button

Bill Everett (art), writer unknown 1950

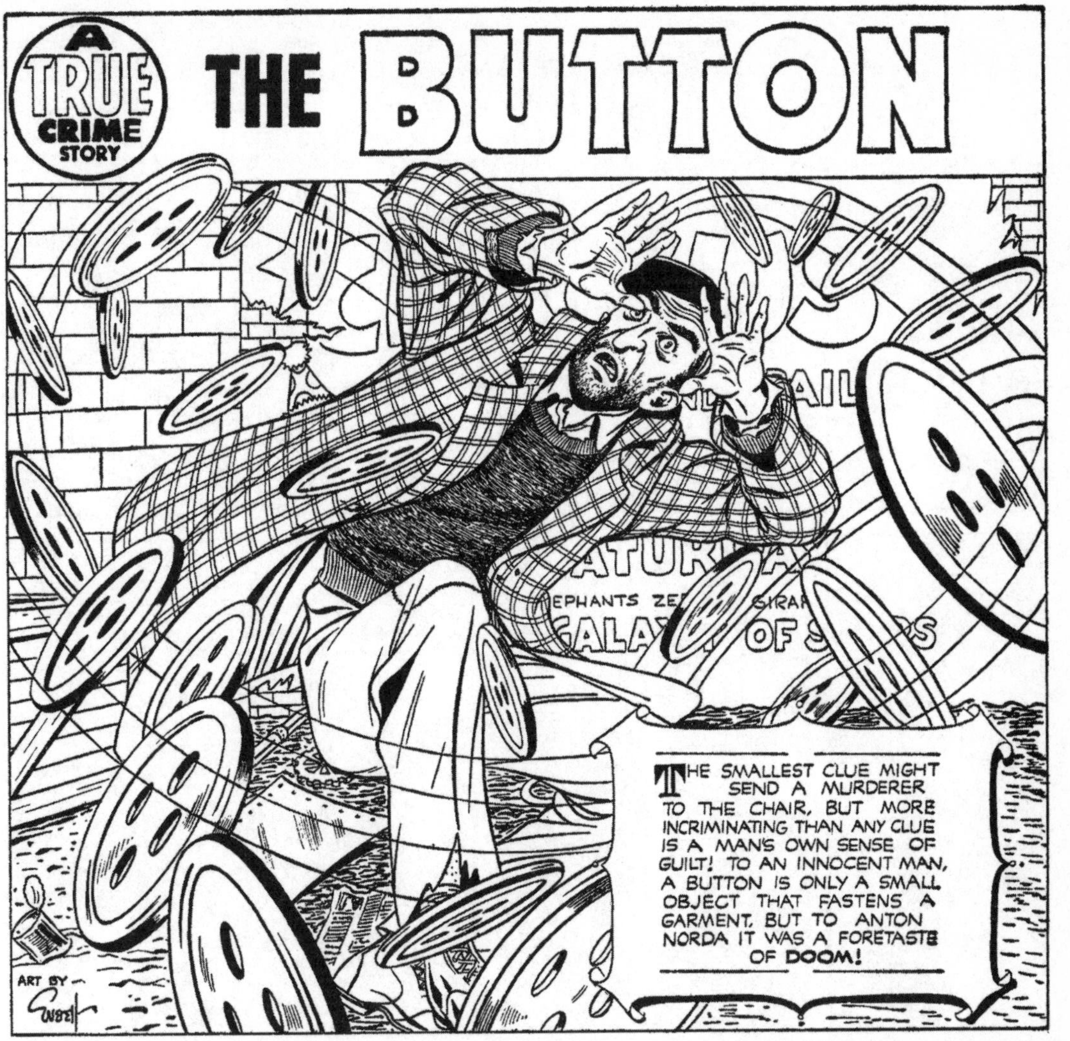
A TRUE CRIME STORY
THE BUTTON
THE SMALLEST CLUE MIGHT SEND A MURDERER TO THE CHAIR, BUT MORE INCRIMINATING THAN ANY CLUE IS A MAN'S OWN SENSE OF GUILT! TO AN INNOCENT MAN, A BUTTON IS ONLY A SMALL OBJECT THAT FASTENS A GARMENT, BUT TO ANTON NORDA IT WAS A FORETASTE OF **DOOM**!
ART BY

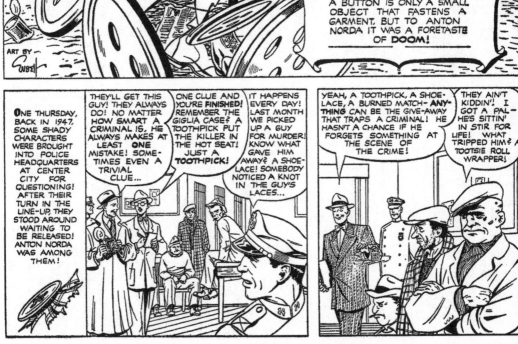

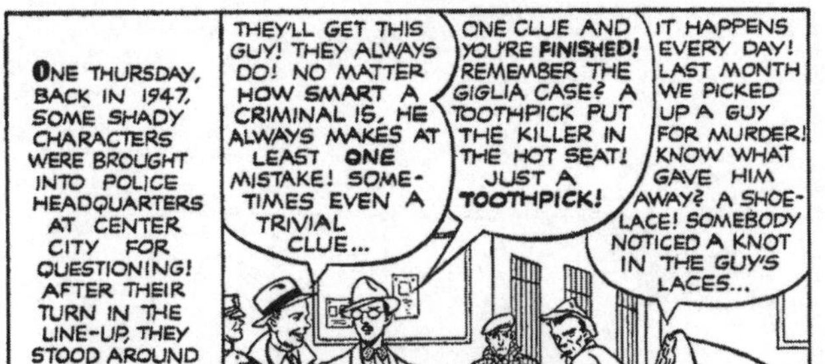
ONE THURSDAY, BACK IN 1947, SOME SHADY CHARACTERS WERE BROUGHT INTO POLICE HEADQUARTERS AT CENTER CITY FOR QUESTIONING! AFTER THEIR TURN IN THE LINE-UP, THEY STOOD AROUND WAITING TO BE RELEASED! ANTON NORDA WAS AMONG THEM!
THEY'LL GET THIS GUY! THEY ALWAYS DO! NO MATTER HOW SMART A CRIMINAL IS, HE ALWAYS MAKES AT LEAST **ONE** MISTAKE! SOMETIMES EVEN A TRIVIAL CLUE...
ONE CLUE AND YOU'RE **FINISHED!** REMEMBER THE GIGLIA CASE? A TOOTHPICK PUT THE KILLER IN THE HOT SEAT! JUST A **TOOTHPICK!**
IT HAPPENS EVERY DAY! LAST MONTH WE PICKED UP A GUY FOR MURDER! KNOW WHAT GAVE HIM AWAY? A SHOE-LACE! SOMEBODY NOTICED A KNOT IN THE GUY'S LACES...

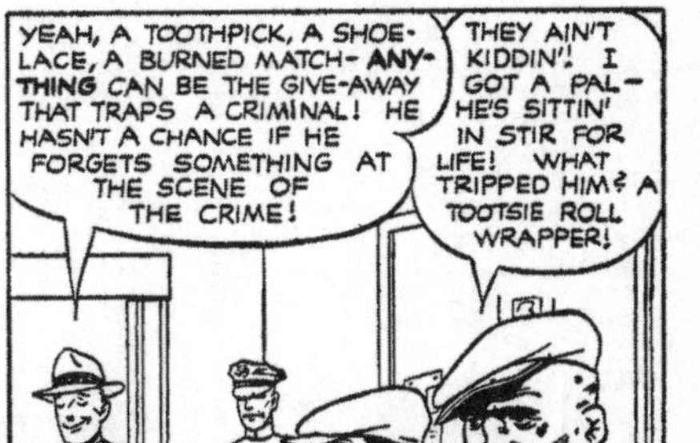
YEAH, A TOOTHPICK, A SHOE-LACE, A BURNED MATCH- **ANYTHING** CAN BE THE GIVE-AWAY THAT TRAPS A CRIMINAL! HE HASN'T A CHANCE IF HE FORGETS SOMETHING AT THE SCENE OF THE CRIME!
THEY AIN'T KIDDIN'! I GOT A PAL- HE'S SITTIN' IN STIR FOR LIFE! WHAT TRIPPED HIM? A TOOTSIE ROLL WRAPPER!

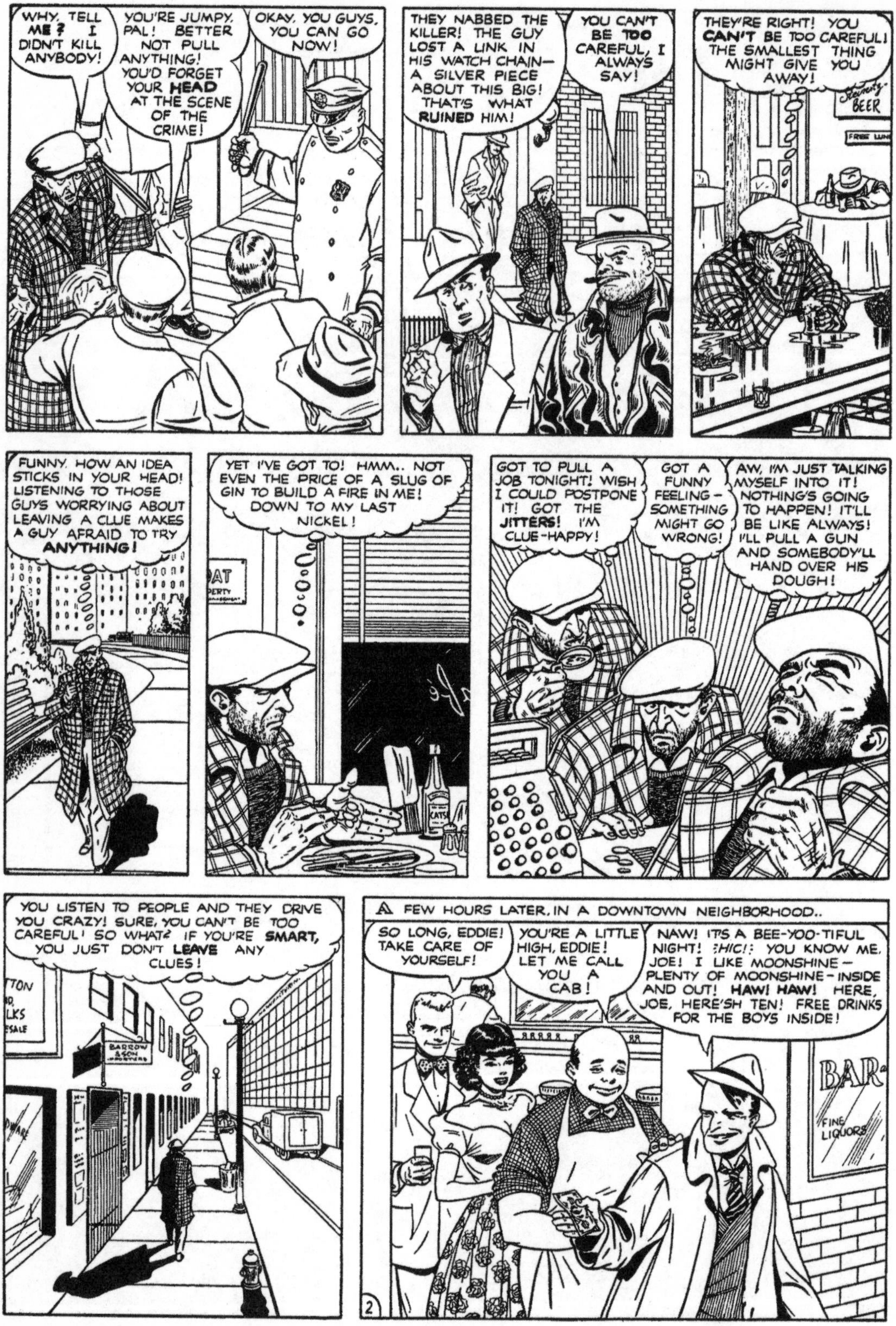
WHY, TELL ME? I DIDN'T KILL ANYBODY!
YOU'RE JUMPY, PAL! BETTER NOT PULL ANYTHING! YOU'D FORGET YOUR HEAD AT THE SCENE OF THE CRIME!
OKAY, YOU GUYS, YOU CAN GO NOW!
THEY NABBED THE KILLER! THE GUY LOST A LINK IN HIS WATCH CHAIN— A SILVER PIECE ABOUT THIS BIG! THAT'S WHAT RUINED HIM!
YOU CAN'T BE TOO CAREFUL, I ALWAYS SAY!
THEY'RE RIGHT! YOU CAN'T BE TOO CAREFUL! THE SMALLEST THING MIGHT GIVE YOU AWAY!
BEER
FUNNY, HOW AN IDEA STICKS IN YOUR HEAD! LISTENING TO THOSE GUYS WORRYING ABOUT LEAVING A CLUE MAKES A GUY AFRAID TO TRY ANYTHING!
YET I'VE GOT TO! HMM.. NOT EVEN THE PRICE OF A SLUG OF GIN TO BUILD A FIRE IN ME! DOWN TO MY LAST NICKEL!
GOT TO PULL A JOB TONIGHT! WISH I COULD POSTPONE IT! GOT THE JITTERS! I'M CLUE-HAPPY!
GOT A FUNNY FEELING— SOMETHING MIGHT GO WRONG!
AW, I'M JUST TALKING MYSELF INTO IT! NOTHING'S GOING TO HAPPEN! IT'LL BE LIKE ALWAYS! I'LL PULL A GUN AND SOMEBODY'LL HAND OVER HIS DOUGH!
YOU LISTEN TO PEOPLE AND THEY DRIVE YOU CRAZY! SURE, YOU CAN'T BE TOO CAREFUL! SO WHAT? IF YOU'RE SMART, YOU JUST DON'T LEAVE ANY CLUES!
A FEW HOURS LATER, IN A DOWNTOWN NEIGHBORHOOD..
SO LONG, EDDIE! TAKE CARE OF YOURSELF!
YOU'RE A LITTLE HIGH, EDDIE! LET ME CALL YOU A CAB!
NAW! IT'S A BEE-YOO-TIFUL NIGHT! *HIC!* YOU KNOW ME, JOE! I LIKE MOONSHINE— PLENTY OF MOONSHINE— INSIDE AND OUT! HAW! HAW! HERE, JOE, HERE'SH TEN! FREE DRINKS FOR THE BOYS INSIDE!
BAR
FINE LIQUORS
2

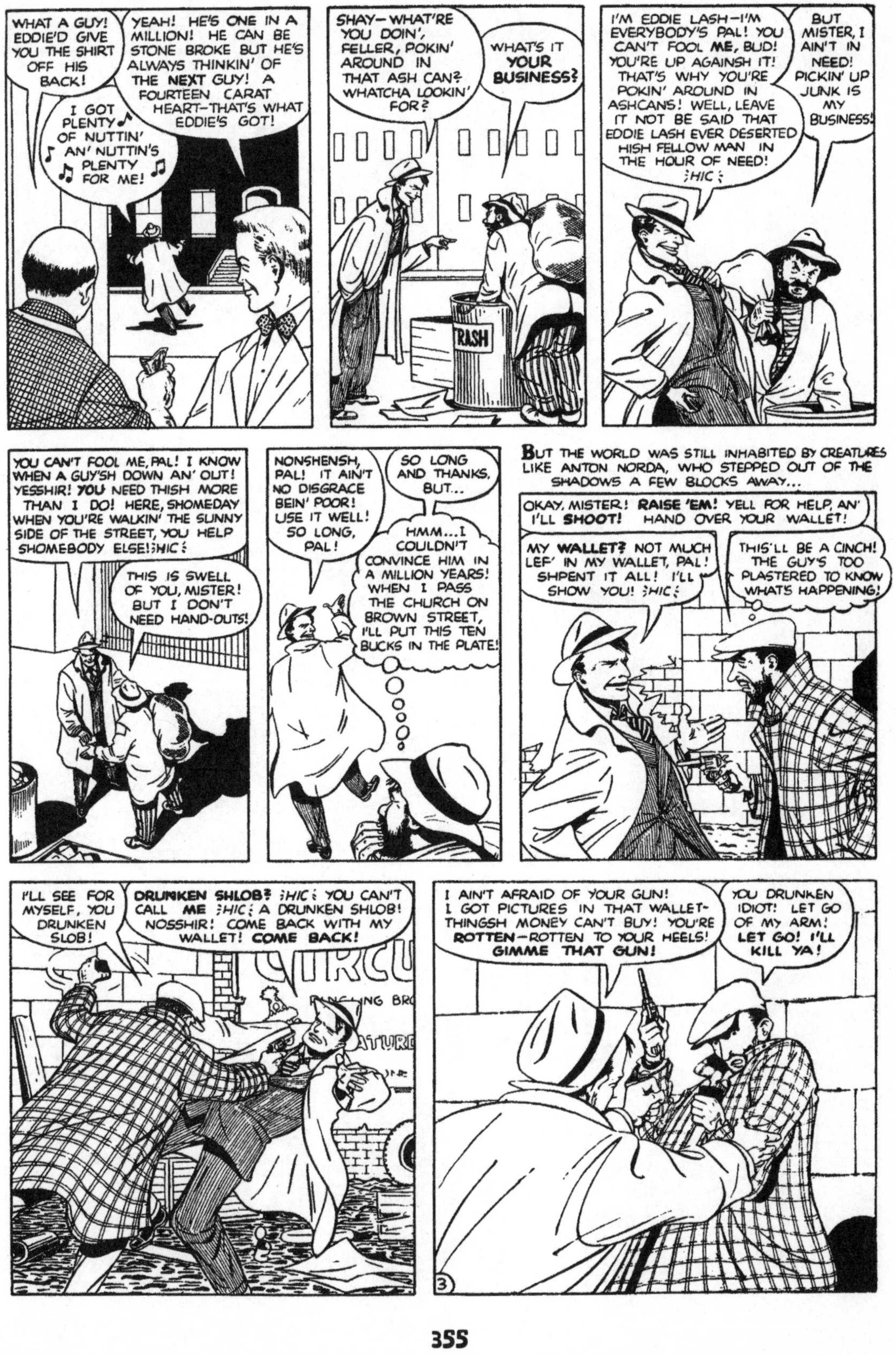
WHAT A GUY! EDDIE'D GIVE YOU THE SHIRT OFF HIS BACK!
YEAH! HE'S ONE IN A MILLION! HE CAN BE STONE BROKE BUT HE'S ALWAYS THINKIN' OF THE NEXT GUY! A FOURTEEN CARAT HEART—THAT'S WHAT EDDIE'S GOT!
I GOT PLENTY OF NUTTIN' AN' NUTTIN'S PLENTY FOR ME!
SHAY—WHAT'RE YOU DOIN', FELLER, POKIN' AROUND IN THAT ASH CAN? WHATCHA LOOKIN' FOR?
WHAT'S IT YOUR BUSINESS?
TRASH
I'M EDDIE LASH—I'M EVERYBODY'S PAL! YOU CAN'T FOOL ME, BUD! YOU'RE UP AGAINSH IT! THAT'S WHY YOU'RE POKIN' AROUND IN ASHCANS! WELL, LEAVE IT NOT BE SAID THAT EDDIE LASH EVER DESERTED HISH FELLOW MAN IN THE HOUR OF NEED! ;HIC;
BUT MISTER, I AIN'T IN NEED! PICKIN' UP JUNK IS MY BUSINESS!
YOU CAN'T FOOL ME, PAL! I KNOW WHEN A GUY'SH DOWN AN' OUT! YESSHIR! YOU NEED THISH MORE THAN I DO! HERE, SHOMEDAY WHEN YOU'RE WALKIN' THE SUNNY SIDE OF THE STREET, YOU HELP SHOMEBODY ELSE! ;HIC;
THIS IS SWELL OF YOU, MISTER! BUT I DON'T NEED HAND-OUTS!
NONSHENSH, PAL! IT AIN'T NO DISGRACE BEIN' POOR! USE IT WELL! SO LONG, PAL!
SO LONG AND THANKS, BUT...
HMM...I COULDN'T CONVINCE HIM IN A MILLION YEARS! WHEN I PASS THE CHURCH ON BROWN STREET, I'LL PUT THIS TEN BUCKS IN THE PLATE!
BUT THE WORLD WAS STILL INHABITED BY CREATURES LIKE ANTON NORDA, WHO STEPPED OUT OF THE SHADOWS A FEW BLOCKS AWAY...
OKAY, MISTER! RAISE 'EM! YELL FOR HELP, AN' I'LL SHOOT! HAND OVER YOUR WALLET!
MY WALLET? NOT MUCH LEF' IN MY WALLET, PAL! SHPENT IT ALL! I'LL SHOW YOU! ;HIC;
THIS'LL BE A CINCH! THE GUY'S TOO PLASTERED TO KNOW WHAT'S HAPPENING!
I'LL SEE FOR MYSELF, YOU DRUNKEN SLOB!
DRUNKEN SHLOB? ;HIC; YOU CAN'T CALL ME ;HIC; A DRUNKEN SHLOB! NOSSHIR! COME BACK WITH MY WALLET! COME BACK!
I AIN'T AFRAID OF YOUR GUN! I GOT PICTURES IN THAT WALLET—THINGSH MONEY CAN'T BUY! YOU'RE ROTTEN—ROTTEN TO YOUR HEELS! GIMME THAT GUN!
YOU DRUNKEN IDIOT! LET GO OF MY ARM! LET GO! I'LL KILL YA!
3

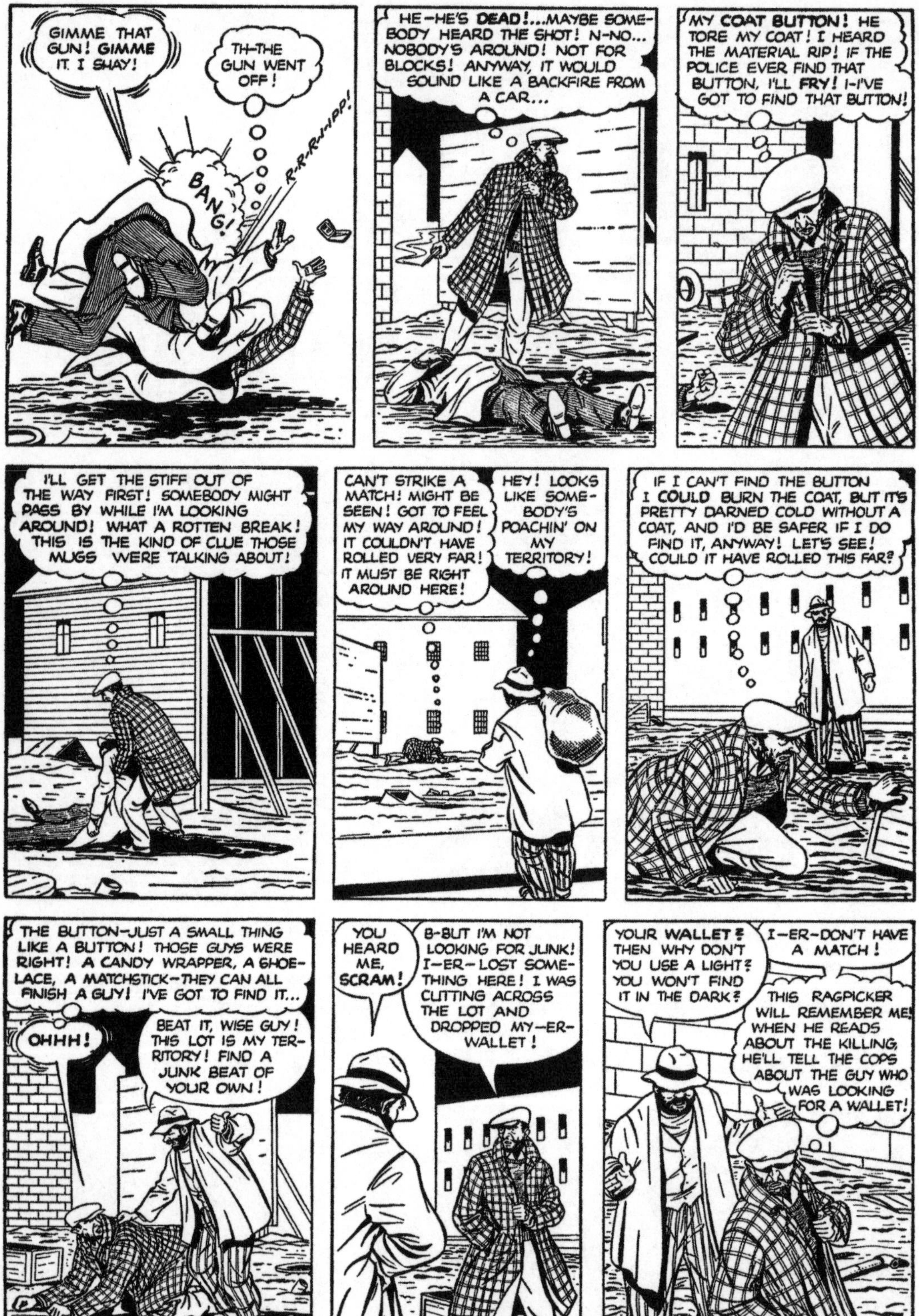
GIMME THAT GUN! GIMME IT. I SHAY!
TH-THE GUN WENT OFF!
BANG!
R-R-Rrrrippp!
HE-HE'S DEAD!...MAYBE SOMEBODY HEARD THE SHOT! N-NO... NOBODY'S AROUND! NOT FOR BLOCKS! ANYWAY, IT WOULD SOUND LIKE A BACKFIRE FROM A CAR...
MY COAT BUTTON! HE TORE MY COAT! I HEARD THE MATERIAL RIP! IF THE POLICE EVER FIND THAT BUTTON, I'LL FRY! I-I'VE GOT TO FIND THAT BUTTON!
I'LL GET THE STIFF OUT OF THE WAY FIRST! SOMEBODY MIGHT PASS BY WHILE I'M LOOKING AROUND! WHAT A ROTTEN BREAK! THIS IS THE KIND OF CLUE THOSE MUGS WERE TALKING ABOUT!
CAN'T STRIKE A MATCH! MIGHT BE SEEN! GOT TO FEEL MY WAY AROUND! IT COULDN'T HAVE ROLLED VERY FAR! IT MUST BE RIGHT AROUND HERE!
HEY! LOOKS LIKE SOMEBODY'S POACHIN' ON MY TERRITORY!
IF I CAN'T FIND THE BUTTON I COULD BURN THE COAT, BUT IT'S PRETTY DARNED COLD WITHOUT A COAT, AND I'D BE SAFER IF I DO FIND IT, ANYWAY! LET'S SEE! COULD IT HAVE ROLLED THIS FAR?
THE BUTTON-JUST A SMALL THING LIKE A BUTTON! THOSE GUYS WERE RIGHT! A CANDY WRAPPER, A SHOE-LACE, A MATCHSTICK-THEY CAN ALL FINISH A GUY! I'VE GOT TO FIND IT...
OHHH!
BEAT IT, WISE GUY! THIS LOT IS MY TERRITORY! FIND A JUNK BEAT OF YOUR OWN!
YOU HEARD ME, SCRAM!
B-BUT I'M NOT LOOKING FOR JUNK! I-ER-LOST SOMETHING HERE! I WAS CUTTING ACROSS THE LOT AND DROPPED MY-ER-WALLET!
YOUR WALLET? THEN WHY DON'T YOU USE A LIGHT? YOU WON'T FIND IT IN THE DARK?
I-ER-DON'T HAVE A MATCH!
THIS RAGPICKER WILL REMEMBER ME! WHEN HE READS ABOUT THE KILLING, HE'LL TELL THE COPS ABOUT THE GUY WHO WAS LOOKING FOR A WALLET!
4

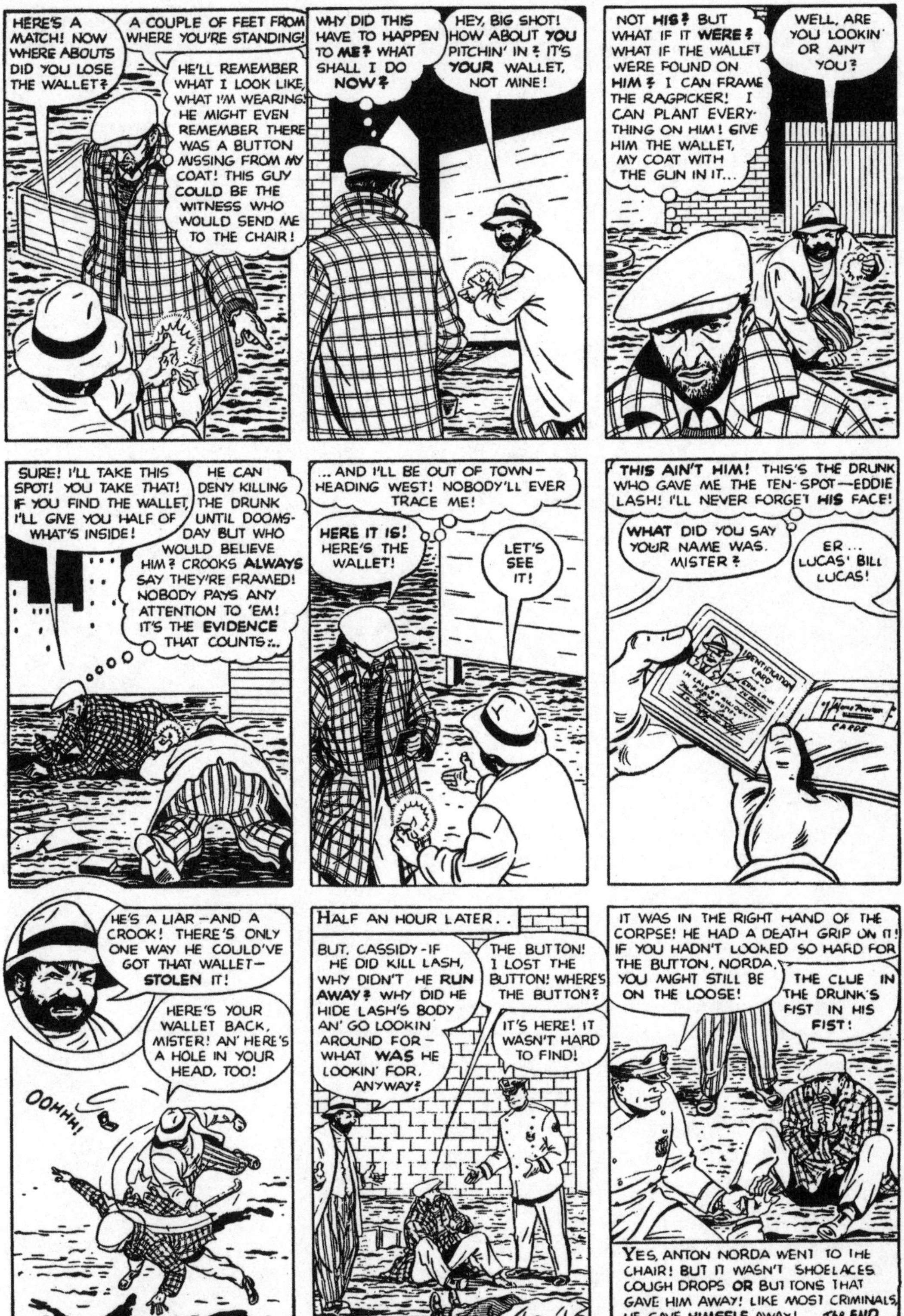
HERE'S A MATCH! NOW WHERE ABOUTS DID YOU LOSE THE WALLET?
A COUPLE OF FEET FROM WHERE YOU'RE STANDING!
HE'LL REMEMBER WHAT I LOOK LIKE, WHAT I'M WEARING! HE MIGHT EVEN REMEMBER THERE WAS A BUTTON MISSING FROM MY COAT! THIS GUY COULD BE THE WITNESS WHO WOULD SEND ME TO THE CHAIR!
WHY DID THIS HAVE TO HAPPEN TO ME? WHAT SHALL I DO NOW?
HEY, BIG SHOT! HOW ABOUT YOU PITCHIN' IN? IT'S YOUR WALLET, NOT MINE!
NOT HIS? BUT WHAT IF IT WERE? WHAT IF THE WALLET WERE FOUND ON HIM? I CAN FRAME THE RAGPICKER! I CAN PLANT EVERYTHING ON HIM! GIVE HIM THE WALLET, MY COAT WITH THE GUN IN IT...
WELL, ARE YOU LOOKIN' OR AIN'T YOU?
SURE! I'LL TAKE THIS SPOT! YOU TAKE THAT! IF YOU FIND THE WALLET, I'LL GIVE YOU HALF OF WHAT'S INSIDE!
HE CAN DENY KILLING THE DRUNK UNTIL DOOMSDAY BUT WHO WOULD BELIEVE HIM? CROOKS ALWAYS SAY THEY'RE FRAMED! NOBODY PAYS ANY ATTENTION TO 'EM! IT'S THE EVIDENCE THAT COUNTS...
...AND I'LL BE OUT OF TOWN—HEADING WEST! NOBODY'LL EVER TRACE ME!
HERE IT IS! HERE'S THE WALLET!
LET'S SEE IT!
THIS AIN'T HIM! THIS'S THE DRUNK WHO GAVE ME THE TEN-SPOT—EDDIE LASH! I'LL NEVER FORGET HIS FACE!
WHAT DID YOU SAY YOUR NAME WAS, MISTER?
ER... LUCAS' BILL LUCAS!
IDENTIFICATION CARD
CARDS
HE'S A LIAR—AND A CROOK! THERE'S ONLY ONE WAY HE COULD'VE GOT THAT WALLET—STOLEN IT!
HERE'S YOUR WALLET BACK, MISTER! AN' HERE'S A HOLE IN YOUR HEAD, TOO!
OOHHH!
HALF AN HOUR LATER..
BUT, CASSIDY-IF HE DID KILL LASH, WHY DIDN'T HE RUN AWAY? WHY DID HE HIDE LASH'S BODY AN' GO LOOKIN' AROUND FOR—WHAT WAS HE LOOKIN' FOR, ANYWAY?
THE BUTTON! I LOST THE BUTTON! WHERE'S THE BUTTON?
IT'S HERE! IT WASN'T HARD TO FIND!
IT WAS IN THE RIGHT HAND OF THE CORPSE! HE HAD A DEATH GRIP ON IT! IF YOU HADN'T LOOKED SO HARD FOR THE BUTTON, NORDA, YOU MIGHT STILL BE ON THE LOOSE!
THE CLUE IN THE DRUNK'S FIST IN HIS FIST!
YES, ANTON NORDA WENT TO THE CHAIR! BUT IT WASN'T SHOELACES COUGH DROPS OR BUTTONS THAT GAVE HIM AWAY! LIKE MOST CRIMINALS, HE GAVE HIMSELF AWAY! THE END

"I've heard
what these guys are like, Steve.
Looking for the slightest hesitation,
waiting for you to slip up.
Catch you out..."

Detective Kane knows that the city of New
Eden is no paradise with crime lord Oscar
Darke back in operation, and his own police
force are no angels either. Kane has become
a pariah since he came back on duty because
of his role in killing his corrupt ex-partner,
instead of keeping quiet and sticking together.
So nobody's happy when Internal Affairs have
to be called in to enquire, after the arrest
of a robbery suspect turns ugly and
the stolen money goes missing. When he
started *Kane* in 1993, British cartoonist
Paul Grist took inspiration from the police
television serial *Hill Street Blues*. His multi-
levelled and experimental page layouts
demand and reward close attention, such as
the symbolic humour of the pest exterminator
or the inset sequences re-telling the raid
from different perspectives. His ensemble
interaction and sophisticated weaving of
plotlines have made *Kane* one of the finest
ongoing cop dramas in current comics.

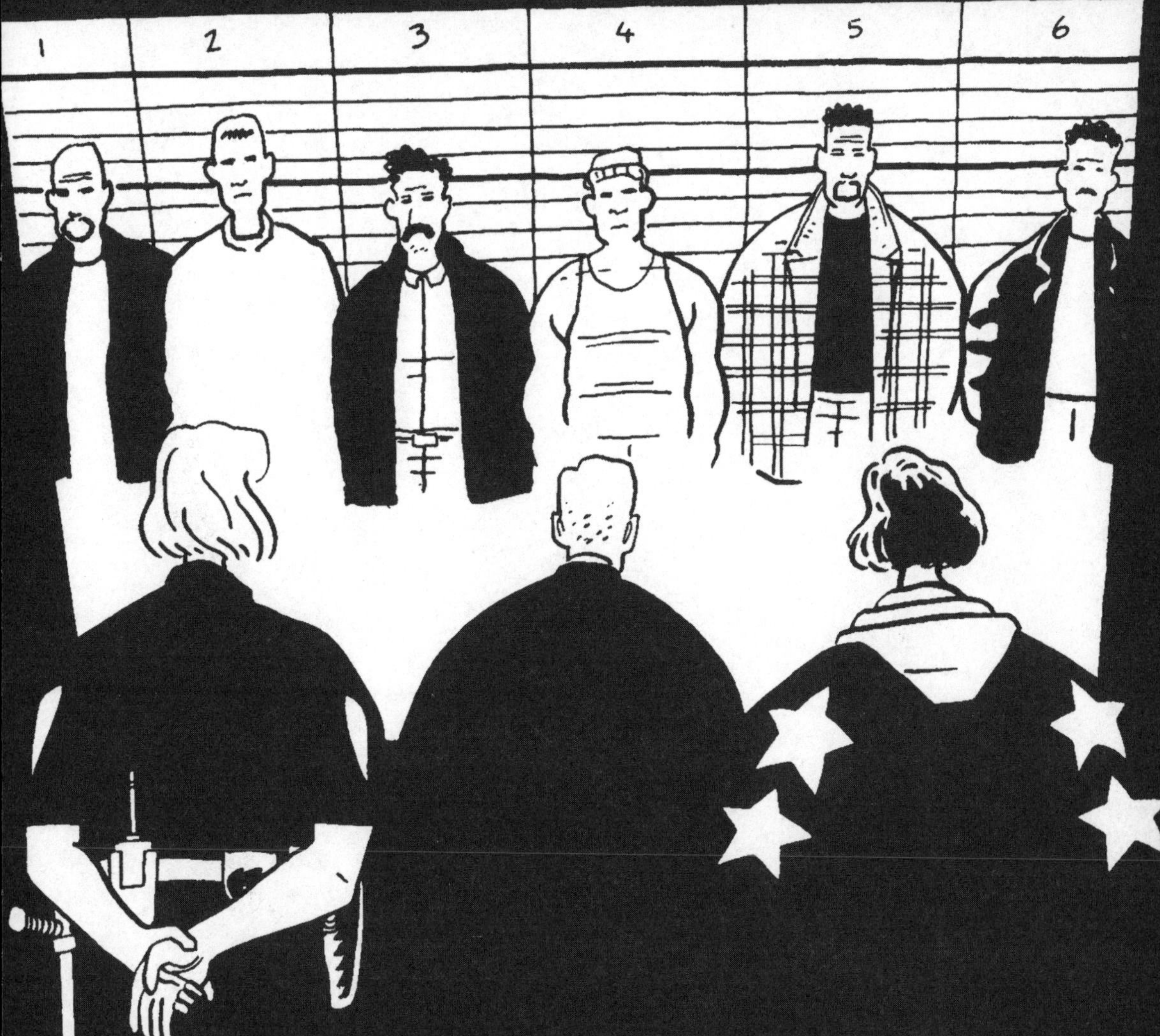
1
2
3
4
5
6

Kane: Rat in the House

Paul Grist (script & art) 1994

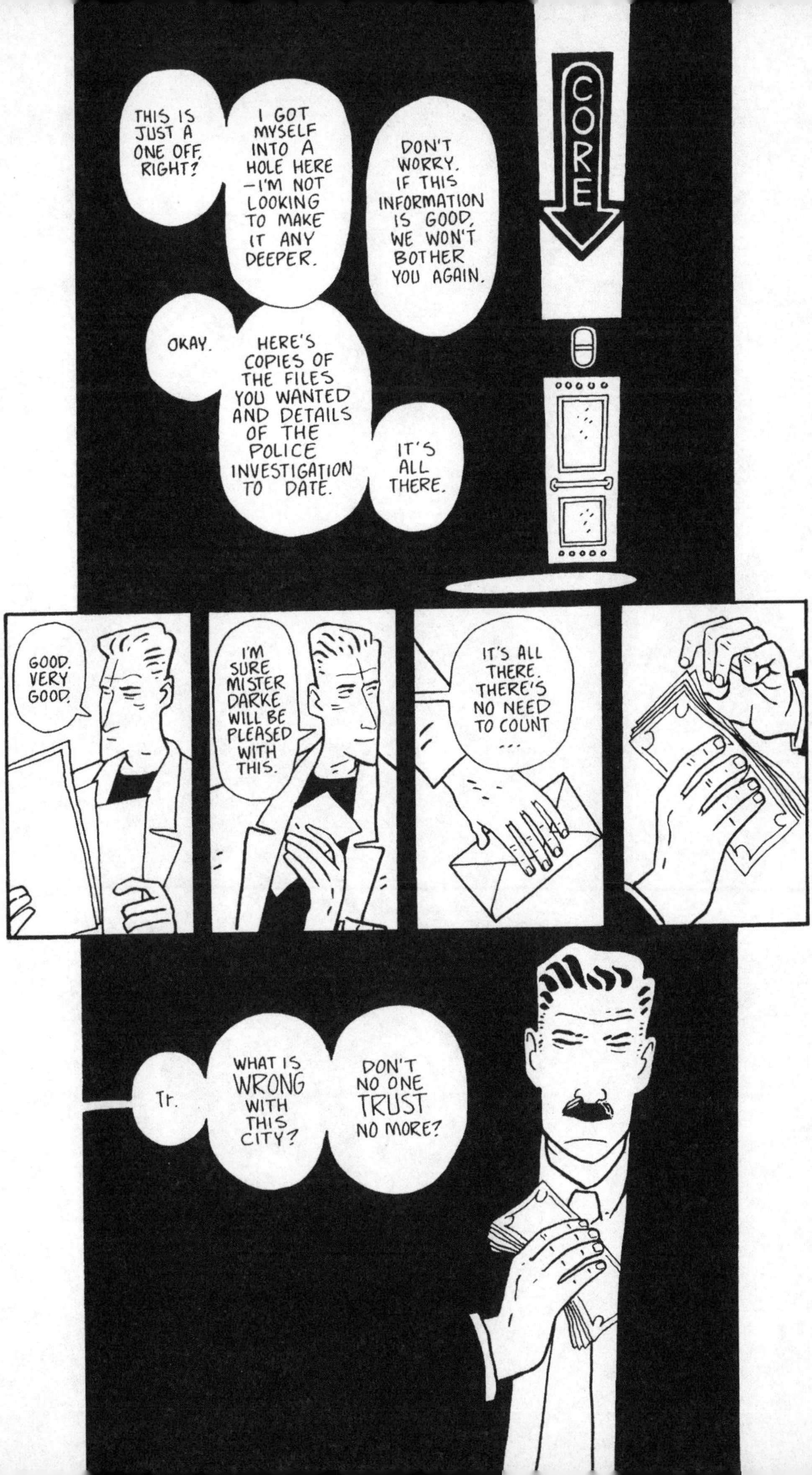
CORE
THIS IS JUST A ONE OFF, RIGHT?
I GOT MYSELF INTO A HOLE HERE —I'M NOT LOOKING TO MAKE IT ANY DEEPER.
DON'T WORRY. IF THIS INFORMATION IS GOOD, WE WON'T BOTHER YOU AGAIN.
OKAY.
HERE'S COPIES OF THE FILES YOU WANTED AND DETAILS OF THE POLICE INVESTIGATION TO DATE.
IT'S ALL THERE.
GOOD. VERY GOOD.
I'M SURE MISTER DARKE WILL BE PLEASED WITH THIS.
IT'S ALL THERE. THERE'S NO NEED TO COUNT ...
Tr.
WHAT IS WRONG WITH THIS CITY?
DON'T NO ONE TRUST NO MORE?

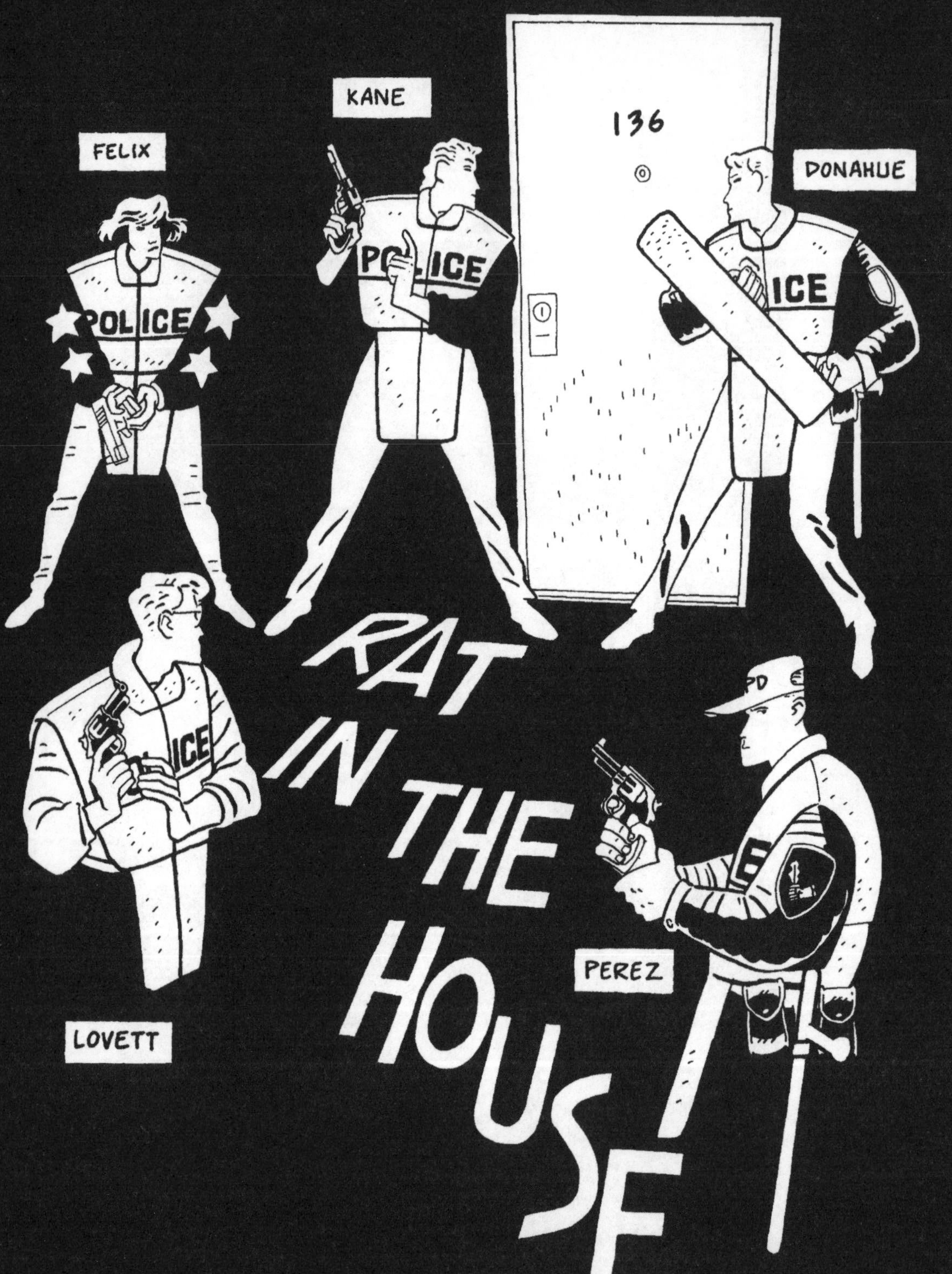

KANE
FELIX
136
DONAHUE
POLICE
POLICE
POLICE
RAT IN THE HOUSE
LOVETT
PEREZ

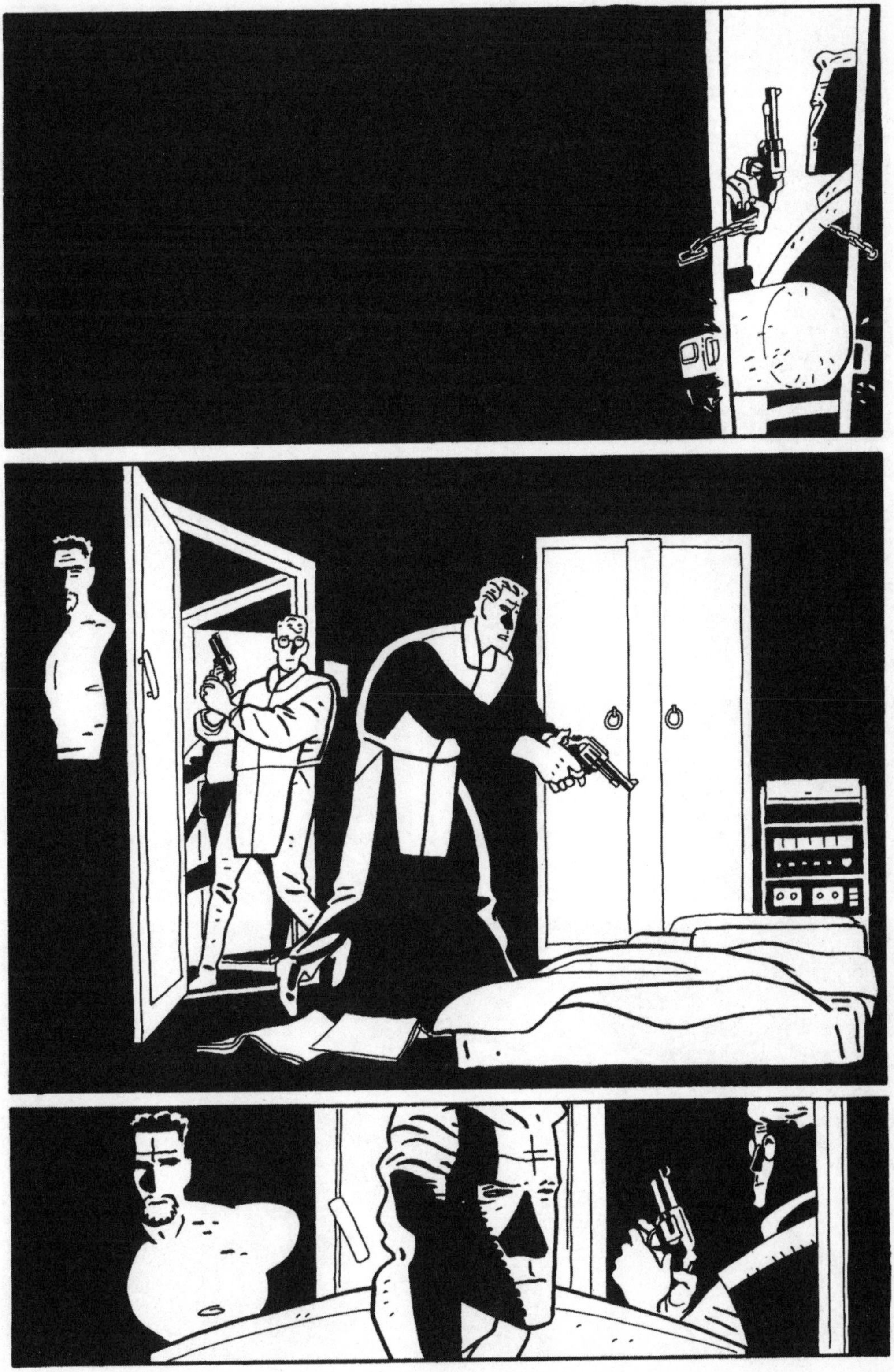

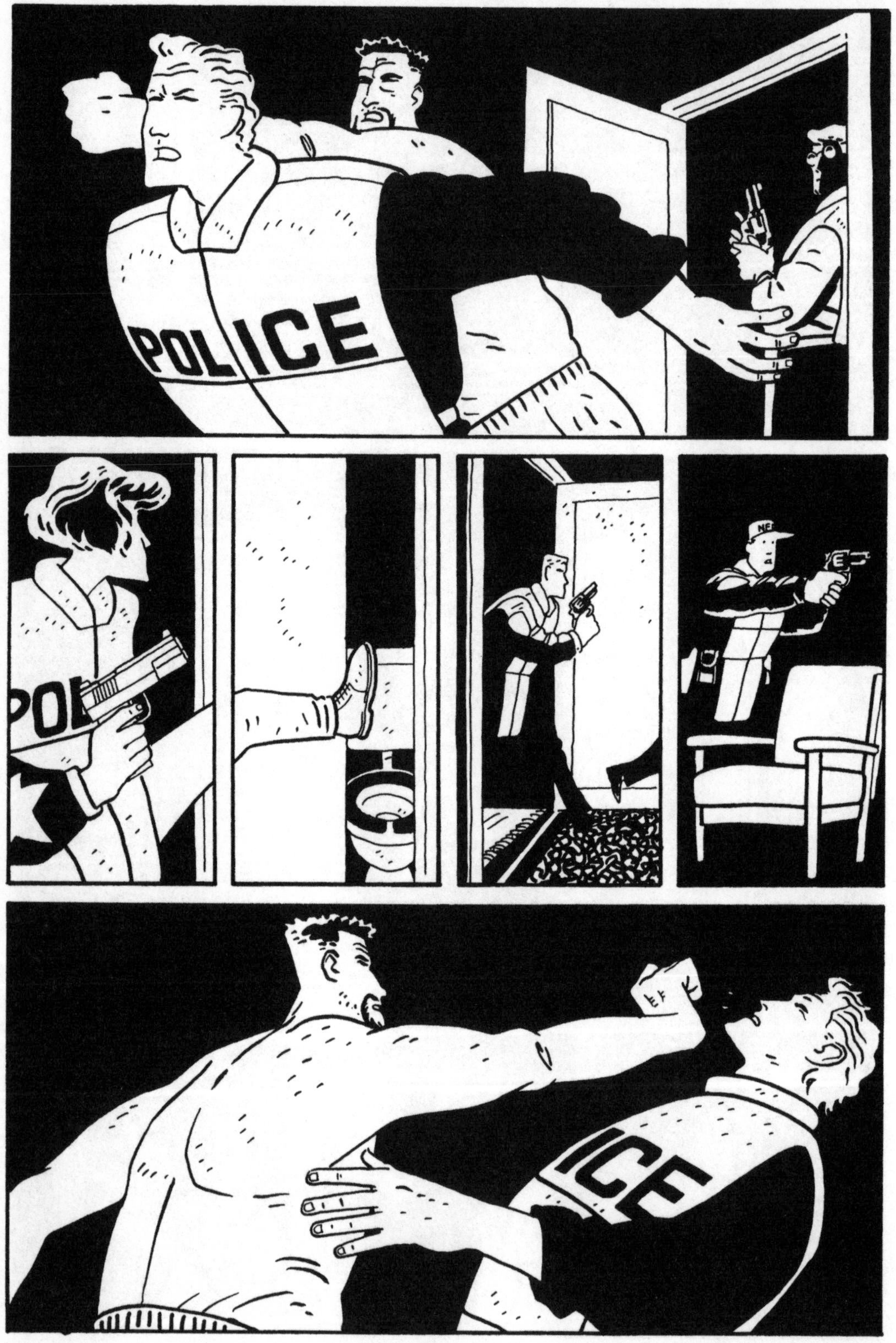
POLICE
POL
ICE

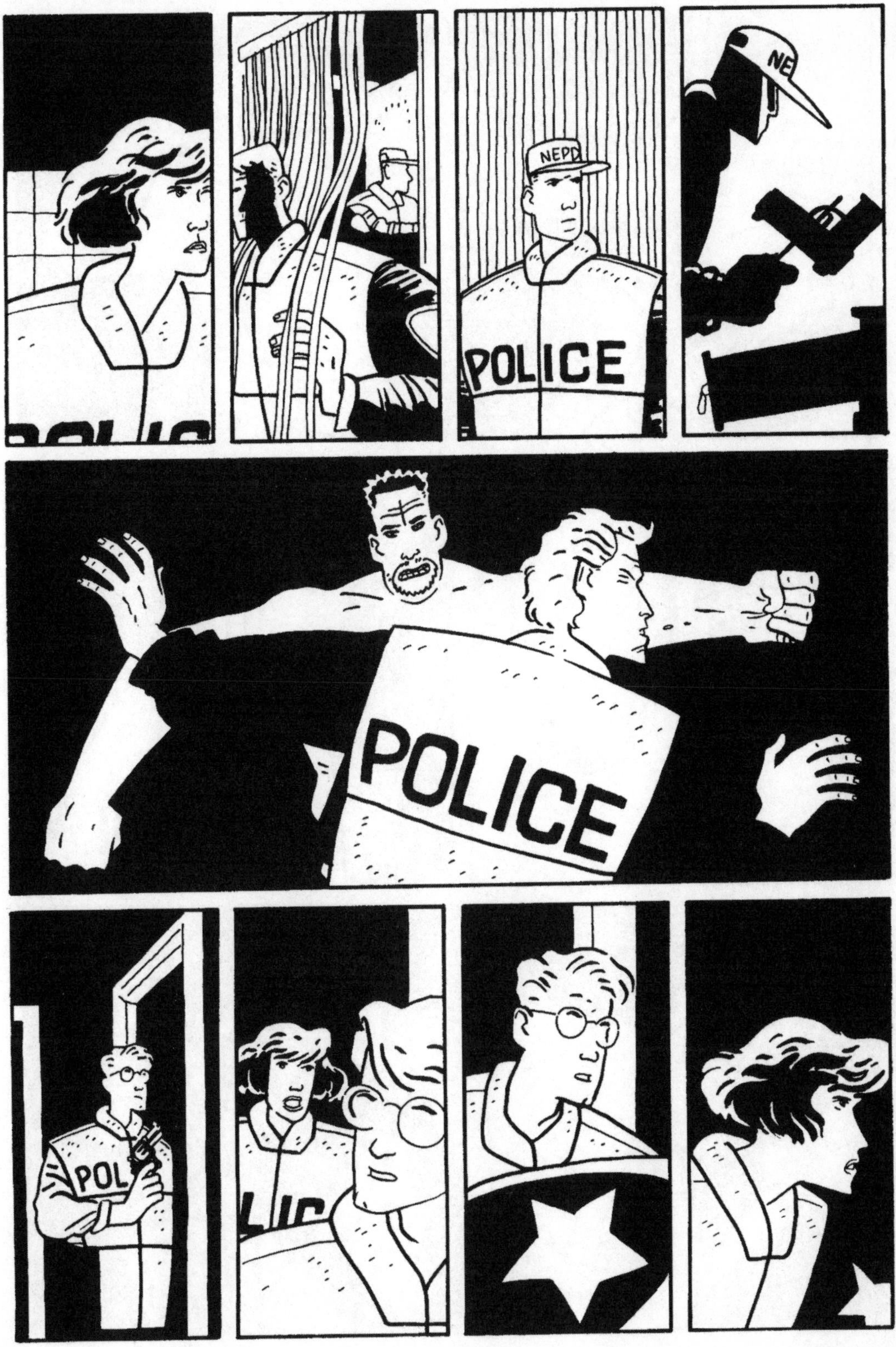
NEPD
POLICE
NE
POLICE
POL

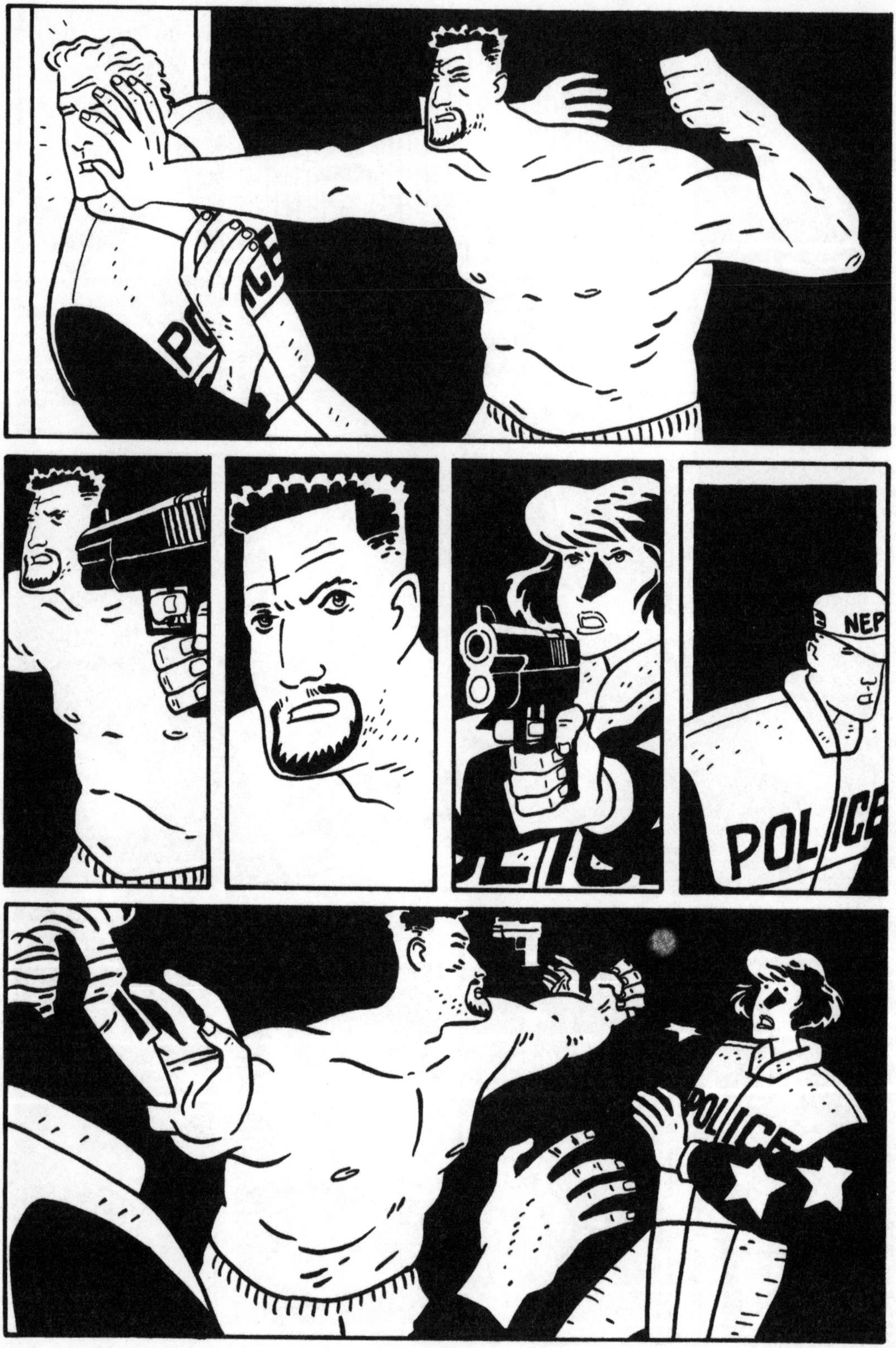
PO
ICE
NEP
POL ICE
POLICE

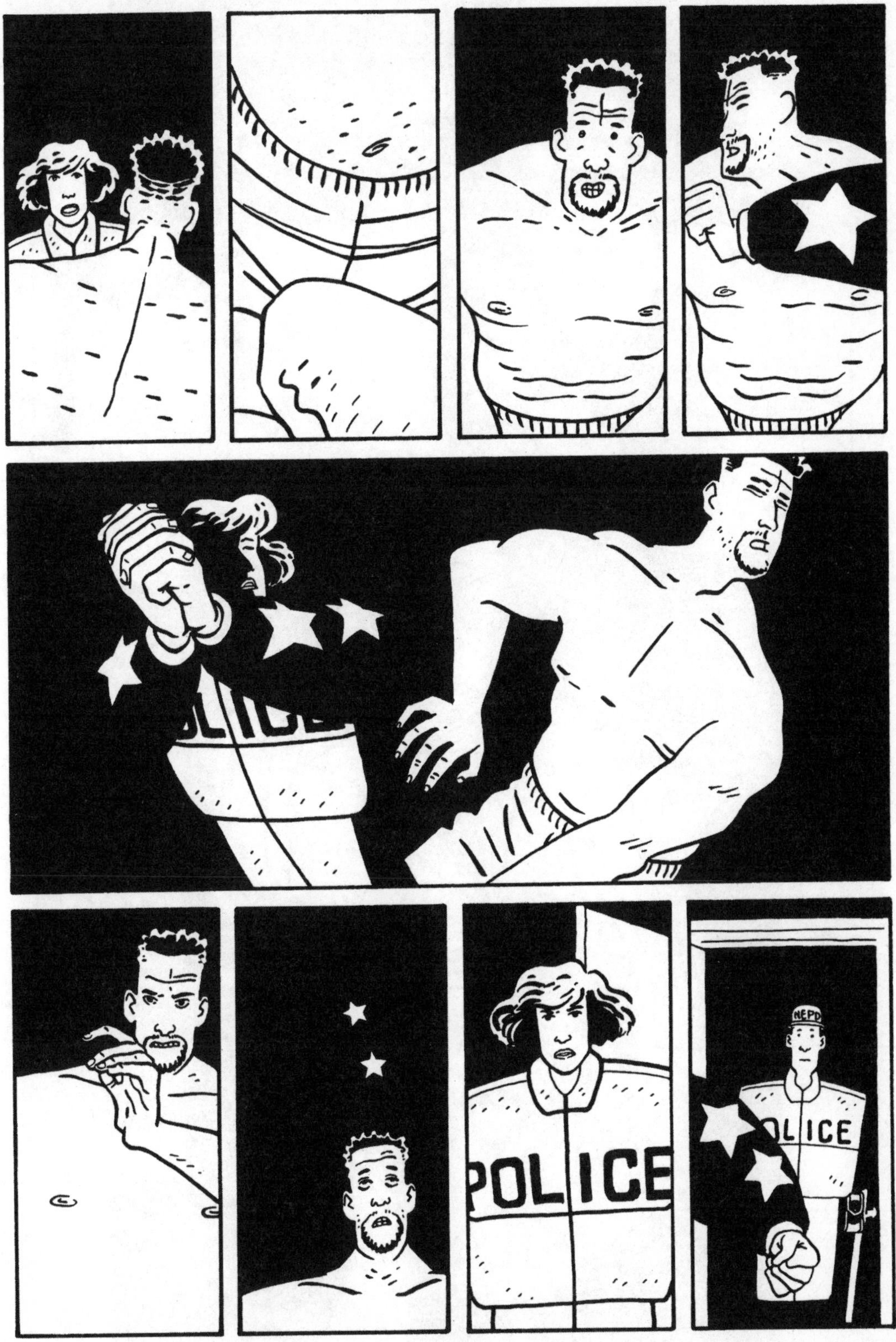
POLICE
NEPD

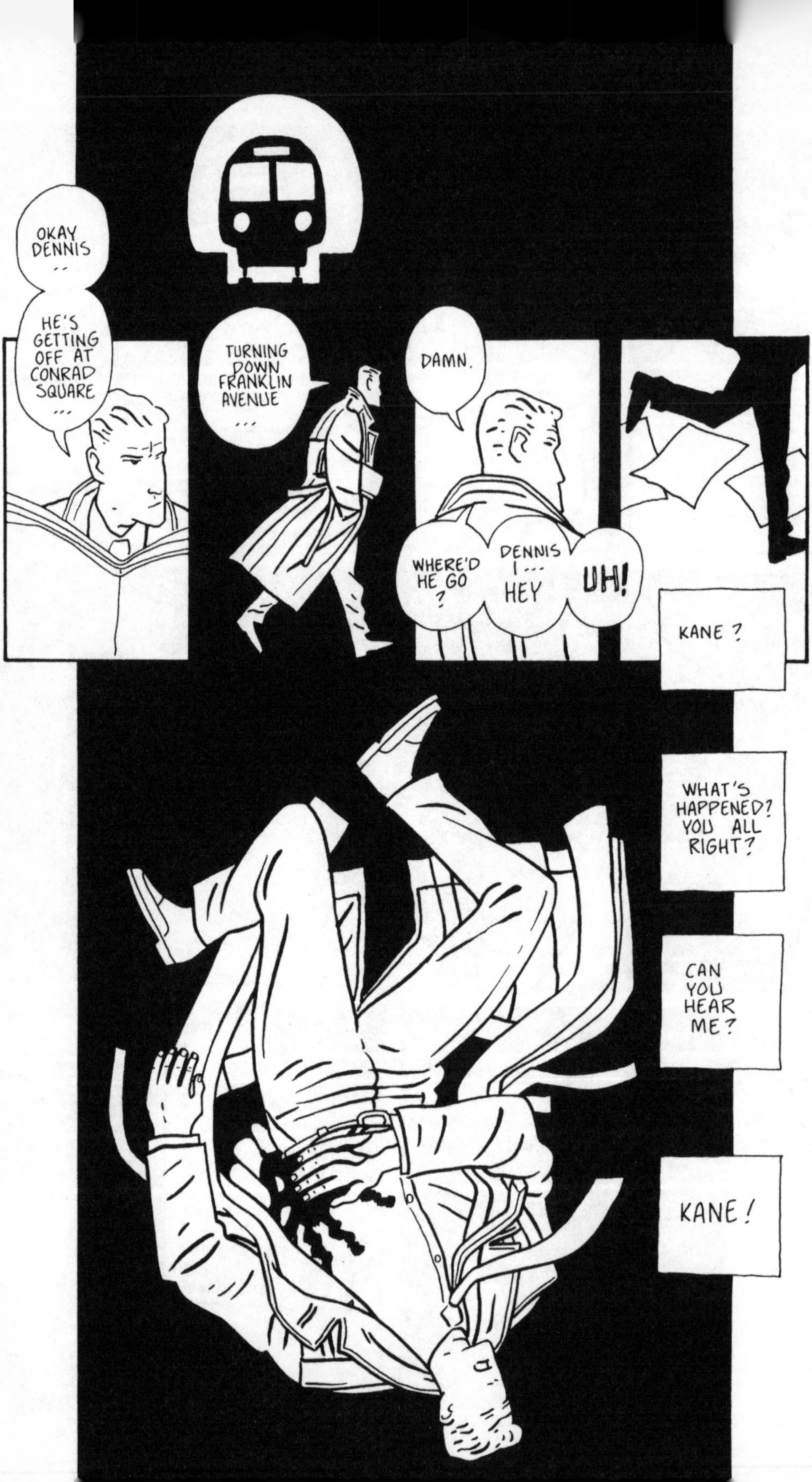
OKAY DENNIS ...
HE'S GETTING OFF AT CONRAD SQUARE ...
TURNING DOWN FRANKLIN AVENUE ...
DAMN.
WHERE'D HE GO ?
DENNIS I ... HEY
UH!
KANE ?
WHAT'S HAPPENED? YOU ALL RIGHT?
CAN YOU HEAR ME?
KANE!

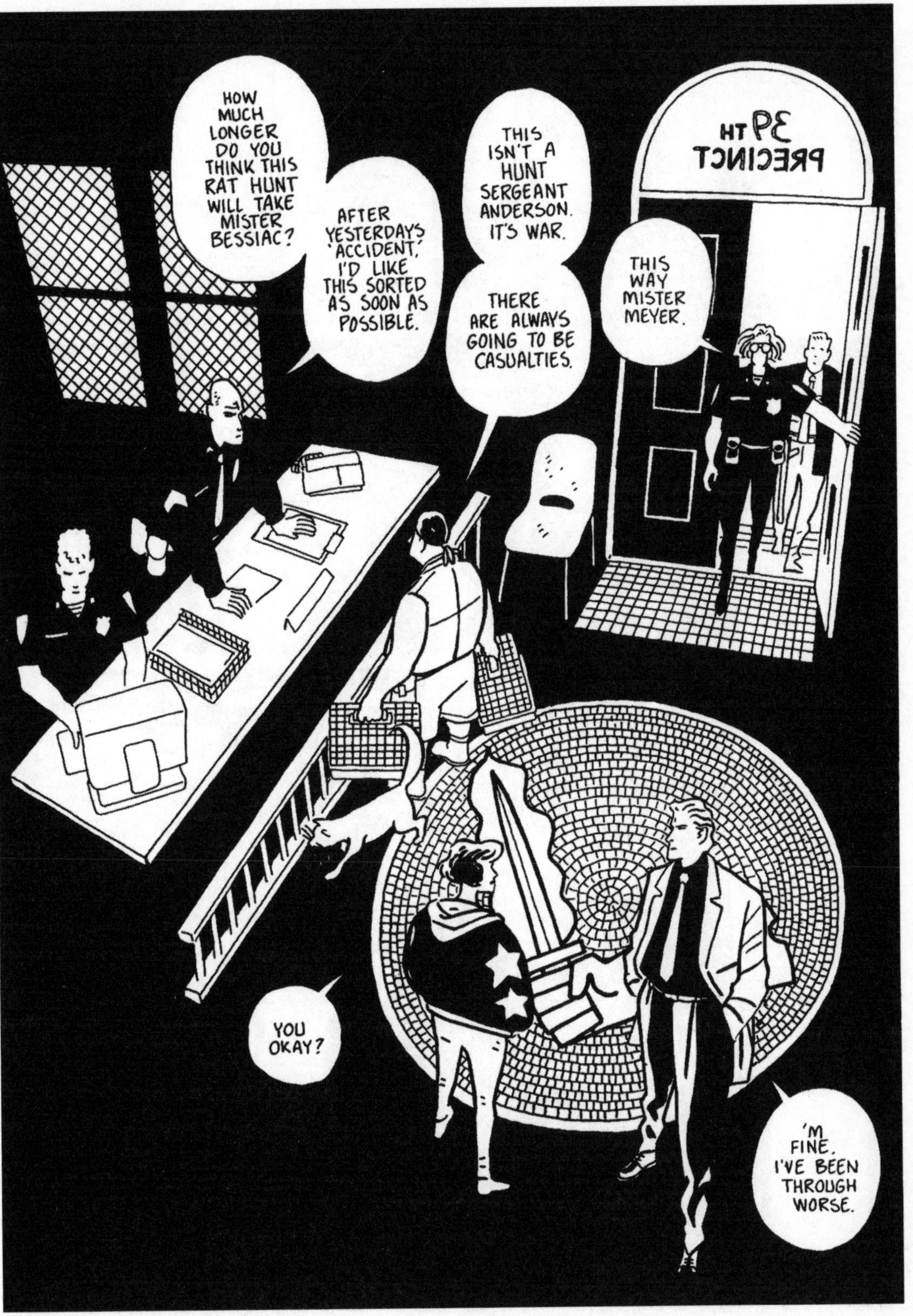

HOW MUCH LONGER DO YOU THINK THIS RAT HUNT WILL TAKE MISTER BESSIAC?
AFTER YESTERDAYS 'ACCIDENT,' I'D LIKE THIS SORTED AS SOON AS POSSIBLE.
THIS ISN'T A HUNT SERGEANT ANDERSON. IT'S WAR.
THERE ARE ALWAYS GOING TO BE CASUALTIES.
39TH PRECINCT
THIS WAY MISTER MEYER.
YOU OKAY?
'M FINE. I'VE BEEN THROUGH WORSE.

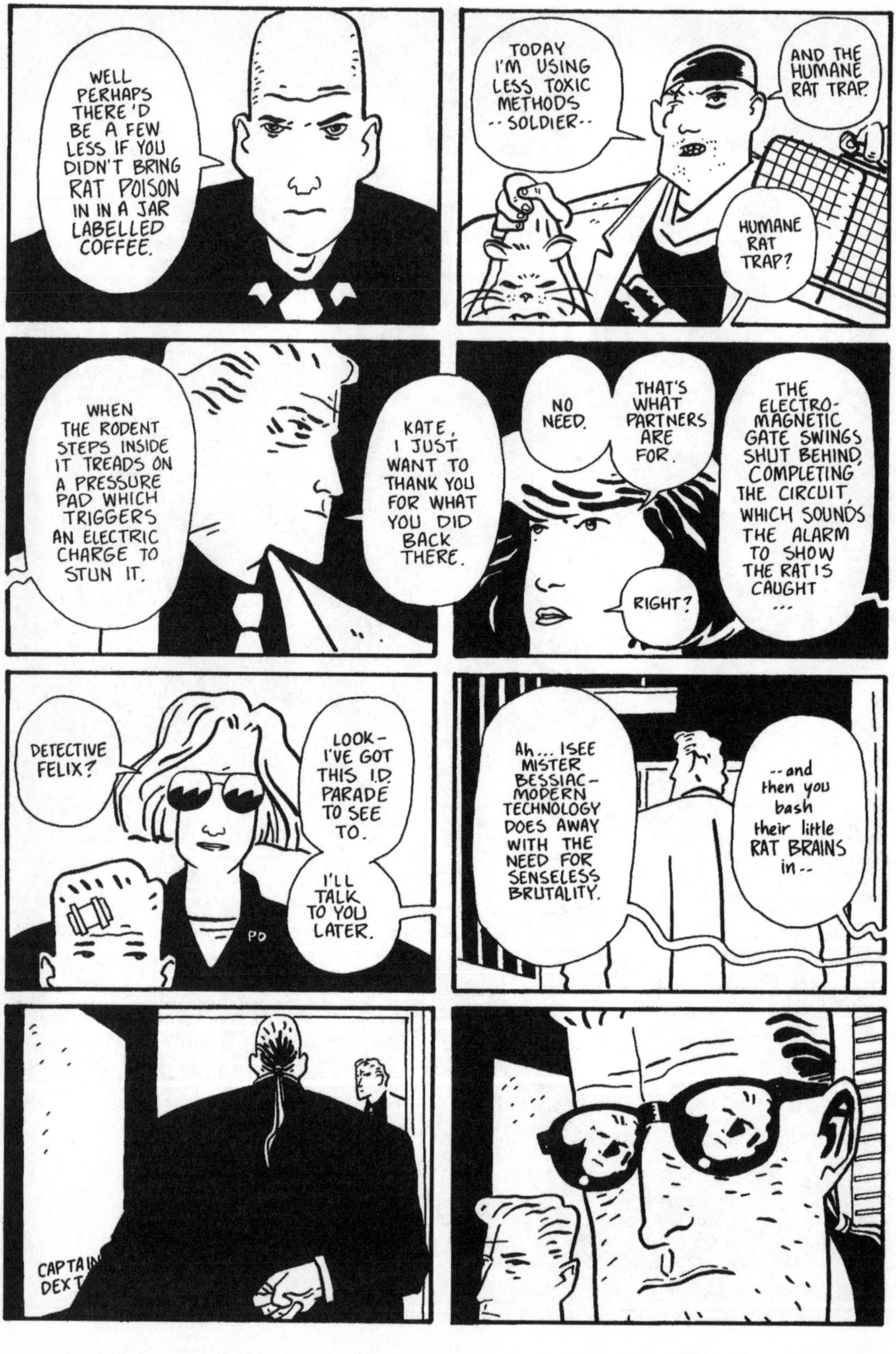
WELL PERHAPS THERE'D BE A FEW LESS IF YOU DIDN'T BRING RAT POISON IN IN A JAR LABELLED COFFEE.
TODAY I'M USING LESS TOXIC METHODS --SOLDIER--
AND THE HUMANE RAT TRAP.
HUMANE RAT TRAP?
WHEN THE RODENT STEPS INSIDE IT TREADS ON A PRESSURE PAD WHICH TRIGGERS AN ELECTRIC CHARGE TO STUN IT.
KATE, I JUST WANT TO THANK YOU FOR WHAT YOU DID BACK THERE.
NO NEED.
THAT'S WHAT PARTNERS ARE FOR.
RIGHT?
THE ELECTRO-MAGNETIC GATE SWINGS SHUT BEHIND, COMPLETING THE CIRCUIT, WHICH SOUNDS THE ALARM TO SHOW THE RAT IS CAUGHT ...
DETECTIVE FELIX?
LOOK- I'VE GOT THIS I.D. PARADE TO SEE TO.
I'LL TALK TO YOU LATER.
PD
Ah... I SEE MISTER BESSIAC- MODERN TECHNOLOGY DOES AWAY WITH THE NEED FOR SENSELESS BRUTALITY.
--and then you bash their little RAT BRAINS in--
CAPTAIN DEXT

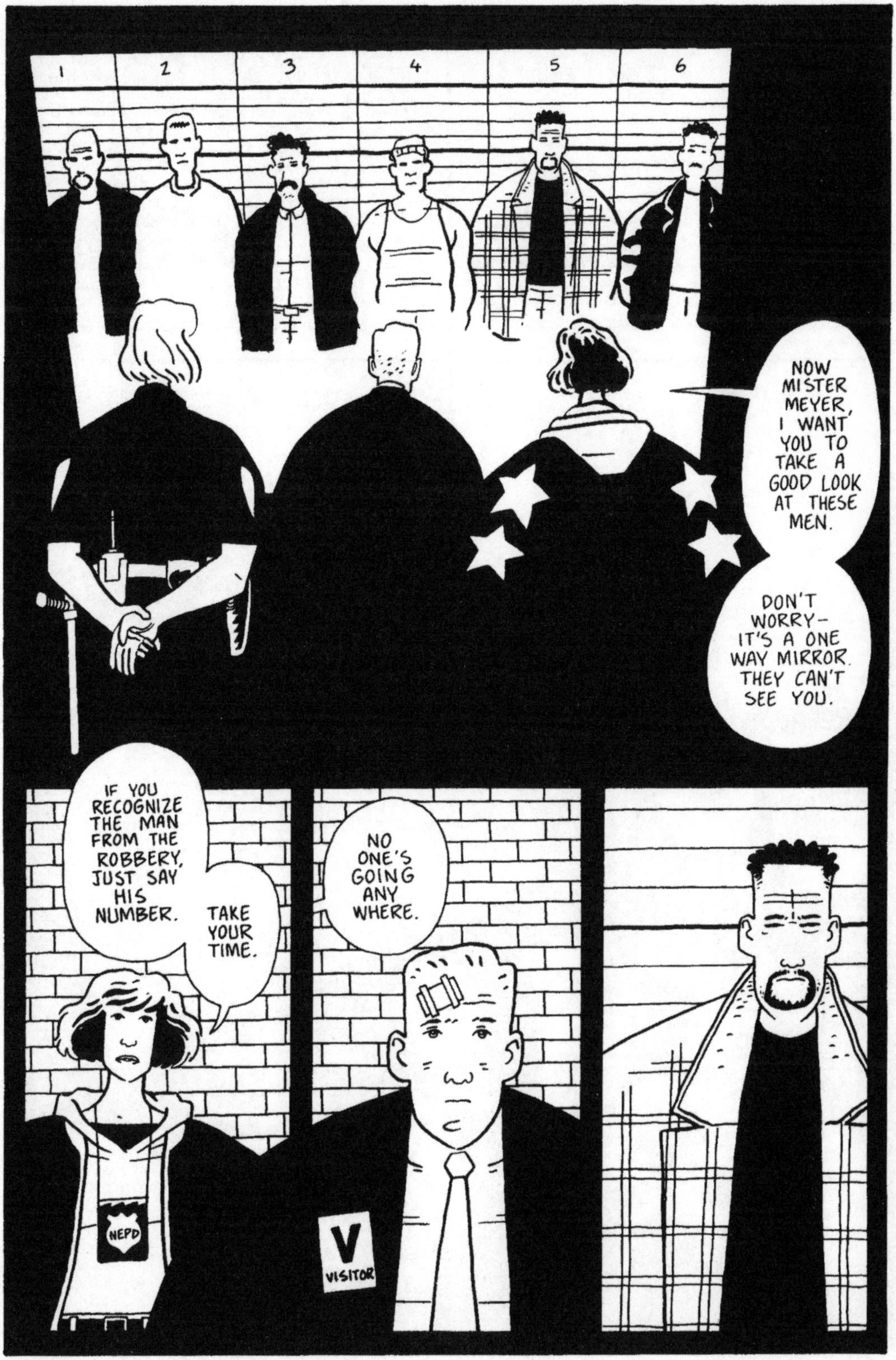
1 2 3 4 5 6
NOW MISTER MEYER, I WANT YOU TO TAKE A GOOD LOOK AT THESE MEN.
DON'T WORRY- IT'S A ONE WAY MIRROR. THEY CAN'T SEE YOU.
IF YOU RECOGNIZE THE MAN FROM THE ROBBERY, JUST SAY HIS NUMBER.
TAKE YOUR TIME.
NEPD
NO ONE'S GOING ANY WHERE.
V
VISITOR

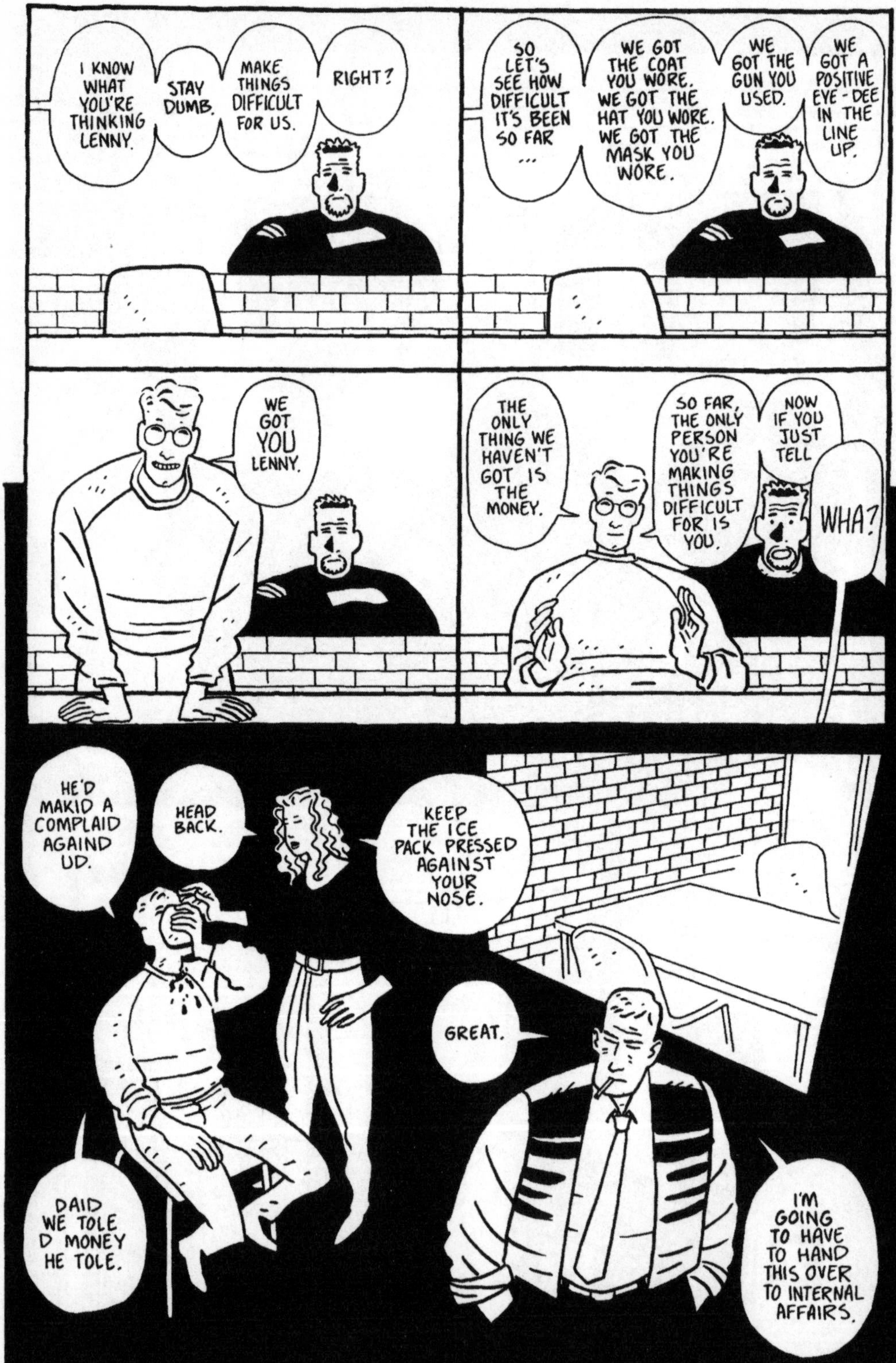
I KNOW WHAT YOU'RE THINKING LENNY.
STAY DUMB.
MAKE THINGS DIFFICULT FOR US.
RIGHT?
SO LET'S SEE HOW DIFFICULT IT'S BEEN SO FAR ...
WE GOT THE COAT YOU WORE. WE GOT THE HAT YOU WORE. WE GOT THE MASK YOU WORE.
WE GOT THE GUN YOU USED.
WE GOT A POSITIVE EYE-DEE IN THE LINE UP.
WE GOT YOU LENNY.
THE ONLY THING WE HAVEN'T GOT IS THE MONEY.
SO FAR, THE ONLY PERSON YOU'RE MAKING THINGS DIFFICULT FOR IS YOU.
NOW IF YOU JUST TELL
WHA?
HE'D MAKID A COMPLAID AGAIND UD.
HEAD BACK.
KEEP THE ICE PACK PRESSED AGAINST YOUR NOSE.
GREAT.
DAID WE TOLE D MONEY HE TOLE.
I'M GOING TO HAVE TO HAND THIS OVER TO INTERNAL AFFAIRS.

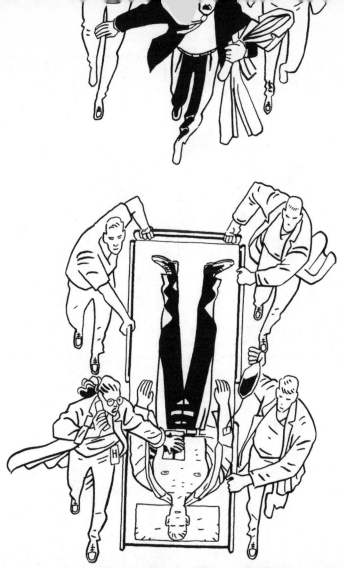

DON'T WORRY SIR. THEY'LL TAKE CARE OF HIM NOW.

PERHAPS YOU COULD GIVE US SOME DETAILS FOR OUR ADMISSION FORMS.

WHAT'S YOUR FRIENDS NAME AND OCCUPATION?

HIS NAME'S KANE. HE'S A POLICE OFFICER.

AND YOU ARE?

DENNIS HARVEY. I'M WITH THE N-E-P-D.

HE'S MY PARTNER.

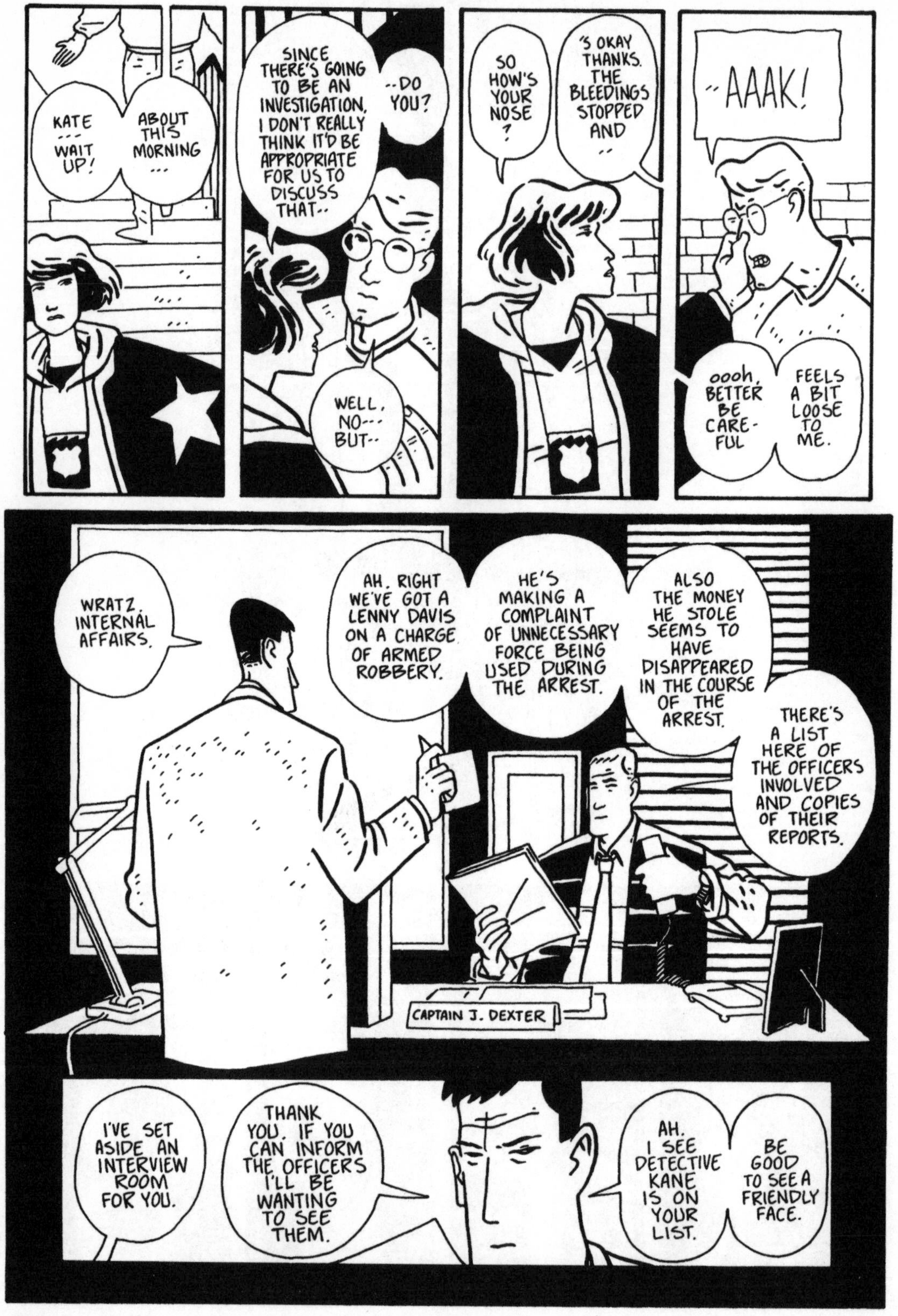
KATE --- WAIT UP!
ABOUT THIS MORNING ...
SINCE THERE'S GOING TO BE AN INVESTIGATION, I DON'T REALLY THINK IT'D BE APPROPRIATE FOR US TO DISCUSS THAT--
--DO YOU?
WELL, NO--- BUT--
SO HOW'S YOUR NOSE ?
'S OKAY THANKS. THE BLEEDINGS STOPPED AND --
--AAAK!
oooh, BETTER BE CARE-FUL
FEELS A BIT LOOSE TO ME.
WRATZ, INTERNAL AFFAIRS.
AH, RIGHT WE'VE GOT A LENNY DAVIS ON A CHARGE OF ARMED ROBBERY.
HE'S MAKING A COMPLAINT OF UNNECESSARY FORCE BEING USED DURING THE ARREST.
ALSO THE MONEY HE STOLE SEEMS TO HAVE DISAPPEARED IN THE COURSE OF THE ARREST.
THERE'S A LIST HERE OF THE OFFICERS INVOLVED AND COPIES OF THEIR REPORTS.
CAPTAIN J. DEXTER
I'VE SET ASIDE AN INTERVIEW ROOM FOR YOU.
THANK YOU, IF YOU CAN INFORM THE OFFICERS I'LL BE WANTING TO SEE THEM.
AH. I SEE DETECTIVE KANE IS ON YOUR LIST.
BE GOOD TO SEE A FRIENDLY FACE.

WRATZ: --IF YOU'LL JUST BEAR WITH ME WHILE I GET THIS SORTED...

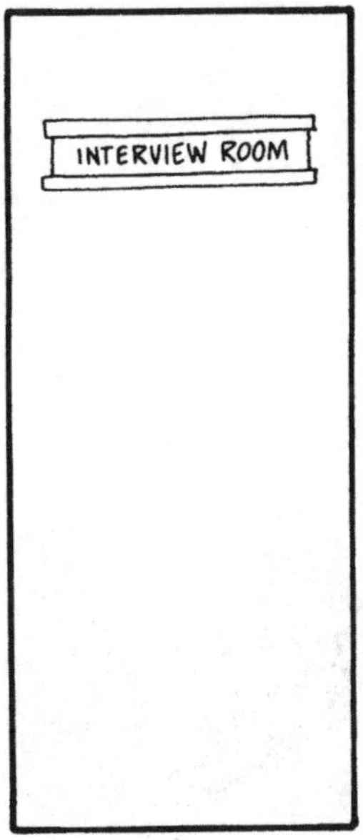
INTERVIEW ROOM

...RIGHT. NOW YOU KNOW THE ROUTINE HERE DETECTIVE. SO IF YOU WANT TO TELL ME ABOUT THIS MORNING ?

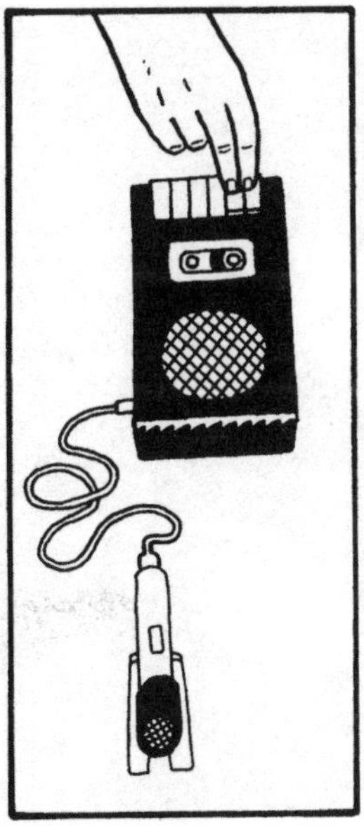

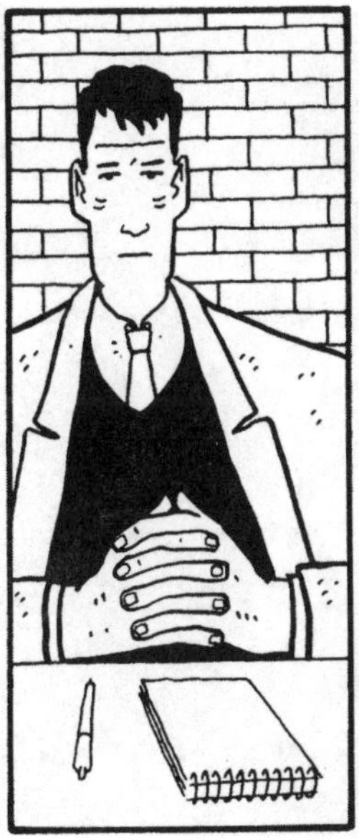

WHENEVER YOU'RE READY DETECTIVE.

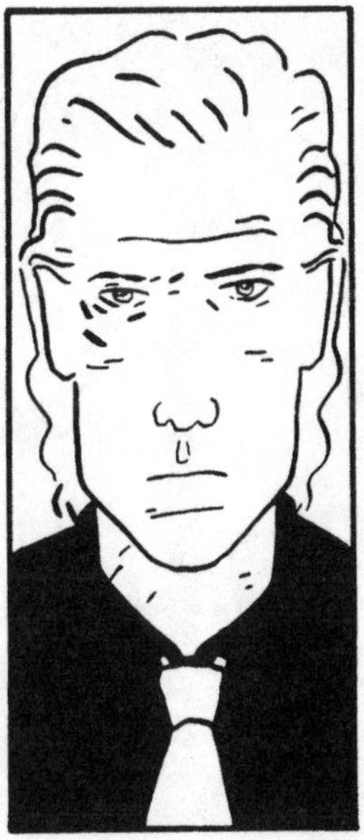

KANE: LENNY DAVIS WAS BELIEVED TO BE RESPONSIBLE FOR AN ARMED ROBBERY ON THE CITY BANK YESTERDAY P.M.

ALONG WITH FOUR OTHER POLICE OFFICERS I LED A SUPRISE RAID ON THE SUSPECTS' APART-MENT.

ON ENTERING HIS BEDROOM I WAS ATTACKED FROM BEHIND BY THE SUSPECT.

WRATZ: WHAT ABOUT YOUR BACKUP? DIDN'T HE ATTEMPT TO PREVENT THE ATTACK? SHOUT A WARNING?

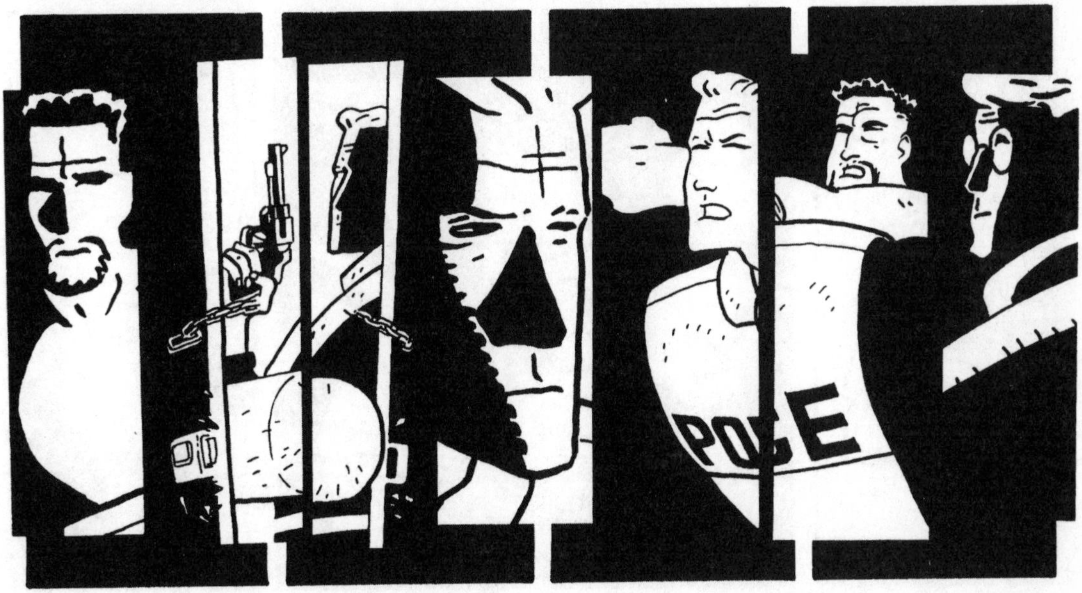

KANE: DETECTIVE FELIX --

WRATZ: I UNDER STOOD DETECTIVE LOVETT WAS COVERING YOU AS YOU ENTERED THE ROOM?

KANE: --RESTRAINED THE SUSPECT.

HE WAS PLACED UNDER ARREST AND BROUGHT DOWN TO THE STATION ALONG WITH EVIDENCE COLLECTED FROM THE APARTMENT.

WRATZ: SO APART FROM THIS ATTACK, THERE WERE NO PROBLEMS WITH THE ARREST?

KANE: NO. NO PROBLEMS AT ALL.

REMEMBER ...

DENNIS HARVEY HAD SOME GOOD FRIENDS IN THIS STATION

AND THAT'S SOMETHING YOU'RE VERY SHORT ON RIGHT NOW.

WELCOME BACK.

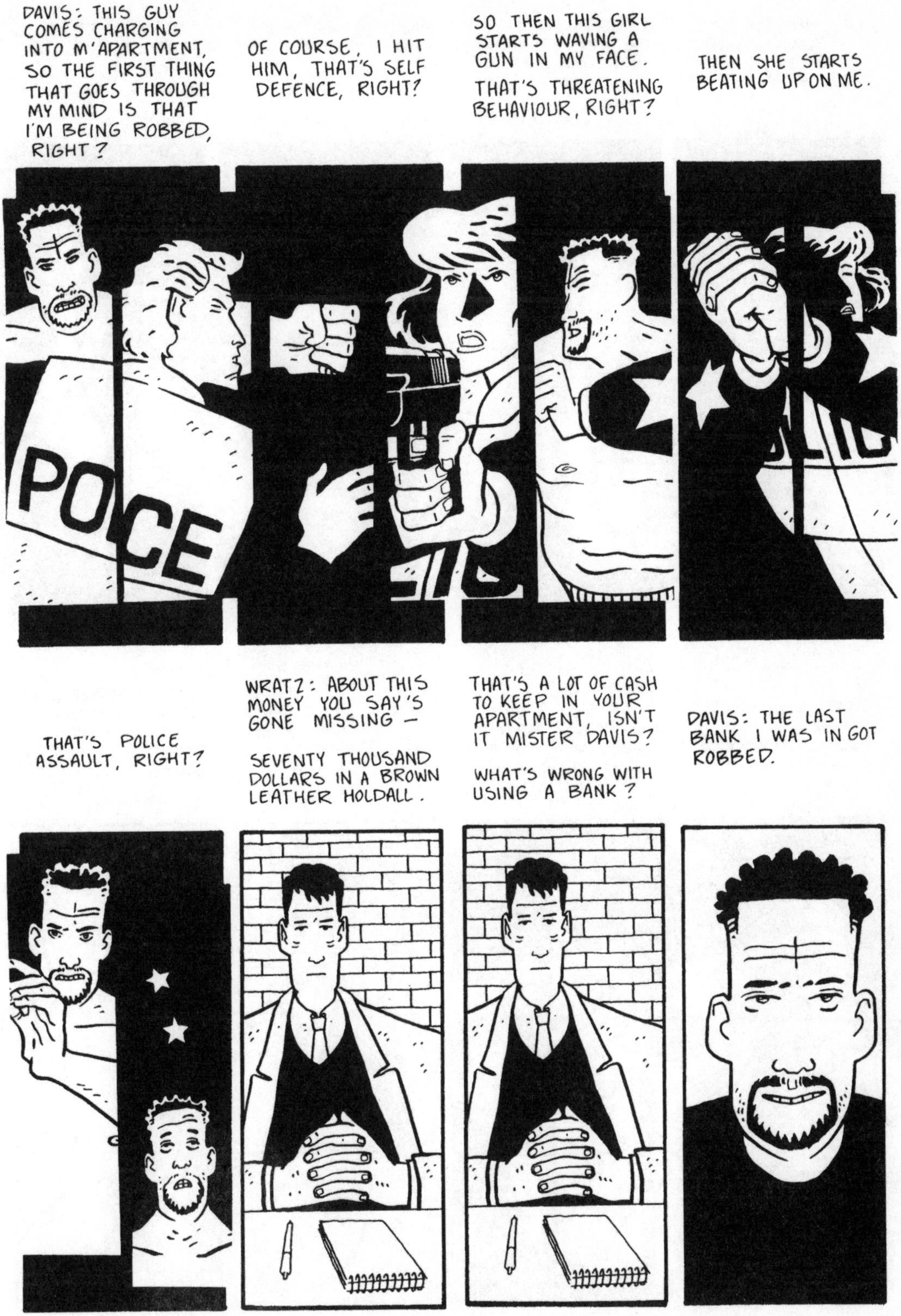
DAVIS: THIS GUY COMES CHARGING INTO M'APARTMENT, SO THE FIRST THING THAT GOES THROUGH MY MIND IS THAT I'M BEING ROBBED, RIGHT?
POCE
OF COURSE, I HIT HIM, THAT'S SELF DEFENCE, RIGHT?
SO THEN THIS GIRL STARTS WAVING A GUN IN MY FACE.
THAT'S THREATENING BEHAVIOUR, RIGHT?
THEN SHE STARTS BEATING UP ON ME.
THAT'S POLICE ASSAULT, RIGHT?
WRATZ: ABOUT THIS MONEY YOU SAY'S GONE MISSING —
SEVENTY THOUSAND DOLLARS IN A BROWN LEATHER HOLDALL.
THAT'S A LOT OF CASH TO KEEP IN YOUR APARTMENT, ISN'T IT MISTER DAVIS?
WHAT'S WRONG WITH USING A BANK?
DAVIS: THE LAST BANK I WAS IN GOT ROBBED.

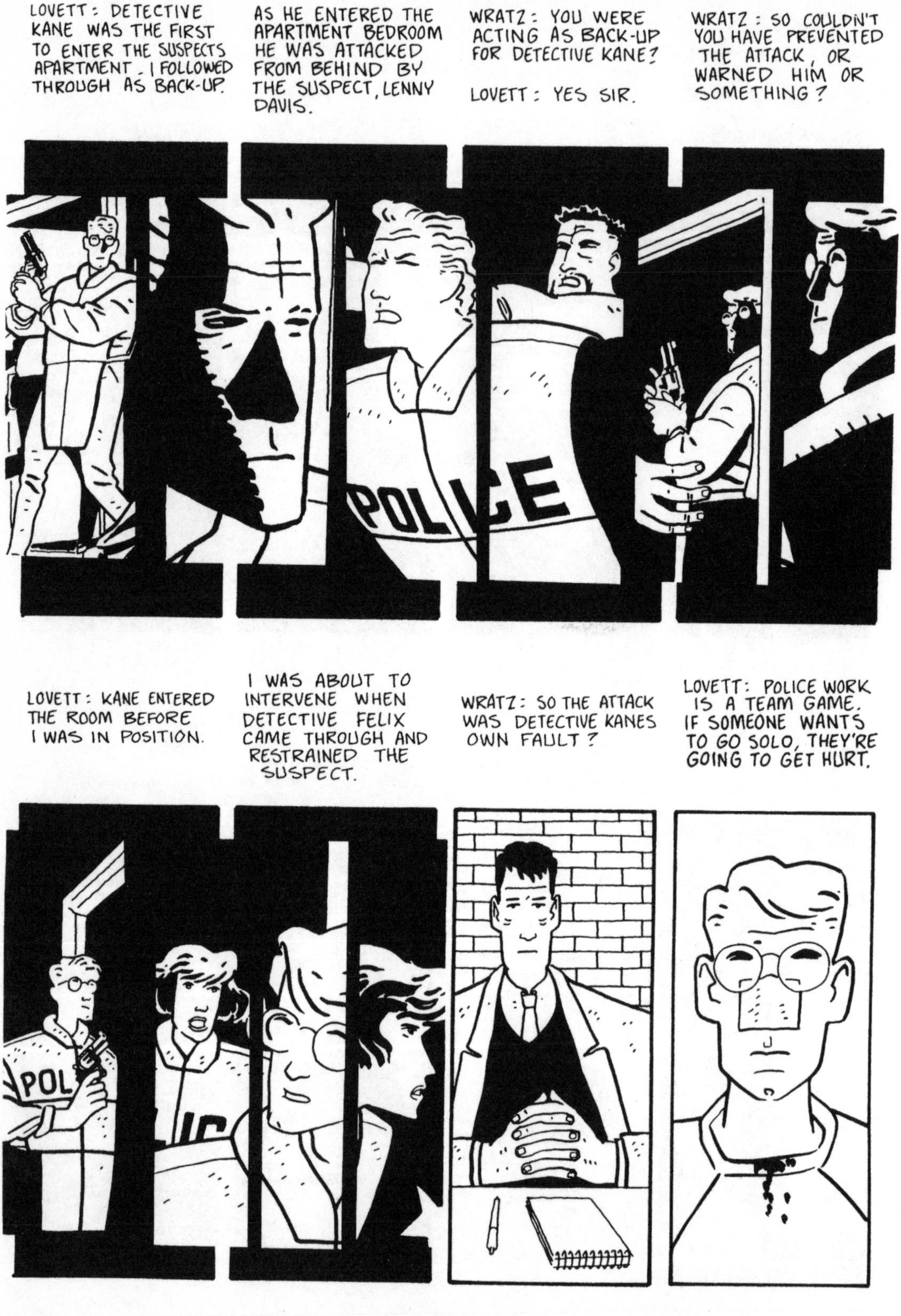
LOVETT: DETECTIVE KANE WAS THE FIRST TO ENTER THE SUSPECTS APARTMENT. I FOLLOWED THROUGH AS BACK-UP.
AS HE ENTERED THE APARTMENT BEDROOM HE WAS ATTACKED FROM BEHIND BY THE SUSPECT, LENNY DAVIS.
WRATZ: YOU WERE ACTING AS BACK-UP FOR DETECTIVE KANE?
LOVETT: YES SIR.
WRATZ: SO COULDN'T YOU HAVE PREVENTED THE ATTACK, OR WARNED HIM OR SOMETHING?
POLICE
LOVETT: KANE ENTERED THE ROOM BEFORE I WAS IN POSITION.
I WAS ABOUT TO INTERVENE WHEN DETECTIVE FELIX CAME THROUGH AND RESTRAINED THE SUSPECT.
WRATZ: SO THE ATTACK WAS DETECTIVE KANES OWN FAULT?
LOVETT: POLICE WORK IS A TEAM GAME. IF SOMEONE WANTS TO GO SOLO, THEY'RE GOING TO GET HURT.

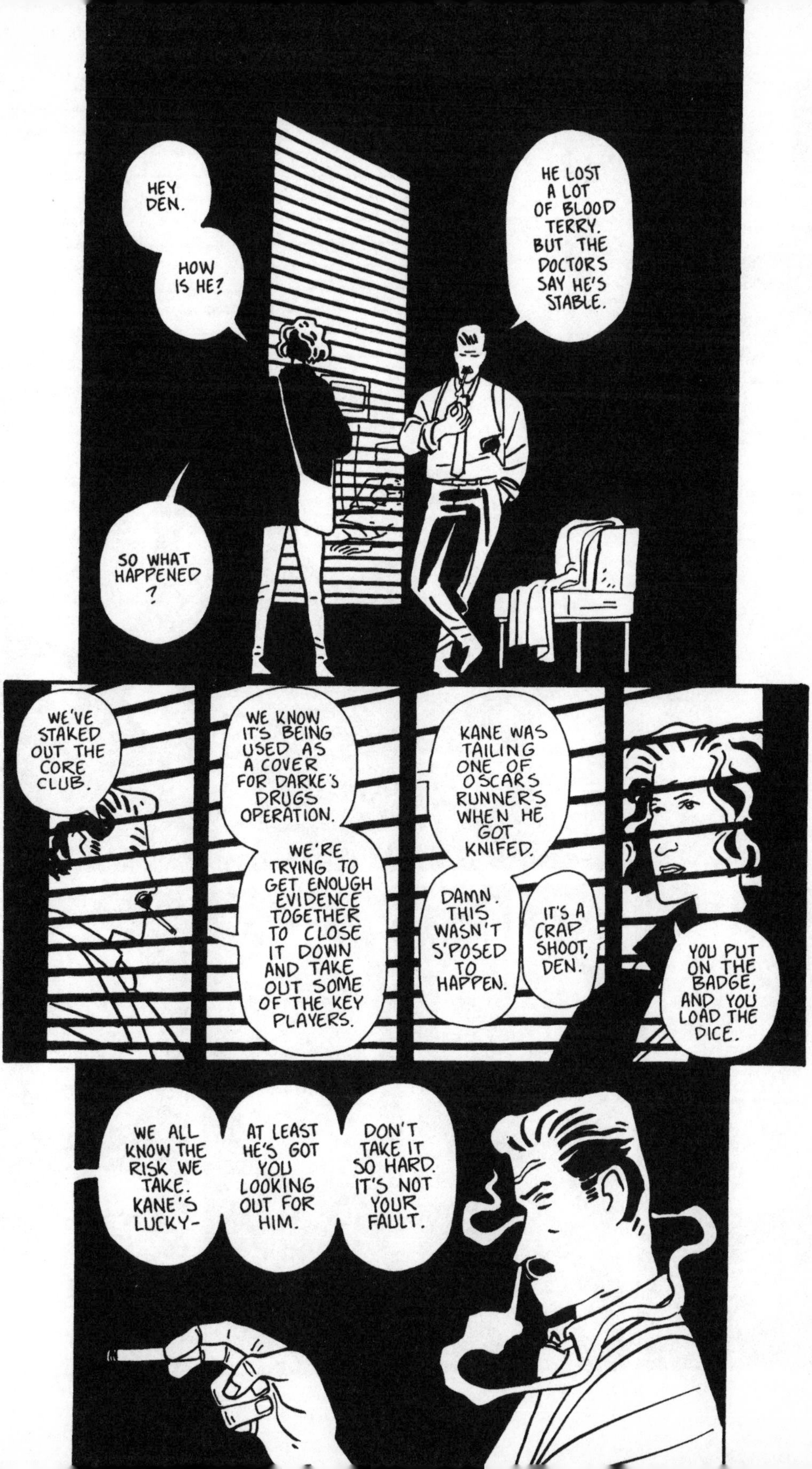
HEY DEN.
HOW IS HE?
HE LOST A LOT OF BLOOD TERRY. BUT THE DOCTORS SAY HE'S STABLE.
SO WHAT HAPPENED ?
WE'VE STAKED OUT THE CORE CLUB.
WE KNOW IT'S BEING USED AS A COVER FOR DARKE'S DRUGS OPERATION.
WE'RE TRYING TO GET ENOUGH EVIDENCE TOGETHER TO CLOSE IT DOWN AND TAKE OUT SOME OF THE KEY PLAYERS.
KANE WAS TAILING ONE OF OSCARS RUNNERS WHEN HE GOT KNIFED.
DAMN. THIS WASN'T S'POSED TO HAPPEN.
IT'S A CRAP SHOOT, DEN.
YOU PUT ON THE BADGE, AND YOU LOAD THE DICE.
WE ALL KNOW THE RISK WE TAKE. KANE'S LUCKY-
AT LEAST HE'S GOT YOU LOOKING OUT FOR HIM.
DON'T TAKE IT SO HARD. IT'S NOT YOUR FAULT.

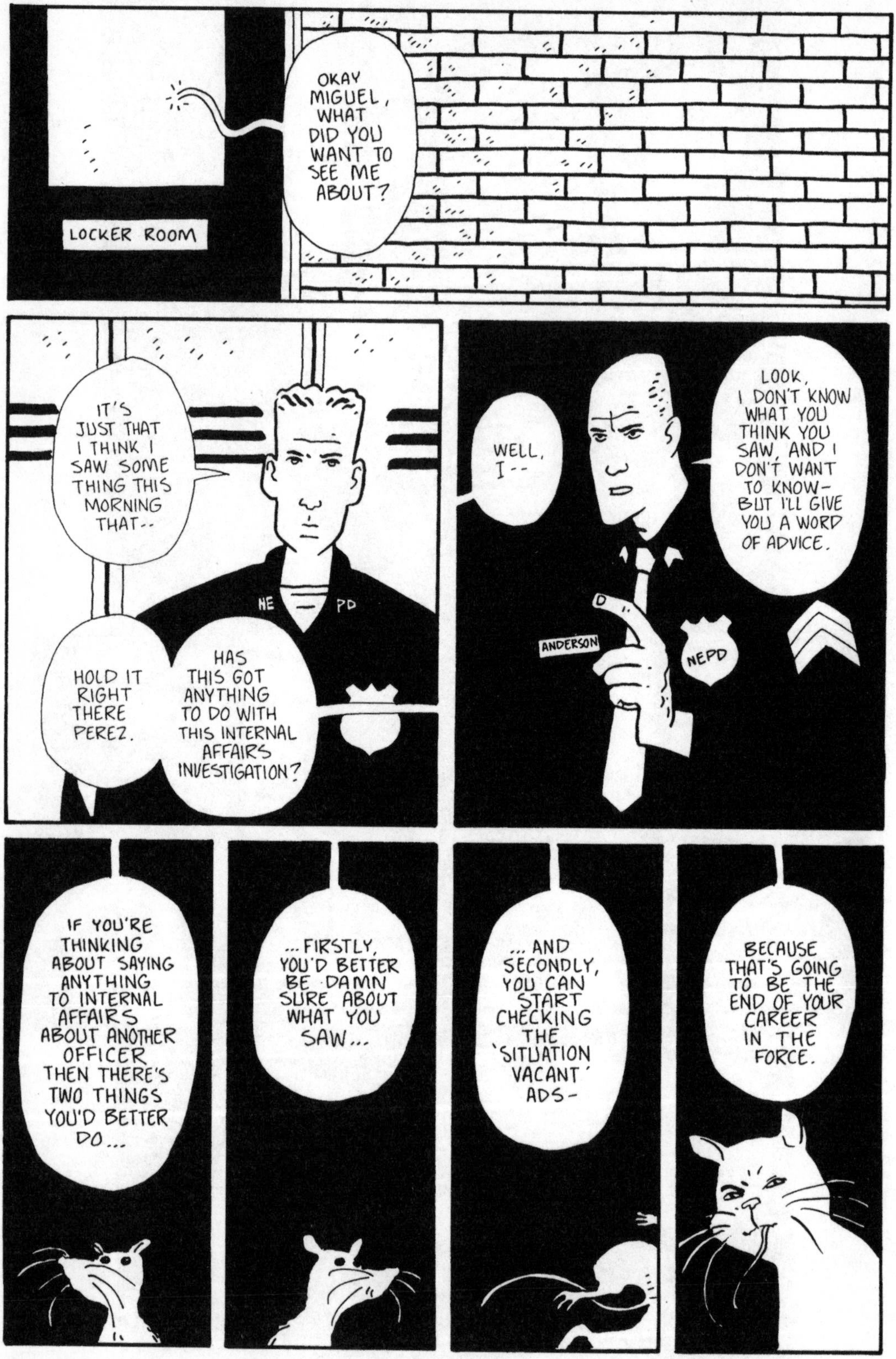
LOCKER ROOM
OKAY MIGUEL, WHAT DID YOU WANT TO SEE ME ABOUT?
IT'S JUST THAT I THINK I SAW SOME THING THIS MORNING THAT--
HE PD
HOLD IT RIGHT THERE PEREZ.
HAS THIS GOT ANYTHING TO DO WITH THIS INTERNAL AFFAIRS INVESTIGATION?
WELL, I--
LOOK, I DON'T KNOW WHAT YOU THINK YOU SAW, AND I DON'T WANT TO KNOW- BUT I'LL GIVE YOU A WORD OF ADVICE.
ANDERSON
NEPD
IF YOU'RE THINKING ABOUT SAYING ANYTHING TO INTERNAL AFFAIRS ABOUT ANOTHER OFFICER THEN THERE'S TWO THINGS YOU'D BETTER DO...
...FIRSTLY, YOU'D BETTER BE DAMN SURE ABOUT WHAT YOU SAW...
...AND SECONDLY, YOU CAN START CHECKING THE 'SITUATION VACANT' ADS-
BECAUSE THAT'S GOING TO BE THE END OF YOUR CAREER IN THE FORCE.

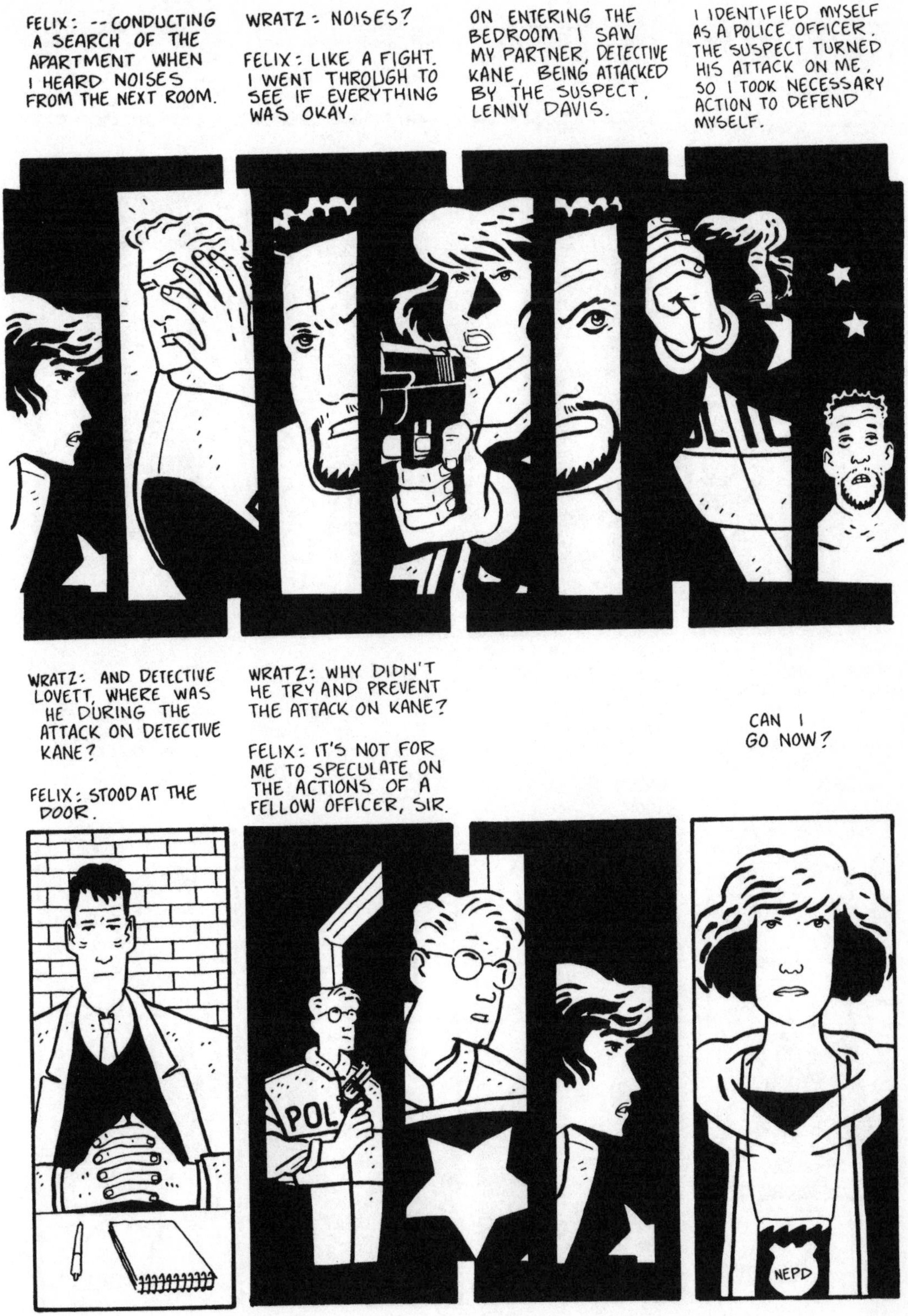
FELIX: --CONDUCTING A SEARCH OF THE APARTMENT WHEN I HEARD NOISES FROM THE NEXT ROOM.
WRATZ: NOISES?
FELIX: LIKE A FIGHT. I WENT THROUGH TO SEE IF EVERYTHING WAS OKAY.
ON ENTERING THE BEDROOM I SAW MY PARTNER, DETECTIVE KANE, BEING ATTACKED BY THE SUSPECT, LENNY DAVIS.
I IDENTIFIED MYSELF AS A POLICE OFFICER. THE SUSPECT TURNED HIS ATTACK ON ME, SO I TOOK NECESSARY ACTION TO DEFEND MYSELF.
WRATZ: AND DETECTIVE LOVETT, WHERE WAS HE DURING THE ATTACK ON DETECTIVE KANE?
FELIX: STOOD AT THE DOOR.
WRATZ: WHY DIDN'T HE TRY AND PREVENT THE ATTACK ON KANE?
FELIX: IT'S NOT FOR ME TO SPECULATE ON THE ACTIONS OF A FELLOW OFFICER, SIR.
POL
CAN I GO NOW?
NEPD

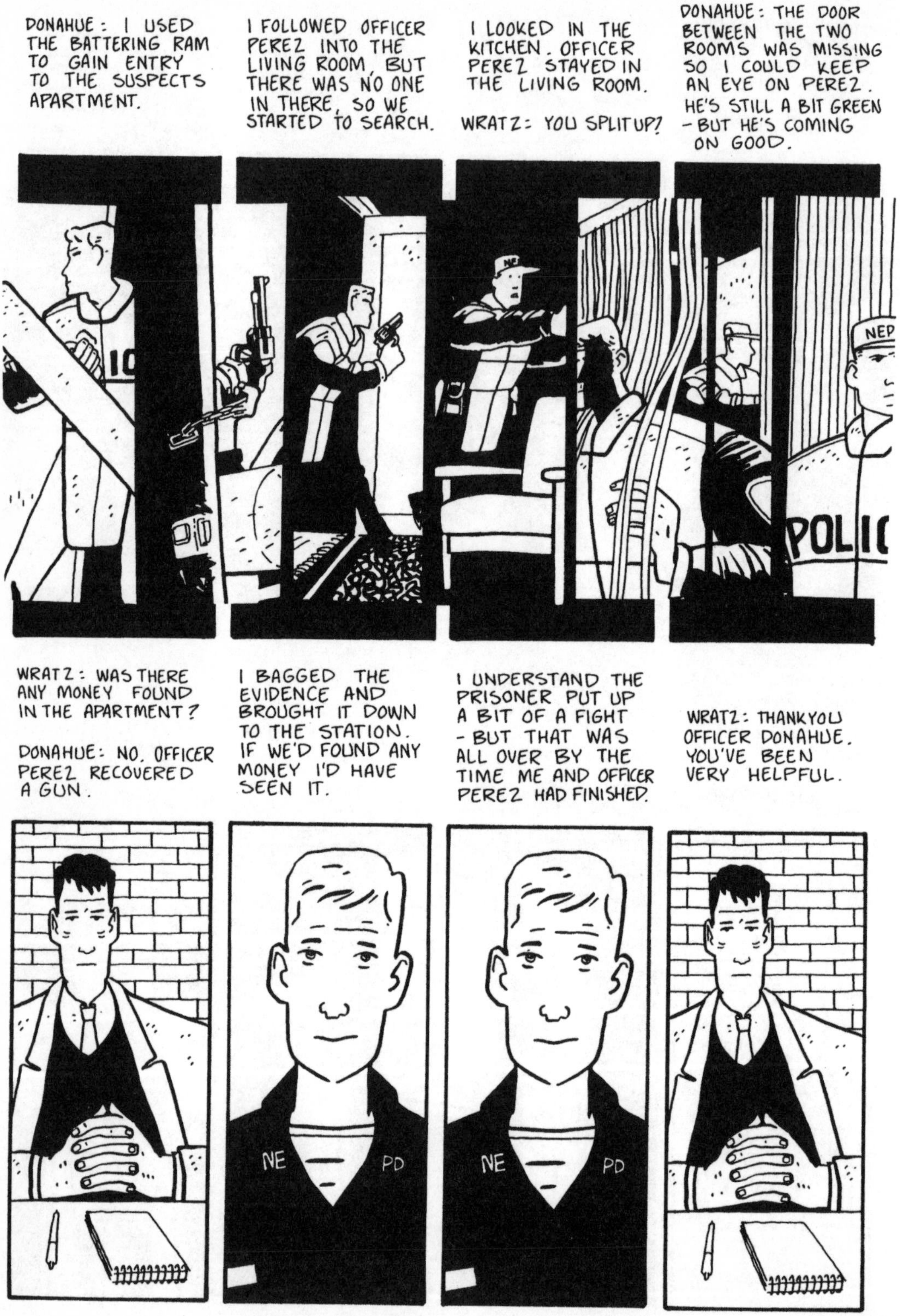
DONAHUE: I USED THE BATTERING RAM TO GAIN ENTRY TO THE SUSPECTS APARTMENT.
I FOLLOWED OFFICER PEREZ INTO THE LIVING ROOM, BUT THERE WAS NO ONE IN THERE, SO WE STARTED TO SEARCH.
I LOOKED IN THE KITCHEN. OFFICER PEREZ STAYED IN THE LIVING ROOM.
WRATZ: YOU SPLIT UP?
DONAHUE: THE DOOR BETWEEN THE TWO ROOMS WAS MISSING SO I COULD KEEP AN EYE ON PEREZ.
HE'S STILL A BIT GREEN - BUT HE'S COMING ON GOOD.
POLIC
WRATZ: WAS THERE ANY MONEY FOUND IN THE APARTMENT?
DONAHUE: NO. OFFICER PEREZ RECOVERED A GUN.
I BAGGED THE EVIDENCE AND BROUGHT IT DOWN TO THE STATION. IF WE'D FOUND ANY MONEY I'D HAVE SEEN IT.
NE PD
I UNDERSTAND THE PRISONER PUT UP A BIT OF A FIGHT - BUT THAT WAS ALL OVER BY THE TIME ME AND OFFICER PEREZ HAD FINISHED.
NE PD
WRATZ: THANKYOU OFFICER DONAHUE. YOU'VE BEEN VERY HELPFUL.

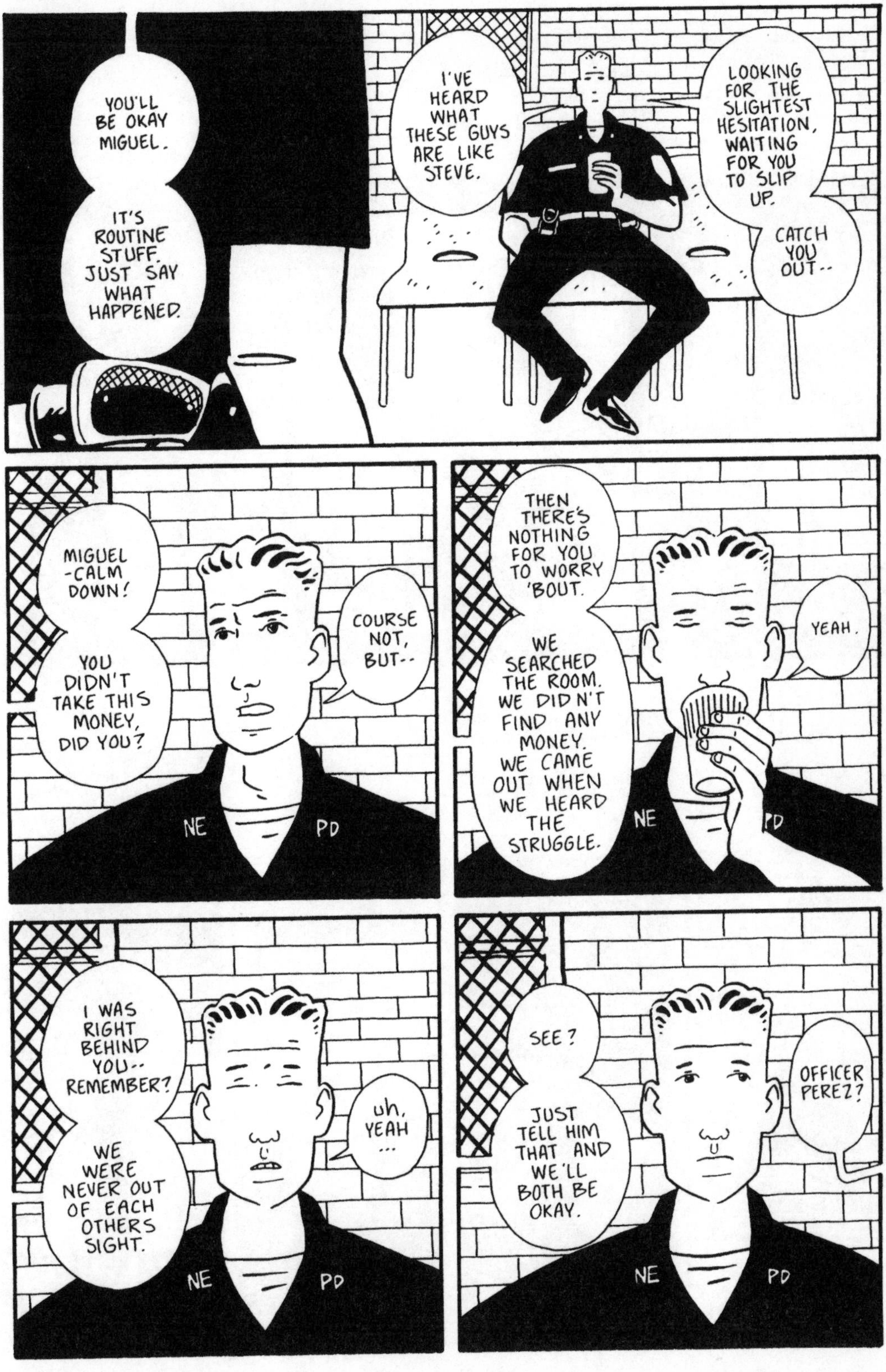
YOU'LL BE OKAY MIGUEL.
IT'S ROUTINE STUFF. JUST SAY WHAT HAPPENED.
I'VE HEARD WHAT THESE GUYS ARE LIKE STEVE.
LOOKING FOR THE SLIGHTEST HESITATION, WAITING FOR YOU TO SLIP UP.
CATCH YOU OUT--
MIGUEL -CALM DOWN!
YOU DIDN'T TAKE THIS MONEY, DID YOU?
COURSE NOT, BUT--
NE PD
THEN THERE'S NOTHING FOR YOU TO WORRY 'BOUT.
WE SEARCHED THE ROOM. WE DIDN'T FIND ANY MONEY. WE CAME OUT WHEN WE HEARD THE STRUGGLE.
YEAH.
I WAS RIGHT BEHIND YOU.. REMEMBER?
WE WERE NEVER OUT OF EACH OTHERS SIGHT.
uh, YEAH ...
SEE?
JUST TELL HIM THAT AND WE'LL BOTH BE OKAY.
OFFICER PEREZ?

WRATZ: NOTHING TO WORRY ABOUT OFFICER. I'M NOT LOOKING TO CATCH YOU OUT. I JUST WANT TO FIND OUT WHAT HAPPENED.

YOU WERE WITH OFFICER DONAHUE?

PEREZ: YES HE WAS IN THE KITCHEN... I SEARCHED THE LIVING ROOM...

WRATZ: SO YOU SPLIT UP THEN?

PEREZ: NO, uh, NOT REALLY, THERE WAS NO DOOR BETWEEN THE TWO ROOMS.

I FOUND THE GUN IN A DRAWER. THERE WAS SOME BANGING GOING OFF IN THE NEXT ROOM, SO WE WENT THROUGH TO SEE WHAT WAS, uh, HAPPENING.

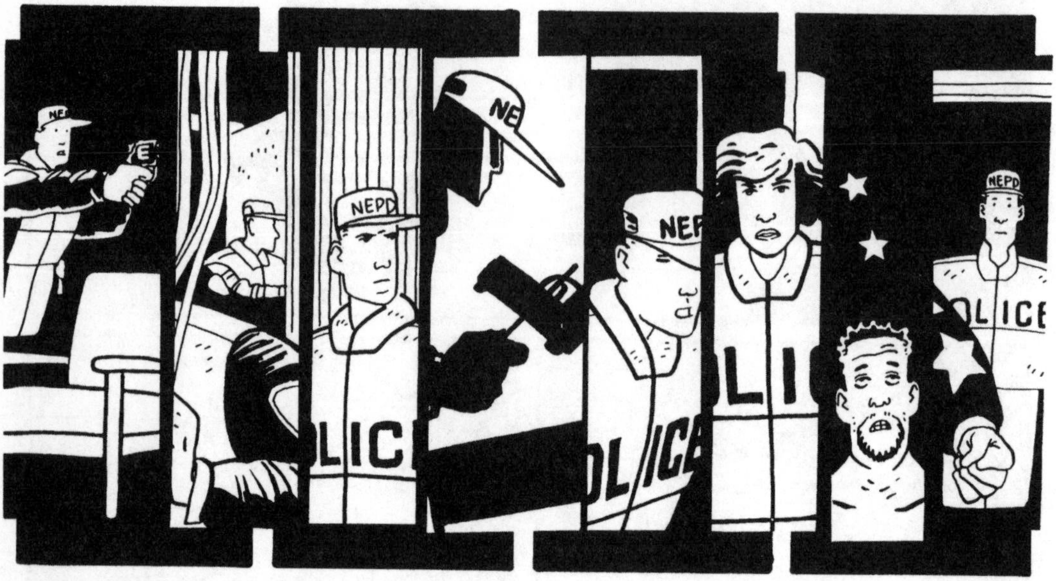

WRATZ: DID YOU SEE ANYONE HIT THE PRISONER?

PEREZ: NO. IT... uh, WAS ALL OVER BY THE TIME I GOT THERE.

WRATZ: YOU SAID 'BY THE TIME I GOT THERE'

...WHERE WAS OFFICER DONAHUE AT THE TIME?

PEREZ: I, uh, HE...

...HE WAS RIGHT BEHIND ME... WE WERE NEVER OUT OF EACH OTHERS SIGHT.

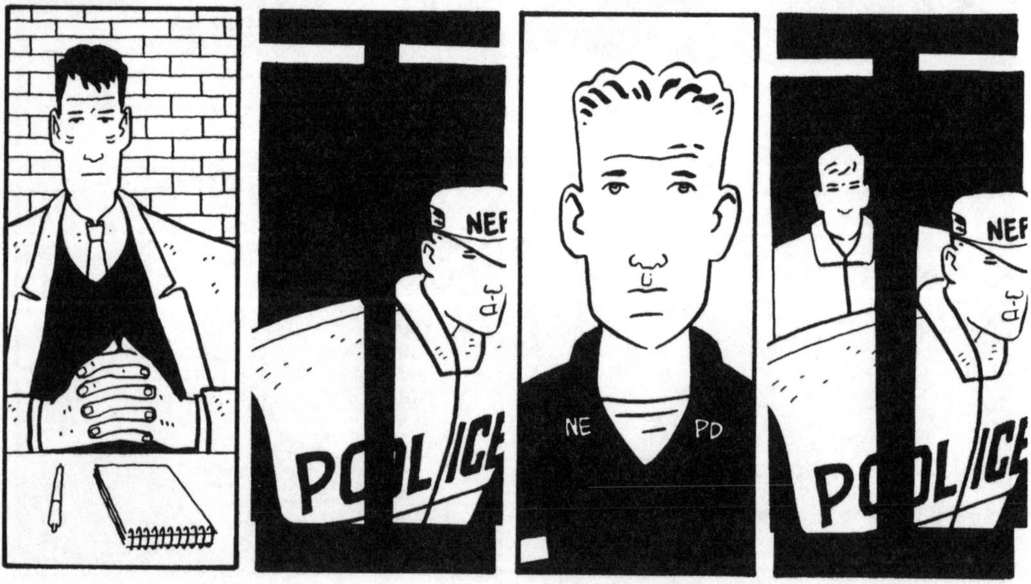

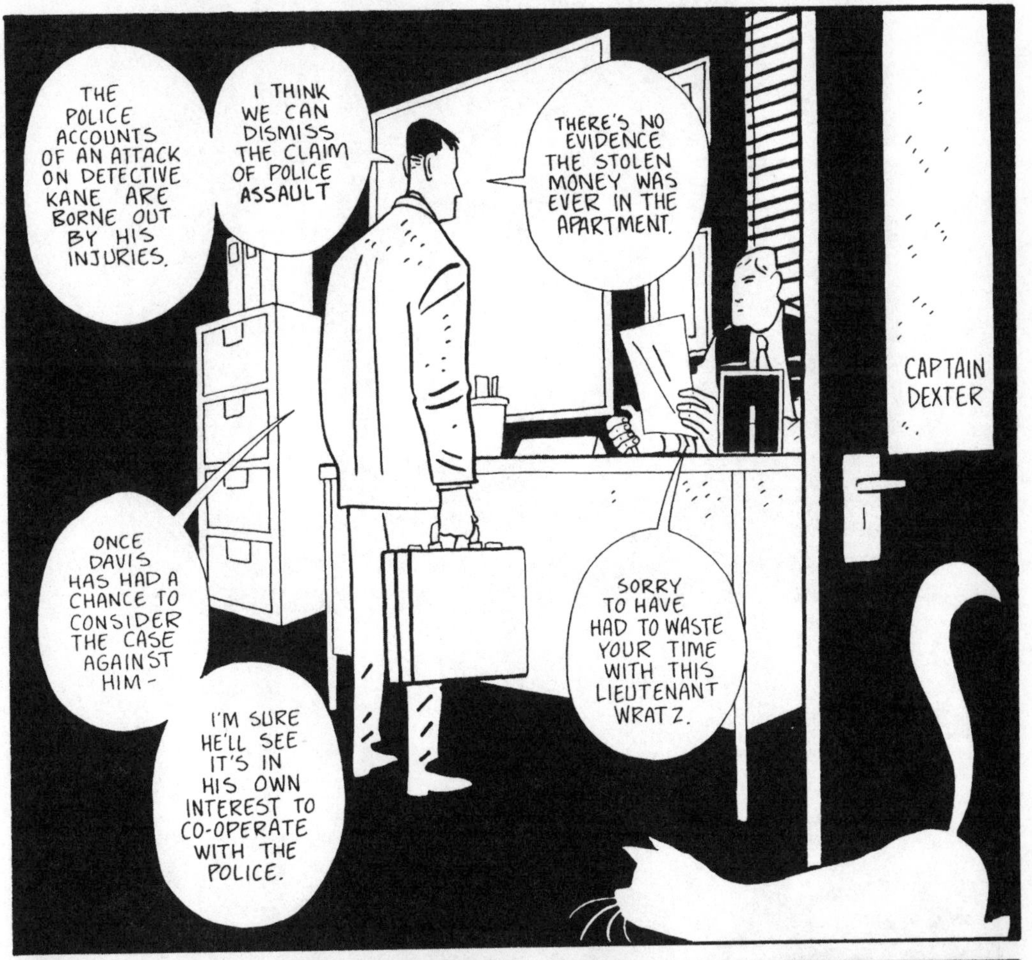
THE POLICE ACCOUNTS OF AN ATTACK ON DETECTIVE KANE ARE BORNE OUT BY HIS INJURIES.
I THINK WE CAN DISMISS THE CLAIM OF POLICE ASSAULT
THERE'S NO EVIDENCE THE STOLEN MONEY WAS EVER IN THE APARTMENT.
CAPTAIN DEXTER
ONCE DAVIS HAS HAD A CHANCE TO CONSIDER THE CASE AGAINST HIM-
I'M SURE HE'LL SEE IT'S IN HIS OWN INTEREST TO CO-OPERATE WITH THE POLICE.
SORRY TO HAVE HAD TO WASTE YOUR TIME WITH THIS LIEUTENANT WRATZ.
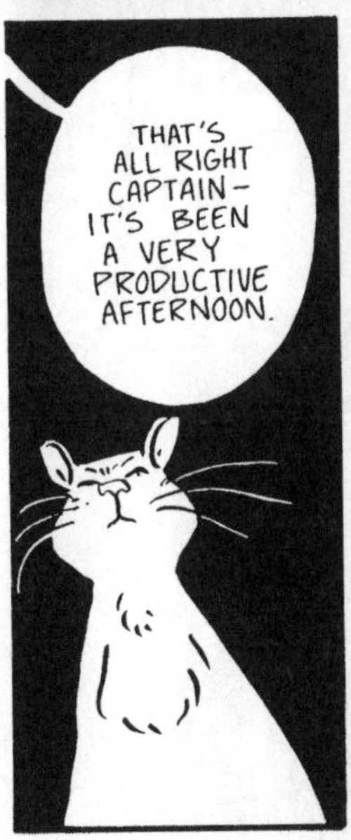
THAT'S ALL RIGHT CAPTAIN - IT'S BEEN A VERY PRODUCTIVE AFTERNOON.
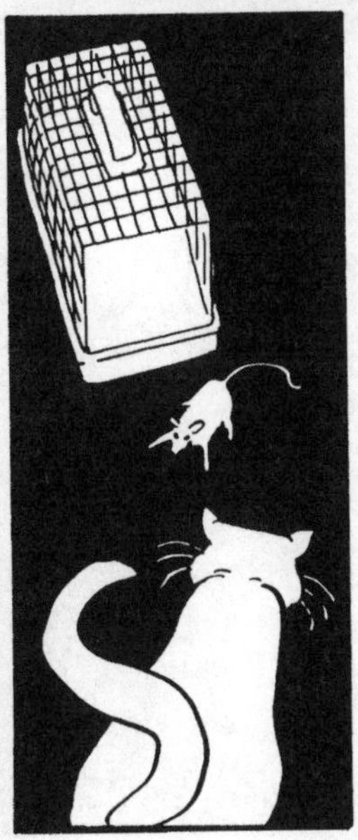
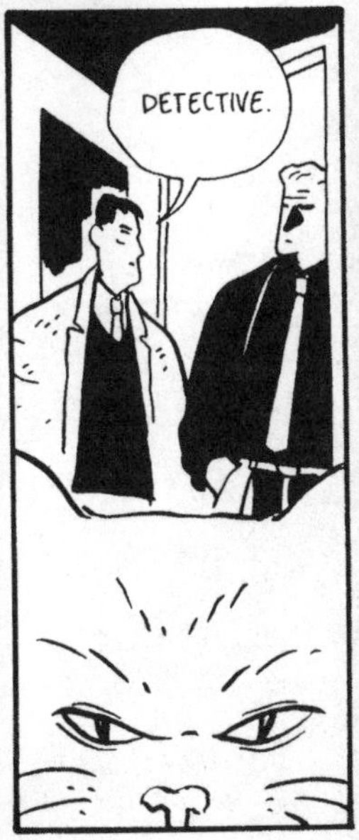
DETECTIVE.
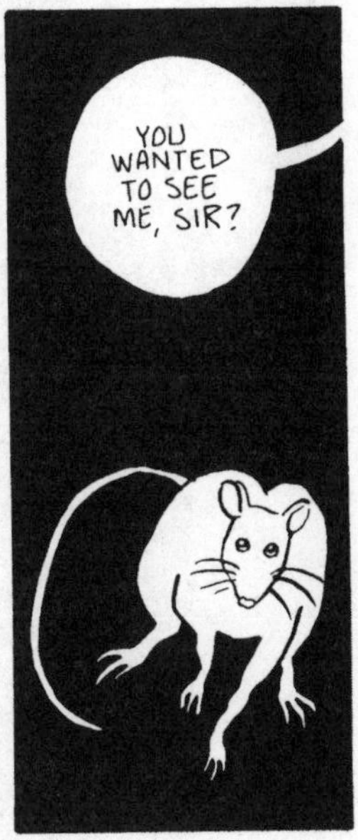
YOU WANTED TO SEE ME, SIR?

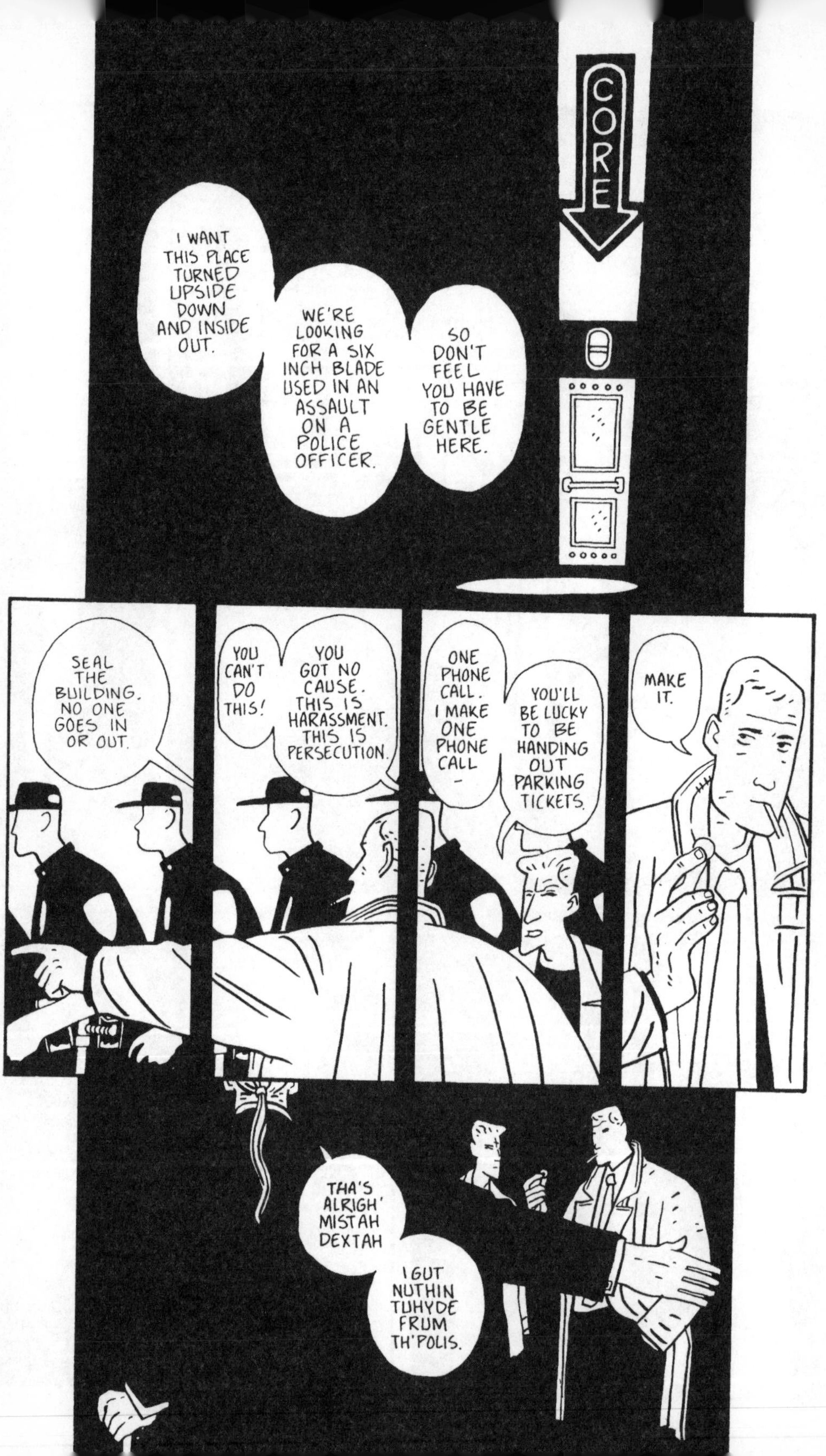
CORE
I WANT THIS PLACE TURNED UPSIDE DOWN AND INSIDE OUT.
WE'RE LOOKING FOR A SIX INCH BLADE USED IN AN ASSAULT ON A POLICE OFFICER.
SO DON'T FEEL YOU HAVE TO BE GENTLE HERE.
SEAL THE BUILDING. NO ONE GOES IN OR OUT.
YOU CAN'T DO THIS!
YOU GOT NO CAUSE. THIS IS HARASSMENT. THIS IS PERSECUTION.
ONE PHONE CALL. I MAKE ONE PHONE CALL –
YOU'LL BE LUCKY TO BE HANDING OUT PARKING TICKETS.
MAKE IT.
THA'S ALRIGH' MISTAH DEXTAH
I GUT NUTHIN TUHYDE FRUM TH'POLIS.

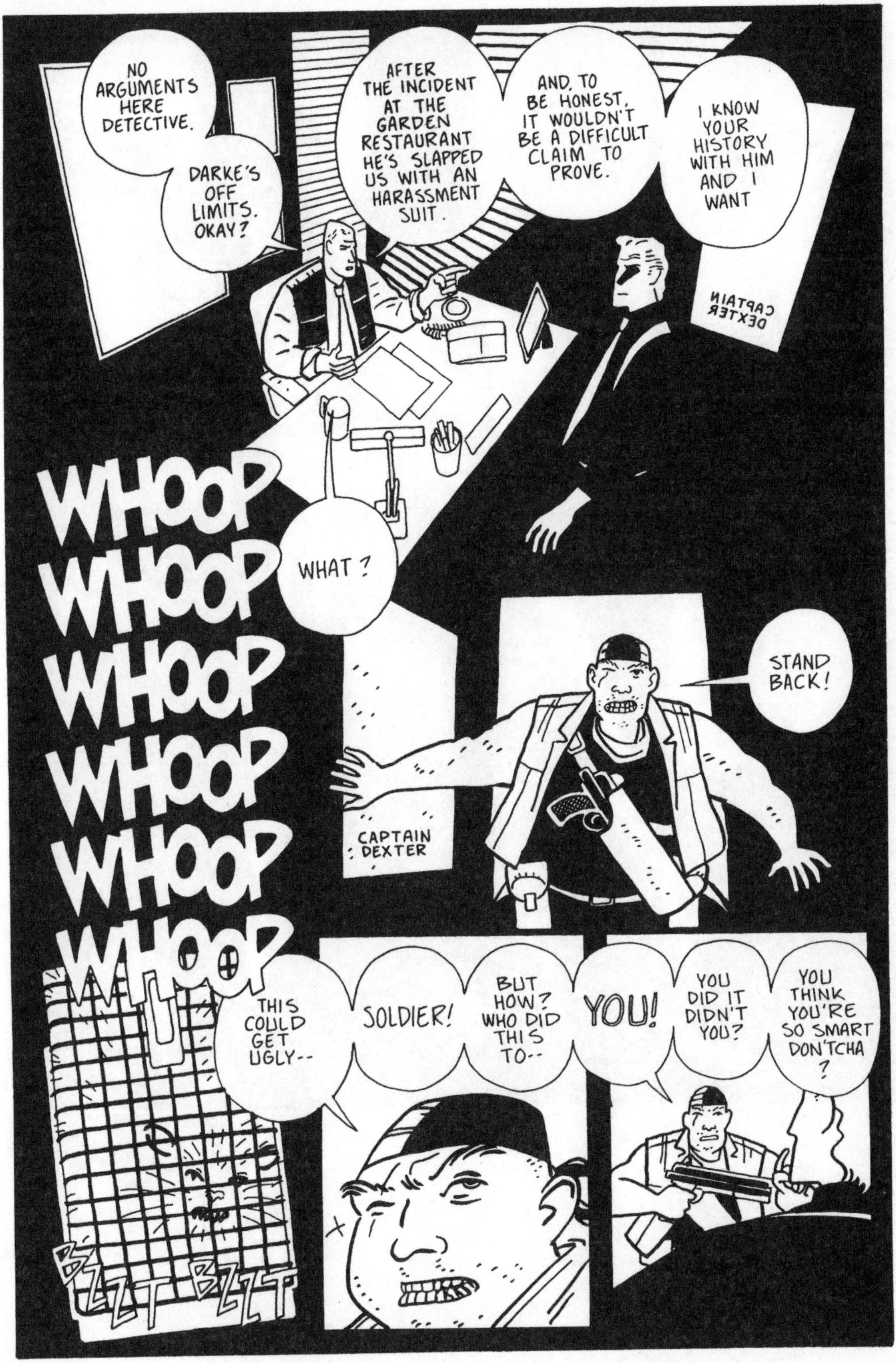
NO ARGUMENTS HERE DETECTIVE.
DARKE'S OFF LIMITS. OKAY?
AFTER THE INCIDENT AT THE GARDEN RESTAURANT HE'S SLAPPED US WITH AN HARASSMENT SUIT.
AND, TO BE HONEST, IT WOULDN'T BE A DIFFICULT CLAIM TO PROVE.
I KNOW YOUR HISTORY WITH HIM AND I WANT
CAPTAIN DEXTER
WHOOP WHOOP WHOOP WHOOP WHOOP WHOOP
WHAT?
CAPTAIN DEXTER
STAND BACK!
BZZT BZZT
THIS COULD GET UGLY--
SOLDIER!
BUT HOW? WHO DID THIS TO--
YOU!
YOU DID IT DIDN'T YOU?
YOU THINK YOU'RE SO SMART DON'TCHA?

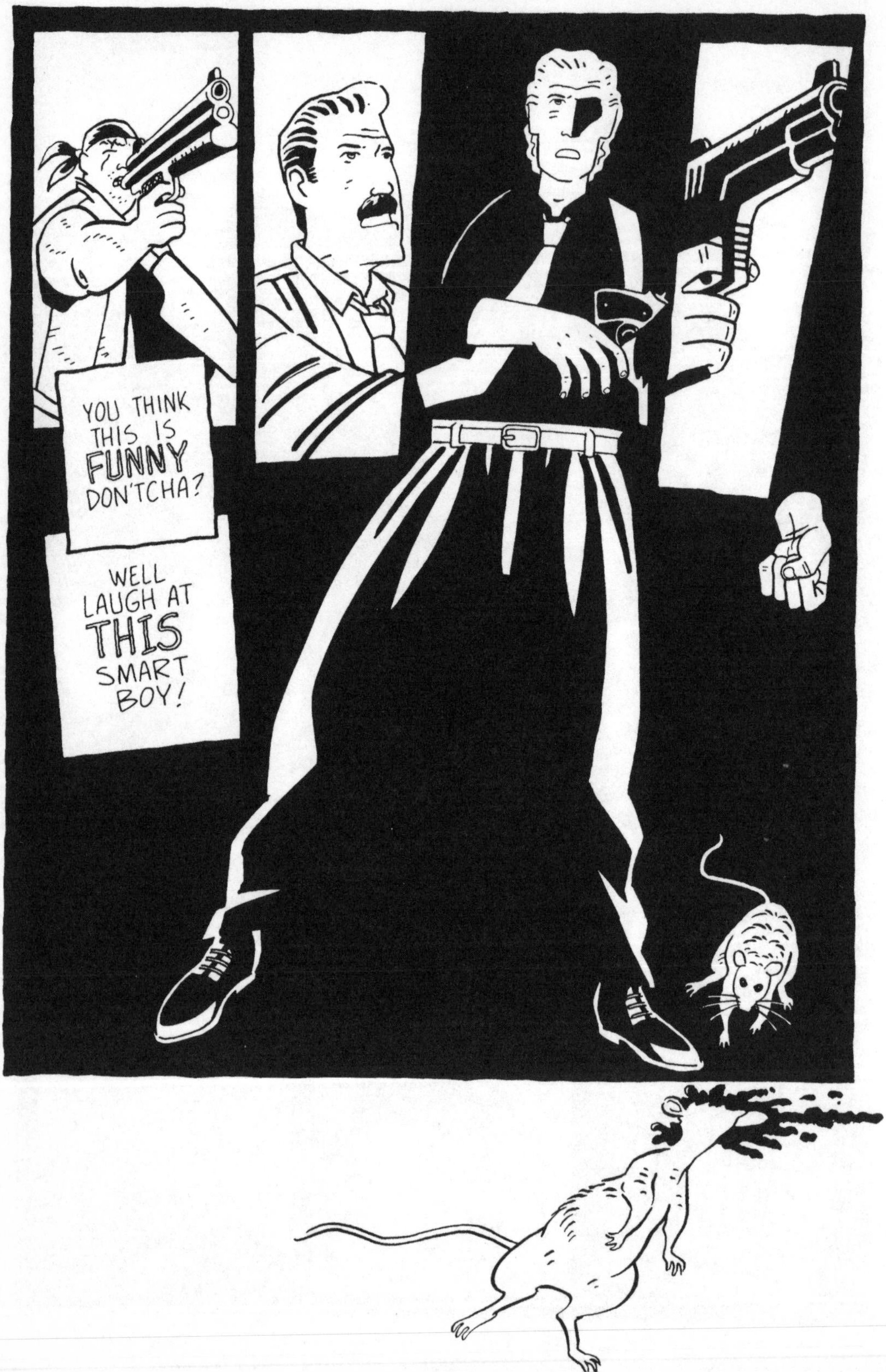
YOU THINK THIS IS FUNNY DON'TCHA?
WELL LAUGH AT THIS SMART BOY!

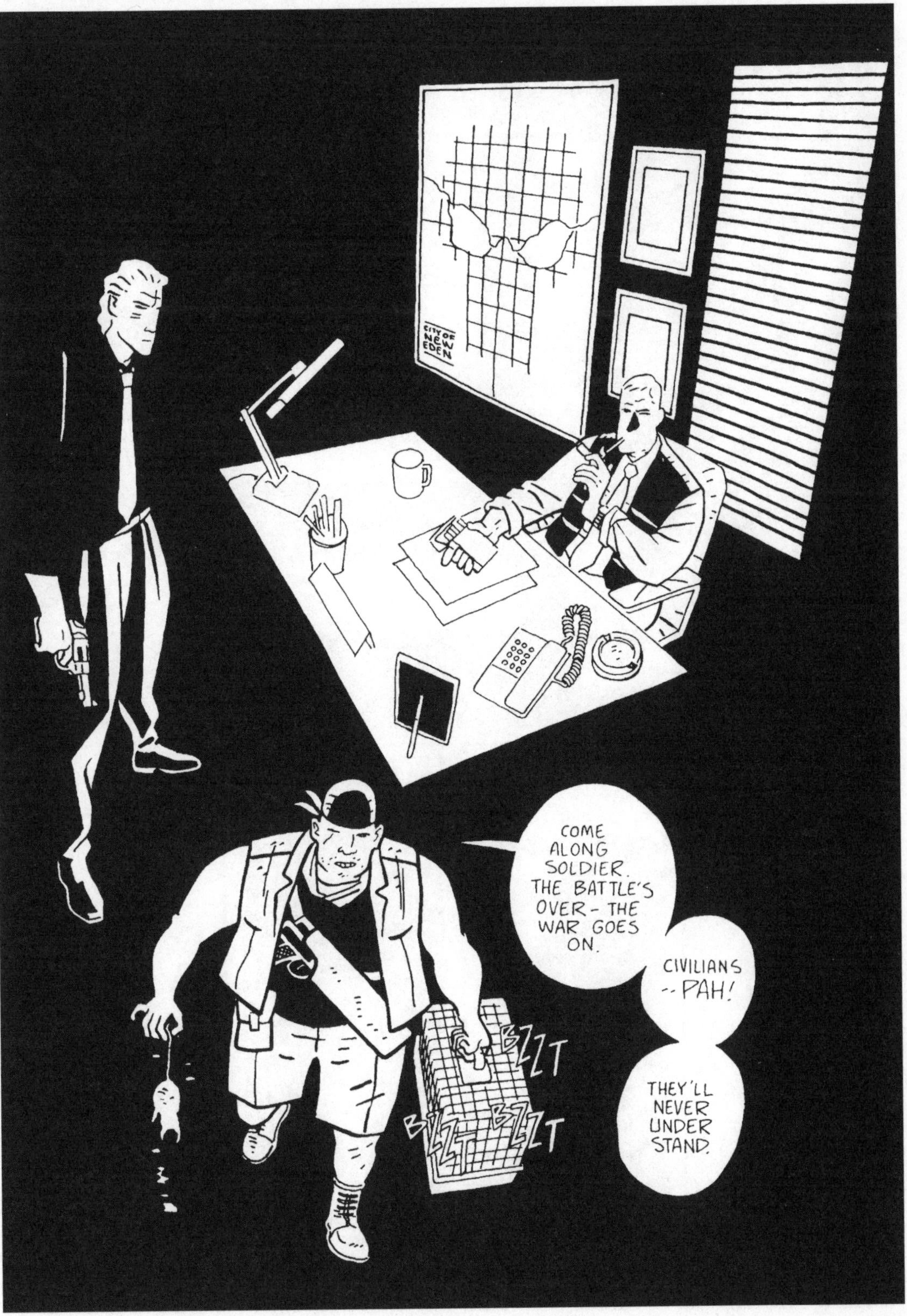
CITY OF NEW EDEN
COME ALONG SOLDIER. THE BATTLE'S OVER - THE WAR GOES ON.
CIVILIANS -- PAH!
THEY'LL NEVER UNDER STAND.
BZZT
BZZT BZZZT

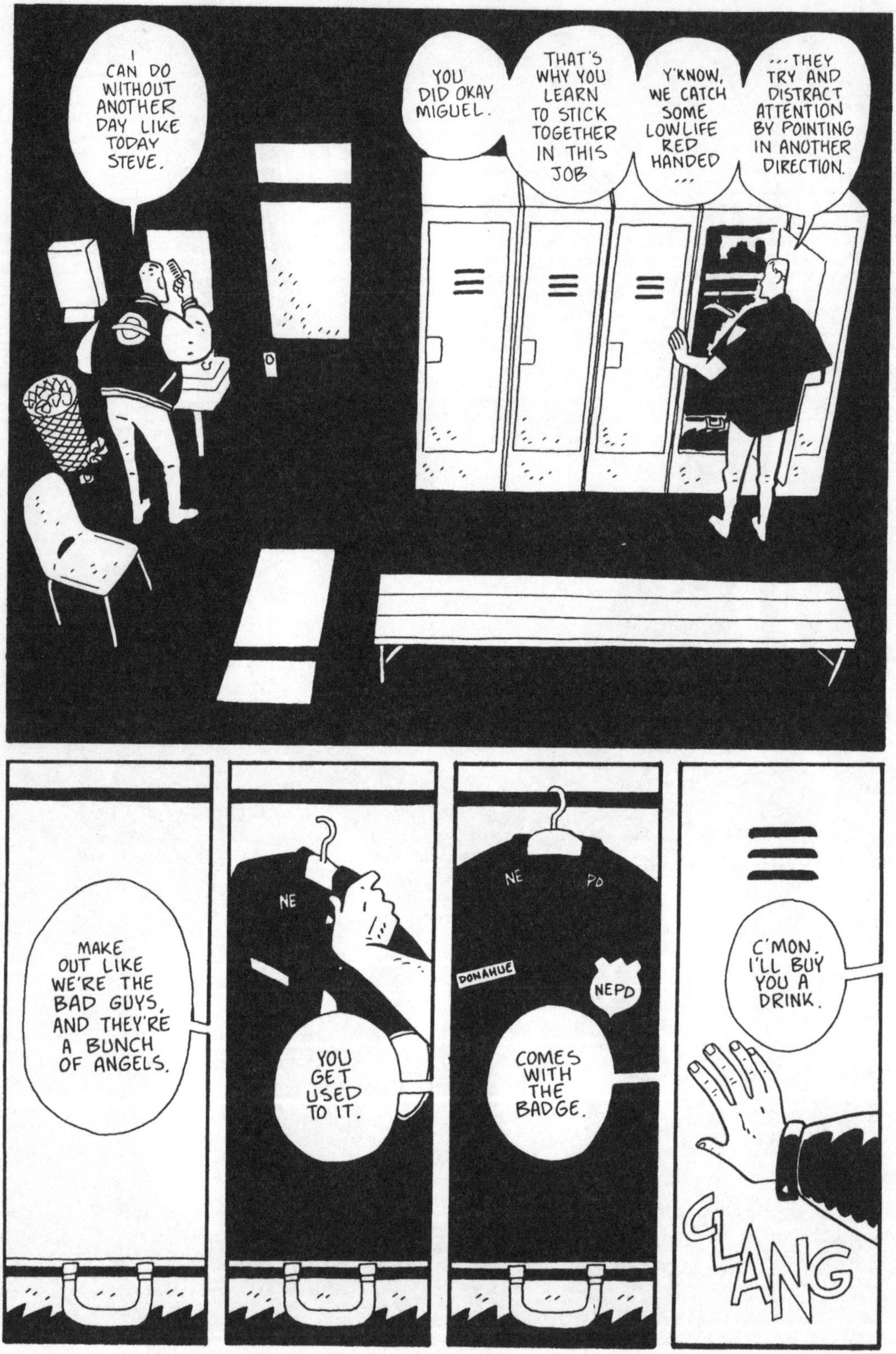
I CAN DO WITHOUT ANOTHER DAY LIKE TODAY STEVE.
YOU DID OKAY MIGUEL.
THAT'S WHY YOU LEARN TO STICK TOGETHER IN THIS JOB
Y'KNOW, WE CATCH SOME LOWLIFE RED HANDED ...
...THEY TRY AND DISTRACT ATTENTION BY POINTING IN ANOTHER DIRECTION.
MAKE OUT LIKE WE'RE THE BAD GUYS, AND THEY'RE A BUNCH OF ANGELS.
NE
YOU GET USED TO IT.
NE PD
DONAHUE
NEPD
COMES WITH THE BADGE.
C'MON. I'LL BUY YOU A DRINK.
CLANG

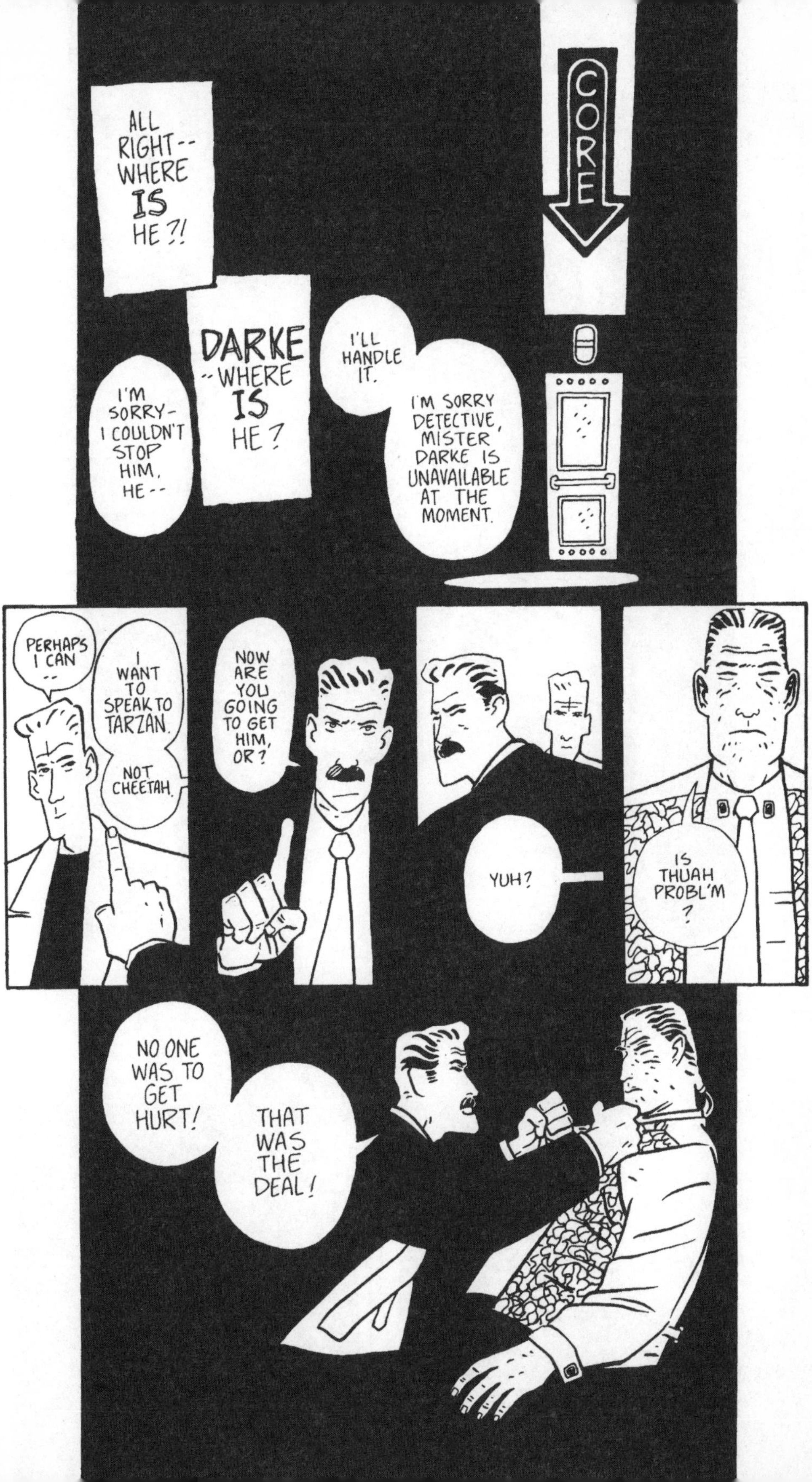
ALL RIGHT-- WHERE IS HE?!
CORE
I'M SORRY- I COULDN'T STOP HIM. HE--
DARKE --WHERE IS HE?
I'LL HANDLE IT.
I'M SORRY DETECTIVE, MISTER DARKE IS UNAVAILABLE AT THE MOMENT.
PERHAPS I CAN --
I WANT TO SPEAK TO TARZAN.
NOT CHEETAH.
NOW ARE YOU GOING TO GET HIM, OR?
YUH?
IS THUAH PROBL'M ?
NO ONE WAS TO GET HURT!
THAT WAS THE DEAL!

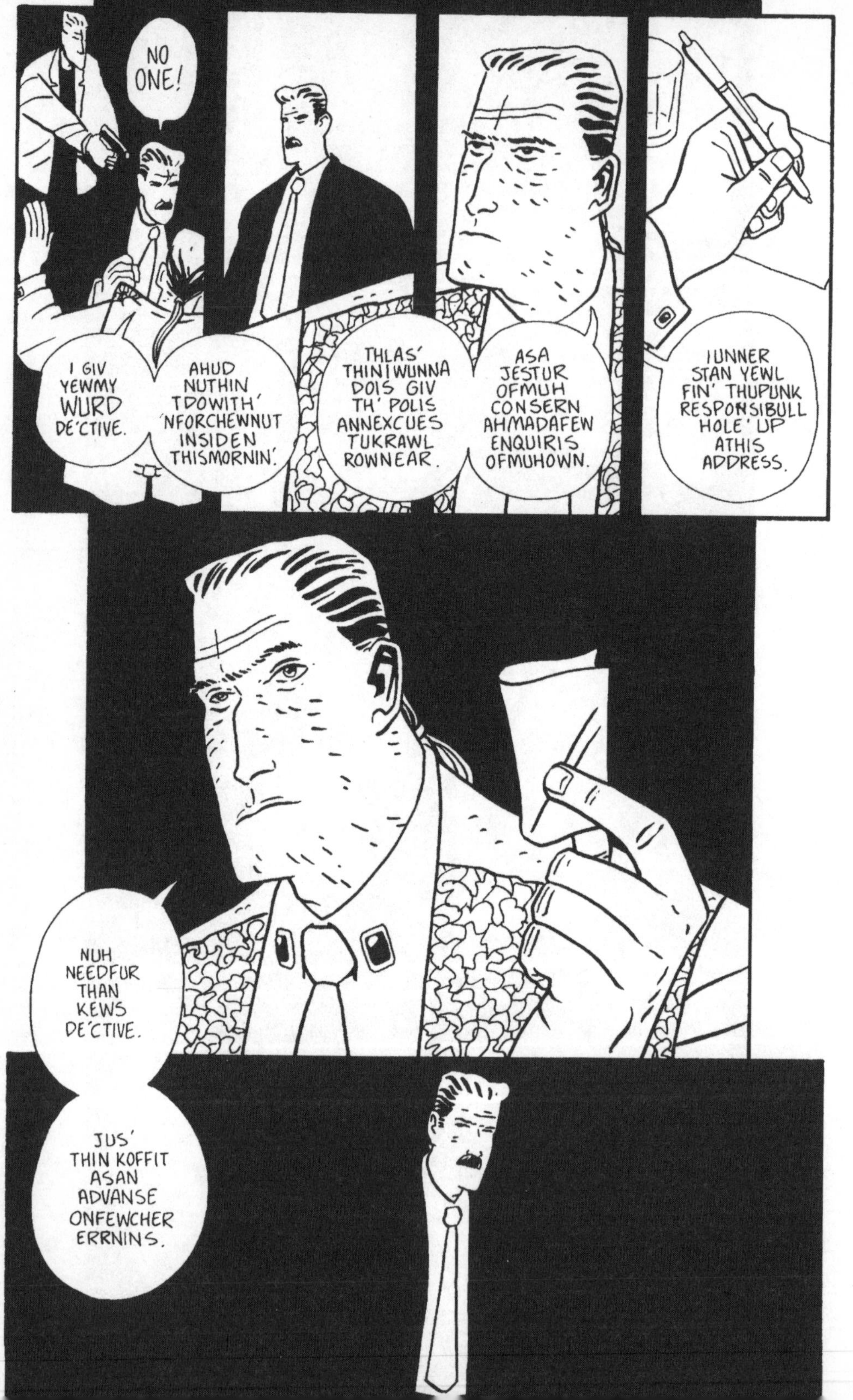
NO ONE!
I GIV YEWMY WURD DE'CTIVE.
AHUD NUTHIN TDOWITH' 'NFORCHEWNUT INSIDEN THISMORNIN'.
THLAS' THINIWUNNA DOIS GIV TH' POLIS ANNEXCUES TUKRAWL ROWNEAR.
ASA JESTUR OFMUH CONSERN AHMADAFEW ENQUIRIS OFMUHOWN.
IUNNER STAN YEWL FIN' THUPUNK RESPONSIBULL HOLE' UP ATHIS ADDRESS.
NUH NEEDFUR THAN KEWS DE'CTIVE.
JUS' THIN KOFFIT ASAN ADVANSE ONFEWCHER ERRNINS.

"Sorry, Genevieve!
If I am saving anybody
—it's going to be me!"

Another highlight of many issues of Crime
Does Not Pay was the "Who Dunnit" puzzle,
which challenged readers to solve a murder
mystery. A lot of plot had to be packed into
the panels and the solution was printed
upside down on the final page. Bile fills
almost every balloon with everyone at each
other's throat, when a double dose of death
strikes a dysfunctional French family. Will
you be as smart as Commissioner Nourvoir of
the Paris Police and identify the killer?

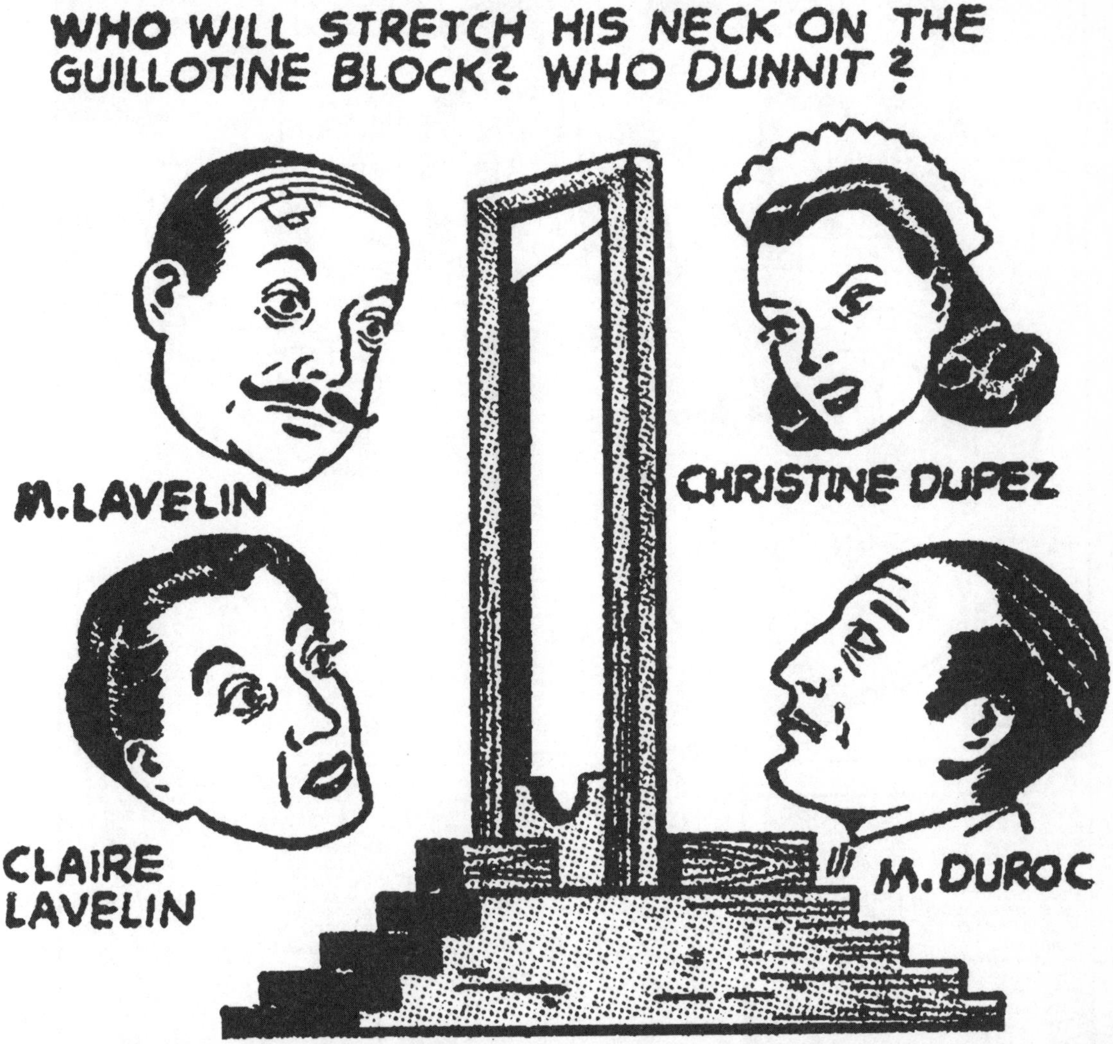
WHO WILL STRETCH HIS NECK ON THE GUILLOTINE BLOCK? WHO DUNNIT?
M. LAVELIN
CHRISTINE DUPEZ
CLAIRE LAVELIN
M. DUROC

Who Dunnit?

Fred Guardineer (art), writer unknown 1948

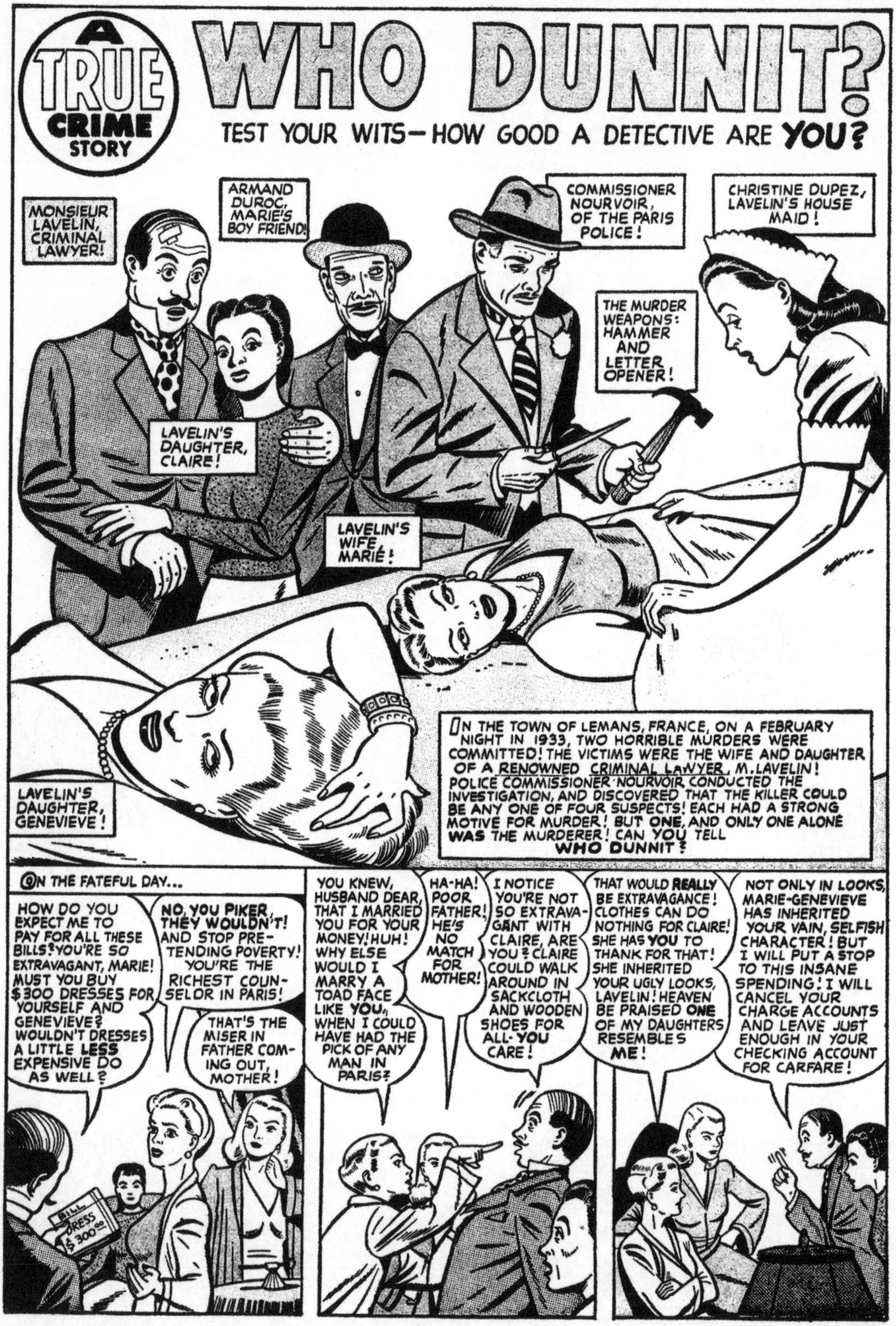
A TRUE CRIME STORY
WHO DUNNIT?
TEST YOUR WITS— HOW GOOD A DETECTIVE ARE YOU?
MONSIEUR LAVELIN, CRIMINAL LAWYER!
ARMAND DUROC, MARIE'S BOY FRIEND!
COMMISSIONER NOURVOIR, OF THE PARIS POLICE!
CHRISTINE DUPEZ, LAVELIN'S HOUSE MAID!
THE MURDER WEAPONS: HAMMER AND LETTER OPENER!
LAVELIN'S DAUGHTER, CLAIRE!
LAVELIN'S WIFE, MARIÉ!
LAVELIN'S DAUGHTER, GENEVIEVE!
IN THE TOWN OF LEMANS, FRANCE, ON A FEBRUARY NIGHT IN 1933, TWO HORRIBLE MURDERS WERE COMMITTED! THE VICTIMS WERE THE WIFE AND DAUGHTER OF A RENOWNED CRIMINAL LAWYER, M. LAVELIN! POLICE COMMISSIONER NOURVOIR CONDUCTED THE INVESTIGATION, AND DISCOVERED THAT THE KILLER COULD BE ANY ONE OF FOUR SUSPECTS! EACH HAD A STRONG MOTIVE FOR MURDER! BUT ONE, AND ONLY ONE ALONE WAS THE MURDERER! CAN YOU TELL WHO DUNNIT?
ON THE FATEFUL DAY...
HOW DO YOU EXPECT ME TO PAY FOR ALL THESE BILLS? YOU'RE SO EXTRAVAGANT, MARIE! MUST YOU BUY $300 DRESSES FOR YOURSELF AND GENEVIEVE? WOULDN'T DRESSES A LITTLE LESS EXPENSIVE DO AS WELL?
NO, YOU PIKER, THEY WOULDN'T! AND STOP PRETENDING POVERTY! YOU'RE THE RICHEST COUNSELOR IN PARIS!
THAT'S THE MISER IN FATHER COMING OUT, MOTHER!
BILL DRESS $300.00
YOU KNEW, HUSBAND DEAR, THAT I MARRIED YOU FOR YOUR MONEY! HUH! WHY ELSE WOULD I MARRY A TOAD FACE LIKE YOU, WHEN I COULD HAVE HAD THE PICK OF ANY MAN IN PARIS?
HA-HA! POOR FATHER! HE'S NO MATCH FOR MOTHER!
I NOTICE YOU'RE NOT SO EXTRAVAGANT WITH CLAIRE, ARE YOU? CLAIRE COULD WALK AROUND IN SACKCLOTH AND WOODEN SHOES FOR ALL YOU CARE!
THAT WOULD REALLY BE EXTRAVAGANCE! CLOTHES CAN DO NOTHING FOR CLAIRE! SHE HAS YOU TO THANK FOR THAT! SHE INHERITED YOUR UGLY LOOKS, LAVELIN! HEAVEN BE PRAISED ONE OF MY DAUGHTERS RESEMBLES ME!
NOT ONLY IN LOOKS, MARIE-GENEVIEVE HAS INHERITED YOUR VAIN, SELFISH CHARACTER! BUT I WILL PUT A STOP TO THIS INSANE SPENDING! I WILL CANCEL YOUR CHARGE ACCOUNTS AND LEAVE JUST ENOUGH IN YOUR CHECKING ACCOUNT FOR CARFARE!

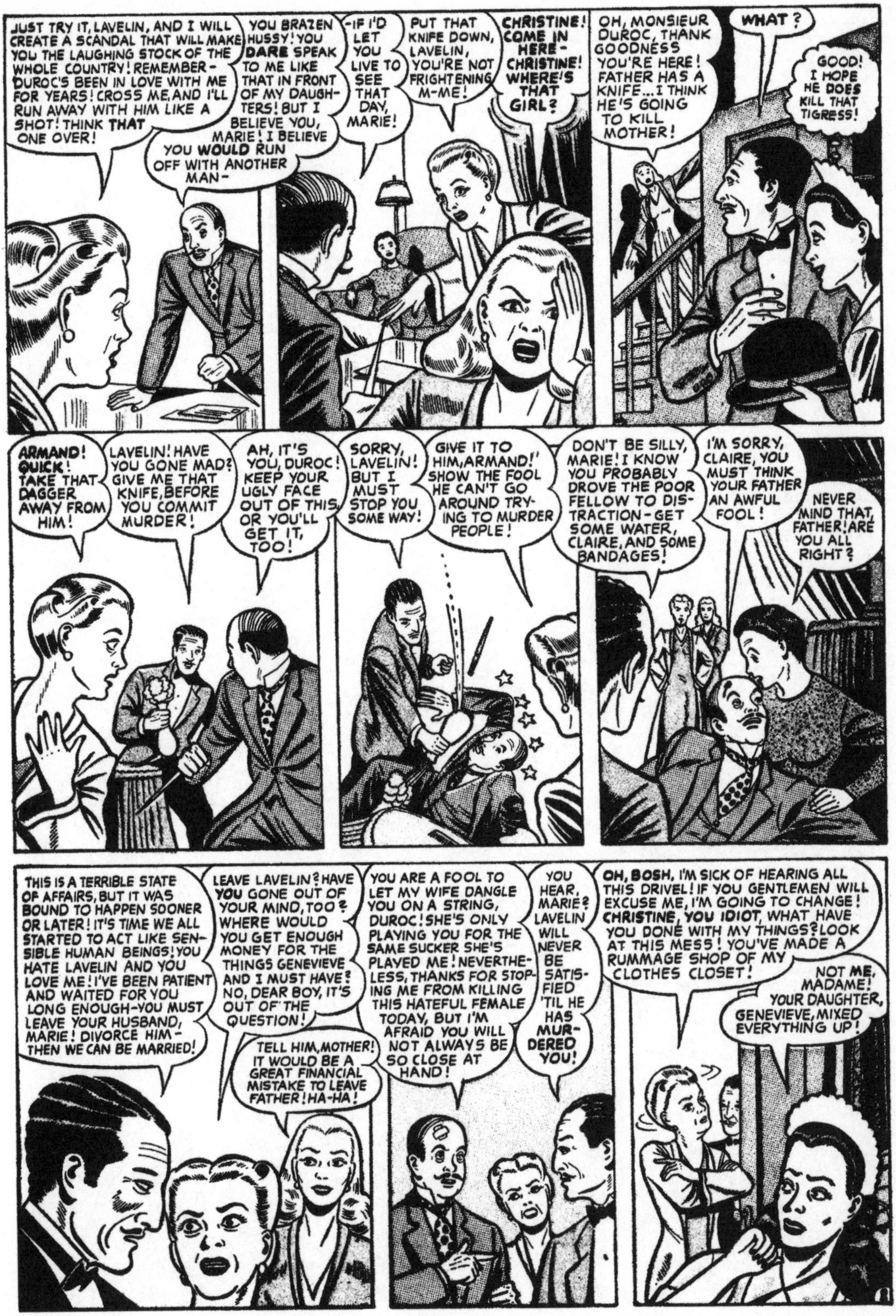
JUST TRY IT, LAVELIN, AND I WILL CREATE A SCANDAL THAT WILL MAKE YOU THE LAUGHING STOCK OF THE WHOLE COUNTRY! REMEMBER - DUROC'S BEEN IN LOVE WITH ME FOR YEARS! CROSS ME, AND I'LL RUN AWAY WITH HIM LIKE A SHOT! THINK THAT ONE OVER!
YOU BRAZEN HUSSY! YOU DARE SPEAK TO ME LIKE THAT IN FRONT OF MY DAUGHTERS! BUT I BELIEVE YOU, MARIE! I BELIEVE YOU WOULD RUN OFF WITH ANOTHER MAN-
-IF I'D LET YOU LIVE TO SEE THAT DAY, MARIE!
PUT THAT KNIFE DOWN, LAVELIN, YOU'RE NOT FRIGHTENING M-ME!
CHRISTINE! COME IN HERE-CHRISTINE! WHERE'S THAT GIRL?
OH, MONSIEUR DUROC, THANK GOODNESS YOU'RE HERE! FATHER HAS A KNIFE...I THINK HE'S GOING TO KILL MOTHER!
WHAT?
GOOD! I HOPE HE DOES KILL THAT TIGRESS!
ARMAND! QUICK! TAKE THAT DAGGER AWAY FROM HIM!
LAVELIN! HAVE YOU GONE MAD? GIVE ME THAT KNIFE, BEFORE YOU COMMIT MURDER!
AH, IT'S YOU, DUROC! KEEP YOUR UGLY FACE OUT OF THIS, OR YOU'LL GET IT, TOO!
SORRY, LAVELIN! BUT I MUST STOP YOU SOME WAY!
GIVE IT TO HIM, ARMAND! SHOW THE FOOL HE CAN'T GO AROUND TRYING TO MURDER PEOPLE!
DON'T BE SILLY, MARIE! I KNOW YOU PROBABLY DROVE THE POOR FELLOW TO DISTRACTION - GET SOME WATER, CLAIRE, AND SOME BANDAGES!
I'M SORRY, CLAIRE, YOU MUST THINK YOUR FATHER AN AWFUL FOOL!
NEVER MIND THAT, FATHER! ARE YOU ALL RIGHT?
THIS IS A TERRIBLE STATE OF AFFAIRS, BUT IT WAS BOUND TO HAPPEN SOONER OR LATER! IT'S TIME WE ALL STARTED TO ACT LIKE SENSIBLE HUMAN BEINGS! YOU HATE LAVELIN AND YOU LOVE ME! I'VE BEEN PATIENT AND WAITED FOR YOU LONG ENOUGH - YOU MUST LEAVE YOUR HUSBAND, MARIE! DIVORCE HIM - THEN WE CAN BE MARRIED!
LEAVE LAVELIN? HAVE YOU GONE OUT OF YOUR MIND, TOO? WHERE WOULD YOU GET ENOUGH MONEY FOR THE THINGS GENEVIEVE AND I MUST HAVE? NO, DEAR BOY, IT'S OUT OF THE QUESTION!
TELL HIM, MOTHER! IT WOULD BE A GREAT FINANCIAL MISTAKE TO LEAVE FATHER! HA-HA!
YOU ARE A FOOL TO LET MY WIFE DANGLE YOU ON A STRING, DUROC! SHE'S ONLY PLAYING YOU FOR THE SAME SUCKER SHE'S PLAYED ME! NEVERTHELESS, THANKS FOR STOPPING ME FROM KILLING THIS HATEFUL FEMALE TODAY, BUT I'M AFRAID YOU WILL NOT ALWAYS BE SO CLOSE AT HAND!
YOU HEAR, MARIE? LAVELIN WILL NEVER BE SATISFIED 'TIL HE HAS MURDERED YOU!
OH, BOSH, I'M SICK OF HEARING ALL THIS DRIVEL! IF YOU GENTLEMEN WILL EXCUSE ME, I'M GOING TO CHANGE! CHRISTINE, YOU IDIOT, WHAT HAVE YOU DONE WITH MY THINGS? LOOK AT THIS MESS! YOU'VE MADE A RUMMAGE SHOP OF MY CLOTHES CLOSET!
NOT ME, MADAME! YOUR DAUGHTER, GENEVIEVE, MIXED EVERYTHING UP!

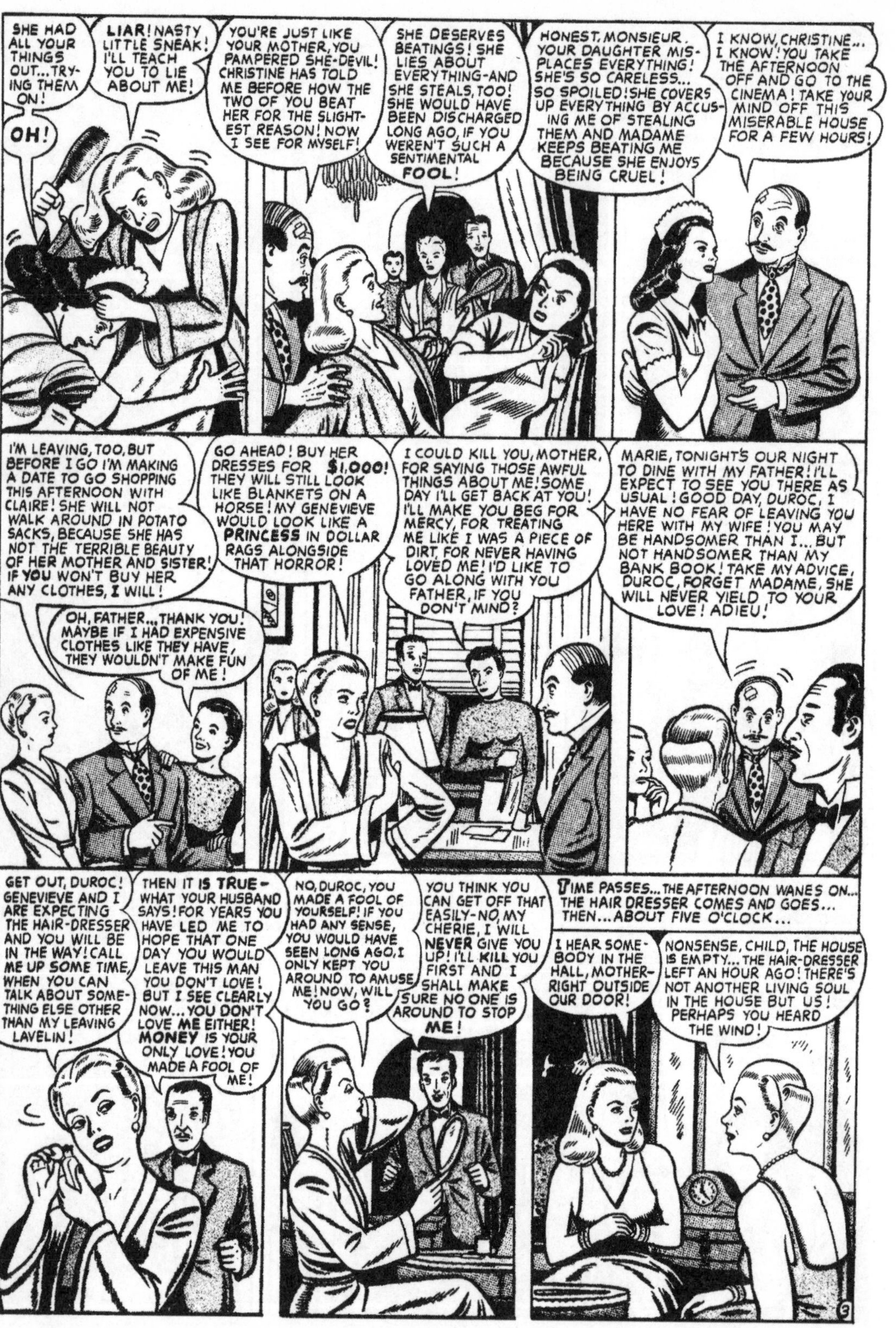
SHE HAD ALL YOUR THINGS OUT...TRYING THEM ON!
LIAR! NASTY LITTLE SNEAK! I'LL TEACH YOU TO LIE ABOUT ME!
OH!
YOU'RE JUST LIKE YOUR MOTHER, YOU PAMPERED SHE-DEVIL! CHRISTINE HAS TOLD ME BEFORE HOW THE TWO OF YOU BEAT HER FOR THE SLIGHTEST REASON! NOW I SEE FOR MYSELF!
SHE DESERVES BEATINGS! SHE LIES ABOUT EVERYTHING-AND SHE STEALS, TOO! SHE WOULD HAVE BEEN DISCHARGED LONG AGO, IF YOU WEREN'T SUCH A SENTIMENTAL FOOL!
HONEST, MONSIEUR. YOUR DAUGHTER MISPLACES EVERYTHING! SHE'S SO CARELESS... SO SPOILED! SHE COVERS UP EVERYTHING BY ACCUSING ME OF STEALING THEM AND MADAME KEEPS BEATING ME BECAUSE SHE ENJOYS BEING CRUEL!
I KNOW, CHRISTINE... I KNOW! YOU TAKE THE AFTERNOON OFF AND GO TO THE CINEMA! TAKE YOUR MIND OFF THIS MISERABLE HOUSE FOR A FEW HOURS!
I'M LEAVING, TOO, BUT BEFORE I GO I'M MAKING A DATE TO GO SHOPPING THIS AFTERNOON WITH CLAIRE! SHE WILL NOT WALK AROUND IN POTATO SACKS, BECAUSE SHE HAS NOT THE TERRIBLE BEAUTY OF HER MOTHER AND SISTER! IF YOU WON'T BUY HER ANY CLOTHES, I WILL!
OH, FATHER... THANK YOU! MAYBE IF I HAD EXPENSIVE CLOTHES LIKE THEY HAVE, THEY WOULDN'T MAKE FUN OF ME!
GO AHEAD! BUY HER DRESSES FOR $1,000! THEY WILL STILL LOOK LIKE BLANKETS ON A HORSE! MY GENEVIEVE WOULD LOOK LIKE A PRINCESS IN DOLLAR RAGS ALONGSIDE THAT HORROR!
I COULD KILL YOU, MOTHER, FOR SAYING THOSE AWFUL THINGS ABOUT ME! SOME DAY I'LL GET BACK AT YOU! I'LL MAKE YOU BEG FOR MERCY, FOR TREATING ME LIKE I WAS A PIECE OF DIRT, FOR NEVER HAVING LOVED ME! I'D LIKE TO GO ALONG WITH YOU FATHER, IF YOU DON'T MIND?
MARIE, TONIGHT'S OUR NIGHT TO DINE WITH MY FATHER! I'LL EXPECT TO SEE YOU THERE AS USUAL! GOOD DAY, DUROC, I HAVE NO FEAR OF LEAVING YOU HERE WITH MY WIFE! YOU MAY BE HANDSOMER THAN I... BUT NOT HANDSOMER THAN MY BANK BOOK! TAKE MY ADVICE, DUROC, FORGET MADAME, SHE WILL NEVER YIELD TO YOUR LOVE! ADIEU!
GET OUT, DUROC! GENEVIEVE AND I ARE EXPECTING THE HAIR-DRESSER AND YOU WILL BE IN THE WAY! CALL ME UP SOME TIME, WHEN YOU CAN TALK ABOUT SOMETHING ELSE OTHER THAN MY LEAVING LAVELIN!
THEN IT IS TRUE- WHAT YOUR HUSBAND SAYS! FOR YEARS YOU HAVE LED ME TO HOPE THAT ONE DAY YOU WOULD LEAVE THIS MAN YOU DON'T LOVE! BUT I SEE CLEARLY NOW... YOU DON'T LOVE ME EITHER! MONEY IS YOUR ONLY LOVE! YOU MADE A FOOL OF ME!
NO, DUROC, YOU MADE A FOOL OF YOURSELF! IF YOU HAD ANY SENSE, YOU WOULD HAVE SEEN LONG AGO, I ONLY KEPT YOU AROUND TO AMUSE ME! NOW, WILL YOU GO?
YOU THINK YOU CAN GET OFF THAT EASILY-NO, MY CHERIE, I WILL NEVER GIVE YOU UP! I'LL KILL YOU FIRST AND I SHALL MAKE SURE NO ONE IS AROUND TO STOP ME!
TIME PASSES... THE AFTERNOON WANES ON... THE HAIR DRESSER COMES AND GOES... THEN... ABOUT FIVE O'CLOCK...
I HEAR SOMEBODY IN THE HALL, MOTHER- RIGHT OUTSIDE OUR DOOR!
NONSENSE, CHILD, THE HOUSE IS EMPTY... THE HAIR-DRESSER LEFT AN HOUR AGO! THERE'S NOT ANOTHER LIVING SOUL IN THE HOUSE BUT US! PERHAPS YOU HEARD THE WIND!

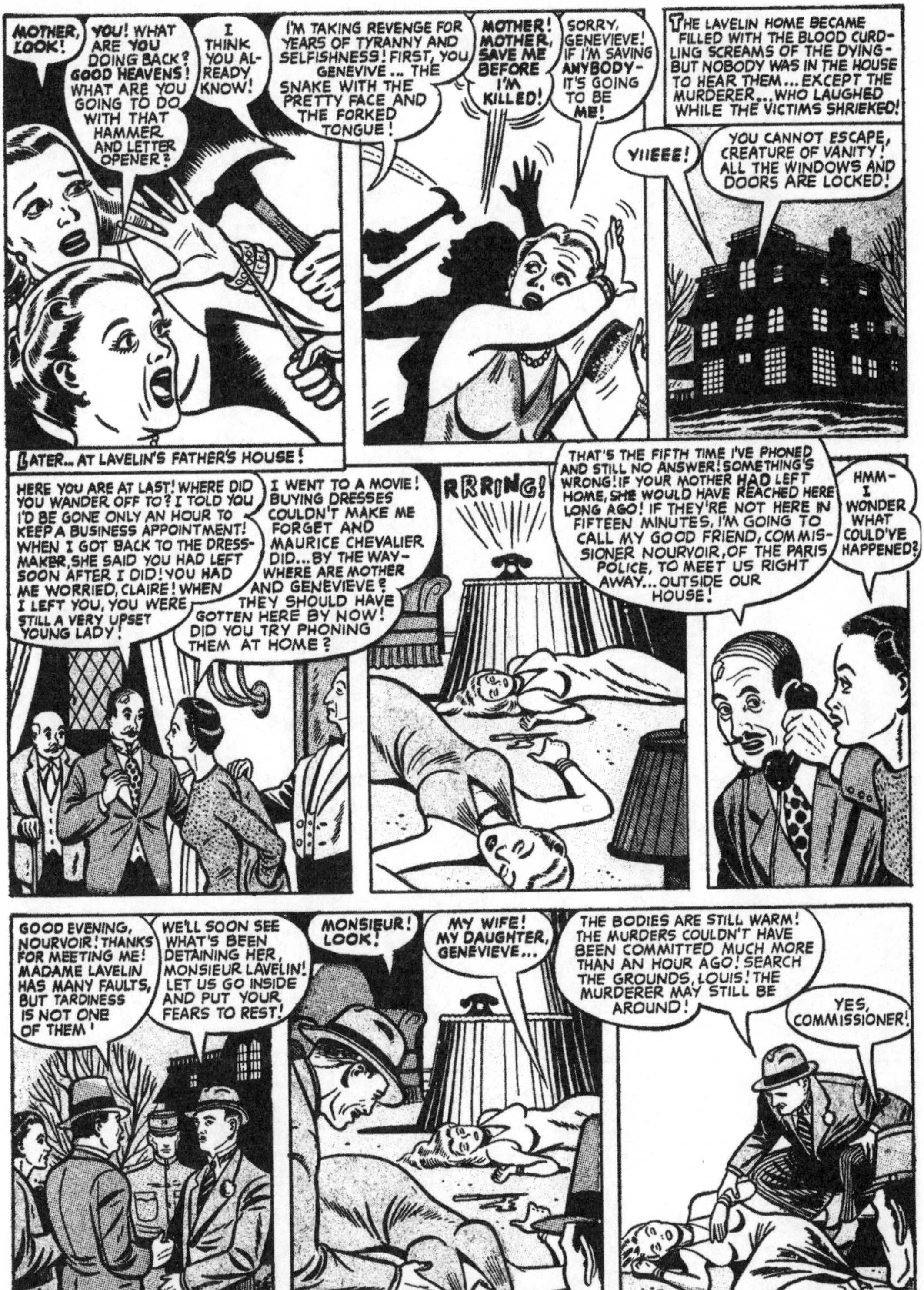

MOTHER, LOOK!
YOU! WHAT ARE YOU DOING BACK? GOOD HEAVENS! WHAT ARE YOU GOING TO DO WITH THAT HAMMER AND LETTER OPENER?
I THINK YOU ALREADY KNOW!
I'M TAKING REVENGE FOR YEARS OF TYRANNY AND SELFISHNESS! FIRST, YOU GENEVIVE... THE SNAKE WITH THE PRETTY FACE AND THE FORKED TONGUE!
MOTHER! MOTHER, SAVE ME BEFORE I'M KILLED!
SORRY, GENEVIEVE! IF I'M SAVING ANYBODY- IT'S GOING TO BE ME!
THE LAVELIN HOME BECAME FILLED WITH THE BLOOD CURDLING SCREAMS OF THE DYING- BUT NOBODY WAS IN THE HOUSE TO HEAR THEM... EXCEPT THE MURDERER... WHO LAUGHED WHILE THE VICTIMS SHRIEKED!
YIIEEE!
YOU CANNOT ESCAPE, CREATURE OF VANITY! ALL THE WINDOWS AND DOORS ARE LOCKED!
LATER... AT LAVELIN'S FATHER'S HOUSE!
HERE YOU ARE AT LAST! WHERE DID YOU WANDER OFF TO? I TOLD YOU I'D BE GONE ONLY AN HOUR TO KEEP A BUSINESS APPOINTMENT! WHEN I GOT BACK TO THE DRESSMAKER, SHE SAID YOU HAD LEFT SOON AFTER I DID! YOU HAD ME WORRIED, CLAIRE! WHEN I LEFT YOU, YOU WERE STILL A VERY UPSET YOUNG LADY!
I WENT TO A MOVIE! BUYING DRESSES COULDN'T MAKE ME FORGET AND MAURICE CHEVALIER DID... BY THE WAY- WHERE ARE MOTHER AND GENEVIEVE? THEY SHOULD HAVE GOTTEN HERE BY NOW! DID YOU TRY PHONING THEM AT HOME?
RRRING!
THAT'S THE FIFTH TIME I'VE PHONED AND STILL NO ANSWER! SOMETHING'S WRONG! IF YOUR MOTHER HAD LEFT HOME, SHE WOULD HAVE REACHED HERE LONG AGO! IF THEY'RE NOT HERE IN FIFTEEN MINUTES, I'M GOING TO CALL MY GOOD FRIEND, COMMISSIONER NOURVOIR, OF THE PARIS POLICE, TO MEET US RIGHT AWAY... OUTSIDE OUR HOUSE!
HMM- I WONDER WHAT COULD'VE HAPPENED?
GOOD EVENING, NOURVOIR! THANKS FOR MEETING ME! MADAME LAVELIN HAS MANY FAULTS, BUT TARDINESS IS NOT ONE OF THEM!
WE'LL SOON SEE WHAT'S BEEN DETAINING HER, MONSIEUR LAVELIN! LET US GO INSIDE AND PUT YOUR FEARS TO REST!
MONSIEUR! LOOK!
MY WIFE! MY DAUGHTER, GENEVIEVE...
THE BODIES ARE STILL WARM! THE MURDERS COULDN'T HAVE BEEN COMMITTED MUCH MORE THAN AN HOUR AGO! SEARCH THE GROUNDS, LOUIS! THE MURDERER MAY STILL BE AROUND!
YES, COMMISSIONER!

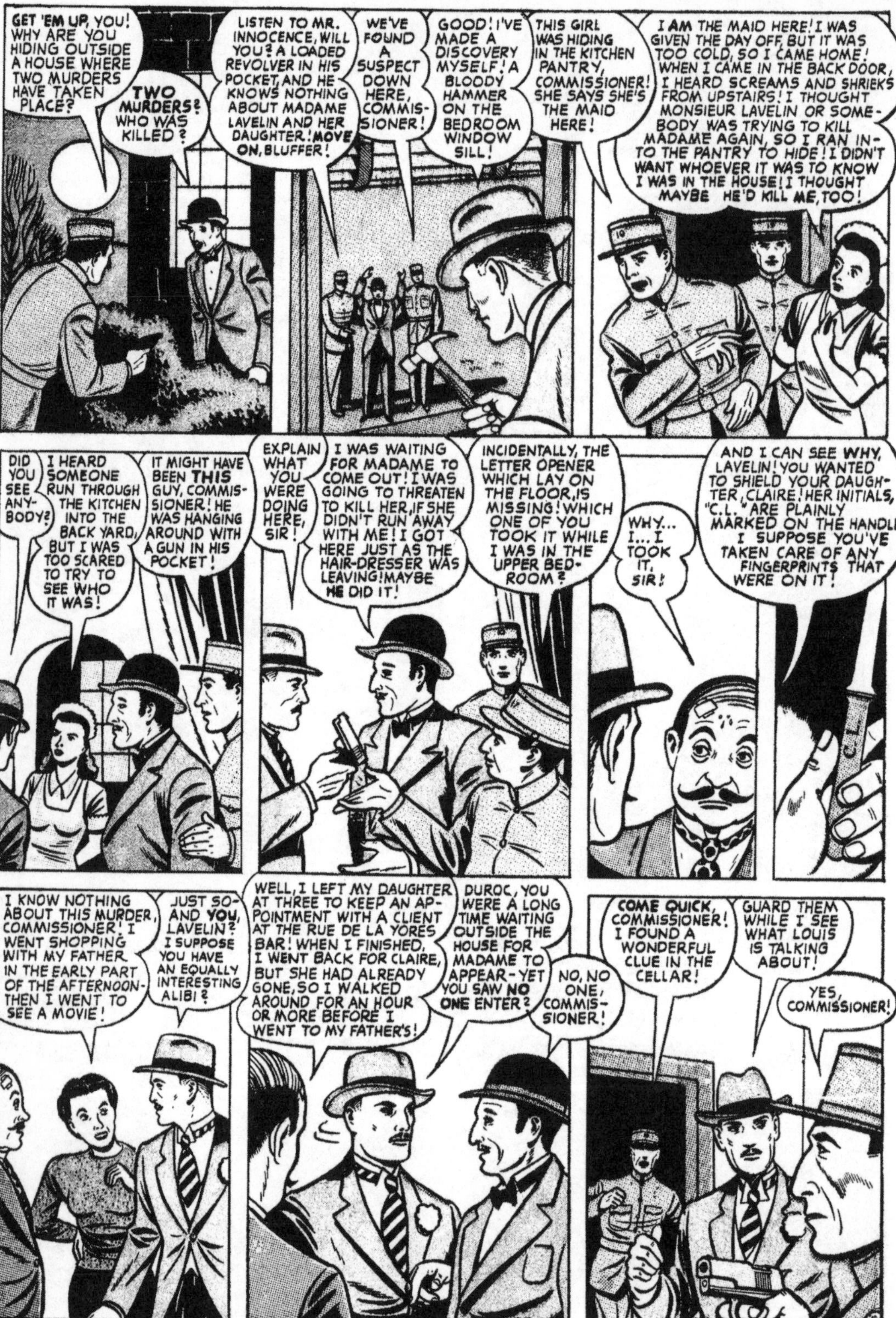
GET 'EM UP, YOU! WHY ARE YOU HIDING OUTSIDE A HOUSE WHERE TWO MURDERS HAVE TAKEN PLACE?
TWO MURDERS? WHO WAS KILLED?
LISTEN TO MR. INNOCENCE, WILL YOU? A LOADED REVOLVER IN HIS POCKET, AND HE KNOWS NOTHING ABOUT MADAME LAVELIN AND HER DAUGHTER! MOVE ON, BLUFFER!
WE'VE FOUND A SUSPECT DOWN HERE, COMMISSIONER!
GOOD! I'VE MADE A DISCOVERY MYSELF! A BLOODY HAMMER ON THE BEDROOM WINDOW SILL!
THIS GIRL WAS HIDING IN THE KITCHEN PANTRY, COMMISSIONER! SHE SAYS SHE'S THE MAID HERE!
I AM THE MAID HERE! I WAS GIVEN THE DAY OFF, BUT IT WAS TOO COLD, SO I CAME HOME! WHEN I CAME IN THE BACK DOOR, I HEARD SCREAMS AND SHRIEKS FROM UPSTAIRS! I THOUGHT MONSIEUR LAVELIN OR SOMEBODY WAS TRYING TO KILL MADAME AGAIN, SO I RAN INTO THE PANTRY TO HIDE! I DIDN'T WANT WHOEVER IT WAS TO KNOW I WAS IN THE HOUSE! I THOUGHT MAYBE HE'D KILL ME, TOO!
DID YOU SEE ANYBODY?
I HEARD SOMEONE RUN THROUGH THE KITCHEN INTO THE BACK YARD, BUT I WAS TOO SCARED TO TRY TO SEE WHO IT WAS!
IT MIGHT HAVE BEEN THIS GUY, COMMISSIONER! HE WAS HANGING AROUND WITH A GUN IN HIS POCKET!
EXPLAIN WHAT YOU WERE DOING HERE, SIR!
I WAS WAITING FOR MADAME TO COME OUT! I WAS GOING TO THREATEN TO KILL HER, IF SHE DIDN'T RUN AWAY WITH ME! I GOT HERE JUST AS THE HAIR-DRESSER WAS LEAVING! MAYBE HE DID IT!
INCIDENTALLY, THE LETTER OPENER WHICH LAY ON THE FLOOR, IS MISSING! WHICH ONE OF YOU TOOK IT WHILE I WAS IN THE UPPER BEDROOM?
WHY... I... I TOOK IT, SIR!
AND I CAN SEE WHY, LAVELIN! YOU WANTED TO SHIELD YOUR DAUGHTER, CLAIRE! HER INITIALS, "C.L." ARE PLAINLY MARKED ON THE HANDLE! I SUPPOSE YOU'VE TAKEN CARE OF ANY FINGERPRINTS THAT WERE ON IT!
I KNOW NOTHING ABOUT THIS MURDER, COMMISSIONER! I WENT SHOPPING WITH MY FATHER IN THE EARLY PART OF THE AFTERNOON- THEN I WENT TO SEE A MOVIE!
JUST SO- AND YOU, LAVELIN? I SUPPOSE YOU HAVE AN EQUALLY INTERESTING ALIBI?
WELL, I LEFT MY DAUGHTER AT THREE TO KEEP AN APPOINTMENT WITH A CLIENT AT THE RUE DE LA YORES BAR! WHEN I FINISHED, I WENT BACK FOR CLAIRE, BUT SHE HAD ALREADY GONE, SO I WALKED AROUND FOR AN HOUR OR MORE BEFORE I WENT TO MY FATHER'S!
DUROC, YOU WERE A LONG TIME WAITING OUTSIDE THE HOUSE FOR MADAME TO APPEAR- YET YOU SAW NO ONE ENTER?
NO, NO ONE, COMMISSIONER!
COME QUICK, COMMISSIONER! I FOUND A WONDERFUL CLUE IN THE CELLAR!
GUARD THEM WHILE I SEE WHAT LOUIS IS TALKING ABOUT!
YES, COMMISSIONER!

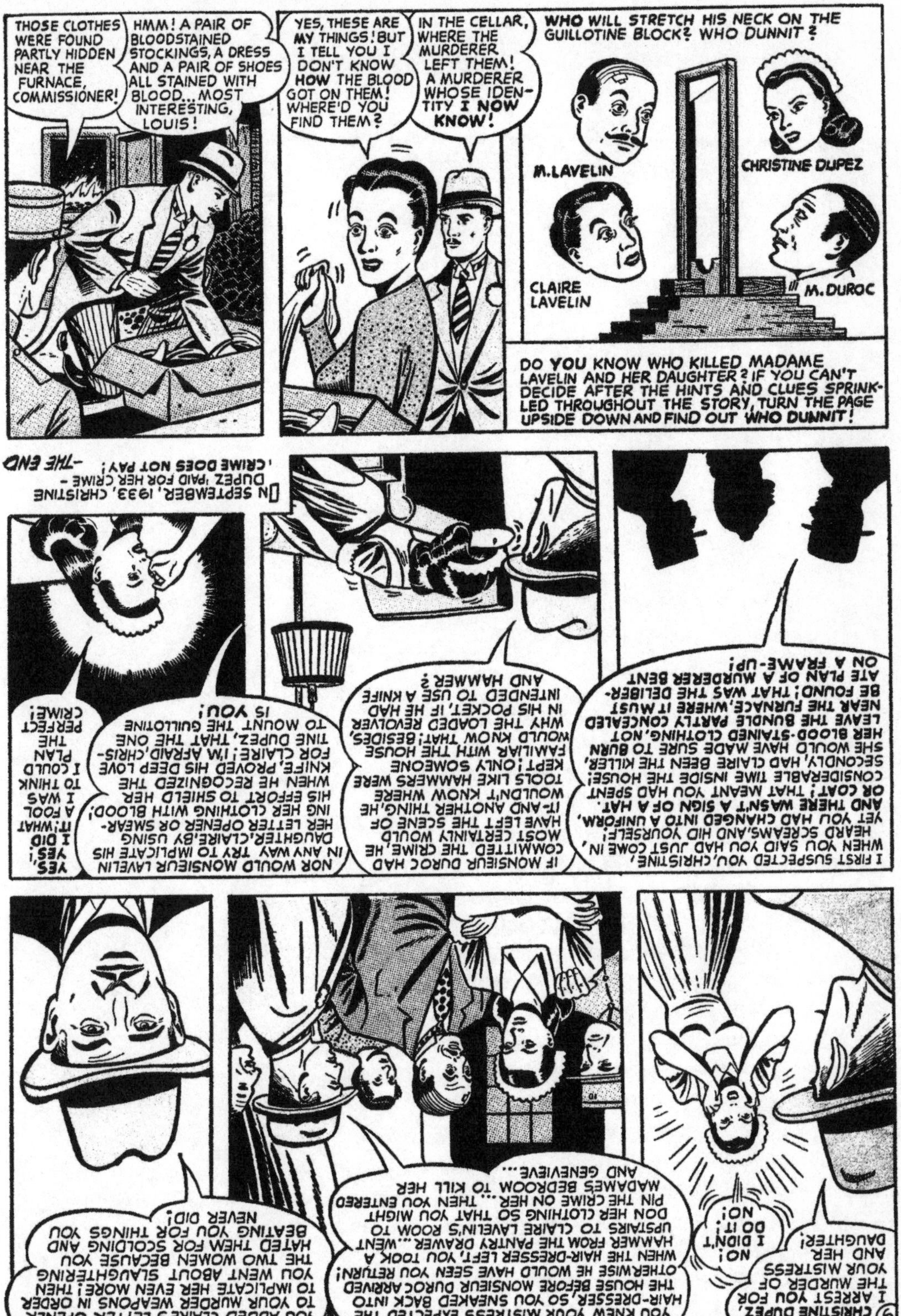

THOSE CLOTHES WERE FOUND PARTLY HIDDEN NEAR THE FURNACE, COMMISSIONER!
HMM! A PAIR OF BLOODSTAINED STOCKINGS, A DRESS AND A PAIR OF SHOES ALL STAINED WITH BLOOD... MOST INTERESTING, LOUIS!
YES, THESE ARE MY THINGS! BUT I TELL YOU I DON'T KNOW HOW THE BLOOD GOT ON THEM! WHERE'D YOU FIND THEM?
IN THE CELLAR, WHERE THE MURDERER LEFT THEM! A MURDERER WHOSE IDENTITY I NOW KNOW!
WHO WILL STRETCH HIS NECK ON THE GUILLOTINE BLOCK? WHO DUNNIT?
M. LAVELIN
CHRISTINE DUPEZ
CLAIRE LAVELIN
M. DUROC
DO YOU KNOW WHO KILLED MADAME LAVELIN AND HER DAUGHTER? IF YOU CAN'T DECIDE AFTER THE HINTS AND CLUES SPRINKLED THROUGHOUT THE STORY, TURN THE PAGE UPSIDE DOWN AND FIND OUT WHO DUNNIT!
9
CHRISTINE DUPEZ, I ARREST YOU FOR THE MURDER OF YOUR MISTRESS AND HER DAUGHTER!
NO! I DIDN'T DO IT! NO!
YOU KNEW YOUR MISTRESS EXPECTED THE HAIR-DRESSER, SO YOU SNEAKED BACK INTO THE HOUSE BEFORE MONSIEUR DUROC ARRIVED OTHERWISE HE WOULD HAVE SEEN YOU RETURN! WHEN THE HAIR-DRESSER LEFT, YOU TOOK A HAMMER FROM THE PANTRY DRAWER... WENT UPSTAIRS TO CLAIRE LAVELIN'S ROOM TO DON HER CLOTHING SO THAT YOU MIGHT PIN THE CRIME ON HER... THEN YOU ENTERED MADAME'S BEDROOM TO KILL HER AND GENEVIEVE...
YOU ADDED CLAIRE'S LETTER OPENER TO YOUR MURDER WEAPONS IN ORDER TO IMPLICATE HER EVEN MORE! THEN YOU WENT ABOUT SLAUGHTERING THE TWO WOMEN BECAUSE YOU HATED THEM FOR SCOLDING AND BEATING YOU FOR THINGS YOU NEVER DID!
I FIRST SUSPECTED YOU, CHRISTINE, WHEN YOU SAID YOU HAD JUST COME IN, HEARD SCREAMS, AND HID YOURSELF! YET YOU HAD CHANGED INTO A UNIFORM, AND THERE WASN'T A SIGN OF A HAT OR COAT! THAT MEANT YOU HAD SPENT CONSIDERABLE TIME INSIDE THE HOUSE! SECONDLY, HAD CLAIRE BEEN THE KILLER, SHE WOULD HAVE MADE SURE TO BURN HER BLOOD-STAINED CLOTHING, NOT LEAVE THE BUNDLE PARTLY CONCEALED NEAR THE FURNACE, WHERE IT MUST BE FOUND! THAT WAS THE DELIBERATE PLAN OF A MURDERER BENT ON A FRAME-UP!
IF MONSIEUR DUROC HAD COMMITTED THE CRIME, HE MOST CERTAINLY WOULD HAVE LEFT THE SCENE OF IT-AND ANOTHER THING, HE WOULDN'T KNOW WHERE TOOLS LIKE HAMMERS WERE KEPT! ONLY SOMEONE FAMILIAR WITH THE HOUSE WOULD KNOW THAT! BESIDES, WHY THE LOADED REVOLVER IN HIS POCKET, IF HE HAD INTENDED TO USE A KNIFE AND HAMMER?
NOR WOULD MONSIEUR LAVELIN IN ANY WAY TRY TO IMPLICATE HIS DAUGHTER, CLAIRE, BY USING HER LETTER OPENER OR SMEARING HER CLOTHING WITH BLOOD! HIS EFFORT TO SHIELD HER WHEN HE RECOGNIZED THE KNIFE, PROVED HIS DEEP LOVE FOR CLAIRE! I'M AFRAID, CHRISTINE DUPEZ, THAT THE ONE TO MOUNT THE GUILLOTINE IS YOU!
YES, YES! I DID IT! WHAT A FOOL I WAS TO THINK I COULD PLAN THE PERFECT CRIME!
IN SEPTEMBER, 1933, CHRISTINE DUPEZ 'PAID FOR HER CRIME - CRIME DOES NOT PAY!
-THE END

"You've done enough killing,
smart guy!
Now take it yourself!"

Not everyone knows that both novelist Frank
Morrison "Mickey" Spillane and his hard-hitting
private eye Mike Hammer started out in comic
books. Spillane used to write anonymously
for the main superhero publishers, but they
turned down his proposal in 1941 for Mike
Danger, convinced that readers would not find
an ordinary, uncostumed hero spectacular
enough to carry a whole solo book. One tale of
his Hammer prototype did see print, however,
the following year as Mike Lancer in *Green
Hornet* Comics. Spillane recalled buying a copy
while in the army stationed in Mississippi and
writing to ask artist Harry Sahle, "What did
you do to Mike Danger?" While the name may
have been changed, Spillane's, and Hammer's,
trademark brutality and fast-paced action
are unmistakeable. As for Mike Danger, he
resurfaced in a pair of tales in 1954 and was
catapulted into the future in a 1995 *Tekno*
Comics series by Spillane and Max Allan Collins.

Mike Lancer
and The Syndicate of Death

Mickey Spillane (script) and Harry Sahle (art)   1942

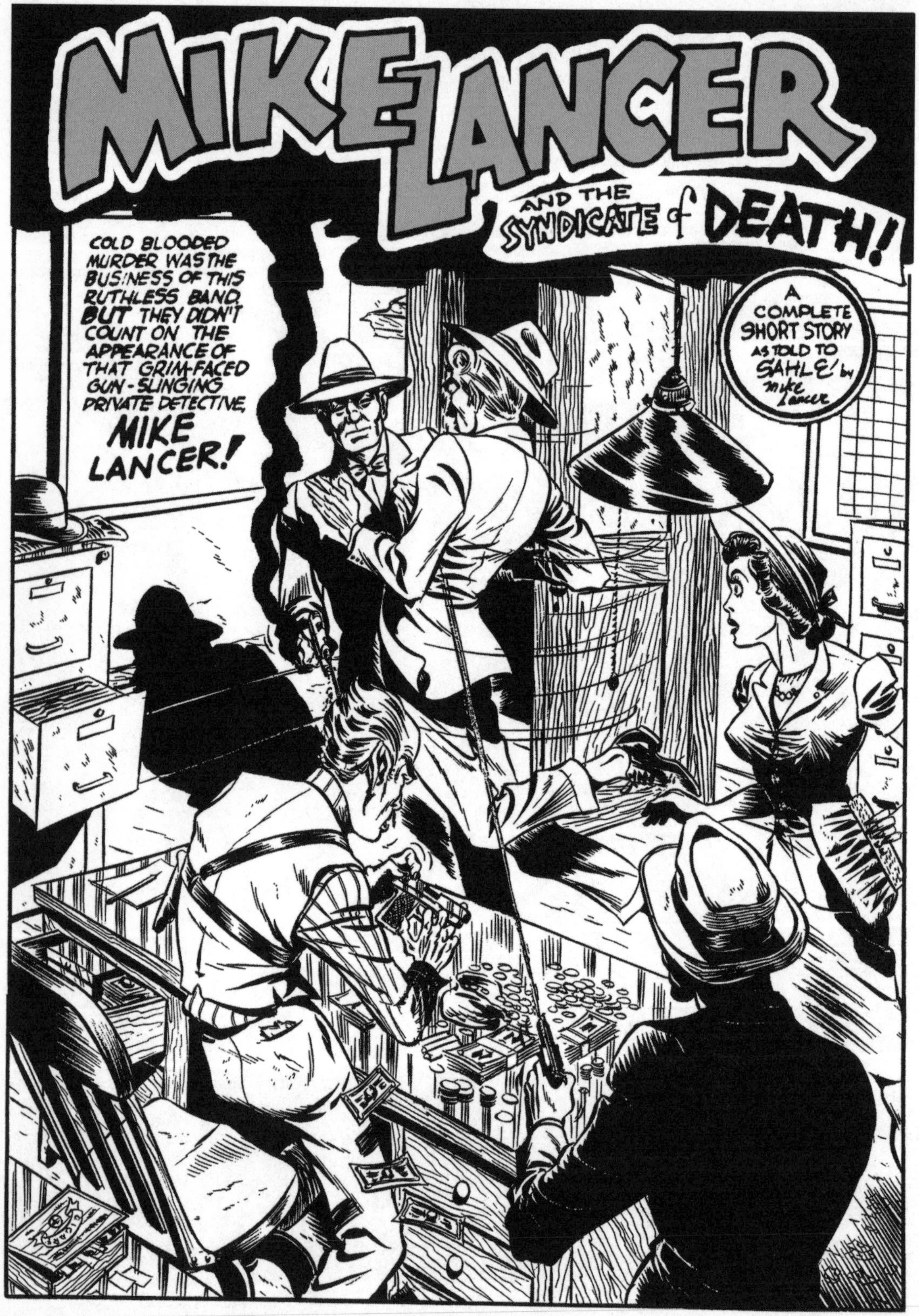
MIKE LANCER
AND THE SYNDICATE of DEATH!
COLD BLOODED MURDER WAS THE BUSINESS OF THIS RUTHLESS BAND, BUT THEY DIDN'T COUNT ON THE APPEARANCE OF THAT GRIM-FACED GUN-SLINGING PRIVATE DETECTIVE, MIKE LANCER!
A COMPLETE SHORT STORY AS TOLD TO SAHLE! by Mike Lancer

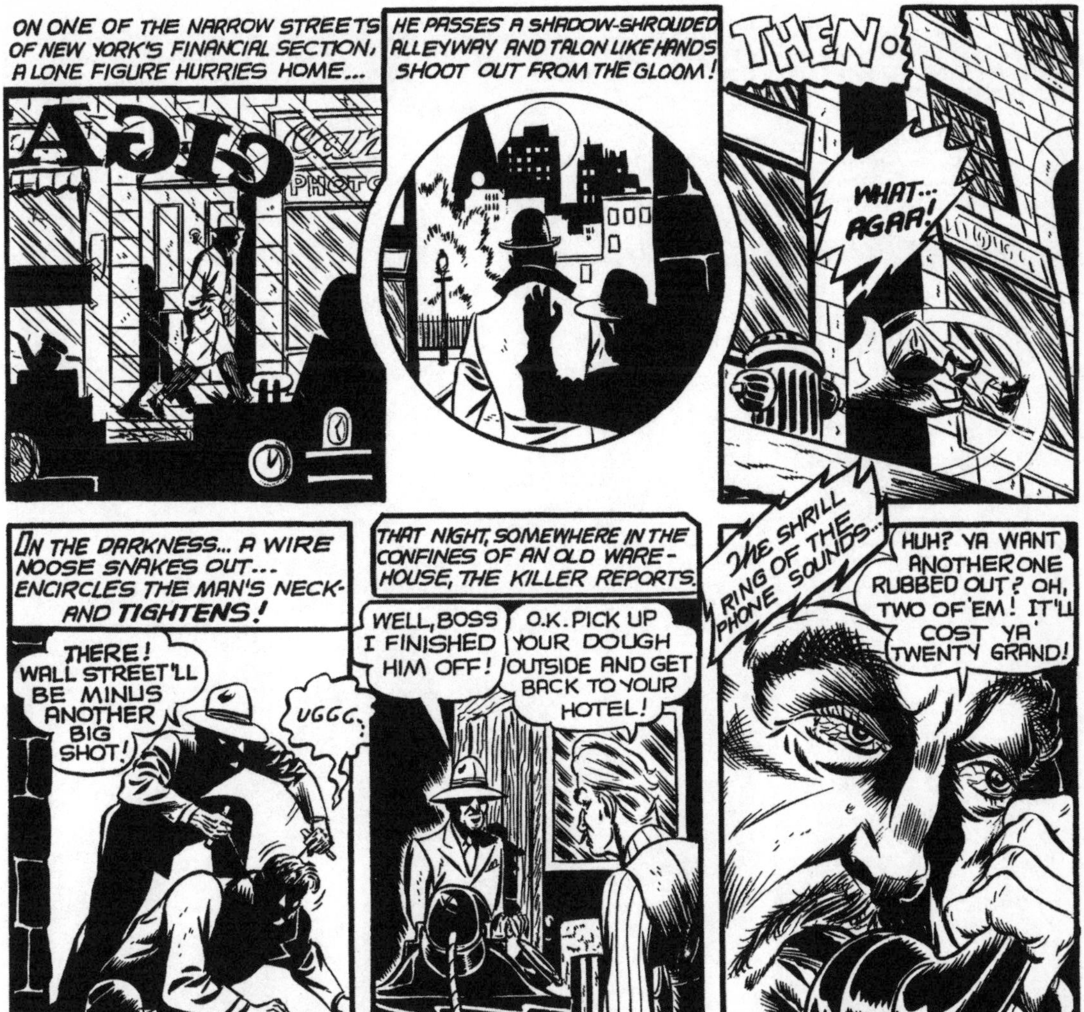

ON ONE OF THE NARROW STREETS OF NEW YORK'S FINANCIAL SECTION, A LONE FIGURE HURRIES HOME...
CIGA
PHOTO
HE PASSES A SHADOW-SHROUDED ALLEYWAY AND TALON LIKE HANDS SHOOT OUT FROM THE GLOOM!
THEN:
WHAT... AGAA!
IN THE DARKNESS... A WIRE NOOSE SNAKES OUT... ENCIRCLES THE MAN'S NECK- AND TIGHTENS!
THERE! WALL STREET'LL BE MINUS ANOTHER BIG SHOT!
UGGG..
THAT NIGHT, SOMEWHERE IN THE CONFINES OF AN OLD WARE-HOUSE, THE KILLER REPORTS.
WELL, BOSS I FINISHED HIM OFF!
O.K. PICK UP YOUR DOUGH OUTSIDE AND GET BACK TO YOUR HOTEL!
THE SHRILL RING OF THE PHONE SOUNDS...
HUH? YA WANT ANOTHER ONE RUBBED OUT? OH, TWO OF 'EM! IT'LL COST YA' TWENTY GRAND!
MEANWHILE, IN UPTOWN MANHATTAN...
GOSH... IF MARTY THE RAT WASN'T SUPPOSED TO BE DEAD, I'D SAY THAT WIRE WORK WAS HIS DOING!
MICHEAL LANCER
DETECTIVE
THE NEW
THIRD WAL
STREET MU
SUDDENLY... THE DOOR BURSTS OPEN! MIKE GOES FOR HIS ROD... BUT IT'S ONLY A GIRL!
PRIVATE
YOU! Y-YOU'RE MIKE LANCER, THE DETECTIVE?
YEAH, BUT GO EASY ON THAT DOOR, SISTER! YOU ALMOST GOT YOURSELF SHOT!

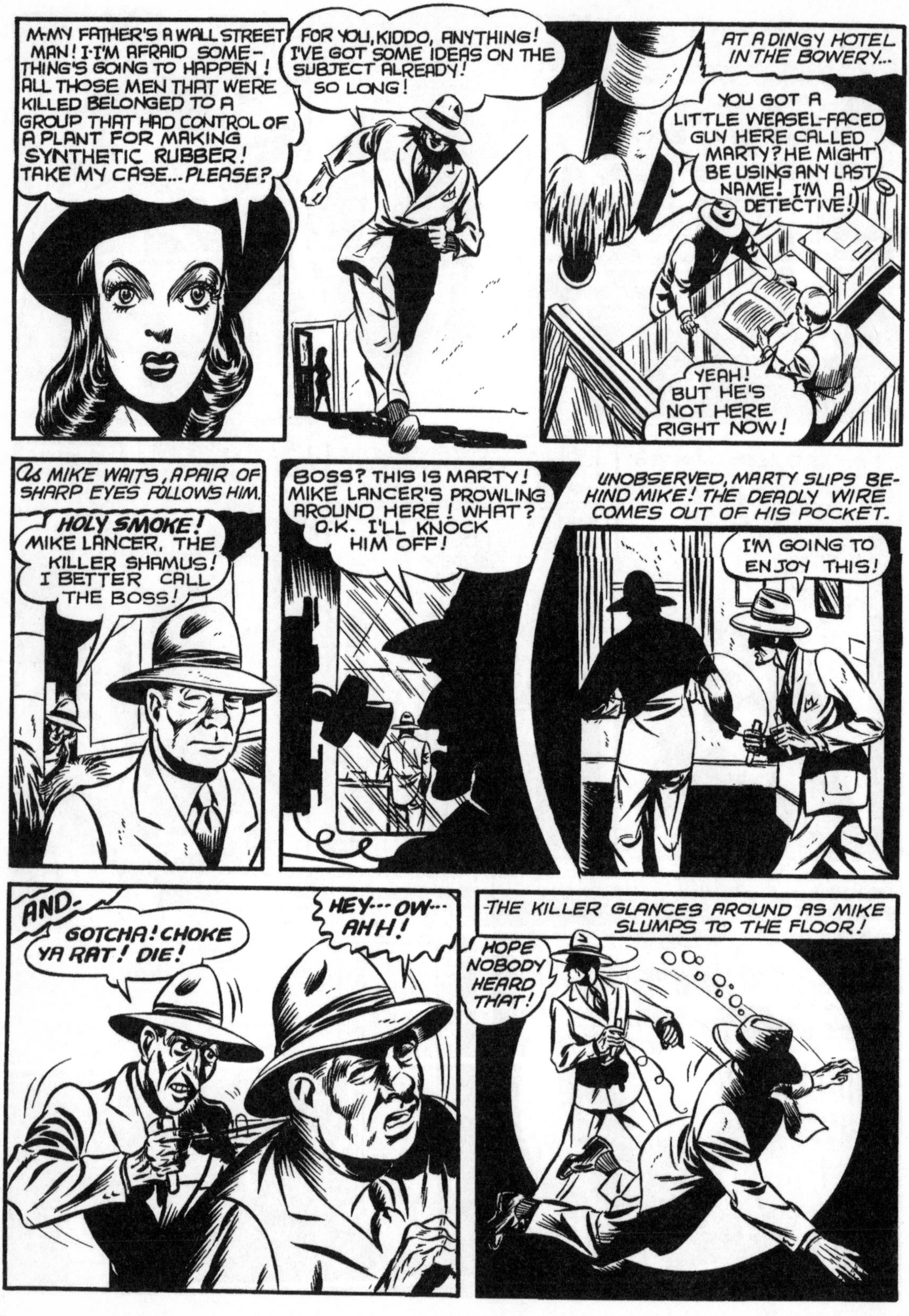
M-MY FATHER'S A WALL STREET MAN! I-I'M AFRAID SOMETHING'S GOING TO HAPPEN! ALL THOSE MEN THAT WERE KILLED BELONGED TO A GROUP THAT HAD CONTROL OF A PLANT FOR MAKING SYNTHETIC RUBBER! TAKE MY CASE...PLEASE?
FOR YOU, KIDDO, ANYTHING! I'VE GOT SOME IDEAS ON THE SUBJECT ALREADY! SO LONG!
AT A DINGY HOTEL IN THE BOWERY...
YOU GOT A LITTLE WEASEL-FACED GUY HERE CALLED MARTY? HE MIGHT BE USING ANY LAST NAME! I'M A DETECTIVE!
YEAH! BUT HE'S NOT HERE RIGHT NOW!
AS MIKE WAITS, A PAIR OF SHARP EYES FOLLOWS HIM.
HOLY SMOKE! MIKE LANCER, THE KILLER SHAMUS! I BETTER CALL THE BOSS!
BOSS? THIS IS MARTY! MIKE LANCER'S PROWLING AROUND HERE! WHAT? O.K. I'LL KNOCK HIM OFF!
UNOBSERVED, MARTY SLIPS BEHIND MIKE! THE DEADLY WIRE COMES OUT OF HIS POCKET.
I'M GOING TO ENJOY THIS!
AND-
GOTCHA! CHOKE YA RAT! DIE!
HEY--- OW--- AHH!
-THE KILLER GLANCES AROUND AS MIKE SLUMPS TO THE FLOOR!
HOPE NOBODY HEARD THAT!

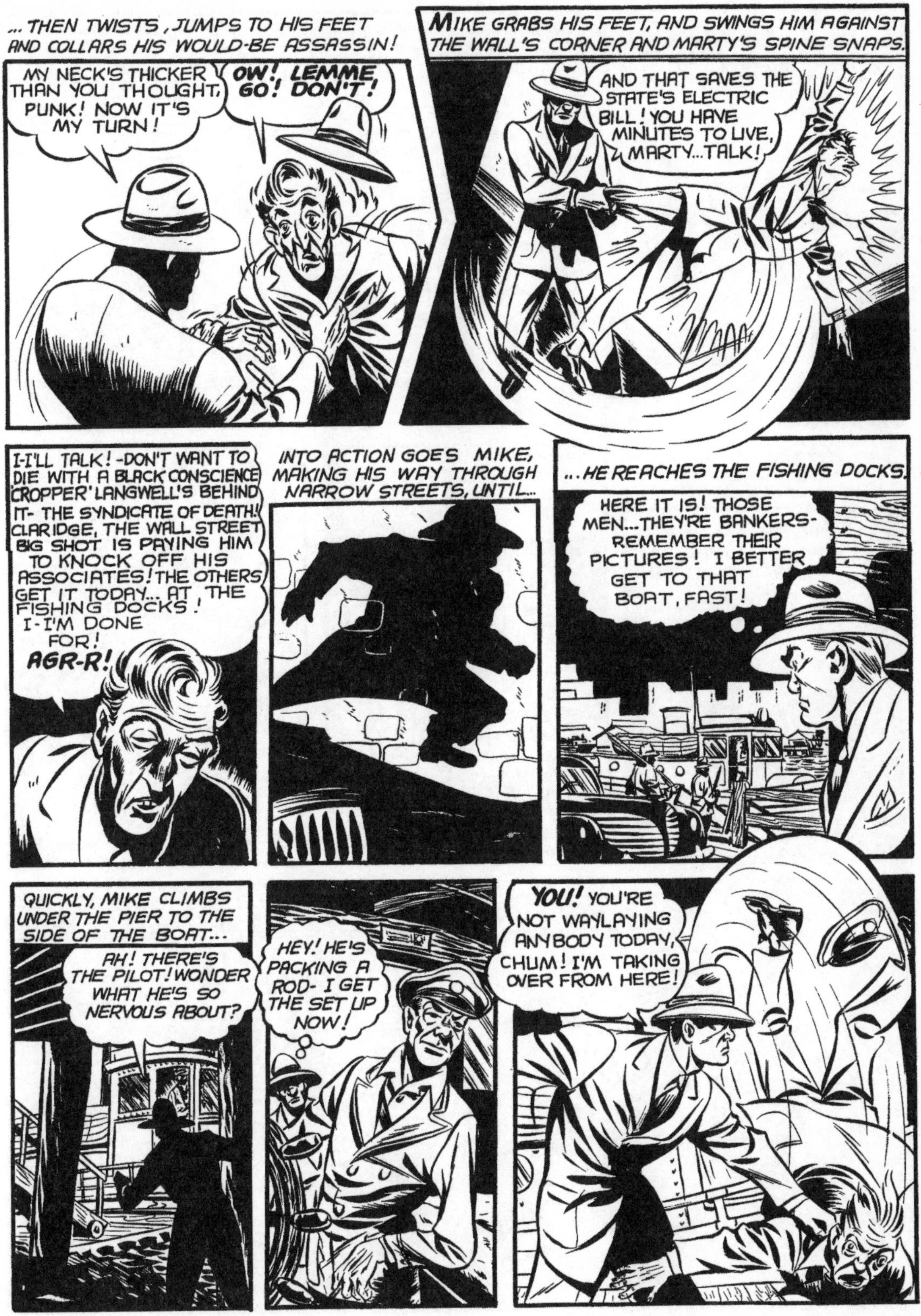
...THEN TWISTS, JUMPS TO HIS FEET AND COLLARS HIS WOULD-BE ASSASSIN!
MY NECK'S THICKER THAN YOU THOUGHT, PUNK! NOW IT'S MY TURN!
OW! LEMME GO! DON'T!
MIKE GRABS HIS FEET, AND SWINGS HIM AGAINST THE WALL'S CORNER AND MARTY'S SPINE SNAPS.
AND THAT SAVES THE STATE'S ELECTRIC BILL! YOU HAVE MINUTES TO LIVE, MARTY...TALK!
I-I'LL TALK! -DON'T WANT TO DIE WITH A BLACK CONSCIENCE 'CROPPER' LANGWELL'S BEHIND IT- THE SYNDICATE OF DEATH! CLARIDGE, THE WALL STREET BIG SHOT IS PAYING HIM TO KNOCK OFF HIS ASSOCIATES! THE OTHERS GET IT TODAY... AT THE FISHING DOCKS! I-I'M DONE FOR! AGR-R!
INTO ACTION GOES MIKE, MAKING HIS WAY THROUGH NARROW STREETS, UNTIL...
...HE REACHES THE FISHING DOCKS.
HERE IT IS! THOSE MEN...THEY'RE BANKERS- REMEMBER THEIR PICTURES! I BETTER GET TO THAT BOAT, FAST!
QUICKLY, MIKE CLIMBS UNDER THE PIER TO THE SIDE OF THE BOAT...
AH! THERE'S THE PILOT! WONDER WHAT HE'S SO NERVOUS ABOUT?
HEY! HE'S PACKING A ROD- I GET THE SET UP NOW!
YOU! YOU'RE NOT WAYLAYING ANYBODY TODAY, CHUM! I'M TAKING OVER FROM HERE!

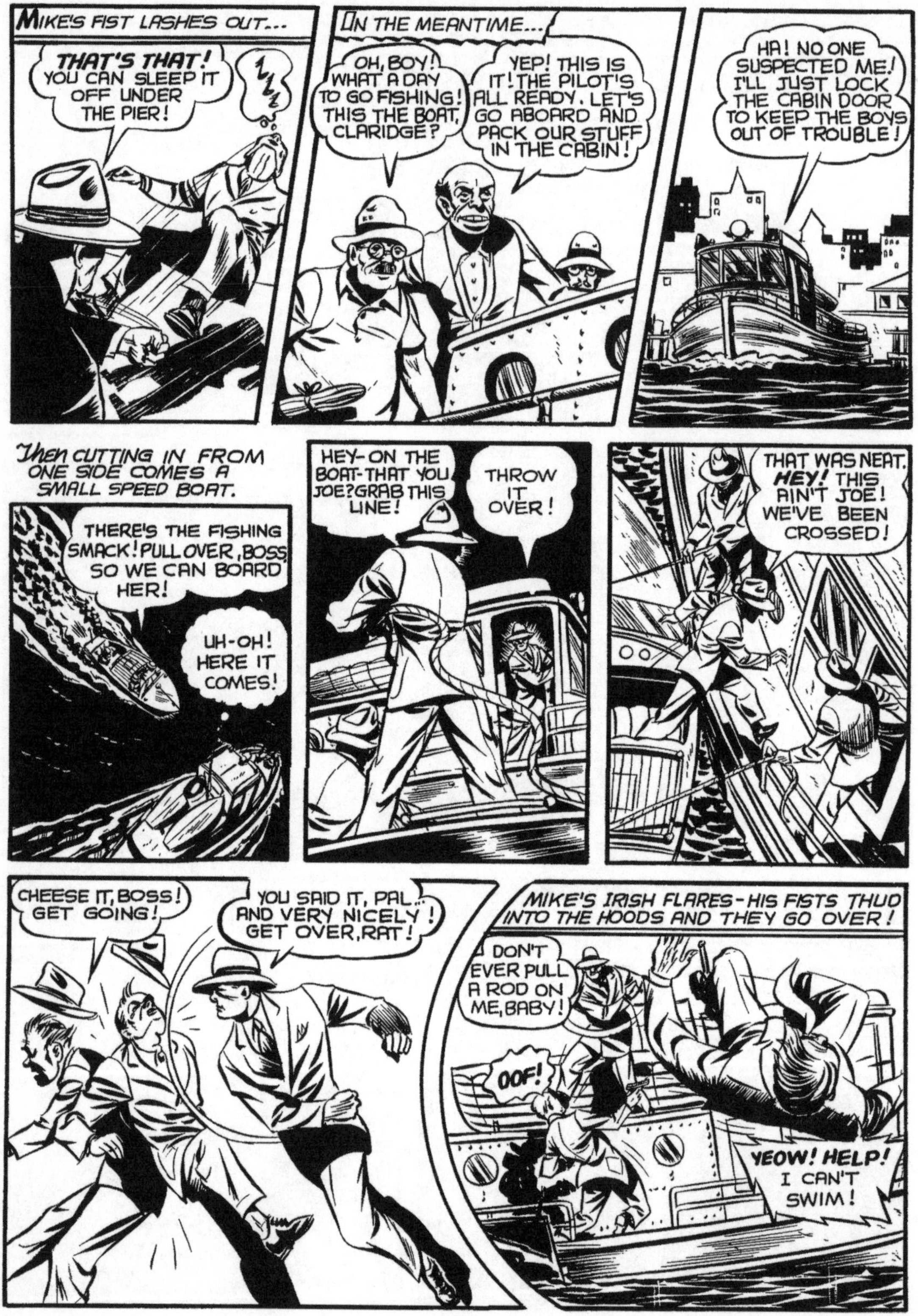
MIKE'S FIST LASHES OUT...
THAT'S THAT! YOU CAN SLEEP IT OFF UNDER THE PIER!
IN THE MEANTIME...
OH, BOY! WHAT A DAY TO GO FISHING! THIS THE BOAT, CLARIDGE?
YEP! THIS IS IT! THE PILOT'S ALL READY. LET'S GO ABOARD AND PACK OUR STUFF IN THE CABIN!
HA! NO ONE SUSPECTED ME! I'LL JUST LOCK THE CABIN DOOR TO KEEP THE BOYS OUT OF TROUBLE!
Then CUTTING IN FROM ONE SIDE COMES A SMALL SPEED BOAT.
THERE'S THE FISHING SMACK! PULL OVER, BOSS, SO WE CAN BOARD HER!
UH-OH! HERE IT COMES!
HEY- ON THE BOAT- THAT YOU JOE? GRAB THIS LINE!
THROW IT OVER!
THAT WAS NEAT. HEY! THIS AIN'T JOE! WE'VE BEEN CROSSED!
CHEESE IT, BOSS! GET GOING!
YOU SAID IT, PAL... AND VERY NICELY! GET OVER, RAT!
MIKE'S IRISH FLARES- HIS FISTS THUD INTO THE HOODS AND THEY GO OVER!
DON'T EVER PULL A ROD ON ME, BABY!
OOF!
YEOW! HELP! I CAN'T SWIM!

"CROPPER" LANGWELL "JUICES" THE ENGINE....THE SPEEDBOAT PULLS AWAY, BUT...

THAT SQUIRT ISN'T GOING TO GET FAR THIS TIME!

BANG

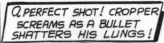

Q. PERFECT SHOT! CROPPER SCREAMS AS A BULLET SHATTERS HIS LUNGS!

EIYII!

THE BOAT SWERVES, HEADS TOWARD AN OLD BARGE, THEN...

CRASH

MIKE STOPS THE BOAT, OPENS THE CABIN AND ENTERS.

HEY--- WHAT DO YOU WANT! WHAT WAS ALL THAT RACKET?

I WANT A KILLER, GENTLEMEN! ONE THAT'S BEEN TRYING TO RUB YOU MEN OUT!

AND YOU, CLARIDGE ARE THE ONE I MEAN!

WHY YOU... I'LL BLAST YOUR FILTHY HEAD OFF!

BUT MIKE FALLS TO THE SIDE, WHIPS OUT HIS AUTOMATIC AND FIRES IT!

YOU'VE DONE ENOUGH KILLING, SMART GUY! NOW TAKE IT YOURSELF!

AND THAT, GENTLEMEN IS THAT! YOUR DAUGHTER, MR. LANE IS THE ONE THAT HIRED ME! YOU OWE HER A VOTE OF THANKS!

WE CERTAINLY DO! AND YOU, TOO! JOIN US FOR A LITTLE FISHING, WON'T YOU?

SO... THEY ALL SETTLE THEMSELVES COMFORTABLY, BUT...

OH, GOSH! I KNEW IT WAS TOO GOOD TO LAST! HERE COME THE COPS AND A MILLION QUESTIONS... JUST WHEN I'M GETTING A BITE!

THE END

"How do I let myself
get feeling like this?
Why...
Better men than you
have begged me to love them."

The first movie adaptation of *I, The Jury*, the
paperback bestseller which had introduced
Mike Hammer to the American public, was
released in 1953. It was perfect timing for
Spillane and Hammer to return to their roots
in a spin-off newspaper strip. The brooding
first-person narration and perverse sexual
dynamics of the novels translate surprisingly
intact to full-page Sunday serials, plotted and
scripted by Spillane himself. *Dark City* became
his final continuity, when a scene of a woman
in a negligé, bound and gagged, enflamed
moral guardians and led to the strip's abrupt
cancellation in 1954. Disappointed, artist Ed
Robbins quit the industry, drawing only a
handful of later comic books. Considering the
censorious climate of the times, it is a wonder
that Hammer made it onto the family funny
pages at all and turned out so well.

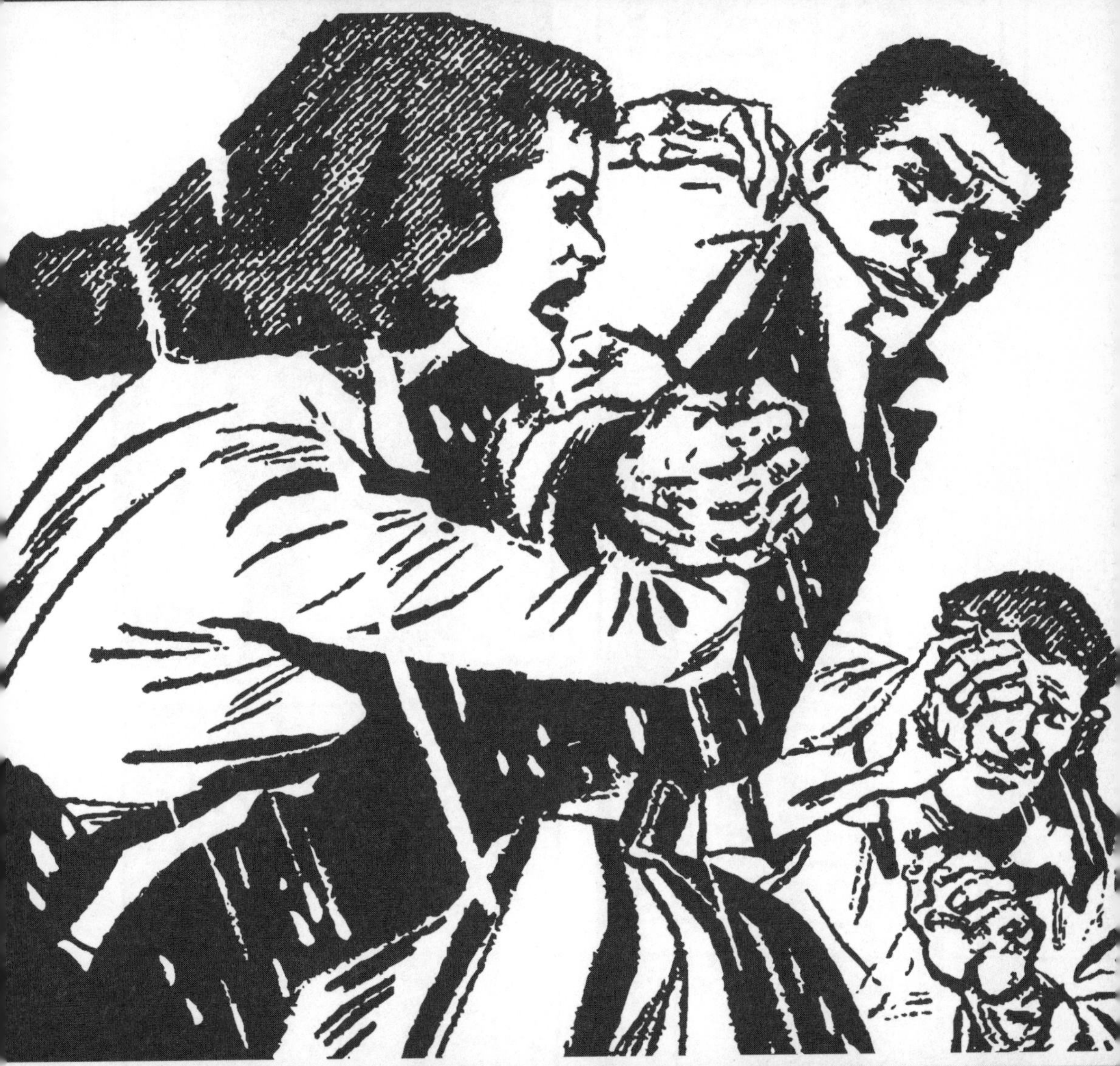

Mike Hammer: Dark City

Mickey Spillane (script) and Ed Robbins (art) 1954

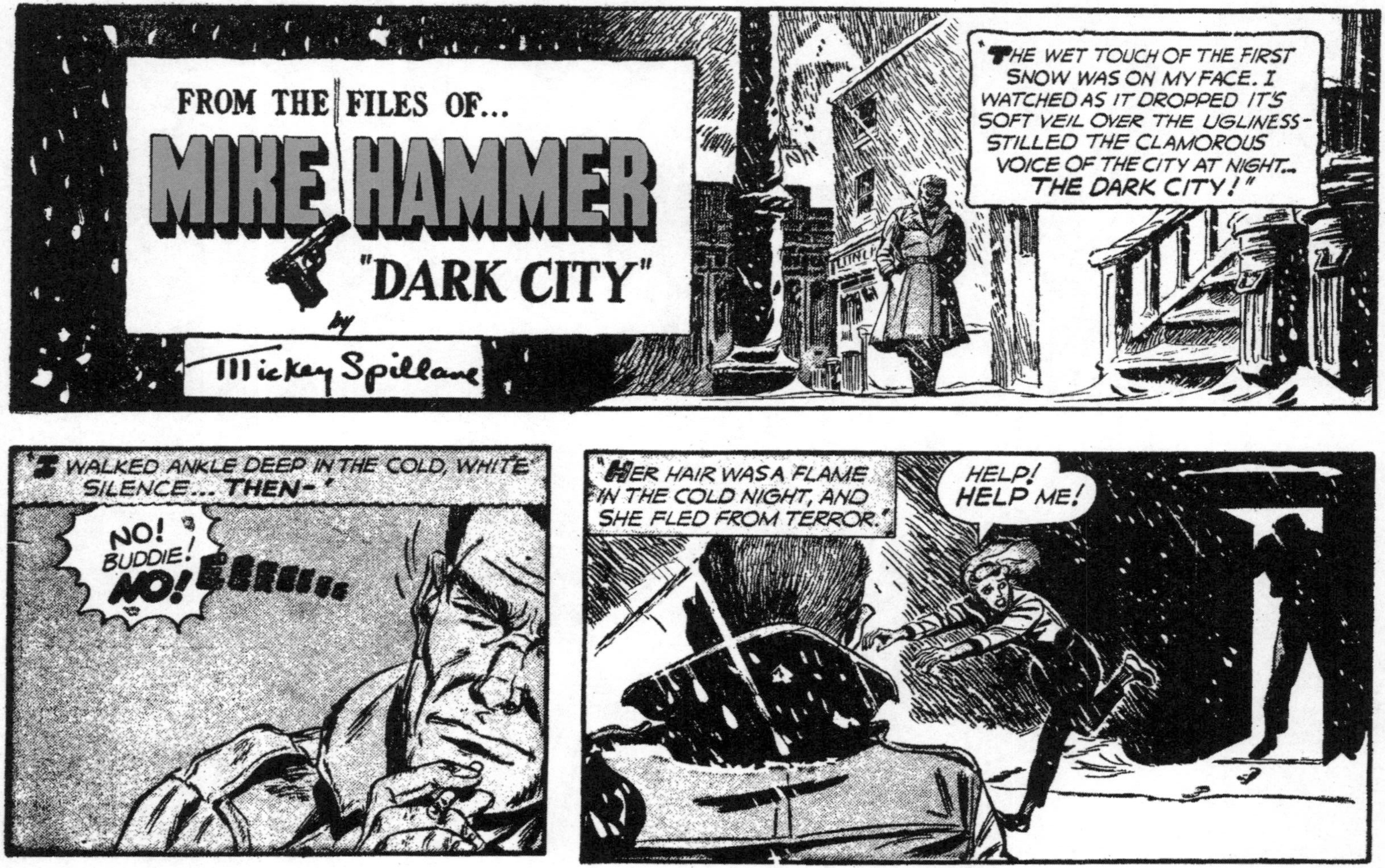

FROM THE FILES OF...
MIKE HAMMER
"DARK CITY"
by Mickey Spillane
"THE WET TOUCH OF THE FIRST SNOW WAS ON MY FACE. I WATCHED AS IT DROPPED IT'S SOFT VEIL OVER THE UGLINESS-STILLED THE CLAMOROUS VOICE OF THE CITY AT NIGHT... THE DARK CITY!"
"I WALKED ANKLE DEEP IN THE COLD, WHITE SILENCE... THEN-"
NO! BUDDIE! NO!
"HER HAIR WAS A FLAME IN THE COLD NIGHT, AND SHE FLED FROM TERROR."
HELP! HELP ME!

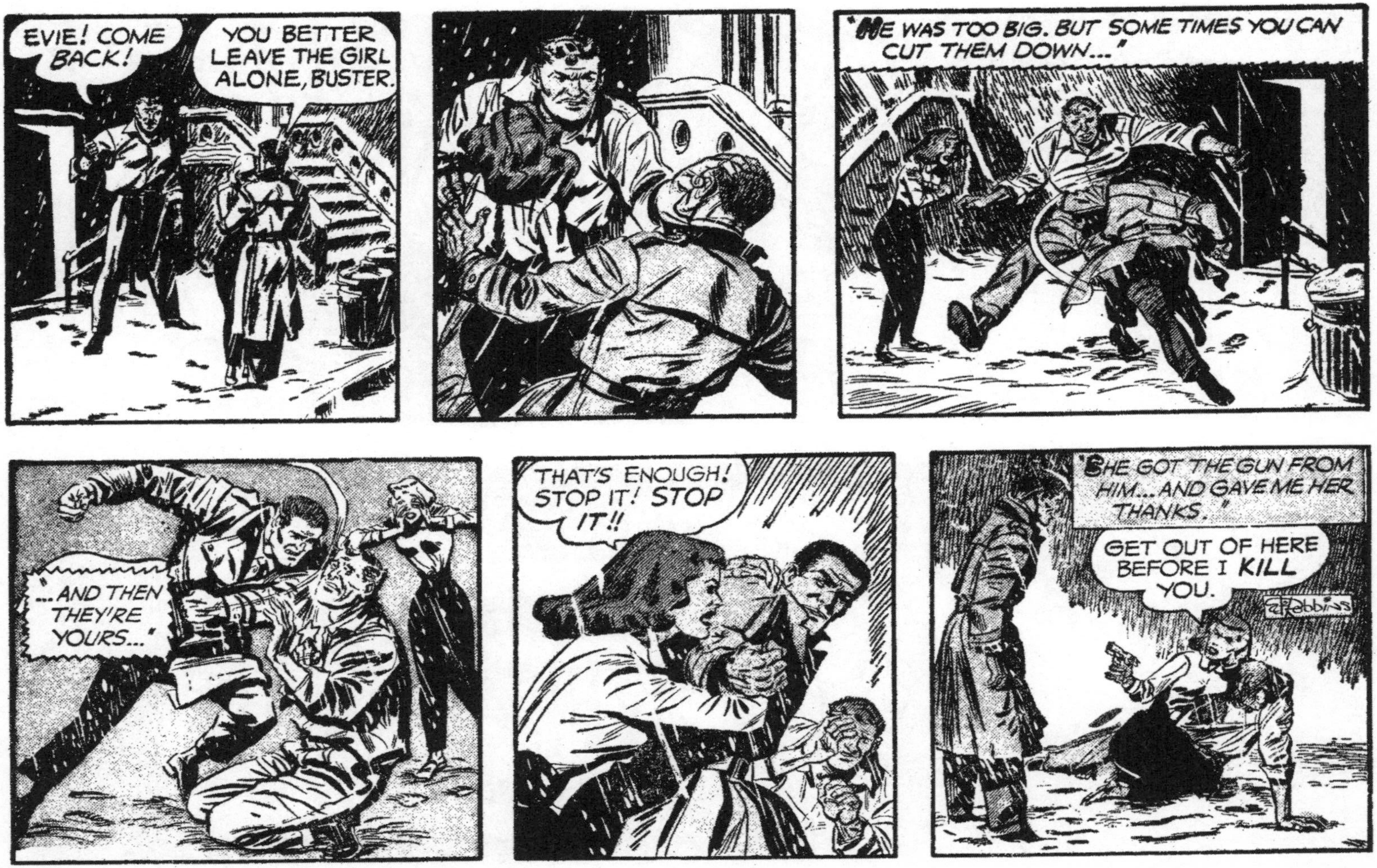
EVIE! COME BACK!
YOU BETTER LEAVE THE GIRL ALONE, BUSTER.
"HE WAS TOO BIG. BUT SOME TIMES YOU CAN CUT THEM DOWN..."
"...AND THEN THEY'RE YOURS..."
THAT'S ENOUGH! STOP IT! STOP IT!!
"SHE GOT THE GUN FROM HIM... AND GAVE ME HER THANKS."
GET OUT OF HERE BEFORE I KILL YOU.
Robbins

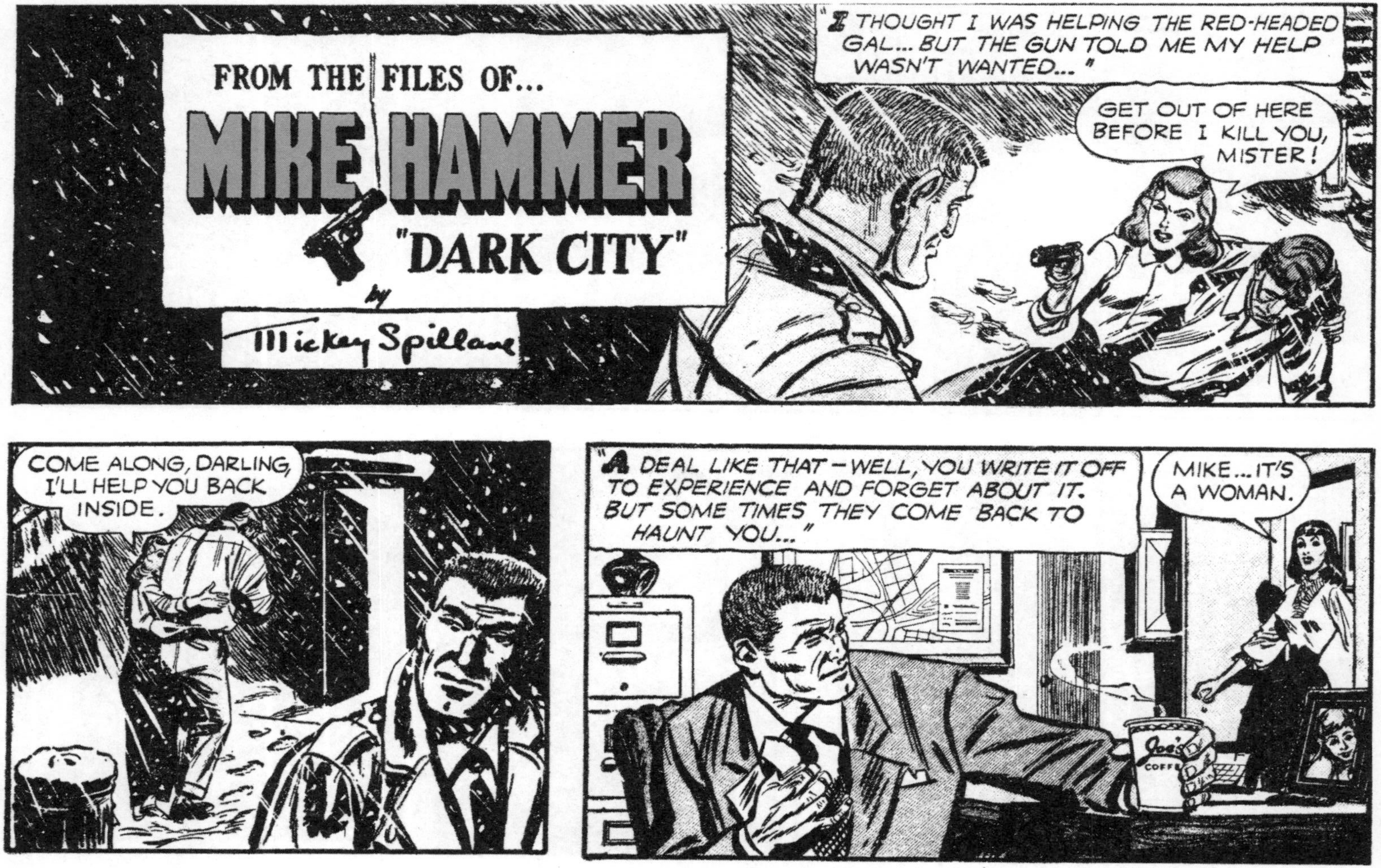
FROM THE FILES OF...
MIKE HAMMER
"DARK CITY"
by Mickey Spillane
"I THOUGHT I WAS HELPING THE RED-HEADED GAL... BUT THE GUN TOLD ME MY HELP WASN'T WANTED..."
GET OUT OF HERE BEFORE I KILL YOU, MISTER!
COME ALONG, DARLING, I'LL HELP YOU BACK INSIDE.
"A DEAL LIKE THAT—WELL, YOU WRITE IT OFF TO EXPERIENCE AND FORGET ABOUT IT. BUT SOME TIMES THEY COME BACK TO HAUNT YOU..."
MIKE... IT'S A WOMAN.

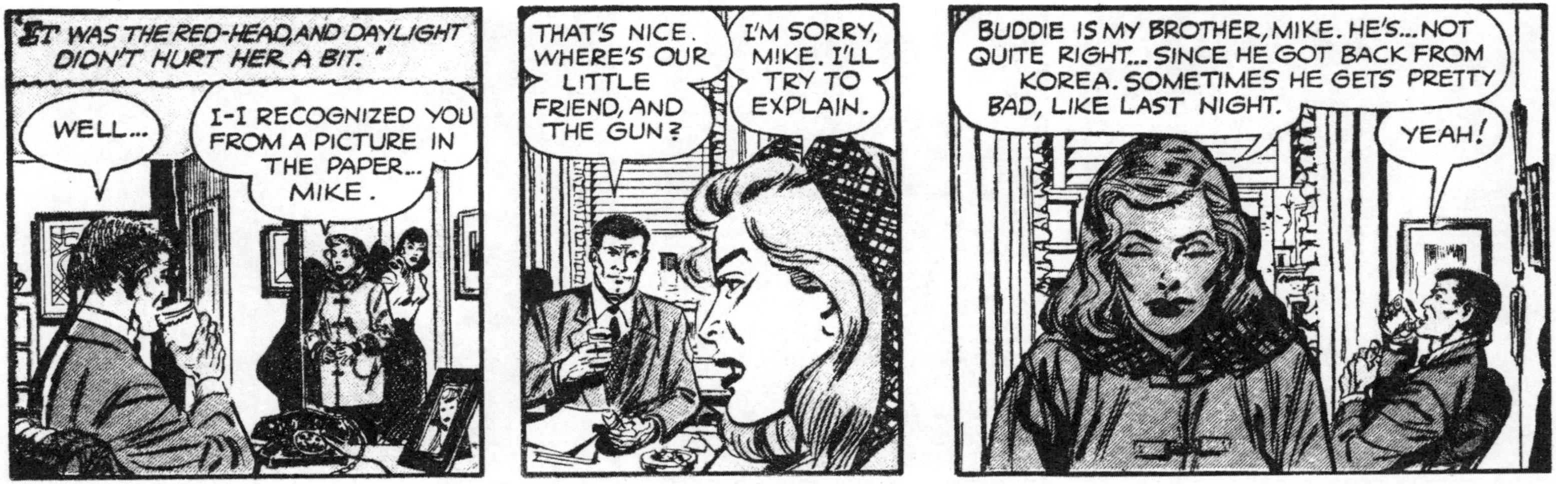
"IT WAS THE RED-HEAD, AND DAYLIGHT DIDN'T HURT HER A BIT."
WELL...
I-I RECOGNIZED YOU FROM A PICTURE IN THE PAPER... MIKE.
THAT'S NICE. WHERE'S OUR LITTLE FRIEND, AND THE GUN?
I'M SORRY, MIKE. I'LL TRY TO EXPLAIN.
BUDDIE IS MY BROTHER, MIKE. HE'S... NOT QUITE RIGHT... SINCE HE GOT BACK FROM KOREA. SOMETIMES HE GETS PRETTY BAD, LIKE LAST NIGHT.
YEAH!

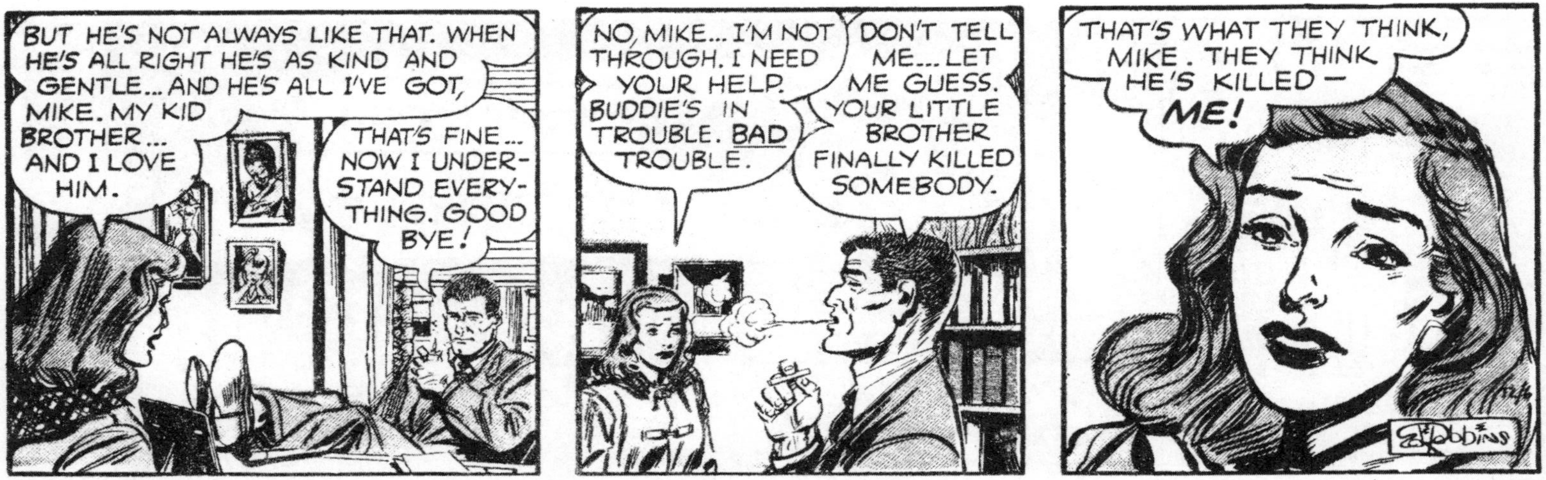
BUT HE'S NOT ALWAYS LIKE THAT. WHEN HE'S ALL RIGHT HE'S AS KIND AND GENTLE... AND HE'S ALL I'VE GOT, MIKE. MY KID BROTHER... AND I LOVE HIM.
THAT'S FINE... NOW I UNDER-STAND EVERY-THING. GOOD BYE!
NO, MIKE... I'M NOT THROUGH. I NEED YOUR HELP. BUDDIE'S IN TROUBLE. BAD TROUBLE.
DON'T TELL ME... LET ME GUESS. YOUR LITTLE BROTHER FINALLY KILLED SOMEBODY.
THAT'S WHAT THEY THINK, MIKE. THEY THINK HE'S KILLED — ME!

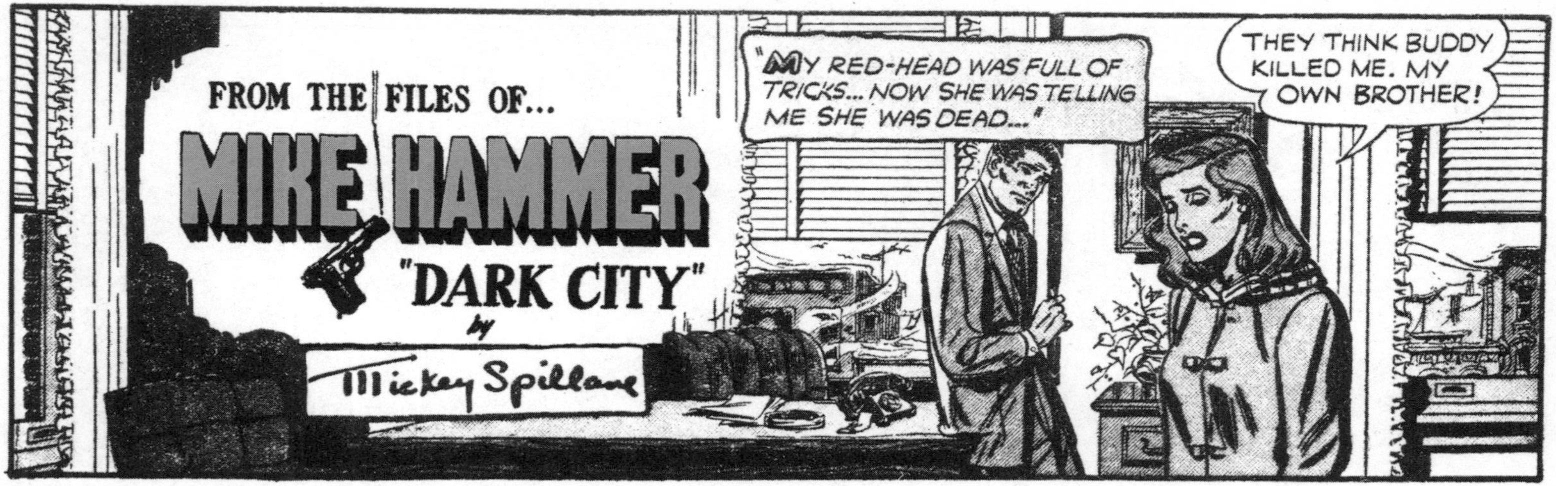
FROM THE FILES OF...
MIKE HAMMER
"DARK CITY"
by
Mickey Spillane
"MY RED-HEAD WAS FULL OF TRICKS... NOW SHE WAS TELLING ME SHE WAS DEAD..."
THEY THINK BUDDY KILLED ME. MY OWN BROTHER!

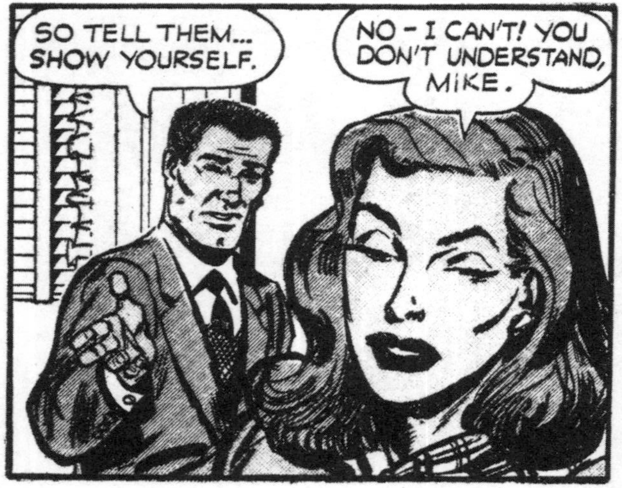
SO TELL THEM... SHOW YOURSELF.
NO - I CAN'T! YOU DON'T UNDERSTAND, MIKE.

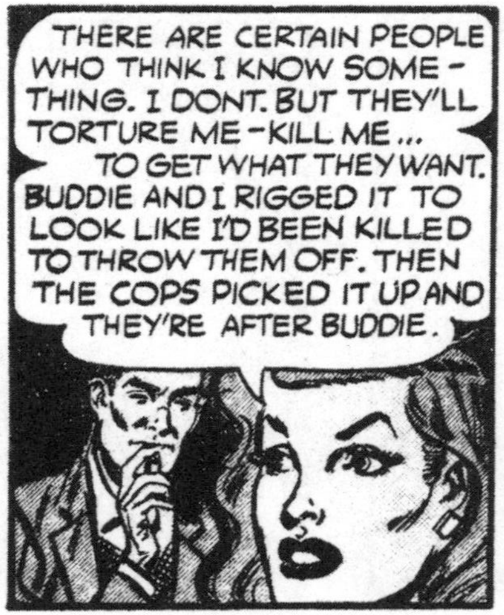
THERE ARE CERTAIN PEOPLE WHO THINK I KNOW SOME - THING. I DONT. BUT THEY'LL TORTURE ME - KILL ME... TO GET WHAT THEY WANT. BUDDIE AND I RIGGED IT TO LOOK LIKE I'D BEEN KILLED TO THROW THEM OFF. THEN THE COPS PICKED IT UP AND THEY'RE AFTER BUDDIE.

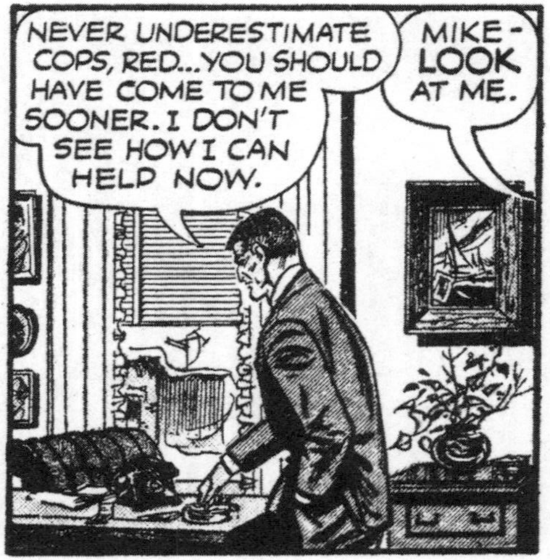
NEVER UNDERESTIMATE COPS, RED... YOU SHOULD HAVE COME TO ME SOONER. I DON'T SEE HOW I CAN HELP NOW.
MIKE - LOOK AT ME.

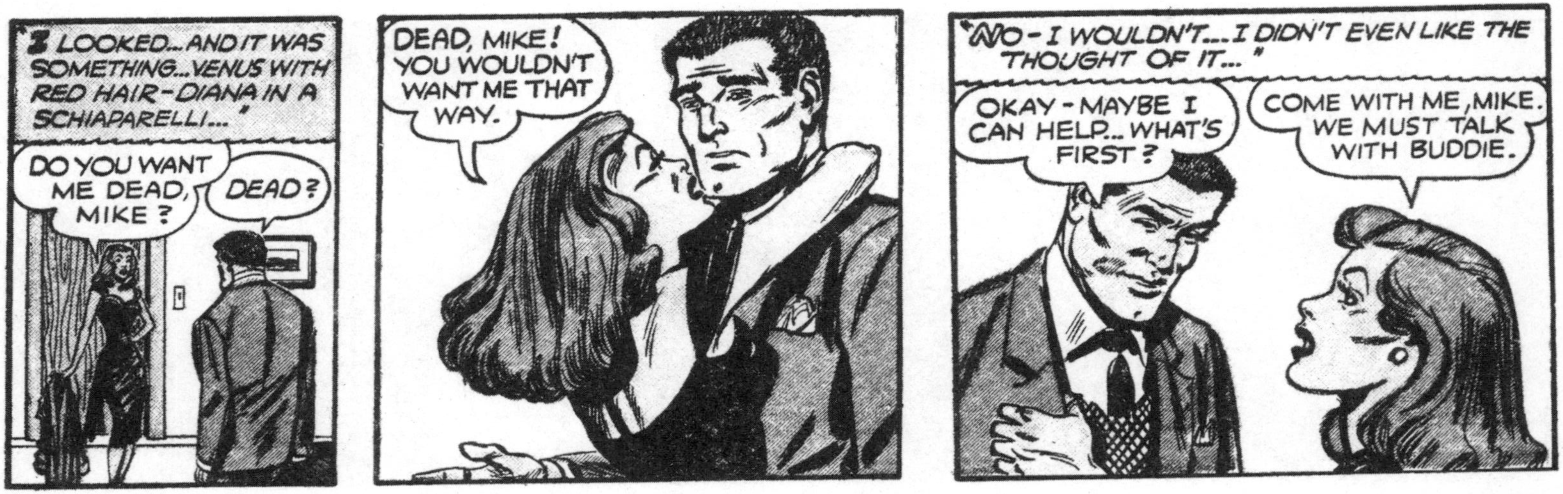
"I LOOKED... AND IT WAS SOMETHING... VENUS WITH RED HAIR-DIANA IN A SCHIAPARELLI..."
DO YOU WANT ME DEAD, MIKE?
DEAD?
DEAD, MIKE! YOU WOULDN'T WANT ME THAT WAY.
"NO-I WOULDN'T... I DIDN'T EVEN LIKE THE THOUGHT OF IT..."
OKAY-MAYBE I CAN HELP... WHAT'S FIRST?
COME WITH ME, MIKE. WE MUST TALK WITH BUDDIE.
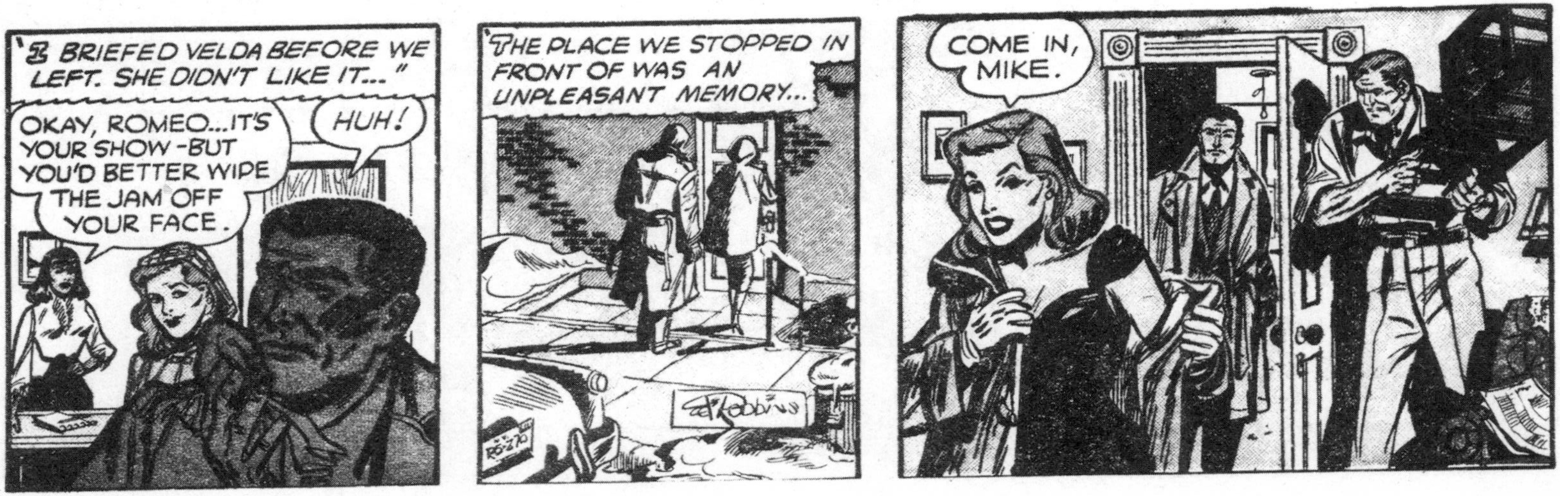
"I BRIEFED VELDA BEFORE WE LEFT. SHE DIDN'T LIKE IT..."
OKAY, ROMEO... IT'S YOUR SHOW-BUT YOU'D BETTER WIPE THE JAM OFF YOUR FACE.
HUH!
"THE PLACE WE STOPPED IN FRONT OF WAS AN UNPLEASANT MEMORY..."
COME IN, MIKE.

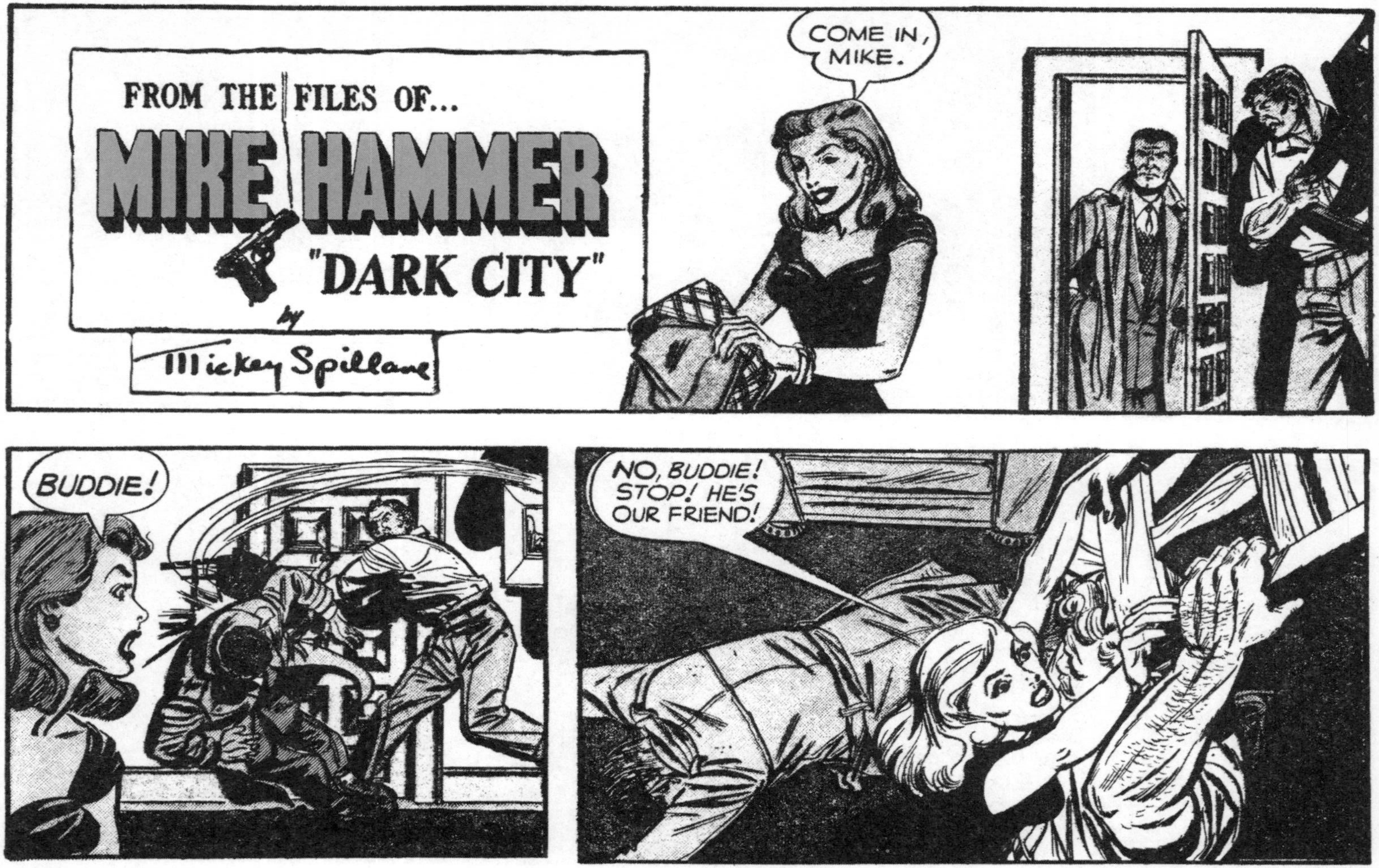
FROM THE FILES OF...
MIKE HAMMER
"DARK CITY"
by Mickey Spillane
COME IN, MIKE.
BUDDIE!
NO, BUDDIE! STOP! HE'S OUR FRIEND!

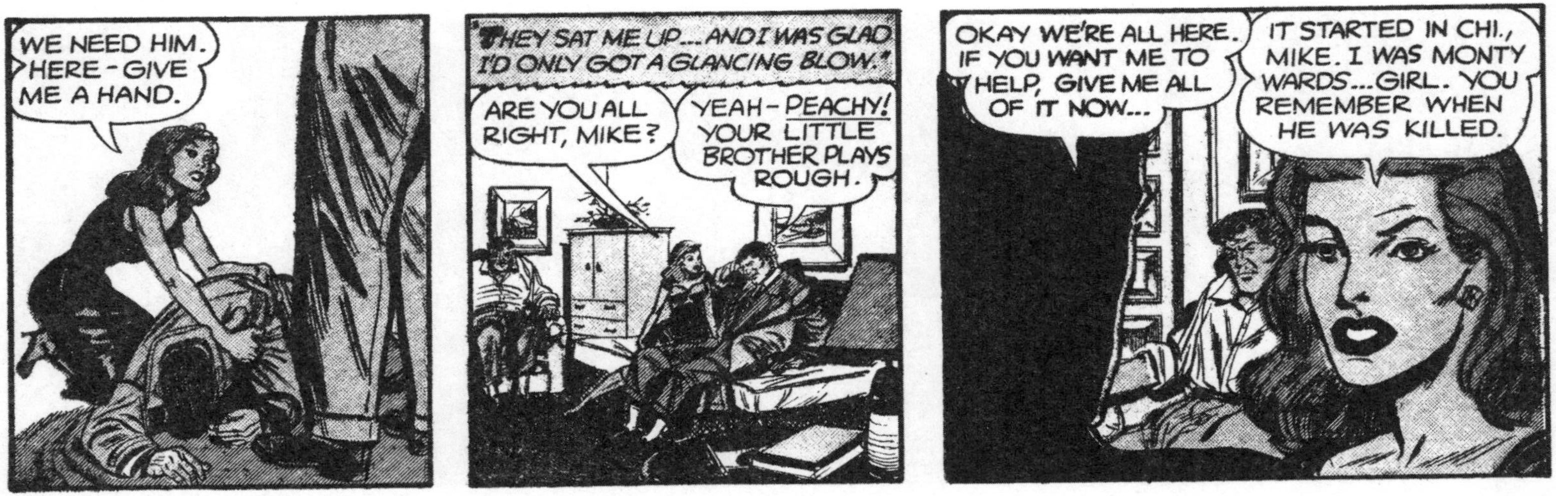
WE NEED HIM. HERE - GIVE ME A HAND.
"THEY SAT ME UP... AND I WAS GLAD I'D ONLY GOT A GLANCING BLOW."
ARE YOU ALL RIGHT, MIKE?
YEAH - PEACHY! YOUR LITTLE BROTHER PLAYS ROUGH.
OKAY WE'RE ALL HERE. IF YOU WANT ME TO HELP, GIVE ME ALL OF IT NOW...
IT STARTED IN CHI., MIKE. I WAS MONTY WARDS... GIRL. YOU REMEMBER WHEN HE WAS KILLED.

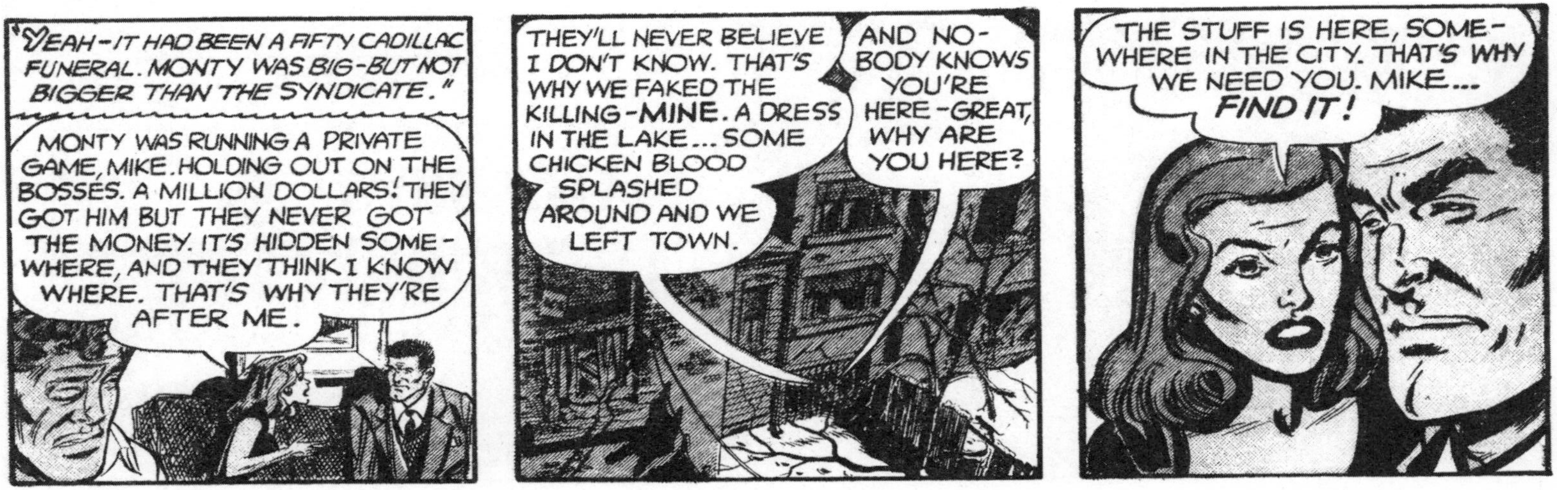
"YEAH - IT HAD BEEN A FIFTY CADILLAC FUNERAL. MONTY WAS BIG - BUT NOT BIGGER THAN THE SYNDICATE."
MONTY WAS RUNNING A PRIVATE GAME, MIKE. HOLDING OUT ON THE BOSSES. A MILLION DOLLARS! THEY GOT HIM BUT THEY NEVER GOT THE MONEY. IT'S HIDDEN SOME-WHERE, AND THEY THINK I KNOW WHERE. THAT'S WHY THEY'RE AFTER ME.
THEY'LL NEVER BELIEVE I DON'T KNOW. THAT'S WHY WE FAKED THE KILLING - MINE. A DRESS IN THE LAKE... SOME CHICKEN BLOOD SPLASHED AROUND AND WE LEFT TOWN.
AND NO-BODY KNOWS YOU'RE HERE - GREAT, WHY ARE YOU HERE?
THE STUFF IS HERE, SOME-WHERE IN THE CITY. THAT'S WHY WE NEED YOU. MIKE... FIND IT!

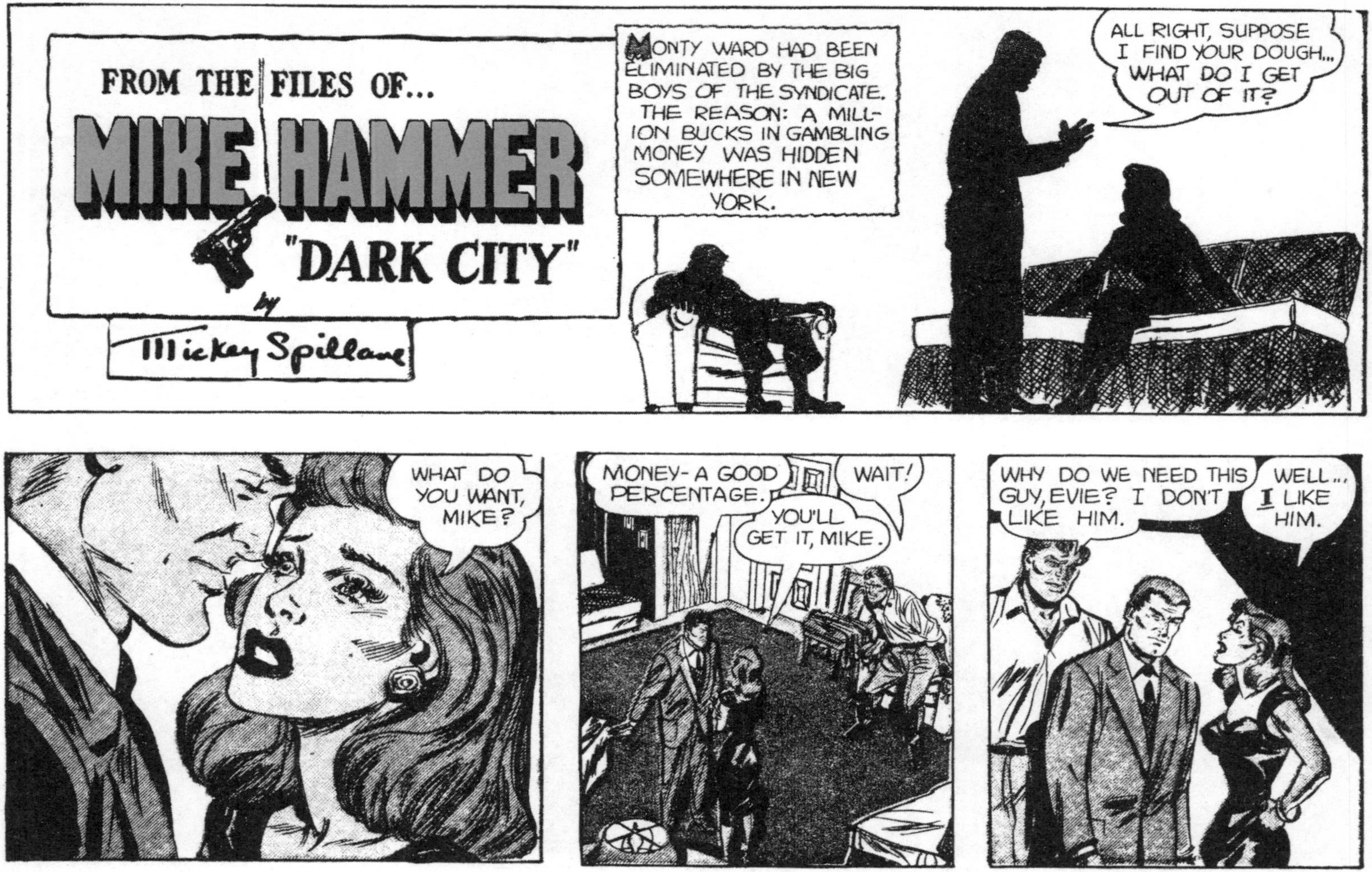
FROM THE FILES OF...
MIKE HAMMER
"DARK CITY"
by Mickey Spillane
MONTY WARD HAD BEEN ELIMINATED BY THE BIG BOYS OF THE SYNDICATE. THE REASON: A MILLION BUCKS IN GAMBLING MONEY WAS HIDDEN SOMEWHERE IN NEW YORK.
ALL RIGHT, SUPPOSE I FIND YOUR DOUGH... WHAT DO I GET OUT OF IT?
WHAT DO YOU WANT, MIKE?
MONEY- A GOOD PERCENTAGE.
YOU'LL GET IT, MIKE.
WAIT!
WHY DO WE NEED THIS GUY, EVIE? I DON'T LIKE HIM.
WELL... I LIKE HIM.

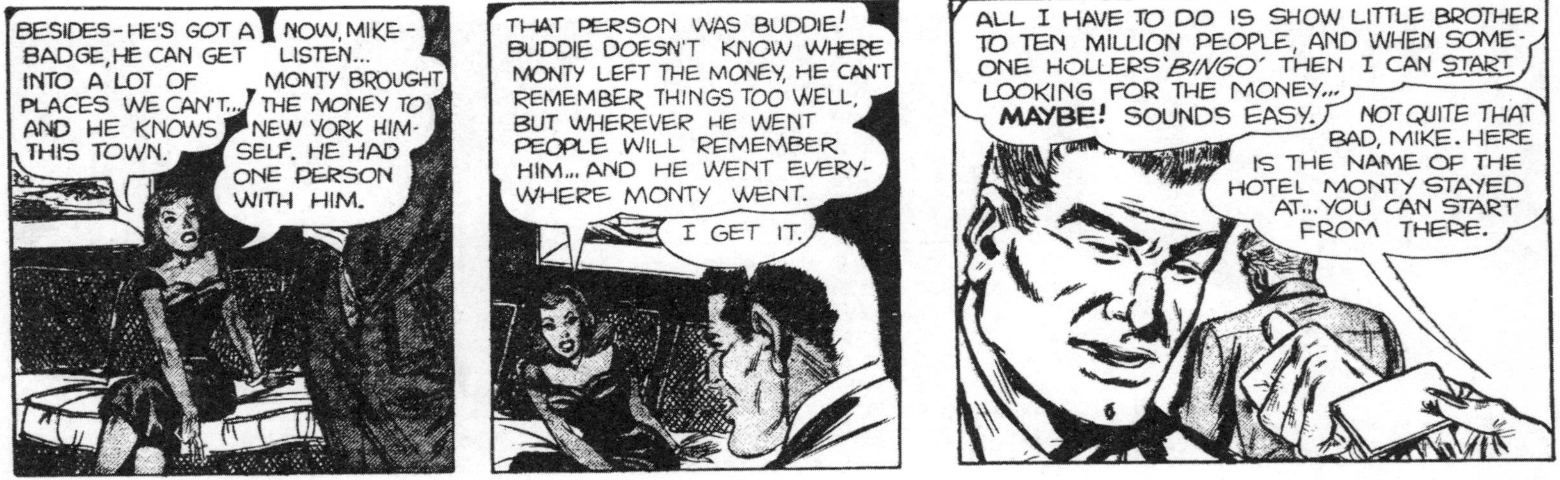
BESIDES - HE'S GOT A BADGE, HE CAN GET INTO A LOT OF PLACES WE CAN'T... AND HE KNOWS THIS TOWN.
NOW, MIKE - LISTEN... MONTY BROUGHT THE MONEY TO NEW YORK HIMSELF. HE HAD ONE PERSON WITH HIM.
THAT PERSON WAS BUDDIE! BUDDIE DOESN'T KNOW WHERE MONTY LEFT THE MONEY, HE CAN'T REMEMBER THINGS TOO WELL, BUT WHEREVER HE WENT PEOPLE WILL REMEMBER HIM... AND HE WENT EVERYWHERE MONTY WENT.
I GET IT.
ALL I HAVE TO DO IS SHOW LITTLE BROTHER TO TEN MILLION PEOPLE, AND WHEN SOMEONE HOLLERS '*BINGO*' THEN I CAN START LOOKING FOR THE MONEY... **MAYBE!** SOUNDS EASY.
NOT QUITE THAT BAD, MIKE. HERE IS THE NAME OF THE HOTEL MONTY STAYED AT... YOU CAN START FROM THERE.

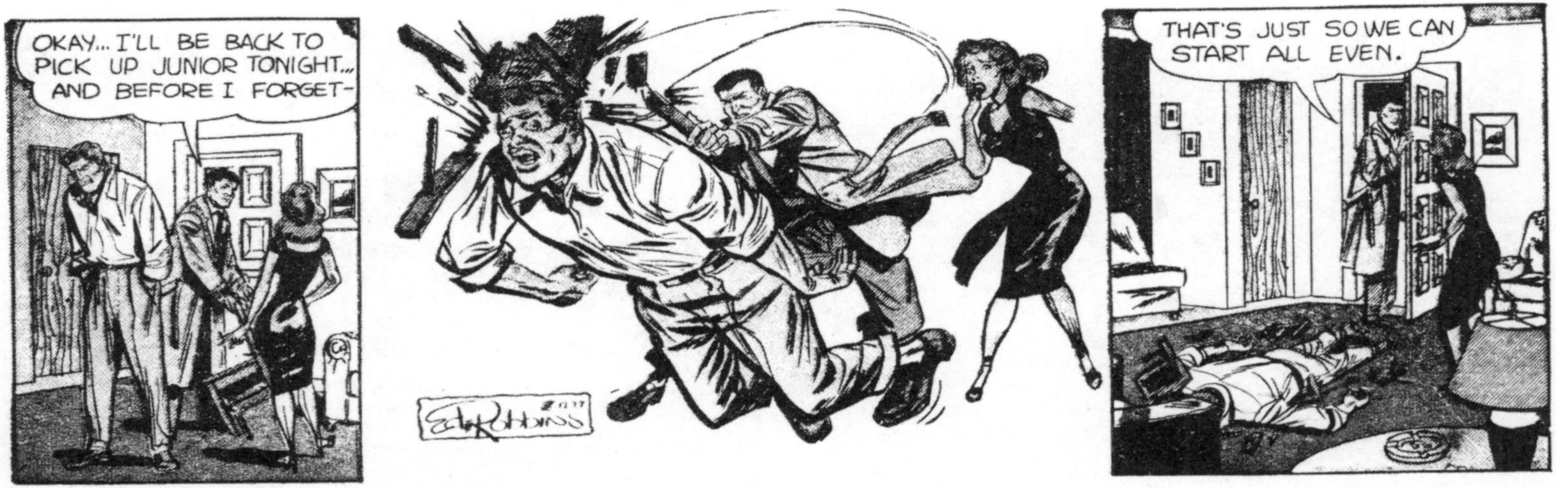
OKAY... I'LL BE BACK TO PICK UP JUNIOR TONIGHT... AND BEFORE I FORGET-
THAT'S JUST SO WE CAN START ALL EVEN.

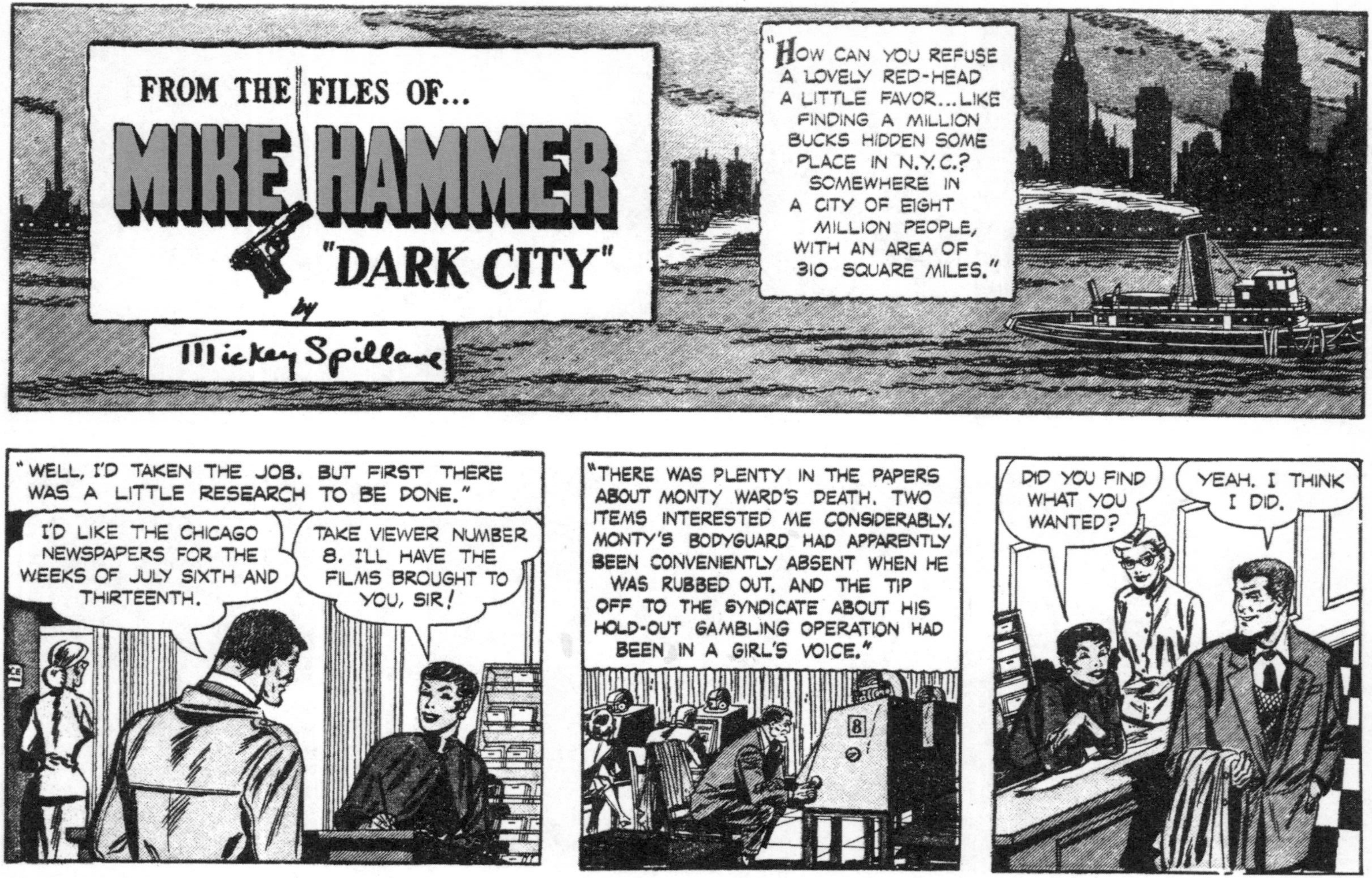
FROM THE FILES OF...
MIKE HAMMER
"DARK CITY"
by Mickey Spillane
"HOW CAN YOU REFUSE A LOVELY RED-HEAD A LITTLE FAVOR...LIKE FINDING A MILLION BUCKS HIDDEN SOME PLACE IN N.Y.C.? SOMEWHERE IN A CITY OF EIGHT MILLION PEOPLE, WITH AN AREA OF 310 SQUARE MILES."
"WELL, I'D TAKEN THE JOB. BUT FIRST THERE WAS A LITTLE RESEARCH TO BE DONE."
I'D LIKE THE CHICAGO NEWSPAPERS FOR THE WEEKS OF JULY SIXTH AND THIRTEENTH.
TAKE VIEWER NUMBER 8. I'LL HAVE THE FILMS BROUGHT TO YOU, SIR!
"THERE WAS PLENTY IN THE PAPERS ABOUT MONTY WARD'S DEATH. TWO ITEMS INTERESTED ME CONSIDERABLY. MONTY'S BODYGUARD HAD APPARENTLY BEEN CONVENIENTLY ABSENT WHEN HE WAS RUBBED OUT. AND THE TIP OFF TO THE SYNDICATE ABOUT HIS HOLD-OUT GAMBLING OPERATION HAD BEEN IN A GIRL'S VOICE."
8
DID YOU FIND WHAT YOU WANTED?
YEAH. I THINK I DID.

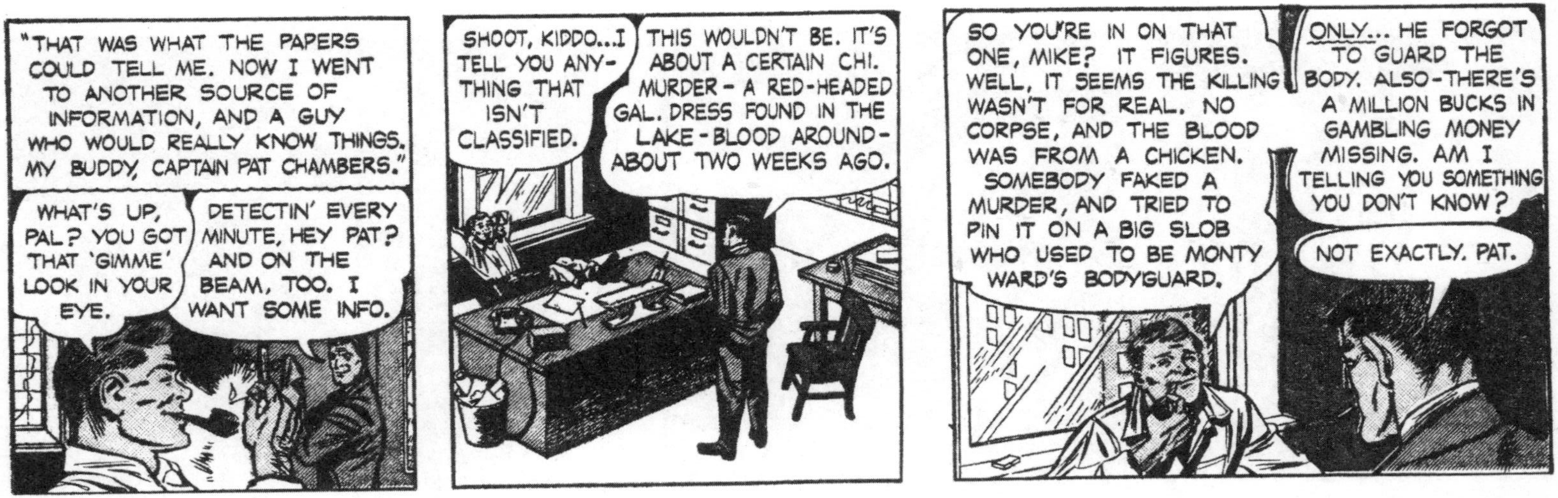
"THAT WAS WHAT THE PAPERS COULD TELL ME. NOW I WENT TO ANOTHER SOURCE OF INFORMATION, AND A GUY WHO WOULD REALLY KNOW THINGS. MY BUDDY, CAPTAIN PAT CHAMBERS."
WHAT'S UP, PAL? YOU GOT THAT 'GIMME' LOOK IN YOUR EYE.
DETECTIN' EVERY MINUTE, HEY PAT? AND ON THE BEAM, TOO. I WANT SOME INFO.
SHOOT, KIDDO...I TELL YOU ANYTHING THAT ISN'T CLASSIFIED.
THIS WOULDN'T BE. IT'S ABOUT A CERTAIN CHI. MURDER - A RED-HEADED GAL. DRESS FOUND IN THE LAKE - BLOOD AROUND - ABOUT TWO WEEKS AGO.
SO YOU'RE IN ON THAT ONE, MIKE? IT FIGURES. WELL, IT SEEMS THE KILLING WASN'T FOR REAL. NO CORPSE, AND THE BLOOD WAS FROM A CHICKEN. SOMEBODY FAKED A MURDER, AND TRIED TO PIN IT ON A BIG SLOB WHO USED TO BE MONTY WARD'S BODYGUARD.
ONLY... HE FORGOT TO GUARD THE BODY. ALSO - THERE'S A MILLION BUCKS IN GAMBLING MONEY MISSING. AM I TELLING YOU SOMETHING YOU DON'T KNOW?
NOT EXACTLY. PAT.

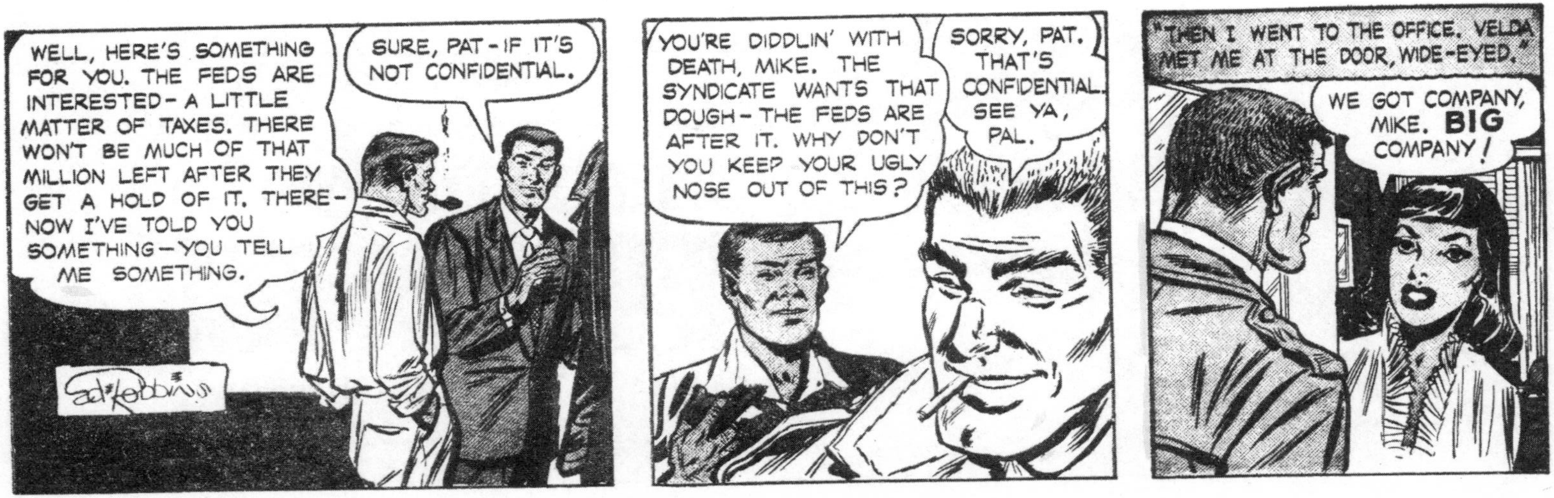
WELL, HERE'S SOMETHING FOR YOU. THE FEDS ARE INTERESTED - A LITTLE MATTER OF TAXES. THERE WON'T BE MUCH OF THAT MILLION LEFT AFTER THEY GET A HOLD OF IT. THERE - NOW I'VE TOLD YOU SOMETHING - YOU TELL ME SOMETHING.
SURE, PAT - IF IT'S NOT CONFIDENTIAL.
Ed Robbins
YOU'RE DIDDLIN' WITH DEATH, MIKE. THE SYNDICATE WANTS THAT DOUGH - THE FEDS ARE AFTER IT. WHY DON'T YOU KEEP YOUR UGLY NOSE OUT OF THIS?
SORRY, PAT. THAT'S CONFIDENTIAL. SEE YA, PAL.
"THEN I WENT TO THE OFFICE. VELDA MET ME AT THE DOOR, WIDE-EYED."
WE GOT COMPANY, MIKE. BIG COMPANY!

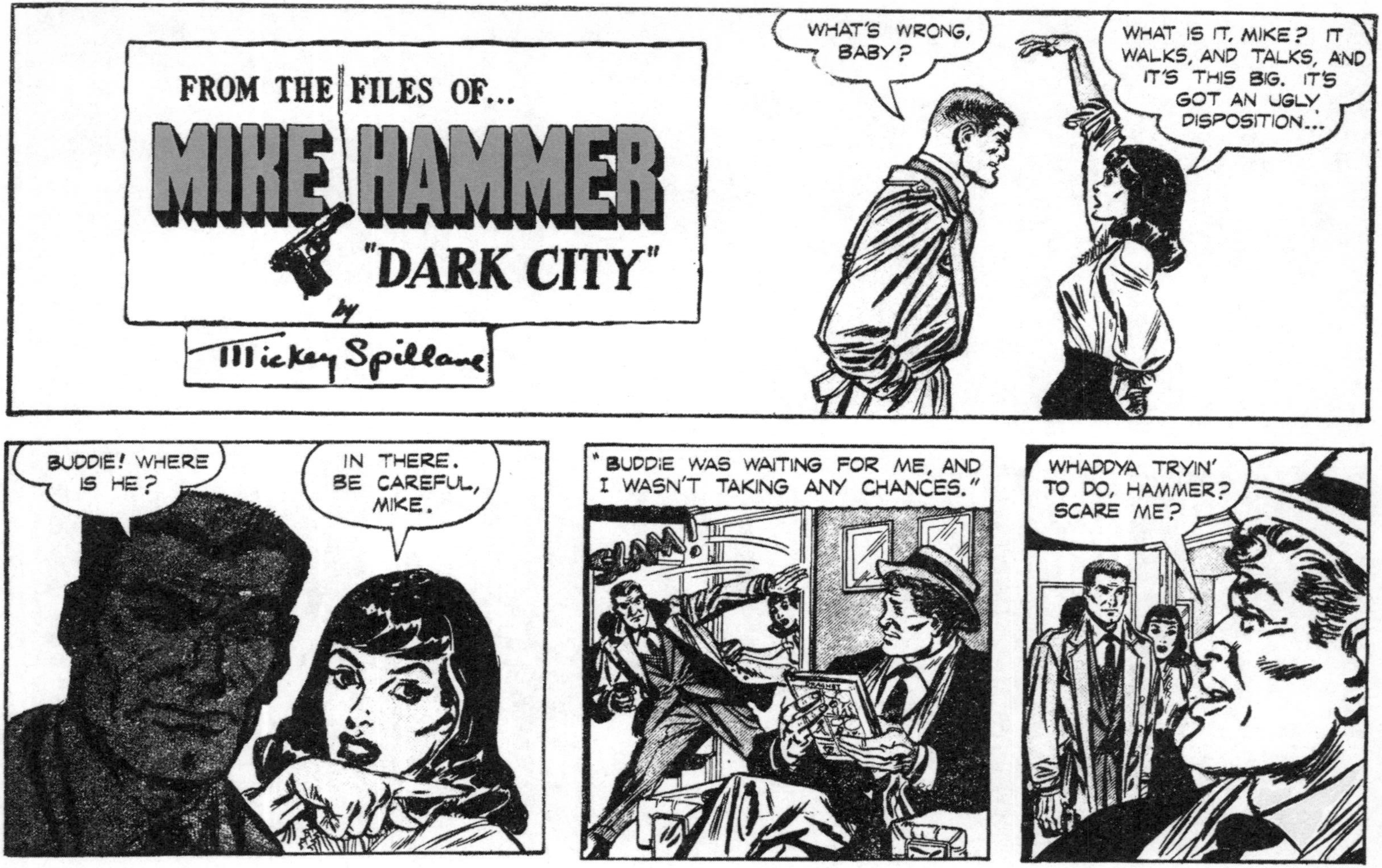
FROM THE FILES OF...
MIKE HAMMER
"DARK CITY"
by Mickey Spillane
WHAT'S WRONG, BABY?
WHAT IS IT, MIKE? IT WALKS, AND TALKS, AND IT'S THIS BIG. IT'S GOT AN UGLY DISPOSITION...
BUDDIE! WHERE IS HE?
IN THERE. BE CAREFUL, MIKE.
"BUDDIE WAS WAITING FOR ME, AND I WASN'T TAKING ANY CHANCES."
SLAM!
WHADDYA TRYIN' TO DO, HAMMER? SCARE ME?

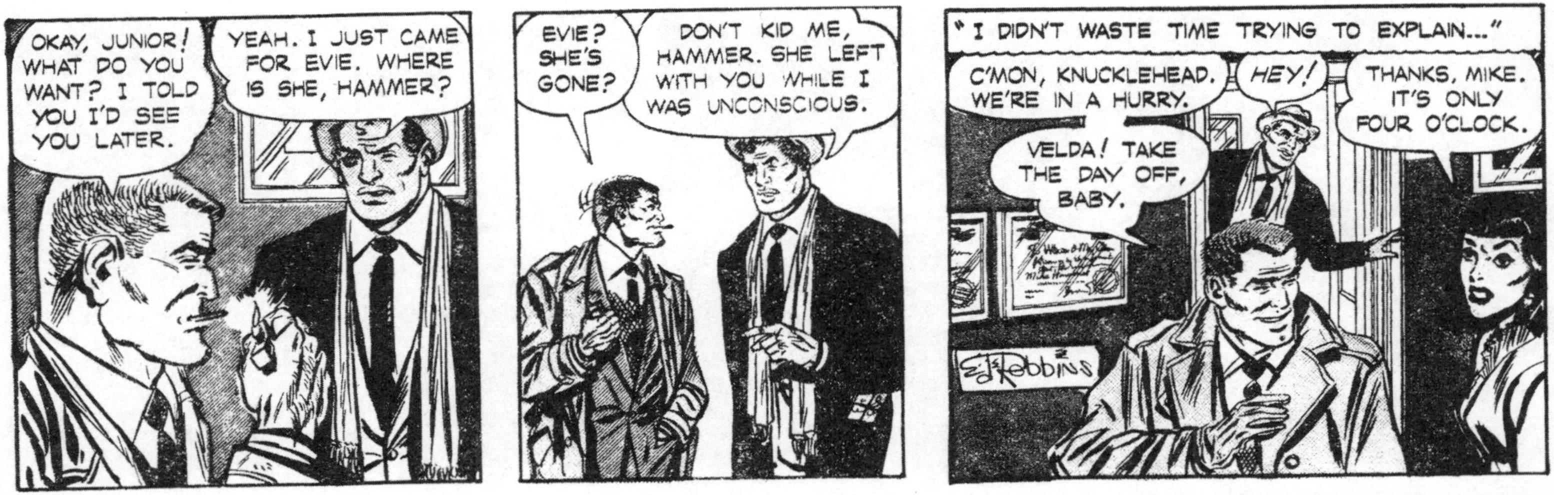
OKAY, JUNIOR! WHAT DO YOU WANT? I TOLD YOU I'D SEE YOU LATER.
YEAH. I JUST CAME FOR EVIE. WHERE IS SHE, HAMMER?
EVIE? SHE'S GONE?
DON'T KID ME, HAMMER. SHE LEFT WITH YOU WHILE I WAS UNCONSCIOUS.
"I DIDN'T WASTE TIME TRYING TO EXPLAIN..."
C'MON, KNUCKLEHEAD. WE'RE IN A HURRY.
HEY!
THANKS, MIKE. IT'S ONLY FOUR O'CLOCK.
VELDA! TAKE THE DAY OFF, BABY.
Ed Robbins

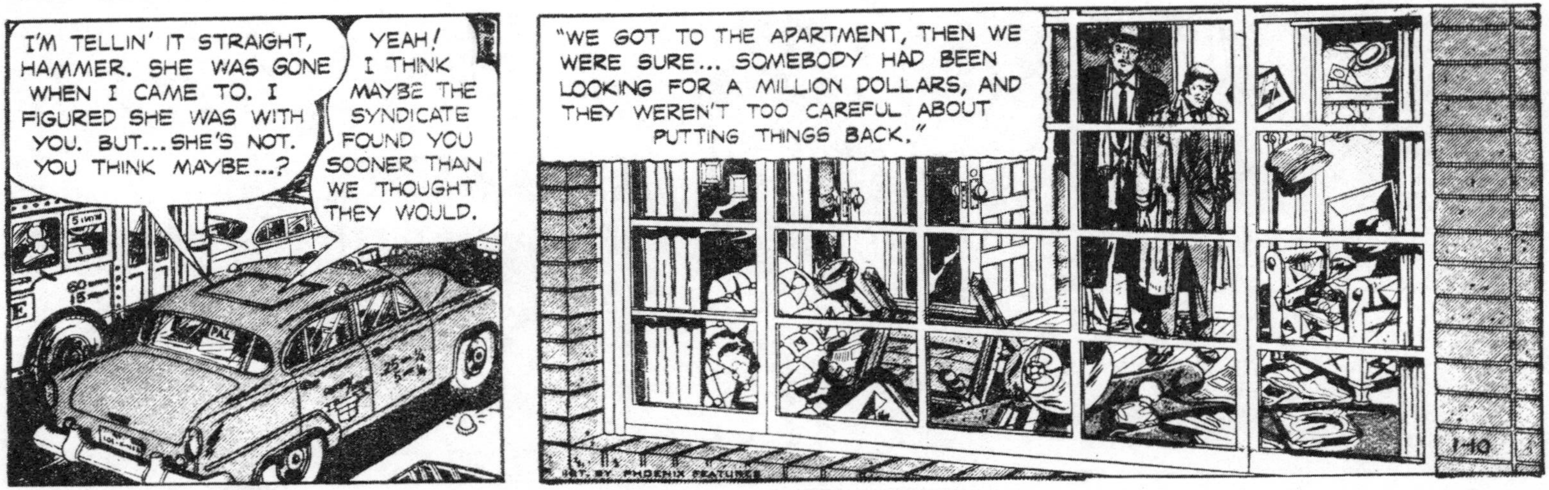
I'M TELLIN' IT STRAIGHT, HAMMER. SHE WAS GONE WHEN I CAME TO. I FIGURED SHE WAS WITH YOU. BUT...SHE'S NOT. YOU THINK MAYBE...?
YEAH! I THINK MAYBE THE SYNDICATE FOUND YOU SOONER THAN WE THOUGHT THEY WOULD.
"WE GOT TO THE APARTMENT, THEN WE WERE SURE... SOMEBODY HAD BEEN LOOKING FOR A MILLION DOLLARS, AND THEY WEREN'T TOO CAREFUL ABOUT PUTTING THINGS BACK."
1-10

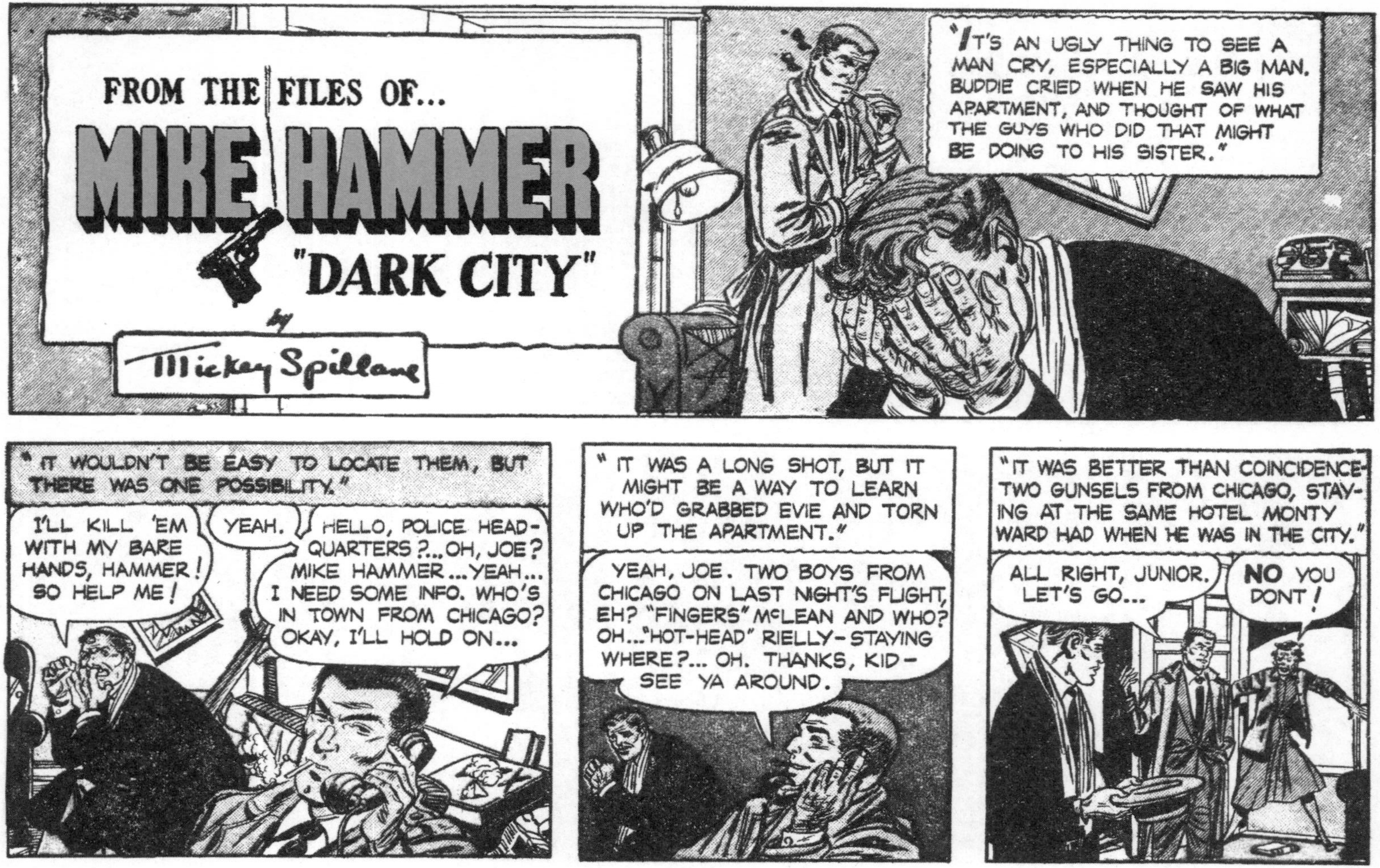
FROM THE FILES OF...
MIKE HAMMER
"DARK CITY"
by
Mickey Spillane
"IT'S AN UGLY THING TO SEE A MAN CRY, ESPECIALLY A BIG MAN. BUDDIE CRIED WHEN HE SAW HIS APARTMENT, AND THOUGHT OF WHAT THE GUYS WHO DID THAT MIGHT BE DOING TO HIS SISTER."
"IT WOULDN'T BE EASY TO LOCATE THEM, BUT THERE WAS ONE POSSIBILITY."
I'LL KILL 'EM WITH MY BARE HANDS, HAMMER! SO HELP ME!
YEAH.
HELLO, POLICE HEAD-QUARTERS?...OH, JOE? MIKE HAMMER...YEAH... I NEED SOME INFO. WHO'S IN TOWN FROM CHICAGO? OKAY, I'LL HOLD ON...
"IT WAS A LONG SHOT, BUT IT MIGHT BE A WAY TO LEARN WHO'D GRABBED EVIE AND TORN UP THE APARTMENT."
YEAH, JOE. TWO BOYS FROM CHICAGO ON LAST NIGHT'S FLIGHT, EH? "FINGERS" McLEAN AND WHO? OH..."HOT-HEAD" RIELLY-STAYING WHERE?... OH. THANKS, KID-SEE YA AROUND.
"IT WAS BETTER THAN COINCIDENCE-TWO GUNSELS FROM CHICAGO, STAY-ING AT THE SAME HOTEL MONTY WARD HAD WHEN HE WAS IN THE CITY."
ALL RIGHT, JUNIOR. LET'S GO...
NO YOU DONT!

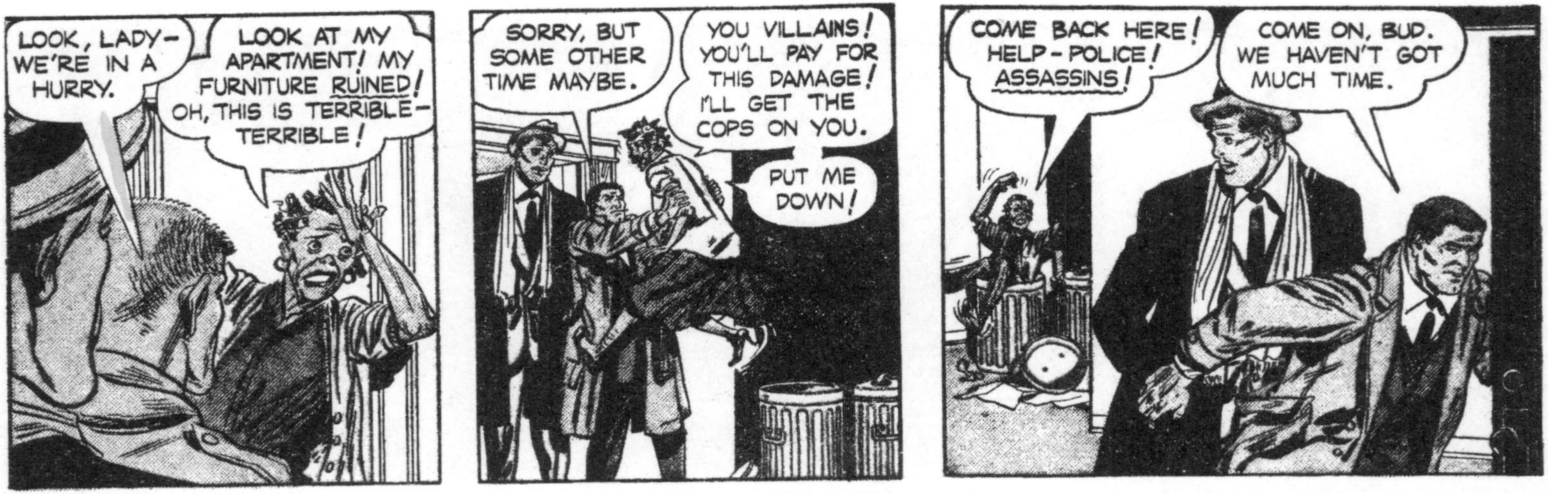
LOOK, LADY- WE'RE IN A HURRY.
LOOK AT MY APARTMENT! MY FURNITURE RUINED! OH, THIS IS TERRIBLE- TERRIBLE!
SORRY, BUT SOME OTHER TIME MAYBE.
YOU VILLAINS! YOU'LL PAY FOR THIS DAMAGE! I'LL GET THE COPS ON YOU.
PUT ME DOWN!
COME BACK HERE! HELP-POLICE! ASSASSINS!
COME ON, BUD. WE HAVEN'T GOT MUCH TIME.
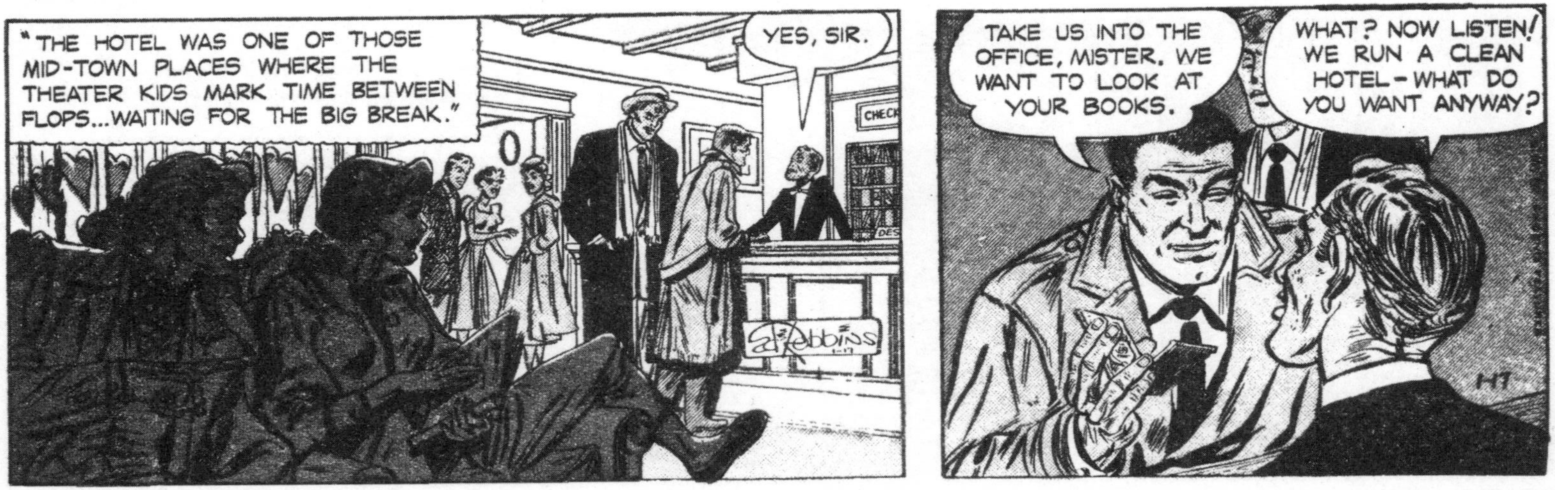
"THE HOTEL WAS ONE OF THOSE MID-TOWN PLACES WHERE THE THEATER KIDS MARK TIME BETWEEN FLOPS...WAITING FOR THE BIG BREAK."
YES, SIR.
CHECK
TAKE US INTO THE OFFICE, MISTER. WE WANT TO LOOK AT YOUR BOOKS.
WHAT? NOW LISTEN! WE RUN A CLEAN HOTEL-WHAT DO YOU WANT ANYWAY?

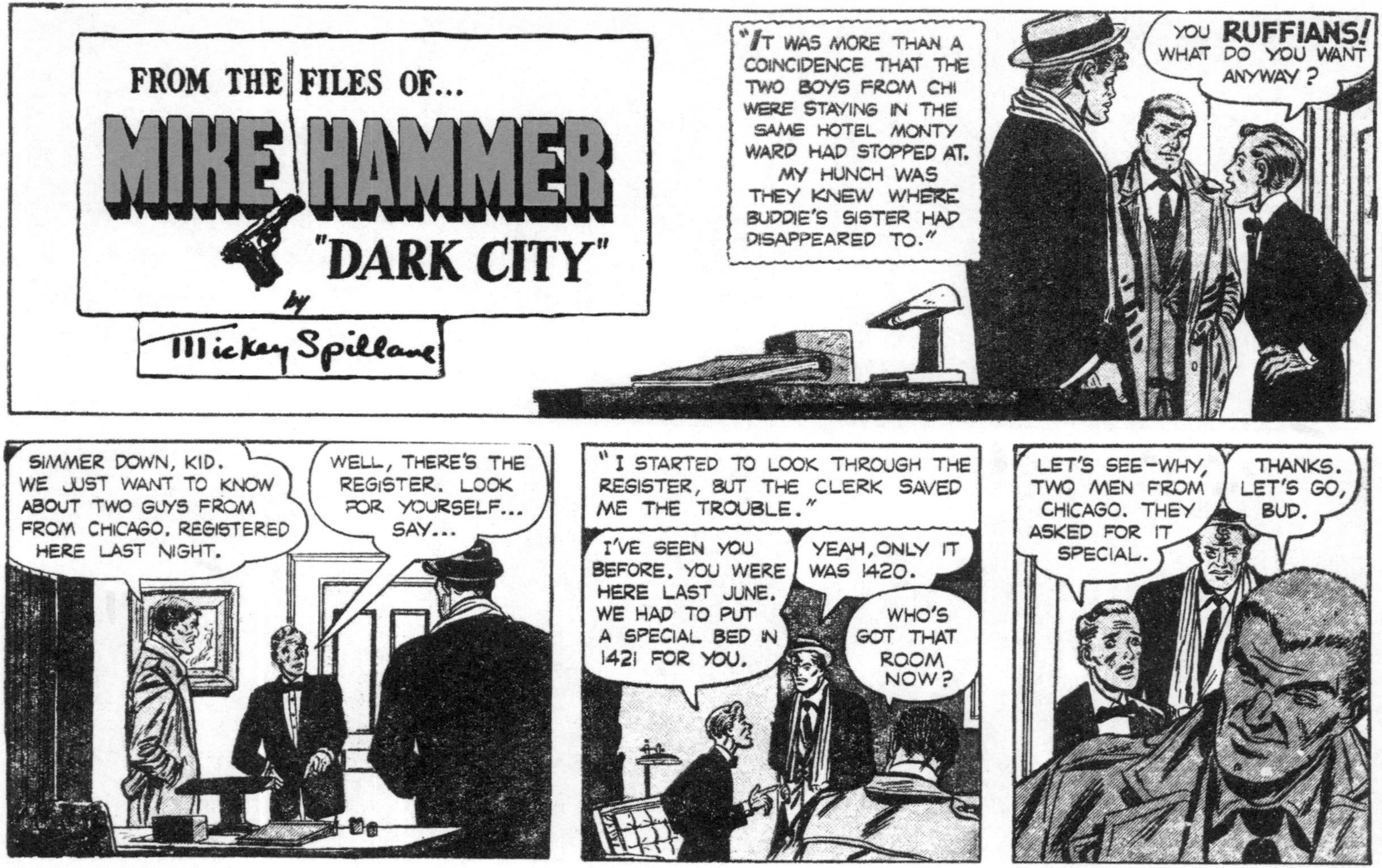
FROM THE FILES OF...
MIKE HAMMER
"DARK CITY"
by
Mickey Spillane
"IT WAS MORE THAN A COINCIDENCE THAT THE TWO BOYS FROM CHI WERE STAYING IN THE SAME HOTEL MONTY WARD HAD STOPPED AT. MY HUNCH WAS THEY KNEW WHERE BUDDIE'S SISTER HAD DISAPPEARED TO."
YOU RUFFIANS! WHAT DO YOU WANT ANYWAY?
SIMMER DOWN, KID. WE JUST WANT TO KNOW ABOUT TWO GUYS FROM FROM CHICAGO. REGISTERED HERE LAST NIGHT.
WELL, THERE'S THE REGISTER. LOOK FOR YOURSELF... SAY...
"I STARTED TO LOOK THROUGH THE REGISTER, BUT THE CLERK SAVED ME THE TROUBLE."
I'VE SEEN YOU BEFORE. YOU WERE HERE LAST JUNE. WE HAD TO PUT A SPECIAL BED IN 1421 FOR YOU.
YEAH, ONLY IT WAS 1420.
WHO'S GOT THAT ROOM NOW?
LET'S SEE-WHY, TWO MEN FROM CHICAGO. THEY ASKED FOR IT SPECIAL.
THANKS. LET'S GO, BUD.

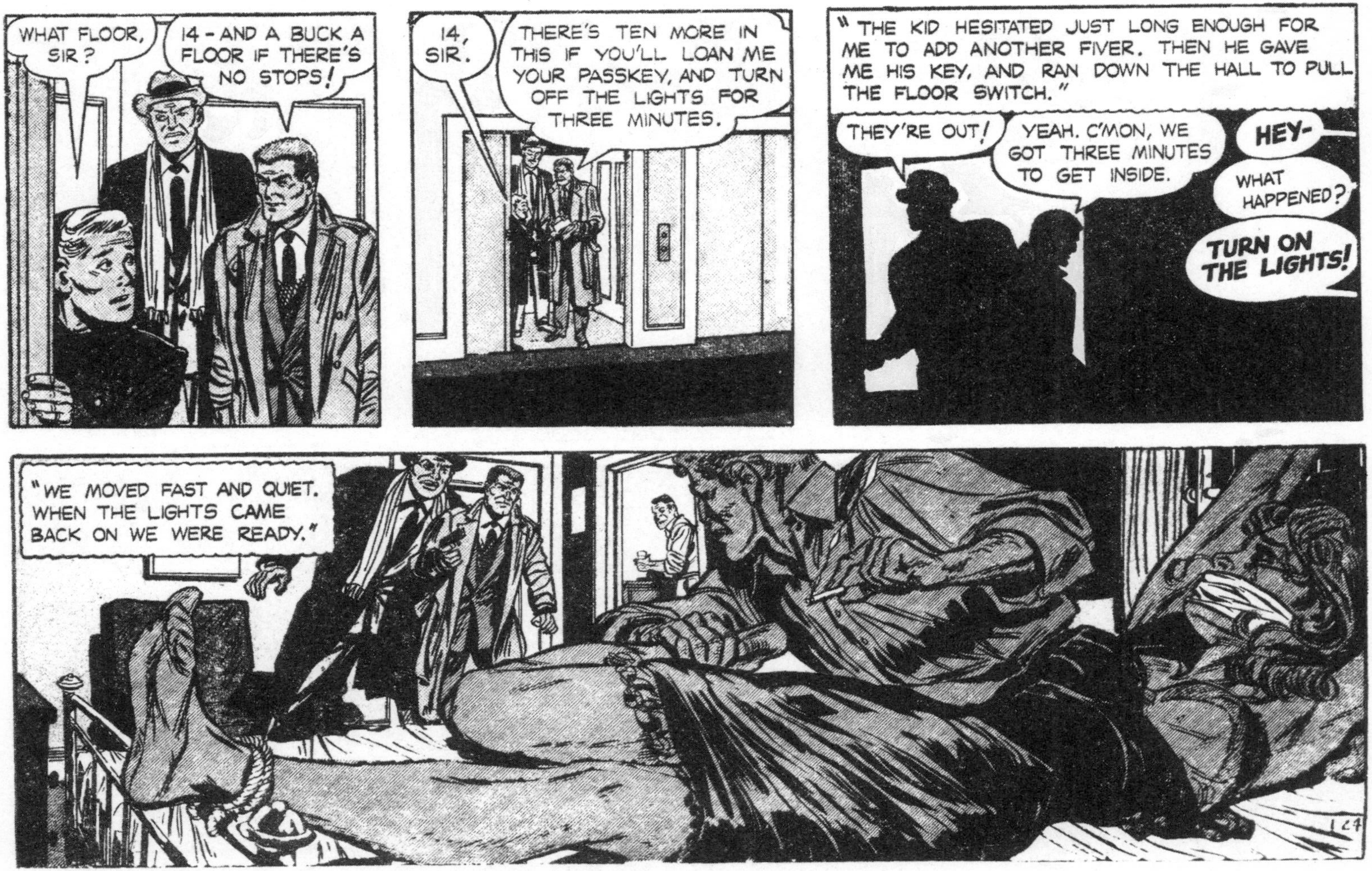
WHAT FLOOR, SIR?
14 - AND A BUCK A FLOOR IF THERE'S NO STOPS!
14, SIR.
THERE'S TEN MORE IN THIS IF YOU'LL LOAN ME YOUR PASSKEY, AND TURN OFF THE LIGHTS FOR THREE MINUTES.
"THE KID HESITATED JUST LONG ENOUGH FOR ME TO ADD ANOTHER FIVER. THEN HE GAVE ME HIS KEY, AND RAN DOWN THE HALL TO PULL THE FLOOR SWITCH."
THEY'RE OUT!
YEAH. C'MON, WE GOT THREE MINUTES TO GET INSIDE.
HEY-
WHAT HAPPENED?
TURN ON THE LIGHTS!
"WE MOVED FAST AND QUIET. WHEN THE LIGHTS CAME BACK ON WE WERE READY."
1 27

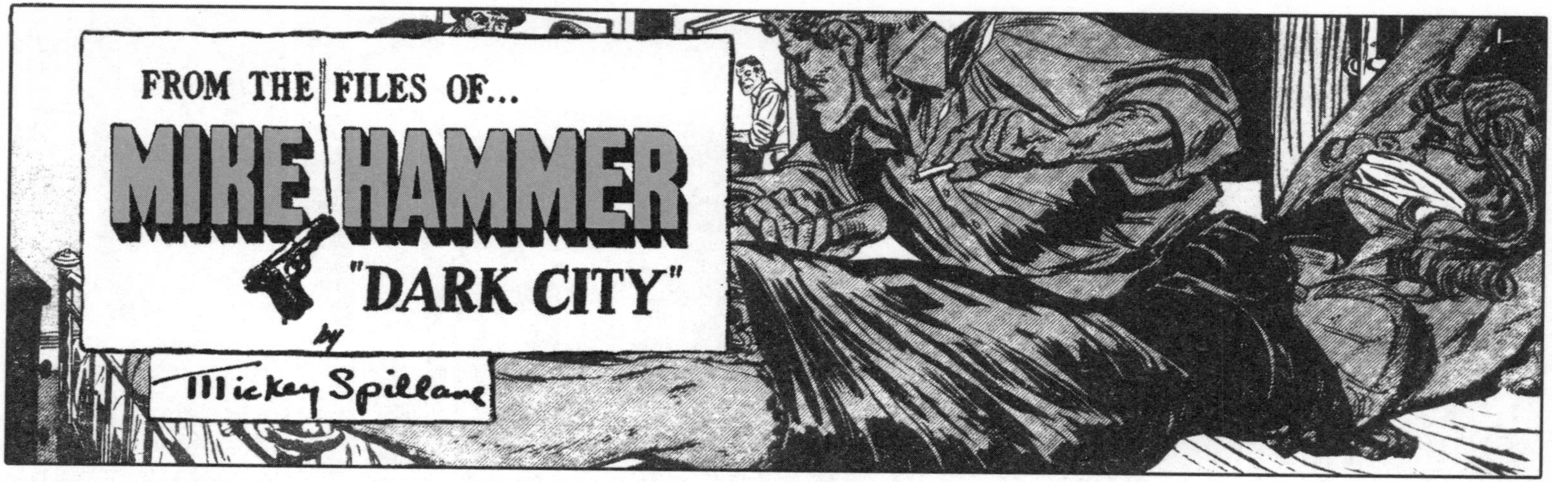
FROM THE FILES OF...
MIKE HAMMER
"DARK CITY"
by
Mickey Spillane

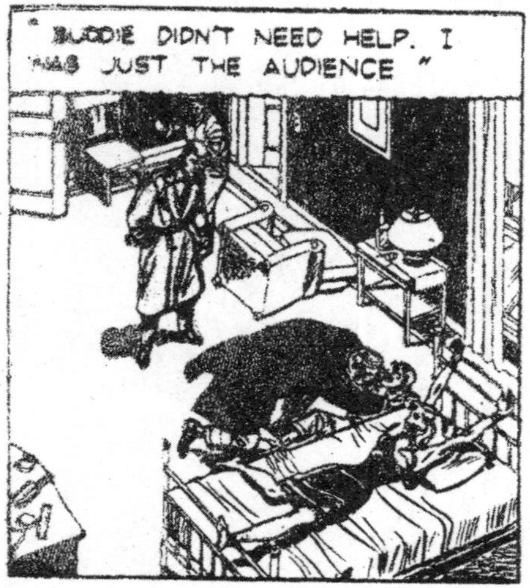
"BUDDIE DIDN'T NEED HELP. I WAS JUST THE AUDIENCE."

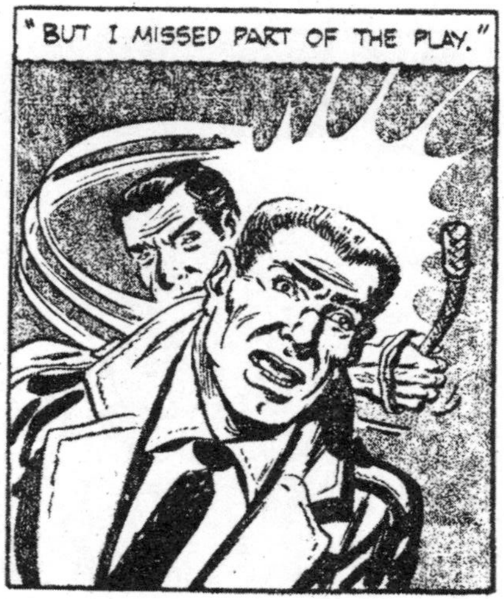
"BUT I MISSED PART OF THE PLAY."

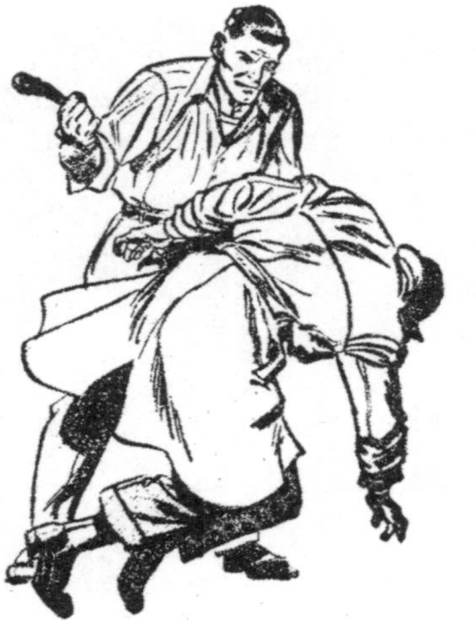

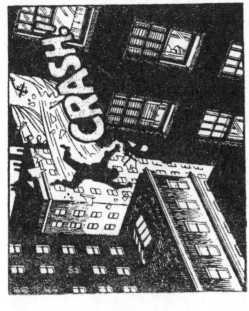

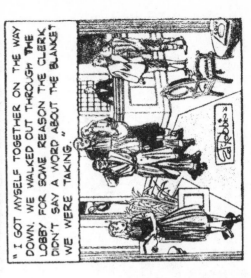

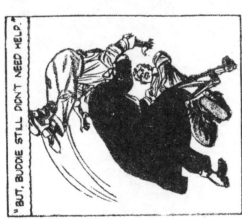

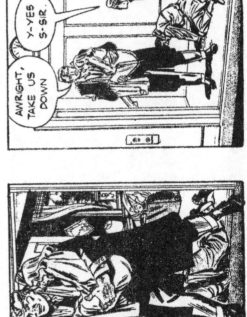

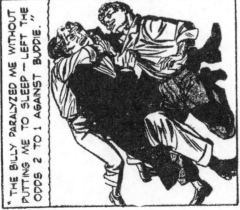

" THE BILLY PARALYZED ME WITHOUT PUTTING ME TO SLEEP — LEFT THE ODDS 2 TO 1 AGAINST BUDDIE. "
"BUT, BUDDIE STILL DIDN'T NEED HELP."
CRASH!
AWRIGHT, TAKE US DOWN
Y-YES S-SIR.
" I GOT MYSELF TOGETHER ON THE WAY DOWN. WE WALKED OUT THROUGH THE LOBBY FOR SOME REASON THE CLERK DIDN'T SAY A WORD ABOUT THE BLANKET WE WERE TAKING. "

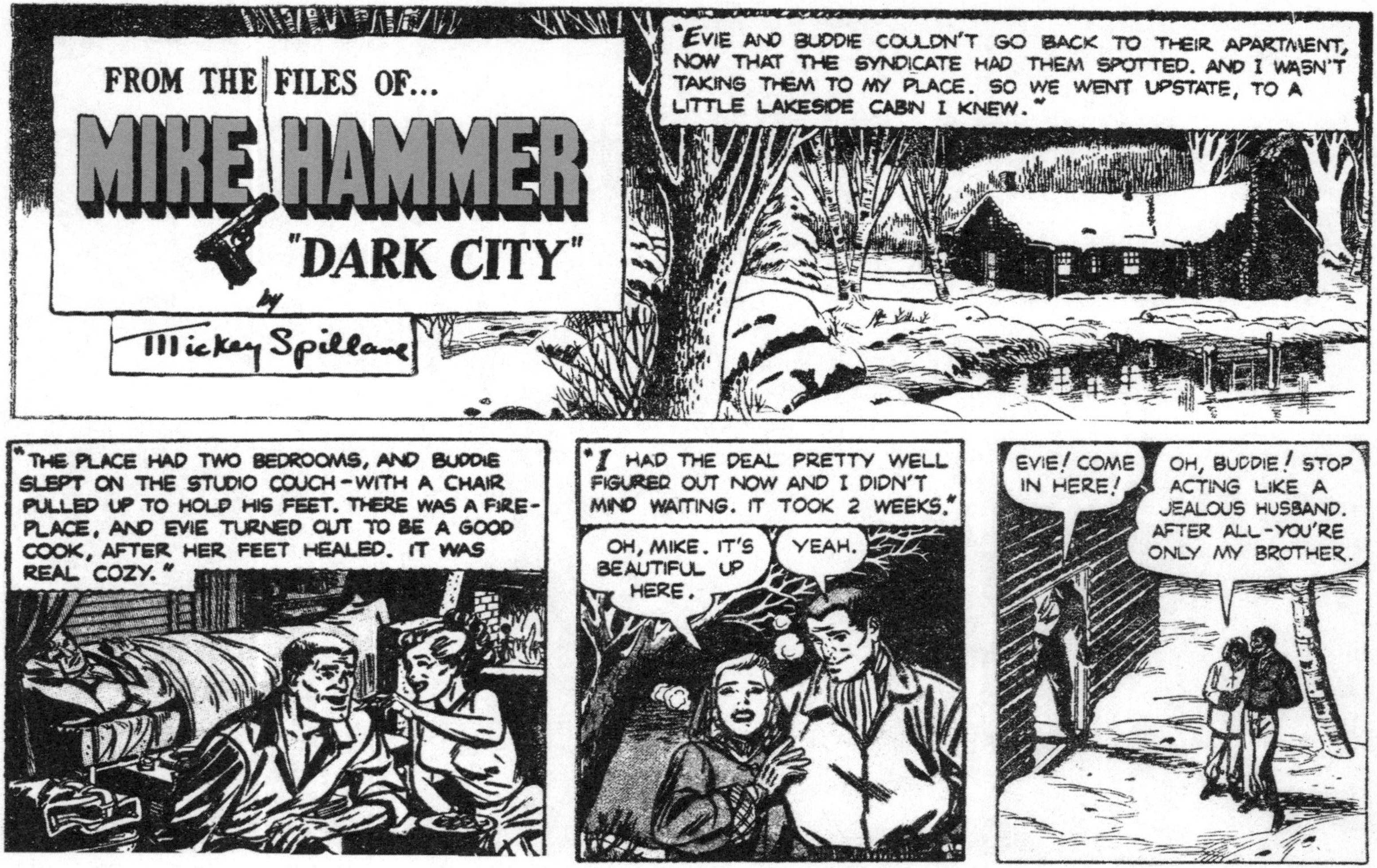
FROM THE FILES OF...
MIKE HAMMER
"DARK CITY"
by Mickey Spillane
"EVIE AND BUDDIE COULDN'T GO BACK TO THEIR APARTMENT, NOW THAT THE SYNDICATE HAD THEM SPOTTED. AND I WASN'T TAKING THEM TO MY PLACE. SO WE WENT UPSTATE, TO A LITTLE LAKESIDE CABIN I KNEW."
"THE PLACE HAD TWO BEDROOMS, AND BUDDIE SLEPT ON THE STUDIO COUCH—WITH A CHAIR PULLED UP TO HOLD HIS FEET. THERE WAS A FIRE-PLACE, AND EVIE TURNED OUT TO BE A GOOD COOK, AFTER HER FEET HEALED. IT WAS REAL COZY."
"I HAD THE DEAL PRETTY WELL FIGURED OUT NOW AND I DIDN'T MIND WAITING. IT TOOK 2 WEEKS."
OH, MIKE. IT'S BEAUTIFUL UP HERE.
YEAH.
EVIE! COME IN HERE!
OH, BUDDIE! STOP ACTING LIKE A JEALOUS HUSBAND. AFTER ALL—YOU'RE ONLY MY BROTHER.

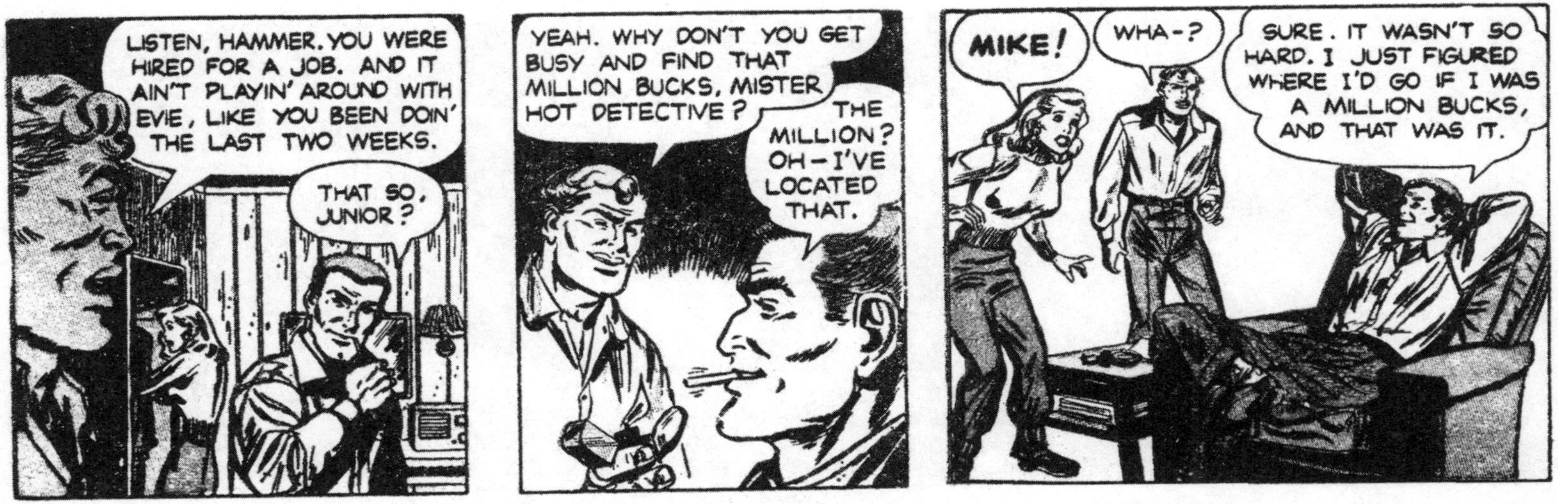
LISTEN, HAMMER. YOU WERE HIRED FOR A JOB. AND IT AIN'T PLAYIN' AROUND WITH EVIE, LIKE YOU BEEN DOIN' THE LAST TWO WEEKS.
THAT SO, JUNIOR?
YEAH. WHY DON'T YOU GET BUSY AND FIND THAT MILLION BUCKS, MISTER HOT DETECTIVE?
THE MILLION? OH – I'VE LOCATED THAT.
MIKE!
WHA-?
SURE. IT WASN'T SO HARD. I JUST FIGURED WHERE I'D GO IF I WAS A MILLION BUCKS, AND THAT WAS IT.

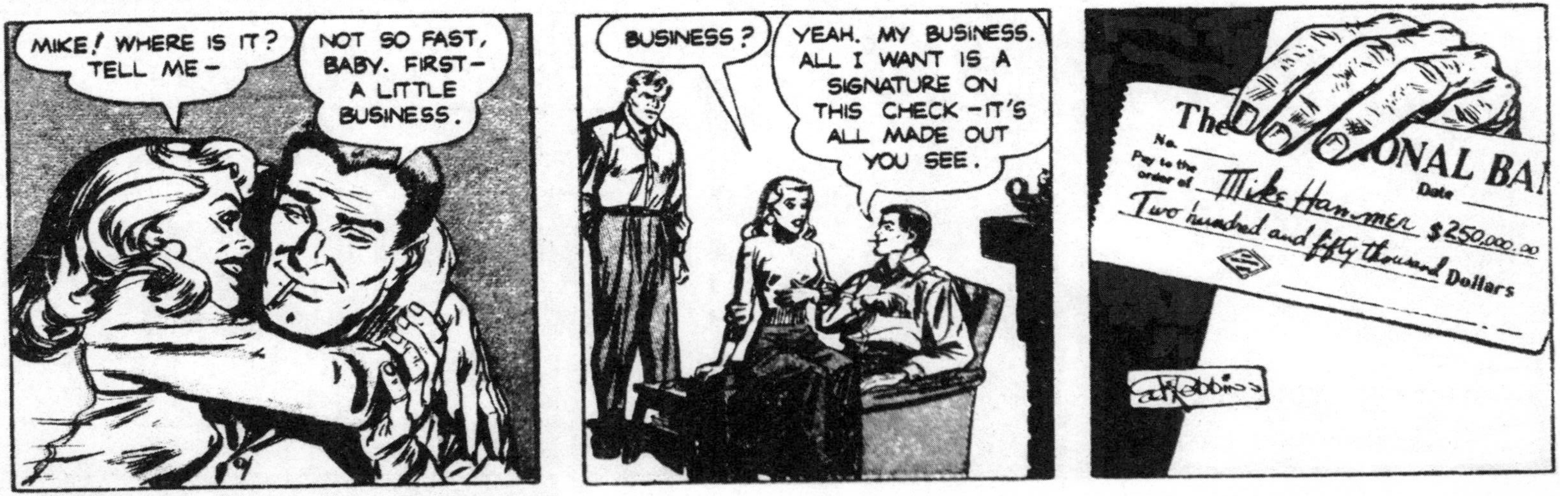
MIKE! WHERE IS IT? TELL ME –
NOT SO FAST, BABY. FIRST – A LITTLE BUSINESS.
BUSINESS?
YEAH. MY BUSINESS. ALL I WANT IS A SIGNATURE ON THIS CHECK – IT'S ALL MADE OUT YOU SEE.
The ONAL BA
No.
Date
Pay to the order of Mike Hammer $250,000.00
Two hundred and fifty thousand Dollars

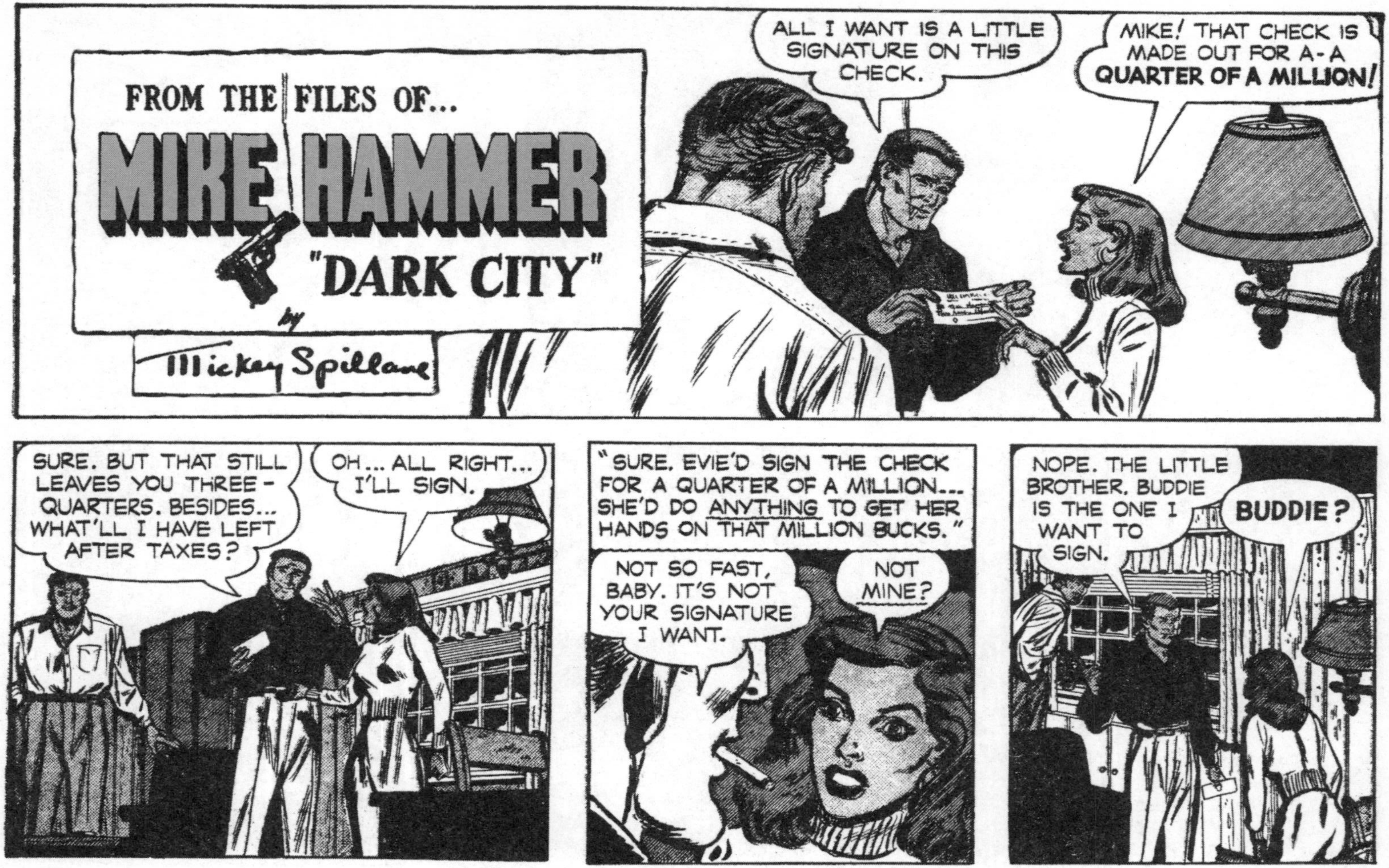
FROM THE FILES OF...
MIKE HAMMER
"DARK CITY"
by Mickey Spillane
ALL I WANT IS A LITTLE SIGNATURE ON THIS CHECK.
MIKE! THAT CHECK IS MADE OUT FOR A-A QUARTER OF A MILLION!
SURE. BUT THAT STILL LEAVES YOU THREE-QUARTERS. BESIDES... WHAT'LL I HAVE LEFT AFTER TAXES?
OH... ALL RIGHT... I'LL SIGN.
"SURE. EVIE'D SIGN THE CHECK FOR A QUARTER OF A MILLION... SHE'D DO ANYTHING TO GET HER HANDS ON THAT MILLION BUCKS."
NOT SO FAST, BABY. IT'S NOT YOUR SIGNATURE I WANT.
NOT MINE?
NOPE. THE LITTLE BROTHER, BUDDIE IS THE ONE I WANT TO SIGN.
BUDDIE?

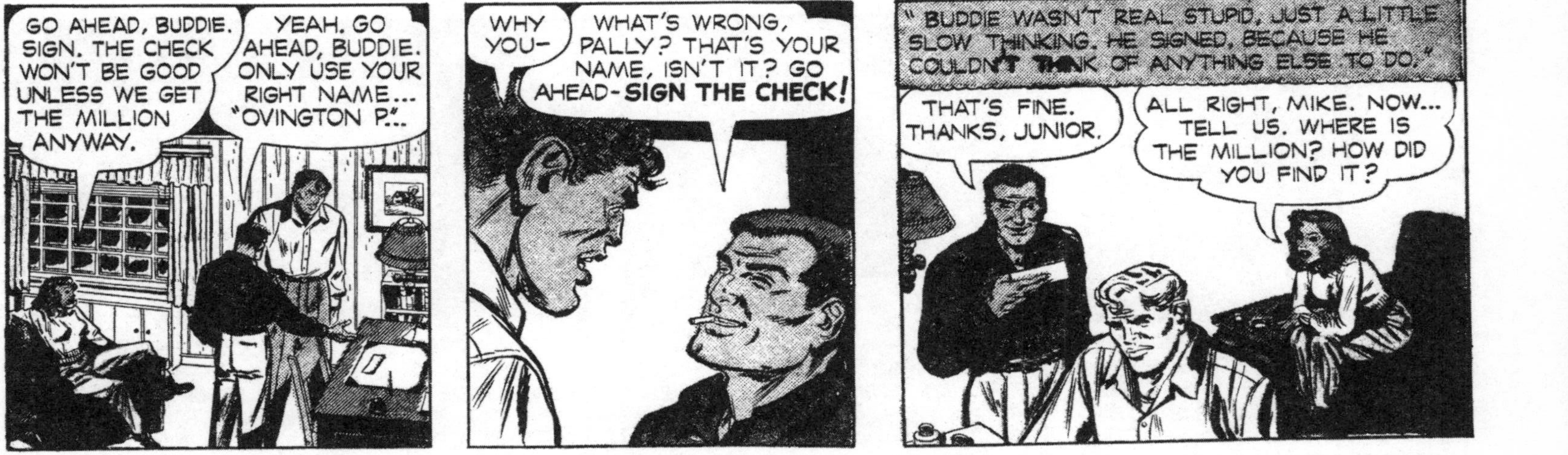
GO AHEAD, BUDDIE. SIGN. THE CHECK WON'T BE GOOD UNLESS WE GET THE MILLION ANYWAY.
YEAH. GO AHEAD, BUDDIE. ONLY USE YOUR RIGHT NAME... "OVINGTON P."...
WHY YOU-
WHAT'S WRONG, PALLY? THAT'S YOUR NAME, ISN'T IT? GO AHEAD- **SIGN THE CHECK!**
"BUDDIE WASN'T REAL STUPID, JUST A LITTLE SLOW THINKING. HE SIGNED, BECAUSE HE COULDN'T THINK OF ANYTHING ELSE TO DO."
THAT'S FINE. THANKS, JUNIOR.
ALL RIGHT, MIKE. NOW... TELL US. WHERE IS THE MILLION? HOW DID YOU FIND IT?

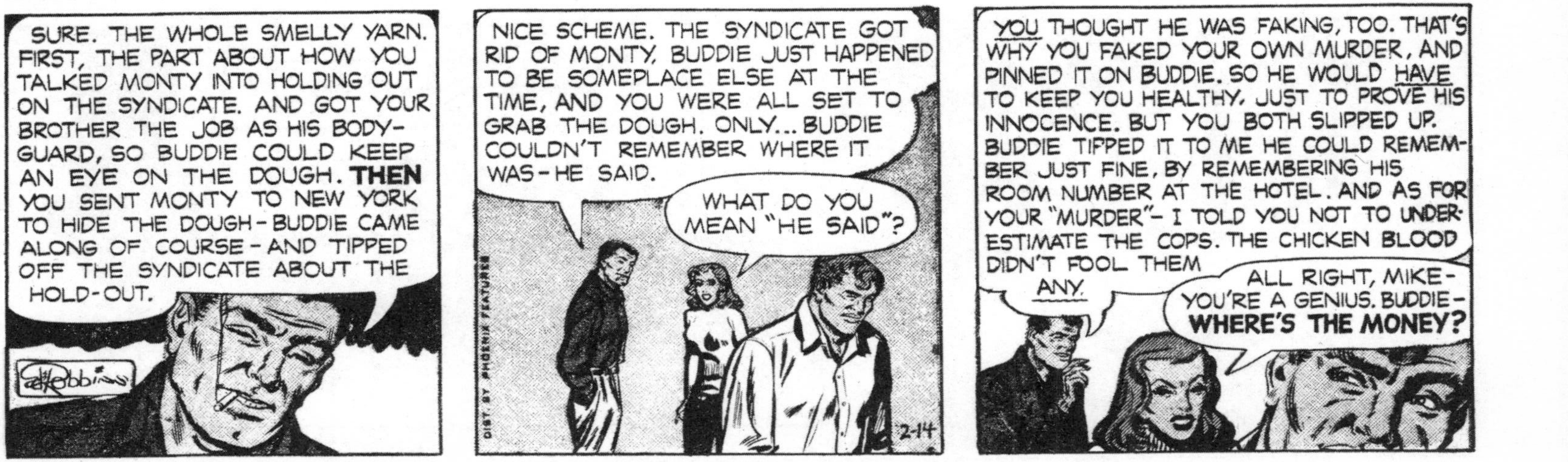
SURE. THE WHOLE SMELLY YARN. FIRST, THE PART ABOUT HOW YOU TALKED MONTY INTO HOLDING OUT ON THE SYNDICATE. AND GOT YOUR BROTHER THE JOB AS HIS BODY-GUARD, SO BUDDIE COULD KEEP AN EYE ON THE DOUGH. **THEN** YOU SENT MONTY TO NEW YORK TO HIDE THE DOUGH - BUDDIE CAME ALONG OF COURSE - AND TIPPED OFF THE SYNDICATE ABOUT THE HOLD-OUT.
NICE SCHEME. THE SYNDICATE GOT RID OF MONTY, BUDDIE JUST HAPPENED TO BE SOMEPLACE ELSE AT THE TIME, AND YOU WERE ALL SET TO GRAB THE DOUGH. ONLY... BUDDIE COULDN'T REMEMBER WHERE IT WAS - HE SAID.
WHAT DO YOU MEAN "HE SAID"?
DIST. BY PHOENIX FEATURES
2-14
YOU THOUGHT HE WAS FAKING, TOO. THAT'S WHY YOU FAKED YOUR OWN MURDER, AND PINNED IT ON BUDDIE. SO HE WOULD HAVE TO KEEP YOU HEALTHY, JUST TO PROVE HIS INNOCENCE. BUT YOU BOTH SLIPPED UP. BUDDIE TIPPED IT TO ME HE COULD REMEMBER JUST FINE, BY REMEMBERING HIS ROOM NUMBER AT THE HOTEL. AND AS FOR YOUR "MURDER" - I TOLD YOU NOT TO UNDERESTIMATE THE COPS. THE CHICKEN BLOOD DIDN'T FOOL THEM ANY.
ALL RIGHT, MIKE - YOU'RE A GENIUS. BUDDIE - **WHERE'S THE MONEY?**

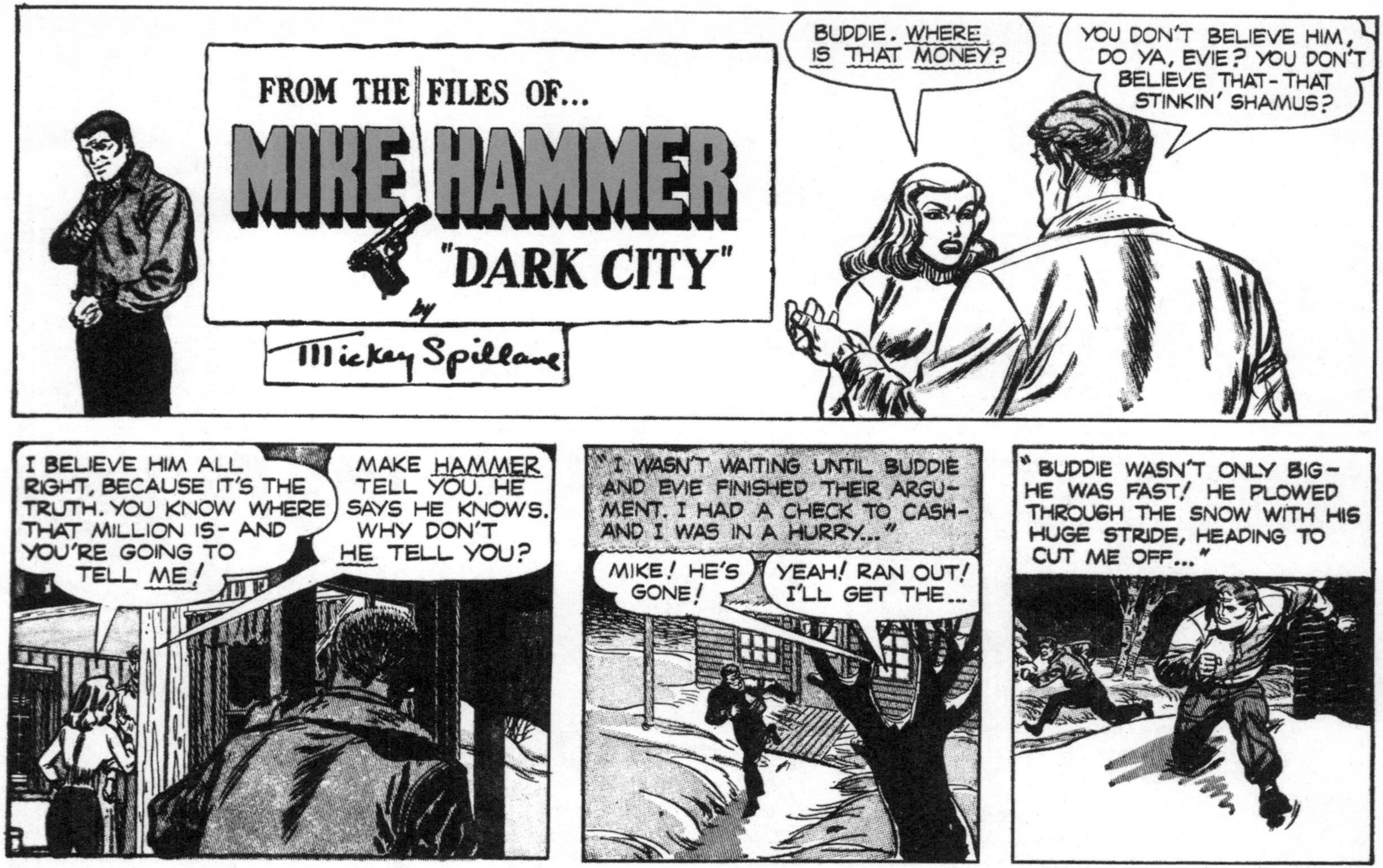
FROM THE FILES OF...
MIKE HAMMER
"DARK CITY"
by Mickey Spillane
BUDDIE. WHERE IS THAT MONEY?
YOU DON'T BELIEVE HIM, DO YA, EVIE? YOU DON'T BELIEVE THAT-THAT STINKIN' SHAMUS?
I BELIEVE HIM ALL RIGHT, BECAUSE IT'S THE TRUTH. YOU KNOW WHERE THAT MILLION IS- AND YOU'RE GOING TO TELL ME!
MAKE HAMMER TELL YOU. HE SAYS HE KNOWS. WHY DON'T HE TELL YOU?
"I WASN'T WAITING UNTIL BUDDIE AND EVIE FINISHED THEIR ARGUMENT. I HAD A CHECK TO CASH- AND I WAS IN A HURRY..."
MIKE! HE'S GONE!
YEAH! RAN OUT! I'LL GET THE...
"BUDDIE WASN'T ONLY BIG- HE WAS FAST! HE PLOWED THROUGH THE SNOW WITH HIS HUGE STRIDE, HEADING TO CUT ME OFF..."

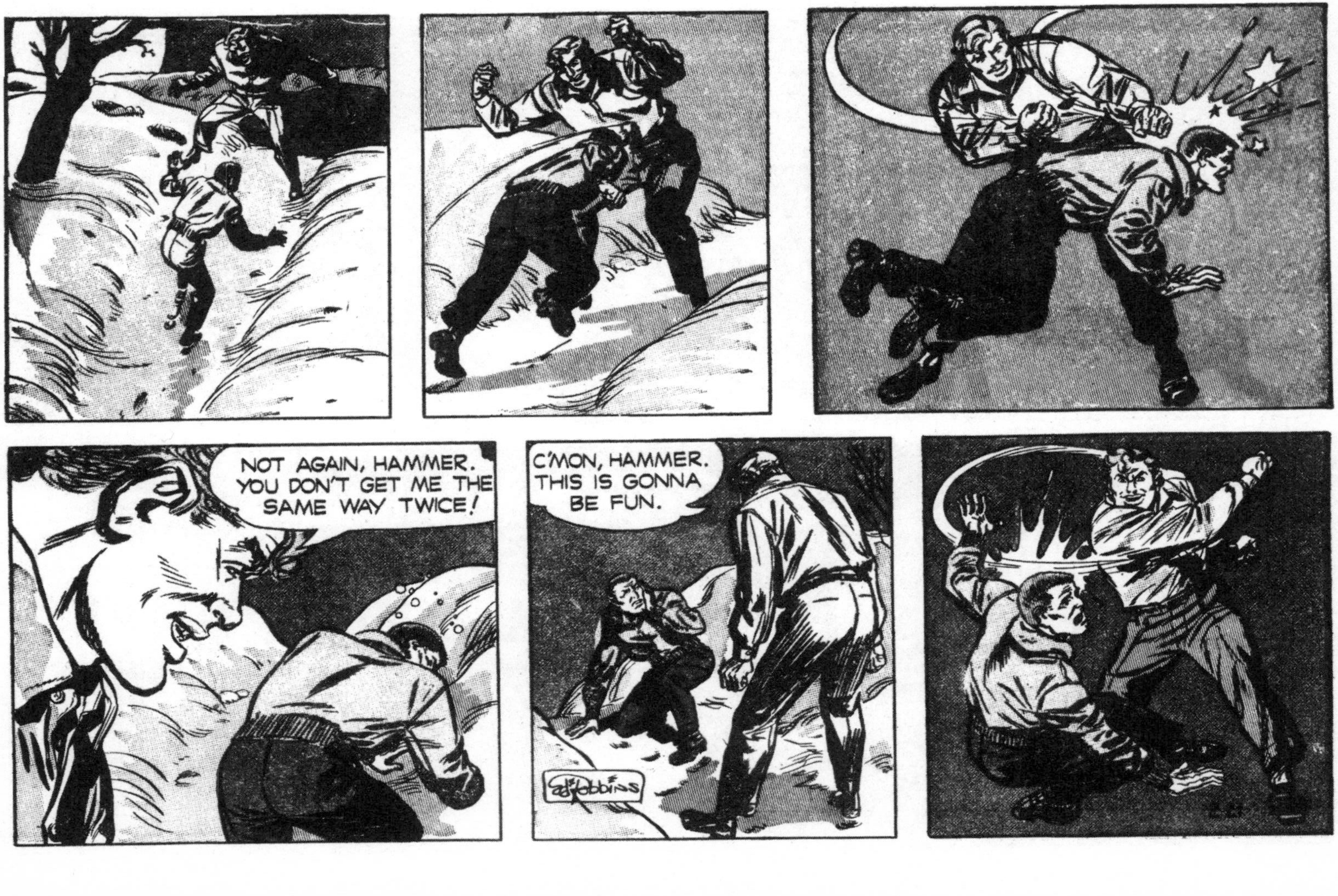
NOT AGAIN, HAMMER. YOU DON'T GET ME THE SAME WAY TWICE!
C'MON, HAMMER. THIS IS GONNA BE FUN.

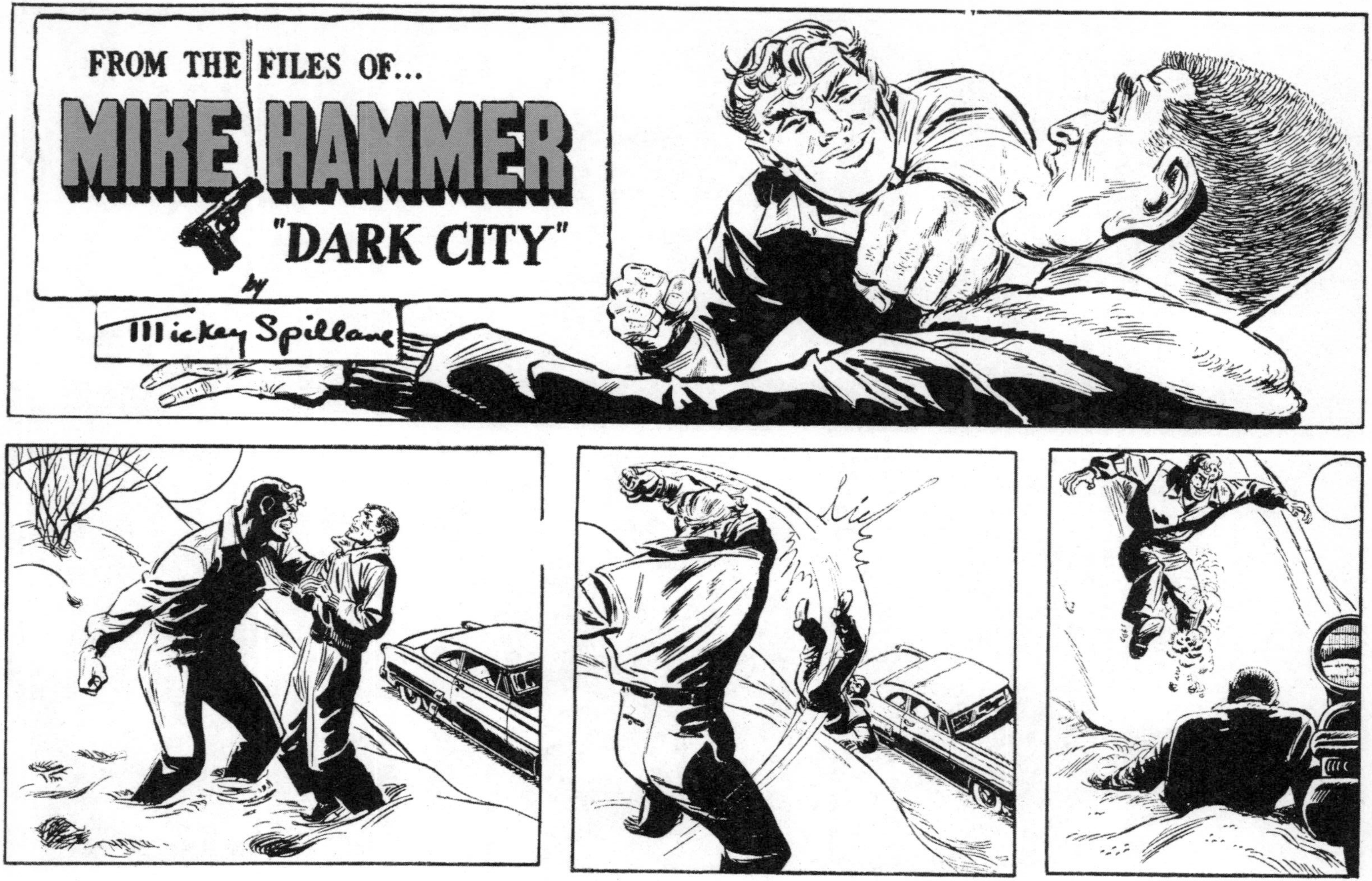
FROM THE FILES OF...
MIKE HAMMER
"DARK CITY"
by
Mickey Spillane

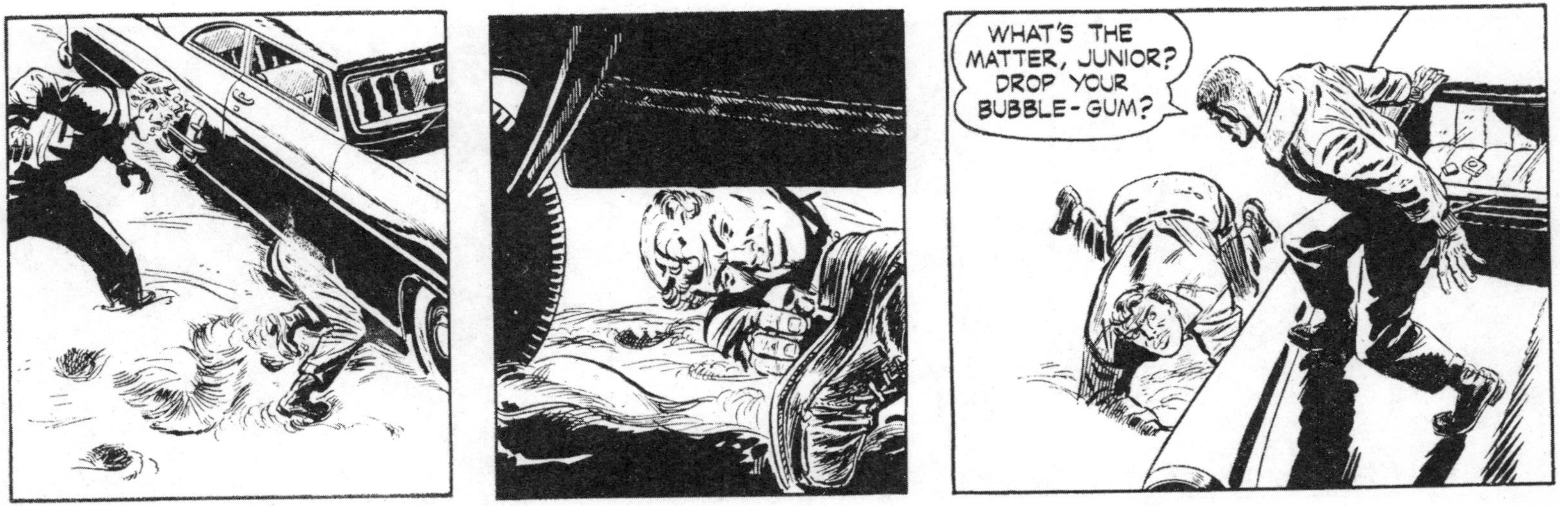
WHAT'S THE MATTER, JUNIOR? DROP YOUR BUBBLE-GUM?

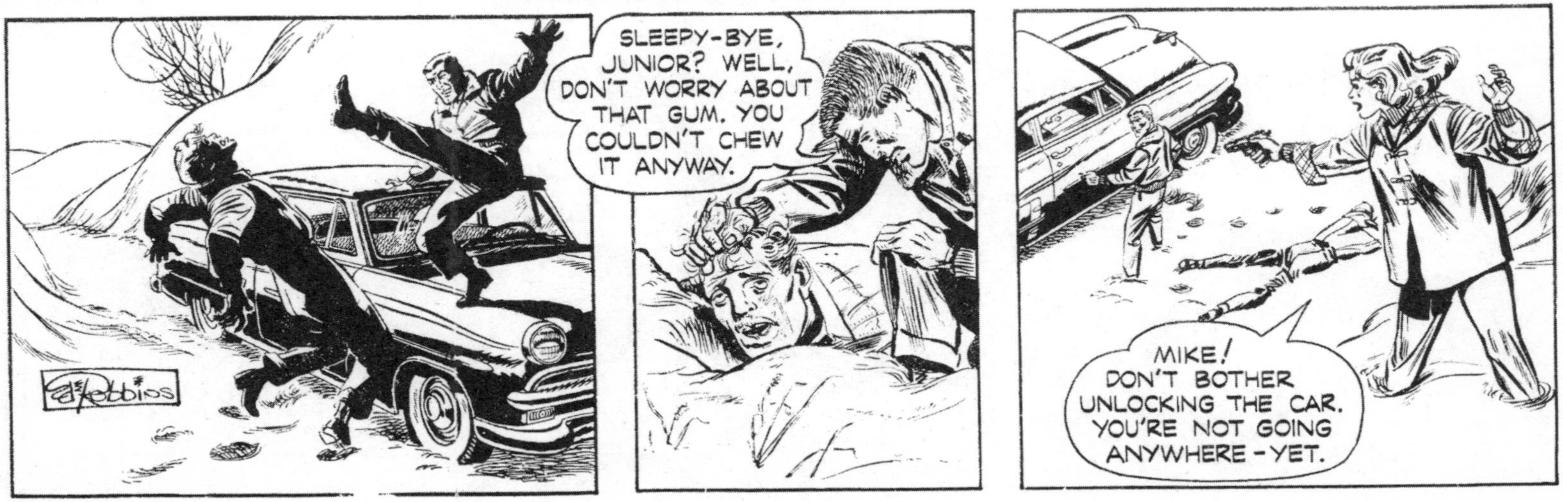
SLEEPY-BYE, JUNIOR? WELL, DON'T WORRY ABOUT THAT GUM. YOU COULDN'T CHEW IT ANYWAY.
MIKE! DON'T BOTHER UNLOCKING THE CAR. YOU'RE NOT GOING ANYWHERE - YET.

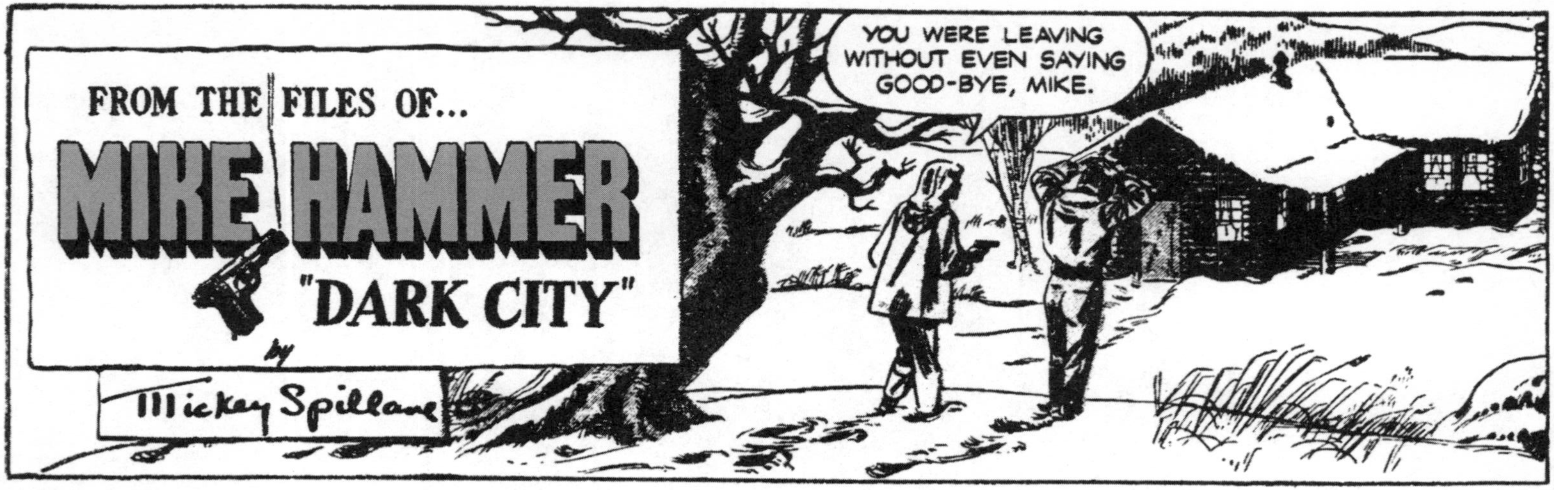
FROM THE FILES OF...
MIKE HAMMER
"DARK CITY"
by Mickey Spillane
YOU WERE LEAVING WITHOUT EVEN SAYING GOOD-BYE, MIKE.
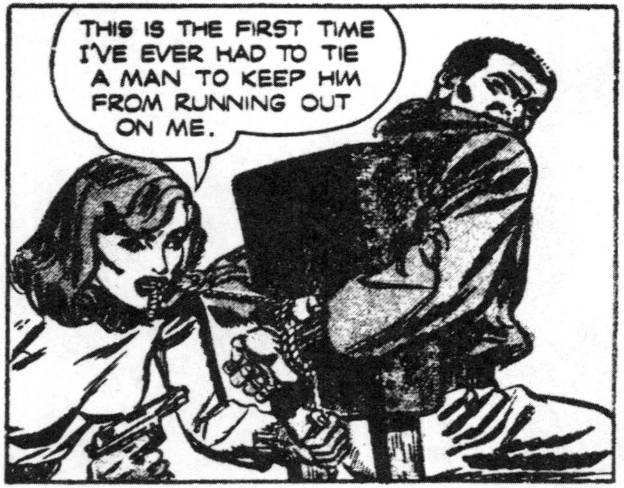
THIS IS THE FIRST TIME I'VE EVER HAD TO TIE A MAN TO KEEP HIM FROM RUNNING OUT ON ME.
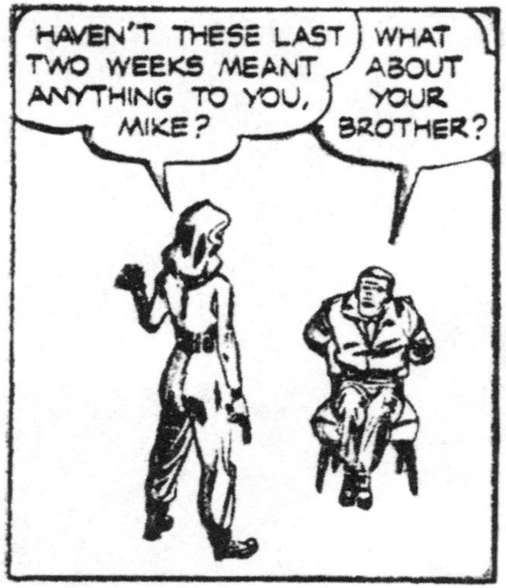
HAVEN'T THESE LAST TWO WEEKS MEANT ANYTHING TO YOU, MIKE?
WHAT ABOUT YOUR BROTHER?
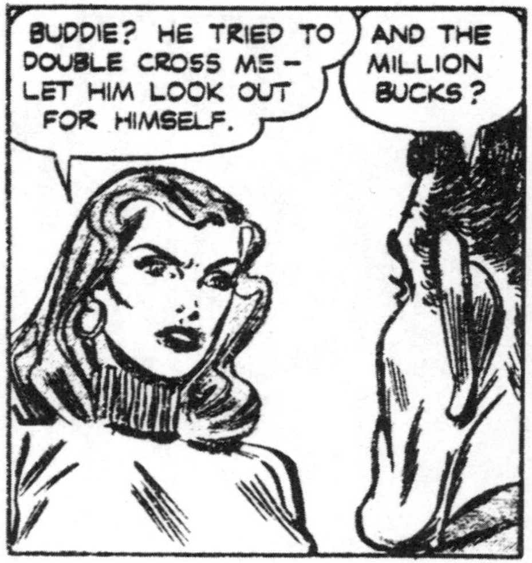
BUDDIE? HE TRIED TO DOUBLE CROSS ME – LET HIM LOOK OUT FOR HIMSELF.
AND THE MILLION BUCKS?

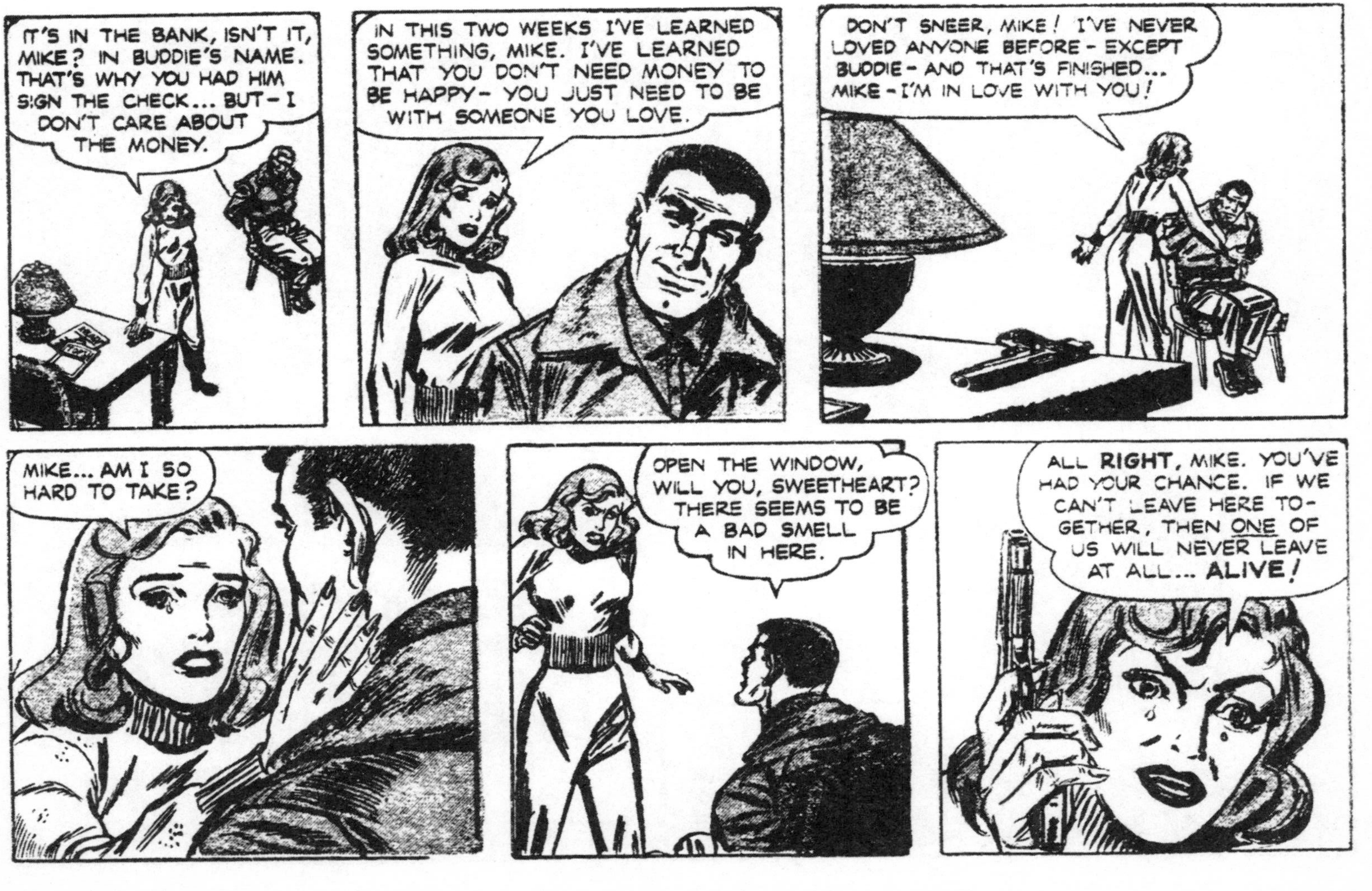
IT'S IN THE BANK, ISN'T IT, MIKE? IN BUDDIE'S NAME. THAT'S WHY YOU HAD HIM SIGN THE CHECK... BUT- I DON'T CARE ABOUT THE MONEY.
IN THIS TWO WEEKS I'VE LEARNED SOMETHING, MIKE. I'VE LEARNED THAT YOU DON'T NEED MONEY TO BE HAPPY- YOU JUST NEED TO BE WITH SOMEONE YOU LOVE.
DON'T SNEER, MIKE! I'VE NEVER LOVED ANYONE BEFORE - EXCEPT BUDDIE - AND THAT'S FINISHED... MIKE - I'M IN LOVE WITH YOU!
MIKE... AM I SO HARD TO TAKE?
OPEN THE WINDOW, WILL YOU, SWEETHEART? THERE SEEMS TO BE A BAD SMELL IN HERE.
ALL **RIGHT**, MIKE. YOU'VE HAD YOUR CHANCE. IF WE CAN'T LEAVE HERE TOGETHER, THEN ONE OF US WILL NEVER LEAVE AT ALL... **ALIVE**!

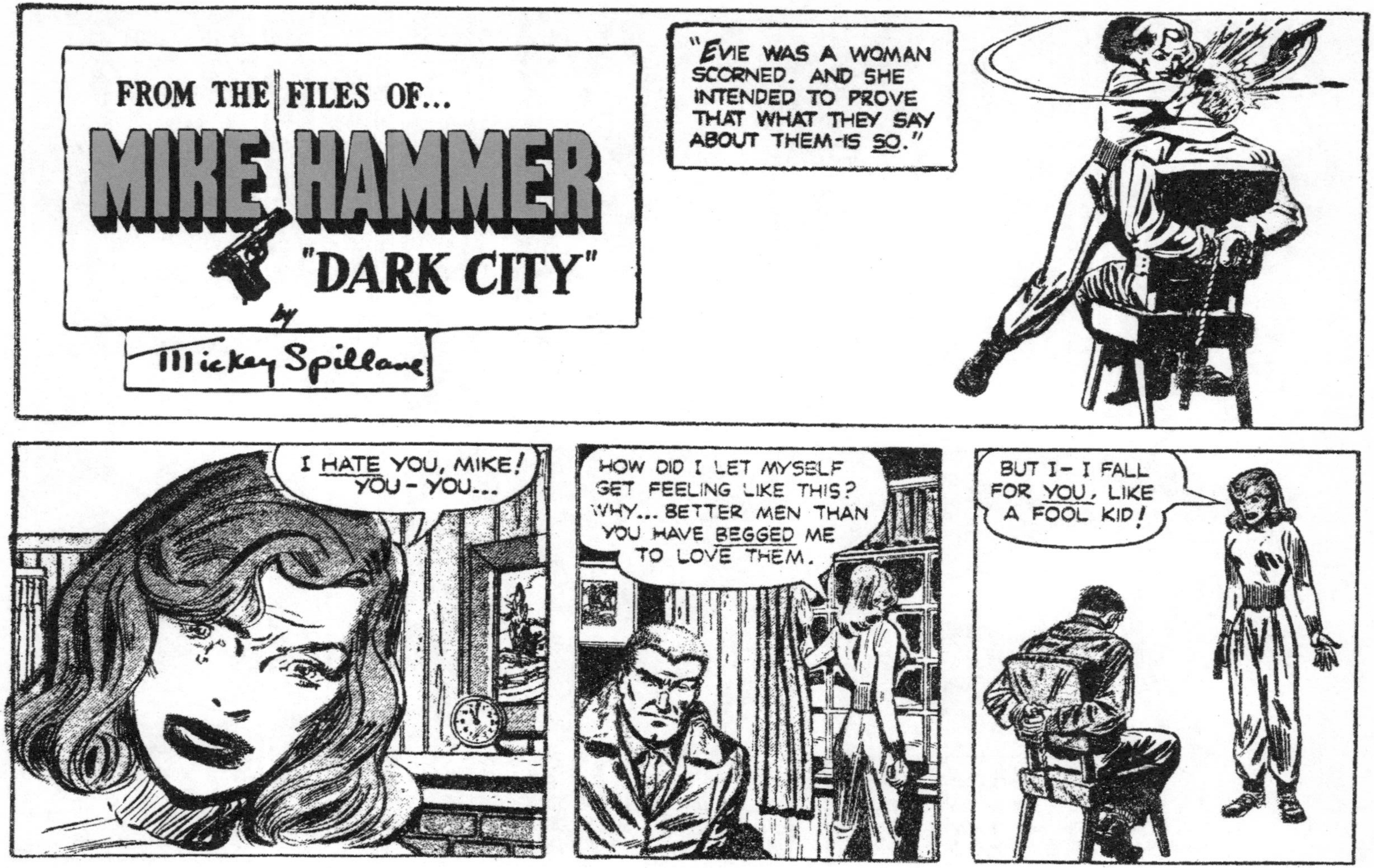
FROM THE FILES OF...
MIKE HAMMER
"DARK CITY"
by Mickey Spillane
"EVIE WAS A WOMAN SCORNED. AND SHE INTENDED TO PROVE THAT WHAT THEY SAY ABOUT THEM-IS SO."
I HATE YOU, MIKE! YOU - YOU...
HOW DID I LET MYSELF GET FEELING LIKE THIS? WHY... BETTER MEN THAN YOU HAVE BEGGED ME TO LOVE THEM.
BUT I- I FALL FOR YOU, LIKE A FOOL KID!

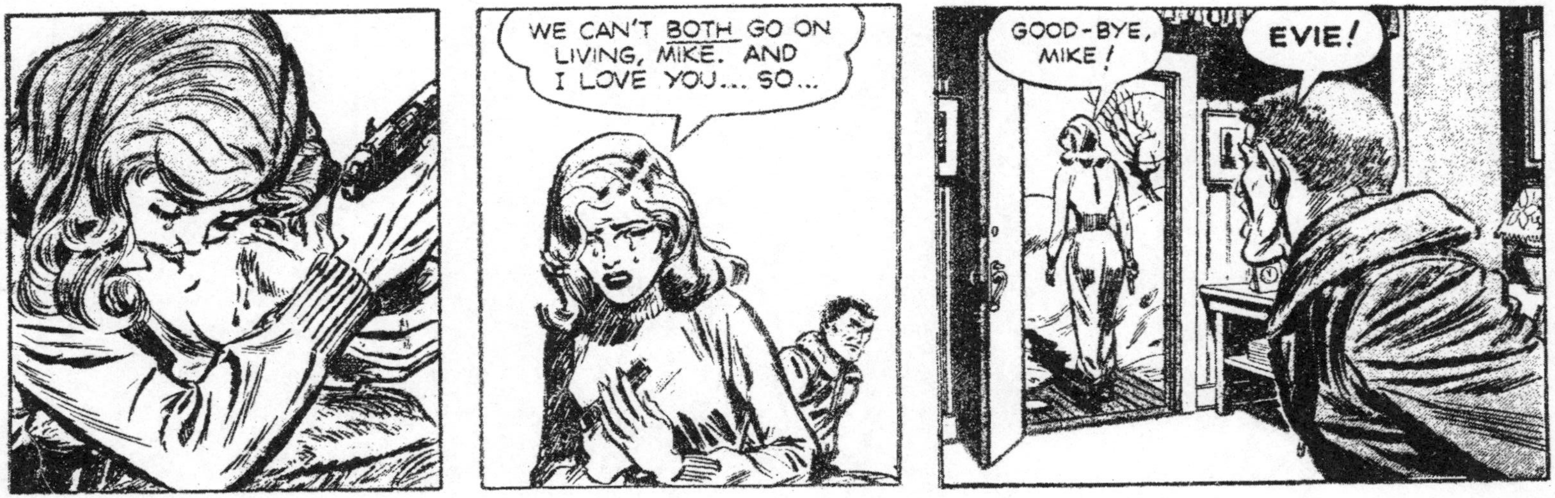
WE CAN'T BOTH GO ON LIVING, MIKE. AND I LOVE YOU... SO...
GOOD-BYE, MIKE!
EVIE!

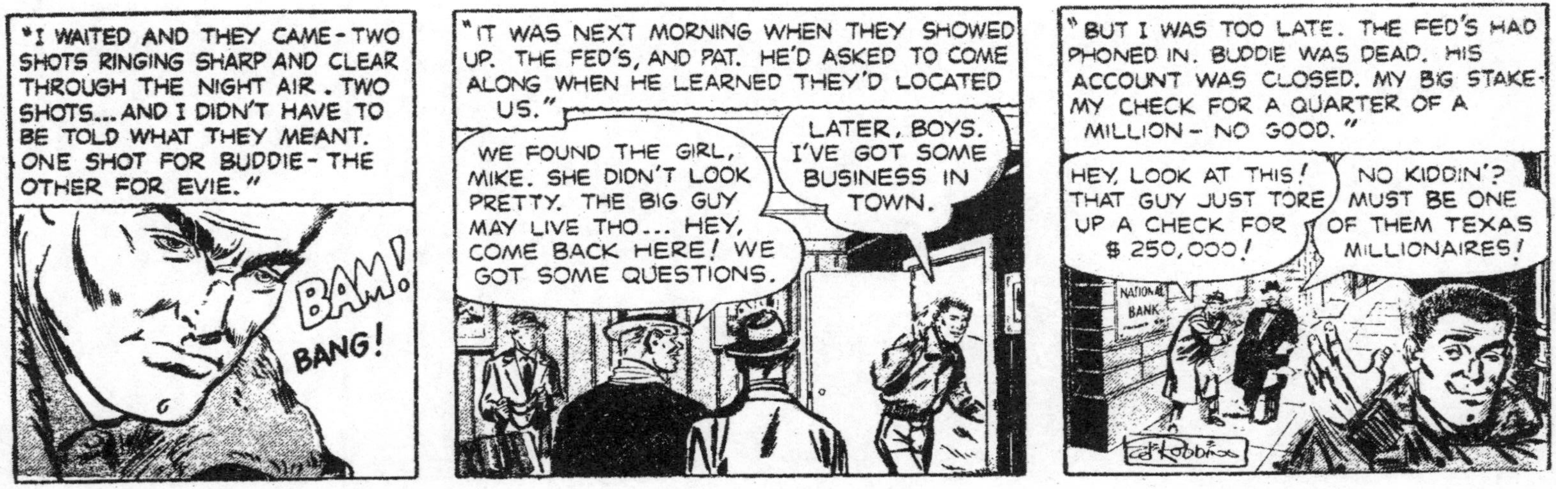
"I WAITED AND THEY CAME - TWO SHOTS RINGING SHARP AND CLEAR THROUGH THE NIGHT AIR. TWO SHOTS... AND I DIDN'T HAVE TO BE TOLD WHAT THEY MEANT. ONE SHOT FOR BUDDIE - THE OTHER FOR EVIE."
BAM!
BANG!
"IT WAS NEXT MORNING WHEN THEY SHOWED UP. THE FED'S, AND PAT. HE'D ASKED TO COME ALONG WHEN HE LEARNED THEY'D LOCATED US."
WE FOUND THE GIRL, MIKE. SHE DIDN'T LOOK PRETTY. THE BIG GUY MAY LIVE THO... HEY, COME BACK HERE! WE GOT SOME QUESTIONS.
LATER, BOYS. I'VE GOT SOME BUSINESS IN TOWN.
"BUT I WAS TOO LATE. THE FED'S HAD PHONED IN. BUDDIE WAS DEAD. HIS ACCOUNT WAS CLOSED. MY BIG STAKE - MY CHECK FOR A QUARTER OF A MILLION - NO GOOD."
HEY, LOOK AT THIS! THAT GUY JUST TORE UP A CHECK FOR $ 250,000!
NO KIDDIN'? MUST BE ONE OF THEM TEXAS MILLIONAIRES!
NATIONAL BANK

"If you know who he is,
he already owns you"

Our guide through London's notorious Earls
Court and beyond is a smooth-talking
East End gangster. Follow him into the
underworld dealings of his impossibly
wealthy boss, a man obsessed with owning
beautiful boys and willing to pay a mysterious
wandering sect any price to buy the
precious ravishing youth they have raised.
Neil Gaiman is a hugely successful novelist
and screenwriter, author of *The Sandman*
graphic novels. He brings his magic-realist
flair and love of arcana and folklore to this
unconventional urban noir, captured by
Warren Pleece's observant penmanship.

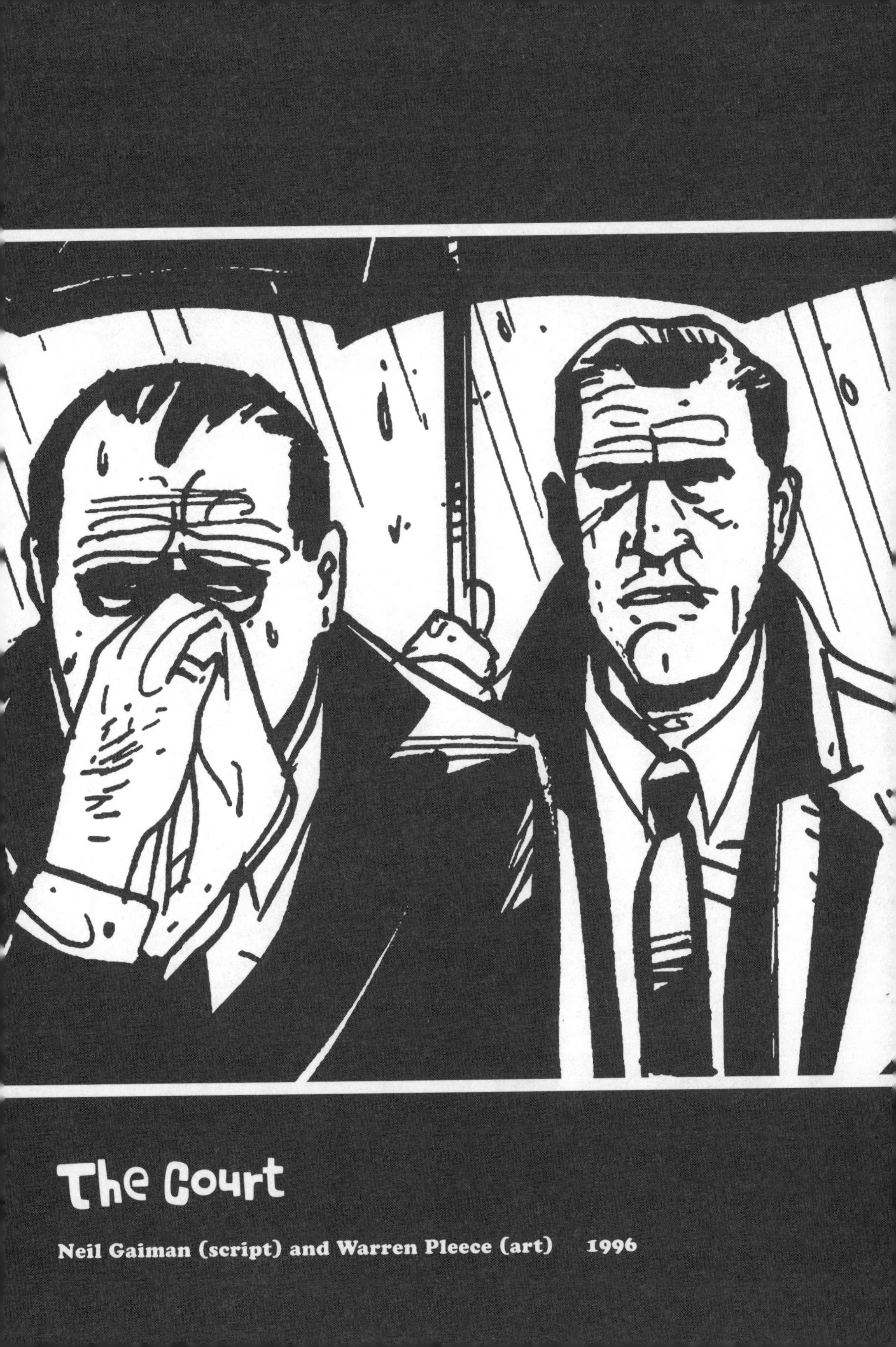

The Court

Neil Gaiman (script) and Warren Pleece (art)   1996

the court

Neil Gaiman
Warren Pleece

One thing I've never understood is why the alcoholics and junkies hang around Earl's Court station.

Well, the junkies are looking for a fix, I suppose.

But why the alcoholics?

You're an alcoholic, no one's going to walk up to you, slip you a can of Guinness scrunched up in a brown paper bag.

They just seem to do it for the company. Why don't they go to pubs? Or sit in the park? Sunny day like today, I'd go to the park. If I was an alcoholic, I wouldn't go to Earl's Court station. And you can take that to the fucking bank.

I'm waiting for my boss.

My boss. This is how rich my boss is: you've never heard of him. Now that takes money. None of your Murdoch, cap-in-hand-to-the-merchant-banks rubbish; you'll never find my boss in the glossy magazines, showing people around his glossy new house.

If you know who he is, he already owns you.

He's owned me since I was fifteen.

Let's call him Mr Alice.

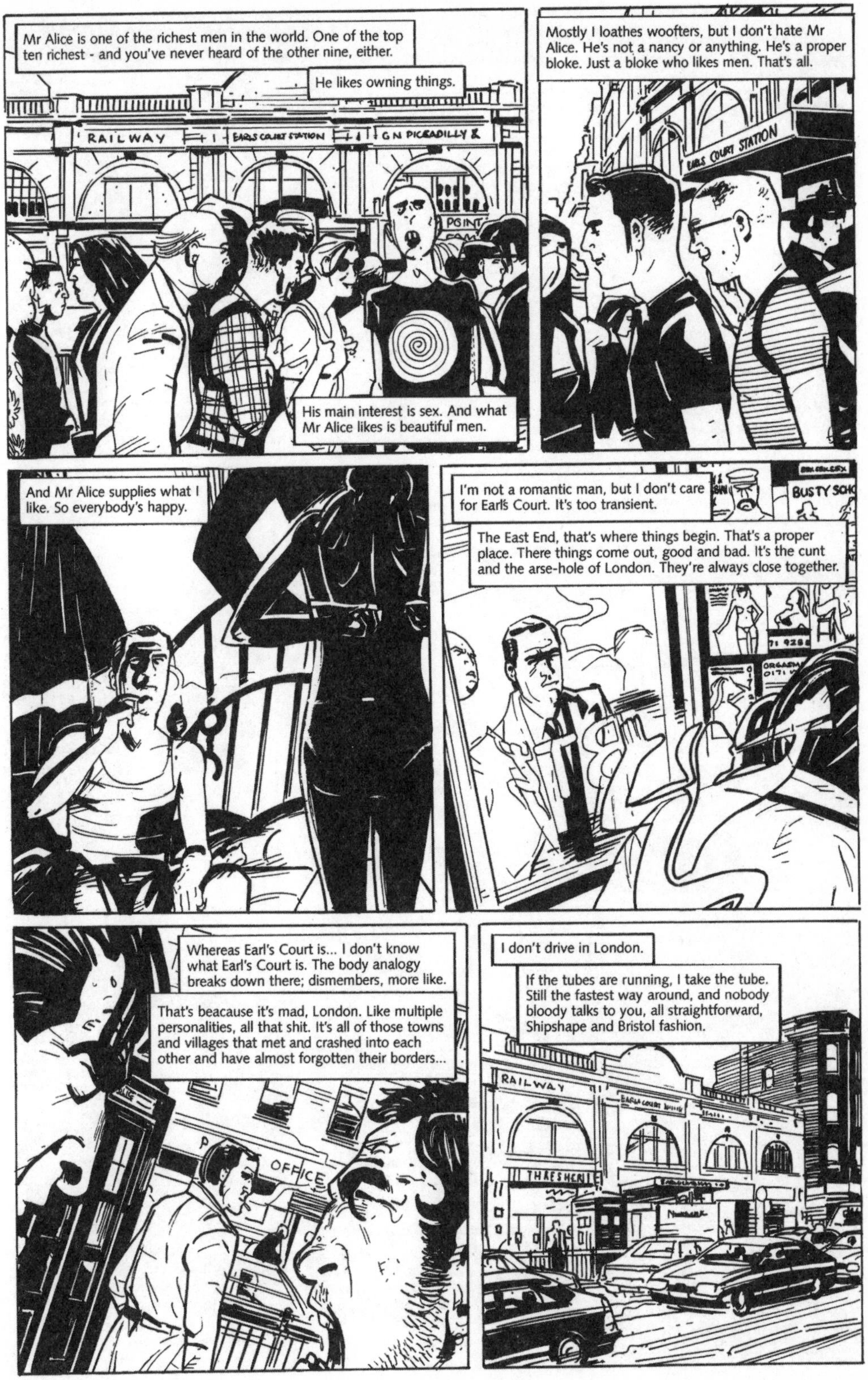
Mr Alice is one of the richest men in the world. One of the top ten richest - and you've never heard of the other nine, either.
He likes owning things.
RAILWAY
EARLS COURT STATION
GN PICCADILLY &
His main interest is sex. And what Mr Alice likes is beautiful men.
Mostly I loathes woofters, but I don't hate Mr Alice. He's not a nancy or anything. He's a proper bloke. Just a bloke who likes men. That's all.
EARLS COURT STATION
And Mr Alice supplies what I like. So everybody's happy.
I'm not a romantic man, but I don't care for Earl's Court. It's too transient.
The East End, that's where things begin. That's a proper place. There things come out, good and bad. It's the cunt and the arse-hole of London. They're always close together.
Whereas Earl's Court is... I don't know what Earl's Court is. The body analogy breaks down there; dismembers, more like.
That's beacause it's mad, London. Like multiple personalities, all that shit. It's all of those towns and villages that met and crashed into each other and have almost forgotten their borders...
OFFICE
I don't drive in London.
If the tubes are running, I take the tube. Still the fastest way around, and nobody bloody talks to you, all straightforward, Shipshape and Bristol fashion.
RAILWAY
THRESHER

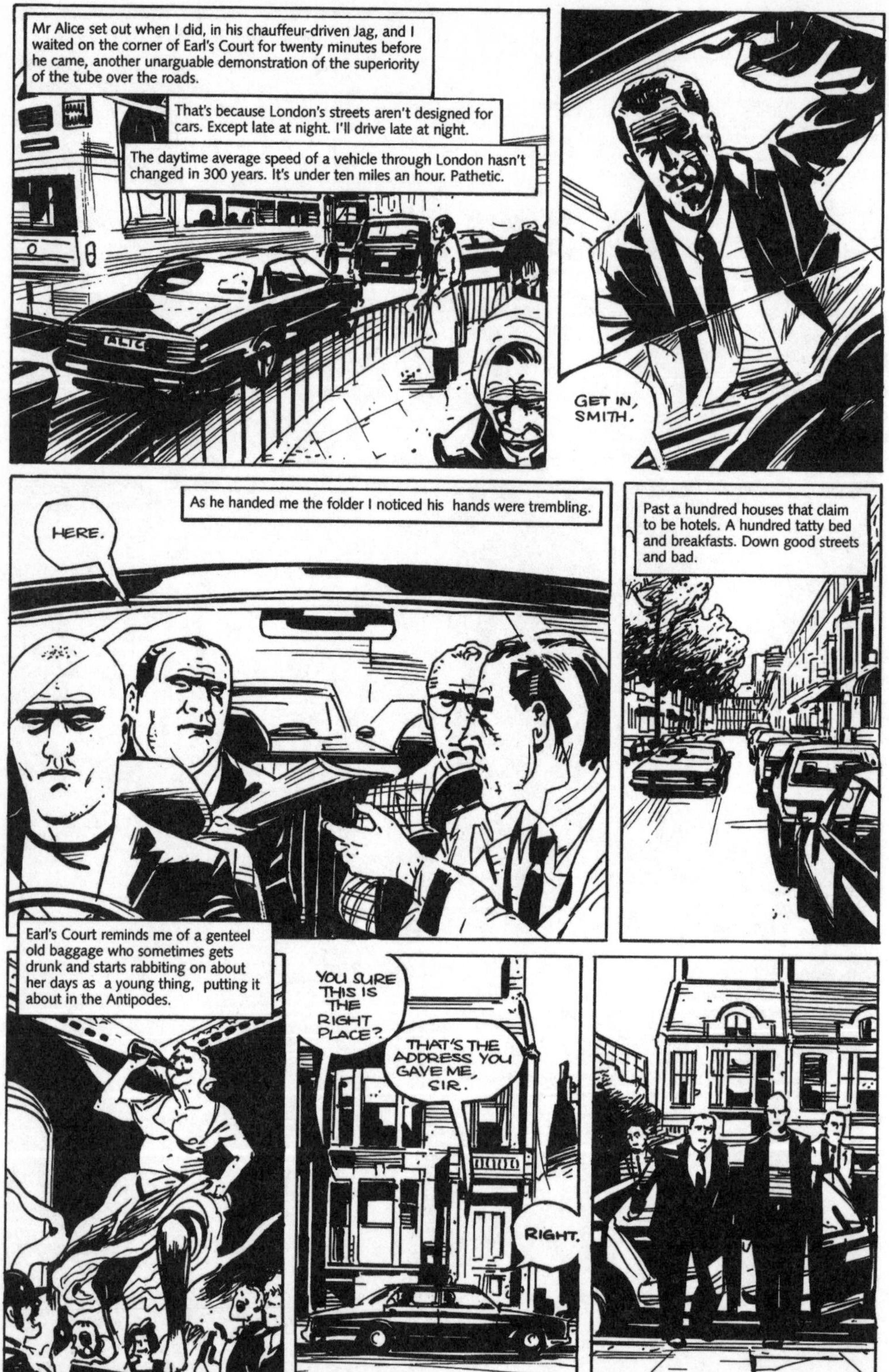
Mr Alice set out when I did, in his chauffeur-driven Jag, and I waited on the corner of Earl's Court for twenty minutes before he came, another unarguable demonstration of the superiority of the tube over the roads.
That's because London's streets aren't designed for cars. Except late at night. I'll drive late at night.
The daytime average speed of a vehicle through London hasn't changed in 300 years. It's under ten miles an hour. Pathetic.
ALICE
GET IN, SMITH.
HERE.
As he handed me the folder I noticed his hands were trembling.
Past a hundred houses that claim to be hotels. A hundred tatty bed and breakfasts. Down good streets and bad.
Earl's Court reminds me of a genteel old baggage who sometimes gets drunk and starts rabbiting on about her days as a young thing, putting it about in the Antipodes.
YOU SURE THIS IS THE RIGHT PLACE?
THAT'S THE ADDRESS YOU GAVE ME, SIR.
RIGHT.

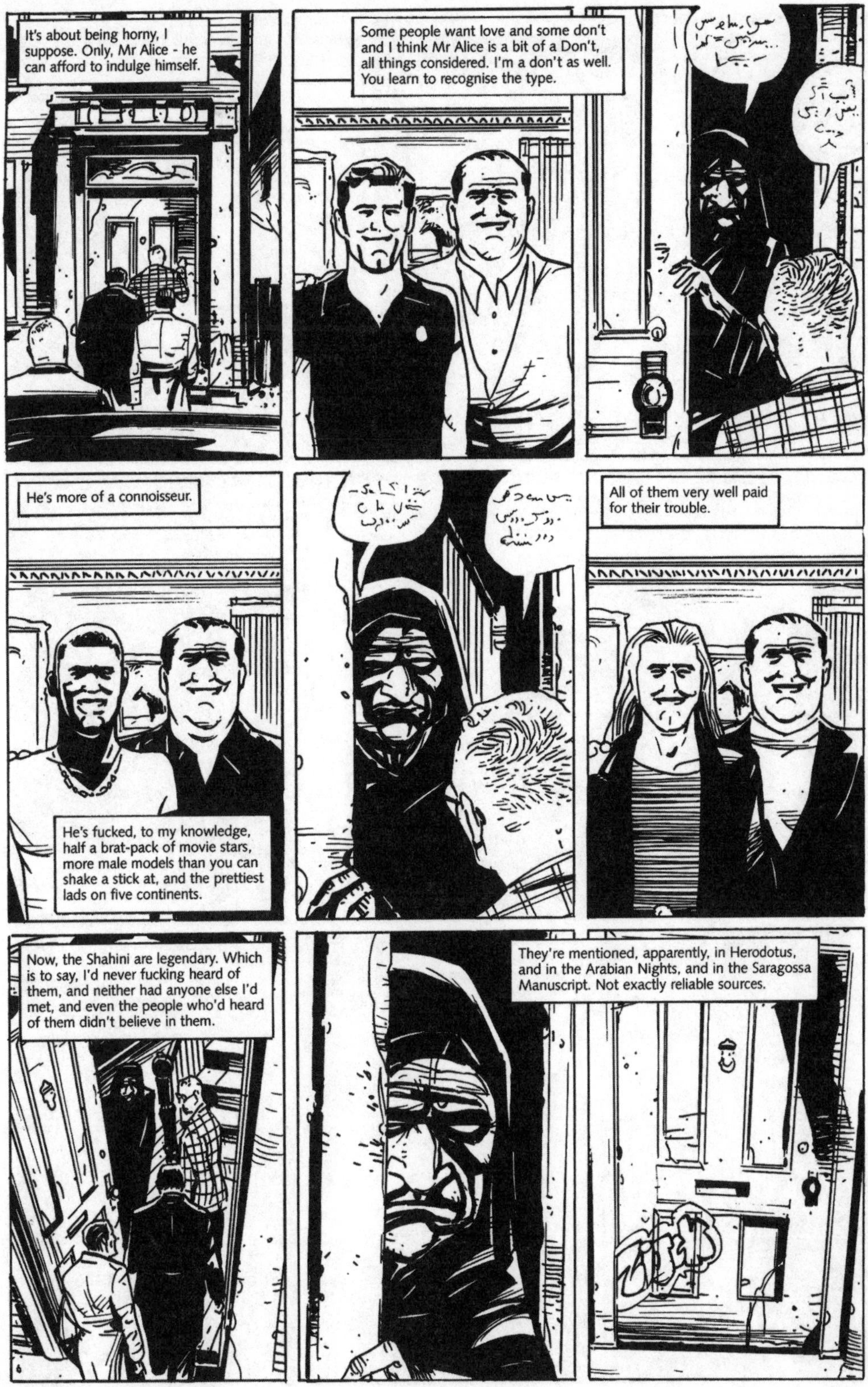
It's about being horny, I suppose. Only, Mr Alice - he can afford to indulge himself.
Some people want love and some don't and I think Mr Alice is a bit of a Don't, all things considered. I'm a don't as well. You learn to recognise the type.
He's more of a connoisseur.
He's fucked, to my knowledge, half a brat-pack of movie stars, more male models than you can shake a stick at, and the prettiest lads on five continents.
All of them very well paid for their trouble.
Now, the Shahini are legendary. Which is to say, I'd never fucking heard of them, and neither had anyone else I'd met, and even the people who'd heard of them didn't believe in them.
They're mentioned, apparently, in Herodotus, and in the Arabian Nights, and in the Saragossa Manuscript. Not exactly reliable sources.

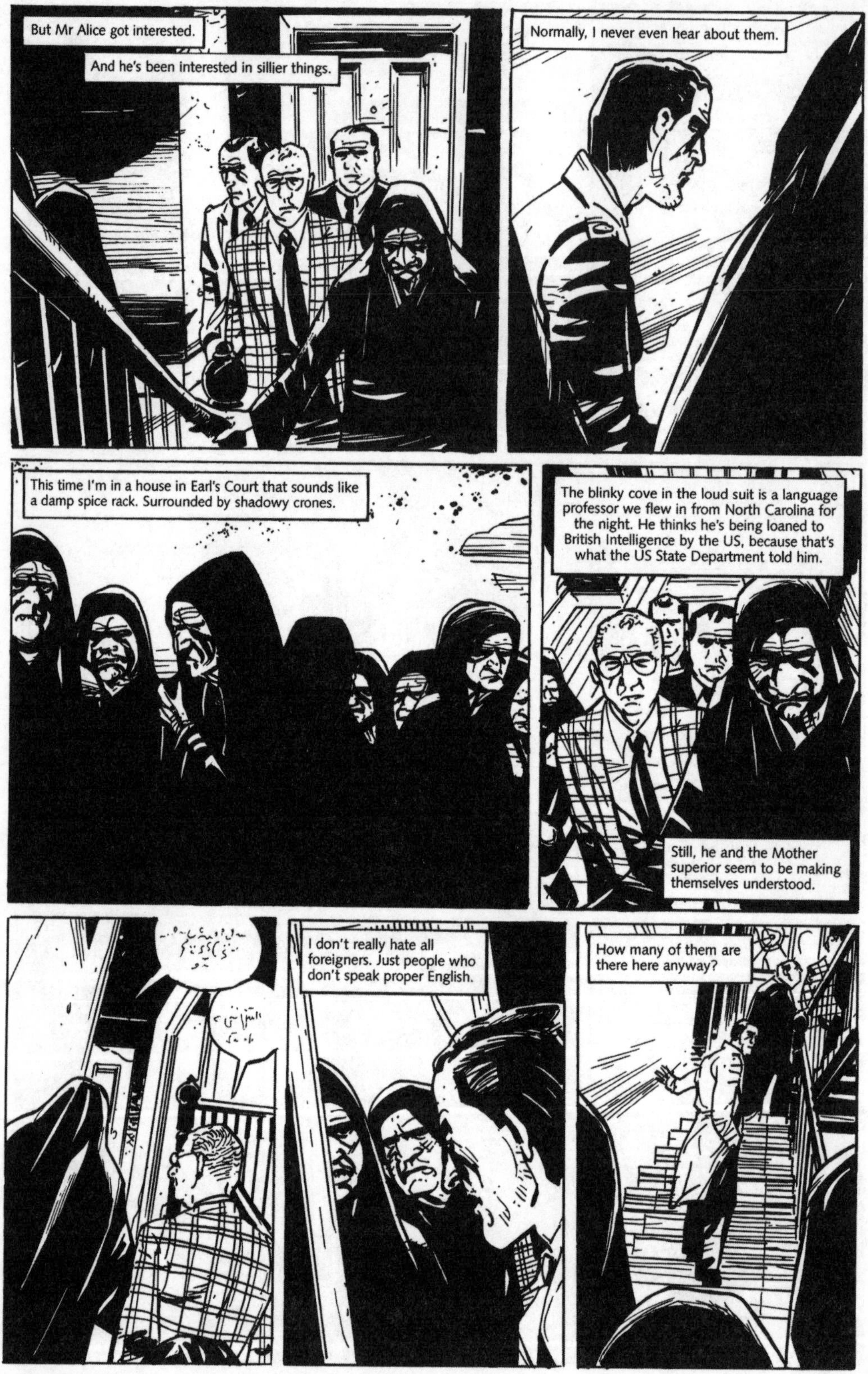
But Mr Alice got interested.
And he's been interested in sillier things.
Normally, I never even hear about them.
This time I'm in a house in Earl's Court that sounds like a damp spice rack. Surrounded by shadowy crones.
The blinky cove in the loud suit is a language professor we flew in from North Carolina for the night. He thinks he's being loaned to British Intelligence by the US, because that's what the US State Department told him.
Still, he and the Mother superior seem to be making themselves understood.
I don't really hate all foreigners. Just people who don't speak proper English.
How many of them are there here anyway?

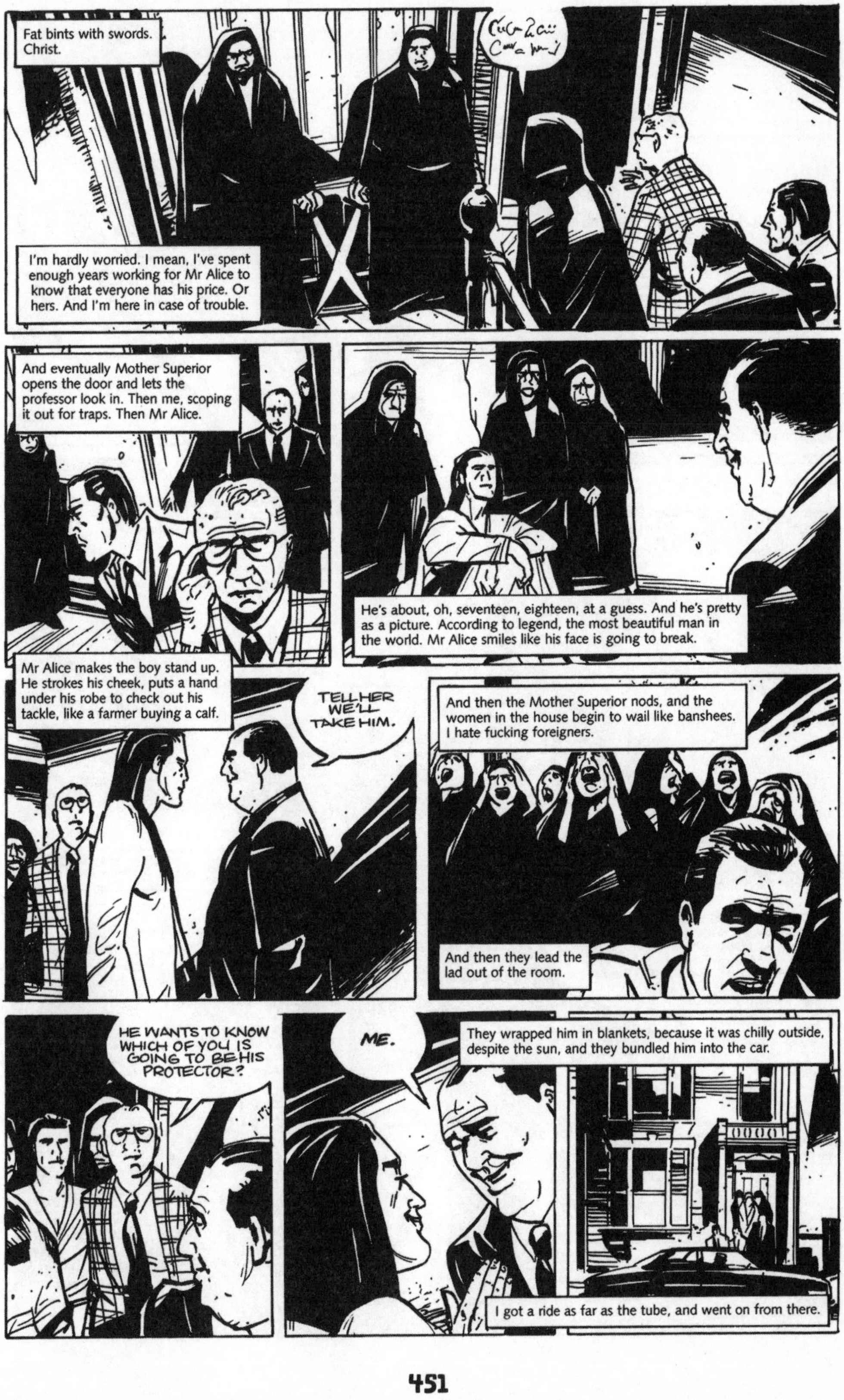
Fat bints with swords. Christ.
I'm hardly worried. I mean, I've spent enough years working for Mr Alice to know that everyone has his price. Or hers. And I'm here in case of trouble.
And eventually Mother Superior opens the door and lets the professor look in. Then me, scoping it out for traps. Then Mr Alice.
He's about, oh, seventeen, eighteen, at a guess. And he's pretty as a picture. According to legend, the most beautiful man in the world. Mr Alice smiles like his face is going to break.
Mr Alice makes the boy stand up. He strokes his cheek, puts a hand under his robe to check out his tackle, like a farmer buying a calf.
TELL HER WE'LL TAKE HIM.
And then the Mother Superior nods, and the women in the house begin to wail like banshees. I hate fucking foreigners.
And then they lead the lad out of the room.
HE WANTS TO KNOW WHICH OF YOU IS GOING TO BE HIS PROTECTOR?
ME.
They wrapped him in blankets, because it was chilly outside, despite the sun, and they bundled him into the car.
I got a ride as far as the tube, and went on from there.

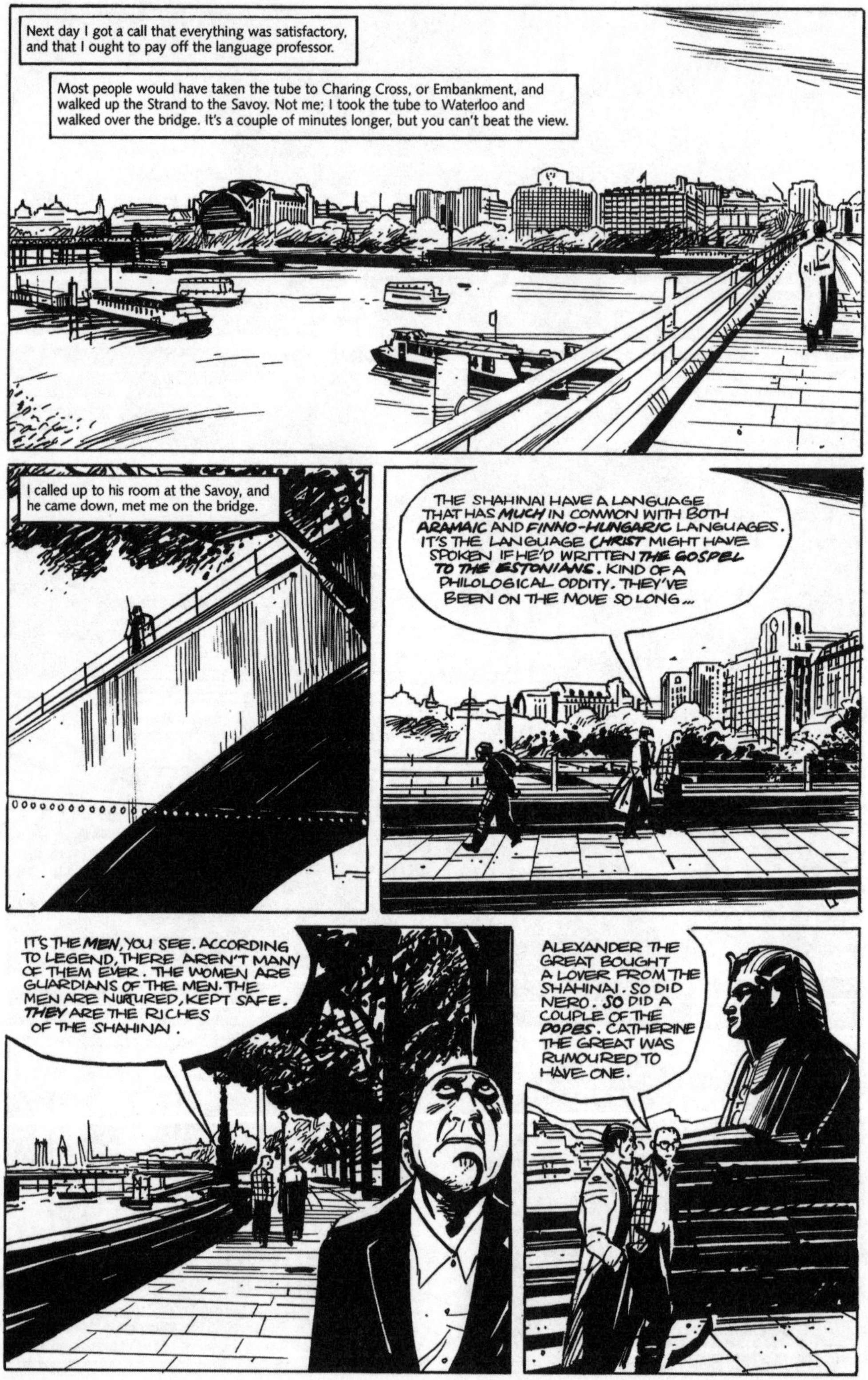
Next day I got a call that everything was satisfactory, and that I ought to pay off the language professor.
Most people would have taken the tube to Charing Cross, or Embankment, and walked up the Strand to the Savoy. Not me; I took the tube to Waterloo and walked over the bridge. It's a couple of minutes longer, but you can't beat the view.
I called up to his room at the Savoy, and he came down, met me on the bridge.
THE SHAHINAI HAVE A LANGUAGE THAT HAS MUCH IN COMMON WITH BOTH ARAMAIC AND FINNO-HUNGARIC LANGUAGES. IT'S THE LANGUAGE CHRIST MIGHT HAVE SPOKEN IF HE'D WRITTEN THE GOSPEL TO THE ESTONIANS. KIND OF A PHILOLOGICAL ODDITY. THEY'VE BEEN ON THE MOVE SO LONG...
IT'S THE MEN, YOU SEE. ACCORDING TO LEGEND, THERE AREN'T MANY OF THEM EVER. THE WOMEN ARE GUARDIANS OF THE MEN. THE MEN ARE NURTURED, KEPT SAFE. THEY ARE THE RICHES OF THE SHAHINAI.
ALEXANDER THE GREAT BOUGHT A LOVER FROM THE SHAHINAI. SO DID NERO. SO DID A COUPLE OF THE POPES. CATHERINE THE GREAT WAS RUMOURED TO HAVE ONE.

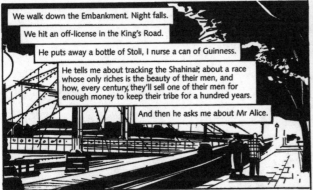

We walk down the Embankment. Night falls.

We hit an off-license in the King's Road.

He puts away a bottle of Stoli, I nurse a can of Guinness.

He tells me about tracking the Shahinai; about a race whose only riches is the beauty of their men, and how, every century, they'll sell one of their men for enough money to keep their tribe for a hundred years.

And then he asks me about Mr Alice.

HE MUST BE *VERY* RICH.

HE IS.

I'M STRAIGHT. BUT I'D FUCK THAT BOY LIKE A SHOT. WHAT ABOUT YOU?

NOT MY CUP OF TEA, REALLY

MM. WHAT IS YOUR CUP OF TEA?

...LITTLE GIRLS.

HOW LITTLE?

ELEVEN, TWELVE, THIRTEEN, FOURTEEN MAYBE. OLDER THAN THAT AND I NORMALLY CAN'T GET IT UP. DOESN'T DO IT FOR ME.

He looked like I'd just told him I liked to fuck dead dogs.

YOU KNOW, BACK IN THE STATES, SOMETHING LIKE THAT WOULD BE ILLEGAL.

YEAH. WELL, THEY AREN'T TOO KEEN ON IT OVER HERE.

DO YOU WANT ANYTHING ELSE TO DRINK?

NO, THANKS. I THINK I OUGHT TO BE GETTING ON BACK.

The cab had been circling for half an hour. I waved it down. It was one of Our Particular Cabs - the kind people get into, and aren't seen getting out of, ever again.

TAX

THE SAVOY, PLEASE.

RIGHT YOU ARE.

I watched it take him away.

Later that night someone checked out of the Savoy, using the professor's credit card, and a pretty good version of his signature.

453

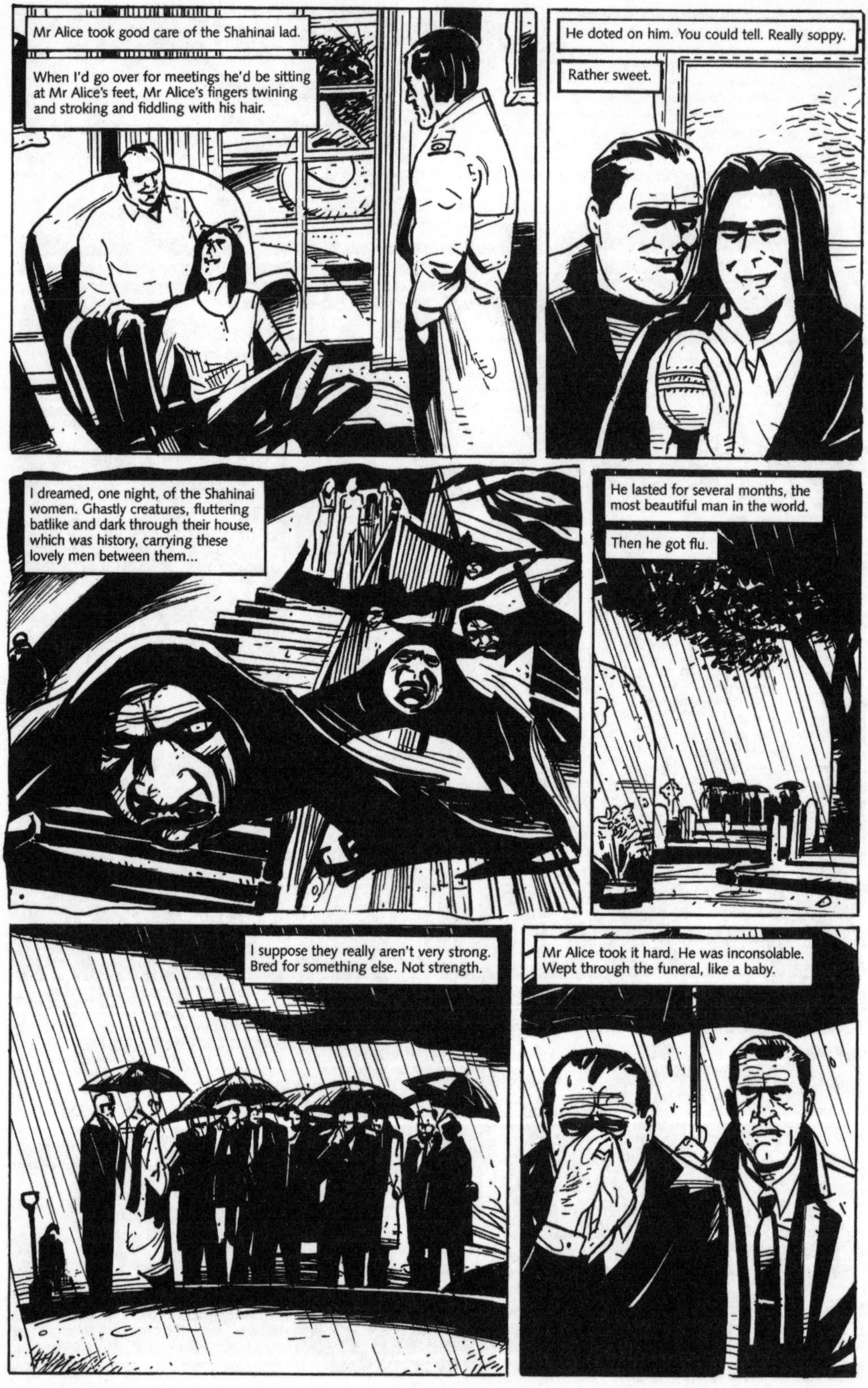
Mr Alice took good care of the Shahinai lad.
When I'd go over for meetings he'd be sitting at Mr Alice's feet, Mr Alice's fingers twining and stroking and fiddling with his hair.
He doted on him. You could tell. Really soppy.
Rather sweet.
I dreamed, one night, of the Shahinai women. Ghastly creatures, fluttering batlike and dark through their house, which was history, carrying these lovely men between them...
He lasted for several months, the most beautiful man in the world.
Then he got flu.
I suppose they really aren't very strong. Bred for something else. Not strength.
Mr Alice took it hard. He was inconsolable. Wept through the funeral, like a baby.

The next day we went back to the house in Earl's Court to see if the Shahinai were still about.

The Shahinai women had gone - replaced by a gaggle of young New Zealanders. We surprised some of them in the kitchen, sucking narcotic smoke from the mouth of a broken lemonade bottle.

We searched the house from top to bottom but we found nothing, and all I took away from the house in Earl's Court was the memory of the breast of a girl sleeping naked in an upper room.

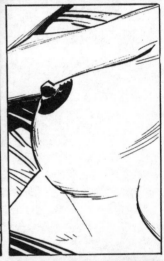

A full, black-nippled breast which curved disturbingly in the sodium light of the street.

THE END

455

"You're a pal George! HIC ...real pal!

Got sumpin, HIC, for me, George?

Whassha got for me, George?

Oh Parm me...

You...

You're Harry"

Of the many imitators of the genre-defining
comic book *Crime Does Not Pay*, *Crime
SuspenStories* from William Gaines' EC
Comics stood apart because it largely ignored
gangster biographies, true or not, and plots
about robbery, kidnapping or blackmail. EC's
writers preferred to mix the twisted twist-
ending, their proven *Tales from the Crypt*
horror formula, with the vicious triangle of
adultery and murder popularized by James M.
Cain, writer of *Double Indemnity. The Sewer*
is a prime example of this by Johnny Craig,
the main cover and lead artist and writer
on the title, and one he was specially proud
of. There is water, water everywhere: the
lashing rainstorm, the spilling bottle of booze,
the bathtub, the tears of hysteria and beads
of sweaty panic, and the horrifying ironic
denouement. Quality like this took time for
Craig to write as well as draw, but his slow,
meticulous care resulted in a select body of
exceptional work.

The Sewer

Johnny Craig (script & art)   1951

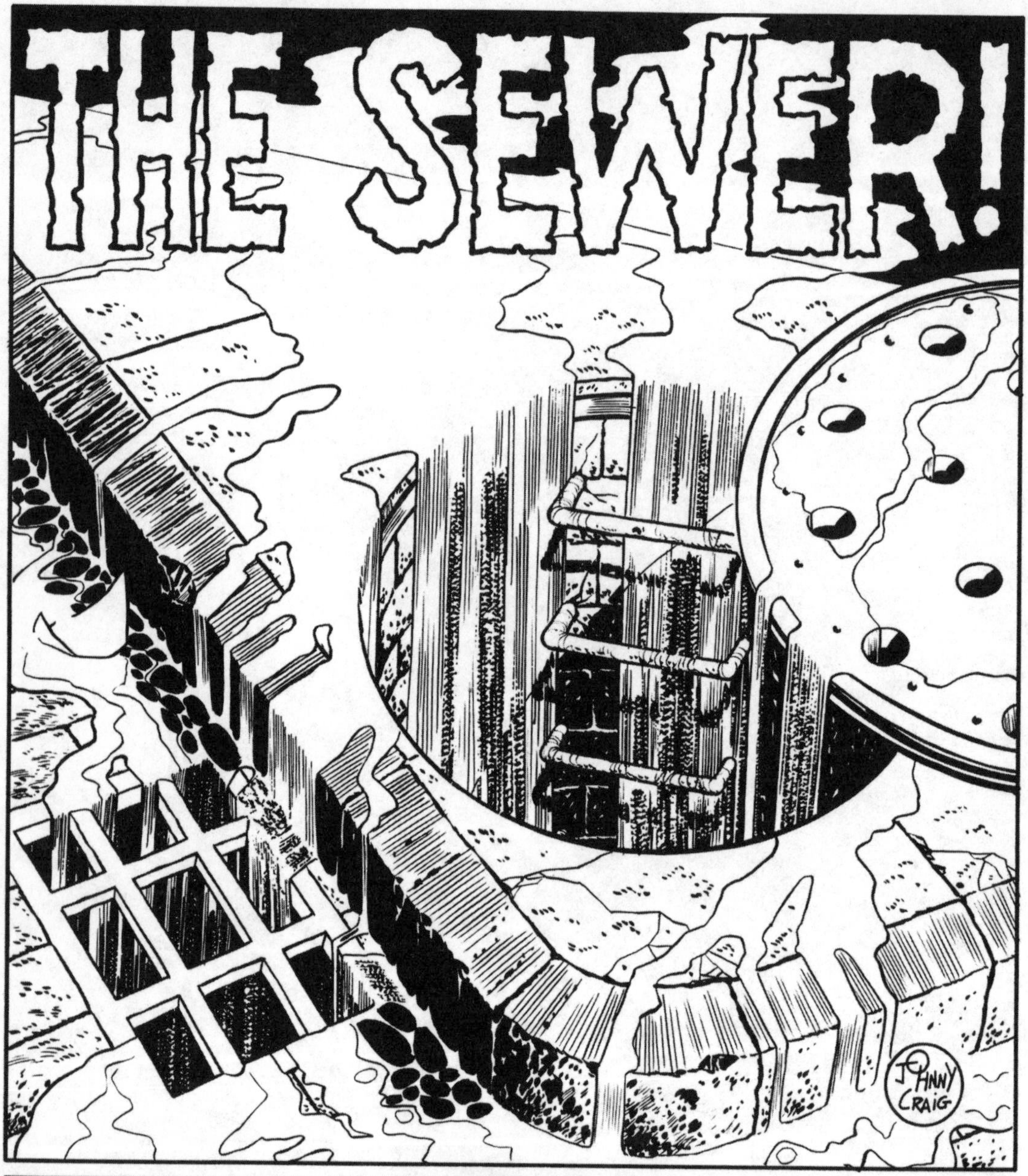
THE SEWER!
JOHNNY CRAIG

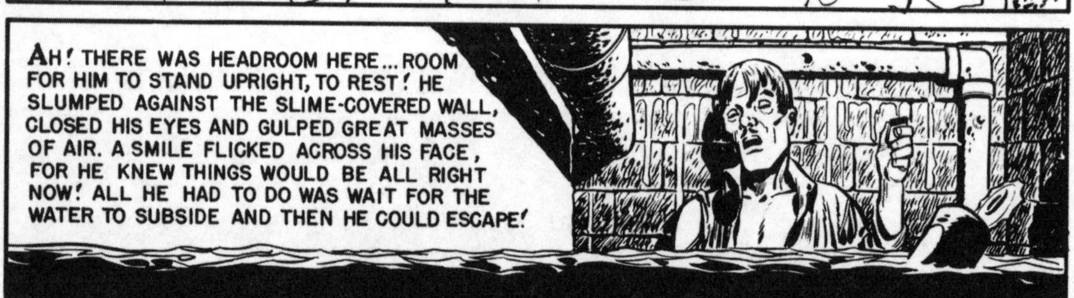
AH! THERE WAS HEADROOM HERE... ROOM FOR HIM TO STAND UPRIGHT, TO REST! HE SLUMPED AGAINST THE SLIME-COVERED WALL, CLOSED HIS EYES AND GULPED GREAT MASSES OF AIR. A SMILE FLICKED ACROSS HIS FACE, FOR HE KNEW THINGS WOULD BE ALL RIGHT NOW! ALL HE HAD TO DO WAS WAIT FOR THE WATER TO SUBSIDE AND THEN HE COULD ESCAPE!
1

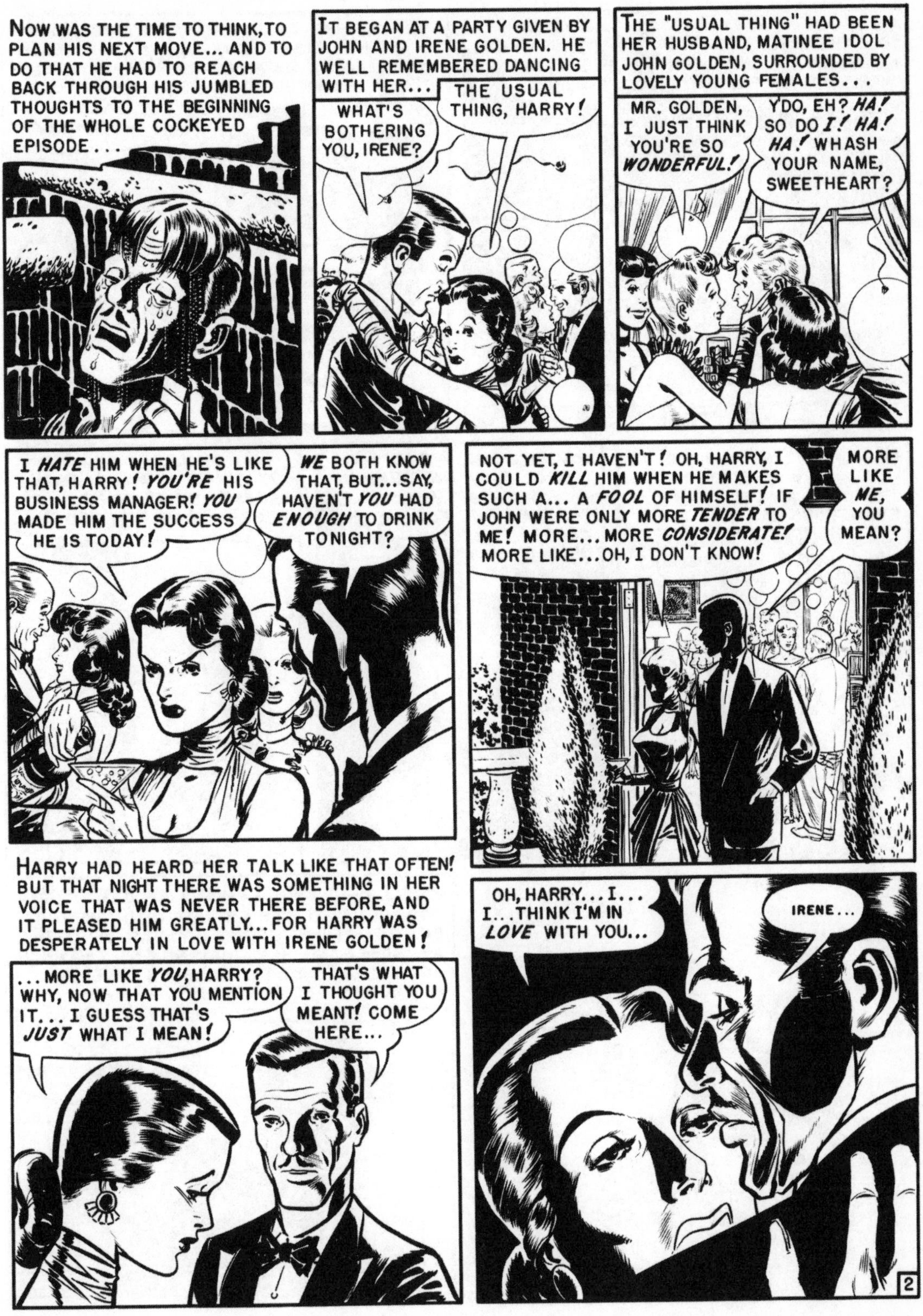
NOW WAS THE TIME TO THINK, TO PLAN HIS NEXT MOVE... AND TO DO THAT HE HAD TO REACH BACK THROUGH HIS JUMBLED THOUGHTS TO THE BEGINNING OF THE WHOLE COCKEYED EPISODE...
IT BEGAN AT A PARTY GIVEN BY JOHN AND IRENE GOLDEN. HE WELL REMEMBERED DANCING WITH HER...
WHAT'S BOTHERING YOU, IRENE?
THE USUAL THING, HARRY!
THE "USUAL THING" HAD BEEN HER HUSBAND, MATINEE IDOL JOHN GOLDEN, SURROUNDED BY LOVELY YOUNG FEMALES...
MR. GOLDEN, I JUST THINK YOU'RE SO WONDERFUL!
Y'DO, EH? HA! SO DO I! HA! HA! WHASH YOUR NAME, SWEETHEART?
I HATE HIM WHEN HE'S LIKE THAT, HARRY! YOU'RE HIS BUSINESS MANAGER! YOU MADE HIM THE SUCCESS HE IS TODAY!
WE BOTH KNOW THAT, BUT... SAY, HAVEN'T YOU HAD ENOUGH TO DRINK TONIGHT?
NOT YET, I HAVEN'T! OH, HARRY, I COULD KILL HIM WHEN HE MAKES SUCH A... A FOOL OF HIMSELF! IF JOHN WERE ONLY MORE TENDER TO ME! MORE... MORE CONSIDERATE! MORE LIKE... OH, I DON'T KNOW!
MORE LIKE ME, YOU MEAN?
HARRY HAD HEARD HER TALK LIKE THAT OFTEN! BUT THAT NIGHT THERE WAS SOMETHING IN HER VOICE THAT WAS NEVER THERE BEFORE, AND IT PLEASED HIM GREATLY... FOR HARRY WAS DESPERATELY IN LOVE WITH IRENE GOLDEN!
...MORE LIKE YOU, HARRY? WHY, NOW THAT YOU MENTION IT... I GUESS THAT'S JUST WHAT I MEAN!
THAT'S WHAT I THOUGHT YOU MEANT! COME HERE...
OH, HARRY... I... I... THINK I'M IN LOVE WITH YOU...
IRENE...
2

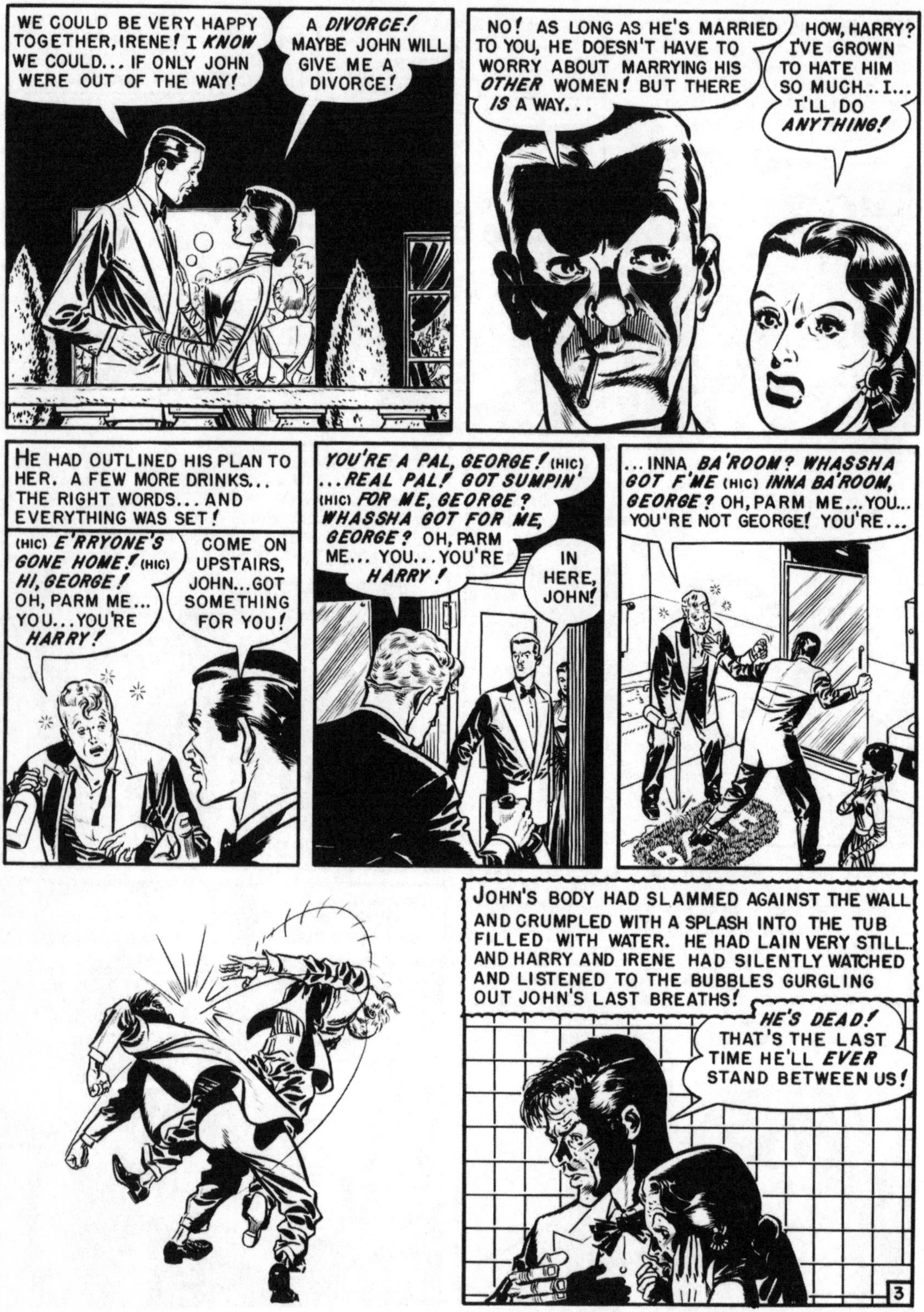
WE COULD BE VERY HAPPY TOGETHER, IRENE! I KNOW WE COULD... IF ONLY JOHN WERE OUT OF THE WAY!
A DIVORCE! MAYBE JOHN WILL GIVE ME A DIVORCE!
NO! AS LONG AS HE'S MARRIED TO YOU, HE DOESN'T HAVE TO WORRY ABOUT MARRYING HIS OTHER WOMEN! BUT THERE IS A WAY...
HOW, HARRY? I'VE GROWN TO HATE HIM SO MUCH... I... I'LL DO ANYTHING!
HE HAD OUTLINED HIS PLAN TO HER. A FEW MORE DRINKS... THE RIGHT WORDS... AND EVERYTHING WAS SET!
(HIC) E'RRYONE'S GONE HOME! (HIC) HI, GEORGE! OH, PARM ME... YOU... YOU'RE HARRY!
COME ON UPSTAIRS, JOHN... GOT SOMETHING FOR YOU!
YOU'RE A PAL, GEORGE! (HIC) ...REAL PAL! GOT SUMPIN' (HIC) FOR ME, GEORGE? WHASSHA GOT FOR ME, GEORGE? OH, PARM ME... YOU... YOU'RE HARRY!
IN HERE, JOHN!
...INNA BA'ROOM? WHASSHA GOT F'ME (HIC) INNA BA'ROOM, GEORGE? OH, PARM ME... YOU... YOU'RE NOT GEORGE! YOU'RE...
JOHN'S BODY HAD SLAMMED AGAINST THE WALL AND CRUMPLED WITH A SPLASH INTO THE TUB FILLED WITH WATER. HE HAD LAIN VERY STILL... AND HARRY AND IRENE HAD SILENTLY WATCHED AND LISTENED TO THE BUBBLES GURGLING OUT JOHN'S LAST BREATHS!
HE'S DEAD! THAT'S THE LAST TIME HE'LL EVER STAND BETWEEN US!
3

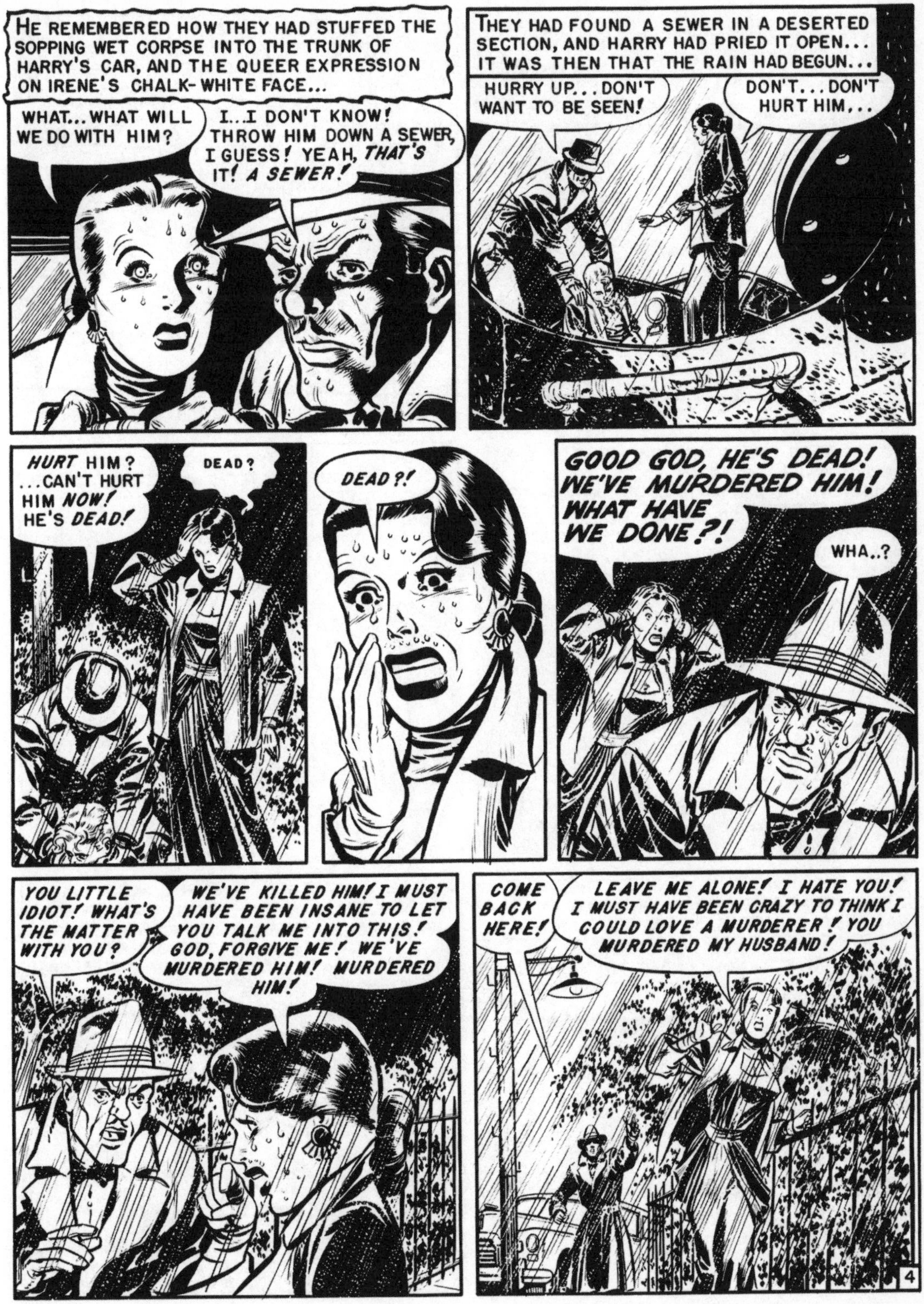
HE REMEMBERED HOW THEY HAD STUFFED THE SOPPING WET CORPSE INTO THE TRUNK OF HARRY'S CAR, AND THE QUEER EXPRESSION ON IRENE'S CHALK-WHITE FACE...
WHAT... WHAT WILL WE DO WITH HIM?
I...I DON'T KNOW! THROW HIM DOWN A SEWER, I GUESS! YEAH, THAT'S IT! A SEWER!
THEY HAD FOUND A SEWER IN A DESERTED SECTION, AND HARRY HAD PRIED IT OPEN... IT WAS THEN THAT THE RAIN HAD BEGUN...
HURRY UP... DON'T WANT TO BE SEEN!
DON'T... DON'T HURT HIM...
HURT HIM? ...CAN'T HURT HIM NOW! HE'S DEAD!
DEAD?
DEAD?!
GOOD GOD, HE'S DEAD! WE'VE MURDERED HIM! WHAT HAVE WE DONE?!
WHA..?
YOU LITTLE IDIOT! WHAT'S THE MATTER WITH YOU?
WE'VE KILLED HIM! I MUST HAVE BEEN INSANE TO LET YOU TALK ME INTO THIS! GOD, FORGIVE ME! WE'VE MURDERED HIM! MURDERED HIM!
COME BACK HERE!
LEAVE ME ALONE! I HATE YOU! I MUST HAVE BEEN CRAZY TO THINK I COULD LOVE A MURDERER! YOU MURDERED MY HUSBAND!
4

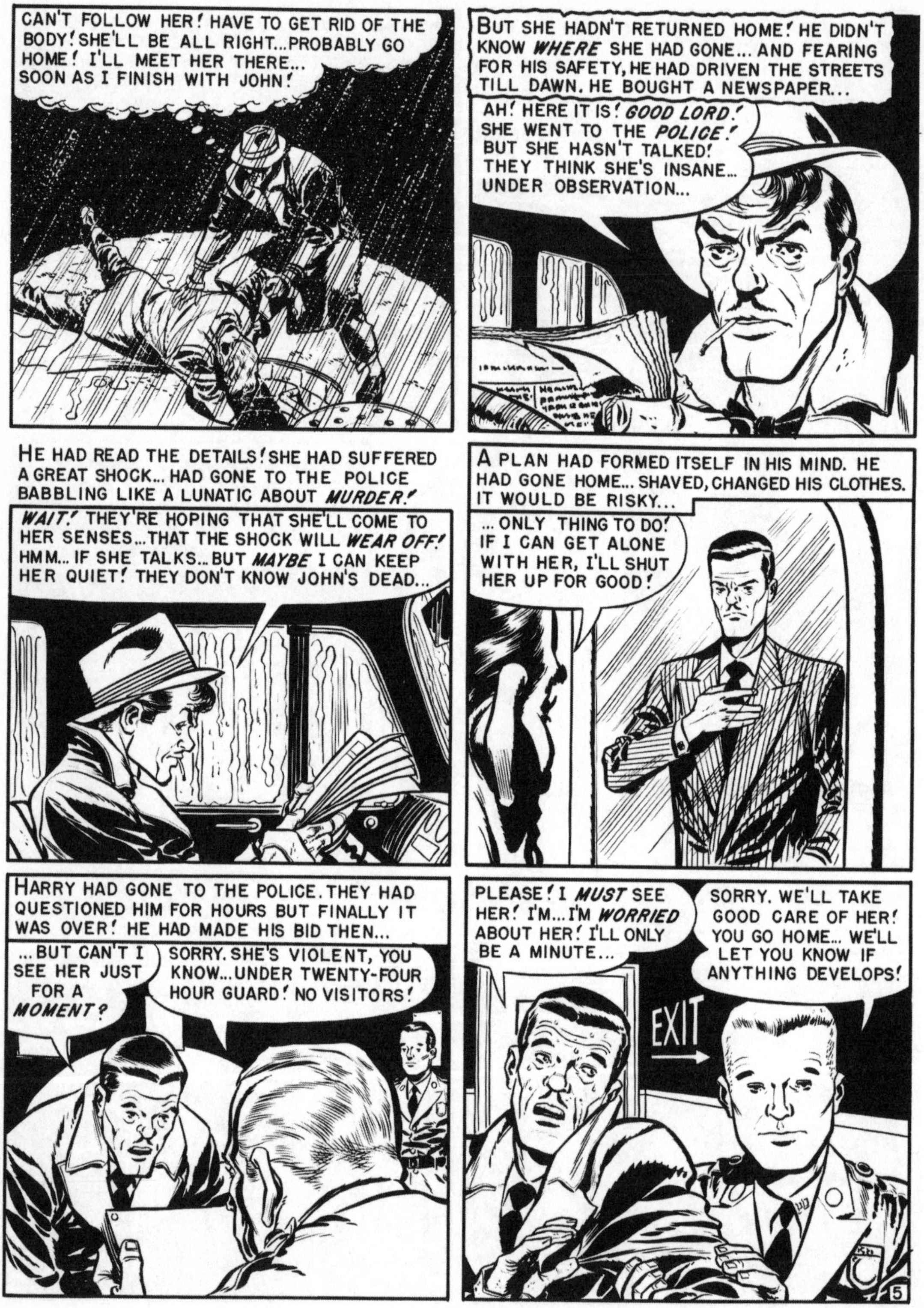
CAN'T FOLLOW HER! HAVE TO GET RID OF THE BODY! SHE'LL BE ALL RIGHT...PROBABLY GO HOME! I'LL MEET HER THERE... SOON AS I FINISH WITH JOHN!
BUT SHE HADN'T RETURNED HOME! HE DIDN'T KNOW *WHERE* SHE HAD GONE... AND FEARING FOR HIS SAFETY, HE HAD DRIVEN THE STREETS TILL DAWN. HE BOUGHT A NEWSPAPER...
AH! HERE IT IS! *GOOD LORD!* SHE WENT TO THE *POLICE!* BUT SHE HASN'T TALKED! THEY THINK SHE'S INSANE... UNDER OBSERVATION...
HE HAD READ THE DETAILS! SHE HAD SUFFERED A GREAT SHOCK... HAD GONE TO THE POLICE BABBLING LIKE A LUNATIC ABOUT *MURDER!*
WAIT! THEY'RE HOPING THAT SHE'LL COME TO HER SENSES...THAT THE SHOCK WILL *WEAR OFF!* HMM... IF SHE TALKS... BUT *MAYBE* I CAN KEEP HER QUIET! THEY DON'T KNOW JOHN'S DEAD...
A PLAN HAD FORMED ITSELF IN HIS MIND. HE HAD GONE HOME... SHAVED, CHANGED HIS CLOTHES. IT WOULD BE RISKY...
... ONLY THING TO DO! IF I CAN GET ALONE WITH HER, I'LL SHUT HER UP FOR GOOD!
HARRY HAD GONE TO THE POLICE. THEY HAD QUESTIONED HIM FOR HOURS BUT FINALLY IT WAS OVER! HE HAD MADE HIS BID THEN...
... BUT CAN'T I SEE HER JUST FOR A *MOMENT?*
SORRY. SHE'S VIOLENT, YOU KNOW... UNDER TWENTY-FOUR HOUR GUARD! NO VISITORS!
PLEASE! I *MUST* SEE HER! I'M... I'M *WORRIED* ABOUT HER! I'LL ONLY BE A MINUTE...
SORRY. WE'LL TAKE GOOD CARE OF HER! YOU GO HOME... WE'LL LET YOU KNOW IF ANYTHING DEVELOPS!
EXIT
5

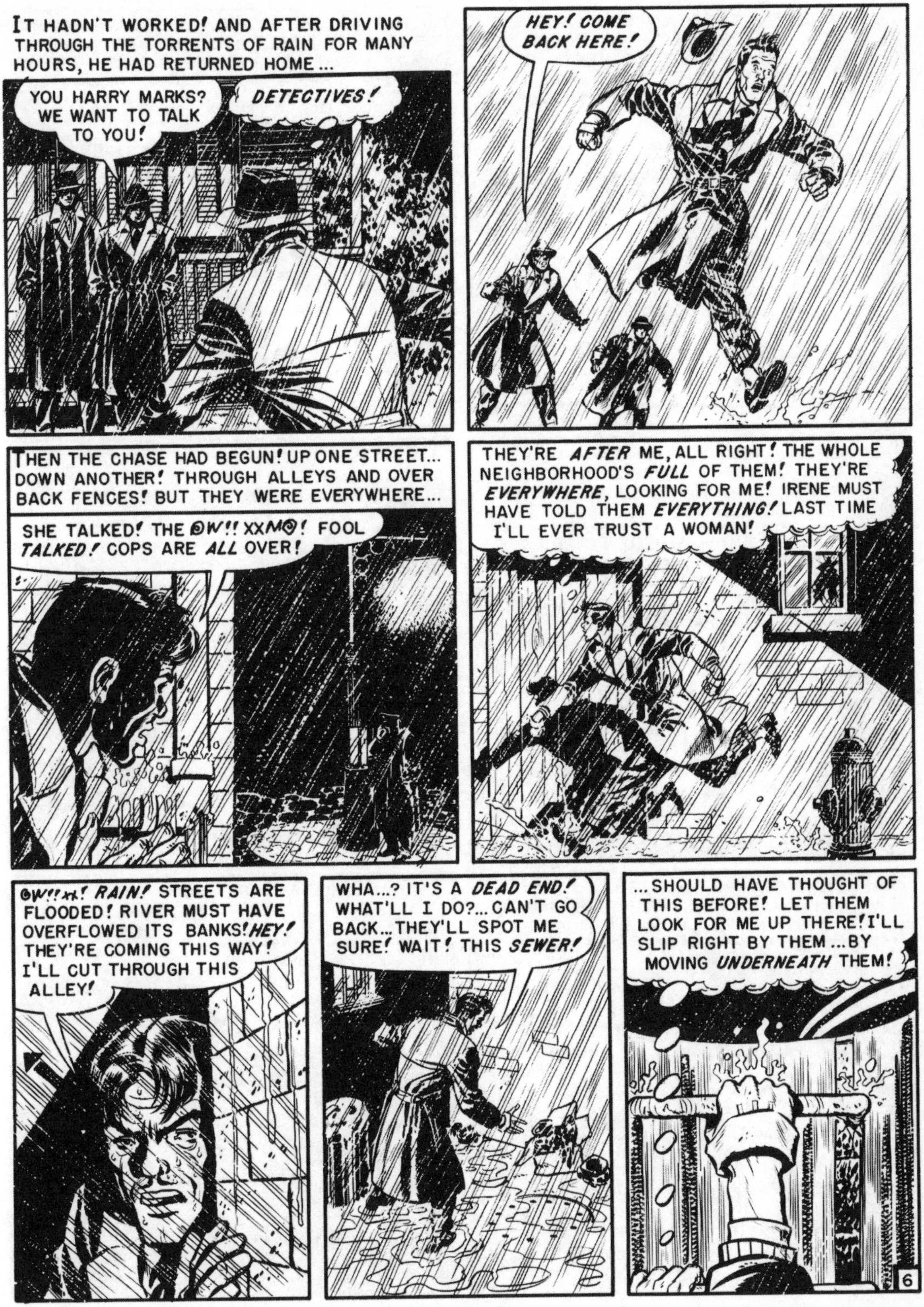
IT HADN'T WORKED! AND AFTER DRIVING THROUGH THE TORRENTS OF RAIN FOR MANY HOURS, HE HAD RETURNED HOME...
YOU HARRY MARKS? WE WANT TO TALK TO YOU!
DETECTIVES!
HEY! COME BACK HERE!
THEN THE CHASE HAD BEGUN! UP ONE STREET... DOWN ANOTHER! THROUGH ALLEYS AND OVER BACK FENCES! BUT THEY WERE EVERYWHERE...
SHE TALKED! THE @W!! XXM@! FOOL TALKED! COPS ARE ALL OVER!
THEY'RE AFTER ME, ALL RIGHT! THE WHOLE NEIGHBORHOOD'S FULL OF THEM! THEY'RE EVERYWHERE, LOOKING FOR ME! IRENE MUST HAVE TOLD THEM EVERYTHING! LAST TIME I'LL EVER TRUST A WOMAN!
@W!!xx! RAIN! STREETS ARE FLOODED! RIVER MUST HAVE OVERFLOWED ITS BANKS! HEY! THEY'RE COMING THIS WAY! I'LL CUT THROUGH THIS ALLEY!
WHA...? IT'S A DEAD END! WHAT'LL I DO?... CAN'T GO BACK... THEY'LL SPOT ME SURE! WAIT! THIS SEWER!
...SHOULD HAVE THOUGHT OF THIS BEFORE! LET THEM LOOK FOR ME UP THERE! I'LL SLIP RIGHT BY THEM... BY MOVING UNDERNEATH THEM!
6

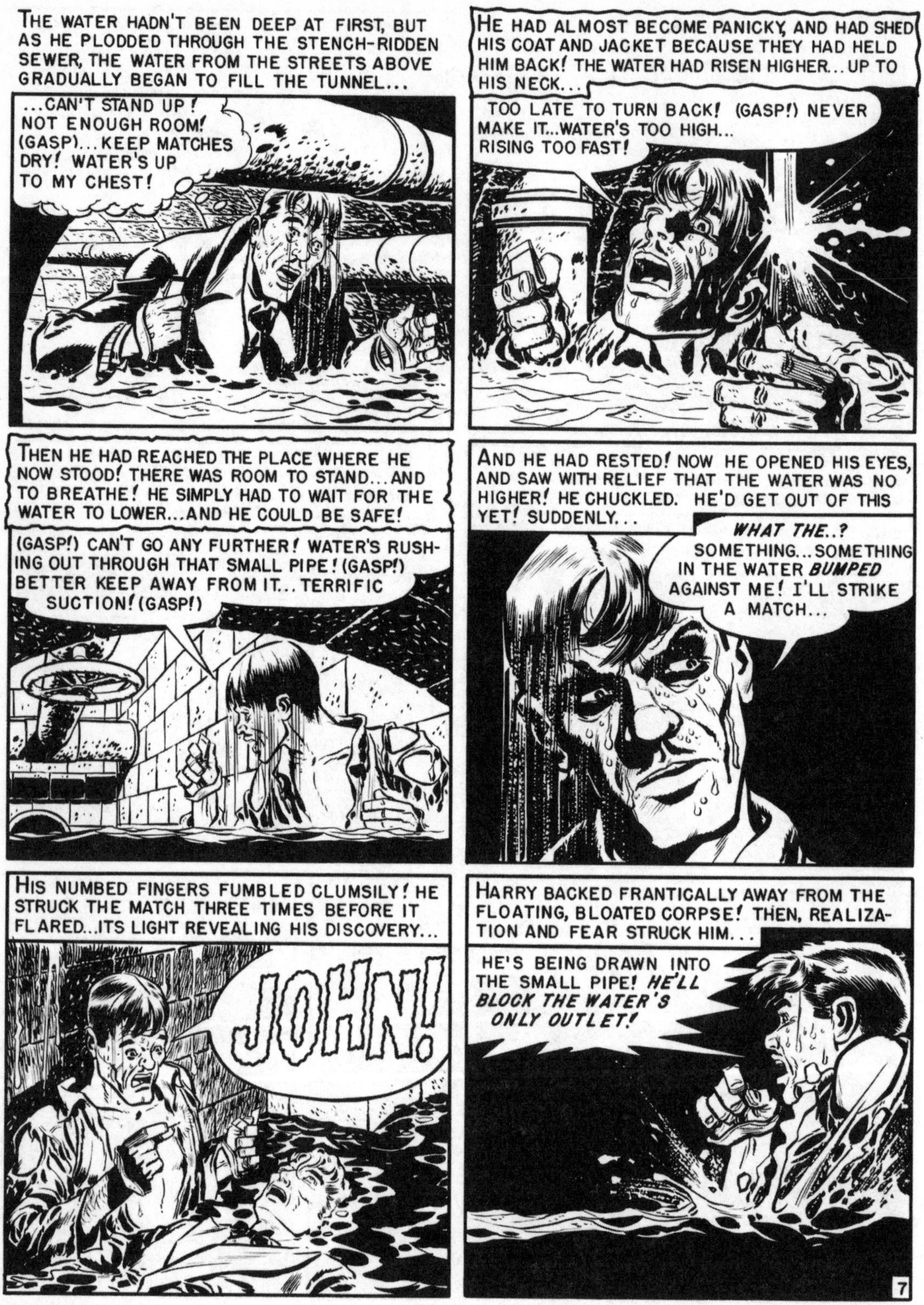
THE WATER HADN'T BEEN DEEP AT FIRST, BUT AS HE PLODDED THROUGH THE STENCH-RIDDEN SEWER, THE WATER FROM THE STREETS ABOVE GRADUALLY BEGAN TO FILL THE TUNNEL...
...CAN'T STAND UP! NOT ENOUGH ROOM! (GASP)... KEEP MATCHES DRY! WATER'S UP TO MY CHEST!
HE HAD ALMOST BECOME PANICKY, AND HAD SHED HIS COAT AND JACKET BECAUSE THEY HAD HELD HIM BACK! THE WATER HAD RISEN HIGHER... UP TO HIS NECK...
TOO LATE TO TURN BACK! (GASP!) NEVER MAKE IT...WATER'S TOO HIGH... RISING TOO FAST!
THEN HE HAD REACHED THE PLACE WHERE HE NOW STOOD! THERE WAS ROOM TO STAND... AND TO BREATHE! HE SIMPLY HAD TO WAIT FOR THE WATER TO LOWER...AND HE COULD BE SAFE!
(GASP!) CAN'T GO ANY FURTHER! WATER'S RUSHING OUT THROUGH THAT SMALL PIPE! (GASP!) BETTER KEEP AWAY FROM IT... TERRIFIC SUCTION! (GASP!)
AND HE HAD RESTED! NOW HE OPENED HIS EYES, AND SAW WITH RELIEF THAT THE WATER WAS NO HIGHER! HE CHUCKLED. HE'D GET OUT OF THIS YET! SUDDENLY...
WHAT THE..? SOMETHING...SOMETHING IN THE WATER *BUMPED* AGAINST ME! I'LL STRIKE A MATCH...
HIS NUMBED FINGERS FUMBLED CLUMSILY! HE STRUCK THE MATCH THREE TIMES BEFORE IT FLARED...ITS LIGHT REVEALING HIS DISCOVERY...
JOHN!
HARRY BACKED FRANTICALLY AWAY FROM THE FLOATING, BLOATED CORPSE! THEN, REALIZATION AND FEAR STRUCK HIM...
HE'S BEING DRAWN INTO THE SMALL PIPE! *HE'LL BLOCK THE WATER'S ONLY OUTLET!*
7

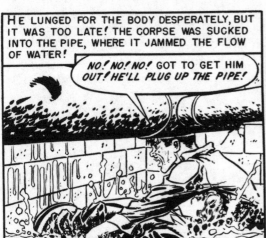

HE LUNGED FOR THE BODY DESPERATELY, BUT IT WAS TOO LATE! THE CORPSE WAS SUCKED INTO THE PIPE, WHERE IT JAMMED THE FLOW OF WATER!

NO! NO! NO! GOT TO GET HIM OUT! HE'LL PLUG UP THE PIPE!

JOHN! F'GOD'S SAKE! COME OUT! COME OUT, @WⒶ×!!Ⓞ! I'LL DROWN!

HIS HYSTERICAL EFFORTS TO SAVE HIMSELF WERE IN VAIN! THE WATER ROSE HIGHER... TO THE CEILING...

ABOVE, IN THE STREETS, THE RAIN HAD STOPPED...

I'D SURE LIKE TO KNOW WHY THAT HARRY MARKS FELLOW RAN AWAY FROM US, SARGE!

DUNNO...HMP!... MAYBE HE THOUGHT WE WERE CROOKS!

BUT WE ONLY WANTED TO WARN HIM THAT IRENE GOLDEN HAD ESCAPED FROM THE PSYCHO WARD, AND HAD THREATENED TO KILL HIM!

IT DOESN'T MATTER NOW. WE CAUGHT HER BEFORE SHE COULD GET HIM!

I GUESS THEY'LL PUT HER AWAY FOR GOOD, HUH, SARGE?

GUESS SO! AT ANY RATE, IT'LL BE THE LAST TIME SHE'LL EVER CAUSE HARRY MARKS ANY TROUBLE!

-THE END-

"**I** wonder if she lingers,
dressed and on her way
to her next venue,
gazing up into
the calm, unknowing
ink-blots of their eyes"

"You have to be so careful what you write about." Alan Moore should know, because for the graphic novel *From Hell* with artist Eddie Campbell, he took over 500 pages to dissect the Victorian murders of Jack the Ripper and expose how his awful legacy still permeates through society. In this sort of coda, Moore confronts the deeply unsettling emotions which the research and promotion for the book stirred up, as a television crew invades the same small Spitalfields pub once frequented by several of the Ripper's prostitute victims. Moore collaborated previously with Argentinian-born artist Oscar Zarate on *A Small Killing*. Here in widescreen expressionist panels they combine, contrast and counterpoint words and images, fiction and real life, to craft a chilling psycho-geography lesson.

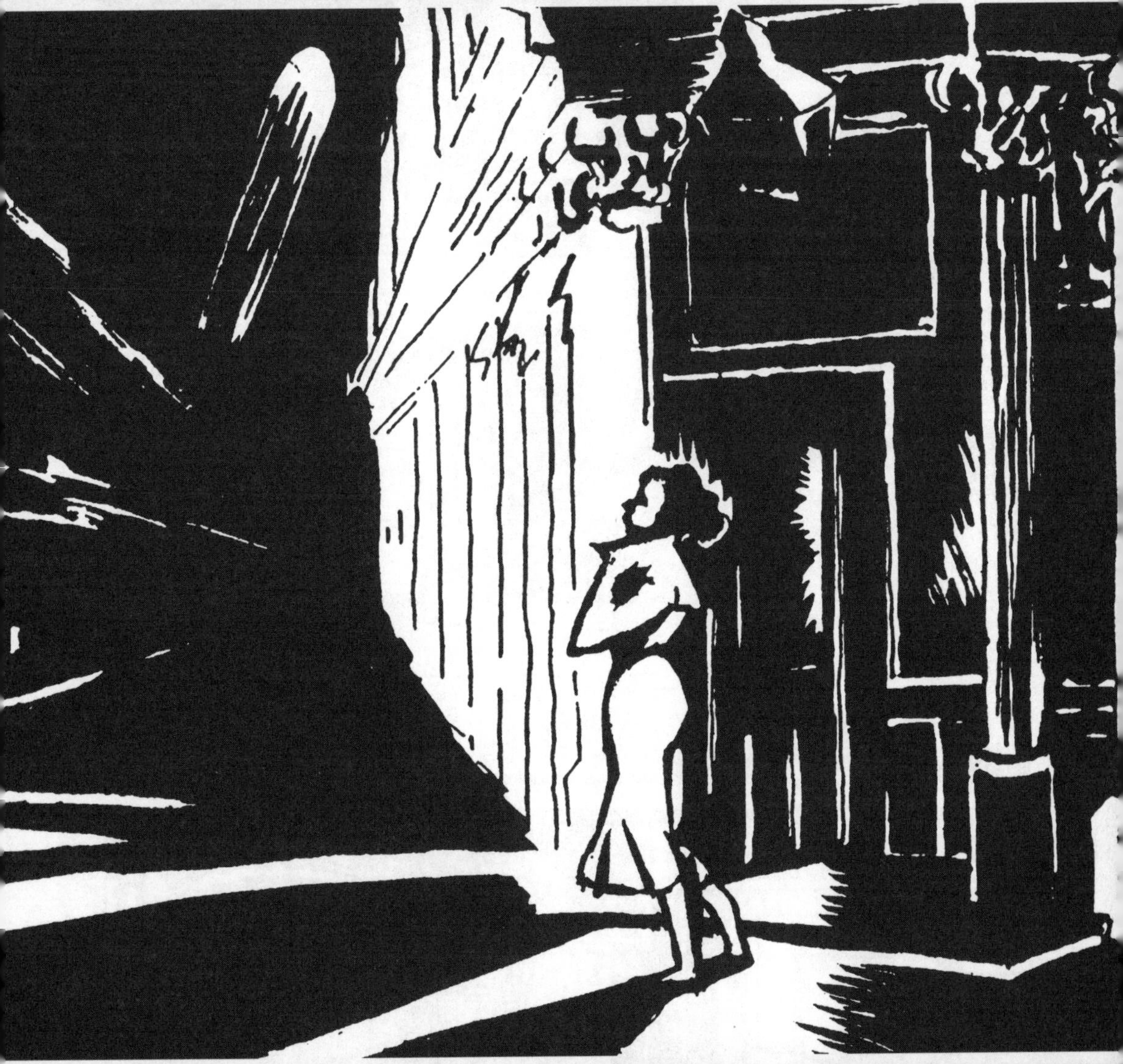

I Keep Coming Back

Alan Moore (script) and Oscar Zarate (art) 1996

I KEEP COMING BACK

ALAN MOORE / OSCAR ZARATE

I KEEP COMING BACK

I DON'T MEAN TO DO IT. IT JUST HAPPENS: WRITE ABOUT A PLACE AND YOU'RE CEMENTED TO IT. THIS TIME A FEATURE FOR B.B.C.2.

TWO DRAG QUEENS CROSS COMMERCIAL STREET BEFORE THE CAMERA UNIT'S VAN, ORCHIDS NOT LONG FOR THIS UNHAPPY CLIMATE.

THEY'VE EMPTIED THE WHOLE EDIFICE FOR US TO FILL WITH REDUNDANT DRY ICE FUMES AND OVERSTATED UNDER-LIGHT.

HOSTON, THE CARETAKER, A STILL AND PRIVATE PRESENCE, IS GENTLY PROTECTIVE OF THE CHURCH, A WEARY HUSBAND WITH HIS SENILE BRIDE.

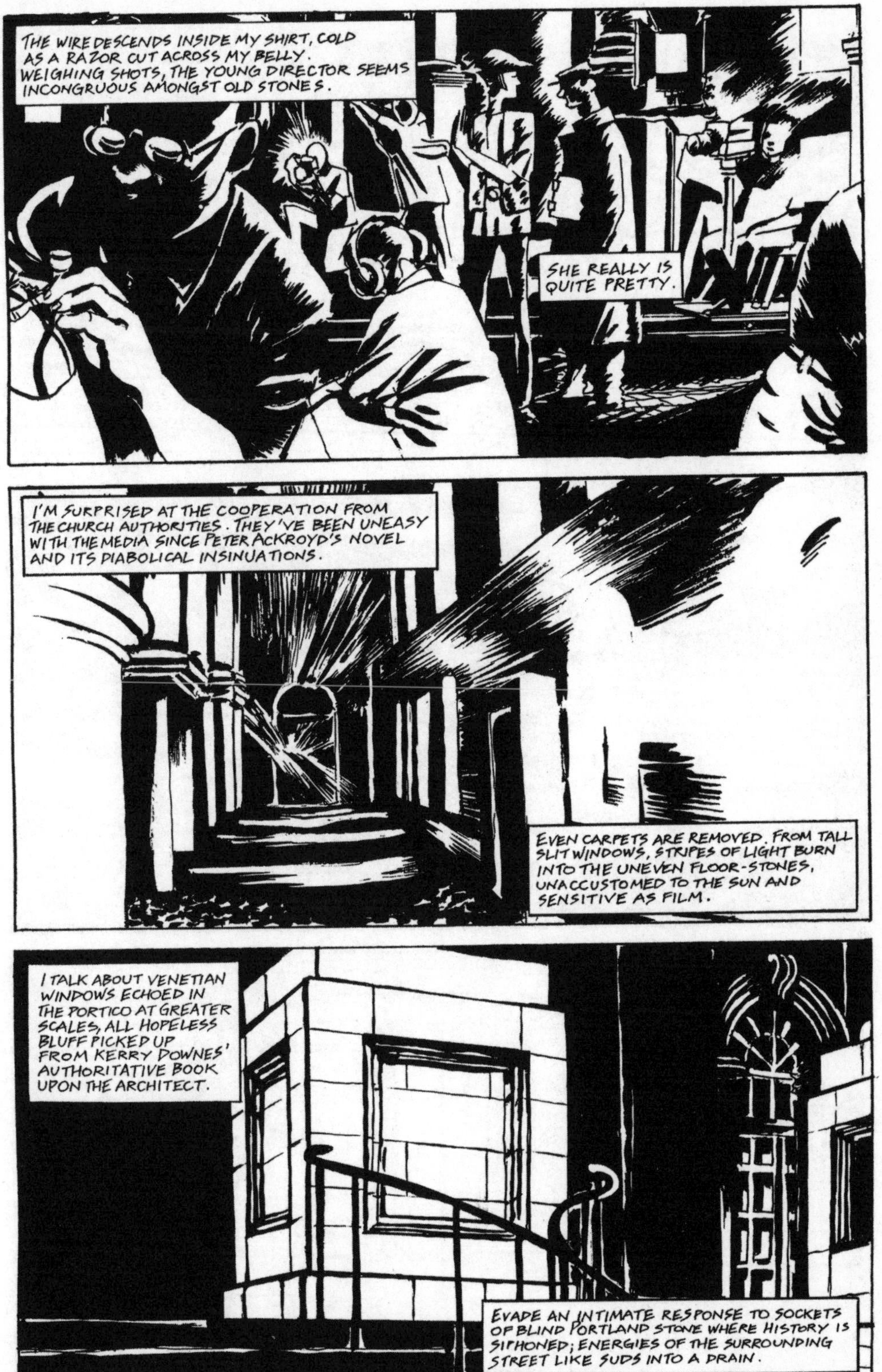

THE WIRE DESCENDS INSIDE MY SHIRT, COLD AS A RAZOR CUT ACROSS MY BELLY. WEIGHING SHOTS, THE YOUNG DIRECTOR SEEMS INCONGRUOUS AMONGST OLD STONES.
SHE REALLY IS QUITE PRETTY.
I'M SURPRISED AT THE COOPERATION FROM THE CHURCH AUTHORITIES. THEY'VE BEEN UNEASY WITH THE MEDIA SINCE PETER ACKROYD'S NOVEL AND ITS DIABOLICAL INSINUATIONS.
EVEN CARPETS ARE REMOVED. FROM TALL SLIT WINDOWS, STRIPES OF LIGHT BURN INTO THE UNEVEN FLOOR-STONES, UNACCUSTOMED TO THE SUN AND SENSITIVE AS FILM.
I TALK ABOUT VENETIAN WINDOWS ECHOED IN THE PORTICO AT GREATER SCALES, ALL HOPELESS BLUFF PICKED UP FROM KERRY DOWNES' AUTHORITATIVE BOOK UPON THE ARCHITECT.
EVADE AN INTIMATE RESPONSE TO SOCKETS OF BLIND PORTLAND STONE WHERE HISTORY IS SIPHONED; ENERGIES OF THE SURROUNDING STREET LIKE SUDS INTO A DRAIN.

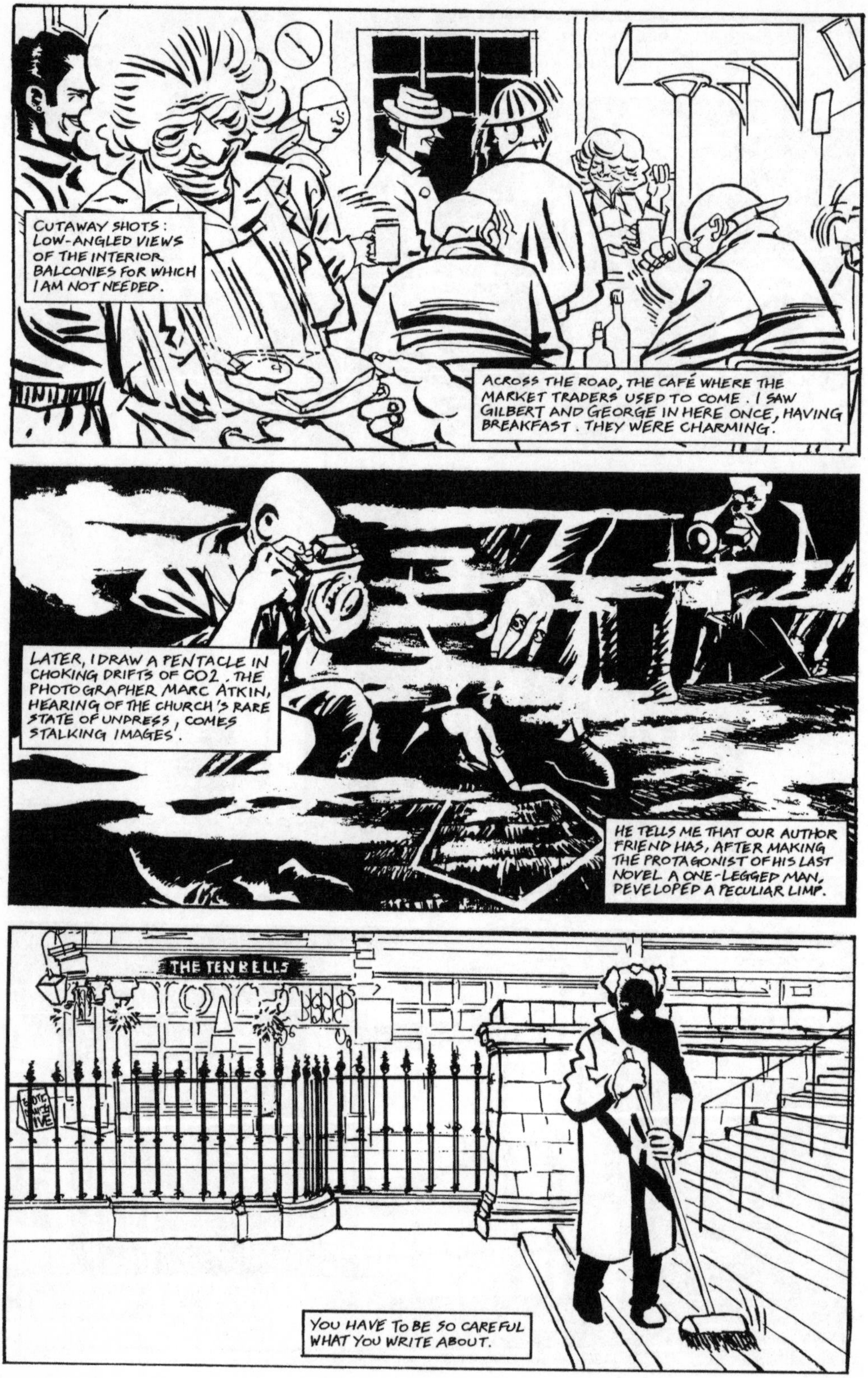
CUTAWAY SHOTS: LOW-ANGLED VIEWS OF THE INTERIOR BALCONIES FOR WHICH I AM NOT NEEDED.
ACROSS THE ROAD, THE CAFÉ WHERE THE MARKET TRADERS USED TO COME. I SAW GILBERT AND GEORGE IN HERE ONCE, HAVING BREAKFAST. THEY WERE CHARMING.
LATER, I DRAW A PENTACLE IN CHOKING DRIFTS OF CO2. THE PHOTOGRAPHER MARC ATKIN, HEARING OF THE CHURCH'S RARE STATE OF UNDRESS, COMES STALKING IMAGES.
HE TELLS ME THAT OUR AUTHOR FRIEND HAS, AFTER MAKING THE PROTAGONIST OF HIS LAST NOVEL A ONE-LEGGED MAN, DEVELOPED A PECULIAR LIMP.
THE TEN BELLS
YOU HAVE TO BE SO CAREFUL WHAT YOU WRITE ABOUT.

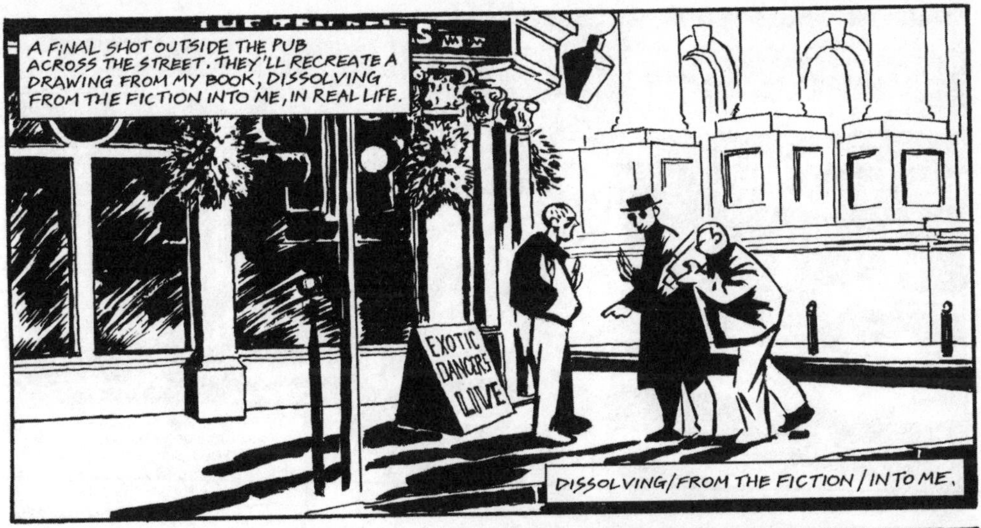
A FINAL SHOT OUTSIDE THE PUB ACROSS THE STREET. THEY'LL RECREATE A DRAWING FROM MY BOOK, DISSOLVING FROM THE FICTION INTO ME, IN REAL LIFE.
EXOTIC DANCERS LIVE
DISSOLVING / FROM THE FICTION / INTO ME.

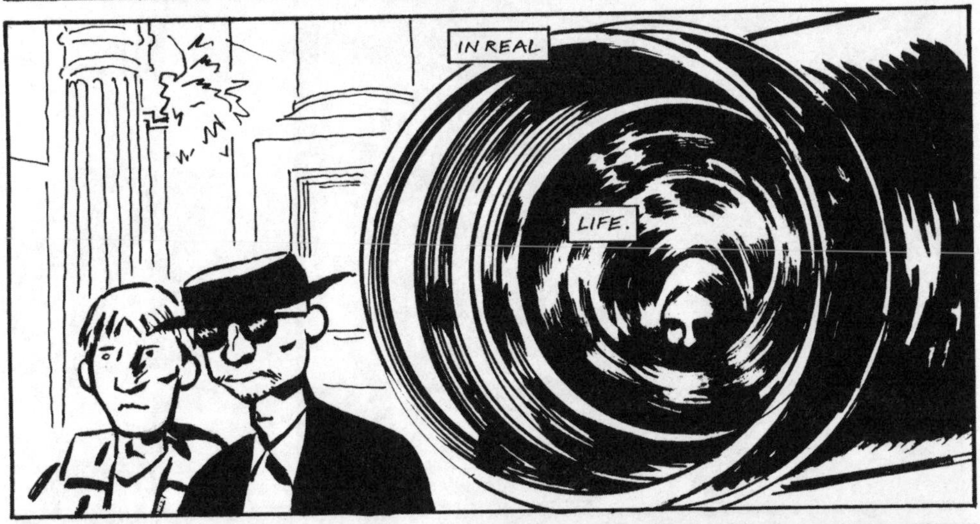
IN REAL
LIFE.

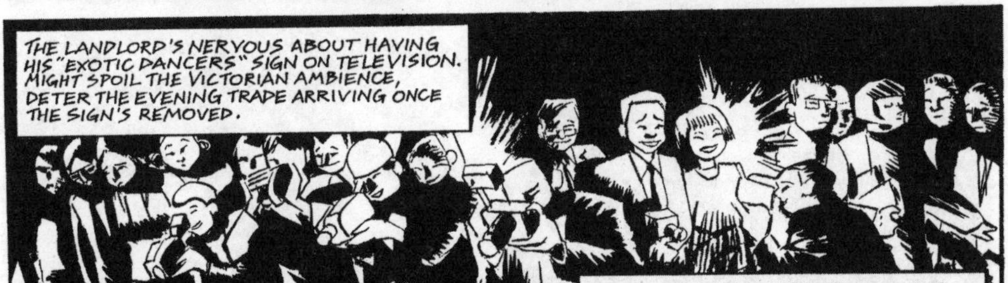
THE LANDLORD'S NERVOUS ABOUT HAVING HIS "EXOTIC DANCERS" SIGN ON TELEVISION. MIGHT SPOIL THE VICTORIAN AMBIENCE, DETER THE EVENING TRADE ARRIVING ONCE THE SIGN'S REMOVED.
EACH NIGHT THE MURDER TOURISTS PHOTOGRAPH THE SACRED GUTTERS WHERE THE BODIES WERE DISCOVERED, FILES OF EARNEST ORIENTALS WHO'VE MISPLACED THEIR PAPER NEW YEAR DRAGON.

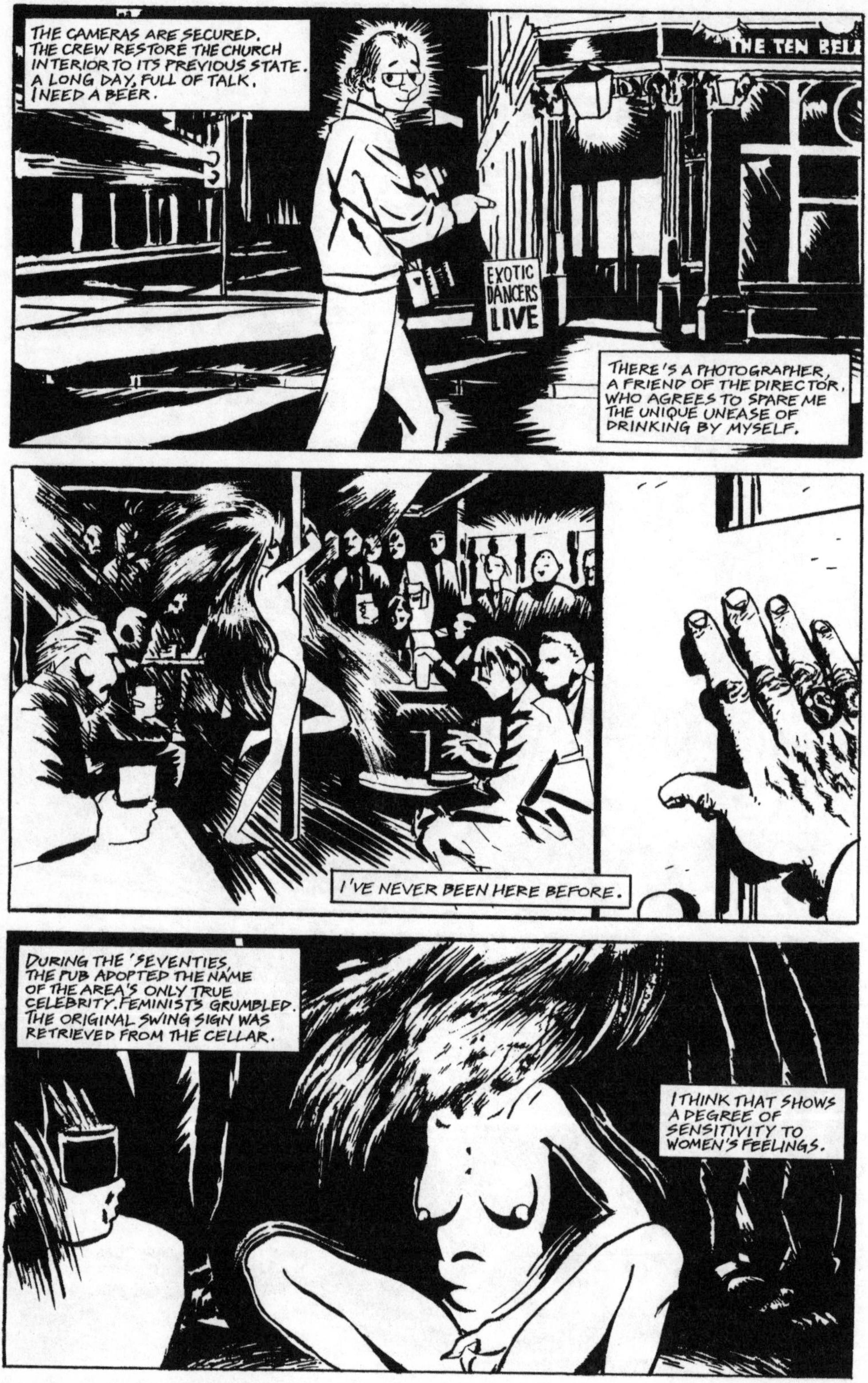
THE CAMERAS ARE SECURED. THE CREW RESTORE THE CHURCH INTERIOR TO ITS PREVIOUS STATE. A LONG DAY, FULL OF TALK. I NEED A BEER.
EXOTIC DANCERS LIVE
THERE'S A PHOTOGRAPHER, A FRIEND OF THE DIRECTOR, WHO AGREES TO SPARE ME THE UNIQUE UNEASE OF DRINKING BY MYSELF.
I'VE NEVER BEEN HERE BEFORE.
DURING THE 'SEVENTIES, THE PUB ADOPTED THE NAME OF THE AREA'S ONLY TRUE CELEBRITY. FEMINISTS GRUMBLED. THE ORIGINAL SWING SIGN WAS RETRIEVED FROM THE CELLAR.
I THINK THAT SHOWS A DEGREE OF SENSITIVITY TO WOMEN'S FEELINGS.

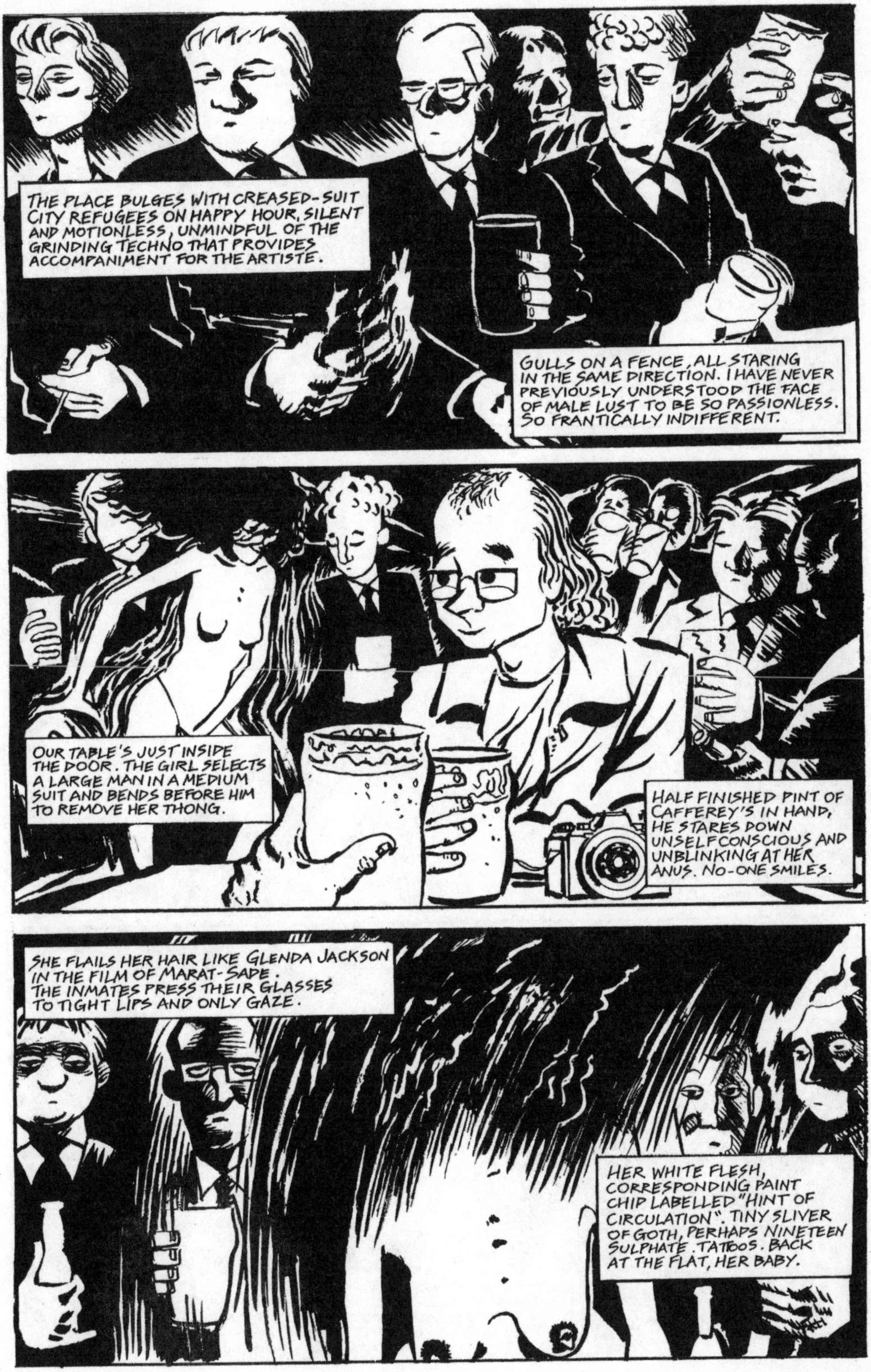
THE PLACE BULGES WITH CREASED-SUIT CITY REFUGEES ON HAPPY HOUR, SILENT AND MOTIONLESS, UNMINDFUL OF THE GRINDING TECHNO THAT PROVIDES ACCOMPANIMENT FOR THE ARTISTE.
GULLS ON A FENCE, ALL STARING IN THE SAME DIRECTION. I HAVE NEVER PREVIOUSLY UNDERSTOOD THE FACE OF MALE LUST TO BE SO PASSIONLESS. SO FRANTICALLY INDIFFERENT.
OUR TABLE'S JUST INSIDE THE DOOR. THE GIRL SELECTS A LARGE MAN IN A MEDIUM SUIT AND BENDS BEFORE HIM TO REMOVE HER THONG.
HALF FINISHED PINT OF CAFFEREY'S IN HAND, HE STARES DOWN UNSELFCONSCIOUS AND UNBLINKING AT HER ANUS. NO-ONE SMILES.
SHE FLAILS HER HAIR LIKE GLENDA JACKSON IN THE FILM OF MARAT-SADE. THE INMATES PRESS THEIR GLASSES TO TIGHT LIPS AND ONLY GAZE.
HER WHITE FLESH, CORRESPONDING PAINT CHIP LABELLED "HINT OF CIRCULATION". TINY SLIVER OF GOTH, PERHAPS NINETEEN SULPHATE. TATTOOS. BACK AT THE FLAT, HER BABY.

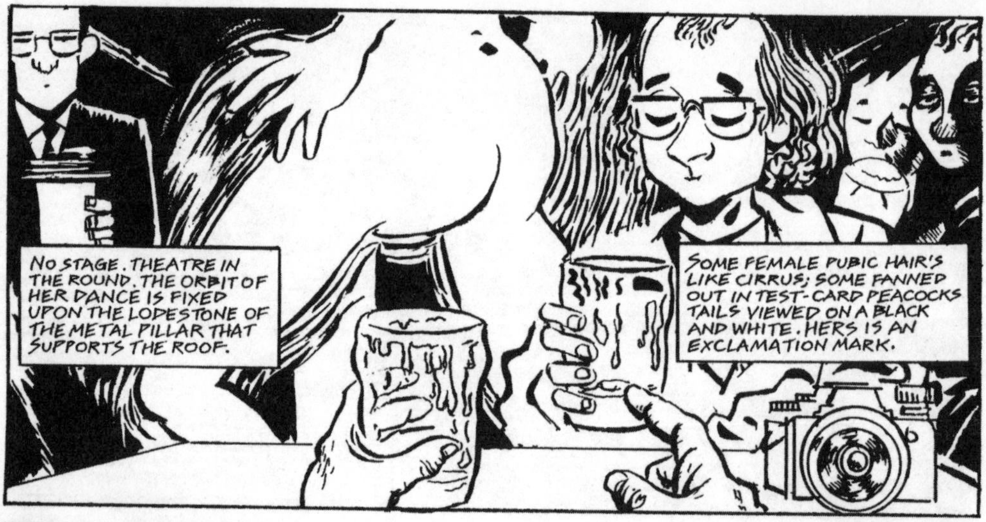
No stage. Theatre in the round. The orbit of her dance is fixed upon the lodestone of the metal pillar that supports the roof.
Some female pubic hair's like cirrus; some fanned out in test-card peacocks tails viewed on a black and white. Hers is an exclamation mark.

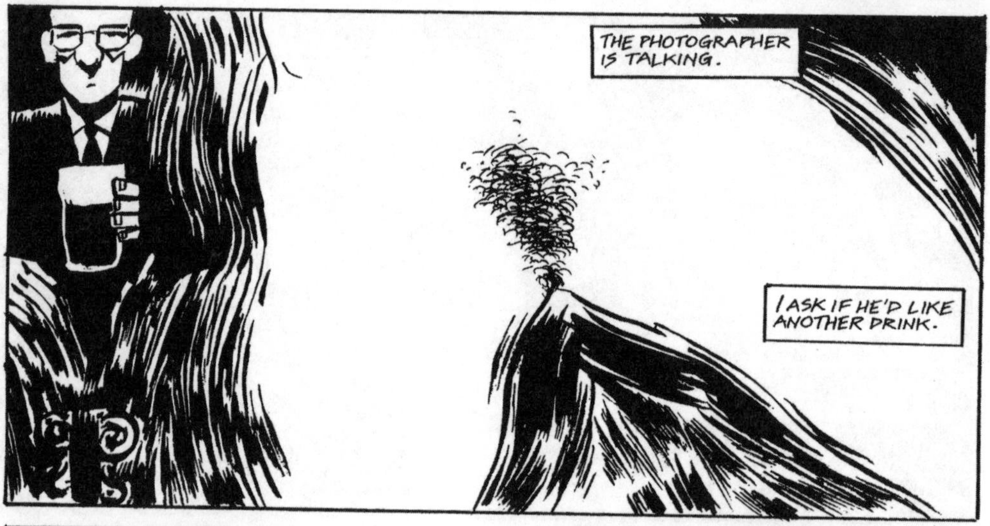
The photographer is talking.
I ask if he'd like another drink.

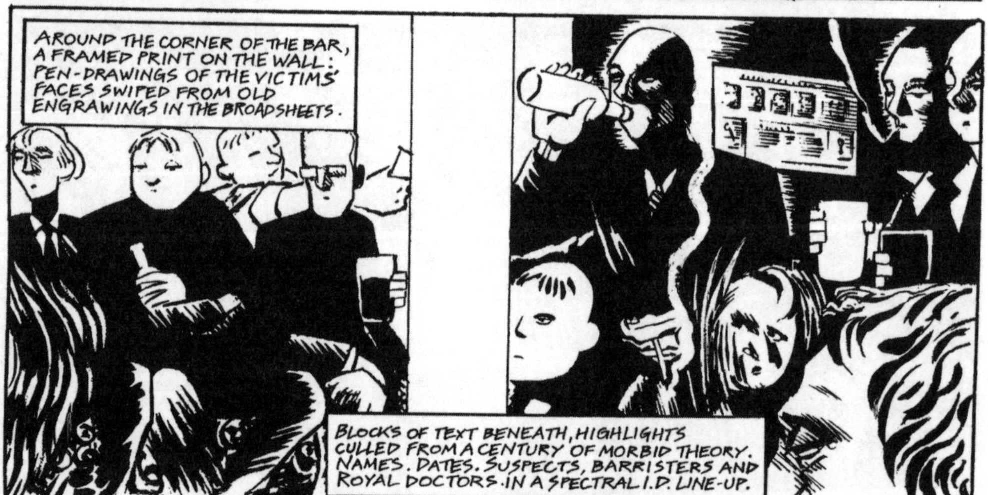
Around the corner of the bar, a framed print on the wall: pen-drawings of the victims' faces swiped from old engrawings in the broadsheets.
Blocks of text beneath, highlights culled from a century of morbid theory. Names. Dates. Suspects, barristers and royal doctors. In a spectral I.D. line-up.

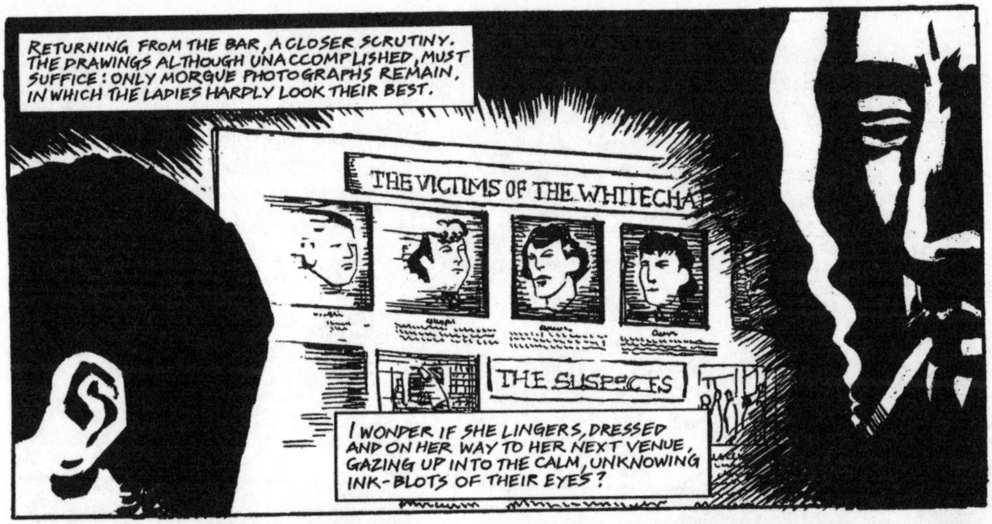
RETURNING FROM THE BAR, A CLOSER SCRUTINY. THE DRAWINGS ALTHOUGH UNACCOMPLISHED, MUST SUFFICE: ONLY MORGUE PHOTOGRAPHS REMAIN, IN WHICH THE LADIES HARDLY LOOK THEIR BEST.
THE VICTIMS OF THE WHITECHA
THE SUSPECTS
I WONDER IF SHE LINGERS, DRESSED AND ON HER WAY TO HER NEXT VENUE, GAZING UP INTO THE CALM, UNKNOWING INK-BLOTS OF THEIR EYES?

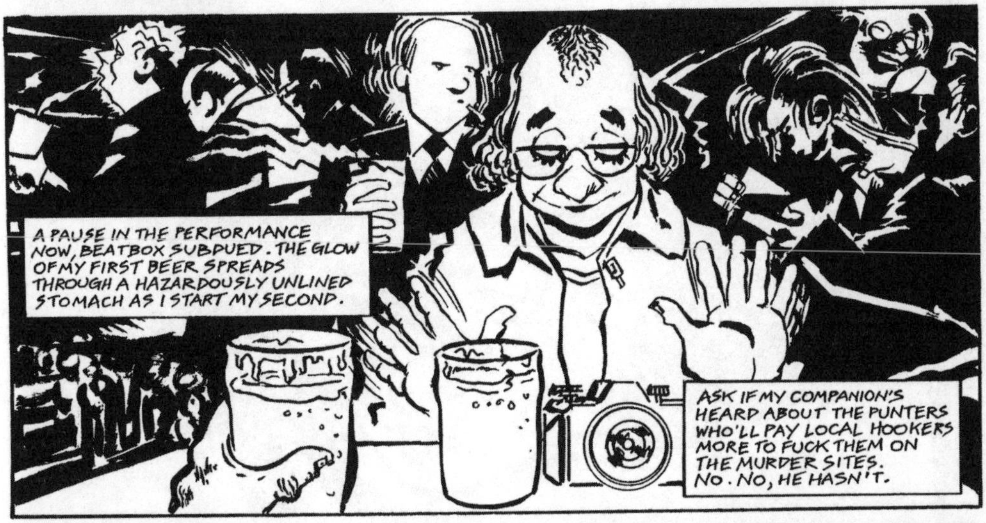
A PAUSE IN THE PERFORMANCE NOW, BEATBOX SUBDUED. THE GLOW OF MY FIRST BEER SPREADS THROUGH A HAZARDOUSLY UNLINED STOMACH AS I START MY SECOND.
ASK IF MY COMPANION'S HEARD ABOUT THE PUNTERS WHO'LL PAY LOCAL HOOKERS MORE TO FUCK THEM ON THE MURDER SITES. NO. NO, HE HASN'T.

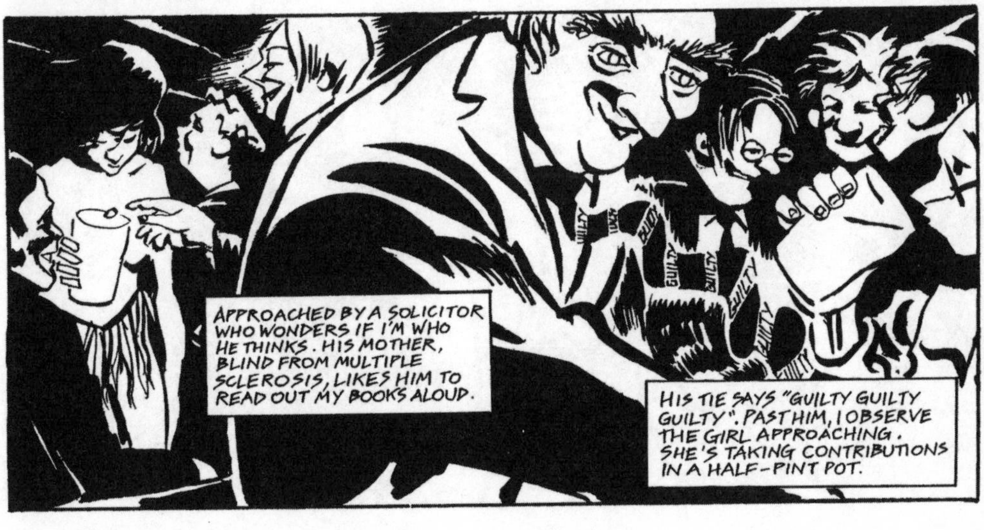
APPROACHED BY A SOLICITOR WHO WONDERS IF I'M WHO HE THINKS. HIS MOTHER, BLIND FROM MULTIPLE SCLEROSIS, LIKES HIM TO READ OUT MY BOOKS ALOUD.
GUILTY
HIS TIE SAYS "GUILTY GUILTY GUILTY". PAST HIM, I OBSERVE THE GIRL APPROACHING. SHE'S TAKING CONTRIBUTIONS IN A HALF-PINT POT.

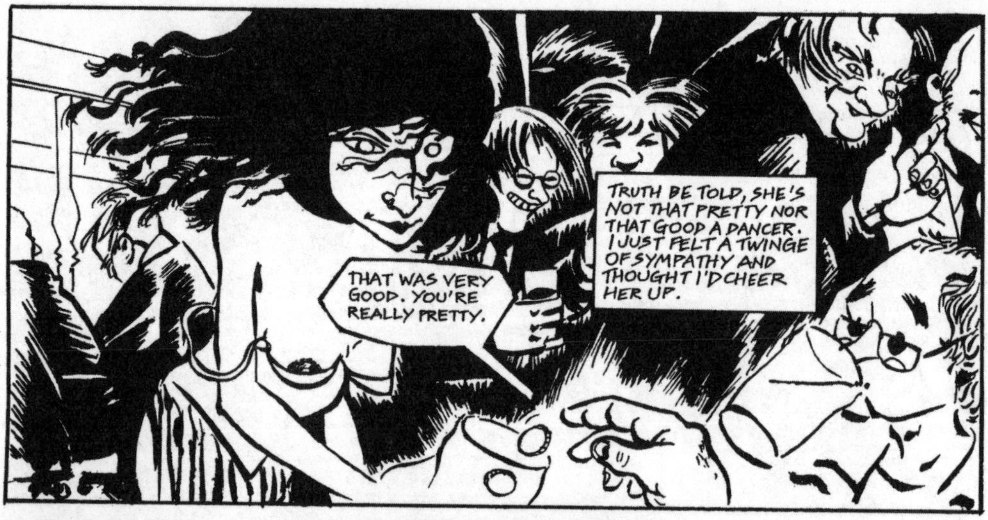
THAT WAS VERY GOOD. YOU'RE REALLY PRETTY.
TRUTH BE TOLD, SHE'S NOT THAT PRETTY NOR THAT GOOD A DANCER. I JUST FELT A TWINGE OF SYMPATHY AND THOUGHT I'D CHEER HER UP.

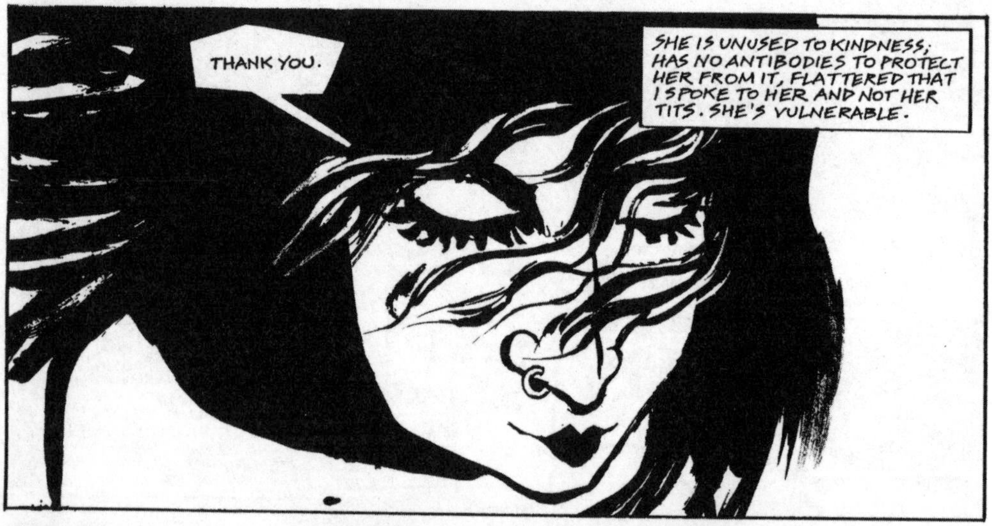
THANK YOU.
SHE IS UNUSED TO KINDNESS; HAS NO ANTIBODIES TO PROTECT HER FROM IT, FLATTERED THAT I SPOKE TO HER AND NOT HER TITS. SHE'S VULNERABLE.

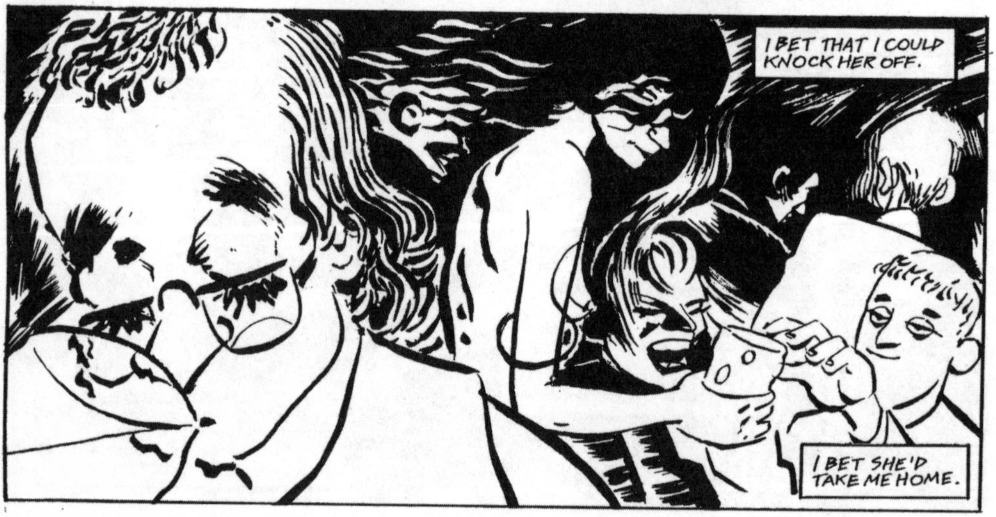
I BET THAT I COULD KNOCK HER OFF.
I BET SHE'D TAKE ME HOME.

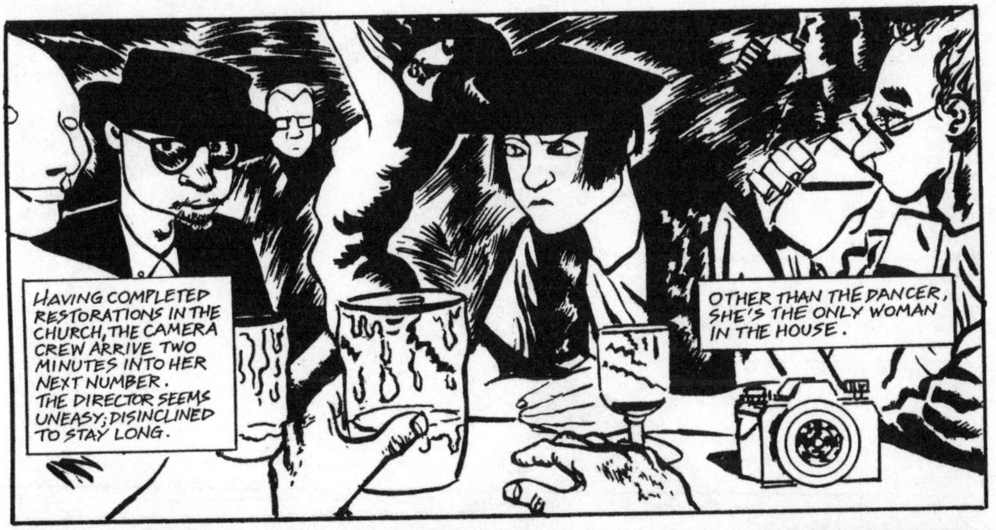
HAVING COMPLETED RESTORATIONS IN THE CHURCH, THE CAMERA CREW ARRIVE TWO MINUTES INTO HER NEXT NUMBER. THE DIRECTOR SEEMS UNEASY; DISINCLINED TO STAY LONG.
OTHER THAN THE DANCER, SHE'S THE ONLY WOMAN IN THE HOUSE.
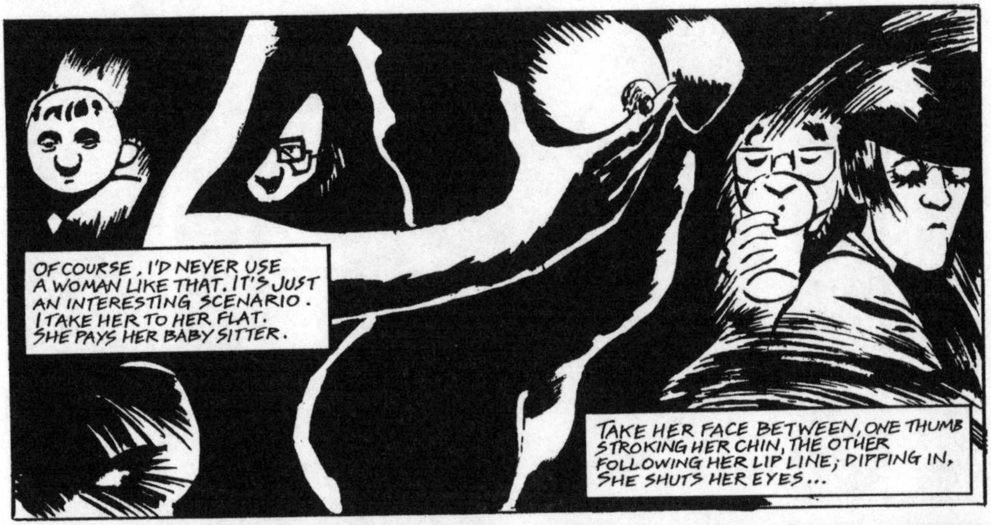
OF COURSE, I'D NEVER USE A WOMAN LIKE THAT. IT'S JUST AN INTERESTING SCENARIO. I TAKE HER TO HER FLAT. SHE PAYS HER BABY SITTER.
TAKE HER FACE BETWEEN, ONE THUMB STROKING HER CHIN, THE OTHER FOLLOWING HER LIP LINE; DIPPING IN. SHE SHUTS HER EYES...
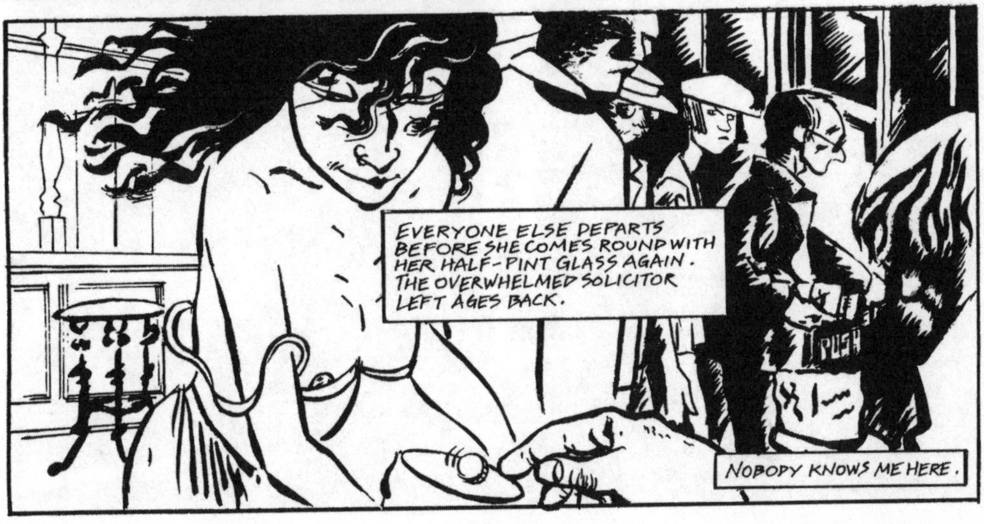
EVERYONE ELSE DEPARTS BEFORE SHE COMES ROUND WITH HER HALF-PINT GLASS AGAIN. THE OVERWHELMED SOLICITOR LEFT AGES BACK.
PUSH
NOBODY KNOWS ME HERE.

WAIT TILL SHE CLOCKS OFF. WALK HER HOME. WE FIND A SIDESTREET SOMEWHERE. MAYBE HANBURY. FACING THE FENCE, SHE MOANS. I REACH INTO MY POCKET.

MAYBE I SHOULD LEAVE.

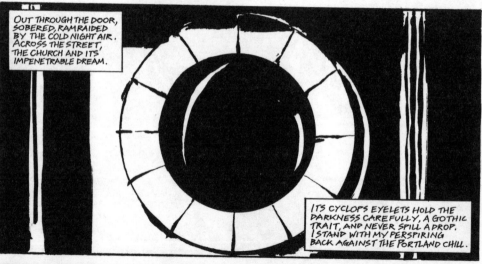

OUT THROUGH THE DOOR, SOBERED, RAMRAIDED BY THE COLD NIGHT AIR. ACROSS THE STREET, THE CHURCH AND ITS IMPENETRABLE DREAM.

ITS CYCLOPS EYELETS HOLD THE DARKNESS CAREFULLY, A GOTHIC TRAIT, AND NEVER SPILL A DROP. I STAND WITH MY PERSPIRING BACK AGAINST THE PORTLAND CHILL.

SOON, ALL THE NECRO-TOURISTS WILL ARRIVE. THE STARK "EXOTIC DANCERS" SIGN'S BEEN TAKEN BACK INSIDE. THE MUFFLE TECHNO DIES, DOES NOT RESUME.

THE TEN BELLS

THE HUDDLED ALLEYS ARE A TEMPLATE OF EVENTS YET TO OCCUR.

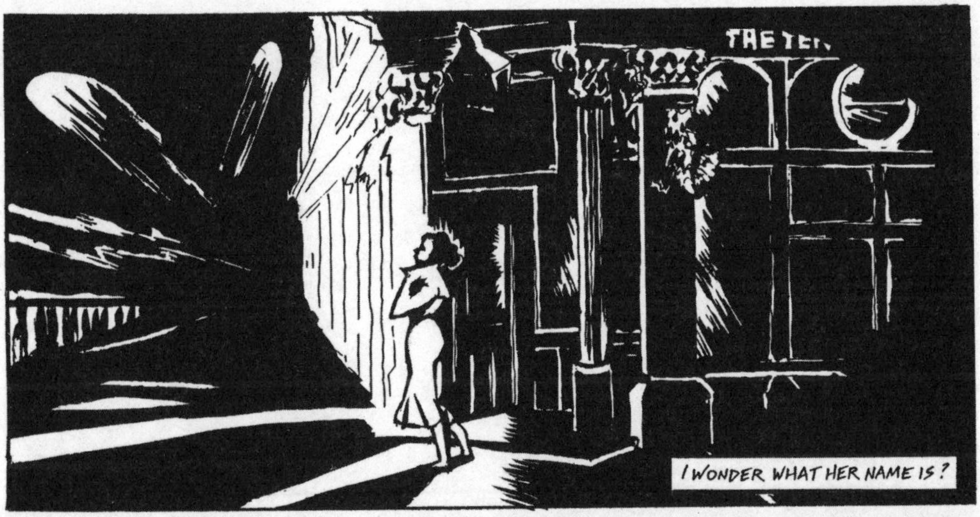
I WONDER WHAT HER NAME IS?

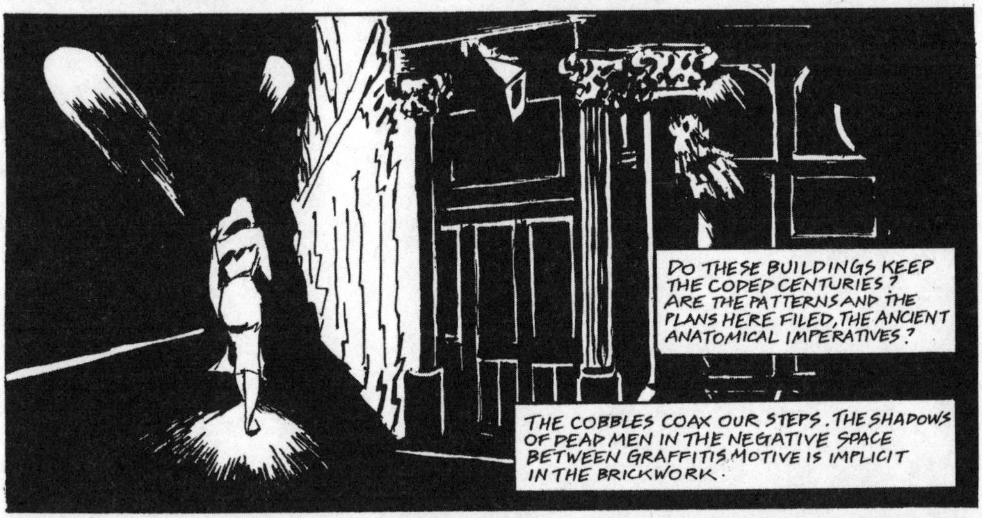
DO THESE BUILDINGS KEEP THE CODED CENTURIES? ARE THE PATTERNS AND THE PLANS HERE FILED, THE ANCIENT ANATOMICAL IMPERATIVES?
THE COBBLES COAX OUR STEPS. THE SHADOWS OF DEAD MEN IN THE NEGATIVE SPACE BETWEEN GRAFFITIS MOTIVE IS IMPLICIT IN THE BRICKWORK.

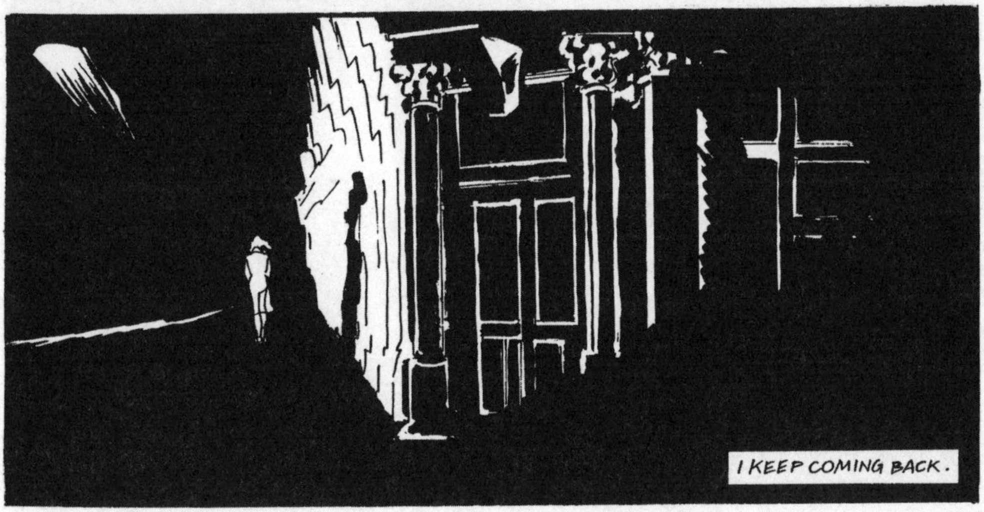
I KEEP COMING BACK.